ARB No.	Date Issued	Title
21	Aug. 1971	Interest on Receivables and Payables
22	Apr. 1972	Disclosure of Accounting Policies
23	Apr. 1972	Accounting for Income Taxes—Special Areas
24	Apr. 1972	Accounting for Income Taxes—Equity Method Investments
25	Oct. 1972	Accounting for Stock Issued to Employees
26	Oct. 1972	Early Extinguishment of Debt
27	Nov. 1972	Accounting for Lease Transactions by Manufacturer or Dealer Lessors
28	May 1973	Interim Financial Reporting
29	May 1973	Accounting for Nonmonetary Transactions
30	June 1973	Reporting the Results of Operations
31	June 1973	Disclosure of Lease Commitments by Lessees

Financial Accounting Standards Board (FASB),
***Statement of Financial Accounting Concepts* (1978–85)**

1	Nov. 1978	Objectives of Financial Reporting by Business Enterprises
2	May 1980	Qualitative Characteristics of Accounting Information
3	Dec. 1980	Elements of Financial Statements of Business Enterprises
4	Dec. 1980	Objectives of Financial Reporting by Nonbusiness Organizations
5	Dec. 1984	Recognition and Measurement in Financial Statements of Business Enterprises
6	Dec. 1985	Elements of Financial Statements (a replacement of *FASB Concepts Statement No. 3*, incorporating an amendment of *FASB Concepts Statement No. 2*)

Financial Accounting Standards Board (FASB), *Statements of Financial Accounting Standards* (1973–88)

1	Dec. 1973	Disclosure of Foreign Currency
2	Oct. 1974	Accounting for Research and Development Costs
3	Dec. 1974	Reporting Accounting Changes in Interim Financial Statements (an amendment of *APB Opinion 23*)
4	Mar. 1975	Reporting Gains and Losses from Extinguishment of Debt
5	Mar. 1975	Accounting for Contingencies
6	May 1975	Classification of Short-Term Obligations Expected to Be Refinanced
7	June 1975	Accounting and Reporting by Development Stage Enterprises
8	Oct. 1975	Accounting for the Translation of Foreign Currency Transactions and Foreign Currency Financial Statements
9	Oct. 1975	Accounting for Income Taxes—Oil and Gas Producing Companies (an amendment of *APB Opinions 11 and 23*)
10	Oct. 1975	Extension of "Grandfather" Provisions for Business Combinations (an amendment of *APB Opinion 16*)
11	Dec. 1975	Accounting for Contingencies—Transition Method (an amendment of *FASB Statement 5*)
12	Dec. 1975	Accounting for Certain Marketable Securities
13	Nov. 1976	Accounting for Leases
14	Dec. 1976	Financial Reporting for Segments of a Business Enterprise
15	June 1977	Accounting by Debtors and Creditors for Troubled Debt Restructurings
16	June 1977	Prior Period Adjustments
17	Nov. 1977	Accounting for Leases—Initial Direct Costs
18	Nov. 1977	Financial Reporting for Segments of a Business Enterprise—Interim Financial Statements
19	Dec. 1977	Financial Accounting and Reporting by Oil and Gas Producing Companies
20	Dec. 1977	Accounting for Forward Exchange Contracts
21	Apr. 1978	Suspension of the Reporting of Earnings per Share and Segment Information by Nonpublic Enterprises
22	June 1978	Changes in the Provisions of Lease Agreements Resulting from Refundings of Tax-Exempt Debt
23	Aug. 1978	Inception of the Lease
24	Dec. 1978	Reporting Segment Information in Financial Statements that Are Presented in Another Enterprise's Financial Report
25	Feb. 1979	Suspension of Certain Accounting Requirements for Oil and Gas Companies (an amendment of *FASB Statement 19*)
26	Apr. 1979	Profit Recognition on Sales-Type Leases of Real Estate (an amendment of *FASB Statement 13*)
27	May 1979	Classification of Renewals or Extension of Existing Sales-Type or Direct Financing Leases (an amendment of *FASB Statement 13*)
28	May 1979	Accounting for Sales with Leasebacks (an amendment of *FASB Statement 13*)
29	June 1979	Determining Contingent Rentals (an amendment of *FASB Statement 13*)
30	Aug. 1979	Disclosure of Information about Major Customers (an amendment of *FASB Statement 14*)
31	Sept. 1979	Accounting for Tax Benefits Related to U.K. Tax Legislation Concerning Stock Relief
32	Sept. 1979	Specialized Accounting and Reporting Principles and Practices in AICPA Statements of Position and Guides on Accounting and Auditing Matters (an amendment of *APB Opinion 20*)
33	Sept. 1979	Financial Reporting and Changing Prices Illustrations of Financial Reporting and Changing Prices, *Statement of Financial Accounting Standards 33*

ARB No.	Date Issued	Title
34	Oct. 1979	Capitalization of Interest Cost
35	Mar. 1980	Accounting and Reporting by Defined Benefit Pension Plans
36	May 1980	Disclosure of Pension Information (an amendment of *APB Opinion 8*)
37	July 1980	Balance Sheet Classification of Deferred Income Taxes (an amendment of *APB Opinion 11*)
38	Sept. 1980	Accounting for Preacquisition Contingencies of Purchased Enterprises (an amendment of *APB Opinion 16*)
39	Oct. 1980	Financial Reporting and Changing Prices: Specialized Assets—Mining and Oil and Gas (a supplement to *FASB Statement 33*)
40	Nov. 1980	Financial Reporting and Changing Prices: Specialized Assets—Timberlands and Growing Timber (a supplement to *FASB Statement 33*)
41	Nov. 1980	Financial Reporting and Changing Prices: Specialized Assets—Income-Producing Real Estate (a supplement to *FASB Statement 33*)
42	Nov. 1980	Determining Materiality for Capitalization of Interest Cost (an amendment for *FASB Statement 34*)
43	Nov. 1980	Accounting for Compensated Absences
44	Dec. 1980	Accounting for Intangible Assets of Motor Carriers (an amendment of Chapter 5 of *ARB 43*, and an interpretation of *APB Opinions 17* and *30*)
45	Mar. 1981	Accounting for Franchise Fee Revenue
46	Mar. 1981	Financial Reporting and Changing Prices: Motion Picture Films
47	Mar. 1981	Disclosure of Long-Term Obligations
48	June 1981	Revenue Recognition When Right of Returns Exists
49	June 1981	Accounting for Product Financing Arrangements
50	Nov. 1981	Financial Reporting in the Record and Music Industry
51	Nov. 1981	Financial Reporting by Cable Television Companies
52	Dec. 1981	Foreign Currency Translation
53	Dec. 1981	Financial Reporting by Producers and Distributors of Motion Picture Films
54	Jan. 1982	Financial Reporting and Changing Prices; Investment Companies
55	Feb. 1982	Determining Whether a Convertible Security Is a Common Stock Equivalent
56	Feb. 1982	Designation of AICPA Guide and SOP 81–1 on Contractor Accounting and SOP 81–2 on Hospital-Related Organizations as Preferable for Applying *APB Opinion 20*
57	Mar. 1982	Related Party Disclosures
58	April 1982	Capitalization of Interest Cost in Financial Statements that Include Investments Accounted for by the Equity Method
59	April 1982	Deferral of the Effective Date of Certain Accounting Requirements for Revision Plans of State and Local Government Units
60	June 1982	Accounting and Reporting by Insurance Enterprises
61	June 1982	Accounting for Title Plant
62	June 1982	Capitalization of Interest in Situations Involving Certain Tax-Exempt Borrowings and Certain Gifts and Grants
63	June 1982	Financial Reporting by Broadcasters
64	Sept. 1982	Extinguishment of Debt Made to Satisfy Sinking Fund Requirements
65	Sept. 1982	Accounting for Certain Mortgage Bank Activities
66	Oct. 1982	Accounting for Sales on Real Estate
67	Oct. 1982	Accounting for Costs and Initial Rental Operations of Real Estate Projects
68	Oct. 1982	Research and Development Arrangements
69	Nov. 1982	Disclosures about Oil and Gas Producing Activities (an amendment of *FASB Statements 19, 25, 33,* and *39*)
70	Dec. 1982	Financial Reporting and Changing Prices: Foreign Currency Translation (an amendment of *FASB Statement 33*)
71	Dec. 1982	Accounting for the Effects of Certain Types of Regulation
72	Feb. 1983	Accounting for Certain Acquisitions of Banking or Thrift Institutions (an amendment of *APB Opinion 17*, an interpretation of *APB Opinions 16* and *17*, and an amendment of *FASB Interpretation 9*)
73	Aug. 1983	Reporting a Change in Accounting for Railroad Track Structures (an amendment of *ABP Opinion 20*)
74	Aug. 1983	Accounting for Special Termination Benefits Paid to Employees
75	Nov. 1983	Deferral of the Effective Date of Certain Accounting Requirements for Pension Plans of State and Local Governmental Units (an amendment of *FASB Statement 35*)
76	Nov. 1983	Extinguishment of Debt (an amendment of *APB Opinion 26*)
77	Dec. 1983	Reporting by Transferors for Transfers of Receivables with Recourse
78	Dec. 1983	Classification of Obligations that Are Callable by the Creditor (an amendment of *ARB 43*, Chapter 3A)
79	Feb. 1984	Elimination of Certain Disclosures for Business Combinations by Nonpublic enterprises (an amendment of *APB Opinion 16*)
80	Aug. 1984	Accounting for Futures Contracts
81	Nov. 1984	Disclosure of Postretirement Health Care and Life Insurance Benefits

INTERMEDIATE ACCOUNTING

The Robert N. Anthony / Willard J. Graham Series in Accounting

INTERMEDIATE ACCOUNTING

Glenn A. Welsch
Charles T. Zlatkovich
both of
The College of Business Administration
The University of Texas at Austin

1989 Eighth Edition

IRWIN
Homewood, IL 64030
Boston, MA 02116

Sponsoring editor: Ron M. Regis
Production manager: Irene H. Sotiroff
Artist: Benoit Design
Compositor: Arcata Graphics/Kingsport
Typeface: 10/12 Palatino
Printer: R. R. Donnelley & Sons Company

Library of Congress Cataloging-in-Publication Data

Welsch, Glenn A.

Intermediate accounting / Glenn A. Welsch, Charles T. Zlatkovich. —8th ed.

p. cm.

Includes index.

ISBN 0-256-06660-4

1. Accounting. I. Zlatkovich, Charles T. II. Title.

HF5635.W46 1989

657'.044—dc19

88–39984
CIP

Printed in the United States of America
1 2 3 4 5 6 7 8 9 0 DO 6 5 4 3 2 1 0 9

PREFACE

Objectives

There are two basic objectives of the eighth edition of this textbook. The first is to comprehensively explain and illustrate the conceptual foundation and rationale that underlie the application procedures for the topical coverage in intermediate accounting courses. The second basic objective is to organize and articulate these concepts, rationales, and procedures in ways that provide (a) maximum flexibility and teachability for faculty purposes; and (b) authoritative, concise, and straightforward textual material for student purposes. To achieve these objectives, the text focuses on student motivation, and understanding the strengths and limitations of accounting. In addition, the text concentrates on how to achieve future success in professional examinations and accounting careers, and how to maximize the usefulness of accounting information for nonaccountants.

Although accounting and external reporting have become increasingly rule-oriented, the authors provide a solid conceptual foundation. This foundation is utilized throughout the text to support and explain the application procedures presented. Our primary emphasis is on **why** and our secondary emphasis is on **how**—this emphasis reduces the need for memorization.

This textbook is designed primarily for students who have successfully completed a reasonably adequate course in the fundamentals of financial accounting. The text is equally adaptable for use by schools that use the semester or the quarter system. Two semesters or three quarters—or their equivalent—are recommended for complete coverage of all chapters.

Revision and New Innovations

This eighth edition continues the leadership and excellence of prior editions that established the highest standards of comprehensiveness, academic excellence, and topical presentation. Rather than a piecemeal revision, this edition represents a major *reorganization and rewrite*. The primary emphasis in preparing this revision was to further enhance the clarity and conciseness of the text while maintaining its long-standing reputation for technical quality. Reviews of the revised manuscript have been exceptionally favorable.

Collectively, intermediate accounting textbooks have tended to follow a common pattern and format established decades ago. As with previous editions, however, this eighth edition continues to depart from that outdated pattern. Some of the recent changes in this textbook are unique among intermediate accounting texts. A major innovation in this eighth edition is the rearrangement of major topics. For example, there are two separate conceptual chapters: Chapter 6, "The FASB Conceptual Framework" (strategically placed after the review chapters), and Chapter 13, "Income Recognition" (logically placed to start the second half of the book). Numerous other innovations have been made throughout the remaining chapters. These changes include the following:

a. Chapter 1—there are some inherent limitations in the first class meeting. Therefore, Chapter 1 is designed primarily for reading in order to give the students a basic understanding of the accounting environment. The chapter also includes a very succinct review of the basic accounting model.

b. The review chapters, Chapters 2, 3 and 4, are lucid and concise with clear-cut and complete relevant illustrations. These chapters provide a comprehensive review to reinforce the students' background knowledge. This review will help the students understand the chapters that follow. Review-type questions, exercises, problems, and cases are provided to to help the students attain this objective.

c. Chapter 5, on PV/FV, contains only minor changes because of its prior wide acclaim for concise presentations and clarity. PV and FV *annuity due* tables are included in the chapter.

d. Chapter 6 is a new, innovative chapter devoted to the FASB conceptual framework. This chapter follows the review chapters which prepare the students for the substantive, conceptual discussion found in Chapter 6. It was written to provide a solid foundation for understanding the topical chapters that follow. Another related conceptual chapter, "Income Recognition" (Chapter 13), is strategically placed to start the second half of the book. These two chapters significantly enhance the students' understanding of the relationships between concepts and practical applications.

e. Chapter 7 has been reorganized to exclude short-term investments, which are discussed in Chapter 18 along with long-term investments. The discussion of inventories encompasses Chapters 8 and 9 (rather than in three chapters as in past editions).

f. Operational assets (property, plant, and equipment) are discussed in Chapters 10 and 11. Chapter 12, which explains intangible assets, concludes the first half of the book.

g. Chapter 13, "Income Recognition," emphasizes the conceptual basis of income. This view contrasts with many presentations that discuss these concepts only on a piecemeal basis throughout numerous chapters. Conceptual distinctions and practical application problems are emphasized in Chapter 13.

h. Chapters 14 and 15 discuss accounting short-term and long-term liabilities for both the borrower and lender. Numerous internal revisions have been made in these chapters.

i. Chapters 16 and 17 on corporations have been revised internally to some extent. However, due to the wide acclaim for these chapters, major revisions have not been made.

j. Chapter 18, on investments in equity securities (Part A) and consolidated financial statements (Part B), received only minor revisions. Many intermediate textbooks do not include Part B, which can be omitted without affecting the remaining chapters. We include Part B because many programs use this widely acclaimed discussion, since many students do not take advanced accounting. Also, time permitting, Part B is an excellent assignment to bridge the gap to the consolidations course.

k. Chapter 19, "Cash Flows," has been widely recognized (in supplement format) for its clarity and comprehensiveness. The chapter is based on *FASB 95;* it is not a patchwork of material based on an early exposure draft.

l. Chapters 20 ("Pensions") and 21 ("Leases") have been widely praised for their completeness and accuracy. The innovative spreadsheets illustrated have been used extensively in teaching and in industry. The spreadsheets make these two complex topics readily teachable and understandable.

m. Chapter 23, "Accounting for Income Taxes," is based strictly on the final pronouncement, *FASB Standard 96.* The chapter is not an assortment of ideas based on a prior exposure draft. One academic review characterized this new chapter as "an outstanding first discussion, with understandable illustrations of a uniquely complex and controversial FASB standard."

n. Chapters 22 ("Earnings Per Share and Financial Statement Analysis"), 24 ("Accounting Changes and Errors"), and 25 ("Changing Price Levels"), received minor internal revisions.

Other primary considerations emphasized in revising this textbook were: (1) a clear, direct, and concise style of writing; (2) integration of concepts and applications; and (3) maximum flexiblity of use. A unique degree of flexibility is attained in the following ways:

____ Subdivision of each chapter into clearly differentiated parts—this includes textual material and all homework material.

____ Numerous end-of-chapter supplements.

____ Careful selection of topical sequence within each chapter. Major categories of topical material are designed to stand alone.

____ Distinctive captions within each chapter (four caption levels).

— Careful design of all homework assignments including an unexcelled inventory of questions, exercises, problems, and cases carefully coordinated with each chapter.

For the instructor, this flexibility has the following advantages: design of a course to accommodate the objectives and time constraints of the curriculum; clearly delineated daily assignments; selective variations in topical sequences; and the option to use expanded, typical, or minimal emphasis of individual topics presented. Given the significantly increasing scope of topics currently included in intermediate accounting courses, maximum flexibility in emphasis is essential.

Chapters are arranged in a teachable and logical sequence and are grouped to facilitate both rearrangement and division of materials over semester or quarter intervals as follows:

Chapters by semester: 1–12 (or 13) and 12 (or 13)–25
Chapters by quarters: 1–9, 10–18, and 19–25.

The major changes and new features of this eighth edition can be summarized as follows:

— Major rewrite of the expository materials to enhance understandability and conciseness; special editing to avoid redundancies.
— Redesigned format—one-column for textual material; boldface and color throughout for emphasis; four caption levels to emphasize topical development.
— New chapter introductions—overview and purpose. Includes explanation of the chapter's relationship to prior and following chapters; concise statement of the purpose of the chapter; and a sequential list, by chapter parts, of the major topics discussed.
— Clarity in presenting and illustrating complex and controversial accounting issues. Does not give oversimplified explanations of such topics. Authoritative and conceptually-sound analyses and responses are given. The text continues to give the innovative, comprehensive exhibits that provide: Panel A—situation; Panel B—analysis; Panel C—accounting entries; and Panel D—reporting.
— Conceptual framework of financial accounting is thoroughly developed and referenced throughout. Emphasis is given to conceptual and practical rationales of the accounting methods and procedures discussed. Preferred terminology is used consistently in the book.
— Text provides approximately 1,500 different units from which to select homework assignments. This textbook maintains an *unusual,* clearcut distinction among the questions, exercises, problems, and cases: **Questions** for discussion (a review objective); **Exercises** (application experience directly related to a specific issue discussed in the chapter); **Problems** (integrate several issues in the chapter and in prior—but not subsequent—chapters); **Cases** (practical situations requiring decisions that are seldom obvious). **Each exercise, problem, and case is introduced by a brief statement of the primary issues involved.**

Aids Available For Adopters Include

For the professor:

1. A comprehensive solution's manual in two volumes that includes several typical assignment schedules and detailed step-by-step computations for each homework item. The solutions manual includes estimated completion time for each exercise, problem, and case.
2. Examination bank—over 4,000 questions classified by chapter. Categories: true-false; multiple-choice nonquantitative; multiple-choice quantitative; matching and short-answer; problems and cases; and selected CPA examination multiple-choice questions. Revised by Sandra and David Byrd, Southwest Missouri State University. Periodic supplements covering FASB statements issued subsequent to publication of the text. Designed for distribution to students.
3. The number of overhead transparencies has been doubled to 700. These transparencies consist of *all* problems in both volumes of the soulutions manual.
4. Selected teaching transparencies.
5. Computest II/Teletest Compugrade II. Either by modem or by telephone order, you can create your own tests efficiently and receive masters within 3 days. An optional disk-based gradebook is included.

For the student:

6. A student study guide prepared by David Spiceland, Memphis State University, in two volumes that incorporates the following features for each chapter: (*a*) a brief overview, (*b*) chapter highlights with illustrations, (*c*) true-false questions, (*d*) review questions and exercises, (*e*) new multiple-choice questions, (*f*) CPA exam questions, and (*g*) solutions to review questions and exercises.
7. A complete set of working papers in two volumes (forms with selected captions provided) for working each exercise and problem. A list of key solution figures (provided upon request of the professor).
8. Intermediate Practice Problem I and II by James Benjamin and Stanley J. Kratchman. The first problem gives students the opportunity to apply and reinforce their knowledge of the accounting cycle for a small retail company. Practice Problem II, for the second half of intermediate accounting courses, reviews the basic accounting cycle and integrates it in intermediate topics. Each of the problems includes a solutions manual with check figures and grading hints.
9. Virginia Plantings, Inc., by Winston Shearon and Janice Benjamin, Texas A&M University, is a computerized practice problem allowing students to review, apply, and reinforce their knowledge of the recording process and accounting cycle while familiarizing themselves with computerized accounting systems.
10. Problem Solvers Volume I and II allows the students to solve selected problems from the text using Lotus 1-2-3.
11. Cases in Financial Accounting by Dyckman (Cornell University and Robert Swieringa (Federal Accounting Standards Board) contains over 85 brief cases based on actual corporate financial reports.

Special Acknowledgement

Because of the long and successful tenure of this outstanding textbook, the publisher—Richard D. Irwin, Inc.—and currently active author, Glenn A. Welsch, express their sincere appreciation to the many dedicated contributors and reviewers that made valuable evaluations and contributions through eight editions.

First edition—1963:
Willard J. Graham, University of North Carolina
George H. Newlove, John Arch White, and C. Aubrey Smith, University of Texas

Second edition—1968:
Faculty: Eldon C. Lewis, Wichita State University

Third edition—1972:
Faculty: Jim G. Ashburne, Lewis L. Davidson, Charles H. Griffin, Gary L. Holstrum, and Kermit D. Larson.

Fourth edition—1976:
Faculty: Allen Bizzell, Lewis L. Davidson, Charles H. Griffin, Kermit D. Larson, Fred Streuling, Edward L. Summers, Larry A. Tomassini, and David L. Wilson. Phyllis Barker, Indiana State University, Kathryn C. Buckner, Georgia State University.

Fifth edition—1979:
Faculty: Allen Bizzell, Gary L. Cunningham, James W. Deitrick, John Fellingham, Louis H. Gilles, Jr., Kermit D. Larson, Edward L. Summers, Lawrence A. Tomassini, and David Wilson.

Sixth edition—1982:
Faculty: J. W. Deitrick, Rebecca Gallun, M. H. Granof, R. L. Kellogg, P. A. Langefeld, K. D. Larson, E. C. Nathan, D. P. Newman, and D. G. Short.

Seventh edition—1986:
Faculty: J. R. Dietrich, J. C. Fellingham, M. H. Granof, W. T. Harrison, K. D. Larson, D. P. Newman, J. C. Olsen, D. G. Short, and R. Thompson.
D. Raymond Bainbridge, Lehigh University, Benzion Barley and Sasson Bar-Yosef, Hebrew University of Jerusalem
Sandra D. Byrd and David Byrd, Southwest Missouri State University
Gary M. Cunningham, Polytechnic Institute and State University
David R. Finley, University of Houston
Robert N. Freeman, University of Florida
Randall B. Hayes, Michigan State University
Dennis L. Knutson, Marquette University
David Nix, Boise State University
Petrea Sandlin, University of Texas at San Antonio
James Volkert, Northeastern University

Acknowledgements for the Eighth Edition

Our thanks and gratitude are extended to the outstanding faculty members who provided criticisms, comments, and constructive suggestions prior to and during the preparation of this eighth edition. These reviewers were:

Frances L. Ayres, University of Oklahoma
Wayne G. Bremser, Villanova University
Lloyd L. Buckwell, Jr., Indiana University, NW
Sandra and David Byrd, Southwest Missouri State University
Charles J. Davis, California State University, Sacramento
Peter Dukes, University of Washington
Paul Frishkoff, University of Oregon
Laverne Gebhard, University of Wisconsin–Milwaukee
H. S. Hendrickson, Florida International University
David O. Jenkins, California State University, Stanilaus
Bruce Johnson, University of Chicago
Gary V. Jorden, California State University–Los Angeles
Ronald M. Mano, Weber State College
D. Paul Newman, University of Texas
Leon Trekell, West Texas State University
Paul R. Welch, University of South Carolina–Columbus
Michael Wilson, University of Wisconsin–Eau Claire

Due to time constraints some innovative suggestions from the above reviewers were not used; however, these suggestions will be especially valuable for the next edition.

Our special appreciation and thanks are extended to the following persons who were actively involved during the revision process for superior editorial and technical assistance: Annick M. Barton, University of Texas; Dr. Robert E. Eganoff, University of Texas at San Antonio; Dr. Petrea Sandlin, University of Texas at San Antonio; and Kathleen A. Springer, Peat Marwick Main & Co.

Sincere thanks is given to Cristina De La Fuente, Deanna C. Lester, Dana Walbert, and Jane Z. Zhou for dedicated and superior editing and proofing. Our thanks also is given to Janie Barker and Tricia M. Gutierrez for competently performing the word-processing tasks.

We are indebted to numerous other colleagues and users whose constructive comments and suggestions have led to the improvements reflected in this latest edition. We appreciate the permissions granted by the Financial Accounting Standards Board, American Accounting Association, and American Institute of CPAs to quote from their pronouncements. The AICPA also permitted us to make liberal uses of selected materials adapted from the Uniform CPA Examinations. We are indebted to The Kimberly-Clark Corporation for permission to reproduce their annual report as an appendix to the text.

We will sincerely appreciate comments and suggestions from all sources.

Glenn A. Welsch

CONTENTS

1 THE ENVIRONMENT OF ACCOUNTING AND THE BASIC ACCOUNTING MODEL

OVERVIEW AND PURPOSE

Today you begin your study of intermediate accounting which often is billed as the toughest accounting course. Also intermediate textbooks are long and heavy, but remember they are for two courses—so divide content, pages, weight, number of chapters, and yes cost, by two! Moreover, we can assure you that your rewards may be great. If you accept the challenge and attain the objectives of these two courses, you will have a foundation that will significantly enhance your success in the other accounting and finance courses.

Some persons believe that accounting is "cut and dried," and that it does not challenge creativity, use of judgment, communication skills, and behavioral competence (how to work with others). Yes, it is true, that assets always equal liabilities plus owners' equity, and debits mean left and credits mean right and they too must be equal! But this is not the essence of accounting. Since you cannot, and should not, try to memorize intermediate accounting you must use creativity in mind, judgment on homework and examinations, and even practice good behavioral relations with your fellow classmates and teachers. Throughout these two courses you will find that accounting always has many conceptual and practical problems to resolve that do not have definitive answers, such as whether an oil company should report the cost of drilling a dry hole as an asset or an expense! Resolution of such accounting problems often is tentative because knowledgeable people, groups, companies, governmental agencies, and yes, elected politicians, in good faith, will have different perspectives (i.e., constituencies), and as a result will propound and support different answers.

During your career, whether or not you are a professional accountant, you may have opportunities to actively participate in resolving such problems which necessarily involve a political process. Moreover, your financial security is maximized because your knowledge of accounting will open many windows of opportunity for you in public, private, and governmental accounting. Also, your success as an employee, the owner of a business, or as a consultant will be enhanced by your knowledge of accounting. Ask any manager about this—those that know accounting will confirm this and those that do not will affirm that such knowledge is essential. Opportunities are also unlimited because the total demand for accountants always increases.

Accounting has a conceptual foundation, which you will study in Chapter 6 and the remaining chapters. Accounting as it is used today is the product of its environmental influences that existed in the distant past and up to the present. These environmental influences have determined the conceptual foundation of accounting, the implementation of an accounting model, how an accounting system works, and the characteristics of financial statements. The purpose of this chapter is to give you an overview of these influences by discussing the following major topics:

1. Objectives of financial reporting.
2. Environmental factors that influence accounting.
3. Development of accounting standards.
4. Review of the basic accounting model.

Financial and Management Accounting Compared

The users of financial information can be classified as either internal or external decision makers. **Internal decision makers** are the managers of an entity. These managers are responsible for planning the future of the entity, implementing those plans, controlling daily operations, and reporting to the owners. Because of their close and direct relationship with the entity, they usually can obtain whatever financial data they need at dates of their choice. Much of this information is not intended to be relayed to outsiders. The process of developing and reporting financial information for internal users is called **management accounting.** The reports are called **internal management reports.** Because of the confidential nature of these reports and their primary focus on internal decision making, there is no requirement (other than that specified by the management) that they conform to generally accepted accounting principles (GAAP).

External decision makers are those groups that do not have direct access to the internal operations of the entity. They make decisions about the entity, such as whether to invest or disinvest and whether to extend credit to the entity.

The external users are owners, lenders, suppliers, investors and creditors, employees, customers, financial analysts and advisers, brokers, underwriters, stock exchanges, lawyers, economists, taxing and regulatory authorities, legislators, financial press and reporting agencies, labor unions, trade associations, business researchers, teachers and students, and the public.[1]

The process of developing and reporting financial information to external decision makers is called **financial accounting;** it is the subject of this textbook. External users, because of their detachment from the entity, often cannot directly command specific financial information from the entity; therefore, they must rely on **general-purpose financial statements.** To meet the information needs of external decision makers, the accounting profession has developed a network of accounting concepts, principles, and procedures to assure that external financial statements are relevant and reliable.[2] This network of concepts, principles, and procedures often is called **generally accepted accounting principles (GAAP).**

Objective of Financial Reporting for External Decision Makers

The **objective** of external financial statements and their disclosure notes is to communicate the economic effects of completed transactions and other events on the entity. Although there are other ways to communicate financial information, such as a prospectus (for security offerings), news releases, and management "letters," the primary means are the periodic financial statements. General-purpose financial statements report financial information relevant to (1) investment decisions (by investors), (2) credit decisions (by creditors), and (3) public

---

[1] Financial Accounting Standards Board, *Statement of Financial Accounting Concepts No. 1*, "Objectives of Financial Reporting by Business Enterprises" (Stamford, Conn., November 1978), p. 11.

[2] FASB, *Statement of Financial Accounting Concepts No. 2*, "Qualitative Characteristics of Accounting Information" (Stamford, Conn., May 1980), identifies relevance and reliability as the two primary qualitative characteristics that accounting information is designed to possess. These and other qualitative characteristics are discussed in Chapter 6.

policy decisions. To accomplish these three objectives, two types of financial statements are used:

1. Statement of financial position (i.e., balance sheet), which reports assets, liabilities, and owners' equity at a specified date.
2. Statements that relate to a specified period of time:
   a. Statement of income, which reports revenues, gains, expenses, losses, and net income.
   b. Statement of cash flows, which reports cash flows from operating, investing, and financing activities.

The purpose of external financial statements has been explained essentially as follows in *FASB Statements of Financial Accounting Concepts 2:*

Financial reporting should provide information that is useful to present and potential investors and creditors and other users in making rational **investment, credit, and other decisions.** The information should be comprehensible to those who have a **reasonable understanding** of business and economic activities and **are willing to study** the information with reasonable diligence [par. 34].

Financial reporting should provide information to help present and potential investors and creditors and other users in assessing the **amounts, timing, and uncertainty of prospective cash receipts** from dividends or interest and the proceeds from the sale, redemption, or maturity of securities or loans. The prospects for those cash receipts are affected by an enterprise's ability to generate enough cash to meet its obligations when due and its other cash operating needs, to reinvest in operations, and to pay cash dividends. They may also be affected by perceptions of investors and creditors generally about that ability, which affect market prices of the enterprise's securities. Thus, financial reporting should provide information to help investors, creditors, and others assess the amounts, timing, and uncertainty of prospective net cash inflows to the related enterprise [par. 37].

Financial reporting should provide information about the **economic resources** of an enterprise, the claims to those resources (obligations of the enterprise to transfer resources to other entities and owners' equity), and the effects of transactions, events, and circumstances that change resources and claims to those resources [par. 40].

Professional Accounting

The environment in which accounting operates reflects a long history. Also, it reflects a unique professional independence that exerts a significant impact on present and future concepts and practices.

Accounting dates back to about 3600 B.C. The first published work describing the double-entry system of accounting was authored by Luca Pacioli in 1494 A.D. in Venice. Pacioli's work described double-entry accounting in much the same way as it is used today. Since that time, the industrial revolutions in Europe and the United States, the emergence of the corporation as a major form of business entity, and many other factors have affected accounting. Today, professional accountants have an important and unique role in society. The professional accountant in industry and public practice is usually a **certified public accountant (CPA)** and/or a **certified management accountant (CMA).**

As with lawyers, physicians, and engineers, accountants engage in many activities. Their primary activities are:

1. **Public accounting.** An independent accountant in public practice (i.e., a CPA) offers services such as *(a)* auditing (the attest function), *(b)* tax planning and determination of tax liability, and *(c)* management consulting services (currently this is the fastest growing service). Accountants in public practice have a unique relationship with their clients. These accountants are independent and impartial auditors of the financial statements. Although independent accountants are paid by the client, the courts and government regulators have extended their responsibilities to third parties as well, such as the users of financial statements.
2. **Management accounting.** Large numbers of CPAs and CMAs are employed by business and accounting firms as management accountants, internal auditors, external auditors, income tax specialists, system experts, controllers, management advisory service consultants, financial vice presidents, and chief executives. Management accounting focuses on the planning and controlling functions in an enterprise with special emphasis on internal management reports and related analyses. These internal reports are prepared to meet the needs of internal management and are not intended to be distributed outside the enterprise. CPAs employed by a company are not considered independent accountants and cannot attest to the company's external financial statements.
3. **Governmental and nonprofit accounting.** CPAs and CMAs serve at all levels of government and not-for-profit entities: local, state, national, and international. **In these capacities, they are not independent accountants.**

What Makes a Successful Accountant

Most intermediate accounting students are accounting majors, and perhaps some aren't sure whether they made the correct choice. After all, everyone knows about the green eyeshade image of the accountant. Writers for television and the movies haven't helped diminish this image either. Some people view accounting as being dull—just debits and credits. It is not.

These people just do not understand accounting and financial statements. The practice of accounting requires considerable professional judgment. In one sense, an accountant is like a historian. Information about transactions and events of an entity is recorded and interpreted. The story about what happened during an accounting period is told in the financial statements. It is an important chapter in the entity's history. Historians often disagree about how events concerning great countries or famous people should be written and interpreted. Similarly, accountants can disagree on how the current chapter in the history of an entity should be written. There are alternative accounting methods that can be used to tell the story about what happened. The method selected will determine how the story is told. Sixty or more years ago the accountant had many choices among alternative accounting methods. Today there is a complex body of accounting concepts, principles, and standards that has eliminated many of the choices among accounting alternatives that once existed. The economic environment has become more complex. New types of business transactions arise each day. It is an increasingly difficult challenge for the accountant to meet the fundamental objective of communicating in the financial statements the economic substance of what happened. To meet the challenge, professional accountants (CPAs and CMAs) need a wide range of knowledge and skills such as the:

1. Ability to calculate and analyze data which requires a facility with numbers.
2. Use of diagnostic skills to recognize problems and gather relevant information.
3. Knowledge of many disciplines such as finance, economics, management, marketing, and statistics in order to interpret information and complex transactions.
4. Decision-making ability to make informed judgments.
5. Technical competence reflecting knowledge of accounting concepts and how to research accounting standards in the accounting literature and computerized data banks.
6. Ability to communicate in a concise and understandable manner.
7. Assurance of integrity.

Intermediate accounting provides the opportunity to make substantial progress in acquiring knowledge and developing many of these skills. Accounting is a challenging career in a fast-changing business environment; therefore, developing these skills becomes a career-long process. Nonaccounting majors will also benefit from the knowledge and skills learned in intermediate accounting.

The Need for Financial Accounting Standards

Investors rely on financial statements as an important source of information about business entities. Financial accounting standards are needed to assure that the information provided is relevant to the type of decisions investors must make. For example, short- and long-term creditors scrutinize this information in an effort to evaluate the entity's ability to meet its future cash obligations. Information about the past is useful to them in predicting an entity's future cash flows. Reported information about current liabilities, long-term debts, and stockholders' equity can be used to compute the ratio of debt to equity, which indicates the portion of the assets invested in the business that were provided by creditors. The reported cash flow from operating activities has been found useful in evaluating a firm's ability to make interest payments and repay debt. Prior to July 15, 1988, companies had a choice of whether to report cash flow from operating activities or working capital from operating activities. Studies showed that a cash flow report provides information with much greater relevance to investor decisions. For example, it could be used as a better predictor of business failure. As a result standards were changed to eliminate the choice and the statement of cash flows is now required (covered in Chapters 4 and 19).

Prices of publicly traded shares of common stock are reported daily in newspapers, accompanied by the ratio of share price to net income per share (price-earnings ratio). Security analysts use information from financial statements and other sources to project future earnings. Studies have shown that investors are very concerned about reported earnings. Share prices do react to reported earnings announcements by corporations. Also, share prices react to forecasts of earnings made by a company's top executives or made by a prominent securities analyst. Consequently, companies are greatly concerned about reported earnings because they desire to keep share values high.

Concerns about reported earnings have caused problems in financial reporting over the years. Many corporations set goals for reported earnings in their planning process for the coming years and often for a period of three to five years as well. They have a strong desire to achieve these goals so that common share prices will be favorable. The chief executive officer (CEO) may even announce an earnings goal or forecast to the financial press. This exerts pressure on the company to reach the goal. Unfortunately there are documented cases where companies, unable to attain earnings goals through operations, have resorted to accounting trickery to report the desired result. Accounting standards have developed over time to prevent blatant accounting trickery. For example, one device for manipulating earnings, which is now prohibited by Financial Accounting Standards in the United States, but still practiced in many countries, is to establish arbitrary "reserves." In one documented case, a company listed on the New York Stock Exchange reported $500,000 in 1912 for depreciation expense; but this amount was increased approximately fivefold the next year so that reported profits would remain flat. In 1914, reported profits doubled because depreciation expense was decreased to $1 million. The common stock's value soared from $11 to $50 per share.

Quality of Earnings

Choices among alternative accounting policies do exist, and a review of a company's significant accounting policies and notes to financial statements will reveal how conservative or liberal the firm is in preparing its financial statements. Generally speaking, accounting policies that report income later and expenses earlier are viewed as being conservative and the earnings are viewed as being of higher quality than earnings measured by policies tending toward the opposite extreme. The phrase **earnings quality** or **quality of earnings** became popular in the mid-1970s among professional securities analysts. Various techniques for assessing earnings quality were developed and incorporated in the overall analysis of valuation of common shares of public companies. In the 1960s there were numerous conglomerate enterprises organized by means of a wave of mergers. These empire builders generally swapped shares of their common or preferred stock for the common shares of the acquired company. To be successful they had to keep their reported net income high or their common stock value would not stay high. Some companies resorted to adopting accounting methods solely on the basis of their effect on reported income, ignoring the criteria of whether they reported economic reality. Security analysts finally realized that an analysis of the accounting methods was needed to assess what the reported income figure really meant. No consensus exists as to where to draw the line between high-quality earnings and medium- (or low-) quality earnings.

Although assessing earnings quality is not an exact science, it is a valuable concept for an intermediate accounting student to learn. When studying accounting methods, it is important to assess the likely impact of the method used on reported net income compared to an alternative method. For example, Chapter 8 discusses the last-in, first-out (LIFO) inventory method, which is an alternative to the first-in, first-out (FIFO) inventory method. Generally, analysts would say that the LIFO method results in higher-quality earnings because expenses are reported on the statement of income sooner; but this is not true in all cases. Another example is income recognition (see Chapter 13). When revenue is recorded, an asset is simultaneously recorded. In assessing earnings quality, the question can be asked: "Is this asset potentially distributable in cash and if so, how soon?" The sooner an asset can be converted to cash, and the more certain that the asset can be converted into cash, the higher the quality of earnings. Also, it is important to be alert for accounting estimates made by management that can be used to report higher earnings. For example, choosing a useful life for a productive asset of 10 years instead of 8 years causes depreciation expense, using the straight-line method, to be reported slower.

Disclosure notes are necessary to facilitate evaluation of financial statements because they tend to explain the quality of the earnings. However, arguments have been made that many financial statement readers will ignore the important information contained in the fine print of the disclosure notes. In the mid-1970s, the Securities and Exchange Commission's chief accountant actually issued a ruling that specified the minimum size of the type that could be used in disclosure notes! Today disclosure notes are an integral part of the financial statements.

Income Smoothing

Earnings volatility affects perceived earnings quality. The stock market dislikes uncertainty because it means a greater risk of being surprised by unpleasant news. An increase in perceived uncertainty about a company typically results in a lower market valuation of its common shares. For this reason many companies try to report a stable pattern of rising earnings over time. Another approach is used to project and attain a desired growth rate, such as 15%. Smooth and growing earnings is typically a winning combination.

Companies often look for opportunities to smooth earnings. In the graph below, panel A, notice that earnings per share (EPS) increased from $1 in year 10 to $2 in year 15 in a volatile pattern. Panel B also shows a doubling of EPS, but a smoother pattern is reported because management took steps to smooth earnings. The smoother pattern of reported earnings was attained by taking actions in years 11 and 13 to lower EPS and in year 12 to raise EPS. The effect of these actions is indicated by the arrows. Of course the ideal pattern is to have EPS on the straight line.

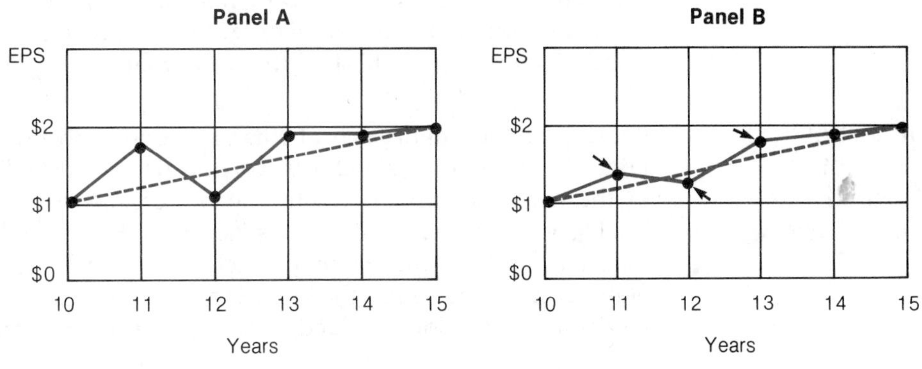

Typically, smoothing actions are taken near the end of the reporting year when management knows whether its EPS will be higher or lower than the goal. To improve EPS, expenses can be deferred until the following year by postponing transactions such as maintenance, and sales can be accelerated into the current year by speeding up shipments at year-end. These actions, if they are completed transactions, are acceptable under accounting standards because they represent changes in economic behavior. Companies have also tried to use accounting techniques to smooth earnings. For example, the desire to minimize expense might influence management's estimate of warranty expense, or the liability for coupons to be redeemed (Chapter 14). The trend in the relatively recent development of accounting standards has been to reduce the opportunities to use accounting techniques to smooth earnings. For example, in the past, companies have had considerable discretion on how they account for research and development costs. If they wanted to lower expenses they would capitalize the costs as an asset and amortize those costs to expense over their estimated useful lives. Meanwhile, other companies in the same industry could be currently expensing all research and development costs. Accounting standards were changed in 1974 (Chapter 12) to require current expensing of all research and development costs; this eliminated the opportunity for income smoothing.

Environmental Factors That Influence Financial Accounting

Accounting is a social science; it is influenced and changed by legal, political, business, and social influences. As a result of these changing influences, accounting concepts, standards and practices often are revised. It is vitally important that accounting evolves to meet the changing needs and demands of society while at the same time it must be a positive cost-benefit activity. That is, the benefits provided by accounting must be in excess of its cost. Also, accounting must be consistent with the current legal and ethical standards of society. Pressures and influences must not be allowed to compromise the ethics of the accounting profession or its measurements of economic events (e.g., business transactions). First and foremost, a professional accountant in public practice must be independent of clients and special interests. Often the reporting of unfavorable economic results may pose major problems for an entity but the results must be accurately and reliably reported. The public interest must predominate. Although accounting is a product of its environment, its first responsibility is to help the environment to be efficient and fair (e.g., not biased). Accounting serves these purposes by providing full and reliable economic information about a broad spectrum of entities. In order for this process to be effective, accounting standards must be established to ensure that the public interest predominates.

Impact of Accounting—Related Organizations

Because of the importance of financial reports to users, there is widespread interest in **accounting standards** and how they are established. Recently, interest in the responses of the accounting profession to its public responsibility to establish accounting standards has increased. For example, accounting standards for oil and gas companies may affect the national energy policy of the United States because they affect the public's awareness of available petroleum reserves. Financial information provided by accountants is important to the effective operation of our economic system. Such information facilitates an efficient allocation of capital in the economy. These are the primary reasons why users of financial statements and the general public are concerned about financial accounting standards.

Among the environmental factors that influence accounting is a group of organizations that expend considerable talents and resources to help develop financial accounting standards (i.e., GAAP). The most influential organizations are described below.

American Institute of Certified Public Accountants (AICPA). The AICPA is the national professional organization of certified public accountants. It responds primarily to the needs of CPAs in public practice. Therefore, its efforts and publications focus on the practice of public accounting. Its primary publications and standard-setting activities include the following:

1. *Journal of Accountancy*—a monthly magazine containing pronouncements, articles, and special sections of interest to independent CPAs.
2. *Accountants' Index*—an annual classified bibliography of the accounting literature published during the year.
3. *Accounting Trends & Techniques*—an annual publication containing a survey of the characteristics of the annual financial reports of 600 corporations.
4. *Accounting Research Studies*—series of early studies that focused on specific accounting issues providing background information, alternative solutions, and in many cases, recommended practices.
5. *Statement of Auditing Standards*—audit practices promulgated by the Auditing Standards Board.
6. Statements that dealt with specific accounting principles, standards, and procedures:
   a. *Accounting Research Bulletins (ARBs)*—During the period between 1938 and 1959, the AICPA's Committee on Accounting Procedure (CAP) was responsible for "narrowing the areas of differences and inconsistencies" in accounting practice. To this end, the Committee issued 51 *Accounting Research Bulletins* and 4 *Accounting Terminology Bulletins;* those not superceded are a part of GAAP.
   b. *Opinions of the Accounting Principles Board (APB)*—In 1959, the AICPA established the Accounting Principles Board (APB) to replace its Committee on Accounting Procedures. The APB designated its pronouncements as *Opinions.* During its existence from 1959 to 1973, the APB issued 31 *Opinions* and 4 *Statements.* In contrast to the *Opinions,* the *Statements* presented recommendations, rather than requirements, for improvement in financial accounting and reporting to external decision makers.[3]
7. Auditing Standards Division, established in 1974, and its Accounting Standards Executive Committee (AcSEC)—Develops *Issue Papers* that iden-

[3] The contents of these *Bulletins, Opinions,* and *Statements* are listed inside the front and back covers of this textbook.

tify, consider alternatives, and present recommendations about current financial reporting issues.

Securities and Exchange Commission (SEC). A number of government regulatory agencies influence accounting and reporting by businesses. Among these agencies are the Internal Revenue Service, Federal Power Commission, Interstate Commerce Commission, and Securities and Exchange Commission. The SEC has a powerful influence on the development of accounting standards.

Because of conditions in the securities market at the beginning of the depression of the 1930s, Congress passed the Securities Act of 1933, the Securities Exchange Act of 1934, and the Public Utility Holding Company Act of 1935. The 1934 act created the Securities and Exchange Commission. The act gave it broad authority to regulate all aspects of the issuance and sale of securities in interstate commerce. Congress gave the Commission authority to prescribe external financial reporting requirements for companies under its jurisdiction. These are the "listed" companies, which means those companies whose shares are sold in interstate commerce. To obtain permission to sell an issue of securities (interstate), a company must submit a prospectus to the SEC.

This prospectus is a public record. The prospectus, which is prepared for a new security issuance, reports information about the company, its officers, and financial affairs. The financial portion of the prospectus must be audited by an independent CPA. After receiving permission to sell securities, the company must file with the SEC, as a matter of public record, audited financial statements each subsequent year (10-K reports) and unaudited quarterly statements (10-Q reports). In most material respects, the annual 10-K reporting requirements are satisfied by the "published financial statements."

The SEC filing and reporting requirements are published as:

1. *Regulation S-X*—This is the original and comprehensive document issued by the Commission, as amended and supplemented. It prescribes the reporting requirements and forms to be filed with the SEC.
2. *Accounting Series Releases (ASRs)*—These releases are amendments, extensions, and additions to *Regulation S-X*.
3. *Special SEC Releases*—These relate to current issues as they arise.
4. *Accounting and Auditing Enforcement Releases (AAERs).*
5. *Accounting Reporting Releases (ARRs).*
6. *Staff Accounting Bulletins (SABs)*—These serve as interpretations of *Regulation S-X* and the *Accounting Series Releases (ASRs).*

These publications continue in force as amended and superseded by the SEC.

The SEC has wide statutory authority to prescribe financial accounting and external reporting requirements for "listed" companies. However, the Commission has relied on the accounting profession to set and enforce accounting standards and to regulate the profession. The working relationship between the SEC and the accounting profession has been positive, and accounting regulation has remained in the private sector. However, on occasion the SEC has forced the accounting profession to move forward in tackling critical problems. These situations occurred in areas where the SEC concluded that the public interest was not being fully served on a timely basis.

American Accounting Association (AAA). The American Accounting Association is an organization primarily for accounting educators; however, its membership includes accountants in public practice, industry, and not-for-profit organizations. Its objectives are to develop accounting theory, encourage and sponsor accounting research, and improve education in accounting. The statements of the AAA do not express GAAP. The Association operates through committees and publishes monographs, committee reports, and periodicals. The periodicals include *The Accounting Review, Accounting Horizons, Issues in Accounting Education,* and other journals published by sections of the AAA. These periodicals contain articles and sections on a wide range of subjects pertaining to accounting research, concepts, and education.

The position papers relating to accounting theory and principles issued by the AAA are normative rather than descriptive. That is, they tend to express what accounting should be, rather than what accounting is as reflected in GAAP. The AAA continues to have a significant impact on accounting standards through its responses to proposed statements of the FASB, and through the teaching, writing, and participating activities of its members.

Governmental Accounting Standards Board (GASB). This Board was created in 1984 to develop accounting standards for governmental units such as state and local entities. It operates under the oversight of the FASB and the Governmental Advisory Council. This textbook focuses primarily on financial reports for businesses rather than on governmental accounting.

Financial Executives Institute (FEI) and the National Association of Accountants (NAA). These organizations have influenced accounting standards favorably in recent years. The FEI publishes the *Financial Executive Magazine* and the NAA publishes *Management Accounting.*

All of these groups and business organizations and industries represent pressure groups that exert influence on the Financial Accounting Standards Board (FASB) and government regulation bodies with federal and state governments.

The Financial Accounting Standards Board is the most influential organization because it is the independent group established to promulgate financial accounting standards. The FASB is discussed in detail later in this chapter and in Chapter 6.

Development of Accounting Standards

There is widespread interest in the process used to develop accounting standards because of *(a)* concern about misleading and inadequate financial reporting, *(b)* the impact of accounting rules on financial statements, and *(c)* a cost-benefit constraint (the cost of producing accounting information versus the benefits to the users). The interested groups are the *(a)* **preparers,** that is, the enterprises that apply accounting standards to develop their own financial statements; *(2)* **auditors,** who give an opinion on the representations in those statements; and *(3)* **users**—the groups that rely on financial statements in decision making. The interests and motivations of these groups often are in conflict because each standing alone may not adequately satisfy the other interested groups and the needs of the general public. Therefore, the standard-setting authority for accounting must reconcile and reach a consensus on these conflicting interests and motivations. The resolution of such conflicts should involve an enlightened **political process.** The objective is to attain a consensus that serves the public interest rather than the self-interest of one or more of the constituent groups. The term **political** often gives a negative impression of self-interest groups. In contrast, the term **political process** is used in the context of attaining a consensus when preparers, auditors, and users negotiate in good faith to resolve their legitimate differences with the general interest dominating. This process should provide a public forum for all inputs, logical analysis, sound judgment, and compromises to serve the general interest.

In addition to the preparers, auditors, and users, a very powerful force—the U.S. Congress—sometimes has become involved in the area of accounting standards and compliance with those standards.[4]

Concern about generally accepted accounting principles arose around 1913 when the first federal income tax was approved by a constitutional amendment. That law posed the question of how net income should be computed. Next, the Great Depression of the 1930s brought into focus the need for generally accepted accounting principles. As a result, in 1938, the AICPA appointed the Committee on Accounting Procedures to provide some definitive accounting principles (see AICPA, page 9). The committee issued the *Accounting Research Bulletins (ARBs)* that set forth what the committee believed GAAP should be. However, the *ARBs* were recommendations only. They were not binding on the preparers and auditors because there was no requirement for adherence.

The committee made a substantive start in developing accounting standards. However, it was a part-time committee and could not devote sufficient time to formulating accounting standards. By the mid-1950s the committee had become inactive. Therefore, in 1959, the **Accounting Principles Board (APB)** was set up by the AICPA. Its basic charge was to *(a)* develop a statement of accounting concepts (i.e., a conceptual foundation of accounting) and *(b)* issue pronouncements on current accounting problems. The APB designated their pronouncements as *Opinions* and issued 31 such *Opinions*.

At the outset, the force of the *APB Opinions,* as had been the case with the *ARBs,* depended on general acceptance. Acceptance was encouraged by **persuasion;** that is, by convincing preparers and independent CPAs that these recommendations were the best solutions to selected accounting problems. By 1964, many leaders of the profession were convinced that persuasion could not reduce the wide range of existing accounting and reporting differences and inconsistencies. In numerous cases, identical transactions could be accounted for by any of several different accounting methods. Net income could be manipulated by selecting a particular accounting approach from among several that were considered to be "generally accepted."

Therefore, a milestone in the development of accounting practice occurred in October 1964. At that time the Council (i.e., the governing body) of the AICPA adopted a requirement that was incorporated into the **rules of ethics** for independent CPAs as follows:

---

[4] "Rep. Dingell to Take Aim at Accountants, SEC in Hearings on Profession's Role as Watchdog," *The Wall Street Journal,* February 19, 1985, p. 4.

Rule 203—Accounting principles. A member shall not express an opinion that financial statements are presented in conformity with generally accepted accounting principles if such statements contain any departure from an accounting principle [[5]] promulgated by the body designated by Council to establish such principles which has a material effect on the statements taken as a whole, unless the member can demonstrate that due to unusual circumstances the financial statements would otherwise have been misleading. In such cases his report must describe the departure, the approximate effects thereof, if practicable, and the reasons why compliance with the principle would result in a misleading statement.

This compliance requirement caused an increased interest in, and concern about, the *APB Opinions* and the *ARBs*. The APB continued the *APB Opinions* and *ARBs* in force because preparers and auditors were required to implement the prescribed accounting standards. Starting in the late 1960s and continuing in the early 1970s, there were many complaints about the process used to develop accounting standards. These complaints criticized *(a)* lack of participation by organizations other than the AICPA, *(b)* "quality" of the *APB Opinions*, *(c)* failure of the APB to develop a "statement of the objectives and principles" underlying external financial reports, and *(d)* insufficient output by the APB.

A major study recommended another more independent standard-setting organization to replace the Accounting Principles Board. This recommendation, approved by the AICPA to be effective July 1, 1973, established the Financial Accounting Standards Board (FASB).

Financial Accounting Standards Board (FASB)

Since July 1, 1973, the Financial Accounting Standards Board has been responsible for establishing the accounting standards that comprise generally accepted accounting principles (GAAP). The FASB is **independent** because it is not affiliated with, nor a part of, any other organization. The report of the special committee to replace the APB with the FASB, as adopted by the AICPA, recommended the following:

1. **Financial Accounting Foundation**—composed of nine trustees appointed by the board of directors of the AICPA. **Responsibilities:** to appoint members of the Financial Accounting Standards Board, to appoint a Financial Accounting Standards Advisory Council, to raise funds to support the new structure, and to periodically review and revise the basic structure.
2. **Financial Accounting Standards Board (FASB)**—composed of seven full-time members. **Responsibilities:** to establish financial accounting standards and to direct a research program to support the standard-setting process.
3. **Financial Accounting Standards Advisory Council**—approximately 35 members. **Responsibilities:** to work closely with the FASB in an advisory

---

[5] This requirement applies to the *FASB Statements of Financial Accounting Standards* and those *Accounting Research Bulletins (ARBs)* and *APB Opinions* that have not been superseded by action of the FASB.

capacity; and to establish priorities, establish task forces, and react to proposed standards.

4. **Research activities**—structured to accomplish specific objectives.[6]

Since its organization in 1973, the FASB has undergone several changes. Currently, its organization and primary activities and other related organizational units are shown in **Exhibit 1–1.**

The first official action of the FASB was to continue in force the then-existing body of GAAP. This body consisted of (1) the *Accounting Research Bulletins (ARBs)* of the Committee on Accounting Procedure (CAP) and (2) the *Opinions* of the Accounting Principles Board (APB). Prior to that time, the CAP and then the APB had been official subentities of the AICPA. To date, the FASB has issued two major categories of pronouncements designated as:

1. *Statements of Financial Accounting Concepts*—The purpose of this series is to provide fundamental concepts on which financial accounting and reporting standards will be based.
2. *Statements of Financial Accounting Standards*—The FASB calls its major pronouncements *Statements of Standards* rather than *Opinions,* which was used by the APB. These statements provide accounting principles and procedures on specific accounting issues.

Currently, the FASB uses "due process" which is open and provides an opportunity for interested parties to express their views. The process used by the FASB involves the following steps:

1. Select and prioritize issues for the Board's agenda.
2. Appoint a representative task force to identify and define the problems and alternatives related to each issue assigned to a task force.
3. Conduct research and analysis about the issue by internal staff and outside experts.
4. Prepare a *Discussion Memorandum* on the issue and distribute it to interested parties, with an invitation to comment.
5. Schedule a public hearing (usually within three months following the *Discussion Memorandum*).
6. Prepare an analysis of all comments received about the issue.
7. Decide whether to issue a standard. If the decision is yes, prepare and distribute to all interested parties an **Exposure Draft** of the standard. An invitation to comment is included.
8. Prepare an analysis of all comments received about the Exposure Draft. Revise the Exposure Draft as needed.

---

[6] AICPA, *Establishing Financial Accounting Standards,* Report of the Study on Establishment of Accounting Principles, American Institute of Certified Public Accountants, March 1972, p. 105 (chair of the Committee, Francis M. Wheat). For a comprehensive and up-to-date description of the mission and operations of the FASB, see Paul B. W. Miller and Rodney J. Redding, *The FASB: The People, the Process, and the Politics* (Homewood, Ill.: Richard D. Irwin, 1986).

Exhibit 1–1
Organizations that have primary responsibilities for setting accounting standards.

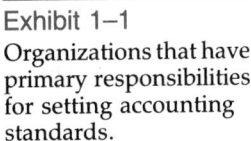

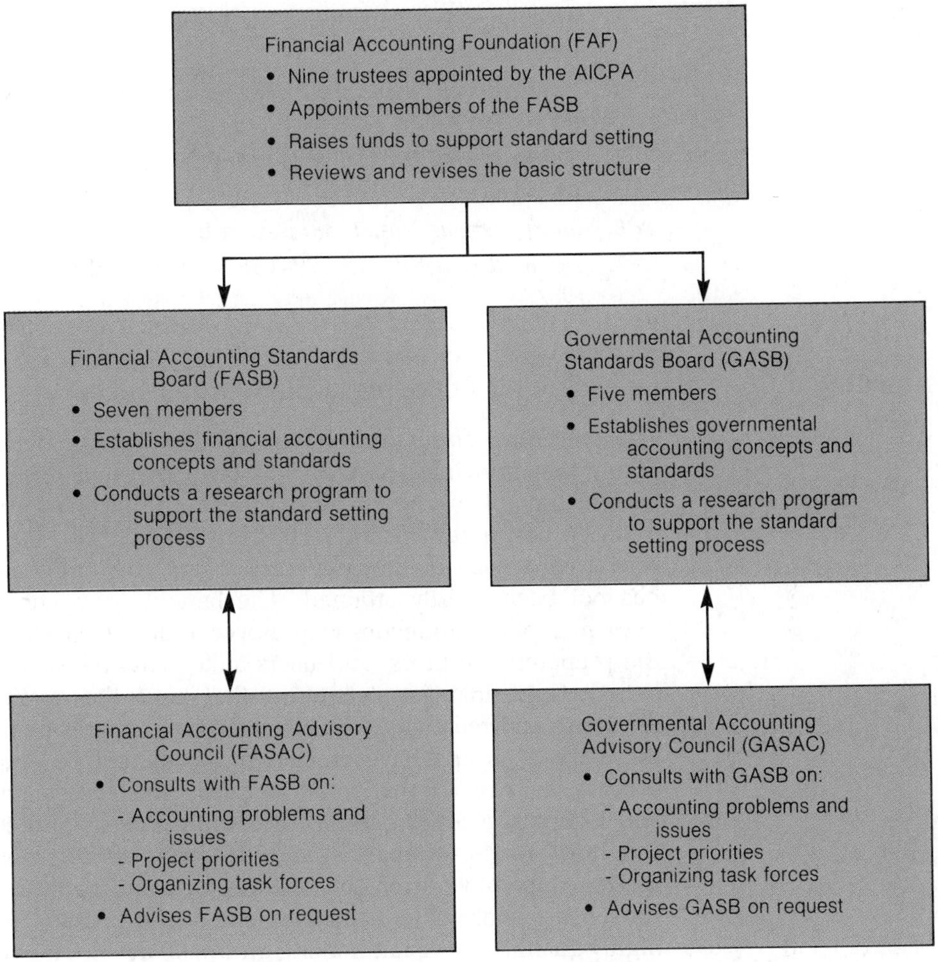

9. Approve (or disapprove) the Exposure Draft as revised, by a vote of at least four of the seven Board members. If approved, distribute the new standard. For complex and controversial issues, some of these steps may be repeated.

Official Accounting Pronouncements Related to GAAP

A list of official pronouncements that are currently in force and the addresses of organizations that are active is given inside the front and back covers. For easy reference by pronouncement, this list gives the *(a)* designated number, *(b)* date issued, and *(c)* title. The pronouncements listed are:

1. *Accounting Research Bulletins (ARBs) Nos. 1–51;* issued by the AICPA, 1939–59.
2. *Accounting Terminology Bulletins Nos. 1–4;* issued by the AICPA, 1953–59.

3. *Accounting Principles Board (APB) Opinions Nos. 1–31;* issued by the AICPA, 1962–73.
4. *Statements of Financial Accounting Concepts Nos. 1–6;* issued by the FASB, 1978–85.
5. *Statements of Financial Accounting Standards Nos. 1–96;* issued by the FASB, 1973–December 31, 1987.
6. *Interpretations Nos. 1–38;* issued by the FASB, 1974–April 1, 1985.
7. *Technical Bulletins Nos. 79–1 to 87–1;* issued by the FASB, 1979–April 1, 1987.

Attaining a Consensus in Setting Accounting Standards

The preceding discussion shows that the development of generally accepted accounting principles (GAAP) has been pursued from the early 1930s to the current time. Throughout those efforts, the primary objective was to develop a conceptual framework and related implementation guidelines that would represent a **consensus** of the preparers, users, and independent CPAs. This goal has not been wholly attained. The benefits of a conceptual framework and implementation guidelines were never in doubt. These guidelines should serve the preparers, auditors, and users alike. That is, each of these groups should benefit from financial statements that have the qualitative characteristics of relevance and reliability. The diverse goals, interests, and influence of each of these three groups have created many difficulties and conflicts. A **political process** is involved that must reconcile the general interest, the conceptual and technical characteristics of accounting itself, and the specific interests of the three groups—preparers, auditors, and users.

The cooperative approach of the preparers, auditors, and users to attain a consensus involved *(a)* establishment of the FASB (1973) as an independent, highly qualified, decision-making group; *(b)* development of a process for resolving accounting issues (see the nine steps summarized above); and *(c)* a requirement that the decisions of the FASB on accounting issues be followed. In the opinion of many people, the success of this process of formulating a consensus on accounting standards depends upon the conceptual soundness, absence of bias, and appropriate cost-benefit trade-offs in the application of the decisions of the FASB.

A directly related issue is **compliance** with the prescribed accounting standards. The FASB has no authority or responsibility to enforce compliance. That responsibility rests with the preparers and the accounting profession primarily through the AICPA, SEC, state boards of accountancy, and the courts. Many observers believe that compliance is a weak link in the chain. This view is supported by *(a)* recurring oversight actions of the SEC, *(b)* increasing litigations in the courts, and *(c)* escalating cost of liability insurance premiums paid by auditing firms.

Throughout the evolution of the standard-setting activities and compliance, the issue persists as to whether these activities should continue to be a responsibility of the private sector or should be taken over by the public sector; that is, by legislative action of the Congress and a federal agency. Many people believe that these activities should reside with the private sector exclusively.

Exhibit 1–2
Participation in attaining a consensus in setting accounting standards.

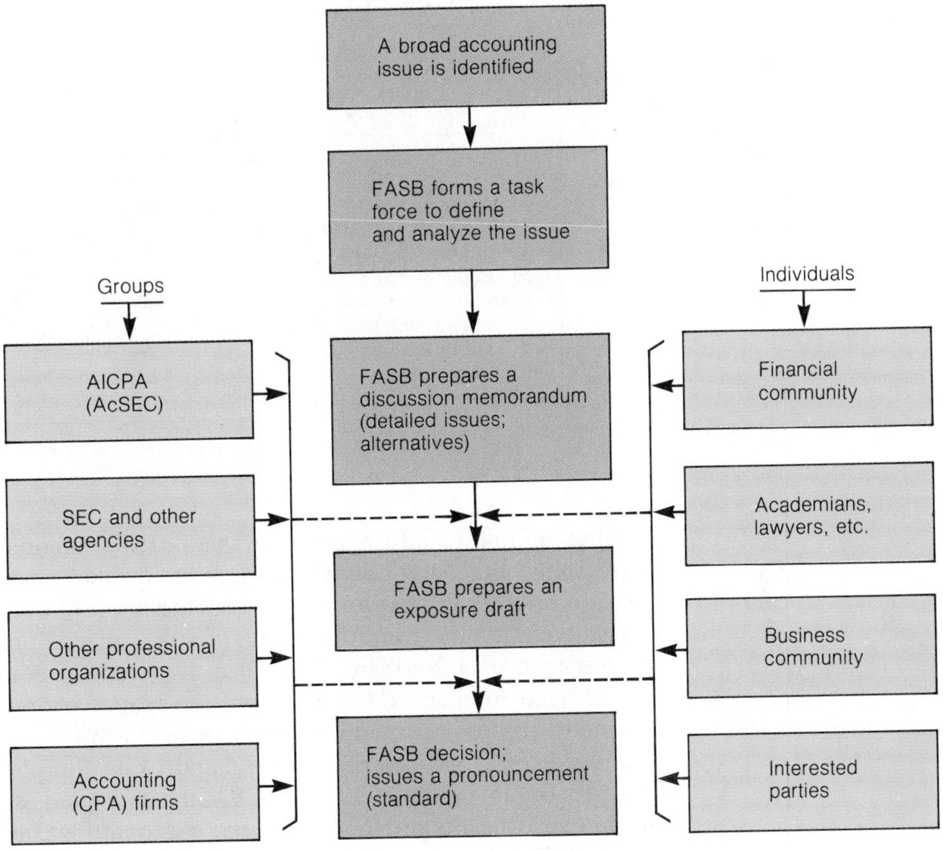

They argue that governmental regulation would not be effective. They believe that the preparers, auditors, and users can provide adequate "policing" action to protect the public interest. They also think that legislative action and a federal agency would result in inflexibility in meeting new challenges, slow reaction time to problems, an ineffective public forum, stereotyped reporting, and a rule-bound environment. Others believe that legislative action and a responsible government agency are necessary to effectively "police" the rule making and enforcement. Still others feel that a cooperative effort by the private and public sectors would be more effective.

The organized units shown in Exhibit 1–1 indicate that the standard setting in accounting remains a responsibility of the public sector. This responsibility is met by a cooperative approach used by the FASB that includes meaningful inputs from preparers, auditors, financial statement users, and other interested groups. This cooperative effort is outlined in **Exhibit 1–2.** Implementation of a cooperative effort, characterized by complex and technical problems and many participants, requires a structured and well-designed process. Currently, to meet this imperative the FASB uses what is called **due process.** The following table shows how the process worked for a recently issued *FASB Statement of Financial Accounting Standards No. 95,* statement of cash flows (October 30, 1987).

The due process is specified in the *FASB Rules of Procedure.* It is designed to ensure public input in the decisions of the FASB. Due process begins with

Nine steps to develop a particular *FASB Standard*

Steps in the FASB due process	Approximate chronology for statement of cash flows*
1. Identify and study the problem	Dec. 1980–Dec. 1983 1984—added to FASB agenda
2. Appoint a task force	1984
3. Issue discussion memorandum	2nd quarter 1984
4. Public comment period	1st quarter 1985
5. Public hearings	2nd quarter 1985
6. Issue exposure draft	July 31, 1986
7. Public comment period	Aug. 1986–Oct. 31, 1986
8. Public hearing	June 1987
9. Issue standard	Oct. 30, 1987—*FASB 95*

*Typically the dates were often changed as unanticipated problems arose during the process.

whether or not to add a topic to the Board's agenda. One member of the Board stated that "the only things that are 'broke' get on the agenda whether they are projects in new areas or reconsideration of old issues."

The average time from the date an issue is placed on the agenda (step 1) to the issuance of a standard (step 9) is two years.[7] A substantial part of this time is used to elicit and analyze written responses received to invitations to comment, discussion memoranda, exposure drafts, and public hearings. The time used for a particular issue is related to its complexity and controversity. Since its organization in 1973, the FASB has issued 96 *Statements of Financial Accounting Standards* and the 6 *Statements of Accounting Concepts*. Of these, approximately 10% have been on new issues, 10% on specific industries, and 80% on old issues revisited. Statements on old issues tend to be the most controversial—one member of the Board identified pension accounting as the most controversial. The controversy mainly was about how much pension liability should be reported on the statement of financial position (discussed in Chapter 20). Some of the controversial issues have been around for more than 50 years. The following is a list of some recurring issues that are still controversial:[8]

1. Capitalization versus expensing:
   Research and development costs.
   Interest costs.
   Software development costs.
   Oil and gas accounting.

---

[7] Adapted from *FASB Viewpoints* a periodic newsletter distributed by the FASB, October 31, 1986.

[8] Paul B. W. Miller and Rodney Redding, *The FASB—The People, the Process and the Politics* (Homewood, Ill.: Richard D. Irwin, 1986).

2. Off-balance sheet financing:
   Leases.
   Pensions.
   Unconsolidated finance subsidiaries.
3. Changing prices.

The Conceptual Framework of Accounting

Accountants have long recognized the need for a definitive explanation of the conceptual framework of accounting. A statement of the conceptual framework of accounting is useful for the following reasons:

- **a.** Standard setting should be consistent with an overall statement of the objectives and concepts of financial reporting.
- **b.** Preparers of financial statements can use the conceptual framework to rationally resolve new accounting problems and practical applications of current GAAP.
- **c.** Users of financial statements (i.e., decision makers) would have better understanding and confidence in financial statements.
- **d.** Financial statements among companies and industries would be more consistent and comparable.
- **e.** Accountants would be better able to assess the validity of different accounting alternatives for similar and dissimilar transactions and events.

For many years considerable attention was given in the accounting literature about various parts of the framework. In fact, there was no single source that articulated a comprehensive and definitive description of a conceptual framework of accounting. When the Accounting Principles Board (APB) was organized (1959) one of its charges was to develop a conceptual framework for accounting. It was unable to complete the project. In turn, the FASB was also given a similar charge. In response, the FASB has published the six *Statements of Financial Accounting Concepts* summarized in **Exhibit 1–3.** This conceptual framework of accounting is a milestone because it is the first such statement. Even though there is not full agreement on the framework, it supports most current GAAP, and points the way for future progress. We will refer to the framework often in this textbook.

What Is GAAP?

GAAP is the widely used acronym for generally accepted accounting principles. This usually is defined as the broad guidelines, conventions, rules, and procedures of accounting. GAAP comes from two main sources as follows:

1. Pronouncements by designated authoritative bodies that must be followed in all applicable cases. The primary designated bodies are the Financial Accounting Standards Board *(Statements),* Accounting Principles Board *(Opinions),* Committee on Accounting Procedures (selected pronounce-

Exhibit 1–3
Overview of the *FASB Statements of Financial Accounting Concepts.**

No.	Date	Title	Primary topics
1	Nov. 1978	Objectives of Financial Reporting by Business Enterprises	1. Financial statement users defined. 2. Objectives of financial statements. 3. Perspective of the conceptual framework.
2	May 1980	Qualitative Characteristics of Accounting Information	1. Primary qualities: *a.* Relevance. *b.* Reliability. 2. Secondary quality: comparability. 3. Threshold of recognition; materiality. 4. Implementation constraints.
3	Dec. 1980	Replaced by No. 6	
6	Dec. 1985	Elements of Financial Statements of Business Enterprises	1. Assets, liabilities, owners' equity, investments and distributions by owners, and comprehensive income. 2. Revenues, expenses, and gains and losses. 3. Accrual accounting.
4	Dec. 1980	Objectives of Financial Reporting by Nonbusiness Organizations	Outside the scope of this textbook.
5	Dec. 1984	Recognition and Measurement in Financial Statements of Business Enterprises	1. Recognition criteria. 2. Measurement criteria. 3. Accounting assumptions, principles, and constraints. 4. A full set of financial statements prospective.

* Discussed in Chapter 6.

ments), and the Securities and Exchange Commission (regulations for listed companies). This part of GAAP is identified in the remaining chapters by references to the sources.

2. Pronouncements developed by respected bodies and industries or have evolved over time. This part of GAAP sometimes is difficult to identify by source; the source may be "general acceptability." Therefore, considerable disagreement exists among accountants about GAAP from these sources. However, a considerable part of this kind of GAAP is formally expressed in such publications as *AICPA Statements of Position, Accounting and Auditing Guides,* and *FASB Technical Bulletins.* In some instances, specific topics not covered by these sources can be found in the accounting literature, including textbooks. Rubin's "The House of GAAP," which is adapted in **Exhibit 1–4,** gives an interesting and valid overview of the

Exhibit 1–4
The House of GAAP.

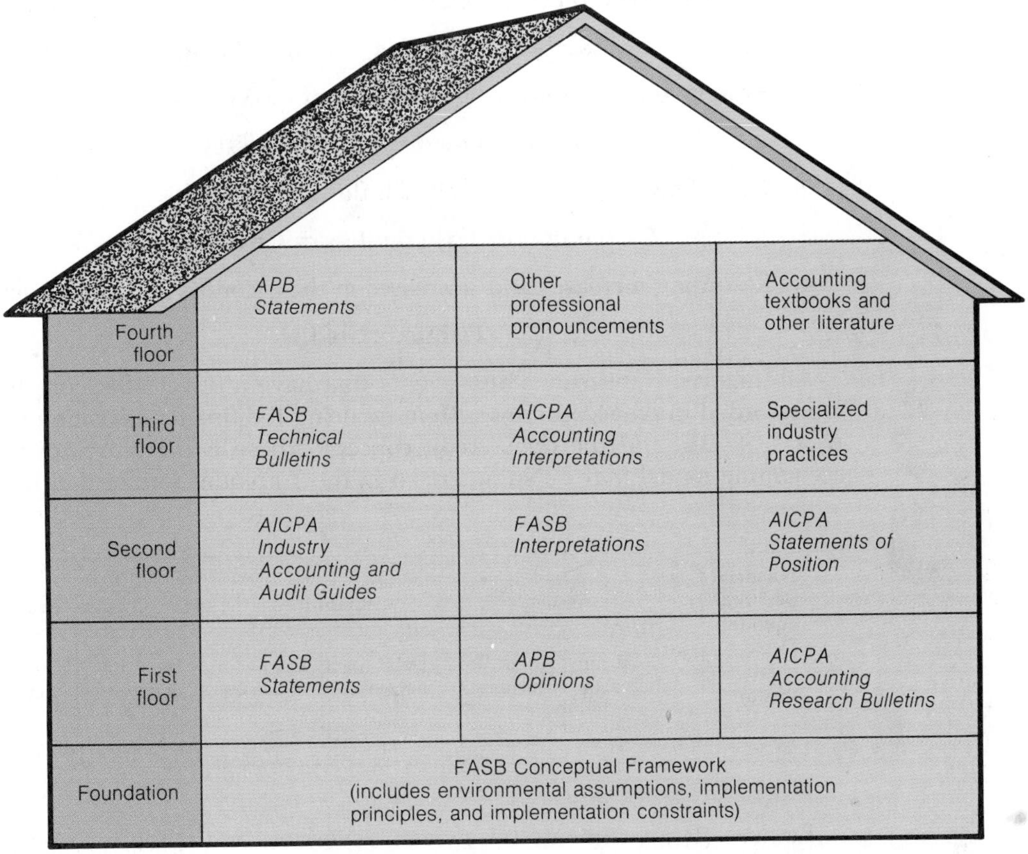

profusion of "statements, opinions, and other pronouncements" about generally accepted accounting principles.[9]

The Basic Accounting Model Reviewed

Current generally accepted accounting principles require three financial statements as a minimum: (1) statement of financial position, (2) statement of income, and (3) statement of cash flows.

These statements are produced by an entity's accounting system (discussed in Chapters 3 and 4). An accounting system is designed to *(a)* collect economic data about each transaction, *(b)* analyze and record the data, and *(c)* produce summarized data which is reported in the periodic financial statements. The data collected are analyzed and recorded, and reported in an accounting format

[9] Steven Rubin, "The House of GAAP," *Journal of Accountancy,* June 1984, p. 123.

which may be called the **basic accounting model.** The primary equations in this model can be outlined as follows for review purposes:[10]

1. **Financial Position** (the statement of financial position equation):

   Assets = Liabilities + Owners' equity

2. **Results of Operations** (the statement of income equation):

   Revenues + Gains − Expenses − Losses = Income

3. **Cash Flow** (the statement of cash flows equation):

   Cash inflow − Cash outflow = Change in cash

4. Recording increases and decreases in the accounts (algebraic balancing):

   Debits = Credits

All financial transactions and events that have a direct effect on the entity are recorded in an accounting system by using the financial position equation: **A = L + OE,** and the debit-credit concept. These two features of the basic accounting model may be summarized in the T-account format that follows:

Financial position equation	**Assets**		=	**Liabilities**		+	**Owners' equity**	
Debit = credit feature	Debit for increases	Credit for decreases		Debit for decreases	Credit for increases		Debit for decreases	Credit for increases

Because (1) investments by owners, revenues, and gains **increase** owners' equity and (2) distributions to owners, expenses, and losses **decrease** owners' equity, the model can be expanded as follows:

Assets		=	**Liabilities**		+	**Owners' equity**	
Debit for increases	Credit for decreases		Debit for decreases	Credit for increases		Debit for decreases: *a.* Distributions to owners. *b.* Expenses. *c.* Losses.	Credit for increases: *a.* Investments by owners. *b.* Revenues. *c.* Gains.

In the preceding diagram, the debits are **always** on the left and the credits are **always** on the right. Therefore, the **increases and decreases are in opposite**

[10] According to *Webster's Ninth New Collegiate Dictionary,* the definition of a model is: "a system of postulates, data, and inferences presented as a mathematical description of an entity or state of affairs."

positions on each side of the equation. That is, debits represent increases to assets and decreases to liabilities and owners' equity, whereas credits represent decreases to assets and increases to liabilities and owners' equity. Expenses and losses are recorded as debits, and revenues and gains as credits. This algebraic arrangement forces debits to always equal credits. Thus, the fundamental accounting model always has a **dual balancing feature:**

1. Assets = Liabilities + Owners' equity.
2. Debits = Credits.

Because of this dual feature, the accounting model often is referred to as a **double-entry accounting system.** The balancing features add reliability to the output of an accounting system by calling attention to those errors which cause an imbalance in the model.

Whether an accounting system is maintained manually, mechanically, or electronically, each entry is recorded in the format of the basic accounting model. Thus, each entry recorded in an accounting system retains the dual-balancing feature standing alone and also on a cumulative basis.

Application of the basic accounting model for seven typical transactions is reviewed in **Exhibit 1–5.** Notice the following aspects of that exhibit:

a. Column B, the accounting analysis of each transaction to determine its effects on assets, liabilities, and owners' equity.
b. Column C, the effects of each transaction, which balance both individually and cumulatively.
c. Column D, the journal entry that records each transaction (discussed below).

We suggest that you study this exhibit to review the methods learned in your principles course.[11]

Nature of Transactions

Two kinds of transactions are **recorded** in an accounting system:

1. External transactions between the entity and one or more external parties that change some combinations of the entity's assets, liabilities, and owners' equity. These transactions may be either *(a)* **reciprocal,** when the entity **both** transfers and receives resources or services (e.g., payment for services received), or *(b)* **nonreciprocal,** when the entity **either** transfers or receives resources (e.g., payment of a cash dividend or receipt of a gift) or nonresources (e.g., a stock dividend).
2. Internal events (within the entity) and external transactions that are not exchange transactions but nevertheless change some combination of the entity's assets, liabilities, or owners' equity (e.g., depreciation of equip-

[11] See G. A. Welsch and D. S. Short, *Fundamentals of Financial Accounting*, 5th ed. (Homewood, Ill.: Richard D. Irwin, 1987).

Exhibit 1–5
Application of the basic accounting model reviewed.

Column A Typical transaction	Column B Transaction analysis	Column C Effect on the statement of financial position			Column D Journal entry into the accounting system		
		A = L + OE			Accounts	Debit	Credit
1. Service Corporation was organized; owners invested $100,000 cash and received nopar common stock.	Asset increased—cash, $100,000	+100,000			Cash	100,000	
					Common stock		100,000
	Owners' equity increased—common stock, $100,000			+100,000			
	Liabilities—no effect.						
Cumulative balance		100,000	-0-	100,000		100,000	100,000
2. Borrowed $50,000 on a note payable.	Asset increased—cash, $50,000	+ 50,000			Cash	50,000	
					Notes payable		50,000
	Liabilities increased—notes payable, $50,000		+50,000				
	Owners' equity—no effect.						
Cumulative balance		150,000	50,000	100,000		150,000	150,000
3. Purchased equipment for use in the business, $40,000; paid cash.	Asset increased—equipment, $40,000	+ 40,000			Equipment	40,000	
					Cash		40,000
	Asset decreased—cash, $40,000	− 40,000					
	Liabilities—no effect.						
	Owners' equity—no effect.						
Cumulative balance		150,000	50,000	100,000		190,000	190,000

4. Services rendered to clients, $20,000, of which $15,000 was collected in cash.	Assets increased—cash, $15,000 .... accounts receivable, $5,000 .... Owners' equity increased—revenue, $20,000 .... Liabilities—no effect.	+ 15,000 + 5,000		+ 20,000	Cash .... Accounts receivable .... Service revenue	15,000 5,000	20,000
Cumulative balance ...	....	170,000	50,000	120,000		220,000	220,000
5. Incurred operating expenses, $11,000, of which $8,000 was paid in cash.	Asset decreased—cash, $8,000 .... Liability increased—accounts payable, $3,000 .... Owners' equity decreased—expense, $11,000	− 8,000	+ 3,000	−11,000	Expenses .... Cash .... Accounts payable ...	11,000	8,000 3,000
Cumulative balance ..	....	162,000	53,000	109,000		221,000	221,000
6. Paid $2,000 on accounts payable (5 above).	Asset decreased—cash, $2,000 .... Liability decreased—accounts payable, $2,000 .... Owners' equity—no effect.	− 2,000	− 2,000		Accounts payable ...... Cash	2,000	2,000
Cumulative balance ..	....	160,000	51,000	109,000		223,000	223,000
7. Depreciation for 1 year on equipment; estimated life, 10 years, no residual value (3 above).	Asset decreased—accumulated depreciation, $4,000 ...... Owners' equity decreased—depreciation expense, $4,000 .... Liabilities—no effect.	− 4,000		− 4,000	Depreciation expense ... Accumulated depreciation, equipment	4,000	4,000
Cumulative balance ..	....	156,000	51,000	105,000		227,000	227,000

ment, use of inventory in the production of other goods, and casualty losses and gains).[12]

Summary

This chapter discussed the environmental influences that affect accounting and the role of various organizations in the accounting environment. The basic accounting model and its use in an accounting system are an important aspect of accounting because each transaction is analyzed, recorded, and its economic effects on the entity are reported in the periodic financial statements. The remaining chapters will continue the emphasis on the basic model.

The next three chapters provide a concentrated review of your prior principles courses. After completing that review (and Chapter 5 on present and future value), we will discuss the conceptual framework developed by the FASB. At that time you will be ready to start "intermediate accounting," learn about the conceptual framework, and understand its application in the chapters that follow.

QUESTIONS

1. Define accounting.
2. Explain the distinction between financial and management accounting. Does this distinction mean that a company should have two accounting systems? Explain.
3. What is meant by general-purpose financial statements? What are their basic components?
4. What is the basic objective of external financial statements?
5. Explain why the emphasis in financial accounting is on communication.
6. What are the primary areas of service provided by certified public accountants (CPAs)?
7. The independent CPA fulfills a unique professional role that involves the concept of independence. Why is that concept important to society in general?
8. The following statements relate to accounting principles, standards, and procedures. For each, you are to briefly explain its primary purpose and current status.
   a. *Accounting Research Bulletins.*
   b. *Opinions* of the APB.
   c. *FASB Statements of Financial Accounting Standards.*
   d. *FASB Interpretations.*
   e. *FASB Statements of Financial Accounting Concepts.*
9. Explain the developments that led to the establishment of the FASB.
10. Briefly explain the role that the SEC has fulfilled in the establishment of accounting standards. What has been its relationship to the accounting profession in this role?
11. What is the AAA? What role has it fulfilled in the development of accounting theory and standards?
12. Explain why there is widespread interest in the development of accounting standards.
13. Briefly explain the "due process" system that is used by the FASB to develop an accounting standard.
14. Why is a consensus important with respect to accounting standards? How is a consensus attained at the present time?

---

[12] The term **transactions** will be used in this textbook to include both transactions and the other events to be recognized.

EXERCISES

E 1–1 (Distinguish between Financial and Management Accounting)

The two basic types of accounting and reporting are called: F—Financial accounting and M—Management accounting. Below are listed 10 characteristics of accounting and reporting. Match the types with the characteristics by entering an F or M in each blank shown to the left. If not applicable enter N.

Type		Characteristics of accounting and reporting
_____	1.	GAAP must be followed in all respects.
_____	2.	External users are of primary concern.
_____	3.	Relates to planning and controlling the operations of an entity.
_____	4.	Does not primarily use general-purpose financial statements.
_____	5.	Information for both internal and external use.
_____	6.	Of particular interest to investors and creditors.
_____	7.	Does not have to conform to GAAP in all respects.
_____	8.	Provides information that is useful to external users in predicting future cash flows.
_____	9.	Internal users are of primary concern.
_____	10.	Seldom, if ever, subject to independent audit.
_____	11.	Does not relate primarily to internal planning and control.
_____	12.	Information primarily for internal use.
_____	13.	Usually not available to external users.
_____	14.	Uses general-purpose financial statements.
_____	15.	Users have direct access to the internal operations.

E 1–2 (Chapter Overview)

Indicate whether each statement is true or false.

T F 1. GAAP must be followed for all items in management accounting and financial accounting reports.

T F 2. Financial accounting focuses primarily on external users of financial statements.

T F 3. General-purpose financial statements are prepared primarily for internal users.

T F 4. Management accounting is directly concerned with stockholders and creditors.

T F 5. Management accounting reports usually are not subject to an independent audit.

T F 6. A CPA always serves in an independent role.

T F 7. CPAs in public accounting practice are not permitted to become involved in management services.

T F 8. The attest and audit functions are the same.

T F 9. Disclosure notes are considered to be an integral part of external financial statements.

T F 10. Management accounting reporting requires a statement of financial position, statement of income, and a statement of cash flows.

T F 11. Internal reporting (i.e., management accounting) must follow GAAP all respects.

T F 12. External financial reports (i.e., financial accounting) are directed primarily to stockholders, creditors, and other similarly situated groups.

E 1–3 (Identify Accounting Organizations)

Listed below are the organizations that are active in setting accounting standards and the designation of some of those standards. To the right are commonly used abbreviations. You are to match the designations with the abbreviations by entering the appropriate letters to the left.

	Designation	Abbreviation
A	Sample: Certified Public Accountant.	A. CPA.
____	1. Accounting Research Bulletin.	B. FASB.
____	2. Accounting Principles Board.	C. GAAP.
____	3. Committee on Accounting Procedures.	D. AICPA.
____	4. Securities and Exchange Commission.	E. CAP.
____	5. Financial Accounting Standards Board.	F. 10-Q report.
____	6. SEC annual reports (required).	G. APB.
____	7. American Institute of CPAs.	H. ARB.
____	8. SEC quarterly report (required).	I. AcSEC.
____	9. Financial Executives Institute.	J. SEC.
____	10. Generally accepted accounting principles.	K. 10-K report.
____	11. Accounting Standards Executive Committee.	L. FEI.
____	12. Internal Revenue Service.	M. IRA.
____	13. National Association of Accountants.	N. NAA.

E 1–4 (Sources of GAAP)

The accounting profession has a long history of developing accounting concepts and their application that constitute generally accepted accounting principles (GAAP). Listed below are some representative documents. You are to identify each document with its source by entering appropriate letters to the left.

	Document	Source
____	1. Accounting Research Bulletins (ARBs).	A. Accounting Principles Board
____	2. Interpretations (of Financial Accounting Standards).	B. AICPA Committee on Accounting Procedures.
____	3. Discussion Memoranda.	C. Securities and Exchange Commission.
____	4. Statement of Basic Accounting Theory.	D. Financial Accounting Standards Board.
____	5. Technical Bulletins.	E. American Accounting Association.
____	6. Accounting Terminology Bulletins.	F. American Institute of Certified Public Accountants.
____	7. Statements of Financial Accounting Standards.	G. AICPA Committee on Terminology.
____	8. Regulation SX.	
____	9. Statements of Financial Accounting Concepts.	

E 1–5 (Consensus Groups in Standard Setting)

The process of attaining a consensus in developing accounting standards involves three major groups, each of which is directly concerned about general-purpose financial statements. Each major group is composed of various subgroups (i.e., organizations, interest groups, and individuals).

The three major groups and some subgroups are listed below. You are to identify the subgroups with the major groups by entering appropriate letters to the left; provide comments when needed to clarify your response.

	Subgroups	Major groups
_____	1. American Institute of CPAs.	A. Preparers.
_____	2. Current stockholder.	B. Auditors.
_____	3. General Motors.	C. Users.
_____	4. WTK Labor Union.	D. None of the above (explain).
_____	5. Financial Executives Institute.	
_____	6. X, Y, Z, Big-8 accounting firm.	
_____	7. Lending institutions.	
_____	8. Securities and Exchange Commission.	
_____	9. OK Bookkeeping Service.	
_____	10. Financial analysts.	
_____	11. Sole owner of a small business.	
_____	12. American Accounting Association.	
_____	13. State Board of Public Accountancy.	
_____	14. Potential investors.	
_____	15. Financial Analysts Federation.	
_____	16. Employees of companies.	
_____	17. Teachers and students.	
_____	18. Taxing and regulatory authorities.	
_____	19. Legislators.	
_____	20. Two-member local CPA firm.	

PROBLEMS

P 1–1 (Review—Transaction Analysis)

Eight 19A transactions of X Corporation are given below. You are to set up an eight-column response form exactly like Exhibit 1–5 in this chapter. In column A, enter the transaction number only and complete the remaining columns.

Transaction:

1. X Corporation was organized and the owners invested $150,000 cash and received 100,000 shares of common stock, par $1. Hint: credit the excess above par to a separately appropriately titled account.
2. Purchased a building and the site (land) for $100,000 cash; 25% of the cost applied to the land.
3. Purchased merchandise for resale, $30,000; paid 80% cash and the balance on credit (periodic inventory system).
4. Sold merchandise for $25,000; received 60% cash and the balance on credit (periodic inventory system).
5. Incurred operating expenses, $15,000; 10% on credit and the balance paid with cash.
6. Depreciated the building for 1 year; 15-year life, no residual value.
7. Paid in full the credit amount in (5).
8. Collected in full the credit amount in (4).

P 1–2 (Review—Transaction Analysis)

Ten 19B transactions of TV Service Company are given below. You are to set up an eight-column response form exactly like Exhibit 1–5 in this chapter. In column A, enter the transaction letters only and complete the remaining columns.

Transaction:

A. Borrowed $100,000 cash on a two-year, 10% note.
B. Rendered services, $100,000; collected 90% cash.

C. Incurred operating expenses, $30,000; paid 80% cash.
D. Collected cash for all of the credit in B.
E. Purchased a new service truck, $20,000; note to finance three-fourths at 12%, balance paid in cash.
F. Paid interest for six months on the note in (A).
G. Made a cash contribution of $50 to the United Fund.
H. Paid all of the credit amount in (C).
I. Paid the local newspaper for a $70 ad.
J. Depreciated the service truck in (E) for a half year; estimated useful life, five years; no residual value.

CASES

C 1–1 (Accounting Principles)

At the completion of the annual audit of the financial statements of AB Corporation, the president of the company asked about the meaning of the phrase **generally accepted accounting principles** that appears in the audit report on the management's financial statements. He observes that the meaning of the phrase must include more than what he considers to be "principles."

You have been asked to respond to the president's question. You have decided to respond in terms of the following:

1. The meaning of the term **accounting principles** as used in audit reports (excluding what "generally accepted" means).
2. How the determination is made as to whether or not an "accounting principle" is generally accepted. Consider sources of evidence to determine whether or not there is substantial authoritative support (do not merely list titles of documents).
3. Diversity in accounting practice will, and should, always exist among companies despite efforts to improve comparability. Discuss arguments that support this statement.

(AICPA adapted)

C 1–2 (Sources of Accounting Standards)

The four primary "sources" of specified accounting standards (GAAP) include the Committee on Accounting Procedures, Accounting Principles Board, Financial Accounting Standards Board, and the Securities and Exchange Commission. This case involves consideration of these sources, their current status, their characteristics, and some assessments of the related successes and shortcomings.

Required:

1. Background—For each of the four sources of specified GAAP, identify the sponsoring, or appointing, organization and give the time period of activity.
2. Background continued—Give the designations of the pronouncements (or publications) issued; the numbers issued; and, in general, their current status.
3. Characterize each of the four sources of accounting standards as either a public or private sector organization. Assess the successes and weaknesses of each source.
4. Explain and assess the following approaches to setting accounting standards: *(a)* private sector exclusively, *(b)* public sector exclusively, and *(c)* jointly. Include a consideration of the "politics" of a standard-setting approach.

2 REVIEW: THE ACCOUNTING INFORMATION PROCESSING SYSTEM

OVERVIEW AND PURPOSE

An accounting system must be designed to (1) collect and measure economic data relating to the entity, (2) classify and process the data, and (3) summarize economic effects in financial reports for decision makers. An accounting system should be tailored to the characteristics of an entity such as size, nature of operations, volume of data to be processed, organizational structure, information needs of the internal and external decision makers, and extent of governmental regulation.

The purpose of this chapter is to **review** the processing of financial data during and at the end of an accounting period, and the reporting of summary information in the periodic financial statements. To accomplish this aim, the chapter is subdivided as follows:

1. The accounting information processing system (11 phases).
2. Adjusting entries.
3. Closing entries.
4. Reversing entries.
5. Information processing for interim reports.

Supplement 2–A: Control Accounts, Subsidiary Ledgers, and Special Journals

1. Control accounts and subsidiary ledgers.
2. Special journals.

The Accounting Information Processing System

An accounting system should provide a systematic and efficient process that records all transactions, classifies the data, and produces the periodic financial statements.[1] Transactions occur and must be recorded each business day. Because the financial statements are produced at the end of the **reporting period,** the accounting processing system involves a series of sequential phases (or steps) that are repeated each accounting period. These sequential phases often are referred to as the **accounting processing cycle.**

Exhibit 2–1 diagrams a typical accounting processing cycle; it shows the sequence in which the various phases usually are completed. Notice that *(a)* Phases 1–4 occur continuously **during** the accounting period, *(b)* Phases 5–10 occur **only** at the **end** of the accounting period, and *(c)* Phase 11 occurs **only** at the **start** of the **next** accounting period.

Collecting Economic Data on Each Transaction (Phase 1)

An accounting system must collect data about each transaction and event that should be recorded by the entity during the reporting year. Economic data are collected from all parts of the entity's operations by means of **source documents.** Because exchange transactions involve external parties, they generate their own source documents—sale invoices, freight bills, notes signed by debtors, purchase invoices, deposit slips, checks, and so on. For nontransaction events, the entity itself will create the source documents. The source documents are important because *(a)* they provide data necessary for transaction analysis (and the resulting journal entry), and *(b)* they constitute a tangible record so that each transaction and event, and the measurement of its effects on the entity, can be subsequently traced and verified when such a need arises.

Analyzing Each Transaction (Phase 2)

The analysis of each transaction during the **reporting period,** based upon the data provided by source documents, involves an assessment of the transaction's economic impact on the entity in terms of its assets, liabilities, owners' equity, revenues, expenses, gains, and losses. This analysis is needed to develop the **accounting entry,** or entries, that must be recorded in the accounting system. Transaction analysis often requires a high degree of accounting knowledge to ensure that the periodic financial statements are reliable. Effective transaction analysis depends upon a sound knowledge of the concepts, principles, and procedures of accounting that will be discussed in Chapter 6.

Journalizing—The Original Data Input (Phase 3)

This phase involves the **original recording** of each transaction during the reporting year in an accounting system. This is called **journalizing.** Each transaction is first recorded in a **journal,** which is a chronological record (i.e., by order of transaction date). Journalizing is the process of recording the effects of transactions in the journal. A journal entry lists the date of the transaction, the account(s) debited and credited (and indented), and their respective amounts. Each entry is recorded so that the duality of the system is maintained: A = L + OE and

---

[1] The term **transactions** will be used to include both transactions and the other events to be recognized.

Exhibit 2–1
Diagram of a typical accounting information processing cycle.[a]

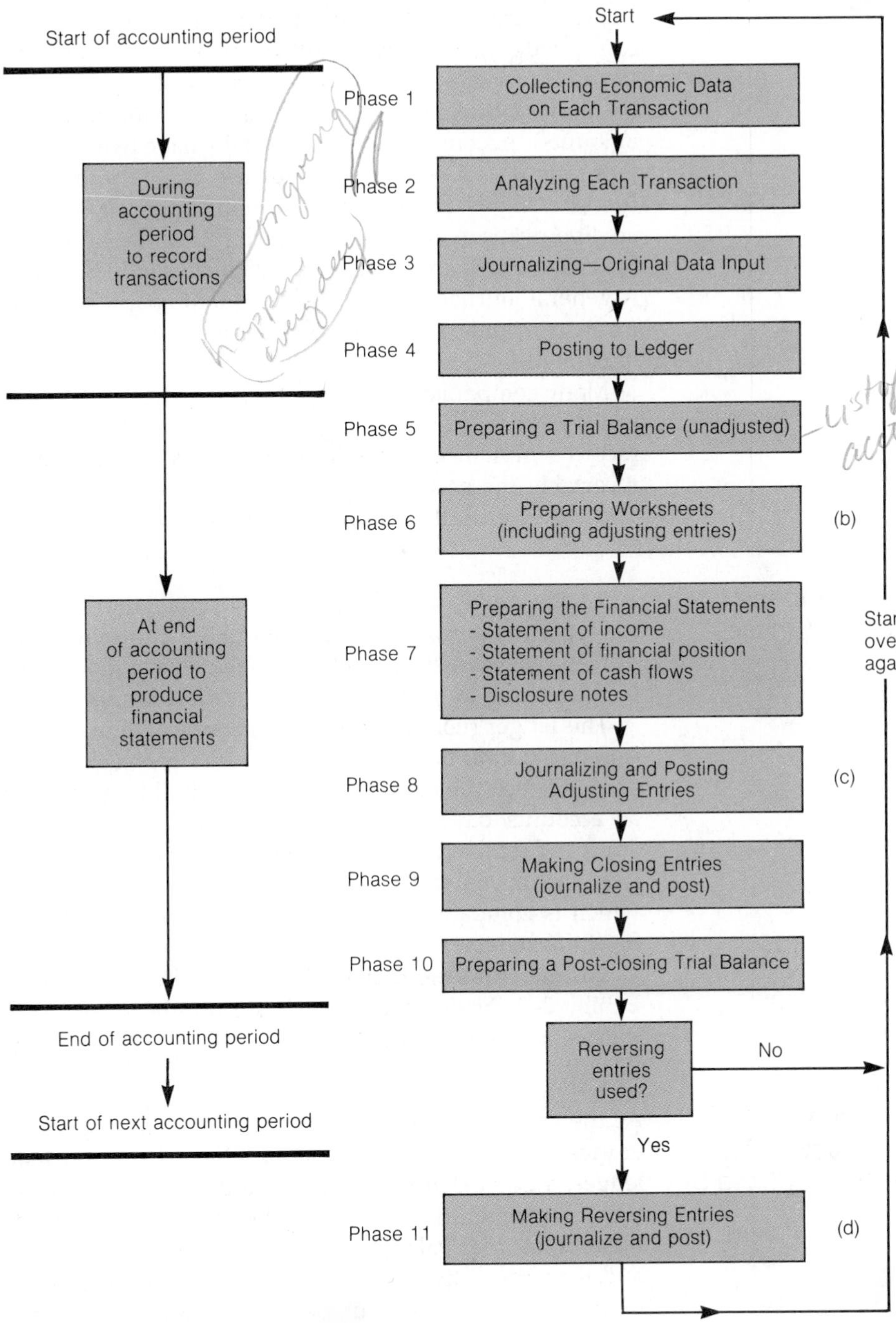

Notes:
(a) See Exhibit 2-9 for a complete summary.
(b) A worksheet is optional. If not used, prepare an adjusted trial balance after Phase 8 as a basis for preparing the financial statements.
(c) Usually completed after the financial statements in order to allow distribution of the financial statements at the earliest possible date.
(d) Reversing entries are optional.

Debits = Credits. Although the journal is not essential (one could input directly to the ledger), it is important because it *(a)* maintains a chronological record of the transactions recognized in the system, which is useful for tracing, and *(b)* shows all aspects of each transaction (i.e., all accounts affected and the amounts). Accounting systems usually have two types of journals: (1) the general journal and (2) several special journals. Special journals are useful for transactions that are highly repetitive. Commonly used special journals are credit sales, credit purchases, cash receipts, cash payments, and the accounts payable journal. Special journals are discussed and illustrated in Supplement 2–A of this chapter. A general journal is used in subsequent chapters because it is especially useful for instructional purposes. The general journal format, with a typical entry, is illustrated in **Exhibit 2–2.**

Many companies use computerized accounting systems that bypass the traditional journal at various stages. For example, the systems used by many retailers record simultaneously at the cash register, the increase in cash or accounts receivable for each sale and the decrease in the inventory of the item sold. Thus, they effectively bypass the journal and record directly in the ledger.

Posting to the Ledger (Phase 4)

After the initial recording in the journal, the next phase that occurs during the reporting period is the **transfer** of the information to the ledger. This transfer process, called **posting,** reclassifies the information from the chronological format in the journal to an account classification format in the **ledger.**

The **ledger** (usually called the **general ledger**) consists of a large number of separate accounts. There are accounts for each kind of asset (such as cash, accounts receivable, investments, land, buildings, and equipment), liability (such as accounts payable and bonds payable), owners' equity (such as common stock and retained earnings), revenue, expense, gain, and loss. Posting amounts from the journal to the ledger results in reclassification of the data by accounts, which is compatible with the classifications of information as reported in the financial statements.

Posting from the general journal to the general ledger also is illustrated in Exhibit 2–2. Notice the use of **folio numbers** (i.e., page numbers) in both the journal and ledger to enhance reliability in the posting process.

Preparing an Unadjusted Trial Balance (Phase 5)

At the end of each accounting (i.e., reporting) period, after all of the regular entries for completed transactions have been journalized and posted to the ledger, a trial balance should be prepared. This trial balance is prepared before the adjusting entries are made; therefore, it is often called the **unadjusted trial balance.** A trial balance is a list of all of the accounts in the general ledger and their respective debit or credit balances. A trial balance, prepared after all of the regular entries but before the adjusting entries, serves the following purposes:

1. It verifies that debits equal credits.
2. It provides important information for development of the:
   a. Worksheet.
   b. End-of-period adjusting entries.

Exhibit 2–2
General journal and general ledger illustrated.

General Journal

Page J-16

Date 19J	Accounts and explanation	Ledger folio*	Amount Debit	Amount Credit
Jan.2	Equipment	150	15,000	
	Cash	101		5,000
	Notes payable	215		10,000
	Purchased equipment for use in the business. Paid $5,000 cash and gave a $10,000, one-year note payable with 15% interest payable at maturity.			

* The figures in this column indicate (1) that the amount has been posted to the ledger and (2) the account number in the ledger to which posted.

General Ledger

CASH — Acct. 101

Date		Debit	Date		Credit
19J Jan.1	balance	18,700	19J Jan.2	J-16†	5,000

EQUIPMENT — Acct. 150

Date		Debit	Date		Credit
19J Jan.1	balance	62,000			
2	J-16†	15,000			

NOTES PAYABLE — Acct. 215

Date		Debit	Date		Credit
			19J Jan.2	J-16†	10,000

† This is the journal page from which the amount was posted.

An unadjusted trial balance for Ace Retailers, Inc., is shown in **Exhibit 2–3.** After the unadjusted trial balance is completed, the **information processing at the end of the period** continues. These phases were shown in Exhibit 2–1.

Permanent and Temporary Accounts. The accounts in the ledger may be classified as follows:

1. **Permanent accounts.** These are the statement of financial position accounts. They are called **permanent** or real accounts because they are not closed at the end of each accounting period. They are the asset,

Exhibit 2–3
Unadjusted trial balance illustrated.

ACE RETAILERS
Unadjusted Trial Balance
December 31, 19J

Account	Debit	Credit
Cash	$ 67,300	
Short-term notes receivable	8,000	
Accounts receivable	45,000	
Allowance for doubtful accounts		$ 1,000
Interest receivable		
Inventory (periodic system)	75,000	
Prepaid insurance	600	
Land	8,000	
Building	160,000	
Accumulated depreciation, building		90,000
Equipment	91,000	
Accumulated depreciation, equipment		27,000
Accounts payable		29,000
Income tax payable		
Interest payable		
Rent revenue collected in advance		
Bonds payable, 6%		50,000
Common stock, par $10		150,000
Contributed capital in excess of par		20,000
Retained earnings		31,500
Sales revenue		325,200
Interest revenue		500
Rent revenue		1,800
Purchases	130,000	
Freight on purchases	4,000	
Purchase returns		2,000
Selling expenses*	104,000	
General and administrative expenses*	23,600	
Interest expense	2,500	
Extraordinary loss	9,000	
Income tax expense		
Totals	$728,000	$728,000

* These broad categories of expenses are used to conserve space. They might represent control accounts.

liability, and owners' equity accounts. The related contra accounts (e.g., Allowance for Doubtful Accounts and Accumulated Depreciation) also are permanent accounts.

2. **Temporary accounts.** These are the statement of income accounts. They are called **temporary** or nominal accounts because they are closed out to a zero balance at the end of each accounting period. They are the revenue, expense, gain, and loss accounts.[2]

A permanent or temporary account may be "mixed" at any specific time because its balance may contain **both** a permanent (i.e., statement of financial position) component and a temporary (i.e., statement of income) component. To illustrate, assume that on January 1, 19J, Ace paid a three-year property insurance premium of $600 which was debited in full to a permanent account called

[2] Revenue, expense, gain, and loss accounts are subaccounts of owners' equity.

Prepaid Insurance. On December 31, 19J, the $600 balance is composed of a temporary component, Insurance Expense, of $200 and a permanent component, Prepaid Insurance, of $400 (an asset). An adjusting entry on December 31, 19J (end of the reporting period), debiting Insurance Expense and crediting Prepaid Insurance for $200, is necessary to transfer from the Prepaid Insurance asset account the temporary component of $200 to a statement of income account, Insurance Expense.

Subsidiary Ledgers and Control Accounts. Most companies use both a **general ledger** and one or more **subsidiary ledgers.** Each subsidiary ledger has a related **control account** in the general ledger. The control account has summary information, whereas the subsidiary ledger has the details that support the control account. The general ledger contains control accounts for all, or some, of the assets, liabilities, and owners' equity accounts, including revenues, expenses, gains, and losses, depending upon the size and complexity of the company.

The subsidiary ledgers provide the details of a particular control account in the general ledger. To illustrate, a department store may have approximately 10,000 credit customers. A separate accounts receivable record must be kept for each customer. Rather than keeping 10,000 different receivable accounts in the general ledger, one controlling account, Accounts Receivable Control, usually is used. An accounts receivable **subsidiary ledger** composed of a separate account for each customer would also be kept. **Each credit sale** would be posted daily to the customer's account in the subsidiary ledger, and the **total of all credit sales** would be posted periodically (e.g., daily or weekly) to the Accounts Receivable Control account in the general ledger. Thus, when posting is complete, the sum of the balances in all of the customer accounts in the subsidiary ledger would agree with the single balance in the Accounts Receivable Control account.

Subsidiary ledgers often are used for cash (when there are numerous cash and bank accounts), accounts receivable, accounts payable, operational assets, revenues, gains, expenses, losses, and common stock. Subsidiary ledgers and control accounts are discussed in Supplement 2–A.

When the **unadjusted trial balance** is completed, the remaining phases of the cycle (see Exhibit 2–1) can be completed in order.

Although Phases 6 through 10 are completed at the end of the accounting (i.e., reporting) period, for practical reasons, the actual work is done early during the next period because they usually require a considerable amount of time to complete.

We will now discuss each of the end-of-period phases.

Preparing a Worksheet (Phase 6)

The financial statements cannot be prepared until all of the necessary **adjusting entries** have been formulated. The **unadjusted** trial balance must be adjusted to incorporate the effects of all of the adjusting entries. This adjustment may be accomplished by either *(a)* recording all of the adjusting entries in the journal followed by immediate posting to the general ledger and then taking an **adjusted** trial balance from the ledger to use in preparing the financial statements, or *(b)* entering the unadjusted trial balance in **worksheet format** (in computer terminology, a spreadsheet), then entering all of the adjusting entries directly on that worksheet. This worksheet can be designed to include the **adjusted** trial balance and the unclassified statement of income, statement of retained earnings, and statement of financial position. A separate worksheet is needed to develop the statement of cash flows (see Chapter 19).

The worksheet technique is widely used because it *(a)* is an organized approach that facilitates a timely distribution of the financial statements, *(b)* provides an opportunity to develop all of the adjusting entries and "clean up" errors that may exist prior to journalizing and posting both the adjusting and closing entries, and *(c)* provides the accounts and amounts for the financial statements. A worksheet or spreadsheet is not a part of the basic accounting records of the entity; it is a separate **facilitating** technique that usually increases efficiency and minimizes processing errors. It does not replace the financial statements or any entries in the accounts.

Exhibit 2–4 illustrates a typical worksheet which can be prepared as follows:[3]

1. Enter the ledger account titles and their balances in the worksheet (this will be the unadjusted trial balance; see Exhibit 2–3). Use the **accounts column** and the first pair of **amount columns** as shown in Exhibit 2–4.
2. Formulate the adjusting entries and enter them in the second pair of columns in the worksheet.
3. Extend the unadjusted balances, plus or minus the adjusting amounts, to the **Adjusted** Trial Balance columns and check for balance (i.e., debit, $746,800 = credit, $746,800).
4. Extend each adjusted amount shown in the Adjusted Trial Balance columns to the right, line by line, to the pair of columns under the financial statement on which each should be reported on the statements of income, retained earnings, or financial position.
5. Check each pair of columns to ensure that debits and credits are equal.

Formulating adjusting entries is a major task in completing a worksheet. Therefore, we will discuss adjusting entries first and then discuss completion of the worksheet.

Adjusting Entries

An adjusting entry is a "catchup" entry usually made at the end of the accounting period. **Accrual** basis accounting requires adjustments to some of the unadjusted account balances because they are not up-to-date at the end of the accounting period. **Adjusting entries** are necessary to adjust certain statement of financial position and statement of income accounts so their balances will conform with the **time period assumption** and the **revenue, cost, and matching principles** discussed in Chapter 6.

There are two possible situations that create the need for adjusting entries. First, some account balances include both permanent and temporary components, which must be separated. Second, some external and internal transactions

[3] If you are not interested in the worksheet technique presented in this chapter, omit the material under the caption "Completion of the Worksheet." However, mastery of techniques for organizing and analyzing large amounts of data is essential in any accounting or financial capacity. Experience with this traditional accounting worksheet technique is helpful in acquiring this skill.

and events have not yet been recorded in the accounts. Adjusting entries are needed for both of these situations. Correcting entries are discussed in later chapters.

The primary characteristics of **adjusting** entries are as follows:

1. They are end-of-period entries only. They are **dated** as of the end of the accounting period; however, the actual work is done early in the next period.
2. They separate permanent (i.e., statement of financial position) amounts from temporary (i.e., statement of income) amounts.
3. They relate to originating transactions that occur in one accounting period with economic effects that extend over more than one accounting period.
4. They are recorded in the journal and posted to the ledger.
5. They always involve a statement of income account and a statement of financial position account. *— if not you're correcting an entry*

Adjusting entries may be classified into three major types: deferred items, accrued items, and cost allocations.

A. **Deferred items**—result from transactions in which cash flow **precedes** recognition of the related expense or revenue. The two general situations are:
 1. **Deferred expense** (an asset account; usually called **prepaid expense**)—cash is **paid before** the related expense should be recognized; for example, insurance premium paid in advance.
 2. **Deferred revenue** (a liability account; usually called **unearned revenue**)—cash is **collected before** the related revenue should be recognized; for example, rent revenue collected in advance of occupancy.
B. **Accrued items**—result from transactions in which cash flow **lags** (i.e., follows) recognition of the related expense or revenue. The two general situations are:
 1. **Accrued expense** (a liability account; usually called **accrued liabilities**)—cash is **paid after** the related expense is incurred; for example, wages earned by an employee but not yet paid.
 2. **Accrued revenue** (an asset account related to revenues other than to sales and services sold on credit; often called **revenue receivable**)—cash is **collected after** the related revenue is earned; for example, interest revenue earned but not yet collected.
C. **Other—internal cost allocations not yet recorded;** for example, estimated bad debt expense and depreciation expense, and cost of goods sold (with a periodic inventory system).

Each kind of adjusting entry is discussed and illustrated below. You should study each adjusting entry illustrated in the worksheet in Exhibit 2–4. If used, the worksheet would be followed by preparation of the financial statements. (Phase 7), then the journalizing and posting of the adjusting entries (Phase 8). If the worksheet technique is not used, these adjusting entries would be directly journalized and posted (Phase 8), followed by preparation of the financial statements (Phase 7).

Exhibit 2–4
Worksheet for Ace Retailers, for the Year Ended December 31, 19J.

Accounts	Unadjusted trial balance		Adjusting entries		Adjusted trial balance		Statement of income		Retained earnings		Statement of financial position	
	Debit	Credit	Debit	Credit	Debit	Credit	Debit	Credit	Debit	Credit	Debit	Credit
Cash	67,300				67,300						67,300	
Short-term notes receivable	8,000				8,000						8,000	
Accounts receivable	45,000				45,000						45,000	
Allowance for doubtful accounts		1,000		(f) 1,200		2,200						2,200
Interest receivable			(d) 100		100						100	
Inventory (periodic system)	75,000		(g) 90,000	(g) 75,000	90,000*						90,000	
Prepaid insurance	600			(a) 200	400						400	
Land	8,000				8,000						8,000	
Building	160,000				160,000						160,000	
Accumulated depreciation, building		90,000		(e) 10,000		100,000						100,000
Equipment	91,000				91,000						91,000	
Accumulated depreciation, equipment		27,000		(e) 9,000		36,000						36,000
Accounts payable		29,000				29,000						29,000
Interest payable				(c) 500		500						500
Rent revenue collected in advance				(b) 600		600						600

Bonds payable, 6%		50,000				50,000						50,000
Common stock, par $10		150,000				150,000						150,000
Contributed capital in excess of par		20,000				20,000						20,000
Retained earnings		31,500				31,500				31,500		
Sales revenue		325,200				325,200		325,200				
Interest revenue		500		(d) 100		600		600				
Rent revenue		1,800	(b) 600			1,200		1,200				
Purchases	130,000			(g) 130,000								
Freight on purchases	4,000			(g) 4,000								
Purchase returns		2,000	(g) 2,000									
Cost of goods sold			(g) 117,000		117,000		117,000					
Selling expenses	104,000		(e) 8,200 (f) 1,200		113,400		113,400					
General and administrative expenses	23,600		(a) 200 (e) 10,800		34,600		34,600					
Interest expense	2,500		(c) 500		3,000		3,000					
Extraordinary loss	9,000				9,000		9,000					
	728,000	728,000	230,600	230,600	746,800	746,800	277,000	327,000				
Income tax expense			(h) 20,000†				20,000					
							297,000	327,000				
Income tax payable				(h) 20,000								20,000
Net income to retained earnings							30,000			30,000		
Retained earnings to statement of financial position									61,500			61,500
Totals							327,000	327,000	61,500	61,500	469,800	469,800

* Periodic inventory system. This is one way to handle inventory on a worksheet. There are several other methods that give the same results.

† (327,000 − \$277,000) × 40% = \$20,000. There are other ways to reflect income tax on a worksheet.

Deferred Expense. A deferred expense, usually called a **prepaid expense,** occurs when services or supplies are paid for in one accounting period but are not fully used or consumed in that period.

To illustrate, on January 1, 19J, Ace Retailers paid a three-year insurance premium of $600 in advance. At that date, the $600 payment was recorded as a debit to Prepaid Insurance and a credit to Cash. On the unadjusted trial balance, the $600 is shown as the debit balance of an asset account, Prepaid Insurance. Because $200 of this service was **used** (in this instance, expired) in 19J, a $400 balance should remain in the **prepaid** expense account. Therefore, on December 31, 19J, an adjusting entry must be made as follows (the letter code to the left is used for reference on the worksheet):

a. December 31, 19J:

Insurance expense (general and administrative expense)	200	
Prepaid insurance		200

The effects of this entry are (1) to adjust the asset account balance to $400, which is then reported on the statement of financial position; and (2) to record the $200 expense component, which is reported on the statement of income.

In the originating entry, a deferred expense can be debited to a permanent (real) account (Prepaid Insurance as above), or to a temporary (nominal) account. In either case, an adjusting entry is required. To illustrate, assume the $600 was initially debited to **Insurance Expense.** The adjusting entry would be: debit Prepaid Insurance, $400; credit Insurance Expense, $400. In either case the net effect on the financial statements is exactly the same.[4]

Deferred Revenue. A deferred revenue, usually called **revenue collected in advance,** occurs when payment for goods or services is collected in one accounting period but is not fully earned in that period.

To illustrate, on January 1, 19J, Ace Retailers leased a small office in its building to Tom Jones. At that time, Ace collected $1,800 cash in advance for 18 months rent. The collection was recorded as a debit to Cash and credit to Rent Revenue. On December 31, 19J, the $1,800 balance in the Rent Revenue account included $600 **unearned** rent revenue. Therefore, the adjusting entry was:

b. December 31, 19J:

Rent revenue	600	
Rent revenue collected in advance*		600

*Sometimes called **Unearned Rent Revenue.**

This entry leaves $1,200 in the Rent Revenue account for 19J and records a liability of $600 for the unearned rent revenue. The $600 is a liability on December 31, 19J, because Ace owes that amount of future "occupancy" to Jones. In 19K, the $600 will be transferred from the liability account to the Rent Revenue account.

[4] The first approach usually is used because the asset account typically continues to exist for a long period of time due to successive renewals.

In the originating entry, a deferred revenue can be credited to a temporary (nominal) account (rent revenue as above) or to a permanent (real) account. In either case, an adjusting entry is required. To illustrate, assume the $1,800 was initially credited to **Rent Revenue Collected in Advance.** The adjusting entry would be: debit Rent Revenue Collected in Advance and credit Rent Revenue for $1,200 each.[5]

Accrued Expense. An accrued expense, usually called an **accrued liability,** is recorded when an expense has been incurred but it is not yet recorded or paid. Incurred means that a transaction or event has occurred that should be recorded as an expense. Therefore, the adjusted entry for an accrued expense should recognize both the **expense** and the related **liability.**

To illustrate, Ace Retailers has a liability for bonds payable of $50,000. These bonds require payments of 6% annual interest on each October 31. Therefore, on December 31, 19J, accrued (unpaid) interest expense was $50,000 × 6% × 2/12 = $500. This accrued interest must be recognized by the following adjusting entry:

c. December 31, 19J:

Interest expense	500	
Interest payable		500

This adjusting entry records (1) 19J expense (interest expense) for statement of income purposes and (2) the liability (interest payable) for the 19J statement of financial position.

Accrued Revenue. Accrued revenue, usually called **uncollected revenue** or revenue earned but not yet collected, occurs when a revenue has been earned and should be recognized but has not yet been collected or recorded. Therefore, the adjusting entry should recognize both **revenue** and the related **receivable.**

To illustrate, Ace Reailers held short-term notes receivable amounting to $8,000. These notes earn 15% annual interest which is collected each November 30. Because interest revenue was earned but not yet collected for the month of December, an adjusting entry must be made as follows:

d. December 31, 19J:

Interest receivable	100	
Interest revenue ($8,000 × 15% × 1/12)		100

This adjusting entry records (1) the asset (interest receivable) for the 19J statement of financial position and (2) 19J revenue (interest revenue) for statement of income purposes.

Internal Cost Allocations Not Yet Recorded. In addition to the adjusting entries for deferrals and accruals, adjusting entries must be made for certain allocations of cost to periodic expense. Usually these adjusting entries are based on

[5] The first approach usually is used because rent revenue typically is credited when rent is collected.

estimated amounts. Examples of such internal cost allocations are: depreciation expense, bad debt expense, and cost of goods sold.

Depreciation Expense. When certain assets, such as a building or equipment, are acquired for use in operating a business (i.e., not for sale), they are "used up" over time through wear and obsolescence. The amount of the **use cost** of such assets is measured each accounting period and recorded as **depreciation expense.** Depreciation expense always is an estimate because the amount recognized depends upon a known amount, the cost of the asset, and two estimates, useful life and residual value (RV).

To illustrate, at the end of 19J, Ace Retailers had the following assets subject to depreciation:

				Proportionate use by function	
Asset	**Cost**	**RV**	**Useful life—years**	**Selling function**	**G & A* function**
Building	$160,000	$10,000	15	46%	54%
Equipment	91,000	1,000	10	40	60

* General and administrative.

The adjusting entry for these two assets is:

e. December 31, 19J:

Selling expense (depreciation)	8,200	
General and administrative expense (depreciation)	10,800	
Accumulated depreciation, building		10,000
Accumulated depreciation, equipment		9,000

Computation:

		Total	Selling	General and administrative
Building: [($160,000 − $10,000) ÷ 15 yrs.]	=	$10,000	× 46% = $4,600	× 54% = $ 5,400
Equipment: [($91,000 − $1,000) ÷ 10 Yrs.]	=	9,000	× 40% = 3,600	× 60% = 5,400
Totals		$19,000	$8,200	$10,800

Depreciation expense was debited to two expense accounts because the company follows the typical policy of **allocating** expense based upon the proportionate use of the assets in each function. This entry (1) records the 19J expense for the statement of income and (2) reduces the book or carrying values of the building and equipment for the 19J statement of financial position. Recall that accumulated depreciation is a contra (i.e., offset) to the related asset account.

Bad Debt Expense. Sales and services sold on **credit** usually result in some losses due to uncollectible accounts receivable (i.e., bad debts). The fact that a specific account will be uncollectible usually is not known for one or more accounting periods subsequent to the period in which the credit was extended. The sale or service is recognized in the period when the transaction is completed in conformity with the **revenue principle.** The **matching principle** requires that all **expenses** associated with sales and service revenue be recognized in the period in which the revenues are reported. Therefore, bad debt expense must be recognized in the revenue-recognition period. This matching can be accomplished only by **estimating** the bad debt expense based on past experience.

To illustrate, Ace Retailers extended credit on sales during 19J amounting to $120,000. Prior experience indicated an expected average bad debt loss rate of 1% of credit sales. Therefore, the following adjusting entry is required:

f. December 31, 19J:

Bad debt expense (selling)	1,200	
Allowance for doubtful accounts		1,200

Computation: $120,000 × 1% = $1,200.

The credit is made to an "allowance" account rather than directly to Accounts Receivable because the identities of the specific customers that will not eventually pay are not known. Bad debt expense is reported on the statement of income, and the allowance account is reported on the statement of financial position as a deduction from accounts receivable (i.e., it is a contra account). When a customer's account is determined to be uncollectible, it is written off by a debit to the allowance account and a credit to Accounts Receivable; this write-off will not change the net book (i.e., carrying) value of accounts receivable.

Cost of Goods Sold. Prior to discussing this adjusting entry, let's review the difference between the perpetual and periodic inventory systems.[6]

Perpetual Inventory System. This system requires the maintenance of a **detailed inventory record** for each kind of item stocked. This record contains data on each purchase and each issue (i.e., cost of goods sold), and an up-to-date inventory balance. The cost of each item purchased is debited directly to the Inventory account (i.e., no Purchases account is used). Under this inventory system, a sale requires two entries: At sales price—debit Cash or Accounts Receivable and credit Sales Revenue; at cost—debit Cost of Goods Sold and credit Inventory. The unadjusted trial balance reflects only the **ending inventory** and the amount of **cost of goods sold;** therefore, **no adjusting entry is required.**

Periodic Inventory System. This system does not maintain a detailed inventory record. Instead, a physical inventory count is taken and valued at cost at the end of each accounting period. This means that cost of goods sold is determined at the end of each accounting period **after** the inventory is counted and valued. The cost of items purchased is debited to Purchases (not inventory), and a sale is recorded only at sales price—debit Cash or Accounts Receivable and credit Sales Revenue.

The **unadjusted** trial balance at the end of the accounting period reflects the beginning (not ending) inventory amount and **does not** reflect cost of goods sold. Therefore, an **adjusting entry is required** to *(a)* remove the beginning inventory amount and replace it with the **ending** inventory amount, and *(b)*

[6] These inventory systems are discussed and illustrated in detail in Chapters 8 and 9.

record **cost of goods sold.**[7] To illustrate, after the ending inventory was counted and valued, Ace Retailers cost of goods sold is computed as follows:

ACE RETAILERS
Periodic Inventory System
December 31, 19J

Beginning inventory (carried over from the prior period)		$ 75,000
Add (from the current-year accounts):		
Purchases	$130,000	
Freight on purchases	4,000	
Purchase returns	(2,000)	
Purchase discounts and allowances	(–0–)	
Net purchases		132,000
Total goods available for sale		207,000
Less: Ending inventory (from physical count)		90,000
Cost of goods sold (as computed)		$117,000

When the periodic inventory system is used, the inventory and cost of goods sold adjusting entry can be made as follows:[8]

g. December 31, 19J:

Inventory (ending)	90,000	
Purchase returns	2,000	
Purchase discounts and allowances	–0–	
Cost of goods sold (balancing amount)	117,000	
Inventory (beginning)		75,000
Purchases		130,000
Freight on purchases		4,000

Completing the Worksheet (Phase 6 Continued)

After the adjusting entries are entered on the worksheet, it is completed by extending each account balance (i.e., the Unadjusted trial balance amount plus or minus any adjusting amounts) to the next columns as illustrated in Exhibit 2–4. Notice that debits are extended as debits and credits as credits. When all of the amounts have been extended, the difference between the debits and credits under the Statement of Income column represents **pretax income.** This amount is needed to compute income tax expense, for which an adjusting entry must be made. To illustrate, for Ace Retailers, Inc., the computation would be as follows, assuming an average 40% income tax rate:

Statement of Income column totals (pretax);	
Credit total	$327,000
Debit total	277,000
Pretax income	50,000
Income tax expense ($50,000 × 40%)	20,000
Net income	$ 30,000

[7] Because this entry has both adjusting and closing characteristics, some accountants consider it to be an adjusting entry, whereas others consider it to be a closing entry; however, the end results are the same.

[8] This compound entry also could be made as a series of individual entries, or groupings, with the same effect.

Exhibit 2–5
Statement of income.

ACE RETAILERS
Statement of Income*
For the Year Ended December 31, 19J

Revenues:		
Sales		$325,200
Interest		600
Rent		1,200
Total revenues		327,000
Expenses:		
Cost of goods sold†	$117,000	
Selling	113,400	
General and administrative	34,600	
Interest	3,000	
Total expenses (excluding income taxes)		268,000
Pretax operating income		59,000
Income taxes ($59,000 × 40%)		23,600
Income before extraordinary items		35,400
Extraordinary loss	9,000	
Less tax saving ($9,000 × 40%)	3,600	5,400
Net income		$ 30,000
EPS:		
Income before extraordinary items ($35,400 ÷ 15,000 shares)		$2.36
Extraordinary loss ($5,400 ÷ 15,000 shares)		(.36)
Net income ($30,000 ÷ 15,000 shares)		$2.00

* This is a single-step statement of income various formats are discussed in Chapter 3.
† Computation of cost of goods sold:

Beginning inventory	$ 75,000
Purchases	130,000
Freight on purchases	4,000
Purchase returns	(2,000)
Total goods available for sale	207,000
Less ending inventory	90,000
Cost of goods sold	$117,000

The adjusting entry for income tax would be as follows:

h. December 31, 19J:

Income tax expense	20,000	
Income tax payable		20,000

After this adjusting entry is made, the extensions can be completed. The amount of net income, $30,000, is entered on the worksheet as a debit to Statement of Income and a credit to Retained Earnings. The ending balance of Retained Earnings is then extended to the statement of financial position and the last two pairs of columns are summed; in the absence of errors, each pair of columns on the worksheet will balance. The worksheet then can be used as a guide for completing the remaining phases in the cycle.

Preparing Financial Statements (Phase 7)

The statements of income, retained earnings, and financial position can be prepared directly from the completed worksheet. A statement of income and statement of financial position, taken directly from the worksheet (Exhibit 2–

Exhibit 2–6
Statement of financial position.

ACE RETAILERS
Statement of Financial Position*
At December 31, 19J

Assets

Current assets:		
Cash		$ 67,300
Accounts receivable	$ 45,000	
Allowance for doubtful accounts	2,200	42,800
Notes receivable		8,000
Interest receivable		100
Inventory		90,000
Prepaid insurance†		400
Total current assets		208,600
Operational assets:		
Land		8,000
Building	160,000	
Accumulated depreciation, building	100,000	60,000
Equipment	91,000	
Accumulated depreciation, equipment	36,000	55,000
Total operational assets		123,000
Total assets		$331,600

Liabilities

Current liabilities:		
Accounts payable		$ 29,000
Income taxes payable		20,000
Interest payable		500
Rent revenue collected in advance		600
Total current liabilities		50,100
Long-term liabilities:		
Bond payable, 6%		50,000
Total liabilities		100,100
Stockholders' Equity		
Contributed capital:		
Common stock, par $10, 15,000 shares issued and outstanding	$150,000	
Contributed capital in excess of par	20,000	
Retained earnings	61,500	
Total stockholders' equity		231,500
Total liabilities and stockholders' equity		$331,600

* Statement of financial position and appropriate supplementary information are discussed in Chapter 4.
† Conceptually, $200 of this amount should not be reported as a current asset because it will extend two years into the future. In practice such differences may not be material in amount, as in this situation; the conceptual distinction is not necessary (refer to the discussion of materiality in Chapter 6).

4), are presented in **Exhibits 2–5** and **2–6,** respectively. Notice the connecting link between the statements of retained earnings and financial position. Phase 7 usually precedes Phase 8 because of the need to distribute the financial statements at the earliest possible date. The issuance date of the financial statements is critical because the longer they are delayed the less relevant they are to decision makers. Financial statements are discussed in more detail in Chapters 3 and 4.

Journalizing and Posting Adjusting Entries (Phase 8)

The adjusting entries, dated the last day of the accounting period, should be entered in the general journal and then posted to the general ledger. The adjusting entries update the ledger accounts by separating the account balances into their permanent (i.e., statement of financial position) and temporary (i.e., statement of income) components. The adjusted temporary accounts are then ready to close. Also, the adjusting entries bring the general ledger accounts into agreement with the financial statements.

If a worksheet, such as Exhibit 2–4, is developed, the adjusting entries can be taken directly from it. Notice that after the adjusting entries are posted to the general ledger, each account will reflect the account balances shown in Exhibit 2–4 in the column labeled Adjusted Trial Balance.

Closing Entries (Phase 9)

After the financial statements are prepared and the adjusting entries have been journalized and posted, the **closing process,** Phase 9, must be completed. The purpose of the closing process is to transfer the balances of all of the **temporary** (i.e., statement of income accounts) to the Retained Earnings account. The result is that *(a)* retained earnings will be increased by the amount of net income, or decreased by net loss, and *(b)* each temporary account will start the next year with a zero balance. The permanent (i.e., statement of financial position) accounts are not affected by the closing process except for the change in retained earnings.

The temporary accounts are used each accounting period to accumulate and classify the revenues, expenses, gains, and losses. At the end of the accounting period, when they have served this temporary information processing purpose, they are closed to zero balances to be ready for **reuse** in the next accounting period.

For closing purposes, a temporary **clearing account,** called **Income Summary,** may be used to aggregate the debits and credits that make up net income or loss. A closing entry transfers a debit balance in an account to Income Summary as a debit, or it transfers a credit balance to an account to Income Summary as a credit. This clearing account is then immediately closed to Retained Earnings as one amount. Cost of goods sold also is used (with a periodic inventory system) in the closing process for a similar reason. These two clearing accounts are used herein primarily for instructional convenience; they are seldom used in practice.

Closing entries are journalized, and dated, only at the end of each accounting period. The closing entries can be *(a)* taken directly from the **worksheet,** or *(b)* developed from the **adjusted** trial balance, if a worksheet is not prepared.

To illustrate, the **closing journal entries** for Ace Retailers, assuming the Cost of Goods Sold and Income Summary clearance accounts are used, would be taken directly from the Statement of Income columns of the worksheet (see Exhibit 2–4):[9]

December 31, 19J:

1. To close the revenue and gain accounts to Income Summary:

Sales revenue	325,200	
Interest revenue	600	
Rent revenue	1,200	
Income summary		327,000

[9] The closing entries can be grouped in various ways, one of which is illustrated here. Alternatively, a separate closing entry can be made for each temporary account. The net effect of all the closing entries would be the same.

2. To close the expense and loss accounts to Income Summary:

Income summary	297,000	
Cost of goods sold		117,000
Selling expenses		113,400
General and administrative expenses		34,600
Interest expense		3,000
Extraordinary loss		9,000
Income tax expense		20,000

3. To close Income Summary (i.e., net income to Retained Earnings):

Income summary	30,000	
Retained earnings		30,000

The closing process is diagrammed in T-account form in **Exhibit 2–7.** Notice that **after the closing process** each statement of income (i.e., temporary) account has a zero balance. Therefore, each account is ready for reuse during the next accounting period.

Preparing a Post-Closing Trial Balance (Phase 10)

The purposes of a trial balance are to *(a)* verify the equality of the debits and credits and *(b)* have the account balances ready for other uses. Two different trial balances have already been discussed: the **unadjusted** trial balance, taken immediately after all of the current entries are journalized and posted for the accounting period but before the adjusting entries; and the **adjusted** trial balance, which reflects the account balances after the adjusting entries. A third trial balance usually is taken after the closing entries have been posted. It is called the **post-closing trial balance.** It is used to verify that the debits and credits are equal at the start of the next accounting period. The post-closing trial balance usually is prepared with a computer rather than preparing a formal listing by some other means.

Reversing Entries (Phase 11)

After the adjusting and closing entries are journalized and posted to the general ledger, the accounts are ready for information inputs of the next period. Prior to entering the new information inputs, many companies journalize and post **reversing entries.** A reversing entry is dated the first day of the next period and simply reverses, or "backs out" of the related accounts, the amounts of an adjusting entry that was made at the end of the prior period. Thus, a reversing entry uses exactly the same accounts and amounts as in the adjusting entry but with the debits and credits reversed. A **reversing entry serves only one purpose, that is, to facilitate (or simplify) a related entry** in the next accounting period. Reversing entries are always optional; the same end result can be obtained whether or not they are used. If used, only certain of the adjusting entries are reversed.

Although it is impossible to provide rigid rules for selecting adjusting entries that may be reversed, some guidelines can be given.

1. **Adjusting entries usually reversed**—As a general rule, only the following adjusting entries should be reversed: *(a)* entries for accured expenses and accrued revenues, and *(b)* entries for deferred expenses and deferred revenues that were originally recorded in a temporary (i.e., statement of income) account.

Exhibit 2–7
Effects of the closing process on the Ledger account balances.

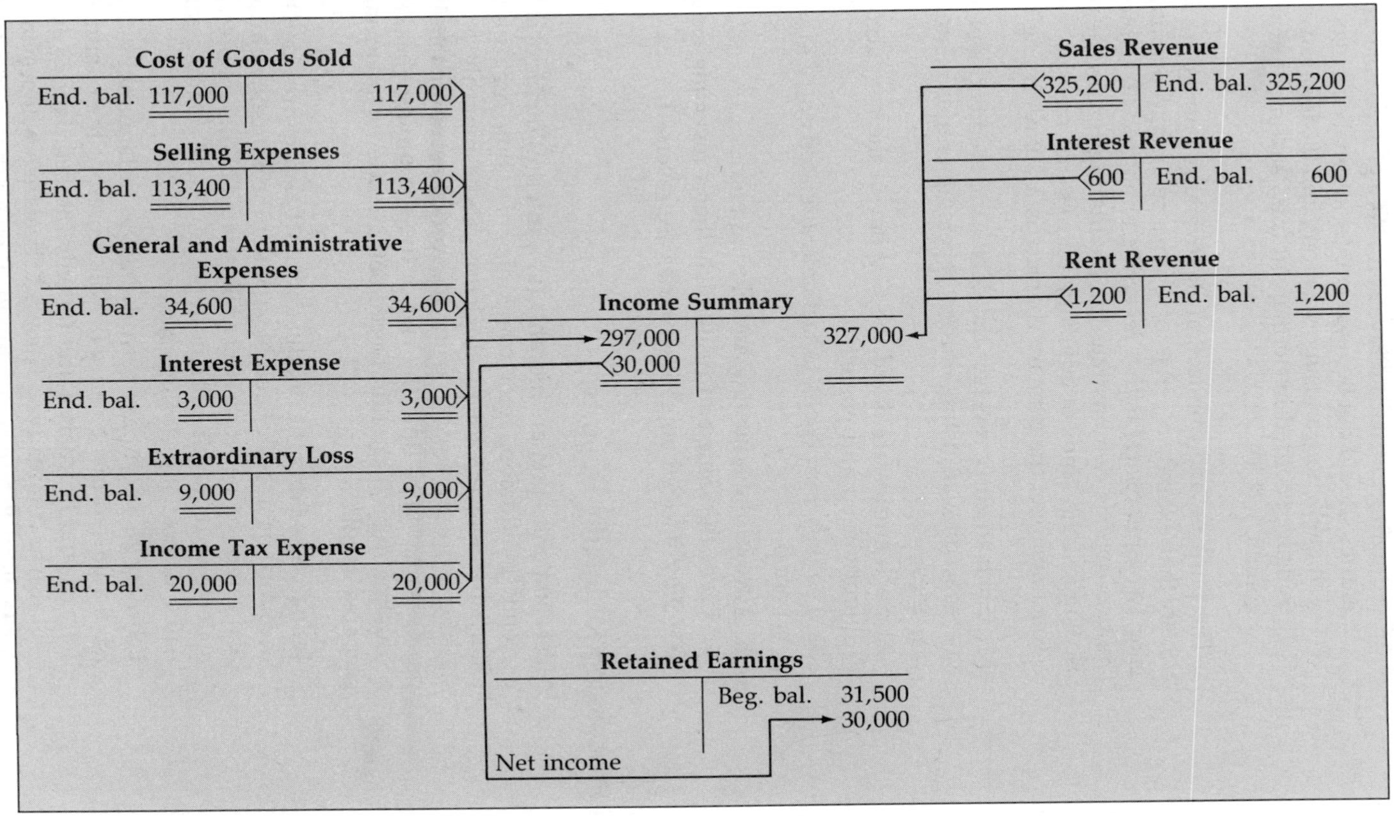

2. **Adjusting entries not reversed**—As a general rule, the following adjusting entries should not be reversed: *(a)* internal cost allocations (e.g., depreciation, depletion, and amortization), and *(b)* deferred expenses and revenues initially recorded in permanent (i.e., statement of financial position) accounts.

The purpose and application of reversing entries are illustrated in **Exhibit 2–8.** In that exhibit, a series of entries related to accrued wages is analyzed using two options: (1) with a reversing entry and (2) without a reversing entry. The two options demonstrate the **facilitating** feature of reversing entries and also suggest the kinds of adjusting entries that may be reversed.

To summarize, the primary characteristics of reversing entries are as follows:

1. Such an entry reverses the debits and credits of one or more immediately preceding adjusting entries; reversing entries relate only to adjusting entries.
2. Such entries are dated the first day of the next accounting period, then journalized and posted.
3. The only purpose is to facilitate a related entry in the next accounting period.
4. Follows the adjusting and closing entries.
5. Gives the same end results whether a reversing entry is used or not.
6. Only selected adjusting entries are reversed.

Information Processing for Interim Reports

Most companies prepare monthly (i.e., interim) financial statements for internal use only. In addition, some companies distribute highly summarized quarterly financial statements for external use. These monthly and quarterly financial statements are prepared by using the **worksheet approach.** However, the closing process is not used until the end of the accounting year. Assuming an annual accounting year that ends December 31, interim financial statements can be prepared as follows:

January 31—Enter the unadjusted trial balance (provided by the general ledger accounts) on a worksheet. Next, enter the adjusting entries on the worksheet and complete the worksheet as illustrated in this chapter. Prepare the January statements of income, financial position, and retained earnings. Do not journalize or post any closing entries.

February 28—Complete a worksheet as in January by using the *(a)* February 28 unadjusted trial balance (it will represent the **cumulative** amounts for January and February), and *(b)* only the February 28 adjusting entries (they will also be cumulative). The worksheet then will provide financial statements for January–February **combined.** Prepare the **February** statement of income by **subtracting** the January amounts previously reported. The February statement of financial position needs no such change because a statement of financial position reports cumulative amounts of assets and liabilities. Do not journalize or post the closing entries.

Exhibit 2–8
Reversing entries illustrated.

KNOX CORPORATION
Annual Accounting Period Ends December 31, 19A

With reversing entry			**Without reversing entry**		
a. Adjusting entry—The last payroll of Knox Corporation was paid on December 28, 19A; the next payroll will be on January 4, 19B. Therefore, at December 31, 19A, accrued wages (i.e., not yet paid or recorded) for three days amounted to $15,000. The following adjusting entry is required:					
December 31, 19A:			December 31, 19A:		
Wage expense	15,000		Wage expense	15,000	
Wages payable		15,000	Wages payable		15,000
b. Closing entry—The revenue and expense accounts are closed to Income Summary.					
December 31, 19A:			December 31, 19A:		
Income summary*	215,000		Income summary*	215,000	
Wages expense		215,000	Wage expense		215,000
* This includes $200,000 wages already paid and recorded.					
c. At this time the adjusting and closing entries have been journalized and posted to the ledger. The information processing cycle for 19A has been completed. On January 1, 19B, the accountant must decide what adjusting entries are to be **reversed** (if any). **Question:** Would a reversing entry for accrued wages on January 1, 19B, simplify or facilitate making the **next payroll entry** on January 4, 19B?					
Decision—make a reversing entry, January 1, 19B			**Decision—no reversing entry to be made**		
Wages payable	15,000				
Wage expense		15,000			
(Note that this entry exactly reverses the adjusting entry made above on 12/31/19A.)					
Effect: The Wages Payable account now reflects a zero balance; Wage Expense reflects a **credit** balance of $15,000.			Effect: The Wages Payable account continues to reflect a **credit** balance of $15,000; Wage Expense reflects a **zero** balance.		
d. Subsequent payroll entry—Payment of $36,000 payroll on January 4, 19B. This amount includes the $15,000 liability (wages payable) carried over from December 19A.					
January 4, 19B, payroll entry (disregarding payroll taxes):					
Wage expense	36,000		Wages payable	15,000	
Cash		36,000	Wage expense	21,000	
			Cash		36,000

Did the prior reversing entry simplify this subsequent entry? The answer is **yes** because when a reversing entry is made (1) the subsequent entry requires one less debit, (2) no time is required to "sort out" the amount of that debit, and (3) when payroll processing is **computerized,** if a reversing entry is not used, a special routine must be written for the first payment which is different from the remaining 51 payrolls during the year.

March 31—Repeat the process, as in February, using the *(a)* March 31 unadjusted trial balance, and *(b)* the March 31 adjusting entries. The worksheet will provide the **quarterly** financial statements. The statement of income for March only can be developed by subtracting **both** the January and February amounts. The quarterly and March statement of financial position are identical.

Summary

Most companies process a large quantity of accounting data each day. This work can be time-consuming and costly. Therefore, a well-designed information processing system is needed to provide an efficient flow of information from the collection of data about each transaction to the preparation of the financial statements. **Exhibit 2–9** summarizes the major sequential phases of the information processing cycle discussed in this chapter.

The processing of accounting information necessarily will vary with the size and complexity of the entity. Information processing may be accomplished (1) manually, when the work is performed by hand; (2) mechanically, when the information is processed by sorting equipment, noncomputerized cash registers, and so on; and (3) electronically, when computers (i.e., maniframes and personal computers) are used. An accounting system may use each of these approaches in varying degrees depending upon the situation. Consideration of these processing approaches is not within the scope of this book. For instructional convenience, the manual approach is used because an understanding of the accounting process is important for accountants.

SUPPLEMENT 2–A: CONTROL ACCOUNTS, SUBSIDIARY LEDGERS, AND SPECIAL JOURNALS

An accounting system usually includes use of information processing procedures called **control accounts, subsidiary ledgers,** and **special journals.** This supplement discusses these procedures.

Control Accounts and Subsidiary Ledgers

The general ledger is the main ledger. It includes an account for each asset, liability, owners' equity, revenue, expense, gain, and loss. To facilitate recordkeeping for accounts that involve a large amount of detail, selected general ledger accounts are designated as **control accounts** to which only summary information is posted. The details related to each control account are maintained in a separate **subsidiary ledger** (one for each control account). As an example, accounts receivable usually is designated as **Accounts Receivable Control** in the general ledger and is supported by a separate **accounts receivable subsidiary ledger** that includes the individual customer accounts. This procedure is illustrated below.

Journals. Both general and special journals are used in most accounting systems. Even when extensive use is made of special journals, a need still exists for a general journal **(Exhibit 2–10)** to record *(a)* those transactions that do not

Exhibit 2–9
Summary of the accounting processing cycle.

Phase (order)	Identification	Objective
During the period (Phases 1–4):		
1	Collecting economic data.	To gather inputs to the accounting system. The inputs are supported by source documents as a basis for *(a)* transaction analysis and *(b)* subsequent verification.
2	Transaction analysis.	To identify, assess, and measure the economic impact on the entity of each transaction recognized. To provide the basis for developing the accounting entry in the journal.
3	Journalizing.	To provide a chronological record (i.e., by date) of the entries in the accounting system that reflect the increases and decreases in each account.
4	Posting.	To transfer the economic effects from the journal to the ledger; to reclassify and accumulate the economic effects for each asset, liability, owners' equity, revenue, expense, gain, and loss.
End of the period (Phases 5–10):		
5	Preparing an unadjusted trial balance.	To provide, in a convenient form, a listing of the accounts and their balances in the general ledger after all current entries have been posted. It serves to *(a)* check the debit-credit equality and *(b)* provide data for use in developing the worksheet and the adjusting entries.
6*	Preparing worksheets	To provide an organized and systematic approach at the end of the accounting period for developing *(a)* the adjusting entries, *(b)* the financial statements, and *(c)* the closing entries. One worksheet suffices for the statements of income and financial position. Another worksheet is needed to develop the statement of cash flows.
7	Preparing financial statements.	To communicate summarized financial information to decision makers.
8	Journalizing and posting adjusting entries.	To update the general ledger and to separate the "mixed" balances into their permanent (i.e., statement of financial position) and temporary (i.e., statement of income) components so the temporary accounts will be ready for the closing process. This phase brings the general ledger account balances into agreement with the amounts reported on the financial statements.
9	Journalizing and posting closing entries.	To close the temporary accounts to retained earnings so they will be ready for reuse during the next period for accumulating and classifying revenues and expenses.
10*	Preparing post-closing trial balance.	To verify the debit-credit accuracy of the general ledger after the closing entries are posted.
Start of next period:		
11*	Making reversing entries.	To facilitate subsequent entries by reversing certain adjusting entries. They are journalized and posted on the first day of the new period.

* Optional.

apply to any of the special journals, *(b)* nonrepetitive current transactions, and *(c)* the adjusting, closing, and reversing journal entries. Occasionally, there will be a complex entry with characteristics that would, in part, qualify for entry in a special journal and, in part, in the general journal. Such entries may be entered only in the general journal or, alternatively, "split" between the general journal and a special journal.

Exhibit 2–10
General journal.

General Journal

Page J-14

Date 19J	Accounts and explanation	Ledger folio	Amount Debit	Amount Credit
Jan. 2	Equipment—trucks	140	9,000	
	Notes payable	214		9,000
	Purchased truck for use in the business. Gave $9,000, 60-day note, interest at 10% per year, payable at maturity.			

Special Journals

A special journal serves the same purpose as a general journal except that it is designed to handle **only one type of transaction** because of the large volume of transactions of that particular type. Each special journal, therefore, is designed specifically to simplify the data processing tasks involved in journalizing and posting a particular type of transaction. The format of each special journal and the number used depend upon the types of frequent transactions recorded by the entity. Commonly used special journals are the following:

1. Merchandise sales on credit—designed for credit sales entries only.
2. Merchandise purchases on credit—designed for credit purchases only.
3. Cash receipts—designed for all cash receipts (including cash sales).
4. Cash payments—designed for all cash payments (including cash purchases).
5. Voucher system journals (replaces **[2]** and **[4]** above when the voucher system is used).
   a. Voucher register—designed to record vouchers payable only. A voucher payable is prepared for each cash payment regardless of the purpose of the payment.
   b. Check register—designed to record all checks written in payment of approved vouchers.

Special Journal for Merchandise Sales on Credit. This journal is designed to accommodate entries for credit sales of regular merchandise only. Therefore, it would handle only the following type of entry (cash sales would not be entered in this journal):

January 2, 19J:

Accounts receivable ($1,000 × 98%)	980	
Sales revenue		980
Credit sale to Adams Company; invoice price, $1,000; terms 2/10, n/30.[10]		

[10] Terms 2/10, n/30, mean that if the account is paid within 10 days after date of sale, a 2% cash discount is permitted to encourage early payment. If not paid within the 10-day discount period, the full amount is past due after the end of 30 days.

Credit sales should be recorded at **net of discount** (rather than at gross) amount, as illustrated above. However, for various reasons, credit sales often are recorded at the gross amount $1,000 (see Chapter 6).

Exhibit 2–11 shows a typical special journal for credit sales for a business that has two sales departments. The general ledger contains an Accounts Receivable Control account. Notice that this special journal provides a convenient format to record all of the relevant data about each credit sale. Also, it can be designed to record sales by department. It is easier to enter a credit sale in this format than in the general journal.

The **posting** of amounts from the special sales journal to the general and subsidiary ledgers is simplified. There are two phases of posting a special journal:

1. **Daily posting**—The amount of **each** credit sale is posted daily to the appropriate individual account in the **accounts receivable subsidiary ledger** to keep it current when the customer pays. Posting is indicated by entering the account number in the ledger Folio column. For example, the number 112.13 entered in the Ledger Folio column in Exhibit 2–11 is the account number assigned to Adams Company and shows that $980 was posted as a debit to the appropriate customer's account in the subsidiary ledger.
2. **Monthly posting**—At the end of each month, the Amount column is summed. This **total is posted to two accounts in the general ledger;** that is, in Exhibit 2–11, the $9,360 was posted (1) as a debit to account No. 112 (Accounts Receivable Control) and (2) as a credit to account No. 500 (Sales Revenue Control). The T-accounts shown in **Exhibit 2–15** illustrate how these postings are reflected in the general ledger and the subsidiary ledger. Notice that the two ledgers show the journal page (i.e., folio) from which each amount was posted.

Exhibit 2–11
Special journal—sales on credit.

SPECIAL JOURNAL-MERCHANDISE SALES ON CREDIT Page S-23

Date 19J	Sales Invoice No.	Accounts Receivable (name)	Terms	Ledger Folio	Receivable and Sale Amount	Dept. Sales	
						Dept. A	Dept. B
Jan. 2	93	Adams Co.	2/10, n/30	112.13	980		
3	94	Sayre Corp.	2/10, n/30	112.80	490		
11	95	Cope & Day Co.	net	112.27	5,734		
27	96	XY Mfg. Co.	2/10, n/30	112.91	1,960	(Not illustrated; the total of each column would also be posted to a sales subsidiary ledger.)	
30	97	Miller, J. B.	2/10, n/30	112.42	196		
31	—	Totals			9,360		
31	—	Posting			(112/500)		

Exhibit 2–12
Special journal—purchases on credit.

SPECIAL JOURNAL · MERCHANDISE PURCHASES ON CREDIT					Page P-19
Date 19J	Purchase Order No.	Accounts Payable (name)	Terms	Ledger Folio	Purchase and Liability Amount
Jan. 3	41	PT Mfg. Co.	1/20,n/30	210.61	990
7	42	Able Suppliers, Ltd.	net	210.12	150
31	—	Totals	—	—	6,760
31	—	Posting	—	—	(612/210)

Special Journal for Merchandise Purchases on Credit In situations where there are numerous credit purchases of merchandise for resale, a special journal may be designed for such transactions as the following:[11]

January 3, 19J:

Purchases ($1,000 × 99%)	990	
Accounts payable (PT Mfg. Co.)		990
Purchased merchandise for resale; invoice price, $1,000; terms 1/20, n/30.		

This transaction, rather than being entered in the general journal, would be entered in the purchases journal as in **Exhibit 2–12.** The purchases are recorded net of discount, however, the gross amount can be used. During the month, each amount would be posted daily as a credit to the accounts of the individual creditors in the **accounts payable subsidiary ledger.**

At the end of the month, the total of the Amount column (i.e., $6,760) would be posted to the general ledger as *(a)* a debit to the Purchases account No. 612 (if a periodic inventory system is used) and *(b)* a credit to the Accounts Payable Control account No. 210.

Special Journal for Cash Receipts. Because a large volume of transactions for cash receipts is typical, a special cash receipts journal often is used. This special journal is designed to accommodate **all cash receipts** including cash sales. Therefore, it must have a column for **cash debit** and several credit columns. Credit columns are for recurring credits, and a Miscellaneous Accounts column is used to record infrequent credits. A typical special cash receipts journal is shown in **Exhibit 2–13.**

During the month, each amount in the Accounts Receivable column is posted daily as a credit to the individual customer accounts in the **accounts receivable subsidiary ledger.** At the end of the month, *(a)* the individual amounts in the Miscellaneous Accounts column are posted as credits to the appropriate general ledger accounts and *(b)* the totals (for Cash, Accounts Receivable, and Sales

[11] This entry assumes periodic inventory procedures. Alternatively, if perpetual inventory procedures are used, the debit would be to the inventory account.

Exhibit 2–13
Special journal—cash receipts.

SPECIAL JOURNAL · CASH RECEIPTS							Page CR-19
			Credits				
Date 19J	Explanation	Debits Cash	Account Title	Ledger Folio	Accounts Receivable	Sales Revenue	Misc. Accounts
Jan. 4	Cash sales	11,200		—		11,200	
7	On acct.	4,490	Sayre Corp.	112.80	4,490		
8	Sale of land	10,000	Land	123			4,000
			Gain on sale of land	510			6,000
10	On acct.	1,000	Adams Co.	112.13	1,000		
19	Cash sales	43,600		—		43,600	
20	On acct.	5,734	Cope & Day Co.	112.27	5,734		
31	Totals	116,224		—	11,224	71,000	34,000
31	Posting	(101)		—	(112)	(500)	(NP)*

* NP—Not posted as one total because the individual amounts are posted as indicated in the Ledger Folio column.

Revenue) are posted to the general ledger as indicated by the folio numbers. The total of the Miscellaneous Accounts column is not posted because the individual amounts have already been posted.

Special Journal for Cash Payments. Because of the large volume of cash disbursements, most companies use a special journal designed to accommodate **all cash payments** including cash purchases of merchandise. The special journal must have a column for cash credits and a number of debit columns. Debit columns are set up for frequently recurring debits, and a Miscellaneous Accounts column is ued for infrequent debits. A typical special cash payments journal, with some common entries, is shown in **Exhibit 2–14.** Posting follows the same procedures explained above for the cash receipts special journal.

Reconciling a Subsidiary Ledger. **The sum of all account balances in a subsidiary ledger must agree with the overall balance reflected in the related control account in the general ledger.** To assure that this equality exists, frequent reconciliations should be made. Clearly, a reconciliation cannot be accomplished unless all posting is complete, both to the control account and to the subsidiary ledger. To illustrate, based upon the information in **Exhibit 2–15,** a reconciliation

Exhibit 2–14
Special journal—cash payments.

SPECIAL JOURNAL · CASH PAYMENTS								Page CP-31
				Debits				
Date 19J	Check No.	Explanation	Credits Cash	Account Name	Ledger Folio	Accounts Payable	Purchases	Misc. Accounts
Jan. 2	141	Pur. mdse.	3,000				3,000	
10	142	On acct.	990	PT Mfg. Co.	210.61	990		
15	143	Jan. rent	660	Rent exp.	612			660
16	144	Pur. mdse.	1,810				1,810	
31	—	Totals	98,400		—	5,820	90,980	1,600
31	—	Posting	(101)		—	(210)	(612)	(NP)

Exhibit 2–15
General ledger and subsidiary ledger.

GENERAL LEDGER (partial)

Cash No. 101

19J			19J		
Jan. 1	balance	18,700	Jan. 31	CP-31	98,400
31	CR-19	116,224			

Accounts Receivable Control No. 112

19J			19J		
Jan. 1	balance	5,000	Jan. 31	CR-19	11,224
31	S-23	9,360			

Equipment No. 140

19J					
Jan. 2	J-14	9,000			

Notes Payable No. 214

			19J		
			Jan. 2	J-14	9,000

Sales Revenue Control No. 500

			19J		
			Jan. 31	S-23	9,360
			31	CR-19	71,000

Exhibit 2–15
(concluded)

SUBSIDIARY LEDGER FOR ACCOUNTS RECEIVABLE (Accts. No. 112)					
Adams Company—Acct. No. 112.13					
Date	Folio	Explanation	Debit	Credit	Balance
19J Jan. 1		balance			1,000
2	S-23		980		1,980
10	CR-19			1,000	980

Cope & Day Company—Acct. No. 112.27					
Jan. 11	S-23		5,734		5,734
20	CR-19			5,734	–0–

Miller, J. B.—Acct. No. 112.42					
Jan. 30	S-23		196		196

Sayre Corporation—Acct. No. 112.80					
Jan. 1		balance			4,000
3	S-23		490		4,490
7	CR-19			4,490	–0–

XY Manufacturing Company—Acct. No. 112.91					
Jan. 27	S-23		1,960		1,960

Reconciliation of Accounts Receivable Subsidiary Ledger (at January 31, 19J)

	Amount
Subsidiary ledger balances:	
112.13 Adams Co.	$ 980
112.42 Miller, J. B.	196
112.91 XY Manufacturing Co.	1,960
Total—agrees with the balance in Accounts Receivable Control ($14,360–$11,224)	$3,136

for **Accounts Receivable Control** and the **accounts receivable subsidiary ledger** would be as follows:

The above discussion reviewed the concepts underlying special journals, control accounts, and subsidiary ledgers. Their design and use depend upon the characteristics of the company. They do not involve new accounting principles because they are only data processing tools. The above discussion also emphasized the four primary efficiencies that may result from their use: (1) journalizing is simplified, (2) posting is simplified, (3) subdivision of work is simplified, and (4) a highly trained person is not needed to maintain a special journal or a subsidiary ledger that involves only one type of transaction.[12]

QUESTIONS

1. Give four examples of internal cost allocations that require adjusting entries.
2. At the end of 19A, Baker Corporation had the following situations:
   a. Prepaid insurance, $150; the policy was acquired on January 1, 19A, and expires on December 31, 19B.
   b. Wages earned on December 29–31, 19A, not yet recorded or paid, $2,400.
   c. Rent collected for January 19B, $400, that was credit to Rent Revenue when collected.
   d. Interest expense of $200 for November–December 19A that will be paid April 30, 19B.
   e. An asset that cost $10,000 (residual value, $1,000) is being depreciated over five years, straight-line (i.e., an equal amount each period).

   Give the 19A adjusting entry for each situation. If none is needed explain why.
3. The following accounts were recorded in the 19X adjusting entries of Jackson Corporation. Classify each account as an asset, liability, revenue, gain, expense, or loss, and explain the classification for each:
   a. Prepaid insurance.
   b. Property taxes payable.
   c. Rent receivable.
   d. Interest payable.
   e. Rent revenue collected in advance.
   f. Accumulated depreciation.
   g. Allowance for doubtful accounts.
4. Briefly explain the differences between perpetual and periodic inventory systems.
5. The following data are available under a periodic inventory system: Purchases, $70,000; Sales, $150,000; Returned sales, $5,000; Returned purchases, $4,000; Freight-in, $7,000; Beginning inventory, $32,000; Selling expenses, $18,000; and Ending inventory, $29,000 (by count). Compute the cost of goods sold.
6. Number the following phases in the accounting information processing cycle to indicate their normal sequence of completion:

[12] Voucher system journals are not discussed because they involve essentially the same procedures as illustrated. The voucher system journals are known as *(a)* the voucher register and *(b)* the check register.

______ Journalize and post reversing entries.	______ Prepare financial statements.
______ Posting.	______ Journalize current transactions.
______ Transaction analysis.	______ Prepare post-closing trial balance.
______ Collection of data.	______ Prepare worksheets.
______ Journalize and post adjusting entries.	______ Prepare unadjusted trial balance.
______ Journalize and post closing entries.	

7. Explain the purpose and nature of closing entries.
8. Give the purpose and nature of reversing entries. Why are they journalized and posted?
9. X Company owes a $4,000, three-year, 9% note payable. Interest is paid each November 30. Therefore, at the end of the accounting period, December 31, the following adjusting entry was made.

Interest expense	30	
Interest payable		30

Would you recommend using a reversing entry in this situation? Explain.

EXERCISES

E 2–1 (Analyze and Record Typical Transactions)
The following selected transactions were completed during the current year by Blue Corporation:

a. Sold 60,000 shares of its own common stock, par $1 per share, for $70,000 cash.
b. Borrowed $20,000 cash on a six-month, 9% note payable (interest is payable at maturity date).
c. Purchased real estate for use in the business at a cash cost of $150,000. The real estate consisted of a small building ($90,000) and the lot on which it was located.
d. Purchased merchandise for resale at a cash cost of $30,000. Assume periodic inventory system; therefore, debit Purchases.
e. Purchased merchandise for resale on credit; terms 3/10, n/30. If paid within 10 days, the cash payment would be $1,940; however, if paid after 10 days, the payment would be $2,000. Because the company takes all discounts, credit purchases are recorded at net of the discount.
f. Sold merchandise for $20,000; collected 60% in cash, and the balance is due in 30 days.
g. Paid the balance due on the purchase in *(e)* within the 10-day period.
h. Paid the note and interest in full for the loan in *(b)* above on due date.
i. Recorded income tax of $9,000 for the current year, which will be paid early next year.
j. Recorded straight-line depreciation for one year on the building; 10-year useful life and estimated residual value, $10,000.

Required:
Analyze each of the above transactions and enter each in a general journal. Use the letter to the left to indicate the date.

E 2–2 (Analyze and Record Typical Transactions)
During the accounting year ended December 31, 19B, Missouri Corporation completed the following selected transactions:

a. Sold 20,000 shares of its own common stock, par $5 for $12 cash per share.
b. Borrowed $100,000 cash on a one-year, 9% interest-bearing note, interest payable at maturity date March 31, 19C.
c. Purchased a small office building for $200,000 cash, of which the land cost was $40,000. Estimated useful life 10 years and $10,000 residual value. The company will use straight-line depreciation.
d. Service revenues, $200,000, of which 20% was on credit.
e. Declared and paid a $20,000 cash dividend.
f. Collected half of the credit revenues (item [*d*] above).
g. Incurred total expenses of $160,000, of which 15% was on credit.
h. Purchased an electric typewriter that had an invoice price of $1,500 for $1,300 cash.
i. Paid two-thirds of the credit expenses (item [*g*]).
j. Recorded interest expense on the note (item [*b*]).
k. Recorded depreciation expense on the office building for six months because it was purchased on July 1, 19B.

Required:
Analyze each of the above transactions and enter each in a general journal.

E 2–3 (Review the Accounting Information Processing Cycle)
The 11 phases that comprise the accounting information processing cycle are listed to the left in scrambled order. To the right is a brief statement of the objective of each phase, also in scrambled order. You are to present two responses.

Required:
1. In the blanks to the left, number the phases in the usual sequence of completion.
2. In the blanks to the right, use the letters to match each phase with its objective.

Sequence (order)	Phases	Matching (with objective)	Objective
______	Journalizing.	______	*a.* Verification after closing entries.
______	Journalize and post reversing entries.	______	*b.* Communication to decision makers.
______	Transaction analysis.	______	*c.* Verification before adjusting entries.
______	Prepare financial statements.	______	*d.* Transfer from journal to ledger.
______	Journalize and post closing entries.	______	*e.* An activity that is based on source documents.
______	Collection of raw data.	______	*f.* Update general ledger by separating "mixed" account balances.
______	Posting.	______	*g.* Assess economic impact of each transaction.
______	Journalize and post adjusting entries.	______	*h.* An original input into the accounting system.
______	Prepare worksheets.	______	*i.* To facilitate subsequent entries.
______	Prepare unadjusted trial balance.	______	*j.* To obtain a zero balance in the revenue and expense accounts.
______	Prepare post-closing trial balance.	______	*k.* A logical and systematic technique that is used in completing the end-of-period procedures.

E 2–4 (Journalize and Post Typical Transactions)
Darby Corporation completed the three transactions given below:

a. January 1, 19A—sold 10,000 shares of its own unissued common stock, par $1 per share, for $50,000 cash.

b. January 3, 19A—purchased a machine that cost $60,000. Payment was $20,000 cash plus a $30,000, one-year, 10% interest-bearing note payable and a $10,000, three year, 12% interest-bearing note payable. Interest on each note is payable every January 2.

c. February 1, 19A—sold two lots that would not be needed for $10,000. Received $4,000 cash down payment and a $6,000, 90-day, 9% interest-bearing note (interest payable at maturity date). The two lots had a book value of $6,500.

Required:

1. Analyze each of the above transactions and enter each in the general journal.
2. Set up T-accounts and post the entries in (1) above. For posting purposes, set up a numbering system for both the journal pages and the ledger accounts. Use these numbers in your posting process.

E 2–5 (Resolve Errors and Correct a Trial Balance)

A clerk for Century Company prepared the following unadjusted trial balance which the clerk was unable to balance:

Account	Debit	Credit
Cash	$ 35,563	
Accounts receivable	31,000	
Allowance for doubtful accounts	(2,000)	
Inventory		$ 18,000
Equipment	181,500	
Accumulated depreciation		12,000
Accounts payable	18,000	
Notes payable		25,000
Common stock, par $10		180,000
Retained earnings (correct)		14,000
Revenues		75,000
Expenses	60,000	
Totals (out of balance by $63)	$324,063	$324,000

Assume you are examining the accounts and have found the following errors:

a. Equipment purchased for $7,500 at year-end was debited to Expenses.

b. Sales on credit of $829 were debited to Accounts Receivable for $892 and credited to Revenues for $829.

c. A $6,000 collection on accounts receivable was debited to Cash and credited to Revenues.

d. The inventory amount is understated by $2,000 (cost of goods is included in expenses).

Required:

Prepare a corrected trial balance. Show computations.

E 2–6 (Journalize Adjusting Entries)

Rivers Corporation adjusts and closes its accounts each December 31. The following situations require adjusting entries at the current year-end. You are requested to prepare the adjusting entries in the general journal for each situation. If no entry is required for any item, explain why.

a. Machine A is to be depreciated for the full year. It cost $90,000, and the estimated useful life is five years, with an estimated residual value of $10,000. Use straight-line depreciation.

b. Credit sales for the current year amounted to $160,000. The estimated bad debt loss rate on credit sales is ½%.

c. Property taxes for the current year have not been recorded or paid. A statement for the current year was received near the end of December for $4,000; if paid after February 1 in the next year, a 10% penalty is assessed.

d. Office supplies that cost $800 were purchased during the year and debited to Office Supplies Inventory. The inventories of these supplies on hand were as follows: $200 at the end of the prior year, and $300 at the end of the current year.

e. Rivers rented an office in its building to a tenant for one year, starting on September 1. Rent for one year amounting to $6,000 was collected at that date. The total amount collected was credited to Rent Revenue.

f. Rivers received a note receivable from a customer dated November 1 of the current year. It is a $12,000, 10%, note, due in one year. At the maturity date, Rivers will collect the amount of the note plus interest for one year.

E 2–7 (Journalize Adjusting Entries)

On December 31, 19D, PV Corporation had the following situations that might affect its annual report. You are to analyze each one and give any required adjusting entries. If no entry is required for any item, explain why.

a. At the end of the year, unpaid and unrecorded wages amounted to $5,000.

b. The company owns a building that is to be depreciated for the full year. It cost $274,000, has an estimated useful life of 20 years, and a residual value of $54,000. Accumulated depreciation at the beginning of the current year was $60,000. Use straight-line depreciation.

c. The company rented some space in its building to a tenant on August 1 of the current year and collected $7,200 cash, which was rent for six months in advance. Rent Revenue was credited for $7,200 on August 1.

d. The company paid a two-year insurance premium in advance on July 1 of the current year amounting to $1,000. The $1,000 was debited to Prepaid Insurance at payment date.

e. Credit sales for the current year amounted to $150,000. The estimated bad debt loss rate is ⅓% of credit sales.

f. On July 1 of the current year, the company received a $30,000, one-year, 9% note from a customer. At maturity date, the company will receive the principal amount plus interest for one year.

E 2–8 (Relationships between Revenue and Cost of Goods Sold)

1. Analyze the relationships and amounts for each of the four cases and complete the following schedule to compute cost of goods sold:

	Case A	Case B	Case C	Case D
Sales revenue	$100,000	$136,000	$128,000	$110,000
Beginning inventory	20,000	25,000	?	26,000
Net income (loss)	10,000	25,000	16,000	(10,000)
Ending inventory	30,000	?	32,000	?
Total expenses	40,000	41,000	44,000	48,000
Purchases	?	60,000	70,000	73,000
Cost of goods sold	?	?	?	?

2. Give the adjusting entry for purchases, inventory, and cost of goods sold assuming that a periodic inventory system is used in Case A.

E 2–9 (Adjusting Entries)

a. On December 31, 19A, the Maintenance Supplies Inventory account showed a balance on hand amounting to $350. During 19B, purchases of office supplies amounted to $1,000. An inventory of maintenance supplies on hand at December 31, 19B, reflected unused supplies amounting to $500. Give the adjusting journal entry that should be made on December 31, 19B, assuming that: Case A—the purchases were debited to the Maintenance Supplies Inventory account, and Case B—the purchases were debited to Maintenance Supplies Expense.

b. On December 31, 19A, the Prepaid Insurance account showed a debit balance of $900, which was for coverage for the three months, January–March. On April 1, 19B, the company obtained another policy covering a two-year period from that date. The two-year premium amounting to $9,600 was paid and debited to Prepaid Insurance. Give the adjusting journal entry that should be made on December 31, 19B, to adjust for the entire year.

E 2–10 (Analysis; Adjusting Entries)

Voss Company adjusts and closes its accounts each December 31. Below are two typical situations involving adjusting entries.

a. During the current year, office supplies were purchased for cash, $750. The inventory of office supplies at the end of the prior year was $150. At the end of the current year, the inventory showed $240 unused supplies remaining on hand. Give the adjusting entry assuming at the time of the purchase that: Case A—$750 was debited to Office Supplies Expense, and Case B—$750 was debited to Office Supplies Inventory.

b. On June 1, the company collected cash, $8,400, which was for rent collected in advance for the next 12 months. Give the adjusting journal entry assuming at the time of the collection that: Case A—$8,400 was credited to Rent Revenue, and Case B—$8,400 was credited to Rent Revenue Collected in Advance.

E 2–11 (Analysis; Adjusting Entries)

Atlantic Company adjusts and closes its books each December 31. It is now December 31, 19A, and the adjusting entries are to be made. You are requested to prepare, in general journal format, the adjusting entry that should be made for each of the following items:

a. Credit sales for the year amounted to $160,000. The estimated loss rate on bad debts is $\frac{3}{8}$%.

b. Unpaid and unrecorded wages incurred at December 31 amounted to $2,400.

c. The company paid a two-year insurance premium in advance on April 1, 19A, amounting to $4,800, which was debited to Prepaid Insurance.

d. Machine A that cost $40,000 is to be depreciated for the full year. The estimated useful life is 10 years, and the residual value, $2,000. Use straight-line depreciation.

e. The company rented a warehouse on June 1, 19A, for one year. They had to pay the full amount of rent one year in advance on June 1, amounting to $4,800, which was debited to Rent Expense.

f. The company received a 9% note from a customer with a face amount of $6,000. The note was dated September 1, 19A; the principal plus the interest is payable one year later. Notes Receivable was debited, and Sales Revenue credited on September 1, 19A.

g. On December 30, 19A, the property tax bill was received in the amount of $2,500. This amount applied only to 19A and had not been previously recorded or paid. The taxes are due, and will be paid, on January 15, 19B.

h. On April 1, 19A, the company signed a $30,000, 10% note payable. On that date, Cash was debited and Notes Payable credited for $30,000. The note is payable on March 31, 19B, for the face amount plus interest for one year.

i. The company purchased a patent on January 1, 19A, at a cost of $5,950. On that date, Patent was debited and Cash credited for $5,950. The patent has an estimated useful life of 17 years and no residual value.

j. The worksheet is being completed, and pretax income has been computed to be $40,000 after all the above adjustments. Assume an average income tax rate of 30%.

E 2–12 (T-accounts; Diagram Closing Entries)

The adjusted trial balance for Ryan Company showed the following on December 31, 19E, which is the end of the annual accounting period:

Sales revenue	$92,000
Interest revenue	4,000
Purchases	44,000
Purchase returns	500
Freight-in (on purchases)	1,500
Beginning inventory (periodic)	17,800
Selling expenses	23,000
Administrative expenses	13,000
Interest expense	400
Income tax expense	1,500
Additional data:	
Ending inventory	19,000

Required:

Set up T-accounts for each of the above; enter the balance in each account, and then draw in lines to diagram and identify any adjusting and closing entries (refer to Exhibit 2–7). Use Cost of Goods Sold, Income Summary, and Retained Earnings accounts.

E 2–13 (Adjusting and Closing Entries)

At December 31, 19B (end of the accounting period), Sara Corporation reflected the following amounts on its worksheet:

Sales revenue	$95,000
Interest revenue	2,000
Beginning inventory (periodic inventory system)	15,000
Ending inventory	17,000
Freight-in (on purchases)	3,000
Purchases	54,000
Sales returns	4,000
Purchase returns	1,000
Operating expenses (including income tax)	26,000

Required:

1. Compute cost of goods sold.
2. Give the adjusting entry for purchases, inventory, and cost of goods sold. If none is required, explain why.
3. Give the closing entries for *(a)* revenues, *(b)* expenses, and *(c)* net income.

E 2–14 (Adjusting and Closing Entries)

Seattle Company has completed its worksheet at December 31, 19B (end of its accounting period). The following accounts and amounts were reflected on the worksheet:

Sales revenue	$110,000
Service revenue	2,000
Operating expenses	24,000
Income tax expense	5,000
Cost of goods sold	53,000
Interest expense	4,000
Ending inventory (perpetual inventory system)	11,000

Required:

1. Give the adjusting entry for inventory and cost of goods sold. If none is required, explain why.
2. Give the closing entries for *(a)* revenues, *(b)* expenses, and *(c)* net income.

E 2–15 **(Reversing Entries)**
At the end of the annual accounting period, Sterling Corporation made the following adjusting entries:

a. Wage expense	8,000	
Wages payable		8,000
b. Bad debt expense	500	
Allowance for doubtful accounts		500
c. Income tax expense	12,000	
Income tax payable		12,000
d. Depreciation expense	25,000	
Accumulated depreciation		25,000

Required:
Give the reversing entries that you think would be preferable on January 1, 19C. For each adjusting entry, explain the analysis you used to decide whether to reverse it.

E 2–16 **(Reversing Entries)**
At the end of the annual accounting period, Rose Corporation made the following adjusting entries:
December 31, 19A:

a. Property tax expense	800	
Property taxes payable		800
(These are paid once each year.)		
b. Rent receivable	4,000	
Rent revenue		4,000
(Rent revenue is collected at various dates each month.)		
c. Patent amortization expense	2,000	
Patents		2,000
d. Warranty expense	600	
Estimated warranty liability		600
e. Wage expense	9,000	
Wages payable		9,000

Required:
Give the reversing entries that should be made on January 1, 19B. Explain, for each adjusting entry, the analysis you used to determine whether to reverse it.

E 2–17 **(Prepare a Monthly Statement of Income)**
Tuffy Corporation prepares monthly interim financial statements for internal use. Its accounting period ends December 31. At the end of each month, the company accountant

prepares a cumulative worksheet that uses the *(a)* unadjusted trial balance at the end of the month and *(b)* adjusting entries based on cumulative amounts to the end of the month.

It is February 28 of the current year 19A, and the worksheet has been completed. Therefore, the following data are available for preparing the statement of income (summarized to simplify):

	Reported in January	Reflected on February 28 worksheet
Sales revenue	$150,000	$365,000
Cost of goods sold	80,000	220,000
Operating expenses	30,000	63,000
Interest revenue	2,000	3,400
Interest expense	5,000	11,100
Gain (loss) on disposal of assets	7,000	(9,000)
Income tax expense	11,000	16,325

Required:

Prepare a summarized statement of income for the month of February. Show computations.

PROBLEMS

P 2–1 (Journalize and Post Unadjusted Trial Balance)

The following selected transactions were completed during year 1 of operations by Rotan Corporation:

a. Sold 20,000 shares of its own common stock, par $1 per share, for $12 per share and received cash in full.

b. Borrowed $100,000 cash on a 9%, one-year note, interest payable at maturity on April 30, year 2.

c. Purchased equipment for use in operating the business at a net cash cost of $164,000; paid in full.

d. Purchased merchandise for resale at a cash cost of $140,000; paid cash. Assume a periodic inventory system; therefore, debit Purchases.

e. Purchased merchandise for resale on credit terms 2/10, n/60. The merchandise will cost $9,800 if paid within 10 days; after 10 days, the payment will be $10,000. The company always takes the discount; therefore, such purchases are recorded at net of the discount.

f. Sold merchandise for $180,000; collected $165,000 cash, and the balance is due in one month.

g. Paid $40,000 cash for operating expenses.

h. Paid three-fourths of the balance for the merchandise purchased in *(e)* within 10 days; the balance remains unpaid.

i. Collected 50% of the balance due on the sale in *(f)*; the remaining balance is uncollected.

j. Paid cash for an insurance premium, $600; the premium was for two years' coverage (debit Prepaid Insurance).

k. Purchased a tract of land for a future building for company operations, $63,000 cash.

l. Paid damages to a customer who was injured on the company premises, $10,000 cash.

Required:

1. Enter each of the above transactions in a general journal; use J1 for the first journal page number. Use the letter to the left to indicate the date.
2. Set up appropriate T-accounts and post the journal entries. Use folio numbers in posting. Assign each T-account an appropriate title, and number each account in statement of financial position order, followed by the statement of income accounts; start with Cash, No. 101.
3. Prepare an unadjusted trial balance.

P 2–2 (Journalize, Post, Unadjusted Trial Balance)

The following selected transactions were completed during year 1 of operations by Karson Corporation.

a. At date of organization, sold and issued 50,000 shares of its common stock, par $1 per share, for $94,000 cash.

b. Purchased a plant site for $100,000. The site included a building valued at $82,000 and land values at $18,000. Payment was made, $70,000 cash and a $30,000 one-year, 10% note, interest payable at maturity.

c. Borrowed $70,000 cash from City Bank; signed a 9% (interest payable at maturity) note due in six months.

d. Purchased equipment for use in the business for $25,000; paid cash.

e. Purchased merchandise for resale at a cost of $80,000; paid $70,000 cash, balance on credit. Assume perpetual inventory system; therefore, debit Merchandise Inventory.

f. Sold merchandise for cash, $65,000; the perpetual inventory records showed that this merchandise cost $30,000 (you should make two entries).

g. Paid operating expenses, $35,000.

h. Sold merchandise for cash, $48,000; cost, $23,000.

i. Purchased merchandise for cash, $22,000.

j. Paid $7,000 of the balance for the merchandise purchased in *(e)*.

k. Sold and issued 30,000 shares of its common stock for $53,000.

l. On due date, paid the local bank the note given in entry *(c)* in the amount of $70,000 plus the interest to maturity date.

m. Paid a two-year premium of $1,400 for an insurance policy on the building and equipment.

Required:

1. Record the above transactions in a general journal; use J1 for the first journal page. Use the letters to the left to indicate dates.
2. Set up appropriate T-accounts and post the entries. Use folio numbers in your posting. Assign each T-account an appropriate descriptive title, and number each account in statement of financial position order, followed by the statement of income accounts; start with Cash, No. 101.
3. Prepare an unadjusted trial balance.

P 2–3 **(Explain Some Adjusting and Closing Entries)**

Below are some unrelated adjusting and closing (but no reversing) entries. Write a suitable explanation for each of the following end-of-period entries:

a. Salary expense	7,000	
Salaries payable		7,000
b. Rent revenue	800	
Unearned rent revenue		800
c. Ending inventory	10,000	
Cost of goods sold	72,000	
Purchases		70,000
Beginning inventory		12,000
d. Interest receivable	900	
Interest revenue		900
e. Supplies expense	400	
Supplies inventory		400
f. Income summary	79,000	
Operating expenses		21,000
Administrative expenses		16,000
Interest expense		2,000
Cost of goods sold		40,000
g. Interest expense	750	
Interest payable		750
h. Income summary	12,500	
Retained earnings		12,500
i. Investment revenue	600	
Unearned investment revenue		600
j. Warranty (guarantee) expense	500	
Estimated warranty liability		500
k. Income tax expense	3,700	
Income taxes payable		3,700
l. Property tax expense	360	
Property taxes payable		360
m. Sales revenue	90,000	
Rent revenue	2,000	
Interest revenue	1,000	
Sales returns		1,500
Income summary		91,500

P 2–4 **(Journalize Adjusting Entries)**

Becker Company adjusts and closes its accounts each December 31. It is December 31, 19D. Prepare, in general journal format, the adjusting entry that should be made at year-end for each of the following items:

a. The company owns a building and the site on which it is situated. The Building account reflects a cost of $500,000; and the Land account, $80,000. The estimated useful life of the building is 20 years, and the residual value, $50,000. Accumulated depreciation to January 1, 19D, was $67,500. Use straight-line depreciation.

b. Property taxes for the city fiscal year, which ends June 30, 19E, have not been recorded or paid. A tax statement was received near the end of December 19D for $6,000. The taxes are due, and will be paid, on February 15, 19E. Property tax expense for the city fiscal year ended June 30, 19D, was $4,800. No property tax expense has been recorded in 19D. Hint: Notice that the city and the company have different fiscal years.

c. The company received a $9,000, 10% note from a customer on May 1, 19D. On that date, Notes Receivable was debited and Sales Revenue credited for $9,000. The face of the note plus interest for one year is payable on April 30, 19E.

d. At December 31, 19D, the Supplies Inventory account showed a debit balance of $1,600. An inventory of unused supplies taken at year-end reflected $300.

e. Sales revenue for the year amounted to $1,500,000, of which $270,000 was on credit. The estimated bad debt loss rate, based on credit sales, was $\frac{1}{3}$% for the year.

f. On August 1, 19D, the company rented some space in its building to a tenant and collected $4,200 cash rent in advance. This was for the six months starting August 1, 19D, and was credited to Rent Revenue.

g. At December 31, 19D, unrecorded and unpaid salaries amounted to $8,000.

h. On April 1, 19D, the company borrowed $20,000 on a one-year 9% note. On that date, Cash was debited and Notes Payable credited for $20,000. At maturity date the face amount plus interest for one year must be paid.

i. On January 1, 19D, the company purchased a patent for use in the business at a cash cost of $3,000, which was debited to Patent. The patent has an estimated remaining economic life of 10 years and no residual value.

j. Inventory: December 31, 19C, $20,000; December 31, 19D, $30,000; Purchases, $800,000; and Purchase returns, $5,000. The company uses the periodic inventory system.

k. The worksheet is being completed; all of the above adjusting entries have been recorded on it. Pretax income has been computed to be $70,000. Assume the average income tax rate is 30%.

P 2–5 (Journalize Adjusting Entries)

The following transactions and events for Sun Manufacturing Corporation are under consideration for adjusting entries at December 31, 19D (end of the accounting period). Give the adjusting entry (or entries) that should be made on December 31, 19D for each item. State any assumptions that you make. If an adjusting entry is not required, explain why.

a. Machine A used in the factory cost $225,000; it was purchased on July 1, 19A. It has an estimated useful life of 12 years and a residual value of $15,000. Straight-line depreciation is used.

b. Sales for 19D amounted to $2,000,000, including $300,000 credit sales. It is estimated, based on experience of the company, that bad debt losses will be $\frac{1}{4}$% of credit sales.

c. At the beginning of 19D, Office Supplies Inventory amounted to $300. During 19D, office supplies amounting to $4,400 were purchased; this amount was debited to Office Supplies Expenses. An inventory of office supplies at the end of 19D showed $200 on the shelves. The January 1 balance of $300 is still reflected in the Office Supplies Inventory account.

d. On July 1, 19D, the company paid a three-year insurance premium amounting to $1,080; this amount was debited to Prepaid Insurance.

e. On October 1, 19D, the company paid rent on some leased office space. The payment of $3,600 cash was for the following six months. At the time of payment, Rent Expense was debited for the $3,600.

f. On August 1, 19D, the company borrowed $60,000 from Sharpstown Bank. The loan was for 12 months at 9% interest payable at maturity date.

g. Finished goods inventory on January 1, 19D, was $100,000; and on December 31, 19D, it was $130,000. The perpetual inventory record provided the cost of goods sold amount of $1,200,000.

h. The company owned some property (land) that was rented to B. R. Speir on April 1, 19D, for 12 months for $4,200. On April 1, the entire annual rental of $4,200 was credited to Rent Revenue Collected in Advance and Cash was debited.

i. On December 31, 19D, wages earned by employees but not yet paid (nor recorded in the accounts) amounted to $9,000. Disregard payroll taxes.

j. On September 1, 19D, the company loaned $30,000 to an outside party. The loan was at 10% per annum and was due in six months; interest is payable at maturity. Cash was credited for $30,000, and Notes Receivable debited on September 1 for the same amount.

k. On January 1, 19D, factory supplies on hand amounted to $100. During 19D, factory supplies that cost $2,000 were purchased and debited to Factory Supplies Inventory. At the end of 19D, a physical inventory count revealed that factory supplies on hand amounted to $400.

l. The company purchased a gravel pit on January 1, 19B, at a cost of $30,000; it was estimated that approximately 60,000 tons of gravel could be removed prior to exhaustion. It was also estimated that the company would take five years to exploit this natural resource. Tons of gravel removed and sold were: 19B—3,000; 19C—7,000; and 19D—5,000. Hint: Amortize on output basis; no residual value.

m. At the end of 19D, it was found that postage stamps that cost $60 were on hand (in a "postage" box in the office). When the stamps were purchased, Miscellaneous Expense was debited and Cash credited.

n. At the end of 19D, property taxes for 19D amounting to $29,500 had been assessed on property owned by the company. The taxes are due no later than February 1, 19E. The taxes have not been recorded on the books because payment has not been made.

o. The company borrowed $60,000 from the bank on December 1, 19D. A 60-day note payable was signed at 9½% interest payable on maturity date. On December 1, 19D, Cash was debited and Notes Payable credited for $60,000.

p. On July 1, 19D, the company paid the city a $500 license fee for the next 12 months. On that date, Cash was credited and License Expense debited for $500.

q. On March 1, 19D, the company made a loan to the company president and received a $15,000 note receivable. The loan was due in one year and called for 6% annual interest payable at maturity date.

r. The company owns three company cars used by the executives. A six-month maintenance contract on them was signed on October 1, 19D, whereby a local garage agreed to do "all the required maintenance." The payment was made for the following six months in advance. On October 1, 19D, Cash was credited and Maintenance Expense was debited for $4,800.

P 2–6 (Adjusting Entries; Correct Financial Statements)

Ace Service Corporation has been in operation since January 1, 19A. It is now December 31, 19B, the end of the annual accounting period. The company has never been audited by an independent CPA. The annual statements given below were prepared by the company bookkeeper at December 31, 19B (additional accounts needed in the solution are provided without amounts):

Statement of Income

Revenues:	
Service revenue	$250,000
Interest revenue	1,000
Total revenues	251,000
Expenses:	
Salary expense	75,000
Wage expense	60,600
Depreciation expense	
Interest expense	2,400
Remaining expenses	50,000
Total operating expenses	188,000
Pretax income	63,000
Income tax expense	
Net income	$ 63,000
EPS	$3.50

Statement of Financial Position

Assets

Cash	$ 40,000
Note receivable (10%)	12,000
Interest receivable	
Inventory, office supplies	2,000
Prepaid insurance	1,500
Equipment	200,000
Accumulated depreciation	(22,500)
Remaining assets	85,500
Total assets	$318,500

Liabilities

Accounts payable	$ 18,000
Wages payable	
Unearned service revenue	
Interest payable	
Income taxes payable	
Notes payable (16%)	40,000
Total liabilities	58,000

Stockholders' Equity

Capital stock, par $10	180,000
Retained earnings	80,500
Total stockholders' equity	260,500
Total liabilities and stockholders' equity	$318,500

An outside accountant was engaged to adjust the statements for any items omitted. As a consequence, the following additional information was developed:

a. No depreciation has been recognized for 19B. The equipment has an eight-year life and residual value of $20,000.

b. Prepaid insurance at the end of 19B was $500. Use "Remaining expenses."

c. Wages unpaid and unrecorded at the end of 19B amounted to $15,000.

d. Interest on the note receivable was collected on the last interest date, October 31, 19B.

e. The inventory count of office supplies at year-end showed $300. Use "Remaining expenses."

f. On December 31, 19B, service revenues collected but unearned amounted to $8,000.
g. Interest on the note payable is paid each August 31.
h. Assume the income tax rate is 20 percent.

Required:

1. Prepare adjusting entries for the above items in general journal form at December 31, 19B.
2. Restate the above statements after taking into account your adjusting entries made in (1) above. Key each adjustment. You need not use additional subclassifications on the statements. Suggestion: Use the following solution format:

Items	Reported amounts	Changes from adjusting entries (use + and −)	Correct amounts
(list the two statements here)			

P 2–7 (Ledger; Periodic Inventory, Closing Entries)

The adjusted trial balance for Bryan Corporation reflected the following on December 31, 19A, end of the annual accounting period:

Cash	$ 27,900	
Accounts receivable	32,000	
Allowance for doubtful accounts		$ 500
Inventory (periodic system)*	18,000	
Prepaid insurance	600	
Equipment	100,000	
Accumulated depreciation, equipment		20,000
Accounts payable		13,400
Wages payable		800
Income taxes payable		5,000
Notes payable, long term		20,000
Common stock, par $10		100,000
Retained earnings		12,400
Sales revenue		116,000
Interest revenue		1,000
Sales returns	3,000	
Purchases	70,000	
Freight-in (on purchases)	2,500	
Purchase returns		900
Operating expenses	18,000	
General expenses (including interest)	13,000	
Income tax expense	5,000	
	$290,000	$290,000

* Inventory count at December 31, 19A, $23,000.

Required:

1. Set up T-accounts only for the Inventory and Cost of Goods Sold accounts, and the accounts that will be closed. Enter the balances given above. Diagram the adjusting entry for inventory and cost of goods sold and all of the closing entries. Use both Cost of Goods Sold and Income Summary accounts (see Exhibit 2–7).
2. The company uses the periodic inventory system. Give the adjusting entry for inventory, purchase accounts, and cost of goods sold.
3. Give the closing entries.

P 2–8 (Complete All Phases of the Accounting Cycle)

The post-closing trial balance of the general ledger of Wilson Corporation at December 31, 19I, reflected the following:

Acct. No.	Account	Debit	Credit
101	Cash	$ 27,000	
102	Accounts receivable	21,000	
103	Allowance for doubtful accounts		$ 1,000
104	Inventory (perpetual inventory system)*	35,000	
105	Prepaid insurance (20 months remaining)	900	
200	Equipment (20-year estimated life; no residual value)	50,000	
201	Accumulated depreciation, equipment		22,500
300	Accounts payable		7,500
301	Wages payable		
302	Income taxes payable (for 19I)		4,000
400	Common stock, par $1		80,000
401	Retained earnings		18,900
500	Sales revenue		
600	Cost of goods sold		
601	Operating expenses		
602	Income tax expense		
700	Income summary		
		$133,900	$133,900

* Ending inventory, $45,000 (at 12/31/19J).

The following transactions occurred during 19J in the order given (use the number at the left to indicate the date):

Date

1. Sales revenue of $30,000, of which $10,000 was on credit; cost provided by perpetual inventory record, $19,500. Hint: When the perpetual system is used, make two entries to record a sale—first, debit Cash and/or Accounts Receivable and credit Sales Revenue; and second, Debit Cost of Goods Sold and credit Inventory.
2. Collected $17,000 on accounts receivable.
3. Paid income taxes payable (19I), $4,000.
4. Purchased merchandise, $40,000, of which $8,000 was on credit.
5. Paid accounts payable, $6,000.
6. Sales revenue of $72,000 (in cash); cost, $46,800.
7. Paid operating expenses, $19,000.
8. On January 1, 19J, sold and issued 1,000 shares of common stock, par $1, for $1,000 cash.
9. Purchased merchandise, $100,000, of which $27,000 was on credit.
10. Sales revenue of $98,000, of which $30,000 was on credit; cost, $63,700.
11. Collected cash on accounts receivable, $26,000.
12. Paid cash on accounts payable, $28,000.
13. Paid various operating expenses in cash, $18,000.

Required:

1. Set up T-accounts in the general ledger for each of the accounts listed in the above trial balance and enter the December 31, 19I, balances.
2. Journalize each of the transactions listed above for 19J; use only a general journal.
3. Post the journal entries; use folio notations.
4. Prepare an unadjusted trial balance.

5. Journalize the adjusting entries and post them to the ledger. Assume a bad debt rate of ½% of credit sales for the period and an average 40% income tax rate. Hint: Income tax expense is $11,784. At December 31, 19J, accrued wages were $300. Use straight-line depreciation.
6. Prepare an adjusted trial balance.
7. Prepare the statements of income and financial position (subclassifications are not required).
8. Journalize and post the closing entries.
9. Prepare a post-closing trial balance.

P 2–9 (Worksheet, Adjusting and Closing Entries; Statements)
Major Corporation adjusts and closes its books each December 31. At December 31, 19C, the following unadjusted trial balance has been developed from the general ledger shown below.

Account	Balances (unadjusted) Debit	Credit
Cash	$139,960	
Accounts receivable	34,000	
Allowance for doubtful accounts		$ 5,400
Inventory (periodic system)	62,000	
Prepaid insurance (15 months remaining as of 1/1/19C)	600	
Long-term note receivable (14%)	12,000	
Investment revenue receivable		
Land	27,000	
Building	240,000	
Accumulated depreciation, building		130,000
Equipment	90,000	
Accumulated depreciation, equipment		50,000
Accounts payable		23,000
Salaries payable		
Income taxes payable		
Interest payable		
Unearned rent revenue		
Note payable, 10%, long term		120,000
Common stock, par $10		200,000
Contributed capital in excess of par		10,000
Retained earnings		27,900
Sales revenue		300,000
Investment revenue		1,260
Rent revenue		6,000
Purchases	164,000	
Purchase returns		4,000
Cost of goods sold		
Selling expenses	51,000	
General and administrative expenses	35,000	
Interest expense	7,000	
Extraordinary loss (pretax)	15,000	
Income tax expense		
	$877,560	$877,560

Additional data for adjustments and other purposes:

a. Estimated bad debt loss rate is ½% of credit sales. Ten percent of 19C sales were on credit. Classify as a selling expense.
b. The company uses the periodic inventory system—ending inventory (December 31, 19C), $70,000.
c. Interest on the long-term note receivable was last collected on September 30, 19C.

d. Estimated useful life on the building was 20 years; residual value, $40,000. Allocate 10% of depreciation expense to administrative expense and the balance to selling expenses. Assume straight-line depreciation (for proportionate usage).

e. Estimated useful life of the equipment was 10 years; residual value, zero. Allocate 10% of depreciation expense to administrative expense and the balance to selling expenses. Assume straight-line depreciation.

f. Unrecorded and unpaid sales salaries at December 31, 19C, were $7,500.

g. Interest on the note payable, long term, was paid last on July 31, 19C.

h. On August 1, 19C, the company rented some space in its building to a tenant and collected $6,000 for 12 months rent in advance, which was credited to Rent Revenue.

i. Adjust for expired insurance. Classify as selling expense.

j. Assume an average 30% corporate income tax rate on all items including the extraordinary loss. Hint: Income tax expense is $3,615.

Required:

1. Enter the above unadjusted trial balance on a worksheet.
2. Enter the adjusting entries (including the adjusting entry for inventory and cost of goods sold) on the worksheet and complete it.
3. Prepare a summary statement of income and financial position (subclassifications are not required).
4. Journalize the closing entries.

P 2–10 (Worksheet, Adjusting and Closing Entries; Statements)

DAR Corporation currently is completing the end-of-the-period accounting process. At December 31, 19D, the following unadjusted trial balance was developed from the general ledger:

Account	Balances (unadjusted) Debit	Credit
Cash	$ 60,260	
Accounts receivable	38,000	
Allowance for doubtful accounts		$ 2,000
Inventory (perpetual inventory system)	105,000	
Sales supplies inventory	900	
Long-term note receivable, 14%	12,000	
Equipment	180,000	
Accumulated depreciation, equipment		64,000
Patent	8,400	
Interest receivable		
Accounts payable		23,000
Interest payable		
Income taxes payable		
Property taxes payable		
Unearned rent revenue		
Mortgage payable, 12%		60,000
Common stock, par $10		100,000
Contributed capital in excess of par		15,000
Retained earnings		32,440
Sales revenue		700,000
Investment revenue		1,120
Rent revenue		3,000
Cost of goods sold	380,000	
Selling expenses	164,400	
General and administrative expenses	55,000	
Interest expense	6,600	
Income tax expense		
Extraordinary gain (pretax)		10,000
	$1,010,560	$1,010,560

Additional data for adjustments and other purposes:

a. Estimated bad debt loss rate is ¼% of credit sales. Credit sales for the year amounted to $200,000; classify as a selling expense.
b. Interest on the long-term note receivable was last collected August 31, 19D.
c. Estimated useful life of the equipment is 10 years; residual value, $20,000. Allocate 10% of depreciation expense to general and administrative expense and the balance to selling expenses to reflect proportionate use. Use straight-line depreciation.
d. Estimated remaining economic life of the patent is 14 years (from January 1, 19D) and no residual value. Use straight-line amortization and classify as selling expense (used in sales promotion).
e. Interest on the mortgage payable was last paid on November 30, 19D.
f. On June 1, 19D, the company rented some office space to a tenant for one year and collected $3,000 rent in advance for the year; the entire amount was credited to Rent Revenue on this date.
g. On December 31, 19D, received a statement for calendar year 19D property taxes amounting to $1,300. The payment is due February 15, 19E. Assume it will be paid on that date and classify it as a selling expense. The $1,300 has not been recorded during 19D.
h. Sales supplies on hand at December 31, 19D, amounted to $300; classify as a selling expense.
i. Assume an average 40% corporate income tax rate on all items including the extraordinary gain. Hint: Income tax expense is $35,132.

Required:

1. Enter the above unadjusted trial balance on a worksheet.
2. Enter the adjusting entries and complete the worksheet.
3. Prepare the statements of income and financial position (subclassifications are not required).
4. Journalize the closing entries.

P 2–11 (Based on Supplement 2A—A Cash Receipts Journal)

Hall Retailers uses special journals. A special cash receipts journal with several selected transactions is given below.

Special Journal—Cash Receipts **Page CR-8**

		Debits	Credits				
Date	Explanation	Cash	Account title	Ledger folio	Accounts receivable	Sales revenue	Misc. accounts
19E:							
Jan. 1	Cash sales	30,000				30,000	
2	On account	4,200	Riley Corp.		4,200		
5	Cash sales	10,000				10,000	
6	On account	1,240	Brown, Inc.		1,240		
8	Sale of short-term investment	7,000	Short-term investments				4,000
			Gain on sale of investments				3,000
11	Cash sales	41,000				41,000	
12	Borrowed cash	10,000	Notes payable				10,000
15	On account	5,500	Watson Co.		5,500		
18	Collected interest	600	Interest revenue				600
31	Cash sales	52,000				52,000	

Required:

1. Sum the special journal (below) and post it to the appropriate accounts in the general ledger (set up the following T-accounts: Cash #101, Accounts Receivable Control #113 (beginning balance, $19,640), Short-term Investments #134, Notes Payable #326, Sales Revenue #500, Interest Revenue #509, and Gain on Sales of Investments #510. Also, set up a subsidiary ledger for Accounts Receivable (with systematic numbers starting with 113.03). Beginning customer balances were: Brown, Inc., $1,240; Riley Corporation, $8,400; and Watson Company, $10,000.
2. Reconcile the subsidiary ledger with its control account.

CASES

C 2–1 (Analysis and a Correct Trial Balance)

Careless Corporation has just completed its third year of operations, December 31, 19C. The newly selected president was amazed, to say the least, when told that the "company's books have never been in balance." In fact, he has learned that they are $14,800 out of balance. Consequently, he has decided to ask an independent CPA to "get things straightened out." You are the lucky CPA! While getting an overview of the situation, you learn that the bookkeeper journalizes and posts all of the daily transactions, but the adjusting and closing entries are entered directly into the ledger accounts. A worksheet is not used. After recording the adjusting entries, the bookkeeper prepares an adjusted trial balance, which is then used to prepare the financial statements.

At your request, the bookkeeper prepared the following post-closing trial balance following his usual procedures:

CARELESS CORPORATION
Post-Closing Trial Balance
December 31, 19C

Accounts	Debit	Credit
Cash	$ 17,800	
Accounts receivable	55,000	
Note receivable, short term	6,000	
Merchandise inventory (periodic system)	120,000	
Prepaid insurance	2,400	
Equipment	240,000	
Land (future plant site)	40,000	
Accounts payable		$ 20,000
Income tax payable		10,000
Mortgage payable		100,000
Common stock, par $10 (20,000 shares outstanding)		320,000
Dividends declared and paid	4,000	
Retained earnings		50,000
To balance	14,800	
Totals	$500,000	$500,000

After spending considerable time digging into the records and files of the company, you discovered the following:

a. Estimates of bad debt expense that total $5,000 have been credited directly to Accounts Receivable.
b. Accrued interest expense of $4,000 was recorded, but the credit was omitted.

c. Depreciation expense, on a straight-line basis (no residual value), is $30,000 each year. Depreciation for 19A and 19B was credited directly to the asset account. No entry has been recorded for 19C.
d. The 19C ending inventory of $140,000 was not recorded; the beginning inventory was $120,000.
e. Prepaid insurance of $2,400 was for two full years, 19C and 19D.
f. Accounts payable of $2,000 were paid, but the debit was not recorded at all.
g. The common stock account needs scrutiny.
h. How should the account, Dividends Declared and Paid, be reported?

Required:

1. Based on your findings, prepare a correct trial balance. Show corrections. Hint: Set up the following headings:

	Trial balance			Correct trial balance	
Accounts	**Debit**	**Credit**	**Corrections**	**Debit**	**Credit**

   Add the following accounts: Allowance for Doubtful Accounts, Accumulated Depreciation—equipment, Interest Payable, and Contributed Capital in Excess of Par.
2. Aside from the lack of accounting knowledge by the bookkeeper, explain why so many continuing mistakes were made in implementing the accounting process.
3. What recommendations would you make concerning the accounting process? Yes, the bookkeeper is no longer on the company payroll!

C 2–2 (Analysis: Correcting Financial Statements)

Fannie Corporation started operations on January 1, 19C. It is now December 31, 19C, the end of the annual accounting period. A company clerk, who maintained the accounting records, has just prepared the following financial statements:

Profit and Loss Statement
December 31, 19C

Service income		$100,000
Costs:		
Salaries and wages	$30,000	
Repairs and maintenance	5,000	
Service	25,000	
Other miscellaneous	10,000	70,000
Profit		$ 30,000

Balance Sheet
December 31, 19C

Assets

Cash	$ 7,500
Note receivable, 16%	1,200
Inventory, supplies	6,000
Equipment	90,000
Other miscellaneous assets	7,300
Total	$112,000

Debts

Accounts payable	$ 8,000
Note payable (15%)	24,000
Total	32,000

Capital

Capital stock, par $10	50,000
Retained earnings	30,000
Total	80,000
Grand total	$112,000

The above statements (unaudited) were presented to a local bank, at the bank's request, to support a major loan. The bank requested that the statements be "examined" by an independent CPA. You are the independent CPA, and among other accounting issues, you found that the following items were not considered by the company in preparing the statement of income and statement of financial position:

a. Service revenue amounting to $2,000 had been collected but not earned at December 31, 19C.

b. At December 31, 19C, wages earned by employees but not yet paid or recorded amounted to $9,000.

c. A count of the inventory of supplies at December 31, 19C, showed $4,000 supplies on hand.

d. Depreciation on the equipment acquired on January 3, 19C, was not recorded. The estimated residual value was $10,000, and the estimated useful life 10 years.

e. The note receivable received from a customer was dated November 1, 19C; the principal plus interest is payable April 30, 19D.

f. The note payable to the local bank was dated June 1, 19C; the principal plus interest is payable May 31, 19D.

g. Assume an average income tax rate of 20% for Fannie Corporation and that no income tax has been recorded.

h. Although you did not do a complete audit of the accounting results, your judgment is that the daily recording of transactions was appropriate.

Required:

1. Recast the statement of income using modern terminology, after giving effect to your findings. Use a format similar to the following to develop the statements:

Items	Reported amount	Changes due to findings				Correct amount
		Key	+ or −	Amount	Comments	
Statement of income: (list the appropriate items here)						
Statement of financial position: (list the appropriate items here)						

2. Write a brief narrative addressed to Fannie Corporation to explain the two corrected statements (not an auditor's opinion).

3. Give any recommendations that you would make to Fannie Corporation concerning its accounting function.

3 REVIEW: THE STATEMENT OF INCOME AND STATEMENT OF RETAINED EARNINGS

OVERVIEW AND PURPOSE

An entity **communicates** financial information to decision makers primarily by using a full set of financial statements at the end of each accounting year. A full set of financial statements must include: (1) a statement of income, (2) a statement of financial position (reviewed in Chapter 4), and (3) a statement of cash flows (discussed in Chapter 19). Also, to assure **full disclosure,** a full financial report almost always includes a statement of retained earnings (or owners' equity) and a series of disclosure notes and schedules.

There are important relationships among the three required financial statements. The statement of income and statement of cash flows are connecting links between the beginning and ending statements of financial position. The statement of income and statement of cash flows explain the causes of changes in financial position during the current accounting period. The statement of income explains the changes due to revenues, expenses, gains, and losses. The statement of cash flows explains the changes in financial position in terms of cash inflows and cash outflows during the current period.

The FASB **Statements of Financial Accounting Concepts** (discussed in Chapter 6) starts the title of each report with the word, **statement,** which will be generally used in the future; however, current usage varies. Therefore, in this textbook we will use the following titles: *(a)* statement of financial position (instead of balance sheet), *(b)* statement of income (instead of income statement), and *(c)* statement of cash flows (instead of cash flow statement). This modern terminology is preferable because it is (1) descriptive of the content of the statements, (2) consistent, and (3) will be used in future FASB pronouncements.

The purpose of this chapter is to review the statement of income from the perspective of both the decision makers who use it and the accountants who prepare it. Therefore, this chapter is subdivided as follows:

Part A: Concepts Underlying the Statement of Income

1. Accounting income.
2. Format and issues of the statement of income.
3. Reporting extraordinary items.
4. Reporting unusual or infrequent gains and losses.
5. Disclosure guidelines for the statement of income.

Part B: Specific Issues Directly Related to the Statement of Income and Statement of Retained Earnings

1. Prior period adjustments.
2. Disclosure of income taxes.
3. Earnings per share.
4. Accounting changes.
5. Statement of retained earnings.
6. Combined statement of income and retained earnings.
7. Actual financial statement illustrated.

PART A: CONCEPTS AND FORMAT OF THE STATEMENT OF INCOME

The relationships among the three required financial statements are shown in **Exhibit 3–1.** The statement of income is important because it provides decision makers with detailed information about the profit performance of a business. This information is useful in predicting the amount, timing, and uncertainty (risks) of *(a)* future incomes (and losses) and *(b)* future cash flows. However, a problem often associated with the statement of income relates directly to the **quality** of the reported earnings discussed in Chapter 1. That is, the amounts reported on the statement (and especially the amount called **net income**) may not be reliable because of selective application of accounting policies which bias the amount too high or too low. For example, a company may over-, or under-estimate such expenses as depreciation, bad debt losses, and cost of goods sold (FIFO versus LIFO). Another way the quality of the reported earnings is affected is by aggregation of diverse kinds of revenues and expenses (such as including nonrecurring items with regularly recurring items) and reporting only the aggregate amount on the statement of income. The generally accepted accounting principles (GAAP) guidelines approved by the APB and FASB to date have significantly reduced the opportunities to manipulate net income.

Accounting Income

most used

The statement of income reports **net income** measured on the **accrual basis** in conformity with GAAP. This means that transactions must be recognized when they occur. This concept of income, commonly called **accounting income,** is a **transactions approach** because each revenue, expense, gain, and loss transaction is recorded when it occurs. In contrast, cash basis accounting, which is not in conformity with GAAP, recognizes these elements only on the dates that the related cash inflows or outflows occur.

Another concept of income, often called **economic income,** measures the income of a business as the amount of "real wealth" that an entity could consume, or use up, during a period and be as well off at the end of that period as it was at the beginning.[1] This definition is often referred to as a capital maintenance approach. Implementation of the concept of economic income would require the use of market values adjusted for the effects of inflation or deflation because real wealth is measured in terms of purchasing power. This concept of income can be shown as follows:

	Market values (adjusted for inflation)
Net assets (assets minus liabilities) at the end of year 19X	$900,000
Net assets at the beginning of 19X	(600,000)
Increase in market value during 19X	300,000
Deduct: Owners' investments in the company during 19X	(100,000)
Add: Withdrawals (i.e., dividends) by owners during 19X	20,000
Income (net increase in real wealth) during 19X	$220,000

[1] See J. R. Hicks, *Value and Capital,* 2d ed. (London: Oxford University Press, 1946), p. 172.

Exhibit 3–1
Relationships among financial statements.

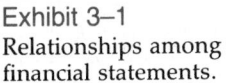

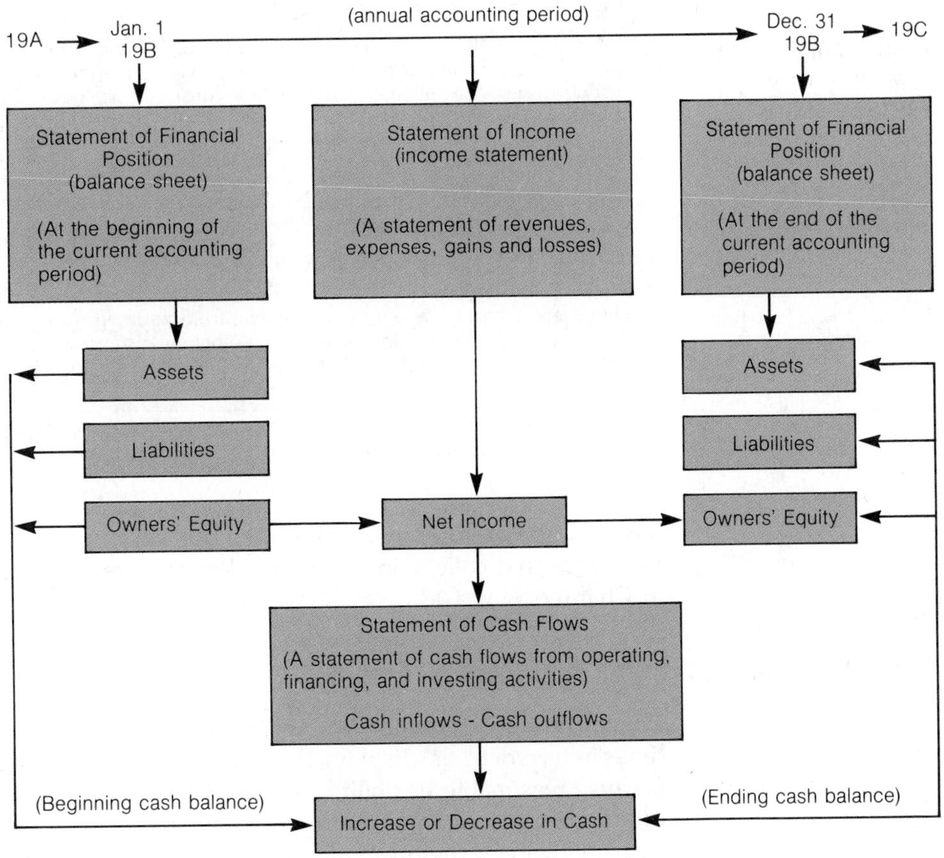

In the broadest sense, accounting income and economic income are consistent. However, the measurement approaches are significantly different. Economic income is based exclusively on wealth changes, whereas accounting income is measured using a **transactions approach** that involves detailed and continuous measurements throughout the reporting period. To provide reliable information to decision makers, the measurements should be verifiable and not subjective. To this end, the transactions approach provides an appropriate accounting approach to income measurement.

The transactions approach was used in your principles of financial accounting course. It is discussed in this textbook because it is in conformity with GAAP. It measures accounting income in terms of the statement of income elements—revenues, expenses, gains, and losses.

FASB Concepts No. 6 defines the **statement of income elements** as those shown in **Exhibit 3–2.** Notice the following: *(a)* gains and losses cannot be included in the "ongoing major or central operations," *(b)* "income" is not a synonym for revenue, and *(c)* "cost" is not a synonym for expense.

Revenue recognition is a primary issue in measuring net income. Revenue is recognized (i.e., recorded) when there is a completed earnings process. An earnings process includes the following: *(a)* a completed transaction to sell goods or services, *(b)* a transfer of ownership of the goods from the seller to the

Exhibit 3–2
FASB definitions of the elements on the statement of income.

Revenues are inflows or other enhancements of assets of an enterprise or settlements of its liabilities (or a combination of both) during a period from delivering or producing goods, rendering services, or other activities that constitute the entity's **ongoing major or central** operations.

Gains are increases in equity (net assets) from **peripheral or incidental** transactions of an entity and from all other transactions and other events and circumstances affecting the entity during a period except those that result from revenues or investments by owners.

Expenses are outflows or other using up of assets or incurrences of liabilities (or a combination of both) during a period from delivering or producing goods, rendering services, or carrying out other activities that constitute the entity's **ongoing major or central** operations.

Losses are decreases in equity (net assets) from **peripheral or incidental** transactions of an entity and from all other transactions and other events and circumstances affecting the entity during a period except those that result from expenses or distributions to owners.

Source: FASB, *Statement of Financial Accounting Concepts No. 6* "Elements of Financial Statements of Business Enterprises" (Stamford, Conn., December 1985).

Not what co. then to do
Cost is sep. from expense

buyer, or the performance of specified services, and *(c)* collection or a reasonable assurance that collection will occur. Revenue recognition is discussed in detail in Chapters 6 and 13.

Format and Issues of the Statement of Income

The accounting profession has not specified a standardized GAAP **format** (sometimes referred to as display) that must be used for the statement of income because reasonable flexibility to adapt to various situations is considered more important than a standard format. As a result, considerable variation in practice exists. However, the presentation of financial information on a typical statement of income must be consistent with the elements defined in Exhibit 3–2. The primary classifications on a statement of income can be summarized as follows:

- **a.** Revenues—such as sales, service, rent, and investment revenue.
- **b.** Expenses—such as wages, services, rent, cost of goods sold, and income tax expense.
- **c.** Gains and losses that are **either** (but not both) unusual or infrequent—such as from the disposal of equipment, sale of investments, and casualties.
- **d.** Gains and losses that are **extraordinary** because they are both unusual and infrequent—such as damage losses from an earthquake in most areas of the world.
- **e.** Net income—the algebraic sum of revenues, expenses, gains, and losses.
- **f.** Earnings per share—income divided by the average number of common shares outstanding during the year.

The statement of income reports all revenues, gains, expenses, and losses for a **specific period of time.** It is "dated" to indicate the period covered, such as **"For the Year Ended December 31, 19XX."** This dating identifies the length and ending date of the **reporting period.**

In addition, a number of *ARBs, APB Opinions,* and *FASB Standards* specify certain **disclosure** requirements that influence statement of income presentation.

Although there is considerable variations in statement of income formats, two formats dominate in practice (with numerous variations of each). These formats usually are designated as (1) single step and (2) multiple step. A recent survey of 600 major companies reported that 46% of them essentially used a single-step format while 54% essentially used a multiple-step format.[2]

Single-Step Format. The single-step format uses two broad classifications: (1) revenues and gains and (2) expenses and losses. It is called a **single-step statement** because only one step is involved in arriving at net income. That is, revenues and gains minus expenses and losses equal net income. However, if the company has extraordinary gains or losses (or other types of gains and losses that warrant separate disclosure), the steps increase.

A single-step statement of income is shown in **Exhibit 3–3** for Graham Retail Company. Notice that it includes an extraordinary item. Numerous variations exist in practice. For example, income tax expense related to operations sometimes is reported as a separate item below "Expenses and losses" but preceding "Income before extraordinary items."

Multiple-Step Format. The multiple-step format makes a distinction between regular or normal operations and irregular and financing activities. It provides multiple classifications and multiple intermediate differences (i.e., multiple steps). It is more informative than the single-step format. A multiple-step statement of income, using the same data as in Exhibit 3–3, is illustrated in **Exhibit 3–4.** The differences between the single-step and multiple-step formats are that the multiple-step format (Exhibit 3–4), but not the single-step format (Exhibit 3–3), reports amounts for the following "income" captions:

1. Gross margin on sales (also called **gross profit**).
2. Income from primary operations.
3. Income before extraordinary items.
4. Net income.

Exhibit 3–5 shows a typical detailed expense schedule that could be included in the disclosure notes. It would supplement either the single- or multiple-step format.

Study Exhibit 3–4 to learn the typical classifications in a multiple-step statement of income. These classifications will be frequently referred to and used in subsequent chapters. Currently the FASB is informally considering whether the statement of income, like the statement of cash flows, should have a higher level of consistency and comparability.

The single-step format has the advantage of simplicity and avoids having to develop captions for the intermediate classifications. The multiple-step format is more useful to decision makers because it better distinguishes the dissimilar items reported.

---

[2] AICPA, *Accounting Trends & Techniques, 1987* (New York, 1987). This is an excellent reference to determine how various companies report the multitude of different items on financial statements.

Exhibit 3–3
Single-step format—statement of income.

GRAHAM RETAIL COMPANY
Statement of Income
For the Year Ended December 31, 19D

Revenues and gains:		
Sales (less returns and allowances of $20,000)		$670,000
Rent revenue		1,200
Interest and dividend revenue		4,800
Gain on sale of operational assets		6,000
Total revenues and gains		682,000
Expenses and losses:		
Cost of goods sold*	$264,000	
Distribution expense*	153,500	
General and administrative expense*	73,500	
Depreciation expense	54,000	
Interest expense	6,000	
Loss on sale of investments	5,000	
Income tax expense ($126,000 × 30%)†	37,800	
Total expenses and losses		593,800
Income before extraordinary items		88,200
Extraordinary item:		
Loss due to earthquake	10,000	
Less: Income tax saving ($10,000 × 30%)	3,000	7,000
Net income		$ 81,200
EPS of common stock (20,000 shares outstanding):		
Income before extraordinary item ($88,200 ÷ 20,000)		$4.41
Extraordinary loss ($7,000 ÷ 20,000)		(.35)
Net income ($81,200 ÷ 20,000)		$4.06

* These expenses may be detailed in the statement or separately in the disclosure notes to the financial statements.
† Assumed average income tax rate, 30%.

Special Issues Related to the Statement of Income

The following special issues related to the statement of income are discussed in this section: *(a)* extraordinary items, *(b)* unusual or infrequent gains and losses, and *(c)* disclosure requirements.

Reporting Extraordinary Items

For accounting purposes, an extraordinary (EO) item is a **transaction or event that is both unusual in nature and infrequent in occurrence.** Extraordinary items are reported as a separate classification on the statement of income to alert users of the financial statements of the extraordinary nature of these gains or losses. Separate reporting signals to users that these gains or losses cannot be expected to recur regularly and, therefore, should have little influence on predictions about the future income and cash flows of the entity.

Extraordinary items are controversial because they are difficult to define precisely. Prior to *APB Opinion 30* (1973), companies often classified gains and losses as ordinary or extraordinary, depending upon their motivations at the end of the accounting period. For example, a company with a low net income

Exhibit 3–4
Multiple-step format—statement of income.

GRAHAM RETAIL COMPANY
Statement of Income
For the Year Ended December 31, 19D

Sales revenue			$690,000
Less: Sales returns and allowances			20,000
Net sales			670,000
Cost of goods sold:			
Beginning inventory (periodic system)		$ 52,000	
Purchases of inventory	$268,000		
Freight-in	1,200		
Cost of purchases	269,200		
Less: Purchase returns and allowances	2,700	266,500	
Total goods available for sale		318,500	
Less: Ending inventory		54,500	
Cost of goods sold			264,000
Gross margin on sales			406,000
Operating expenses:			
Distribution expense*		153,500	
General and administrative expense*		73,500	
Depreciation expense		54,000	
Total operating expenses			281,000
Income from continuing (or primary) operations†			125,000
Other revenues and gains:			
Rent revenue	1,200		
Interest and dividend revenue	4,800		
Gain on sale of operational assets	6,000	12,000	
Other expenses and losses:			
Interest expense	6,000		
Loss on sale of investments	5,000	11,000	1,000
Income before income tax and extraordinary items			126,000
Income tax expense ($126,000 × 30%)‡			37,800
Income before extraordinary item			88,200
Extraordinary item:			
Loss due to earthquake		10,000	
Less: Income tax saving ($10,000 × 30%)		3,000	7,000
Net income			$ 81,200
EPS of common stock (20,000 shares outstanding):			
Income before extraordinary item ($88,200 ÷ 20,000)			$4.41
Extraordinary loss ($7,000 ÷ 20,000)			(.35)
Net income ($81,200 ÷ 20,000)			$4.06

* These expenses may be detailed in the statement or separately in the **disclosure notes** to the financial statements.
† Also, variously labeled, such as **Income from primary operations** and **Income from operations.**
‡ Assumed average income tax rate, 30%.

would select one or more large losses on the statement of income and reclassify them as extraordinary in order to report a high income **before** extraordinary items. In other situations, large extraordinary gains would be classified as **ordinary** gains to increase income **before** extraordinary items. The tendency was to classify gains as ordinary and losses as extraordinary.

To prevent such manipulations, the APB issued *Opinion 30* to define extraordinary items precisely. The result was to significantly reduce the number of items

Exhibit 3–5
Detailed expense schedule.

GRAHAM RETAIL COMPANY
Schedule of Operating Expenses
For the Year Ended December 31, 19D

Operating expenses:		
Distribution expenses:		
Advertising	$58,500	
Salaries	45,000	
Commissions	31,000	
Freight-out (on sales)	10,000	
Insurance on inventory	1,000	
Other selling expenses	8,000	$153,500
Administrative expenses:		
Office expenses	24,800	
Office payroll	42,100	
Rent	3,600	
Bad debt expense	3,000	73,500
Depreciation expense		54,000
Total operating expense		$281,000

that can be classified as extraordinary. Extraordinary items are defined in *APB Opinion 30* as follows (emphasis added):

> Extraordinary items are events and transactions that are distinguished by their **unusual nature and by the infrequency of their occurrence.** Thus, both of the following criteria should be met to classify an event or transaction as an extraordinary item:
>
> *a.* **Unusual nature**—The underlying event or transaction should possess a high degree of abnormality and be of a type clearly unrelated to, or only incidentally related to, the ordinary and typical activities of the entity, taking into account the environment in which the entity operates.
>
> *b.* **Infrequency of occurrence**—The underlying event or transaction should be of a type that would not reasonably be expected to recur in the foreseeable future, taking into account the environment in which the entity operates.[3]

Two aspects of the above definition should be emphasized. First, **both** criteria, unusual and infrequent, must be met. Thus, an item that meets **either,** but not both, is not an extraordinary item. Second, the **environment in which the entity operates** often is controlling. For example, earthquake damage usually would be extraordinary—it is unusual and occurs infrequently in most parts of the world. However, if one were to locate a plant on a fault where earthquakes occur regularly, earthquake damage would not be extraordinary in that particular environment; the damage would be considered "usual **or** frequent." Thus, whether an event or transaction is extraordinary depends not only on the characteristics of the event or transaction itself, but also on the environment in which it occurs. The *Opinion* cites only three different kinds of events that may be classified as extraordinary: (1) a major casualty, such as an earthquake; (2)

[3] AICPA, *APB Opinion No. 30,* "Reporting the Results of Operations" (New York, June 1973), par. 20.

expropriation by a foreign government; and (3) prohibition under a newly enacted law or regulation. However, this list was not intended to be exclusive.

The *Opinion* states that the following should not be considered as extraordinary items because they are expected during the customary and continuing business activities of any entity:

a. Write-down or write-off of receivables, inventories, equipment leased to others, or other intangible assets.
b. Gains or losses from exchange or translation of foreign currencies, including those related to major devaluations or revaluations.
c. Gains or losses on disposal of a segment of a business.
d. Other gains or losses from sale or abandonment of property, plant, or equipment used in the business.
e. Effects of a strike, including those against competitors and major suppliers.
f. Adjustments of accruals on long-term contracts.[4]

Extraordinary items must be reported on the statement of income under a separate classification **net of any income tax effect caused by their occurrence.** If subject to income tax, an extraordinary gain causes an increase in income tax and an extraordinary loss creates a tax saving. In both situations, the tax effect is subtracted from the gain or loss. Exhibits 3–3 and 3–4 illustrate the required reporting of extraordinary items between the captions "Income before extraordinary items" and "Net income," and their inclusion in EPS reporting.

The reporting of extraordinary items is simple and straightforward; however, in practice the classification decision is still subjective as is evident in many financial statements.

Also, the APB and the FASB have made exceptions to the above definition to specify that certain items be classified as extraordinary; these are certain gains and losses from (1) extinguishment of debt (discussed in Chapter 15) and (2) income tax loss carryforwards (discussed in Chapter 10). These exceptions require that certain items be reported as extraordinary, although they may not meet the two criteria—unusual and nonrecurring.

Finally, the **amount** of a gain or loss is not a criterion for determining whether an item should be designated as extraordinary. The only criteria are that the item be *(a)* unusual in nature and *(b)* infrequent in occurrence. However, as with other amounts, an extraordinary gain or loss that clearly is not material in **amount** is not required to be reported as an extraordinary item. However, lack of materiality does not preclude the opportunity to appropriately report an item.

Reporting Unusual or Infrequent Gains and Losses

We have referred to events or transactions that are either unusual or infrequent, but not both. They do not qualify as extraordinary items; however, the prevailing view is that they should be called to the attention of the statement user to **full disclosure.** Therefore, *APB Opinion 30* requires that the effects of such events or transactions be **reported separately on the** statement of income as follows (emphasis supplied):

[4] Ibid., par. 23.

> A material event or transaction that is unusual in nature or occurs infrequently, but not both, and therefore does not meet both criteria for classification as an extraordinary item, should be **reported as a separate component of income from continuing operations.** Such items should not be reported. . . . net of income taxes.[5]

The *Opinion* stated that these items should not be reported **net of income tax** because *(a)* reporting net of tax is a feature of extraordinary items, *(b)* other items above "Income before extraordinary items" are not usually reported net of tax, and *(c)* intraperiod income tax allocation might become overly complex (discussed in Part B).

Exhibit 3–6 illustrates one way to report unusual or infrequent items.

Disclosure Guidelines for the Statement of Income

A statement of income must satisfy **full disclosure,** which requires that all relevant information relating to the economic affairs of the entity must be reported in the statement or in the supporting notes and schedules. Therefore, the typical statement of income is supplemented with a number of **disclosure notes to the financial statements.** Typically, these notes contain schedules and written explanations to communicate more fully information about the amounts reported in the tabular portions of the statements. For example, Exhibit 3–5 presents a detailed expense schedule to supplement the statement of income of Graham Retail Company illustrated in Exhibit 3–4.

APB Opinion 22, "Disclosure of Accounting Policies," August 1972, paragraph 8, states that "a description of all significant accounting policies of the reporting entity should be included as an integral part of the financial statements." Examples are those policies related to the basis of consolidation, depreciation methods, amortization of intangibles, inventory costing, accounting for research and development costs, translation of foreign currencies, recognition of profit on long-term construction contracts, and revenue from leasing transactions.

The objective of disclosure notes is to present information that cannot be effectively communicated in another way. **Disclosure notes are an integral part of the financial statements.** Generally, pronouncements of the profession on reporting specific items specify that they may, or in some case must, be included in disclosure notes when it is impractical to present the information in the tabular portions of the statements. For example, two specific statement of income items that must be disclosed separately are *(a)* depreciation expense and *(b)* income tax expense.

Disclosure of Depreciation. *APB Opinion 12,* paragraph 5, requires that *(a)* the amount of depreciation expense for the period and *(b)* the method or methods of depreciation used, be disclosed either in the financial statements or in the notes thereto. This requirement was specified because depreciation often is a major noncash expense. The amount of depreciation expense depends, in part, upon the depreciation policies of the enterprise rather than solely on external

[5] Ibid., par. 23.

Exhibit 3–6
Reporting unusual or infrequent gains and losses and extraordinary items.

LUCKY OIL CORPORATION
Statement of Income (partial)
For the Year Ended December 31, 19X

Revenues (not detailed in this example)			$990,000
Expenses (not detailed in this example)			878,000
Income from primary operations (pretax)			112,000
Unusual or infrequent items (Note 10):			
Loss on disposal of long-term investment		$ 43,000	
Gain on disposal of farming equipment		31,000	12,000
Income before income tax and extraordinary items			100,000
Income tax expense (40% tax rate assumed)			40,000
Income before extraordinary item			60,000
Extraordinary item:			
Gain, offshore drilling salvage (Note 11)		500,000	
Less: Income tax (40% tax rate assumed)		200,000	300,000
Net income			$360,000
EPS (10,000 common shares outstanding):			
Income before extraordinary items	$ 6.00		
Extraordinary gain	30.00		
Net income	$36.00		

Note 10. The loss on disposal is due to the sale of the only long-term investment held by the company in the timber industry. The company has no plans to reinvest in this industry. The company has discontinued the use of farm equipment that orignally was acquired for rent to landowners with whom the company had leasing activities.
Note 11. The extraordinary gain is due to discovery of a sunken ship during offshore drilling operations. The artifacts salvaged were sold.

transactions; therefore, the amount of depreciation is subject to considerable latitude. To realistically assess future cash flows, statement users need to know both the amount of depreciation expense and the depreciation method(s) used.

In manufacturing enterprises, much of the depreciation expense may be included in the ending inventory and cost of goods sold amounts (it is not specifically identified). Therefore, reporting the method of depreciation used and total depreciation in disclosure notes is characteristic of these companies.

Disclosure of income tax is discussed in Part B of this chapter.

PART B: SPECIFIC ISSUES DIRECTLY RELATED TO THE STATEMENT OF INCOME AND STATEMENT OF RETAINED EARNINGS

Prior Period Adjustments

Prior period adjustments must be reported on the statement of retained earnings. This GAAP requirement means that prior period adjustments **never** flow through the statement of income.

FASB Standard 16, paragraph 11, defines and prescribes the accounting for prior period adjustments in terms of only two items, as follows (emphasis added):

> Items of gain and loss related to the following shall be accounted for and reported as prior period adjustments and excluded from the determination of net income for the current period:
>
> *a.* **Correction of an error** in the financial statements of a prior period and
>
> *b.* **Adjustments** that result from realization of income tax benefits of preacquisition operating loss carryforwards of purchased subsidiaries.

FASB Standard 16 requires that all other items of revenue, expense, gain, and loss recognized during the period be included in the determination of reported net income for that period.

To illustrate the recording of a prior period adjustment for an error correction, assume a machine that cost $10,000 (with a 10-year estimated useful life and no residual value) was purchased on January 1, 19A. Further, assume that the total cost was erroneously debited to an expense account in 19A. The error was discovered December 29, 19D. The following correcting entry would be required in 19D, assuming any income tax effects are recorded separately.

December 29, 19D:

Machinery	10,000	
Depreciation expense, straight line (for 19D)	1,000	
Accumulated depreciation (19A through 19D)		4,000
Prior period adjustment, error correction		7,000

Any income tax effect of the prior period adjustment could be included in the above entry or recorded separately. Assuming the same error was made on the income tax return, the entry to record the income tax effect of the prior period adjustment, assuming a 30% income tax rate, would be:

Prior period adjustment, error correction ($7,000 × 30%)	2,100	
Income tax payable		2,100

The Prior Period Adjustment, Error Correction account balance would be closed directly to Retained Earnings on December 31, 19D.

A prior period adjustment (net of its income tax effect) is **reported** on the statement of retained earnings as a **correction of the beginning balance** of retained earnings as illustrated in **Exhibit 3–7.**

Disclosure of Income Taxes

Income taxes are assessed on profit-making corporations (but not on sole proprietorships or partnerships). Also, stockholders must pay income taxes on dividends received. Income tax paid by corporations is an expense (except when it relates to a prior period adjustment that has tax effects). APB *Opinion 11* prescribes the reporting of two separate and distinctly different types of income tax allocations. These are:

1. Intraperiod tax allocation. This is an allocation of **total** income tax **within the current accounting period** to various specified components on the current financial statements. This allocation is discussed below.
2. Interperiod tax allocation. This is an allocation of income taxes on taxable items **among accounting periods.** It occurs when there are items of revenue

Exhibit 3–7
Statement of retained earnings.

GRAHAM RETAIL COMPANY
Statement of Retained Earnings
For the Year Ended December 31, 19D

Retained earnings, 1/1/19D		$378,800
Prior period adjustments:		
Correction of error from prior period, a credit	$7,000	
Less: Income tax effect	2,100*	4,900
Balance as adjusted		383,700
Add: Net income, 19D (from the statement of income, Exhibit 3–3)		81,200
		464,900
Deduct: Cash dividends declared in 19D		30,000
Retained earnings, 12/31/19D (Note 7)		$434,900

Notes to financial statements:
Note 7. Retained earnings—Of the $434,900 ending balance in retained earnings, $280,000 is restricted from dividend availability under the terms of the bond indenture. When the bonds are retired, the restriction will be removed.
* This reporting of income tax is an example of intraperiod tax allocation; average income tax rate, 30%.

and/or expense on the statement of income for the current period that, because of the tax laws, are reported on the income tax return for an earlier or later accounting period. Interperiod tax allocation causes deferred income taxes, which are reported on the statement of financial position. This kind of allocation is discussed in Chapter 23.

Although intraperiod and interperiod tax allocation are different types, they are not mutually exclusive. Both types are concurrently required because each serves a different reporting purpose.[6]

Intraperiod Income Tax Allocation

The concept underlying **intraperiod** income tax allocation is that **all income tax consequences should be reported along with the transaction, or group of transactions, that caused the tax effect.** Thus, total income tax for the current period must be allocated (1) in the statement of income *(a)* to income before extraordinary items and *(b)* extraordinary items, and (2) on the statement of retained earnings to prior period adjustments.[7]

The need for **intraperiod** income tax allocation arises because financial statement users want information that is useful for **predicting the future cash flows of an entity.** Because extraordinary gains and losses are not as predictable as income before extraordinary items, investors should evaluate a company on the basis of its **income before extraordinary items.** Therefore, it is important to report separately the amounts of income tax expense applicable to (1) income before extraordinary items, (2) extraordinary items, and (3) prior period adjustments.

---

[6] Intraperiod tax allocations are discussed in this chapter because it is used in illustrations and problems prior to Chapter 23, where tax allocation is discussed in detail.

[7] Although rare, certain direct entries to stockholders' equity accounts also may have income tax effects requiring intraperiod tax allocation.

Exhibit 3–8
Intraperiod income tax allocation, X Corporation.

X Corporation's accounts provided the following data for 19B:
Case data:

1. Income before income tax and before extraordinary items, $115,000.
2. Extraordinary gain (specified), $40,000 (taxable).
3. Beginning balance, retained earnings, $130,000.
4. Cash dividends declared and paid, $50,000.
5. Prior period adjustment, error correction, $7,000 debit (subject to income tax).
6. Income tax rates: First $25,000, 20%; all above $25,000, 40%.

Requirement 1—Compute total income tax for 19B.
Response:
Taxable income: $115,000 + $40,000 − $7,000 = $148,000

Total income tax to be allocated: ($25,000 × 20%) + [($148,000 − $25,000) × 40%] = $54,200

Requirement 2—Prepare *(a)* a partial statement of income starting with "income before income tax and before extraordinary items" and *(b)* a complete statement of retained earnings, both of which include intraperiod income tax allocation.

Response:
a. Partial statement of income:

Income before income tax and extraordinary items		$115,000
• Less: Applicable income tax expense*		41,000
Income before extraordinary items		74,000
Extraordinary items:		
Extraordinary gain (specified)	$40,000	
Less: Applicable income tax expense ($40,000 × 40%)	16,000	
• Extraordinary gain, net of applicable income tax		24,000
Net income		$ 98,000

Note: Income tax allocated to the statement of income, $41,000 + $16,000 = $57,000.

b. Statement of retained earnings:

Beginning balance (1/1/19B)		$130,000
Prior period adjustment:		
Error correction, a debit	$ 7,000	
• Less: Income tax saving ($7,000 × 40%)	2,800	4,200
Balance as corrected		125,800
Add: 19B net income (from statement of income)		98,000
		223,800
Deduct: Cash dividends		50,000
Ending balance (12/31/19B)		$173,800

Note: Income tax (saving) allocated to the statement of retained earnings, $2,800.

Requirement 3—Prove the intraperiod income tax allocation.
Response: Total income tax allocated, $41,000 + $16,000 − $2,800 = $54,200

* Computation of intraperiod tax allocation:
Tax on ordinary income:

$25,000 × 20% =	$ 5,000
$90,000 × 40% =	36,000
Total	$41,000

Revenues, gains, and prior period adjustments (if credits) usually increase income tax expense. In contrast, expenses, losses, and prior period adjustments (if debits) usually result in tax savings because they decrease income tax expense. The amount of such a tax reduction often is called a **tax saving.**

Exhibit 3–8 illustrates intraperiod income tax allocation for X Corporation.

Exhibit 3–9
Intraperiod income tax allocated, Graham Retail Company.

Intraperiod income tax allocation:

Exhibit	Taxable item	Income tax amount	
3–4	Income before extraordinary items	$37,800	
3–4	Extraordinary loss (a tax saving)	(3,000)	
	Total income tax reported on the statement of income		$34,800
3–7	Prior period adjustment (on the statement of retained earnings)		2,100
	Total income tax reported ($126,000 − $10,000 + $7,000) × 30%		$36,900

Journal entry to record income tax:

Income tax expense (on income before EO loss, $37,800 − income tax saving on EO loss, $3,000)	34,800	
Prior period adjustment (income tax on the error)	2,100	
Income tax payable		36,900

In this illustration, total income tax for 19B was $54,200, which is allocated to three items in the following order: (1) income before extraordinary items, $41,000; (2) extraordinary gain, $16,000; and (3) prior period adjustment, $2,800 (a tax saving because the prior period adjustment—debit—reduced total income tax).

In this example, it would be misleading to allocate total income tax of $54,200 to income before extraordinary items (which would cause income before extraordinary items to be $60,800) because $16,000 of the income tax expense was caused by the extraordinary gain and the prior period adjustment caused a $2,800 tax saving. If an investor were to evaluate X Corporation based on the $60,800 income before extraordinary items instead of the correct amount of $75,000, the predicted income potential of the company probably would be understated.

Intraperiod income tax allocation also is illustrated in Exhibits 3–4 (statement of income) and 3–7 (statement of retained earnings). In the case of Graham Retail Company there is an **extraordinary loss** which causes an **income tax saving** (i.e., this loss reduces total income tax). The income tax allocation for Graham is summarized in **Exhibit 3–9** along with the related journal entry to record income tax.

Earnings per Share (EPS)

Earnings per share (EPS) is the relationship computed by dividing *(a)* reported income (available to the holders of common stock) by *(b)* the average number of common shares outstanding (during the year). EPS is not computed on preferred stock. To compute EPS on the common stock only, income must be reduced by any preferred stock dividend claim (a priority).

EPS is important to decision makers because it *(a)* relates the income of the entity to a single share of stock, *(b)* helps investors in making relevant profit performance comparisons among companies with different numbers of common shares outstanding, and *(c)* makes possible comparisons of relative profitability of companies on the basis of a single share of stock. *APB Opinion 15* requires companies to report per share data on *(a)* income before extraordinary items and *(b)* net income.[8]

Calculation of Earnings per Share

In this chapter, we will review only the fundamentals of EPS for companies with **simple capital structures.**[9]

To illustrate the calculation of EPS in simple situations, four separate cases are presented in **Exhibit 3–10.** These cases will provide sufficient background for the discussions and homework prior to the detailed EPS discussion in Chapter 22. The four cases are summarized as follows:

Case A. This is the least complex case. It involves common and preferred stock with no changes in the number of common shares outstanding during the year and no extraordinary items on the statement of income. In such a situation, calculation of EPS involves dividing net income applicable to common stock by the number of common shares outstanding, as illustrated in Exhibit 3–10.

Case B. A slight complexity occurs when there is an extraordinary gain or loss on the statement of income. In this case, EPS amounts are calculated and reported for *(a)* income before extraordinary items, *(b)* extraordinary items, and *(c)* net income, as illustrated in Exhibit 3–10.

Case C. Another complexity occurs when there is a change during the period in the number of common shares outstanding because of the sale and issuance of common stock or the purchase of such shares as treasury stock. This complexity requires calculation of the weighted-average number of shares outstanding during the year. The weighted average, calculated as illustrated in Exhibit 3–10, is divided into the income amounts.

Case D. Another complexity occurs when the company issues more shares of its common stock because of a stock dividend or stock split. In these cases, the shares issued are treated in EPS computations as though they had been outstanding for the entire period, as illustrated in Exhibit 3–10.

Additional complexities occur when a company has outstanding preferred stock or bonds payable that are convertible into common stock. These complexities involve the concepts of common stock equivalents and fully diluted EPS, which are discussed in Chapter 22. *FASB Standard 21,* "Suspension of Earnings

---

[8] AICPA, *APB Opinion No. 15,* "Earnings per Share" (New York, May 1969), does not require reporting of EPS for extraordinary items. EPS for *(a)* income before extraordinary items and *(b)* net income are required. In this textbook, we usually illustrate reporting EPS for the three amounts, for completeness and because most companies follow this practice.

[9] Under certain conditions (i.e., complex capital structures), *APB Opinion 15* requires two presentations of EPS on the statement of income: (1) primary EPS and (2) fully diluted EPS. Primary EPS relates income to the company's outstanding common stock, and fully diluted EPS relates income to the maximum number of shares of common stock that could conceivably become outstanding. Therefore, fully diluted EPS is an estimate of the company's minimum EPS under its existing capital structure. This topic is discussed in Chapter 22.

(handwritten marginalia at top of page):
15,000 × 4 = 140,000
50,000 × 8 = 400,000
540,000

Exhibit 3–10
Calculation of earnings per share (EPS).

Assumptions	Calculating and reporting of EPS	
Case A: 30,000 common shares outstanding throughout the year; net income for the year, $106,000; dividends applicable to preferred stock, $10,000.	Net income applicable to common stock ($106,000 − $10,000) .	$96,000
	Earnings per share ($96,000 ÷ 30,000 shares)	$ 3.20
Case B: 30,000 common shares outstanding throughout the year; income applicable to common stock, before extraordinary item, $96,000; extraordinary loss less applicable tax saving, $21,000; net income for the year, $75,000.	Income before extraordinary item	$96,000
	Extraordinary loss (less applicable tax saving) .	21,000
	Net income .	$75,000
	Earnings per share: Income before extraordinary item	$ 3.20
	Extraordinary loss .	(.70)
	Net income	$ 2.50
	$96,000 ÷ 30,000 shares = $3.20 (21,000) ÷ 30,000 shares = (.70) 75,000 ÷ 30,000 shares = 2.50	
Case C: 30,000 common shares outstanding from January 1 through April 1, on which date an additional 10,000 common shares were sold and issued; other data as in Case B.	Income before extraordinary item	$96,000
	Extraordinary loss (less applicable tax saving) .	21,000
	Net income .	$75,000
	Earnings per share: Income before extraordinary item	$ 2.56
	Extraordinary loss .	(.56)
	Net income .	$ 2.00
	Calculation of weighted-average number of shares:	

Dates	Months	Shares	Weighted shares
Jan. 1–Apr. 1	3	× 30,000 =	90,000
Apr. 1–Dec. 31	9	× 40,000 =	360,000
	12		450,000

Average: 450,000 ÷ 12 = 37,500.
$96,000 ÷ 37,500 shares = $2.56
(21,000) ÷ 37,500 shares = (.56)
 75,000 ÷ 37,500 shares = 2.00

Assumptions	Calculating and reporting of EPS	
Case D: 30,000 common shares outstanding from January 1 through April 1, on which date an additional 20,000 common shares were issued as a stock dividend; other data as in Case B (no additional shares were sold).	Income before extraordinary item	$96,000
	Extraordinary loss (less applicable tax saving) .	21,000
	Net income .	$75,000
	Earnings per share: Income before extraordinary item	$ 1.92
	Extraordinary loss .	(.42)
	Net income .	$ 1.50
	As provided in APB *Opinion 15*, when there is a stock dividend, the divisor is the average number of shares outstanding at year-end (including all stock dividends, as if they had been outstanding for the entire year). In this case, this is 30,000 + 20,000 = 50,000.	
	$96,000 ÷ 50,000 shares = $1.92 (21,000) ÷ 50,000 shares = (.42) 75,000 ÷ 50,000 shares = 1.50

per Share and Segment Information by Nonpublic Enterprises," exempts corporations that are not publicly held from the EPS disclosure requirement.

Accounting Changes

APB Opinion 20 defines three types of accounting changes essentially as follows:[10]

1. **Changes in estimates**—The use of estimates (such as in determining depreciation expense or bad debt expense) is a natural consequence of the accounting process. However, experience and additional information may make it possible to later improve prior estimates. For example, the estimated useful life of an operational asset, after having been used (and depreciated) for 6 years, may be changed from the original 10-year estimated life to a 15-year estimated life. Changes of this type are referred to as **changes in estimates** and are clearly distinguished from the next type of change—changes in accounting principle.
2. **Changes in accounting principle**—Because of a change in circumstances, or the development of a new accounting principle, a change in the recording and reporting approach for a particular transaction may be necessary. For example, a change in circumstances may make it desirable to change from straight-line depreciation to sum-of-the-years'-digits (SYD) depreciation. This would be a change in accounting principle, **a change from one acceptable principle to another acceptable principle.**
3. **Change in accounting entity** (see Chapter 24).

Accounting changes are discussed in detail in Chapter 24. **Changes in estimates** occur frequently in the discussions prior to Chapter 24; therefore, this type of change will be reviewed to provide background for the interim topics and homework.

Changes in Estimates

Revisions of estimates, such as useful lives and/or residual value of depreciable assets, the loss rate for bad debts, and warranty costs, are called **changes in estimates.** As a company gains experience in such areas as depreciable assets, receivables, and warranties, it may have a sound basis for revising one or more of its prior accounting estimates. *APB Opinion 20* states that, in such instances, the **prior accounting results are not to be disturbed. Instead, the new estimate should be used over the current and remaining periods.** Thus, a change in estimate is made on a **prospective** (i.e., future-oriented) basis.

To illustrate the accounting for a change in estimate, assume a machine that cost $24,000 is being depreciated on a straight-line basis over a 10-year estimated useful life with no residual value. Early during the 7th year, on the basis of more experience with the machine, it is determined that the total useful life should have been 14 years (and no residual value). Thus, the remaining life becomes 8 years from the start of the year in which the revised estimate was made (year 7 in the example). This change in estimate does not require

---

[10] Accounting changes **are not** due to accounting errors. They are approved accounting approaches for the three situations described. Correction of **accounting errors** will be discussed in detail in Chapter 24.

an entry to correct the prior depreciation already recorded (years 1–6 in the example). Rather, new depreciation amounts will be recorded at the end of the current year (year 7) and each year during the remaining useful life of the asset. The new depreciation amounts, starting with the year of change, would be based upon *(a)* the then **undepreciated** amount of the asset and *(b)* the new **remaining** useful life of the asset.

To illustrate, the new depreciation amounts would be computed and recorded as follows:

End of years 7–14 (8 years' remaining life):

Depreciation expense	1,200	
Accumulated depreciation, machinery		1,200

Computations (straight-line):	
Original cost	$24,000
Accumulated depreciation to date of change ($24,000 × 6/10)	14,400
Difference—depreciated over 8 years remaining life	$ 9,600
Annual depreciation over remaining life: ($9,600 ÷ 8 years)	$ 1,200

Statement of Retained Earnings

A statement of retained earnings often is presented as a supplement to the statements of income and financial position to provide full disclosure. However, many companies present a **statement of owners' equity** instead which shows all changes in owners' equity, including retained earnings (see Chapters 16 and 17).

The purposes of the statement of retained earnings are to report all changes in retained earnings during the accounting period, to reconcile the beginning and ending balances of retained earnings, and to provide a connecting link between statement of income and the statement of financial position. The ending balance of retained earnings is reported on the statement of financial position as one element of owners' equity (refer to Chapter 4). In conformity with *APB Opinion 9* and *FASB Standard 16,* the major segments of a statement of retained earnings are (1) prior period adjustments, (2) net income or loss for the period, and (3) dividends.

Appropriations and Restrictions of Retained Earnings

Appropriations of, and restrictions on, retained earnings limit the availability of retained earnings to support dividends.

Restrictions result from *(a)* **legal requirements,** as when a state statute requires that retained earnings be restricted for dividend purposes by the cost of any treasury stock held; or *(b)* **contractual agreements,** as when a bond agreement (i.e., indenture) requires that retained earnings of a specified amount be withheld from dividend purposes until the bonds are retired.

Appropriations of retained earnings result from decisions by the corporation to set aside, or appropriate, a specific amount of retained earnings (temporarily or permanently). The effect of an appropriation is to remove the specified amount of retained earnings from dividend availability. For example, corporations often set up appropriations such as "retained earnings appropriated for future plant expansion."

The primary purposes of restrictions and appropriations are to *(a)* "protect"

Exhibit 3–11
Combined statement of income and retained earnings.

GRAHAM RETAIL COMPANY
Combined Statement of Income and Retained Earnings
For the Year Ended December 31, 19D

Details of statement of income as illustrated in Exhibit 3–3 (single step) or Exhibit 3–4 (multiple step).

Net income	$ 81,200
Retained earnings, January 1, 19D	378,800
Prior period adjustment, correction of error (net of income tax of $2,100) (Note 6)	4,900
Cash dividends declared and paid during 19D	(30,000)
Retained earnings, December 31, 19D (Note 7)	$434,900*

Notes to financial statements:
Note 6. Prior period adjustments—During the year, the company discovered that an expenditure made in 19A was incorrectly expensed. This error caused net income of that period to be understated. The prior period adjustment of a $7,000 credit corrects the error.
Note 7. Restrictions—Of the $434,900 ending balance in Retained Earnings, $280,000 is restricted from dividend availability under the terms of the bond indenture. When the bonds are retired, the restriction will be removed.
* Notice that this amount agrees with the ending balance in Exhibit 3–7.

the cash position of the company by constraining cash dividends, *(b)* reduce the risk of nonpayment to creditors, and *(c)* inform statement users that a portion of retained earnings is set aside for a specific purpose (usually long term).

Exhibit 3–11 illustrates a restriction of $280,000 on the retained earnings of Graham Retail Company. In this situation, the unrestricted balance of retained earnings is $154,900 (i.e., $434,900 − $280,000 = $154,900). Graham recorded the restriction, on the date it was imposed, as follows:

Retained earnings (unappropriated)	280,000	
Retained earnings appropriated (as required by the bond indenture)		280,000

When a restriction or appropriation is removed (a debit), the amount is returned to the Retained Earnings (unappropriated) account (a credit). Restrictions and appropriations usually are reported in a note (as illustrated in Exhibit 3–7). Retained earnings is discussed in detail in Chapter 17.

Combined Statement of Income and Retained Earnings

The statements of income and retained earnings may be presented together as a **combined statement.** The primary advantage of such a format is that it brings together related and relevant information for the statement user. A combined statement is illustrated in Exhibit 3–11.

Actual Financial Statements Illustrated

Throughout this chapter, hypothetical examples were used for instructional purposes. To enable you to gain confidence in understanding financial statements, the **Appendix following Chapter 25** presents a complete set of actual financial statements for a well-known company. We suggest that you carefully examine these statements and relate them to the topics discussed in this chapter.

Summary

This chapter reviewed the statements of income and retained earnings. The statement of income reports a company's operations (i.e., revenues and expenses) and its gains and losses for a specified period of time (e.g., For the Year Ended December 31, 19XX). The statement must be prepared on the accrual basis to be in conformity with GAAP. The statement of income may be presented using either a single-step or a multiple-step format. Earnings per share (income applicable to common stock ÷ average number of common shares outstanding) must be reported on the statement of income. Extraordinary items, which are both unusual and infrequent, must be separately reported, net of income tax, on the statement of income.

A statement of income must show income tax along with the items that caused the tax; that is, income tax related to *(a)* income before extraordinary items and *(b)* extraordinary items. This allocation of income tax in financial statements is called **intraperiod** income tax allocation.

A statement of retained earnings, although not required, usually is presented to ensure full disclosure. This statement reports the following: *(a)* the beginning balance of retained earnings, *(b)* prior period adjustments (net of income tax), *(c)* net income or loss, *(d)* dividends, and *(e)* the ending balance of retained earnings.

QUESTIONS

Part A

1. Briefly explain how the statement of income is a connecting link between the beginning and ending statements of financial position.
2. Briefly explain the difference between economic income and accounting income.
3. Explain the basic difference between revenues and gains.
4. Explain the basic difference between expenses and losses.
5. Briefly explain the two formats used for statements of income. Explain why actual income statements usually are a combination of these two formats.
6. Explain how gross margin is computed for a retail business. How would gross margin be computed for a service organization?
7. Explain how cost of goods sold is reported on a single-step statement of income and on a multiple-step statement of income.
8. List the four major "income" captions, in their order of appearance, on a typical multiple-step statement of income.
9. Explain why the total amount of depreciation expense should be disclosed in the financial statements.
10. Define an extraordinary item. How should extraordinary items be reported on *(a)* a single-step and *(b)* a multiple-step statement of income?
11. How are items that are either unusual or infrequent, but not both, reported on the statement of income?
12. Outline a situation when a large hurricane or tornado loss could *(a)* be extraordinary and *(b)* not be an extraordinary item.
13. Does the amount of a gain determine whether it is an extraordinary item or not? Explain.

Part B

14. Briefly define a prior period adjustment. How is a prior period adjustment reported?
15. Briefly distinguish between intraperiod and interperiod tax allocation.
16. TK Corporation computed total income tax expense for 19B of $16,640. The following pretax amounts were used: *(a)* income before extraordinary loss, $60,000; *(b)* extraordinary loss, $12,000; and *(c)* prior period adjustment, $4,000 (a credit). The average income tax rate on all items was 32%. Compute the intraperiod income tax allocation amounts.
17. Define earnings per share (EPS). Why is it required as an integral part of the statement of income?
18. Fluke Company reported the following amounts at the end of 19D:

Extraordinary gain	$90,000
Net income	50,000

Average number of common shares outstanding, 25,000.

Prepare the EPS presentation. Which EPS amount is likely to be the most relevant? Explain.

19. What are the three types of accounting changes discussed in *APB Opinion 20?* Explain what is meant by a change in estimate. Explain the basic approach used to account for and report a change in estimate.
20. VEE Company has a machine that cost $21,000 when acquired at the beginning of year 1. It has been depreciated using straight line, on the basis of a 10-year useful life and a $1,000 residual value. At the start of year 5, the residual value was changed to $3,000. Compute the amount of depreciation expense per year that should be recorded for the remaining useful life of the machine.
21. What items are reported on a statement of retained earnings? Explain how it provides a link between the current statement of income and statement of financial position.
22. What is meant by appropriations and restrictions on retained earnings? How are such items usually reported?

EXERCISES

Part A: Exercises 3–1 to 3–8

E 3–1 (Market Value Statement of Income)
Oro Corporation has been operating for five years. The 19E detailed statement of income, prepared in conformity with generally accepted accounting principles (i.e., the transactions approach on the accrual basis), reported income of $17,600. The principal owner, who is the chief executive officer (CEO), believes that the company earned much more than that amount. To support this contention, the CEO developed the following schedule:

	Market values	
	End 19D	End 19E
Total assets (70% plant and equipment)	$270,000	$360,000
Total liabilities	100,000	110,000
Contributions of owners during 19E		20,000
Dividends paid to owners		6,000

Required:

1. Prepare a 19E statement of income using the CEO's data.
2. How would you label this income amount?
3. What reservations would you have about this way of measuring income?

E 3–2 (Classifications on the Statement of Income)

Fifteen transactions are listed below (left) that may or may not affect the statement of income. Statement of income classifications are listed by letters to the right. You are to match each transaction with the appropriate letter to indicate the usual classification that should be used. Provide comments when appropriate.

Answer	Selected transactions
______	1. Sales of goods and services.
______	2. Prepaid insurance premium.
______	3. Loss on disposal of service trucks.
______	4. Cash dividends received on an investment in African diamond mine.
______	5. Wages accrued (unpaid and unrecorded).
______	6. Cost of moving the only plant the company owns from state X to state A (a major expenditure).
______	7. Cost of goods sold.
______	8. Services rendered.
______	9. Gain (characterized as unusual or infrequent).
______	10. Rent collected in advance.
______	11. Fire loss (characterized as unusual).
______	12. Loss due to a rare freeze which destroyed the citrus trees in the Rio Grande Valley.
______	13. Gain on sale of short-term investments.
______	14. Cash dividend declared and paid.
______	15. Loss due to meteor which completely destroyed the factory.

Statement of income classification

A. Revenues
B. Expenses
C. Gains (ordinary)
D. Gains (unusual or infrequent)
E. Loss (ordinary)
F. Loss (unusual or infrequent)
G. Gain (extraordinary)
H. Loss (extraordinary)
I. None of the above

E 3–3 (Formats of Statement of Income; EO Item; Periodic Inventory)

The following items were taken from the adjusted trial balance of Kasper Manufacturing Corporation at December 31, 19B:

Sales revenue	$950,000
Cost of goods manufactured (including depreciation, $52,000)	580,000
Dividends received on investment in stocks	6,500
Finished goods inventory, 1/1/19B (periodic inventory system)	48,000
Interest expense	4,200
Extraordinary item: fire loss (pretax)	48,000
Distribution expenses	135,300
Common stock, par $10	200,000
General and administrative expenses	113,000
Interest revenue	2,500
Finished goods inventory, 12/31/19B	53,000
Income tax, assume average 30% tax rate	?

Required:

1. Prepare a single-step statement of income (includes EPS). Set up cost of goods sold as a separate schedule to include the inventory amounts and cost of goods manufactured.

2. Prepare a multiple-step statement of income. Include computation of cost of goods sold within the statement.

E 3–4 (Revenue Recognition)

The following selected transactions were completed by Avis Company during the year 19C. The accounting period ends December 31.

1. On December 21, 19C, merchandise was sold for $15,000 cash. The customer took possession of two thirds of the merchandise on that date. The balance will be picked up on January 3, 19D.
2. Services were rendered to a customer starting on December 27, 19C. The services will be completed around January 8, 19D, at which time $32,000 cash in full will be collected. Assume eight working days are involved of which two were in 19C.
3. During 19C, the company sold 10 TV sets and collected $6,000 cash in full. The company gives a one-year guarantee. It is estimated that the average warranty cost per set under the guarantee is $20. Assume by the end of 19C, that half of the guarantees on the 10 sets have been satisfied.
4. On December 31, 19C, a used truck was sold by the company. The truck had been used in operating the business and had a book value of $1,000. The sale price was $2,400, which was payable six months from date of the sale plus 15% interest per annum.
5. On December 27, 19C, the company received an income tax refund of $1,000 after four years of negotiations with the Internal Revenue Service.

Required:

For each transaction, give the following (including the basis for your decisions): *(a)* when revenue and/or expense should be recognized, and *(b)* the amount(s) that should be recognized in 19C.

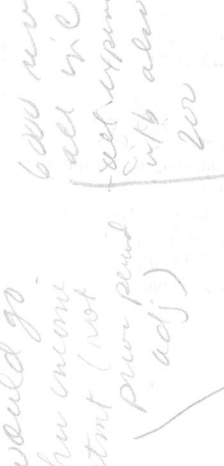

E 3–5 (Formats of the Statement of Income; EO Item; Periodic Inventory)

Storm Company's records provided the following information at December 31, 19B (end of the accounting period):

Sales revenue	$95,000
Service revenue	35,000
Gain on sale of short-term investments	11,000
Distribution expense	18,000
General and administrative expense	12,000
Depreciation expense	6,000
Interest expense	4,000
Income tax expense (30% rate on all items)	?
Rare tornado loss on building (infrequent and unusual)	15,000
Loss on sale of store fixtures (infrequent but not unusual)	3,000
Beginning inventory (periodic inventory system)	20,000
Ending inventory	23,000
Purchases (including freight-in)	50,000
Purchase returns	2,000

Common stock shares outstanding, 10,000 shares.

Required:

1. Prepare a single-step statement of income (show cost of goods sold computations in a separate supporting schedule).
2. Prepare a multiple-step statement of income. Include computation of cost of goods sold within the statement.

E 3–6 (Formats of the Statement of Income; EO Item; Perpetual Inventory)

AAA Sales and Service Company's accounts provided the following information at December 31, 19C (end of the accounting period):

Sales revenue	$199,000
Service revenue	33,000
Sales returns and allowances	1,500
Interest revenue	2,500
Gain on sale of short-term investments	1,000
Distribution expenses	56,700
General and administrative expenses	32,500
Depreciation expense	18,500
Income tax expense (40% rate on all items)	?
Loss on disposal of service trucks (assume infrequent but not unusual)	4,000
Gain (assume both unusual and infrequent)	10,000
Cost of goods sold (perpetual inventory system)	54,000
Interest expense	4,300
Common stock, par $5	100,000

Required:

1. Prepare a single-step statement of income.
2. Prepare a multiple-step statement of income.

E 3–7 (Revenue Recognition)

The following selected transactions were completed by JB Company during the year 19J; the accounting period ends December 31:

1. On December 30, 19J, sold $10,000 merchandise; terms 3/10, n/30.
2. On December 30, 19J, paid $3,000 for advertising in the local paper. The ads related only to a clearance sale that would run from January 1–31, 19K.
3. Performed services each working day for a customer from December 27, 19J, through January 5, 19K. Assume eight working days are involved, of which four were in 19J. Cash collected was $2,000 (in full) on December 27, 19J.
4. Sold a used TV set for $200 on December 28, 19J, and collected $125 cash. The balance is due in six months; however, collection of the balance is very doubtful, and the set will not be worth repossessing again. It is now carried in the inventory of used sets at $80. Credit Inventory because the perpetual inventory system is used.
5. On December 1, 19J, borrowed $6,000 cash and gave a one-year, 10% note payable for $6,000. Interest is payable at maturity.

Required:

For each transaction, give the following (including the basis of your decisions): *(a)* when revenue and/or expense should be recognized, and *(b)* the amount that should be recognized in 19J.

E 3–8 (Formats of the Statement of Income; EO Items; Perpetual Inventory)

The following items were taken from the adjusted trial balance of Big T Trading Corporation on December 31, 19K. Assume an average 30% income tax on all items (including the casualty loss). The accounting period ends December 31.

Sales revenue	$645,200
Rent revenue	2,400
Interest revenue	900
Gain on sale of operational assets (an ordinary item)	2,000
Distribution expenses	136,000
General and administrative expenses	110,000
Interest expense	1,500
Depreciation for the period	6,000
Extraordinary item: casualty loss (pretax)	22,000
Common stock (par $10)	100,000
Cost of goods sold (perpetual inventory system)	330,000

Required:

1. Prepare a single-step statement of income.
2. Prepare a multiple-step statement of income.

Part B: Exercises 3–9 to 3–15

E 3–9 (Statements of Income and Retained Earnings)

The following pretax amounts were taken from the adjusted trial balance of Como Corporation on December 31, 19B, end of the annual accounting period:

Balance, retained earnings, 1/1/19B	$ 45,000
Sales revenue	300,000
Cost of goods sold (perpetual inventory system)	105,000
Distribution expenses	36,000
Administrative expenses	34,000
Extraordinary gain (pretax)	10,000
Prior period adjustment, correction of error from prior period, pretax (a debit)	20,000
Dividends declared and paid	16,000

For problem purposes, assume the income tax rate for all items is 30%. The average number of common shares outstanding during the year was 20,000.

Required:

1. Prepare a complete multiple-step statement of income.
2. Prepare a statement of retained earnings.
3. Give the entry to record income taxes payable (assume not yet paid).

E 3–10 (Statements of Income and Retained Earnings)

The following pretax amounts were taken from the adjusted trial balance of Watson Corporation at December 31, 19C, end of the annual accounting period:

Dividends declared and paid	$ 35,000
Sales revenue	300,000
Cost of goods sold (perpetual inventory system)	100,000
Operating expenses	60,000
Extraordinary loss (pretax)	22,000
Prior period adjustment, correction of error from prior period, pretax (a credit)	10,000
Common stock (par $5)	200,000
Beginning retained earnings, 1/1/19C	60,000

Required:

1. Prepare a complete single-step statement of income assuming the income tax rate is 30% on all items.
2. Prepare a statement of retained earnings.
3. Give the entry to record income taxes payable (assume not yet paid).

E 3–11 (Statements of Income and Retained Earnings; EPS)

The following pretax amounts were taken from the adjusted trial balance of Olsen Corporation at December 31, 19J, end of the annual accounting period:

Sales revenue	$260,000
Cost of goods sold (perpetual inventory system)	110,000
Operating expenses	80,000
Extraordinary gain (pretax)	20,000
Prior period adjustment, correction of error from prior period, pretax (a debit)	32,000
Retained earnings, balance 1/1/19J	30,000
Dividends declared and paid	25,000
Common stock (par $10):	Shares
Outstanding 1/1/19J	15,000
Sold and issued 4/1/19J	5,000
Sold and issued 10/1/19J	7,000
Outstanding 12/31/19J	27,000

Required:
1. Prepare a complete single-step statement of income. Assume an average 30% tax rate on all items.
2. Prepare a statement of retained earnings.

E 3–12 (Statement of Income; Unusual or Infrequent Items)
The following pretax amounts were taken from the adjusted trial balance of Cortez Corporation at December 31, 19B, end of the annual accounting period:

Sales revenue	$220,000
Service revenue	50,000
Cost of goods sold (perpetual inventory system)	130,000
Operating expenses	88,000
Unusual item, gain on sale of operational asset (pretax)	25,000
Extraordinary item, loss (pretax)	20,000
Prior period adjustment, correction of error from prior period, pretax (a debit)	5,000
Common stock (par $1), 10,000 shares outstanding.	

Assume an average 30% corporate tax rate on all items.

Required:
1. Prepare a single-step statement of income.
2. Give the journal entry to record income tax (assume not yet paid).

E 3–13 (Depreciation; Change in Estimate)
Knight Company purchased a machine that cost $40,000 on January 1, 1983. The estimated useful life was 12 years, and the estimated residual value was $4,000. Straight-line depreciation is used. On December 31, 1988, prior to the adjusting entry, the company's chief accountant decided that the machine should be depreciated over a 15-year total useful life and that the estimated residual value at the end of the 15th year should be $1,000.

Required:
1. Give the adjusting entry at the end of 1988 for depreciation expense. Show computations.
2. Give the correcting entry required at the end of 1988. If none is required, so state and give the reasons.

E 3–14 (Change in Estimate; Error Correction)
It is December 31, 1988, and Owner Company (not a corporation) is preparing adjusting entries at the end of the accounting year. The company owns two trucks of different types. The following situations confront the company accountant:

Truck No. 1 cost $7,700 on January 1, 1986. It is being depreciated on a straight-line basis over an estimated useful life of 10 years with a $700 residual value. At December 31, 1988, it has been determined that the total useful life should have been 6 years instead of 10, with a revised residual value of $900.

Truck No. 2 cost $4,550 on January 1, 1985. It is being depreciated on a straight-line basis over an estimated useful life of seven years with a $350 residual value. At December 31, 1988, it was discovered that no depreciation had been recorded on this truck for 1985 or 1986.

Required:
1. For each truck, give the required adjusting entry for depreciation expense at December 31, 1988. Show computations.
2. For each truck, give the appropriate correcting entry and show computations. If no correcting entry is needed, give the reasons (ignore income tax effects).

E 3–15 (Combined Statements of Income and Retained Earnings)

The following pretax amounts were taken from the accounts of Scott Corporation at December 31, 19C, end of the annual accounting period:

Sales revenue	$170,000
Cost of goods sold (perpetual inventory system)	85,000
Distribution and administrative expenses	45,000
Extraordinary gain (pretax)	15,000
Prior period adjustment, correction of error from prior period, pretax (a debit)	8,000
Interest expense	1,000
Cash dividends declared and paid	5,000
Retained earnings, 1/1/19C	51,400

Common stock (par $5), 10,000 shares outstanding.

Assume an average 30% tax rate on all items, including the extraordinary gain.

Required:

Prepare a combined single-step statement of income and retained earnings, including intraperiod income tax allocation and EPS.

PROBLEMS

Part A: Problems 3–1 to 3–6

P 3–1 (Formats of the Statement of Income; EO Item; Periodic Inventory)

The following pretax information was taken from the adjusted trial balance of Atra Corporation at December 31, 19D, end of the accounting period:

Sales revenue	$957,000
Inventory, 12/31/19C	80,000
Inventory, 12/31/19D	92,000
Sales returns	7,000
Gain on sale of equipment (unusual but not infrequent)	8,000
Depreciation expense	25,000
Distribution expense	140,000
General and administrative expenses	92,300
Rent revenue	18,000
Investment revenue	7,000
Gain on sale of land (pretax)	6,000
Interest expense	9,000
Extraordinary gain (pretax)	80,000
Loss on sale of long-term investments, ordinary item (pretax)	10,000
Cost of goods sold	550,000
Loss due to leak in roof (infrequent but not unusual)	4,000
Extraordinary loss (pretax)	30,000

The company uses a periodic inventory system. Assume an average 35% income tax rate on all items. There are 40,000 shares of common stock outstanding.

Required:

1. Prepare a single-step statement of income.
2. Prepare a multiple-step statement of income.

P 3–2 (Formats of the Statement of Income; EO; Periodic Inventory)

The following data were taken from the adjusted trial balance of Miami Retail Corporation at December 31, 19B, end of the accounting period:

Merchandise inventory, 1/1/19B (periodic inventory system)	$ 71,000
Purchases	121,400
Sales revenue	405,000
Purchase returns	3,400
Sales returns	5,000
Common stock (par $10)	200,000
Depreciation expense (70% administrative expense, 30% distribution expense)	50,000
Rent revenue	4,000
Interest expense	6,000
Investment revenue	2,500
Distribution expenses (exclusive of depreciation)	105,500
General and administrative expenses (exclusive of depreciation)	46,000
Gain on sale of noncurrent asset (an ordinary gain)	6,000
Loss on sale of long-term investments (ordinary)	3,600
Income tax expense (not including the extraordinary item)	?
Extraordinary item: Flood loss (pretax)	10,000
Freight paid on purchases	1,000
Merchandise inventory, 12/31/19B	88,000

Assume an average 35% income tax rate on all items, including gains and losses on assets sold and extraordinary items.

Required:

1. Prepare a single-step statement of income and a separate schedule of cost of goods sold to support it.
2. Prepare a multiple-step statement of income (include cost of goods sold computation within the statement).

P 3–3 (Financial Statement Classifications)

Listed below are the primary financial statement classifications coded with letters. Also, a list of 25 selected transactions is given along with a space for your response.

For each transaction enter one code letter to indicate the usual classification. Comment on doubtful items.

Code	Financial statement classification
	Statement of Income
A	Revenue
B	Expense
C	Unusual or infrequent (but not both) gain or loss
D	Extraordinary item
	Statement of retained earnings
E	An addition or deduction
F	Addition to retained earnings
G	Deduction from retained earnings
H	Note to the financial statements
	Statement of financial position
I	Appropriately classified

Response	Transaction (summarized)
1. ______	Estimated warranties payable.
2. ______	Allowance for doubtful accounts.
3. ______	Gain on sale of operational asset.
4. ______	Hurricane damages.
5. ______	Payment of $30,000 additional income tax assessment (on prior year's income).
6. ______	Earthquake damages.
7. ______	Distribution expenses.
8. ______	Total amount of cash and credit sales for the period.
9. ______	Gain on disposal of long-term investments in stocks (nonrecurring).
10. ______	Net income for the period.

11. ______ Insurance gain on casualty (fire)—insurance proceeds exceeded the book value of the assets destroyed.
12. ______ Cash dividends declared and paid.
13. ______ Rent collected on office space temporarily leased.
14. ______ Interest expense of the year paid plus interest accrued on liabilities.
15. ______ Dividends received on stocks held as an investment.
16. ______ Damages paid as a result of a lawsuit by an individual injured while shopping in the store; the litigation covered three years.
17. ______ Loss due to expropriation of a plant in a foreign country.
18. ______ A $10,000 bad debt is to be written off—the receivable had been outstanding for five years. Use the allowance method.
19. ______ Adjustment due to correction during current year of an error; the error was made two years earlier (discussed in Part B of the chapter).
20. ______ On December 31 of current year, paid rent expense in advance for the next year.
21. ______ Cost of goods sold.
22. ______ Interest collected on November 30 of the current year from a customer on a 90-day note receivable, dated September 1 of the current year.
23. ______ Year-end bonus of $50,000 paid to employees for performance during the year.
24. ______ Depreciation on a machine used in operations.
25. ______ A meteor smashes the plant to smithereens ($5 million book value, no insurance).

P 3–4 (Identify Reporting Deficiencies; Redraft Statement of Income)

Buffer Company prepared the following statement of income at the end of its annual accounting period, December 31, 19C:

BUFFER COMPANY
Profit and Loss Report
December 31, 19C

Sales income		$ 98,000
Inventory	$ 12,000	
Merchandise	34,000	
Freight	1,000	
Inventory	(15,000)	
Cost of sales		32,000
Gross profit		66,000
Costs:		
Labor	15,000	
Depreciation	6,000	
Sales	21,000	
Overhead	8,000	
Interest	3,000	
Extraordinary	5,000	
Sale of used equipment	4,300	(61,400)
Other incomes:		
Service	3,600	
Interest	1,400	5,000
Taxable profit		9,600
Tax (25%)		2,400
Net profit		$ 7,200

EPS—$7,200 ÷ 5,000 shares = $1.40.

Required:

1. List all of the defects that you can identify on the above statement.
2. Recast the above statement in good format and terminology. Use the multiple-step format.

P 3–5 (Analysis; Revenue and Expense Recognition)

During the current year, 19X, Arizona Company completed the selected transactions given below that posed questions as to when revenue and/or expense should be recognized. The annual accounting period ends December 31.

a. Merchandise (TV sets) was sold on credit during 19X for $240,000. The terms were 25% down payment plus six monthly payments. The collection experience on such sales, although not as good as on regular credit sales (due at end of month of sale), has been consistently satisfactory.

b. On December 24, 19X, the company sold a used TV set for $110, which had been repossessed and was set up in used goods inventory at $60. At the date of sale, $70 cash was collected with the balance due in six months. There is a high probability that collection will not be made, and the TV set probably will not be worth repossessing again. Hint: Use cash basis only.

c. During 19X, the company sold 30 TV sets for a total of $15,000 and collected cash in full. The sets were guaranteed for 12 months from date of sale. It was estimated that the guarantee will cost the company, on the average, $20 per set. Cash paid for warranties during the year was $320.

d. On December 14, 19X, received a $20,000 income tax refund from prior years. The negotiations with the IRS extended over a three-year period.

e. Services were rendered to a customer starting on December 28, 19X, and will be completed January 15, 19Y. Cash in full ($6,000) will be collected at date of completion of the services. Assume 12 working days, of which 4 were in 19X.

f. On July 1, 19X, paid a two-year insurance premium in advance, $600.

g. On December 30, 19X, sold merchandise for $5,000; terms 2/10, n/30 (i.e., 2% discount if paid within 10 days). The company always takes the discount.

h. On December 1, 19X, sold a customer merchandise for $1,000. Collected $400 cash and received a $600, 10% note for the remainder; principal plus interest is due in three months.

i. On November 15, 19X, the court assessed damages against the company amounting to $25,000 cash. The suit was filed in 19W, as a result of an accident in the company store. Payment in full will be made on January 10, 19Y.

j. On December 23, 19X, purchased merchandise for resale that cost $18,000; terms, 2/10, n/30.

Required:

For each transaction, give the year in which revenue and/or expense should be recognized. Give the basis for your decision. Based on your analysis, also give the appropriate entry, if any, in 19X for each transaction.

P 3–6 (Relationships among the Statements of Income and Financial Position)

Analyze the relationships and amounts for each case and complete the following schedule by entering the appropriate amount in the blank spaces:

1.

Case	Owners' equity at start of period	Additional investment by owners	Withdrawals by owners	Owners' equity at end of period	Net income (loss)
A	$10,000	$2,000	$1,000	$17,400	$____
B	28,000	3,000	____	22,000	4,700
C	____	1,200	800	30,000	(2,200)
D	15,500	600	____	12,950	(2,000)
E	18,000	____	2,700	22,000	4,700

2.

Case	Sales revenue	Beginning inventory	Purchases	Ending inventory	Cost of goods sold	Gross margin	Total remaining expenses	Net income
F	$____	$25,000	$60,000	$____	$67,000	$23,000	$____	$1,000
G	80,000	____	48,000	2,000	____	23,000	18,000	____
H	____	20,000	____	36,000	59,000	18,000	____	8,000

Part B: Problems 3–7 to 3–11

P 3–7 **(Combined Statements of Income and Retained Earnings)**
The following amounts were taken from the accounting records of Walker Corporation at December 31, 19B, end of the annual accounting period:

Sales revenue	$340,000
Service revenue	64,000
Cost of goods sold (perpetual inventory system)	170,000
Distribution and administrative expenses	86,000
Investment revenue	6,000
Interest expense	4,000
Infrequent item: Loss on sale of long-term investment (pretax)	10,000
Extraordinary item: Earthquake loss (pretax)	14,000
Cash dividends declared and paid	8,000
Prior period adjustment, correction of error from prior period, pretax (a debit)	12,000
Balance, retained earnings, 1/1/19B	80,300

Common stock (par $5), 30,000 shares outstanding.
Restriction on retained earnings, $50,000 per bond payable indenture.

Assume an average 35% income tax rate on all items.

Required:
Prepare a combined single-step statement of income and retained earnings, including tax allocation and EPS. Show computations.

P 3–8 **(Analytical; Give Correct Entries)**
Unitas Corporation is undergoing its annual audit by the independent CPA at December 31, 1988 (end of the annual accounting period). During the audit, the following situations were found that needed attention:

a. On December 29, 1986, an asset that cost $12,000 was debited in full to 1986 Operating Expenses. The asset has a six-year estimated life and no residual value. The company uses straight-line depreciation.

b. Late in 1988, the company constructed a small warehouse using their own employees at a total cost of $90,000. However, before the decision was made to self-construct it, Unitas obtained a $100,000 bid from a contractor. Upon completion of the warehouse, Unitas made the following entry in the accounts:

Warehouse (an operational asset)	100,000	
Cash		90,000
Other income (nonoperating)		10,000

c. Prior to recording 1988 depreciation expense, the management decided that a large machine that originally cost $128,000 should have been depreciated over a useful life of 14 years instead of 20 years. The machine was acquired January 2, 1983. Assume the residual value of $8,000 was not changed. Give the 1988 adjusting entry and any other entries incident to the change in useful life.

d. During December 1988, the company disposed of an old machine for $6,000 cash. Annual depreciation was $2,000. At the beginning of 1988, the accounts reflected the following:

Machine (cost)	$18,000
Accumulated depreciation	13,000

At date of disposal, the following entry was made:

Cash	6,000	
Machine		6,000

No depreciation has been recorded for 1988.

e. A patent that originally cost $3,400 is being amortized over its legal life of 17 years at $200 per year. After the 1987 adjusting entry, it had been amortized down to a book value of $800. At the end of 1988, it was determined in view of a competitor's patent, that the patent will have no economic value to the company by the end of 1989. Straight-line amortization is used.

Required:
For each of the above situations, briefly explain the nature of each item and what should have been recorded in the accounts. If a journal entry is needed to correct the accounts, provide it along with supporting computations. Ignore income tax considerations.

P 3–9 (Combined Statements of Income and Retained Earnings; Intraperiod Income Tax Allocation)

The following pretax amounts were taken from the accounts of Jarvis Corporation at December 31, 19C, end of the annual accounting period:

Sales revenue	$550,000
Cost of goods sold (perpetual inventory system)	280,000
Distribution expenses	100,000
Administrative expenses	70,000
Interest revenue	1,000
Interest expense	3,000
Unusual item: Gain from sale of noncurrent asset (pretax; an ordinary gain)	20,000
Extraordinary item: Casualty (pretax loss)	40,000
Balance, retained earnings, 1/1/19C	95,000
Cash dividends declared and paid	15,000
Prior period adjustment, correction of error from prior period, pretax (a debit)	8,000

Common stock (par $1), 40,000 shares outstanding.

Restriction on retained earnings amounting to $25,000 as required by the indenture agreement on bonds payable.

Assume an average 35% income tax rate on all items.

Required:
Prepare a combined multiple-step statement of income and retained earnings, including intraperiod income tax allocation and EPS. Show computations.

P 3–10 (Identify Statement Deficiencies; Explain)

The following financial statements have come to you for review:

FAST PRODUCTION COMPANY
Profit and Loss Statement
December 31, 19K

Incomes:			
Gross sales		$256,800	
Less: Sales returns		5,120	
Net sales			$251,680
Costs and expenses:			
Cost of goods sold:			
Inventory, Jan. 1		98,500	
Purchases	$132,600		
Less: Purchase returns	2,780	129,820	
		228,320	
Inventory, Dec. 31		102,300	
Cost of goods sold			126,020
Gross profit			125,660
Operating costs:			
Selling		38,000	
General and administrative:			
General	20,000		
Depreciation	8,800		
Bad debts	1,080	29,880	
Total operating costs			67,880
Profit from operations			57,780
Other income:			
Interest income			970
Profit			58,750
Less taxes			28,720
Net			$ 30,030

FAST PRODUCTION COMPANY
Earned Surplus Statement
At December 31, 19K

Balance from last year		$267,600
Corrections:		
Additions:		
Depreciation overstated		3,400
Adjusted		271,000
Additions:		
Profit	$30,030	
Profit on sale of land	8,200	38,230
		309,230
Deductions:		
Dividends	30,000	
Loss on sale of machinery	9,650	39,650
Earned surplus (to balance sheet)		$269,580

Required:

Critically evaluate the above financial statements. Cite items to support your response. List and explain all of the aspects of the above statements that you would change in order to conform to appropriate reporting, terminology, and format.

P 3–11 (Identify Statement Deficiencies; Redraft Statements)

The following income statement and statement of retained earnings were prepared by the bookkeeper for Lax Corporation:

LAX CORPORATION
Statement of Profit
December 31, 19W

Sales income		$123,000
Service income		20,000
Total		143,000
Cost of sales (periodic inventory system):		
Inventory	$ 34,000	
Purchases (net)	71,000	
Inventory	(40,000)	65,000
Gross profit		78,000
Costs:		
Salaries, wages, etc.	35,000	
Depreciation and write-offs	7,000	
Rent	3,000	
Taxes, property	500	
Utilities	2,100	
Promotion	900	
Sales returns	2,000	
Sundry	6,700	(57,200)
Special items:		
Profit on asset sold		6,000
Inventory shortage		(2,800)
Pretax profit		24,000
Income tax		3,200
Net profit		$ 20,800

LAX CORPORATION
Earned Surplus
December 31, 19W

Balance, earned surplus		$27,000
Add:		
Profit		20,800
Correction of inventory error of 19V (pretax)		5,000
Total		52,800
Deduct:		
Earthquake loss (pretax)	$13,000	
Dividends	10,000	
Earned surplus to capital	5,000	27,000
Balance		$25,800

Required:

1. List each item on the above statements that you believe should be changed and give your recommendations with respect to appropriate reporting, terminology, and format. The average income tax rate is 20%, and 10,000 shares of common stock are outstanding. For problem purposes, assume the earthquake loss is extraordinary.
2. Prepare a complete multiple-step statement of income and a complete statement of retained earnings.

CASES

C 3–1 (Analytical; Discuss Statement Classifications)

During the 19D audit, the independent CPA encountered the following situations that caused serious concern as to proper classifications on the financial statements of selected clients. Assume all amounts are material.

a. A client was assessed additional income taxes of $100,000 plus $36,000 interest related to the past three years.

b. A client suffered a casualty loss (a fire) amounting to $500,000. The client occasionally experiences a fire, but this was significantly more than any such loss ever experienced by the client company.

c. A client company paid $175,000 damages assessed by the courts as a result of an injury to a customer on the company premises three years earlier.

d. A client sold a large operational asset and reported a gain of $70,000.

e. The major supplier of raw materials to a client company experienced a prolonged strike. As a result, the client company reported a loss of $150,000. This is the first such loss; however, the client has three major suppliers and strikes are not unusual in those industries.

f. A client owns several large blocks of common stock of other corporations. The shares have been held for a number of years and are viewed as a long-term investment. During the past year, 20% of the stock was sold to meet an unusual cash demand. Additional sales of the stock are not anticipated.

Required:

1. Briefly define *(a)* ordinary business operations, *(b)* unusual or infrequent gains and losses, *(c)* extraordinary gains and losses, and *(d)* prior period adjustments. Explain how the effects of each should be reported.
2. For each transaction, indicate how the financial effects should be classified; that is, classify as *(a)* ordinary business operations; *(b)* unusual or infrequent (but not both) gains and losses; *(c)* extraordinary; or *(d)* prior period adjustments. Explain the basis for your decision for each situation.

C 3–2 **(Analyze and Discuss EO Items)**

The following information was taken from an article in the *Journal of Accountancy:**

Case A:

"XYZ Company's fruit crop was destroyed by a severe freeze. The loss was $40,000. A freeze in XYZ's location is very rare. . . . ABC Company's fruit crop was also destroyed by a severe freeze. The loss was $40,000. A severe freeze in ABC's locale occurs about every two years."

Case B:

"Company A sold 100 shares of XYZ Company common stock for a gain of $5,000. This is the only stock that Company A owned or will ever own. . . . Company B also sold 100 shares of XYZ Company common stock for a gain of $5,000. Company B has several other investments in its common stock portfolio and is frequently involved in stock transactions."

Required:

1. Give the definition of an extraordinary item.
2. For Case A, explain how, and why, XYZ Company and ABC Company should report the $40,000 loss.
3. For Case B, explain how, and why, Company A and Company B should report the $5,000 gain.

---

* Bill D. Jarnigan, "Extraordinary Items: An Update," *Journal of Accountancy*, April 1984, pp. 42–44.

C 3–3 **(Analysis of Actual Financial Statements)**

Kimberly-Clark

The Appendix following Chapter 25 gives an actual set of financial statements for Kimberly-Clark. Examine them carefully and respond to the following questions (for 1987 only, unless otherwise specified):

a. Are the statements comparative? Why are comparative statements usually presented?
b. Are the statements consolidated? What do you understand this to mean?
c. Is this a retail, financial, or a manufacturing company? Explain.
d. How many different kinds of revenue were reported? How many different kinds of expenses were reported?
e. How were interest expense and interest revenue reported on the statement of income?
f. Was the total amount of depreciation expense separately reported on the statement of income? If not, where was it presented?
g. Were any unusual or infrequently occurring (but not both) items reported on the statement of income in 1986 or 1987?
h. Were any extraordinary items reported on the 1986 or 1987 statement of income? What were they? Were they net of tax?
i. Was there any indication of an accounting change? If so, explain how it was reported and what type of change it was.
j. How many EPS amounts were reported?
k. What "differences" were reported on the statement of income? Gross margin? Income from continuing operations? Income before extraordinary items? Net income? Others (list)?
l. What was the profit margin (net income divided by revenue) for 1987?
m. What basis was used for valuing inventories?
n. How does this company define "funds" in the SCF? What amount of "funds" was provided from operations in 1987?
o. What was the primary depreciation method used for accounting purposes?
p. What was the amount of income tax expense for 1987?
q. In 1987, what was the total amount of cash dividends declared on *(a)* common stock and *(b)* preferred stock?
r. What were the total amounts of net sales and net income reported for the first quarter of 1987?
s. Did the auditor's report express any reservations about the financial statements? Explain.

4 REVIEW: THE STATEMENT OF FINANCIAL POSITION AND THE STATEMENT OF CASH FLOWS

OVERVIEW AND PURPOSE

The statement of financial position is an accrual basis report; it is the primary statement because it is based on the fundamental accounting model: Assets = Liabilities + Owners' equity. Chapters 1 and 2 reviewed this model and focused on its application in transaction analysis, recording transactions, and producing the statements of income, retained earnings, and financial position. Understanding the interrelationships and the connecting links among these three statements and the statement of cash flows is important. These relationships were summarized in Exhibit 3–1. The statements of income and cash flows can be viewed as "change" statements because they give insights into what caused the financial position of an entity to change from the beginning to the end of the reporting period. The statement of income links directly to retained earnings and the statement of cash flows links directly to cash and cash equivalents. The statement of income reports the revenues, expenses, gains, and losses, on the accrual basis, from the entity's operating activities. In contrast, the statement of cash flows reports the detailed cash inflows and outflows from operating, investing, and financing activities. It is the only cash-basis financial statement that is required.

The purpose of this chapter is to review the underlying concepts, format, and usefulness of the statement of financial position and statement of cash flows. To accomplish this purpose, the chapter is organized as follows:

Part A: Review of the Statement of Financial Position (SFP)

1. Underlying concepts.
2. Valuations.
3. Format and classifications.
4. Usefulness and limitations.

Part B: Introduction to the New Statement of Cash Flows (SCF)

1. Objectives.
2. Characteristics and classifications.
3. Illustration.
4. Usefulness.
5. Additional reporting issues.

PART A: REVIEW OF THE STATEMENT OF FINANCIAL POSITION

The statement of financial position is based on the basic accounting model: **Assets (A) = Liabilities (L) + Owners' equity (OE).** The statement of financial position is a more descriptive (and preferable) title than balance sheet because the statement provides economic information about an entity's resources (assets), claims against those resources (liabilities), and the interests of the owners (owners' equity). The traditional designation, balance sheet, simply refers to the fact that the statement "balances" in conformity with the equation: A = L + OE.[1]

Concepts that Underlie the Statement of Financial Position

The primary terms used in the financial position model, A = L + OE, should be carefully defined. The accounting profession has developed various definitions. The latest "official" definitions are given in *FASB Statement of Financial Accounting Concepts No. 6* as shown in **Exhibit 4–1.** An asset may be tangible (such as a machine) or intangible (such as a patent). A liability may be short term (such as an account payable) or long term (such as a 10-year mortgage note payable). Owners' equity may include capital stock (for a corporation) or partners' interests (for a partnership).

Valuations Reported on the Statement of Financial Position

Fundamentally, a statement of financial position (SFP) *(a)* **lists** the assets, liabilities, and components of owners' equity, and *(b)* **reports** a specific dollar amount (i.e., valuation) for each item listed. Assigning a valuation to each item poses a basic conceptual issue. The issue is: Should the valuations at each SFP date represent *(a)* **current market** values or *(b)* **historical cost** values determined at the originating transaction dates? Some accountants and financial analysts argue that market values are more relevant to decision makers—investors, creditors, and other interested parties—because current values are more useful than historical cost values in assessing financial strength and in projecting future cash flows of the entity.

Despite the relevance of market values, the SFP primarily reports **historical cost** valuations because they are considered to be more **reliable.** The market value of an asset often can be known reliably only when the asset is bought or sold in a completed transaction. Such a transaction involves parties that have **different economic interests** (i.e., an arm's-length transaction where the seller wants a high price and the purchaser wants a low price). At SFP date, this situation does not exist; therefore, determination of market values generally is viewed as subjective and susceptible to manipulation, bias, and misrepresentation. In contrast, historical cost values are **objective, measurable, and verifiable.** It is important that decision makers clearly understand what SFP valuations mean, and equally important, what they do not mean.

[1] The 1987 edition of AICPA, *Accounting Trends & Techniques,* reported that 93% of the 600 companies used the title *balance sheet,* and the remainder used more descriptive titles.

Exhibit 4–1
Definitions of the primary elements on a statement of financial position.

Assets are probable future economic benefits obtained or controlled by a particular entity as a result of past transactions or events.

Liabilities are probable future sacrifices of economic benefits arising from present obligations of a particular entity to transfer assets or provide services to other entities in the future as a result of past transactions or events.

Equity [i.e., owners' equity] is the residual interest in the assets of an entity that remains after deducting its liabilities. In a business enterprise, the equity is the ownership interest.

Source: FASB, *Statement of Financial Accounting Concepts No. 6,* "Elements of Financial Statements of Business Enterprises" (Stamford, Conn., December 1985).

Subsequent to acquisition date, **assets** are reported at their **book or carrying value,** which may be *(a)* their cost (i.e., cash-equivalent cost) or *(b)* an amount less than cost due to market value impairment, depreciation, depletion, and amortization of the original cost caused by use, exploitation, or expiration. In general, cash is reported at its current value, and accounts receivable at expected **net realizable value** (i.e., accounts receivable less the allowance for doubtful accounts). Inventories and marketable equity securities usually are reported at lower of cost or market (discussed later), and plant and equipment are reported at cost less accumulated depreciation.

Liabilities are reported on the SFP at their carrying or book value which is their maturity value or discounted present value.

Owners' equity is a residual amount. It does not report the current market value of the business; rather, it is a measurement of the owners' interest that follows directly from the measurements used for the assets and liabilities in conformity with generally accepted accounting principles (GAAP). Valuation issues will be discussed in detail in subsequent chapters.

Format of the Statement of Financial Position

Full disclosure (discussed later) requires a complete statement of financial position with relevant subclassifications of assets, liabilities, and owners' equity. However, GAAP does not prescribe detailed specifications regarding an appropriate statement of financial position format. Current practice reflects two overall formats: *(a)* the account, or horizontal, format that lists the assets on the left and the liabilities plus owners' equity on the right, and *(b)* the report, or vertical, format. The report format, illustrated in this chapter, dominates in current practice.

To aid decision makers, SFP items usually are grouped according to common characteristics. **Assets usually are grouped in decreasing order of liquidity (i.e., nearness to cash), liabilities by time to maturity, and owners' equity in decreasing order of permanence.** Classifications of information used in a statement of financial position, and the array of items under each classification, are determined by GAAP. However, the classifications used are strongly influenced by the characteristics of each industry and of the enterprise. For example, the SFP of a financial institution, such as a bank, will reflect classifications different from those of a manufacturing company. Format and classifications should be designed for a particular enterprise and should comply with full

Exhibit 4–2
Classifications in a typical statement of financial position (SFP).

Assets:
1. Current assets.
2. Investments and funds.
3. Operational (or fixed) assets—tangible (often called **property, plant and equipment**).
4. Operational assets—intangible.
5. Other assets.
6. Deferred charges.

Liabilities:
1. Current liabilities (including short-term deferred credits).
2. Long-term, or noncurrent, liabilities (including long-term deferred credits).

Owners' equity:
1. Contributed capital (or paid-in capital):
   a. Capital stock.
   b. Contributed (or paid in) capital in excess of the par or stated value of capital stock (or premium on capital stock).
   c. Other contributed (or paid in) capital.
2. Retained earnings.
3. Unrealized losses and gains.

disclosure, which specifies that reporting be informative and not misleading. Therefore, flexibility in format and classifications is deemed to be desirable; however, a reasonable degree of uniformity is essential.

The classifications shown in **Exhibit 4–2** are typical of current reporting practices and terminology. Such a format provides a major caption for each SFP element—assets, liabilities, and owners' equity. Under each element caption, several subclassifications, such as those listed, commonly are used. As a position statement, the SFP must be dated **at a specific date,** such as "At December 31, 19XX." In contrast, the statement of income and the statement of cash flows are dated to cover a specific period of time, such as "For the Year Ended December 31, 19XX." These dates identify the end of the **reporting period.**

Exhibit 4–3 shows an actual statement of financial position adapted for instructional use. You should refer to it when preparing homework solutions and for other purposes in subsequent chapters.

Review of Classifications on the Statement of Financial Position

Current Assets

Current assets include (1) cash and (2) other assets that are **reasonably expected** to be realized in cash, or to be sold or consumed during the normal operating cycle of the business or within one year from the SFP date, whichever is longer.

The **normal operating** cycle of a business is the average period of time between the expenditure of cash for goods and services and the date those goods and services are converted into cash. Thus, it is the average length of time from cash expenditure, to inventory, to sale, to accounts receivable, and back to cash.

Most companies use one year as the time period for classifying items as current or long-term because *(a)* the operating cycle usually is less than one year, or *(b)* the length of the operating cycle may be difficult to measure reliably.

Current assets usually are presented on the SFP in order of **decreasing liquid-**

ity (i.e., nearness to cash conversion). The major items included in current assets, in order of liquidity, are cash, short-term investments, receivables, inventories, and prepaid expenses (see Exhibit 4–3).

Assets that are similar to but **not** classified as current assets are: (1) cash and claims to cash that are **restricted for uses other than current operations,** (2) receivables with an **extended** maturity date, and (3) **long-term** prepayments of expenses.

Exhibit 4–3
Statement of financial position illustrated.

JOY CORPORATION
Statement of Financial Position (Balance Sheet)
At December 31, 19X

Assets			
Current assets:			
Cash			$ 35,200
Short-term investments (current market value, $35,000)			20,000
Accounts receivable (trade)		$ 43,100	
Less: Allowance for doubtful accounts		1,300	41,800
Merchandise inventory (FIFO, LCM)			120,000
Prepaid expenses:			
Prepaid insurance			3,000
Total current assets			220,000
Investments and funds:			
Investment in stock of Y Corporation (at cost)	$ 77,000		
Less: Allowance to reduce to market value	7,000	70,000	
Plant expansion fund		80,000	150,000
Land, building and equipment:			
Land		24,000	
Building	200,000		
Less: Accumulated depreciation	80,000	120,000	
Equipment and fixtures	140,000		
Less: Accumulated depreciation	56,000	84,000	228,000
Intangible assets:			
Patent (cost, $42,500, less accumulated amortization, $17,500)			25,000
Other assets:			
Land held for future building site			37,000
Deferred charges:			
Rearrangement costs			8,000
Total assets			$668,000
Liabilities			
Current liabilities:			
Accounts payable (trade)			$ 48,700
Notes payable			30,000
Rent revenue collected in advance			1,800
Wages payable			2,000
Income taxes payable			12,500
Total current liabilities			95,000
Long-term liabilities:			
Bonds payable, 6%, due 19Z		175,000	
Less: Unamortized discount		4,000	171,000
Total liabilities			266,000

Exhibit 4–3
(concluded)

Stockholders' Equity		
Contributed capital:		
Preferred stock, par $10, 9% cumulative, nonparticipating, authorized 20,000 shares, issued and outstanding 5,000 shares	$ 50,000	
Common stock, nopar, authorized 100,000 shares, issued and outstanding 75,000 shares	150,000	
Additional contributed capital:		
In excess of par value of preferred stock	40,000	
Total contributed capital	240,000	
Retained earnings (Note A)	169,000	
Total contributed capital and retained earnings	409,000	
Less: Unrealized loss on long-term investment	7,000	
Total stockholders' equity		$402,000
Total liabilities and stockholders' equity		$668,000

Notes to financial statements:
Note A. Under the terms of the bond indenture (i.e., agreement), a part of retained earnings, determined by a formula, is restricted from dividend availability. The formula, computed for 19X, restricts retained earnings in the amount of $61,000. This amount will be increased each year as provided by the bond indenture formula. When the bonds are retired, the restriction will be automatically removed.

The definition of current assets is clear cut. However, problems are encountered in implementation. The phrases **normal operating cycle** and **reasonably expected to be realized in cash** involve judgments. Companies can **use** this judgment to incorrectly classify certain items as current assets to produce a desired effect on working capital (current assets minus current liabilities). For example, an investment in marketable securities may be classified as a current or noncurrent asset, depending upon the **stated intention** of management as to the planned holding period. An intention to hold the investment beyond the period specified for current assets would require its classification as a noncurrent asset. Thus, a simple change in **intention** of management can be used to justify an arbitrary change in the classification of the investment.

Prepaid expenses is another area with variation in classification. A short-term prepayment should be classified as a current asset (i.e., a prepaid expense), whereas a long-term prepayment should be classified as noncurrent (i.e., a deferred charge). Prepaid expenses are current assets because an "investment" is made by paying expenses in advance and cash outlays for the **next** reporting period are thereby reduced.

Some companies and industries do not use the current asset category. For example, financial institutions, such as banks and mutual funds, have no current asset caption because it would be pointless due to the nature of their asset structures.

Cash set aside in savings accounts or other investments should be reported as short- or long-term investments (discussed later in this chapter). Restrictions that require minimum cash balances in checking accounts should be disclosed.

Short-term investments should be valued on a lower-of-cost-or-market (LCM) basis (discussed in Chapter 8).

Merchandise inventories usually are reported at LCM as shown in Exhibit 4–3 (discussed in Chapter 9).

Current Liabilities

The definition of current liabilities parallels the definition of current assets. **Current liabilities are short-term liabilities "whose liquidation is reasonably expected to require the use of existing resources properly classified as current assets, or the creation of other current liabilities."**[2] This definition relates to current assets as a total rather than to specific current assets (e.g., a specific customer's account receivable).

Current liabilities include the following items:

1. Accounts payable for goods and services that enter into the operating cycle of the business (sometimes called **trade payables**).
2. Special short-term payables for nonoperating items and services.
3. Short-term notes payable.
4. Current maturities of long-term liabilities.
5. Collections in advance for unearned revenue (such as rent revenue collected in advance).
6. Accrued expenses for payrolls, interest, and taxes (e.g., unpaid income taxes and property taxes).

Liabilities that are similar to but are not classified as current liabilities include long-term notes, bonds, and obligations that will not be paid out of current assets. For example, a bond issue payable during the next reporting period would not be classified as a current liability if it is to be paid out of a special noncurrent fund. Similarly, currently maturing bonds payable that are to be refunded (i.e., paid off by issuing a new series of bonds) usually should not be classified as a current liability, as specified in *FASB Standard 6*. Liabilities usually are classified in the order in which they will be paid.

Working Capital. Working capital is defined as **current assets minus current liabilities.** The computation of working capital, and the working capital ratio, for Joy Corporation (Exhibit 4–3) would be as follows:

Current assets	$220,000
Current liabilities	95,000
Difference—working capital	$125,000

Working capital ratio (also called the **current ratio**):
$220,000 ÷ $95,000 = 2.32.

Notice that the above definition of working capital only explains how it is computed. More explicitly, if the current assets were converted to cash at their **book value** and the current liabilities paid at their **book value,** working capital would be the amount of cash remaining.

Although the concept of working capital is widely used in the business community, no one ever receives or pays working capital. In fact, a company may

[2] AICPA, *Accounting Research and Terminology Bulletins, Final Edition* (New York, 1961), p. 21.

report an excellent working capital position and at the same time have a serious cash deficiency. The amount of working capital and the working capital ratio are viewed as measures of liquidity; that is, the ability of the enterprise to meet its short-term obligations. For example, the working capital **ratio** computed for Joy Corporation shows that at book value the current assets were 2.32 times the current liabilities, or that for each $1 of current liabilities, there was $2.32 in current assets. Because of the use of working capital as an index of liquidity, the independent auditor sometimes encounters attempts to misclassify some noncurrent assets as current and some current liabilities as noncurrent. These manipulations would make it possible for the company to report a better working capital position than actually exists.

In financial reporting, offsetting current assets and liabilities is improper. This practice avoids full disclosure and would permit a business to show a more favorable current ratio than actually exists. For example, if Joy Corporation were to offset a current liability of $45,000 against current assets, the current ratio would be computed as follows: ($220,000 − $45,000 = $175,000) ÷ ($95,000 − $45,000 = $50,000) = 3.5 instead of the correct ratio of 2.32 shown above.

Offsetting is permissible only when a legal right to offset exists. For instance, it would be permissible to offset a $5,000 overdraft in one bank account against another account reflecting $8,000 on deposit in **that same bank** because the bank can offset the two deposit accounts.

Investments and Funds

The investments and funds classification includes **noncurrent** investments and cash set aside in special-purpose funds for long-term use as needed. This classification usually is reported directly under the current assets section. The long-term assets reported under this caption are:

1. Long-term investments in the capital stock of another company.
2. Long-term investments in the bonds of another company; any unamortized premium is added to the investment, and any unamortized discount is subtracted (see Chapter 15).
3. Investments in subsidiaries, including long-term receivables from subsidiaries.
4. Funds set aside for long-term future use, such as bond sinking funds (to retire bonds payable), expansion funds, stock retirement funds, and long-term savings deposits.
5. Cash surrender value of life insurance policies carried by the company.
6. Long-term investments in tangible assets, such as land and buildings, which are not used in current operations (long term includes operational assets that are only temporarily idle).

The important distinctions between current investments and funds and the above long-term assets are that *(a)* the long-term items are not used in the central ongoing and major operations of the entity, and *(b)* management plans to retain the long-term items beyond one year from the SFP date, or the operating cycle if it is longer.

Long-term investments reported under this caption usually are shown at their original cost. Funds included under this caption are shown at the accumulated amount in the fund. This valuation amount usually includes all contributions to the fund plus all interest accumulations added to the fund balance to date.

Operational Assets

Operational assets are long-term, noncurrent assets used in the continuing operations of the entity; they are not held for resale. Thus, operational assets are different from inventories (e.g., raw materials, work in process, finished goods, and supplies). Historically, operational assets were called **fixed assets** because of their relative permanence or long-term nature. Operational assets are subclassified as follows:

1. **Tangible**—Those assets used in operating the business that have **physical substance,** such as land, buildings, machinery, equipment, furniture, fixtures, and natural resources.
2. **Intangible**—Those assets used in operating the business that do not have physical substance but have value **because of the rights conferred by their ownership.** Examples include patents, copyrights, trademarks, brand names, leaseholds, and goodwill.

Operational Assets—Tangible. This group of operational assets is reported on the SFP under various captions depending upon the business. Manufacturing enterprises often use a caption such as **Property, plant, and equipment.** Other companies use a caption such as **Property and equipment,** or simply **Property.**

Tangible operational assets include items that are *(a)* depreciable, such as buildings, machinery, and fixtures, and *(b)* not subject to depreciation, such as land. Therefore, land should be reported separately.

APB Opinion 12 requires that the SFP, or the related notes, report *(a)* balances of major classes of depreciable assets by nature or function; *(b)* accumulated depreciation, either by major classes of depreciable assets or in total; and *(c)* a description of the methods used in computing depreciation for the major classes of operational assets. The term **Reserve for depreciation** should not be used to refer to accumulated depreciation because no "reserve" exists; instead, the appropriate term is **Accumulated depreciation.**

Tangible operational assets are shown on the SFP at their original cash equivalent cost, less any accumulated depreciation or depletion to date (see Exhibit 4–3).

Operational Assets—Intangible. This classification is reported separately on the SFP under the title **Intangible assets.** Major items should be listed separately, and the accumulated amount of **amortization** also should be disclosed. By convention, the contra account, accumulated amortization, seldom is separately listed. This contrasts to the usual treatment given tangible operational assets (see Exhibit 4–3).

Intangible operational assets are reported on the SFP at their original cash-equivalent cost, less accumulated amortization to date.

Other Assets

The **other assets** classification is used for assets that cannot be included under alternative asset classifications. Examples include long-term receivables from employees and idle operational assets (such as an idle plant). An asset should be analyzed carefully before it is classified as "other assets" because there is often a logical basis for classifying it elsewhere. If an asset has no future economic benefit, it should be written off and reported on the statement of income as a loss in the period in which the write-off occurs.

Deferred Charges

Deferred charges are caused by the **prepayment** of long-term expenses. These expenses have reliably determinable future economic benefits useful in earning future revenues. On this basis, they are viewed as assets until they are "used." The **only** conceptual difference between a prepaid expense (classified as a current asset) and a deferred charge is the **length of time** over which the deferred amount will be amortized.

The following accounts typify the "Deferred charges" caption: Machinery Rearrangement Costs, Organization Costs, Pension Costs Paid in Advance, and Insurance Prepayments (long-term prepayments not properly classified as a current asset). Deferred charges sometimes are inappropriately reported as "Other assets."

Long-Term Liabilities

A long-term liability is an obligation that will not require the use of current assets for payment during the next operating cycle or during the next reporting year, whichever is longer. Long-term liabilities initially are recorded at their "cost" (i.e., the value received). If such cost cannot be determined reliably, then the long-term liability is recorded at the discounted present value of all of its required future cash flows. The "cost" and maturity amount of a long-term liability may coincide (see discussion in Chapters 14 and 15).

A bond liability issued at more than its maturity amount is issued at a premium; if issued for less than its maturity amount, it is issued at a discount. Any unamortized debt premium should be added to the debt. Any unamortized debt discount should be subtracted (see Chapter 15).

All liabilities not appropriately classified as current liabilities are reported under this caption. Typical long-term liabilities are bonds payable, long-term notes payable, and long-term lease obligations.

Deferred Credits

A company may include the caption "Deferred credits" between long-term liabilities and owners' equity. This caption is not an appropriate classification because the financial position equation (Assets = Liabilities + Owners' equity) does not include it. At best, "Deferred credits" is a catchall SFP classification of long-term credit balance accounts that are difficult to classify elsewhere. Typical deferred credits are long-term deferred income taxes, deferred revenues (i.e., revenues collected in advance), and deferred investment tax credits. Most of the items reported under this caption are long-term liabilities or proper components of owners' equity.

Owners' Equity

Owners' equity for a corporation is called **stockholders' equity;** for a partnership, partners' equity; and for a sole proprietorship, proprietor's equity. Owners' equity is the owners' residual interest in the entity; it is always total assets minus total liabilities. This classification is used to report the various kinds of capital of an entity, such as contributed (or paid-in) capital and accumulated earnings.

Because of legal requirements, owners' equity is subclassified to reflect detailed sources. For a corporation, the following sources commonly are reported:

1. Contributed capital (or paid-in capital):
   a. Capital stock.
   b. Contributed (or paid-in) capital in excess of the par or stated value of capital stock (or premium on capital stock).
   c. Other contributed (or paid-in) capital.
2. Retained earnings.
3. Unrealized losses and gains.

Contributed Capital (or Paid-In Capital). *Capital Stock.* This caption reports the sources of owners' equity that are represented by the stated or legal capital (i.e., the par value of the issued or outstanding preferred and common stock) of the corporation. **Legal capital** is specified by state law and in the Articles of Incorporation (i.e., the Charter) of the corporation. In some states it is based on issued shares; in other states it is based on outstanding shares. Each class of stock, common and preferred, must be reported at its par or stated amount, or in the case of nopar stock, the total amount paid in (those specifications vary depending upon the law of the state of incorporation). Details of each class of capital stock should be reported separately. These details include number of shares authorized, issued, outstanding, and subscribed; conversion features; callability; preferences; and any other special features.

Contributed Capital in Excess of Par or Stated Value. This source sometimes is called **additional paid-in capital** or premium on stock. It reports the amounts received by the corporation in excess of the par or stated value of the capital stock outstanding. These amounts usually arise when the corporation sells its stock above its par or stated amount per share, or issues stock dividends (discussed in Chapters 16 and 17).

Other Contributed Capital. This source of contributed capital arises from such transactions as assets donated to the company (i.e., donated capital), treasury stock, and retirements and conversion of stock (discussed in Chapter 17).

Retained Earnings. Retained earnings is the corporation's accumulated earnings, less accumulated losses and dividends from inception. It reports the amount of resources (from undistributed earnings) that the corporation has retained for use in the enterprise. In most corporations, retained earnings is the **major source** of owners' equity. In the long term, most corporations distribute dividends to the stockholders amounting to less than the corporation's earnings. This policy establishes a continuing source of internally generated funds. Indirectly, retained earnings represents additional investments by the stockholders because they have foregone dividends equal to the cumulative balance of retained earnings. A negative balance in retained earnings usually is called a **deficit.**

A portion of the total amount of retained earnings may be **restricted or appropriated.** This means that during the period of restriction or appropriation, the restricted or appropriated amount is not available for dividends. For example, Joy Corporation (Exhibit 4–3) had total retained earnings of $169,000. However,

$61,000 of that amount was restricted for a specific period of time. After the restriction is removed, the $61,000 may be included in the amount available for dividends.

A restriction on retained earnings may be **contractual,** as in Exhibit 4–3, in which the bond indenture restricts the amount of retained earnings available for dividend declaration. Alternatively, a restriction may result from a **legal requirement,** such as a restriction by state law equal to the cost of any treasury stock held. The purpose of such laws is to protect the creditors of the corporation. Finally, the board of directors may exercise its **discretion** and **"appropriate"** a portion of retained earnings, as in the case of "retained earnings appropriated for future plant expansion."

Restrictions or appropriations of retained earnings may be reported in two ways. One way is to report restrictions or appropriations in notes, such as Note A in Exhibit 4–3. Another approach is to make an **entry** in the accounts to reflect the restriction or appropriation. For example, the $61,000 restriction on retained earnings reported by Joy Corporation (Exhibit 4–3) could be recorded and reported as follows:

Entry to **record** the appropriation in the accounts:

Retained earnings	61,000	
Retained earnings restricted by bond indenture		61,000

Reporting on the statement of financial position then could be:

Retained earnings:	
Unappropriated	$108,000
Appropriated by bond indenture	61,000
Total retained earnings	$169,000

Each additional appropriation, or increase in a prior appropriation, reduces the unappropriated balance and increases the total appropriated by the same amount.

Unrealized Capital (Losses and Gains)

This component of owners' equity is used mainly for recording and reporting **unrealized** losses resulting from the application of the LCM rule to long-term equity investments in capital stock, under the requirements of *FASB Standard 12.* This *Standard* requires that the cumulative amount of unrealized loss be reported separately as an **unrealized element of owners' equity** (i.e., a reduction in owners' equity as shown in Exhibit 4–3). A **realized** gain or loss is recognized only when an actual transaction occurs. In contrast, an **unrealized gain** or loss is recognized in the absence of an actual transaction. Assume a company owns a tract of land that cost $50,000. If it sells the land for $80,000, a $30,000 **realized** gain is recognized. Assume instead that the land is not sold but is written up to its market value of $80,000. Then a $30,000 **unrealized** gain would be recognized. This discussion is not intended to imply that writeups of assets to market value currently are in accordance with GAAP. However, there are a few exceptions as explained in Chapters 8, 10, 18, and 25.[3]

[3] Other items, not appropriate for review purposes, are discussed in later chapters. They include contingency gains and losses, accounting policies, contractual arrangements, and post-SFP events.

Usefulness and Limitations of the Statement of Financial Position

The statement of financial position is an important financial report, particularly when used with a statement of income and a statement of cash flows. Collectively, these statements and their related disclosure notes and schedules are very useful. In particular, they help decision makers assess the past performance of an enterprise and assess and project the future cash flows of that enterprise.

The statement of financial position has some limitations that often are overlooked. First, a SFP reports on a **historical cost** basis; it does not report the current market value of the business. Second, a SFP reports some **estimates** such as the estimated loss from uncollectible receivables, and accumulated depreciation, depletion, and amortization. Finally, certain liabilities often must be estimated such as income taxes and contingencies. Other SFP estimates (e.g., pension liabilities) are discussed in subsequent chapters.

PART B: INTRODUCTION TO THE NEW STATEMENT OF CASH FLOWS (SCF)

Objectives

In addition to the statements of income and financial position, a statement of cash flows is required by *FASB Standard 95.* This standard is dated November 1987 and is effective "for annual financial statements for fiscal years ending after July 15, 1988." The basic purpose of the statement of cash flows (SCF) is to provide relevant information about the cash inflows and outflows of an entity. Cash flow information is needed to help investors, creditors, and others assess and project the future net cash flows of an entity. In turn, these projections help investors, creditors, and others project their own net cash flows from investments in, and loans to, an entity.[4]

Characteristics of a Statement of Cash Flows

A statement of cash flows reports only cash data; it does not report accrual amounts. For cash flow purposes, *FASB Standard 95* defines cash as "cash plus cash equivalents." Cash equivalents are defined in *FASB Standard 95* as "short-term highly liquid investments" held by an entity, such as Treasury bills, money market funds, and similar commercial paper. Cash equivalents must be clearly defined by company policy which is seldom changed.

Standard 95 specifically defines six items that must be reported on the SCF. These six items, or classifications, are shown in **Exhibit 4–4** (A–F) with summary amounts for Barton Company. The major classifications on the SCF are **cash flows from an entity's operating, investing, and financing activities.** Notice in Exhibit 4–4 that the new SCF **does not** have **major** captions for cash inflows

---

[4] *FASB Standard No. 95* superseded *APB Opinion No. 19,* which required a statement of changes in financial position (SCFP). Prior to *Standard 95,* the SCFP could be prepared on either a working capital or a cash basis. The new SCF must be on a cash basis. This part of the chapter is more than a review because it provides a brief discussion of the new statement of cash flows, which is discussed comprehensively in Chapter 19.

Exhibit 4–4
Overview of a statement of cash flows, Barton Company, December 31, 1988.

A.	Cash flows from **operating** activities:		
	1. Cash inflows (detailed)	$10,700	
	2. Cash outflows (detailed)	(7,750)	
	3. Net cash inflow (outflow) from operating activities		$ 2,950
B.	Cash flows from **investing** activities:		
	1. Cash inflows (detailed)	13,300	
	2. Cash outflows (detailed)	(17,100)	
	3. Net cash inflow (outflow) from investing activities		(3,800)
C.	Cash flows from **financing** activities:		
	1. Cash inflows (detailed)	2,925	
	2. Cash outflows (detailed)	(875)	
	3. Net cash inflow (outflow) from financing activities		2,050
D.	Effect of foreign exchange rates		100
E.	Net increase (decrease) in cash during the period		1,300
	Cash balance at the beginning of the period		14,000
	Cash balance at the end of the period		$15,300
F.	**Noncash** investing and financing activities—Either clearly identified in the statement or set out separately in disclosure notes.		

(i.e., cash receipts) and cash outflows (i.e., cash payments) because **each** of the three major classifications must show **both the cash inflows and outflows** related to each activity. The summary amounts shown in Exhibit 4–4 (for instructional purposes only) are discussed later. At this point notice that *(a)* the net increase (decrease) in cash during the period is the algebraic sum of four amounts and *(b)* the net increase (decrease) in cash (i.e., classification E) ties in directly to the statement of financial position. The key, or check, amount (classification F) on the SCF is known in advance because the statement of financial position is prepared first.

Classifications on a Statement of Cash Flows Defined

The classifications used on the SCF are defined in *Standard 95* essentially as follows:

a. **Cash flows from operating activities.** This includes all transactions and events not defined as investing or operating activities. This classification reports **both** the cash inflows and cash outflows that are directly related to net income reported on the statement of income. The usual cash flows under this classification are:

Inflows—cash received from:	Outflows—cash paid for:
Customers.	Purchase of goods for resale.
Interest on receivables.	Interest on liabilities.
Dividends on investments.	Income taxes, duties, fines, etc.
Gains on discontinued operations.	Losses on discontinued operations.
Refunds from suppliers.	Salaries and wages.

A gain or loss on an extraordinary item or a discontinued operations gain or loss sometimes must be "removed" from operating activities. The **full** cash effect is included in investing or financing activities, whichever is the dominant source.

The difference between the above inflows and outflows is called the **net cash inflow (outflow) from operating activities.** Typically, the net amount will be an inflow because in the long term, revenues necessarily must exceed expenses.

b. **Cash flows from investing activities.** This major classification on the SCF reports both cash inflows and outflows that are related to the use of cash for obtaining the productive facilities used by the company and other noncash assets. The **cash outflows** under this classification represent the "investments" of cash by the entity to acquire its noncash assets. The **cash inflows** under this classification occur only when cash is received back from the prior investments. The typical cash flows under this classification are:

Outflows—cash paid for:
- Property, plant and equipment.
- Investment in debt and equity securities.
- Lending to other parties.
- Other assets used in productive activities, such as a patent (excluding inventories which are operating activities).

Inflows—cash received from:
- Disposal of property and plant equipment.
- Disposal of investments in securities.
- Collection of a loan (excluding interest which is an operating activity).
- Disposal of other assets used in productive activities (excluding inventories).

The difference between the above cash inflows and outflows is called **net cash inflow (outflow) from investing activities.**

c. **Cash flows from financing activities.** This major classification on the SCF represents **both** cash inflows and outflows that are related to **how cash was obtained** to finance the enterprise (including its operations). The **cash inflows** under this classification represent the financing activities used to obtain cash for the entity. The **cash outflows** occur only when cash is paid back to the owners and creditors for their prior cash-providing activities. The usual cash flows under this classification are:

Inflows—cash received from:
- Owners—issuing equity securities.
- Creditors—borrowing on notes, mortgages, bonds, etc.

Outflows—cash paid to:
- Owners for dividends and other distributions.
- Owners for treasury stock purchased.
- Payment of principal amounts borrowed (excluding interest, which is an operating activity).

The difference between the above cash inflows and outflows is called **net cash inflows (outflows) from financing activities.**

d. **Effect of foreign exchange rates.** This classification applies only to companies that have foreign operations or foreign currency transactions. This classification reports the effect of exchange rate changes on cash balances held in foreign currencies. These changes affect the amount of cash reported on the statement of financial position.

e. **Reconciling balances.** *FASB Standard 95* requires reporting of the three related amounts: (1) net increase (decrease) in cash, (2) beginning cash balance, and ending cash balance, as shown in Exhibit 4–4.

f. **Noncash investing and financing activities.** These are the investing and financing transactions that involve some noncash effects. There are two types: (1) no cash is received or paid (such as settling a debt in full by issuing the company's capital stock to the creditor) and (2) part cash and part noncash (such as settling a debt with 30% cash and 70% capital stock (the noncash activity is 70%)). These noncash activities must be reported in a separate schedule or set out separately in the disclosure notes.

Statement of Cash Flows Illustrated

The SCF for Barton Company is shown in **Exhibit 4–5,** which is a detailed expansion of the overview provided in Exhibit 4–4. Before considering how the SCF is prepared, notice the following important characteristics of a statement of cash flows:

a. **Cash flows from operating activities**—cash inflows from revenues; cash outflows for expenses, and net cash flows from operating activities. Basically, this caption shows net income (accrual basis) restated to a strict cash basis.

b. **Cash flows from investing activities**—cash used (outflows) to acquire noncash assets and cash received (inflows) from subsequent disposals of those assets. (Note—we have shown cash outflows first to indicate the normal sequence [timing] involved in this activity; however, for reporting purposes cash inflows usually are reported first under each activity [as shown in Exhibit 4–4].) Interest or dividends earned on investing activities are included in **operating activities** because such amounts are reported on the statement of income.

c. **Cash flows from financing activities**—cash inflows from borrowing and issuance of company stock and cash outflows to pay debt principal and cash dividends. Interest on debt is reported as an operating activity because it is reported on the statement of income.

d. Classification E ties in (and proves) the **net increase (decrease) in cash** during the year with the beginning and ending cash balances.

e. **Disclosure notes:**

Note A—reports a "noncash" transaction which was part cash ($425) and part noncash ($575). Notice that the SCF reported **only** the cash part (under financing activities because it involved the payment of a debt).

Note B—reconciles net income with cash flow from **operating** activities. *Standard 95* requires this reconciliation because it is considered to be

Exhibit 4–5
Statement of cash flows (direct method).

BARTON COMPANY
Statement of Cash Flows (direct method)
For the Year Ended December 31, 1988

A. **Cash flows from operating activities:**		
Cash inflows from operating activities:		
From customers	$ 8,600	
Interest received (on investments)	50	
Cash outflows from operating activities:		
Cash paid to suppliers (cash for CGS)	(4,550)	
Cash paid for remaining expenses	(1,000)	
Cash paid for interest expense	(100)	
Cash paid for income tax	(50)	
Net cash inflow (outflow) from operating activities		$2,950
B. **Cash inflows (outflows) from investing activities:**		
Cash outflows (investments in the following):		
Property, plant, and equipment	(4,900)	
Purchase of securities for investment	(4,700)	
Cash loan to CRB	(7,500)	
Cash inflows (cash collections related to "investments"):		
Sale of property plant and equipment	2,500	
Sale of investment securities	5,000	
Collections on loan (excluding interest)	5,800	
Net cash inflow (outflow) from investing activities		(3,800)
C. **Cash inflows (outflows) from financing activities:**		
Cash inflows (obtained from the following sources):		
Cash deposits by customers	1,100	
Cash from short-term debt	75	
Cash from long-term debt	1,250	
Issuance of company stock	500	
Cash outflows (cash payments related to financing):		
Payment on long-term debt (Note A)	(425)	
Dividends paid (cash to owners)	(450)	
Net cash inflow (outflow) from financing activities		2,050
D. Net cash inflow (outflow) from currency exchange rate changes		100
E. Net increase (decrease) in cash during the period		1,300
Cash balance, January 1, 1988*		14,000
Cash balance, December 31, 1988*		$15,300

Note A. Paid a long-term note with stock and cash as follows:

Cash paid	$ 425
Common stock issued	575
Note paid in full	$1,000

A reconciliation of net income, $3,300, with net cash increase during the period, $1,300: (This disclosure requirement is discussed in Chapter 19.)

* Agrees with the statement of financial position.

useful information for investors, creditors, and others. Discussion of this reconciliation is deferred to Chapter 19 because it is the only complex computation related to the SCF.

f. Finally, notice that the **heading for the SCF** includes "(direct method)." *FASB Standard 95* provides that either of two methods can be used to report **cash flows from operations.** These alternative methods are called the (1) **direct method** and (2) **indirect method.** Except for reporting cash flows from operating activities, the SCF is identical under both methods. The direct method is (1) much more simple than the indirect method, and (2) strongly recommended in *Standard 95*. Therefore, we use the direct method in this chapter. Both methods are discussed in Chapter 19.

Preparing an SCF

The SCF can be prepared by using either a schedule approach (for simple cases) or a spreadsheet approach (for complex cases). This chapter uses the **schedule approach** and Chapter 19 discusses both approaches. Under either approach there are three steps as follows:

1. Obtain the current statements of income and comparative statement of financial position (i.e., for the current and the prior year). Develop an analysis of selected accounts from the statement of financial position that involved cash flows during the year.
2. Prepare schedules for the operating, investing, and financing activities, or prepare a spreadsheet.
3. Prepare the SCF by using data provided by the schedules or spreadsheet.

Next we illustrate how Barton Company prepared the 1988 SCF shown in Exhibit 4–5 by following the three steps listed above.

Step 1—Data related to the SCF for Barton Company for the Year Ended December 31, 1988

1. Statement of income (accrual basis):

Sales revenue	$ 9,000
Interest revenue	400
Total revenues	9,400
Cost of goods sold	(4,100)
Depreciation expense	(1,500)
Interest expense	(200)
Income tax expense	(200)
Remaining expenses*	(1,000)
Total expenses	(7,000)
Gain on sale of property, plant and equipment	600
Gain on sale of securities	300
Net income	$ 3,300

* All cash.

2. Comparative statement of financial position (selected accounts):

Selected accounts	Balances December 31, 1987	Balances December 31, 1988	Increase (decrease)
Cash	$14,000	$15,300	$1,300
Accounts receivable	500	900	400
Interest receivable	0	350	350
Inventory	1,000	1,250	250
Accounts payable	300	100	(200)
Interest payable	80	180	100
Income tax payable	50	200	150

3. Analysis of selected accounts for 1988:
   a. Property, plant and equipment—Purchased equipment for $4,900; cash paid in full payment.
   b. Property, plant and equipment—Sold old equipment for cash and made the following entry:

Cash	2,500	
Accumulated depreciation	8,500	
Equipment		10,400
Gain on disposal		600

   c. Investment—Purchased debt securities of XYZ Company for cash, $4,700 (January 3, 1988).
   d. Received cash deposit from a customer to apply on a future contract (a debt), $1,100.
   e. Issued company stock for $500 cash.
   f. Cash collected on a short-term note, $75.
   g. Cash loan made to CRB customer, $7,500.
   h. Paid a long-term debt in full by issuing capital stock and paying cash, recorded as follows:

Long-term note	1,000	
Common stock		575
Cash		425

   i. Collection of principal on a long-term note receivable, $5,800.
   j. Sold investment securities for cash and made the following entry:

Cash	5,000	
Investment securities		4,700
Gain on sale of investments		300

   k. Barton Company paid a cash dividend of $450.
   l. Effect of foreign currency exchange rate changes (cash increase), $100.

Step 2—Prepare schedules for operating, investing, and financing activities. Barton Company prepared two schedules: A for operating activities, and B for investing and financing activities—as follows:

Schedule A—Statement of Income Converted to Cash Basis, Barton Company

Accrual basis		Cash basis: Conversion computation—See Step 1 data		Amount
a. Sales revenue	$9,000	Accounts receivable increase	$−400	$ 8,600
b. Interest revenue	400	Interest receivable increase	−350	50
Deduct expenses:				
c. Cost of goods sold	4,000	Inventory increase	+250	
		Accounts payable decrease	+200	(4,550)
d. Depreciation expense	1,500	Noncash expense		–0–
e. Interest expense	200	Interest payable increase	−100	(100)
f. Income tax expense	200	Income tax payable increase	−150	(50)
g. Remaining expenses	1,000	All cash for remaining expenses		(1,000)
h. Gain on sale of property, plant and equipment	600	Included in investing activities		–0–
i. Gain on sale of securities	300	Included in investing activities		–0–
Net income	$3,300			
Net cash inflow from operating activities				$ 2,950

Explanation of the conversion computations *(a–f)* in Schedule A:

a.–b. Sales revenue and interest revenue on the statement of income (accrual basis) are converted to a cash basis by using the changes during the period in accounts receivable and interest receivable as follows:

(1) Receivable increases—deduct (−) from the related revenue because the change amount was "on credit."

(2) Receivable decreases—add (+) to the related revenue because the change amount "on credit" was collected.

c. Cost of goods sold (CGS) on the statement of income (accrual basis) is converted to a cash basis by considering changes in both inventory and accounts payable. This conversion computes the total amount of cash purchases for the period. It requires a two-step conversion as follows (minus means deduct and plus means add):

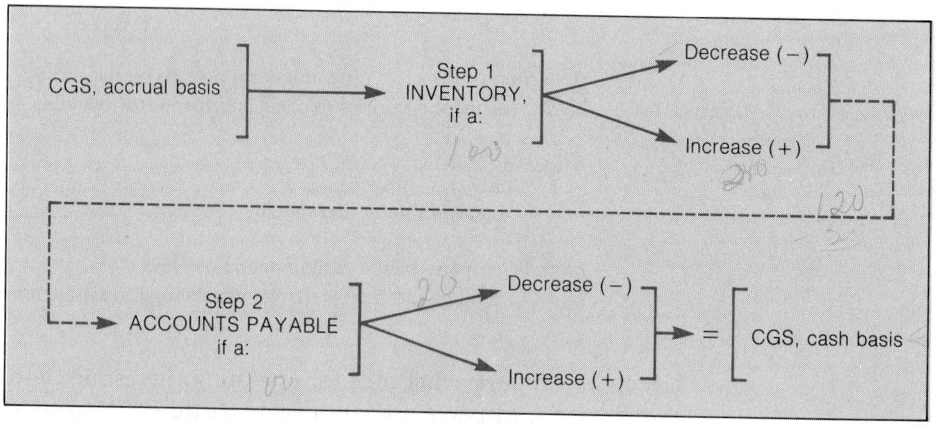

The "key" to this two-step conversion is: Cash is required to increase inventory and decrease accounts payable (and vice versa).

d. Depreciation, depletion, and amortization, and bad debt expense reported on the statement of income are all noncash—omit from cash basis.

e.–g. Expenses reported on the statement of income (accrual basis) are converted to a cash basis by using the change in the related payables (e.g., accounts payable and income taxes payable) as follows:

(1) Payables increase—deduct (−) from the related expense because the change "on credit" amount was not paid during the current period.

(2) Payables decrease—add (+) to the related expense because the change "on credit" amount was paid this period.

Note: If a prepaid expense is involved the signs reverse.

h.–i. Gains and losses on disposal of noncash items:

(1) Disregard because the **total** cash received is appropriately reported under investing or financing activities.

The investing and financing cash inflows and outflows are shown below in Schedule B, which was based on the data (given above under Step 1), from the statement of financial position and the analysis of selected accounts:

Schedule B—Cash Flows from Investing and Financing Activities

		Investing		Financing		
Transaction	**Cash amount**	**Inflow**	**Outflow**	**Inflow**	**Outflow**	**Noncash**
a. Purchased equipment	$4,900		✓			
b. Sold old equipment	2,500	✓				
c. Purchased debt securities	4,700		✓			
d. Customer deposit received	1,100			✓		
e. Issued company stock	500			✓		
f. Collected short-term note, principal	75			✓		
g. Loan to CRB	7,500		✓			
h. Long-term note paid	425				✓	$575
i. Long-term note collected, principal	5,800	✓				
j. Sale of investment securities	5,000	✓				
k. Paid cash dividend	450				✓	
l. Effect of foreign currency exchange rate changes*	100					

* Separate category of cash inflow (outflow).

Usefulness of the Statement of Cash Flows

There is general agreement that a statement of cash flows is needed to give investors, creditors, and other interested parties feedback about cash inflows and outflows for each major activity—operating, investing, and financing. Information about the cash available from various sources for debt payments, dividends, investments by the entity, and the support of future growth is important to decision makers. Moreover, decision makers are particularly interested in the amount of cash that the entity generates from its operating activities. The operating activities necessarily must be the primary long-term cash source because operations must eventually pay for the company's debts, dividends, and growth. Also, the SCF provides useful information about the company's borrowing and repayments (i.e., financing activities), and new investments by owners (a source of interest-free cash) and dividends (i.e., investing activities).

On a broader scale, the SCF helps decision makers assess the financial strength of a business. The **financial strength** of a company is reflected primarily by *(a)* its financial flexibility and *(b)* its financial liquidity. In general, financial strength is evidenced by the relationship between the company's assets and liabilities and the company's credit standing with financial institutions and other lenders. **Financial flexibility** refers to the ability of a company to effectively respond to unexpected cash demands and new opportunities to enhance its earnings and assets. **Financial liquidity** refers to the time that is needed by an entity to *(a)* convert noncash assets to cash and *(b)* pay maturing liabilities.

The purpose of this brief discussion of the new statement of cash flows is to familiarize you with its characteristics—particularly its format and what it reports—even though the techniques used in complex situations to construct the SCF are not discussed in this chapter. Chapter 19 is a comprehensive discussion of the new SCF, including both the direct and indirect methods and the schedule and spreadsheet approaches.

Additional Reporting Issues

We will conclude the review of information processing and the financial statements with a brief discussion of additional reporting issues that often are encountered.

Terminology

Accounting has developed its own jargon and the same word or phrase often is used to mean different things. In preparing reports, accountants should refrain from using vague terminology. Captions and titles should be selected carefully because the statements will be used by a wide range of decision makers. From time to time, pronouncements such as the *ARBs, APB Opinions,* and *FASB Statements* have recommended improved terminology. For example, *FASB Concepts Statement 6* created a new term, **comprehensive income.** This term encompasses a wider range of revenues, expenses, gains, and losses than is contemplated by conventional net income. At some time in the future, the FASB may define this term more precisely and incorporate it in the statement of income.

An example of careless terminology is using the term **reserve** to refer to *(a)* a contra asset account, such as "reserve for depreciation," instead of the more descriptive term **accumulated depreciation;** *(b)* an estimated liability, such as "reserve for warranties" instead of "estimated warranty liability"; and *(c)* an appropriation of retained earnings, such as "reserve for future expansion" instead, of "Retained earnings appropriated for future expansion." However, *Accounting Terminology Bulletin No. 1* recommended that the term be restricted to the last usage. Even in this context, the authors do not believe that the word **reserve** is suitable to describe the nature of a restriction or appropriation of retained earnings.

The terminology bulletin recommended using the terms **retained earnings** instead of earned surplus and **net income** instead of net profit. Confusion of the terms **cost** and **expense** and **revenue** and **income** discussed in Chapter 3, is another example of careless terminology. **Throughout this textbook we discuss and use preferred terminology because the effectiveness of accounting communication and precision in discussing accounting concepts and their implementation depends largely upon consistent use of precise and descriptive terminology.**

Comparative Statements

To help predict the future success, or failure, of an enterprise, comparable financial information for two or more periods should be used. For prediction purposes, trends are much more revealing than information for only one period. In recognition of this fact, *ARB 43* states:

> The presentation of comparative financial statements in annual and other reports enhances the usefulness of such reports and brings out more clearly the nature and trends of current changes affecting the enterprise. Such presentation empha-

sizes the fact that statements for a series of periods are far more significant than those for a single period and that the accounts for one period are but an installment of what is essentially a continuous history.[5]

Comparative financial statements for the current and prior reporting periods are essential for **full disclosure.** In 1980, the SEC began requiring three-year comparative statements, in lieu of the customary two-year statements, for "listed" companies. The actual statements shown in the Appendix following Chapter 25 display comparative amounts.

In addition to comparative statements, many companies present a special tabulation of selected financial items for time spans of 5 to 20 or more years. Items often included are total revenues, income before extraordinary items, net income, depreciation expense, EPS, dividends, total assets, total owners' equity, and average number of shares of common stock outstanding. These long-term summaries are particularly useful in trend analysis.

Subsequent Events

Subsequent events are important events or transactions that occur **subsequent** to the statement of financial position date but **prior** to the actual issuance of the financial statements (ordinarily one to four months later), and that have a material effect on the financial statements. Subsequent events must be reported in the financial statements of the current reporting period if they occur before these statements are issued. They involve information that could influence the statement users' interpretation and evaluation of the future prospects of the enterprise. Auditing standards define these events and specify that they must be reported either in the (1) tabular portion of the statements or (2) notes to the statements, depending upon their nature.

The effects of subsequent events should be reported in the **tabular portion of the statements** if they *(a)* provide additional evidence about conditions **that existed at** the date of the statement of financial position (SFP), *(b)* affect estimates inherent in the process of preparing the financial statements, and *(c)* require adjustments to the financial statements resulting from the estimates. An example would be a material loss on an uncollectible receivable because of a customer's deteriorating financial condition. The deteriorating financial condition presumably was occurring at the SFP date, but recent information made it more evident.

Subsequent events should be **disclosed in the notes** to the statements if they *(a)* result from conditions that did not exist at the SFP date, *(b)* arose subsequent to that date, and *(c)* do not merit adjustment to the current financial statements. Examples listed in *Codification of Statements on Auditing Standards*, AU Sec. 560.06, are sale of a bond or capital stock issue, litigation based on an event subsequent to the date of the statement of financial position, inventory losses due to casualty, and losses caused by a condition that arose subsequent to the SFP date (such as a fire or flood). The fire or flood did not "exist" at the SFP date.

This topic is considered in depth in auditing texts and courses.

---

[5] AICPA, *Accounting Research Bulletin No. 43*, "Restatement and Revision of Accounting Research Bulletins" (New York, 1953), chap. 2, sec. A.

Full Disclosure

Full disclosure requires complete reporting of all information relating to the economic affairs of the enterprise to avoid **misleading** financial statements. Full disclosure requires, in addition to the information reported in the tabular portions of the financial statements, additional information in the notes and schedules that supplement the financial statements.

Disclosure notes are narrative explanations relating to such items as accounting policies used by the company, pension plans, maturity dates on payables and receivables, restrictions relating to long-term debt, and the effects of subsequent events and contingencies (e.g., lawsuits pending). A note may refer to a single amount on one of the three basic statements or to several amounts on two or more of them, or to a situation that is not directly reflected on any of them. The guideline for deciding when a note is required, other than when specifically required, is largely judgmental.

A number of *APB Opinions* and *FASB Statements* require disclosures in the notes to the financial statements. For example, *APB Opinion 22,* "Disclosure of Accounting Policies," requires that information about **important** accounting policies adopted by the enterprise, including their identification and description, be disclosed "in a separate *Summary of Significant Accounting Policies* preceding the notes to the financial statements or as the initial note." The summary should include policies that involve *(a)* a selection from existing alternatives, *(b)* principles and methods peculiar to the industry, and *(c)* unusual or innovative applications of GAAP.

Supporting schedules often are presented separately or are incorporated into the notes. Supporting schedules are typical for large and complex companies, and in situations where a particular item involves a number of complex changes during the period. We mentioned in Chapter 3 that when there have been numerous changes in owners' equity, the statement of retained earnings often is replaced with a more comprehensive schedule. For example, in the 1987 financial statements of the Kimberly-Clark Corporation, given in the Appendix following Chapter 25, Note 8 presents a "Schedule of Shareholders' Equity."

Parenthetical notes are often used in the tabular portions of the financial statements to disclose information such as the method of inventory costing and valuation; for example, Inventory (FIFO, applied on LCM basis). **Contra items,** such as accumulated depreciation and allowance for doubtful accounts, are reported as separate line deductions or parenthetically.

The Kimberly-Clark statements presented in the Appendix following Chapter 25 include typical disclosures.

Auditors' Report

The auditors' report also is called the **accountants' report** or the **independent accountants' report.** It often is the last item in the financial statements.

The independent auditors' primary function is to express the **auditors' professional opinion** on the financial statements. Although the auditors have sole responsibility for their opinion expressed in the auditors' report, **the management of the enterprise** has the **primary responsibility for the financial statements** (including the supporting notes). The financial statements are management's; the auditors affirm or disaffirm the statements in the **opinion.**

The auditors' report includes (1) a **scope** paragraph and (2) an **opinion** paragraph. The standard format of the auditors' report is as follows:

(Scope paragraph)

We have examined the statement of financial position of X Company as of (at) December 31, 19XX, and the related statements of income, retained earnings and cash flows for the year then ended. Our examination was made in accordance with generally accepted auditing standards and, accordingly, included such tests of the accounting records and such other auditing procedures as we considered necessary in the circumstances.

(Opinion paragraph)

In Our opinion, the financial statements referred to above present fairly the financial position of X Company as of (at) December 31, 19XX, and the results of its operations, and the changes in its financial position and the related cash flows for the year then ended, in conformity with generally accepted accounting principles applied on a basis consistent with that of the preceding year.[6]

Eight key elements in the auditors' report have special significance:[7]

1. Date.
2. Salutation.
3. Identification of the statements examined.
4. Statement of scope of the examination.
5. Opinion introduction.
6. Reference to fair presentation in conformity with generally accepted accounting principles.
7. Reference to consistency.
8. Signature of the CPAs.

When the audit is finished, the auditors are required to draft the **opinion** paragraph to communicate their professional opinion about the financial statements by giving one of the following types of opinions.

1. **Unqualified opinion**—An unqualified opinion is given when the CPA has formed the opinion that the statements (1) "present fairly" the results of operations, financial position, and the related cash flows; (2) conform to GAAP, applied on a consistent basis; and (3) meet full disclosure requirements so that the statements are not misleading.
2. **Qualified opinion**—A qualified opinion is given when the requirements for an unqualified opinion are not met and the auditor has limited exceptions to the client's financial statements. A qualified opinion must clearly explain the reasons for the "exception" and its effect on the financial statements.
3. **Adverse opinion**—An adverse opinion is given when the financial statements do not "fairly present." Also, material exceptions require an adverse opinion on the statements.
4. **Disclaimer of opinion**—When the auditors have not been able to obtain sufficient competent evidential matter, auditors must state that they are unable to express an opinion (i.e., they issue a disclaimer). Auditors must explain the reasons for not giving an opinion.

---

[6] AICPA, *Codification of Statements on Auditing Standards* (New York, 1977), AU Sec. 509.07.

[7] AICPA, *The Auditors' Report—Its Meaning and Significance* (New York, 1967), p. 2.

A comprehensive discussion of the responsibilities of independent auditors is beyond the scope of this book. The above summary is provided to describe the range of possible auditors' opinions regarding the extent to which the financial statements of a client company conform to GAAP.

The auditors' opinion is intended to assure that the financial statements conform to GAAP. The importance of this assurance can be seen in the context of the investment of lending decision of an outside party. For example, without assurance that the financial statements conform to GAAP, the investor or creditor could be misled by such actions as the omission of certain liabilities, inclusion of nonexistent assets, or misclassification of current and long-term items. In conclusion, the auditors' report should be viewed as a critical part of an annual financial report because it indicates whether the report is **reliable.**

Summary

The statement of financial position (SFP) uses the accrual basis to report the assets, liabilities, and owners' equity as of a specified date. It reflects the fundamental accounting model—Assets = Liabilities + Owners' equity. Basically, the valuations reported on the SFP are historical cost adjusted for depreciation, depletion, and amortization. Certain assets, such as inventory, are measured at lower-of-cost-or-market (LCM). The SCF links directly with the (a) statement of income (through retained earnings) and (b) statement of financial position (through cash balance).

The statement of cash flows (SCF) is the only required cash-basis statement. It does not report any accrual-basis amounts unless they are strictly cash-basis when incurred. It reports the cash inflows and outflows from the following activities of a business: (a) operating, (b) investing, and (c) financing. The SCF is dated the same as the statement of income—"for the year ended xxxx" because they are for the entire year rather than at only a specific date. The SCF is particularly useful to investors and creditors in projecting the future cash flows of a company. A projection for the company helps investors and creditors project their own cash flows.

QUESTIONS

1. What is the basic purpose of a statement of financial position?
2. What is a statement of financial position? Why is it dated differently from the statement of income and the statement of cash flows?
3. Basically, what valuations are reported on the statement of financial position?
4. Define assets.
5. Define liabilities.
6. Explain the relationship between the statement of financial position and full disclosure.
7. Define current assets and current liabilities and emphasize their interrelationship.
8. Define working capital. What is the working capital ratio?

9. Distinguish between short-term investments and the investments classified as investments and funds. Under what conditions could an investment be reclassified from current assets to investments and funds and vice versa?
10. Is it proper to offset current liabilities against current assets? Explain.
11. Define the "Investments and funds" caption on a statement of financial position.
12. What are operational assets? Distinguish between tangible and intangible operational assets.
13. Why is it sometimes necessary to use the caption "Other assets"? Give two examples of items that might be reported under this classification.
14. Explain the term **deferred charge** and contrast it with a prepaid expense.
15. Distinguish between current and noncurrent liabilities. Under what conditions would a noncurrent liability amount be reclassified as a current liability?
16. What is a deferred credit? Explain why this classification, reported on a statement of financial position between liabilities and owners' equity, is difficult to defend conceptually.
17. What is owners' equity? What are the main components of owners' equity?
18. What is a restriction, or appropriation, of retained earnings? How are restrictions and appropriations reported?
19. What is the purpose of the SCF?
20. Explain the three major captions on the SCF.
21. What two items are included in cash on the SCF?
22. What is meant by "noncash investing and financing activities" on the SCF?
23. Explain the relationship between the balance in the cash account and the SCF.
24. Explain the position of the accounting profession with respect to use of the terms **reserves, surplus,** and **net profit.** Why is careful attention to terminology important in financial statements?
25. What are comparative financial statements? Why are they important?
26. What is meant by subsequent events? Why are they reported? How are they reported?
27. In general, why are notes to the financial statements important? How does the accountant determine when a note should be included?
28. What is the auditors' report? Basically, what does it include? Why is it especially important to the statement user?
29. Are the financial statements the representations of the management of the enterprise, the independent accountant, or both? Explain.

EXERCISES

Part A (Exercises 4–1 to 4–11)

E 4–1 (Terminology)

Give the best answer for each of the following (explain any qualifications):

1. Which of the following is not a current asset?
   a. Office supplies inventory.
   b. Short-term investment.
   c. Petty cash (undeposited cash).
   d. Cash surrender value of life insurance policies.

2. The distinction between current and noncurrent assets and liabilities is based primarily upon—
   a. One year; no exceptions.
   b. One year or operating cycle, whichever is shorter.
   c. One year or operating cycle, whichever is longer.
   d. Operating cycle; no exceptions.
3. Under GAAP, unexpired insurance usually is a—
   a. Noncurrent asset.
   b. Deferred charge.
   c. Prepaid expense.
   d. Short-term investment.
4. Working capital means—
   a. Current assets minus current liabilities.
   b. Total current assets.
   c. Capital contributed by stockholders.
   d. Capital contributed by stockholders plus retained earnings.
5. Which of the following is not a current liability?
   a. Accrued (unpaid) interest on notes payable.
   b. Accrued interest on bonds payable.
   c. Rent revenue collected in advance.
   d. Premium on long-term bonds payable, a credit (unamortized).
6. A deficit is synonymous with—
   a. A net loss for the current reporting period.
   b. A cash overdraft at the bank.
   c. Negative working capital at the end of the reporting period.
   d. A debit balance in retained earnings at the end of the reporting period.
7. The statement of financial position is an expression of the model—
   a. Assets = Liabilities + Owners' equity.
   b. Assets = Liabilities − Owners' equity.
   c. Assets + Liabilities = Owners' equity.
   d. Working capital + Operational assets − Long-term liabilities = Contributed capital.
8. Acceptable usage of the term **reserve** is reflected by—
   a. Deduction from an asset to reflect accumulated depreciation.
   b. Description of a known liability for which the amount is estimated.
   c. Restriction or appropriation of retained earnings.
   d. Deduction on the statement of income for an expected loss.
9. Which terminology essentially is synonymous with "statement of financial position"?
   a. Operating statement.
   b. SCF.
   c. Statement of financial value of the business.
   d. Balance sheet.
10. The "operating cycle concept"—
    a. Causes the distinction between current and noncurrent items to depend upon whether they will affect cash within one year.
    b. Permits some assets to be classified as current even though they are more than one year removed from becoming cash.
    c. Is becoming obsolete.
    d. Affects the statement of income but not the statement of cash flows.

E 4–2 (Valuations on the SFP)

Below left are some items from a typical statement of financial position for a corporation. Below right are some brief statements of the valuations usually reported on the statement of financial position for specific items.

Required:

Use the code letters given below to the right to indicate the usual valuation reported on the statement of financial position. Comment on any doubtful items. Some code letters may be used more than once or not at all. The first item is an example.

Statement of financial position items

1. __C__ Land (held as investment).
2. _____ Merchandise inventory, FIFO.
3. _____ Short-term investments.
4. _____ Accounts receivable (trade).
5. _____ Long-term investment in bonds of another company (purchased at a discount; the discount is a credit balance).
6. _____ Plant site (in use).
7. _____ Plant and equipment (in use).
8. _____ Patent (in use).
9. _____ Accounts payable (trade).
10. _____ Bonds payable (sold at a premium; the premium is a credit balance).
11. _____ Common stock (par $10 per share) sold at par.
12. _____ Contributed capital in excess of par.
13. _____ Retained earnings.
14. _____ Land (future plant site).
15. _____ Idle plant (awaiting disposal).
16. _____ Natural resource.

Valuations usually reported

A. Amount payable when due (usually no interest because short term).
B. Lower of cost or market.
C. Original cost when acquired.
D. Market value at date of the statement of financial position, whether it is above or below cost.
E. Original cost less accumulated amortization over estimated economic life.
F. Par value of the issued shares.
G. Face amount of the obligation plus unamortized premium.
H. Realizable value expected.
I. Principal of the asset less unamortized discount.
J. Cost when acquired less accumulated depreciation.
K. Accumulated income less accumulated losses and dividends.
L. Excess of issue price over par or stated value of common stock.
M. No valuation reported (explain).
N. Expected net disposal proceeds, if below book value, otherwise net book value.
O. Cost less accumulated depletion.
P. None of the above (when this response is used, explain the valuation usually used).

E 4–3 (Classifications on the SFP)

A typical statement of financial position has the following subcaptions:

A. Current assets.
B. Investments and funds.
C. Operational assets (property, plant, and equipment).
D. Intangible assets.
E. Other assets.
F. Deferred charges.
G. Current liabilities.
H. Long-term liabilities.
I. Capital stock (common or preferred).
J. Additional contributed capital.
K. Retained earnings.

Required:
Use the code letters above to indicate the usual classification for each statement of financial position item listed below. If an item is a contra amount (i.e., a deduction) under a caption, place a minus sign before the lettered response.

1. __−C__ Accumulated depreciation (example).
2. ____ Bonds payable (due in 10 years).
3. ____ Accounts payable (trade).
4. ____ Investment in stock of X Company (long term).
5. ____ Plant site (in use).
6. ____ Restriction of appropriation of retained earnings.
7. ____ Office supplies inventory.
8. ____ Loan to company president (collection not expected for two years).
9. ____ Accumulated income less accumulated dividends.
10. ____ Unamortized bond discount (on bonds payable; a debit balance).
11. ____ Bond sinking fund (to retire long-term bonds).
12. ____ Prepaid insurance.
13. ____ Accounts receivable (trade).
14. ____ Short-term investment.
15. ____ Allowance for doubtful accounts.
16. ____ Building (in use).
17. ____ Common stock (par $10).
18. ____ Interest revenue earned but not collected.
19. ____ Patent.
20. ____ Land, held for investment.
21. ____ Land, idle plant site held for sale.

E 4–4 (Classifications on the SFP)
A typical statement of financial position has the following subcaptions:

A. Current assets.
B. Investments and funds.
C. Operational assets (property, plant, and equipment).
D. Intangible assets.
E. Other assets.
F. Deferred charges.
G. Current liabilities.
H. Long-term liabilities.
I. Capital stock (common or preferred).
J. Additional contributed capital.
K. Retained earnings.

Required:
Use the code letters above to indicate the usual classification for each statement of financial position item listed below. If an item is a contra amount (i.e., a deduction) under a caption, place a minus sign before the lettered response.

1. __A__ Accounts receivable, trade (example).
2. ____ Unamortized premium (on bonds payable; a credit balance).

3. _____ Short-term investments.
4. _____ Cash dividends payable (within six months).
5. _____ Rent revenue collected in advance.
6. _____ Accumulated depreciation.
7. _____ Premium on common stock issued.
8. _____ Idle plant held for final disposal.
9. _____ Deferred costs being amortized over five years.
10. _____ Inventory of supplies.
11. _____ Preferred stock.
12. _____ Unamortized discount on long-term investment in bonds of another company (the discount is a credit balance).
13. _____ Installment payment due in six months on long-term note payable.
14. _____ Accrued interest on note payable.
15. _____ Rent revenue receivable.
16. _____ Allowance for doubtful accounts.
17. _____ Investment in bonds of another company (long term).
18. _____ Undeposited cash (for making change).
19. _____ Bonds payable, long term.
20. _____ Idle plant site (held for early sale).
21. _____ A deficit for the current reporting period.

E 4–5 (Prepare a Classified SFP)

The following data, in no particular order, were provided by the accounts of Small Corporation, December 31, 19B, end of the current reporting year. All amounts are correct, all of the accounts have typical balances, and debits equal credits. The amounts are given in thousands.

Accounts payable (trade)	$ 3
Debt retirement fund (long term)	20
Accounts receivable	16
Income taxes payable	1
Short-term investments, marketable securities (cost)	5
Bonds payable (long term)	50
Accumulated depreciation, equipment and furniture	16
Common stock, par $1 (100,000 shares authorized)	70
Cash	15
Retained earnings, January 1, 19B	17
Allowance for doubtful accounts	1
Unearned rent revenue (or rent revenue collected in advance)	2
Cash dividends payable	3
Merchandise inventory (December 31, 19B)	30
Land held for future business site	18
Equipment and furniture	80
Net income for 19B	35
Dividends (cash) declared (a debit)	3
Prepaid expenses (short term)	1
Unamortized bond premium (bonds payable, a credit)	1
Patent	4
Deferred rearrangement costs	2
Investment in capital stock of T Corporation (long term)	10
Premium on common stock	5

Required:

Prepare a complete statement of financial position (in thousands), assuming Small Corporation uses the captions illustrated in Exhibit 4–3. Use the account titles as given. Show computation of the ending balance of retained earnings.

E 4–6 (Prepare a Classified SFP; Ratios)

The ledger of Missouri Manufacturing Company reflects obsolete terminology, but you find its accounts have been, on the whole, accurately kept. After closing the books at December 31, 19B, the following accounts were submitted to you for preparation of a statement of financial position:

Accounts payable	$33,200
Accounts receivable	9,500
Accrued expenses (credit)	800
Bonds payable, 14%	25,000
Capital stock ($100 par)	70,000
Cash	15,000
Earned surplus	xx,xxx
Factory equipment	31,200
Finished goods	12,100
Investments	13,000
Office equipment	9,500
Raw materials	9,600
Reserve for bad debts	500
Reserve for depreciation	9,000
Rent expense paid in advance (a debit)	3,000
Sinking fund	7,000
Land held for future plant site	15,000
Note receivable	6,600
Work in process	18,300

You ascertain that two thirds of the depreciation relates to factory equipment and one third to office equipment. Of the balance in the Investments account, $4,000 will be converted to cash during the coming year; the remainder represents a long-term investment. Rent paid in advance is for the next year. The note receivable is a loan to the company president on October 1, 19B, and is due in 19D when the principal amount ($6,600) plus 8% interest per annum will be paid to the company. The sinking fund is being accumulated to retire the bonds at maturity.

Required:

1. Prepare a statement of financial position using preferred format, classifications, and terminology.
2. Compute *(a)* the amount of working capital and *(b)* the current (working capital) ratio.

E 4–7 (Prepare a Classified SFP; Terminology)

The following trial balance was prepared by Vance Corporation as of December 31, 19F. The adjusting entries for 19F have been made, except for any specifically noted below.

Cash	$20,000	
Accounts receivable	15,000	
Inventories	12,000	
Equipment	22,400	
Land	6,400	
Building	7,600	
Deferred charges	1,100	
Accounts payable		$ 5,500
Note payable, 9%		8,000
Capital stock (par $10)		38,500
Earned surplus		32,500
	$84,500	$84,500

You find that certain errors and omissions are reflected in the above trial balance, including the following:

1. The $15,000 balance in accounts receivable represents the entire amount owed to the company; of this amount, $12,400 is from trade customers, and 5% of that amount

is estimated to be uncollectible. The remaining amount owed to the company represents a long-term advance to its president.

2. Inventories include $1,000 of goods incorrectly valued at double their cost (i.e., reported at $2,000). No correction has been recorded. Office supplies on hand of $500 also are included in the balance of inventories.
3. When the equipment and building were purchased new on January 1, 19A (i.e., 6 years earlier), they had, respectively, estimated lives of 10 and 25 years. They have been depreciated using the straight-line method on the assumption of zero residual values, and depreciation has been credited directly to the asset accounts. Depreciation has been recorded for 19F.
4. The balance in the Land account includes a $1,000 payment made as a deposit of earnest money on the purchase of an adjoining tract. The option to buy it has not yet been exercised and probably will not be exercised during the coming year.
5. The interest-bearing note dated April 1, 19F, matures March 31, 19G. Interest on it has been ignored.
6. Common stock shares outstanding, 2,500.

Required:
Prepare a correct statement of financial position with appropriate captions and subcaptions; use preferred terminology and the vertical format. Show the computation of the ending balance in retained earnings.

E 4–8 (Prepare Statements of Income and Financial Position)
The following adjusted trial balance was prepared by Western Corporation at December 31, 19X:

Debits

Cost of goods sold	$230,000
Distribution and administrative expenses (including interest)	130,000
Income tax expense	41,500
Cash	44,000
Short-term investments	12,000
Accounts receivable	70,000
Merchandise inventory*	72,000
Office supplies inventory	2,000
Investment in bonds of X Corp. (long term), cost (market value, $35,000)	33,000
Land (plant site in use)	10,000
Plant and equipment	120,000
Franchise (less amortization)	8,000
Rearrangement costs†	15,000
Idle equipment held for disposal	7,500
Dividends declared and paid during 19X	40,000
	$835,000

Credits

Sales revenue	$480,000
Accumulated depreciation, plant and equipment	40,000
Accounts payable	50,000
Income taxes payable	11,000
Bonds payable	50,000
Allowance for doubtful accounts	3,000
Premium on bonds payable (unamortized)	1,000
Common stock, par $10 (authorized 50,000 shares)	150,000
Excess of issue price over par of common stock	18,000
Retained earnings, 1/1/19X	32,000
	$835,000

* Perpetual inventory system.
† Amortization period is three years; this is the unamortized balance.

87500

Required:

1. Prepare a single-step statement of income.
2. Prepare a statement of financial position with appropriate captions and terminology.

E 4–9 (Stockholders' Equity; Classifications)

Based upon the following information, prepare the stockholders' equity section of the statement of financial position for Raleigh Corporation at December 31, 19C.

Preferred stock, par $15, authorized 20,000 shares	$270,000
Cash received above par of preferred stock	15,000
Common stock, nopar, 60,000 shares issued (100,000 shares authorized)	200,000
Retained earnings:	
Unappropriated	80,000
Restricted by special contract	60,000

E 4–10 (Analyzing and Reporting; SFP)

Dawson Corporation is preparing the statement of financial position at December 31, 19K. The following items are at issue:

a. Note payable, long term, $80,000. This note will be paid in installments. The first installment of $10,000 will be paid August 1, 19L.

b. Bonds payable, 12%, $200,000; at December 31, 19K, unamortized premium amounted to $6,000.

c. Bond sinking fund, $40,000; this fund is being accumulated to retire the bonds at maturity. There is a restriction on retained earnings required by the bond indenture equal to the balance in the bond sinking fund.

d. Rent revenue collected in advance for the first quarter of 19L, $6,000.

e. After the statement of financial position date, but prior to issuance of the 19K balance sheet, one third of the merchandise inventory was destroyed by flood (date, January 13, 19L); estimated loss, $150,000.

f. Ending balance of unappropriated retained earnings (December 31, 19K), $35,000.

Required:

Show, by illustration, with appropriate captions, how each of these items should be reported on the December 31, 19K, statement of financial position.

E 4–11 (Terminology; "Reserves")

The records of Scott Corporation provided the following selected data on December 31, 19B:

Preferred stock, par $10, 100,000 shares authorized	$350,000
Common stock, no par, 200,000 shares authorized of which 100,000 are outstanding	300,000
Premium on preferred stock	90,000
Earned surplus (free) at end of 19B (excluding all appropriations)	40,000
Reserves at end of 19B for:	
Bad debts	11,000
Depreciation	90,000
Patent amortization	6,000
Warranty obligations	14,000
Income tax obligations	31,000
Future plant expansion (management decision plans are to remove this appropriation within five years after completion)	70,000
Retirement of bonds payable (required by the bond indenture; automatically ends when the bonds are paid)	60,000
Bond sinking fund	60,000

Required:

1. Prepare the stockholders' equity section of the statement of financial position using preferred terminology and format.
2. If any of the above items do not belong in the stockholders' equity section, explain how they should be reported.

Part B (Exercises 4–12 to 4–15)

E 4–12 (SCF; Classifications)

The main parts of a statement of cash flows are shown below with letter identifications. Next, several transactions are given preceded by a blank space. You are to match the transactions with the statement parts by entering a letter in each blank space.

Statement of Cash Flows

A. Net cash inflows (outflows) from operating activities.
B. Net cash inflows (outflows) from investing activities.
C. Net cash inflows (outflows) from financing activities.

Transactions

____ 1. Acquisition of operational assets; paid cash.
____ 2. Cash dividends paid.
____ 3. Proceeds from note payable.
____ 4. Sale of operational assets.
____ 5. Loan on note receivable.
____ 6. Purchase of a long-term security as an investment.
____ 7. Collections on notes receivable (principal only).
____ 8. Change in inventory.
____ 9. Depreciation expense.
____ 10. Payment of debt, 60% cash and 40% stock issued.
____ 11. Issuance of the company's capital stock, for cash.
____ 12. Sales revenue, cash.
____ 13. Purchase of treasury stock, cash.
____ 14. Payment on notes payable.
____ 15. Paid cash dividend.

E 4–13 (Prepare a SCF)

Selected 19X data from the accounts of Hypothetical Company are given below. The amounts are in thousands.

Statement of financial position:	
Borrowed cash, signed a long-term note payable	$ 20
Collection on note receivable	3
Decrease in accounts payable	2
Purchased a new machine	9
Issued the company's capital stock for cash	2
Paid a cash dividend	1
Depreciation expense	6
Sold an old machine (book value, $5)	4
Loaned cash on note receivable	8
Increase in accounts receivable	2
Payment on note payable	4
Decrease in inventory	3
Issued capital stock for cash and to settle a $2 debt	5
Sold long-term securities (carrying value, $12)	13

Statement of income data:	
Sales revenue	$ 60
Cost of goods sold	(30)
Depreciation expense	(6)
Remaining expenses (all cash)	(12)
Gain on sale of long-term securities	1
Loss on sale of operational assets	(1)
Net income	$ 12

Required:
Prepare a SCF for 19X similar to Exhibit 4–5 in this chapter.

E 4–14 (Prepare a SCF)
The records of Ranger Company provided the selected data given below for the reporting period ended December 31, 19C.

Statement of financial position:	
Paid cash dividend	$ 18,000
Established an external construction fund at 8% interest (building)	50,000
Increased inventory of merchandise	14,000
Borrowed on a long-term note	25,000
Acquired five acres of land for a future site for the company; paid in full by issuing 3,000 shares of Ranger capital stock, par $10, when the quoted market price per share was $15	—
Increase in prepaid expenses	3,000
Decrease in accounts receivable	7,000
Payment of bonds payable in full	97,000
Increase in accounts payable	5,000
Cash from disposal of old operational assets (sold at book value)	12,000
Decrease in rent receivable	2,000

Statement of income data:	
Sales revenue	$ 400,000
Rent revenue	10,000
Cost of goods sold	(190,000)
Depreciation expense	(20,000)
Remaining expenses	(97,000)
Net income	$ 103,000

Required:
Prepare a SCF similar to Exhibit 4–5 in this chapter (in thousands).

E 4–15 (Recast a Deficient SCF)
The following statement was incorrectly prepared by Vista Corporation.

VISTA CORPORATION
Cash Statement
December 31, 19B

Cash received:	
From operations:	
Net income	$ 102,000
Depreciation expense	40,000
Amortization of patent	9,000
Decrease in accounts receivable balance	5,000
Increase in inventory balance	(10,000)
Increase in wages payable balance	4,000
Machinery, old (sold at book value on credit)	7,000
Long-term note given for land purchased	25,000
Total funds received	$ 182,000

Cash spent:	
Retirement of mortgage	$ 60,000
Cash dividends	20,000
Machinery (new)	50,000
Acquired land; issued capital stock in full payment (6,000 shares, par $5)*	36,000
Invested in capital stock of B Corporation	10,000
Increase in cash balance	6,000
Total funds spent	$ 182,000
Statement of income data:	
Sales revenue	$ 320,000
Cost of goods sold	(120,000)
Depreciation expense	(40,000)
Amortization of patent	(9,000)
Salaries and wages	(11,000)
Remaining expenses (all cash)	(38,000)
Net income	$ 102,000

* Market price per share, $6.

Required:
Recast the above statement (in 000's) using the format and terminology shown in Exhibit 4–5.

PROBLEMS

Part A (Problems 4–1 to 4–6)

P 4–1 **(Valuations on a SFP)**
Below left are some typical items from a statement of financial position for a corporation. Below right are some brief statements of valuations usually reported on a statement of financial position for different items.

Statement of financial position items

1. __N__ Cash (example).
2. ______ Short-term investments.
3. ______ Accounts receivable (trade).
4. ______ Notes receivable (short term).
5. ______ Merchandise inventory.
6. ______ Prepaid expenses (such as prepaid insurance).
7. ______ Long-term investment in bonds of another company (purchased at a premium).
8. ______ Long-term investment in stock of another company (less than 20% of the outstanding shares purchased).
9. ______ Plant site (in use).
10. ______ Plant equipment (in use).
11. ______ Patent (used in operations).
12. ______ Deferred charge.
13. ______ Accounts payable (trade).
14. ______ Income taxes payable.
15. ______ Notes payable (short term).
16. ______ Bonds payable (sold at a discount).
17. ______ Common stock (no par).
18. ______ Preferred stock (par $10 per share).
19. ______ Contributed capital in excess of par.
20. ______ Retained earnings.
21. ______ Land held for speculation.
22. ______ Land held for a future plant site.
23. ______ Damaged merchandise (goods held for sale).

Valuations usually reported

A. Lower-of-cost-or market.
B. Principal amount collectible at maturity.
C. Total amount paid in by stockholders when issued.
D. Cost to acquire the asset.
E. Excess of issue price over par value of stock.
F. Accumulated income less accumulated losses and dividends.
G. Cost to acquire less amortization to date.
H. Estimated net realizable value (amount billed less estimated loss due to uncollectibility).
I. Par value of shares issued.
J. Cost less expired or used portion.
K. Cost at date of investment.
L. Replacement cost.
M. Principal amount plus unamortized premium.
N. Current market value.
O. Amount payable when due (short term).
P. Maturity amount of the obligation less unamortized discount.
Q. Cost to acquire less accumulated depreciation.
R. Market value at the date of the balance sheet, whether it is above or below cost.
S. No valuation reported (explain).
T. None of the above (when this response is used, explain the valuation usually used).

Required:
Use the code letters to the right to indicate, for each statement of financial position item listed, the usual valuation reported on the statement of financial position. Provide explanatory comments for each doubtful item. Some code letters may be used more than once or not at all.

P 4–2 (Classification on the SFP)
Typical statement of financial position classifications along with a code letter for each classification are as follows:

A. Current assets.
B. Investments and funds.
C. Operational assets, tangible (property, plant, and equipment).
D. Intangible assets.
E. Other assets.
F. Deferred charges.
G. Current liabilities.
H. Long-term liabilities.
I. Capital stock.
J. Additional contributed capital.
K. Retained earnings.

Typical statement of financial position items are as follows:

1. __A__ Cash (example).
2. ______ Cash set aside to meet long-term purchase commitment.
3. ______ Land (used as plant site).
4. ______ Accrued salaries.
5. ______ Investment in the capital stock of another company (long term; not a controlling interest).
6. ______ Inventory of damaged goods.
7. ______ Idle plant being held for disposal.
8. ______ Investment in bonds of another company.
9. ______ Cash surrender value of life insurance policy.
10. ______ Goodwill.
11. ______ Natural resource (timber tract).
12. ______ Allowance for doubtful accounts.
13. ______ Stock subscriptions receivable (no plans to collect in near future).
14. ______ Organization costs.
15. ______ Discount on bonds payable.
16. ______ Service revenue collected in advance.
17. ______ Accrued interest payable.
18. ______ Accumulated amortization on patent.
19. ______ Prepaid rent expense.
20. ______ Short-term investment (common stock).
21. ______ Rent revenue collected but not earned.
22. ______ Net of accumulated revenues, gains, expenses, losses and dividends.
23. ______ Trade accounts payable.
24. ______ Current maturity of long-term debt.
25. ______ Land (held for speculation).
26. ______ Notes payable (short term).
27. ______ Special cash fund accumulated to build plant five years hence.
28. ______ Bonds issued—to be paid within six months out of bond sinking fund.
29. ______ Long-term investment in rental building.
30. ______ Copyright.
31. ______ Accumulated depreciation.
32. ______ Deferred plant rearrangement costs.
33. ______ Franchise.
34. ______ Revenue earned but not collected.
35. ______ Premium on bonds payable (unamortized).
36. ______ Common stock (at par value).
37. ______ Petty cash fund.
38. ______ Deficit.
39. ______ Contributed capital in excess of par.
40. ______ Earnings retained in the business.

Required:
Enter the appropriate code letter for each item to indicate its usual classification on the statement of financial position. When it is a contra item (i.e., a deduction), place a minus sign before the lettered response.

(AICPA adapted)

P 4–3 (Redraft a Deficient SCF; "Reserves")
The statement of financial position given below, which was submitted to you for review, has been prepared for inclusion in the published annual report of the Careless Company for the year ended December 31, 19X:

CARESLESS COMPANY

Balance Sheet

December 31, 19X

(in thousands)

Assets			
Current:			
Cash			$ 1,900
Accounts receivable		$3,900	
Less: Reserve for bad debts		50	3,850
Inventories—at the lower of cost (determined by the first-in, first-out method) or market			3,500
Total current			9,250
Investment in raw land			250
Fixed:			
Land—at cost		200	
Buildings, machinery and fixtures—at cost	$4,200		
Less: Reserves for depreciation	1,490	2,710	2,910
Deferred charges and other assets:			
Cash surrender value of life insurance		15	
Prepaid costs of major plant rearrangements		12	
Plant assets held for early resale		20	47
Total assets			$12,457
Liabilities			
Current:			
Notes payable to bank			$ 750
Current maturities of first-mortgage note			600
Accounts payable—trade			1,900
Reserve for income taxes for the year ended 12/31/19X			700
Accrued expenses			550
			4,500
Funded debt:			
9% first-mortgage bonds payable in annual installments of $600		$4,200	
Less: Current maturity		600	3,600
Reserves:			
Reserve for various unexpected damages in the future on uninsured assets		50	
Reserve for possible future inventory losses		300	
Reserve for general contingencies		500	
Reserve for additional federal income taxes that may occur		100	950
Capital:			
Common stock—authorized, issued and outstanding 100,000 shares of $10 par value		1,000	
Capital surplus paid in		300	
Earned surplus		2,107	3,407
Total liabilities			$12,457

Additional Information:

1. The reserve for damages was set up by a debit to 19X expense and a credit to the reserve for damages possibly payable by the company as a defendant in a lawsuit in progress at the SFP date. The lawsuit was subsequently settled for $50,000 prior to issuance of the statement.
2. The reserve for possible future inventory losses was set up in prior years, by action of the board of directors, as debits to earned surplus and credits to the reserve. No change occurred in the account during the current fiscal year.

3. The reserve for contingencies was set up by debits to earned surplus and credits to the reserve over a period of several years by the board of directors to provide for a possible future recession in general business conditions.
4. The reserve for federal income taxes was set up in a prior year as a debit to earned surplus and a credit to the reserve. It relates to additional taxes which the Internal Revenue Service contended that the company owed. The company now has good evidence that settlement will be effected for the $100,000.
5. The capital surplus consists of the difference between the par value of $10 per share of capital stock and the price at which the stock was actually issued.

Required:

1. Redraft the above SFP using appropriate format, major captions, subcaptions, titles, and terminology. Use thousands of dollars. Report both appropriated and unappropriated retained earnings amounts.
2. What is the *(a)* amount of working capital and *(b)* working capital ratio?
3. Explain when and how the four "reserves" will be zero.

(AICPA adapted)

P 4–4 (Prepare SFP; Analytical Questions)

The following data were provided by the accounts of Fuere Corporation, December 31, 19C, end of the current reporting year:

Cash	$ 21,000
Accounts receivable, trade	36,000
Short-term investment in marketable securities (cost $41,000)	40,000
Inventory of merchandise (cost $92,000), FIFO	90,000
Prepaid expense (short term)	1,000
Bond sinking fund (to pay bonds at maturity)	35,000
Advances to suppliers (short term)	4,000
Dividends (cash) declared during 19C	15,000
Rent revenue receivable	2,000
Investment in stock of V Corporation (long term, at cost, which approximates market)	22,000
Unamortized discount on bonds payable	3,000
Loans to employees (company president; payment date uncertain)	25,000
Land (building site in use)	30,000
Building	400,000
Equipment	60,000
Franchise (used in operations)	12,000
Deferred equipment rearrangement cost (long term)	4,000
Total debits	$800,000
Mortgage payable, long term	$ 50,000
Accounts payable, trade	6,000
Dividends (cash) payable (payable March 1, 19D)	15,000
Deferred rent revenue	3,000
Interest payable	4,000
Accumulated depreciation, building	160,000
Accumulated depreciation, equipment	20,000
Allowance for doubtful accounts	1,000
Bonds payable (maturity 19W)	100,000
Common stock, nopar (30,000 shares outstanding)	200,000
Preferred stock, par $10	80,000
Premium on preferred stock	16,000
Retained earnings, January 1, 19C	17,000
Net income for 19C	88,000
Appropriation of retained earnings for plant expansion (set up prior to 19C)	40,000
Total credits	$800,000

Required:

1. Prepare a complete statement of financial position, assuming the company uses the captions illustrated in Exhibit 4–3. Assume all amounts are correct and round to the nearest thousand dollars. Use the account titles as given. Show computation of the ending balance in retained earnings and include any restrictions on retained earnings on the statement.
2. Interpretation—Refer to your response to Requirement 1 and respond to the following:
   a. Give the amount of working capital and the working capital ratio.
   b. Give the amount of total retained earnings.
   c. By what percent was the building depreciated?
   d. What were the per share issue prices of the preferred and common stock?
   e. Give the entry that was made to record the 19C dividend declaration.
   f. Give the entry that was made for the appropriation of retained earnings.
   g. Give the entry that probably was made to record the issuance of the (1) preferred stock and (2) common stock. Assume cash transactions.
   h. Give the entry that was made for the advances to suppliers. Assume cash transactions.
   i. Give the adjusting entry that probably was made for rent revenue receivable.
   j. Give the adjusting entry that probably was made for deferred rent revenue.
   k. Give the probable closing entry for net income.

P 4–5 (Statements of Income and Financial Position; Obsolete Terminology)
The adjusted trial balance for Bird Corporation, and other related data, at December 31, 19C, are given below. Although the company uses obsolete terminology, the amounts are correct (but certain amounts may have to be reported separately). Assume that a perpetual inventory system is used.

Adjusted Trial Balance, December 31, 19C

Debits

Cash	$ 43,600
Land (used for building site)	29,000
Cost of goods sold	110,500
Short-term securities (stock of S Co.)	42,000
Goodwill (unamortized cost)	12,000
Merchandise inventory	30,000
Office supplies inventory	1,000
Patent	7,000
Operating expenses	55,000
Income tax expense	17,500
Bond discount (unamortized)	7,500
Prepaid insurance	900
Building (at cost)	150,000
Land (held for speculation)	31,000
Accrued interest receivable	300
Accounts receivable (trade)	17,700
Note receivable, 16% (long-term investment)	20,000
Cash surrender value of life insurance policy	9,000
Deferred store rearrangement costs (assume a deferred charge)	6,000
Dividends, paid cash during 19C	15,000
Prior period adjustment (correction of error from prior year—no income tax effect)	16,000
	$621,000

Credits

Reserve for bad debts	$ 1,100
Accounts payable (trade)	15,000
Revenues	230,000
Reserve for income taxes	7,500
Note payable (short term)	12,000
Common stock, par $10, authorized 50,000 shares	100,000
Reserve for depreciation, building	90,000
Retained earnings, 1/1/19C	38,000
Accrued wages	2,100
Reserve for estimated damages (set up in 19B)	10,000
Premium on common stock	15,000
Reserve for patent amortization	4,000
Cash advance from customer	3,000
Accrued property taxes	1,300
Note payable (long term)	16,000
Rent revenue collected in advance	1,000
Bonds payable, 11% ($25,000 due 6/1/19D)	75,000
	$621,000

Additional Information (no accounting errors are involved):

a. Market value of the short-term marketable securities, $46,000.

b. Merchandise inventory is based on FIFO, lower-of-cost-or-market (LCM).

c. Goodwill is being amortized (i.e., written off) over a 20-year period. The amortization for 19C has already been recorded (as a direct credit to the Goodwill account and a debit to expense). Amortization of other intangibles is recorded in this manner except for the patent (a contra account is used for it).

d. Reserve for income taxes represents the estimated income taxes payable at the end of 19C. Reserve for estimated damages was recorded as a credit to this reserve account and a debit to Retained Earnings during 19B. The $10,000 was the estimated amount of damages that would have to be paid as a result of a damage suit against the company. At December 31, 19C, the appeal was still pending. The $10,000 represents an appropriation, or restriction, placed on retained earnings by management.

e. Operating expenses as given include interest expense, and revenues include interest and investment revenues.

f. The cash advance from customer was for a special order that will not be completed and shipped until March 19D; the sales price has not been definitely established because it is to be based upon cost (no revenue should be recognized for 19C).

Required:

1. Prepare a single-step statement of income and a separate statement of retained earnings.
2. Prepare a statement of financial position including appropriate disclosures. Use preferred terminology, captions, subcaptions, and format.

P 4–6 (Statements of Income and Financial Position; Disclosure)

The adjusted trial balance for Truefit Manufacturing Corporation at December 31, 19X, is given below in no particular order. Debits and credits are not indicated; however, debits equal credits. All amounts are correct. Assume the usual type of balance in each account and a perpetual inventory system, FIFO, LCM.

Work in process inventory	$ 24,000
Accrued interest on notes payable	1,000
Accrued interest receivable	1,200
Accrued income on short-term investments	1,000
Common stock, nopar, authorized 100,000 shares, issued 40,000	150,000

Cash in bank	40,000
Trademarks (unamortized cost)	1,400
Land held for speculation	17,000
Supplies inventory	600
Goodwill (unamortized cost)	20,000
Raw materials inventory	13,000
Bond sinking fund	10,000
Accrued property taxes	1,200
Accounts receivable (trade)	19,000
Accrued wages	2,300
Mortgage payable (due in three years)	10,000
Building	130,000
Prepaid rent expense	1,700
Organization expenses (unamortized cost—assume a deferred charge)	7,800
Deposits (cash collected from customers on sales orders to be delivered next quarter; no revenue yet recognized)	1,000
Long-term investment in bonds of K Corp. (at cost)	60,000
Patents (unamortized cost)	12,000
Reserve for bond sinking fund*	10,000
Reserve for depreciation, office equipment	1,600
Reserve for depreciation, building	5,000
Premium on preferred stock	8,000
Cash on hand for change	400
Preferred stock, par $100, authorized 5,000 shares, 10% noncumulative	60,000
Precollected rent income	900
Finished goods inventory	48,000
Note receivable (short term)	4,000
Bonds payable, 12% (due in 6 years)	50,000
Accounts payable (trade)	17,000
Reserve for bad debts	1,400
Notes payable (short term)	7,000
Office equipment	25,000
Land (used as building site)	8,000
Short-term investments (at cost)	15,500
Retained earnings, unappropriated (1/1/19X)	13,200
Cash dividends on preferred and common stock declared and paid during 19X	20,000
Revenues during 19X	400,000
Cost of goods sold for 19X	210,000
Expenses for 19X (including income taxes)	90,000
Income taxes payable	40,000

* This is a restriction on retained earnings required by the bond indenture equal to the bond sinking fund that is being accumulated to retire the bonds.

Required:

1. Prepare a single-step statement of income; use preferred terminology. To compute EPS, deduct $6,000 of net income as an allocation to nonconvertible preferred stock.
2. Prepare a complete statement of financial position; use preferred terminology, format, captions and subcaptions.
3. Assume that between December 31, 19X, and issuance of the financial statements, a flood damaged the finished goods inventory in an amount estimated to be $20,000. This event has not been and should not have been recorded in 19X. However, disclosure in the 19X statements is required. Prepare the necessary disclosure.

Part B Problems 4–7 to 4–8

P 4–7 **(Prepare a SCF; Net Loss)**

At the end of the current reporting year, December 31, 19K, Fisher Company's executives were very concerned about the ending cash balances of $2,500 (the beginning cash balance of $32,500 also had been considered serious at that time).

During 19K, management undertook numerous actions to attain a better cash position. In view of the decreasing cash balance, they asked the chief accountant to prepare a cash flow report (for the first time). The following information was developed from the accounting records:

a. Debt:
  (1) Borrowing on long-term (LT) note, $10,000.
  (2) Payments on maturing long-term debt, $100,000.
  (3) Settled short-term debt of $50,000 by issuing Fisher capital stock at par (which approximated market value).
  (4) Increase in accounts payable, $20,000.

b. Cash payments:
  (1) Regular cash dividends, $28,000.
  (2) Purchase of new operational assets, $22,000.

c. Cash received:
  (1) Sold and issued Fisher capital stock, $11,000.
  (2) Sold old operational assets at their book value, $1,000.
  (3) Sold investment (long term) in stock of T Corporation and made the following entry:

Cash	90,000	
Loss on sale of investment	30,000	
Investment in T Corporation stock		120,000

d. Relevant statement of financial position accounts:
  (1) Decrease in income tax payable, $10,000.
  (2) Decrease in inventory, $38,000.
  (3) Increase in accounts receivable, $5,000.

e. Statement of income data:

Sales	$ 150,000
Cost of goods sold	(140,000)
Depreciation expense	(58,000)
Amortization of patent	(2,000)
Income tax expense	(4,000)
Remaining expenses	(41,000)
Loss on sale of long-term investment	(30,000)
Net income (loss)	$(125,000)

Required:
Based on the above data, prepare a statement of cash flows (in thousands).

P 4–8 (Prepare a SCF; Analytical Questions)
Cristina De La Fuente, the president of De La Fuente Corporation, has asked the company controller for a statement of cash flows for the reporting year just ended, December 31, 19B. The company has not previously prepared such a statement. The following data has been obtained from the accounting records:

Statement of financial position data:

a. Cash account balances: January 1, 19B, $43,000; December 31, 19E, $18,000.

b. The balance in accounts receivable decreased by $5,000 during the year. Wages payable decreased by $5,000.

c. Inventory increased $9,000, and accounts payable increased $3,000 during the year.

d. Income tax payable increased $4,000 during the year.

e. During December 19B, the company settled a $10,000 note payable by issuing shares of its own capital stock with equivalent value.

f. Cash expenditures during 19B were: (1) payment of long-term debts, $64,000; (2) purchase of new operational assets, $79,000; (3) payment of a cash dividend, $16,000; and (4) purchase of land as an investment, $25,000.

g. Sale and issuance of shares of De La Fuente capital stock for $20,000 cash.

h. Issuance of a long-term mortgage note, $30,000.

i. Sale of some old operational assets; the following entry was made:

Cash	5,000	
Accumulated depreciation	12,000	
Operational asset		15,000
Gain on sale of operational assets		2,000

Statement of income data:	
Sales revenue	$ 295,000
Cost of goods sold	(140,000)
Depreciation expense	(12,000)
Patent amortization	(1,000)
Income tax expense	(7,000)
Remaining expenses	(42,000)
Gain on sale of operational assets	2,000
Net income	$ 95,000

Required:
Prepare a SCF (in thousands of dollars). Follow the format given in this chapter, Exhibit 4–5.

CASES

C 4–1 **(Criticize a Deficient SFP)**
The president of Apple Manufacturing Company is a personal friend of yours, and she tells you the company has never had an audit and is contemplating having one principally because it is suspected that the financial statements are not well prepared. As an example, the president hands you the following statement for review:

APPLE MANUFACTURING COMPANY
Balance Sheet
For the Year Ended December 31, 19X

Resources

Liquid assets:	
Cash in banks	$12,500
Receivables from various sources net of reserve for bad debts ($200)	5,000
Inventories	6,000
Cash for daily use	500
Total	24,000
Permanent assets:	
Treasury stock, par	4,000
Fixed assets (net of depreciation)	26,000
Grand total	$54,000

Obligations and Net Worth

Short-term:	
Trade payables	$ 3,000
Salaries accrued	1,000
Total	4,000
Fixed:	
Mortgage	8,000
Net worth:	
Capital stock, par $10	30,000
Earned surplus	12,000
Total	42,000
Grand total	$54,000

Required:

1. List and explain your criticisms of the above statement.
2. Using the above data, prepare a statement of financial position that meets your specifications in terms of format, terminology, and classification of data. If necessary make realistic assumptions. *Hint:* Total assets are $50,000.

C 4–2 (Criticize a Deficient SFP)

The following statement has come to your attention:

EASY CORPORATION
Balance Sheet Statement
For Year Ended December 31, 19C

Assets			
Liquid assets:			
Cash		$ 31,000	
Receivables	$ 29,000		
Less: Reserve for bad debts	700	28,300	
Inventories		42,000	
			$101,300
Investments and funds:			
Petty cash fund		200	
Sinking fund		70,000	
			70,200
Permanent assets:			
Land and building	140,000		
Less: Reserve for depreciation	9,000	131,000	
Equipment	84,000		
Less: Reserve for depreciation	29,000	55,000	
			186,000
Deferred charges:			
Prepaid expenses		2,700	
Accrued sinking fund income (interest)		600	
			3,300
Total			$360,800
Obligations			
Short term:			
Accrued interest on mortgage payable		$ 700	
Accounts payable		36,500	
Reserve for income taxes	$ 13,000		
Less: U.S. government bonds	8,000	5,000	
			$ 42,200
Long term:			
Mortgage payable*			74,000
Net Worth			
Capital stock		150,000	
Earned surplus		52,400	
Reserve for contingencies		66,400	
		268,800	
Less: Treasury stock		24,200	
			244,600
Total			$360,800

* The mortgage payable matures 4/18/19D, and is funded by the sinking fund.

Required:

Constructively criticize the above statement. Set up your responses in the following format:

Specific criticism (list)	Explanation of criticism	Recommended treatment
1.		
Etc.		

C 4–3 **(Criticize a Deficient SFP; Redraft)**

The most recent balance sheet of Brown Corporation appears below:

BROWN CORPORATION
Balance Sheet
For the Year Ended December 31, 19B

Assets

Current:			
Cash		$ 12,000	
Marketable securities		10,000	
Accounts receivable		30,000	
Merchandise		25,000	
Supplies		5,000	
Stock of Co. W (not a controlling interest)		17,000	$ 99,000
Investments:			
Cash surrender value of life insurance		45,000	
Treasury stock (2,500 shares)		37,500	82,500
Tangible:			
Building and land ($10,000)	$56,000		
Less: Reserve for depreciation	10,000	46,000	
Equipment	15,000		
Less: Reserve for depreciation	10,000	5,000	51,000
Deferred:			
Prepaid expenses		2,000	
Discount on bonds payable		3,000	5,000
Total			$237,500

Debt and Capital

Current:		
Accounts payable	$ 16,000	
Reserve for income tax	17,000	
Customers' accounts with credit balance	100	$ 33,100
Fixed (interest paid at year-end):		
Bonds payable (due at end of 19L), 7%	45,000	
Mortgage, 11%	12,000	57,000
Reserve for bad debts		900
Capital:		
Capital stock, authorized 10,000 shares, par $15	112,500	
Earned surplus	25,000	
Capital surplus	9,000	146,500
Total		$237,500

Required:

1. List and explain your criticisms of the above statement.
2. Prepare a complete statement of financial position; use appropriate format, captions, and terminology. The capital stock was sold par. Deduct treasury stock from stockholders' equity.

C 4–4 **(Analysis of Actual Financial Statements)**

Kimberly-Clark

The Appendix following Chapter 25 gives the Kimberly-Clark financial statements. Examine them carefully and respond to the following questions (respond for 1987 unless directed otherwise):

a. Are they comparative statements? Briefly explain.
b. Are they consolidated statements?
c. What is the date of the end of the fiscal or reporting year?
d. How many years' data are reported on the three required financial statements?
e. What title is used on the "funds flow" statement?
f. Is the statement that you gave in (e) based on working capital or on cash? What are the major captions?
g. What title classifications were used on the statement of financial position?
h. What was the amount of (1) cash and (2) working capital reported at the end of the current year?
i. What was the income tax obligation at the end of the current year?
j. How many different long-term liabilities are outstanding?
k. What percent of total assets was provided by (1) creditors and (2) owners?
l. How much did cash and cash equivalents increase (decrease) each year?
m. What item represented the highest use of cash?
n. What was the largest source of cash?
o. What kind of opinion did the auditor give? Explain.
p. Who is responsible for the preparation and integrity of the company's financial statements? Support your answer.
q. What are the responsibilities of the Audit Committee?

5 INTEREST—CONCEPTS OF FUTURE AND PRESENT VALUE

OVERVIEW AND PURPOSE

Interest on debt or assets is important in many accounting issues. **Interest is the cost of using money over time;** therefore, it often is referred to as the time value of money.

A dollar at a given date will represent different amounts of resources at earlier and later dates when interest is considered. For example, given a 10% interest rate, you would prefer receiving $10,000 cash today rather than receiving that same amount 10 years from today (assuming no inflation or deflation). The strength of this preference would be based on the additional $15,937 compound interest that you could earn on the $10,000 if it was received at the earlier date.

Measurement of the time value of money involves the basic concepts of the **future value** and **present value** of a dollar. Higher interest rates and longer time periods increase the interest amount. As a consequence, the accounting and reporting implications become more significant. Knowledge of these concepts is essential for accountants because they are applied to such diverse accounting topics as receivables, investments, funds, depreciation, goodwill, installment contracts, liabilities, bonds, pensions, leases, business combinations, and investment decisions (these applications of interest concepts are discussed in later chapters). In addition, knowledge about the concepts of future and present value is useful in making your personal investing and financing decisions, such as purchasing a home or investing in securities.

The purpose of this chapter is to present *(a)* a concise discussion of interest concepts, and *(b)* some typical illustrations of their application in accounting. To accomplish this purpose, the chapter is organized as follows:

Part A: Basic Interest Concepts and Future and Present Values of 1

1. Interest concepts.
2. Overview of future and present value concepts.
3. Future value of 1.
4. Present value of 1.
5. Selecting an interest rate.

Part B: Annuities—Future and Present Values

1. Concept of an annuity.
2. Future value of an annuity of 1.
3. Present value of an annuity of 1.
4. Using multiple present and future amounts.

PART A: BASIC INTEREST CONCEPTS AND FUTURE AND PRESENT VALUES OF 1

Concept of Interest

Conceptually, interest is the **time value of money.** It is the "rent" paid or collected for the use of money. It is measured by the excess of resources (usually cash) received or paid over the amount of resources loaned or borrowed at a different date. The amount loaned or borrowed usually is called the **principal.** The outflow of resources for the time value of money is called **interest expense.** The inflow of resources for the time value of money is called **interest revenue.** At various times, entities make decisions that involve either *(a)* receiving funds, goods, or services currently with a promise to make payments over one or more future periods, or *(b)* disbursing funds for operating assets or investments to obtain returns over one or more future periods. In both cases, the time value of money is fundamental to the decision-making process and in measuring and reporting the financial effects of those decisions.

To illustrate the measurement of interest in a simple situation, assume XY Company borrowed $10,000 cash and promised to repay $11,200 one period later; that is, the maturity date. The interest on this contract would be measured as the difference in resources as follows:

Resources borrowed	$10,000
Resources repaid at maturity	11,200
Interest (i.e., time value of money)	$1,200
Analysis:	
Interest in dollars	$1,200
Interest rate for the one period ($1,200 ÷ $10,000)	12%

Consistent Interest Periods and Rates

Interest usually is expressed as a **rate per year,** such as 12%. However, contracts that require interest often specify interest periods of less than one year, such as monthly, quarterly, or semiannually.[1] Thus, a 12% annual interest rate may be specified as 1% per month, 3% quarterly, or 6% semiannually assuming interest is paid monthly, quarterly, or semiannually, respectively. However, if compound interest is specified, the compound interest rate must be clearly specified. For example, interest of 1% compounded each month turns out to be 12.68% per year.[2] If an interest rate is specified with no indication of an interest period of less than one year, annual interest should be assumed. The amount of interest in investing and financing transactions is determined by the (1) principal amount, (2) interest rate, and (3) number of interest periods.

Simple versus Compound Interest

Contracts that require interest will specify either simple interest or compound interest. **Simple interest** is computed for each interest period on the same

[1] Throughout this textbook and in the problem materials, short-term periods are used to facilitate comprehension. Also, amounts usually are rounded to the nearest dollar for instructional convenience.

[2] Some federal and state laws require disclosure of the true annual rate of interest on loans. For example, 1% per month would be disclosed as *(a)* for simple interest, 12% per year, and *(b)* for compound interest, 12.68% per year.

amount of **principal** each period, regardless of any interest accrued in the past. For example, a $10,000 loan that specifies 12% simple interest would require the payment of $1,200 interest each year the loan is outstanding. If there are three interest periods, total interest would be $3,600. The equation for computing simple interest can be expressed as follows:

Interest amount = Principal × Interest rate × Time
(P) *(i)* *(n)*

Compound interest is computed on the amount of **principal** for the period **plus all prior interest accumulated** and not paid or withdrawn. Thus, in addition to interest on principal, compound interest includes interest on interest. Interest amounts that are more than the simple interest amount occur only when there are two or more interest periods. For example, the $10,000 loan, cited above, at 12% compound interest for three interest periods would produce $4,049 of interest, computed as follows:

Period 1—$10,000 × 12%	$1,200
Period 2—($10,000 + $1,200) × 12%	1,344
Period 3—($10,000 + $1,200 + $1,344) × 12%	1,505
Total compound interest	$4,049

Notice that the simple interest amount was $3,600; the difference of $449 (i.e., $4,049 − $3,600) is caused by the inclusion of interest on interest.

Overview of Future Value and Present Value Concepts

Future value (FV) and present value (PV) concepts relate to compound interest; that is, they include interest on principal and interest on the prior accumulated interest. **Future value** involves a current amount that is **increased** in the future by interest **compounding. Present value** involves a future amount which is **decreased** from the future to the present by compound interest discounting.

Future value and present value concepts also include two different situations in regard to the principal. In the simplest situation, the FV or PV amount involves a **single principal** amount. In the other situation, called an **annuity,** the FV or PV is represented by a series of equal principal amounts (usually called **rents**) for each annuity period; that is, one such amount of each annuity period. Therefore, there are four basic FV and PV **values.** These four values, based on $1, for a range of periods *(n)* and interest rates *(i)* are presented in Tables 5–1, 5–2, 5–3, and 5–4 (given on pp. 175–80 of this chapter). These four values may be summarized as follows:

Values of 1—a single principal amount:

1. **Future value of 1**—the future value of a **single** principal amount of 1 after a specified number of periods *(n)* when increased at *i* compound interest rate. The symbol that we will use for this future value is *f* and the formula is: $f = (1 + i)^n$. **Table 5–1** gives *f* values, based on $1, for various *n* and *i* values.
2. **Present value of 1**—the present value of a **single** principal amount of 1 due *n* periods in the future when discounted (i.e., decreased) back to

the present time at i compound interest rate. The symbol we will use is p and the formula is:

$$p = \frac{1}{(1 + i)^n}$$

Table 5–2 gives p values, based on $1, for various n and i values.

Annuities—a series of equal periodic amounts (receipts or payments—called **rents**) each annuity period. There are two kinds of annuities—ordinary annuity and annuity due (discussed later).

3. **Future value of an annuity of 1**—the future value of a series of n equal periodic rents (or contributions) of 1 when **increased** at i compound interest rate. The symbols we will use are F_0 and F_d. The formula for F_0 is:[3]

$$F_0 = \frac{(1 + i)^n - 1}{i}$$

Table 5–3 gives F_0 values, based on rents of $1 each period, for various n and i values and **Table 5–5** gives the comparable F_d values.

4. **Present value of an annuity of 1**—the present value of a series of n equal periodic rents (or contributions) of 1 in the future when **discounted** (i.e., decreased) back to the present time at i compound interest rate. The symbols we use are P_0 and P_d. The formula for P_0 is (see footnote 3):

$$P_0 = \frac{1 - \frac{1}{(1 + i)^n}}{i}$$

Table 5–4 gives P_0 values, based on rents of $1 each period, for various n and i values and **Table 5–6** gives the comparable P_d values.

The remainder of this chapter will discuss and illustrate the application of each of these situations. We suggest that you briefly examine the six FV/PV tables given earlier in this chapter. They will be referred to frequently in the discussions that follow. Notice the following characteristics of each table:

1. Each table heading identifies the specific values presented and the formula.
2. Interest rates *(i)* are given as column headings. These are rates **per interest period** regardless of whether the interest period is annual, semiannual, quarterly, monthly, or daily.
3. Periods *(n)* are given in the left column. The n values may be viewed as annual, semiannual, quarterly, monthly, or daily periods.
4. The table values are based on 1 unit of currency (in the United States, this is $1).
5. The table values express the effect of interest.

---

[3] The subscript o refers to **ordinary** annuities as contrasted with d for annuities due (discussed in Part B). Also, notations used vary considerably. FV and PV often are used as abbreviations for future and present value, respectively.

Table 5–1
Future value of 1, $f = (1 + i)^n$

n Periods	2%	2½%	3%	4%	5%	6%	7%	8%	9%	10%
1	1.02000	1.02500	1.03000	1.04000	1.05000	1.06000	1.07000	1.08000	1.09000	1.10000
2	1.04040	1.05063	1.06090	1.08160	1.10250	1.12360	1.14490	1.16640	1.18810	1.21000
3	1.06121	1.07689	1.09273	1.12486	1.15763	1.19102	1.22504	1.25971	1.29503	1.33100
4	1.08243	1.10381	1.12551	1.16986	1.21551	1.26248	1.31080	1.36049	1.41158	1.46410
5	1.10408	1.13141	1.15927	1.21665	1.27628	1.33823	1.40255	1.46933	1.53862	1.61051
6	1.12616	1.15969	1.19405	1.26532	1.34010	1.41852	1.50073	1.58687	1.67710	1.77156
7	1.14869	1.18869	1.22987	1.31593	1.40710	1.50363	1.60578	1.71382	1.82804	1.94872
8	1.17166	1.21840	1.26677	1.36857	1.47746	1.59385	1.71819	1.85093	1.99256	2.14359
9	1.19509	1.24886	1.30477	1.42331	1.55133	1.68948	1.83846	1.99900	2.17189	2.35795
10	1.21899	1.28008	1.34392	1.48024	1.62889	1.79085	1.96715	2.15892	2.36736	2.59374
11	1.24337	1.31209	1.38423	1.53945	1.71034	1.89830	2.10485	2.33164	2.58043	2.85312
12	1.26824	1.34489	1.42576	1.60103	1.79586	2.01220	2.25219	2.51817	2.81266	3.13843
13	1.29361	1.37851	1.46853	1.66507	1.88565	2.13293	2.40985	2.71962	3.06580	3.45227
14	1.31948	1.41297	1.51259	1.73168	1.97993	2.26090	2.57853	2.93719	3.34173	3.79750
15	1.34587	1.44830	1.55797	1.80094	2.07893	2.39656	2.75903	3.17217	3.64248	4.17725
16	1.37279	1.48451	1.60471	1.87298	2.18287	2.54035	2.95216	3.42594	3.97031	4.59497
17	1.40024	1.52162	1.65285	1.94790	2.29202	2.69277	3.15882	3.70002	4.32763	5.05447
18	1.42825	1.55966	1.70243	2.02582	2.40662	2.85434	3.37993	3.99602	4.71712	5.55992
19	1.45681	1.59865	1.75351	2.10685	2.52695	3.02560	3.61653	4.31570	5.14166	6.11591
20	1.48595	1.63862	1.80611	2.19112	2.65330	3.20714	3.86968	4.66096	5.60441	6.72750
21	1.51567	1.67958	1.86029	2.27877	2.78596	3.39956	4.14056	5.03383	6.10881	7.40025
22	1.54598	1.72157	1.91610	2.36992	2.92526	3.60354	4.43040	5.43654	6.65860	8.14027
23	1.57690	1.76461	1.97359	2.48472	3.07152	3.81975	4.74053	5.87146	7.25787	8.95430
24	1.60844	1.80873	2.03279	2.56330	3.22510	4.04893	5.07237	6.34118	7.91108	9.84973
25	1.64061	1.85394	2.09378	2.66584	3.38635	4.29187	5.42743	6.84848	8.62308	10.83471

n Periods	11%	12%	14%	15%	16%	18%	20%	22%	24%	25%
1	1.11000	1.12000	1.14000	1.15000	1.16000	1.18000	1.20000	1.22000	1.24000	1.25000
2	1.23210	1.25440	1.29960	1.32250	1.34560	1.39240	1.44000	1.48840	1.53760	1.56250
3	1.36763	1.40493	1.48154	1.52088	1.56090	1.64303	1.72800	1.81585	1.90662	1.95313
4	1.51807	1.57352	1.68896	1.74901	1.81064	1.93878	2.07360	2.21533	2.36421	2.44141
5	1.68506	1.76234	1.92541	2.01136	2.10034	2.28776	2.48832	2.70271	2.93163	3.05176
6	1.87041	1.97382	2.19497	2.31306	2.43640	2.69955	2.98598	3.29730	3.63522	3.81470
7	2.07616	2.21068	2.50227	2.66002	2.82622	3.18547	3.58318	4.02271	4.50767	4.76837
8	2.30454	2.47596	2.85259	3.05902	3.27841	3.75886	4.29982	4.90771	5.58951	5.96046
9	2.55804	2.77308	3.25195	3.51788	3.80296	4.43545	5.15978	5.98740	6.93099	7.45058
10	2.83942	3.10585	3.70722	4.04556	4.41144	5.23384	6.19174	7.30463	8.59443	9.31323
11	3.15176	3.47855	4.22623	4.65239	5.11726	6.17593	7.43008	8.91165	10.65709	11.64153
12	3.49845	3.89598	4.81790	5.35025	5.93603	7.28759	8.91610	10.87221	13.21479	14.55192
13	3.88328	4.36349	5.49241	6.15279	6.88579	8.59936	10.69932	13.26410	16.38634	18.18989
14	4.31044	4.88711	6.26135	7.07571	7.98752	10.14724	12.83918	16.18220	20.31906	22.73737
15	4.78459	5.47357	7.13794	8.13706	9.26552	11.97375	15.40702	19.74229	25.19563	28.42171
16	5.31089	6.13039	8.13725	9.35762	10.74800	14.12902	18.48843	24.08559	31.24259	35.52714
17	5.89509	6.86604	9.27646	10.76126	12.46768	16.67225	22.18611	29.38442	38.74081	44.40892
18	6.54355	7.68997	10.57517	12.37545	14.46251	19.67325	26,62333	35.84899	48.03860	55.51115
19	7.26334	8.61276	12.05569	14.23177	16.77652	23.21444	31.94800	43.73577	59.56786	69.38894
20	8.06231	9.64629	13.74349	16.36654	19.46076	27.39303	38.33760	53.35764	73.86415	86.73617
21	8.94917	10.80385	15.66758	18.82152	22.57448	32.32378	46.00512	65.09632	91.59155	108.42022
22	9.93357	12.10031	17.86104	21.64475	26.18640	38.14206	55.20614	79.41751	113.57352	135.52527
23	11.02627	13.55235	20.36158	24.89146	30.37622	45.00763	66.24737	96.88936	140.83116	169.40659
24	12.23916	15.17863	23.21221	28.62518	35.23642	53.10901	79.49685	118.20502	174.63064	211.75824
25	13.58546	17.00006	26.46192	32.91895	40.87424	62.66863	95.39622	144.21013	216.54199	264.69780

Table 5–2

Present value of 1, $p = \dfrac{1}{(1+i)^n}$

n Periods	2%	2½%	3%	4%	5%	6%	7%	8%	9%	10%
1	.98039	.97561	.97087	.96154	.95238	.94340	.93458	.92593	.91743	.90909
2	.96117	.95181	.94260	.92456	.90703	.89000	.87344	.85734	.84168	.82645
3	.94232	.92860	.91514	.88900	.86384	.83962	.81630	.79383	.77218	.75131
4	.92385	.90595	.88849	.85480	.82270	.79209	.76290	.73503	.70843	.68301
5	.90573	.88385	.86261	.82193	.78353	.74726	.71299	.68058	.64993	.62092
6	.88797	.86230	.83748	.79031	.74622	.70496	.66634	.63017	.59627	.56447
7	.87056	.84127	.81309	.75992	.71068	.66506	.62275	.58349	.54703	.51316
8	.85349	.82075	.78941	.73069	.67684	.62741	.58201	.54027	.50187	.46651
9	.83676	.80073	.76642	.70259	.64461	.59190	.54393	.50025	.46043	.42410
10	.82035	.78120	.74409	.67556	.61391	.55839	.50835	.46319	.42241	.38554
11	.80426	.76214	.72242	.64958	.58468	.52679	.47509	.42888	.38753	.35049
12	.78849	.74356	.70138	.62460	.55684	.49697	.44401	.39711	.35553	.31863
13	.77303	.72542	.68095	.60057	.53032	.46884	.41496	.36770	.32618	.28966
14	.75788	.70773	.66112	.57748	.50507	.44230	.38782	.34046	.29925	.26333
15	.74301	.69047	.64186	.55526	.48102	.41727	.36245	.31524	.27454	.23939
16	.72845	.67362	.62317	.53391	.45811	.39365	.33873	.29189	.25187	.21763
17	.71416	.65720	.60502	.51337	.43630	.37136	.31657	.27027	.23107	.19784
18	.70016	.64117	.58739	.49363	.41552	.35034	.29586	.25025	.21199	.17986
19	.68643	.62553	.57029	.47464	.39573	.33051	.27651	.23171	.19449	.16351
20	.67297	.61027	.55368	.45639	.37689	.31180	.25842	.21455	.17843	.14864
21	.65978	.59539	.53755	.43883	.35894	.29416	.24151	.19866	.16370	.13513
22	.64684	.58086	.52189	.42196	.34185	.27751	.22571	.18394	.15018	.12285
23	.63416	.56670	.50669	.40573	.32557	.26180	.21095	.17032	.13778	.11168
24	.62172	.55288	.49193	.39012	.31007	.24698	.19715	.15770	.12640	.10153
25	.60953	.53939	.47761	.37512	.29530	.23300	.18425	.14602	.11597	.09230

n Periods	11%	12%	14%	15%	16%	18%	20%	22%	24%	25%
1	.90090	.89286	.87719	.86957	.86207	.84746	.83333	.81967	.80645	.80000
2	.81162	.79719	.76947	.75614	.74316	.71818	.69444	.67186	.65036	.64000
3	.73119	.71178	.67497	.65752	.64066	.60863	.57870	.55071	.52449	.51200
4	.65873	.63552	.59208	.57175	.55229	.51579	.48225	.45140	.42297	.40960
5	.59345	.56743	.51937	.49718	.47611	.43711	.40188	.37000	.34111	.32768
6	.53464	.50663	.45559	.43233	.41044	.37043	.33490	.30328	.27509	.26214
7	.48166	.45235	.39964	.37594	.35383	.31393	.27908	.24859	.22184	.20972
8	.43393	.40388	.35056	.32690	.30503	.26604	.23257	.20376	.17891	.16777
9	.39092	.36061	.30751	.28426	.26295	.22546	.19381	.16702	.14428	.13422
10	.35218	.32197	.26974	.24718	.22668	.19106	.16151	.13690	.11635	.10737
11	.31728	.28748	.23662	.21494	.19542	.16192	.13459	.11221	.09383	.08590
12	.28584	.25668	.20756	.18691	.16846	.13722	.11216	.09198	.07567	.06872
13	.25751	.22917	.18207	.16253	.14523	.11629	.09346	.07539	.06103	.05498
14	.23199	.20462	.15971	.14133	.12520	.09855	.07789	.06180	.04921	.04398
15	.20900	.18270	.14010	.12289	.10793	.08352	.06491	.05065	.03969	.03518
16	.18829	.16312	.12289	.10686	.09304	.07078	.05409	.04152	.03201	.02815
17	.16963	.14564	.10780	.09293	.08021	.05998	.04507	.03403	.02581	.02252
18	.15282	.13004	.09456	.08081	.06914	.05083	.03756	.02789	.02082	.01801
19	.13768	.11611	.08295	.07027	.05961	.04308	.03130	.02286	.01679	.01441
20	.12403	.10367	.07276	.06110	.05139	.03651	.02608	.01874	.01354	.01153
21	.11174	.09256	.06383	.05313	.04430	.03094	.02174	.01536	.01092	.00922
22	.10067	.08264	.05599	.04620	.03819	.02622	.01811	.01259	.00880	.00738
23	.09069	.07379	.04911	.04017	.03292	.02222	.01509	.01032	.00710	.00590
24	.08170	.06588	.04308	.03493	.02838	.01883	.01258	.00846	.00573	.00472
25	.07361	.05882	.03779	.03038	.02447	.01596	.01048	.00693	.00462	.00378

Table 5–3

Future value of ordinary annuity of n rents of 1 each (F_0): $F_0 = \frac{(1+i)^n - 1}{i}$

n Periods	2%	2½%	3%	4%	5%	6%	7%	8%	9%	10%
1	1.00000	1.00000	1.00000	1.00000	1.00000	1.00000	1.00000	1.00000	1.00000	1.00000
2	2.02000	2.02500	2.03000	2.04000	2.05000	2.06000	2.07000	2.08000	2.09000	2.10000
3	3.06040	3.07563	3.09090	3.12160	3.15250	3.18360	3.21490	3.24640	3.27810	3.31000
4	4.12161	4.15252	4.18363	4.24646	4.31013	4.37462	4.43994	4.50611	4.57313	4.64100
5	5.20404	5.25633	5.30914	5.41632	5.52563	5.63709	5.75074	5.86660	5.98471	6.10510
6	6.30812	6.38774	6.46841	6.63298	6.80191	6.97532	7.15329	7.33593	7.52333	7.71561
7	7.43428	7.54753	7.66246	7.89829	8.14201	8.39384	8.65402	8.92280	9.20043	9.48717
8	8.58297	8.73612	8.89234	9.21423	9.54911	9.89747	10.25980	10.63663	11.02847	11.43589
9	9.75463	9.95452	10.15911	10.58280	11.02656	11.49132	11.97799	12.48756	13.02104	13.57948
10	10.94972	11.20338	11.46388	12.00611	12.57789	13.18079	13.81645	14.48656	15.19293	15.93742
11	12.16872	12.48347	12.80780	13.48635	14.20679	14.97164	15.78360	16.64549	17.56029	18.53117
12	13.41209	13.79555	14.19203	15.02581	15.91713	16.86994	17.88845	18.97713	20.14072	21.38428
13	14.68033	15.14044	15.61779	16.62684	17.71298	18.88214	20.14064	21.49530	22.95338	24.52271
14	15.97394	16.51895	17.08632	18.29191	19.59863	21.01507	22.55049	24.21492	26.01919	27.97498
15	17.29342	17.93193	18.59891	20.02359	21.57856	23.27597	25.12902	27.15211	29.36092	31.77248
16	18.63929	19.38022	20.15688	21.82453	23.65749	25.67253	27.88805	30.32428	33.00340	35.94973
17	20.01207	20.86473	21.76159	23.69751	25.84037	28.21288	30.84022	33.75023	36.97370	40.54470
18	21.41231	22.38635	23.41444	25.64541	28.13238	30.90565	33.99903	37.45024	41.30134	45.59917
19	22.84056	23.94601	25.11687	27.67123	30.53900	33.75999	37.37896	41.44626	46.01846	51.15909
20	24.29737	25.54466	26.87037	29.77808	33.06595	36.78559	40.99549	45.76196	51.16012	57.27500
21	25.78332	27.18327	28.67649	31.96920	35.71925	39.99273	44.86518	50.42292	56.76453	64.00250
22	27.29898	28.86286	30.53678	34.24797	38.50521	43.39229	49.00574	55.45676	62.87334	71.40275
23	28.84496	30.58443	32.45288	36.61789	41.43048	46.99583	53.43614	60.89330	69.53194	79.54302
24	30.42186	32.34904	34.42647	39.08260	44.50200	50.81558	58.17667	66.76476	76.78981	88.49733
25	32.03030	34.15776	36.45926	41.64591	47.72710	54.86451	63.24904	73.10594	84.70090	98.34706

n Periods	11%	12%	14%	15%	16%	18%	20%	22%	24%	25%
1	1.00000	1.00000	1.00000	1.00000	1.00000	1.00000	1.00000	1.00000	1.00000	1.00000
2	2.11000	2.12000	2.14000	2.15000	2.16000	2.18000	2.20000	2.22000	2.24000	2.25000
3	3.34210	3.37440	3.43960	3.47250	3.50560	3.57240	3.64000	3.70840	3.77760	3.81250
4	4.70973	4.77933	4.92114	4.99338	5.06650	5.21543	5.36800	5.52425	5.68422	5.76563
5	6.22780	6.35285	6.61010	6.74238	6.87714	7.15421	7.44160	7.73958	8.04844	8.20703
6	7.91286	8.11519	8.53552	8.75374	8.97748	9.44197	9.92992	10.44229	10.98006	11.25879
7	9.78327	10.08901	10.73049	11.06680	11.41387	12.14152	12.91590	13.73959	14.61528	15.07349
8	11.85943	12.29969	13.23276	13.72682	14.24009	15.32700	16.49908	17.76231	19.12294	19.84186
9	14.16397	14.77566	16.08535	16.78584	17.51851	19.08585	20.79890	22.67001	24.71245	25.80232
10	16.72201	17.54874	19.33730	20.30372	21.32147	23.52131	25.95868	28.65742	31.64344	33.25290
11	19.56143	20.65458	23.04452	24.34928	25.73290	28.75514	32.15042	35.96205	40.23787	42.56613
12	22.71319	24.13313	27.27075	29.00167	30.85017	34.93107	39.58050	44.87370	50.89495	54.20766
13	26.21164	28.02911	32.08865	34.35192	36.78620	42.21866	48.49660	55.74591	64.10974	68.75958
14	30.09492	32.39260	37.58107	40.50471	43.67199	50.81802	59.19592	69.01001	80.49608	86.94947
15	34.40536	37.27971	43.84241	47.58041	51.65951	60.96527	72.03511	85.19221	100.81514	109.68684
16	39.18995	42.75328	50.98035	55.71747	60.92503	72.93901	87.44213	104.93450	126.01077	138.10855
17	44.50084	48.88367	59.11760	65.07509	71.67303	87.06804	105.93056	129.02009	157.25336	173.63568
18	50.39594	55.74971	68.39407	75.83636	84.14072	103.74028	128.11667	158.40451	195.99416	218.04460
19	56.93949	63.43968	78.96923	88.21181	98.60323	123.41353	154.74000	194.25350	244.03276	273.55576
20	64.20283	72.05244	91.02493	102.44358	115.37975	146.62797	186.68800	237.98927	303.60062	342.94470
21	72.26514	81.69874	104.76842	118.81012	134.84051	174.02100	225.02560	291.34691	377.46477	429.68087
22	81.21431	92.50258	120.43600	137.63164	157.41499	206.34479	271.03072	356.44323	469.05632	538.10109
23	91.14788	104.60289	138.29704	159.27638	183.60138	244.48685	326.23686	435.86075	582.62984	673.62636
24	102.17415	118.15524	158.65862	184.16784	213.97761	289.49448	392.48424	532.75011	723.46100	843.03295
25	114.41331	133.33387	181.87083	212.79302	249.21402	342.60349	471.98108	650.95513	898.09164	1054.79118

Table 5–4

Present value of ordinary annuity of rents of 1 each (P_o): $P_o = \dfrac{1 - \dfrac{1}{(1+i)^n}}{i}$

n Periods	2%	2½%	3%	4%	5%	6%	7%	8%	9%	10%
1	.98039	.97561	.97087	.96154	.95238	.94340	.93458	.92593	.91743	.90909
2	1.94156	1.92742	1.91347	1.88609	1.85941	1.83339	1.80802	1.78326	1.75911	1.73554
3	2.88388	2.85602	2.82861	2.77509	2.72325	2.67301	2.62432	2.57710	2.53129	2.48685
4	3.80773	3.76197	3.71710	3.62990	3.54595	3.46511	3.38721	3.31213	3.23972	3.16987
5	4.71346	4.64583	4.57971	4.45182	4.32948	4.21236	4.10020	3.99271	3.88965	3.79079
6	5.60143	5.50813	5.41719	5.24214	5.07569	4.91732	4.76654	4.62288	4.48592	4.35526
7	6.47199	6.34939	6.23028	6.00205	5.78637	5.58238	5.38929	5.20637	5.03295	4.86842
8	7.32548	7.17014	7.01969	6.73274	6.46321	6.20979	5.97130	5.74664	5.53482	5.33493
9	8.16224	7.97087	7.78611	7.43533	7.10782	6.80169	6.51523	6.24689	5.99525	5.75902
10	8.98259	8.75206	8.53020	8.11090	7.72173	7.36009	7.02358	6.71008	6.41766	6.14457
11	9.78685	9.51421	9.25262	8.76048	8.30641	7.88687	7.49867	7.13896	6.80519	6.49506
12	10.57534	10.25776	9.95400	9.38507	8.86325	8.38384	7.94269	7.53608	7.16073	6.81369
13	11.34837	10.98318	10.63496	9.98565	9.39357	8.85268	8.35765	7.90378	7.48690	7.10336
14	12.10625	11.69091	11.29607	10.56312	9.89864	9.29498	8.74547	8.24424	7.78615	7.36669
15	12.84926	12.38138	11.93794	11.11839	10.37966	9.71225	9.10791	8.55948	8.06069	7.60608
16	13.57771	13.05500	12.56110	11.65230	10.83777	10.10590	9.44665	8.85137	8.31256	7.82371
17	14.29187	13.71220	13.16612	12.16567	11.27407	10.47726	9.76322	9.12164	8.54363	8.02155
18	14.99203	14.35336	13.75351	12.65930	11.68959	10.82760	10.05909	9.37189	8.75563	8.20141
19	15.67846	14.97889	14.32380	13.13394	12.08532	11.15812	10.33560	9.60360	8.95011	8.36492
20	16.35143	15.58916	14.87747	13.59033	12.46221	11.46992	10.59401	9.81815	9.12855	8.51356
21	17.01121	16.18455	15.41502	14.02916	12.82115	11.76408	10.83553	10.01680	9.29224	8.64869
22	17.65805	16.76541	15.93692	14.45112	13.16300	12.04158	11.06124	10.20074	9.44243	8.77154
23	18.29220	17.33211	16.44361	14.85684	13.48857	12.30338	11.27219	10.37106	9.58021	8.88322
24	18.91393	17.88499	16.93554	15.24696	13.79864	12.55036	11.46933	10.52876	9.70661	8.98474
25	19.52346	18.42438	17.41315	15.62208	14.09394	12.78336	11.65358	10.67478	9.82258	9.07704

n Periods	11%	12%	14%	15%	16%	18%	20%	22%	24%	25%
1	.90090	.89286	.87719	.86957	.86207	.84746	.83333	.81967	.80645	.80000
2	1.71252	1.69005	1.64666	1.62571	1.60523	1.56564	1.52778	1.49153	1.45682	1.44000
3	2.44371	2.40183	2.32163	2.28323	2.24589	2.17427	2.10648	2.04224	1.98130	1.95200
4	3.10245	3.03735	2.91371	2.85498	2.79818	2.69006	2.58873	2.49364	2.40428	2.36160
5	3.69590	3.60478	3.43308	3.35216	3.27429	3.12717	2.99061	2.86364	2.74538	2.68928
6	4.23054	4.11141	3.88867	3.78448	3.68474	3.49760	3.32551	3.16692	3.02047	2.95142
7	4.71220	4.56376	4.28830	4.16042	4.03857	3.81153	3.60459	3.41551	3.24232	3.16114
8	5.14612	4.96764	4.63886	4.48732	4.34359	4.07757	3.83716	3.61927	3.42122	3.32891
9	5.53705	5.32825	4.94637	4.77158	4.60654	4.30302	4.03097	3.78628	3.56550	3.46313
10	5.88923	5.65022	5.21612	5.01877	4.83323	4.49409	4.19247	3.92318	3.66186	3.57050
11	6.20652	5.93770	5.45273	5.23371	5.02864	4.65601	4.32706	4.03540	3.77569	3.65640
12	6.49236	6.19437	5.66029	5.42062	5.19711	4.79322	4.43922	4.12737	3.85136	3.72512
13	6.74987	6.42355	5.84236	5.58315	5.34233	4.90951	4.53268	4.20277	3.91239	3.78010
14	6.98187	6.62817	6.00207	5.72448	5.46753	5.00806	4.61057	4.26456	3.96160	3.82408
15	7.19087	6.81086	6.14217	5.84737	5.57546	5.09158	4.67547	4.31522	4.00129	3.85926
16	7.37916	6.97399	6.26506	5.95423	5.66850	5.16235	4.72956	4.35673	4.03330	3.88741
17	7.54879	7.11963	6.37286	6.04716	5.74870	5.22233	4.77463	4.39077	4.05911	3.90993
18	7.70162	7.24967	6.46742	6.12797	5.81785	5.27316	4.81219	4.41866	4.07993	3.92794
19	7.83929	7.36578	6.55037	6.19823	5.87746	5.31624	4.84350	4.44152	4.09672	3.94235
20	7.96333	7.46944	6.62313	6.25933	5.92884	5.35275	4.86958	4.46027	4.11026	3.95388
21	8.07507	7.56200	6.68696	6.31246	5.97314	5.38368	4.89132	4.47563	4.12117	3.96311
22	8.17574	7.64465	6.74295	6.35866	6.01133	5.40990	4.90943	4.48822	4.12998	3.97049
23	8.26643	7.71843	6.79206	6.39884	6.04425	5.43212	4.92453	4.49854	4.13708	3.97639
24	8.34814	7.78432	6.83514	6.43377	6.07263	5.45095	4.93710	4.50700	4.14281	3.98111
25	8.42174	7.84314	6.87293	6.46415	6.09709	5.46691	4.94759	4.51393	4.14742	3.98489

Table 5–5

Future value of an annuity due (F_d) of n rents of 1 each: $\left[F_0 = \frac{(1+i)^n - 1}{i}\right] \times (1+i) = F_d$

n Periods	2%	2½%	3%	4%	5%	6%	7%	8%	9%	10%
1	1.02000	1.02500	1.03000	1.04000	1.05000	1.06000	1.07000	1.08000	1.09000	1.10000
2	2.06040	2.07563	2.09090	2.12160	2.15250	2.18360	2.21490	2.24640	2.27810	2.31000
3	3.12161	3.15252	3.18363	3.24646	3.31013	3.37462	3.43994	3.50611	3.57313	3.64100
4	4.20404	4.25633	4.30914	4.41632	4.52563	4.63709	4.75074	4.86660	4.98471	5.10510
5	5.30812	5.38774	5.46841	5.63298	5.80191	5.97532	6.15329	6.33593	6.52333	6.71561
6	6.43428	6.54743	6.66246	6.89829	7.14201	7.39384	7.65402	7.92280	8.20043	8.48717
7	7.58297	7.73612	7.89234	8.21423	8.54911	8.89747	9.25980	9.63663	10.02847	10.43589
8	8.75463	8.95452	9.15911	9.58280	10.02656	10.49132	10.97799	11.48756	12.02104	12.57948
9	9.94972	10.20338	10.46388	11.00611	11.57789	12.18079	12.81645	13.48656	14.19293	14.93742
10	11.16872	11.48347	11.80780	12.48635	13.20679	13.97164	14.78360	15.64549	16.56029	17.53117
11	12.41209	12.79555	13.19203	14.02581	14.91713	15.86994	16.88845	17.97713	19.14072	20.38428
12	13.68033	14.14044	14.61779	15.62684	16.71298	17.88214	19.14064	20.49530	21.95338	23.52271
13	14.97394	15.51895	16.08632	17.29191	18.59863	20.01507	21.55049	23.21492	25.01919	26.97498
14	16.29342	16.93193	17.59891	19.02359	20.57856	22.27597	24.12902	26.15211	28.36092	30.77248
15	17.63929	18.38022	19.15688	20.82453	22.65749	24.67253	26.88805	29.32428	32.00340	34.94973
16	19.01207	19.86473	20.76159	22.69751	24.84037	27.21288	29.84022	32.75023	35.97370	39.54470
17	20.41231	21.38635	22.41444	24.64541	27.13238	29.90565	32.99903	36.45024	40.30134	44.59917
18	21.84056	22.94601	24.11687	26.67123	29.53900	32.75999	36.37896	40.44626	45.01846	50.15909
19	23.29737	24.54466	25.87037	28.77808	32.06595	35.78559	39.99549	44.76196	50.16012	56.27500
20	24.78332	26.18327	27.67649	30.96920	34.71925	38.99273	43.86518	49.42292	55.76453	63.00250
21	26.29898	27.86286	29.53678	33.24797	37.50521	42.39229	48.00574	54.45676	61.87334	70.40275
22	27.84496	29.58443	31.45288	35.61789	40.43048	45.99583	52.43614	59.89330	68.53194	78.54302
23	29.42186	31.34904	33.42647	38.08260	43.50200	49.81558	57.17667	65.76476	75.78981	87.49733
24	31.03030	33.15776	35.45926	40.64591	46.72710	53.86451	62.24904	72.10594	83.70090	97.34706
25	32.67091	35.01171	37.55304	43.31175	50.11345	58.15638	67.67647	78.95442	92.32398	108.18177

n Periods	11%	12%	14%	15%	16%	18%	20%	22%	24%	25%
1	1.11000	1.12000	1.14000	1.15000	1.16000	1.18000	1.20000	1.22000	1.24000	1.25000
2	2.34210	2.37440	2.43960	2.47250	2.50560	2.57240	2.64000	2.70840	2.77760	2.81250
3	3.70973	3.77933	3.92114	3.99338	4.06650	4.21543	4.36800	4.52425	4.68422	4.76563
4	5.22780	5.35285	5.61010	5.74238	5.87714	6.15421	6.44160	6.73958	7.04844	7.20703
5	6.91286	7.11519	7.53552	7.75374	7.97748	8.44197	8.92992	9.44229	9.98006	10.25879
6	8.78327	9.08901	9.73049	10.06680	10.41387	11.14152	11.91590	12.73959	13.61528	14.07349
7	10.85943	11.29969	12.23276	12.72682	13.24009	14.32700	15.49908	16.76231	18.12294	18.84186
8	13.16397	13.77566	15.08535	15.78584	16.51851	18.08585	19.79890	21.67001	23.71245	24.80232
9	15.72201	16.54874	18.33730	19.30372	20.32147	22.52131	24.95868	27.65742	30.64344	32.25290
10	18.56143	19.65458	22.04452	23.34928	24.73290	27.75514	31.15042	34.96205	39.23787	41.56613
11	21.71319	23.13313	26.27075	28.00167	29.85017	33.93107	38.58050	43.87370	49.89495	53.20766
12	25.21164	27.02911	31.08865	33.35192	35.78620	41.21866	47.49660	54.74591	63.10974	67.75958
13	29.09492	31.39260	36.58107	39.50471	42.67199	49.81802	58.19592	68.01001	79.49608	85.94947
14	33.40536	37.27971	42.84241	46.58041	50.65951	59.96527	71.03511	84.19221	99.81514	108.68684
15	38.18995	41.75328	49.98035	54.71747	59.92503	71.93901	86.44213	103.93450	125.01077	137.10855
16	43.50084	47.88367	58.11760	64.07509	70.67303	86.06804	104.93056	128.02009	156.25336	172.63568
17	49.39594	54.74971	67.39407	74.83636	83.14072	102.74028	127.11667	157.40451	194.99416	217.04460
18	55.93949	62.43968	77.96923	87.21181	97.60323	122.41353	153.74000	193.25350	243.03276	272.55576
19	63.20283	71.05244	90.02493	101.44358	114.37975	145.62797	185.68800	236.98927	302.60062	341.94470
20	71.26514	80.69874	103.76842	117.81012	133.84051	173.02100	224.02560	290.34691	376.46477	428.68087
21	80.21431	91.50258	119.43600	136.63164	156.41499	205.34479	270.03072	355.44323	468.05632	537.10109
22	90.14788	103.60289	137.29704	158.27638	182.60138	243.48685	325.23686	434.86075	581.62984	672.62636
23	101.17415	117.15524	157.65862	183.16784	212.97761	288.49448	391.48424	531.75011	722.46100	842.03295
24	113.41331	132.33387	180.87083	211.79302	248.21402	341.60349	470.98108	649.95513	897.09164	1053.79118
25	126.99877	149.33393	207.33274	244.71197	289.08827	404.27211	566.37730	794.16526	1113.63363	1318.48898

Table 5–6

Present value of an annuity due (P_d) of n rents of 1 each: $\left[P_0 = \dfrac{1 - \dfrac{1}{(1+i)^n}}{i} \right] \times (1+i) = P_d$

n Periods	2%	2½%	3%	4%	5%	6%	7%	8%	9%	10%
1	1.00000	1.00000	1.00000	1.00000	1.00000	1.00000	1.00000	1.00000	1.00000	1.00000
2	1.98039	1.97561	1.97087	1.96154	1.95238	1.94340	1.93458	1.92593	1.91743	1.90909
3	2.94156	2.92742	2.91347	2.88609	2.85941	2.83339	2.80802	2.78326	2.75911	2.73554
4	3.88388	3.85602	3.82861	3.77509	3.72325	3.67301	3.62432	3.57710	3.53130	3.48685
5	4.80773	4.76197	4.71710	4.62990	4.54595	4.46511	4.38721	4.31213	4.23972	4.16987
6	5.71346	5.64583	5.57971	5.45182	5.32948	5.21236	5.10020	4.99271	4.88965	4.79079
7	6.60143	6.50813	6.41719	6.24214	6.07569	5.91732	5.76654	5.62788	5.48592	5.35526
8	7.47199	7.34939	7.23028	7.00205	6.78637	6.58238	6.38929	6.20637	6.03295	5.86842
9	8.32548	8.17014	8.01969	7.73274	7.46321	7.20979	6.97130	6.74664	6.53482	6.33493
10	9.16224	8.97087	8.78611	8.43533	8.10782	7.80169	7.51523	7.24689	6.99525	6.75902
11	9.98259	9.75206	9.53020	9.11090	8.72173	8.36009	8.02358	7.71008	7.41766	7.14457
12	10.78685	10.51421	10.25262	9.76048	9.30641	8.88687	8.49867	8.13896	7.80519	7.49506
13	11.57534	11.25776	10.95400	10.38507	9.86325	9.38384	8.94269	8.53608	8.16073	7.81369
14	12.34837	11.98319	11.63496	10.98565	10.39357	9.85268	9.35765	8.90378	8.48690	8.10336
15	13.10625	12.69091	12.29607	11.56312	10.89864	10.29498	9.74547	9.24424	8.78615	8.36669
16	13.84926	13.38139	12.93794	12.11839	11.37966	10.71225	10.10791	9.55948	9.06069	8.60608
17	14.57771	14.05500	13.56110	12.65230	11.83777	11.10590	10.44665	9.85137	9.31256	8.82371
18	15.29187	14.71220	14.16612	13.16567	12.27407	11.47726	10.76322	10.12164	9.54363	9.02155
19	15.99203	15.35336	14.75351	13.65930	12.68959	11.82760	11.05909	10.37189	9.75563	9.20141
20	16.67846	15.97889	15.32380	14.13394	13.08532	12.15812	11.33560	10.60360	9.95012	9.36492
21	17.35143	16.58916	15.87747	14.59033	13.46221	12.46992	11.59401	10.81815	10.12855	9.51356
22	18.01121	17.18455	16.41502	15.02916	13.82115	12.76408	11.83553	11.01680	10.29224	9.64869
23	18.65805	17.76541	16.93692	15.45112	14.16300	13.04158	12.06124	11.20074	10.44243	9.77154
24	19.29220	18.33211	17.44361	15.85684	14.48857	13.30338	12.27219	11.37106	10.58021	9.88322
25	19.91393	18.88499	17.93554	16.24696	14.79864	13.55036	12.46933	11.52876	10.70661	9.98474

n Periods	11%	12%	14%	15%	16%	18%	20%	22%	24%	25%
1	1.00000	1.00000	1.00000	1.00000	1.00000	1.00000	1.00000	1.00000	1.00000	1.00000
2	1.90090	1.89286	1.87719	1.86957	1.86207	1.84746	1.83333	1.81967	1.80645	1.80000
3	2.71252	2.69005	2.64666	2.62571	2.60523	2.56564	2.52778	2.49153	2.45682	2.44000
4	3.44371	3.40183	3.32163	3.28323	3.24589	3.17427	3.10648	3.04224	2.98130	2.95200
5	4.10245	4.03735	3.91371	3.85498	3.79818	3.69006	3.58873	3.49364	3.40428	3.36160
6	4.69590	4.60478	4.43308	4.35216	4.27429	4.12717	3.99061	3.86364	3.74538	3.68928
7	5.23054	5.11141	4.88867	4.78448	4.68474	4.49760	4.32551	4.16692	4.02047	3.95142
8	5.71220	5.56376	5.28830	5.16042	5.03857	4.81153	4.60459	4.41551	4.24232	4.16114
9	6.14612	5.96764	5.63886	5.48732	5.34359	5.07757	4.83716	4.61927	4.42122	4.32891
10	6.53705	6.32825	5.94637	5.77158	5.60654	5.30302	5.03097	4.78628	4.56550	4.46313
11	6.88923	6.65022	6.21612	6.01877	5.83323	5.49409	5.19247	4.92318	4.68186	4.57050
12	7.20652	6.93770	6.45273	6.23371	6.02864	5.65601	5.32706	5.03540	4.77569	4.65640
13	7.49236	7.19437	6.66029	6.42062	6.19711	5.79322	5.43922	5.12737	4.85136	4.72512
14	7.74987	7.42355	6.84236	6.58315	6.34322	5.90951	5.53268	5.20277	4.91239	4.78010
15	7.98187	7.62817	7.00207	6.72448	6.46753	6.00806	5.61057	5.26456	4.96160	4.82408
16	8.19087	7.81086	7.14217	6.84737	6.57546	6.09158	5.67547	5.31522	5.00129	4.85926
17	8.37916	7.97399	7.26506	6.95424	6.66850	6.16235	5.72956	5.35673	5.03330	4.88741
18	8.54879	8.11963	7.37286	7.04716	6.74870	6.22233	5.77463	5.39077	5.05911	4.90993
19	8.70162	8.24967	7.46742	7.12797	6.81785	6.27316	5.81219	5.41866	5.07993	4.92794
20	8.83929	8.36578	7.55037	7.19823	6.87746	6.31624	5.84350	5.44152	5.09672	4.94235
21	8.96333	8.46944	7.62313	7.25933	6.92884	6.35275	5.86958	5.46027	5.11026	4.95388
22	9.07507	8.56200	7.68696	7.31246	6.97314	6.38368	5.89132	5.47563	5.12117	4.96311
23	9.17574	8.64465	7.74294	7.35866	7.01133	6.40990	5.90943	5.48822	5.12998	4.97049
24	9.26643	8.71843	7.79206	7.39884	7.04425	6.43212	5.92453	5.49854	5.13708	4.97639
25	9.34814	8.78432	7.83514	7.43377	7.07263	6.45095	5.93710	5.50700	5.14281	4.98111

Future and Present Value of 1 Compared

Future value of 1 and present value of 1 are the same in one respect—they both relate to a **single** principal amount. The future value of 1 looks **forward** from present dollars to future dollars. The present value of 1 looks **back** from future dollars to present dollars. This distinction is shown by "time lines" in **Exhibit 5–1;** it is important to notice the direction of the arrows in each instance. We suggest time-line diagramming to analyze PV and FV cases.

Exhibit 5–1
Future value of 1 and present value of 1 compared.

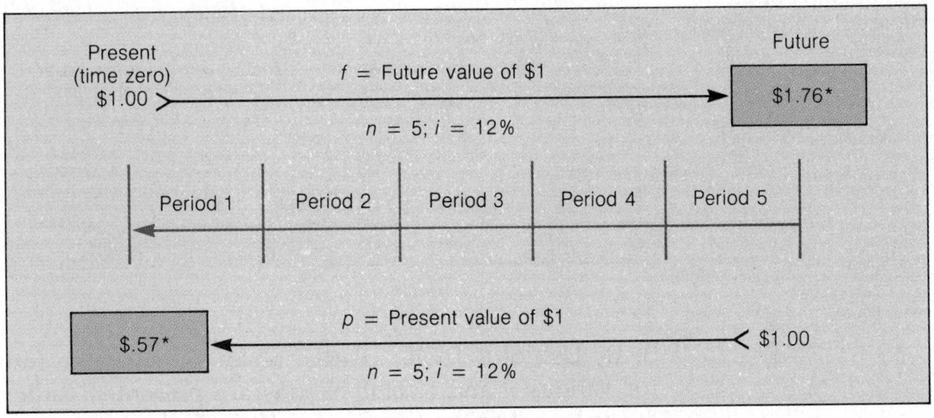

*Rounded. Notice the reciprocal relationship $1.00 ÷ $1.76 = $.57, rounded (explained on page 185).

Future Value of 1

The concept of future value of 1 (the symbol used herein is **f**) often is called **compound interest.** The future value is the single principal amount plus all subsequent accumulated compound interest. For example, $1,000 deposited in a savings account on January 1, 19A, compounded each interest period of one year at 12% interest, would amount (accumulate) to $1,762 at the end of the fifth year (December 31, 19E). The increase of $762 is the accumulated compound interest during the five years. The future value of 1 always will be more than 1 by the compound interest accumulation.

To increase our knowledge of the concept of a future value of 1 (a single amount), we will consider four ways that it can be computed. Assume we want to compute the future value of $1, invested for five years at 12% compound interest each year (i.e., PV of principal = $1, n = 5, i = 12%). The future value of 1 can be computed as follows:

1. **By Successive Interest Computations.** Multiply the principal ($1) by the interest rate (12%) and add to the principal the 12 cents interest for the first period; the sum ($1.12) is the amount at the end of the first period. This amount then becomes the **interest-bearing** amount for the second period. This sum is principal plus interest ($1 + i$) and may be used as the multiplier of the balance at the start of the second period to determine the compounded amount at the end of that period. The tabulation below in (1) uses this multiplier to illustrate successive interest computations to derive our answer, $1.76 (rounded). The FV of any amount of 1 can be computed in this way by substituting the amount in place of $1.

Future value always more than 1 — implies growth

2. By Formula. Substitute into a formula which states that for n interest periods at i rate of interest the future value of 1 is $f = (1 + i)^n$. Substituting, \$1 invested at 12% annual compound interest for five years = $(\$1 + .12)^5$, or \$1.76. See (2) in the tabulation for period 5. The FV of any amount can be computed in this way by multiplying the amount by $(1 + i)^n$.

Computation of future value of 1 (without table values).

	(1) By successive computations			(2) By formula
Period	Balance at start of period	× Multiplier $(1 + i)$	= Amount at end of period	Alternate computation at end $(1 + i)^n$
1	\$1	1.12	\$1.12	$(1.12)^1$ = \$1.12
2	1.12	1.12	1.2544	$(1.12)^2$ = 1.2544
3	1.2544	1.12	1.40493	$(1.12)^3$ = 1.40493
4	1.40493	1.12	1.57352	$(1.12)^4$ = 1.57352
5	1.57352	1.12	1.76234	$(1.12)^5$ = 1.76234

3. By Use of a Table. Partial tables showing the future and present values for various n and i combinations are presented earlier in this chapter. Table 5–1 is based on the formula $f = (1 + i)^n$; therefore, it presents the future value of 1 values (for a limited number of periods and interest rates). Reference to Table 5–1, down the 12% column and across on the five-period line, shows the future value of 1 to be 1.76234 (the same as computed in the above tabulation). Table 5–1 is titled **Future Value of 1,** and the underlying formula is $f = (1 + i)^n$. Tables make computation of future and present values easier because any amount to be used is multiplied by the appropriate table value for \$1. When the table value is to be applied to a large amount, rounding of **table values** can cause a material error in the resulting amount computed. The table values presented in this chapter are carried to five places.

4. By Use of a Calculator. Many calculators are programmed to compute FV and PV. To compute an f value, the following inputs are used: n, i, and PV amount.

Each of the four approaches requires that the n and i values be consistent for the interest periods and rates (see page 172). For most accounting purposes you should be able to use approaches 3 and 4.

Accounting Applications of Future Value of 1

Case A. On January 1, 19A, Able Company deposited \$100,000 in a special construction fund. The fund will earn 10% interest, compounded annually. Interest earned each period will be added to the fund.

Required:

1. Compute the amount that will be in the fund at the end of 19C.

$$\$100{,}000 \times f_{n=3;\,i=10\%} \text{ (Table 5–1, 1.331)} = \underline{\underline{\$133{,}100}}$$

2. What is the total amount of accumulated interest?

$$\$133{,}100 - \$100{,}000 = \$33{,}100.$$

use to make your journal entries from

3. Prepare a fund accumulation schedule.

Fund accumulation schedule

Date	Interest earned	Fund balance
January 1, 19A		$100,000
December 31, 19A	$100,000 × 10% = $10,000	110,000
December 31, 19B	110,000 × 10% = 11,000	121,000
December 31, 19C	121,000 × 10% = 12,100	133,100

4. Give the journal entries related to the fund.

January 1, 19A:

	Debit	Credit
Special construction fund	100,000	
Cash		100,000

Each December 31:

	19A		19B		19C	
Each December 31:						
Special construction fund	10,000		11,000		12,100	
Investment revenue		10,000		11,000		12,100

Case B. On January 1, 19A, Baker Company deposited $100,000 in a special savings account. The fund will earn 10% interest compounded quarterly for three years. Interest earned will be added to the fund.

Required:

1. Compute the amount that will be in the fund at the end of 19C.

$$\$100{,}000 \times f_{n=12;\, i=2\frac{1}{2}\%} \text{ (Table 5–1, 1.34489)} = \underline{\underline{\$134{,}489}}.$$

Notice that the three years encompass 12 interest periods, and the interest rate for each quarterly interest period is: 10% ÷ 4 = 2½%.

2. What is the total amount of accumulated interest?

$$\$134{,}489 - \$100{,}000 = \underline{\underline{\$34{,}489}}.$$

Notice the difference between the accumulated interest amounts in Case A versus Case B (i.e., $33,100 versus $34,489). More frequent compounding leads to a higher amount of accumulated interest.

Determination of an Unknown Interest Rate or Unknown Number of Periods

Cases may be encountered when either the interest rate *(i)* or the number of periods *(n)* is not known, but sufficient data are available for their determination. For example, in Case A above, three values were provided: *(a)* principal, $100,000; *(b)* interest rate, 10%; and *(c)* periods, 3. These three values were used to compute the future value *(f)* of $133,100. Thus, there were a total of **four** variables. Now let's examine two situations, using the same case, where the unknown variable is not the future value *(f)*.

FV = PV × Factor

FV = F

PV

n = period

i = int

Situation 1—the interest rate is unknown.

Given: Present value, $100,000; future value, $133,100, interest periods, 3. To compute the implicit interest **rate:**

a. $133,100 ÷ $100,000 = 1.33100, which is the table value of $1, for three periods.

b. Use Table 5–1 and read **across** for three interest periods to find this table value.

c. Table value 1.33100 is found under the 10% column.

d. The interest rate, therefore, is 10%.

Situation 2—the number of interest periods is unknown.

Given: Present value, $100,000; future value, $133,100, interest rate, 10%. To compute the **number of interest periods:**

a. $133,100 ÷ $100,000 = 1.33100, which is the table value of $1, at 10% interest.

b. Use Table 5–1 and read **down** the 10% column to find this table value.

c. Table value 1.33100 is found on the line for three periods.

d. The implied number of interest periods, therefore is 3.

Interpolation of Table Values. To determine an unknown interest rate, or number of periods, interpolation often is necessary. This is because the table values, computed in situations 1 and 2 above, usually will be between two interest rates or two periods. Assume $5,000 is deposited in a savings account at compound interest, with an expected balance of $15,000 at the end of year 10. Question: What is the implicit interest rate, assuming annual compounding?

Computation:

a. $15,000 ÷ $5,000 = 3.00000.

b. Table 5–1 indicates that when n equals 10, 11% = 2.83942 and 12% = 3.10585. Therefore, by inspection the implicit rate is between 11% and 12%—a little closer to 12%—approximately six-tenths of the way between them.

c. We usually would use 12%, or 11.6%, as close approximations.

d. If more precision is desired, we could use linear interpolation and derive 11.603% as follows:[4]

$$11\% = 2.83942$$
$$?\ = 3.00000 \quad \Delta = .16058$$
$$12\% = 3.10585 \qquad\qquad \Delta = .26643$$

$$11\% + \left[\left(\frac{.16058}{.26643}\right) \times (12\% - 11\%)\right] = 11.603\%$$

[4] This is an illustration of linear interpolation. A more precise answer can be obtained by using a calculator and the following procedure:

$$\$5,000\ (1 + i)^{10} = \$15,000$$
$$(1 + i)^{10} = \$15,000 ÷ \$5,000$$
$$(1 + i)\ = (3.0)^{1/10}$$
$$i\ = 11.612\%$$

Present Value of 1

The concept of present value of 1 (the symbol used herein is p) often is called **compound discounting.** The **present value** of a single principal amount is the future principal less all compound interest discounted to the present date at the specified interest rate. The present value of $1 always will be less than $1 by the amount of the compound interest discount. For example, a single principal amount of $10,000 discounted at 10% interest for three years is $7,513 (rounded).

All present value of 1 amounts are reciprocals of their comparable future value amounts because one (i.e., f) adds accumulated compound interest and the other (i.e., p) subtracts accumulated compound interest (i.e., discounting). That is, $f = (1 + i)^n$ and $p = \frac{1}{(1 + i)^n}$ as shown in the headings of Tables 5–1 and 5–2, respectively (this relationship was illustrated on page 181).

Calculation of Present Value of 1

Present value of 1 amounts can be computed four different ways as follows:

1. Successive discounting by dividing each period's beginning f amount by $(1 + i)$.
2. Dividing the equivalent f value in Table 5–1 into 1 (p is a reciprocal to f).
3. Use of an available present value of 1 table such as Table 5–2.
4. Use of a pocket calculator programmed to compute FV and PV values.

For most accounting purposes you should be able to use approaches 3 and 4.

Accounting Application of Present Value of 1

On January 1, 19A, Cary Company purchased a machine. Payment was $25,000 cash and a $50,000 noninterest-bearing note, due on December 31, 19B. The $50,000 includes all accumulated interest. The implied interest rate is 10%.

Required:

1. Compute the cost of the machine.

Cash paid	$25,000
Note at present value, $50,000 \times p_{n=2; i=10\%}$ (Table 5–2, .82645)	41,323
Cost of the machine	$66,323

Notice that if the note had been interest-bearing, the machine would have cost $75,000 and in addition, interest would be paid on $50,000. A so-called noninterest-bearing note (also called a **discounted note**) has implicit interest. The cash received is the same as the face of the note less the implicit interest (see Chapter 14).

2. Give the entry to record the acquisition of the machine.

Machine	66,323	
Cash		25,000
Note payable		41,323*

*This note could be recorded at $50,000 with a debit for the interest of $8,677 to Discount on Note Payable. The results would be the same (discussed in Chapter 14).

3. Prepare a debt payment schedule.

Debt payment schedule

Date	Interest expense incurred (payable at maturity)	Liability (note payable) Increase	Balance
January 1, 19A			$41,323
December 31, 19A	$41,323 × 10% = $4,132	$4,132	45,455
December 31, 19B	45,455 × 10% = 4,545	4,545	50,000

4. Give the entries related to this case.

	December 31 19A		19B	
Interest expense	4,132		4,545	
Note payable		4,132		4,545
Note payable			50,000	
Cash				50,000

Selecting an Interest Rate

The results of future and present value computations are significantly influenced by the interest rate used, particularly when the rates are high and the time period is long. For example, the future value of $100,000 for 20 periods at 10% per period is $672,750. If the interest rate is 8%, the future value is $466,096—a significant difference.

Generally, an interest rate has three components: (1) a pure no-risk component with no inflation or deflation effects included, (2) a credit risk component that varies among borrowers, security pledged and types of loans, and (3) an expected inflation or deflation component. Conceptually the interest rate is the sum of these three components. However, this concept assumes a competitive free market with fully informed borrowers. "What the traffic will bear" is thought by some people to be operative in some situations. Consequently, each of the three components is very difficult, if not impossible, to determine in a given situation.

In recognition of (1) the difficulty in selecting a realistic interest rate and (2) the opportunity to select an interest rate to manipulate FV and PV results for accounting purposes, *APB Opinion 21*, paragraphs 13 and 14, provides a general guideline. The guideline states that the rate selected should approximate "the rate which would have resulted if an independent borrower and an independent lender had negotiated a similar transaction under comparable terms and conditions with the option to pay the cash price upon purchase or to give a note for the amount of the purchase which bears the prevailing rate of interest to maturity." The rate described in this quotation usually is called the **going, prevailing,** or **market rate** for the transaction under consideration. It is the rate that generally should be used for "GAAP applications."

PART B: ANNUITIES—FUTURE AND PRESENT VALUES

Annuities Defined

Annuities involve periodic payments or receipts of cash during a specified period of time. For all specific purposes, including accounting, annuities must be precisely defined to conform to the mathematical formulas used.

Annuities involve the future and present value concepts discussed in Part A of this chapter. **Annuities differ from amounts of 1 (*f* or *p*) in one way; instead of a single amount, all annuities include a series of equal periodic amounts. There is one amount for each annuity period over the life of the annuity.** These principal amounts usually are called **rents;** they may be cash payments or cash receipts. An annuity has three essential **characteristics:**[5]

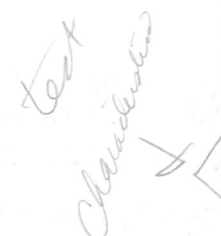

1. Equal time periods (called **annuity periods**).
2. Equal rents each annuity period, either at the end or the beginning of each annuity period.
3. Equal interest rates compounded or discounted each interest period.

When one or more of these characteristics changes, a different annuity must be used because these characteristics are **explicit** in all interest table values, including FV/PV computer programs. Also, they are explicit in the table formulas given in the headings of Tables 5–3, 5–4, 5–5, and 5–6. For example, these three characteristics are encompassed in the equal monthly payments on an auto loan. An auto loan usually is an annuity that requires equal periodic cash payments by the borrower and provides the same periodic cash receipts for the lender.

The **future value** of an annuity is the sum of all of its principal amounts (i.e., its rents) **plus** all of the accumulated compound interest on those rents. The **present value** of an annuity is the sum of all of its principal amounts (i.e., its rents) **less** all of the accumulated compound discount on those rents.

Annuities are either **ordinary** or **due.** The classification depends upon the **timing of the rents** during each annuity period that the annuity is in existence. An **ordinary annuity** (also called an **annuity in arrears**) is an end-of-period annuity. Its rents occur at the **end of each** annuity period that the annuity is in existence. An **annuity due** (also called an **annuity in advance**) is a beginning-of-period annuity. Its rents occur at the **beginning of each** annuity period that the annuity is in existence.

To illustrate the difference between an ordinary annuity and an annuity due, assume that a $15,000, 10%, three-year debt is incurred on April 1, year 1. The debt is to be paid in three equal annual installments that include compound interest. Case A: Assume payments of $6,032 are to be made each March 31, for three annuity periods. This specification creates an **ordinary annuity** because

---

[5] These are sometimes called **standard** or **consistent** annuities. They conform to the formulas given in all annuity tables (e.g., Tables 5–3, 5–4, 5–5, and 5–6). In a broader sense, the term **annuities** often is used to refer to situations that involve principal and compound interest with periodic rents, but the interest rate, periodic rent, or annuity periods may be specified to change during the life of the annuity. These kinds of annuities require a separate computation for each specification.

diff – 1 unit period (compounding)

the payments are to be made at the **end** of each annuity period. Case B: Assume instead that payments of $5,483 are to be made April 1, years 1, 2, and 3. This specification creates an **annuity due** because the payments are to be made at the **beginning** of each annuity period (i.e., in advance). Notice the significant difference in the periodic payments (i.e., ordinary, $6,032 = due, $5,438 = $594). This difference is interest because each of the annual payments under the annuity due is paid one year earlier than under the ordinary annuity (i.e., the principal is paid off earlier which means less interest is paid). The characteristics and applications of the future value and present value of annuities are discussed and illustrated in the remainder of this chapter.

Future Value of an Annuity of 1

The future value of an annuity, designated *F* herein, is the sum of all of its periodic rents **plus** the accumulated compound interest in each of those rents. The formula for the future value of an ordinary annuity is: $F_0 = \frac{(1+i)^n - 1}{i}$. If the rents are at the **end** of each annuity period, its future value is an ordinary annuity; if the rents are at the beginning of each annuity period, its future value is an annuity due. The difference between these two annuities is one period's compound interest. The timing of their respective rents is different by one period.

Exhibit 5–2 shows two time lines and compares the future value of an ordinary annuity with the future value of an annuity due of $1 at 10% compound interest for three annuity periods (and three rents). The symbol "F_0" is used to designate the future value of an **ordinary annuity** and F_d" to designate an **annuity due.** Panel B of Exhibit 5–2 identifies the differences between F_0 and F_d annuities.

Because of the difference in the timing of the periodic rents, the future value of the ordinary annuity illustrated in Exhibit 5–2 involves three rents (i.e., one in each annuity period) but there are only two compounding (i.e., interest) periods. The annuity due involves three rents and three compounding periods. Therefore, for each of the three annuity values illustrated, $F_0 \times (1 + i) = F_d$. This relationship means that if an F_0 value is known, it can be multiplied by $(1 + i)$ to determine its comparable F_d value.[6] Tables 5–5 and 5–6 earlier in this chapter give annuity due values.

Determination of the Future Value of an Annuity of 1

The future value of an **ordinary** annuity can be determined by using any one of four approaches. To illustrate, assume rents of $1, n = 3, and i = 10%. The four approaches, **each of which computes the future value as of the date of the last rent** (i.e., an ordinary annuity), are as follows:

1. Successive computations of the future value of 1 (Table 5–1):

[6] Another procedure frequently used when the **future value of an annuity due** is needed, and an annuity due table is not available, is to determine the future table value of an ordinary annuity for **one more rent** (i.e., n + 1) than the number of rents specified in the annuity problem, and then subtract 1.0 from that table value. The effect of this is to add one more period of compound interest while keeping the rents the same. This procedure frequently is expressed as: (n + 1 rents) − 1.0. If the **present value of an annuity due** is needed, the relationships are essentially the opposite; thus, the procedure is: (n + 1 rents) + 1.0. Calculators often are programmed to compute both ordinary annuity and annuity due.

Exhibit 5–2
Future value of ordinary annuity distinguished from future value of annuity due.

Panel A - Future of Ordinary Annuity and Annuity Due Illustrated:

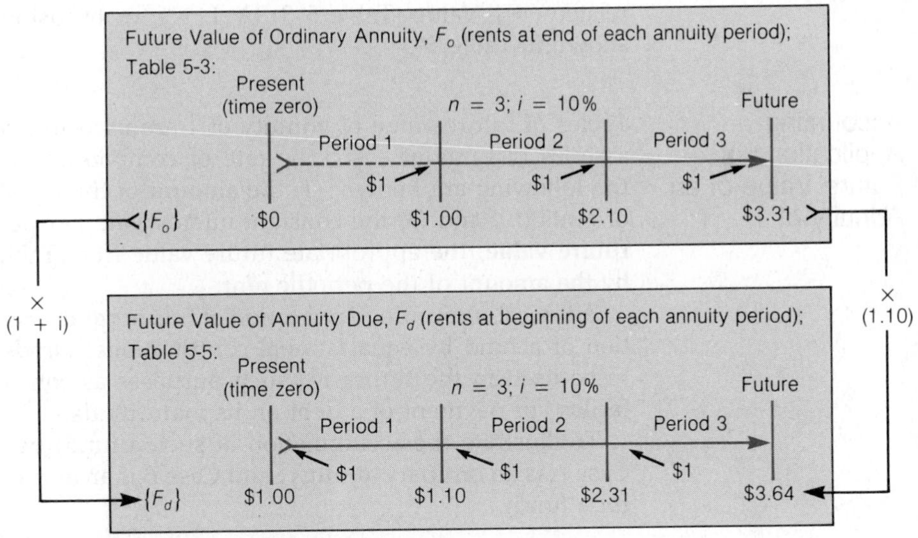

Panel B - Future Value of Ordinary Annuity and Annuity Due Differentiated:

	Type of Future Value Annuity	
Characteristic	F_o - Ordinary	F_d - Due
1. Timing of each rent	End of each period	Beginning of each period
2. Number of rents (n)	Three } n = 3	Three } n = 3
3. Number of compounding periods (i)	Two } i = 2	Three } i = 3
4. Point in time of the future value	On date of last rent	One compounding period after the last rent

Rent*	×	Table value, "f"	=	F_0
1		(n = 2; i = 10%) = 1.210	=	1.210
1		(n = 1; i = 10%) = 1.100	=	1.100
1		(n = 0; i = 10%) = 1.00	=	1.000
F_0—future value of ordinary annuity				$3.310

* Notice that the first rent is compounded for two periods, the second rent for one period, and the third rent for zero periods because the rents are at the **end** of each period.

2. By formula:

$$F_0 = \frac{(1+i)^n - 1}{i} = \frac{(1+.10)^3}{.10} = \frac{.33100}{.10} = 3.310$$

3. By using a prepared FV table of ordinary annuities: Table 5–3, (n = 3; i = 10%) = 3.310, as of the date of the third and last rent.

4. Pocket calculator programmed for annuities:

Input: n = 3; i = 10%, pmt. $1; press FV = 3.310

For all practical purposes, the last two approaches should be used.

The future value of an **annuity due** can be determined by: multiplying the related "F_0" value (Table 5–3) by $1 + i$, or by using an annuity due table as shown in Table 5–5.

Accounting Applications of Future Value of an Annuity of 1

Tables of future value of annuity of 1 are used to calculate the future value of a series of rents at a specific rate of compound interest. In most situations, the following are known: (1) the amount of the equal rent (R), (2) the number of rents (n), and (3) the constant interest rate per period (i). To determine the **future value,** the appropriate future value from Table 5–3 or 5–5 is multiplied by the amount of the periodic rent.

A typical accounting application of future value of an annuity is the accumulation of a fund by equal annual contributions. Funds typically are established to be used in the future for such purposes as construction or expansion of a facility, or payment of a debt on its maturity date.

To illustrate the accumulation of such a fund, two cases will be presented. Case A is an ordinary annuity, and Case B is an annuity due (the usual situation for a fund).

Case A. On April 1, 19A, AB Company decided to accumulate a **fund** to pay a debt that matures on March 31, 19D. The company decided to deposit $10,000 cash in this debt retirement fund each March 31, 19B, 19C, and 19D. The fund will earn 10% compound interest which will be added to the fund balance on March 31, 19C, and 19D. The company's accounting period ends December 31. Notice that the debt matures on the date of the last deposit, which is when the annuity terminates.

Required:

1. Is this an ordinary annuity or an annuity due?

   This is an ordinary annuity because the rents are deposited at the **end** of each of the three annuity periods. This is evident because the **last rent is deposited on the last day that the annuity is in existence**—March 31, 19D.

   The time line for this **ordinary annuity** is:

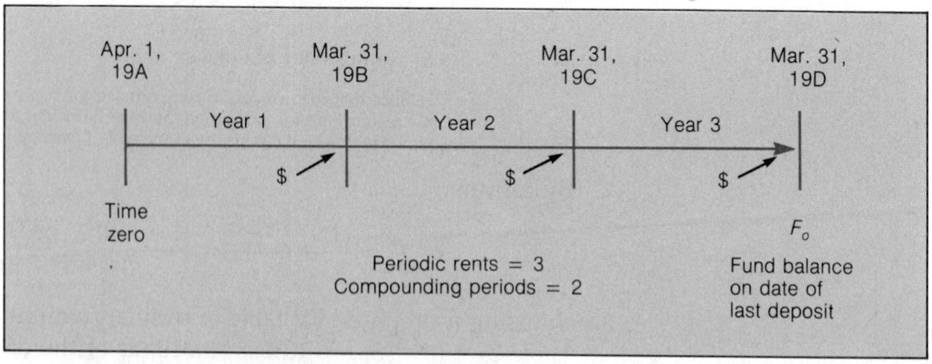

2. What amount will be in the fund at the end of the annuity's existence?

$$\$10{,}000 \times F_{0_{n=3;\,i=10\%}} \text{ (Table 5–3, 3.31000)} = \underline{\underline{\$33{,}100}}$$

3. Prepare the fund accumulation schedule.

Case A: Fund Accumulation Schedule—Ordinary Annuity

Month and annuity year	Cash deposit	Interest revenue	Fund Change	Fund Balance
March 31, 19B	$10,000		+$10,000	$10,000
March 31, 19C	10,000	$10,000 × 10% = $1,000	+ 11,000	21,000
March 31, 19D	10,000	21,000 × 10% = 2,100	+ 12,100	33,100*
Totals	$30,000	$3,100	$33,100	

* Ordinary annuity balance, which is as of the date of the last deposit.

4. Give the journal entries required at each year-end, March 31.

	19B		19C		19D	
Debt retirement fund	10,000		11,000		12,100	
Cash		10,000		10,000		10,000
Interest revenue				1,000		2,100

5. Give the journal entry to record withdrawal of the fund balance on March 31, 19D.

Cash (or debt retired)	33,100	
Debt retirement fund		33,100

Case B. Assume the same facts as in Case A, except that the annual deposits are made at the beginning of each interim annuity period on April 1, 19A, 19B, and 19C.

Required:

1. Is this an ordinary annuity or an annuity due?
   This is an annuity due because the rents are deposited at the **beginning** of each of the three annuity periods. This is evident because the last rent is deposited one interest or compounding period **prior** to the date on which the annuity ceases to exist, March 31, 19D.

The time line for this **annuity due** is:

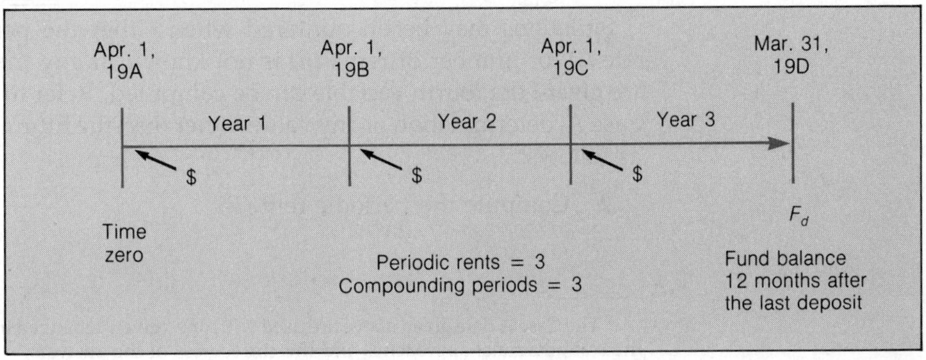

2. What amount will be in the fund at the end of the annuity's existence?

$$\$10{,}000 \times F_{d_{n=3;\,i=10\%}} \text{ (Table 5–5, 3.64100)} = \underline{\underline{\$36{,}410}}.$$

3. Prepare the fund accumulation schedule.

Case B: Fund Accumulation Schedule—Annuity Due

Month and annuity year	Cash deposit	Interest revenue	Fund: Change	Fund: Balance
April 1, 19A	$10,000		+$10,000	$10,000
March 31, 19B		$10,000 × 10% = $1,000	+ 1,000	11,000
April 1, 19B	10,000		+ 10,000	21,000
March 31, 19C		21,000 × 10% = 2,100	+ 2,100	23,100
April 1, 19C	10,000		+ 10,000	33,100
March 31, 19D		33,100 × 10% = 3,310	+ 3,310	36,410*
Totals	$30,000	$6,410	$36,410	

* Annuity due balance, which is 12 months after the last deposit.

4. Give the journal entries for this annuity due, for *(a)* April 1, 19A and March 31, 19B, and *(b)* March 31, 19D, when the fund balance is withdrawn.

	Debit	Credit
a. April 1, 19A:		
Debt retirement fund	10,000	
Cash		10,000
March 31, 19B:		
Debt retirement fund	1,000	
Interest revenue		1,000
b. March 31, 19D (maturity date):		
Debt retirement fund	3,310	
Interest revenue		3,310
Cash (or debt retired)	36,410	
Debt retirement fund		36,410

Determination of Other Values Related to Future Value of an Ordinary Annuity

In the preceding example—Case A, ordinary annuity—**three** values were given: (1) periodic rent, $R = \$10{,}000$; (2) number of periodic rents, $n = 3$; and (3) periodic interest rate, $i = 10\%$. A fourth value, future value of an ordinary annuity was unknown; however, it was computed as follows:

1. $\$10{,}000 \times F_{o_{n=3;\,i=10\%}}$ (Table 5–3, 3.31000) = $\underline{\underline{\$33{,}100}}$.

Situations may be encountered when either the periodic rent *(R)*, interest rate *(i)*, or number of rents *(n)* is not known. If any three of the four variables are given, the fourth variable can be computed. Refer to the preceding example, Case A; determination of any value (other than the future value) can be computed as follows:[7]

2. Compute the periodic rent *(R)*:

[7] The Case A data given above are used with one "given" changed in each instance to demonstrate the computational approaches and the correctness of the answers.

Given: future value of ordinary annuity, \$33,100; $n = 3$; $i = 10\%$.

$$R = \$33,100 \div F_{O_{n=3;\,i=10\%}} \text{ (Table 5–3, 3.310)} = \underline{\underline{\$10,000}}.$$

3. Compute the periodic interest rate (i):

   Given: future value of ordinary annuity, \$33,100; rent, \$10,000; and $n = 3$.

   $$\$33,100 \div \$10,000 = 3.310, \text{ the Table 5–3 value for } n = 3.$$

   Reference to the Table 5–3 **line** for $n = 3$ indicates a periodic interest rate of $\underline{\underline{10\%}}$. See the discussion below for an **annuity due.**

4. Compute the number of rents (n):

   Given: future value of an ordinary annuity, \$33,100; rent, \$10,000; and $i = 10\%$.

   $$\$33,100 \div \$10,000 = 3.310, \text{ the Table 5–3 value for } i = 10\%.$$

   Reference to the Table 5–3 **column** for $i = 10\%$ indicates the number of rents to be 3. If this were an **annuity due,** the annuity due amount given in Exhibit 5–5 would be used in the above computations.

Present Value of an Annuity of 1

The present value of an annuity, designated ***P*** herein, is the sum of all of the periodic rents **minus** the accumulated compound **discount** on each of those rents. The formula for the present value of an ordinary annuity is:

$$P_0 = \frac{1 - \dfrac{1}{(1+i)^n}}{i}$$

If the rents are at the end of each annuity period, its present value is an ordinary annuity. If the rents are at the **beginning** of each annuity period, its present value is an annuity due. The difference between these two annuities is one period's compound discount because the timing of their respective rents is different by one compounding or interest period.

Exhibit 5–3 shows two time lines and compares the present value of an ordinary annuity with an annuity due of \$1 at 10%. The symbol P_o is used to designate the present value of an **ordinary annuity** and P_d designates an **annuity due.** Panel B of Exhibit 5–3 identifies the four differences between P_o and P_d annuities.

Because of the difference in the timing of the periodic rents, the value of the **ordinary annuity** illustrated in Exhibit 5–3 involves **three rents and three discounting periods.** In contrast, **the annuity due involves three rents but only two discounting periods.** The annuity due is discounted for one less period than the ordinary annuity, which means that the ordinary annuity amount will be less than the comparable annuity due amount by $(1 + i)$; therefore, $P_o \times (1 + i) = P_d$. This relationship means that if a P_o value is known, it can be multiplied by $(1 + i)$ to determine its comparable P_d value. Table 5–4 gives the present value amounts for an ordinary annuity, and Table 5–6 gives the comparable annuity due amounts.

Determination of the Present Value of an Annuity

The present value of an ordinary annuity can be determined by (1) successive discounting (using Table 5–2, ***p*** values), (2) formula (given above), (3) using a prepared present value of annuity of 1 table, such as Table 5–4, or (4) a PV-programmed calculator.

The present value of an annuity due usually is determined by multiplying the related "P_o" value (Table 5–4) by $(1 + i)$, or by using an annuity due table as shown in Table 5–6.

Accounting Applications of Present Value of an Annuity of 1

Tables of present value of an annuity of 1 are used to calculate the present value of a series of future rents at a specific compound discount rate. In most cases, the following variables are known: (1) the amount of each equal rent (R), (2) the number of rents (n), and (3) the constant rate of interest per discounting period (i). To determine the **present value** in a specific situation, the appropriate present value factor from Table 5–4 or 5–6 is multiplied by the amount of the periodic rent.

Exhibit 5–3
Present value of ordinary annuity distinguished from present value of annuity due.

Panel A - Present Value of Ordinary Annuity and Annuity Due Illustrated:

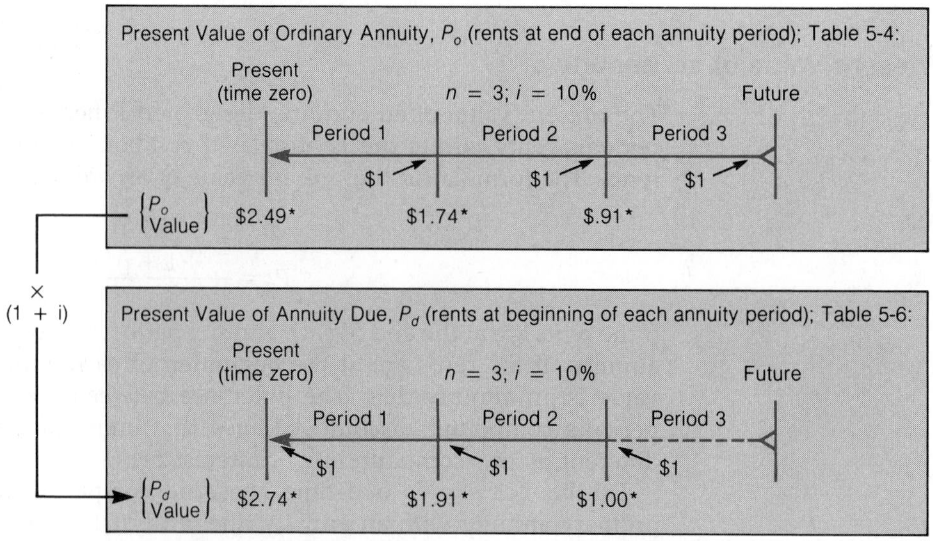

*Present values of the annuity on the date indicated.

Panel B - Present Value of Ordinary Annuity and Annuity Due Differentiated:

	Type of Present Value Annuity	
Characteristic	P_o - Ordinary	P_d - Due
1. Timing of each rent	End of each annuity period	Beginning of each annuity period
2. Number of rents (n)	Three $n = 3$	Three $n = 3$
3. Number of discounting periods (i)	Three $i = 3$	Two $i = 2$
4. Point in time of the first rent	End of first discounting period	Present date

An accounting application of the present value of an annuity is the payment of a debt (e.g., incurred to purchase an asset on credit) in equal future installments (i.e., an annuity).

To illustrate such a situation, two cases will be presented. Case C is an ordinary annuity, and Case D is an annuity due.

Case C. On April 1, 19A, CD Company owed a $15,000 liability (a present value amount). Because of CD's cash flows problem, the creditor agreed to allow CD Company to pay the debt in three equal installments at 10% compound interest. The payments of $6,032 are payable March 31, 19B, 19C, and 19D.

Required:

1. Is this an ordinary annuity or an annuity due? Explain.
   This is an ordinary annuity because the three rents are payable at the year-end during the three-year extended credit period. The first payment is to be made 12 months after the debt payment was extended.

   The time line for this ordinary annuity is:

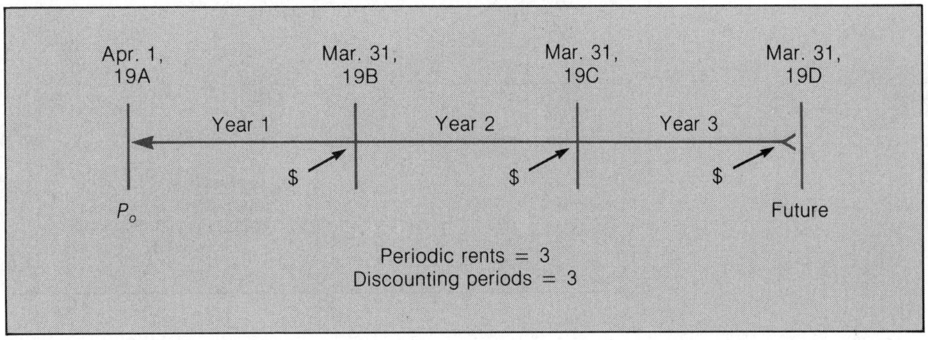

2. What is the present value of the three rents?

   $\$6{,}032 \times P_{o\,n=3;\,i=10\%}$ (Table 5–4, 2.48685) = $15,000.

3. How was the amount of each equal annual payment computed?

   $\$15{,}000 \div P_{o\,n=3;\,i=10\%}$ (Table 5–4, 2.48685) = $6,032.

4. Prepare the debt payment schedule.

Case C: Debt Payment Schedule—Ordinary Annuity

Month and annuity year	Cash payment	Interest expense	Liability Change	Liability Balance
April 1, 19A				$15,000
March 31, 19B . . .	$ 6,032	$15,000 × 10% = $1,500	−$ 4,532	10,468
March 31, 19C . . .	6,032	10,468 × 10% = 1,047	− 4,985	5,483
March 31, 19D . . .	6,032	5,483 × 10% = 549*	− 5,483	-0-
Totals	$18,096	$3,096	$15,000	

* Rounded to come out even.

5. Give the entries required on each March 31.

	19B		19C		19D	
Interest expense	1,500		1,047		549	
Liability	4,532		4,985		5,483	
Cash		6,032		6,032		6,032

Case D. Assume the same facts as in Case C, except that three equal annual payments of $5,483 are to be made on each April 1, years 19A, 19B, and 19C.

Required:

1. Is this an ordinary annuity or an annuity due? Explain.
   This is an annuity due because the rents are payable at the beginning of each year; the first payment is paid immediately.

   The time line for this annuity due is:

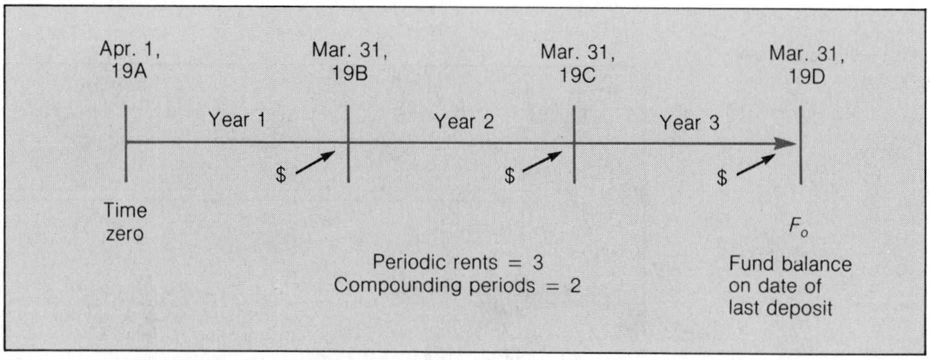

2. What is the present value of the three rents?

   $\$5,483 \times P_{d_{n=3;\, i=10\%}}$ (Table 5–6, 2.73554) = $15,000.

3. How was the amount of each equal annual payment computed?

   $\$15,000 \div P_{d_{n=3;\, i=10\%}}$ (Table 5–6, 2.73554) = $5,483

4. Prepare the debt payment schedule.

Case D: Debt Payment Schedule—Annuity Due

Date	Cash payment	Interest expense	Liability Change	Liability Balance
April 1, 19A				$15,000
April 1, 19A	$ 5,483		−$ 5,483	9,517
March 31, 19B . . .		$9,517 × 10% = $ 952	+ 952	10,469
April 1, 19B	5,483		− 5,483	4,986
March 31, 19C . . .		4,986 × 10% = 497*	+ 497	5,483
April 1, 19C	5,483		− 5,483	-0-
Totals	$16,449	$1,449	$15,000	

* Rounded to come out even.

5. Give the entries required on each April 1 and March 31.

April 1:	19A		19B		19C	
Liability	5,483		5,483		5,483	
Cash		5,483		5,483		5,483
March 31:			**19B**		**19C**	
Interest expense			952		497	
Liability				952		497

Determination of Other Values Related to an Annuity Due

Determination of an implicit interest rate for an annuity due is done the same way as for an ordinary annuity (see page 192). To illustrate, assume an overdue debt of $83,398 will be paid in five equal installments of $20,000 each. The first payment is to be paid immediately; therefore, this involves the **PV of an annuity due.** What is the implicit compound interest rate?

Solution:

$83,398 ÷ $20,000 = 4.1699, table value for PV of an annuity due, $n = 5; i = ?$

Reference to Table 5–6 for line $n = 5$ indicates a periodic interest rate of approximately 10% (read footnote 4).

Proof: $20,000 × $P_{d_{n=5;i=10\%}}$ (Table 5–6, 4.16987) = $83,398 (rounded).

Using Multiple Present and Future Value Amounts

There are cases that require the application of two or more future or present value amounts (i.e., table values for f, p, F, and P). Problems that use two or more of these values require a careful analysis of the situation and a precise knowledge of what each "table" value means.

Two situations are given below, with solutions, to illustrate the application of multiple future and present values.

Situation 1—On January 1, 19A, TG Company deposited $100,000 in a special fund to provide five annual equal payments in the future to Employee Doe who was injured while working. The fund will earn 11%, which will increase the fund starting on December 31, 19A. Doe is to receive the five annual payments each January 1, starting in 19E, the year in which Doe will retire.

Required:
1. Compute the amount of the annual payments that Doe will receive.
2. Prepare a fund schedule for the period January 1, 19A, through January 1, 19I.

Solution:
Requirement 1 (diagrammed for instructional purposes and computation):

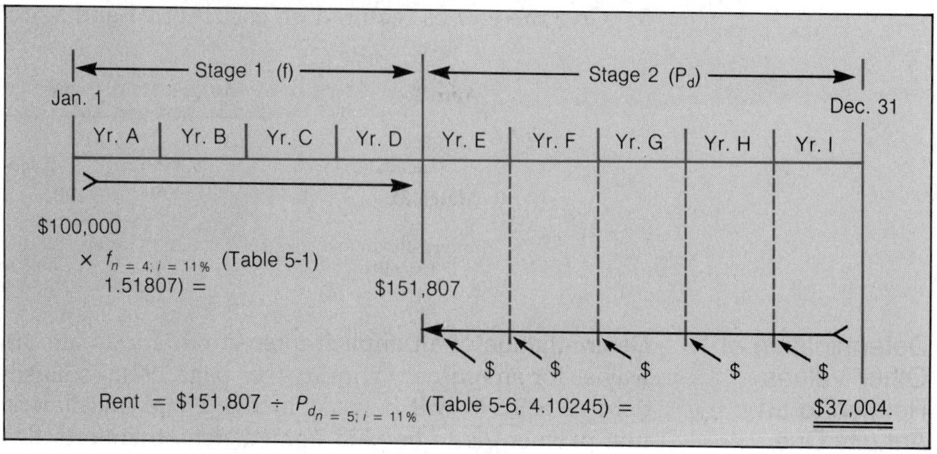

Requirement 2:

Fund Schedule

Date	Interest revenue	Fund change	Fund balance
January 1, 19A	Single deposit	+$100,000	$100,000
December 31, 19A . .	$100,000 × 11% = $11,000	+ 11,000	111,000
December 31, 19B . . .	$111,000 × 11% = 12,210	+ 12,210	123,210
December 31, 19C . .	$123,210 × 11% = 13,553	+ 13,553	136,763
December 31, 19D . .	$136,763 × 11% = 15,044	+ 15,044	151,807
January 1, 19E	Payment	− 37,004	114,803
December 31, 19E . . .	$114,803 × 11% = 12,628	+ 12,628	127,431
January 1, 19F	Payment	− 37,004	90,427
December 31, 19F . . .	$ 90,427 × 11% = 9,947	+ 9,947	100,374
January 1, 19G	Payment	− 37,004	63,370
December 31, 19G . .	$ 63,370 × 11% = 6,971	+ 6,971	70,341
January 1, 19H	Payment	− 37,004	33,337
December 31, 19H . .	$ 33,337 × 11% = 3,667	+ 3,667	37,004
January 1, 19I	Payment	− 37,004	-0-

Situation 2—ST Construction Company is negotiating to purchase 4 acres of land with a deposit of gravel that is suitable for exploitation. ST Company and the seller are negotiating the price. ST Company has completed an extensive study that provided reliable estimates as follows:

Expected net cash revenues over life of resource:	
End of year 1	$ 5,000
End of years 2–5 (per year)	30,000
End of years 6–9 (per year)	40,000
End of year 10 (last year—resource exhausted)	10,000
Estimated sales value of 4 acres after exploitation and net of land-leveling costs (end of 10th year)	2,000

Required:

Compute the amount ST Construction Company should offer for the land assuming it expects a 12 percent return on the investment. Assume all amounts are at year-end and that the above amounts are net of income taxes.

Solution:

This problem requires computation of the present value of the futute expected cash inflows.

The amount that should be offered is the sum of the present values of the net cash revenues for the various years. The complexity in this situation arises because *(a)* $5,000 for year 1, $10,000 for year 10, and the $2,000 estimated value at the end of year 10 involve use of the present value of 1 concept; and *(b)* the equal amount revenues for years 2–5 and 6–9 involve the use of the present value of two different annuities.

Complex situations such as this one demonstrate the need to diagram most future and present value situations in terms of *(a)* the timing of the resource flows (rents), *(b)* the interest assumptions, and *(c)* the value to be derived. Moveover, this problem also illustrates the three basic decisions that must be made to solve all future and present value problems:

1. Identification of whether the situation involves future value or present value concepts.
2. Identification of whether the situation involves a single sum or an annuity. Situations often involve single sums and annuities in combination.
3. If the situation involves an annuity, do the rents occur at the end of each annuity period (an ordinary annuity) or at the beginning of each period (an annuity due)? Situations may involve ordinary annuities and annuities due in combination.

For ST Company the primary focus is on **present value** because estimated future cash inflows are provided and the amount that the company should be willing to pay is the present value of those future expected cash inflows. Because equal future cash inflows are expected for years 2–5 and 6–9, two annuities are involved. Because these two cash inflows are assumed to be at year-end, the annuities are ordinary.

Because of its complexities, this problem is best solved in two steps, one for each element in the solution, as follows:

Step 1—Prepare a time-line diagram, which reveals the *(a)* timing of the resource flows, *(b)* interst assumption, and *(c)* value to be derived. A time-line diagram of this situation can be drawn as follows (amounts in thousands of dollars):

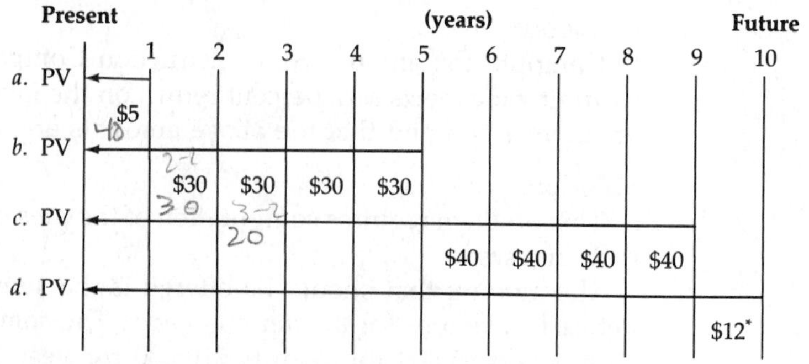

Σ PV = offering price; value to be derived.

* $10 + $2 = $12.

Step 2—Compute the present values of each annuity and single-sum amounts in order:

PV item	Computation	Present value
a.	Year 1—PV of a single sum:	
	\$5,000 × $p_{n=1;i=12\%}$ (Table 5–2, .89286)	\$ 4,464
b.	Years 2–5—PV of ordinary annuity, deferred one year:	
	\$30,000 × ($P_{o_{n=5;i=12\%}} - P_{o_{n=1;i=12\%}}$)[(Table 5–4) 3.60478($n$ = 5) − .89286(n = 1) = 2.71192]	81,358
c.	Years 6–9—PV of ordinary annuity, deferred 5 years:	
	\$40,000 × ($P_{o_{n=9;i=12\%}} - P_{o_{n=5;i=12\%}}$)[(Table 5–4) 5.32825($n$ = 9) − 3.60478 (n = 5) = 1.72347]	68,939
d.	Year 10—PV of a single sum:	
	(\$10,000 + \$2,000) × $p_{n=10;i=12\%}$ (Table 5–2, .32197)	3,864
	Offering price (PV of all future cash flows)	\$158,625

Summary

This chapter presented the concepts of future and present value. It illustrated their relevance in certain accounting problems. At the beginning of the chapter, the primary accounting applications were listed. Those applications often are required to conform to GAAP. Because of the wide range of accounting applications, accountants need a thorough understanding of FV and PV concepts. These concepts also have considerable relevance in financial analyses, capital budgeting, and alternative choice problems which accountants often encounter in public, private, and governmental accounting. Throughout the later chapters, and in subsequent business administration courses, the concepts of present and future value are widely used.[8]

A summary of the interest concepts discussed in this chapter is presented on page 201.

---

[8] The discussion of present and future value is in Chapter 5 because it is primarily for review purposes. However, when the quarter system is used it often is deferred to follow Chapter 9. In this way the first quarter ends with the chapter on inventories completed. This change does not affect coordination among the topics and homework in any manner.

Summary of interest concepts.

Title	Symbol	Basic concept summarized	Formula	Table	Illustrative table values: $n = 5; i = 10\%$	Illustrative table values: $n = 6; i = 10\%$
Simple interest	i	Interest on principal only, regardless of any prior accrued interest.	$P \times i \times n$	—	—	—
FV of 1	f	FV of a single principal amount increased by compound interest i for n periods.	$(1 + i)^n$	5–1	1.61051 (always more than 1)	1.77156 (more by compound i for 1 period)
PV of 1	p	PV of a single principal amount decreased by compound discount i for n periods. A reciprocal of FV of 1.	$\frac{1}{(1 + i)^n}$	5–2	.62092 (always less than 1)	.56447 (less by i discount for 1 period)
FV of annuity of 1:						
Ordinary annuity	F_0	FV of a series of n equal **end-of-period** rents at compound interest i. One less compounding period than rents.	$\frac{(1 + i)^n - 1}{i}$	5–3	6.10510 (always more than sum of rents)	7.71561 (more by 1 rent, plus compound interest for 1 period)
Annuity due	F_d	FV of a n series of equal **beginning-of-period** rents at compound interest i. Same number of compounding periods as rents.	$\frac{(1 + i)^n - 1}{i} \times (1 + i)$	5–5	6.71561 or (6.10510 × 1.10)	8.48717 or (7.71561 × 1.10)
PV of annuity of 1:						
Ordinary annuity	P_o	PV of a series of n equal **end-of-period** rents in the future decreased at compound discount i. Same number of discounting periods as rents.	$\frac{1 - \frac{1}{(1 + i)^n}}{i}$	5–4	3.79079 (always less than sum of rents)	4.35526 (more by 1 rent, less discount for 1 period)
Annuity due	P_d	PV of a series of n equal **beginning-of-period** rents in the future decreased at compound discount i. One less discounting period than rents.	$\frac{1 - \frac{1}{(1 + i)^n}}{i} \times (1 + i)$	5–6	4.16987 or (3.79079 × 1.10)	4.79079 or (4.35526 × 1.10)

QUESTIONS

Part A

1. Explain what is meant by the time value of money.
2. Assuming the annual rate of interest is specified as 9%, what would simple interest rates be for the following periods: *(a)* semiannual, *(b)* quarterly, and *(c)* monthly?
3. What is the fundamental difference between simple interest and compound interest?
4. Briefly explain each of the following:
   a. Future value of 1.
   b. Present value of 1.

c. Future value of annuity of n rents of 1 each.
d. Present value of annuity of n rents of 1 each.

5. Assume $6,000 is borrowed on a two-year, 15% note payable. Compute the total amount of interest that would be paid on this note assuming *(a)* simple interest and *(b)* compound interest.
6. Match columns 2 and 3 with column 1 by entering the appropriate letter from column 1:

Column 1	Column 2	Column 3
A. Future value of 1.	F_0 ______	$\frac{1}{(1+i)^n}$ ______
B. Present value of 1.	P_0 ______	$(1+i)^n$ ______
C. Future value of an ordinary annuity of 1.	p ______	$\frac{1-\frac{1}{(1+i)^n}}{i}$ ______
	f ______	
D. Present value of an ordinary annuity of 1.		$\frac{(1+i)^n-1}{i}$ ______

7. Match the following by entering the appropriate letter (n and i are the same for each value):

A. Future value of 1.	17.51851 ________
B. Present value of 1.	4.60654 ________
C. Future value of annuity of 1 (ordinary).	.26295 ________
D. Present value of annuity of 1 (ordinary).	3.80296 ________
E. Future value of annuity of 1 (due).	20.32147 ________
F. Present value of annuity of 1 (due).	5.34359 ________

8. Contrast a future value of 1 with a present value of 1.
9. The future value of 1 at 13% interest for 15 years is 6.25427. *(a)* What is the present value of 1 in this situation? *(b)* If the present value of 1 at 17% interest for 12 years is .15197, what is the future value of 1 at 17% for 12 years?
10. *(a)* If the table value for a future value of 1 is known, how may it be converted to the table value for present value of 1? *(b)* Show the computations to convert the following future values of 1 to the equivalent present values of 1 as follows: 1.46933; 3.18547; and 216.54199.
11. If $10,000 is deposited in a savings account at 8% compound interest, what would be the balance in the savings account at the end of *(a)* 9 years? *(b)* 15 years? *(c)* 25 years?
12. Assume you have a legal contract which specifies that you will receive $150,000 cash in the future. Assuming a 9% interest rate, what would be the present value of that contract if the amount will be received: *(a)* 7 years, *(b)* 15 years, or *(c)* 24 years from now?
13. Assume you deposited $10,000 in a savings account for a three-year period. How much cash would you receive at the end if 8% simple interest per annum is accumulated in the fund at the end of each quarter?
14. Assume you will receive $50,000 cash from a trust fund six years from now. What is the present value of the $50,000 assuming 8% interest on a quarterly basis?

Part B

15. What are the three characteristics of an annuity? Explain what would happen if any of these characteristics are changed.
16. Table 5–3 gives a future value of an ordinary annuity of 1 of 3.09 (rounded) for $n = 3$; $i = 3\%$. Explain the meaning of this table value.
17. If \$10,000 is deposited in a savings account at the end of each of n annual periods and will earn 9%, what would be the balance in the savings account at the date of the last deposit (i.e., an ordinary annuity), assuming $n = 7$ years, 15 years, and 24 years?
18. Explain the difference between *(a)* future value of an ordinary annuity and *(b)* future value of an annuity due.
19. Explain the difference between *(a)* present value of an ordinary annuity and *(b)* present value of an annuity due.
20. Compute the present value of an annuity of five rents of \$6,000 each using an 8% interest rate, assuming *(a)* an ordinary annuity and *(b)* an annuity due. Explain why the two amounts are different.
21. Compute the future value of an annuity of six rents of \$4,000 each using an 8% interest rate, assuming *(a)* an ordinary annuity and *(b)* an annuity due. Explain why the two amounts are different.
22. XR Company will create a building fund by contributing \$15,000 per year to it for 10 years; the fund will be increased each year at a 7% compound interest rate. Assume the current year is 19A. *(a)* Explain how you would determine whether this situation is an ordinary annuity or an annuity due. *(b)* In each instance, how many rents and compounding periods would be involved?
23. If an annuity value of 1 is computed by formula or read from an annuity table, explain the implicit dates for both a future value and present value, assuming *(a)* an ordinary annuity and *(b)* an annuity due.
24. J. Blow purchased a Mercedes with a cash "bargain" price of \$40,000. Cash of \$10,000 was paid at purchase date and the remainder was paid in eight quarterly payments (ordinary annuity) of \$4,274 each. The "going" rate of annual interest used for this deal was 12%. How much did JB pay for the auto, excluding interest? How much interest did JB pay?

EXERCISES

Part A: Exercises 5–1 to 5–14

E 5–1 **(Compounding for Periods Less than One Year)**
Rox Company plans to deposit \$60,000 today into a special building fund that will be needed at the end of 5 years. A financial institution will serve as the fund trustee and will pay 8% interest on the fund balance.

Required:
Compute the fund balance at the end of year 6, assuming:

Case A—Annual compounding.

Case B—Semiannual compounding.

Case C—Quarterly compounding.

E 5–2 (Compounding for Periods Less than One Year)
The two situations below are independent.

1. Rice Company will need about $300,000 cash to renovate some old equipment four years from now. A local financial institution will increase a fund at 8% annual interest. Compute the amount of cash that would have to be deposited now to meet the future need, assuming (show computations):

   Case A—Annual compounding.

   Case B—Semiannual compounding.

   Case C—Quarterly compounding.

2. On January 1, 19A, BR Company has a contract whereby the company is due to receive $70,000 cash on December 31, 19F. The company is short of cash and desires to discount (sell) this claim. WT is willing to accept a 7% annual discount. Under these conditions, how much cash would BR receive on January 1, 19A?

E 5–3 (Compounding for Periods Less than One Year)
Each of the following situations is independent.

1. You invested $10,000 in a savings account at 8% compound interest. What balance would be in your savings account at the end of five years assuming:
   a. Annual compounding?
   b. Semiannual compounding?
   c. Quarterly compounding?
   Explain why these amounts are different.
2. You have agreed to accumulate a fund of $40,000 at the end of six years by making a single deposit now. The fund will earn 8% compound interest. What amount must you deposit now to accumulate the $40,000 fund assuming:
   a. Annual compounding?
   b. Semiannual compounding?
   c. Quarterly compounding?
   Explain why these amounts are different.

E 5–4 (Present Value; Fund Accumulation; Schedule)
Each of the following situations is independent.

1. KA Corporation plans a plant expansion that will require approximately $300,000 at December 31, 19C. Because it has some idle cash on hand now, January 1, 19A, it desires to know how much it would have to invest as a lump sum now to accumulate the required amount, assuming 9% annual compound interest is added to the fund each December 31.

   Required:
   a. Compute the amount that must be invested on January 1, 19A.
   b. Prepare an accumulation schedule for the plant expansion fund.
2. On January 1, 19A, KA Corporation signed a noninterest-bearing $200,000 note that is due on December 31, 19D (the $200,000 includes both principal and interest). According to the agreement, KA has the option to pay the $200,000 at maturity date or to pay the obligation in full on January 1, 19A, with a 12% compound interest discount. What would be the amount of cash required on January 1, 19A, to settle the debt in full under the early payment option?

E 5–5 **(Fund Accumulation; Schedule; Entries)**
Small Company has on hand $150,000 cash that will not be needed in the near future. However, the company will expand operations within the next three to five years. The company has decided to establish a savings account locally which will earn 10% interest compounded annually. The interest will be added to the fund each year. The deposit of $150,000 is made on January 1, 19A.

Required:
1. Compute the balance in the fund at the end of year 3.
2. Prepare a fund accumulation schedule.
3. Give the journal entries for the fund for 19A.

E 5–6 **(Fund Accumulation; Schedule; Entries)**
B. Ball has a small child. Ball has decided to set up a fund to provide for the child's college education. A local financial institution will handle the fund and increase it each year on a 10% annual compound interest basis. Ball desires to make a single deposit on January 1, 19A, and specifies that the fund must have a $90,000 balance at the end of the 16th year.

Required:
1. Compute the amount of cash that must be deposited on January 1, 19A.
2. Prepare a fund accumulation schedule through December 31, 19C (three years).
3. Give the journal entries for the fund for 19A.

E 5–7 **(PV; Acquisition of Equipment; Cost; Debt Schedule; Entries)**
AC Company purchased some additional equipment that was needed because of a new contract. The equipment was purchased on January 1, 19A. Because the contract would require two years to complete and AC was short of cash, the vendor agreed to accept a down payment of $10,000 and a two-year, noninterest-bearing note for $45,000 (this amount includes the principal and all interest) due December 31, 19B. Assume the going rate of interest for this debt was 20% because of the extremely high risk.

Required:
1. Compute the cost of the equipment. Show computations.
2. Give the entry at date of acquisition of the equipment.
3. Prepare a debt payment schedule.
4. Give all additional entries related to the debt.

E 5–8 **(Savings Account; Simple and Compound Interest Compared)**
Assume you deposit $30,000 in a special savings account on January 1, 19A; the interest rate is 9%.

Required:
1. Compute the balance in the savings account at the end of 19E, assuming *(a)* simple interest and *(b)* compound interest.
2. Calculate and explain the cause of the difference.

E 5–9 **(Fund Accumulation; Interest Rate or Time Unknown)**
The two following cases are independent.

1. BR Company, at the present date, has $40,000 which will be deposited in a savings account until needed. It is anticipated that $111,000 will be needed at the end of

nine years to expand some manufacturing facilities. What approximate rate of interest would be required to accumulate the $111,000, assuming compounding on an annual basis? Show computations; no need to interpolate.

2. BR Company is planning an addition to its office building as soon as adequate funds can be accumulated. The company has estimated that the addition will cost approximately $250,000. At the present time $90,600 cash is on hand that will not be needed in the near future. A local savings institution will pay 7% interest (compounded annually). How many periods would be required to accumulate the $250,000? Show computations; no need to interpolate.

E 5–10 (Debt Retirement; Interest Rate Not Known)
The two following cases are independent.

1. On September 1, year 1, BX Company decided to deposit $200,000 in a debt retirement fund. The company needs $337,000 cash to pay a debt on August 31, year 5. What rate of compound interest must the fund earn to meet the cash requirement to pay the debt?
2. TV Company owes a $200,000 debt (this amount includes both principal and interest) that is payable three years from now. TV wants to pay the debt in full immediately. The creditor has agreed to settle the debt in full for $177,800 cash. What rate of compound discount is the creditor applying to the note?

E 5–11 (Compounding with Increasing Interest Rate; Compute Expected Selling Price)
The two cases that follow are independent.

1. You have decided to invest $10,000 today in a mutual fund. You anticipate leaving this investment in the fund for 12 years. The fund will be increased each year-end by specified compound interest rates as follows: years 1–4 inclusive, 8%; 5–8 inclusive, 9%; and 9–12 inclusive, 10%.
Compute the balance that will be in the fund at the end of year 12.
2. You own a special kind of property that cost $6,000 five years ago. Now you want to sell it for cash. You estimate reliably that this property will produce two net cash inflows as follows: End of year 5 from now, $120,000; and end of year 8 from now, $80,000. You deem it reasonable to use compound discounting interest rates of 6% for the $120,000 cash inflow and 10% for the $80,000 cash inflow (it is riskier to the buyer). Given these estimates, compute the approximate selling price that you should expect.

E 5–12 (Applications of Future and Present Value of 1)
Each of the following cases is independent.

1. A compound interest table (or formula) value for $n = 9$ and $i = 9\%$ is .46043. Is this a future value of 1 or a present value of 1? Explain.
2. What table value should be used to compute the balance in a fund at the end of year 11, if $100,000 is deposited at the date the fund is established, assuming 8% annual compound interest, and semiannual compounding?
3. What table value should be used to compute the present value of $50,000, assuming 8% compound interest, quarterly compounding and six years of discounting?
4. A fund is established by depositing $5,000 at compound interest; the fund will have a balance of $19,980 at the end of 18 years. What is the approximate annual rate of interest?
5. A discounted note payable of $20,000 (including both principal and interest) is due three years hence. Assuming 7% annual compound interest rate, at what amount should this debt be settled today (i.e., three years before maturity) on a cash basis?

E 5–13 **(Application of Future and Present Value of 1)**
Each of the following cases is independent.

1. Approximately how long will it take a $10,000 fund to double at 10% interest, assuming *(a)* simple interest and *(b)* compound interest?
2. A $100 utility deposit is made; the utility company must pay 5% compound interest on all such deposits. How much would the customer receive if the utility service was discontinued at the end of year 8?
3. What amount should be deposited in a savings account today, at 8% annual compound interest, to have a $30,000 balance in the account at the end of year 10?
4. On January 1, 19A, a machine is purchased with a "sticker price" of $8,000. Credit arrangements stated that the $8,000 (including any interest) is payable in full on December 31, 19B. The going rate of compound interest on this kind of credit is 15%. What was the cost of the machine?
5. VT Company owed a debt of $2,895, which is now due. Arrangements were made whereby VT can extend the debt by signing a four-year noninterest-bearing note of $6,000 (including principal and interest). What approximate rate of compound interest is implicit in the note?

E 5–14 **(Fund Balance with Changing Interest Rate)**
On January 1, 19A, you invested $10,000 cash in a special savings account. It will be increased by the compound interest each year-end. The fund will earn 6% for the first three years, 8% for the next three years, and 10% for the last four years.

Required:
Compute the balance in the fund at the end of year 10.

Part B: Exercises 5–15 to 5–25

E 5–15 **(Ordinary and Annuity Due Compared)**
United Company has decided to accumulate a fund by making equal periodic contributions. The fund will be increased each interest period by 8% compound interest. The current date is January 1, 19A.

Required:

1. Complete the following tabulation to compare an ordinary annuity with an annuity due:
   a. Ordinary (end-of-period) annuity:

Compounding	Rent	*n*	*i*	Table value	Fund balance
Annual	$5,000	5	______	______	$______
Semiannual	2,500	______	______	______	______
Quarterly	1,250	______	______	______	______

   b. Annuity due (beginning of period):

Compounding	Rent	*n*	*i*	Table value	Fund balance
Annual	$5,000	______	______	______	______
Semiannual	2,500	______	______	______	______
Quarterly	1,250	______	______	______	______

2. Explain why the ordinary annuity and annuity due fund balances are different.
3. Give the journal entry at the end of the first compounding period for each of the six situations above (indicate dates and use simple interest because of insignificant differences).

E 5–16 **(Understanding Future and Present Value Concepts)**
Complete the following table assuming $n = 7$; $i = 16\%$ for column 3 (16% is used to simplify computations):

Concept	Symbol	Formula	"Value" based on $1	Table
1. Future value of 1.	____	____	____	____
2. Present value of 1.	____	____	____	____
3. Future value of ordinary annuity of n rents of 1 each.	____	____	____	____
4. Present value of ordinary annuity of n rents of 1 each.	____	____	____	____
5. Future value of annuity due of n rents of 1 each.	____	____	____	____
6. Present value of annuity due of n rents of 1 each.	____	____	____	____

E 5–17 **(Ordinary and Annuity Due Compared; Schedules)**
The following two cases are independent.

Case 1:

On January 1, year 1, SB Company decided to create an expansion fund by making equal annual deposits of $66,000. The fund is required on December 31, year 5. Interest at 12% compounded annually will be added to the fund. Five deposits are planned. Two alternative dates are under consideration:

Alternative A—Make the annual deposits on each December 31 starting in year 1.

Alternative B—Make the annual deposits on each January 1 starting in year 1.

Required:
Complete the following schedule:

Alternative	Type of annuity	Balance in the fund at end of 19E	
		Computations	Amount
A			
B			

Case 2:

TV Company agreed on January 1, year 1, to deposit $120,000 cash with a trustee. The trustee will increase the fund on a 10% compound interest basis on the fund balance each successive year. The trustee is required to pay out the fund in 10 equal annual installments to a former employee of TV so that the fund is completely exhausted at the end of that time. Two alternative payment dates are under consideration:

Alternative A—Make the annual payments to the former employee each December 31 starting in year 1.

Alternative B—Make the annual payments to the former employee each January 1 starting in year 1.

Required:
Complete the following schedule:

Alternative	Type of annuity	Amount of the equal annual payments	
		Computations	Amount
A			
B			

E 5–18 (Fund; Ordinary Annuity; Schedule; Entries)

SEC Company has decided to accumulate a debt retirement fund by making three equal annual deposits of $22,000 on each December 31, starting at the end of 19A. Assume the fund will accumulate annual compound interest at 7% per year which will be added to the fund balance.

Required:

1. What kind of annuity is this? Why?
2. What will be the balance in the fund on December 31, 19C (immediately after the last deposit)?
3. Prepare an accumulation schedule for this fund.
4. Prepare the journal entries for the period January 1, 19A, through December 31, 19C.
5. What would be the balance in the fund on December 31, 19C, if it were set up on an annuity due basis?

E 5–19 (Debt Payment; Annuity Due; Schedule; Entries)

On September 1, 19A, Sault Company incurred a $60,000 debt. Arrangements have been made to pay this debt in three equal annual installments starting on September 1, 19A; the compound interest is 10%.

Required:

1. Is this an ordinary annuity or annuity due? Explain.
2. Compute the amount of the equal annual payments.
3. Prepare a debt payment schedule.
4. Give the journal entries related to the debt.
5. Compute the annual payment if the debt payments were made annually beginning on August 31, 19B.

E 5–20 (Debt Payment; Ordinary Annuity; Schedule; Entries)

On May 1, 19A, JSB Company owes a $90,000 debt that will be paid in three equal annual payments. The first payment is to be made on April 30, 19B. The interest rate is 10%.

Required:

1. Is this an ordinary annuity or an annuity due? Explain.
2. Compute the amount of the equal annual payments.
3. Prepare a debt payment schedule.
4. Give the journal entries related to the fund.
5. Compute the annual payment if the debt payments were made annually beginning on May 1, 19A.

E 5–21 (Debt; Annuity; Schedule; Entries)

GNU Company has decided to establish a debt retirement fund with three equal annual contributions of $15,000, starting on January 1, 19A. The fund will be increased at each year-end at 9% per annum. The $53,000 debt must be paid on December 31, 19C.

Required:

1. Is this an ordinary annuity or an annuity due? Explain.
2. What will be the balance of the fund on December 31, 19C?
3. Prepare a fund accumulation schedule.
4. Give the journal entries related to the fund.
5. What balance would be in the fund if it had been set up on an ordinary annuity basis, with the first annual contribution on December 31, 19A?

E 5–22 (Debt and Fund; Annuity; Interest Rate or Time Not Known)

The following two cases are independent.

Case 1:

Oliver Company plans to establish a debt retirement fund, beginning December 31, 19A, to accumulate $90,120. End-of-period contributions of $20,000 will be made to a trustee each December 31, so that the desired amount will be available on December 31, 19D, the date of the last rent. Compute the required interest rate that must be earned by the fund on an annual compound basis to satisfy these requirements. Show your computations to demonstrate that your answer is correct.

Case 2:

Polus Company has decided to create a plant expansion fund by making equal annual deposits of $30,000 on each January 1. Interest at 10% compounded annually will be added to the fund balance each year-end. The company wants to know how many deposits will be required to accumulate a fund of $313,077. Show your computations to demonstrate that your answer is correct.

E 5–23 (Understanding Present and Future Value Cases)

Each of the following cases is independent (interest rates selected to simplify the computations).

Case 1:

You have $50,000 in a fund that earns 10% annual compound interest. If you desire to withdraw it in five equal annual amounts, starting today (i.e., beginning of period) how much would you receive each year?

Case 2:

You will deposit $500 each semiannual period starting today (i.e., beginning of period); this savings account will earn 6% compounded each semiannual period. What will be the balance in your savings account at the end of year 10?

Case 3:

You purchased a new automobile that cost $14,000. You received a $4,000 trade-in allowance for your old auto and signed a 12% note for $10,000. The note requires eight equal quarterly payments starting at the end of the first quarter from date of purchase. What is the amount of each payment?

12,456 ÷ 2,000 = F 6.228 n=5 Approx 11%

Case 4:

You deposited $2,000 at the end of each year in a savings account for five years at compound interest. The fund had a balance of $12,456 at the date of the last deposit. What rate of interest did you earn? ord. annuity n5 i =

Case 5:

On January 1, 19A, you owed a debt of $15,131.14. An agreement was reached that you would pay the debt plus compound interest in 24 monthly installments of $800, the first payment to be made at the end of January 19A. What rate of annual interest are you paying? Monthly rate 2% 24%

E 5–24 (Funds; Single Plus Periodic Deposits)

WV Company established a construction fund on July 1, 19A, by making a single deposit of $250,000. Also, at the end of each year, starting at the end of June 19B, the company will make $20,000 deposits in the fund. The fund will earn 9% compound interest each year, which will be added to the fund balance.

Required:

1. Compute the balance that will be in the fund at the end of five years (on June 30, 19F).
2. Give the journal entries that would be made for the first year starting on July 1, 19A, and through June 30, 19B.

E 5–25 (Compute the Price of a Used Machine)

Rye Company is considering purchasing a used machine that is in excellent mechanical condition. The company plans to keep the machine for 10 years, at which time the residual value will be zero. An analysis of the capacity of the machine and the costs of operating it (including materials used in production) provided an estimate that the machine would increase aftertax net cash inflow by approximately $100,000 per year.

Required:

1. Compute the approximate amount that Rye should be willing to pay now for the machine assuming a target earnings rate of 15% per year. Assume also that the revenue is realized at each year-end. Show your computations.
2. What price should be paid assuming a $20,000 residual value at the end of the 10 years?

PROBLEMS

Part A: Problems 5–1 to 5–6

P 5–1 (Future Values; Different Compounding Periods)

Avis Company deposited $300,000 in a special expansion fund on May 1, 19A, for future use as needed. The fund will accumulate 12% compounded interest per year.

Required:

1. Complete the following table by entering, into each cell, the balance that would be in the fund at the end of the intervals indicated:

Compounding assumption	Periodic interest rate	Fund balance at end of	
		Two years	Four years
Annual			
Semiannual			
Quarterly			

2. Prepare a fund accumulation schedule based on the first cell (annual, for two years).
3. Give journal entries for the fund based on the first cell (annual, for two years).

P 5–2 (How Much to Deposit to Build a Fund; Different Compounding Periods)
Story Company anticipates that it will need $200,000 cash for an expansion in the next few years. Assume an annual compound interest rate of 8%. The company desires to make a single contribution now, January 1, 19A, so that the $200,000 will be available when needed.

Required:
1. Complete the following schedule by entering into each cell the amount that must be deposited now to meet the above specifications:

		Amount to be deposited now			
		Two years		Three years	
Compounding assumption	Interest rate	n	$	n	$
Annual	______	______	$______	______	$______
Semiannual	______	______	$______	______	$______

2. Prepare a fund accumulation schedule based on $n = 2$; $i = 8\%$.
3. Give journal entries for 19A and 19B based on $n = 2$, $i = 8\%$.

P 5–3 (Building a Fund; Three Cases; Unknown Time or Rate; Schedule)
The following three cases are independent.

Case 1:

On January 1, 19A, Investor A deposited $8,000 in a savings account that would accumulate at 8% annual compound interest for three years.

Required:
a. Compute the balance that would be in the savings account at the end of the third year.
b. Prepare a fund accumulation schedule for this case.

Case 2:

On March 1, 19A, Investor B deposited $8,000 in a savings account that would accumulate to $9,800 at the end of three years, assuming annual compound interest.

Required:
a. Compute the interest rate that would be necessary. Show computations.
b. Prepare a fund accumulation schedule for this case.

Case 3:

On September 1, 19A, Investor C deposited $7,000 in a savings account that would accumulate to $11,108, assuming 8% annual compound interest.

Required:

a. Compute the number of periods that would be necessary. Show computations.

b. Prepare a fund accumulation schedule for this case.

P 5–4 **(Fund; Compute Balances; Schedule; Entries)**

Fox Company deposited $100,000 in a special expansion fund for use in the future as needed. The fund will accumulate at 7% annual compound interest. The fund was started on March 1, 19A, and the interest will be added to the fund balance on an annual compound interest basis.

Required:

1. Compute the balance that will be in the fund at the end of 3 years, 5 years, and 10 years, respectively.
2. Prepare a fund accumulation schedule for three years.
3. Give the journal entries for Fox Company for the first three years. Disregard adjusting and closing the entries.
4. What adjusting entry would be made on December 31, 19A, assuming this is the end of the accounting period for Fox Company?

P 5–5 **(Funds; Time or Rate Unknown; Fund Balance)**

The following three cases are independent.

Case 1:

On September 1, year 1, Investor A deposited $40,000 in a savings account that was expected to accumulate $43,600 at August 31, year 1.

Required:

a. Compute the implicit compound annual interest rate.

b. What would be the balance in the fund at the end (i.e., August 31) of years 5, 10, and 20?

Case 2:

On May 1, year 1, Investor B deposited $100,000 in a savings account that would accumulate to $125,971 on April 30, year 3.

Required:

a. Compute the implicit compound annual interest rate.

b. Prepare the three-year fund accumulation schedule.

Case 3:

On October 1, year 1, Investor C deposited $10,000 in a savings account and expects the fund to have a balance of $25,000 at the end of year 10.

Required:

a. Compute the implicit interest rate. Show the interpolation that would be required to obtain the approximate interest rate to two decimal places.

b. What would be in the fund at the end of year 20? (Hint: Use calculator programmed for FV, if available; otherwise round your answer in *a.* to the nearest percent.)

P 5–6 **(Settle Old Debts with New Debt; Present and Future Values)**
NIX Company is trying to "clean up" some of its debts. On January 1, 1988, the company has savings accounts as follows:

Date established	Amount deposited (a single deposit for each)	Annual compound interest rate
1/1/77	$20,000	8%
1/1/83	30,000	10%

The outstanding debts on January 1, 1988, to be paid off are as follows:

Due date	Type of note	Face of note*
12/31/91	Noninterest bearing	$ 60,000
12/31/98	Noninterest bearing	200,000

* These amounts include both principal and all interest thereon. The amount given for each note is the single sum to be paid at maturity date.

Required:
1. Compute the amount of cash that Nix can get from the two savings accounts on January 1, 1988.
2. Compute the amount for which the two debts can be settled on January 1, 1988, assuming a going rate of interest of 18%.
3. Assuming all cash is withdrawn from the savings accounts and all payments are made on the debts, would Nix have a cash shortage or an excess? How much?

Part B: Problems 5–7 to 5–18

P 5–7 **(Annuity: Ordinary and Due Compared; Schedules; Entries)**
Alvin Company will establish a special debt retirement fund amounting to $70,000. A trustee has agreed to handle the fund and to increase it each year on a 10% annual compound interest basis. Alvin will make equal annual contributions to the fund during the years 19A through 19D.

Required:
1. Compute the amount of the required annual deposit assuming that they are made on *(a)* December 31 and *(b)* January 1. If your answers are different, explain why.
2. Prepare a fund accumulation schedule for each starting date; *(a)* and *(b)* above.
3. Give the journal entries related to each starting date for 19A through 19D. Date each entry. Hint: To save time you can use a tabulation similar to the following:

Date	Fund (debit)	Cash (credit)	Interest revenue (credit)

P 5–8 **(Special Fund; Annuity Compute; Schedule; Entries)**
Catherine Company is contemplating the accumulation of a special fund to be used for expanding sales activities into the western part of the country. It is January 1, 19A, and the fund will be needed at the beginning of 19D, according to present plans. The fund will earn 6% interest compounded annually. Annual contributions will be $50,000. The management has not yet decided whether to start the deposits on January 1, 19A, or December 31, 19A.

Required:

1. Compute the amount of the fund balance at the beginning of 19D, assuming three annual deposits are made on *(a)* January 1 and *(b)* December 31. If your answers are different, explain why.
2. Prepare a fund accumulation schedule for each starting date; *(a)* and *(b)* above.
3. Give the journal entries related to each starting date for 19A through 19C. Date each entry. *Hint:* To save time you can use a tabulation similar to the following:

Date	Fund (debit)	Cash (credit)	Interest revenue (credit)

P 5–9 **(Annuity; Debt; Schedule; Entries)**

It is January 1, 19E, and RX Company owes an $80,000 past-due debt to City Bank. The bank has agreed to permit RX to pay the debt in three equal installments, each payment to include principal and compound interest at 10%. One issue has not yet been settled. The bank desires that the first installment be paid immediately; however, because of a cash liquidity problem, RX is asking to make the first payment at year end, December 31, 19E.

Required:

1. Compute the amount of the three equal annual payments if *(a)* the first payment is on January 1, 19E, and *(b)* the first payment is on December 31, 19E. If the amounts are different, explain why.
2. Prepare a debt payment schedule for each payment.
3. Give the journal entries related to each payment date through the last payment. Hint: To save time you can use a tabulation similar to the following:

Date	Interest expense (debit)	Liability		Cash (credit)
		Debit	Credit	

P 5–10 **(Annuity; Debt; Schedule; Entries)**

Rapid Construction Company can purchase a used machine for $30,000. The machine will be needed on a new job that will continue for approximately three years. It is January 1, 19A, and the machine is needed immediately. Because of a shortage of cash, Rapid has asked the vendor for credit terms. The vendor charges 11% annual compound interest. The machine can be purchased under these terms by making three equal payments.

Required:

1. Compute the amount of the three equal payments assuming they are to be paid on *(a)* January 1, 19A, B, and C; and *(b)* December 31, 19A, B, and C. If your answers are different, explain why.
2. Prepare a debt payment schedule for *(a)* and *(b)* above.
3. Give the journal entries for *(a)* and *(b)* through 19C. Date each entry. To save time you can use a tabulation similar to the following:

Date	Interest expense (debit)	Liability		Cash (credit)
		Debit	Credit	

4. What amount should be recorded as the cost of the machine in *(a)* and *(b)* above?

P 5–11 (Annuity; Fund; Schedule)

On January 1, 19A, Wick Company agreed with its president, J. Smith, to make a single deposit immediately, to establish a fund with a trustee that will pay Smith $50,000 per year for each of the three years following retirement. Smith will retire on January 1, 19K, and the equal annual payments are to be made by the trustee each December 31 starting in 19K. The trustee will add to the fund 12% annual compound interest each year-end. The fund is to have a zero balance on December 31, 19M, immediately after the last payment to Smith.

Required:

1. Compute the single amount that Wick Company must deposit in the fund on January 1, 19A, to meet the specified payments to Smith.
2. Prepare a fund payout schedule to show the use of the fund during the payout period from January 1, 19K, through December 31, 19M. Use captions similar to the following: Date; Cash payments to Smith; Interest revenue earned on the fund; Net fund decreases, and Fund balance.
3. How much of the amount paid to Smith during the payout period was provided by interest earned during the payout period?

P 5–12 (Debt; Compute Periodic Payments; Schedule)

Richie Student is considering the purchase of a Super Sail Boat which has a cash price of $6,726. Terms can be arranged for a $2,000 cash down payment and payment of the remaining $4,726, plus interest at 15% compound interest per annum, in three equal payments. Assume purchase on January 1, 19A, and payments on each December 31 thereafter.

Required:

1. Compute the amount of each annual payment.
2. What did Richie pay for the boat? What was the total amount of interest paid?
3. Prepare a debt payment schedule using the following format:

Date	Cash payment	Interest expense	Liability	
			Decrease	Balance

4. Upon graduation (end of 19C) Richie sold the sailboat for three equal annual payments of $1,000 each; the first payment was paid on the date that the boat was transferred, January 1, 19D. Assume a 9% going rate of interest. What selling price did Richie get?

P 5–13 (Annuities Compared; Ordinary and Due; Compute)

For each of the independent cases given below, assume the interest rate is 12% and compounding is semiannual.

Case 1:

How much will accumulate by the end of six years, if $2,000 is deposited each interest period in a savings account at the *(a)* end of each period and *(b)* at the start of each period? Verify your answers, one with the other.

Case 2:

What will be the periodic payments each period on a $35,000 debt that is to be paid in semiannual installments over a four-year period, assuming compound interest, if payments are made at the *(a)* beginning of each period and *(b)* end of each period?

Case 3:

A special machine is purchased that had a list price of $38,000. Payment in full was: cash, $8,000; and five equal semiannual payments of $5,000 each. The first payment will be made at the end of the first semiannual period from purchase date. How much should be recorded in the accounts as the cost of the machine?

Case 4:

A special investment is being contemplated. This investment will produce an estimated end-of-period income of $16,000 semiannually for five years. At the end of its productive life it will have an estimated recovery value of $3,500. Determine a reasonable estimate of the value of the investment.

P 5–14 (Annuity; Debt; Computation; Entry)

Each case that follows is independent of the other.

Case 1:

On June 1, 19C, RV Company owed a $40,000 overdue debt. The bank agreed to allow payment of it over the next three years at 16% compound interest; payments to be made each quarter. Compute the periodic payments assuming *(a)* the first payment is made August 31, 19C, and *(b)* the first payment is made June 1, 19C. If you get different answers, explain why they are different.

Case 2:

RV Company rents a warehouse from Owner Jones for $12,000 annual rent, payable in advance on each January 1. RV Company proposed to sign a three-year lease and to pay the three years' rent in advance. The owner agreed to the proposal with the stipulation that the $36,000 be paid immediately (i.e., on January 1). RV Company has this proposal under consideration because it expected some discount in view of the fact that funds currently are earning about 9% per annum. Develop a counter proposal as to the amount that RV Company should pay. Give the entry that RV Company should make on January 1 to record your proposal, assuming it is accepted by Jones.

P 5–15 (Understanding Annuities; Six Cases)

Refer to the tables of future and present values given in the chapter to respond to the following independent cases (no need to interpolate):

Case 1:

XT Company deposited $12,500 cash in a fund that will increase at compound interest to $53,880 in 14 years. What is the approximate interest rate?

Case 2:

XT Company owes a $20,400 noninterest-bearing note payable, which is due several years hence. The payee (i.e., creditor) has offered to settle the note today for $5,364 cash. Compute the approximate term to maturity (in years) from today, assuming a 16% interest rate.

Case 3:

XT will deposit $5,000 in a fund at the end of each year for 20 years. Compound interest will be added to the fund at the end of each period. The balance of the fund on the date of the last deposit will be $228,810. Compute the approximate interest rate that the fund earned each year.

Case 4:

XT Company owes a $17,950 debt that is being paid in equal installments at 15% compound interest. The annual year-end payments are $4,000 each (rounded to the nearest $). Compute the number of payments that XT Company will make.

Case 5:

XT Company will deposit $4,000 in a fund at the beginning of each year for six years. Compound interest will be added to the fund each year-end. The balance in the fund at the end of year 6 will be $30,616. Compute the approximate interest rate that this fund will earn. Prove your answer.

Case 6:

XT Company owes a $20,200 debt that is being paid off in equal beginning of the year payments of $3,192 (rounded). The payments include 12% compound interest. Compute the number of payments that XT Company will make. Prove your answer.

P 5–16 (Annuity; Fund Accumulation; Fund Payout; Schedule)

Daddy Lane has a motivated daughter, Lois, who is 15 years old today. For her birthday, Lane invests $20,000 toward her college education. Lane stipulates that Lois may withdraw four equal annual amounts from the fund, the first withdrawal to be made on her 18th birthday. The savings and loan association in which Lane placed the investment will add to the fund annual compound interest at the rate of 14% at the end of each year.

Required:

1. Compute the amount of each of the four withdrawals by Lois which will completely deplete the fund on the date of the final withdrawal. Hint: Diagram the problem situation.
2. Prepare a schedule that reflects the *(a)* accumulation of the fund balance and *(b)* withdrawal period (i.e, from the 15th birthday through the 21st birthday). *Hint:* Use captions similar to the following:

			Fund	
Date	**Cash**	**Interest revenue**	**Changes**	**Balance**

P 5–17 (Compute Offering Price for Plant; Entries)

East Corporation is negotiating to purchase a plant from another company that will complement East's operations. They have just completed a careful study of the plant and have developed the following estimates:

Expected net cash inflow:	
End of years 1–5 (per year)	$50,000
End of years 6–10 (per year)	40,000
End of year 11	30,000
End of year 12	10,000
Expected net residual value at end of year 12	3,000

Required:

1. Compute the amount that East should be willing to pay for the plant assuming a 16% return on the investment. Assume all amounts are at year-end and are given net of expenses and income taxes.
2. Assume the down payment is $150,000. East will pay this, and the bank will lend East the balance at 16% per annum, payable in equal annual payments (including interest and principal) over five years. The payments will be at each year-end, starting one year after the date of purchase. Compute the amount of the equal annual payments on the loan. Compute the total interest that will be paid.
3. Give the entries (or entry) to record the purchase in (1) above, and the loan in (2) above using the amounts you computed.

4. Give entries at the end of year 1 to record *(a)* net revenue from the plant, assuming the estimate was correct, *(b)* interest expense, and *(c)* the loan payment.

P 5–18 (Overview of Future and Present Value Applications)

Compute each of the following amounts (each one is independent of the others). Round to the nearest dollar or percent.

a. On January 1, 19A, $20,000 is deposited in a fund at 8% compound interest. At the end of year 5, the fund balance will be, assuming—
(1) Annual compounding $______
(2) Semiannual compounding $______
(3) Quarterly compounding $______

b. On January 1, 19A, a machine is purchased at an invoice price of $10,000. The full purchase price is to be paid on December 31, 19E. Assuming 16% compound interest, what did the machine cost if compounding is:
(1) Annual $______
(2) Semiannual $______
(3) Quarterly $______

c. If $5,000 is deposited in a fund and it will increase to $13,598 by the end of year 13, the implicit compound interest rate is ______%.

d. If the present value of $15,000 is $5,864 at 11% compound annual discount, the number of periods is ______.

e. On January 1, 19A, a company decided to establish a fund by making 10 equal annual deposits of $4,000, starting on December 31, 19A. The fund will be increased by 8% compounded interest. What will be the fund balance at the end of year 10 (i.e., immediately after the last deposit)?

f. On January 1, 19A, a company decided to establish a fund by making 10 equal annual deposits of $4,000, starting on January 1, 19A. The fund will be increased by 8% compound interest. What will be the balance in the fund at the end of year 10?

g. John Doe is at retirement and has a large amount of ready cash. He wants to deposit enough cash in a fund to receive back $20,000 each December 31 for the next five years, starting on December 31, 19A. Assuming 10% compound interest, how much cash must Doe deposit on January 1, 19A?

h. Ace Company is considering the purchase of a unique asset on January 1, 19A. The asset will earn $7,000 net cash inflow each January 1 for five years, starting January 1, 19A. At the end of year 5, the asset will have no value. Assuming a 14% compound interest rate, what should Ace be willing to pay for this unique asset on January 1, 19A?

i. In 19A, XT Company decided to build a fund by the end of 19G of $446,140 by making seven equal annual deposits of $50,000, starting on December 31, 19A. What is the implicit compound interest rate for this fund?

j. The present value of several future equal annual cash payments at year-end of $30,000 each is $141,366; assuming 11% compound discount. What is the implicit number of cash payments?

k. M. Moe will retire 10 years from now and wants to establish a fund now that will pay him $30,000 cash at the end of each of the first five years after retirement. Specific dates are: date of a single deposit by Moe, January 1, year 1; date of first cash payment from the fund to Moe, December 31, year 11. The fund will pay 10% compound interest. How much cash must Moe deposit on January 1, year 1, to provide the five equal annual year-end cash payments from the fund?

CASES

C 5–1 (Select Your Bonus)
You are an executive of VP Company and have earned a performance bonus. You have the option of taking the $15,000 bonus now, or to take $30,170 five years from now. Which option would you elect? Explain why.

C 5–2 (Which Insurance Indemnity Should Be Selected?)
Caster Corporation had a $200,000 life insurance policy at the time of the death of its president. The company is the beneficiary and can receive the $200,000 cash immediately, or elect any one of the following options:

a. Withdraw the $200,000, plus 10% compound interest, in equal annual payments over the next five years. The first payment would be made immediately.
b. Withdraw $100,000 cash now, and withdraw the remainder, plus 10% compound interest, in equal annual payments over the next five years. The first payment would be made one year from now.
c. Withdraw $50,000 at years-end 1, 2, and 3, and then withdraw the balance at the end of year 5; all including 10% compound interest.

Required:
1. Complete the following schedule. Show all computations (round to the nearest $).

Option	Cash to be received in year					Total cash
	1	2	3	4	5	
a.	$	$	$	$	$	$
b.						
c.						

2. *a.* How much interest did each option earn?
   b. Give any logical reasons for withdrawing the $200,000 immediately.

C 5–3 (Compare the Cost of Two Alternatives)
Viable Corporation purchases large machines for use in its plant. Machine Type A is typical of these machines. Currently, Viable is considering the purchase of a new Type A machine. Two different brand names are being considered as follows:

	Brand A	Brand B
Cost (cash basis)	$100,000	$85,000
Operating expense to operate the machine (per year)	$ 6,000	$ 8,000
Estimated useful life (years)	8	8
Estimated residual value (% of cost)	20%	10%

Viable expects a 20% return on its investments.

Required:
1. Prepare an analysis to compare the relative cost of the two brands (assume all variables, other than the four listed above, are the same for both brands).
2. Which machine should Viable purchase? Why (consider other factors along with your computations)?

C 5–4 (Compute an Implicit Interest Rate)

Slick Real Estate Tax Shelters, Inc., advertised that its special tax-shelter partnerships "earn 21% interest for the investor each year." An independent analysis of the actual figures (obtained from a prior partner after considerable effort) showed that an individual who invested \$100,000 would receive a projected return of \$310,000 at the end of year 10 (from investment date) (adapted from "How to Fool with Averages," *Forbes Magazine*, December 7, 1984, pp. 33–34).

Required:

1. Compute the actual interest rate implicit in the tax shelter (round to the nearest percent).
2. Was the advertised rate of return of 21% correct or was it misleading? Explain why.

6 A CONCEPTUAL FRAMEWORK AND THE IMPLEMENTATION PRINCIPLES OF ACCOUNTING

OVERVIEW AND PURPOSE

Chapter 1 discussed the objectives of financial reporting and how accounting standards are currently set. That chapter emphasized the role of the Financial Accounting Standards Board (FASB) and the **process** that it uses to help attain a consensus about accounting standards. Notice that in Chapter 1, Exhibit 1–1 shows an overview of that process—it starts with an accounting issue and ends with an FASB decision. An understanding of the accounting concepts and guidelines is useful to preparers, auditors, and users of financial statements. Also, as a student you should understand the concepts and implementation standards, which is the primary subject matter of this book.

The purpose of this chapter is to discuss one primary phase of the FASB's activities—a **conceptual framework of accounting** and its related **implementation** principles (or guidelines). To date the FASB has issued six *Statements of Financial Accounting Concepts*, which are outlined in Exhibit 6–2. Discussion of the FASB conceptual framework was deferred to this chapter because the review of the financial statements (Chapters 2–4) will help you to *(a)* understand the conceptual framework and *(b)* appreciate its importance when studying the subsequent chapters. The discussion in this chapter will cite some examples from the review chapters. Now you are ready to start your study of intermediate accounting by studying the conceptual framework. This discussion of concepts will be expanded in Chapter 13.

This chapter discusses the following conceptual topics:

1. Overview of the FASB conceptual framework.
2. Qualitative characteristics of accounting information.
3. Elements of financial statements of business enterprises.
4. Recognition and measurement criteria.
5. Continuation of current GAAP for financial statements.
6. Supplement 6A—A prospective set of financial statements.

Overview of the FASB Conceptual Framework

Theory, in general, can be defined as a coherent set of hypothetical, conceptual, and pragmatic principles forming a general frame of reference for a field of inquiry. Concepts can be viewed as components of theory; they are generalizations about the environment, observable events, and an existing body of knowledge. Accounting concepts are human-made; therefore, they change with the evolving social and economic environment within which the accounting process is applied. Thus, accounting concepts involve continuous changes. The organizations and the "political process" discussed in Chapter 1 will continue to be influential in the development of accounting concepts and standards.

Accounting concepts are based upon inductive and deductive reasoning, economic theory, experience, pragmatism, and general acceptability. Because accounting concepts are human-made, they cannot be derived from, nor proven by, the laws of nature as can be done in mathematics and the natural sciences. A prominent academician explained one view of the background as follows:[1]

> Attempts to formulate a conceptual framework of accounting have been going on now for at least 50 years, and to get the board's project into perspective it is important to see it as only the latest in a series of attempts to formulate what W. A. Paton and A. C. Littleton in 1940 called "a coherent, coordinated, consistent body of doctrine." There have been many steps along the road from the American Accounting Association's 1936 *Tentative Statement of Accounting Principles Underlying Corporate Financial Statements* to Concepts Statement no. 5, with Accounting Principles Board Statement no. 4 (1970) and the American Institute of CPAs Trueblood report (1973) among the major landmarks.

The latest effort to develop a conceptual framework of accounting was a primary responsibility of the FASB. In response the FASB developed the conceptual framework of accounting that encompasses the five statements of concepts shown in **Exhibit 6–1.** This framework is explained in the *FASB Statements of Financial Accounting Concepts,* which is summarized in **Exhibit 6–2.** A conceptual framework is needed for the following reasons:

1. The accounting standards on each accounting issue should be consistent with a conceptual framework developed by a prior consensus. This process assures consistency among the guidelines and procedures used in accounting.
2. New and unique accounting problems on which there are no current guidelines can be more consistently resolved by statement preparers in conformity with a conceptual framework.
3. The relevance and reliability of financial statements may be enhanced significantly.
4. Users of financial statements can benefit because of a better understanding of the information that financial statements communicate.

On the following pages we discuss each of the *FASB Statements of Financial Accounting Concepts* (i.e., the five conceptual levels) in the order listed in Exhibits 6–1 and 6–2.

---

[1] David Solomons, "The FASB's Conceptual Framework: An Evaluation," *Journal of Accountancy,* June 1986, pp. 114–24.

Exhibit 6–1
Overview of the FASB conceptual framework and implementation guidelines for accounting.

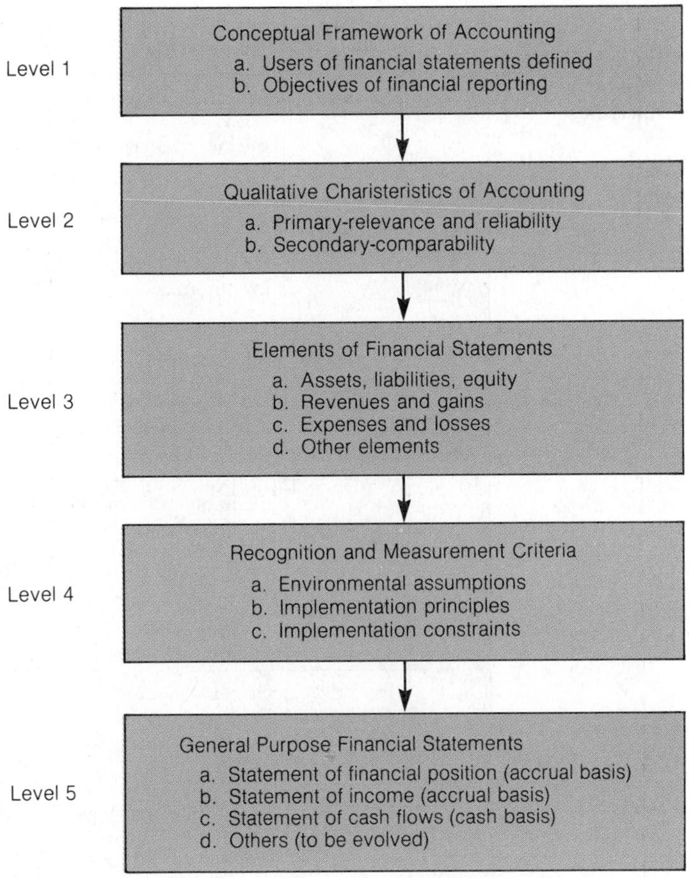

Objectives of Financial Reporting by Business Enterprises (FASB Statement of Financial Accounting Concepts 1)

This concepts statement defines: *(a)* the users of financial statements, *(b)* objectives of financial statements, and *(c)* perspective of the conceptual framework. These three topics provide the fundamental basis for financial accounting and reporting (refer to Exhibit 6–2).

Users of Financial Statements

External decision makers use accounting information. At one end of the spectrum is the investor who seldom looks at even the pictures in the annual financial report and never analyzes the financial statements. At the other end of the spectrum is the professional chartered financial analyst (CFA) who advises investors. Because of this diversity, accounting information realistically cannot be directed at users at either end of the spectrum, nor can it be directed at any **one** group. Rather, *FASB Concepts No. 1* established accounting standards to meet the information needs of the large group of external users. These users "lack the authority to prescribe the information they want and must rely on information management communicates to them." Also, they "have a reasonable understanding of business and economic activities and are willing to study

Exhibit 6–2
Overview of the *FASB Statements of Financial Accounting Concepts**.

No.	Date	Title	Primary topics
1	Nov. 1978	Objectives of Financial Reporting by Business Enterprises	1. Financial statement users defined. 2. Objectives of financial statements. 3. Perspective of the conceptual framework. Elaboration: Exhibit 6–3
2	May 1980	Qualitative Characteristics of Accounting Information	1. Primary qualities: *a.* Relevance. *b.* Reliability. 2. Secondary quality: comparability. 3. Threshold of recognition; materiality. 4. Implementation constraints. Elaboration: Exhibit 6–3.
3	Dec. 1980	Replaced by No. 6	
6	Dec. 1985	Elements of Financial Statements of Business Enterprises	1. Assets, liabilities, owners' equity, investments and distributions by owners, and comprehensive income. 2. Revenues, expenses, and gains and losses. 3. Accrual accounting. Elaboration: Exhibit 6–4.
4	Dec. 1980	Objectives of Financial Reporting by Nonbusiness Organizations	Outside the scope of this textbook.
5	Dec. 1984	Recognition and Measurement in Financial Statements of Business Enterprises	1. Recognition criteria 2. Measurement criteria 3. Accounting assumptions, principles, and constraints. 4. A full set of financial statements prospective.

* Previously shown as Exhibit 1–3; repeated for convenience.

the information with reasonable diligence." *FASB Concepts No. 1* identifies these users as "investors and creditors" . . . and "also those who advise or represent them." By selecting these users as the focus for the objectives of financial reporting, the FASB defined their conception of the "average prudent investor" to be a reasonably sophisticated decision maker. The users include investors (and those who advise investors), creditors, employees, and other potential users such as managers, directors, customers, stock exchanges, lawyers, taxing authorities, researchers, teachers, students, and the public.

Financial Reporting Objectives

FASB Concepts No. 1 discusses the objectives of financial reporting by business enterprises. These objectives focus on the decision makers (financial statement users) identified in the preceding paragraph. The objectives state that financial reporting should provide information—

1. That is useful to present and potential investors and creditors and other users in making **rational investment, credit, and similar decisions.**

2. To help current and potential investors and creditors and other users in assessing the amounts, timing, and uncertainty of prospective cash receipts from dividends or interest and the proceeds from the sale, redemption, or maturity of securities or loans. Investors' and creditors' cash flows are related to enterprise cash flows; therefore, financial reporting should provide information to help investors, creditors, and others assess the amounts, timing, and uncertainty of **prospective net cash flows** of the enterprise.
3. About the economic resources of the enterprise, the claims to those resources (obligations of the enterprise to transfer resources to other entities) and the effects of transactions, events, and circumstances that change its resources and claims to those resources.

FASB Concepts No. 1 implicitly recognizes an investment decision model that investors and creditors often use to value an investment. That model helps investors predict the future net cash receipts they can expect from an investment in, or loan to, a particular business enterprise. It may be useful for you to think in terms of a discounted cash flow analysis in which the investor or creditor will purchase an investment for a price that is equal to the present value (discounted at the expected rate of return) of the future net cash receipts expected from the investment or loan (see Chapter 5). To project the net cash flows, investors usually need information about (1) the timing and amounts of expected net cash flows of the enterprise, and (2) the risk that the business may or may not realize the expected cash flows (see Chapter 4, Part B), and (3) the appropriate rate of interest for discounting. This statement has had a positive effect primarily because of its specification of users and the objectives of financial statements.

A Perspective of the Conceptual Framework

The discussions above focused on the users and objectives of general-purpose financial statements. A conceptual framework must also include an identification of the qualities of accounting information that are needed to attain the objectives. Also the elements of financial statements, recognition and measurement of those elements, and their display (i.e., how reported) on financial statements must be specified. These matters are the subject of subsequent *FASB Statements of Financial Accounting Concepts.*

Qualitative Characteristics of Accounting Information *(FASB Statement of Financial Accounting Concepts 2)*

FASB Concepts Statement 2 continues the emphasis of *FASB Concepts No. 1.* The purpose of *FASB Concepts No. 2* is to identify and define a "hierarchy" of **characteristics of accounting information** to enhance its usefulness for decision making. **Exhibit 6–3** summarizes in context the primary and secondary qualitative characteristics of the conceptual framework.

Primary Qualities—Relevance and Reliability

FASB Concepts No. 2 emphasizes the importance of decision usefulness and identifies relevance and reliability as the two primary qualities that make accounting information useful for decision making.

Exhibit 6–3
Qualitative characteristics of accounting.

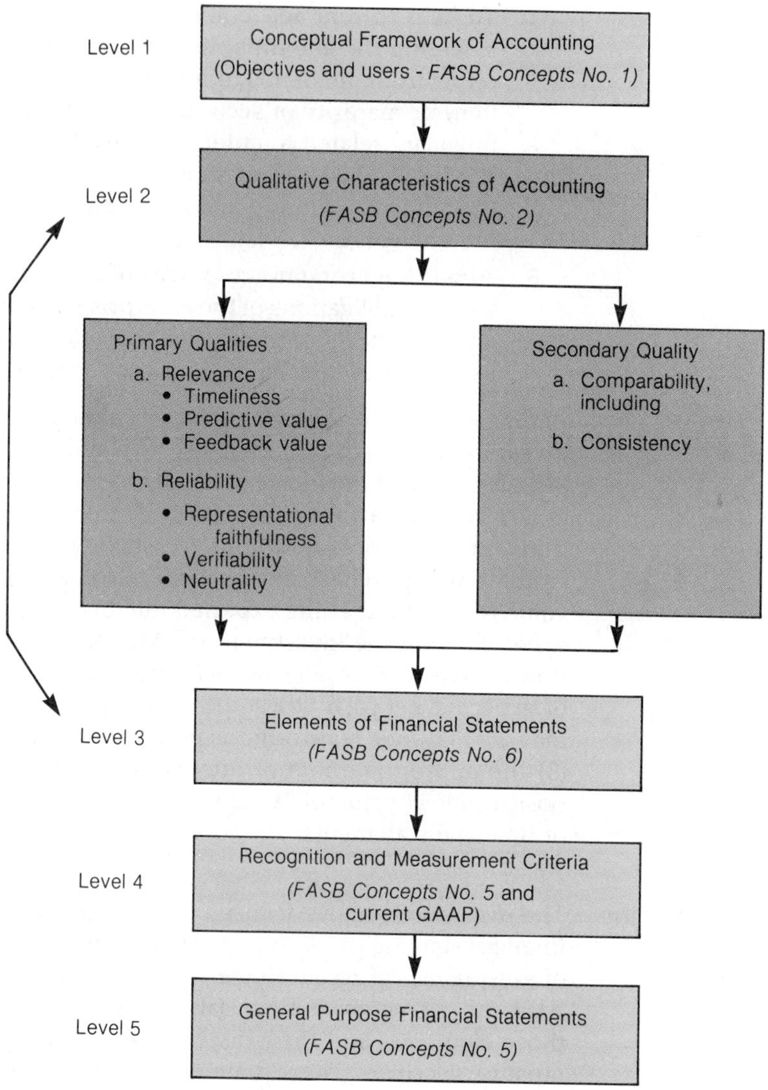

Relevance. Relevance can be simply defined as bearing upon the matter at hand. Relevance is the capacity of accounting information to make a difference in decisions by helping users to make predictions about the outcomes of past, present, and future events (i.e., predictive value) or to confirm or correct prior expectations (i.e., feedback value).

Relevance depends upon three ingredients as follows:

1. **Timeliness**—having relevant information available to a decision maker before it loses its capacity to influence decisions. Lack of timeliness can reduce the level of relevance.
2. **Predictive value**—having relevant information that helps users increase the likelihood of correctly predicting the ultimate outcome of past or

present events. Users prefer information that has the highest predictive value in attaining their objectives.

3. **Feedback value**—having relevant information that helps users to confirm or correct prior expectations.

Reliability. Reliability is the quality of accounting information which assures that it is reasonably free from error and bias and faithfully represents what it purports to represent (i.e, the information is believable). Users must be confident that they can depend on the information contained in financial statements.

Reliability depends upon three ingredients as follows:

1. Representational faithfulness—correspondence or agreement between a measure or description and the phenomenon that it purports to represent (sometimes called **validity**). Accounting information must report in words and numbers the economic substance of a transaction rather than its form or a misleading description.
2. Verifiability—the capacity to confirm or substantiate. It involves the ability through consensus (i.e., confirmation) among measurers to ensure that accounting information is, and can be verified as, what it purports to represent.
3. Neutrality—absence of bias in reported information with no intention to attain a predetermined result or to induce a particular mode of behavior. Accounting information should not be biased toward or against a particular viewpoint, predetermined result, particular party, nor should it be consistently too high or too low.[2]

The two primary qualities should be evident in the financial statement information provided to users. For example, the statement of cash flows (SCF) that you reviewed in Chapter 4 (Exhibit 4–5) has relevance for decision makers (i.e., users) because it provides information about current cash flows that is essential to assess and predict future cash flows. However, it is relevant only if it *(a)* is current (i.e., not too out of date), *(b)* presents information that is properly classified and understandable to users, and *(c)* presents the information in ways that are in conformity with the decision maker's decision models (i.e., to help users confirm or correct past expectations). Moreover, the SCF must be reliable. This means it must *(a)* report only what it purports to report (i.e., cash flows), *(b)* be verifiable (i.e, capable of being audited), and (c) not be biased.

Secondary Quality—Comparability

FASB Concepts No. 2 summarizes comparability as follows:

> Information about a particular enterprise gains greatly in usefulness if it can be compared with similar information about other enterprises and with similar informa-

[2] Bias is used in the definitions of reliability, verifiability, and neutrality. In measurement, bias is the tendency of a measure to fall more often on one side than the other of what it represents instead of being equally likely to fall on either side. Bias in accounting measures means a tendency to be consistently too high or too low.

Error is used in the definitions of reliability and verifiability. Error in accounting usually is defined as deviation from truth or accuracy, as in a mistake, either intentional or unintentional. Another kind of error of concern to decision makers is called **statistical measurement error,** which is a difference between estimated and actual values.

> tion about the same enterprise for some other period or some other point in time. Comparability between enterprises and consistency in the application of methods over time increases the informational value of comparisons of relative economic opportunities or performance.

Comparability involves the comparison of accounting information of an enterprise with similar information about other enterprises and with similar information about the same enterprise for some other period.

Consistency is the application of accounting concepts and principles from period to period in the same manner. *APB Opinion 20,* "Accounting changes," states that "there is a presumption that an accounting principle once used should not be changed." However, if consistency is carried too far, relevance may be adversely affected. A change to a preferred accounting principle is permitted, although this would impair consistency. This conflict is resolved by supplemental note disclosures to retain consistency (and comparability) between the financial statements before and after the change. For example, the statement of income reviewed in Chapter 3 (Exhibit 3–4) should be designed from year to year so that it can be reasonably compared with *(a)* revenue and expense information about other companies (e.g., in the same industry), and *(b)* past and future revenue and expense information for the same company. This concept requires that the accounting concepts and principles be applied on the statement of income in a consistent manner.

Elements of Financial Statements of Business Enterprises *(FASB Statement of Financial Accounting Concepts 6)*

The primary medium used to communicate accounting information about a business enterprise is its periodic financial statements. The building blocks of the accrual-basis financial statements are called **elements.** *FASB Concepts No. 6,* which replaced *FASB Concepts No. 3,* defines the 10 elements shown in **Exhibit 6–4** (also refer to Exhibit 6–2). The first four elements (revenues, expenses, gains, and losses) relate directly to the statement of income; and the next three elements (assets, liabilities, and equity) relate directly to the statement of financial position. The definitions of these seven elements are particularly relevant because they provide authoritative definitions of the major classifications used in current financial statements.

The next two elements, investments by owners and distributions to owners, are related to the statement of financial position. In contrast, the last element listed in Exhibit 6–4, comprehensive income, is unique because *(a)* it does not appear in the current statement of income and *(b)* it adds a new dimension to the traditional statement of income.

FASB Concepts No. 6 uses the term **elements** to mean the classes of items that financial statements should contain. The definitions of elements, given in Exhibit 6–4, will often be referred to throughout this textbook. For example, *FASB Concepts No. 6* requires that all of the companies that you reviewed—Ace Retailers (Exhibits 2–5 and 2–6), Graham Retail Company (Exhibits 3–3 and 3–7), and Joy Corporation (Exhibit 4–3)—use identical definitions of the elements defined in Exhibit 6–4.

FASB Concepts No. 6 has had a major impact because its definitions of the elements of financial statements are distinct improvements over prior definitions. As one prominent accountant stated: "Not surprisingly, therefore, when the

Exhibit 6–4
Elements of financial statements.

Statement of income (discussed in Chapter 3):

1. **Revenues** are inflows or other enhancements of assets of an entity or settlements of its liabilities (or a combination of both) during a period from delivering or producing goods, rendering services, or other activities that constitute the entity's ongoing major or central operations.
2. **Expenses** are outflows or other using up of assets or incurrences of liabilities (or a combination of both) during a period from delivering or producing goods, rendering services, or carrying out other activities that constitute the entity's ongoing major or central operations.
3. **Gains** are increases in equity (net assets) from peripheral or incidental transactions of an entity and from all other transactions and other events and circumstances affecting the entity during a period except those that result from revenues or investments by owners.
4. **Losses** are decreases in equity (net assets) from peripheral or incidental transactions of an entity and from all other transactions and other events and circumstances affecting the entity during a period except those that result from expenses or distributions to owners.

Statement of financial position (discussed in Chapter 4):

5. **Assets** are probable future economic benefits obtained or controlled by a particular entity as a result of past transactions or events.
6. **Liabilities** are probable future sacrifices of economic benefits arising from present obligations of a particular entity to transfer assets or provide services to other entities in the future as a result of past transactions or events.
7. **Equity** (i.e., owners' equity) is the residual interest in the assets of an entity that remains after deducting its liabilities. In a business enterprise, the equity is the ownership interest.

Other elements:

8. **Investments by owners** are increases in net assets of a particular enterprise resulting from transfers to it from other entities of something of value to obtain or increase ownership interests (or equity) in it. Assets are most commonly received as investments by owners, but that which is received may also include services or satisfaction or conversion of liabilities of the enterprise.
9. **Distributions to owners** are decreases in net assets of a particular enterprise resulting from transferring assets, rendering services, or incurring liabilities by the enterprise to owners. Distributions to owners decrease ownership interests (or equity) in an enterprise (discussed in Chapter 17).
10. **Comprehensive income** is the change in equity (net assets) of an entity during a period from transactions and other events and circumstances from **nonowner sources.** It includes all changes in equity during a period except those resulting from investments by owners and distributions to owners.

Source: FASB, *Statement of Financial Accounting Concepts No. 6,* "Elements of Financial Statements of Business Enterprises," (Stamford, Conn., December 1985).

FASB seriously tries to use the conceptual framework to structure debate on accounting issues, it turns to the definitions."[3]

Recognition and Measurement Criteria *(FASB Statements of Financial Accounting Concepts 5)*

FASB Concepts No. 5 is summarized in context with the other concepts statements in **Exhibit 6–5,** which discusses the following issues:

[3] Dale L. Gerboth, "The Conceptual Framework: Not Definitions, But Professional Values," *Accounting Horizons,* September 1987, pp. 1–8.

1. Recognition of financial statement items such as assets, liabilities, equity, revenues, gains, expenses, and losses.
2. Measurement in units of money.
3. Assumptions, principles, and constraints.
4. A full set of financial statements.

Recognition Criteria

FASB Concepts No. 5 provides the conceptual basis for accrual basis recognition. The statement defines recognition as **the process of recording and reporting an item as an asset, liability, revenue, gain, expense, loss, and change in owners' equity. A recognized item is expressed in both words and numbers.** Recognition applies to **all** financial statement elements in all companies.

FASB Concepts No. 5 (pars. 58–63) states that recognition of an item is required when all four of the following criteria are met:

1. **Definitions**—the item must meet the definition of an element of financial statements as defined in *FASB Concepts No. 6*.
2. **Measurability**—the item has a relevant attribute (i.e., characteristic) that is reliably measurable.
3. **Relevance**—the information about the item is capable of making a difference in user decisions.

Exhibit 6–5
Recognition and measurement criteria.

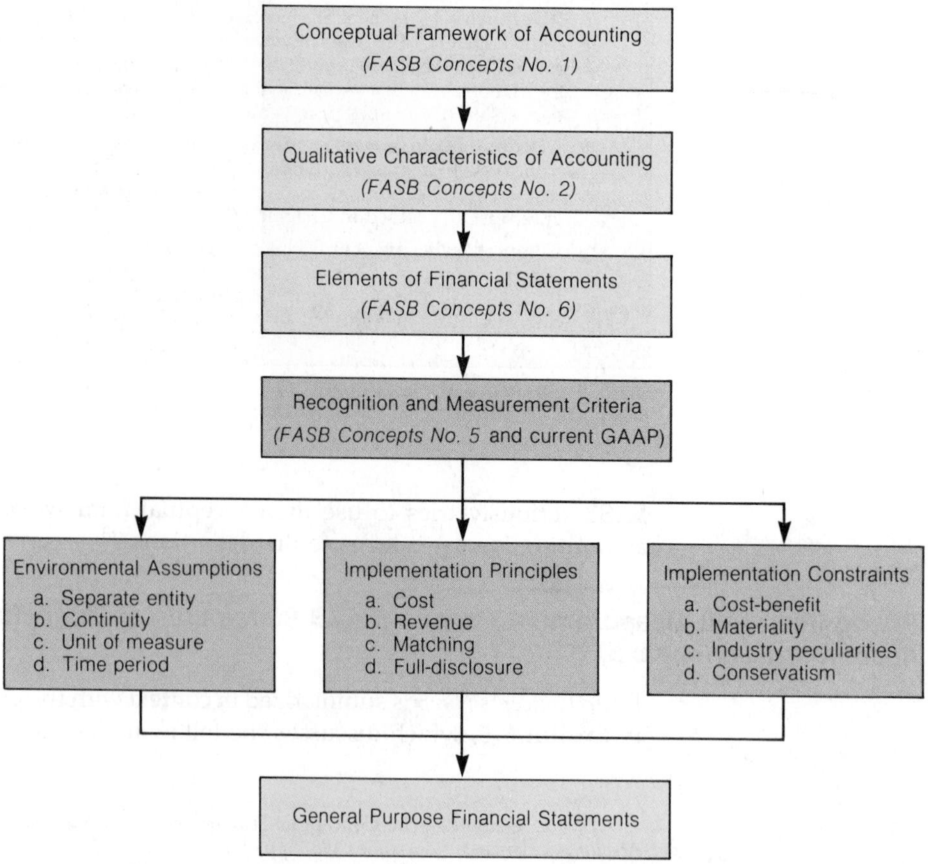

4. **Reliability**—the information about the item is representationally faithful, verifiable, and neutral (i.e., not biased).

Measurement Criteria

FASB Concepts No. 5 states that all monetary measurements should be based on historical cost (unadjusted for inflation or deflation), and the measurements used currently under GAAP should be continued. These will be discussed in the remaining chapters.

To return to our prior example about "elements," *FASB Concepts No. 6* specifies that each of the companies reviewed—Ace, Graham, Joy, etc.—should conform to the four recognition criteria and the measurement criteria.

A Prospective Set of Financial Statements

FASB Concepts No. 5 indicates that, at some time in the future, a full set of financial statements for a reporting period should show as a minimum: *(a)* financial position (i.e., the statement of financial position), *(b)* earnings (i.e., the statement of income), *(c)* comprehensive income (a new view), *(d)* cash flows (i.e., the statement of cash flows), and *(e)* investments by and distributions to the owners (i.e., a statement of owners' equity). Supplement 6–A discusses and illustrates some notion about how the prospective set of financial statements may evolve in the future.

Continuation of Current GAAP for Financial Statements

The FASB *Statements of Financial Accounting Concepts* discuss the conceptual framework of accounting. To implement that framework certain GAAP guidelines (usually called **principles**) that have evolved in recent years are used. These guidelines usually are identified as shown in Exhibit 6–5: *(a)* environmental assumptions, *(b)* implementation principles, and *(c)* implementation constraints.

Environmental Assumptions

Four basic environmental assumptions significantly affect the recording, measuring, and reporting of accounting information. These assumptions, called *(a)* separate entity, *(b)* continuity, *(c)* unit of measure, and *(d)* time period, are discussed below.

Separate Entity Assumption. Accounting deals with specific and separate entities. Each enterprise is considered an **accounting unit separate and apart from its owners and from other entities.** A corporation and its stockholders are separate entities for accounting purposes. Also, partnerships and sole proprietorships are treated as separate and apart from their owners although this distinction is not made in the legal sense.

Under the separate entity assumption, all accounting records and reports are developed from the viewpoint of the particular entity. This assumption provides a basis for clear-cut differentiation (or separation) of the transactions of the enterprise from those of its owners. For example, the personal residence of an individual owner is not considered an asset for the business to report, although the residence and the business have a common owner. Ace Retailers' financial statements (Exhibits 2–5 and 2–6) do not include any financial data that relate directly to the separate transactions of its owner or owners.

Continuity Assumption. The continuity assumption frequently is called the **going-concern** assumption. Under this assumption, the business is not expected to liquidate in the foreseeable future. The assumption does not imply that accounting assumes permanent continuance; rather there is a presumption of continuity for a period of time **sufficient to carry out contemplated operations, contracts, and commitments.** This concept establishes the rationale of accounting on a **nonliquidation basis.** Also it provides the conceptual basis for many of the classifications used in accounting. For example, the classification of assets and liabilities as current or long term relies upon this assumption. If continuity were not assumed, all assets and liabilities would become current, and the current/long-term distinction would lose its significance.

If an entity expects probable liquidation, conventional accounting based on the continuity assumption would not be appropriate for reporting the enterprise's elements. Such cases call for **liquidation** accounting, wherein all elements are accounted for at estimated net realizable amounts.

Unit-of-Measure Assumption. The unit-of-measure assumption specifies that accounting should measure and report the results of the economic activities of the entity in terms of a monetary unit (e.g., dollars). It recognizes that the monetary unit is an effective means of communicating financial information. Thus, money is the common denominator—the meterstick—used in accounting.

Unfortunately, use of a monetary unit for measurement purposes poses an accounting dilemma. Unlike the meterstick, which is always the same length, the monetary unit (i.e., the dollar) changes in real value (or purchasing power). Therefore, during inflation or deflation, dollars of different size (i.e., with different purchasing power) are entered in the accounts and intermingled as if they were of equal purchasing power. Because of the practice of ignoring changes in the purchasing power of a dollar, accounting assumes that the magnitude of changes in the value of the monetary unit is not material. Chapter 25 discusses techniques that the accounting profession uses to report the effects of changes in prices.

Time Period Assumption. Although the results of operations of a specific business enterprise cannot be known with certainty until the business has completed its life span and gone through final liquidation, short-term financial reports are necessary because financial statement users need relevant (i.e., timely) financial information. Thus, the environment—the business community and government—has imposed on accounting a **calendar constraint,** that is, the necessity to assign changes in the economic elements of an enterprise to a series of short time periods. These **reporting periods** vary; however, a year is the most common. Some companies adhere to the calendar year, whereas other companies use a business year that ends near the lowest point of business activity in each 12-month period—regardless of its relation to the calendar year. In addition to annual reports, companies also report summarized financial information on an **interim** basis, usually quarterly (discussed in Chapter 22).

The time period assumption recognizes the need of decision makers for short-term financial information. This assumption underlies the use of **accruals** and **deferrals** that distinguish accrual basis accounting from cash basis accounting. If a demand for periodic reports did not exist during the life span of a business, accruals and deferrals of revenues and expenses would not be necessary. Notice that all of the financial statements that you reviewed in Chapters 2, 3, and 4 were precisely dated. The statement of financial position at a specific date (e.g., At December 31, 19XX), and the statements of retained earnings, income, and cash flows for a specified time period (e.g., For the year ended December 31, 19XX).

Implementation Principles

At the operational level, preparers use implementation principles for recognizing (i.e., recording) and reporting revenues, expenses, gains, and losses. The implementation principles are the cost, revenue, matching, and full-disclosure principles.

These principles focus on the accounting term recognition. **Recognition** is the formal process of recording in the accounts and reporting in the financial statements the **elements** of financial statements. These elements are assets, liabilities, investments by owners, withdrawals by owners, revenues, expenses, and gains and losses. A recognized item is depicted in both words and numbers, with the amount included in financial statement totals *(FASB Concepts No. 5).*

Income is defined as revenues plus gains minus expenses and losses; therefore the revenue, cost, and matching principles are the fundamental building blocks of income recognition. **Chapter 13 discusses income recognition and focuses on implementation of these three principles.**

Cost Principle. The cost principle specifies that cash-equivalent cost is the most useful basis for **initial** accounting recognition of the elements recorded in the accounts and reported on the financial statements. It is important to note that the cost principle applies to the **initial** recording of transactions and events.

The cost principle assumes *(a)* a completed **arm's-length** business transaction, and *(b)* that the market value of the **resources given up** in the transaction provides reliable evidence of the valuation of the item acquired in the transaction. The cost principle requires that all of the four recognition criteria listed above be met.

When a noncash consideration is involved, cost is measured as the market value of the resources given, or the market value of the item received, whichever is more **reliably** determinable. For example, an asset may be acquired with a debt given as settlement. Cost in this instance is the **present value** of the amount of cash to be paid in the future, as specified by the terms of the debt. The cost principle applies to all of the elements of financial statements, including liabilities.

The cost principle provides guidance at the initial recognition date. However, the original cost of some items acquired is subject to depreciation, depletion, amortization, and write-down in conformity with the matching principle and the conservatism constraint (discussed in the sections that follow). For example, the statement of financial position of Joy Corporation (Exhibit 4–3) showed the following:

Building (cost principle applied when acquired)	$200,000	
Less: Accumulated depreciation (matching principle applied as used)	80,000	
Book or carrying value		$120,000

Revenue Principle. The revenue principle requires the **accrual basis** for revenues. It specifies when revenue should be recognized in the accounts and reported in the financial statements. It requires that all four of the recognition criteria—definition, measurability, relevance, and reliability—must be met (see page 232). Also, there must be *(a)* a completed transaction and *(b)* a completed earnings process. A completed earnings process includes the following: *(a)* there is a completed transaction to sell goods or services, *(b)* there is a transfer of ownership of the goods from the seller to the buyer, or specified services have been performed, and *(c)* collection has been made or is assured.

Revenue Defined. Revenue is defined in *FASB Concepts No. 6* (see Exhibit 6–4) as "inflows of other enhancements of assets of an entity or settlements of its liabilities (or a combination of both) during a period from delivering or producing goods, rendering service, or other activities that constitute the entity's ongoing major or central operations." Revenues "represent actual or expected cash inflows (or the equivalent) that have occurred or will eventually occur as a result of the enterprise's ongoing major or central operations during the period."

Measurement of Revenue. Revenue is measured as the market value of the resources received or the product or service given, whichever is the more reliably determinable. The revenue principle requires that all discounts be viewed as adjustments of the amount of revenue earned. For example, in determining the net cash exchange value of sales subject to a discount, sales discounts should be subtracted from gross sales revenue in measuring the net amount of sales revenue.

Under the revenue principle, revenue from the sale of **goods** is recognized in conformity with the **sales method** (i.e., at the time of sale) because the earning process usually is complete at the time of sale. At that time, the relevant information about the asset inflows to the seller would be known with reliability.

The conditions for **completion of the earning process** are *(a)* collection from the buyer is reasonably assured and *(b)* the expenses of making the sale can be determined reliably. Condition *(a)*—reasonable assurance of collection—provides the basis for the conclusion that the transaction provided a "probable future economic benefit" (i.e., an asset) to the seller. Without this condition, the concept of revenue recognition would be altogether lacking in substantive economic content. Condition *(b)*—reliable determination of related expenses—provides the basis for measurement of the net economic benefit of the transaction. Without this condition, measurement of the effect of the revenue would ignore the related expenses required by the matching principle, which is discussed next.

Under the revenue principle, revenue from the sale of **services** is recognized on the basis of performance because performance determines the extent to which the earning process is complete.

The revenue principle requires **accrual basis** accounting rather than cash basis accounting for revenues. Therefore, completed transactions for the sale of goods or services on credit usually are recognized as revenue in the period in which the sale or service occurred rather than in the period in which the cash is eventually collected. For example, the statement of income of Graham Retail Company (Exhibit 3–4) showed the following:

Net sales (revenue principle applied)		$670,000
Cost of goods sold (matching principle applied)	$264,000	
Distribution expense (matching principle applied)	153,000	

Other types of revenue transactions that pose problems of revenue recognition are installment sales, long-term construction contracts, sales of land with minimal down payments, and sales of franchises that require a certain level of performance on the part of the purchaser. In these and many other cases, both determination of when the earning process is complete and measurement of the amount of revenue are difficult tasks. A detailed discussion of revenue recognition is provided in Chapter 13.

Matching Principle. The matching principle requires the **accrual basis** for recognizing expenses. It states that for a given reporting period revenues should be recognized in conformity with the revenue principle; then the expenses incurred in earning that revenue should be recognized during the same period. If revenue is carried over from a prior period or deferred to a future period in conformity with the revenue principle, all identifiable expenses related to that revenue likewise should be carried over from the prior period or deferred to the future period. Many expenditures are first recognized as assets because they help earn **future** revenues. In this case, the matching principle requires that as the revenues are earned, those assets sold or consumed (used) must be recognized and reported as **expenses** of the period in which the related revenue is recognized.

The pattern of expense recognition varies. Some expenses reflect a **direct cause-and-effect** relationship with revenues. That is, the revenue and expense occur simultaneously. Examples are cost of goods sold, sales commission expense, and delivery expense. Other expenses are recognized on a **time basis** because their asset counterparts expire over time rather than reflecting direct cause-and-effect relationships with revenues. Examples are depreciation expense of the home office building, interest expense, and property tax expense. For some expenses, there is no direct relationship with **either revenue or time.** Therefore, these expenses must be allocated to reporting periods on some subjective basis. Examples are expenditures for advertising, research and development, and charitable contributions. A common system of allocation is to recognize such costs as expense in full in the period in which they are incurred.

To illustrate the matching principle, assume a home appliance was sold for cash during 19B (the annual accounting period). It was guaranteed for 12 months from date of sale. The sales revenue should be recognized as earned during 19B. The expense of honoring the warranty also should be recognized in 19B, although the actual warranty cost may not be known until the next year. Therefore, at the end of 19B, the warranty expense must be estimated, recorded, and reported. In this way, the warranty expense is **matched** with the 19B revenue to which it is related.

These relationships can be summarized as follows:

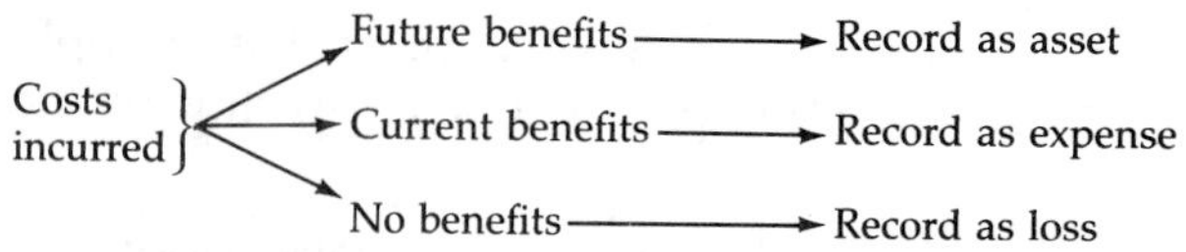

The matching principle is the expense analog to the revenue principle. Because of the wide diversity and large number of types of expenses, it is one of the most pervasive principles of accounting in terms of the number of accounting judgments that it affects.

The matching principle requires the use of **accrual basis** accounting (as opposed to cash basis accounting) to record and report expenses. Thus, **adjusting entries** (discussed in Chapter 2) must be recorded at the end of each period to update certain expenses for the period. Examples are depreciation expense, wage expense earned but not paid, and estimated warranty expense. An expanded discussion of expense recognition under the matching principle is provided in Chapter 13.

Full-Disclosure Principle. The full-disclosure principle requires that the financial statements of a business clearly report all of the relevant information about the economic affairs of the enterprise. This principle rests upon the primary characteristic of relevance (see Exhibit 6–3). Full disclosure requires *(a)* that all information that can make a difference in a decision is reported and *(b)* that the accounting information reported must be understandable (i.e., not susceptible to misleading inferences). Full disclosure also requires that the major accounting policies and any special accounting policies used by the company be explained in the notes to the financial statements.

Accounting information may be reported in the *(a)* financial statements themselves, *(b)* disclosure notes to those statements, or *(c)* supplementary schedules and other presentations.

The full-disclosure principle requires the financial report to place **substance over form;** that is, the primary objective is to report the economic substance of a transaction, rather than its form. This means that the substance should not be made vague or hidden by using the mechanics, rules, and technical terminology. For example, Joy Corporation's statement of financial position (Exhibit 4–3) that you reviewed shows five different full disclosure items in parentheses within the statement and one supplementary note about the bond indenture.

Implementation Constraints

The conceptual framework, environmental assumptions, and implementation principles have been discussed. Throughout those discussions, the **implementation constraints** identified were: *(a)* cost-benefit, *(b)* materiality, *(c)* industry peculiarities, and *(d)* conservatism. These constraints exert a modifying influence on financial accounting and reporting.

Cost-Benefit Constraint. *FASB Concepts Nos.* 2 and 5 discuss a cost-benefit constraint that often affects accounting information. The underlying concept is that the **benefits** to be derived by **users** from specific information should exceed the cost of providing it. Although the concept is important, it is difficult to quantify either the benefits or the costs. The FASB viewed this concept at two levels: *(a)* a standard-setting body must "do its best" to communicate the intent of the conceptual framework in the standard-setting process, and *(b)* individual businesses should apply the intent of the framework in the accounting and reporting of information (for external users). This constraint is also called **utility constraint.**

Materiality Constraint. Materiality is defined in *FASB Concepts No. 2* as "The magnitude of an omission or misstatement of accounting information that, in the light of surrounding circumstances, makes it probable that the judgment of a reasonable person relying on the information would have been changed or influenced by the omission or misstatement."

This quotation means that the omission or inclusion of an immaterial item or amount would not change or influence the decision of a rational decision maker. **The materiality threshold does not mean that immaterial items and amounts do not have to be accounted for or reported.** Rather, it means that strict adherence to the related accounting standard is not required. To illustrate, in conformity with GAAP, discounts and premiums on bonds payable should be amortized using the interest method (based on the effective interest rate). However, straight-line amortization can be used provided the results are not materially different. Similarly, a low-cost asset, such as a $9.95 pencil sharpener, can be recorded as an expense in full when purchased (i.e., not recorded as an asset nor depreciated) because the amount is not material. Moreover, under this principle, Graham Retail Company (Exhibit 3–5) would include this $9.95 in office expenses rather than as a separate item.

Materiality judgments are situation specific. This means that an amount which is material in one situation may be immaterial in another situation due to the nature of the item (e.g., an illegal payment in all cases is material) or to the magnitude of the related amount such as income, total assets, and total liabilities. Because of the uniqueness of specific materiality judgments, the FASB has not been able to specify **general** materiality guidelines that apply to a wide variety of situations. In practice, materiality guidelines such as "5% of net income" or "5% of total assets" sometimes are used. This constraint also is called a **threshold for recognition.**

Industry Peculiarities. Because accounting focuses on usefulness the peculiarities and practices of an industry (such as the utility, railroad, banking, mutual funds, insurance, and extractive industries) may warrant selective exceptions to accounting principles and practices. This constraint permits special accounting for specific items where there is a clear precedent in the industry based on uniqueness, usefulness, substance over form, and representational faithfulness.

Some differences in accounting also occur in response to legal requirements. This is especially true for companies subject to significant and pervasive regulatory controls (e.g., public utilities). Another exception permits the use of a principle or procedure that is at variance with an official pronouncement if it can be clearly shown that it is more useful and is necessary to avoid misleading inferences. In such cases, the departure must be fully disclosed including the reasons.

Conservatism. The conservatism constraint holds that where two alternatives equally satisfy conceptual and implementation principles for a transaction, the alternative having the **least favorable** effect on net income and/or total assets should be used. In recognizing **assets** where two alternative valuations are acceptable, the lower valuation should be used. In recognizing **liabilities,** the higher of two alternative liability amounts should be recorded. In recording revenues, expenses, gains, and losses where there is reasonable doubt as to the appropriateness of alternative amounts, the one having the least favorable effect on net income should be used.

Conservatism implies that when the "correct" treatment or amount is not determinable, the users of financial statements usually are better served by understatement rather than overstatement of net income and assets. Accountants must make many accounting decisions based on judgment in selecting alternatives, making estimates, and applying accounting principles. These choices often affect net income, assets and owners' equity, and they do not always have a single "correct" answer.

The concept of conservatism provides a time-tested guideline for making these choices. Examples of the use of conservatism are the use of lower of cost or maarket in valuing inventories and equity investments, minimizing the estimated life and residual value of depreciable assets, and the classification of gains as extraordinary and losses as ordinary in the same situation (e.g., debt restructuring).

Summary

This chapter discussed the conceptual framework of accounting and is intended to provide a frame of reference for your study of subsequent chapters. Rather than presenting these concepts piecemeal throughout the textbook, the authors have chosen to discuss them in this early chapter. Of particular importance are the relationships portrayed in Exhibits 6–1 through 6–5 which summarize the conceptual and implementation foundation. The remaining chapters discuss and illustrate numerous examples of the implementation of this foundation. As a result, the emphasis on the qualitative characteristics, elements, assumptions, principles, and financial statements is continued in those chapters.

Finally, it has been said that:[4]

> The conceptual framework is better understood as a political document than as a purely conceptual effort. The concepts statements have emerged from the same political processes—with the same need to compromise—that are used for setting standards. Inevitably, then, the framework lacks the conciseness of some other conceptual structures. But this potential shortcoming must be considered in light of the fact that the framework enjoys much more authoritative support and potential for affecting practice than any of its predecessors.

---

[4] Paul B. Miller, "The Conceptual Framework: Myths and Realities," *Journal of Accountancy*, March 1985, pp. 62–71.

SUPPLEMENT 6–A

A Prospective Set of Financial Statements (nor GAAP Currently)

Exhibit 6–4 lists prospective financial statements that comprise the full set of interrelated statements envisioned for the future in *FASB Concepts No. 5.* This concepts statement does not illustrate the five individual statements; nor does it indicate an expected implementation time. This supplement discusses and briefly illustrates some ideas about how the restructured statements may evolve.

Statement of Financial Position

This statement will continue to report assets, liabilities, and owners' equity. The subclassifications will change and owners' equity will reflect a major restructuring because of the importance that will be given the **change** statements. For example, the restructured statement of financial position (old title, balance sheet) may evolve to look like this:

Statement of Financial Position (summarized)
At December 31, 19X
(in thousands)

Assets:		
(By new classifications not yet specified)		$611
Liabilities:		
(By new classifications not yet specified)		$150
Owners' equity:		
Accumulated equity contributed by owners	$387*	
Accumulated comprehensive income	74†	
Total owners' equity		461
Total liabilities and owner's equity		$611

* From the statement of investments by and distributions to owners (page 243).
† From the statement of comprehensive income (page 242).

Statement of Earnings

The statement of earnings (a change statement) described in *FASB Concepts No. 5* corresponds to the traditional statement of income now used **except** that it will be limited to continuing operations, unusual and/or infrequent items, and extraordinary items. It will exclude items that are extraneous to the current reporting period, such as the cumulative effect of a change in accounting principle (discussed in Chapter 23). The statement of earnings (or income) may look like this:

Statement of Earnings (summarized)
For the Year Ended December 31, 19X
(in thousands)

Revenues		$100
Expenses		(80)
Gain from unusual source		3
Income from continuing operations		23
Loss on discontinued operations:		
Income from operating discontinued segment	$ 10	
Loss on disposal of discontinued segment	(12)	(2)
Income before extraordinary items		21
Extraordinary loss		(6)
Earnings		15*

Earnings per share (to be specified):

* Carried to the statement of comprehensive income, shown below.

Statement of Comprehensive Income

This will be a new financial statement (a change statement) that will replace the traditional statement of retained earnings. **Comprehensive income** (a new concept) is defined in *FASB Concepts No. 5* (par. 30) as comprising **all recognized changes in equity (net assets) of the entity during the period from transactions and other events except those resulting from investments by owners and distributions to owners.** This new statement may be something like this (notice in particular how comprehensive income is computed):

Statement of Comprehensive Income
For the Year Ended December 31, 19X
(in thousands)

Balance from prior period		$60
Earnings (from statement of earnings, given above)	$15	
Cumulative accounting adjustments:		
Cumulative effect of a change in accounting principle	(2)	
Other nonowner changes in owners' equity:		
Donated assets	1	
Comprehensive income		14
Ending balance, cumulative comprehensive income		$74*

* Carried to statement of financial position (page 241).

Statement of Investments by and Distributions to Owners

This statement is briefly described in *FASB Concepts No. 5*, pars. 55–57. It reports the "ways the equity increased or decreased from transactions with owners as owners during a period." **Investments by owners** establish or increase owners' equity and "may be received in the form of cash, goods or services, or satisfaction or conversion of the entity's liabilities." **Distributions to owners** decrease owners' equity by means of cash and property dividends when declared and "transactions such as reacquisitions of the entity's equity securities." This statement will summarize all capital changes. It will start with the beginning balance of each category of the capital stock accounts and end with the balances at the end of the reporting period. It will be another change statement. The following statement continues the preceding examples:

Statement of Investments by and Distributions to Owners (summarized)
For the Year Ended December 31, 19X
(in thousands)

Items	Common stock (par $1)	Contributed capital	Treasury stock	Dividends	Total equity contributed by owners
Balance from prior period	$100	$200	$(10)		$290
Investments by owners:					
Stock issued	50	60			110
Treasury stock sold		2	5		7
Total investments	150	262	(5)		407
Distributions to owners:					
Cash dividend				$(20)	(20)
Stock dividend	30	36		(66)	-0-
Total distributions	30	36		(86)	(20)
Balance, December 31, 19X	$180	$298	$ (5)	$(86)	$387*

* Carried to statement of financial position (page 241).

Statement of Cash Flows

This required statement reports an entity's cash inflows and outflows classified by operating, investing, and financing activities during the reporting period. *FASB Concepts No. 5* did not provide guidance about the details of this statement. However, *FASB Concepts No. 5* specified the basis for the statement of cash flow and discontinuance of the traditional statement of working capital flows. *FASB Statement of Financial Accounting Standard 95* requires a statement of cash flows and provides detailed guidelines for its format, classifications, and terminology. The new statement of cash flow is discussed in Chapter 19.

QUESTIONS

1. What are the basic objectives of external financial reporting?
2. Identify and briefly explain the primary qualities of accounting information.
3. What is the secondary quality of accounting information? Briefly explain what it means.
4. Explain the difference between a revenue and a gain.
5. Explain the difference between an expense and a loss.
6. Explain the four basic environmental assumptions that underlie implementation of accounting.
7. What is the basic accounting problem created by the unit-of-measure assumption when there is significant inflation?
8. Explain why the time period assumption causes accruals and deferrals in accounting.
9. Relate the continuity assumption to periodicity of financial statements.
10. Which assumption or principle discussed in this chapter is most affected by the phenomenon of inflation? Give reasons for your choice.

11. Relate the continuity assumption to use of accrual basis accounting.
12. Explain the cost principle. Why is it used in the basic financial statements instead of a current value model?
13. How is cost measured in noncash transactions?
14. Define the revenue principle and explain each of its three aspects: *(a)* definition, *(b)* measurement, and *(c)* realization.
15. How is revenue measured in transactions involving noncash items (exclude credit situations)?
16. Explain the matching principle. What is meant by "the expense should follow the revenue"?
17. Explain why the matching principle usually necessitates the use of adjusting entries. Use depreciation expense and unpaid wages as examples.
18. Relate the matching principle to the revenue and cost principles.
19. Briefly explain the continuity assumption.
20. Briefly explain the technical term generally accepted accounting principles (GAAP) as used by the accounting profession.
21. What accounting principle or assumption is manifested in each situation below?
    a. Prepayment for an annual license is allocated equally to expense over the next 12 months.
    b. Jerry Jenkins owns a shoe repair shop, a restaurant, and a service station. Different and independent statements are prepared for each business.
    c. Inventories at King Store are valued at lower of cost or market (LCM).
    d. Although the inflation rate for the most recent fiscal year of Clyde's Auto Dealership was 9%, no cognizance was taken of it in the year-end statements.
    e. While making a delivery, the driver for Cross Appliance Store collided with another vehicle causing both property damage and personal injury. The party sued Cross for damages that could exceed Cross's insurance coverage. Existence of the suit was disclosed on Cross's most recent financial statements.

EXERCISES

Exercises 6–1 to 6–9

E 6–1 (Topics of *FASB Statements of Financial Accounting Concepts*)
The *FASB Statements of Financial Accounting Concepts* related to this textbook are as follows:

No.	Title
1.	Objectives of Financial Reporting by Business Enterprises
2.	Qualitative Characteristics of Accounting Information
5.	Recognition and Measurement in Financial Statements of Business Enterprises
6.	Elements of Financial Statements of Business Enterprises

Listed below are primary topics of the above *Statements*. You are to match the topics with the *Statements* by entering the appropriate *Statement* numbers in the blanks to the left.

No.	Primary topics	No.	Primary topics
1	Example: Defines statement users.	______	*j.* Revenues and expenses (defined).
______	*a.* Recognition criteria.	______	*k.* Comprehensive income (defined).
______	*b.* Defines assets, liabilities, and owners' equity.	______	*l.* Cost-benefit.
______	*c.* Threshold for recognition.	______	*m.* Primary qualities of accounting information.
______	*d.* Quality constraint.	______	*n.* Guidance in applying recognition criteria.
______	*e.* Reliability.	______	*o.* Accrual accounting.
______	*f.* Objectives of financial statements.	______	*p.* Materiality.
______	*g.* Consistency.	______	*q.* Gains and losses (defined).
______	*h.* Comparability.	______	*r.* Secondary quality of accounting information.
______	*i.* Financial statements (described).		

E 6–2 (FASB Qualitative Characteristics)

FASB Concepts No. 2 identifies the following "Hierarchy levels of qualitative characteristics of accounting" (lettered for response purposes):

Hierarchy levels

A. Purpose of accounting information.
B. Primary qualities.
C. Ingredients of the primary qualities.
D. Secondary quality.
E. Threshold for recognition.
F. Utility constraint.
G. None of the above is correct.

Listed below are the individual qualitative characteristics that relate to the hierarchy levels. You are to match these characteristics with the hierarchy levels by entering the appropriate letters in the blanks to the left.

Qualitative characteristics

______ 1. Comparability.
______ 2. Relevance.
______ 3. Feedback value.
______ 4. Accrual basis accounting.
______ 5. Timeliness.
______ 6. Cost-benefit.
______ 7. Includes consistency.
______ 8. Verifiability.
______ 9. Materiality.
______ 10. Representational faithfulness.
______ 11. Reliability.
______ 12. Predictive value.
______ 13. Cost principle.
______ 14. Neutrality.
______ 15. Decision usefulness.

E 6–3 (Definitions—Relevance and Reliability)

FASB Concepts No. 2 sets forth relevance and reliability as the primary qualitative characteristics of accounting information. Each primary quality has three "ingredients." This conceptual framework is listed below. You are to provide a brief definition of each hierarchy level listed by using the following format.

Hierarchy level	Brief definition
A. Relevance.	
1. Timeliness.	
2. Predictive value.	
3. Feedback value.	
B. Reliability.	
1. Representational faithfulness.	
2. Verifiability.	
3. Neutrality.	

E 6–4 (Elements of Financial Statements)

FASB Concepts No. 6 defines the elements of financial statements listed to the left below. To the right, some primary distinctions in the definitions are listed. You are to match the distinctions with the elements by entering appropriate letters in the blanks. More than one letter can be placed in a blank.

Elements of financial statements

A. Revenues.
B. Expenses.
C. Gains.
D. Losses.
E. Assets.
F. Liabilities.
G. Owners' equity.
H. Investments by owners.
I. Distributions to owners.
J. None of the above.

Primary distinctions in the definition

____ 1. Residual interest in the assets after deducting liabilities.
____ 2. Decreases ownership interests.
____ 3. Constitute the entity's ongoing major or central operations.
____ 4. Probable future economic benefits obtained by an entity.
____ 5. Using up of assets or incurrence of liabilities.
____ 6. Cash dividends declared and paid.
____ 7. Enhancement of assets or settlements of liabilities.
____ 8. From peripheral or incidental transactions of the entity.
____ 9. Probable future sacrifices arising from present obligations.
____ 10. Issuance of a stock dividend.
____ 11. Increases in equity from peripheral or incidental activities.
____ 12. Increases in net assets for an ownership interest.
____ 13. Decreases in net assets by transferring assets to entity owners.
____ 14. Purchase of treasury stock.
____ 15. Sold operational assets above book value.
____ 16. Sold treasury stock.

E 6–5 (Examples of Assumptions, Principles and Constraints)
Listed below are the implementation assumptions, principles, and constraints, lettered for response purposes.

Assumptions, principles, and constraints

A. Separate entity assumption.
B. Continuity assumption.
C. Unit-of-measure assumption.
D. Time period assumption.
E. Cost principle.
F. Revenue principle.
G. Matching Principle.
H. Full-disclosure principle.
I. Cost-benefit constraint.
J. Materiality.
K. Industry peculiarities.
L. Conservatism.

Below is a list of key phrases directly related to the above list. You are to match these phrases with the above list by entering the appropriate letters to the left.

Key phrase

____ 1. Criteria—definition, measurability, relevance, and reliability must be met.
____ 2. Least favorable effect on income and/or total assets.
____ 3. Common denominator—the meterstick.
____ 4. Expenses incurred in earning the period's revenues.
____ 5. Preparation cost versus value of benefit to the user.
____ 6. Separate and apart from its owners and other entities.
____ 7. Report all relevant information.
____ 8. Reporting periods—usually one year.
____ 9. Cash-equivalent expenditures to acquire.
____ 10. Going concern basis.
____ 11. Relative amount of an item that would not have changed or influenced the judgment of a reasonable person.
____ 12. Exception to accounting principles and practices because of uniqueness of the entity.

E 6–6 (Questions on Concepts)
Indicate whether each statement is true or false.

______ 1. The users of financial statements that are recognized in the *FASB Statements of Financial Accounting Concepts* are limited to owners and creditors.
______ 2. Materiality is identified as the threshold for recognition.
______ 3. Comparability (including consistency) is a primary quality of accounting information.
______ 4. Neutrality in accounting means that the information reported is not biased either in favor of a particular party nor is it consistently too high or too low.
______ 5. Comparability and consistency are defined in the same way (as qualitative characteristics of accounting information).
______ 6. The declaration and issuance of a stock dividend is an element on the financial statements called distributions to owners.
______ 7. Both gains and losses relate to peripheral or incidental transactions of the entity.
______ 8. All items (resulting from a transaction) must be recognized if they meet the definition of a financial statement element.
______ 9. The matching principle is completely independent of the cost principle.

E 6–7 **(Cash versus Accrual Basis)**
The following summarized data were taken from the records of Moby Company at December 31, 19B, end of the accounting year:

a. Sales: 19B cash sales, $150,000; and 19B credit sales, $110,000.
b. Cash collections during 19B: on 19A credit sales, $30,000; on 19B credit sales, $80,000; and on 19C sales (collected in advance), $20,000.
c. Expenses: 19B cash expenses, $180,000; and 19B credit expenses, $70,000.
d. Cash payments during 19B: for 19A credit expenses, $10,000; for 19B credit expenses, $40,000; and for 19C expenses (paid in advance), $7,000.

Required:
1. Complete the following statements for 19B as a basis for evaluating the difference between cash and accrual accounting.

	Cash basis	Accrual basis
Sales revenue	$ 280,000	$ 260,000
Expenses	237,000	250,000
Net income	43,000	10,000

2. Which basis is in conformity with GAAP? Explain the basis for your answer.

E 6–8 **(Concepts Violated?)**
The *FASB Statements of Financial Accounting Concepts* are intended to provide guidance in analyzing and recording certain transactions and events. Below are several such cases. Indicate the concept that applies to each case and state whether the concept was followed or violated.

Case A—Company T used FIFO in 19A; LIFO in 19C; and FIFO in 19D.

Case B—A tract of land was acquired on credit by signing a $55,000, one-year, noninterest-bearing note. The asset account was debited for $55,000. The going rate of interest was 10%.

Case C—This company always issues its annual financial report nine months after the end of the annual reporting period.

Case D—This company recognizes all sales revenues on the cash basis.

Case E—This company records interest expense only on the payment dates.

Case F—This retail company includes among its financial statement elements an apartment house owned and operated by the owner of the company.

Case G—This company never uses notes or supplemental schedules as a part of its financial reports.

E 6–9 **(Application of Concepts)**

During the year 19X5, an auditor for a CPA firm (independent CPA) encountered the transactions and the related journal entries given below that had been made by clients. You are to (1) identify any accounting concept(s) violated and (2) give the journal entry that should have been made.

Transaction A—The company failed to record depreciation in 19X4 of $10,000; therefore it made the following 19X5 entry: (ignore income tax):

Depreciation expense	20,000	
Accumulated depreciation		20,000

Transaction B—The company sold an old machine (no longer used in operations). It originally cost $30,000 (no residual value) and was 90% depreciated. Therefore, the company made the following entry:

Cash	4,500	
Gain on sale of machine		4,500

Transaction C—The company sold 1,000 shares of its own stock (par. $1) for cash and made the following entry:

Cash	3,000	
Capital stock (1,000 shares)		1,000
Gain on sale of capital stock		2,000

Transaction D—The company paid and recorded routine advertising costs incurred in 19X5, as follows:

Prepaid advertising costs	12,000	
Cash		12,000

Transaction E—The company owed 19X4 income taxes of $3,000. During 19X5 the company paid the Internal Revenue Service, $12,000 income tax. Therefore, the company made only the following entry which recognized 19X5 income tax expense in full (except for $1,000):

Income tax expense	12,000	
Cash		12,000

PROBLEMS

Problems 6–1 to 6–6

P 6–1 **(Qualitative Characteristics)**

During an audit of Carlin Company, the cases given below were found to exist. For each case you are to *(a)* identify and briefly explain the qualitative characteristic of accounting information that is directly involved in each situation, and *(b)* indicate what the company should do in the future by way of any change in accounting policy.

Case A:

The company recorded a $19.98 pencil sharpener as expense when purchased, although it had a three-year estimated life and no residual value.

Case B:

For inventory purposes, the company switched from FIFO to LIFO to FIFO during a five-year period.

Case C:

The company recognizes earnings on long-term construction contracts at the end of each year of the construction period (based on estimates), while major competitors recognize earnings only at the date the contract is completed (based on actual results).

Case D:

The company follows a policy of depreciating plant and equipment on the straight-line basis over a period of time that is 50% longer than the reliably estimated useful life.

Case E:

As an accounting policy, interest expense is reported at the end of each reporting period as the amount of interest expense less interest revenue.

P 6–2 **(Application of Assumptions, Principles, and Constraints)**

The list of statements given below poses conceptual issues. For each statement *(a)* indicate whether it is correct or incorrect; *(b)* identify the implementation assumption, principle, or constraint that is controlling; and *(c)* provide a brief discussion of its implications.

1. The accounting entity is considered to be separate and apart from the owners.
2. A transaction involving a very small amount does not need to be recorded because of materiality.
3. The monetary unit is not stable over time.
4. GAAP always requires supplementary notes to the financial statements.
5. GAAP often requires that LCM be used in valuing inventories.
6. The cost principle relates only to the statement of income.
7. Revenue should be recognized only when the cash is received.
8. Accruals and deferrals are necessary because of the separate entity assumption.
9. Revenue should be recognized as early as possible and expenses as late as possible.
10. Relevance and reliability dominate all of the qualitative characteristics of accounting information.

P 6–3 **(Application of Concepts)**

Bad Luck Corporation was experiencing a bad year because it was operating at a loss. To minimize the loss, the company recorded certain transactions as indicated below. Determine for each transaction what accounting principle was violated (if any) and explain the nature of the violation and give the journal entry that should have been made.

a. At the beginning of the year, a new machine was purchased for $80,000 cash for use in the business. The estimated useful life was 10 years, and the estimated residual value was $10,000. The following depreciation entry was made at the end of the reporting period:

Depreciation expense	3,500	
Accumulated depreciation		3,500

b. A patent was being amortized over a 17-year useful life. The amortization entry at the end of the current year was:

Retained earnings	500	
Patent		500

c. Two delivery trucks were repaired (engine tune-up, new tires, brakes relined, front end realigned) at a cost of $2,300. The follow entry was made:

Operational asset—trucks	2,300	
Cash		2,300

d. The bad debt loss rate did not change; therefore, an adjusting entry was not made for the estimate of $2,000.

e. Goods for resale (inventory) were being purchased at $1 per unit. However, the company located a good deal and acquired 10,000 units for $7,500 cash. The company recorded the purchase as follows:

Inventory	10,000	
Cash		7,500
Revenue		2,500

f. The company sold its long-term investment in the capital stock of another company for $32,000 cash. The book value of the investment when sold was $20,000. The company made the following entry:

Cash	32,000	
Sales revenue		32,000

P 6–4 (Application of Assumptions, Principles, Constraints)

An inspection of the annual financial statements and the accounting records revealed that the company had violated some implementation assumptions, principles, and constraints. The following transactions were involved:

a. Merchandise purchased for resale was recorded as a debit to Inventory for the invoice price of $10,000 (Accounts Payable was credited for the same amount); terms were 2/10, n/30. Ten days later the account was paid (Cash was credited for $9,800).

b. Accounts receivable of $60,000 was reported on the statement of financial position; this amount included a $20,000 loan to the company president. The maturity date on the loan was not specified.

c. Usual and ordinary repairs on operational assets were recorded as follows: debit Operational Assets, $12,000; credit Cash, $12,000.

d. The company sustained a $20,000 storm damage loss during the current year (no insurance). The loss was recorded and reported as follows:

Statement of income: Extraordinary item—storm loss, $2,000.
Statement of financial position (assets): Deferred charge, storm loss, $18,000.

e. Treasury stock (i.e., stock of the company that was sold and subsequently bought back from the stockholders) was properly debited to Treasury Stock and was reported on the statement of financial position as an asset at the purchase cost, $18,000.

f. Depreciation expense of $41,000 was recorded as a debit to Retained Earnings and was deducted directly from retained earnings on the statement of financial position.

g. Income tax expense of $48,000 was recorded as a debit to Retained Earnings and was deducted directly from retained earnings on the statement of financial position.

Required:

For each transaction, identify the inappropriate treatment and the assumptions, principles, and constraints violated. Also, give the entry that should have been made and the appropriate reporting.

P 6–5 (Implementation of Principles)

The transactions summarized below were recorded as indicated during the current year. Determine for each transaction what implementation accounting principle was violated (if any) and explain the nature of the violation. Also, in each instance, indicate how the transaction should have been recorded.

a. The company needed a small structure for temporary storage. A contractor quoted a price of $650,000. The company decided to build it itself. The cost was $550,000, and construction required three months. The following entry was made:

Buildings—warehouse	650,000	
Cash		550,000
Revenue		100,000

b. The company owns a plant that is located on a river that floods every few years. As a result, the company suffers a flood loss regularly. During the current year, the flood was severe causing an uninsured loss of $12,000, which was the amount spent to repair the flood damage. The following entry was made:

Retained earnings, flood loss	12,000	
Cash		12,000

c. The company originally sold and issued 50,000 shares of $10 par value common stock. During the current year, 45,000 of these shares were outstanding and 5,000 were held by the company as treasury stock (they had been repurchased from the stockholders in prior years). Near the end of the current year, the board of directors declared and paid a cash dividend of $2 per share. The dividend was recorded as follows:

Retained earnings	100,000	
Cash		90,000
Investment income		10,000

d. The company purchased a machine that had a quoted price of $20,000. The company paid for the machine in full by issuing 1,000 shares of its common stock, par $10 (market price $18). The purchase was recorded as follows:

Machine	10,000	
Capital stock		10,000

e. On December 28, the company collected $11,000 cash in advance for merchandise to be available and shipped during February of the next accounting year (the accounting period ends December 31). This transaction was recorded on December 28 as follows:

Cash	11,000	
Sales revenue		11,000

P 6–6 (Accrual and Cash Basis Compared)

The following summarized data were taken from the records of Trippett Corporation at the end of the annual accounting period, December 31, 19B:

Sales for cash	$261,000
Sales on account	84,000
Cash purchases of merchandise for resale	170,000
Credit purchases of merchandise for resale	40,000
Expenses paid in cash (includes any prepayments)	71,000
Accounts receivable:	
Balance in account on 1/1/19B	23,000
Balance in account on 12/31/19B	30,000
Accounts payable:	
Balance in account on 1/1/19B	14,000
Balance in account on 12/31/19B	16,000
Merchandise inventory:	
Beginning inventory, 1/1/19B	50,000
Ending inventory, 12/31/19B	60,000
Accrued (unpaid) wages at 12/31/19B (none at 1/1/19B)	2,000
Prepaid expenses at 12/31/19B (none at 1/1/19B)	3,000
Operational assets—equipment:	
Cost when acquired	100,000
Annual depreciation	10,000

Required:

1. Based on the above data, complete the following statements of income for 19B in order to evaluate the difference between cash and accrual basis (show computations):

	Accrual basis		Cash basis	
Sales revenue		$____		$____
Less expenses:				
Cost of goods sold	$____		$____	
Depreciation expense	____		____	
Remaining expenses	____		____	
Total expenses		____		____
Pretax income		$____		$____

2. Which basis is in conformity with GAAP? Give support for your answer.

CASES

C 6–1 Discuss; Any Conceptual Violations?)

Two independent cases given below violate some parts of the conceptual framework of accounting. For each case, explain *(a)* the nature of the incorrect accounting and reporting, and *(b)* what parts of the conceptual framework were directly violated.

Case A:

The financial statements of Phillips Corporation included the following note: "During the current year, plant assets were written down by $6,000,000 to make possible substantial savings to the company in the future. Depreciation and other expenses in future years will be lower as a result; this will benefit profits of future years."

Case B:

During an audit of Bliss Company, you find certain liabilities, such as taxes, which appear to be overstated. Also some semiobsolete inventory items seem to be undervalued, and the tendency is to expense rather than to capitalize as many items as possible.

In talking with the management about the policies, you are told that "the company has always taken a very conservative view of the business and its future prospects." Management suggests that they do not wish to weaken the company by reporting any more earnings or paying any more dividends than are absolutely necessary, because they do not expect business to continue to be good. They point out that the undervaluation of assets, and so on, does not lose anything for the company and creates reserves for "hard times."

C 6–2 (Materiality Analyzed; a Practical Problem)
At the end of 19X, Bronson Corporation reported the following (summarized):

Statement of financial position

Total assets	$100,000
Total liabilities	30,000
Total equity	70,000

Statement of income

Sales revenue	$180,000
Expenses	150,000
Net income	30,000

Required:

1. This problem focuses on the concept of materiality. Define materiality.
2. On the basis of your definition, use your best judgment to respond to each of the following examples. For each example make a choice as to materiality and give your reason.
   (a) At the beginning of the accounting year, an operational asset, with an estimated useful life of five years and no residual value, was purchased. If the cost is not capitalized, it will be expensed as incurred. The cost of the asset is material if the amount is (check for "yes" response):

______$ 100	______$ 10,000
______ 500	______ 20,000
______ 1,000	______ 50,000
______ 5,000	______ 100,000

   (b) At the end of the accounting year, the amount of accrued wages payable is material if the amount is (check for "yes" response):

______$ 100	______$ 10,000
______ 500	______ 20,000
______ 1,000	______ 50,000
______ 5,000	______ 100,000

   (c) At the end of the accounting year, unearned revenue (cash collected in advance) is material if the amount is (check for "yes" response):

______$ 100	______$ 10,000
______ 500	______ 20,000
______ 1,000	______ 50,000
______ 5,000	______ 100,000

C 6–3 (Full Disclosure)
Explain how each of the following items, as reported on Cate Corporation's statement of financial position violated (if it did) the full-disclosure principle.

a. There was no comment or explanation of the fact that the company changed its inventory method from FIFO to LIFO at the beginning of the current reporting period. A large changeover difference was involved.

b. Owners' equity reported only two amounts: capital stock, $100,000; and retained earnings, $80,000. The capital stock has a par value of $100,000 and originally sold for $150,000 cash.

c. Sales revenue was $900,000 and cost of goods sold, $500,000; the first line reported on the statement of income was revenues, $400,000.

d. No earnings per share (EPS) amounts were reported.

e. Current assets amounted to $200,000 and current liabilities, $180,000; the statement of financial position reported as a single amount, working capital, $20,000.

f. The statement of income showed only the following classifications:
Gross revenues
Costs
Net profit

(AICPA adapted)

C 6–4 (Qualitative Characteristics)

The following quotation is from *Forbes* magazine, November 7, 1983, p. 106:

Last summer followers of Rockwell International, the $7.4 billion conglomerate, probably noticed a *Wall Street Journal* article giving painful details of the company's computer-leasing fiasco with OPM Leasing Service. The story said that Rockwell has not revealed the amount of the losses, calling them "immaterial." But tucked away was the *Journal's* assertion that a member of the company's outside accounting firm, Deloitte, Haskins & Sells, told the paper that fraud-related losses that are less than 10% of the company's $2.2 billion in shareholder equity might properly be considered not material. Both Rockwell and Deloitte insist that the comment in question was taken out of context.

Required:

1. Explain the qualitative characteristic of accounting information that is at issue in this quotation.
2. Assess the situation as described in the quotation.

C 6–5 (Analyzing Actual Financial Statements)

Kimberly-Clark

This case relates to the 1987 financial statements of Kimberly-Clark (given in the Appendix immediately following Chapter 25).

Required:

1. To become familiar with the 1987 financial statements respond to the following:
   a. Date the annual reporting period ends is: _____.
   b. Net sales for 1987 were: $_____.
   c. Net increase (decrease) in cash and cash equivalents for 1987 was: $_____.
   d. Total assets at the end of the 1987 reporting period was: $_____.
   e. Note No. 1 to the consolidated financial statements was titled as follows: _____. How many notes were provided? _____.
   f. What is the name of the auditing firm?
2. The following questions relate to the conceptual framework:
   a. What recent FASB Standards are discussed? What is the expected future impact on the financial statements?
   b. What does the financial statements (including the notes) say about GAAP?
   c. How does the company apply the matching principle to (1) start-up and preoperating costs; (2) advertising and promotion expenses, (3) depreciation, (4) inventories, and (5) pension expense for the transition adjustment?

7 CASH AND RECEIVABLES

OVERVIEW AND PURPOSE

We have reviewed the accounting process, the financial statements, and the concepts related to interest. The prior chapter discussed the conceptual framework of accounting. In this chapter we start our discussion of one of the statement of financial position (SFP) elements—Assets (see Exhibit 6–4). Assets usually are reported on a statement of financial position in order of liquidity; that is, nearness to cash. Financial liquidity and financial flexibility were discussed in Chapter 4 (page 143) because these are issues about which information is provided in a statement of cash flows (SCF). The SCF is an especially significant report because unfavorable cash flows over an extended period of time often result in bankruptcy.

The purpose of this chapter is to discuss two highly liquid assets—cash and receivables. Discussion of another highly liquid asset—short-term (or temporary) investments—is deferred to Chapter 17 because of its similarities to long-term investments. This chapter is subdivided as follows:

Part A: Cash

1. Characteristics of cash and cash equivalents.
2. Control of cash by use of bank accounts.
3. Reconciliation of bank and book cash balances.

Part B: Receivables

1. Receivables defined.
2. Measurement of bad debt expense and accounts receivable.
3. Use of accounts receivable to obtain immediate cash.
4. Accounting for notes receivable.
5. Nontrade receivables.

Supplement 7–A: Comprehensive Bank Reconciliation

PART A: CASH

Characteristics of Cash and Cash Equivalents

Cash is the medium of exchange; it is used to express most of the measurements in accounting. Because of its pervasive use by society, cash as a specific term is understood by nearly everyone. **Cash** inflows and outflows are recorded in an accounting system in one or more **cash accounts.** For **accounting** purposes, cash should include **only** those items that are available for use as a medium of exchange. Thus, cash includes balances in bank checking accounts, currency, and certain negotiable instruments that are accepted by banks for immediate deposit and withdrawal. These negotiable documents, called **immediate cash equivalents,** include ordinary checks, bank drafts, cashier's checks, certified checks, and money orders.[1] These documents are recorded as cash for accounting purposes. Other cash equivalents, such as balances in savings accounts, money market funds, Treasury bills, commercial paper, and certificates of deposit (CDs), usually are recorded as short-term investments because there often is a delay or penalty for conversion to immediate cash. Cash **excludes** such items as postage stamps (a prepaid expense), receivables from company employees, cash advances paid to employees and outsiders, and postdated checks.

For **external** reporting purposes (i.e., on the statement of financial position), companies often combine cash and cash equivalents, such as short-term investments. A typical example of **cash reporting** (not recording) is as follows:

THE FLUOROCARBON COMPANY
(in thousands)

	1987	1986
Current assets:		
Cash and cash equivalents (Note 1)	$ 8,406	$13,259
Accounts receivable, less allowance for doubtful accounts of $556 in 1987 and $476 in 1986	13,282	15,351
Current portion notes receivable	3,875	736
Inventories	12,464	11,879
Income taxes receivable	452	—
Prepaid expenses and other assets	1,330	950
Total current assets	39,809	42,175

Notes to consolidated financial statements:
Note 1. Summary of Significant Accounting Policies Cash and Cash Equivalents (in part)
The company's policy is to invest cash in excess of operating requirements, arising primarily from the proceeds of the subordinated debt offering, in income-producing investments. Temporary cash investments of $6,944,000 at January 31, 1987, and $18,000,000 at January 31, 1986, include money market and commercial paper amounts stated at cost, which approximates market. Included in selling, general, and administrative costs is interest and dividend income from temporary investments of $846,000 in fiscal 1987, $58,000 in fiscal 1986, and $13,000 for fiscal 1985.

A continuing survey of the accounting practices of 600 large companies reported the following:

[1] For statement of cash flow purposes, cash equivalents are defined more broadly to include short-term or temporary "highly liquid" investments. (See Chapter 4.)

Cash—balance sheet captions	Number of companies 1986	1985	1984	1983
Cash	235	233	266	293
Cash and equivalents	117	106	89	86
Cash includes certificates of deposit or time deposits	47	55	60	59
Cash combined with marketable securities	201	206	185	162
Total companies	600	600	600	600

Source: AICPA, *Accounting Trends & Techniques, 1987* (New York, 1987), p. 109.

Checks that have not been mailed or otherwise delivered to the payees by the end of the accounting period should not be deducted from the balance of the Cash account. Entries already made to record such checks should be reversed before preparing the financial statements. To illustrate, one large company included the following notes to its 1987 financial statements:

> Under the company's cash management program, checks in transit are not considered reductions of cash or accounts payable until presented to the appropriate banks for payment. At December 31, 1987 and 1986, checks in transit amounted to $25 million and $20 million, respectively.

An **overdraft** in a bank account should be shown as a current liability. However, if a depositor has overdrawn one account with Bank A but has positive balances in other accounts in that bank, it is appropriate accounting to offset the negative balance in one account against the positive balance in the other account. The net asset or liability should be reported on the statement of financial position because the single bank is in a position to protect both accounts. It is incorrect to offset an overdraft in Bank A against a balance on deposit in Bank B because the positive account is open to withdrawals without knowledge by the other bank.

Petty cash funds (discussed later) and cash held by branches or divisions should be included in cash because such funds ordinarily are used to meet current operating expenses and to liquidate current liabilities.

Items properly included in cash seldom present valuation problems because cash is recorded and reported at its "face" value. Foreign currency balances cause valuation problems since they must be translated to their current dollar equivalents, which often causes translation gains and losses (see Exhibit 4–5).

A **compensating balance** occurs when a bank lends funds to a customer and requires that a minimum balance be retained at all times in the customer's checking account. The practical effects are to *(a)* limit the amount of funds effectively borrowed and *(b)* increase the **effective** interest rate on the loan. For example, if you borrow $10,000 at 10% and must keep $1,000 of it as a minimum in your bank account, you can use only $9,000 but you pay interest on $10,000. This increases your interest rate to 11.1%. Strictly viewed, a compensating balance should not be included in the cash balance. If compensating balances are not disclosed, misleading inferences about the company's liquidity and interest costs may occur. Therefore, compensating balances should be *(a)* reported on the statement of financial position as a noncash current asset, or *(b)* clearly disclosed in the notes to the financial statements.[2]

[2] The SEC requires that **legally restricted deposits** held as compensating balances against short-term borrowing arrangements be reported as noncash current assets, and if long-term borrowing, as noncurrent assets.

Internal Control of Cash

Cash management involves the planning and control of cash to efficiently *(a)* meet the day-to-day cash needs of the company, *(b)* invest temporarily idle cash to earn interest revenue, and *(c)* safeguard cash from theft.

Safegarding cash from theft is critical in most businesses. Cash is *(a)* easy to conceal and transport and *(b)* desired by everyone. This phase of the control of cash is closely related to the accounting system. Free access to the accounting system makes it easy to conceal cash theft. Therefore, careful control of cash receipts and payments is essential.

Control of Cash Receipts

Cash inflows in businesses come from numerous sources; therefore, the control procedures must vary among companies. However, the following procedures apply in most situations:

1. **Separate the responsibilities** for the cash-handling and cash-recording functions. This separation assures that an individual cannot steal cash and conceal the theft by making fictitious journal entries.
2. **Assign cash-handling and cash-recording responsibilities** to ensure a continuous and uninterrupted flow of cash from initial receipt to deposit in an authorized bank account. This control requires *(a)* immediate counting, *(b)* immediate recording, and *(c)* timely deposits of all cash received.
3. **Maintain continuous and close supervision** of all cash-handling and cash-recording functions. This control should include both routine and surprise internal audits and required daily reports of cash receipts, payments, and balances.

Control of Cash Disbursements

The cash outflows in most businesses involve many purposes or uses. Many of the cash thefts in the disbursements process occur because disbursements are numerous and it is relatively easy to conceal disbursement cash thefts. The most effective control is to use a strict internal control system for all cash payments.

Although each control system for cash disbursements should be tailored to the situation, several fundamentals are essential; these are:

1. **Separate the responsibilities** for cash disbursement documentation, check writing, check signing, check mailing, and record-keeping.
2. **Make all cash disbursements by check.** An exception can be made for small amounts from a petty cash fund.
3. **Establish a petty cash fund** with tight controls and close supervision.
4. **Prepare and sign checks** only when supported by adequate documentation and verification.
5. **Supervise** all cash disbursement and record-keeping functions.

Petty Cash System

Cost-effective control of cash disbursements often can be facilitated by using a **petty cash (or imprest) fund** to make small cash disbursements because it usually is not cost effective to process a check for each payment. Examples of such payments are those made for the daily paper for the office, small express shipments, local taxi fares, special postage charges on delivery, supplies for the coffee maker, and other minor office supplies. A petty cash system should operate as follows:

1. A reliable employee is designated as the petty cash **custodian.** This person is given a specified amount of petty cash at the outset. The custodian then disburses the cash as needed, receives adequate documentation for each petty cash disbursement, maintains a running record of the petty cash on hand, and periodically reports the total amount of cash spent supported by the **documentation** for each disbursement. The record maintained, in addition to the documentation, often is called the **petty cash record.** To illustrate, assume J. Doe is selected as the petty cash custodian with a petty cash fund of $300. A regular check drawn to "Petty Cash" is cashed and the cash is given to Doe for safekeeping in a designated place. The initiating entry is:

Petty cash (or imprest cash fund)	300	
Cash		300

2. When the amount of petty cash runs low due to expenditures, and also at the end of the accounting period, the custodian submits a request for replenishment. This request must be supported by the documentation of expenditures for the amount of petty cash spent since the last replenishment date. At each of these dates, a regular check is drawn for the amount spent; the custodian is provided cash for the amount of the check in order to maintain the specified petty cash balance. To illustrate, at the end of the first month, J. Doe submitted a replenishment request for $260. It was supported by documentation that reflected the following payments from the petty cash fund: postage, $90; office supplies, $70; taxi fares, $80; and daily papers, $20. The following replenishment entry must be made:

Postage expense	90	
Office supplies expense	70	
Transportation expense	80	
Administrative expense	20	
Cash (not Petty Cash)		260

The effects of this entry are to *(a)* replenish the amount of petty cash held by the custodian to $300, which is the specified balance maintained in the Petty Cash account in the ledger and *(b)* record expenses incurred by using petty cash.

Recording Cash Shortages and Overages. Cash shortages and overages may be caused by (1) theft, (2) unintentional errors in counting cash when there is a large volume of cash transactions, and (3) inappropriate accounting. Cash shortages and overages usually should be recorded in a Cash Shortage and Overage account. A debit balance in this account is an expense or loss and a credit balance represents a revenue or gain depending on the circumstances (see Exhibit 6–4). In contrast, when theft is discovered, the amount involved should be recorded as a credit to the regular Cash account and as a debit to *(a)* a receivable if recovery is expected from the individual involved or from an insurance or bonding company, or *(b)* a loss account on the presumption that recovery is improbable.

Control of Cash by Use of Bank Accounts

One of the most important cash controls is provided by bank accounts. Typically, a small business has one or two bank accounts—usually in the same bank. In contrast, large companies often have a number of bank accounts in diverse locations. An essential control activity is the monthly bank reconciliation for each bank account. The reconciliation is a check to determine whether the bank account and the company's cash are in agreement after taking into account such items as outstanding checks and deposits.

Large companies with widely dispersed activities often use multiple bank accounts in diverse locations to facilitate the collection of cash and to reduce collection float. **Float** is the period of time between the time a customer mails a check and the time it is received and deposited by the company. A variation of this procedure is available with a lockbox account. The company rents a box at a local post office and instructs customers to mail their payments to that address. A local bank is authorized (for a fee) to empty the box daily and deposit the funds in a lockbox account for the company. In this way, the company has immediate use of the cash. Also, electronic transfer of cash between banks by telephone, wire, or computer is being used to reduce float time (and to maximize interest earned on cash in excess of immediate needs, or to reduce borrowing).

Reconciliation of Bank and Book Cash Balances

Monthly reconciliation of the bank balance, as reported on the monthly **bank statement,** with the depositor's **Cash account** balance is an important cash control procedure.

If the bank statement and the depositor's Cash account are current, the two balances will be in agreement. In this case they will reflect the **correct cash balance** for that particular bank account and the depositor's Cash account. This condition will seldom occur; therefore, a reconciliation of bank and book balances will require identification of the various items that are not yet reflected in both balances.

On receipt of the monthly bank statement, the cash balance reported in the bank statement should be reconciled with the cash balance shown in the Cash account in the company books for that bank account. Reconciliation of bank and book balances has three basic purposes: (1) it establishes a **control,** that is, it checks the accuracy of the records of both the bank and the company; (2) it establishes the correct ending cash balance; and (3) it provides information for entries in the company accounts for items shown in the bank statement that have not yet been recorded in the company's Cash account, such as a bank service charge.

Reconciliation of the bank balance with the book balance of the Cash account requires an analysis of the **monthly bank statement and the cash records maintained by the company.** Usually the bank and book cash balances will differ for the following reasons:

a. Items recorded as cash receipts in the company books but not added to the bank balance on the bank statement.

Examples:

1. Deposits outstanding (traditionally called **deposits in transit**)—cash deposits made by the company that have not been added by the bank to the bank balance.
2. Cash on hand and petty cash (i.e., cash not on deposit in the bank.) Some companies do not include cash on hand in a bank reconciliation for two reasons: *(a)* two or more bank accounts are maintained and the cash on hand does not relate to either one (companies usually relate it to the main bank account), and *(b)* they prefer to keep it separate (in which case the bank and book balances will not agree unless it is compensated for in some other way). Petty cash also can be included or excluded in a similar manner.

b. Amounts added by the bank to the bank balance but not yet recorded as cash receipts in the company books.

Examples:

1. Interest earned by the company that was added by the bank to the bank balance but has not yet been recorded as a cash receipt in the company books.
2. Collections of notes receivable by the bank on behalf of the company; these amounts have been added by the bank to the bank balance but have not yet been recorded as cash receipts in the company books.

c. Amounts recorded as cash disbursements in the company books but not yet deducted by the bank from the bank balance.

Example:

Checks outstanding—checks written and recorded as cash disbursements in the company books that have not been cleared through the bank and, as a result, have not been deducted by the bank from the bank balance.

d. Amounts subtracted by the bank from the bank balance but not yet recorded as cash disbursements in the company books.

Examples:

1. Bank service charge.
2. Nonsufficient funds (i.e., a NSF, or "hot, rubber, or bounced," check received from a customer).

e. Errors in the bank's records or in the company's cash account.

Reconciliation Procedures

Reconciliation of the bank balance with the book balance of cash can be accomplished in any of the three following formats:

1. Reconciliation of the book balance to the bank balance. This format starts with the related Cash account balance, then analyzes the differences, and ends with the bank balance.
2. Reconciliation of both the book and bank balances to the true or correct cash balance. This format has two parts, one for the **bank balance,** and another for the **book balance.** The last line for each part is the **correct cash balance.**

3. A comprehensive, proof of cash or audit, format that reconciles the beginning balances, cash receipts, cash payments, and ending balances for **both** the bank and the books (discussed in Supplement 7–A).

The second format is used in this chapter because *(a)* it facilitates the analysis of differences, *(b)* it provides data for the adjusting entries needed to update the company's Cash account, and *(c)* it provides the correct balance of the Cash account that should be reported on the statement of financial position.

Bank Reconciliation Illustrated

The August reconciliation of the bank balance with the book balance for West Company is shown in **Exhibit 7–1.** The August 31 bank statement reported an **ending** cash balance of $38,900. The company's Cash account showed an **ending** cash balance of $35,300. The bank reconciliation reconciles both the bank balance and the book balance to the correct cash balance of $35,890.

Exhibit 7–1 presents panel A, the case data, panel B, the **bank reconciliation,** and panel C, the entries needed to update the company's Cash account to the correct cash balance. Notice that the reconciliation has two parts—bank balance and book balance. Each part starts with the unreconciled **ending** balance for the reconciliation period (August 31 in this example). Each part also provides for **additions** and **deductions** for the reconciling items. Notice that the bottom line on the reconciliation is the correct cash balance. Both the bank and the books would reflect this balance if all items were recognized by both the bank and the depositor. This fact is the key used to decide which additions and deductions should be entered under "bank balance" and which should be entered under "book balance." The only items entered under "bank balance" are those that eventually will change the "bank balance." Only those that will cause another change in the Cash account are entered under "book balance."

Five items on the bank reconciliation given in Exhibit 7–1 need explanation:

1. **Deposits outstanding**—A deposit made and recorded by the company late in the period that was not yet included on the bank statement. This amount **is determined by comparing company deposits with the deposits listed on the bank statement.** Alternately, the amount can be determined as a proof or shortcut as follows:

Deposits outstanding at end of prior period	$ 5,000
Deposits for the current period (per books)	75,300
Total that could have been deposited	80,300
Deposits shown in bank statement	(77,300)
Deposits outstanding at end of current period	$ 3,000

2. **Checks outstanding**—Checks that have not yet cleared the bank. This amount **is determined by comparing checks written with checks cleared.** Alternately, the amount can be determined as a proof or shortcut as follows:

Checks outstanding at end of prior period	$ 8,000
Checks written during current period (shown in books)	70,000
Total checks that could have cleared	78,000
Checks cleared shown in bank statement	(71,000)
Checks outstanding at end of current period	$ 7,000

Exhibit 7–1
Bank reconciliation to the correct cash balance—West Company.

Panel A—Case Data at August 31, 19X:

Bank Statement		Company's Cash Account	
August 1 balance	$ 32,000	August 1 balance	$ 30,000
Deposits recorded in August	77,300	August deposits	75,300
Checks cleared in August	(71,000)	August checks	(70,000)
Note collected (including $100 interest)	1,100	August 31 balance	$ 35,300
NSF check, J. Fox	(300)		
August service charges	(200)		
August 31 balance	$ 38,900		

Additional data, end of July: Deposits outstanding, $5,000 and checks outstanding, $8,000 (these amounts were taken from the July bank reconciliation). End of August: Cash on hand (undeposited), $990.

Panel B—Reconciliation of Bank and Book Balances, August 31, 19X:

Bank Balance		Book Balance	
Ending bank balance, August 31	$38,900	Ending book balance, August 31	$35,300
Additions:		Additions:	
Cash on hand (undeposited)	990	Note collected by bank:	
Deposits outstanding, August 31 ($5,000 + $75,300 − $77,300)	3,000	Principal	1,000
Deductions:		Interest	100
Checks outstanding ($8,000 + $70,000 − $71,000, August 31)	(7,000)	Deductions:	
Total	35,890	NSF check, J. Fox	(300)
Cash shortage		Bank service charges	(200)
Correct cash balance	$35,890	Total	35,900
		Cash shortage*	(10)
		Correct cash balance	$35,890

* Discovered in making the reconciliation.

Panel C—Entries Required to Update the Cash Account to the Correct Balance of $35,890:

1. Cash	1,100	
Note receivable		1,000
Interest revenue		100
2. Special receivable, J. Fox, NSF	300	
Expense, bank service charge	200	
Cash shortage	10	
Cash		510

3. **NSF (nonsufficient funds) check**—The company received a $300 check from customer J. Fox, debited that amount to the Cash account, and deposited it. The bank received the check and increased the company's bank balance. The check was returned to the company's bank as a "hot" check; the bank reduced the company's checking account. Therefore, it is no longer in the company's bank account. It is still included as a debit in the company's Cash account. The debit must be removed from the Cash account and debited to a special receivable account as in Exhibit 7–1, panel C. This is what would be done when a bank receives a dishonored check and immediately notifies the depositor, and also reduces the customer's bank balance. This reduction will show on the next bank statement. If the customer also immediately makes an entry to record the returned check, a correcting entry at the end is not needed; otherwise, a correcting entry is needed when the reconciliation is completed.

4. **Cash shortages and overages**—After all of the above items were verified and entered on the bank reconciliation, the bank and book **correct balances** did not agree by $10. The logical conclusion was a cash **shortage** because the books totaled $10 more cash than shown as the correct cash balance. It appears that cash on hand was $10 short; therefore, the book balance was reduced and a cash shortage was recorded.
5. **Entries required by the bank reconciliation** to update the company's Cash account are shown in Exhibit 7–1, panel C. The five required entries were combined into two entries for practical reasons. Notice that these entries **recorded each addition and deduction shown on the book balance section of the reconciliation.** The additions and deductions in the bank balance section do not affect the company's books because they already have been recorded by the company.

The importance of the control implications of preparing a bank reconciliation for each bank statement received cannot be overemphasized. Moreover, it provides information needed for the journal entries to recognize those items shown on the bank statement that have not yet been recorded in the depositor's accounts.

Comprehensive Bank Reconciliation

This bank reconciliation format is variously called **a comprehensive bank reconciliation, a proof of cash, a cash reconciliation, a four-column reconciliation,** and **an audit-based reconciliation.** This format contains separate parts for **bank** and **book.** It is a comprehensive reconciliation because it reconciles *(a)* beginning bank and book balances, *(b)* cash receipts, *(c)* cash payments, and *(d)* ending (or correct) cash balances. A comprehensive bank reconciliation is discussed and illustrated in Supplement 7–A.

PART B: RECEIVABLES

Receivables Defined

Receivables include all of an entity's claims for money, goods, services, and other noncash assets from other entities. Receivables may be classified as current assets or noncurrent assets depending on their time to maturity or expected collection date. Receivables may be informal, such as an "open" account, or be represented by a formal contract, such as a note receivable. For discussion purposes, receivables are classified herein as follows:

a. Accounts receivable (trade receivables).
b. Notes receivable (short term and long term).
c. Nontrade receivables (short term and long term).

Accounts Receivable

Trade receivables are amounts owed by customers for goods and services sold in the entity's normal course of business. **Accounts receivable** (also called **trade accounts receivable**) include amounts that are expected to be collected within the year following the statement of financial position date or the operating cycle of the entity, whichever is longer. Trade receivables include "open" accounts, usually called **accounts receivable,** and written agreements usually called **notes receivable, trade.** Various terms used for current trade receivables are indicated by the following tabulation based on the financial reports of 600 major companies:

	Number of companies			
Trade receivable captions	**1986**	**1985**	**1984**	**1983**
Accounts receivable	237	222	210	207
Receivables	150	168	171	162
Accounts and notes receivable	102	106	115	118
Trade accounts receivable	111	104	105	113
Total companies	600	600	600	600

Source: AICPA, *Accounting Trends & Techniques, 1987* (New York, 1987), p. 118.

At the date of a credit sale, an account receivable is debited and Sales Revenue is credited. This initial entry should record the amount of **cash** that is expected to be collected from the customer. Often this is the amount that is billed to the customer. However, companies sometimes offer a **cash discount** (also called a **sales discount**) to encourage early payment by the customer. Typical terms are 2/10, n/30; that is, 2% cash discount if paid within 10 days from the sale date and the gross amount due in 30 days. Another commonly used credit term is 2/10; n/EOM (i.e., end of month). Most companies pay such accounts early to avoid the additional cash payment, which involves a very high interest rate on an annualized basis (approximately 36½% in the above example). When a cash discount is offered, the question arises as to whether the sale should be recorded at its *(a)* gross amount, or *(b)* net of allowed discount amount. To illustrate, on December 28, 19A, a sale of $1,000 was made with terms 2/10, n/30. Should this sale be recorded at the **gross** amount of $1,000 or at the **net** amount of $980 (i.e., $1,000 × .98)? Given the high annualized interest rate of 36½%, the usual expectation is that the net amount will be collected. Both the gross and net approaches are used in industry. The net approach is conceptually preferable because the discount is properly viewed as interest earned for late payments made by customers. The gross approach often is viewed as more practical because of a minor clerical advantage at the time of sale; however, many accountants believe that it overstates an asset (receivables) and understates interest revenue. An application of the two approaches is presented in **Exhibit 7–2.** The evaluation at the end of the exhibit indicates the conclusion that the net method generally is preferable.

Subsequent to the initial recording of accounts receivable, this current asset is carried at its **net realizable value,** which is the cash amount expected to be collected. This valuation reflects the effects of *(a)* cash discounts allowed for early payment and *(b)* estimated bad debt losses.

Trade discounts are used to change the sale price *(a)* when quoting sales prices, such as in catalogs (without changing the catalog), and *(b)* by giving quantity discounts. For example, an item priced at $50 with a trade discount

Exhibit 7–2
Recording credit sales and subsequent collections.

Case Data: December 28, 19A—Sale, $1,000; credit terms 2/10, n/30. End of annual reporting period, December 31.

Net approach			Gross approach		
19A—To record the credit sale:					
Accounts receivable	980		Accounts receivable	1,000	
Sales revenue		980	Sales revenue		1,000
19B—To record collection if within the 10-day discount period:					
Cash	980		Cash	980	
Accounts receivable		980	Sales discounts	20	
			Accounts receivable		1,000
19C—To record collection if after the 10-day discount period:					
Cash	980		Cash	1,000	
Interest revenue		20	Accounts receivable		1,000
Accounts receivable		980			

Evaluation:

a. Conceptual—The 2% discount is interest (time value of money), not sales revenue. Sales revenue in 19A is $980, not $1,000. The interest should be recognized only if the full amount, $1,000, is actually paid. The receivable at the end of 19A should be the net cash expected to be received ($980) because the discounts usually are taken. The net method attains all of these conceptual objectives. Even if the discounts are not taken, the net method should be used.

b. Conceptually, an **adjusting entry** at the end of 19A can be supported on balance under each approach: Net approach—for discounts already forfeited; and gross approach—for discounts that can still be taken. Lack of materiality usually precludes such adjusting entries in both cases.

c. Practical—Comparing the above entries for each approach and the adjusting entry issue in *(b)*, the clerical differences appear to be insignificant. Observation: A perceptive cash customer could get the item for $980 by buying on credit, then immediately pay the credit department $980 to settle the debt!

of 40% would cost the retailer $30. Also, a company may give customers a discount, such as 10%, on a unit price of $100 if 10 or more items are purchased at the same time. The unit price would be $90. In summary, trade discounts are used as pricing mechanisms, whereas, cash discounts are used to encourage early payment of a debt.

Measurement of Bad Debt Expense and Accounts Receivable

When credit is extended some uncollectible receivables are inevitable. These bad debt expenses are considered a normal operating expense of the business. Measurement of such items involves the concurrent estimation of *(a)* the amount of **bad debt expense** for the period and *(b)* **valuation of accounts receivable** at net realizable value.

A special valuation account (i.e., a contra asset), Allowance for Doubtful Accounts (or Allowance for Bad Debts), is used to report the estimated bad debts included in Accounts Receivable at the end of each reporting period.

The residual amount, Accounts Receivable less Allowance for Doubtful Accounts, is intended to represent the **estimated net realizable value** of accounts receivable. An adjusting entry is used to record bad debt expense and concurrently to adjust the allowance account as follows:

Bad debt expense (or estimated bad debt expense)	6,000	
Allowance for doubtful accounts		6,000

The basic accounting question is when should the loss due to an uncollectible account (i.e., bad debt expense) be recognized. The primary issues are (1) how to **measure** bad debt expense in conformity with the **matching principle,** and (2) how to measure accounts receivable in conformity with the definition of a **current asset**—its expected net realizable value. These measurements require the use of estimates.[3]

Estimating Bad Debt Expense

The **matching principle** requires that bad debt expense be estimated at the end of each accounting period. The estimate is needed in order to **match** expected bad debt losses with the revenues of the period that **caused** those losses.

The sales revenue of the period from **credit sales** is known at the end of the period; however, the specific accounts receivable that ultimately will be uncollectible often will not be known until future periods. The **matching principle** requires that bad debt expense be matched against the sales revenue of the period in which the sales revenue is recognized. Therefore, it is necessary for each period to **estimate** the amount of bad debt expense and record it in an adjusting entry, similar to the one above. This estimate is prepared before the ultimate determination of whether the individual accounts receivable of the period will be collected.

Two methods are commonly used to estimate the adjustment to the Bad Debt Expense and the Allowance for Doubtful Accounts:

Method 1. Percent of credit sales—This method emphasizes the **matching principle.** The net realizable value of accounts receivable is secondary. Based on experience, the average percentage relationship between actual bad debt losses and net credit sales is estimated. This percentage then is applied to the actual net credit sales of the period to determine both the Bad Debt Expense and the concurrent addition to the Allowance for Doubtful Accounts.

Method 2. Net realizable value—This method uses net realizable value of the ending balance of accounts receivable and a bad debt percentage. This method emphasizes the statement of financial position and the definition of a current asset—accounts receivable. The balance in accounts receivable is multiplied by the appropriate bad debt percent(s) to determine the balance that is required to be in the allowance account. **The balance in the allowance account then is adjusted so that it equals the total amount of the estimated uncollectible accounts.** The bad debt percent(s) used in this method can be either *(a)* a composite (i.e., single) rate, or *(b)* a series of rates based on an aging schedule.

---

[3] *APB Opinion No. 21,* "Interest on Receivables and Payables," does not require that accounts receivable be valued by present-value discounting.

The two methods, *(a)* **percent of credit sales** and *(b)* **net realizable value,** are acceptable under current generally accepted accounting principles (GAAP). Some companies use both methods as explained later.

Bad Debt Expense Based on Credit Sales. To illustrate accounting for bad debt expense and uncollectible receivables, assume the following data for X Company for the year ended December 31, 19B:

January 1, 19B, balances:	
Accounts receivable (debit)	$101,300
Allowance for doubtful accounts (credit)	3,300
Transactions during 19B:	
Credit sales	500,000
Cash sales	700,000
Collections on accounts receivable	420,000
Prior accounts to be written off as uncollectible during 19B	3,800

The 19B entry to write off the prior uncollectible accounts is:

Allowance for doubtful accounts	3,800	
Accounts receivable (specific accounts)		3,800

After posting this entry, Accounts Receivable will reflect a debit balance of $177,500 (i.e., $101,300 + $500,000 − $420,000 − $3,800). The write-off of individual accounts as uncollectible would occur as a result of a review by the credit department during the period and would precede the end-of-period adjusting entries. In some cases, such as after a large write-off or when currently created receivables are written off before the end of the period, the allowance account may have a temporary **debit** balance prior to the adjusting entry ($500 in this example, i.e., $3,300 − $3,800).

An analysis of the actual uncollectible accounts related to actual credit sales for the past three years showed that an average of 1.2% of credit sales was not collected and that this relationship is expected to continue. The required 19B adjusting entry is:

Bad debt expense ($500,000 × 1.2%)	6,000	
Allowance for doubtful accounts		6,000

After posting this entry, the allowance account will reflect a credit balance of $5,500 (i.e., $3,300 − $3,800 + $6,000). The entry is made without regard to the prior balance in the allowance account.

Method 1, percent of credit sales, emphasizes the statement of income because its primary focus is on bad debt **expense** and it only incidentally measures accounts receivable at net realizable value. The conceptual basis for the estimation of bad debt expense by this method is the **matching principle.** It is simple and economical to implement. Its primary disadvantage is that it does not reconsider prior estimates in the short term; thus, it does not compensate in the short term for prior estimating deficiencies.

Bad Debt Expense Based on Net Realizable Value of Accounts Receivable. This method is based on the relationship between **accounts receivable** and the balance in the allowance for doubtful accounts. It emphasizes the statement of financial position because its primary focus is on the net realizable value of a current asset—accounts receivable. Its conceptual basis is the **full disclosure principle** and it compensates for prior estimating deficiencies in both the short and long term. This approach has two variations: *(a)* the use of a composite (or single) rate or *(b)* the use of an "aging" approach.

Estimate Based on a Composite or Single Percent of Accounts Receivable. An analysis of prior actual uncollectible accounts related to the prior ending balances of accounts receivable showed that an average of 3½% of the ending balance was uncollectible. Assuming this relationship is expected to continue, an ending balance in Accounts Receivable of $177,500, and a debit balance of $500 in the Allowance for Doubtful Accounts, then the required 19B entry would be:

Bad debt expense [($177,500 × 3½%) + $500*]	6,713	
Allowance for doubtful accounts		6,713

* Debit balance in the allowance account.

This variation is simple to apply; however, the single average may be nonrepresentative of both the net realizable value of the receivables and bad debt expense.

Estimate Based on Aging Schedule of Accounts Receivable. This approach is based on an aging of the current receivables. It involves two phases: (1) preparation of an aging schedule of accounts receivable and (2) estimation of the collection loss percentages for each age category.

Phase 1. Aging Accounts Receivable—Aging accounts receivable involves an analysis of each individual account to determine the amounts not due, currently due, and past due. More than three classifications often are used, measured in terms of days or months. Classification of receivable amounts by age (i.e., length of time uncollected) is important because experience indicates that the older an account, the higher the probability of uncollectibility. Aging requires the preparation of an *aging schedule* similar to **Exhibit 7–3.**

Phase 2. Estimating the Collection Loss Percentages—On completion of the aging schedule, each past-due amount (e.g., Field's account in Exhibit 7–3) is reviewed by the credit department to determine its probable collectibility. The purpose of this analysis is to develop an estimated collection loss percentage for each **age category.** This estimate is based on the previous loss experience of the company for each age category. The results of this analysis by X Company are shown in **Exhibit 7–4.**

Based on the computation in Exhibit 7–4, at December 31, 19B, the Allowance for Doubtful Accounts would be adjusted to a credit balance of $5,690, as follows:

Bad debt expense	6,190	
Allowance for doubtful accounts		6,190

Computation:

To adjust to the desired creidt balance as follows:

Desired balance (see Exhibit 7–4)	$5,690
Debit balance in allowance before adjustment	500
Amount of credit needed	$6,190

Exhibit 7–3
Aging schedule for accounts receivable, X Company, December 31, 19B.

SPECIAL JOURNAL - MERCHANDISE PURCHASES ON CREDIT Page P-19

Date 19J	Purchase Order No.	Accounts Payable (name)	Terms	Ledger Folio	Purchase and Liability Amount
Jan. 3	41	PT Mfg. Co.	1/20,n/30	210.61	990
7	42	Able Suppliers, Ltd.	net	210.12	150
31	—	Totals	—	—	6,760
31	—	Posting	—	—	(612/210)

Exhibit 7–4
Estimating doubtful accounts based on aging schedule, X Company, December 31, 19B.

Status	Total balances*	Uncollectible experience percentage	Amount estimated to be uncollectible
Not past due	$110,000	.2%	$ 220
1–30 days past due	31,000	1.0	310
31–60 days past due	29,500	8.0	2,360
Over 60 days past due	7,000	40.0	2,800
	$177,500		$5,690

* Amounts agree with amounts on "Total" line in Exhibit 7–3.

The aging schedule approach is preferable to the composite percentage approach because the former involves a more comprehensive analysis of accounts receivable. The composite approach does not directly consider the age of accounts receivables.

In practice, both the credit sales and accounts receivable methods often are used together. That is, for interim financial statements, many companies base monthly or quarterly adjusting entries on the credit sales method because of the low cost of applying this method. At the end of the year, however, many companies age their accounts receivable as a check on the reasonableness of the balance in the allowance account. If the balance in the allowance account (before the year-end adjustment) differs materially from the balance implied by the aging schedule, the company must make a judgment about the appropriate amount to record in the year-end adjusting entry.

In the past, aging accounts receivables was a costly process. It required credit department personnel to analyze each account receivable individually. The aging method is used more frequently now because computer software has lowered the cost of implementing the aging method. Also, cash flow problems in recent years have prompted companies to monitor their receivables closely to save interest charges and reduce losses, and aging is the primary way accounts receivable are analyzed.

In the preceding illustration, the $3,800 write-off of receivables during the current period caused the allowance account to have a debit balance of $500 before the end-of-period adjustment. This result does not necessarily indicate that past estimates of bad debt losses were too low. It is possible that the $3,800 write-off includes some receivables created during the same period. However, if the allowance account were to have a debit balance soon after making the end-of-period adjustment, an inadequate provision for bad debts probably is indicated. When it is determined that bad debt estimates have been too low or too high, current and future rates should be adjusted accordingly. This would be accounted for as a change in accounting estimate as prescribed in *APB Opinion No. 20*, "Accounting Changes" (see Chapters 3 and 24). A change in estimate does not use a correction entry; rather, the effects of the change are spread over the current and future reporting periods by using a new collection loss percentage.

Both the credit sales and the accounts receivable methods must be adapted to changes in credit policy, changes in economic conditions, or any other factor which might affect the ability of customers to pay their debts. After one of these methods is selected for use, it should be continuously reviewed by the accountant and the officers of the company so that the estimated loss rates can be revised to attain reliable results.

Bad Debts Collected. When an account is written off as uncollectible, continuing collection efforts are not discontinued. When these efforts are successful, the customer's account previously written off should be debited for the amount actually collected and the allowance account should be credited for the same amount. (This reverses the write-off entry.) This entry will cause the debtor's account to reflect a detailed record of the credit and related collections. The entry also will correct the allowance account. The **collection** then is recorded as a debit to Cash and a credit to Accounts Receivable.

Customers' Credit Balances. Individual accounts receivable for customers with material **credit** balances (from prepayments or overpayments) should be reclassified and reported as liabilities. Credit Balance of Customers' Accounts is a suitable liability account title.

Direct Write-Off of Uncollectible Accounts. Some small nonpublic companies apply a "direct or specific write-off" procedure because it is acceptable for income tax purposes. Under this procedure, bad debt expense is recorded only when individual customers' accounts are determined to be uncollectible. At that time, Accounts Receivable is credited for the uncollectible balance and Bad Debt Expense is debited. This procedure does not require the use of estimates. It has the advantage of simplicity. It also is used by companies in which bad debt losses are not material in amount from year to year. The direct write-off procedure is subject to severe criticism on three counts: (1) Receivables are reported at more than their net realizable value; there is no allowance to deduct even though it is virtually certain that not all receivables will be collected (a violation of the disclosure principle). (2) The period in which the write-off occurs is often later than the period in which the receivable was created. The reported amounts of bad debt expense are not in conformity with the **matching principle**—the expenses of extending credit should be recognized in the period when the revenue is recognized. (3) It allows manipulation of income by arbitrary selection of the period of write-off. For these reasons, the **specific write-off method is not in conformity with GAAP,** except when there is absolutely no reliable method to estimate the loss, or the amounts involved are clearly not material.

Use of Accounts Receivable to Obtain Immediate Cash

Companies usually collect accounts receivable in the normal manner. However, to get immediate cash, companies often **sell** accounts receivable. They also may **borrow money** and pledge accounts receivable as collateral for the loan. Such **transfer arrangements** to advance the cash inflow from accounts receivable involve a wide range of contracts referred to as factoring, selling, assigning, or pledging receivables. The scope of the use of accounts receivables to obtain early cash is indicated in the following tabulation from a survey of 600 companies:

Receivables used for financing	Number of companies 1986	1985	1984	1983
Receivables sold to finance subsidiary	56	60	59	57
Receivables sold to independent entity	47	46	38	39
Receivables used as collateral	35	26	29	34
Total references	138	132	126	130
Reference to receivable financing	132	125	118	121
No reference to receivable financing	468	475	482	479
Total companies	600	600	600	600

Source: AICPA, *Accounting Trends & Techniques, 1987* (New York, 1987), p. 123.

For example, one prominent company reported the following:

SEARS MERCHANDISE GROUP
(in millions)

	1986	1985
Current assets:		
Cash	$ 593.4	$ 405.6
Retail customer receivables (Note 1)	12,726.2	12,502.3
Less: Allowance for uncollectible accounts and unearned finance charges	317.8	242.2
	12,408.4	12,260.1

Note 1. Retail Customer Receivables (in part)

The Group sold selected revolving charge account balances, with proceeds of $1.8, $2.2 and $1.3 billion received in 1986, 1985, and 1984, respectively. As of Dec. 31, 1986 and 1985, the aggregate outstanding balances in such accounts were $2.2 billion and $2.4 billion, respectively.

Receivables are currently sold with a limited repurchase liability for balances ultimately determined to be uncollectible. The purchaser receives all cash collections and finance charge revenues and the Group earns a fee for administering the accounts sold.

The sale of accounts receivable, or borrowing money on them, will either be *(a)* with recourse or *(b)* without recourse. **With recourse** means that the transferor (i.e., the borrower) of the accounts receivables agrees to reimburse the transferee (i.e., the lender) for contractually specified **collection losses.**

These include *(a)* failure of the customers to pay their accounts in full and *(b)* adjustments to the receivables for cash discounts and sales returns. Thus, **without recourse** means that the transferor assumes no obligation to guarantee such losses; the transferee must assume the collection losses.

Also, the agreement to transfer accounts receivable for early cash will specify either *(a)* notification or *(b)* nonnotification. **Notification** means that the debtors (i.e., the customers) are notified of the transfer and that they will be billed and must make payments on the receivables directly to the transferee. **Nonnotification** means that the debtors are **not** notified of the transfer; thus, they will continue to be billed by, and make payments on the receivables to, the transferor. The transferor has the responsibility to remit the cash to the transferee as collected.

Accounting for the Transfer of Accounts Receivable

For the **transferor's** accounting purposes, a transfer of accounts receivables to obtain early cash must be classified as either a "sale" or "borrowing" transaction. A transfer is categorized as:

a. A sale of the receivables, similar to the sale of any other assets for cash, if **all** of the following conditions are met:[4]

1. The transferor surrenders **control** of the future economic benefits of the receivables (control is absent if transferor retains a later repurchase option).
2. The transferor's obligation under the recourse provisions can be **reasonably estimated** (e.g., bad debt losses, collection expenses, discounts, and repossessions).
3. The transferee cannot require the transferor to **repurchase** the receivables except pursuant to the recourse provisions.

b. A borrowing transaction and the recording of a **liability** for the amount of cash received if **any one** of the three conditions listed above is not met. In this situation, the receivables involved remain in the accounts of the transferor as "pledged" assets to support the loan agreement.

Transfers **with** recourse typically qualify as either a sale transaction or a borrowing transaction with neither clearly dominating. Transfers **without** recourse usually qualify as a sale transaction. They usually involve a high discount rate (and a consequent loss on sale).

Illustrations of the Transfer of Accounts Receivable to Obtain Early Cash

It is impractical to illustrate all of the contractual specifications found in the use of accounts receivable to obtain early cash. Therefore, for practical reasons, three simplified cases are illustrated to emphasize the primary accounting distinctions involved.[5] The following basic case is assumed:

> On January 2, 19A, Transferor Company transferred or assigned accounts receivable of $40,000 to Transferee Finance Company to obtain immediate cash. The related Allowance for Doubtful Accounts was $1,000.

---

[4] The discussion that follows is based on the provisions of FASB, *Statement of Financial Accounting Standards No. 77*, "Reporting by Transferors of Transfer of Receivables with Recourse" (Stamford, Conn., December 1983).

[5] Ibid., par. 5.

Stnd #77

Case A—Sale without Recourse; Meets All Three Conditions for a Sale as Listed Above. The sale price is $30,000 cash; notification basis.

January 2, 19A—To record sale of accounts receivable:

Cash	30,000	
Allowance for doubtful accounts	1,000*	
Loss on sale of accounts receivable	9,000*	
Accounts receivable		40,000

* In some cases, the total (i.e., $1,000 + $9,000) would be debited to the allowance account, as in the case where prior estimates of bad debt losses included transactions involving sale of the receivables.

Subsequently, the debtors will pay cash on the accounts directly to Transferee Finance Company. The transferee will assume all bad debt losses and related collection costs.

Case B—Sale with Recourse; Meets All Three Conditions for a Sale as Listed Above. The sale price is $34,000 cash; notification basis. Estimated collection cost of obligations under the recourse provision is $1,500 (e.g., for uncollectible accounts, discounts, and sales returns and allowances).

January 2, 19A—To record sale of accounts receivable, with recourse:

Cash	34,000	
Allowance for doubtful accounts	1,000*	
Loss on sale of accounts receivable	6,500	
Accounts receivable		40,000
Liability—estimated collection loss on accounts receivable sold		1,500

* See note in Case A.

Subsequently, the debtors will pay cash on the accounts directly to Transferee Finance Company. Collection losses will be billed by Transferee Finance Company and will be paid by Transferor Company. To illustrate, on January 30, 19A, Transferee Finance Company billed the following collection losses: Cash discounts allowed debtors, $300, and sales allowances for defective merchandise, $500. Consequently, Transferor Company would make the following entry:

Liability—estimated collection loss on accounts receivable sold	800	
Cash		800

Case C—Borrowing Transaction and the Recording of a Liability for the Amounts Borrowed (Not All of the Three Conditions for a Sale as Listed Above Are Met). Typical terms are "with recourse, nonnotification." In this case, the accounts receivable **assigned** (i.e., not sold) serve as collateral for the loan (usually a note payable). To illustrate, the loan agreement specifies that Transferee Finance Company would advance cash equal to 75% of the gross receivables advanced (i.e., $40,000 in this case) and charge 24% annual interest (payable monthly) on the outstanding receivables at the end of each month. The customers will continue to pay directly to Transferor Company who will remit the appropriate amount of cash as payments on the loan. When the loan and interest are paid in full, any remaining assigned accounts receivable revert to the transferor. Typical transactions and journal entries for Transferor Company are shown in **Exhibit 7–5.**

Exhibit 7–5
Borrowing cash on accounts receivable assigned as collateral for the loan (entries).

Transaction	Entries by Transferor Company		
a. January 2: Assigned $40,000 accounts receivable; advance received, 75%; gave note payable in favor of Transferee Finance Company.	Accounts receivable assigned	40,000	
	Accounts receivable		40,000
	Cash ($40,000 × 75%)	30,000	
	Notes payable (Transferee Finance Co.)		30,000
b. January 3–30: Collected $20,500 of the assigned accounts less sales returns and allowances, $800.	Cash	19,700	
	Sales returns and allowances	800	
	Accounts receivable assigned		20,500
c. January 31: Remitted collections to Transferee Finance Company plus $600 interest (i.e., $30,000 × 24% × 1/12).	Interest expense	600	
	Notes payable (Transferee Finance Co.)	19,700	
	Cash		20,300
d. February 1–27: Collected balance of the assigned accounts, except $200 written off as uncollectible.	Cash	19,300	
	Allowance for doubtful Accounts	200	
	Accounts receivable assigned		19,500
e. February 28: Remitted balance due Transferee Finance Company ($30,000 − $19,700 = $10,300) plus $206 interest (i.e., $10,300 × 24% × 1/12) = $10,506.	Interest expense	206	
	Notes payable (Transferee Finance Co.)	10,300	
	Cash		10,506

Note: Alternatively, if the exact amount of the collections is remitted directly to the finance company (not deposited by Transferor Company into their own bank account), entries *(b)* and *(c)* and *(d)* and *(e)*, respectively, would be combined into two entries.

To summarize, when accounts receivable are used to obtain early cash (i.e., before their expected collection dates), the agreement between the two parties involved—the transferor and transferee—must be analyzed. The analysis is to determine whether the transaction is *(a)* the sale of an asset (the receivables) or *(b)* a borrowing transaction with the accounts receivable used as collateral for a loan. GAAP prescribes three criteria to determine whether the transaction is a sale (all three criteria must be met) or a borrowing (if any one of the three criteria is not met). If the transaction qualifies as a sale, the transferor must record a sale of the receivables in the same manner as the cash sale of any other asset. Cases A and B above illustrate sale situations. Alternatively, if the transaction qualifies as a borrowing, the transferor must record a liability for the loan and keep the receivables in the accounts (but separate them as assigned because they are collaterized or pledged). Case C above illustrates a borrowing situation.

When the transferor agrees to a "with recourse" provision, all collection losses (e.g., uncollectible accounts, discounts, and sale returns and allowances) are assumed by, and recorded in the accounts of, the transferor.

Accounting for Notes Receivable

A note receivable is a written promise to pay the payee (or holder) a specified amount at a specified future date, or dates. Unless forbidden by the note agreement, it is negotiable or transferable to other parties. All commercial notes bear interest; however, notes are classified as either interest bearing or noninterest bearing. An interest-bearing note requires the payment of interest **in addition** to the face amount of the note. In contrast, in a noninterest-bearing note (often called a **discounted note**) the interest is **included** in the face amount of the note.

The **principal amount** of a note receivable is the cash equivalent amount loaned, or the price of goods and services sold; it is the **amount subject to interest** except when there is compound interest. The **face amount** of a note receivable is the amount specified on the face of the note. This amount will be collected at maturity date; it may be the same as, or different from, the principal amount depending on whether the note is interest bearing or noninterest bearing. The **maturity amount** of a note receivable is the amount to be collected on the maturity date, excluding any **separate** interest collections due on that date. Interest on a note (i.e., simple interest) is computed as:

$$\text{Principal amount} \times \text{Stated interest rate} \times \text{Time to maturity} = \text{Interest amount}$$

The **stated** rate of interest on a note is specified in the debt instrument. It is used to compute the amount of **cash** interest to be paid on the principal amount. Short-term notes usually involve simple interest, while long-term notes often specify compound interest (see Chapter 5).

Conceptually, all notes should be recognized at the present value of all specified future cash flows. The discounting, illustrated in Chapter 5, should be at the "going" or market rate of interest commensurate with the risks involved.[6] The rate applicable when the note is received is used; later rate changes are disregarded. Under GAAP, **short-term notes are recorded at their face amount** but long-term notes **must** be recorded at their present value *(APB Opinion No. 21)*.

Short-term notes usually involve simple interest. They often are received from customers, and debtors for money loaned. Long-term notes often require equal cash payments that include both principal and interest (i.e., an annuity).

Accounting for notes receivable involves *(a)* recognition at origination date, *(b)* valuation and interest during the time to maturity, and *(c)* disposal, if it occurs before maturity date.

---

[6] *APB Opinion No. 21,* "Interest on Receivables and Payables," explains this rate as follows: The prevailing rates for similar instruments of issuers with similar credit ratings will normally help determine the appropriate interest rate for determining the present value of a specific note at its date of issuance. In any event, the rate used for valuation purposes will normally be at least equal to the rate at which the debtor can obtain financing of a similar nature from other sources at the date of the transaction. The objective is to approximate the rate which would have resulted if an independent borrower and an independent lender had negotiated a similar transaction under comparable terms and conditions with the option to pay the cash price on purchase or to give a note for the amount of the purchase which bears the prevailing rate of interest to maturity.

Short term always face
Long term always discounted at PV

Accounting for Notes Receivable Illustrated

Case A—Short-Term, Interest-Bearing Note. On April 1, 19A, WV Company sold merchandise on credit and received a $3,000, one-year trade note receivable; stated interest rate, 10%. The annual reporting period for WV Company ends on December 31.

The required journal entries over the term of the note are as follows:

April 1, 19A—To record the sale and the interest-bearing note:

Notes receivable, trade	3,000	
Sales revenue		3,000

December 31, 19A—Adjusting entry:

Interest receivable ($3,000 × 10% × 9/12)	225	
Interest revenue		225

March 31, 19B—Collection of face of note plus interest (no prior reversing entry):

Cash [$3,000 + ($3,000 × 10%)]	3,300	
Notes receivable, trade		3,000
Interest receivable (above)		225
Interest revenue ($3,000 × 10% × 3/12)		75

Case B—Short-Term, Noninterest-Bearing Note Receivable. Noninterest-bearing commercial notes always involve interest. The face amount of a noninterest-bearing note **includes both the principal amount and the interest amount of a single amount that will be collected on maturity date.** Typically, no stated interest rate is specified on the note itself. However, an interest rate may have to be imputed for accounting purposes.

On April 1, 19A, WV Company sold merchandise on credit and received a noninterest-bearing note receivable, face amount, $3,300, due in one year. The face of the note includes 10% interest on the principal amount of $3,000 (i.e., $3,300 ÷ 1.10 = $3,000). The sale price of the merchandise is the present **value** of the face amount of the note; the $300 difference is interest revenue. The accounting period ends December 31. Such notes can be recorded at "net" or "gross"; both give the same results. Either approach is acceptable in all respects. For this reason, you should understand both approaches.

April 1, 19A—To record the sale and noninterest-bearing note using the **net approach:**[7]

---

[7] *Gross approach:*

April 1, 19A:		
Notes receivable, trade	3,300	
Discount on notes receivable*		300
Sales revenue		3,000
December 31, 19A:		
Discount on notes receivable*	225	
Interest revenue		225
March 31, 19B (no reversing entry on January 1, 19B):		
Cash	3,300	
Discount on notes receivable*	75	
Interest revenue		75
Notes receivable, trade		3,300

* Contra account to Notes Receivable.

Notes receivable, trade (face $3,300; recorded net of interest)	3,000	
Sales revenue		3,000

December 31, 19A—Adjusting entry:

Interest receivable ($3,000 × 10% × 9/12)	225	
Interest revenue		225

March 31, 19B—Collection of face of note of $3,300 (no reversing entry on January 1, 19B):

Cash	3,300	
Note receivable, trade (above)		3,000
Interest receivable (above)		225
Interest revenue ($3,000 × 10% × 3/12)		75

Case C—Long-Term, Interest-Bearing Note Receivable with Simple Interest. On April 1, 19A, LT Company loaned $12,000 cash and received a three-year, 10% note. Interest is payable each March 31 and the principal is payable at the end of the third year.

	19A		19B		19C	
April 1, 19A—Originating entry:						
Note receivable	12,000					
Cash		12,000				
December 31, Adjusting entry:						
Interest receivable	900		900		900	
Interest revenue		900		900		900
March 31, Interest collection (no						
Cash			1,200		1,200	
Interest receivable				900		900
Interest revenue				300		300

March 31, 19D—Collection of principal and interest:

Cash	13,200	
Note receivable		12,000
Interest receivable		900
Interest revenue		300

Case D—Long-Term, Interest-Bearing Note Receivable with Equal Annual Payments Including Principal and Compound Interest. On April 1, 19A, ANN Company sold merchandise for $12,000 and received a $12,000, three-year, 10% note. The principal and interest is to be paid in equal annual payments each March 31, starting in 19B. Refer to Chapter 5.

a. To compute the equal payments: $12,000 ÷ $P_{o_{n=3;\,i=10\%}}$ (2.48685, Table 5–4) = $4,825.

b. To prepare the note receivable collection schedule:

Date	Periodic collection	Interest revenue	Receivable: Reduction	Receivable: Balance
4-1-19A				$12,000
3-31-19B	$ 4,825	$12,000 × 10% = $1,200	$ 3,625†	8,375
3-31-19C	4,825	8,375 × 10% = 838	3,987	4,388
3-31-19D	4,825	4,388 × 10% = 437*	4,388	-0-
	$14,475	$2,475	$12,000	

* Rounded to come out even.
† $4,825 − $1,200 = $3,625, etc.

c. April 1, 19A—Originating entry:

Note receivable	12,000	
Sales revenue		12,000

d. December 31, 19A—Adjusting entry:

Interest receivable ($12,000 × 10% × 9/12)	900	
Interest revenue		900

e. March 31, 19B—Periodic collection (no prior reversing entry on January 1, 19B):

Cash	4,825	
Note receivable		3,625
Interest receivable (from above)		900
Interest revenue ($12,000 × 10% × 3/12)		300

Accounting for Notes Receivable with an Unrealistic Interest Rate

Sometimes accountants must deal with a note that has an unrealistically low interest rate. In such cases, if the note is more than one year to maturity, a realistic interest rate must be used to account for the note so that the economic essence of the transaction is reported. For example, Fox Company has a two-year, $10,000 note receivable that has a stated interest rate of 3%. The interest is payable each December 31 and the entire principal is payable on maturity date, December 31, 19B. This note was received for goods sold. The going or market rate of interest for this note is about 10%. Therefore, a question arises about the amount of sales revenue that should be recognized under the revenue principle—$10,000 or some other amount.

The revenue principle specifies that, when a noncash consideration is received, the market value of the item sold, or of the consideration received, whichever is the more reasonably determinable, should be recognized. For Fox Company, the present value of the note is assumed to be the market value of the consideration received and it should be recorded as specified in *APB Opinion No. 21*, "Interest on Receivables and Payables." In this case the present value of cash flows from the note is computed as shown in *(a)* below. Next, the schedule of collections *(b)* and the related entries *(c)* can be completed.

if long term need to get real rate

a. Principal:

$$\$10,000 \times p_{n=2; i=10\%} \text{ (.82645, Table 5–2)} \dots\dots\dots\dots\dots\dots\dots\dots\dots \$8,265$$

Interest:

$$(\$10,000 \times 3\% = \$300) \times \mathbf{P}_{o_{n=2; i=10\%}}$$
$$(1.73554, \text{ Table 5–4}) \dots\dots\dots\dots\dots\dots\dots\dots\dots\dots\dots\dots 521$$
Total—present value of the note (at 10%) . $8,786

b. The accounting for this interest-bearing note with an unrealistic rate should be as follows:

Schedule of collections

Date	Cash interest (at stated rate, 3%)	Interest revenue (at effective rate, 10%)	Note receivable (Net) Increase	Note receivable (Net) Balance
1-1-19A	Present value of the note			$ 8,786
12-31-19A	$300	$8,786 \times 10\% = \$ 879$	$ 579†	9,365
12-31-19B	300	$9,365 \times 10\% = 935*$	635	10,000
	$600	$1,814	$1,214	

* Rounded to come out even.
† $879 − $300 = $579.

c. Journal entries (based on the above schedule):

January 1, 19A—Originating entry:
Note receivable* . 8,786
 Sales revenue . 8,786
* These entries could be at gross with the same results (see page 278).

December 31—Interest date:

	19A	19B
Cash ($10,000 × 3%) .	300	300
Note receivable .	579	635
Interest revenue .	879	935

December 31, 19B—Collection of the note principal on maturity date:

Cash . 10,000
 Note receivable . 10,000

To illustrate another transaction that has an unrealistic interest rate, assume HYP Company sold merchandise on January 1, 19A, at a quoted price of $15,000. Considerations received were cash $5,000 and a $10,000, 4% note receivable which is payable in four equal annual installments (starting on December 31, 19A) of $2,755 (computation, $10,000 ÷ $P_{o_{n=4; i=4\%}}$, 3.62990, Table 5–4). The going rate for notes with comparable risk was reliably estimated to be 10%. First, the present value of the four payments at 10% interest must be computed as shown in (*a*) below. Next a schedule of collections (*b*) and the related entries (*c*) can be completed.

a. Present value of the note: $2,755 × $P_{o_{n=4; i=10\%}}$ (3.16987, Table 5–4) = $8,733.

b. Schedule of collections:

Date	Cash collection	Interest revenue (10%)	Note receivable	
			Reduction	Balance
1-1-19A	(at present value)			$8,733
12-31-19A	$2,755	$8,733 × 10% = $ 873	$1,882†	6,851
12-31-19B	2,755	6,851 × 10% = 685	2,070	4,781
12-31-19C	2,755	4,781 × 10% = 478	2,277	2,504
12-31-19D	2,755	2,504 × 10% = 251*	2,504	-0-
	$11,020	$2,287	$8,733	

* Rounded to come out even.
† $2,755 − $873 = $1,882.

c. Entries:

January 1, 19A—To record sale		
Cash	5,000	
Note receivable (net)	8,733	
Sales revenue		13,733
December 31, 19A—First collection (from the above schedule)		
Cash	2,755	
Interest revenue		873
Note receivable		1,882

Notice that, in conformity with the revenue principle, sales revenue was recognized at the "fair" value of the considerations received (cash + present value of the note). Interest revenue was not included in sales revenue.

Sale (Discounting) of Notes Receivable

If a note receivable is sold (transferred by endorsement) to a third party before maturity, the original payee receives cash before maturity. The sale of a note receivable often is referred to as **discounting.** The original payee assumes a **contingent liability** if the note is endorsed **with recourse.** In contrast, there is no contingent liability if it is endorsed **without recourse.** "Contingent liability" means that if the maker of the note defaults at maturity date, the endorser (i.e., original payee in this situation) must reimburse the new payee for the principal and interest due on the note, plus any protest fee charged by the last holder of the note. Because an investor usually is unwilling to purchase a note without recourse, most notes sold create a contingent liability.[8]

The cash received from the sale of a note receivable (either interest bearing or noninterest bearing) is computed as follows:

Principal of note + **Total interest to maturity** − **Interest charged by new payee** = **Cash proceeds**

[8] However, if the discount rate is high enough, third parties can be induced to purchase notes without recourse.

Example:
WV Company sold (i.e., discounted) a $3,000, 10% interest-bearing one-year note receivable, dated April 1, 19A. The note was sold to National Finance Company on August 1, 19A, at a 15% discount rate. Notice that this note had been held by WV for four months and will be held by the bank for the eight remaining months. This means that **the cash proceeds** to be paid by the finance company to WV Company is the total amount the finance company will receive at maturity ($3,000 principal plus $300 total interest) less the interest the finance company charges. This interest is computed on the $3,300 total maturity value. **The carrying value** of the note for WV Company at the time of the sale is the principal of the note ($3,000) plus the interest receivable accrued for the four months WV Company held the note ($3,000 × 10% × 4⁄12 = $100). **The difference between the cash proceeds WV receives and the carrying value WV gives up is the gain or loss on the sale.** These computations are as follows:

a. To compute the cash proceeds:

Principal of the note	$3,000
Total interest at maturity ($3,000 × 10%)	300
Total maturity value (subject to the discount rate)	3,300*
Interest charged by the new payee ($3,300 × 15% × 8⁄12)	330
Cash proceeds on date sold	$2,970

b. To compute gain (loss) on the sale of the note:

Carrying value of the note receivable, $3,000 + ($3,000 × 10% × 4⁄12 = $100)	$3,100
Cash proceeds	2,970
Gain (loss) on disposal of note	($ 130)

*If this had been a **noninterest-bearing** note the face of the note would be the "total maturity value," $3,300, because it already would include the total interest amount.

The accrued interest revenue at the date of the discounting transaction and the sale of the note are recorded as follows:

Interest (or note) receivable ($3,000 × 10% × 4⁄12)	100	
Interest revenue (i.e., interest earned)		100
Cash [(*a*) above]	2,970	
Loss on disposal of note [(*b*) above]	130	
Note receivable (face amount)		3,000
Interest (or note) receivable (prior entry)		100

Note: These two entries may be combined into one.

Disclosure of a contingent liability on a note receivable that has been sold usually is made by a disclosure note such as: "The company is contingently liable for discounted notes receivable amounting to $3,000." Other ways to report the contingent liability are as follows (assuming $10,000 notes receivable held prior to discounting the $3,000 note):

1. Current assets:
   Notes receivable (contingent liability for notes receivable discounted, $3,000) $7,000

2. Current assets:

Notes receivable	$10,000	
Less: Notes receivable discounted	3,000	$7,000

Contingencies of all types, including contingent liabilities, are discussed in more detail in Chapter 14, Part A.

Dishonored Notes Receivable

When a note receivable is not renewed or collected at maturity, it is dishonored. The accounting procedure followed depends on *(a)* whether the note was held or sold (discounted), and *(b)* if sold, whether endorsed with or without recourse. A dishonored note whether discounted or not usually is transferred from the Note Receivable account to a special receivable account.

After dishonor, interest accrues on the face amount plus any accrued interest and any protest fees at the **legal** rate of interest (usually specified by state laws). However, if the note is uncollectible, the total claim should be written off as a bad debt.

Examples:

a. **Dishonored note receivable not previously sold:**
On March 31, 19B, WV Company's $3,000, 10%, one-year note receivable, dated April 1, 19A, was dishonored. The default would be recorded as follows (see page 282):

Special receivable, dishonored note	3,300	
Notes receivable, trade		3,000
Interest receivable ($3,000 × 10% × 9/12)		225
Interest revenue ($3,000 × 10% × 3/12)		75

b. **Dishonored note receivable previously sold and endorsed with recourse** (in such cases banks charge a fee to cover the added clerical costs; usually called a protest fee). Protest fee charged by the bank, $15:

Special receivable, dishonored note	3,315	
Cash		3,315*

* Principal, $3,000 + interest, $300 + protest fee, $15.

c. **Dishonored note receivable previously sold and endorsed without recourse:**
No entry is recorded because the note will not revert to the original holder.

If a dishonored note is uncollectible, the total claim (including all of the related account balances) should be written off as a bad debt. If it is a **trade** note receivable, the "loss" should be debited to the allowance for doubtful accounts because all "trade" losses are included in the estimated balance in that account.

Nontrade Receivables

Nontrade receivables (other than accounts and notes receivable that arise from the usual customer transactions) often are called **special receivables.** They include "open" accounts, notes, and special transactions such as the following (there are numerous other examples):

Receivables other than trade receivables	Number of companies 1986	1985	1984	1983
Tax refund claims	67	84	73	91
Contracts	51	48	44	44
Investees	27	34	38	35
Installment notes or accounts	14	18	21	20
Employees	7	6	9	10
Sale of assets (nontrade)	13	11	16	9

Source: AICPA, *Accounting Trends & Techniques, 1987* (New York, 1987), p. 118.

Nontrade receivables are classified in the statement of financial position as *(a)* current assets in conformity with the definition of that category, or *(b)* as long-term assets under captions such as "Investments and funds"[9] or "Other assets." Losses on nontrade receivables are not debited to the allowance for doubtful accounts. In some cases, a special allowance account is established only for these kinds of receivables. Special receivables are recorded at the time of the originating transaction in conformity with the cost principle. Subsequently, they should be valued in terms of their probability of collection.

Summary

This chapter discussed recognition and reporting of cash and receivables. Cash is the most liquid asset; it includes all cash owned by the company plus negotiable instruments such as money orders and checks. Planning and controlling cash is needed to ensure that it is used efficiently and to avoid its misappropriation. Internal control of cash primarily includes separate control of cash receipts and cash disbursements, often a petty cash system, and reconciliation of each of the periodic bank statements with the cash accounts of the company. The reconciliation often requires that certain entries be made that affect the company's cash account.

Receivables include accounts, notes, and nontrade receivables. Each receivable is classified as short term (i.e., current) or long term. Accounts receivable (i.e., from credit sales) usually should be coupled with bad debt estimates, to apply the matching principle, and to measure bad debt expense and the net realizable value of accounts receivable. Accounts receivable sometimes are sold or assigned to get early cash. Notes receivable (both short term and long term) can require accounting for both simple and compound interest.

SUPPLEMENT 7–A: COMPREHENSIVE BANK RECONCILIATION

The comprehensive bank reconciliation format often is used as a "proof of cash" by auditors. It encompasses four reconciliations in one worksheet, that is:

1. The bank reconciliation of the **prior period** (column 1 in **Exhibit 7–6).**
2. Reconciliation of the bank's cash receipts with the company's cash receipts (column 2 in Exhibit 7–6).

[9] "Advances to subsidiaries" normally would be reported under "Investments and funds."

Exhibit 7–6
Comprehensive bank reconciliation, West Company, August 31.

Items	Prior (July 31) balances	August receipts	August payments	August 31 reconciled balances
Bank:				
Per bank statement (unreconciled)	$32,000	$78,400	$71,500	$38,900
Cash on hand:				
July 31	1,000	(1,000)[a]		
August 31		990[b]		990
Deposits outstanding:				
July 31	5,000	(5,000)[c]		
August 31		3,000[d]		3,000
Checks outstanding:				
July 31	(8,000)		(8,000)[e]	
August 31			7,000[f]	7,000
Correct cash balance	$30,000	$76,390	$70,500	$35,890
Books:				
Per Cash account (unreconciled)	$30,000*	$75,300	$70,000	$35,300
Note collected by bank (August)		1,100[g]		1,100
NSF check, J. Doe			300[h]	(300)
Bank service charge (August)			200[i]	(200)
Cash shortage (August)		(10)[j]		(10)
Correct cash balance	$30,000	$76,390	$70,500	$35,890

* After July 31, entries from July bank reconciliation. Inclusion of cash on hand is optional.
Explanation of inner extensions:

Bank:
a. A July balance, deducted to remove it from August receipts.
b. An August balance, added to include it in August receipts.
c. A July deposit, deducted to remove it from August receipts.
d. An August deposit, added to include the amount in August receipts.
e. July checks, deducted to remove the amount from August payments.
f. August checks, added to include the amount in August payments.

Books:
g. August receipt, added to include it in August receipts.
h. **and i.** August payments, added to include them in the August payments.
j. Cash shortage deducted, reduced cash receipts.
Check: Both correct cash balances agree in total for each of the four columns.

3. Reconciliation of the bank's cash disbursements with the company's cash disbursements (column 3 in Exhibit 7–6).
4. The bank reconciliation for the **current period** (column 4 in Exhibit 7–6).

To illustrate a comprehensive bank reconciliation, the data used in Part A of the chapter are restated as follows:

a. July bank reconciliation—West Company, July 31:

Items	Bank balance	Book balance
Ending balances, July 31	$32,000	$29,550
Deposits outstanding, end of July	5,000	
Cash on hand (undeposited), end of July	1,000	
Checks outstanding, end of July	(8,000)	
Note collected for the company		600
Bank service charge for July		(150)
Correct cash balance, July 31	$30,000	$30,000

b. August transactions:

Bank statement	
August 1 balance	$ 32,000
Deposits recorded in August	77,300
Checks cleared in August	(71,000)
Note collected (including $100 interest)	1,100
NSF check, J. Doe	(300)
August service charges	(200)
August 31 balance	$ 38,900

Company's cash account	
August 1 balance	$ 30,000
August deposits	75,300
August checks	(70,000)
August 31 balance	$ 35,300

c. End of August: Cash on hand (undeposited), $990.

Based on the above data only, the comprehensive bank reconciliation shown in Exhibit 7–6 was prepared. The sequential preparation steps were as follows:

Step 1:
Enter the prior (July 31, in the example) **bank** reconciliation data in the **bank part of the first** column and the current bank statement data (August 31) across the first line of the **bank** part of the format.

Step 2:
Enter the unreconciled amounts from the current Cash account (for August) across the first line of the **book** part of the format. Also, enter unreconciled ending balance in the first column, on the "Correct cash balance" line. (Thus, under "books" the same cash amount will be reflected on the first and last lines of the first column, $30,000)

Step 3:
Prepare the bank reconciliation for the current period (August 31 in the example) in the last (i.e., fourth) column of the worksheet; use the "correct cash balance" approach.

Step 4:
Complete the two inner columns to reconcile "total receipts" and "total payments" of the bank and book parts. The purpose of this phase of the reconciliation is to test for internal correctness by reconstructing the elements in both the receipts and payments.

The final test of correctness is met in all respects when (1) vertically, each of the four column totals agree for the bank and book lines "correct cash balance" and (2) horizontally, beginning balances plus receipts less payments equal ending balances for both the bank and book reconciliations.

Another format sometimes used for the comprehensive reconciliation starts with "balance per bank statement" and ends with "balance per books." This format has two major disadvantages: (1) it does not show the correct cash balance and (2) it is more complex because of the way the inner extensions must be entered. However, when there are only two or three reconciling items (e.g., outstanding checks, deposits outstanding and a service charge) it is simple and time saving.

QUESTIONS

Part A

1. Define cash as it is used for accounting purposes.
2. In what circumstances, if any, is it permissible to offset a bank overdraft against a positive balance in another bank account?
3. Define a compensating balance and explain the related reporting requirements.
4. If you were called upon to establish a petty cash system that would be particularly effective from the standpoint of internal control, briefly describe the important features that you would incorporate into it.
5. Which of the following items should not be recorded in the Cash account?

   a. Money orders.
   b. Postdated checks.
   c. Ordinary checks.
   d. Postage stamps.
   e. Currency.
   f. Cash deposited in savings accounts.
   g. Certificates of deposit.
   h. Deposits in checking accounts.

6. Where (if at all) do items *(a)* through *(g)* belong in the following bank reconciliation?

Balance from bank statement, June 30	$ x,xxx.xx
Additions	
Deductions	
June 30 correct cash balance	$ 9,600.00
Balance from company cash account, June 30 . . .	$ x,xxx.xx
Additions	
Deductions	
June 30 correct cash balance	$ 9,600.00

   a. Note collected by bank for the depositor on June 29; notification was received July 2 when the June 30 bank statement was received.
   b. Checks drawn in June which had not cleared the bank by June 30.
   c. Check of a depositor with a similar name which was returned with checks accompanying June 30 bank statement and which was subtracted from the company's bank account.
   d. Bank service charge for which notification was received on receipt of bank statement.
   e. Deposit mailed June 30 which reached bank July 1 (not yet included in the bank statement).
   f. Notification of charge for imprinting the company's name on blank checks was received with the June 30 bank statement.
   g. Upon refooting the cash receipts journal, the company discovered that one receipt was omitted in arriving at the total which was posted to the Cash account in the ledger.

7. Briefly explain the three basic purposes of a bank reconciliation.
8. Define the following terms related to accounting for cash:
   a. Deposits outstanding.
   b. Checks outstanding.
   c. NSF check.
   d. Correct cash balance.
   e. Cash shortage and cash overage.
9. How should cash shortages and overages be recorded and reported?
10. Explain a "lockbox" bank account.

Part B

11. Define receivables and briefly explain their classifications.
12. RS Company sold merchandise for $500; terms 2/10, n/30. Explain these terms and give the journal entry under the net approach and gross approach. Which approach is preferable? Why?
13. Briefly describe the different methods of estimating bad debt expense and the allowance for doubtful accounts for trade receivables. State which financial statement each method emphasizes. What is the conceptual basis for each emphasis?
14. It sometimes happens that a receivable that has been written off as uncollectible is subsequently collected. Describe the accounting procedures in such an event.
15. What is the difference between a cash discount and a trade discount?
16. How should customer accounts with credit balances be reported in the financial statements?
17. Company X has a credit balance in allowance for doubtful accounts of $600. The amount of credit sales for the period is $80,000 and the balance in accounts receivable is $15,000. Assume the bad debt estimates are *(a)* related to accounts receivable, 9%, and *(b)* related to credit sales, ½%.

    Complete the following tabulation after the adjusting entry is made for bad debts.

Account	(a) Based on accounts receivables	(b) Based on credit sales
Bad debt expense	$______	$______
Allowance for doubtful accounts	$______	$______

18. Illustrate the differences between a one-year note received for a sale on credit of $5,000 and a going rate of interest of 12%, assuming *(a)* an interest-bearing note and *(b)* a noninterest-bearing note.
19. T Company received, from a customer, a $1,000, 9% interest-bearing note that will mature in three months. After holding it two months, the note was sold by T to the bank at 12%. Compute T's proceeds. Give the required journal entry made by T at the time the note was sold.
20. RV Company sold accounts receivable of $10,000 (allowance for doubtful accounts, $300) for $9,000, with recourse. Estimated obligations due to the "with recourse" provision amounted to $700 (uncollectible accounts, discounts, and sales returns). Give the required entry.

EXERCISES

Part A: Exercises 7–1 to 7–10

E 7–1

Match the descriptions given below with the terms listed to the left by entering one capital letter in each blank space:

Term

_____ 1. Petty cash
_____ 2. Checks outstanding
_____ 3. Bank reconciliation
_____ 4. Compensating balance
_____ 5. Cash debits
_____ 6. Immediate cash equivalents
_____ 7. Deposits outstanding
_____ 8. Lockbox system
_____ 9. NSF
_____ 10. Overdraft in bank
_____ 11. Cash that is not reported as a current asset
_____ 12. CDs
_____ 13. Cash credits
_____ 14. Cash shortage and overage
_____ 15. Comprehensive bank reconciliation

Brief description

A. Cash inflows.
B. Negotiable instruments that are accepted by a bank for immediate deposit and withdrawal.
C. Certificates of deposit.
D. A special cash fund used to make small payments.
E. A negative balance in a bank account.
F. Caused by theft, unintentional counting errors, and inappropriate accounting.
G. Checks drawn and mailed but have not yet cleared the bank.
H. A loan constraint that requires a minimum balance at all times in a bank account.
I. Cash outflows.
J. A deposit made but not included on the periodic bank statement.
K. A system to reduce the mail time for delivery of collections from customers; uses a post office box number.
L. A "hot" check.
M. A schedule that shows the correct cash balance for both the bank and the company.
N. A four-column bank reconciliation.
O. A cash fund set aside to pay a long-term debt.

E 7–2 (Petty Cash Entries)

Ever Company decided to use a petty cash system for making small payments. The following transactions were completed during December 19XX.

Transaction:

On December 1, 19XX the company treasurer prepared a $200 check payable to petty cash, the cash was given to the custodian.

Expenditures by the custodian (and signed receipts received) through December 20: Postage, $40; Office supplies, $35; Newspapers, $18; Office equipment repairs, $60; Coffee room supplies, $15; and Miscellaneous items, $12.

December 20, the treasurer fully replenished the fund with a check (i.e., cash).

Expenditures by the custodian through December 31:
Postage, $13; Office supplies, $18; Newspapers, $7; Office equipment repairs, $21; Coffee room supplies, $10; and Miscellaneous items, $6.

Required:

1. Give all of the journal entries that should be made relating to the petty cash fund through December 31, 19XX (end of the annual accounting period) assuming petty cash expenditures were for administrative expenses.
2. Show how the petty cash fund should be reported on the statement of financial position. The regular cash account showed an ending cash balance of $93,000.
3. How should the petty cash transactions affect the 19XX statement of income?

E 7–3 (Define Cash)

VW Company is preparing its December 31 Bank A reconciliation (end of the annual accounting period), and it must determine the proper balance sheet classification of the items listed below. You have been asked to complete the tabulation provided.

Item	Statement of financial position classification	
	Include in cash amount	Classification if not cash
1. Coins and currency, $500.		
2. Checks on hand received from customers, $6,000.		
3. Certificates of deposit (CDs), $8,000.		
4. Petty cash fund, $400.		
5. Postage stamps, $60.		
6. Bank A, checking account balance, $21,000.		
7. Postdated check, customer, $100.		
8. Money order, from customer, $150.		
9. Cash in savings account, $10,000.		
10. Bank draft from customer, $400.		
11. Cash advance received from customer, $80.		
12. Utility deposit to the gas company, refundable, $50.		
13. Certified check from customer, $1,000.		
14. NSF check, R. Roe, $200.		
15. Cash advance to company executive, collectible upon demand, $20,000.		
16. Bank B, checking account, overdraft, $2,000.		
17. IOUs from employees, $120.		

E 7–4 (Define Cash)

Maze Company is preparing its 19D financial statements; the accounting period ends December 31. The following items, related to cash, are under consideration. You have been asked to indicate how each item should be reported on the statement of financial position and to explain the basis for your responses.

1. A $900 check received from a customer dated February 1, 19E, is on hand.
2. A customer's check was included in the December 20 deposit. It was returned by the bank stamped "NSF." Not entry has yet been made by Maze to reflect the return.
3. A $20,000 CD on which $1,000 of interest accrued to December 31 has just been recorded by debiting Interest Receivable and crediting Interest Revenue. The chief accountant proposes to report the $20,000 as "Cash in Bank."
4. Maze has a $200 petty cash fund. As of December 31, the fund cashier reported expense vouchers covering various expenses in the amount of $167 and cash of $32.
5. Postage stamps that cost $30 are in the cash drawer.
6. A cashier's check of $200 payable to Maze Company is in the cash drawer; it is dated December 29.
7. Three checks, dated December 31, 19D, totaling $465, payable to vendors who have sold merchandise to Maze Company on account were not mailed by December 31, 19D. They have not been entered as payments in the check register and ledger.
8. Prior to December 30, Maze Company left a note that matures December 31, 19D, with its bank for collection. The note is for $20,000 and bears interest at 9%, having been outstanding for three months. As yet, Maze has not heard from the bank about collection but is confident of a favorable outcome because of the high credit rating of the maker of the note. The company plans to include the $20,000 plus interest in its cash balance.

E 7–5 **(Define Cash)**

Each of the following items is independent of the others. For each item you are to compute the amount that should be included in "cash" that will be reported on the year-end statement of financial position.

a. Balance in general checking account, Bank H, $60,000; an overdraft in special checking account, Bank H, $2,000. IOU held from company president for $4,000, received six weeks ago because of a cash loan.

b. Balance in Bank P checking account, $45,000. Refundable deposit paid to state treasurer to guarantee performance on a highway contract, $25,000. Balance in foreign bank (converted to U.S. dollars), $9,000.

c. Cash on hand, $800; cash in Bank C checking account, $29,000; cash held by salespersons as advances on expense accounts, $800. Postage stamps on hand received from mail-order customers, $50.

d. Balance in checking account, $33,000. Certificates of deposit, $5,000. Cash in bond sinking fund, $25,000. Cash on hand, $1,000.

e. Cash in checking account, $18,000. Cash on hand, $400. Various instruments on hand as follows:

Checks from customers:	
In payment of overdue account	$ 500
In payment for goods sold	700
NSF check, previously deposited then returned	300
Postdated (February 1, next year)	400
American Express Travelers Check	100
Signed IOUs for loans to employees	600
Receipt for deposit in savings account	1,000
Receipt for postage stamps (not yet used)	60

E 7–6 **(Petty Cash Entries)**

As a part of their newly designed internal control system, DOT Corporation established a petty cash fund. Transactions for the first month were as follows:

a. Wrote a check for $500 on August 1 and gave the cash to the custodian.

b. Summary of the petty cash expenditures made by the custodian:

	August 1–15	August 16–31
Postage used	$ 40	$ 58
Supplies purchased and used	265	190
Delivery expense	98	178
Miscellaneous expenses	35	40
Totals	$438	$466

c. Fund replenished on August 16.

d. Fund replenished on August 31 and increased by $300.

Required:

Give all of the entries indicated through August 31.

E 7–7 **(Bank Reconciliation and Journal Entries)**

Foster Company, as a matter of policy, deposits all cash receipts and makes all payments by check. The following data were taken from the cash records of the company:

	May 31	June 30
Deposits outstanding	$2,200	$3,900
Checks outstanding	1,400	800

June transactions:

	From bank	From books
Balance, June 1	$ 5,000	$ 5,800
June deposits	10,600	12,300
June checks	14,500	13,900
June note collected (including 10% interest)	2,200	—
June bank charges	10	—
Balance, June 30	3,290	4,200

Required:

1. Based on the above data only, show how to prove the deposits outstanding and checks outstanding as of June 30.
2. Reconcile the bank account as of June 30.
3. Give any journal entries that should be made based on the June bank reconciliation.

E 7–8 (Bank Reconciliation, Hot Check, Journal Entries)

Reconciliation of Crabtree Company's bank account at May 31 was as follows:

Balance from bank statement	$10,000
Deposits outstanding	1,500
Checks outstanding	(150)
Correct cash balance	$11,850
Balance from books	$11,864
Bank service charge	(14)
Correct cash balance, May 31	$11,850

June transactions:

	Bank	Books
Checks recorded	$11,500	$11,800
Deposits recorded	8,100	9,000
Service charges recorded	12	—
Collection by bank ($2,000 note plus interest)	2,100	—
NSF check returned with June 30 statement (will be redeposited; assumed to be good)	50	—
Balances, June 30	9,138	9,050

Required:

1. Compute deposits outstanding and checks outstanding at June 30 by comparing bank and books for deposits and checks.
2. Prepare a bank reconciliation for June.
3. Give all journal entries that should be made based on the June bank reconciliation.

E 7–9 (Bank Reconciliation, Cash Overage or Shortage, Entries)

Davis Company has its checking account with First National Bank. The company is ready to reconcile its May bank and book balances. The following data are available:

a. From the April 30 bank reconciliation:
   Deposits outstanding, $150.
   Checks outstanding: No. 698, $30; No. 699, $80; and No. 702, $25.
b. Cash on hand, $50 (by actual count).
c. Davis Company Cash account for May:

Balance, April 30 (correct)	$ 10,958
Cash receipts during May	14,210
Checks processed during May	(13,812)
Balance, May 31	$ 11,356

d. Bank statement for May:

Balance, April 30	$ 10,900
Deposits during May	13,940
Checks cleared during May	(13,742)
Note collected for Davis (including $50 interest)	550
Bank service charge	(14)
Balance, May 31	$ 11,634

e. At May 31, the following checks were outstanding: No. 702, $25; No. 735, $100; No. 738, $60; and No. 740, $20. May 31 receipts amounting to $420 were mailed to the bank at the close of business that day and were not included in the May bank statement.

Required:

1. Prepare the May bank reconciliation.
2. Give all required journal entries based on the bank reconciliation.

E 7–10 (Bank Reconciliation Based on a Computer Prepared Bank Statement and Cash Account)

a. First Commerce Bank, Any location, Address and Phone, Customer Jones Company, Address; Date, June 30, 19X1:

Statement summary:	
Balance June 1, 19X1	$23,000 +
Deposits and other credits	11,600 +
Checks and other debits	12,120 −
Interest earned on this statement	100 +
Ending balance, June 30, 19X1	$22,580 +

Account transactions:

Deposits		Checks			
6–1	$ 2,000	6–2 #61	$ 1,000	6–17 #65	$ 400
6–8	3,000	6–7 #63	2,000	6–23 #60	1,100
6–17	4,500	6–9 #66	3,000	6–27 #67	2,100
6–22	2,100	6–14 #64	1,420	6–28 #59	1,100
Total	$11,600				$12,120

b. **Cash Account**

Balance June 1, 19X1	23,900	Checks	13,220
Deposits	12,300	60 $1,100 65 $ 400	
6–8 $3,000		61 1,000 66 3,000	
6–17 4,500		62 900 67 2,100	
6–22 2,100		63 2,000 68 1,300	
6–30 2,700		64 1,420	

c. Bank reconciliation at May 31, 19x1:

Bank balance, $23,000, add deposit outstanding, $2,000,
deduct check #59 outstanding, $1,100 =
book balance, $23,900.

Required:

Prepare the June bank reconciliation and give any entries required.

Part B: Exercises 7–11 to 7–27

E 7–11 (Correcting Ledger Accounts for Receivables)

During the annual audit of TAR Corporation, you encountered the following account entitled "Receivables and Payables":

Items	Debit	Credit
Due from customers	$78,000	
Payables to creditors for merchandise		$31,000
Note receivable, long term	40,000	
Expected cumulative losses on bad debts		2,000
Due from employees, current	1,100	
Cash dividends payable		12,000
Special receivable, dishonored note*	11,000	
Accrued wages		1,200
Deferred rent revenue		800
Insurance premiums paid in advance	600	
Mortgage payable, long term		20,000

* Collection probable some time in the future.

Required:

1. Give the journal entry to eliminate the above account and to set up the appropriate accounts to replace it.
2. Show how the various items should be reported on a current statement of financial position.

E 7–12 (Accounting for Sale on Credit; Net versus Gross Methods)

On December 29, 19A, Sabre Company sold merchandise for $8,000 on credit terms, 3/10, n/60. The accounting period ends December 31.

Required:

1. Give the following entries under two different accounting approaches: *(a)* the net approach and *(b)* the gross approach:
   a. To record the 19A sale.
   b. To record collection of the account:
      Assumption A—On January 5, 19B.
      Assumption B—On April 1, 19B.
2. Show what should be reported on the 19A and 19B statements of financial position and income under each approach and for each assumption for the above transactions only.

E 7–13 (Recording Bad Debt Expense Based on Credit Sales)

At January 1, 19B, the credit balance in the Allowance for Doubtful Accounts of the Master Company was $400,000. The provision (i.e., expense) for doubtful accounts is based on a percentage of net credit sales. Total sales revenue for 19B amounted to $150 million of which one third was on credit. Based on the latest available facts, the 19B provision (i.e., expense) needed for doubtful accounts is estimated to be three fourths of 1% of net credit sales. During 19B, uncollectible receivables amounting to $440,000 were written off.

Required:

1. Prepare a schedule to compute the balance in Master's Allowance for Doubtful Accounts at December 31, 19B. Show supporting computations.
2. Give all 19B entries related to doubtful accounts. (AICPA adapted)

E 7–14 **(Bad Debt Estimates Based on Credit Sales, Accounts Receivable, and Aging)** At December 31, 19B, end of the annual reporting period, the accounts of Bader Company showed the following:

a. Sales revenue for 19B, $360,000 of which one sixth was on credit.
b. Allowance for doubtful accounts, balance January 1, 19B, $1,800 credit.
c. Accounts receivable, balance December 31, 19B (prior to any write-offs of uncollectible accounts during 19B), $36,100.
d. Uncollectible accounts to be written off, December 31, 19B, $2,100.
e. Aging schedule at December 31, 19B, showed the following:

Status	Amount
Not past due	$20,000
Past due 1–60 days	8,000
Past due over 60 days	6,000

Required:

1. Give the 19B entry to write off the uncollectible accounts.
2. Give the 19B adjusting entry to record bad debt expense for each of the following independent assumptions concerning bad debt loss rates:
   a. On credit sales, 1½%.
   b. On total receivables at year-end, 2½%.
   c. On aging schedule: Not past due, ½%; past due 1–60 days, 1%; and past due over 60 days, 8%.
3. Show what would be reported on the 19B statement of financial position relating to accounts receivable for each assumption.

E 7–15 **(Bad Debt Estimates Based on Aging, Computation, Entries, Reporting)** On December 31, 19C, end of the annual reporting period, the accounts receivable records of Company X provided the following information about its customers (only four are used to minimize the clerical task):

Customer Jones: Balance of account, $16,000; all is current (i.e., not past due) except two older invoices—one for $2,000 is 20 days past due and the other for $5,000 is 50 days past due.

Customer Simon: Balance of account, $17,000; all is current except one invoice for $4,000 which is 64 days past due.

Customer Tanner: Balance of account, $23,000; all is current except for three older invoices—one for $4,000 is 28 days past due; another invoice for $3,000 is 50 days past due; and the last one for $1,000 is 75 days past due.

Based on past experience, the following bad debts loss percentages on credit sales have been developed; not past due, ½%; 1–30 days past due, 1¼%; 31–60 days past due, 3%; and more than 60 days past due, 20%.

The balance in the allowance for doubtful accounts on December 31, 19C, is $3,720, prior to writing off the account of Customer Zen of $4,000 determined to be uncollectible.

Required:

1. Prepare an aging schedule including computation of the estimated loss on accounts receivable.
2. Based on the above data and your response to Requirement 1, give all journal entries related to bad debts.
3. Show how the items related to bad debts should be reported on the 19C statement of income and statement of financial position.

E 7–16 (Note Receivable, Short Term, Simple Interest, Interest-Bearing; Entries and Reporting)

On April 15, 19A, Botch Company sold merchandise to Customer Smith for $9,000; terms 2/10; n/EOM (i.e., end of month). Because of nonpayment by Smith, Botch received a $9,000, 15%, 12-month note dated May 1, 19A. The annual reporting period ends December 31. Customer Smith paid the note in full on its maturity date.

Required:

1. Give all entries related to the above transactions.
2. Show what should be reported on the 19A statement of income and statement of financial position.

E 7–17 (Note Receivable, Short Term, Noninterest-Bearing, Simple Interest; Entries and Reporting)

On May 1, 19A, Darby Company sold merchandise to Customer Domo and received a $13,200 (face amount), one year, noninterest-bearing note. The going (i.e., market) rate of interest in this situation is 10%. The annual reporting period for Darby Company ends on December 31. Customer Domo paid the note in full on its maturity date.

Required:

1. Give all entries related to the above transactions.
2. Show what should be reported on the 19A statement of income and statement of financial position.

E 7–18 (Notes Receivable, Interest Bearing and Noninterest Bearing; Entries at Net and Gross and Reporting)

On November 1, 19A, Rouse Company sold merchandise on credit to Customer A for $14,000 and received a six-month, 12%, interest-bearing note. On this same date, Customer B purchased the same merchandise for the same price and credit terms except that the note received by Rouse was noninterest bearing (the interest was included in the face of the note). The annual accounting period for Rouse ends December 31.

Required:

1. Give all required entries for each note from the date of sales of the merchandise through the maturity dates of the notes. For the noninterest-bearing note, give the entries for both the "net" and "gross" alternatives.
2. Show how the effects of these two notes should be reported on the 19A statement of income and statement of financial position.

E 7–19 (Discounting an Interest-Bearing Note; Entries)

On May 1, 19A, Mark Company sold merchandise to Customer K for $20,000, credit terms 2/10; n/EOM (i.e., end of month). At the end of May, Customer K could not make the payment. Instead, a six-month, 12%, note receivable of $20,000 was received by Mark (dated June 1, 19A). Mark Company's accounting period ends December 31. On August 1, 19A, Mark discounted (i.e., sold) this note, with recourse, to City Bank at 14% interest. On maturity date, Customer K paid the bank in full for the note.

Required:

Give all required entries for Mark Company on May 1, 19A, through the maturity date, November 30, 19A. Record sales at net.

E 7–20 (Discounting an Interest-Bearing Note; Entries)

Bay Company completed the following 19A transactions related to a special note receivable:

debit ✓ a land 30,000 gain on sale 70,000

February 1, 19A—Received a $100,000, 9%, interest-bearing, six-month note from Capps Company for a tract of land that had a carrying value of $30,000.

March 1, 19A—Discounted (sold with recourse) the note to Local Bank at a 12% interest rate.

July 31, 19A—Maturity date of the note:

Case A—Capps Company paid the bank for the note and all interest.

Case B—Capps Company defaulted on the note. The bank charged a $500 protest fee.

Required:

Give all journal entries that Bay Company should make for the term of the note, February 1, 19A, through July 31, 19A.

E 7–21 (Sale of Accounts Receivable with and without Recourse; Entries)

On April 1, 19A, DOS Company transferred $10,000 accounts receivable to SLK Finance Company to obtain immediate cash. The related allowance for doubtful accounts was $400.

Required:

1. The financial agreement specified a price of $8,000 on a "without recourse, notification basis." Give the entry(s) that DOS Company should make. Explain the basis for your response.

2. The financial agreement specified a price of $8,500 on a "with recourse, notification basis." DOS estimated $200 transfer obligations related to the "with recourse" provision. Give the entry(s) that DOS should make. Explain the basis for your response.

E 7–22 (Assignment of Accounts Receivable with Recourse; Entries)

Ink, Inc., assigned $60,000 of its receivables to Pen Finance Company. A note payable was executed. The contract provided that Pen would advance 85% of the gross amount of the receivables. The contract specified recourse and nonnotification; therefore, Ink's debtors continue to remit directly to it; the cash (including finance charges) is then remitted to the finance company.

During the first month, customers owing $41,000 paid cash, less sales returns and allowances of $1,600. The finance charge at the end of the first month was $350.

During the second month, the remaining receivables were collected in full except for $400 written off as uncollectible. Final settlement was effected with the finance company, including payment of an additional finance charge of $150.

Required:

1. Give the entries for Ink to record (a) the assignment of the receivables and (b) the note payable.

2. Give the entries for Ink to record (a) the collections and (b) the payment to Pen for the first month.

3. Give the entries for Ink to record (a) the collections for the second month and (b) the final payment to Pen.

E 7–23 (Accounting for an Account Receivable over a Six-Year Period)

Given below is the history of a sale on credit by AB Company to J. Doe:

December 24, 19X1—Sold merchandise to J. Doe, $2,000, terms 2/10, n/30.

January 2, 19X2—Doe paid half of the receivable and was allowed the discount.

December 31, 19X4—Because of the disappearance of Doe, AB Company wrote Doe's account off as uncollectible.

December 31, 19X6—Doe reappeared and paid the debt in full including 6% annual interest (not compounded, compute to the nearest month).

Required:

1. Give the entry(s) that AB Company should make at each of the above dates. Record at net.
2. Show how Doe's account should be reported each December 31 (end of AB Company's annual reporting period).

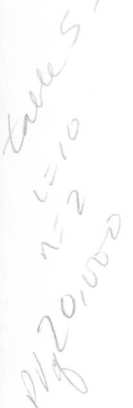

E 7–24 **(Long-Term Note, Simple Interest; Interest-Bearing versus Noninterest-Bearing)** Story Company sells large construction equipment. On January 1, 19X1, the company sold BG Builder a machine at a quoted price of $30,000. Story collected cash $10,000 and received a $20,000, two-year, 10% note (simple interest payable each December 31).

Required:

1. Give Story's required entries for the two years assuming an interest-bearing note, face $20,000.
2. Give Story's required entries for the two years assuming a noninterest-bearing note, face $20,000.
3. Compare the interest revenue, sales revenue, and asset cost under each requirement.

E 7–25 **(Long-Term Note; Interest-Bearing; Entries)** Felix Company sold a pickup truck to RV Company on January 1, 19X1, at a quoted price of $24,000. Felix collected $6,000 cash and received a $18,000 note. The note is payable in three equal (December 31) installments that include both principal and compound interest at 10%.

Required:

1. Compute the equal periodic collections.
2. Prepare a collection schedule and give the entries for Felix Company.

E 7–26 **(Note Receivable; Imputed Interest; Entries)** On January 1, 19X1, EUD Company sold a special machine that had a list price of $39,995. The purchaser paid $9,995 cash and signed a $30,000 note prepared by EUD. The note specified that it would be paid off in three equal annual payments of $13,798 each (starting on December 31, 19X1).

Required:

1. Compute the imputed rate of interest on the note (see Chapter 5).
2. Prepare a collection schedule for EUD.
3. Give all entries for EUD through 19X3.

E 7–27 **(Note Receivable with Unrealistic Interest Rate)** On July 1, 19X1, SMX Company sold a large machine that had a list price of $18,000. The customer paid $3,000 cash and signed a three-year, $15,000 note that specified a stated interest rate of 3%. Annual interest on the full amount of the principal is payable each June 30. The principal is payable on June 30, 19X4. The market (going) rate of interest for this transaction is 10%.

Required:

1. Compute the present value of this note.
2. Prepare a collection schedule for this note.
3. Give all entries required through maturity date.

PROBLEMS

Part A: Problems 7–1 to 7–7

P 7–1 **(Bank Reconciliation; Errors; Journal Entries)**
It is March 31, 19E, and Fry Company is ready to prepare its March bank reconciliation. The following information is available:

(1) **Company Cash account**

March 1 balance	14,175	Checks	26,500
Deposits	25,734		

(2) Bank statement, March 31:

Balance, March 1	$15,400
Deposits	25,599
Checks cleared	(27,059)
NSF check (Customer X)	(50)
Note collected for depositor (including interest, $40)	840
Interest on bank balance	18
Bank service charge	(7)
Balance, March 31	$14,741

3. Additional information:
   a. One deposit by the company was $10 overstated by the company; it was recorded correctly by the bank.
   b. The bank cleared an $89 check as $98; it has not been corrected by the bank.
   c. End of February: Deposits outstanding, $775; checks outstanding, $2,000.

Required:
1. Based on the data given above, compute the March 31 deposits outstanding and checks outstanding.
2. Prepare a bank reconciliation for March. (Hint: A check figure, $14,200.)
3. Give all journal entries that should be made based on your bank reconciliation.

P 7–2 **(Bank Reconciliation; Error; Journal Entries)**
VT Company is ready to prepare its March 31 bank reconciliation. The following data are available:

a. From the February bank reconciliation:
   Deposits outstanding, $170.
   Checks outstanding, $390.
b. March data:

	From bank	From books
Balance, February 28	$7,414	$7,194
March deposits	4,760	4,900
March checks	(6,170)*	(6,100)
Note collected (including $20 interest)	2,020	—
Service charge	(12)	—
Balance, March 31	$8,012	$5,994

* Erroneously includes a check drawn by AB Company for $150.

Required:
1. Compute the deposits outstanding and checks outstanding at March 31.
2. Prepare the March 31 bank reconciliation.
3. Give all of the required entries based on your bank reconciliation.

P 7–3 (Reconciliation; Errors; NSF; Collection; Deduction; Entries)

PT Company is ready to prepare its May 31, 19B, bank reconciliation. The following data are available:

a. Bank statement for May:

Balance, April 30, 19B	$34,300
Deposits during May	79,700
Checks cleared during May	(77,350)
Note receivable collected for PT Company (including 10% interest for six months)	5,250
NSF check, Customer Young	(80)
Deduction for United Fund (per deduction form signed by PT Company)	(50)
Bank service charge	(15)
Balance, May 31, 19B	$41,755

b. PT Company Cash account:

Balance, April 30, 19B	$33,320
Deposits	80,000
Checks written, signed, and delivered	(77,000)
Balance	$36,320

c. *Additional information:*

(1) April 30, 19B: deposits outstanding, $3,000; checks outstanding, $4,000.

(2) Inspection of the canceled checks included in the May bank statement revealed that the $77,350 erroneously included a $150 check written by TPP Company.

(3) Petty cash balance, May 31, 19B, $400 (not included in the book balance).

Required:

1. Compute the May 31 deposits outstanding and checks outstanding.
2. Prepare the May 31 bank reconciliation. (Hint: Be alert for a cash shortage.)
3. Give all of the journal entries that should be made based on your bank reconciliation.

P 7–4 (Reconciliation; Errors; Deduction; NSF; Transfer; Shortage; Entries)

ZT Company carries its checking account with Fidelity Bank. The company is ready to prepare its December 31, 19B, bank reconciliation. The following data are available:

a. ZT Company Cash account for December:

Balance, November 30 (includes $400 cash for change held back each day)	$20,900
Deposits during December	93,400
Checks written during December	(82,000)
Balance, December 31, 19B	$32,300

b. Bank statement for December:

Balance, November 30	$20,000
Deposits during December	92,300
Checks cleared during December	(82,150)
Funds (in dollars) transferred from foreign operations revenue (not yet recorded by ZT Co.)	25,000
United Fund (per withholding form signed by ZT Company)	(50)
NSF check, Customer T	(180)
Bank service charges	(20)
Balance, December 31, 19B	$54,900

c. *Additional data:*
   (1) Balance in Petty Cash account, $200 (not included in ZT Cash account).
   (2) The deposits of $93,400 by ZT Company are overstated by $100; the bank recorded the correct amount.
   (3) The checks cleared by the bank of $82,150 erroneously included a $300 check drawn by AT Corporation; the bank has not yet corrected this error.
   (4) November 30, 19B: deposits outstanding, $2,000, and checks outstanding, $1,500.

Required:
1. Compute the December 31, 19B, deposits outstanding and checks outstanding.
2. Prepare the December bank reconciliation.
3. Give all of the journal entries that should be made based on your bank reconciliation.

P 7–5 (Reconciliation, Collection, Deduction, Transfer, Entries)
AB Company carries its checking account with Commerce Bank. The company is ready to prepare its December 31, 19G, bank reconciliation. The following data are available:

a. The November 30, 19G, bank reconciliation showed the following: (1) cash on hand (held back each day by AB Company for change), $400 (included in AB's Cash account); (2) deposit outstanding, #51, $2,000; and (3) checks outstanding, #121, $1,000; #130, $2,000; and #142, $3,000.

b. AB Company Cash account for December, 19G:

Balance, December 1, 19G	$ 64,000
Deposits: #52–#55, $186,500; #56, $3,500	190,000
Checks: #143–#176, $191,000; #177, $2,500; #178, $3,000; and #179, $1,500	(198,000)
Balance, December 31, 19G (includes $400 cash held each day for change)	$ 56,000

c. Bank statement, December 31, 19G:

Balance, December 1, 19G	$ 67,600
Deposits: #51–#55	188,500
Checks: #130, $2,000; #142, $3,000; #143–#176, $191,000	(196,000)
Note collected for AB Co. (including $720 interest)	6,720
Fund transfer received for foreign revenue (not yet recorded by AB Co.)	10,000
NSF check, Customer B	(200)
United Fund (per transfer authorization signed by AB Co.)	(50)
Bank service charges	(20)
Balance, December 31, 19G	$ 76,550

Required:
1. Identify by number and dollars the December 31, 19G, *(a)* deposits outstanding and *(b)* checks outstanding.
2. Prepare the December 31, 19G, bank reconciliation.
3. Give all journal entries that should be made at December 31, 19G, based on your bank reconciliation.

P 7–6 (Based on Supplement 7–A—Four-Column Reconciliation)
Rae Company is ready to reconcile its bank and book balances at March 31, 19X. The following information is available:

a. February bank reconciliation:

	Bank balance	Book balance
Ending balances, February 28	$49,550	$51,050
Additions:		
Deposits outstanding	3,100	
Deductions:		
Checks outstanding	(1,650)	
Bank service charge		(50)
Correct cash balance, February 28	$51,000	$51,000

b. Company Cash account for March:

Balance, March 1 (after February 28 entry)	$ 51,000
Deposits during March	52,800
Checks written during March	(54,150)
Balance, March 31	$ 49,650

c. Bank statement for March:

Balance, March 1	$ 49,550
Deposits recorded during March	53,850
Checks cleared during March	(53,800)
Note collected for Rae Co. (including interest, $200)	5,200
Service charge	(100)
Balance, March 31	$ 54,700

Required:

1. Compute the March 31 amounts for *(a)* deposits outstanding and *(b)* checks outstanding.
2. Prepare a comprehensive bank reconciliation for March.
3. Give all journal entries that should be made on March 31 based on your bank reconciliation.

P 7–7 **(Based on Supplement 7–A—Four-Column Reconciliation)**
Springer Company has assembled the data needed to prepare the September 30, 19X2, bank reconciliation. The following data are available (in thousands):

a. August 31, 19X2, bank reconciliation:

	Bank	Book
Ending cash balance, August 31	$340	$291
Cash on hand	1	
Deposits outstanding	10	
Checks outstanding	(7)	
Bank service charge		(2)
Note collected (including interest, $5)		55
Correct cash balance, August 31	$344	$344

b. Company cash account for September:

Balance, September 1, 19X2 (before reconciliation)	$344
Deposits during September	400
Checks written during September	(413)
Balance, September 30	$331

c. Bank statement for September:

Balance, September 1, 19X2	$340
Deposits recorded	375
Clerks cleared	(390)
Bank service charge	(3)
NSF check (Person X)	(2)
Deduction for union dues	(1)
Balance, September 30	$319

d. Cash on hand, September 30, $1.

Required:

1. Prepare a comprehensive (four-column) bank reconciliation.
2. Give the entries required by the September bank reconciliation.

Part B: Problems 7–8 to 7–17

P 7–8 **(Classification of Receivables)**

When examining the accounts of Saad Company, you ascertain that balances relating to both receivables and payables are included in a single controlling account (called Receivables), which has a $46,100 debit balance. An analysis of the details of this account revealed the following:

Items	Debit	Credit
Accounts receivable—customers	$80,000	
Accounts receivable—officers (current collection expected)	5,000	
Debit balances—creditors	900	
Expense advances to salespersons	2,000	
Capital stock subscriptions receivable	9,200	
Accounts payable for merchandise		$38,500
Unpaid salaries		6,600
Credit balances in customer accounts		4,000
Cash received in advance from customers for goods not yet shipped		900
Expected bad debts, cumulative		1,000

Required:

1. Give the journal entry to eliminate the above account and set up the appropriate accounts to replace it.
2. How should the items be reported on Saad Company's statement of financial position?

P 7–9 **(Comparison of Four Ways to Estimate Bad Debt Expense)**

The accounting records of GM Company provided the following data for 19F:

Cash sales	$1,200,000
Credit sales	900,000
Balance in accounts receivable, January 1, 19F	180,000
Balance in accounts receivable, December 31, 19F	200,000
Balance in allowance for doubtful accounts, January 1, 19F	3,000 (cr.)
Accounts already written off as uncollectible during 19F	5,000

Recently GM's management has become concerned about various estimates used in their accounting system, including those relating to receivables and bad debts. The company is considering various alternatives with a view to selecting the most appropriate approach and related estimates.

For analytical purposes, the following 19F alternative estimates have been developed for consideration:

a. Bad debt expense approximates ⅗% of credit sales.
b. Bad debt expense approximates ¼% of net sales (cash plus credit sales).
c. Two percent of the uncollected receivables at year-end will be bad at any one time.
d. Aging of the accounts at the end of the period indicated that three fourths of them would incur a 1% loss while the other one fourth would incur a 6% loss.

The reporting period ends December 31.

Required:

1. For each of the four alternatives listed above, give the following: 19F adjusting entry; ending 19F balance in the allowance account; and an evaluation of the alternative.
2. Which alternative would you recommend for GM Company? Why?

P 7–10 **(Comparison and Evaluation of Three Ways to Estimate Bad Debt Expense)**
The accounts of Long Company provided the following 19C information at December 31, 19C, end of the annual reporting period:

Accounts receivable balance, January 1, 19C	$51,000
Allowance for doubtful accounts balance, January 1, 19C	3,000
Total sales revenue during 19C (⅙ on credit)	960,000
Uncollectible accounts to be written off during 19C (ex-customer Slo)	1,000
Cash collected on accounts receivable during 19C	170,000

Estimates of bad debt losses based on:

a. Credit sales, 1%.
b. Ending balance of accounts receivable, 8%.
c. Aging schedule:

Age	Accounts receivable	Probability of noncollection
Less than 30 days	$28,000	2%
31–90 days	7,000	10
91–120 days	3,000	30
More than 120 days	2,000	60

Required:

1. Give the entry to write off customer Slo's long overdue account.
2. Give all entries related to accounts receivable and the allowance account for the following three cases:

Case A—Bad debt expense is based on credit sales.
Case B—Bad debt expense is based on the ending balance of accounts receivable.
Case C—Bad debt expense is based on aging.

3. Show how the results of applying each case above should be reported on the 19C statement of income and statement of financial position.
4. Briefly explain and evaluate each of the three methods used in Cases A, B, and C.
5. On August 1, 19D, customer Slo paid his long-overdue account in full. Give the required entry.

P 7–11 **(Establish an Allowance for Doubtful Accounts)**
Pawn Company has been in business for five years but has never had an audit of its financial statements. Engaged to make an audit for 19E, you find that the company's statement of financial position carries no allowance for doubtful accounts; instead, uncollectible accounts have been expensed as written off and recoveries have been credited to income as collected. The company's policy is to write off, at December 31 of each

year, those accounts on which no collections have been received for three months. The credit terms usually provide for equal monthly collections over two years from date of sale.

Upon your recommendation the company agreed to revise its accounts for 19E in order to account for bad debts on the allowance basis. The allowance is to be based on a percentage of credit sales which is derived from the experience of prior years.

Statistics for the past five years are as follows:

Year	Credit sales	Accounts written off and year of sale			Recoveries and year of sale
19A	$100,000	(19A) $ 550			
19B	250,000	(19A) 1,500	(19B) $1,000		(19A) $300
19C	300,000	(19A) 500	(19B) 4,000	(19C) $1,300	(19B) 850
19D	325,000	(19B) 1,200	(19C) 4,500	(19D) 1,500	(19C) 500
19E	275,000	(19C) 2,700	(19D) 5,000	(19E) 1,400	(19D) 600

Accounts receivable at December 31, 19E, were as follows:

19D sales	$ 15,000
19E sales	135,000
	$150,000

Required:

Prepare the journal entry or entries, with appropriate explanations, to establish the Allowance for Doubtful Accounts. Debit Prior Period Adjustment because this is the correction of an accounting error. Support each item with computations; ignore income tax implications. The books have been adjusted but not closed at December 31, 19E.

(AICPA adapted)

P 7–12 (Assignment of Accounts Receivable; Entries)

VT Company finances some of its current operations by assigning accounts receivable to Ace Finance Company. On July 1, 19A, VT Company assigned, with recourse, notification basis, accounts amounting to $50,000, the finance company advancing 80% of the accounts assigned (20% of the total to be withheld until the finance company has made full recovery), less a commission charge of ½% of the total accounts assigned.

On July 31, VT Company received a statement from the finance company that it had collected $26,000 of these accounts and, in conformity with the contract, an additional charge of ½% of the total accounts outstanding as of July 31 was deducted.

On August 31, VT Company received a second statement from the finance company, together with a check for the amount due. The statement indicated that the finance company had collected an additional $16,000 and had made a charge of ½% of the balance outstanding as of August 31.

Required:

1. Give VT's entry to record *(a)* the assignment of the accounts and *(b)* the liability on July 1, 19A.
2. Give VT's entry to record the data from the July 31 report from the finance company.
3. Reconstruct the report submitted to VT by Ace Finance Company on August 31; show details to explain cash remitted and the uncollected accounts still held by the finance company.

4. Give VT's entry to record the data in the report of August 31.
5. Explain how the items should be reported on the statement of financial position of VT Company at July 31 and August 31.
6. Give the entry to record the collection of the remaining assigned accounts receivables on September 15, 19A.

P 7–13 **(PV of a Note; Collection Schedule, Entries)**

SAD Company sold a building and the land on which it is located on January 1, 19A, and received a $150,000 noninterest-bearing note receivable that matures December 31, 19C. The $150,000 is to be paid in full on maturity date. The sale was recorded as follows by SAD Company:

Note receivable	150,000	
Accumulated depreciation, building	100,000	
Building		150,000
Land		60,000
Gain on sale of assets		40,000

It has been determined that 12% is a realistic interest rate for this particular note. The annual reporting period ends December 31. The accounts have not been adjusted and closed for 19A.

Required:
1. Compute the present value of the note. Use compound interest.
2. Prepare a correction and collection schedule as follows:

		Note receivable	
Date	**Explanation and interest revenue**	**Change**	**Balance**
1–1–19A	Originally recorded		$150,000
12–31–19A	Corrections to present value	?	?

3. Give all entries through 19C.

P 7–14 **(Note Receivable, Equal Collections; Note Receivable, Long-Term, Unrealistic Interest Rate)**

During the annual reporting period (ends on December 31) Koke Company received two notes receivable related to the sale of products (commercial autos). These notes are identified as Note A and Note B.

Note A:

On August 1, 19X1, Koke Company sold a special van with a price of $31,000. Koke received cash, $11,000 and a $20,000 six-month note that matures January 31, 19X2. This note specifies equal monthly payments of $3,451, starting on August 31, 19X1, which included principal and interest. The going or market rate of interest for this loan is 12%.

Required:
1. Prepare a schedule of collections that shows by date, cash collections, interest revenue, and note receivable (reduction and balance).
2. Give all entries from August 1, 19X1 through January 31, 19X2.

Note B:

On March 1, 19X1, Koke Company sold a large vehicle equipped with a special crane mounted to it. The quoted price was $80,000. Koke Company received $20,000 cash and a $60,000, five-year note receivable. The note had a stated rate of 3%, although the imputed (going or market) rate for this transaction was 9%. The interest concession was made to "beat a strong competitor." The note is payable in five equal annual payments starting on February 28, 19X2.

Required:
1. Compute the annual cash collections and the present value of the note.
2. Prepare a schedule of collections to show by date, cash collections, interest revenue and note receivable (reduction and balance).
3. Give all entries from March 1, 19X1 through February 28, 19X2.

P 7–15 **(Discounting Notes: Interest-Bearing and Noninterest-Bearing)**
On October 15, 19A, Farb Company sold identical merchandise for $12,000 on credit terms 2/10; n/30, to two different customers, designated as Customer X and Customer Y. Farb's annual reporting period ends December 31. These sales were recorded as follows:

	Customer X		Customer Y	
Accounts receivable	11,760		11,760	
Sales revenue		11,760		11,760

The events that followed for each customer were:

Customer X:

11/1/19A Could not pay the account; signed a note payable for $12,000, 10% interest bearing, due in six months, on April 30, 19B.

12/1/19A Sold (discounted) the "X" note to State Bank, with recourse, at 12% interest per annum.

4/30/19B Customer X defaulted and the bank charged a $20 protest fee.

7/31/19B Collected in full on the defaulted note plus an additional interest charge of 10% per annum.

Customer Y:

11/1/19A Could not pay the account; signed a $12,600 noninterest-bearing note; maturity date, on April 30, 19B.

12/1/19A Sold (discounted) the "Y" note to State Bank, with recourse, at 12% interest per annum.

4/30/19B Customer Y paid the note in full on maturity date.

Required:
1. Give all of the entries related to the Customer X note from date initiated through July 31, 19B.
2. Give all of the entries related to the Customer Y note from date initiated through its final settlement, assuming *(a)* the net approach is used and *(b)* the gross approach is used. No need to recompute when the same as (1).
3. Show the effect of each note on the 19A statement of income and statement of financial position of Farb Company. Set up the following column headings and side captions:

Items	Customer X note	Customer Y note	
		Net basis	Gross basis
Statement of income:			
(List items)			
Statement of financial position:			
(List items)			

P 7–16 (Overview of Notes; Four Different Notes)

REV Company had a critical cash problem related to collections from four customers—Smith, Johnson, Karnes, and Cates. The transactions, in order of date, are given below. You will notice discounting, defaults, and extensions. But finally, everyone paid in full. REV's annual accounting period ends December 31.

May 1	Received an $8,000, 90-day, 9% interest-bearing note from E. M. Smith, a customer, in settlement of an account receivable for that amount.
June 1	Received a $12,000, six-month, 9% interest-bearing note from M. Johnson, a customer, in settlement of an account receivable for that amount.
Aug. 1	Discounted (i.e., sold), with recourse, the Johnson note at the bank at 10%.
Aug. 2	Smith defaulted on the $8,000 note.
Sept. 1	Received a one-year, noninterest-bearing note from D. Karnes, a customer, in settlement of a $5,000 account receivable. The face of the note was $5,400, and the imputed going rate of interest was 8% (use the net method).
Oct. 1	Received a $20,000, 90-day note from R. M. Cates, a customer. The note was in payment for goods Cates purchased and was interest bearing at 15%.
Oct. 1	Collected the defaulted Smith note plus accrued interest to September 30 (10% per annum on the total amount due for two months).
Dec. 1	Johnson defaulted on the $12,000 note. REV Company paid the bank the total amount due plus a $25 protest fee.
Dec. 30	Collected Cates note in full.
Dec. 30	Collected Johnson note in full including additional interest on the full amount due at the legal rate of 10% since default date.
Dec. 31	Accrued interest on outstanding notes.

Required:

1. Give REV's entry to record each of the above transactions. Show computations.
2. Show how the outstanding notes at December 31, 19B, would be reported on the 19B statement of financial position.

P 7–17 (Notes Receivable with Unrealistic Interest Rate)

Howe Service Company completed a major renovation contract and billed the customer $28,000 on January 1, 19A. Cash of $8,000 was collected and a 5% note was received for the remaining $20,000, payable in three equal annual installments (including principal plus interest) each December 31. The going rate of interest for notes with comparable risk is 12%.

Required:

1. Compute the amount of the annual payments.
2. Compute the present value of the note.
3. Prepare a schedule of collections.
4. Give the entries on January 1, 19A, December 31, 19A, December 31, 19B, and December 31, 19C (use the net method).

CASES

C 7–1 (Data from Two Well-Known Companies; Analyze Accounts Receivable and Any Related Contingencies)

The annual financial reports of two corporations included the following notes to the financial statements:*

* Source: AICPA, *Accounting Trends & Techniques, 1984* (New York, 1984), p. 119.

1. Marathon sells certain of its accounts receivable to financial institutions. These accounts receivable sold are transferred subject to defined recourse provisions. Marathon collects the proceeds from the accounts receivable, and collection transfers are made in accordance with provisions of the agreements. As defined by the agreements, Marathon is required to calculate on a monthly basis the value of accounts receivable to be conveyed to the institutions. Accounts receivable sold as of December 31, 19X2, and December 31, 19X1, amounted to $260 million and $417 million, respectively, of which $173 million and $304 million, respectively, were subject to recourse.
2. Tonka Corporation: Note C—Sale of Accounts receivable:

In December 19X2, accounts receivable of approximately $14,558,000 were sold to a bank under an agreement without recourse which provided for replacement in certain circumstances. Net proceeds to the company were approximately $14,306,000.

Required (round amounts to the nearest million):

1. What were the amounts of accounts receivable sold by each company in 19X1 and 19X2?
2. What were the amounts of cash received from the sale of accounts receivable by each company in 19X1 and 19X2?
3. To whom were the accounts receivable sold?
4. Were the sales of accounts receivable on a notification or on a nonnotification basis? Explain.
5. Did each company incur a contingent liability as a result of the sale of accounts receivable? Explain.

C 7–2 **(Analysis of Actual Financial Statements)**

Kimberly-Clark

Refer to the 1987 financial statements of Kimberly-Clark (see the Appendix immediately following Chapter 25) and respond to the following for 1987 unless specifically indicated otherwise:

1. Reconcile the cash change during 1987 as reported on the statement of financial position and the change in funds shown on the statement of cash flows.
2. Explain the treatment of "depreciation and amortization" on the 1987 statement of cash flows.
3. Explain the treatment of "accounts receivable" on the 1987 statement of financial position.
4. Complete the following for 1987:
   a. Cash equivalents.
   b. Accounts receivable.
   c. Allowance for doubtful accounts.
   d. Receivables, net of allowance.
5. What long-term investments were reported? Explain.

8 INVENTORY MEASUREMENT, COST OF GOODS SOLD, AND DV LIFO

OVERVIEW AND PURPOSE

Accounting for inventories involves *(a)* measuring a current asset—inventories—that is reported on the statement of financial position, and *(b)* measuring an expense—cost of goods sold (and other "uses" of inventories)—that is reported on the statement of income in conformity with the matching principle. Measuring an inventory basically involves determination of physical quantity (units) and unit cost ($). Measurement of inventories poses major problems for managers and accountants because of the relatively large inventory investment which exists in a typical business. The importance of measuring, safeguarding, and controlling investment levels has caused accountants to give particular attention to inventories.

The purposes of this chapter are to discuss the characteristics of inventories and the typical inventory and cost of goods sold measurement approaches. Special inventory approaches and problems are discussed in Chapter 9. To accomplish these purposes this chapter is subdivided as follows:

Part A: Application of the Cost and Matching Principles in Measuring Inventories

1. Characteristics and measurement of inventories.
2. Measurement of physical quantities in an inventory; periodic and perpetual.
3. Measurement of inventory values for accounting purposes.
4. Inventory cost flow methods.

Part B: LIFO Inventory Issues and Dollar Value LIFO

1. Initial adoption of LIFO.
2. LIFO inventory liquidation—a special problem.
3. Recording LIFO in the accounts.
4. Comparison of FIFO with LIFO.
5. Dollar value LIFO method.

Supplement 8–A: Miscellaneous Cost Flow Methods

PART A: APPLICATION OF THE COST AND MATCHING PRINCIPLES IN MEASURING INVENTORIES

Characteristics and Measurement of Inventories

Inventories are assets consisting of goods owned by the business and held for future sale or for use in the manufacture of goods for sale. No other asset includes such an extensive variety of properties under a single heading; practically all kinds of tangible goods and properties are found in the inventories of one business or another. Machinery and equipment are operational assets of the business using them. However, at one time they were part of the inventory of the manufacturer of such equipment. Even a building, during the construction period, is an inventory item of the builder.

In many companies, inventories are a significant portion of current assets or even total assets. Inventories usually represent an "active" asset because they are constantly used and replaced. Although many inventory items are small, they frequently have considerable value; therefore, the problem of safeguarding inventories is similar to protecting cash. The need to adequately stock items for sale, coupled with the risk of loss and cost of overstocking, are critical management planning and control problems. Failure to control physical inventories and to properly account for inventory costs may lead to business failure.[1]

Inventories may be classified as follows:

1. **Merchandise inventory**—goods on hand purchased by a **trading entity** for resale. The physical form of the goods is not altered prior to resale.
2. **Manufacturing inventory**—the combined inventories of a **manufacturing entity** consisting of—
   a. **Raw materials inventory**—tangible goods purchased or obtained in other ways (e.g., by mining) and on hand for direct use in the manufacture of goods for resale. Parts or subassemblies manufactured prior to use are sometimes classified as raw materials inventory or **component parts inventory.**
   b. **Work in process inventory**—goods requiring further processing before completion and sale. Work (goods) in process inventory usually is valued at the sum of **direct material, direct labor, and allocated manufacturing overhead costs** incurred to date.
   c. **Finished goods inventory**—manufactured items completed and held for sale. Finished goods inventory usually is valued at the sum of **direct material, direct labor,** and **allocated manufacturing overhead costs** related to its manufacture.
   d. **Manufacturing supplies inventory**—items on hand such as lubrication oils for the machinery, cleaning materials, and other items that comprise an insignificant part of the finished product (such as the thread and glue used in binding this book).

---

[1] For an introductory discussion of accounting for inventories, refer to G. A. Welsch and D. G. Short, *Fundamentals of Financial Accounting*, 5th ed. (Homewood, Ill.: Richard D. Irwin, 1987), chap. 6.

3. **Miscellaneous inventories**—items such as office supplies, janitorial supplies, and shipping supplies. Inventories of this type typically are used in the near future and usually are recorded as selling or general expense when used.

The major classifications of inventories depend on the operations of the business. A trading entity (i.e., wholesale or retail) acquires merchandise for resale. A manufacturing entity acquires raw materials and component parts, manufactures finished products, and then sells them. The flow of inventory costs through these different entities is shown in **Exhibit 8–1** (assuming a perpetual inventory system).

Many inventory accounting problems occur because the amount of goods sold during a reporting period often differs from the amount of inventory produced or bought during that period. Therefore, the typical case is one in which the physical inventory increases or decreases during the period. This increase or decrease in the physical quantity of inventory creates the need for a corresponding **allocation of the total cost of goods available** between *(a)* **expense,** for the goods that were sold or used (i.e., cost of goods sold) and *(b)* **assets,** for the goods that remain on hand (i.e., the ending inventory). This allocation involves **two distinct phases:**

1. Identification and measurement of the **quantity of physical goods** (items and quantities) that should be included in inventory at the end of the accounting period.

Exhibit 8–1
Flow of inventory costs.

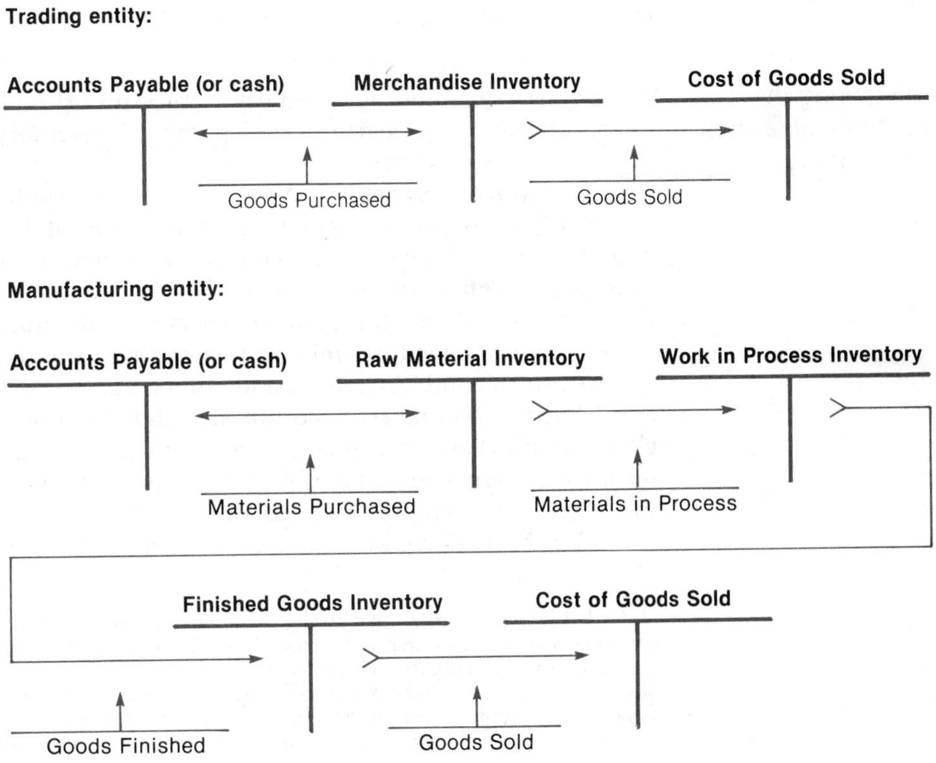

2. Measurement of the **accounting value** assigned to the physical goods included in inventory at the end of the period.

Items That Should Be Included in Inventory

To identify the items that should be included in inventory, accountants apply the general rule that all goods the entity **owns** at the inventory date should be included, regardless of their location. At the end of an accounting period, a business may *(a)* hold goods that it does not own or *(b)* own goods that it does not hold. Therefore, care must be exercised to identify the goods properly includable in inventory.

Goods purchased and in transit should be included in the inventory of the purchaser provided **ownership** to such goods has passed to the purchaser. Application of the "passage of ownership" rule usually is determined as follows: if the goods are shipped FOB (free on board) destination, ownership passes when the purchaser receives the goods from the common carrier; if the goods are shipped **FOB shipping point,** ownership passes when the seller delivers them to the common carrier.

Goods **out on consignment,** those held by agents, and those located at branches, should be **included** in inventory.[2] On the other hand, goods **held** (but owned by someone else) for sale on commission or on consignment, and those received from a vendor but rejected and awaiting return to the vendor for credit, should be **excluded** from inventory.

To identify items that should be included in inventory, when a question exists as to whether ownership has passed, the accountant must use judgment in light of each situation. Legal ownership should be recognized; however, a strict legal determination often is impractical. In such cases, the sales agreement, industry practices, and other evidence of intent should be considered.

Measuring the Quantity of Goods in Inventory

The physical quantities in inventory may be measured by use of *(a)* **a periodic (physical) inventory system** or *(b)* **a perpetual inventory system.**

Periodic Inventory System.

When a periodic inventory system is used, an actual **physical count** of the goods on hand is taken at the end of each accounting period for which financial statements are prepared. The goods are counted, weighed, or otherwise measured, and then extended at unit costs to value the inventory. Under the periodic system, a continuous inventory record is not kept of the inventory units and amounts purchased, sold (or issued), and the balance on hand. Therefore, under the periodic inventory system purchases are debited to a purchases account and end-of-period entries are made to *(a)* close the purchases account, *(b)* close out the beginning inventory, and *(c)* record the ending inventory as an asset (i.e., the ending inventory replaces the beginning inventory in the accounts).

Under the periodic system, cost of goods sold is computed as a **residual**

[2] Consignment is a marketing arrangement whereby the consignor (the owner of the goods) ships merchandise to another party, known as a **consignee,** who acts as a sales agent only. The consignee does not purchase the goods but assumes responsibility for their care and sale. Upon sale, the consignee remits the proceeds (less specified expenses and a commission) to the consignor. Goods on consignment, because they are owned by the consignor until sold, should be excluded from the inventory of the consignee and included in the inventory of the consignor.

amount and for all practical purposes cannot be verified independently of the inventory count. To illustrate:

Computation of Cost of Goods Sold:

Beginning inventory (carried forward from the prior period)	$ 50,000
Merchandise purchases (accumulated in the Purchases account)	200,000
Total goods available for sale during the period	250,000
Less: Ending inventory (determined by a physical count)	60,000
Cost of goods sold (a residual amount)	$190,000

The accounting entries and external financial reporting under the periodic inventory system were reviewed in Chapters 3 and 4.

Perpetual Inventory System. When a perpetual inventory system is used, **detailed perpetual inventory records,** in addition to the usual ledger accounts, are maintained for each inventory item. An **Inventory Control** account is maintained in the general ledger on a current basis. The perpetual inventory record for **each** item must provide for recording *(a)* receipts, *(b)* issues, and *(c)* balances on hand, usually in **both quantities (units)** and dollar amounts. Thus, the physical quantity and valuation of goods on hand at any time are available from the accounting records. Therefore, a physical inventory count is unnecessary except to check on the accuracy of the perpetual inventory records. Such checks (physical counts) usually are made annually on a rotation basis (cycle counts).

When a difference is found between the perpetual inventory records and the physical count, the perpetual inventory records are adjusted to the physical count. In such cases, the inventory account is debited or credited as necessary for the correction, and an inventory correction account such as Inventory Shortages (loss) or Overages (gain) is debited or credited. The inventory correction account is closed to Income Summary at the end of the period. The balance in the inventory shortage account usually is reported separately on internal financial statements. However, it is combined with the cost of goods sold amount on external statements.

For control purposes, many companies rely on a perpetual inventory system. This control need is critical for inventory items of high unit value and in situations where it is important to have certain quantities of inventory on hand to avoid overstocking and understocking. A perpetual system is useful for *(a)* controlling and safeguarding inventory and *(b)* preparing monthly and other interim statements without counting and costing the ending inventory each time. A perpetual system is one of the characteristics of a good cost accounting system. The only negative feature of a perpetual system is the cost of implementation; however, advances in computer technology have reduced these costs to levels that make it economically feasible for even small entities to use a perpetual system. **Exhibit 8–2** illustrates a **perpetual inventory record** for item X during 19J. The accounting procedures for the **periodic** and **perpetual** inventory systems are illustrated in **Exhibit 8–3.** This exhibit emphasizes three procedural differences between the two inventory systems:

Exhibit 8–2
Perpetual inventory record.

SUBSIDIARY LEDGER

PERPETUAL INVENTORY RECORD

Verification Dates

Article: Item X | Unit: Pounds | Maximum: 1,600

Location: 1-15 | Bin No.: 32 | Reorder Level: 800

	Ordered		Received or Completed					Issued or Sold				Balance on Hand		
Date 19J	Order No.	Units	Order No.	Ref.	Units	Unit Cost	Total Cost	Ref.	Units	Unit Cost	Total Cost	Units	Unit Cost	Total Cost
(1)												500	4.00	2,000
(2)			17		1,000	4.00	4,000					1,500	4.00	6,000
(3)									900	4.00	3,600	600	4.00	2,400
(4)	18	700												

1. **Entries at date of purchase**—When the **periodic** system is used, purchases of goods during the period are debited to the **Purchases** account to accumulate total purchases for the period. When the **perpetual** system is used, purchases are debited directly to the Inventory Control account (and concurrently entered into the subsidiary inventory records as shown in Exhibit 8–3).
2. **Entries at date of sale**—When the **periodic** system is used, only **one** entry is made to record a sale. **No** entry is made at this time to record the related **cost of goods sold** amount because this amount is not directly available. When the **perpetual** system is used, **two** entries are required to record a sale—one for the revenue (at sales price) and one for cost of goods sold (at cost price). Only the perpetual system provides a current accounting for the cost of goods sold amount at the date of each sale.
3. **Inventory balances**—When the **periodic** system is used, the **beginning balance** in the Inventory account remains unchanged throughout the accounting period; detailed records of the current amount of goods on hand are not maintained. When the **perpetual** system is used, the **cost** of current sales of inventory (CGS) is credited to the Inventory account as sales are made; thus, the Inventory account carries a perpetual, or continuing, balance of the goods on hand at all times.

Exhibit 8–3
Periodic and perpetual inventory systems compared.

Panel A—Case Data:

Item X	Units	Unit amount
Merchandise inventory, beginning	500	$4 (cost)
Merchandise purchases during the period	1,000	4 (cost)
Total goods available for sale	1,500	
Merchandise sold during the period	900	6 (sales price)
Merchandise inventory, ending	600	

Panel B—Comparative Entries:

Periodic inventory system			Perpetual inventory system		
a. Merchandise purchased for resale:					
Purchases (1,000 × $4)	4,000		Inventory	4,000	
Cash		4,000	Cash		4,000
b. Merchandise sold:					
Cash (900 × $6)	5,400		Cash	5,400	
Sales revenue		5,400	Sales revenue		5,400
			Cost of goods sold	3,600	
			Inventory (900 × $4)		3,600
c. Entries at end of the accounting period:					
To transfer Purchases account balance:					
Cost of goods sold	4,000		None		
Purchases		4,000			
To transfer beginning inventory amount:					
Cost of goods sold	2,000		None		
Inventory (beginning)		2,000			
To record ending inventory amount:					
Inventory (ending)	2,400		None		
Cost of goods sold		2,400			
Closing entry:					
Income summary	3,600		Income summary	3,600	
Cost of goods sold		3,600	Cost of goods sold		3,600

Panel C—Reporting:
Statement of income (partial):

Periodic			Perpetual	
Sales revenue		$5,400	Sales revenue	$5,400
Cost of goods sold:*				
Beginning inventory	$2,000			
Purchases	4,000			
Goods available for sale	6,000			
Ending inventory (by physical count)	2,400			
Cost of goods sold		3,600	Cost of goods sold*	3,600
Gross margin		$1,800	Gross margin	$1,800
Statement of financial position (partial):				
Current assets:				
Merchandise inventory		$2,400	Merchandise inventory	$2,400

* Cost of goods sold is shown both in detail and as one amount to emphasize the different ways that it is **derived** under the two systems. It can be **reported** the same under either system.

Measurement of Inventory Values for Accounting Purposes

At date of acquisition, inventory items are recorded at their **cash equivalent cost** in conformity with the **cost principle.** Subsequently, when an item is sold, its cost is matched with revenue in conformity with the **matching principle.** Inventory items remaining on hand at the end of an accounting period are assigned an accounting value. This value is based on the **cost principle** except when their value has declined below cost because of damage, obsolescence, decrease in replacement cost, or similar factors. In this case, the items in inventory are assigned an accounting value in conformity with the **conservatism constraint** (for example, lower-of-cost-or-market or net realizable value).

The **accounting value** of merchandise and finished goods inventories results from an allocation of the total cost of goods **available for sale** between that portion sold (i.e., cost of goods sold) and that portion held as an asset for subsequent sale (i.e., ending inventory). The nature of this allocation is shown below (based on the data given in Exhibit 8–3):

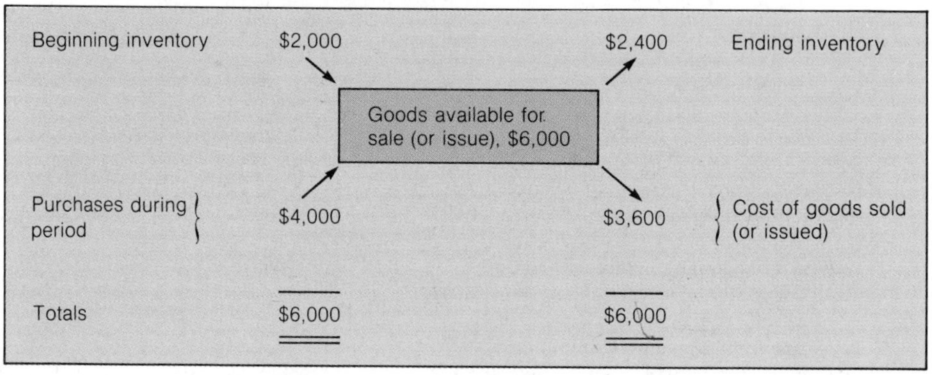

A number of procedures used for measuring the accounting value of inventories satisfy conceptual requirements. The variety of acceptable procedures reflects the wide variation in inventory characteristics and conditions, depending upon particular company situations and objectives.

Basically, the accounting values for inventories serve two different objectives. Each objective implies procedures that may not be appropriate for the other objective. One objective is to develop a monetary value for the inventory reported on the **statement of financial position.** The second objective, focusing on the **statement of income,** is to measure the inventory value in order to achieve a proper matching of cost of goods sold with the sales revenue of the period. Measurement of acceptable accounting **values** for (1) inventory and (2) cost of goods sold involves two distinct problems:

1. **Inventory unit cost**—selection of an appropriate **unit cost** for valuation of the items in inventory. The principal **inventory valuation methods** are:
   a. Cost basis.
   b. Departure from cost basis (discussed in Chapter 9):
      1. Lower-of-cost-or market (LCM).
      2. Net realizable value.

3. Current cost.
4. Selling price.

2. **Inventory flow**—selection of an inventory flow method using the cost basis; that is, selection of an **assumed flow** of inventory unit costs during the accounting period. The principal **inventory flow methods** (discussed in this chapter) are:
   a. Specific cost.
   b. Average cost.
   c. First-in, first-out (FIFO).
   d. Last-in, first-out (LIFO).

Content of Inventory Cost

The **cost principle** provides the conceptual foundation for measuring the cost of inventory and cost of goods sold.[3] Inventory cost is measured by the total cash equivalent outlay made to acquire the goods and to prepare them for sale. These costs include the purchase cost and incidental costs incurred on the goods up to the time they are ready for use or for sale to the customer.

In conformity with the **cost-benefit constraint and materiality,** some incidental costs, although theoretically a cost of goods purchased, often are not included in inventory valuation but are reported as a separate expense; the cost of allocating such costs may not be warranted by the related benefits. In such cases, **consistency** in application is particularly important. For example, general administrative and distribution expenses usually are not included in determining inventory costs because they are not directly related to the purchase or manufacture of goods for sale. General and administrative (G&A) expenses often are treated as **period** expenses because they relate more directly to accounting periods than to inventory. Therefore, they are recognized on the statement of income in the period incurred.

Freight-In (freight on purchases). In conformity with the **cost principle,** freight and other incidental costs paid in connection with the purchase of inventory are additions to unit cost. When such costs can be identified with specific goods, they should be added as part of the cost of such goods. However, in some cases identification is impractical. Therefore, such costs often are recorded in a special account such as Freight-In, which is reported as an addition to cost of goods sold in the case of a trading entity and to cost of materials used in a manufacturing entity. This practical procedure may overstate cost of goods sold and understate inventory by the amount of such costs that should be allocated to inventory (as opposed to including the full amount in cost of goods sold). Conceptually, freight-in should be apportioned between cost of goods sold and the ending inventory.

Cash Discounts on Credit Purchases. Many companies offer cash discounts on credit purchases to encourage early payment. Under the cost principle, the cost of an item is the **net cash equivalent** paid for it. Payments made for the extension of credit should not be added to inventory cost but should be accounted

[3] AICPA, *Accounting Research Bulletin No. 43,* "Restatement and Revision of Accounting Research Bulletins" (New York, 1961), chap. 4, statement 3.

for as **interest expense.**[4] Conceptually, all cash discounts permitted, **whether taken or not,** should be omitted from cost. On payment of invoices, any discounts not taken constitute interest expense. Therefore, credit purchases should be recorded **net of discount** to reflect the **correct cash equivalent cost.** However, purchases sometimes are recorded at the **gross amount** for practical reasons or because the cash discount is immaterial. When the gross method is used, purchases and accounts payable are overstated pending payment. When payment is made, a credit must be recorded as a purchase discount. This account

Exhibit 8–4

Recording and reporting inventory at net and gross amounts compared (perpetual inventory system).

Panel A—Case Data:

1. Merchandise was purchased for $1,000 on credit, terms of 2/10, n/30.
2. Three fourths of the $1,000 was paid within the 10-day discount period. The remainder was paid after the discount period expired.

Net of Discount Approach (conceptually preferable)			Gross Amount Approach (acceptable)		
Panel B—Recording:					
To record the purchase (perpetual inventory system):					
Inventory	980		Inventory	1,000	
Accounts payable (net)		980	Accounts payable (gross)		1,000
To record payment of three fourths of the liability within discount period:					
Accounts payable (net)	735		Accounts payable (gross)	750	
Cash		735	Cash		735
($980 × ¾ = $735).			Discount on purchases		15
To record payment of one fourth of the liability after the discount period:					
Accounts payable (net)	245		Accounts payable (gross)	250	
Interest expense*	5		Cash		250
Cash		250			
* Alternative title: Purchase discounts lost.					
To record sale of half the inventory for $1,500 cash:					
Cash	1,500		Cash	1,500	
Sales revenue		1,500	Sales revenue		1,500
Cost of goods sold	490		Cost of goods sold	500	
Inventory		490	Inventory		500
($980 × ½ = $490).			($1,000 × ½ = $500).		

Panel C—Reporting (notice the different amounts that result from the two approaches):

Statement of income:			
Cost of goods sold	$490	Cost of goods sold ($500 less purchase discount, $15)	$485
Interest expense	5		
Statement of financial position:			
Inventory	490	Inventory	500

[4] *FASB, Statement of Financial Accounting Standards No. 34* "Capitalization of Interest Cost" (Stamford, Conn., October 1979), par. 10. An exception to this general rule requires capitalization of interest on one class of inventory as follows: "[a]ssets intended for sale that are constructed or otherwise produced as discrete projects (e.g., ships or real estate developments)" (see par. 96).

balance is *(a)* subtracted from cost of goods sold (with no effect on the inventory), or *(b)* reported as "financial" revenue (which illogically creates revenue by paying the bill, even though the goods may still be in inventory). Recording and reporting under the net and gross approaches are illustrated in **Exhibit 8–4.** This discussion does not include trade discounts. Trade discounts are used for price quotations, such as a unit cost reduction for purchases in excess of 1,000 units.

Inventory Cost Flow Methods

Underlying Concepts of Cost Flow

A basic problem associated with accounting for inventories is the allocation of the cost of goods **available for sale or use** between goods sold or used and inventory on hand at the end of the period. The purchase or manufacture of inventory during a period incurs costs. These costs, combined with the cost of inventory on hand at the beginning of the period, determine the total cost of goods available for sale or use during a period. The sale or issuance of inventory changes some of these costs into an expense. The remaining costs become the cost of inventory on hand at the end of the period. An appropriate cost **allocation** procedure must be selected to allocate the total cost of goods available for sale for each period between goods sold and goods on hand. If inventory unit costs are constant during the reporting period, the allocation is not complex. However, items typically are manufactured or purchased at different unit costs, creating a need to use an explicit **cost flow assumption** to allocate cost of goods available for sale.

Inventory cost flow methods may be consistent with the physical flow of goods in a specific case. However, the accounting emphasis is on the **flow of costs** rather than on the flow of physical goods. On this issue *Accounting Research Bulletin No. 43* states:

> Cost for inventory purposes may be determined under any one of several assumptions as to the flow of cost factors (such as first-in, first-out, average, and last-in, first-out); the major objective should be to choose the one which, under the circumstances, most clearly reflects periodic income.[5]

The inventory cost flow methods discussed in this chapter conform to the **cost principle.** The central issue is the **order** in which the actual unit costs incurred are assigned to the ending inventory and cost of goods sold. The selection of an inventory flow method applies the **matching principle** to determine cost of goods sold, which is deducted from sales revenue for the period. Under GAAP, the method selected should be the one that most clearly reflects periodic income in each situation. The data given in **Exhibit 8–5** are used to illustrate cost allocation to inventory and cost of goods sold.

Application of some of the inventory costs flow methods varies depending on whether a **periodic** or **perpetual** inventory system is used. The following discussion distinguishes between these systems because they affect the application of the inventory cost flow method.

---

[5] AICPA, *Accounting Research Bulletin No. 43*, "Restatement and Revision of Accounting Research Bulletins" (New York, 1961), chap. 4, statement 4.

Exhibit 8–5
Data used to illustrate cost flows in the inventory methods.

Panel A—Situation–Inventory Data:

Transactions	Received (purchased) Units	Received (purchased) Unit cost	Units issued (sold)	Units on hand
Jan. 1 Inventory [at $1]				200
9 Purchase	300	$1.10		500
10 Sale			400	100
15 Purchase	400	1.16		500
18 Sale			300	200
24 Purchase	100	1.26		300

Panel B—Illustration of the Cost Flow Problem:

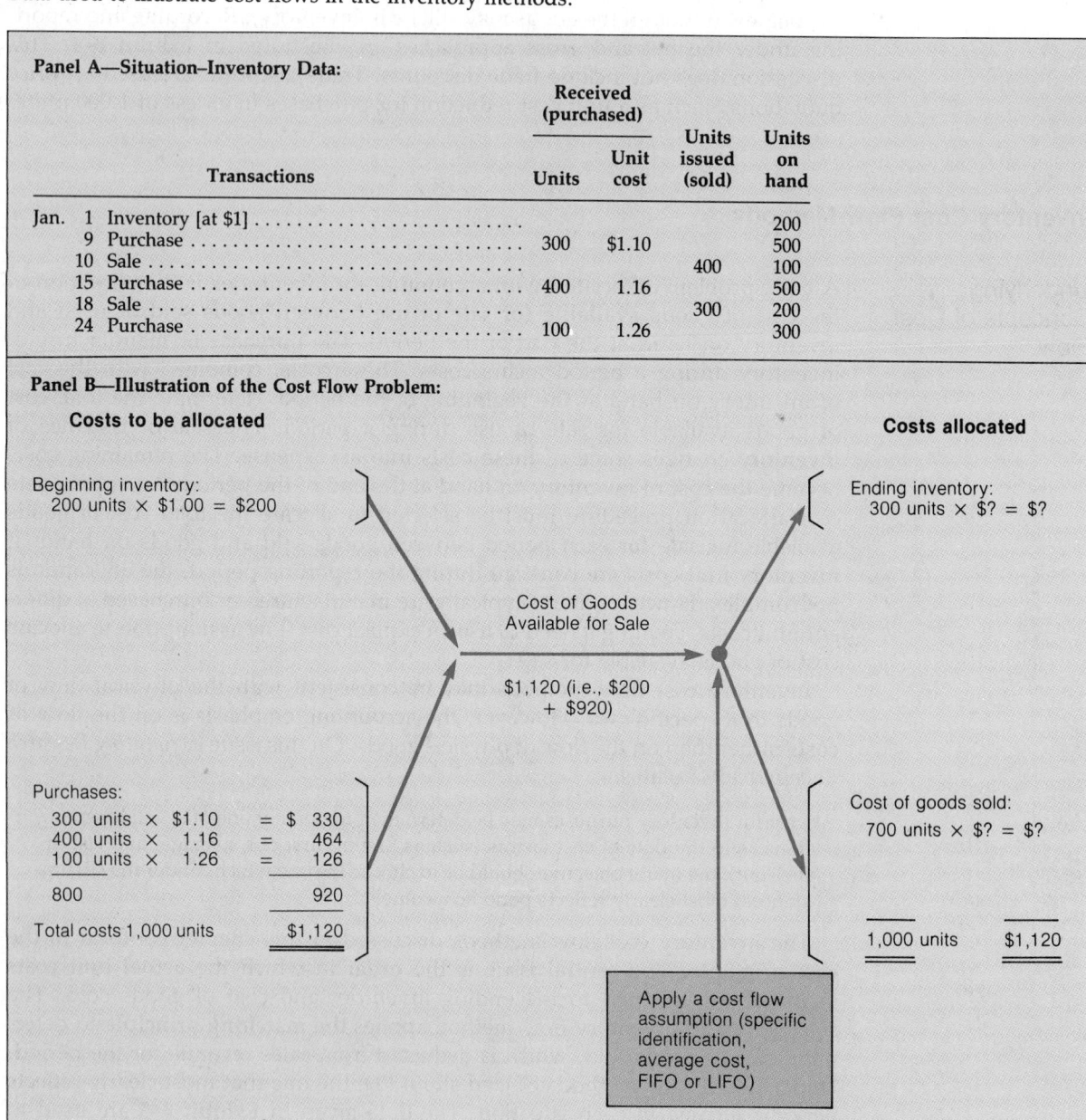

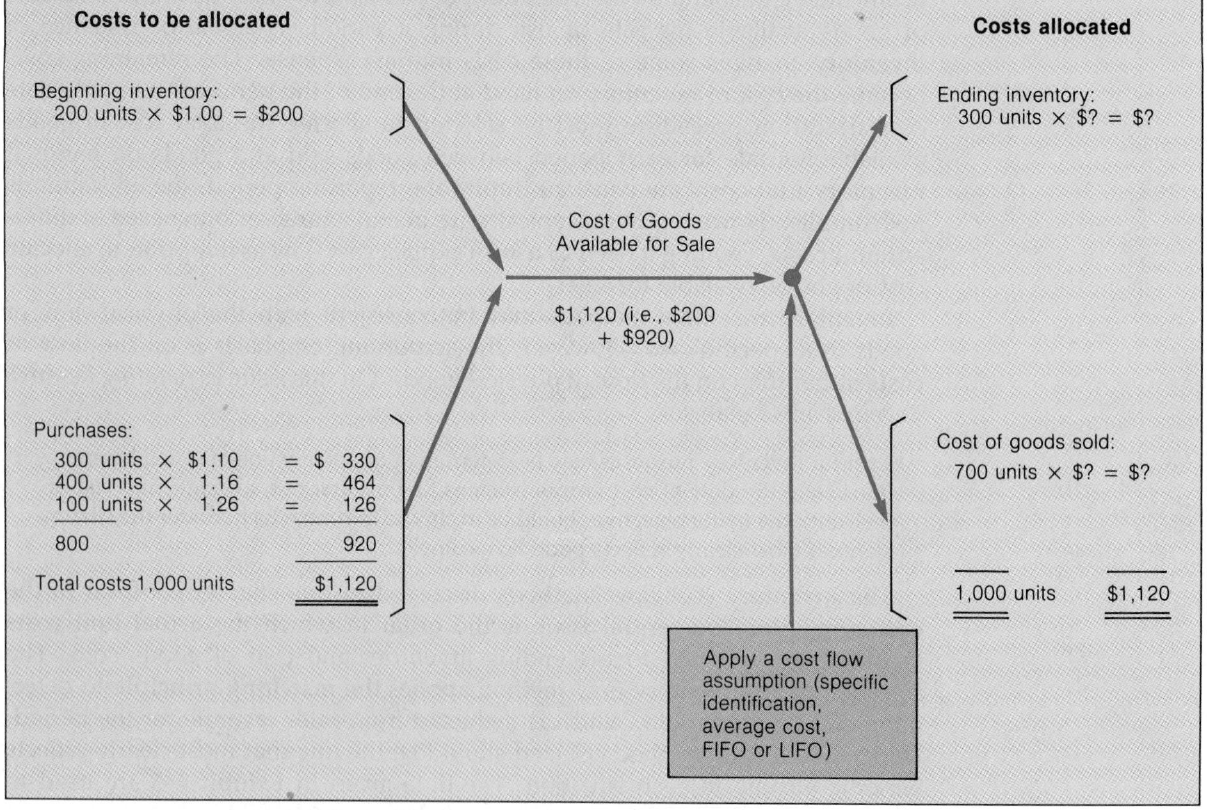

Under a **periodic inventory system,** the quantity of the ending inventory is determined solely by a physical unit count at the end of the period. The unit costs then are applied to derive the ending inventory valuation by using one of the flow methods discussed next. Cost of goods sold (or used) is determined by subtracting the ending inventory valuation from the **cost of goods available** amount.

Under a **perpetual inventory system,** each receipt and each issue of an inventory item is recorded in the inventory records to maintain an up-to-date perpetual inventory balance at all times. Thus, the perpetual inventory records provide the amounts of ending inventory and cost of goods sold. The unit costs applied to each issue or sale are determined by the cost flow method which is used.

The remaining sections in Part A will discuss four inventory cost flow methods—specific identification, average cost, FIFO and LIFO.

Specific Cost Identification Method

This method requires that each item stocked be specifically marked so that its unit cost can be identified at any time. When the items involved are large or expensive and small quantities are handled, it may be feasible to tag or number each item when purchased or manufactured. This method makes it possible to identify at date of sale the specific unit cost of each item sold and each item remaining in inventory. Thus, the specific cost identification method relates the cost flow with the specific **flow of physical goods.**

Evaluation of Specific Cost Identification Method. The specific cost method requires careful identification of each item, which causes a practical limitation created by the detailed records that are required. However, computerized inventory systems can help resolve this problem.

Another undesirable feature of the method is the opportunity to manipulate income by arbitrary selection of items at time of sale. Assume three identical stereo sets are for sale. Their costs are $800, $850, and $900. One is sold for $1,500. In this instance, reported cost of goods sold (and reported income) would depend on the unit arbitrarily selected for this particular sale. Thus, the specific cost method can easily be applied subjectively. This method is essential in cases where individual units have unique characteristics that, by their relative appeal to customers, determine which unit is sold. For example, with rare gems, this method often is used because the unique characteristics of such items reduce the opportunity for income manipulation.

Average Cost Method

The average cost method is based on the view that the cost of inventory on hand at the end of a period and the cost of goods sold during a period should be representative of all costs incurred during the period. The average cost method can be applied in two ways, depending on the inventory system used: *(a)* **periodic** inventory system—**weighted-average unit cost** for the entire accounting period; and *(b)* **perpetual** inventory system—**moving average unit cost.**

Weighted-Average Cost (Periodic Inventory System). The weighted-average cost method is used with the periodic inventory system because the average cost can be computed only at the end of the period. A weighted-average unit cost is computed by dividing the sum of the beginning inventory plus current purchase **costs** by the number of **units** in the beginning inventory plus units purchased during the period. The weighted unit cost is then applied to *(a)* the units in the ending inventory and *(b)* the units sold (to compute cost of goods sold). **Exhibit 8–6** illustrates application of the weighted-average method, using the data given in Exhibit 8–5, panel A.

Exhibit 8–6
Weighted-average inventory cost method (periodic inventory system).

	Units	Unit price	Total cost
Goods available:			
Jan. 1 Beginning inventory	200	$1.00	$ 200
9 Purchase	300	1.10	330
15 Purchase	400	1.16	464
24 Purchase	100	1.26	126
Total available	1,000	1.12*	1,120
Ending inventory at weighted-average cost:			
Jan. 31	300	1.12	336
Cost of goods sold at weighted-average cost:			
Sales during January	700†	1.12	$ 784

* Weighted-average unit cost ($1,120 ÷ 1,000 = $1.12).
† 400 units on January 10 plus 300 units on January 18.

Evaluation of the Weighted-Average Cost Method. The weighted-average cost method is generally viewed as objective, consistent, not subject to easy manipulation, and easy to apply. The method is appropriate for **periodic** inventory systems because *(a)* the inventory of physical units is not counted until the end of the period and *(b)* the weighted-average unit cost can be determined only at the end of the period. Thus, the measurements needed to compute ending inventory and cost of goods sold are determined at the same time, at the end of the accounting period.

Moving Average Cost (Perpetual Inventory System). When a perpetual inventory system is used, the weighted-average approach cannot be applied because a weighted-unit cost cannot be calculated until the end of the period. To avoid this problem, a **moving** average unit cost is used. The **moving** average provides a new unit cost **after each purchase.** Thus, when goods are sold or issued, the moving average unit cost at that time is used. Application of the moving average concept in a **perpetual inventory system** is shown in **Exhibit 8–7** (based on data from Exhibit 8–5). Notice that a **new** moving average unit cost is computed after **each purchase** (actually it is a short term weighted-average cost). This facilitates the current costing of items sold or issued during the period. For example, on January 9, the $1.06 moving average cost was derived by dividing the total cost ($530) by the total units (500). The ending inventory of 300 units is costed at the latest moving average unit cost of $1.18 (total $354). Cost of goods sold for the period is the sum of the Sales, Total cost column, $766 (i.e., $424 + $342).

Evaluation of Moving Average Cost Method. The moving average method is generally viewed as objective, consistent, and not subject to easy manipulation. It is appropriate for **perpetual** inventory systems because it provides a current average cost on a continuous basis.

Overall Evaluation of the Average Cost Methods. The average cost methods do not match the **latest** unit costs with current sales revenues. Rather, they

Exhibit 8–7
Moving average cost (perpetual inventory system).

Date	Purchases			Sales (issues)			Inventory Balance		
	Units	Unit cost	Total cost	Units	Unit cost	Total cost	Units	Unit cost	Total cost
Jan. 1							200*	$1.00	$200
9	300	$1.10	$330				500	1.06(a)	530
10				400	$1.06	$424	100	1.06	106
15	400	1.16	464				500	1.14(b)	570
18				300	1.14	342	200	1.14	228
24	100	1.26	126				300	1.18(c)	354

* Beginning inventory.
(a) $530 ÷ 500 = $1.06.
(b) $570 ÷ 500 = $1.14.
(c) $354 ÷ 300 = $1.18.

match the average costs of the period against revenues and value the ending inventory at average cost. Therefore, when unit costs are steadily increasing or decreasing, they provide inventory and cost of goods sold amounts between the LIFO and FIFO extremes. The amounts reported in the statement of financial position (ending inventory) and the statement of income (cost of goods sold) are valued consistently because the same unit costs are used on both statements. Many accountants favor the average cost method (versus FIFO or LIFO) because unit values for inventory and cost of goods sold are consistent.

First-In, First-Out Cost Method

The first-in, first-out method (FIFO) is based on the view that the first goods purchased or manufactured should be the first units costed out on sale or issuance. Because the costs flow out in the same order they flowed in, goods sold (or issued) are valued at the **oldest** unit costs. The goods remaining in inventory are valued at the **most recent** unit cost amounts. Application of FIFO requires the identification of **inventory layers** for the different unit costs. FIFO can be used with either a periodic or a perpetual inventory system.

Periodic Inventory System. Using the data given in Exhibit 8–5 and assuming a physical inventory count at the end of the period, FIFO results are shown in **Exhibit 8–8.**

Perpetual Inventory System. Application of FIFO with a perpetual inventory system is illustrated in **Exhibit 8–9.** Notice that the maintenance of **inventory layers** by unit costs throughout the period is needed to assign the appropriate cost to each issue.

When FIFO is used with a **perpetual** inventory system, the issues on the inventory record may be costed out either *(a)* currently throughout the period (i.e., each time there is a withdrawal) or *(b)* all at the end of the period, with the same results. In Exhibit 8–9, issues from inventory on January 10 and 18

Exhibit 8–8
FIFO inventory costing (periodic inventory system).

	Beginning inventory (200 units at $1)		$ 200
	Add purchases during period (computed as in Exhibit 8–5)		920
	Cost of goods available for sale		1,120
	Deduct ending inventory (300 units per physical inventory count):		
Inventory Computation (FIFO)	100 units at $1.26 (most recent purchase)	$126	
	200 units at $1.16 (next most recent purchase)	232	
	Total ending inventory cost		358
	Cost of goods sold (or issued)		$ 762*

* (200 units at $1 plus 200 units at $1.10 on January 10) plus (100 units at $1.10 plus 200 units at $1.16 on January 18) = $762.

(FIFO basis) were costed out as they occurred (i.e., currently). FIFO produces the same cost of ending inventory regardless of whether a periodic or a perpetual system is used (compare Exhibits 8–8 and 8–9). FIFO is the only method for which this is true.

Evaluation of FIFO Cost Method. FIFO is often used for inventory costing purposes because *(a)* it is easy to apply with either periodic or perpetual inventory systems, *(b)* it produces an inventory value for the statement of financial position that approximates current cost, *(c)* the flow of costs **tends** to be consistent with the usual physical flow of goods, *(d)* it is systematic and objective, and *(e)* it is not subject to manipulation. A criticism of FIFO sometimes made is that it does not match the **current cost** of goods sold with current revenues; rather, the oldest unit costs are matched with current sales revenue. Thus,

Exhibit 8–9
FIFO costing (perpetual inventory system).

	Purchases			Sales (issues)			Inventory Balance		
Date	Units	Unit cost	Total cost	Units	Unit cost	Total cost*	Units	Unit cost	Total cost
Jan. 1							200†	$1.00	$200
9	300	$1.10	$330				200 300	1.00 1.10	200 330
10				200 200	$1.00 1.10	$200 220	100	1.10	110
15	400	1.16	464				100 400	1.10 1.16	110 464
18				100 200	1.10 1.16	110 232	200	1.16	232
24	100	1.26	126				200 100	1.16 1.26	232 126 $358

* Total cost of goods sold for January = $200 + $220 + $110 + $232 = $762.
† Beginning inventory.

when costs are rising, reported income under FIFO is **higher** than under LIFO or average cost.[6] This result often is called **inventory profit,** which is the difference between actual cost of goods sold at FIFO cost and cost of goods sold measured at the current cost of goods sold.

The income tax implications of FIFO are important. When inventory costs are rising, companies that use FIFO report more income than those using LIFO or average cost, when all other factors are constant. Therefore, FIFO users pay more income taxes when prices are rising.

Last-In, First-Out Cost Method

The last-in, first-out (LIFO) method of inventory costing is based on the view that the latest unit acquisition cost should be matched with current sales revenue. Therefore, under LIFO, the order of cost **outflows** recognized is the inverse of the order of cost **inflows** (the opposite of FIFO). The units remaining in **ending** inventory are costed at the **oldest** unit costs available; the units in **cost of goods sold** are costed at the **most recent** unit costs available. LIFO application requires the use of inventory layers for the different unit costs.

The LIFO inventory concept may be applied by using either of two approaches:

1. **Unit cost approach**—Units are multiplied by unit cost for each separate product (discussed below).[7]
2. **Dollar value LIFO approach**—Large inventory pools (i.e., groups of similar products) and index prices are used to compute the LIFO inventory (discussed in Part B).

lowers tax liability

Unit Cost Approach for LIFO. This section will present the concept of LIFO applied by using units and unit costs for each individual product. For instructional purposes, a single product is used. LIFO may be applied with either a periodic or perpetual inventory system. However, the cost of goods sold amount and the ending inventory balance are usually different depending on the inventory system used.

Periodic Inventory System. Assuming a **periodic inventory system** and a physical inventory of units at the **end of the period,** LIFO results are determined as shown in **Exhibit 8–10.** Notice that the ending inventory is costed at the

Exhibit 8–10
LIFO costing (periodic inventory system).

	Cost of goods available (see Exhibit 8–5)		$1,120
End-of-Period Inventory Computation (LIFO)	Deduct ending inventory (300 units per physical inventory count):		
	200 units at $1 (oldest costs available; from January 1 inventory)	$200	
	100 units at $1.10 (next oldest costs available; from January 9 purchase)	110	
	Ending inventory		310
	Cost of goods sold		$ 810

[6] When costs are falling, reported income is lower under FIFO than under LIFO or average cost.

[7] This application also is called the **quantity, specific goods,** or **unit** LIFO method of applying the LIFO concept.

Exhibit 8–11
LIFO costing (perpetual inventory system).

	Purchases			Sales (issues)			Inventory Balance		
Date	Units	Unit cost	Total cost	Units	Unit cost	Total cost	Units	Unit cost	Total cost
Jan. 1							200	$1.00	$200
9	300	$1.10	$330				200 300	1.00 1.10	200 330
10				300 100	$1.10 1.00	$330 100	100	1.00	100
15	400	1.16	464				100 400	1.00 1.16	100 464
18				300	1.16	348	100 100	1.00 1.16	100 116
24	100	1.26	126				100 100 100	1.00 1.16 1.26	100 116 126
Ending inventory									$342
Cost of goods sold						$778			

oldest unit costs. Cost of goods sold is determined by deducting ending inventory from the cost of goods available for sale.

Perpetual Inventory System. When LIFO is applied with a **perpetual inventory system,** the sales (issues) are costed **currently** throughout the period (i.e., each time a sale occurs).[8] The **internal** application of LIFO with a **perpetual** inventory system (i.e., costed currently during the period) is shown in **Exhibit 8–11.** It also illustrates the tedious nature of LIFO inventory computations. However, difficulties in using LIFO may be reduced by using computerized inventory systems.

Notice that both cost of goods sold and ending inventory differ by $32 (i.e., $342 – $310) under the two systems shown in Exhibits 8–10 and 8–11, which is a result of costing at year-end (periodic system) versus costing during the year (perpetual system).

A variation of the unit cost approach, called a **pooled approach,** groups similar products into inventory pools. Each such pool is treated as one product—units of the products in a pool are added together and are costed at the average unit cost on a LIFO basis. The pooled approach originally was developed to save clerical time; however, the extensive use of computers for inventory purposes has largely negated this advantage. The pooled approach is subject to

[8] Throughout this discussion, we used the term **sale** to refer to the event that decreases the balance of inventory on hand. The term **issue** is synonymous with **sale** in this context. Therefore, **cost of goods sold** is synonymous with **cost of issues.**

manipulation to avoid actual LIFO-cost liquidation and to affect reported income. This is done by intentionally having combinations of diverse products in the inventory pools and by shifting products among the various pools.

During periods of rising inventory costs, LIFO costed at the end of the period will provide a lower pretax income than current costing. Therefore, a company using LIFO for tax purposes would cost at the end of the period to minimize taxable income. Because of this, if a perpetual LIFO system costed currently is used for internal purposes, the results usually are restated to an end-of-period costing basis for both income tax and external reporting purposes. When inventory unit prices are increasing, and units sold are not decreasing, LIFO often is used for income tax purposes to obtain a cash flow advantage. This advantage occurs because the LIFO cost method causes cost of goods sold to be higher and taxable income to be lower.

The lower income tax payments reduce cash outflow. The IRS has consistently taken a strong position to prevent what is called **LIFO abuses.** For example, many companies wanted to use LIFO for income tax purposes and another approach such as FIFO for internal purposes and for external reporting. First, the IRS specified an income tax conformity rule which states that a company can use LIFO for income tax purposes only if it also uses LIFO for financial reporting purposes. The IRS also specified strict rules that require LIFO companies to maintain detailed LIFO records to facilitate IRS income tax audits.

In response to the income tax conformity rule, companies began giving supplemental data in disclosure notes about "net income on a FIFO basis." This tactic raised IRS objections. However, because of considerable pressure, the IRS relaxed the LIFO conformity rule somewhat. The basic requirement that LIFO can be used for tax purposes only if it is used for external reporting purposes was not changed, but supplemental disclosure about income under FIFO or average is permitted (but not on the statement of income). These rules do not apply to the other inventory methods.

An evaluation of LIFO, and a comparison of LIFO with FIFO, are given in Part B.

PART B: LIFO INVENTORY ISSUES AND DOLLAR VALUE LIFO

The unit cost approach to LIFO discussed in Part A has four major problems as follows:

1. Liquidation of LIFO inventory layers.
2. The reluctance of companies to use it for internal planning and control purposes.
3. Complications when old products are dropped and new products are introduced.
4. The complexity involved in costing inventory and cost of goods sold differently for interim, year-end, and income tax purposes.

These problems have been the primary reasons for the development of an innovative, short-cut way to approximate LIFO results, called the **dollar value**

LIFO method (DV LIFO). This method uses dollars and a price index to compute LIFO cost for inventory and cost of goods sold.[9]

Initial Adoption of LIFO

Income tax regulations permit taxpayers to use LIFO for all or part of the total inventory of goods (e.g., for manufacturers—raw materials, work in process, finished goods; for retailers and wholesalers—merchandise for sale). In the typical LIFO situation, the company has changed from some other method to LIFO for **tax** and **external reporting** purposes.

The switch to LIFO involves a **change in accounting principle** as described in *APB Opinion No. 20*, "Accounting Changes." Paragraph 20 of that *Opinion* requires that the **cumulative** effect of a change in accounting principle be reported between the captions Income before extraordinary items and Net income. However, the *Opinion* does not require measurement of the cumulative effect when it is impossible to measure (par. 26). The specific example given in the *Opinion* is a change from FIFO to LIFO. Usually it is virtually impossible to reconstruct the exact composition of old inventory cost layers that the company would have reported in prior periods if it had been using LIFO. The difficulty of computing the cumulative effect of a change to LIFO is due to the arbitrariness of deciding how far back in time to go to identify the base layer of LIFO inventory. Ideally, the company would go all the way back to its origin, but in most cases that is not feasible. Therefore, when a company changes to LIFO, the base year is the year in which the change is made. The **base year LIFO cost** for the beginning inventory of the year of change (and subsequent years) is the ending inventory for the prior year based on FIFO or whatever method was then used. The base layer of LIFO inventory must be changed to cost regardless of the prior method used due to income tax regulations. This requirement means that write-downs of the prior year's ending inventory below cost (such as to LCM) must be eliminated because in this context LCM is not applied to LIFO. For example, at the start of 19D, X Company changed from FIFO, LCM to LIFO for income tax purposes. It will continue to use FIFO (but not LCM) in its accounts. The 19C ending FIFO inventory was: at cost, $100,000, at LCM, $90,000. Therefore, X Company would make the following entry assuming LCM was recorded in the accounts (otherwise no such entry would be needed):

January 1, 19D:		
Inventory*	10,000	
Change in Accounting Principle FIFO to LIFO†		10,000

* This assumes the direct inventory method of recording LCM is used. If the allowance method is used this would be "Allowance to Reduce Inventory to LCM" (discussed in Chapter 9, Part A).
† This account is reported as explained immediately above.

LIFO allowances (often inappropriately called **reserves**) are used by some companies to reflect the difference, on a cumulative basis, between the inventory costing method used in the accounts, such as FIFO, and the method used in the income tax return, such as LIFO. For example, in the X Company case

[9] This part, or any topic in it, can be omitted because it does not impact on any subsequent discussions or homework assignments.

above, this may be done for each year subsequent to the change to LIFO for income tax purposes. The "allowance" procedure may be used in either of two ways as follows:

a. Report only—the difference (in the accounts) and LIFO (on the tax return) at each year-end between FIFO is reported as a contra inventory account "Allowance to Reduce Inventories to LIFO Cost." Under this procedure no entry is made in the accounts for the "allowance."
b. Record and report—the difference is recorded in the accounts at the end of each year by revising the allowance balance so that the account reflects the current year-end balance. The other part of the entry is to cost of goods sold. For example, if the difference at the end of 19D for X Company (above) is $6,000, the following entry would be made:

Cost of goods sold	6,000	
Allowance to reduce FIFO inventory to LIFO basis		6,000

If the difference between FIFO and LIFO is $4,000 at the end of 19E, the entry would be:

Allowance to reduce FIFO inventory to LIFO basis	2,000	
Cost of goods sold		2,000

Computation:	
Balance in the allowance account	$6,000
Balance needed in the allowance account	4,000
Difference—reduction in the allowance account	$2,000

A special problem occurs under LIFO procedures when a company fails to maintain the **base layer** of inventory (i.e., the **beginning** inventory of the period when LIFO was first adopted by the company). To illustrate **LIFO inventory liquidation,** assume the following:

	Units	Unit cost	Total cost
Beginning inventory (assumed to be the base layer of LIFO inventory [year 1])	10,000	$1.00	$10,000
Purchases	40,000	1.50	60,000
Total available for sale	50,000		70,000
Sales (44,000 units, costed on LIFO basis) from:			
Purchases	40,000	1.50	60,000
Base inventory layer	4,000	1.00	4,000*
Total	44,000		64,000
Ending inventory	6,000	1.00	$ 6,000

* Base layer partially used.

In this example, the company did not maintain the base year inventory of 10,000 units. This may have been due to:

a. **Voluntary inventory liquidation**—Management may have decided to reduce normal inventory quantity for some reason, such as a decline in demand, in anticipation of a decline in inventory replenishment costs, or in anticipation of improvement in the product.[10]

b. **Involuntary inventory liquidation**—An inventory reduction may have been forced by uncontrollable causes, such as shortages, strikes, delayed delivery dates, or unexpected customer demand.

As a result of the liquidation of part of the base inventory, cost of goods sold includes 4,000 units with an old cost ($1 per unit) matched against current revenue. This liquidation of part of the LIFO base layer distorts reported income relative to income under the normal LIFO relationship of cost and revenue. Assuming the inventory liquidation is temporary, should the 4,000 units be costed out at $1 per unit or at some other cost? If the 4,000 units will be replaced in the next period at a higher cost, at $1.60 per unit, for example, should the restoration of the base inventory position be at $1 per unit or at $1.60 per unit? One approach that some companies use involves increasing Cost of Goods Sold with the estimated replacement cost, decreasing Inventory at LIFO cost, and crediting the difference to a temporary account as follows (assuming a perpetual inventory system):

Cost of goods sold (40,000 × $1,50) + (4,000 × $1.60)	66,400	
Inventory (40,000 × $1.50) + (4,000 × $1)		64,000
Excess of replacement cost of LIFO inventory temporarily liquidated (4,000 × $.60)		2,400

When the base position is restored at $1.60 per unit, the following entry is made:

Inventory (4,000 × $1)	4,000	
Excess of replacement cost of LIFO inventory temporarily liquidated (4,000 × $.60)	2,400	
Accounts payable (4,000 × $1.60)		6,400

If replacement occurs at a unit cost different from the estimate of $1.60 per unit, the difference is accounted for as a change in estimate. *APB Opinion No. 20*, "Accounting Changes," requires that changes in estimates be accounted for prospectively. Therefore, the difference between the actual replacement cost and the estimated replacement cost is included in cost of goods sold for the year of replacement. If this occurs, the last entry given above would include a debit or credit to Cost of Goods Sold.

The credit balance (i.e., $2,400) in the Excess of Replacement Cost of LIFO Inventory Temporarily Liquidated account should be reported as a current liability. It represents an amount that will have to be spent to replace inventory.

No official pronouncement specifies how LIFO inventory liquidation should be accounted for when it is due to uncontrollable causes. Accountants do not agree as to the validity of the procedure illustrated immediately above. When LIFO liquidation occurs for reasons beyond the control of the company, some accountants believe that it is a reasonable accounting solution to the problem. In such cases, they believe it is justified to protect the integrity of the LIFO

[10] A criticism of LIFO is that it is subject to income manipulation. For example, a year-end purchasing policy can be used to (1) reduce reported income by heavy buying if prices have increased and (2) increase reported income by permitting inventories to decline and "old" low prices to be included in cost of goods sold.

concept. Other accountants disagree on the basis that it introduces subjective values into the accounts and financial statements. In addition, the argument that cost of goods sold should be reflected at inventory replacement cost could be applied to any liquidation of old layers, not just the base inventory layer. However, few companies use the replacement cost method described above when liquidating recently added layers only. As a practical matter, companies try to avoid liquidating old layers of LIFO inventory during periods of rising prices since it causes their income tax payments to increase.[11]

Recording LIFO in the Accounts

Many companies that report inventory at LIFO cost do not use LIFO for **internal** accounting and control purposes.[12] For internal and control purposes, most companies use either FIFO, average, standard, or variable costing. At the end of the period, these results are converted to LIFO for income tax purposes and for **external financial reporting.** Usually this conversion is external to the accounts. However, in some cases the results of the conversion to LIFO are entered into the accounts as a single amount by using an inventory allowance account (Allowance to Reduce Inventory to LIFO Basis).[13] This allowance is a contra account to the Inventory account. The Internal Revenue Code permits a company to use LIFO on the income tax return only if it maintains sufficient records to facilitate a tax return audit. This does not mean that LIFO must be used for internal purposes and entered into the accounts.

Comparison of LIFO with FIFO

We have seen that LIFO versus FIFO can cause significant differences in the statement of income and statement of financial position. The **comparative effects will depend on the *direction* of the change in unit costs.** If unit costs remain constant, the two methods give the same results. With rising costs, FIFO matches low (older) costs with sales revenue. Also, it provides an inventory valuation approximating higher current cost. In contrast, LIFO matches high (newer) costs with sales revenue and provides an inventory valuation on a low (older) cost basis.

Conversely, with **declining** costs, FIFO matches high (older) costs with sales revenue and provides an inventory valuation approximating lower current cost. By contrast, LIFO matches low (newer) costs with sales revenue and provides an inventory valuation on a high (older) cost basis.

With respect to the **cash flow** effects, when costs are rising and inventory quantities are not decreasing, LIFO results in lower pretax income and, consequently, less income tax; therefore, in terms of cash flows, LIFO provides an advantage over FIFO. These effects can be seen in **Exhibit 8–12.** The data given in that exhibit assume rising inventory costs. Note the impact of LIFO on income taxes, net income, cash, and inventory.

---

[11] Some companies liquidated parts of their LIFO layers of inventory during the early 1980s in response to high interest rates that increased the cost of acquiring and carrying inventory.

[12] When LIFO is used for internal purposes and entered in the accounts, issues usually are costed currently; management will not delay interim costing of inventory and cost of goods sold until year-end because these amounts are needed throughout the period for internal reports.

[13] This allowance sometimes is called a **LIFO Reserve.** The authors regard this as a misuse of the term **reserve** because the account is a valuation adjustment to reduce inventory to LIFO cost. No "reserve" exists.

Exhibit 8–12
LIFO costing compared with FIFO costing.

Basic data assumed

Beginning cash balance	$ 2,000
Beginning inventory balance, 5,000 units at $5 (base inventory)	
Purchases during period, 5,000 units at $7	
Sales during period, 5,000 units at $18	
Expenses (excluding income taxes)	35,000
Income tax rate, 40%	

Comparative results

	First-in, first-out			Last-in, first-out			
	Units	per unit	Amount	Units	per unit	Amount	Increase (decrease) from FIFO to LIFO
Statement of income:							
Sales revenue	5,000	$18	$90,000	5,000	$18	$90,000	$ -0-
Cost of goods sold	5,000	5	25,000	5,000	7	35,000	10,000
Gross margin			65,000			55,000	(10,000)
Expenses			35,000			35,000	-0-
Pretax income			30,000			20,000	(10,000)
Income taxes (at 40%)			12,000			8,000	(4,000)*
Net income			$18,000			$12,000	$ (6,000)*
Statement of financial position (limited to above transactions):							
Cash (assuming all transactions were cash)			$10,000†			$14,000†	$ 4,000 *
Inventory			35,000			25,000	(10,000)*
Net difference (same as difference in net income)							$ (6,000)

* Critical differences.
† Beginning cash balance + Sales − Purchases − Expenses − Income taxes = Ending cash balance.
$2,000 + $90,000 − $35,000 − $35,000 − $12,000 = $10,000 (FIFO).
$2,000 + $90,000 − $35,000 − $35,000 − $8,000 = $14,000 (LIFO).

Selection of LIFO versus FIFO by Management. An interesting paradox is evident in Exhibit 8–12. FIFO produces the higher inventory and income amounts. However, LIFO produces more cash because it results in less income tax. If cash flows were the dominant factor, LIFO would be used by most companies during periods when inventory costs are expected to increase. If reported income were the dominant factor, most companies would use FIFO. The table below shows that many companies continue to use FIFO rather than LIFO.

	Number of disclosures*			
Methods	1986	1985	1984	1983
First-in, first-out (FIFO)	383	381	377	366
Last-in, first-out (LIFO)	393	402	400	408
Average cost	223	223	223	235
Other	53	48	54	52
Total inventory method disclosures	1,052	1,054	1,054	1,061

* Some companies use more than one method.
Source: AICPA, *Accounting Trends & Techniques, 1987* (New York, 1987), table 2–8, p. 126.

Several factors may account for the use of FIFO (or other inventory costing methods) rather than LIFO. One such factor is a contractual arrangement, such as a debt agreement, which specifies that the borrower must *(a)* maintain a certain minimum current ratio (i.e., Current assets ÷ Current liabilities) or *(b)* not exceed a certain **maximum** ratio of long-term debt to owners' equity. When inventory prices are rising, the use of FIFO (versus LIFO) provides more favorable ratio values, which allows management greater flexibility in managing the business.

A second possible factor in the selection of FIFO is a management compensation plan under which executives receive a bonus based on reported income (executive stock options are discussed in Chapter 17). Because FIFO (versus LIFO) increases reported income, it may increase managers' compensation and, thus, motivate managers to use the FIFO method.

A third possible factor in the selection of FIFO is management's desire to report higher income in the belief that this will lead to higher prices for the company's stock.

A fourth possible factor influencing managers to select FIFO is the anticipation of future inventory declines or inventory liquidations. Because companies cannot change accounting methods each year based on current economic conditions, selection of LIFO may result in higher taxable income than FIFO in years in which either *(a)* inventory costs decline or *(b)* "old" low-cost inventory layers are voluntarily or involuntarily liquidated.

Evaluation of LIFO Cost Method. Because of a continuing worldwide inflationary trend and the pervasiveness of income taxes, an increasing number of companies are using LIFO. In addition to the tax factor discussed above, arguments sometimes given **for LIFO** are (1) it provides a matching of current costs with current revenue, and (2) it reflects the usual pricing policy of an enterprise—raise selling prices when replacement cost increases even though there are goods still on hand at the old lower cost.

The primary arguments cited **against LIFO** are (1) the inventory on the statement of financial position is costed at old, out-of-date unit costs; (2) it does not precisely match replacement cost with revenue; (3) it is subject to manipulation—profits can be affected by changing usual purchasing patterns (e.g., in a period of rapidly rising prices, a company can decrease its reported income by making large purchases at year-end or increase reported income by delaying purchases); (4) it is subject to involuntary inventory liquidation, which can cause reported and taxable income to increase significantly; (5) cost flows do not correspond to the physical flow of goods; and (6) it is complex and costly to apply.

The tax advantage of LIFO is transitory when old layers of inventory are liquidated. Because LIFO (like FIFO and average cost methods) is based on **cost,** a company that uses LIFO has the same **total** pretax income over time as a company that uses FIFO or average cost if all inventory layers are ultimately liquidated. However, to the extent that old layers remain in ending inventory (i.e., are never liquidated), the tax advantage of LIFO remains intact. Therefore, the tax advantage of LIFO involves the timing of the recognition of expense (i.e., cost of goods sold), and hence is often advantageous primarily because of the **time value of money.**

Dollar Value LIFO Method

Dollar Value LIFO Concepts

The dollar value (DV) LIFO method (1) uses **price indexes** related to the inventory, instead of units and unit costs, and (2) is applied to large groups of products, called **inventory pools,** rather than to each individual product stocked. These features of DV LIFO simplify the application of LIFO because most of the detailed computations of the unit cost LIFO method are avoided.

The purpose of our discussion is to present the basic application of DV LIFO, rather than the complexities that may arise from a wide variety of situations.

The term **dollar value** emphasizes that the LIFO inventory each period is determined for **pools of inventory dollars.** The units and unit costs of individual products included in the inventory pool lose their identities.

Application of the DV LIFO Method

The DV LIFO method groups a large number of products into each **inventory pool,** and then uses an inventory **price index** for each year to determine the DV LIFO inventory amount for the pool. LIFO **inventory** layers are identified by year with the price index for each year instead of in terms of units and unit costs for each separate product.

The DV LIFO method is applied only when the company's internal inventory records provide an ending inventory based on either the FIFO method or the average cost method (both non-LCM). DV LIFO **is not a distinctly different inventory method; rather, it is an approach to convert a FIFO or average inventory amount to LIFO cost.** The conversion to LIFO is not recorded internally in the company's accounts. This approach determines the LIFO amounts of the **ending inventory** and, as a result, **cost of goods sold** for (1) income tax and (2) external reporting purposes. The company continues to implement and use either the FIFO or average cost results for internal purposes.

The annual **price index** used for each inventory pool may be derived in either of the following ways:

1. **Internal index**—An internal index is computed using either *(a)* the entire FIFO inventory pool or *(b)* a statistical sample of the inventory pool. Both of these index computations are the same except for the number of products included. The statistical sample approach can be used when determination of detailed unit data for each item in the entire inventory pool is impractical (because of technological changes, wide variety of items, or extreme fluctuations in the variety of items). The statistical sampling approach is computed by using a representative portion of the inventory pool, or by use of other sound and consistent statistical methods. Under both approaches, the internal price index for each year is computed by costing the ending inventory in two ways: at current year FIFO cost and at base year FIFO cost. The current year's price index is derived from a ratio of these two costs in this manner:

$$\frac{\text{FIFO ending inventory at current year cost}}{\text{FIFO ending inventory at base year cost}} = \text{Current year inventory price index}$$

2. **External index**—In situations where **neither** the entire ending inventory pool nor statistical sampling of the pool is feasible for computing an internal index, an **appropriate external price index** may be used. This situation often is difficult to justify to the IRS. The selection of an external price index avoids detailed index computations. The use of an **external conversion price index** in the DV LIFO method sometimes is called **indexing.** External price indexes are prepared and published by the Bureau of Labor Statistics (BLS).

The **inventory pools** used in DV LIFO may be either:

a. **A single pool**—A single pool is used for the entire company when (1) the company is a manufacturer or processor and (2) overall operations constitute a "natural business unit." Thus, an automobile manufacturer may use a single pool that includes raw materials, component parts, work in process, and finished goods (as if the pool were one inventory item).
b. **Multiple pools**—A separate inventory pool is formed for each "natural business" **subunit** of the company. Each pool includes a group of inventory items that are **similar** in respect to raw materials, manufacturing, and distribution. Income tax regulations specify that manufacturers may use either single pool or multiple pools; however, retailers, wholesalers, and jobbers must use multiple pools. For example, a large department store may use separate inventory pools for mens' clothing, ladies' clothing, home appliances, and so on.

Because of the higher degree of aggregation and the attendant likelihood of avoiding some liquidation of the base layer, a single pool usually is preferred to multiple pools when there is a choice.

Application of the DV LIFO method involves three sequential steps as follows:

Step 1—Identify the inventory pool and then obtain data about the FIFO, or average, cost (not LCM) for the beginning and ending inventories of the current period.

Step 2—Obtain a price index relevant to the inventory pool which can be either *(a)* internally computed, or *(b)* selected from an appropriate external source.

Step 3—Restate the ending FIFO, or average cost, inventory (in dollars) to a LIFO basis by using the price index derived in Step 2 (units and unit cost data are not used).

For instructional purposes we will use an inventory pool that includes two inventory items and FIFO costing in the accounts. Also, for instructional purposes, two illustrations are provided: Exhibit 8–13—a simplified one-year case with an **external** price index, and Exhibits 8–14 and 8–15—an extended example with **internally computed** price indexes by year.

Notice in **Exhibit 8–13** that *(a)* the inventory pool already has been defined and the relevant FIFO data are given, *(b)* the 19D price index (1.10) was obtained from an external source, and *(c)* the conversion process (panel B) is simple. When the inventory method is changed from FIFO to DV LIFO, the beginning FIFO inventory amount for the year of change is used as the beginning **base**

Exhibit 8–13
Conversion of a FIFO inventory to a DV LIFO inventory.

Panel A—Case Data:
On January 1, 19D, AA Corporation changed from FIFO to DV LIFO for income tax and external reporting purposes. AA Corporation continued using FIFO in the accounts for internal purposes. 19D data from the company records were:

	Units	Unit cost	Total cost
FIFO inventory (non-LCM):			
January 1, 19D	10,000	$2.00	$20,000
December 31, 19D	10,200	2.20	22,440
Price index for 19D, 1.10*			

* From an external source.

Panel B—Conversion of FIFO to DV LIFO:
The conversion of the FIFO ending inventory of $22,440 to a DV LIFO basis of $20,440 is done as follows:

	Inventory at base year cost (in common dollars)*		Conversion price index		DV LIFO cost (in current dollars)
(1) 19D ending FIFO inventory ($22,440 ÷ 1.10)	$ 20,400				
(2) Base inventory layer (1/1/19D)	(20,000)	×	1.00	=	$20,000
(3) 19D inventory layer added	$ 400	×	1.10	=	440
(4) 19D DV LIFO ending inventory					$20,440 †

* Basic year cost in this example is the cost of inventory in terms of prices at the beginning of the first year in which LIFO is used.
† Reported on the income tax return, statement of financial position and statement of income.

Note: Another format for this conversion schedule, which gives the same results, is as follows:

	Inventory at base year cost		Conversion price index		DV LIFO cost
(1) Base inventory layer (1/1/19D)	$20,000	×	1.00	=	$20,000
(2) 19D inventory layer added	400	×	1.10	=	440
(3) 19D ending FIFO inventory ($22,440 ÷ 1.10)	$20,400				
(4) 19D DV LIFO ending inventory					$20,440

year LIFO inventory amount. It is called the **base (or base year) inventory.** This process starts (line 1) with the current (19D) ending FIFO inventory of $22,440, which is divided by the 19D external price index (1.10) to **restate** it into common base year dollars ($20,400). This restatement removes the 19D price change (.10, or 10%) from the ending inventory to make it comparable with the 19D beginning FIFO inventory amount ($20,000). Line 3 is the difference (in common dollars) between the beginning and ending FIFO inventories. Finally, to compute DV LIFO on line 4, lines 2 and 3 must be multiplied by the current 19D price index (last column) and then added to derive the 19D DV LIFO ending inventory ($20,440) in 19D dollars. This ending LIFO inventory amount will be reported in the 19D statement of financial position and may be reported in the statement of income as a component of cost of goods sold.

An Extended Illustration of DV LIFO

This extended case is given to show the linkage from year to year in both *(a)* computing an internal price index and *(b)* the DV LIFO conversion process. This case has an inventory pool that includes two products in a single department. An internal price index is **computed** each year based on the FIFO inventory data taken directly from the inventory records. This computation uses the formula given on page 336. For example, the computation in this case for year 19B is as follows:

FIFO ending inventory at **current year** cost from the inventory records, $8,940 (Exhibit 8–14).	÷	FIFO ending inventory at **base year** cost computed at the base unit cost, $7,320 (Exhibit 8–15).	=	Current year price index, 1.221.

This computation holds units (quantity) constant and the price is the variable. Therefore, it measures the ratio (or percentage) that prices increased. The conversion process then starts (Exhibit 8–15, panel B), with common or constant dollars to measure the inventory layers. Next, these common dollars, by inventory layer, are restated in current dollars by using the annual price index which corresponds to each layer.

Exhibit 8–14 gives the case data for BB Corporation, years 19A, B, and C. **Exhibit 8–15,** panel A, shows the computation of the price indexes for 19B and 19C. For convenience, the **ending** inventory for the year prior to the adoption of LIFO (which is also the beginning inventory for the year of adoption) usually is assigned an index of 1.000. Notice in Exhibit 8–15, under the conversion price index column, that the base year inventory is always related to 1.000. The computed internal indexes are used in exactly the same way in the conversion process as was illustrated in Exhibit 8–13 for external price indexes. Exhibit 8–15, panel B, shows the conversion process for each year—19B and 19C. This conversion process also is diagrammed in **Exhibit 8–16.**

Exhibit 8–14
Inventory data, BB Corporation.

Case Data:
On January 1, 19B, BB Corporation changed from FIFO to DV LIFO for income tax and external reporting purposes. BB Corporation will continue using FIFO (not LCM) in its accounts and for internal purposes. BB has one inventory pool comprised of two products—A and B. The 19A, B, and C FIFO inventory costs, taken directly from the FIFO inventory records, were:

	Product A			**Product B**			
	Units	**Cost**	**Total**	**Units**	**Cost**	**Total**	**Total amount**
End of 19A (base year):							
Ending inventory (FIFO)*							
Layer 1	1,000	$1.00	$1,000	2,000	$2.00	$ 4,000	
Layer 2				500	2.20	1,100	
	1,000	$1.00	$1,000	2,500	$2.04	$ 5,100	$6,100
Year 19B (year of LIFO adoption):							
Purchases†	3,000	$1.20	$3,600	4,000	$2.50	$10,000	
Sales	(2,800)			(3,500)			
Ending inventory: FIFO (internal)	1,200	1.20	1,440	3,000	2.50	7,500	$8,940
Year 19C:							
Purchases†	3,300	1.30	4,290	4,200	2.60	10,920	
Sales	(3,200)			(4,200)			
Ending inventory: FIFO (internal)	1,300	1.30	1,690	3,000	2.60	7,800	$9,490

* Beginning inventory for the year of adoption of LIFO.
† Totals for the year; thus, the unit purchase costs are annual averages.

Exhibit 8–15
DV LIFO—Computation of periodic price indexes and conversion from FIFO to DV LIFO.

Panel A—Computation of Price Indexes:
At end of base year 19A 1.000

End of Year 19B:	**Product A**	**Product B**	**Total**
FIFO inventory at current year cost*	1,200 × $1.20 = $1,440	3,000 × $2.50 = $7,500	$8,940
Inventory at base year cost	1,200 × 1.00 = 1,200	3,000 × 2.04 = 6,120	7,320
Price index, 19B; $8,940 ÷ $7,320 = 1.221			
End of Year 19C:			
FIFO inventory at current year cost*	1,300 × $1.30 = $1,690	3,000 × $2.60 = $7,800	$9,490
Inventory at base year cost	1,300 × 1.00 = 1,300	3,000 × 2.04 = 6,120	7,420
Price index, 19C; $9,490 ÷ $7,420 = 1.279			

Taken from Exhibit 8–14.

Panel B—Conversion of FIFO to DV LIFO Inventory:
Conversion schedule at end of 19B:

	Inventory at base year cost		Conversion price index		DV LIFO cost
19B ending FIFO inventory ($8,940 ÷ 1.221)	$ 7,320				
Base inventory layer	(6,100)	×	1.000	=	$6,100
Difference: 19B additional layer	$ 1,200	×	1.221	=	1,490
19B DV LIFO ending inventory					$7,590*

Conversion schedule at end of 19C:

	Inventory at base year cost		Conversion price index		DV LIFO cost
19C ending FIFO inventory ($9,490 ÷ 1.279)	$ 7,420				
Base inventory layer	(6,100)	×	1.000	=	$61,000
19B inventory layer	(1,220)	×	1.221	=	1,490
Difference: 19C additional layer	$ 100	×	1.279	=	128
19C, DV LIFO ending inventory					$ 7,718†

* Reported on 19B statement of financial position and statement of income.
† Reported on 19C statement of financial position and statement of income.

Notice in Exhibit 8–15 that all prior inventory layers were retained in both 19B and 19C. This was because the total inventory **increased** each year—$6,100 to $7,320 in 19B, and to $7,420 in 19C. Also, notice that the price indexes for prior years are never changed.

When the total inventory **decreases,** some (or part) of the layers of prior years are "used" and the LIFO assumption is that they are used in inverse order; that is, the last layer is used first and so forth. To illustrate, assume that the total FIFO inventory for 19C was $8,900 (instead of $9,490). That is, the FIFO inventory decreased from $8,940 to $8,900. Under this assumption no 19C layer was added; in fact, some of the 19B layer was used. This assumption would be shown in Exhibit 8–15, panel B as follows:

Exhibit 8–16

Diagram of the conversion of a FIFO inventory to a DV LIFO inventory (Refer to Exhibit 8–15, panel C).

Year-End	Inventory at FIFO cost (in current dollars)	Current price index	Inventory at base year cost (in common dollars)	Conversion FIFO to LIFO	Inventory at DV LIFO cost (in current dollars)
19A	$6,100	÷ 1.00 ⟶	$6,100		
19B	$8,940	÷ 1.221 ⟶	Base layer 19B layer added Total	$7,320 (6,100) × 1.00 ⟶ (1,220) × 1.221 ⟶	$6,100 1,490 $7,590
19C	$9,490	÷ 1.279 ⟶	Base layer 19B layer 19C layer added Total	$7,420 (6,100) × 1.00 ⟶ (1,220) × 1.221 ⟶ (100) × 1.279 ⟶	$6,100 1,490 128 $7,718

Year 19C	Inventory at base year cost	Conversion price index	DV LIFO cost
19C ending FIFO inventory ($8,800 ÷ 1.279)	$ 6,959		
Base inventory layer	(6,100)	× 1.000	$6,100
19B inventory layer ($6,959 − $6,100)	(859)	× 1.221	1.049
Difference: 19C additional layer	$ –0–		–0–
19C DV LIFO ending inventory			$7,149

Notice that (a) no 19C layer was added, (b) a good portion of the 19B layer was used (i.e., sold), and (c) the base inventory layer remained the same. Since no 19C layer was added there will never be a 19C layer in the future. A layer once reduced or eliminated, or not originally established in its current year, will never be restored or established. Also, notice that a decrease in inventory is always taken out in LIFO order; that is, starting with the most recent layer and working backward in time. To reemphasize, the original price indexes used for prior years are never changed.

Exhibit 8–17 compares the FIFO and DV LIFO inventory and cost of goods sold results for 19C. The comparison reflects a lower 19C ending inventory amount and a higher 19C cost of goods sold amount for DV LIFO than for

Exhibit 8–17
FIFO and DV LIFO results compared, BB Corporation.

	Year 19C—Cost of goods sold compared	
	FIFO—for internal purposes	DV LIFO—for external purposes
Beginning inventory	$ 8,940	$ 7,590
Purchases	15,210	15,210
Total	24,150	22,800
Ending inventory	9,490	7,718
Cost of goods sold	$14,660	$15,082

FIFO, as would be expected when inventory costs are rising. This difference causes lower pretax income and lower income tax under DV LIFO.

Advantages of DV LIFO

The above illustrations of DV LIFO demonstrates that the application of LIFO to pools of inventory dollars has three major advantages:

1. It reduces the probability of liquidating an old LIFO layer of inventory. When LIFO ending inventory is less than beginning inventory, older costs from prior periods are reflected in cost of goods sold. When prices are rising, this inventory liquidation can cause a significant **decrease** in cost of goods sold and **increase** in reported income, relative to normal LIFO results (i.e., in the absence of liquidation). Because the tax consequences of LIFO liquidation can be severe, companies often apply LIFO costing to inventory pools to reduce the probability of liquidation. The logic of the pool concept is that, within an inventory pool, the amounts of some items may increase and the amounts of other items may decrease. If the size of the pool is stable or increasing, liquidation will not occur for the pool.
2. It reduces the accounting cost of applying LIFO. The complexity of applying LIFO to individual units was not apparent in the illustrations in Part A. When applied to many different types of items, each type of which may be represented by thousands of individual items, the accounting costs may be significant and the chance for error may be large. In contrast, the application of LIFO to pools of similar items reduces accounting costs by reducing the level of detail.
3. It preserves FIFO or average cost for internal uses.

Variations in Applying the DV LIFO Method. Two variations of the DV LIFO method are known as the (1) double-extension and (2) link-chain approaches.[14] The presentations in this chapter are based on the double-extension approach, which is more common.

The term **double extension** is based on the fact that under DV LIFO, the ending inventory each period must be double costed (i.e., at base year costs and at current year costs).

[14] The link-chain method was designed for restrictive situations in which the double-extension method is not satisfactory (e.g., significant technlogical changes in the inventory, discussed later).

Technological Changes in LIFO Inventories. The problem caused by technological changes in LIFO inventories can be viewed as a special case of inventory liquidation. That is, as technology advances, older products (and product lines) are dropped and new products are added. When LIFO is applied using the unit cost approach (Part A) and liquidation of older LIFO layers occurs, the older costs are moved out of inventory to cost of goods sold. The effect of this liquidation is mitigated under DV LIFO because of the grouping of inventory into pools. For this reason, DV LIFO, and its concept of inventory pools, represents a practical solution to inventory liquidation caused by technological changes in inventories.

Summary

Accounting for inventories is important for reporting and controlling inventory levels and the cash invested in those inventories. Accounting for inventories primarily involves the cost and matching principles. Inventories are current assets and are classified as merchandising, manufacturing, raw materials, work in process, finished goods, and various supplies acquired in advance of usage. To qualify as an asset, ownership of an item (not mere possession) is controlling.

A major problem in accounting for inventories is *(a)* determination of the inventory items available for sale or use (i.e., beginning inventory plus purchases) and *(b)* allocation of that total between inventory remaining on hand and cost of goods sold (or other uses). The primary methods used to resolve this problem are the cost flow methods—specific identification, average cost, FIFO, and LIFO.

LIFO presents several problems, such as inventory liquidation, current versus noncurrent costing of issues, and other effects of its internal inconsistency. LIFO can be applied on *(a)* the unit cost basis, or *(b)* the DV LIFO basis. The latter does not use product units and unit costs for converting FIFO to LIFO. Rather, it uses FIFO dollar amounts and an annual price index to derive LIFO amounts for the ending inventory.

The discussion in Part B explained the primary complexities in applying LIFO. LIFO has received much attention from governmental agencies such as the SEC and the IRS because *(a)* income can be manipulated under LIFO by altering purchasing patterns near year-end, and *(b)* LIFO reduces income tax liabilities when prices are rising. Also, for the same reasons, accounting firms have devoted much research to the study of LIFO. To reduce the possibility of income manipulation, accountants insist that LIFO can be applied consistently and that the financial statements adequately disclose effects such as *(a)* the impact of LIFO liquidation, *(b)* the extent of usage of LIFO, *(c)* differences between LIFO cost and the cost of another inventory method when inventory methods are changed, and *(d)* the income effects of accounting changes involving inventory. These items were discussed under the captions Initial Adoption of LIFO and LIFO Allowances.

It is safe to predict that the use of LIFO will become more widespread because of its tax advantage during periods of inflation. The tabulation on page 334 indicates that of the companies included in *Accounting Trends & Techniques, 1987* (p. 126), LIFO and FIFO were used with about equal frequency in 1986 (383 used FIFO, 393 used LIFO). A shift toward LIFO has occurred and is continuing. From an accounting standpoint, LIFO matches current expense (i.e., cost of goods sold) with the revenue of the period better than the other inventory costing methods.

SUPPLEMENT 8–A: MISCELLANEOUS COST FLOW METHODS

This supplement discusses four inventory cost methods used less often than FIFO, LIFO, and average cost. The four methods discussed are next-in, first-out; base stock; standard costing; and variable, or direct, costing. These methods are discussed in this supplement primarily for reference purposes.

Next-In, First-Out (NIFO) Method

NIFO is an inventory cost method under which cost of goods sold is costed at the unit cost anticipated for the next purchase of a like volume. The concept attempts to measure cost of goods sold as the actual replacement cost of the goods sold. Proponents of NIFO maintain that LIFO fails to precisely match replacement cost with current revenues because the method employs the cost of the latest purchase prior to the actual sale. NIFO currently is **not** acceptable under GAAP.

Base Stock Method

The base stock (or normal stock) method is viewed as the predecessor of the LIFO method. The method assumes that there is a normal or base stock of goods that should be maintained at all times. The base stock represents a permanent commitment of resources, similar to an operational asset, that is costed at a "normal" price. This price is viewed as the original cost—usually the lowest cost experienced by the company. Goods must be maintained above the minimum base stock for operational purposes. These goods are viewed as temporary increments and are recorded at cost; issues should be costed out of the increment on a LIFO basis, although FIFO or average cost sometimes is used for practical reasons. The base stock method is illustrated below.

The accounting purpose of using the base stock method is similar to that of LIFO, that is, the matching of current costs with current revenues. The base stock method is not generally used because of the arbitrary nature of both the quantity and unit values of the assumed base stock. Similar results may be obtained under LIFO as shown below. Like LIFO, the base stock method is subject to manipulation through selective purchasing. Erosion of the **base stock** would be treated in a manner similar to that shown on page 331 for LIFO liquidation. The base stock method is neither permitted for income tax purposes nor by current GAAP.

Base stock inventory method

	Units	Unit cost	Amount
Base stock	10,000	$ .50	$ 5,000
Extra stock	2,000	1.20	2,400
Total beginning inventory	12,000		7,400
Purchases:			
First	2,000	1.30	2,600
Second	6,000	1.40	8,400
Total available	20,000		18,400
Ending inventory (11,000 units per count):			
Base stock	10,000	.50	5,000
Extra stock	1,000	1.20	1,200
Total	11,000		6,200
Cost of goods sold	9,000		$12,200

Standard Cost Method

In manufacturing entities using a standard cost system, the inventories are valued, recorded, and reported for internal purposes on the basis of a standard unit cost. The standard cost approximates an ideal or expected cost. Its use prevents the overstatement of inventory values because it excludes from inventory those losses and expenses due to inefficiency, waste, and abnormal conditions. Under this method, the **differences** between actual cost (which **includes** losses due to inefficiencies, etc.) and standard cost (which **excludes** losses due to inefficiencies, etc.) are recorded in separate variance accounts, which are written off as a current period "loss" rather than being capitalized in inventory. Standard costing may be applied to raw materials, work in process, and finished goods inventories. Standard costing is used more often in manufacturing situations because of its usefulness for cost control. To illustrate, assume a manufacturing company has just adopted standard cost procedures and that the beginning inventory is zero. During the current period, the company makes two purchases and one issue and records them as follows:

1. To record the purchase of 10,000 units of raw material at $1.10 actual cost; standard cost has been established at $1:

Raw materials (10,000 units × $1)	10,000	
Raw materials purchase price variance (10,000 units × $.10)	1,000	
Accounts payable (10,000 units × $1.10)		11,000

2. To record issuance of 8,000 units of raw material to the factory for processing:

Material in process	8,000	
Raw materials (8,000 units × $1)		8,000

3. To record the purchase of 2,000 units of raw materials at 95 cents:

Raw materials (2,000 units × $1)	2,000	
Raw materials purchase price variance (2,000 units × $.05)		100
Accounts payable (2,000 units × $.95)		1,900

Results for the period:		
Purchases at actual cost:		
10,000 units at $1.10	$11,000	
2,000 units at $.95	1,900	
Total		$12,900
Issues at standard cost:		
8,000 units at $1	8,000	
Ending inventory at standard cost:		
4,000 units at $1	4,000	12,000
Raw materials purchase price variance (debit—charged against current income as a loss) ($1,000 − $100)		$ 900

Under the procedures shown above for raw material, there would be no need to consider inventory flow methods such as LIFO, FIFO, and average, because only one cost—standard cost—appears in the records. In addition, perpetual inventory records could be maintained in **units only** because all issues and inventory valuations are at the same standard cost. Standard cost represents a departure from the cost principle and therefore is **not** acceptable under GAAP. Therefore, for external reporting, the standard cost inventory usually is restated by applying one of the generally accepted methods discussed above. Standard costs are widely used for **internal management** planning and control. A detailed discussion of standard cost procedures can be found in cost accounting textbooks.

Variable, or Direct, Cost Method

For **internal management** planning and control purposes, the concept of variable, or direct, costing often is used in manufacturing companies. Under this concept, fixed costs (i.e., those that relate to time, such as salaries) and variable costs (i.e., those that vary with productive activities, such as direct material and direct labor) are segregated. This separation is useful for internal management planning and control. One important aspect of this concept is that the cost of goods manufactured is the sum of the variable costs only. These include direct materials, direct labor, and variable manufacturing overhead. All fixed costs, including fixed manufacturing overhead, are treated as period costs and are deducted from revenues of the period when incurred rather than being capitalized and carried forward in inventory. Hence, fixed costs are not reported as part of cost of inventory or cost of goods sold.

Valuation of inventories at only variable production costs, although highly useful for internal management purposes, is **not** GAAP for external financial reporting purposes. Also, it cannot be used for tax purposes except in special circumstances. Therefore, for external reporting and tax purposes, companies using variable costing internally convert the inventory and cost of goods sold to "actual" cost by using other costing methods discussed in this chapter.

QUESTIONS

1. In general, why should accountants and management be concerned with inventories?
2. List and briefly explain the usual inventory classifications.

3. What general rule is applied by accountants in determining what goods should be included in inventory? How does the location of inventory affect this rule?
4. Complete the following:

	Include in inventory	
	Yes	No
a. Goods held by our agents for us.	___	___
b. Goods held by us for sale on commission.	___	___
c. Goods held by us but awaiting return to vendor because of damaged condition.	___	___
d. Goods returned to us from buyer, reason unknown to date.	___	___
e. Goods out on consignment.	___	___
f. Goods held on consignment.	___	___
g. Merchandise at our branch for sale.	___	___
h. Merchandise at conventions for display purposes.	___	___

5. Assume you are in the process of adjusting and closing the books at the end of the accounting period (for the purchaser of inventory). For inventory purposes, how would you treat the following goods in transit: *(a)* invoice received for $10,000, shipped FOB shipping point? *(b)* invoice received for $18,000, shipped FOB destination? and *(c)* invoice received for $6,000, shipped FOB shipping point and delivery refused on the last day of the period because of damaged condition?
6. Explain the principal features of a periodic inventory system.
7. Why is cost of goods sold sometimes characterized as a residual amount? In which inventory system is this characterization appropriate?
8. In determining unit cost for inventory purposes, how should the following items be treated?
   a. Purchase returns.
   b. Cash discounts on credit purchases.
   c. Freight on goods purchased.
9. Should cash discounts on credit purchases be *(a)* deducted in part on the statement of income and in part from inventory on the statement of financial position or *(b)* deducted in total on the statement of income for the period in which the discounts arose? Assume that three fourths of the goods purchased were sold by year-end. Explain.
10. What is meant by the accounting value of inventory? What accounting principles predominate in measuring this value?
11. Assuming the LIFO method, what is meant by inventory liquidation? Why is it a serious problem for LIFO but not FIFO?
12. What are the primary purposes to be considered in selecting a particular inventory cost flow method? Why is the selection important?
13. Briefly explain the differences between periodic and perpetual inventory systems. Under what circumstances is each generally used?
14. Does the adoption of a perpetual inventory system eliminate the need for physical count or measurement of inventories? Explain.
15. Explain the specific cost identification method and when the method is not appropriate.
16. Distinguish between a weighted average and a weighted moving average in determining inventory unit cost. When is each generally used? Explain.
17. Explain the essential features of first-in, first-out (FIFO). What are the primary advantages and disadvantages of FIFO? Explain the difference in the application

of FIFO under *(a)* periodic and *(b)* perpetual inventory systems. In contrast with LIFO, how does FIFO affect cash flow?

18. Explain the essential features of last-in, first-out (LIFO). What are the primary advantages and disadvantages of LIFO? Explain the differences in application of LIFO under *(a)* periodic inventory and *(b)* perpetual inventory systems.
19. What is meant by inventory layers? Why are they significant with respect to the FIFO and LIFO methods?
20. Compare the statement of financial position and statement of income effects of FIFO versus LIFO *(a)* when prices are rising, and *(b)* when prices are falling.
21. Explain why a company's management may be reluctant to use LIFO in a period of rising inventory costs even though such use would reduce the company's current income tax liability.
22. What is meant by the unit cost LIFO method? What type of entity would be most likely to use unit cost (versus dollar value) LIFO?
23. In describing a company's inventory position, the phrase "LIFO Reserve" is sometimes used. What is meant by LIFO Reserve? What alternative phrase is more appropriate?

EXERCISES

Part A: Exercises 8–1 to 8–12

E 8–1 **(Items Included in Inventory)**

Listed below for Hance Corporation are some items of inventory that are in question. The company stores a substantial portion of the merchandise in a separate warehouse and transfers damaged goods to a special inventory account. The company policy is "satisfied customers."

a.	Items in receiving department returned by customer, no communication received from customer	$ 200
b.	Items ordered and in receiving department, invoice not yet received from supplier	500
c.	Items counted in warehouse by the inventory crew	70,000
d.	Invoice received for goods ordered, goods shipped but not received (Hance pays freight)	800
e.	Items shipped today, FOB destination, invoice mailed to customer	70
f.	Items currently used for window displays	200
g.	Items on counters for sale per inventory count (not in [c])	12,000
h.	Items in shipping department, invoice not mailed to customer	140
i.	Items in receiving department, refused by Hance because of damage (not in [c])	100
j.	Items shipped today, FOB shipping point, invoice mailed to customer	400
k.	Items included in warehouse count, damaged, not returnable	200
l.	Items included in warehouse count, specifically crated and segregated for shipment to customer in five days per sales contract, with return privilege	1,800

Required:

Complete the following tabular to compute the correct inventory:

Item	Exclude or include in inventory	Amount	Explanation
c. Items counted in warehouse	Include	$70,000	Items on hand
Etc.			
Total inventory valuation		$	

E 8–2 (Items to Include in Inventory; Classification, Correction)

On December 31, 19A, Davis Company computed an ending inventory valuation of $250,000 based on a periodic inventory system. The accounts for 19A have been adjusted and closed. Subsequently, the independent auditor located several discrepancies in the 19A ending inventory. These were discussed with the company accountant who then prepared the following schedule:

a. Merchandise in store (at 50% above cost)	$250,000
b. Merchandise out on consignment at sales price (including markup of 60% on selling price)	10,000
c. Goods held on consignment from Brown Electrical Co. at sales price (sales commission, 20% of sales price, included)	3,000
d. Goods purchased, in transit (shipped FOB shipping point; estimated freight, not included, $600), invoice price	5,000
e. Goods out on approval, sales price, $1,500, cost, $1,000	1,500
Total inventory as corrected	$269,500

Average income tax rate, 40%.

Required:

1. The auditor did not agree with the "corrected" inventory amount of $269,500. Compute the correct ending inventory amount (show computations) by modifying the "corrected" balance of $269,500.
2. List the items on the statement of income and statement of financial position for 19A that should be corrected for the above errors, and give the amount of the error in the balance of each item affected.
3. The accounts have been closed for 19A. Therefore, a correcting entry in January 19B is needed. Give the required correcting entry.

E 8–3 (Perpetual and Periodic Inventory; Statement of Income; Closing Entries)

The records of Laurel Company reflected the following data: sales revenue, $110,000; purchases, $80,000; net income as a percentage of sales revenue, 10%; beginning inventory, $9,000; and expenses including income tax, $24,000.

Required:

1. Reconstruct the statement of income. Assume a periodic inventory system.
2. Give the required journal entries at the end of the period for the inventories and the closing entries for revenues and expenses, assuming Case A—a periodic inventory system; and Case B—a perpetual inventory system.

E 8–4 (Periodic and Perpetual Inventory; Journal Entries)

The records for Estacado Company at December 31, 19A, reflected the following:

	Units	Unit price
Sales during period (for cash)	10,000	$10 (sales price)
Inventory at beginning of period	2,000	6 (cost)
Merchandise purchased during period (for cash)	16,000	6 (cost)
Purchase returns during period (cash refund)	100	6 (cost)
Inventory at end of period	?	6 (cost)
Total expenses (excluding cost of goods sold), $30,000		

Required:

In parallel columns, give entries for the above transactions, including all entries at the end of the period assuming:

Case A—Periodic inventory system.
Case B—Perpetual inventory system.

Use the following format:

Accounts	Case A	Case B

E 8–5 **(Credit Purchases Recorded "Net" versus "Gross")**
Ace Boot Company purchased merchandise on credit for $50,000; terms 2/10, n/30. Payment was made within the discount period. At the end of the reporting period, one fourth of this merchandise was unsold.

Required:
Determine (1) the cost of goods sold that would be reported on the statement of income and (2) the ending inventory valuation for this particular lot of merchandise assuming:

a. Purchases and accounts payable are recorded at gross, and cash discounts are deducted in total from purchases on the statement of income.
b. Purchases and accounts payable both are recorded at net.
c. Purchases and accounts payable are recorded at gross, and cash discounts are reported on the statement of income as "Other income."

Evaluate the various approaches. Which approach is preferable conceptually? Why?

E 8–6 **(Credit Purchases; Net versus Gross; Entries)**
M and R Corporation purchased merchandise on credit for $50,000; terms 2/15, n/30. Payment for one-half of the recorded liability was made during the discount period; the balance was paid after the discount period. The company uses a perpetual inventory system.

Required:
Give entries in parallel columns to record the purchase and payments on the liability assuming:

a. Net of discount approach is used for cash discounts.
b. Gross amount is used for cash discounts. Which approach is preferable conceptually? Why?

E 8–7 **(Perpetual Inventory; Shortage; Entries)**
Perot Company uses a perpetual inventory system. The items on hand are inventoried on a rotation basis throughout the year so that all items are checked twice each year. At the end of the year, the following data relating to goods on hand are available:

Product	From perpetual inventory: Units	From perpetual inventory: Unit cost	From physical count (units)
A	210	$9	190
B	1,500	2	1,520
C	2,000	3	1,900
D	8,000	1	8,000
E	13,000	4	12,800

Required:
Determine the amount of the net inventory overage or shortage and give the adjustment to the perpetual inventory records. Give any entry needed to record the final disposition of any discrepancy.

E 8–8 (Inventory Cost with a Rebate)

Volume Stores, Inc., a dealer in radio and television sets, buys large quantities of a television model that costs $500. The contract reads that if 100 or more are purchased during the year, a rebate of $25 per set will be made. On December 15, the records showed that 150 sets had been purchased and that 10 remained on hand in inventory. A request for the rebate was made, and a check was received on January 20 after Volume's books were closed.

Required:

1. At what valuation should the inventory be shown on December 31? Why?
2. What entry should be made relative to the rebate on December 31? Why?
3. What entry would be made on January 20? Why?

E 8–9 (Inventory and CGS; Five Cost Methods)

The inventory records of Mishan Corporation showed the following data relative to inventory item A (assume the transactions occurred in the order given):

Transaction	Units	Unit cost
1. Inventory	300	$2.00
2. Purchase	400	2.10
3. Sale	600	
4. Purchase	600	2.20
5. Sale	500	
6. Purchase	600	2.30

Required:

Compute the cost of goods sold for the period and the ending inventory assuming (round unit costs to nearest cent):

a. Weighted average (periodic inventory system).
b. Moving average (perpetual inventory system).
c. FIFO.
d. LIFO (unit basis, 300 units in base layer, periodic inventory system).
e. LIFO (unit base, 300 units in base layer, perpetual inventory system).

E 8–10 (Inventory and CGS; Four Cost Methods)

The inventory records of Gilman Company provided the following data for one item of merchandise for sale (assume the six transactions occurred in the order of the number given):

	Units	Unit cost	Total amount
Goods available for sale:			
Beginning inventory	500	$6.00	$ 3,000
Purchases:			
(1)	600	6.10	3,660
(3)	600	6.20	3,720
(5)	400	6.30	2,520
	2,100		$12,900

Sales in units: (2), 900; (4), 500; and (6), 300.

Required:

1. Complete the following schedule (round unit costs to nearest cent and total amounts to nearest dollar):

Costing method	Valuation: Ending inventory	Valuation: Cost of goods sold
a. FIFO	$____	$____
b. LIFO (unit cost basis, periodic inventory system, assume base inventory is 500 units)	$____	$____
c. Weighted average	$____	$____
d. LIFO (same as [b] except perpetual inventory system)	$____	$____

2. Compute the amount of pretax income and rank the methods in order of the amount of pretax income (highest first) assuming FIFO pretax income is $50,000.
3. Which method is preferable in this instance? Explain your choice.

E 8–11 (Inventory and CGS; Five Cost Methods)

Dyer Company's inventory records showed the following data relative to a particular item sold regularly (assume transactions in the order given):

Transaction	Units	Unit cost
1. Inventory	2,000	$5.00
2. Purchases	18,000	5.20
3. Sales (at $13 per unit)	7,000	
4. Purchases	6,000	5.50
5. Sales (at $13.50 per unit)	16,000	
6. Purchases	3,000	6.00

Required:

1. Complete the following schedule (round unit costs to nearest cent and total costs of inventory to the nearest $10):

	Ending inventory	Cost of goods sold	Gross margin
a. FIFO	____	____	____
b. Weighted average	____	____	____
c. LIFO (unit cost basis, periodic inventory system, 2,000 units in base layer)	____	____	____
d. LIFO (unit cost basis, perpetual inventory system, 2,000 units in base layer)	____	____	____
e. Moving average (show computations)	____	____	____

2. What method would be preferable? Explain the basis for your choice.

E 8–12 (Ending Inventory; Three Cost Methods)

Lorie Company was formed on December 1, 19A. The following information is available from the company's inventory records for Product A:

	Units	Unit cost
January 1, 19B (beginning inventory)	800	$ 9.00
Purchases:		
January 5, 19B	1,500	10.00
January 25, 19B	1,200	10.50
February 16, 19B	600	11.00
March 26, 19B	900	11.50

A physical inventory taken on March 31, 19B, showed 1,500 units on hand. Lorie uses a periodic inventory system.

Required:
Prepare schedules to compute the ending inventory at March 31, 19B, under each of the following inventory flow methods: (1) FIFO, (2) LIFO, and (3) weighted average. Show supporting computations.

Part B: Exercises 8–13 to 8–19

E 8–13 **(Initial Adoption of LIFO)**
On January 1, 19X5, Harper Corporation decided to change from FIFO to LIFO for income tax purposes. However, the company will continue to use FIFO in its accounts for internal purposes. The following data are available:

a. Ending inventory, 19X4 (as shown in the accounts)	
FIFO at LCM (FIFO cost, $75,000)	$70,000
b. Ending inventory, 19X5:	
FIFO at cost	80,000
LIFO at cost	74,000
c. Ending inventory 19X6:	
FIFO at cost	83,000
LIFO at cost	79,000

Required:
Give the journal entries related to the change from FIFO, LCM to LIFO on *(a)* January 1, 19X5, and the subsequent entries on *(b)* December 31, 19X5, and *(c)* December 31, 19X6.

E 8–14 **(DV LIFO, Conversion from FIFO)**
Wolfson Company manufactures a single product. On December 31, 19A, Wolfson adopted the DV LIFO inventory method. The inventory on that date using the dollar value LIFO inventory method was determined to be $300,000. Inventory data for succeeding years are as follows:

Year ended December 31,	Inventory at year-end prices	Relevant price index (base year 19A)
19B	$368,000	1.15
19C	420,000	1.20
19D	440,000	1.25

Required:
Compute the inventory amounts at December 31, 19B, 19C, and 19D, using the DV LIFO inventory method for each year. (AICPA adapted)

E 8–15 **(DV LIFO, Conversion from FIFO)**
On January 1, 19C, Poole Company changed from FIFO to LIFO for income tax and external reporting purposes. At that date, the beginning FIFO inventory (the base inventory for LIFO purposes) was $130,000. The following information is available from Poole's records for the years 19C through 19F:

Year	Ending inventory on a FIFO basis	LIFO conversion index
19C	$150,000	1.10
19D	160,000	1.20
19E	180,000	1.30
19F	190,000	1.25

Required:
Compute the ending inventory on a DV LIFO basis for each year, 19C through 19F.

E 8–16 **(DV LIFO; Conversion; External Index)**
On January 1, 19B, Miller Company adopted LIFO for income tax and external reporting purposes. The ending inventory for 19A (FIFO basis) amounted to $260,000. The physical inventory taken at the end of 19B, at 19B costs, was valued at $400,000 (FIFO basis). The external price index analysis indicated a 25% increase in prices during 19B.

Required:
1. Use the external index to compute the 19B LIFO inventory amount assuming the DV LIFO approach.
2. Under what special conditions is the external index approach appropriate for converting a FIFO basis inventory to the DV LIFO basis?

E 8–17 **(DV LIFO, Conversion from FIFO)**
Diamond Company uses LIFO for income tax and external reporting purposes. The LIFO base inventory (at end of 19A) for inventory pool No. 1 amounted to $170,000. The periodic inventory of pool No. 1 taken at the end of 19B, priced at 19B costs on a FIFO basis, amounted to $220,000. Analysis of a statistical sample of the inventory and related computations showed a price index for 19A of 100 and for 19B of 110.

Required:
1. Use the internal indexes given above to compute the 19B ending DV LIFO inventory.
2. Under what conditions is the statistical sample approach for DV LIFO appropriate?

E 8–18 **(FIFO and LIFO Reporting)**
At the end of the annual accounting period, the inventory records of Baird Company reflected the following:

	19D	19E
Ending inventory at FIFO	$50,000	$90,000
Ending inventory at LIFO	20,000	40,000

The company uses FIFO for internal purposes and LIFO for income tax and external reporting purposes.

Required:
1. Assume the inventory difference is recognized in the accounts. Give the appropriate journal entry for each year.
2. Show how the inventories should be shown on the 19D–19E comparative statement of financial position.

E 8–19 **(FIFO and LIFO, Disclosure)**
On January 1, 19C, Schwartz Company changed from FIFO to LIFO for income tax and external reporting purposes. The ending inventory for 19B (FIFO basis) was $155,000 (this will be the base inventory amount for LIFO). At the end of 19C the LIFO inventory amount, computed using the dollar value approach, was $180,000; had the company continued using FIFO, this amount would have been $202,000. The average income tax rate is 40%.

Required:

1. Compute the difference in net income for 19C attributable to the change from FIFO to LIFO. Show computations.
2. Prepare an appropriate note to the financial statements for 19C.

PROBLEMS

Part A: Problems 8–1 to 8–11

P 8–1 **(Recording Credit Purchases, Gross and Net)**

Nevada Company purchased merchandise during 19B on credit for $52,000 (includes $2,000 freight charges paid in cash); terms 2/10, n/30. All of the purchase liability, except $20,000, was paid within the discount period; the remainder was paid within the 30-day term. At the end of the annual accounting period, December 31, 19B, 80% of the merchandise had been sold and 20% remained in inventory. The company uses a perpetual system.

Required:

1. Give entries in parallel columns for the purchase and the two payments on the liability assuming *(a)* purchases and accounts payable are recorded at gross and *(b)* purchases and accounts payable are recorded at net.
2. What amounts would be reported for the ending inventory and cost of goods sold under *(a)* and *(b)* in (1) above? Assume cash discounts under the gross method are reported as a deduction from cost of goods sold. Explain in general terms why the amounts are different between the two methods.
3. Which method is preferable? Why?

P 8–2 **(Items to Include/Exclude in Inventory)**

Assume you are the independent auditor for Medal Manufacturing Corporation. The ending inventory for the year ended December 31, 19A, is under consideration. The following problems related to the inventory have arisen, and the company accountant requests your advice on them:

Part A

	Units	
	Material X at $3	**Material Y at $5**
Raw material unit inventory data on 12/31/19A—Items counted in warehouse (excluding items below)	18,000	4,000
a. Items set aside for return to vendor next period per agreement 12/20/19A; not up to guaranteed specifications, returned 1/2/19B		200
b. Items issued to factory and returned in damaged condition, not returnable to vendor		50
c. Purchase invoice received, items not received (FOB shipping point)		300
d. Items from shipment partly damaged when received, returnable to vendor per agreement; shipped 1/3/19B		40
e. Items purchased, on receiving dock, refused because of damage	30	
f. Items purchased, on receiving dock, invoice not received	200	300
g. Items to be returned to vendor per agreement, rejected for incorrect specs	150	
h. Purchase invoice received, items not received (FOB destination)	20	100

Part B

	Units	
	Product A at $10	Product B at $20
Finished goods unit inventory data on 12/31/19A—Items counted in warehouse (excluding items below)	25,000	12,000
a. Items shipped to customer on 1/1/19B, invoice mailed 12/31/19A (FOB shipping point)		500
b. Items completed by factory, counted in work in process inventory; not transported to warehouse	1,000	
c. Items on receiving dock, returned by customer because of major damage, notification from customer received		100
d. Items on trucking company dock, invoice mailed to customer, buyer pays freight	450	
e. Items in damaged condition	40	25
f. Items in shipping department, invoice not mailed to customer	80	
g. Items shipped 12/31/19A (FOB destination), invoice mailed to customer 1/2/19B	100	
h. Items on consignment to Smith Distributing Co.	400	800
i. Items specifically segregated and crated for shipment to Medal Branch No. 10 (not a separate company)	100	100
j. Items used for display purposes	10	30
k. Items specifically segregated and crated and held for shipment to customer 1/10/19B, per contract of sale for December 19A		600
l. Items on receiving dock, returned by customer, no notification received (not damaged)	20	

Required:
Compute the value of the ending inventory of finished goods and raw materials, indicating specifically what items you would include and exclude. Give the reasons that you would present to the company for any doubtful items. The following format is recommended (same format for Products A and B):

		Inventory valuation				
		Material X		Material Y		
Item	Inventory include/exclude	Units	Amount	Units	Amount	Explanation

P 8–3 (Perpetual and Periodic Inventory Systems Compared; Entries)
Alfred Company completed the following selected transactions during 19B for product A:

	Units	Unit price
Beginning inventory	6,000	$18 (cost)
Purchases	20,000	18 (cost)
Purchase returns	1,000	18 (cost)
Sales (gross)	18,000	25 (selling price)
Sales returns	100	25 (selling price)
Ending inventory per physical count	6,900	
Inventory shortage	?	

Expenses (excluding cost of goods sold and income taxes), $47,800.

Required:
1. In parallel columns, give entries for the above transactions including entries at the end of the accounting period, December 31, 19B, for (assume a 40% income tax rate and cash transactions):

Case A—Periodic inventory system.
Case B—Perpetual inventory system.

2. Prepare a multiple-step statement of income assuming a periodic inventory system and 10,000 shares of common stock outstanding.
3. What amounts, if any, would be different on the statement of income assuming a perpetual inventory system is used? Explain.

P 8–4 (Inventory, CGS, Gross Margin; Five Inventory Methods)
The records of Barnett Company showed the following transactions, in the order given, relating to the major inventory item:

	Units	Unit cost
1. Inventory	3,000	$7.00
2. Purchase	5,000	7.20
3. Sales (at $15)	4,000	
4. Purchase	7,000	7.50
5. Sales (at $15)	9,000	
6. Purchase	8,000	7.70
7. Sales (at $18)	9,000	
8. Purchase	6,000	7.80

Required:
Complete the following schedule for each independent assumption (round unit costs to the nearest cent for inventory; show computations):

Independent assumptions	Units and amounts: Ending inventory	Goods sold	Gross margin
a. FIFO.			
b. LIFO, periodic inventory system (base inventory, 1,000 units).			
c. LIFO, perpetual inventory system (base inventory, 1,000 units).			
d. Weighted average, periodic inventory system.			
e. Moving average, perpetual inventory system.			

P 8–5 (Inventory, Cost Flow Issues; Four Methods; Two Inventory Systems)
The records of Baker Company showed the following data about one raw material used in the manufacturing process. Assume the transactions occurred in the order given.

	Units	Unit cost
1. Inventory	4,000	
2. Purchase No. 1	3,000	7.60
3. Issue No. 1	5,000	
4. Purchase No. 2	8,000	8.00
5. Issue No. 2	7,000	
6. Purchase No. 3.	3,000	8.50

Required:
1. Compute cost of materials issued (to work in process) and the valuation of raw materials ending inventory for each of the following independent assumptions (round unit costs to the nearest cent for inventory; show computations):
   a. FIFO.
   b. LIFO, periodic inventory system (base inventory, 4,000 units).
   c. Weighted average, periodic inventory system.
   d. Moving average, perpetual inventory system.

2. In parallel columns, give all entries indicated for FIFO assuming a count of the raw material on hand at the end showed 6,000 units.

Case A—Periodic inventory system.
Case B—Perpetual inventory system.

P 8–6 (Inventory, CGS, Gross Margin; Three Inventory Methods)
The records of Bosworth Company showed the following data relative to one of the major items being sold. Assume the transactions occurred in the order given.

	Units	Unit cost
Beginning inventory	8,000	$4.00
Purchase No. 1	6,000	4.20
Sale No. 1 (at $12)	9,000	
Purchase No. 2	8,000	4.50
Sale No. 2 (at $13)	4,000	

Required:
1. Complete the following schedule under each independent assumption given (round unit costs to nearest cent):

	Units and amount		
Independent assumptions	Ending inventory	Cost of goods sold	Gross margin
a. Weighted-average cost, periodic inventory system.			
b. FIFO, perpetual inventory system.			
c. LIFO, periodic inventory system (base inventory, 7,000 units).			

2. Give all transaction entries indicated by the above data assuming FIFO and a perpetual inventory system ([*b*] above).

P 8–7 (Ending Inventory, CGS, Five Methods; Two Inventory Systems)
Kim Corporation's records showed the following transactions, in order of occurrence, relative to inventory item A:

	Units	Unit cost
1. Inventory	400	$5.00
2. Purchase	600	5.50
3. Sale	700	
4. Purchase	900	5.60
5. Sale	800	
6. Purchase	200	5.75

Required:
Compute the cost of goods sold and ending inventory in each of the following independent situations (round unit costs to the nearest cent for inventory; show computations):

	Units and amount	
Assumption	Ending inventory	Cost of Goods sold
a. Weighted average.		
b. Moving average.		
c. FIFO.		
d. LIFO, perpetual inventory system.		
e. LIFO, periodic inventory system.		

P 8–8 (Ending Inventory, CGS, Income; Three Cost Methods)

Patterson Corporation maintains a periodic inventory system. The following transactions occurred during 19B for its major inventory item (in order of occurrence):

	Units	Unit cost
1. Beginning inventory	1,000	$50
2. Purchase	900	40
3. Sale (at $100)	800	
4. Purchase	800	51
5. Sale (at $100)	200	

Other expenses (excluding income taxes) during 19B were $20,000. Patterson's tax rate is 40%.

Required:

1. Complete the following schedule for each of the independent assumptions given (show supporting computations):

Independent assumptions	Ending inventory	Cost of goods sold	Net income
a. Weighted average			
b. FIFO			
c. LIFO			

2. Which method results in the highest tax liability? Explain why this occurred.

P 8–9 (FIFO to LIFO; Reporting the Change)

Deitrick Company decided at the beginning of 19B to change from FIFO to LIFO. The records of the company showed the following data for 19B relative to one major inventory item distributed:

	Units	Unit cost
Beginning inventory (LIFO base inventory) 1/1/19B	10,000	$3.10
Purchases and sales (in order given):		
1. Purchase	8,000	3.20
2. Sold (at $8)	9,000	
3. Sold (at $8.25)	5,000	
4. Purchase	7,000	3.20
5. Purchase	6,000	3.40
6. Sold (at $8.75)	8,000	
7. Purchase	3,000	3.50

Expenses (excluding income taxes), $40,000.
Average income tax rate, 40%.

Required:

1. Prepare an statement of income for 19B, unit cost LIFO basis, periodic inventory system. Assume 10,000 shares of common stock outstanding.
2. Prepare an appropriate footnote, and any other required supporting data, for the change in 19B from FIFO to LIFO.
3. What would be disclosed in 19C relative to the change? Why?

P 8–10 (A Hypothetical Inventory Riddle to Solve!)

Stigler Corporation sells two main products. The records of the company showed the following information relating to one of the products:

	Units	Unit cost
Beginning inventory	500	$3.00
Purchases and sales (in order given):		
Purchase No. 1	400	3.10
Purchase No. 2	600	3.15
Sale No. 1	1,000	
Purchase No. 3	800	3.25
Sale No. 2	700	
Sale No. 3	500	
Purchase No. 4	700	3.30

In considering a change in inventory policy, the following summary was prepared:

	Illustration			
	(1)	(2)	(3)	(4)
Sales	$16,000	$16,000	$16,000	$16,000
Cost of goods sold	7,110	6,996	6,905	6,930
Gross margin	$ 8,890	$ 9,004	$ 9,095	$ 9,070

Required:
Identify the inventory flow method used for each illustration assuming only the ending inventory was affected. Show computations. (AICPA adapted)

P 8–11 **(An Overview; Perpetual Inventory; Entries, Partial Statement of Income)**
Wagner Company maintains perpetual inventory records on a FIFO basis for the three main products distributed by the company. A physical inventory is taken at the end of each year in order to check the perpetual inventory records.

The following information relating to one of the products, Product A, for the year 19B was taken from the records of the company:

	Units	Unit cost
Beginning inventory	9,000	$8.10
Purchases and sales (in order given):		
Purchase No. 1	5,000	8.15
Sale No. 1	10,000	
Purchase No. 2	16,000	8.20
Sale No. 2	11,000	
Purchase No. 3	4,000	8.30
Purchase No. 4	7,000	8.20
Sale No. 3	14,000	
Purchase No. 5	5,000	8.10
Ending inventory (per count)	10,500	
Replacement cost (per unit), $8.10.		

Required:
1. Reconstruct the perpetual inventory record for Product A.
2. Give all entries indicated by the above data assuming selling price is $18 per unit and that the company employs the inventory allowance method (holding losses separately identified) in recognizing LCM.
3. Prepare the statement of income through gross margin for this product.

Part B: Problems 8–12 to 8–18

P 8–12 **(DV LIFO, Conversion from FIFO)**
Brady Company has been using FIFO for all internal and external reporting purposes. At the start of 19B, it adopted DV LIFO for external financial statement and income tax purposes. The FIFO inventory records reported the following for one inventory pool:

	FIFO basis
19A ending inventory	$100,000
19B ending inventory	120,000
19C ending inventory	128,000
19D ending inventory	130,000

Internal price index derived: 19A—1.00; 19B—1.10; 19C—1.15; and 19D—1.20.

Required:
Convert the ending FIFO inventory amounts to a LIFO basis for 19B, 19C, and 19D, assuming the DV LIFO method, using the internal price index values given above.

P 8–13 (DV LIFO, Conversion from FIFO)
Ohio Corporation maintains its internal inventory records on a FIFO basis. On January 1, 19B, Ohio changed to DV LIFO for external reporting and income tax purposes. The following data are available regarding Ohio's inventory:

	19B	19C	19D
Ending inventory at current year cost	$140,000	$160,000	$175,000
LIFO conversion index*	1.20	1.30	1.45

* Computed internally.

Ohio's base inventory is $100,000.

Required:
1. Compute the ending inventory on a DV LIFO basis for the years 19B, 19C, and 19D.
2. Assume the 19E ending inventory on a DV LIFO basis is $144,195, and the 19E LIFO conversion index is 1.50. What is the ending inventory on a current cost basis?

P 8–14 (DV LIFO, Conversion from FIFO; Calculate Price Index)
Little Corporation has been using FIFO since its organization for *(a)* internal management reports and control, *(b)* external reporting to shareholders, and *(c)* income tax purposes. On January 1, 19B, management decided to change from FIFO to DV LIFO for external reporting and income tax purposes. FIFO will continue in use for internal purposes.

The company has a number of LIFO inventory pools; however, this problem deals with only one of them. The company will apply the dollar value approach for converting the FIFO results to a LIFO basis and will use an internal conversion index computed each year.

The FIFO results for a three-year period, taken directly from the accounts and internal reports for inventory pool No. 1 (composed of five similar items in a "natural business unit") are shown below.

	Year 19A			Year 19B			Year 19C		
	Units	Unit cost	Total	Units	Unit cost	Total	Units	Unit cost	Total
Sales revenue			$18,200			$24,280			$30,920
Cost of goods sold (FIFO):									
Beginning inventory	800	$2.50	2,000	600	$3.00	1,800	700	$3.60	2,520
Purchases	2,000	3.00	6,000	2,500	3.60	9,000	4,000	4.00	16,000
Ending inventory	(600)	3.00	(1,800)*	(700)	3.60	(2,520)	(900)	4.00	(3,600)
Cost of goods sold	2,200		6,200	2,400		8,280	3,800		14,920

* Base inventory.

Required:
1. Compute the conversion price indexes needed for the DV LIFO application in 19B and 19C. Show computations and round conversion ratios to two decimal places.

2. Convert the FIFO results to a LIFO basis for 19B and 19C using the DV approach. Show computations.
3. Assuming $8,000 operating expenses, a 30% average tax rate, and 4,000 shares of common stock outstanding, prepare statements of income for 19B and 19C with two headings for each year: *(a)* for internal reports (FIFO basis), and *(b)* for external reports and tax returns (LIFO basis).

Suggestion:

Use one set of side captions and four money columns.

P 8–15 **(DV LIFO, Conversion from FIFO; Disclosure; Calculate Price Index)**
Stein Corporation sells two main products. FIFO, with a perpetual inventory system, is used for internal cost accounting and management purposes. On January 1, 19B, the company adopted DV LIFO for external reporting and income tax purposes; FIFO will continue to be used for internal purposes. The FIFO inventory records are shown below.

Perpetual Inventory Record

	Purchases			Issues			FIFO balance		
	Units	Cost	Total	Units	Cost	Total	Units	Cost	Total
Product X:									
December 31, 19A							200	$100	$20,000
19B: Purchases	400	$130	$52,000						
Sales				{200	$100	$20,000			
				{200	130	26,000	200	130	26,000
19C: Purchases	500	140	70,000						
Sales				200	130	26,000	500	140	70,000
19D: Purchases at	300	145	43,500						
Sales				500	140	70,000	300	145	43,500
Product Y:									
December 31, 19A							300	$ 90	$27,000
19B: Purchases	400	$ 92	$36,800						
Sales				300	$ 90	$27,000	400	92	36,800
19C: Purchases	100	95	9,500						
Sales				400	92	36,800	100	95	9,500
19D: Purchases	400	98	39,200						
Sales				{100	95	9,500			
				{100	98	9,800	300	98	29,400

Required:
Assume the two products form one pool for inventory purposes. Convert the ending inventory at FIFO to a DV LIFO basis for 19B, 19C, and 19D. Round conversion indexes to two places.

P 8–16 **(DV LIFO, Conversion from FIFO, Reporting)**
Westshore Corporation sells three main products regularly. The products form one pool for inventory purposes. The company used FIFO through 19A for all purposes. After 19A, FIFO was continued for internal management and accounting purposes; however, at the start of 19B, DV LIFO was adopted for income tax and external reporting purposes. The following data (for the three products combined) were taken from the records for the three years following the adoption of LIFO:

	FIFO basis per accounts		
	Units	Cost	Total
19A:			
Ending inventory	2,000	$3.00	$ 6,000
19B:			
Purchases	7,000	3.30	$23,100
Sales	6,000		
Ending inventory	3,000	3.30	9,900
19C:			
Purchases	10,000	3.50	$35,000
Sales	6,000		
Ending inventory	7,000	3.50	24,500
19D:			
Purchases	5,000	4.00	$20,000
Sales	8,000		
Ending inventory	4,000	4.00	16,000

Required:

1. Convert the ending inventory at FIFO to a DV LIFO basis for 19B, 19C, and 19D. Round conversion indexes to two decimal places.
2. Prepare a schedule (which includes inventory, tax, and income) that compares the results of the methods, FIFO and LIFO. For analytical purposes, assume *(a)* an average tax rate of 40% and *(b)* a pretax income amount of $5,000 each year under FIFO. Which method should be used? Why?
3. Prepare an appropriate footnote to the financial statements for 19B assuming LIFO is used for external reporting and tax purposes.

P 8–17 (DV LIFO, Conversion from FIFO, Reporting)

Sonoma Company sells two main products. The products form one pool for inventory purposes. The company used FIFO through 19B for all purposes. Starting in 19C, DV LIFO was adopted for external reporting and income tax purposes. The inventory pool (the two products combined) records at FIFO reflected the information shown below.

	Purchases			Sales			Balance (FIFO)		
19B:									
Ending inventory . . .							400	$1.00	$400
19C:									
Purchases	700	$1.20	$840				400	1.00	400
							700	1.20	840
Sales				400	$1.00	$400			
				100	1.20	120	600	1.20	720
19D:									
Purchases	600	1.35	810				600	1.20	720
							600	1.35	810
Sales				600	1.20	720			
				200	1.35	270	400	1.35	540
19E:									
Purchases	500	1.50	750				400	1.35	540
							500	1.50	750
Sales				500	1.35	675	400	1.50	600

Required:

1. Convert the ending inventory at FIFO to a DV LIFO basis for 19C, 19D, and 19E. Round conversion indexes to two decimal places.

2. Prepare a schedule (that includes inventory, tax, and income) to compare the results for FIFO and LIFO. For analytical purposes, assume *(a)* an average tax rate of 40% and *(b)* a pretax income amount of $300 (FIFO basis) for each year. Which method should be used? Why?
3. Prepare a suitable footnote for the financial statements for 19C assuming LIFO is used for external reporting and income tax purposes.

P 8–18 (Supplement 8–A: Standard Costs)

Orr Manufacturing Company manufactures one main product. Two raw materials are used in the manufacture of this product. The company uses standard costs in the accounts and carries the raw material, work in process, and finished goods inventories at standard. The records of the company showed the following:

	Material A	Material B
Beginning inventory (units)	8,000	5,000
Standard cost per unit	$2.00	$7.00
Purchases during period:		
No. 1	10,000 at $2.00	7,000 at $7.00
No. 2	20,000 at 1.90	8,000 at 7.20
Issues during period (units)	28,000	16,000
Ending inventory per physical count (units)	10,000	3,900

Required:

1. Give all entries indicated relative to raw materials assuming standard costs (assume a perpetual system).
2. Determine the value of the ending inventory and cost of issues for each raw material.
3. Accumulate the amount of the variations from standard for each raw material, and explain or illustrate the reporting and accounting disposition of these amounts.

CASES

C 8–1 (LIFO, Profit Manipulation)

Bauer Company uses a periodic inventory system and LIFO, unit basis, to cost the ending inventory for income tax and external reporting purposes. Near the end of 19A, the records and related estimates provided the following annual data for one item sold regularly:

	Units	Unit cost
Beginning inventory (LIFO basis):		
Base inventory (normal minimum level)	10,000	$20
Increment No. 1	5,000	30
Purchases (actual)	60,000	37
Sales* (at $50 per unit)	65,000	
Expenses* (excluding income taxes), $880,000.		
Average income tax rate, 30%.		

* Including estimates for remainder of 19A.

On December 26, 19A, the company has an opportunity to purchase not less than 30,000 units of the above item at $33 (a special price) with 10-day credit terms. Delivery is immediate, and the offer will expire January 3, 19B. The question has been posed as to whether the purchase (and delivery) should be consummated in 19A or 19B; the management has tentatively decided to make the purchase in 19A.

Required:

1. What is your recommendation as to the purchase date? Support your recommendation with reasons and pro forma (as if) statement of income and statement of financial position data. Include computations. Assume 40,000 shares of common stock are outstanding.
2. Explain and illustrate why EPS would be changed if the purchase is made in 19A.
3. Would you suspect profit manipulation in this situation if Bauer elected to make the purchase in 19A? Explain.

C 8–2 (LIFO, Profit Manipulation)

R. Babinski, S. Chasnoff, and T. Doland formed a partnership to import furniture. Their initial partnership agreement provided for equal investments, equal sharing of responsibilities, equal work, equal salaries, and equal shares of the partnership income. After a few years of operation, sales "took off" and the business prospered. On January 1, 19T, they incorporated as BCD, Inc., with each of the former partners owning 33⅓% of the stock of the corporation. The board of directors of BCD, Inc., was comprised of Babinski, Chasnoff, and Doland. The board elected Chasnoff as chairman of the board of directors, Babinski as president of the corporation in charge of operations, and Doland as vice president and controller (Doland was a CPA). Annual compensation of the three officers was set as follows:

Chasnoff . . .	$130,000	plus bonus equal to 2% of annual net income
Babinski	135,000	plus bonus equal to 1% of annual net income
Doland	140,000	plus 5% of annual decrease in income tax payments

The compensation plan was intended as an incentive device as well as to reflect the relative contributions of the three officers to corporate success. In particular, the bonus plan was intended to motivate Chasnoff and Babinski (who represented the corporation in the business community) to increase sales and to encourage Doland (the accountant) to decrease income tax payments. During 19U, 19V, and 19W, sales and income increased steadily. In the year ended December 31, 19W, net income of the corporation was $500,000, which put the annual earnings of all three officers at $140,000 (this amount cannot be verified). Income tax payments for 19W were $150,000. During 19X, net income, computed on the basis of the FIFO inventory method, which BCD used, increased to $750,000. This increase in corporate income was destined to put Chasnoff's annual earnings at $145,000 and Babinski's at $142,500, but to leave Doland's at $140,000 (neither Babinski nor Chasnoff were aware of this). A major reason for the increase in corporation income was Doland's skill at controlling costs; however, the compensation plan did not adequately reflect this factor. Doland tried to persuade Chasnoff and Babinski to renegotiate his salary, but they refused because they knew very little about finance and accounting and, therefore, were unable to appreciate Doland's effectiveness at controlling expenses. They were convinced the reason for the success of BCD was their superlative sales and management skills.

The cost to BCD, Inc., of its imported furniture was rising rapidly near the end of 19X, but, due to increased competition, the outlook for the company's sales was not bright for 19Y. Without notifying Chasnoff or Babinski, Doland changed inventory methods from FIFO to LIFO, effective January 1, 19X. Also, near year-end 19X, Doland, who controlled all purchases of inventory, stocked up on inventory in response to a pending 20% cost increase announced by BCD's suppliers; the price increase was to become effective in January 19Y. Because of the change to LIFO, income tax payments for 19X decreased to $70,000.

Required:

1. What was the likely effect of the change in inventory method on reported income of BCD for 19X? On the annual bonuses of Babinski and Chasnoff?
2. What was the likely effect of stocking up of inventory on reported income of 19X? On the annual earnings of Babinski and Chasnoff?
3. What was the effect of Doland's actions on his annual bonsus?
4. What conclusions can you draw from this situation about accounting income?

9 INVENTORY: LOWER OF COST OR MARKET, ESTIMATING METHODS, AND DV LIFO RETAIL

OVERVIEW AND PURPOSE

Because of implementation and practical problems, the accounting profession has established GAAP guidelines for certain methods of valuing inventory. In fact, you studied one inventory estimating method in Chapter 8—DV LIFO.

Inventory values often must be determined by using an estimate because a valuation at cost may be too costly or impossible to obtain. For example, inventory estimates may be required for interim reporting when a physical inventory count is impractical and a perpetual inventory system is not used. Also, certain industries, such as retail department stores, use accepted estimating methods to convert inventories valued at retail to a cost basis.

Inventory estimating methods have gained wide acceptance in these circumstances. Among these procedures are the gross margin method of estimating inventory and the retail method of converting inventories from retail value to cost. The purpose of this chapter is to discuss inventory estimating methods. To accomplish this purpose, the chapter is subdivided as follows:

Part A: Lower-of-Cost-or-Market and Inventory Estimating Methods

1. Lower-of-cost-or-market (LCM).
2. Gross margin method to estimate inventory.
3. Retail inventory method to estimate inventory.

Part B: Retail Inventory, DV LIFO, and Additional Inventory Issues

1. Retail inventory method, DV LIFO.
2. Additional inventory issues.
3. Relative sales value method.
4. Losses on purchase commitments.
5. Effects of inventory errors.

PART A: LOWER-OF-COST-OR-MARKET AND INVENTORY ESTIMATING METHODS

Lower-of-Cost-or-Market (LCM)

In conformity with the conservatism constraint (page 240), losses due to a decrease in the market value (i.e., current replacement cost) of inventory below cost, although not actually incurred in completed transactions, are recognized in the period of the market value decline. In contrast, market value gains not evidenced by completed transactions are not recognized until realized (i.e., when sold). Therefore, under the LCM rule, the unit cost of inventory is identified as the **lower** of *(a)* **original cost** when purchased or *(b)* the **current replacement cost** (i.e., the current cost to replace or reproduce the ending inventory, **not** its current selling price) at the end of the current period. Thus, an item purchased in June 19A for $50 that is still on hand at the end of 19A, at which time it could be purchased for $45, is reported in the 19A ending inventory at a unit cost of $45. The $5 loss is reported as an expense on the 19A statement of income, and the current replacement cost of $45 becomes the inventory cost for future accounting. Therefore, $45 is included in cost of goods sold for the period when the item is sold. The net effect of the LCM application is to shift the $5 loss from 19B (the period of sale) to 19A (the period the replacement cost decreased).

The LCM rule was adopted on the basis of *(a)* the matching principle, so that a decline in utility of the goods on hand (evidenced by the decrease in current replacement cost) is recognized as a loss in the period in which the decline took place; and *(b)* the concept of conservatism, which results in the asset inventory being reported at the lower amount in the statement of financial position.

reason for adoption
Conservatism
& Matching Principle

To apply LCM, certain **constraints** were recognized by the AICPA Committee on Accounting Procedure, which issued the definitive pronouncement on LCM. That is, while **"market"** usually means current replacement cost (or current reproduction cost, as the case may be),

(1) Market should not exceed the net realizable value (i.e., estimated selling price in the ordinary course of business less reasonably predictable costs of completion and disposal); and
(2) Market should not be less than net realizable value reduced by an allowance for an approximately normal profit margin.[1]

Net realizable value and **net realizable value less normal profit** may be illustrated as follows for one unit of inventory item A:

Inventory item A, at original cost		$ 70
Inventory item A, at estimated current selling price in present condition		$100
Less: Estimated costs of completion and cost to sell*		40
Net realizable value		60
Less: Allowance for normal profit (10% of sales price)		10
Net realizable value less normal profit		$ 50

* For goods already completed, as in a retail company, this would be "cost of repair and cost to sell."

[1] *ARB 43*, chap. 4, statement 6.

The deduction of estimated completion and selling costs of the inventory is necessary to prevent valuation of the inventory at more than its current realizable value.

The constraints quoted above for net realizable value and net realizable value less normal profit effectively establish a "ceiling" and a "floor" for measuring the **market value,** which is compared with original **cost** in applying LCM. **Exhibit 9–1** shows how LCM is determined in four different cases for a single unit where the "ceiling" and "floor" are calculated (the same procedure would apply to an entire inventory).

Notice in Exhibit 9–1 that "market" as used under LCM is never higher than the "ceiling" (net realizable value), nor lower than the "floor" (net realizable value less a normal profit). That is, market is always the middle amount of

Exhibit 9–1
Determination of lower-of-cost-or-market (LCM) illustrated.

	Case I	Case II	Case III	Case IV
a. Cost (per unit)	$1.00	$1.00	$1.00	$.45
b. Current replacement cost (per unit)	.55	.65	.45	.40
c. Ceiling (net realizable value, i.e., estimated sales price less predictable costs of completion and sale; see additional data below)	.60	.60	.60	.60
d. Floor (net realizable value less a normal profit margin; see additional data below)	.51	.51	.52	.52
e. Market (selected from [*b*], [*c*], and [*d*] values)	.55	.60	.52	.52
f. Inventory valuation under LCM rule (selected from [*a*] and [*e*])*	.55	.60	.52	.45

* The "key" is as follows:

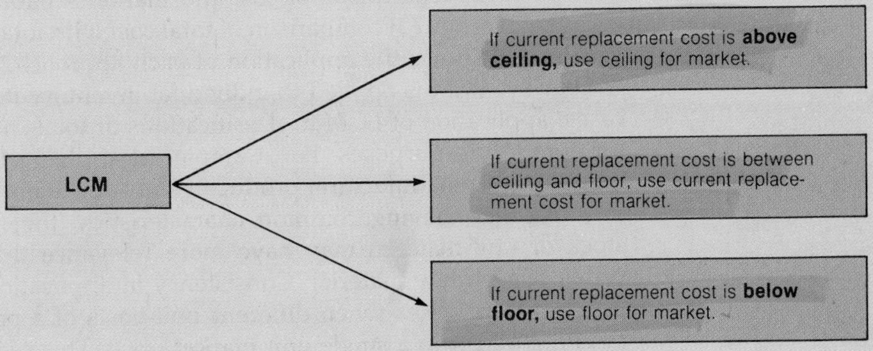

LCM
If current replacement cost is **above ceiling,** use ceiling for market.
If current replacement cost is between ceiling and floor, use current replacement cost for market.
If current replacement cost is **below floor,** use floor for market.

Additional data to verify ceiling and floor:

	I	II	III	IV
Estimated selling price (later period)	$ .85	$ .90	$ .80	$ .75
Less: Estimated cost to complete and sell	.25	.30	.20	.15
Net realizable value (ceiling)	.60	.60	.60	.60
Less: Estimated normal profit†	.09	.09	.08	.08
Net realizable value less profit (floor)	$ .51	$ .51	$ .52	$ .52

† 10% of sales price; rounded for instructional convenience.

the three possible figures. The market valuation thus derived is compared with cost to determine the appropriate inventory valuation.

The limits (ceiling and floor) are used to measure the economic utility of the items in inventory. For example, in Case II in Exhibit 9–1, current replacement cost is \$.65 and the net realizable value (ceiling) is \$.60. To value the inventory at its current replacement cost of \$.65, which is higher than the net realizable value, would result in a deduction of \$.35 (i.e., \$1 – \$.65) from current income, which is less than the anticipated loss of \$.40 (i.e., \$1 – \$.60). Hence, the reported income and inventory value of each period would be incorrect.

In Case III, Exhibit 9–1, the net realizable value less normal profit (floor, \$.52) is higher than current replacement cost; therefore, the floor value should be carried forward in inventory. To value the inventory at \$.45 (i.e., current replacement cost) would result in an understatement of the inventory because at the floor value of \$.52, a normal profit margin (\$.08) will be earned when the item is sold for \$.60. Therefore, if current replacement cost (\$.45) were carried forward in this case, future income earned on the inventory items would be overstated and current period income would be understated.

Accounting Problems in Applying LCM

In applying LCM, the following accounting problems arise:

1. How should LCM be applied to determine the overall inventory valuation?
2. How should the resulting inventory valuation be recorded in the accounts and reported on the financial statements?

Determination of Overall Inventory Valuation.

To apply LCM to determine the overall inventory valuation, three approaches are available (*ARB 43*, chap. 4, statement 7): (1) comparison of cost and market separately for each item of inventory, (2) comparison of cost and market separately for each **classification** of inventory, and (3) comparison of **total** cost with **total** market for the inventory. **Exhibit 9–2** shows the application of each approach.

Usually, LCM is applied to individual inventory items.[2] However, in certain cases, application of LCM to classifications or totals may have greater relevance for accounting purposes. For example, in applying LCM to the raw materials inventory of a manufacturer producing only one major product and using several raw materials having common characteristics, the market value of the total stock of raw material may have more relevance than the individual market prices of each raw material. Consistency in application is essential.

A problem arises when different unit costs of a particular commodity must be compared with a single unit **market** price. This case frequently occurs when the first-in, first-out cost flow assumption (discussed in Chapter 8) is used. In such cases, the aggregate cost for the commodity should be compared with the aggregate market, as shown under "Total" in Exhibit 9–2.

Recording and Reporting Lower of Cost or Market (LCM).

Purchases are recorded at cost; therefore, the introduction of LCM valuation of the inventory each period raises the question of how the **difference** between actual cost and LCM should be recorded and reported. This difference arises only because inventory

---

[2] Ibid., chap. 4, statement 7.

Exhibit 9–2
Application of LCM to inventory categories.

			LCM applied to		
Inventory	Cost	Market	Individual items	Classification	Total
Classification A:					
Item 1	$10,000	$ 9,500	$ 9,500		
Item 2	8,000	9,000	8,000		
	18,000	18,500		$18,000	
Classification B:					
Item 3	21,000	22,000	21,000		
Item 4	32,000	29,000	29,000		
	53,000	51,000		51,000	
Total	$71,000	$69,500			$69,500
Inventory valuation . .			$67,500	$69,000	$69,500

items on hand can now be replaced for less than their original cost. This difference usually is called an **inventory holding loss.** The basic issue is whether the inventory holding loss should be **separately recorded** in the accounts and **separately reported** on the financial statements or **merged** into cost of goods sold. The following two methods of recording and reporting the effects of the application of LCM are used in practice.

1. **Direct inventory reduction method**—Under this method, the inventory holding loss is **not** separately recorded and reported. Only the LCM amount, rather than the actual cost, of the inventory is recorded and reported each period. **Thus, the inventory holding loss is automatically included in the ending inventory and cost of goods sold amounts.**
2. **Inventory allowance method**—Under this method, the inventory holding loss is **separately recorded and reported** each period. This separation is recorded by using a **contra inventory** account, Allowance to Reduce Inventory to LCM. Thus, *(a)* the inventory and cost of goods sold amounts are recorded and reported at actual cost, and *(b)* the inventory holding loss is **separately** recognized.

Both of the above methods derive exactly the same income and total asset amounts; the two methods differ only with respect to the detail in the entries and disclosures on the statement of income and statement of financial position. Both methods are shown in **Exhibit 9–3.** Panel A gives data for three consecutive years. Panel B illustrates the related accounting entries under both methods (assuming a periodic inventory system). Panel C presents the related statement of financial position and statement of income amounts as they would be reported in the financial statements.

Under the **direct inventory reduction** method, the LCM amount of the ending inventory, rather than the actual inventory cost, is *(a)* recorded directly in the accounts and *(b)* reported on the financial statements. The amount of ending inventory at LCM is carried forward to the next period as the beginning inventory. Thus, **both** of the beginning and ending inventory amounts are reflected at LCM. These characteristics are evident in Exhibit 9–3, panels B and C, under the heading "Direct Inventory Reduction Method."

In contrast, under the **inventory allowance method,** the entries and financial statements *(a)* retain actual costs for inventory and cost of goods sold and *(b)* record and report the holding loss each period in a contra inventory account, Allowance to Reduce Inventory to LCM. The net holding loss (i.e., the net effect of the holding losses in the beginning and ending inventories) is reported separately on the statement of income. These characteristics are evident in Exhibit 9–3, panels B and C, under the heading "Inventory Allowance Method."

A net holding gain is also possible if market declines below cost in one period and increases above cost in a subsequent period. For example, if the market value of the 19C ending inventory described in Exhibit 9–3 was $32 (instead of $26), a holding gain of $3 would be recognized (either in cost of goods sold or in a separate holding gain account). Holding gains (or holding

Exhibit 9–3
Recording and reporting LCM (periodic inventory system).

Panel A—Case Data (in thousands of dollars):

	19A		19B		19C	
	Beginning	**Ending**	**Beginning**	**Ending**	**Beginning**	**Ending**
A. Cost	-0-	$10	$10	$20	$20	$30
B. Market (replacement)	-0-	11	11	17	17	26
C. LCM (lower of A, B)	-0-	10	10	17	17	26

Panel B—End-of-Period Inventory Entries:

	Direct inventory reduction method		**Inventory allowance method**	
19A (no holding loss):*				
a. Beginning inventory—none				
b. Ending inventory:				
Inventory (ending)	(cost) 10		(cost) 10	
Income summary (cost of goods sold)		10		10
19B (holding loss, $3):				
a. Beginning inventory—to close:				
Income summary (cost of goods sold)	(cost 10		(cost) 10	
Inventory (beginning)		10		10
b. Ending inventory—to record:				
Inventory (ending)	(LCM) 17		(cost) 20	
Income summary (cost of goods sold)		17		20
c. To record holding loss in ending inventory:				
Holding loss on inventory ($20 – $17)			3	
Allowance to reduce inventory to LCM				3
19C (holding loss, $1):				
a. Beginning inventory—to close:				
Income summary (cost of goods sold)	(LCM) 17		(cost) 20	
Inventory (beginning)		17		20
b. Ending inventory—to record:				
Inventory (ending)	(LCM) 26		(cost) 30	
Income summary (cost of goods sold)		26		30
c. To record holding loss on ending inventory:				
Holding loss on inventory			1	
Allowance to reduce inventory to LCM†				1

* Note: no entry for holding loss in 19A because market is above cost.
† 19C balance required in allowance account, $ (i.e., $30 – $26), less 19B balance in allowance account, $3, = $1.

Exhibit 9–3
(concluded)

Panel C—Financial Statement—Reporting LCM for Inventory: Direct Inventory Reduction and Inventory Allowance Methods Compared:

REPORTING LCM—DIRECT INVENTORY REDUCTION METHOD
Inventory Holding Loss Merged with Inventory and Cost of Goods Sold

	Year 19A		Year 19B		Year 19C	
Statement of financial position:						
Current assets:						
Merchandise inventory		$ 10		$ 17		$ 26
Statement of income:						
Sales revenue (assumed)		$ 50		$ 65		$ 81
Cost of goods sold:						
Beginning inventory (at LCM)	$ 0		$ 10		$ 17	
Purchases (assumed)	40		47		61	
Total goods available for sale	40		57		78	
Ending inventory (at LCM)	(10)		(17)		(26)	
Cost of goods sold		30		40*		52*
Gross margin		20		25		29
Expenses (assumed)		(10)		(13)		(16)
Income (pretax)		$ 10		$ 12		$ 13

REPORTING LCM—INVENTORY ALLOWANCE METHOD
Holding Losses Reported Separately from Inventory and Cost of Goods Sold

	Year 19A		Year 19B		Year 19C	
Statement of financial position:						
Current assets:						
Merchandise inventory (at cost)	$ 10		$ 20		$ 30	
Less: Allowance to reduce inventory to LCM	(0)	$ 10	(3)	$ 17	(4)	$ 26
Statement of income:						
Sales revenue (assumed)		$ 50		$ 65		$ 81
Cost of goods sold:						
Beginning inventory (at cost)	$ 0		$ 10		$ 20	
Purchases (assumed)	40		47		61	
Total goods available for sale	40		57		81	
Ending inventory (at cost)	(10)		(20)		(30)	
Cost of goods sold (at cost)		30		37		51
Gross margin		20		28		30
Expenses (assumed)		(10)		(13)		(16)
Deduct net holding loss effect:						
19A		-0-				
19B				(3)		
19C						(1)
Income (pretax)		$ 10		$ 12		$ 13

* The holding loss merged with these amounts is: 19B, $3; and 19C, $1.

loss recovery) cannot exceed previously recognized holding losses under the LCM rule.

The **direct inventory reduction method** is widely used because *(a)* it is less complex than the allowance method when the periodic system is used, *(b)* the inventory holding loss amount for the period often is not material or unusual, and *(c)* disclosure notes can be used to report the holding loss information. In contrast, the **inventory allowance method** is used because it *(a)* provides full disclosure of the effects of LCM on inventories (the direct inventory reduction method does not), *(b)* is required under certain conditions,[3] *(c)* is less complex than the direct inventory reduction method when the perpetual inventory system is used (perpetual records usually are maintained at cost, not LCM), and *(d)* provides insight into the interperiod effects of using LCM.

Gross Margin Method to Estimate Inventory

The gross margin method (often called the **gross profit method**) is used to **estimate** the value of an inventory independent of a physical count of goods. It also is used as a test check on the accuracy of the results of other inventory methods. The method is based on the assumption that the gross margin rate (gross margin divided by sales), based on recent past performance, will be approximately constant in the short run. The gross margin method has two basic characteristics: *(a)* it requires the development of an estimated gross margin rate; and *(b)* numerous items typically are grouped for its application (such as all items sold in the sports department of a large retail store).

Estimating the ending inventory by the gross margin method requires the following steps: (1) Estimate the gross margin rate. (2) Compute total **cost of goods available for sale** in the usual manner (i.e., beginning inventory plus purchases), based on actual data provided by the accounts. (3) Compute the **estimated gross margin** by multiplying sales by the estimated **rate** of gross margin. (4) Compute **cost of goods sold** by subtracting the computed gross margin from sales. (5) Compute **ending inventory** by subtracting the computed cost of goods sold from the cost of goods available for sale. Application of the gross margin method is shown in **Exhibit 9–4.** Panel A gives the case data. Panel B shows the computations.

The gross margin method has two significant limitations: *(a)* the estimated gross margin rate, based on data from past period(s), may not appropriately reflect markup changes relating to the current or future periods; and *(b)* the average gross margin rate may include widely varying markup rates on different types of inventory. Most companies carry a number of different lines of merchandise, each having a different markup rate. A change during the period in the markup rate on one or more lines, or a shift in the relative quantities of each line sold, will change the **average** gross margin rate (markup). This affects the reliability of the results derived by the method.

When the gross margin method is applied in a situation that involves broad aggregations of inventory items with significantly different markup rates, the computations should be developed for each separate class. Then the estimate of the total inventory can be determined by summing the estimates for the separate classes.

---

[3] Ibid., chap. 7, statement 7, par. 14, states: "When substantial and unusual losses result from the application of this rule [LCM], it will frequently be desirable to disclose the amount of the loss **in the income statement as a charge separately identified from . . . cost of goods sold"** (emphasis supplied). The inventory allowance method provides for separate reporting of the holding loss. The direct inventory reduction method merges the holding loss with cost of goods sold automatically; therefore, to some accountants it does not appear compatible with this quotation from *ARB 43* when the difference is substantial in amount and unusual.

Exhibit 9–4
Gross margin method applied.

Panel A—Case Data:

1. Net sales revenue during the period, \$10,000.
2. Beginning inventory, \$5,000.
3. Purchases during the period, \$8,000.

(Items 1–3: Provided by the accounting records.)

4. Estimated gross rate, computed as a percent of sales, 40% (based on recent past performance).

Panel B—Gross Margin Method Applied:

	Known data		Computations*	Order of computation (step)
Net sales revenue (base amount)		\$10,000	100%	
Cost of goods sold:				
Beginning inventory ..	\$ 5,000			
Add: Purchases	8,000			
Goods available for sale	13,000			
Less: Ending inventory	?		(\$13,000 − \$6,000) = \$7,000	3
Cost of goods sold		?	60% × \$10,000 = \$6,000	2
Gross margin (estimated as percent of sales) ..	40%	?	40% × \$10,000 = \$4,000	1

* Given in statement of income format to place it in context. These simple computations can be arranged in numerous ways. The most abbreviated one is: \$13,000 − [\$10,000 × (1.00 − .40) = \$6,000] = \$7,000, ending inventory.

The gross margin method accommodates different inventory cost flow assumptions (FIFO, LIFO, average cost) because the computed gross margin rate is based implicitly on the cost method used by the company.

Some problems relating to the gross margin method give a **cost** percentage (cost of goods sold divided by sales) rather than the gross margin percentage (gross margin divided by sales). If either percentage is known, the other can be determined because **the two percentages must sum to 100 percent.** In the above example, the rate of gross margin is 40% of sales; therefore, the cost percentage is 60% (100% − 40%) of sales.

Also, the gross margin rate, or **markup,** may be given (i.e., in homework, CPA exams, etc.) as a percent of **selling price** (or sales) or cost (or cost of goods sold). In Exhibit 9–4, for example, markup was given as a percent of selling price (i.e., 40%). We can readily compute the needed ratio with formulas often used by retailers.

a. When markup on cost is known, it can be converted to markup on sales as follows:*

$$\text{Gross margin on selling price} = \frac{\text{Percentage markup on cost}}{100\% + \text{Percentage markup on cost}}$$

$$40\% = \frac{66\tfrac{2}{3}\%}{100\% + 66\tfrac{2}{3}\% = 1.66\tfrac{2}{3}\%}$$

b. When markup on sales is known, it can be converted to markup on cost as follows:

$$\text{Gross margin on cost} = \frac{\text{Percentage markup based on selling price}}{100\% - \text{Markup based on selling price}}$$

$$66\tfrac{2}{3}\% = \frac{40\%}{100\% - 40\% = 60\%}$$

* These formulas can be readily verified by starting with the relationship: Selling price − Cost = Gross margin. Many pocket calculators are programmed to make these computations.

Applications of the Gross Margin Method

The gross margin method is used in the following situations:

1. To test the reasonableness of an inventory valuation provided by some other person or determined by some other means such as a physical inventory count or from perpetual inventory records. For example, assume the company in Exhibit 9–4 submitted to an auditor an ending inventory valuation of $10,000. The gross margin method provides an approximation of $7,000, which suggests that the inventory should be examined because it may be overvalued.
2. To estimate the ending inventory for interim financial reports (e.g., monthly or quarterly statements) prepared during the year when *(a)* it is impractical to physically count the inventory and *(b)* a perpetual inventory system is not used.
3. To estimate the cost of inventory destroyed by a casualty, such as fire or storm. This application is limited to cases in which the accounting records are not destroyed because certain data from the accounts are essential. Valuation of inventory lost through casualty is necessary to *(a)* estimate its replacement cost to account for the casualty and *(b)* establish a basis for related insurance claims and/or income tax computation.
4. To develop budget estimates of cost of goods sold, gross margin, and inventory consistent with a sales revenue budget.

Retail Inventory Method to Estimate Inventory

The retail method of estimating inventory often is used by retail stores, particularly department stores, which sell a wide variety of items. In such situations, perpetual inventory procedures may be impractical, and it is unusual to take a complete physical inventory count more often than annually. The method also can be used for income tax purposes.

Two features of department store operation that make it possible to use the retail inventory method are: *(a)* items sold within a department often have essentially the same markup rate; and *(b)* articles purchased for resale are priced immediately and the sales prices are displayed.

The retail inventory method is not a quantity of goods (unit costs) method; rather **it is based only on dollar amounts.** The retail inventory method (1) uses both **retail value** (i.e., selling price) and **actual cost** data provided by the accounts to compute a **ratio of cost to retail** (referred to as the **cost ratio**), (2) calculates the ending inventory at retail value, and (3) converts that retail value to a cost value by using the computed cost ratio.

Application of the retail inventory method requires that internal records be kept to provide the following data:

1. Sales revenue.
2. Beginning inventory valued at **both** cost and retail.
3. Purchases during the period valued at **both** cost and retail.
4. Adjustments to the original retail price, such as additional markups, markup cancellations, markdowns, markdown cancellations, and employee discounts.
5. Data relating to other adjustments, such as interdepartmental transfers, returns, breakage, and damaged goods.

This method is similar to the gross margin method in that the inventory valuation is based on the **ratio of cost to selling price.** The gross margin method uses an estimate of the gross margin rate for the current period based upon historical cost. The retail inventory method, however, uses a computed cost ratio based on the **actual** relationship between cost and retail for the **current** period.

Because the cost and retail data required for the retail method are not estimates, the cost ratio is certain. However, because the computed cost ratio is an average (i.e., not specific to each kind of goods sold), the computed inventory amount is an estimate.

The retail inventory method is illustrated in **Exhibit 9–5.** Panel A presents the case data, and panel B shows the computation of the cost of ending inventory. In this exhibit, the amounts needed for computation of the cost ratio [i.e., goods available for sale at cost ($300,000)] are provided by the accounting records. The sales amount (i.e., $260,000 at retail) is taken from the Sales Revenue account and is subtracted from goods available for sale at retail (i.e., $300,000).

Exhibit 9–5
Retail inventory method illustrated, average cost.

Panel A—Case Data (from the accounting records):

1. Beginning inventory (January 1, 19B):
   a. At cost, $15,000.
   b. At retail, $25,000.
2. Purchases during January 19B:
   a. At cost, $195,000.
   b. At retail, $275,000.
3. Sales revenue, $260,000.

Panel B—Retail Method Applied:*

	At cost	At retail
Goods available for sale:		
Beginning inventory (January 1, 19B)	$ 15,000	$ 25,000
Purchases during January 19B	195,000	275,000
Total goods available for sale	$210,000	300,000
Cost ratio:		
$210,000 ÷ $300,000 = .70 (average, January 19B)		
Deduct January sales at retail		260,000
Ending inventory (January 31, 19B):		
At retail		$ 40,000
At cost ($40,000 × .70)	$ 28,000	

* Average cost basis used for this illustration.

The remainder (i.e., $40,000) is the **retail value** of ending inventory. It is multiplied by the computed cost ratio, .70 (i.e., $210,000 ÷ $300,000), to estimate ending inventory at cost, $28,000 (i.e., $40,000 × .70).

The validity of an inventory amount determined by the retail inventory method depends upon the accuracy with which changes in the original sales price are reported by the merchandising personnel to the accounting department. The importance of the markup/markdown distinction will be illustrated in the following applications.

Markups and Markdowns. The data used in Exhibit 9–5 assumed no changes in the **original** marked sales price. Frequently, the original sales price on some of the merchandise is raised or lowered, particularly at the end of the selling season or when replacement costs are changing. The retail method requires that a careful record be kept of all changes to the **original** sales price because these changes affect the inventory cost computation. To apply the retail inventory method, it is important to distinguish among the following terms:

Original sales price—sale price **first marked** on the merchandise.

Markup—the **original** or initial amount that the merchandise is marked up **above cost.** It is the difference between the purchase cost and the original sales price. It may be expressed as a dollar amount or a percent of either cost or sale price. Sometimes it is called **initial** markup or markon.

Additional markup—any increase in the sales price **above the original sales** price. Note that the original sales price is the base from which additional markup is measured.

Additional markup cancellations—cancellation of all, or some, of an **additional** markup. Additional markup less additional markup cancellations usually is called **net additional markup.**

Markdown—a reduction in the original sales price.

Markdown cancellation—after a reduction in the original sales price (i.e., after a markdown), an increase in the sales price that does not exceed the

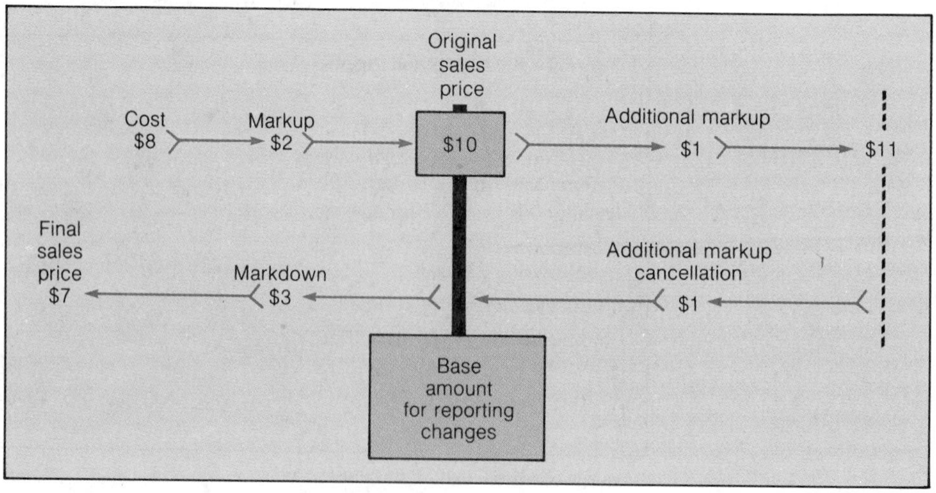

Exhibit 9–6
Data used to illustrate the retail inventory method.

	At cost	At retail
Inventory at beginning of period	$ 550	$ 900
Purchases during period	6,290	8,900
Additional markups during period		225
Additional markup cancellations during period		25
Markdowns during period		600
Markdown cancellations during period		100
Sales revenue for the period		8,500

original sales price (if it exceeds the original sales price, the increase is an additional markup).

The definitions may be illustrated by assuming an item that cost $8 is originally marked to sell at $10. It is subsequently marked to sell at $11, then marked down to $10, and finally reduced to sell at $7:

Application of the Retail Inventory Method

The retail inventory method can be applied in different ways to estimate the cost of ending inventory under different inventory cost flow assumptions. These applications are: *(a)* FIFO cost, LCM; *(b)* average cost, LCM; and *(c)* LIFO cost.

To illustrate the FIFO and average cost bases, the information given in **Exhibit 9–6** is used; it was provided by the accounting records at the end of the accounting period. Note that **units are not used, only dollars.**

Key Procedures Used in Applying the Retail Inventory Method

FIFO Cost Basis. To estimate the FIFO cost of ending inventory, the cost and retail amounts of the beginning inventory are **excluded** from the computation of the cost ratio because under FIFO the cost of the ending inventory is assumed to come from the purchases of the current period, not from the beginning inventory. Thus, this cost ratio effects the relationship of cost to retail values for current period purchases only.

Average Cost Basis. To estimate the cost of ending inventory on an average cost basis, the cost ratio is computed on total goods available for sale (i.e., the sum of beginning inventory plus purchases) because the cost of the ending inventory is assumed to come from the total goods available for sale during the period. Thus, this cost ratio reflects the relationship of cost to retail values for all inventory items available for sale, including the beginning inventory.

LCM Basis. To estimate the LCM of ending inventory, **the cost ratio excludes net markdowns.** The reason is that exclusion of net markdowns from computation of the **retail** value of goods available (markups and markdowns do not affect cost) causes the retail value of goods available (the denominator of the cost ratio) to be **higher** than if net markdowns were subtracted from goods available. In turn, this **decreases the cost ratio** and, thus, produces a **conservative** (i.e., LCM) estimate of the value of ending inventory. As indicated in **Exhibit**

9–7, LCM is applied to FIFO and average cost. **LCM is not applied to LIFO** under the retail method (discussed in Part B of this chapter).

Retail Method, FIFO with LCM Illustrated

When FIFO is used, the ending inventory is costed at the **current** period's unit costs; therefore, the costs in the beginning inventory are included in cost of goods sold rather than in the ending inventory. To accomplish this effect with the retail method, the beginning inventory is **excluded** from the computation of the cost ratio. The result will approximate the FIFO cost of the ending inventory. Then to approximate LCM, net markdowns are excluded from the cost ratio. The LCM computations on the FIFO basis are shown in Exhibit 9–7 (it also shows Average, LCM, discussed under "Retail Method, Average cost with LCM Illustrated"). FIFO, LCM and average cost, LCM are the conventional retail methods. For our purposes, FIFO, LCM is meant when the "retail method" is used without qualification. When the retail inventory method is used, cost of goods sold is computed in the usual manner (i.e., goods available for sale minus ending inventory at cost). Cost of goods sold is **not** computed by multiplying sales revenue by the cost ratio.

Retail Method, Average Cost with LCM Illustrated

Under the retail method, average cost basis, the cost ratio is derived by dividing total goods available for sale at **cost** by total goods available for sale at **retail;** both totals include the beginning inventory. Therefore, if the cost ratio is calcu-

Exhibit 9–7
Retail inventory method illustrated—Beta Corporation FIFO, LCM and Average, LCM).

	At cost		At retail
Goods available for sale:			
Beginning inventory	$ 550		$ 900
Purchases during period	6,290		8,900
Additional markups during period		$225	
Less: Additional markup cancellations		(25)	
Net additional markups			200
Markdowns		(600)	
Less: Markdown cancellations		100	
Net markdowns			(500)
Total goods available for sale	$6,840		9,500
Deduct:			
Sales			(8,500)
Ending inventory:			
At retail			$1,000
At approximate FIFO cost, LCM ($1,000 × .691[a])	$ 691		
At approximate average cost, LCM ($1,000 × .684[b])	$ 684		

Computation of cost ratios:

a. FIFO, LCM cost ratio: $\frac{\$6,290}{\$8,900 + \$225 - \$25} = .691$

Based on current period costs and retail values; beginning inventory excluded from numerator and denominator; net markdowns excluded from denominator in computation of cost ratio.

b. Average, LCM cost ratio: $\frac{\$6,290 + \$550}{\$8,900 + \$900 + \$225 - \$25} = .684$

Based on average costs and retail values; beginning inventory included in numerator and denominator; net markdowns excluded from denominator in computation of cost ratio.

lated on the basis of totals, including the beginning inventory, the retail method approximates average cost. To approximate LCM, net markdowns are excluded from the cost ratio. The LCM computation, average cost basis, for Beta Corporation is shown in Exhibit 9–7.

The retail inventory methods of estimating the LCM of inventory, shown in Exhibit 9–7, assume **markdowns** occur because the utility of the merchandise has declined. That is, the current purchase of identical new goods decreased or, stated differently, the goods had a replacement cost that was lower than historical cost. The decrease in replacement cost could result from such factors as obsolescence, spoilage, or excess supply. Therefore, to value the inventory at LCM, the **net markdowns** are omitted from computation of the **cost ratio;** this **lowers** the computed cost ratio because the denominator is higher than it would be if markdowns were included.

Notice in Exhibit 9–7 that the inventory amount at retail, $1,000, is the same under FIFO and average. However, the **cost ratios differ** because the cost ratio excludes the cost and retail prices of the beginning inventory under FIFO and includes these amounts under average cost.

Special Items Related to the Retail Inventory Method

Several factors may complicate computation of the ending inventory by the retail inventory method. In resolving these issues it is essential to protect the integrity of *(a)* the computed "normal" cost ratio and *(b)* the amount of ending inventory at retail. Six complicating factors, and the way each usually is treated, are as follows:

1. **Freight-in**—This expenditure adds to the **cost** of merchandise; therefore, it should be added to goods available for sale (or directly to purchases) at **cost** but not at retail.
2. **Purchase returns**—Because purchase returns, as distinguished from allowances, reduce the amount of goods available for sale, they should be deducted from goods available for sale at both **cost** and **retail.**
3. **Abnormal casualty losses** and missing merchandise arising from unusual or infrequent events (such as a fire or theft) should be deducted from goods available for sale at both **cost** and **retail** because they will not be sold; removal from both cost and retail eliminates their effect on the cost ratio as if they had not been purchased in the first place. The damaged merchandise should be set up in a special inventory account at its net realizable value.
4. **Sales Returns and Allowances**—Because this is a contra account to the Sales Revenue account, Sales Returns and Allowances should be deducted from gross sales. If the returned merchandise is placed back into inventory for resale, no change in the "At cost" column is needed because its cost is already properly included in the purchases amount. However, if the merchandise is not returned to inventory (because of damage, for example), then its cost should be deducted in the "At cost" column on the sales line after the cost ratio (because net sales has been reduced, the cost also should be reduced).
5. **Discounts to employees and favored customers**—These discounts result from selling merchandise below the "normal" sales price and are not

occasioned by market value decreases; therefore, they are different from markdowns. The amount of the discounts is computed as the number of units sold at a discount multiplied by the difference between the marked selling price and the discount price. Such discounts always must be **deducted below the cost ratio,** along with sales. This procedure is followed because they are concessions to the recipients and do not reflect general market value decreases. If such discounts were deducted in deriving the cost ratio, the cost ratio would be overstated. As a result, the ending inventory would be overstated.

6. **Normal spoilage** (including shrinkage and breakage)—This term is measured for retail inventory purposes as the number of units lost multiplied by the marked detail price. This amount must always be **deducted below the cost ratio,** along with sales, because the **expected** cost of normal spoilage implicitly is included in determining the selling price and it does not reflect market value changes. Deduction of normal spoilage in arriving at the cost ratio would overstate the cost ratio and the estimated cost of the ending inventory.

These six items are illustrated in **Exhibit 9–8** and are numbered in the order given above to facilitate study.

The preceding discussion of the retail inventory method assumed that the goods included in a single set of computations are similar in terms of their *(a)* markup percentage and *(b)* relative proportion of the total inventory of the

Exhibit 9–8
Retail inventory method (average cost, LCM), with special items illustrated.

		At cost	At retail
Goods available for sale:			
Beginning inventory		$ 6,050	$ 11,000
Purchases		57,120	102,000
Freight-in (1)		1,020	
Purchase returns (2)		(560)	(1,000)
Net additional markups			600
Casualty loss:* (3)			
At cost		(3,630)	
At retail			(6,600)
Total		$60,000	106,000
Cost ratio: $60,000 ÷ $106,000 = .566			
Deduct:			
Gross sales	$71,200		
Sales returns (merchandise returned to stock) (4)	1,200		
Net sales			(70,000)
Discounts to employees (5)			(200)
Normal spoilage (6)			(1,300)
Net markdowns			(4,500)
Ending inventory			
At retail			$ 30,000
At average cost, LCM ($30,000 × .566)		$16,980	

* The casualty loss could have been recorded as follows per the assumed fact situation:

Cash (from insurance company)	2,000	
Casualty loss (fire damage)	1,630	
Purchases (or cost of goods sold)		3,630

company. In individual departments this usually is the case; however, on a storewide basis it often is not. For example, three fourths of the total inventory may have a markup of 80% and one fourth of the inventory may have a markup of 50%. Therefore, the essential data should be accumulated for each sales department. The retail inventory computations then should be made on a **departmental** basis. The departmental inventories are summed to derive the total ending inventory.

PART B: RETAIL INVENTORY, DV LIFO, AND ADDITIONAL INVENTORY ISSUES

Retail Inventory Method, DV LIFO

This section discusses the application of LIFO by companies that also use the retail inventory method to estimate their inventory costs. This method is acceptable for interim financial reports, external financial reports, and for income tax purposes (subject to specific constraints in the tax regulations).[4]

The dollar value LIFO retail method (abbreviated, DV LIFO retail method) requires that the FIFO retail method (not LCM) be used. The results then are converted to a LIFO basis by applying the DV LIFO conversion process discussed in Chapter 8, Part B. The DV LIFO retail method is the only acceptable way to convert the retail data to a LIFO basis. This method requires that *(a)* a distinction be maintained between the base year inventory and subsequent incremental layers, and *(b)* the subsequent layers be costed by applying two different ratios: (1) a conversion price index and (2) a cost ratio for the year the layer was added.

Treasury regulations specify that "variety" stores using the DV LIFO retail method for income tax purposes must use an **internally computed price index.** On the other hand, retailers that qualify as "department" stores (as defined for tax purposes) may use a published external index. In the discussions and illustrations that follow, we will assume a **published price index** is used for conversion purposes.

The **DV LIFO retail method** is similar to DV LIFO (discussed in Chapter 8, Part B) because it uses dollars only (not units and unit costs) and an **inventory price index.** The DV LIFO retail method may be outlined as follows:

Step 1. For each period, first apply the **FIFO retail method without considering LCM** to compute that period's cost ratio. Thus, net markdowns must be included in the computation of the FIFO cost ratio, thereby ignoring the adjustment for LCM. The FIFO method, which excludes amounts of the beginning inventory from the cost ratio, **must** be used. The average cost method, which includes the amounts of the beginning inventory, **cannot** be used.

Step 2. At the end of each period, the **retail inventory** amount is converted to a **LIFO cost** basis by using the dollar value approach. The **beginning base year inventory** for the year of change to DV LIFO is the **ending**

[4] Income tax regulations have a significant impact upon financial accounting for inventory at LIFO cost.

FIFO (not LCM) inventory carried over from the year prior to the change.

At the end of each period, conversion of the **retail** inventory to a **LIFO cost** basis involves two distinct phases as follows:

Step 3. Compute an **internal** conversion price index (for variety stores) for the current period, or select an **external** price index for conversion purposes (by department stores). This step was illustrated in Chapter 8.

Step 4. Convert the ending inventory amount, **at retail,** to a LIFO cost basis by using (1) the conversion price index related to each layer of inventory and (2) the FIFO cost ratio of the period. The LIFO effect is attained by assuming the last layers of inventory purchased are the first layers sold.

Step 4 starts with the ending inventory, valued at retail, stated in the **current year's dollars.** This retail amount then is **restated** to retail in the **base year's dollars by dividing** it by the current year conversion price index. The result is the total ending inventory for the current year valued at retail but stated in base year dollars. This **base year retail value** then is identified in terms of the base layer and any additional layers added in years subsequent to the year of the base layer. Each layer then is converted to LIFO costs by multiplying the base year retail amount by (1) **its conversion price index** to convert base year retail dollar values into dollars of the year the layer was added and (2) **its cost ratio** to restate those retail dollar values to cost amounts. The sum of the costs of the various layers, as converted, provides the ending inventory at LIFO cost. This amount is reported on the statement of financial position and used on the statement of income to compute cost of goods sold.

Notice the logic in the DV LIFO retail inventory method. The current period's incremental inventory layer is first determined in terms of **base year retail prices.** The base year retail values for the current layer then must be converted to the **retail values** of the current year (i.e., by multiplying by the conversion price index) because the cost ratio of the current year is based on the relationship of the current year's costs and retail values. Finally, the **FIFO** cost ratio is applied, because the FIFO ratio considers **only** the current year's cost-to-retail relationship (an average cost ratio would include some elements from prior years).

Conversion computations will be illustrated using the data given in **Exhibit 9–9.** The computations are shown separately for each year in **Exhibits 9–10, 9–11, and 9–12.** The exhibits should be studied carefully because they are designed to be self-explanatory.

Notice in phase B (i.e., the bottom part) of Exhibit 9–10 that at the end of 19B, Gamma Corporation had two layers of inventory, with costs of $17,400 and $6,120 (total cost, $23,520). At the end of 19C (see Exhibit 9–11), Gamma Corporation had three layers of inventory, with costs of $17,400, $6,120, and $4,484 (total cost, $28,004). During 19D (see Exhibit 9–12), part of the 19C layer was liquidated, and at the end of 19D, Gamma Corporation had only two layers, with costs of $17,400 and $5,007 (total cost, $22,407). **Layers (or parts of layers) once liquidated are never restored. New layers are added at their actual cost.**

Exhibit 9–9
Data from inventory records to illustrate DV LIFO retail computation—Gamma Corporation.

1. The company has been using the retail inventory method (FIFO, not LCM) for *(a)* internal reporting and control purposes, *(b)* external reporting to shareholders, and *(c)* income tax purposes. Starting on January 1, 19B, the company decided to use the DV LIFO retail method for the latter two purposes.
2. The ending inventory at December 31, 19A, using the retail inventory method, FIFO basis (not LCM), was:
   At retail, $30,000
   At cost ($30,000 × cost ratio, .58), $17,400
3. Detailed data subsequent to December 31, 19A (date of the change):*

	19B		19C		19D	
	At cost	At retail	At cost	At retail	At cost	At retail
Purchases	$90,480	$147,000	$101,500	$169,000	$115,800	$186,800
Net additional markups		8,800		9,000		7,000
Net markdowns		5,000		6,000		4,000
Sales		140,000		162,800		197,800
4. Selected external price index (19A = 100)	102		106		110	

5. *Required:*
   a. Compute the ending inventory of Gamma Corporation for 19B, 19C, and 19D using the retail inventory method, FIFO (not LCM) to provide the data for conversion.
   b. Convert the FIFO retail results (computed in [2] above) to DV LIFO cost.

* A three-year period is used to illustrate initial adoption of LIFO, buildup of additional layers, and subsequent liquidation (in LIFO order) of parts of layers.

Based upon the LIFO costs shown in 19D in Exhibit 9–12 (beginning inventory, $28,004; ending inventory, $22,407), Gamma Corporation would make the following entries at the end of 19D (assuming a periodic inventory system and use of LIFO cost):

Cost of goods sold	28,004	
Inventory (beginning)		28,004

2. To record the 19D ending inventory:

Inventory (ending)	22,407	
Cost of goods sold		22,407

Evaluation of the Retail Inventory Method

The retail inventory method has been sponsored by the National Retail Merchants Association and approved by the Internal Revenue Service. Therefore, it has become an important method of inventory determination. Like the gross margin method, the retail inventory method is an approach for **estimating** the amount of the ending inventory and cost of goods sold. It can be used for both financial accounting and income tax purposes.

Because the retail inventory method provides only an estimate of the ending inventory, a physical inventory count should be taken at least annually as a check on the accuracy of the estimated inventory amounts. Differences between the inventory valuations based on the (1) physical inventory count and (2) retail inventory estimate should be analyzed because a difference may indicate

Exhibit 9–10
Application of DV LIFO retail—Gamma Corporation, 19B.

I. Computation of Ending Inventory at FIFO Cost:
a. Base layer (carried over from 19A): Retail $30,000 × .58 = Cost $17,400.
b. Computation of 19B ending FIFO inventory (not LCM):

	At FIFO cost		At retail		Cost ratio
Goods available for sale:					
Inventory, 1/1/19B (Exhibit 9–9)	$ 17,400		$ 30,000		
Purchases (Exhibit 9–9)	90,480		147,000		
Net additional markups (Exhibit 9–9)			8,800		
Net markdowns (Exhibit 9–9)			(5,000)		
Subtotal (excluding beginning inventory due to FIFO)	90,480	÷	150,800	=	.60
Total goods available for sale	$107,880		180,800		
Deduct: Sales			140,000		
Ending 19B inventory: At retail			$ 40,800		
At FIFO cost ($40,800 × .60)	$ 24,480				

II. Conversion to LIFO Cost (involves two phases):
Phase A—Conversion:
Use external price index for 19B = 1.02

Phase B—Conversion of ending inventory at retail ($40,800) to LIFO cost:

	At base year retail	Conversion price index	Cost ratio		DV LIFO cost
Ending inventory at retail converted to base year retail, $40,800 ÷ 1.02	$40,000				
Comprised of: Base inventory layer	$30,000	×1.00	×.58	=	$17,400
19B additional inventory layer	10,000*	×1.02	×.60	=	6,120
Ending 19B inventory at LIFO cost					$23,520

* Multiplication of this retail amount by the current year conversion price index restates it to current year prices (i.e., $10,000 × 1.02 = $10,200); multiplication of the result by the current year cost ratio restates this 19B layer to 19B cost (i.e., $10,200 × .60 = $6,120).

(a) inventory losses due to breakage, loss, or theft; *(b)* incorrect application of the retail method; *(c)* failure of departmental managers to correctly report markdowns, additional markups, or cancellations; *(d)* errors in the inventory records; *(e)* errors in the physical inventory; or *(f)* inventory manipulation. The inventory accounts, in case of error, must be changed to the actual count by using a correcting entry (discussed comprehensively in Chapter 24).

Uses of the Retail Inventory Method. The primary uses of the retail inventory method are as follows:

1. To provide estimates of inventory cost for interim periods (e.g., monthly or quarterly) when it is not practical to physically count the inventory and a perpetual inventory system is not used. The method provides estimated inventory valuations needed for interim statements, analyses, and purchasing policy considerations.
2. To provide a means for converting inventory amounts determined by a physical count of inventory, priced at retail, to a cost basis. To eliminate the necessity of marking the cost on the merchandise, or referring to invoices, some retail establishments, after physically counting the inven-

Exhibit 9–11
Application of DV LIFO Retail—Gamma Corporation, 19C.

I. Computation of Ending Inventory at FIFO Cost:

a. Beginning DV LIFO inventory carried over from end of 19B (from Exhibit 9–10):

	At base year retail	Conversion price index	Cost ratio		DV LIFO cost
Base inventory layer	$30,000	×1.00	×.58	=	$17,400
19B additional layer	10,000	×1.02	×.60	=	6,120
Total	$40,000				$23,520

b. Computation of 19C ending FIFO inventory (not LCM):

	At FIFO cost		At retail		Cost ratio
Goods available for sale:					
Inventory, 1/1/19C (Exhibit 9–10)	$ 24,480		$ 40,800		
Purchases (Exhibit 9–9)	101,500		169,000		
Net additional markups (Exhibit 9–9)			9,000		
Net markdowns (Exhibit 9–9)			(6,000)		
Subtotal (excluding beginning inventory)	101,500	÷	172,000	=	.59
Total goods available for sale	$125,980		212,800		
Deduct: Sales			162,800		
Ending 19C inventory: At retail			$ 50,000		
At FIFO cost ($50,000 × .59)	$ 29,500				

II. Conversion to LIFO Cost (involves two phases):

Phase A—Conversion price index for 19C =1.06

Phase B—Conversion of ending inventory at retail ($50,000) to LIFO cost:

	At base year retail	Conversion price index	Cost ratio		DV LIFO cost
Ending inventory at retail converted to base year retail, $50,000 ÷ 1.06	$47,170				
Comprised of: Base inventory layer	$30,000	×1.00	×.58	=	$17,400
19B inventory layer	10,000	×1.02	×.60	=	6,120
19C additional inventory layer	$ 7,170	×1.06	×.59	=	4,484
Ending 19C inventory at LIFO cost					$28,004

tory, extend the inventory sheets at retail. The retail value then is converted to cost by applying the retail inventory method without reference to the costs of individual items.

3. To provide a basis for **control** of inventory, purchases, theft, markdowns, and additional markups when neither a traditional periodic nor perpetual inventory system is used for these interim purposes.
4. To provide inventory cost data for external financial reports.
5. To provide inventory cost data for income tax purposes.
6. To provide a test of the overall reasonableness of a physical inventory costed in the normal manner.

Exhibit 9–12
Application of DV LIFO, retail—Gamma Corporation, 19D.

I. Computation of Ending Inventory at FIFO Cost:

a. Beginning DV LIFO inventory carried over from end of 19C (from Exhibit 9–11):

	At base year retail	Conversion price index	Cost ratio		DV LIFO cost
Base inventory layer (see note below)	$30,000	×1.00	×.58	=	$17,400
19B additional layer	10,000	×1.02	×.60	=	6,120
19C additional layer	7,170	×1.06	×.59	=	4,484
Total	$47,170				$28,004

b. Computation of 19D ending FIFO inventory (not LCM):

	At FIFO cost		At retail		Cost ratio
Goods available for sale:					
Inventory, 1/1/19D (Exhibit 9–11)	$ 29,500		$ 50,000		
Purchases (Exhibit 9–9)	115,800		186,800		
Net additional markups (Exhibit 9–9)			7,000		
Net markdowns (Exhibit 9–9)			(4,000)		
Subtotal (excluding beginning inventory	115,800	÷	189,800	=	.61
Total goods available for sale	$145,300		239,800		
Deduct: Sales			197,800		
Ending 19D inventory: At retail			$ 42,000		
At FIFO cost ($42,000 × .61)	$ 25,620				

II. Conversion to LIFO Cost (involves two phases):

Phase A—Conversion price index for 19D = 1.10

Phase B—Conversion of ending inventory at retail ($42,000) to LIFO cost:

	At base year retail	Conversion price index	Cost ratio		DV LIFO cost
Ending inventory at retail converted to base year retail, $42,000 ÷ 1.10	$38,182				
Comprised of: Base inventory layer	$30,000	×1.00	×.58	=	$17,400
19B inventory layer remaining	8,182*	×1.02	×.60	=	5,007
Ending 19D inventory at LIFO cost					$22,407

* After subtracting the base layer of $30,000, $8,182 remained. Therefore, all of the 19C layer was liquidated, and $8,182 of the 19B layer remained. Notice that layers are liquidated in **LIFO order** and that both the conversion price index and the cost ratio are **always** identified with the layer created at those ratios. **A layer once liquidated is never restored.**

Note: Preferably the base year should be set at 1.00 because subsequent changes are easier to assess. This can be done easily as follows:

Year	Index as given as computed	Conversion to Base Year Index 1.00
Base year	1.20	1.20 ÷ 1.20 = 1.00
1	1.32	1.32 ÷ 1.20 = 1.10
2	1.44	1.44 ÷ 1.20 = 1.20
3	1.50	1.50 ÷ 1.20 = 1.25

Additional Inventory Issues

This section concludes our discussion of inventories with four topics: *(a)* inventory valuation at current replacement cost, net realizable value, and selling price, *(b)* relative sales value method, *(c)* losses on purchase commitments, and *(d)* effects of inventory errors.

Inventory Valuation at Current Replacement Cost, Net Realizable Value, and Selling Price

Special inventory categories often contain items that are not in "new condition for resale" because they are damaged, shopworn, obsolete, defective, trade-ins, or repossessions. These inventory items must be assigned a reliable cost related to their **current condition.** In such cases, for inventory valuation purposes, **current replacement cost** is used as a substitute if it can be determined reliably in an established market for the items in their current condition.

Current replacement cost (RC) is defined for "used" inventory valuation purposes as the price for which the items can be **purchased** in their present condition. To illustrate a typical situation in which the current replacement cost can be determined reliably, assume ABC Appliance Company has on hand a repossessed TV set that cost $650. It was originally sold for $995 and was repossessed when $500 was owed on it by the customer. Also, assume that similar used TV sets could be purchased in the used market for $240. The repossessed item should be recorded as follows:

Inventory, repossessed merchandise (RC)	240	
Loss on repossession*	260	
Account receivable		500

* In some situations this may be a gain. If losses, such as the one above, are included in bad debt estimates, Allowance for doubtful accounts is debited.

Assume further that during the following year the repossessed TV set was sold for $270 cash. The entry to record the sale could be recorded as follows (assuming a perpetual inventory system):

Cash	270	
Sales revenue, repossessed merchandise		270
Cost of goods sold (RC)	240	
Inventory, repossessed merchandise		240

When the RC cannot be determined reliably, such items should be valued for inventory purposes at their **estimated net realizable value** (NRV). NRV is defined for inventory valuation purposes as the estimated **sale price** less all costs expected to be incurred in *(a)* preparing for sale and *(b)* selling. To illustrate accounting for inventory at NRV when replacement cost cannot be determined reliably, assume Acme Company suffered fire damages to 100 units of its regular inventory. Item W, which originally cost $10 per unit (as reflected in the perpetual inventory records), was marked to sell for $18 per unit. The RC of each item W in its present condition cannot be determined reliably because no established used market exists. Therefore, the company should value item W for inventory purposes at its NRV. Acme Company estimated that after cleaning the items and making repairs, they would sell for $7 per unit; the estimated cost of the repairs is $150, and estimated selling costs is 20% of the new selling price. Based on these data, the total inventory valuation for item W was computed as follows:

Estimated sale price (100 × $7)		$ 700
Less: Estimated cost to repair	$150	
Estimated selling costs ($700 × 20%)	140	(290)
NRV for inventory		$ 410

Assuming no insurance indemnity, the casualty loss and the inventory would be recorded as follows (assuming a perpetual inventory system):

Inventory, damaged merchandise (NRV)	410	
Casualty loss, fire damage	590	
Inventory (regular merchandise) (100 × $10)		1,000

Inventories Valued at Selling Price

Under unusual circumstances, an inventory item may be valued at selling price. The GAAP specification is as follows:

> It is generally recognized that income accrues only at the time of sale, and that gains may not be anticipated by reflecting assets at their current sales prices. For certain articles, however, exceptions are permissible. Inventories of [commodities for which] there is an effective government-controlled market at a fixed monetary value are ordinarily reflected at selling prices. A similar treatment is not uncommon for inventories representing agricultural, mineral, and other products, units of which are interchangeable and have an immediate marketability at quoted prices and for which appropriate costs may be difficult to obtain. Where such inventories are stated at sales prices, they should of course be reduced by expenditures to be incurred in disposal, and the use of such basis should be fully disclosed in the financial statements.[5]

Under the **selling price method,** when a **decrease** in selling price occurs, a **holding loss** is reported; when an **increase** in selling price occurs, a **holding gain** is reported. Thus, income includes the gross margin and the holding gain or loss for the period. Assume the following simplified data:

Year	Sales	Purchases at cost	Ending inventory at selling price	Expenses
19A	$ -0-	$1,000	$1,750	$300
19B	1,700	-0-	-0-	300

The financial statements with inventory valued at selling price would appear as shown below; the cost basis statement data are shown for comparison.

	Cost basis		Selling price basis	
	19A	19B	19A	19B
Statement of financial position:				
Inventory	$1,000	-0-	$1,750	-0-
Statement of income:				
Sales revenue	$ -0-	$ 1,700	$ -0-	$ 1,700
Cost of goods sold	-0-	(1,000)	-0-	(1,750)
Expenses	(300)	(300)	(300)	(300)
Holding gain	-0-	-0-	750*	-0-
Net income (loss)	$ (300)	$ 400	$ 450	$ (350)

* $1,750 − $1,000 = $750.

[5] Ibid., chap. 4, statement 9.

Relative Sales Value Method

Two or more different kinds of inventory items may be purchased for a lump sum. A separate cost for each kind is required for accounting purposes. Thus, the total joint cost must be apportioned to individual kinds of items. The apportionment of the total cost should be related to the economic utility of each kind or group of items. Because the **sales value** of a particular item may be a reasonable indication of its relative utility, apportionment of the joint cost of such "basket purchases" usually is made on the basis of the **relative sales value** of the several items. Also, additional joint costs incurred subsequent to purchase may be allocated on the basis of relative sales value.

Assume a packing plant purchased 1,000 bushels of apples (ungraded) for $2,000. After purchase, the apples were sorted into three grades at a cost of $70, with the following results: grade A, 200 bushels; grade B, 300 bushels; and grade C, 500 bushels. The sorted apples were selling at the following prices per unit: grade A, $5; grade B, $4; and grade C, $2.50. The cost apportionment may be made as shown in **Exhibit 9–13.**

In joint cost allocations, quantities lost due to shrinkage or spoilage should be assigned no cost, thus increasing the unit cost for the remaining units. In the case of real estate developments, improvements such as streets and parks are apportioned to the cost of the salable areas as joint costs.

Losses on Purchase Commitments

To "lock in" specific prices for needed items of inventory, companies often contract with a supplier to purchase a specified **quantity** of materials during a future **period** at an agreed **unit cost.** Some purchase commitments (contracts) are subject to revision or cancellation before the end of the contract period, whereas others are not. Each case requires different accounting and reporting procedures.

In the case of purchase contracts **subject to revision or cancellation** where a future loss is **possible** and the amount of the commitment can be **reasonably**

Exhibit 9–13
Relative sales value method applied.

Grade	Quantity (bushels)	Unit sales price	Total sales value	Fraction of total sales value	Apportioned cost
A	200	$5.00	$1,000	$1,000/$3,450	$ 600*
B	300	4.00	1,200	1,200/ 3,450	720
C	500	2.50	1,250	1,250/ 3,450	750
	1,000		$3,450		$2,070

* ($1,000 ÷ $3,450) × $2,070 = $600. Or alternatively, $2,070 ÷ $3,450 = 60%; $1,000 × 60% = $600; $1,200 × 60% = $720; and $1,250 × 60% = $750.

Entry indicated (assuming a perpetual inventory system:

Inventory—grade A apples, 200 units	600	
Inventory—grade B apples, 300 units	720	
Inventory—grade C apples, 500 units	750	
Cash		2,070

estimated, and is **material** in amount, the full-disclosure principle requires note disclosure of the contingency. To illustrate, XY Company entered into a purchase contract during October 19J that stated: "During 19K, 50,000 units of Material X will be purchased at $5 each (i.e., $250,000). On 60 days' notice, this contract is subject to revision or cancellation by either party." If the current cost of the inventory (under contract for purchase) at the end of 19J was $240,000, a disclosure note similar to the following should be included in the financial statements for 19J:

> Note 1. At the end of 19J, a contract was in effect that will require the Company to pay $250,000 for materials during 19K. The purchase contract can be revised or canceled upon 60 days' notice by either party. At the end of 19J, the materials under contract had a current replacement cost of $240,000.

This note should give the relevant aspects of the contingency. No entry is required for the $10,000 (i.e., $250,000 − $240,000) contingent loss because the loss is not **probable** (contingencies are discussed in Chapter 14).

When purchase contracts are **not subject to revision or cancellation,** and when a loss is **probable** and the loss amount can be **reasonably estimated** and is **material** in amount, the loss and related liability should be **recorded** in the accounts and reported in the financial statements. In the above example, assume the $240,000 current replacement cost is measured reliably and is probable. In such cases, the loss on the purchase commitment should be recorded as follows:

Estimated loss on purchase commitment ($250,000 − $240,000)	10,000	
Estimated liability on noncancellable purchase commitment		10,000

The estimated loss is reported on the 19J statement of income, and the liability is reported on the statement of financial position.[6] When the goods are acquired in 19K, Merchandise Inventory (or Purchases) is debited at the current replacement cost and the estimated liability account is debited. Assume the above materials have a replacement cost at date of delivery of $235,000. The purchase entry would be:

Materials inventory (or purchases)	235,000	
Estimated liability on noncancellable purchase commitment	10,000	
Loss on purchase contract	5,000	
Cash		250,000

This treatment records the loss in the period when it became probable and is consistent with the provisions of *ARB 43*, chap. 4, statement 10, and *FASB Standard 5*, "Accounting for Contingencies" (see Chapter 14).

Effects of Inventory Errors

Errors in measuring inventory quantities or values occur because of the size of the inventory, the number of different kinds of items, their physical characteris-

---

[6] Even if no loss is probable, *FASB Standard 47*, "Disclosure of Long-Term Obligations," requires disclosure, either in a note or by way of entries in the accounts, as appropriate, of the *(a)* nature and term of the obligation, *(b)* fixed amount of the obligation, and *(c)* amounts purchased to date under the obligation.

tics, and their means of storage. This section discusses the effect of inventory errors on the financial statements. A periodic inventory system is used.

Overstatement of the **ending** inventory overstates pretax income by the same amount. Understatement of the ending inventory understates pretax income by the same amount. Conversely, an overstatement of the **beginning** inventory understates pretax income, and an understatement of the beginning inventory overstates pretax income. Overstatement of purchases (with correct measurement of beginning and ending inventories) overstates cost of goods sold and understates pretax income by the same amount.

Inventory overstatement or understatement will cause errors in the statement of income and statement of financial position (SFP). Often the inventory amount may not be consistent with the amounts recorded in accounts payable (i.e., credit sales). The inventory and purchases errors discussed below are common.[7] **Exhibit 9–14,** using the periodic inventory system, shows the pretax effects of such errors.

Ending inventory **overstated:**

Case A. Ending inventory is overstated but the purchases amount is correct. This error causes cost of goods sold to be understated and both gross margin and income to be overstated by the same amount.

Case B. Ending inventory and purchases are both overstated by the same amount. These two errors go in the opposite direction; therefore, gross margin and income are correct. However, on the SFP, both inventory and accounts payable are overstated by the same amount.

Exhibit 9–14

Effects of inventory errors illustrated—Periodic Inventory System (in thousand $).

	Statement of income								SFP
		Cost of goods sold							Asset
	Sales –	(BI +	PUR –	EI =	CGS) =	GM –	EXP =	NI	EI
Correct →	10	3	12	8	7	3	1	2	8
Error									
A. EI, 1*	10	3	12	9*	6†	4*	1	3*	9*
B. EI and PUR, 1*	10	3	13*	9*	7	3	1	2	9*
C. EI, 1†	10	3	12	7†	8*	2†	1	1†	7†
D. EI & PUR, 1†	10	3	11†	7†	7	3	1	2	7†
E. BI, 1*	10	4*	12	8	8*	2†	1	1†	8
F. BI, 1†	10	2†	12	8	6†	4*	1	3*	8

* Overstated.
† Understated.
Abbreviations: BI = beginning inventory; PUR = purchases; EI = ending inventory; GM = gross margin; EXP = expenses; NI = net income; CGS = cost of goods sold.

[7] Some of the effects of these errors will differ depending upon the cost flow method used, that is, FIFO, LIFO, etc.

Ending inventory **understated:**

Case C. Ending inventory is understated, but total purchases is correct. This error causes cost of goods sold to be overstated and both gross margin and income to be understated by the same amount.
Case D. Ending inventory and purchases are both understated by the same amount. These two errors have opposite effects; therefore, gross margin and income are correct. However, on the SFP, both inventory and accounts payable are understated by the same amount.

Errors similar to those illustrated above not only cause the financial statements for the current period to be in error but also frequently cause future amounts to be wrong. That is, an error in the ending inventory, if not corrected, will cause a **counterbalancing** error in the next period because the ending and beginning inventories have opposite effects on income amounts of the two consecutive periods. Cases E and F in Exhibit 9–14 show the effects of errors in the beginning inventory. Notice that these effects are the opposite of Cases A and C.

Keep in mind that the inventory figure carries over; for example, ending inventory at 12/31/X2 becomes the beginning inventory on 1/1/X3. If ending inventory is overstated in one year, then beginning inventory is overstated by the same amount for the next year, if no correction is made. So, if net income for **19X2** is **overstated** by $2,000 because 19X2 ending inventory was overstated by $2,000, net income for **19X3** will be **understated** by $2,000, but the **combined** income for the two-year time span of 19X2 and 19X3 will be **correct;** however, cost of goods sold and net income for each year are incorrect by the same amount. A comprehensive discussion of accounting errors is provided in Chapter 24.

A related issue to inventory errors is the effect of errors made in determining sales revenue. There are two types of errors (that carry over to the next accounting period) in sales revenue—sales price and sales quantity mistakes. An error in sales price only (one not involving units sold) has a direct effect (equal amount) on pretax income. In contrast, an error that involves units sold (one not involving unit sales prices) affects cost of goods sold for one amount and income for another amount.

Summary

The cost and matching principles dominate in accounting for inventories. However, because of practical implementation problems, inventories are sometimes estimated and certain departures from the cost principle are required or permitted by GAAP. Lower of cost or market is required to provide a conservative inventory valuation when inventory items can be currently replaced at less than their original recorded cost. Inventory estimating methods, such as the gross margin and the retail inventory methods, provide estimated rather than actual inventory costs. The DV LIFO inventory method is the only way to convert a FIFO retail inventory cost to a LIFO basis. It starts with a FIFO (not LCM) amount and then applies a price index to compute an estimated DV LIFO ending inventory amount.

QUESTIONS

1. Why is the LCM rule applied to inventory valuation?
2. Why are the "ceiling" and "floor" values used in determining "market" in the application of the LCM concept?
3. What is the holding loss (gain) recognized using the LCM, inventory allowance method, for each of the following years:

	Cost	Market
19A Beginning inventory	$ -0-	$ -0-
Ending inventory	12,000	14,000
19B Ending inventory	15,000	13,000
19C Ending inventory	18,000	17,000
19D Ending inventory	20,000	16,000
19E Ending inventory	22,000	23,000

4. What basic assumption is implicit in the gross margin method?
5. Approximate the valuation of the ending inventory assuming the following data are available:

Cost of goods available for sale	$170,000
Sales	150,000
Gross margin rate (on sales)	30%

6. Assume the gross margin rate in (5) is based on cost of goods sold. Approximate the valuation of the ending inventory.
7. Distinguish between *(a)* gross margin rate on sales, *(b)* gross margin percentage on cost of goods sold, *(c)* cost percentage, *(d)* markup on cost, and *(e)* markup on sales.
8. List four uses of the gross margin method.
9. Why is it frequently desirable to apply the gross margin method by classes of merchandise?
10. Explain the basic approach of the retail method of estimating inventories (FIFO and Average). What data must be accumulated in order to apply the retail method?
11. The ending inventory estimated by the retail inventory method was $90,000. A physical inventory of the merchandise on hand extended at retail showed $75,000. Suggest possible reasons for the discrepancy.
12. What are the primary uses of the retail method of estimating inventories?
13. When are markdowns and markdown cancellations excluded in computing the cost ratio in the retail inventory method?
14. Explain the difference between the FIFO cost, LCM and the average cost, LCM, methods under the retail method of estimating inventories.
15. What are two primary differences between the retail inventory method under FIFO and average cost versus the DV LIFO retail method?
16. Explain why the FIFO (not LCM) retail cost ratio must be used in combination with DV LIFO retail to attain LIFO retail results.
17. When dollar value LIFO retail is adopted, why must the ending inventory of the period prior to the base year often be recomputed?
18. What are the primary differences and limitations of the quantity of goods LIFO method versus the DV LIFO method?
19. Why does a change to LIFO present a greater accounting problem than a change from LIFO? How is this problem resolved? What accounting principle governs the extent of disclosure of the effect of the change?

20. What are the basic features of the DV LIFO method?
21. What is indexing in the context of applying the DV LIFO approach? When can an external, rather than an internal, price index be used?
22. How should damaged or obsolete merchandise on hand at the end of the period be valued for inventory purposes?
23. What types of inventory does GAAP allow to be measured at selling price in excess of cost?
24. What are the basic assumptions underlying the relative sales value method when used in allocating costs for inventory purposes?
25. Briefly outline the accounting and reporting of losses on purchase commitments when *(a)* the purchase contract is subject to revision or cancellation and *(b)* it is noncancellable and a loss is probable.
26. Explain the effect of each of the following errors in the ending inventory of a retail business (ignore income taxes):
    a. Incorrectly excluded 300 units of commodity C, valued at $3 per unit, from the ending inventory; the purchase was recorded.
    b. Incorrectly excluded 400 units of commodity D, valued at $4 per unit, from the ending inventory; the purchase was not recorded.
    c. Incorrectly included 100 units of commodity A, valued at $5 per unit, in the ending inventory; the purchase was recorded.
    d. Incorrectly included 200 units of commodity B, valued at $3 per unit, in the ending inventory; the purchase was not recorded.
27. Assume that inventory, cost, $1,000, was sold on credit for $1,200 and held pending pickup by the customer. The goods were incorrectly included in the ending inventory. What is the pretax effect of this error if *(a)* the sale was not recorded? *(b)* the sale was correctly recorded? Assume that a periodic inventory system is used.

Part A: Exercises 9–1 to 9–15

E 9–1 (LCM; Maximum and Minimum)

Clark Company had 1,000 units of product A in inventory at the end of the accounting period. The unit cost was $60; estimated distribution costs, $3 per unit; and the "normal" profit is $4 per unit. Compute the unit valuation of the inventory based on LCM under each separate case listed below.

Case	Anticipated sales price	Current replacement cost
a	$61	$53
b	66	57
c	68	61
d	50	44
e	59	57
f	56	50
g	73	59
h	65	61
i	70	62
j	60	58

E 9–2 (LCM; Maximum and Minimum)

The management of Tarry Hardware Company has taken the position that under the LCM procedure the two items listed below should be reported in the ending inventory at $16,600 (total). Do you agree? If not, indicate the correct inventory valuation by item. Show computations.

"Handyman" edgers: 300 on hand; cost, $22 each; replacement cost, $16; estimated sales price, $30; estimated distribution cost, $3 each; and normal profit, 10% of the sales price.

"Handyman" hedge clippers: 200 on hand; cost, $50 each; replacement cost, $36 each; estimated sales price, $90; estimated distribution cost, $28; and normal profit, 20% of the sales price.

E 9–3 (LCM; Compute the Holding Gain or Loss)

The records of Volatility Company showed the following inventory data:

		Cost	Market
19A	Beginning inventory	$ -0-	$ -0-
19A	Ending inventory	5,000	6,000
19B	Ending inventory	8,000	7,500
19C	Ending inventory	4,000	3,000
19D	Ending inventory	12,000	10,000
19E	Ending inventory	8,000	7,500
19F	Ending inventory	10,000	11,000

Required:

Compute the holding gain or loss recognized by Volatility in each year due to the use of the LCM, inventory allowance method.

E 9–4 (LCM; Direct and Allowances Compared)

The inventories for the years 19A and 19B are shown below for Boston Corporation.

Inventory date	Original cost	LCM	Difference
1/1/19A	$6,000	$6,000	-0-
12/31/19A	7,000	6,600	$400
12/31/19B	9,000	9,000	-0-

Required:

1. Give the journal entries to apply the LCM procedure to the inventories for 19A and 19B assuming the company uses the inventory allowance method and periodic inventory procedures.
2. Give the journal entries to apply the LCM procedure to the inventories for 19A and 19B assuming the company uses the direct inventory reduction method and periodic inventory procedures.
3. What are the primary advantages and disadvantages of each method?

E 9–5 (Gross Margin Method; Estimate the Ending Inventory)

You are auditing the records of Franklin Corporation. A physical inventory has been taken by the company under your observation. However, the valuation extensions have not been completed. The records of the company provide the following data: sales, $315,000 (gross); return sales, $5,000 (returned to stock); purchases (gross), $155,000; beginning inventory, $50,000; freight-in, $5,000; and purchase returns and allowances, $2,000. The gross margin last period was 35% of net sales; you anticipate that it will be 40% for the year under audit.

Required:

Estimate the cost of the ending inventory using the gross margin method. Show computations.

E 9–6 (Gross Margin Method; Results Evaluated)

The records of Shain Company provided the following data for January for two products sold:

	Product A	Product B
Beginning inventory, January 1	$ 50,000	$ 60,000
Purchases during January	147,000	180,000
Freight on purchases	3,000	4,000
Sales revenue during January	300,000	400,000

The gross margin rates on sales for the prior year were: company overall, 45%; product A, 42%; and Product B, 47%.

Required:

1. Estimate the cost of the ending inventory separately by products and in the aggregate.
2. Under what conditions would one of your responses to (1) above be suspect?

E 9–7 (Gross Margin Method; Estimate a Fire Loss)

On November 15, 19A, a fire destroyed Young Corporation's warehouse where Product A was stored. It is estimated that $10,000 can be realized from sale of usable damaged inventory. The accounting records concerning Product A reveal:

Inventory at 11/1/19A	$120,000
Purchases from 11/1/19A to 11/15/19A	140,000
Net sales from 11/1/19A to 11/15/19A	220,000

Based on recent history the gross margin has averaged 40% of net sales.

Required:

Prepare a schedule to calculate the estimated loss of inventory based on the gross margin method. Show supporting computations. (AICPA adapted)

E 9–8 (Gross Margin Method; Markup on Sales and Cost Compared)

Assume the following data for Burke Company for a particular period:

Sales revenue	$120,000
Beginning inventory	16,000
Purchases	80,000

Required:

For each of the separate situations below, estimate the ending inventory (round all ratios to three decimal places):

a. Markup is 50% on cost.
b. Markup is 60% on sales.
c. Markup is 30% on cost.
d. Markup is 40% on sales.
e. Markup is 57% on cost.

E 9–9 (Gross Margin Method; Estimate Inventory Loss; Markup on Sales versus Costs)

The books of Leigh Company provided the following information:

Inventory, January 1	$ 10,000
Purchases to July 19	100,000
Net sales to July 19	85,000

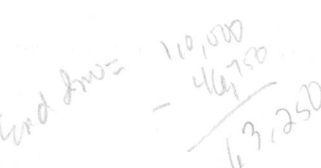

Before opening for business on July 20, the assets of the company were totally destroyed by fire. The insurance company adjuster found that the average rate of gross margin for the past few years had been 45%.

Required (round all ratios to two decimal places):
What was the approximate value of the inventory destroyed assuming the gross margin percentage given was based on (1) sales and (2) cost of goods sold?

E 9–10 **(Retail Inventory Method: Average LCM)**
Dan's Clothing Store values its inventory using the retail inventory method at the lower of average cost or market. The following data are available for the month of June 19A:

	Cost	Selling price
Inventory, June 1	$ 53,800	$ 80,000
Markdowns		21,000
Markups		29,000
Markdown cancellations		10,000
Markup cancellations		9,000
Purchases	173,200	223,600
Sales		250,000
Purchase returns and allowances	3,000	3,600
Sales returns and allowances		10,000

Required:
Prepare a schedule to compute the estimated inventory at June 30, 19A, at the lower of average cost or market using the retail inventory method. Round the cost ratio to three decimals. (AICPA adapted)

E 9–11 **(Retail Inventory Method; FIFO and Average)**
Chic Department Store uses the retail method of inventory. At the end of June, the records of the company provided the following information:

Purchases during June: at cost, $250,000; at retail, $430,000.
Sales during June: $350,000.
Inventory, June 1: at cost, $40,000; at retail, $75,000.

Required:
Estimate the ending inventory and cost of goods sold for June assuming *(a)* FIFO cost basis and *(b)* average cost basis. Show all computations (round cost ratios to two decimals).

E 9–12 **(Retail Inventory Method; FIFO and Average)**
The records of Blue Retailers showed the following data for January: beginning inventory at cost, $20,000, and $26,000 at selling price; purchases at cost, $150,000, and $300,000 at selling price; gross sales, $310,000; return sales, $6,000 (returned to stock); purchase returns at cost, $4,000, and $7,000 at selling price; and freight-in, $7,000.

Required (round all cost ratios to three decimal places):
Determine the approximate valuation of the ending inventory using the retail inventory method *(a)* at average cost and *(b)* at FIFO. Show all computations. Which is lower? What may have accounted for the result? Was LCM applied implicitly by Blue? If yes, explain.

E 9–13 **(Retail Inventory Method; FIFO and Average; LCM)**
Use the retail inventory method to estimate the ending inventory *(a)* at average cost, LCM and *(b)* FIFO cost, LCM for Post Corporation based on the following data (round all cost ratios to three decimal places):

	At cost	At retail
Beginning inventory	$ 91,000	$150,000
Purchases	330,000	561,000
Purchases returned	6,000	10,000
Freight-in	8,000	
Additional markups		12,000
Additional markup cancellations		5,000
Markdowns		9,000
Markdown cancellations		2,000
Sales		540,000
Sales returned (and restored to inventory)		6,000

How is LCM introduced into the computations? Explain the logic of this procedure. Will LCM always produce a lower inventory cost estimate under the retail method than FIFO or average without LCM?

E 9–14 (Retail Inventory Method; Average LCM; Discrepancy)

Franklin Retail Company has just completed the annual physical inventory, which involved counting the goods on hand and then pricing them at selling prices. The inventory valuation derived in this manner amounted to $106,000. The records of the company provided the following data: Beginning inventory, $80,000 at retail, and $50,000 at cost; purchases (including freight-in and returns), $750,000 at retail, and $500,000 at cost; additional markups, $20,000; additional markup cancellations, $8,000; gross sales, $733,000; return sales (restored to inventory), $13,000; and markdowns, $10,000.

Required (round all costs ratios to three decimal places):

1. Estimate the cost of the ending inventory assuming average cost, LCM.
2. Note any discrepancies and give possible reasons for them.

E 9–15 (Retail Inventory Method; LCM with Shrinkage)

Boley Department Store uses the retail inventory method. Information relating to the computation of inventory for 19B is as follows:

	At cost	At retail
Beginning inventory	$ 40,000	$ 80,000
Sales		600,000
Purchases	300,000	590,000
Freight on purchases	8,000	
Markups		60,000
Markup cancellations		10,000
Markdowns		25,000
Markdown cancellations		5,000

Estimated normal shrinkage is 1% of sales.

Required (round all cost ratios to three decimal places):

Calculate the estimated ending inventory for 19B at the lower of average cost or market. Show supporting calculations. (AICPA adapted)

Part B: Exercises 9–16 to 9–27

E 9–16 (DV LIFO Retail; Entry to Restate FIFO)

Anderson Company used the retail inventory method for a number of years. On January 1, 19C, the company changed to DV LIFO retail for external reporting and income tax purposes. The following data were provided by the inventory records for the accounting year ended December 31, 19B:

	At cost	At retail
January 1, 19B, inventory	$48,000	$ 95,000
Purchases	80,000	170,000
Net additional markups		4,000
Net markdowns		8,000
Sales revenue		190,000

Required (round all cost ratios to three decimal places):

1. Compute the December 31, 19B, retail inventory results assuming: *(a)* Average, LCM; *(b)* FIFO, LCM; and *(c)* FIFO.
2. Give the adjusting entry to restate the inventory to FIFO (not LCM) to be used as the base inventory for the DV LIFO retail method assuming Anderson had been using: *(a)* Average, LCM; *(b)* FIFO, LCM.

E 9–17 **(DV LIFO Retail; Conversion from FIFO)**

Riley Retail Store used the retail inventory method, determined on the average cost, LCM basis, for a number of years for all purposes. On January 1, 19D, the company changed to DV LIFO retail for external reporting and income tax purposes, but retained average cost, LCM, for internal purposes.

At the end of 19C and 19D, the retail inventory computations (average, LCM) for internal purposes were as shown below.

	Year 19C		Year 19D	
	At cost	At retail	At cost	At retail
Beginning inventory, January 1	$ 17,000	$ 30,000	$ 28,000	$ 50,000
Purchases	151,000	268,000	180,000	321,789
Net additional markups		2,000		3,000
Total	$168,000	300,000	$208,000	374,789
Cost ratio ($168,000 ÷ $300,000 = .56)	.56		.55	
Sales		(245,000)		(305,789)
Net markdowns		(5,000)		(9,000)
Inventory, December 31:				
At retail		$ 50,000		$ 60,000
At cost (average, LCM)	$ 28,000		$ 33,000	

Conversion price indexes: 12/31/19C, 125; and 12/31/19D, 140.

Required (round all cost ratios to two decimal places):

1. Compute the inventory values (at cost and at retail) that should be used as the base inventory and the ending inventory for 19D for conversion purposes. Why are the above inventory values not appropriate for this purpose?
2. Convert the FIFO retail inventory results, computed in (1) above, to the DV LIFO retail basis for the external reports and income tax use at the end of 19D.
3. Complete the following tabulation for 19D:

	Year 19D		
	Average, LCM	FIFO	DV LIFO
Sales revenue	$_____	$_____	$_____
Cost of goods sold:			
Beginning inventory	_____	_____	_____
Purchases	_____	_____	_____
Total	_____	_____	_____
Ending inventory	_____	_____	_____
Cost of goods sold	_____	_____	_____
Gross margin	_____	_____	_____

E 9–18 (DV LIFO Retail; Conversion from FIFO)

Manne Company uses FIFO retail for internal purposes and the DV LIFO retail method to convert those results for external reporting and for income tax purposes (starting January 1, 19B). The base year, 19A, index is 100%.

The following data were provided by the inventory records for the year ended December 31, 19B:

	At cost	At retail
January 1, 19B, base inventory (carried over from 19A)	$ 6,000	$10,000
Data at end of 19B:		
Sales revenue (net of returns)		80,000
Purchases (net of returns)	65,000	85,000
Net additional markups		7,000
Net markdowns		3,000
Total administrative and selling expenses	10,000	

Assume the conversion price index numbers are: December 31, 19A, 120; and December 31, 19B, 126. Average income tax rate, 35%.

Required (round all cost ratios to three decimal places):

1. Compute the FIFO retail inventory results that would be used for internal purposes at the end of 19B.
2. Convert the FIFO retail inventory results to a DV LIFO basis for external reporting and income tax purposes.
3. Prepare a statement of income using the following format:

	Year 19B	
	FIFO basis	LIFO basis
Sales revenue	$____	$____
Less expenses:		
Cost of goods sold:		
Beginning inventory	____	____
Purchases	____	____
Total	____	____
Ending inventory	____	____
Cost of goods sold	____	____
Administrative and selling expenses	____	____
Total expenses	____	____
Pretax income	____	____
Income taxes	____	____
Net income	____	____

E 9–19 (Net Realizable Value of Damaged Goods; Entries)

A fire damaged some of the merchandise held for sale by AAA Appliance Company. Seven television sets and six stereo sets were damaged. They were not covered by insurance. The sets will be repaired and sold as used sets. Data are as follows:

	Per set	
	Television	Stereo
Inventory (at cost)	$400	$200
Estimated cost to repair	50	30
Estimated cost to sell	20	20
Estimated sales price	200	90

Required:

1. Compute the appropriate inventory net realizable value for each set.
2. Give the separate entries to record the damaged merchandise inventory for the television and stereo sets. Assume a perpetual inventory system.

3. Give the entries to record the subsequent repair of the television sets and the stereo sets (credit cash).
4. Give the entry to record sale for cash of two television sets and one stereo set; credit distribution costs in the entry to record the sale (it will be necessary to record payment of the distribution costs in a separate entry). Assume the actual sales prices equaled the estimated sales prices.

E 9–20 (Relative Sales Value Method)

Tough Nut, Inc., purchased 1,000 bags of pecans that cost $4,200. In addition, the company incurred $300 for transportation and grading. The pecans graded out as follows:

Grade	Quantity	Current market price per bag
A	350	$7
B	500	6
C	100	4
Waste	50	

Required:

Assuming the relative sales value method is used to apportion the joint costs, give:

1. The entry for purchase assuming a perpetual inventory system (show computations).
2. Valuation of ending inventory assuming the following quantities are on hand: grade A, 100 bags; grade B, 80 bags; and grade C, 40 bags.
3. The entry for sale of 20 bags of the grade A pecans at the above market price for cash.

E 9–21 (Relative Sales Value Method; Entries)

Arizona Land Developers purchased and subdivided a tract of land that cost $900,000. The subdivision was divided on the following basis:

10% used for streets, alleys, and parks.
50% divided into 100 lots to sell for $4,000 each.
30% divided into 200 lots to sell for $3,000 each.
10% divided into 100 lots to sell for $2,000 each.

Required:

1. Give the entry for the purchase of the lots. Use the relative sales value method to apportion the total cost of $900,000 to the three categories of lots. Assume a perpetual inventory system.
2. During the final month of the year, the paving was completed (included in the $900,000 cost), and sales were made. At the end of the first year, 20, $4,000 lots; 50, $3,000 lots; and 10, $2,000 lots are on hand. Compute the valuation of the inventory at year-end, and record the sales and cost of goods sold amounts for each category of lots. Assume cash sales only.

E 9–22 (Relative Sales Value Method; Land; Entries)

DDD Development Company purchased a tract of land for development purposes. The tract was subdivided as follows: 30 lots to sell at $6,000 per lot and 80 lots to sell at $9,000 per lot. The tract cost $335,000, and an additional $25,000 was spent in general development costs, including streets and alleys.

Required:

Assuming cost apportionment is based on the relative sales value method, give entries for (1) purchase of the tract and payment of the develoment costs, (2) sale of one $6,000 lot, and (3) sale of one $9,000 lot. DDD uses a perpetual inventory system. Assume cash transactions.

E 9–23 (Relative Sales Value Method; Entry)

Quick Company purchased 2,630 bushels of ungraded apricots at $2 per bushel. The apricots were sorted as follows: grade one, 1,000 bushels; grade two, 700 bushels; grade three, 900 bushels; and spoilage, 10 bushels. Handling and sorting costs amounted to $140. The current market prices for graded apricots were: grade one, $4 per bushel; grade two, $3 per bushel; and grade three, $1 per bushel. The company uses a perpetual inventory system.

Required:

What entry should be made to record the purchase? Show computations of total costs for each grade assuming the relative sales value method of cost apportionment is used.

E 9–24 (Loss on Purchase Commitment)

During 19A, Delta Company signed a contract with Alpha Corporation to "purchase 15,000 subassemblies at $30 each during 19B."

Required:

1. On December 31, 19A, end of the annual accounting period, the financial statements are to be prepared. Under what additional contractual and economic conditions should disclosure of the contract terms be made only by means of a note in the financial statements? Prepare an appropriate note. Assume the cost of the subassemblies is dropping and the estimated current replacement cost is $400,000.
2. What contractual and economic conditions would require accrual of a loss? Give the accrual entry.
3. Assume the subassemblies are received in 19B when their cost was at the estimate given in (1) above. The contract was paid in full. Give the required entry.

E 9–25 (Loss on Purchase Commitments)

On November 1, 19A, XIT Corporation entered into a purchase contract (not subject to revision or cancellation) to purchase 10,000 units of Material X at $6 per unit (to be used in manufacturing). The contract period extends through February 19B. XIT's accounting period ends December 31. On December 31, 19A, Material X was being sold at a firm price of $5 per unit. On January 25, 19B, XIT purchased the 10,000 units; however, the market price per unit of Material X on this date was $4.75. The company uses a perpetual inventory system.

Required:

Give all relevant entries or disclosure notes on November 1, 19A, December 31, 19A, and January 25, 19B. Explain the basis for each entry.

E 9–26 (Correct Four Inventory Errors)

The independent CPA for JP Corporation found the following errors in the records of the company:

a. Inclusion in the ending inventory of goods costing $2,000, although a purchase was not recorded. The goods in question were being held on consignment from Wilson Company.
b. Incorrect exclusion from the ending inventory of items costing $5,000 for which the purchase was not recorded.
c. Incorrect exclusion of $8,000 from the inventory count at the end of the period. The goods were in transit (FOB shipping point); the invoice had been received, and the purchase was recorded.

d. Inclusion of items on the receiving dock that were being held for return to the vendor because of damage. In counting the goods in the receiving department, these items were incorrectly included. With respect to these goods, a purchase of $6,000 had been recorded.

The records (uncorrected) showed the following amounts: *(a)* purchases, $180,000; *(b)* pretax income, $20,000; *(c)* accounts payable, $28,000; and *(d)* inventory at the end of the period, $50,000.

Required:
Set up a schedule to reflect the uncorrected balances, changes caused by correction of the errors, and the corrected balances for (1) purchases, (2) pretax income, (3) accounts payable, and (4) ending inventory. Hint: Set up four amount columns.

E 9–27 (Correct Four Inventory Errors on the Statement of Income)
The records of Varga Company reflected the following:

Sales revenue		$205,000
Cost of goods sold:		
Beginning inventory	$ 10,000	
Purchases	105,000	
Goods available for sale	115,000	
Ending inventory	25,000	90,000
Gross margin		115,000
Expenses		60,000
Income (pretax)		$ 55,000

The following errors were found that had not been corrected:

a. Revenues collected in advance amounting to $5,000 are included in the sales revenue amount.
b. Accrued expenses not recognized, $6,000.
c. Goods costing $10,000 were incorrectly included in the ending inventory (they were being held on consignment from Carter Company). No purchase was recorded.
d. Goods costing $5,000 were correctly included in the ending inventory; however, no purchase was recorded (assume a credit purchase).

Required:
1. Prepare the statement of income on a correct basis.
2. What amounts would be incorrect on the statement of financial position if the errors are not corrected?

Part A: Problems 9–1 to 9–12

P 9–1 (LCM; Three Ways to Apply)
The information shown below relating to the ending inventory was taken from the records of Quick Print Company.

Inventory classification	Quantity	Per unit Cost	Per unit Market
Paper:			
Stock X	200	$300	$330
Stock Y	60	250	230
Ink:			
Stock D	20	70	65
Stock E	10	60	62
Toner fluid:			
Stock A	8	75	70
Stock B	4	90	80
Stock C	7	100	110

Required:

1. Determine the valuation of the above inventory at cost and at LCM assuming application by *(a)* individual items, *(b)* classifications, and *(c)* total inventory. The unit costs of the three categories are significantly different; however, within each category the unit costs are similar.
2. Give the entry to record the ending inventory for each approach assuming periodic inventory and the allowance method.
3. Of the three applications described in (1) above, which one appears preferable in this situation? Explain.

P 9–2 (LCM, Allowance Method; Recording and Reporting)

The records of Scofield Company provide the following data relating to inventories for the years 19B and 19C:

Inventory date	Original cost	At LCM
1/1/19B	$40,000	$40,000
12/31/19B	50,000	46,000
12/31/19C	46,000	45,000

Other data available are as follows:

	19B	19C
Sales	$220,000	$245,000
Purchases	135,000	150,000
Administrative and selling expenses	49,000	61,000

The company values inventories on the basis of LCM and uses the periodic inventory system. For problem purposes, ignore income taxes.

Required:

1. Give, in a parallel columns, for 19B and 19C, the entries to apply the LCM procedure under the allowance method.
2. Prepare a statement of income for 19B and 19C, and show the inventory amounts for the statement of financial position. Follow the format illustrated in the chapter.

P 9–3 (LCM, Allowance and Direct Methods Compared)

David Corporation uses a perpetual inventory system. The following data are available from David's records:

	19A	19B
Sales revenue	$80,000	$120,000
Cost of goods sold	40,000	60,000
Remaining expenses	20,000	35,000

The cost of goods sold is based on inventories valued at cost. Additional information regarding inventories are:

	Cost	Market
January 1, 19A	$ 6,000	$7,000
December 31, 19A	10,000	8,000
December 31, 19B	12,000	9,000

Required:

1. In parallel columns, for 19A and 19B, give the entries to apply the LCM procedure under the allowance method. Prepare a statement of income for 19A and 19B. Ignore income taxes.
2. In parallel columns, for 19A and 19B, give the entries to apply the LCM procedure

under the direct inventory reduction method. Prepare a statement of income for 19A and B. Ignore income taxes.

P 9–4 (LCM, Allowance and Direct Methods Compared)
York Corporation's summarized statements of income for 19A and 19B are shown below. The inventories given below were valued at cost.

	19A	19B
Sales	$107,000	$97,000
Cost of goods sold:		
Beginning inventory	25,000	20,000
Purchases	75,000	73,000
Total	100,000	93,000
Ending inventory	20,000	15,000
Cost of goods sold	80,000	78,000
Gross margin	27,000	19,000
Less: Operating expenses	14,000	12,000
Pretax income	$ 13,000	$ 7,000

The inventories valued at LCM would have been: at the beginning of 19A, $25,000 (the same as cost); end of 19A, $17,000; and end of 19B, $10,000.

Required:
1. Restate the 19A and 19B statements of income applying the LCM rule for each of the following procedures (use a format similar to that illustrated in the text). Disregard income taxes.
   a. Direct inventory reduction method where the inventory holding loss is not reported separately.
   b. Allowance method.
2. Which procedure is preferable? Why?

P 9–5 (GM; Inventory Fire Loss; Evaluation)
The records of Eger Company provided the following information on September 1, 19A:

Inventory, 1/1/19A	$ 50,000
Purchases, January 1 to September 1	300,000
Sales, January 1 to September 1	400,000
Purchase returns and allowances	3,000
Sales returns (goods returned to stock)	5,000
Freight-in	4,000

A fire completely destroyed the inventory on September 1, 19A, except for goods marked to sell at $6,000, which had an estimated residual value of $4,000, and for goods in transit to which Eger had ownership; the purchase had been recorded. Invoices recorded on the latter show merchandise cost, $2,000, and freight-in, $100. The average rate of gross margin on sales in recent years has been 35%.

Required:
1. Compute the inventory fire loss.
2. Under what conditions would your response to (1) above be questionable?

P 9–6 (GM; Use in Profit Planning)
Neiman Company is developing a profit plan. The following data were estimated for 19C and 19D:

a. January 1, 19C, estimated inventory, $90,000.
b. Estimated average rate of gross margin on sales, 25%.

Required:
Complete the following profit plan:

	Profit plan estimates 19C	19D
Sales planned	$160,000	$190,000
Cost of goods sold:		
Beginning inventory	?	?
Purchases budget	110,000	130,000
Total goods available	?	?
Less: Ending inventory	?	?
Cost of goods sold	?	?
Gross margin planned	?	?

P 9–7 (GM; Inventory Burned; Indemnity)
Wood Wholesaler Company's warehouse burned on April 1, 19D. The following information (up to the date of the fire) was taken from the records of the company: inventory, January 1, $30,000; gross sales, $160,000; purchases, $90,000; sales returns (restored to stock), $5,000; purchase returns and allowances, $2,000; and freight-in, $8,000. The cost of goods sold and gross margin for the past three years were as follows:

Year	Cost of goods sold	Gross margin
19A	$500,000	$125,000
19B	435,000	120,000
19C	470,000	120,000

Required:
1. Estimate the cost of the inventory destroyed in the fire.
2. Under what conditions would your response to (1) above be questionable?
3. The insurance company pays indemnity on "market value" at date of the fire. What amount would you recommend that Wood submit as an insurance claim? Explain.

P 9–8 (GM; Inventory Records Destroyed; Statement of Income)
In the past, SWT Corporation valued inventories at cost. At the end of the current period, the inventory was valued at 40% of selling price as a matter of convenience. However, the cost ratio is not 40%. The current financial statements have been prepared, and the inventory sheets inadvertently destroyed; consequently, you find it impossible to reconstruct the ending inventory at actual cost per the physical count. Fortunately, the following data are available.

Sales	$300,000
Ending inventory (at 40% of selling price)	25,000
Purchases (at cost)	190,000
Pretax income	40,000
Beginning inventory (at cost)	20,000

Required:
Prepare a corrected (and detailed) statement of income. Show computations and round the cost ratio to four decimal places.

P 9–9 (Retail Inventory Method; Average, FIFO; LCM)

Young Department Store uses the retail inventory method. Data for the year ended January 31, 19B, for one department appear below:

Inventory, 1/31/19A:	
Cost	$ 30,000
Sales price	54,000
Purchases for year ended 1/31/19B (gross):	
Cost	140,000
Sales price	275,000
Sales for year (gross)	250,000
Freight on merchandise purchased	6,000
Returns:	
Purchases:	
Cost	1,000
Sales price	2,000
Sales (merchandise restored to inventory)	5,000
Additional markups	4,000
Additional markup cancellations	1,000
Markdowns	2,000
Markdown cancellations	1,000
Employee discounts	1,000

Required:

1. Estimate the January 31, 19B, inventory valuation using the retail inventory method under each of the following methods (carry cost ratios to three decimal places):
   a. Average cost and LCM.
   b. FIFO cost and LCM.
   c. Average cost (without LCM).
   d. FIFO cost (without LCM).
2. Because sales returns reenter Young's inventory after the customer returns the goods, why are sales returns not added back to goods available for sale at cost and at retail?

P 9–10 (Retail Inventory Method; Average, FIFO: LCM)

The records of Diskount Department Store provided the following data for 19A:

Sales (gross)	$800,000
Return sales (restored to inventory)	2,000
Additional markups	9,000
Additional markup cancellations	5,000
Markdowns	7,000
Purchases:	
At retail	850,000
At cost	480,000
Purchase returns:	
At retail	4,000
At cost	2,200
Freight on purchases	6,000
Beginning inventory:	
At cost	45,000
At retail	80,000
Markdown cancellations	3,000

Required:

Estimate the valuation of the ending inventory and cost of goods sold assuming (show computations, carry cost ratios to four decimal places, and round inventory to the nearest dollar):

Case A—Average cost (for illustrative purposes only).

Case B—Average cost, LCM.

Case C—FIFO cost (for illustrative purposes only).

Case D—FIFO cost, LCM.

P 9–11 (Retail Inventory Method; an Audit Test)

Auditors are examining the accounts of Detroit Retail Corporation. They were present when Detroit's personnel physically counted the Detroit inventory; however, the auditors made their own tests. Detroit's records provided the following data for the current year:

	At retail	At cost
Inventory, January 1	$ 300,000	$180,500
Net purchases	1,473,000	973,500
Freight-in		15,000
Additional markups	16,000	
Additional markup cancellations	9,000	
Markdowns	8,000	
Employee discounts	2,000	
Sales	1,300,000	
Inventory, December 31 (per physical count valued at retail)	475,000	

Required:

1. Compute the ending inventory at average cost and LCM as an audit test of the overall reasonableness of the physical inventory count. Round the cost ratio to three decimals.
2. Note any discrepancies indicated. What factors should the auditors consider in reconciling any difference in results from the analysis?
3. What accounting treatment should be accorded the discrepancy (if any)?

P 9–12 (Overview; Inventory Concepts, Recording, Adjusting, Closing, Reporting)

Fame Company completed the following selected (and summarized) transactions during 19A:

a. Merchandise inventory on hand January 1, 19A: $105,000 (at cost, which was the same as LCM).

b. During the year, purchased merchandise for resale at quoted price of $200,000 on credit, terms 2/10, n/30. Immediately paid 85% of the cash cost.

c. Paid freight on merchandise purchased, $9,000 cash.

d. Paid 40% of the accounts payable within the discount period. The remaining payables were unpaid at the end of 19A and were still within the discount period.

e. Merchandise that had a quoted price of $3,000 (terms 2/10, n/30) was returned to a supplier. A cash refund of $2,940 was received because the items were unsatisfactory.

f. During the year, sold merchandise for $370,000, of which 10% was on credit, terms n/30.

g. A television set caught fire and was damaged internally; it was returned by the customer because it was guaranteed. The set was originally sold for $600, of which $400 cash was refunded. The set cost the company $420. Estimates are that the set, when repaired, can be sold for $240. Estimated repair costs are $50, and selling costs are estimated to be $10.

h. Operating expenses (administrative and distribution) paid in cash, $115,000 (includes the $10 in [*g*]).
i. Excluded from the purchase given in *(b)* and from the ending inventory was a shipment for $7,000 (net of discount). This shipment was in transit, FOB shipping point at December 31, 19A. The invoice was on hand.
j. Paid $50 cash to repair the damaged television set (see [*g*] above).
k. Sold the damaged television set for $245; selling costs allocated, $10.
l. The ending inventory (as counted) was $110,000 at cost, and $107,000 at market. Assume an average income tax rate of 40%.

Accounting policies followed by the company are (1) the annual accounting period ends December 31; (2) a periodic inventory system is used; (3) purchases and accounts payable are recorded net of cash discounts; (4) freight charges are allocated to merchandise when purchased; (5) all cash discounts are taken; (6) used and damaged merchandise is carried in a separate inventory account; and (7) inventories are reported at LCM and the allowance method is used.

Required:
1. Give the entries for transactions *(b)* through *(k)*.
2. Give the end of the period entries (adjusting and closing).
3. Prepare a multiple-step statement of income (19A). Assume 20,000 shares of common stock outstanding.
4. Show how the ending inventory should be reported on the statement of financial position at December 31, 19A.

Part B: Problems 9–13 to 9–21

P 9–13 (DV LIFO Retail; Price Indexes Given; Conversion; Three Years)
Casey Retailers has used the FIFO retail method, LCM basis, of inventory for all purposes. On January 1, 19D, the company decided to use the DV LIFO retail method to convert the inventory to the LIFO basis. The results will be used for external reporting and for income tax purposes. The base inventory at the start of 19D was as follows: 1/1/19D, base inventory (carried over from 12/31/19C), at cost, $31,000; at retail, $50,000.

Data from the inventory records for 19D–19F are given below.

	19D		19E		19F	
	At cost	At retail	At cost	At retail	At cost	At retail
Sales (net)		$120,000		$140,000		$150,000
Purchases (net)	$100,800	143,000	$112,000	164,000	$121,600	180,000
Net additional markups		7,000		11,000		5,000
Applicable price index (19C = 100)	104		107		111	
Administrative and selling expenses	25,000		27,000		36,000	

Required:
1. Compute the inventory values (at cost and at retail) that should be used for 19D, 19E, and 19F to determine cost ratios.
2. Convert the inventory results for each year, computed in (1) above, to DV LIFO retail for use in developing the external financial statements and the income tax return (round all cost ratios to three decimal places).
3. Complete the following tabulation for 19F:

	Year 19F	
	FIFO basis	DV LIFO basis
Sales revenue	$____	$____
Less expenses:		
Cost of goods sold:		
Beginning inventory	____	____
Purchases	____	____
Total	____	____
Ending inventory	____	____
Cost of goods sold	____	____
Administrative and selling expenses	____	____
Total expenses	____	____
Pretax income	____	____
Income taxes (assume a 33% rate)	____	____
Net income	____	____
Reduction in cash outflows by using DV LIFO	$____	

P 9–14 (DV LIFO Retail Conversion; Price Indexes Given)

Lester Retailers keeps its internal inventory records on a FIFO (not LCM) basis. At interim reporting dates, Lester's accountants convert the book balances to a LIFO basis for reporting purposes by using the DV LIFO retail method. The following data for the quarter ended March 31, 19E, are available:

	Quarter ended 3/31/19E	
	At cost	At retail
Base layer from 19C (when LIFO was adopted); index = 100	$ 19,750	$ 38,500
Additional LIFO layer added in 19D; index = 104; cost ratio = .60	30,900	51,500
Beginning inventory, 19E; index = 110	49,500	90,000
Purchases (net)	231,000	400,000
Net additional markups		30,000
Net markdowns		10,000
Return sales		6,000
Sales (gross)		392,000
Price index at end of March 19E = 124.		

Required:

Compute the ending inventory at March 31, 19E, at DV LIFO cost using the retail inventory method. Show all computations in order and round all cost ratios and price index ratios to the nearest three decimal places.

P 9–15 (DV LIFO Retail; Price Indexes Given; Conversion)

White Company changed to the DV LIFO retail method for external reporting and income tax purposes on January 1, 19B. The following data are available from White's records for the year ended December 31, 19C:

	At cost	At retail
Purchases	$70,000	$100,000
Net additional markups		4,000
Net markdowns		4,000
Sales		80,000

The December 31, 19B, ending inventory was $88,000 at retail and $51,450 at DV LIFO cost. Relevant external price indexes are: 19A (base year), 110; 19B, 121; and 19C, 132.

Required (round all cost ratios to three decimal places):
Compute the December 31, 19C, ending inventory using the DV LIFO retail method.

P 9–16 (DF LIFO Retail; Overview Three Years; Price Indexes Given)
Miller Department Store has been using the retail inventory method (average, LCM) for a number of years. After extensive consideration the company decided to change to DV LIFO retail for all purposes. Thus, after the change, instituted on January 1, 19D, FIFO retail cost basis will be computed each period, then these results will be converted to DV LIFO retail for external reporting and income tax purposes.

The inventory records for the year 19C showed the following computations (i.e., for the year prior to the change):

	At cost	At retail
Inventory, 1/1/19C	$ 55,000	$ 74,000
Purchases	530,000	700,000
Net additional markups		6,000
Total	$585,000	780,000
Cost ratio: $585,000 ÷ $780,000 = .750.		
Sales		(700,000)
Net markdowns		(10,000)
Inventory, 12/31/19C:		
At retail		$ 70,000
At average cost, LCM ($70,000 × .750)	$ 52,500	

Data for the three years 19D–19F were as shown in the following schedule:

	19D		19E		19F	
	At cost	At retail	At cost	At retail	At cost	At retail
Purchases	$500,000	$618,000	$580,000	$700,000	$600,000	$750,000
Net additional markups		16,000		10,000		10,000
Net markdowns		9,000		11,000		7,000
Sales		600,000		650,000		725,000
Applicable price index (19C = 120)	132		144		150	
Administrative and selling expenses	45,000		48,000		50,000	

Required (round all cost ratios to three decimal places):

1. Compute the inventory value that should be used as the base inventory on January 1, 19D.
2. Compute the inventory values (at cost and at retail) that should be used as the ending inventories for 19D, 19E, and 19F for conversion purposes (and for internal use).
3. In view of the change from average, LCM, the company decided to adjust the inventory account to the FIFO cost basis for internal purposes. Give the entry to effect this change at the start of the 19D.
4. Convert the FIFO inventory results for each year, computed in (2) above, to DV LIFO retail for use in developing the external financial statements and the income tax return.
5. Complete the schedule for 19F shown on page 414.

	Year 19F	
	FIFO basis	DV LIFO basis
Sales revenue	$ ______	$ ______
Less expenses:		
Cost of goods sold:		
Beginning inventory	______	______
Purchases	______	______
Total	______	______
Ending inventory	______	______
Cost of goods sold	______	______
Administrative and selling expenses	______	______
Total expenses	______	______
Pretax income	______	______
Income taxes (assume a 34% rate)	______	______
Net income	______	______
Reduction in cash outflows by using DV LIFO	$ ______	

P 9–17 **(DV LIFO Retail; Comprehensive)**

Shirts, Incorporated, has used the conventional retail inventory method, average (LCM) basis for a number of years for all purposes. The company has decided to use DV LIFO retail results for external reporting and income tax purposes. The change is to be effective January 1, 19F. Relevant data subject to the change and the next three years are given below.

a. From the internal inventory records—computation of the retail inventory (average, LCM basis) for 19E:

	At cost	At retail
Inventory, 1/1/19E	$ 37,000	$ 60,000
Purchases	227,000	413,000
Net additional markups		7,000
Total	$264,000	480,000
Cost ratio: $264,000 ÷ $480,000 = .55		
Sales		(416,000)
Net markdowns		(14,000)
Inventory, 12/31/19E:		
At retail		$ 50,000
At average cost, LCM ($50,000 × .55)	$ 27,500	

b. Data for 19F–19H are shown below. The company will use the retail inventory method FIFO cost basis (not LCM) for internal purposes starting with 19F.

	19F		19G		19H	
	At cost	At retail	At cost	At retail	At cost	At retail
Purchases	$231,000	$400,000	$262,200	$450,000	$271,600	$470,000
Net additional markups		30,000		17,000		20,000
Net markdowns		10,000		7,000		5,000
Sales		380,000		410,000		485,000
Applicable price index (19E = 110)	116.6		132.0		143.0	
Administrative and selling expenses	70,000		80,000		100,000	

Required:

1. Compute the inventory value that should be used as the base inventory on January 1, 19F. Round all cost ratios to two decimal places.
2. Compute the inventory values (at cost and retail) that should be used as the ending inventories for 19F, 19G, and 19H for conversion purposes (and for internal use).
3. In view of the change from average, LCM, the company decided to adjust the inventory account to the FIFO cost basis (not LCM) for internal purposes. Give the entry to effect this change at the start of 19F.
4. Convert the FIFO inventory results for each year, computed in (2) above, to DV LIFO retail for use in developing the external financial statements and the income tax return.
5. Complete the following tabulation for 19H:

	Year 19H	
	FIFO basis	DV LIFO basis
Sales revenue	$271,666	$485,000
Less expenses:		
Cost of goods sold:		
Beginning inventory	79,866	140,000
Purchases	271,600	470,000
Total	351,400	625,000
Ending inventory	78,400	140,000
Cost of goods sold	____	____
Administrative and selling expenses	____	____
Total expenses	____	____
Pretax income	____	____
Income taxes (assume 40% rate)	____	____
Net income	____	____
Reduction in cash outflows by using DV LIFO	$____	

P 9–18 **(Relative Sales Value Method)**

Valley Grocers Co-op purchased a large quantity of mixed grapefruit for $41,000, which was graded at a cost of $1,000, as indicated below. Sales (at the sales prices indicated) and losses (frozen, rotten, etc.) are also listed.

Grade	Baskets bought	Sales price per basket	Baskets sold	Baskets spoiled
A	5,000	$4.00	2,000	50
B	4,000	3.00	3,000	60
C	10,000	2.00	8,000	40
Culls	1,000	.50	900	
Loss	100			

Required:

1. Give the entry for the purchase assuming a perpetual inventory system. Show computations.
2. Give entries to record the sales and cost of goods sold.
3. Give the entry for the losses assuming the losses are recorded separately from cost of goods sold.
4. Determine the valuation of the ending inventory.
5. Compute the direct contribution to pretax income for each grade of grapefruit. (Disregard operating, administrative, and selling expenses.)

P 9–19 (Relative Sales Value Method; Land)

On January 1, 19A, Graham and Will each invested $100,000 cash in a partnership for the purpose of purchasing and subdividing a tract of land for residential building purposes.

On June 1, they purchased 30 acres comprising the subdivision, at $5,000 per acre, paying $50,000 in cash and giving a one-year, 15% interest-bearing note (with mortgage) for the balance. Development costs amounted to an additional $92,000 (paid in cash).

The property was subdivided into 300 lots, 200 of which were to sell at $4,000 each and the balance at $3,000 each.

During July through December 19A, the following sales were made for half cash and half interest-bearing notes receivable due in six months from date of sale.

	Lots
Group A (sold at $4,000 each)	50
Group B (sold at $3,000 each)	60

Cash collections on the notes receivable up to December 31, 19A, amounted to $49,000 principal plus $1,000 interest. Accrued interest recorded at December 31, 19A, amounted to $1,000.

Operating and selling expenses amounted to $125,000 by the end of December 19A. No payment was made on the note payable.

Required:

1. Give the entries for all of the above transactions. Disregard income taxes.
2. Prepare a statement of income for 19A.
3. Compute the valuation of the inventory of unsold lots on December 31, 19A.

P 9–20 (Correcting Errors on a Statement of Income)

Bass Company has completed the statement of income and statement of financial position (summarized and uncorrected shown below) at December 31, 19A. Subsequently, during an audit, the following items were discovered:

a. Expenses amounting to $5,000 were not accrued.
b. A conditional sale on credit for $12,000 was recorded on December 31, 19A. The goods, which cost $8,000, were included in the ending inventory; they had not been shipped because the customer's address was not known and the credit had not been approved. Ownership had not passed.
c. Merchandise purchased on December 31, 19A, on credit for $8,000 was included in the ending inventory because the goods were on hand. A purchase was not recorded because the accounting department had not received the invoice from the vendor.
d. The ending inventory was overstated by $10,000 due to an addition error on the inventory sheet.
e. A sale return (on account) on December 31, 19A, was not recorded: sales amount, $15,000; and cost, $8,000. The ending inventory did not include the goods returned.

Required:

Set up a schedule similar to the one below; make the corrections and derive the corrected amounts. Indicate increases and decreases for each transaction. Explain any assumptions made with respect to doubtful items. Disregard income taxes.

	Uncorrected amounts	Items for correction (a)	(b)	(c)	(d)	(e)	Corrected amounts
Statement of income:							
Sales revenue	$90,000						
Cost of goods sold	50,000						
Gross margin	40,000						
Expenses	30,000						
Pretax income	$10,000						
Statement of financial position:							
Accounts receivable	$42,000						
Inventory	20,000						
Remaining assets	30,000						
Accounts payable	11,000						
Remaining liabilities	6,000						
Common stock	60,000						
Retained earnings	15,000						

P 9–21 (Correcting Inventory Errors)

On January 3, 19B, Jonah Corporation engaged an independent CPA to perform an audit for the year ended December 31, 19A. The company uses a periodic inventory system. The CPA did not observe the inventory count on December 31, 19A; as a result, a special examination was made of the inventory records.

The financial statements prepared by the company (uncorrected) showed the following: ending inventory, $72,000; accounts receivable, $60,000; accounts payable, $30,000; sales, $400,000; net purchases, $160,000; and pretax income, $51,000.

The following data were found during the audit:

a. Merchandise received on January 2, 19B, costing $800 was recorded on December 31, 19A. An invoice on hand showed the shipment was made FOB supplier's warehouse on December 31, 19A. Because the merchandise was not on hand at December 31, 19A, it was not included in the inventory.

b. Merchandise that cost $18,000 was excluded from the inventory, and the related sale for $23,000 was recorded. The goods had been segregated in the warehouse for shipment; there was no contract for sale but a "tentative order by phone."

c. Merchandise that cost $10,000 was out on consignment to Bar Distributing Company and was excluded from the ending inventory. The merchandise was recorded as a sale of $25,000 when shipped to Bar on December 2, 19A.

d. A sealed packing case containing a product costing $900 was in Jonah's shipping room when the physical inventory was taken. It was included in the inventory because it was marked *"Hold for customer's shipping instructions."* Investigation revealed that the customer signed a purchase contract dated December 18, 19A, but that the case was shipped and the customer billed on January 10, 19B. A sale was recorded on December 18, 19A.

e. A special item, fabricated to order for a customer, was finished and in the shipping room on December 31, 19A. The customer had inspected it and was satisfied. The customer was billed in full on that date. The item was included in inventory at cost, $1,000, because it was shipped on January 4, 19B.

f. Merchandise costing $1,500 was received on December 28, 19A. The goods were excluded from inventory, and a purchase was not recorded. The auditor located the related papers in the hands of the purchasing agent; they indicated, *"On consignment from Baker Company."*

g. Merchandise costing $2,000 was received on January 8, 19B, and the related purchase invoice recorded January 9. The invoice showed the shipment was made on December 29, 19A, FOB destination. The merchandise was excluded from the inventory.
h. Merchandise that cost $11,000 and sold on December 31, 19A, for $16,000 was included in the ending inventory. The sale was recorded. The goods were in transit; however, a clerk failed to note that the goods were shipped FOB shipping point.
i. Merchandise that cost $6,000 was excluded from the ending inventory and not recorded as a sale for $7,500 on December 31, 19A. The goods had been specifically segregated. According to the terms of the contract of sale, ownership will not pass until actual delivery.
j. Merchandise that cost $15,000 was included in the ending inventory. The related purchase has not been recorded. The goods had been shipped by the vendor FOB destination; and the invoice, but not the goods, was received on December 30, 19A.
k. Merchandise in transit that cost $7,000 was excluded from inventory because it was not on hand. The shipment from the vendor was FOB shipping point. The purchase was recorded on December 29, 19A, when the invoice was received.
l. Merchandise in transit that cost $13,000 was excluded from inventory because it had not arrived. Although the invoice had arrived, the related purchase was not recorded by December 31, 19A. The merchandise was shipped by the vendor FOB shipping point.
m. Merchandise that cost $8,000 was included in the ending inventory because it was on hand. The merchandise had been rejected because of incorrect specifications and was being held for return to the vendor. The merchandise was recorded as a purchase on December 26, 19A.

Required:
1. Prepare a schedule with one column for each of the six financial statement items (starting with the uncorrected balances), plus a column for explanations. Show the specific corrections to each balance and the corrected balances. Explain the basis for your decision on all items.
2. Give the entry to correct the accounts assuming the accounts for 19A have been closed.

(AICPA adapted)

CASES

C 9–1 (Estimate the Inventory of Books)

The manager of Seton Book Company, a book retailer, requires an estimate of the inventory cost for a quarterly financial report to the owner on March 31, 19D. In the past, the gross margin method was used due to the difficulty and expense of taking a physical inventory at interim dates. The company sells both fiction and nonfiction books. Due to their lower turnover rate, nonfiction books are typically marked up at a 60% rate on cost. Fiction, on the other hand, has a 40% markup rate on cost. The manager has used an average markup of 50% to estimate interim inventories.

You have been asked by the manager to estimate the book inventory cost as of March 31, 19D. The following data is available from Seton's accounting records:

	Fiction	Nonfiction	Total
Inventory, 1/1/19D	$100,000	$ 40,000	$140,000
Purchases	600,000	200,000	800,000
Freight	5,000	2,000	7,000
Sales	580,000	160,000	740,000

Required (round gross margin ratios to two decimal places):

1. Using an estimated markup on cost of 50%, compute the estimate of inventory as of March 31, 19D based on the gross margin method applied to combined fiction and nonfiction books.
2. Compute the estimate of ending inventory as of March 31, 19D, based on the gross margin method applied separately to fiction and nonfiction books.
3. Which method is preferable in this situation? Explain.

C 9–2 **(What about the Competitor?)**

The manager of Jolie's, a retail department store, is concerned about declining sales. She is particularly worried that a competitor is consistently undercutting Jolie's prices. A recent financial statement of the competitor reflects the following inventory data:

	December 31, 19B	December 31, 19A
Inventory	$1,560,000	$1,342,000

The competitor uses the DV LIFO retail method for inventories and reported retail value for inventories on 12/31/19B and 12/31/19A of $4,108,000 and $3,530,000, respectively. The manager of Jolie's estimated that the external price indexes used by the competitor are similar to those used by Jolie's, which were 1.15 for 19B and 1.10 for 19A (both relative to the base year index, which is the same for both companies).

Required:

1. Compute the 19B cost ratio used by the competitor based on the assumptions given above.
2. If Jolie's 19B cost ratio is .45 and the cost of inventory to both Jolie's and its competitor are the same, is the manager's concern justified? Explain.

C 9–3 **(Repurchase Commitment; Probable Loss)**

Stauffer Chemical Company is a major agricultural chemical supplier. The following excerpts are from an article in *The Wall Street Journal* (August 14, 1984, page 2):

> Stauffer, which relies on agricultural chemicals for more than half its profits, has been hammered in the past three years by bad weather, depressed farm prices, and lowered farm output caused by a federal price-support program. In the summer of 1982, "aware that agricultural chemical sales for its 1982–83 season would probably fall off sharply," Stauffer undertook a plan to accelerate sales of certain products to dealers during fiscal 1982, according to the SEC.
>
> The commission charged that the plan was "tantamount to consignment sales which shouldn't have been recognized in 1982," and that Stauffer's annual report to shareholders for that year failed to reflect this fact.
>
> Stauffer, the SEC charged, offered its dealers incentives to take products during the fourth quarter of 1982. As a result, the company reported $72 million of revenue that ordinarily wouldn't have been booked until early 1983. By March 1983, according to the commission, Stauffer realized that it would have to "offer its distributors relief" from the oversupply of unsalable products. Stauffer offered dealers refunds for as much as 100% of unsold products taken in 1982, compared with 32% the previous year.
>
> Stauffer ended up refunding nearly 40% of its 1982 agricultural chemical sales, but failed to disclose the "substantial uncertainties" surrounding the sales in the annual report it filed with the SEC in April 1983. The omission was "materially false and misleading," according to the SEC.
>
> "Their business was down and they wanted to accelerate sales," said a government official familiar with the year-long SEC investigation.

H. Barclay Morley, Stauffer's chief executive officer, conceded that fears about the fading popularity of the company's best-selling farm products had prompted some of the accounting policies questioned by the SEC. "Our theory was that if the distributor had title on the product he would have more incentive to move it," Mr. Morley said. But he declined to comment on the SEC charge that the company was aware of severe problems with a substantial portion of its agricultural chemical sales when it filed its annual report.

Required:
Discuss the appropriate accounting treatment and disclosures by Stauffer for its agricultural chemical inventories and sales in 1982.

C 9–4 (Analysis of Actual Financial Statements)

Kimberly-Clark

Refer to the 1987 financial statements of Kimberly-Clark (Appendix immediately following Chapter 25) and respond to the following:

Required:
1. What did the company report as the inventory valuations for 1987 and 1986?
2. What are the accounting policies related to inventories?
3. Summarize any note disclosures related to inventories.

10 OPERATIONAL ASSETS: PROPERTY, PLANT, AND EQUIPMENT

OVERVIEW AND PURPOSE

This chapter and the next two chapters focus on a broad category of assets often described as operational assets because they are used in the operations of the business and are not held for resale. For accounting purposes, operational assets, also called **property, plant** and **equipment** or **fixed assets,** may be classified as tangible or intangible. Tangible assets have physical substance while intangible assets have value solely because of the rights that ownership confers. Chapter 11 discusses depreciation and depletion and Chapter 12 discusses intangible assets.

The purpose of this chapter is to discuss the concepts and accounting principles used to record (i.e., recognize) and report the acquisition and disposition of tangible operational assets, To accomplish this purpose, the chapter is organized as follows:

Part A: Acquisition of Operational Assets

1. Classifications related to operational assets.
2. Principles underlying accounting for property, plant, and equipment.
3. Operational assets acquired for cash.
4. Operational assets acquired on credit.
5. Operational assets acquired in exchange for securities.
6. Operational assets acquired in exchange for assets other than securities.
7. Departures from cost in accounting for operational assets.

Part B: Special Problems in Accounting for Operational Assets

1. Assets constructed for own use.
2. Capitalization of interest during the construction period.
3. Expenditures subsequent to acquisition.
4. Disposal of operational assets.

PART A: ACQUISITION OF OPERATIONAL ASSETS

Classifications Related to Operational Assets

For accounting purposes operational assets usually are classified as follows:

1. **Tangible property, plant, and equipment** have five characteristics as follows: *(a)* actively used in operations, *(b)* not held as an investment or for resale, *(c)* relatively long lived, *(d)* have physical substance, and *(e)* provide measurable future benefits to the entity. These operational assets are described by the terms **property, plant, and equipment; plant assets; capital assets; or tangible fixed assets.** This group of assets is divided into the following three classes;
   a. Those subject to depreciation, such as buildings, equipment, tools, and furniture.
   b. Those subject to depletion, such as mineral deposits and timber tracts.
   c. Those not subject to depreciation or depletion, such as land for a plant site.
2. **Intangibles** are similar to tangible operational assets. However, intangibles have no physical substance; their value is represented solely by grants or business rights that confer some operating, financial, or income-producing benefit on the owner. The cost of an intangible asset is periodically amortized to expense over the asset's useful life. Examples include goodwill, patents, copyrights, and trademarks.

Accounting for expenditures related to the acquisition and use of operational assets also requires that they be classified as either **capital expenditures** or **revenue expenditures.**[1] **Capital expenditures** are incurred assets which provide benefits to the entity over one or more accounting periods beyond the period of acquisition. Therefore, such expenditures are recorded in appropriate **asset** accounts. The cost of an asset acquired through a capital expenditure is allocated to future periods through depreciation, amortization, or depletion. An expenditure that is debited to an asset account or to Accumulated Depreciation has been **capitalized.**

Revenue expenditures are expenses because they relate to the acquisition of property or other benefits that do **not** extend beyond the current accounting period. Therefore, they are recorded in appropriate **expense** accounts for the current period. The term **revenue expenditure** indicates that such expenditures are matched against the revenue of the period in which they are incurred. Thus, **expense expenditure** is a more descriptive term.

Correct classification between capital and revenue expenditures is crucial. An incorrect classification may affect reported income for the entire life of an asset (land is an exception). In cases in which the *(a)* capital expenditure is relatively small, *(b)* future benefit is insignificant, or *(c)* measurement of the future benefit is not reliable, the materiality and conservatism constraints (see Chapter 6) provide that the outlay may be expensed.

---

[1] Expenditures related to acquisition of an operational asset include, but are not limited to, transactions that require *(a)* payment of cash, *(b)* transfer of noncash assets, or *(c)* incurrence of a liability. See FASB, *Statement of Financial Accounting Standards No. 34,* "Capitalization of Interest Cost" (Stamford, Conn., 1979), par. 16.

Principles Underlying Accounting for Property, Plant, and Equipment

Accounting for property, plant, and equipment is based on the **cost and matching principles.** At acquisition date, property, plant, and equipment are recorded in the accounts **at cost in conformity with the cost principle.** The acquisition cost is measured by the cash outlay made to acquire such assets. If a consideration other than cash is given for the asset, the market value of such a consideration at the time of the transaction is recorded as the cost of the asset. When the market value of the consideration given cannot be reliably determined, the asset acquired is recorded at its own market value. When the market values of both items must be estimated, the more reliable estimate is used to determine the cost of the asset acquired. All costs incurred to place an asset in service and test it are additions to the cost of the asset.

Subsequent to acquisition, **in conformity with the matching principle,** operational assets are carried in the accounts and reported at *(a)* cost when their economic value in use does not decline as revenues are earned, or *(b)* cost less accumulated depreciation, amortization, or depletion when their economic value in use declines as revenues are earned.

Operational Assets Acquired for Cash

If a tangible operational asset is purchased for cash, all outlays required to purchase the asset and place it in service, including cost of installation and making it ready for use, should be capitalized, in conformity with the **cost principle.** The capitalizable costs include the invoice price (less discounts), plus other costs such as sales tax, insurance during transit, freight, duties, ownership searching, ownership registration, installation, and break-in costs. All available discounts, **whether taken or not,** should be deducted from the invoice cost. Discounts not taken should be recorded as discounts lost and reported as interest expense.

Operational Assets Acquired on Credit (Debt Securities)

In conformity with the **cost principle,** the cost of an asset purchased on credit is either *(a)* its cash equivalent price or *(b)* the **present value** of the future cash payments required by the debt security or agreement discounted at the current (going) rate of interest and considering the level of risk for that particular debt *(APB Opinion No. 21).* Also, see Chapter 5. The cost principle specifies that a tangible operational asset acquired on credit should be recorded at its cash equivalent price, excluding all interest and financing charges on the debt. Interest and other finance charges should be debited to Interest Expense when incurred, and not treated as part of the asset cost (see the Part B section captioned "Capitalization of Interest during the Construction Period").

If the debt contract does not specify interest and financing charges, such amounts should be estimated and excluded from the cost of the asset. If the current cash price for the asset is determinable, the excess to be paid under the debt contract should be treated as interest expense and apportioned over the period covered by that contract. If no cash price for the asset is determinable, a realistic amount of interest should be recognized in recording the purchase *(APB Opinion, No. 21).*

To illustrate the purchase of an operational asset on credit, assume a machine was purchased with a debt agreement that required payment of $8,615 at the end of each of three years, when the annual interest rate was 14% on liabilities of this risk and duration. Notice that this debt contract does not separately identify the amount or rate of interest. Thus, the **face** amount of the note is $25,845 (i.e., $8,615 × 3). To record the asset at $25,845 would include in the asset cost the interest expense implicit in the debt contract. Because no cash equivalent cost is known, the cost of the asset should be recorded at the **present value** of the three payments discounted at 14% as follows:

PV = Annual payment × $\boldsymbol{P}_{o_{n=3;\,i=14\%}}$ (Table 5–4; 2.32163)
= $8,615 × 2.32163 (present value of an ordinary annuity of 3 rents of 1 each at 14%)
= $20,000 (rounded).

Therefore, the indicated entries are as follows:

a. At date of purchase:[2]

Asset—machinery	20,000	
Note payable on machinery		20,000

b. At payment dates (see the debt payment schedule below):

	1st year		2d year		3d year	
Interest expense	2,800		1,986		1,059	
Note payable on machinery	5,815		6,629		7,556	
Cash		8,615		8,615		8,615

Debt payment schedule

End of period	Annual payment (cash credit)	Interest expense (debit)	Payment on principal (debit)	Unpaid principal
Start	initial value			$20,000
1	$ 8,615	$2,800[(a)]	$ 5,815[(b)]	14,185[(c)]
2	8,615	1,986	6,629	7,556
3	8,615	1,059*	7,556	-0-
	$25,845	$5,845	$20,000	

(a) $20,000 × 14% = $2,800.
(b) $8,615 − $2,800 = $5,815.
(c) $20,000 − $5,815 = $14,185.
* Rounded to come out even.

[2] Alternatively, this entry could be made with the same end result on a "gross" basis as follows:

Asset—machinery	20,000	
Discount on installment payable*	5,845	
Payable on machinery ($8,615 × 3)		25,845

* The unamortized portion of this amount would be shown contra to "Payable on machinery" on the statement of financial position, thus reporting the liability at its present value.

The payment entries would be different; the first payment entry would be as follows:

Interest expense ($20,000 × 14%)	2,800	
Payable on machinery	8,615	
Discount on installment payable		2,800
Cash		8,615

Operational Assets Acquired in Exchange for Equity Securities

The proper valuation of tangible operational assets received in exchange for **equity securities** of the acquiring company often is difficult to determine because of:

1. The lack of a readily determinable market value for *(a)* the securities (e.g., the common stock of a privately held company) or *(b)* the operational assets involved (e.g., used assets).
2. The absence of arm's-length bargaining between the parties to the exchange (e.g., operational assets contributed by the organizers in return for the common stock of a newly formed corporation).
3. The nature of the assets involved (e.g., unexplored or unproven mineral deposits, manufacturing rights, patents, chemical formulas, and mining claims).
4. The current market price of the security may be based on a market volume considerably below the volume of shares involved in the exchange (i.e., a "thin" market).

The costs of assets acquired through exchange of securities should be measured as follows:

1. Determine the market value of the securities given. If the securities have an established market price, it should be used as long as the market would absorb the volume of securities involved at that price.
2. If the market value of the securities (in the volume exchanged) cannot be determined reliably, the market value of the assets acquired should be used if it can be determined reliably. In the absence of a recent cash basis sale of the assets involved, an independent appraisal by a professional appraiser may be recorded as the cost of the assets acquired.
3. If a reliable market value for neither the securities given nor the assets received can be determined, values established by the board of directors of the corporation may be used. The directors have considerable discretion in establishing values in this situation, except in cases where fraudulent intent on the part of the directors can be shown.

When assets are acquired in exchange for equity securities, any actual or implied discounts or premiums on the securities should be accounted for in the usual manner (see Chapter 18). Operational assets acquired for a combination of cash **and** securities should be capitalized at the sum of the cash and the market value of securities.

Operational Assets Acquired in Exchange for Assets Other than Securities

Operational assets often are acquired by exchanging (i.e., trading in) another asset in full or partial payment. Some transactions involve an exchange of two or more **nonmonetary** assets. In other cases, an asset is acquired by exchanging another asset plus a payment or receipt of cash (often referred to as **boot**).

Prior to *APB Opinion No. 29*, "Accounting for Nonmonetary Transactions," companies accounted for operational assets acquired through **exchanges** of nonmonetary assets in a variety of ways. These exchanges **were** variously recorded by debiting the asset account for the item acquired at (1) its quoted list price, (2) the cash paid plus the book value of the old asset exchanged, or (3) its market value.

APB Opinion No. 29 specifies the accounting approach for various nonmonetary transactions, including those involving the acquisition of tangible operational assets. Although the *Opinion* also applies to items held for resale (inventory), this chapter focuses only on its application to **productive assets.** The **basic principle** established in the *Opinion,* paragraph 18, is:

> Accounting for nonmonetary transactions should be based on the fair values of the assets (or services) involved which is the same as that used in monetary transactions.

This principle assumes that the transaction involves the culmination of an **earnings process** for the asset given up. That is, the old asset will no longer create earnings for the company and the newly acquired asset will start a new earnings process. In such a transaction, the asset acquired should be recorded on the basis of **market value.** If the transaction does not culminate an earnings process, the newly acquired asset should assume the **book value** of the asset given up. In this context, *APB Opinion 29* specifies that a direct exchange (i.e., a swap) transaction may be accounted for as follows:

a. **Earnings process culminated**—this happens when **dissimilar** assets are exchanged; therefore, use the **market value** approach.
b. **Earnings process not culminated**—this happens when **similar** productive assets are exchanged; therefore, use the **book value** approach.

Similar productive assets are defined as "assets that are of the same general type, that perform the **same function,** or that are employed in the same line of business." All other productive assets are classified as **dissimilar.** For example, the exchange of an old truck for another truck involves similar assets. In contrast, the exchange of a tract of speculative land for a truck involves dissimilar assets because they perform different functions for the entity.

Accounting Procedures for Exchanges

Dissimilar Assets Exchanged. Exchanges of **dissimilar** assets are recorded on a **market value** basis; that is, the cost of the asset acquired is measured by its market value.[3] When a cash difference is **paid** in an exchange of **dissimilar** assets, the cost of the asset acquired is the **cash paid plus the market value of the asset surrendered.** When a cash difference is **received** the cost of the asset acquired is the **market value of the asset surrendered minus the cash received.**

Similar Assets Exchanged. When **similar** assets are exchanged and no cash difference is paid or received, both parties record the exchange on a **book value** basis. Such exchanges do **not** culminate an earnings process. When a cash difference is paid or received and the assets are similar, the book value

[3] Recall that the market value of the asset(s) surrendered is used to estimate the market value of the asset purchased unless the market value of the asset(s) surrendered is not reliably determinable.

basis is altered as illustrated in 2 and 3 below. In **no case (involving either similar or dissimilar assets) is the asset received recorded at a cost in excess of its market value if its market value is known.** Thus, **all related losses are recognized** when the exchange occurs.

Illustrations of Accounting for Exchanges

Dissimilar Assets. Apply the market value concept.

Example: Company A has a large crane that cost $50,000; accumulated depreciation to date, $45,000 (i.e., its carrying value is $5,000). It is exchanged for a tract of speculative land held by Company B; in addition, $12,000 cash was **paid** by Company A. The market value of the crane being exchanged is determined to be $13,000.

To record the exchange for Company A:

Land (market value, $13,000 + cash, $12,000)	25,000*	
Accumulated depreciation (crane)	45,000	
Machinery (crane)		50,000
Cash		12,000
Gain on disposal of machinery †		8,000

* Cannot exceed market value of the land if it is known.
† Market value of the crane recognized, $13,000, less its book value, $5,000, is a gain of $8,000.

Similar Assets. Apply the **book value** approach. Recording an exchange of similar assets depends upon whether a cash difference is paid or received. Three possible situations are as follows:

1. **Similar assets exchanged and no cash difference is paid or received**—The asset acquired is recorded at the **book value** of the asset given up. However, the acquired asset cannot be recorded at more than its market value. Therefore, a loss, but not a gain, could be recognized in an exchange of this type.

Example: Company A exchanged a large crane that cost $50,000, accumulated depreciation to date, $45,000, for a small crane with a current cash price (i.e., market price) of $8,000. No cash difference was paid or received. The exchange would be recorded as follows:

Machinery (small crane, at book value of the large crane)	5,000*	
Accumulated depreciation (large crane)	45,000	
Machinery (large crane)		50,000

* Cannot exceed its market value. Notice that the market value of the asset given up was greater than the book value and was therefore ignored.

2. **Similar assets exchanged and a cash difference is paid**—The asset acquired is recorded at the sum of the **cash paid plus the book value** of the asset given up. However, the asset acquired cannot be recorded at more than its market value. Therefore, no gain can be recorded, however, if the market value of the asset received is less than the sum of the cash paid plus the book value of the asset given up, a loss must be recorded.

Example: Company A exchanged a large crane that cost $50,000, accumulated depreciation, $45,000, for a small crane having a current cash price of $8,000, and **paid** $1,000 in cash. The transaction would be recorded as follows:

Machinery (small crane, $1,000 + $5,000)	6,000	
Accumulated depreciation (large crane)	45,000	
Machinery (large crane)		50,000
Cash		1,000

Had the cash difference been $4,000, the asset acquired would have been recorded at $8,000 and a $1,000 loss would have been recognized.

3. **Similar assets exchanged and a cash difference is received**—This transaction is viewed as a **sale of part** of the asset surrendered and an **exchange of the remainder** of that asset. In such a transaction, *APB Opinion 29* requires that a **gain be recognized on the part of the asset sold** (i.e., given up) if the cash received exceeds the book value of the portion of the asset considered sold. **The asset acquired is recorded at an amount equal to that proportion of the book value of the asset considered to have been exchanged.** Thus, this transaction is recorded in part at market value and in part at book value.

Example: Company A exchanged a large crane that cost $50,000, accumulated depreciation, $45,000, for a small crane with a cash price (i.e., market value) of $8,000, and **received** a cash difference of $2,000. The transaction would be recorded as follows:[4]

Cash	2,000	
Machinery (small crane)*	4,000	
Accumulated depreciation (large crane)	45,000	
Machinery (large crane)		50,000
Gain on disposal of machinery (large crane)†		1,000

Computations:

* Cost of small crane—book value of large crane less the proportion of book value of the large crane sold:

Book value, large crane ($50,000 − $45,000)	$5,000
Proportion of book value of the large crane sold for cash:	

$$\text{Book value of large crane} \times \frac{\text{Cash realized on part sale}}{\text{Cash realized on part sale} + \text{MV of asset acquired on part exchange}}$$

$\$5{,}000 \times \dfrac{\$2{,}000}{\$2{,}000 + \$8{,}000}$	1,000
Difference—cost asset acquired	$4,000

† Gain on disposal of asset given up—cash received less proportion of book value of asset given up that is considered sold:

Cash received	$2,000
Proportion of book value of large crane sold (per above)	1,000
Difference—gain on sale of large crane	$1,000

---

[4] The entry to record the exchange can be separated into two component entries, as shown below:

a. To record sale of 20% of the asset given up [$2,000 ($8,000 + $2,000) = 20%]:

Cash	2,000	
Accumulated depreciation ($45,000 × 20%)	9,000	
Machinery (large crane) ($50,000 × 20%)		10,000
Gain on disposal of machinery (large crane)		1,000

b. To record exchange of 80% of the large asset for another similar asset (at book value):

Machinery (small crane)	4,000	
Accumulated depreciation ($45,000 × 80%)	36,000	
Machinery (large crane) ($50,000 × 80%)		40,000

In case of a **loss,** the *Opinion* requires recognition of the full amount of such loss. Assume in the preceding example that the accumulated depreciation was $39,000. The transaction would be recorded as follows:

Cash	2,000	
Accumulated depreciation (large crane)	39,000	
Loss on disposal of machinery (large crane)	1,000*	
Machinery (small crane)	8,000†	
Machinery (large crane)		50,000

* Computation of loss:	
Value received ($8,000 + $2,000)	$10,000
Less: Book value of asset given up ($50,000 − $39,000)	11,000
Loss	$(1,000)

† Cannot exceed its market value.

Notice that the full amount of the loss is recognized because the asset acquired cannot be recorded at more than its market value (i.e., $8,000 in this case). Thus, there is no need to calculate the proportionate part of the large crane sold. A loss is reported because the book value of the asset given up (i.e., $11,000) is greater than its market value (i.e., $2,000 + $8,000 = $10,000), as reflected in the exchange transaction.

The *Opinion* does not recognize the list or "sticker" price of an asset acquired as the measure of its cost unless list price is the actual cash equivalent (i.e., market) value of the asset. The list price often is merely a basis for bargaining rather than a genuine cash cost. To determine market value in exchanges of operational assets, *APB Opinion 29* states that market values should be determined by "quoted market prices, independent appraisals, estimated fair values of assets or services received in exchange, and other available evidence."

If a business acquires several generations of **similar** assets by trading the next-to-newest asset as part payment for the newest asset, the effect of accounting for the exchanges at book value under the provisions of *APB Opinion 29* can be to accumulate past errors into the book value of the newest asset. Examples of such errors that can affect this book value include past errors in depreciation and expenditures for repairs. The cycle is broken in the event of a loss on exchange of assets, in which case the new asset is recorded at its market value.

Accounting for exchanges of dissimilar and similar assets is summarized in **Exhibit 10–1.**

Lump-Sum Purchases of Several Assets. Often a business may acquire several different assets for a single lump sum. This type of acquisition, frequently called a **basket, group,** or **lump-sum purchase,** poses the problem of allocating the single lump-sum cost to the several different assets acquired. The apportionment is necessary to conform to the cost principle for each asset. The allocation of the purchase price should be based on some realistic indicator of the relative values of the several assets involved, such as current appraised values, tax assessment, cost savings, or the present value of estimated future earnings.

Assume $90,000 was paid for property that included land, a building, and some machinery. An independent appraisal showed the following appraised values: land, $30,000; building, $50,000; and machinery, $20,000. The cost appor-

Exhibit 10–1
Accounting for exchanges of similar and dissimilar assets.*

I. Dissimilar Assets
In accounting for operational assets acquired by trading in another asset and paying or receiving cash, the asset acquired is recorded at cost (i.e., at market value) in conformity with the cost principle and a gain or loss on disposition of the asset is recognized. This accounting is used when the asset acquired and the asset given up are dissimilar.

II. Similar Assets
APB Opinion 29 makes an exception to the above principle if the asset acquired and the asset given up are similar. The "rules" for similar assets are as follows:

A. No cash involved.
   1. MV of asset received > Book value (BV) of asset given up:
      a. No gain is recognized.
      b. Asset acquired is recorded at BV of asset given up.
   2. MV of asset received < BV of asset given up:
      a. Loss is recognized.
      b. Asset acquired is recorded at its MV.

B. Cash paid in addition to the exchanged asset.
   1. MV of asset received > BV of asset given up + Cash:
      a. No gain is recognized.
      b. Asset acquired is recorded at BV of asset given up + Cash.
   2. MV of asset received < BV of asset given up + Cash:
      a. Loss is recognized.
      b. Asset received is recorded at its MV.

C. Cash received in addition to the exchanged asset.
   1. MV of asset received + Cash > BV of asset given up:
      a. Partial gain is recognized (for portion of asset sold for cash).
      b. Asset received is recorded at BV of exchange portion of asset given up.
   2. MV of asset received + Cash < BV of asset given up:
      a. Loss is recognized.
      b. Asset received is recorded at its MV.

*This summary is based on the assumption that the MV of assets received equals the MV of assets given up.

tionment of the single lump-sum cost and the entry to record the transaction are shown below:

Asset	Appraised value	Apportionment of cost	Apportioned cost
Land	$ 30,000	3/10 × $90,000	$27,000
Building	50,000	5/10 × 90,000	45,000
Machinery	20,000	2/10 × 90,000	18,000
Total	$100,000		$90,000

To record the purchase:

Land	27,000	
Building	45,000	
Machinery	18,000	
Cash		90,000

Make-Ready Costs. Subsequent to acquisition, but prior to the use of an operational asset, all costs incurred to ready the asset for use should be capitalized as part of the cost of the asset. Prior to the operational use, a secondhand asset often requires substantial outlays for repairs, reconditioning, remodeling, and installation, all of which should be capitalized. Reinstallation and rearrangement costs of machinery, rearrangement of building partitions, renovation of buildings, and similar outlays **directly related** to operational assets purchased new or in used condition should be capitalized as part of the cost. During a period of renovation, overhead expenditures such as insurance, taxes, supervisory salaries, and similar incidental expenditures directly related to a used asset also should be capitalized. Depreciation should not be recorded on such costs prior to the period of use of the asset.

Departures from Cost in Accounting for Operational Assets

Accounting for operational assets is based on the **cost principle;** however, departure from the cost principle is allowed in special cases. These departures relate to the following:

1. Donation of assets to the company.
2. High and unexpected discovery value of assets owned by the company.
3. Significant and permanent impairment of use value to the company.
4. Revaluations due to quasi-reorganization of the company (discussed in Supplement 17–A).

Donated Assets. Assets occasionally are donated to a company by municipalities or other nonprofit organizations as an inducement to locate a plant or other facility in the area. Often such donations are conditional upon some particular performance by the company, such as the employment of a certain number of individuals by a specified date. Donations of assets also are made occasionally by the owners of the company.

Strict adherence to the cost principle would result in recording donated assets at only the amount of incidental costs incurred in acceptance of the asset and in fulfilling the related agreements. However, accountability for the resources of the entity and measurement of its earning power suggest that each operational asset acquired and used by the entity be recorded at its cash equivalent value, regardless of its origin. *APB Opinion 29* states that "a nonmonetary asset received in a **nonreciprocal transfer** should be recorded at the fair market value of the asset received." Donated assets exemplify "nonreciprocal transfers," that is, transfers in which the donor receives few resources or none at all. An independent and realistic appraisal of the current market value of the donated asset should be recorded, provided the donation is unconditional. Should the donor impose restrictions, any "negative values" arising from such conditions should be estimated and deducted from the market value of the asset in determining the valuation to be recorded. Depreciable assets received by donation should be depreciated in the normal manner on the basis of the valuation recorded in the accounts. To illustrate, assume a building, including the land on which it is located, is given by a city to XYZ Corporation as an inducement to establish a plant in that locale. The related transactions are recorded as follows:

a. To record the market value, based on an appraisal at the date of donation and a $5,000 transfer cost:

Plant building	400,000	
Plant land	100,000	
Cash		5,000
Contributed capital—donated plant building and land		495,000

b. To record depreciation on the building for the first year assuming a 10-year life and no residual value:

Depreciation expense	40,000	
Accumulated depreciation—plant building		40,000

If the donation is contingent upon the fulfillment of some contractual obligation by the recipient, the asset should be treated as a contingent asset until the contingent condition has been met. In such a case, *FASB Standard 5,* "Accounting for Contingencies," specifies that the donated asset be disclosed in the financial statements by note only. Any cash paid that is directly related to the contingency should be debited to a deferred charge account and fully explained in the disclosure notes.

Discovery Value. Property owned by a company may significantly increase in value after its acquisition date as a result of the discovery of valuable mineral or other natural resources. In such cases, the original cost of the property may not provide a reasonable basis for accountability. Both the FASB and the Securities and Exchange Commission (SEC) have considered discovery value accounting for oil and gas companies. Discovery value is usually defined as the "best estimate" of the underground market value of the reserves found. This value would be reestimated at each year-end. In 1978, the SEC issued *Accounting Series Release 253,* requiring that Reserve Recognition Accounting, which is a form of discovery value accounting, be used to account for oil and gas reserves. In 1981, the SEC dropped the requirement. The accounting profession has been reluctant to recognize accounting values other than cost for natural resources in the basic financial statements.[5]

Write-Down of Operational Assets Due to Impairment of Use Value. As a general accounting guideline, operational assets should not be reported at a book value materially in excess of their economic value in use. If the assets are not in use, they should not be carried in excess of their net realizable value.

If an operational asset suffers **permanent impairment of its operational value by a material amount,** it should be written down or written off as the circumstances warrant. For example, a plant may become idle due to such factors as continuing decline in demand, obsolescence of its products, or inadequate transportation facilities. As a result, it may have little or no resale value and its decreased value, if any, can only be realized as salvage. In such cases, GAAP **requires** an immediate write-down to net realizable value and recognition of the **impairment loss** in the write-down period. Normally the write-down should be accomplished with a credit to the accumulated depreciation account (in recognition of obsolescence) and a debit to a nonrecurring loss in the period of the write-down.

---

[5] However, *FASB Standards 33* and *69* allow or recommend certain supplemental disclosures of the current cost of some natural resource reserves.

PART B: SPECIAL PROBLEMS IN ACCOUNTING FOR OPERATIONAL ASSETS

Assets Constructed for Own Use

Some companies construct operational assets for their own use. For example, a utility may use its work crews to extend transmission facilities and construct pipelines. Other companies that normally would not construct their own facilities may do so when their personnel and properties would otherwise be idle. All labor and material costs **directly** identified with such construction projects should be capitalized as a cost of the constructed asset. Determining the amount of **general overhead** cost that should be allocated to the construction project is controversial. Two accounting problems arise: (1) What overhead costs can be incrementally (i.e., directly) identified with the new construction? (2) Should general company overhead be allocated to self-constructed assets on the same basis as to regular production for inventory?

Some accountants believe the only sound basis for allocating overhead costs is to assign self-constructed assets only the **incremental overhead cost** caused by the project. Other accountants believe self-construction projects should bear the incremental overhead cost and, in addition, the same proportion of general overhead costs that would be assigned to regular production. In their view, if general overhead is allocated on the basis of labor-hours, and 8% of labor-hours are associated with self-construction, then 8% of **total** general overhead should be included as a cost of the self-constructed assets. Those favoring allocating general overhead on this basis maintain that self-constructed assets should be accounted for on the same basis as inventory. They argue that if the same basis is not followed, special treatment is granted to self-constructed assets. In particular, not allocating some portion of the general overhead to self-construction may result in an undervaluation of self-constructed assets and an overstatement of inventory and cost of goods sold on regular production. The counterargument by those who favor allocating only the **incremental** overhead to self-constructed assets is that allocation of overhead to self-constructed assets when idle capacity exists should not affect the cost of normal production. In this view, capitalization of overhead other than that caused by the self-construction results in overstatement of the cost of self-constructed assets and understatement of inventory and cost of goods sold. Perhaps as a compromise, the usual policy for self-constructed assets is to capitalize *(a)* all incremental overhead and *(b)* a part of general overhead to the extent that idle capacity is used.

Excess Costs of Construction. The actual cost of a self-constructed asset may differ from its cost if acquired from outsiders. When a company determines that its cost to self-construct an asset **exceeds** the prospective cost of acquiring a similar asset of equal capacity and quality from outsiders, the company should include the excess cost in expense (or loss) of the period in which the self-construction is completed. Failure to do so carries forward cost elements that have no future benefit. On the other hand, when the cost of a self-constructed asset is less than its prospective cost if acquired from outsiders, the asset should be recorded at actual cost. Writing it up to the prospective cost and recognition of the cost saving as revenue or a gain of the current period is not permitted under GAAP.

Capitalization of Interest during the Construction Period

Whether an asset is self-constructed or acquired from outsiders, there is often a lengthy period from an authorization, to the start of a project, and to its completion. A controversial question is whether to capitalize (i.e., debit the Asset account) the interest cost during the construction period, or to account for it as interest expense. There is general agreement that time-related costs, such as taxes and insurance, during construction should be added to the cost of the asset under construction rather than recognized as current expenses. Consistent logic supports capitalization of interest during the construction period (interest costs incurred before and after construction is completed always should be expensed). However, capitalization of interest causes complications. For example, unless the funds were borrowed specifically to finance the construction, it is difficult to determine the proper amount of interest to capitalize.

Public utilities traditionally have capitalized interest during construction. Instead of matching interest on funds borrowed to finance construction with current revenue (i.e., as interest expense), they have capitalized it as a cost of the assets built. The argument is that utility customers are charged regulated rates designed to *(a)* give utility company stockholders a "fair" rate of return on their investment and *(b)* provide equitable utility rates for present and future utility customers. If interest is recognized as current expense, current customers would have to pay increased utility rates to cover the added expense and, in effect, would be financing facilities that will benefit future customers. By including the interest in the cost of the constructed assets (thereby raising future depreciation amounts), future customers who benefit from the assets pay for the interest incurred to create the assets and the related utility service.

Capitalization of interest during construction by nonutility companies has not been widespread, but the practice grew in the early 1970s. Consequently, in 1979, the FASB issued *Statement of Financial Accounting Standards 34,* "Capitalization of Interest Cost," which governs the capitalization of interest (as revised by *FASB Standard 42,* November 1980, and *FASB Standard 62,* June 1982). These *Standards* provide the following guidelines (adapted from *FASB Standard 34*):

1. **Underlying concept**—The historical cost of acquiring an asset includes all costs incurred to bring it to the condition and location necessary for its **intended use** (i.e., for operational assets, readiness for use, and for inventory readiness for sale).
2. **Qualifying assets**—Interest **shall be capitalized** on expenditures for the following types of assets:
   a. Assets that are constructed or otherwise produced for an enterprise's **own use** (including assets constructed or produced for the enterprise by others for which deposits or progress payments have been made).
   b. Assets intended for **sale or lease** that are constructed or otherwise produced as **discrete** projects (e.g., ships or real estate developments).

3. **Interest not capitalized**—Interest is not capitalized for the following:[6]
   a. Inventories that are routinely manufactured or produced in large quantities on a **repetitive** basis.
   b. Assets that are already **in use or are ready for their intended use** in the earning activities of the enterprise.
   c. Assets that are **not being used** in the earning activities of the enterprise and that are not undergoing the activities necessary to get them ready for use.
   d. Land that is **not undergoing activities** necessary to get it ready for its intended use (e.g., operational assets for own use, or inventory for resale).
4. **Interest capitalization period**—The beginning and end of the entire **capitalization** period are as follows:
   a. The capitalization period **begins** when **all** of three conditions are present:
      (1) Qualifying expenditures (defined below) for the qualifying asset actually have been made.
      (2) Activities that are necessary to get the asset ready for its intended use are actually in progress.
      (3) Interest cost actually is being incurred.
   b. Interest capitalization **continues** only so long as these three conditions are present.
   c. The capitalization period **ends** when the asset is substantially complete and ready for its intended use or in conformity with (4*b*) above.

For accounting purposes the entire capitalization period, if an extended time (e.g., longer than three months), should be subdivided into **interim** interest capitalization periods (of one year or less).

Amount of Interest Capitalized

Conceptually, the amount of interest to be capitalized is the interest that could have been avoided if the expenditures for the assets have not been made. Application of this concept requires determination of two amounts: *(a)* average accumulated expenditures, and *(b)* the interest rate(s) to be used (often called the **capitalization rate**). *FASB Standard 34* defines these two amounts as follows:

a. **Average accumulated expenditures each interim capitalization period**—the payments made to contractors (and other parties involved in the construction process) of cash, the transfer of other assets, or the incurring of a liability on which interest is recognized. For each interim capitalization period a weighted average of these expenditures must be computed.[7]
b. **Average interest rate for capitalization**—the average interest rate on all outstanding debts during an interim capitalization period. This excludes

[6] *FASB Standard 62* (par. 5) specifies that interest should not be capitalized for assets acquired with gifts and grants that are restricted by the donor or grantor to acquisition of those assets to the extent that funds are available from such gifts and grants.

[7] Notice that the emphasis is on the accrual basis, not on cash exclusively, for both weighted-average expenditures and interest rates.

short-term debts that specify no interest such as accounts payable and wages payable.[8] **For each interim capitalization period a weighted-average interest rate must be computed.**

Computation of interest capitalized each interim capitalization period. Subject to a limitation (usually called the **capitalization "cap"**) the amount of interest **capitalizable** each capitalization period is **calculated by multiplying the weighted-average accumulated expenditures** ([*a*] above) **by the weighted-average interest rate.**[9]

Limitation on interest capitalized each capitalization period. A "cap" is specified by *FASB Standard 34* for the total amount of interest that can be capitalized **each accounting period** as follows: "The total amount of interest cost capitalized in an **accounting period shall not exceed the total amount of interest cost incurred** by the enterprise in that period." Notice that this constraint emphasizes the "accounting period," not the "capitalization period." The effect of this "cap" is to prevent the capitalization of interest on owners' equity.

Computing and recording the **interest to be capitalized** for each interim capitalization period involves four steps as follows:

Step 1—Computation of the weighted-average accumulated expenditures.
Step 2—Computation of the weighted-average capitalization rate(s).
Step 3—Computation of the amount of interest to be capitalized. Basically, this is done by multiplying the amount computed in Step 1 by the interest rate (i.e., capitalization rate) computed in Step 2 and checking the "cap" constraint.
Step 4—Preparation of the journal entry to record construction expenditures including capitalization of interest.

Exhibit 10–2 gives an overview of these four steps. *FASB Standard 34* does not give detailed guidelines for computation of the weighted-average *(a)* accumulated expenditures and *(b)* interest rate for each capitalization period. However, the term **weighted average** is used in the traditional way—weighted by amount and time (as in computing weighted-average common shares in EPS computations). *FASB Standard 34* does not specify the length of the interim capitalization periods. If the construction project involves less than one year, the entire capitalization period generally is used. If the construction period is longer than one year, monthly or quarterly interim capitalization periods often are used. For instructional purposes, we will illustrate annual and quarterly interim capitalization periods. However, it should be noted that quarterly or monthly computations assure conformity with the purpose of the "cap" constraint when related to an accounting period that is not the same as the capitalization period.

---

[8] *FASB Standard 62* disallows the offset of interest earned against interest cost in determining either capitalization rates or the limit on interest capitalized except in situations involving acquisition of qualifying assets financed with the proceeds of tax-exempt borrowings if those funds are externally restricted to finance acquisition of specified qualifying assets or to service the related debt. When tax exempt debt is involved, the amount of interest to be capitalized is the interest cost of the debt less any interest earned on related interest-bearing investments acquired with the proceeds of the debt from the date of the borrowing until the assets are ready for their intended use (pars. 3–4).

[9] *FASB Standard 34* permits two approaches in the use of interest rates which involve some minor differences. One approach, usually called the **weighted-average approach,** is assumed here. The other approach, called the **specific approach,** is discussed later.

Exhibit 10–2
Capitalization of Interest during construction.

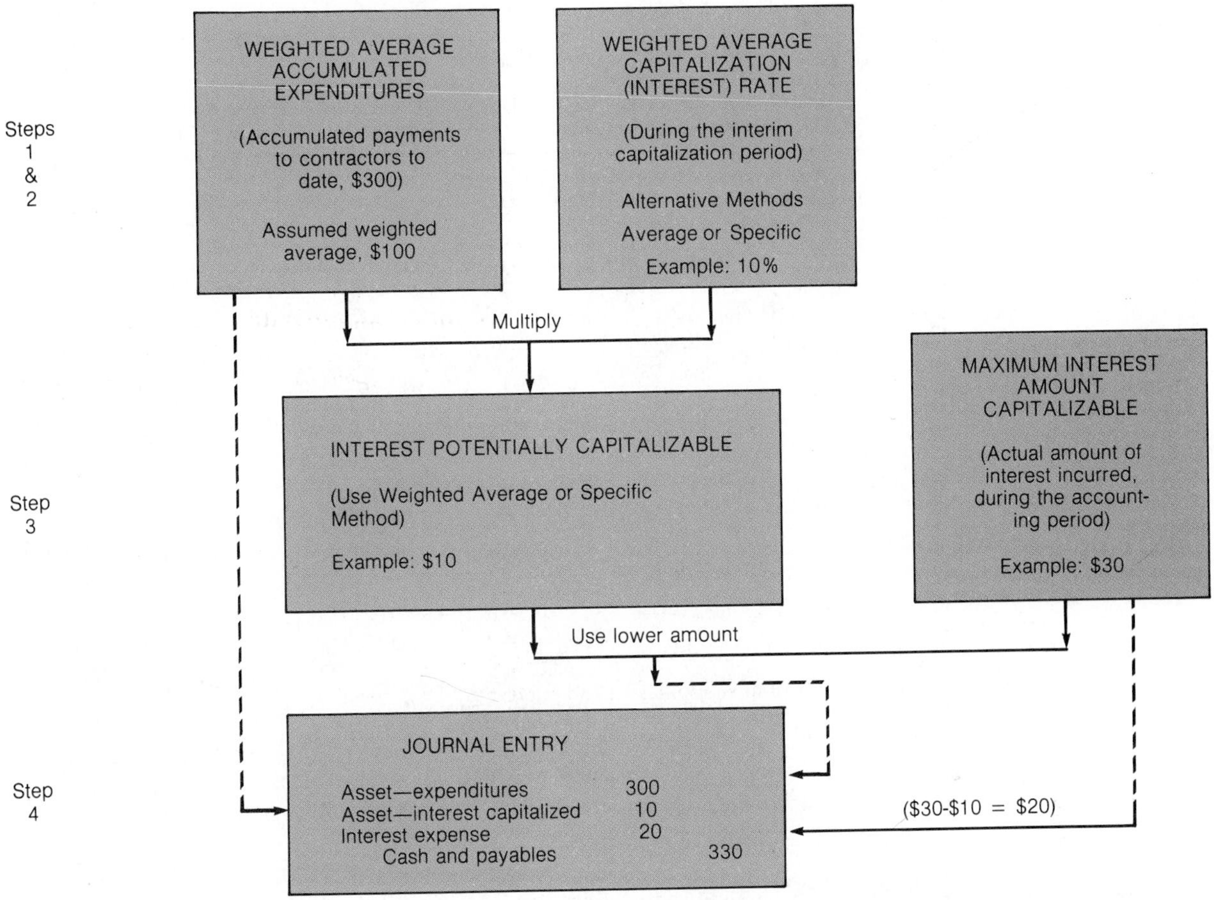

Illustrations of Interest Capitalization

To illustrate capitalization of interest we use two cases—Simple Company (using an annual capitalization period) and Complex Company (using quarterly capitalization periods). Both companies use the weighted-average method (rather than the **specific method** which is discussed later).

Exhibit 10–3 gives the case data and the solution for Simple Company. Notice that two weighted averages—expenditures and interest rate—were computed. The product of these two averages was compared with the cap to determine the amounts of interest to be capitalized and expensed. Based on these computations the required entry was made. If the construction project continued for another year with exactly the same basic data, the schedule would be exactly the same. The point is, for each interim capitalization period this same computation must be made, taking into account the accumulated expenditures to date and the outstanding debt during the new interim capitalization period.

Now we will consider the case of Complex Company during the construction of an office building. This case is complex only because **quarterly** interim capitalization periods are used. Instead of one set of computations (as shown for Simple Company) four separate computations must be made—one for each

Exhibit 10–3
Simple Company, annual capitalization period (weighted average).

Panel A—Case data:
Simple Company contracted with Super-Builders to build a warehouse on land acquired some years earlier. The following data relate to this project:

a. Start of construction, January 1, 19X1; completion date, December 31, 19X1.
b. Cash payments during 19X1 to the contractor were in (000s): January 1, $60; June 30, $180; and December 31, $60.
c. The outstanding debt during 19X1 was: January 1–December 31, construction note payable, $50, 12% interest; remaining debts, $250, 9.6% interest.

Panel B—Capitalization computations and journal entry:
Step 1—Computation of the **weighted-average** accumulated payments to the contractor:

Date	Expenditure	Months to Dec. 31	Dollar-months
Jan. 1	$ 60	12	$ 720
June 30	180	6	1,080
Dec. 31	60	0	-0-
Total	$300	18	$1,800 Average: $1,800 ÷ 18 = $100

Step 2—Computation of the **weighted-average** capitalization (i.e., interest) rate:

Debt	Time	Principal amount	Actual interest Rate	Actual interest Amount
Note payable	Jan. 1–Dec. 31	$ 50	× 12% =	6
Remaining debts	Jan. 1–Dec. 31	250	× 9.6% =	24
Total		$300		$30 Average: $30 ÷ $300 = 10%

Step 3—Interest to be capitalized and interest to be expensed:

Interest potentially capitalizable ($100 × 10%)	$10*	
Maximum capitalizable (actual) interest (from Step 2) . .	30	
Interest to be **capitalized** (lower amount)		$10
Interest to be **expensed** ($30 – $10)		$20

Step 4—Entries for 19X1 (combined):

Building (payments to contractor, $60 + $180 + $60)	300	
Building (interest capitalized, from Step 3)	10	
Interest expense (from Step 3)	20	
Cash and payables ($300 to contractor + $30 interest)		330

* Based on the two computed averages.

quarter. Other than this difference, the computations each quarter are identical with annual computations shown above for Simple Company. To provide an organized presentation of the four steps listed above, we present two facing exhibits as follows:

Exhibit 10–4—Case data and entries for capitalization of interest.
Exhibit 10–5—Computation of interest to be capitalized and expensed (quarterly), weighted-average method.

Exhibit 10–4, panel A, gives the data for Complex Company. Panel B shows the entry each quarter to record the following costs: *(a)* acquisition of a site, *(b)* payments to the building contractor, *(c)* interest capitalized in the cost of the building, and *(d)* interest expense (not capitalizable). The first entry shown

Exhibit 10–4
Complex Company, quarterly capitalization periods (weighted-average method).

Panel A—Case data:
Complex Company contracted with Handy Builders, Inc. to construct an office building. The following data relates to the construction project which will start on January 5, 19C:

a. January 1, 19C, Complex purchased a site for the building that cost $40,000; paid 10% cash and signed a $36,000, two-year, 9% interest-bearing note. Interest is payable each December 31.
b. Other debt outstanding; note payable, dated June 1, 19A, $400,000, 12%; maturity date, September 30, 19C.
c. July 1, 19C, Complex borrowed $800,000 on a construction note at 10% interest; maturity date, June 30, 19E.
d. During the construction period, which ended on December 28, 19C, Complex made the following payments to the contractors (total for 19C, $3,541,000):

1st Quarter		2d Quarter		3d Quarter		4th Quarter	
Jan. 31	$ 90,000*	Apr. 30	$150,000	Jul. 31	$ 50,000	Oct. 31	$2,185,000
Feb. 28	96,000	May 31	-0-	Aug. 31	40,000	Nov. 30	70,000
Mar. 31	180,000	Jun. 30	280,000	Sep. 30	260,000	Dec. 31	140,000
Total	$366,000		$430,000		$350,000		$2,395,000

Required:
Give the entry to record the transactions related to the construction project at the end of each quarter. Use the weighted-average method applied on a quarterly basis. To save space provide answer in thousands.

Panel B—Solution, journal entries:

	1st Quarter		2d Quarter		3d Quarter		4th Quarter	
Land (payments)	40.0							
Building (payments) ..	326.0†		430.0		350.0		2,395.0	
Building (interest)†	2.7		8.1		11.4		20.8	
Interest expense‡	10.1		4.7		21.4		-0-	
Cash and payables		378.8		442.8		382.8		2,415.8

* Includes the $40,000 expenditure for the land.
† $366.0 − land, $40.0 = $326.0
‡ Computations to support these amounts are shown in Exhibit 10–5.

in Exhibit 10–4 records the land cost as a debit to Land, and the payments to the contractors to Building. These amounts were taken directly from the quarterly payments given in Exhibit 10–4. The four quarterly entries also record **actual** interest cost for each interim period allocated in part to building (i.e., interest capitalized) and in part to interest expense (which is zero in the last quarter). Computation of the quarterly amounts of interest *(a)* capitalized and *(b)* expensed is shown in **Exhibit 10–5.** Exhibit 10–5 shows that the interest on the cost of the land is capitalized as part of the cost of the building (i.e., it is not included in the cost of the land) because the land was acquired as the building site. Exhibit 10–5, panel A, indicates that, for the first quarter of 19C, the average accumulated expenditures (including the land expenditure) on which interest should be capitalized was $92,000. The weighted-average interest rate for the first quarter was 2.9 percent, and the interest potentially capitalizable for the first quarter was $2,700 (i.e., $92,000 × 2.9 percent, in thousands). The total interest for the first quarter was $12,800. Because total interest exceeds the interest potentially capitalizable (i.e., by $2,700), the amount of interest to be

Exhibit 10–5
Complex Company, computation of interest to be capitalized; weighted-average method applied quarterly.

Panel A—Interest to be capitalized (weighted-average method):
First quarter 19C (in 000s):
Step 1—Average accumulated expenditures:

	Actual payments	Remaining months	Dollar-months		Weighted average
January 31	$ 90*	× 2	$180		
February 28	96	× 1	96		
March 31	180	× 0	-0-		
	$366	3	$276	÷ 3	= $ 92

* Includes the land expenditure.

Step 2—Average capitalization rate:

	Principal	Weight	Actual interest		
Prior year note	$400	12% × 3/12	$12.0		
Land note	36	9% × 3/12	.8		
	$436		$12.8	÷ $436 =	2.9%

Step 3—Interest potentially capitalizable	$92 × 2.9% =	$ 2.7	
Maximum capitalizable (actual interest)		12.8	
Interest to be capitalized (lower)			$ 2.7
Interest expense ($12.8 − $2.7)			$ 10.1

Second quarter:
Step 1—Average accumulated expenditures:

From prior quarter	$366	× 3	$1,098		
April 30	150	× 2	300		
June 30	280	× 0	-0-		
	$796	5	$1,398	÷ 5	= $279.6

Step 2—Average capitalization rate (same as first quarter) 2.9%

Step 3—Interest potentially capitalizable	$279.6	× 2.9% =	$ 8.1	
Maximum capitalizable (actual interest, from Step 2)			12.8	
Interest to be capitalized (lower)				$ 8.1
Interest expense ($12.8 − $8.1)				$ 4.7

capitalized for the first quarter is the $2,700; the remaining actual interest, $10,100 is reported as interest expense. If the total interest for the first quarter had been less than capitalizable interest (say $2,500), only that amount of interest cost would have been capitalized as part of the cost of the building and no interest expense would be reported. Notice that for the year, interest of $43,000 was capitalized and interest of $36,200 was expensed.

Exhibit 10–5 shows the interest computations for each quarter and the related

Exhibit 10–5
(concluded)

Third quarter:
Step 1—Average accumulated expenditures:

From prior quarter	$ 796	× 3	$2,388		
July 31	50	× 2	100		
August 31	40	× 1	40		
September 30	260	× 0	-0-		
	$1,146	6	$2,528 ÷	6	= $ 421.3

Step 2—Average capitalization rate:

Prior note	$ 400	12% × 3/12	$12.0	
Land note	36	9% × 3/12	.8	
Construction note	800	10% × 3/12	20.0	
	$1,236		$32.8 ÷ $1,236 =	2.7%

Step 3—Interest potentially capitalizable	$421.3 × 2.7% = $11.4	
Maximum capitalizable (actual interest, from above)	32.8	
Interest to be capitalized (lower)		$ 11.4
Interest expense ($32.8 − $11.4)		$ 21.4

Fourth quarter:
Step 1—Average accumulated expenditures:

From prior quarter	$1,146	× 3	$3,438		
October 31	2,185	× 2	4,370		
November 30	70	× 1	70		
December 31	140	× 0	-0-		
	$3,541	6	$7,878 ÷	6	= $1,313

Step 2—Average capitalization rate:

Land note	$ 36	9% × 3/12	$ .8	
Construction note	800	10% × 3/12	20.0	
	$836		$20.8 ÷ $836 =	2.5%

Step 3—Interest potentially capitalizable	$1,313 × 2.5% = 32.8	
Maximum capitalizable (actual interest, from above)	20.8	
Interest to be capitalized (lower)		$20.8
Interest expense (all capitalized)		$ -0-

journal entries. The interest computation for each quarter involves three steps as follows:

Step 1—Compute the weighted-average expenditure based exclusively on the **payments to the contractors.**

Step 2—Compute the weighted-average interest (i.e., capitalization) rate based exclusively on **qualifying debts.**

Step 3—Multiply the weighted-average expenditures (computed in Step 1) by the weighted-average interest rate (computed in Step 2) to determine the amount of **actual interest to be *(a)* capitalized and *(b)* expensed.**

Specific Method of Computing Interest to Be Capitalized. The two prior cases for Simple and Complex Companies illustrated the weighted-average method. The other method, called the **specific method** (see page 436), computes the weighted-average accumulated expenditures exactly like the weighted-average method. The only computations in the specific method that are different relate directly to the capitalization (interest) rate. The weighted-average method includes all outstanding debt in the computation; therefore, only one interest rate is computed for each interim capitalization period. In contrast, the specific method uses two rates for each interim capitalization period which has *(a)* debt(s) specifically related to the construction project, and *(b)* other outstanding debt(s). Interest to be capitalized then is computed for each of the two debt layers: (1) the interest that relates to the specific debt and (2) the remaining amount of the average accumulated expenditures that relate to the other outstanding debt(s). To illustrate, the specific method for Simple Company would be applied as follows (refer to Exhibit 10–3 for Step 1):

Simple Company, specific method, annual capitalization period.

Step 1—Average accumulated expenditures (already computed in Exhibit 10–3)			$100
Step 2—Specific interest rate and average rate:			
Specific construction loan, $50			12%
Average rate on $250 remaining debts			9.6%
Step 3—Interest to be capitalized and interest to be expensed:			
Interest potentially capitalizable:			
On specific loan ($50 × 12%)	$6		
On remaining debt ($100 − $50) × 9.6%	4.8	$10.8	
Maximum capitalizable (actual) interest			
$50 × 12% = $6) + ($250 × 9.6% = $24)		$30	
Interest to be capitalized (lower amount)			$10.8
Interest to be expensed ($30 − $10.8)			$19.2
Step 4—Entries for 19C (combined):			
Building (payments to contractor)		300	
Building interest (capitalized)		10.8	
Interest expense:		19.2	
Cash and payables ($300 + $30)			330

Selection of the weighted-average method or the specific method would depend on *(a)* whether the specific loans outstanding have higher or lower rate(s) than the weighted-average rate on the remaining loans outstanding, and *(b)* whether the company desires to maximize or minimize the amount of interest capitalized. The **consistency principle** precludes "willy-nilly" changes from one method to the other to manipulate the amount of interest capitalized and the net income for the period. This method is seldom used; it does not involve any new concepts—only a minor priority distinction.

Expenditures Subsequent to Acquisition

After acquisition, numerous costs are incurred related to the **use** of operational assets. Examples include repairs, maintenance, betterments, and replacements. The problem of which outlays should be debited to the Asset account, to the Accumulated Depreciation account, to expense, or to some combination of these accounts is important because of the difficulty in distinguishing between the different types of outlays, such as ordinary repairs as opposed to extraordinary repairs. It is also important because each type of outlay requires different accounting and financial reporting.

Maintenance and Ordinary Repairs

Maintenance expenses are those expenditures for lubrication, cleaning, adjustment, and painting, incurred on a continuous basis to keep operational assets in usable condition. **Ordinary repairs** (as distinguished from major repairs) are outlays for parts, labor, and related supplies necessary to keep the asset in operating condition but neither *(a)* add materially to the use value of the asset, nor *(b)* immediately prolong its life significantly. Ordinary repairs are recurring expenses and usually involve relatively small expenditures. Examples of ordinary repairs are repairing a broken chain or electrical circuit and replacing spark plugs. Because maintenance costs and ordinary repairs are similar, they usually are combined for accounting purposes.

Ordinary repair and maintenance expenses are called **revenue expenditures;** they may be accounted for by using either of two approaches:

1. **Incurred approach**—This approach is based on **actual** amounts. Expense is debited for each outlay as incurred. Because use of the asset precedes repairs, sometimes it is argued that the matching principle is not adequately implemented. However, immateriality of any difference in the amount of expense recorded under the incurred approach versus the allocation approach (see below) and the short time between use and recurring repairs mitigate this violation of strict theory.
2. **Allocation approach**—This approach is based on **estimated** amounts. For a new asset, repairs and maintenance initially will be low, increasing in amount as the asset is utilized. Repair costs also tend to vary with use. Rather than debiting operating expense as the repairs are incurred, sometimes it is preferable to use an allocation approach. The allocation approach requires an advance estimate of the total cost of repairs and maintenance during *(a)* the life of the asset or *(b)* during the current year, depending upon the period over which allocation is desired. The amount of estimated repairs is allocated to each interim period on the basis of time (e.g., an equal amount each month or year, as the case may be) or preferably on the basis of production or output depending on the situation. Repair and Maintenance Expense is recognized each period, and a liability account is created for the estimated amount. Actual expenditures for ordinary repairs and maintenance then are offset against the liability account when incurred. To illustrate the allocation approach, estimated ordinary repairs and maintenance for the year was $18,000. This amount will be allocated equally to each month. The total repairs and maintenance cost incurred for the first month was $1,100. The indicated entries are as follows:

a. To record the estimated ordinary repair and maintenance expense and the related liability for the month:

Repair and maintenance expense ($18,000 ÷ 12 months)	1,500	
Estimated liability for repairs and maintenance		1,500

b. To record actual outlays for the first month for ordinary repairs and maintenance:

Estimated liability for repairs and maintenance	1,100	
Cash or payables		1,100

The statement of income would report repair and maintenance expense of $1,500 for the month. The $400 credit balance in the liability account would be reported on the interim statement of financial position as a current liability because it reflects a future demand on current assets. At the end of the year, any balance in the liability account would be removed and the offset would be to the related expense account. That is, repair and maintenance expense would be adjusted at year-end to reflect the actual cost of repairs for the year.

The allocation approach for ordinary repairs and maintenance has been accorded general acceptability by the accounting profession. In seasonal businesses, when possible, repair activities often are deferred to the end of the busy season for a repair "catchup." In such circumstances, matching is better served under the allocation rather than the incurred method. However, in some situations the allocation method may be used inappropriately to manipulate income, particularly when a long allocation period is used (such as 10 years).

Extraordinary Repairs and Renewals

Extraordinary or major repairs involve large dollar expenditures, are not recurring in nature, and usually increase the **use value** (efficiency and use utility) or the service life of the asset beyond what it was before the repairs. Examples of extraordinary repairs are major overhauls, major improvements in the electrical system, and strengthening the foundation of a building. Such repairs are called **capital expenditures.** Traditionally, two **alternative** approaches are used to account for extraordinary repairs:

1. **Increase the asset account**—If the expenditure serves primarily to increase the asset's use value (utility), the cost is debited to the related asset account.
2. **Reduce the accumulated depreciation account**—If the expenditure serves primarily to increase the service life of the asset (and perhaps the residual value), the cost is debited to the related accumulated depreciation account.

In either case, the revised book value (cost minus accumulated depreciation) is the **same.** The revised book value, taking residual value into consideration, is depreciated over the estimated remaining life.

Both approaches are used because of the difficulty of making a realistic distinction between an increase in utility and an increase in useful life as a result of extraordinary repairs. The two approaches give the same net results on the statement of financial position and statement of income (with the same set of facts).

Replacements and Betterments

Replacement involves the removal of a major part or component of plant or equipment and the substitution of a new part or component of essentially the **same type and performance capabilities.** Replacement may involve specific subunits or a number of major items similar to an extraordinary repair. In fact, the line between replacements and extraordinary repairs often is difficult to draw.

In contrast, a **betterment,** or improvement, involves the removal of a major part or component of plant or equipment and the substitution of a different part or component having significantly **improved and superior performance capabilities.** The improved substitute increases the overall efficiency of the asset and increases the **useful life** of the primary asset. The replacement of an old shingle roof with a modern fireproof tile roof, installing a more powerful engine in a shrimp boat, and replacement with an improved electrical system in a building, are examples of betterments.

Replacements and betterments are **capital expenditures.** Because of the different circumstances in which **replacements and betterments** are made, three different accounting approaches are used:

1. **Substitution**—This method appropriately assumes a disposal of the old unit and acquisition of a new unit. Therefore, these two events are recorded as follows:

   a. The cost of the old unit replaced is removed from the asset account, the accumulated depreciation on the old unit is removed, and a loss is recognized.

   b. The cost of the new replacement unit is debited to the asset account.

   To illustrate, assume the old shingle roof on Building A, original cost $20,000, 80% depreciated, is replaced by a fireproof tile roof that cost $60,000. The two entries (which could be combined) are as follows:

   a. To remove old roof from the accounts:

Accumulated depreciation (old roof, $20,000 × 80%)	16,000	
Loss on asset replacement	4,000	
Building (old roof)		20,000

   b. To record acquisition of new roof:

Building (new roof)	60,000	
Cash		60,000

   This method is conceptually sound; however, it can be applied only when the cost of the old subunit and the related accumulated depreciation amount are known or can be reliably estimated.

2. **Increase asset account**—This approach is used when the old costs and related accumulated depreciation amounts are not known, and when the primary effect is to increase efficiency (i.e., a betterment), rather than to lengthen the economic life of the basic asset. The cost of the betterment is debited to the primary asset account in conformity with the cost principle. In this approach, the cost and accumulated depreciation on the unit replaced are not removed from the accounts because they cannot be determined reliably. Often the depreciation rate must be revised.

3. **Reduce accumulated depreciation**—This approach is used when the primary effect is to lengthen the remaining life of the related asset (a replacement). However, it is used as an acceptable alternative for approach (2) above. The cost of the replacement is debited to the related accumulated depreciation account on the basis that it is a recovery of past depreciation and that the life of the primary asset is lengthened. The cost and accumulated depreciation on the unit replaced are not removed from the accounts. Often the depreciation rate must be revised.

In their 1987 annual report, NCH Corporation disclosed that the company capitalizes the cost of extraordinary repairs, renewals, and betterments, and expenses the cost of ordinary repairs and maintenance.[10]

Additions

Additions are extensions, enlargements, or expansions made to an existing asset. Examples are an extra wing or room added to a building and the addition of a production unit to an existing machine. An addition is a **capital expenditure.** It should be recorded in the operational asset accounts at acquisition cost. Work done on the existing structure, such as shoring up the foundation for the addition or the cutting of an entranceway through an existing wall, is a part of the cost of the addition and should be capitalized. If the addition is an integral part of the older asset, its cost, less any estimated residual value, normally should be depreciated over its own service life or the remaining life of the original asset, whichever period is shorter. If not an integral part, it should be depreciated over its own useful life.

Pollution control devices have been added by many entities to comply with laws and court or administrative orders. Sometimes, either because the original assets (which are the source of the pollution) were acquired when prices were low or because of stringent control regulations, the antipollution devices are costly in relation to the costs of the original assets. In this case, the devices are separately capitalized and depreciated as plant additions.

A question arises as to the accounting classification of fines, damages, or penalties assessed for earlier pollution. Some accountants argue that such costs should be expensed in the current period; others contend the costs should be capitalized as a cost of the related asset and depreciated over future periods. The authors prefer the current expense alternative.

Rearrangement of Assets. The costs of reinstallation, rerouting, or rearrangement of factory machinery to increase efficiency are **capital expenditures** if the benefits of the rearrangement will extend beyond the current accounting period. Such costs should be capitalized as a **deferred charge** and amortized over the ensuing periods benefiting from the rearrangement. If either the future benefits from such outlays or the periods benefited cannot be estimated reliably, such expenditures should be expensed as incurred.

---

[10] The company's annual report provides details in the "Disclosure of Accounting Policies."

Disposal of Operational Assets

The disposal of operational assets may be voluntary as in a sale, trade, or abandonment—or involuntary as a result of a casualty, such as a fire or storm. If the asset is subject to depreciation, it should be depreciated to the date of disposal. Likewise, taxes, insurance premium costs, and similar costs should be accrued up to the date of disposal. At the date of disposal the cost of the asset and its related accumulated depreciation should be removed from the accounts. For example, a truck that cost $32,000 on February 1, 19A, is sold on July 1, 19E, for $8,000. Straight-line depreciation has been recorded on the basis of an estimated service life of five years and an estimated residual value of $2,000. The company's fiscal year-end is December 31. The entries at date of sale are as follows:

1. Depreciation expense	3,000	
Accumulated depreciation—equipment		3,000

To record six months' depreciation for 19E at $500 per month computed as follows:

Amount to be depreciated ($32,000 − $2,000)	$30,000
Service life—5 years or 60 months.	
Depreciation ($30,000 × 6/60)	3,000

2. Cash	8,000	
Accumulated depreciation—equipment ($30,000 × 53/60)	26,500	
Delivery equipment		32,000
Gain on disposal of equipment*		2,500

To record retirement of old truck by sale:

*Sales price			$8,000
Less book value of asset sold:			
Original cost		$32,000	
Accumulated depreciation:			
19A—11 months	$5,500		
19B—12 months	6,000		
19C—12 months	6,000		
19D—12 months	6,000		
19E— 6 months	3,000	26,500	5,500
Gain on disposal			$2,500

If an operational asset is abandoned or disposed of because it has no value, the cost and accumulated depreciation amounts should be removed from the accounts. Any loss on abandonment, including costs of disposal, should also be recognized.

Outlays made to restore and repair uninsured assets damaged through fire, storm, or other casualty should be recorded as losses.[11] Outlays made subsequent to casualty damage, which significantly enhance the operating condition that existed prior to the casualty, should be apportioned between losses and the asset on a reasonable basis. Damaged assets not restored should be reduced to a carrying value consistent with the decrease in going-concern utility.

---

[11] When the casualty loss is both *(a)* unusual and *(b)* occurs infrequently, as defined in *APB Opinion 30*, it must be reported as an extraordinary item.

Disclosures of operational assets for Univar Corporation are shown below. Notice the accounting policies disclosed in the notes regarding sale or retirement of properties and expenditures for maintenance, repairs, renewals, and improvements.

UNIVAR CORPORATION
Consolidated Balance Sheets
(in thousand dollars)

	February 28	
	1987	**1986**
Assets:		
Property, plant and equipment (Notes 1, 3 & 10):		
Land	$ 14,146	$ 7,392
Buildings	52,528	30,724
Equipment	83,173	37,000
Leased property under capital leases	7,493	3,989
Construction in progress	8,091	1,553
	$165,431	$80,658
Less accumulated depreciation	28,815	21,325
Net property, plant, and equipment	$136,616	$59,333

Notes to Consolidated Financial Statements:

Note 1: Summary of Accounting Policies (in part).

Property, Plant & Equipment

Expenditures for property, plant and equipment and for renewals and betterments which extend the originally estimated economic lives of assets are capitalized. Expenditures for maintenance, repairs and other renewals are charged to expense. The Corporation's property accounts are maintained, for the most part, in multiple asset accounts. In the case of normal dispositions, the cost of property sold or retired is removed from the property account and charged to accumulated depreciation and no gain or loss is recorded. In the case of significant dispositions, gain or loss is recognized.

For financial reporting purposes, depreciation has been provided using the straight-line method over the estimated useful lives of the related assets. For income tax purposes, depreciation on certain assets is computed using accelerated methods.

Depreciation expense charged against operations in the accompanying consolidated statements of income amounted to $8,184,000 in 1987, $4,844,000 in 1986, and $4,262,000 in 1985.

In accordance with *FASB Statements of Financial Accounting Standards Nos. 34* and *62*, interest costs have been capitalized on major construction projects while in progress. Interest costs of $75,000, $75,000, and $213,000 for fiscal years 1987, 1986, and 1985, respectively, have been capitalized in the cost of new facilities.

Summary

This chapter discussed the acquisition and disposition of operational assets in conformity with the cost principle. The original cost of an operational asset basically is the cash paid, plus all noncash considerations valued at the market value of the consideration given, or of the asset received, whichever is more reliably determinable. If the noncash consideration is debt, the present value of the debt should be used. The acquisition of operational assets may involve, in addition to cash, a trade-in of old assets. Basically, the new asset is recorded at market value (which is the case when the asset received and the asset given up are dissimilar). However, when the two assets are similar a book value approach is used. In this case the asset received is recorded as the book value of the asset given up plus any cash paid.

Interest should not be capitalized as part of the cost of an operational asset unless it meets specified criteria **during the construction period.** Interest capitalized during construction may be computed using either the weighted-average method or the specific method. The specified criteria for capitalization of interest relates to the kind of asset, the length of the construction period, actual interest incurred, and interest to be capitalized.

Expenditures made on operational assets after their acquisition should be classified as either *(a)* **capital expenditures** (debited to the related asset account or accumulated depreciation) and depreciated over the remaining life of the asset, or *(b)* **revenue expenditures** (expensed as incurred). Expenditures for repairs, renovation, replacements, and betterments should be accounted for in conformity with this guideline.

The disposal of an operational asset involves two types of entries:

1. Adjust the balances of all related accounts up to the date of disposal (e.g., accumulated depreciation, property taxes, and insurance premiums).
2. Record the disposal of the asset and recognize a gain or loss on disposal.

QUESTIONS

Part A

1. Operational assets are classified as tangible or intangible; distinguish between the two, and give examples. Under what statement of financial position caption are tangible operational assets reported? Give at least one synonym for whatever title you specify.
2. How does the cost principle apply to the acquisition of operational assets? What implications does the matching principle have for operational asset accounting?
3. Distinguish between capital and revenue expenditures. What accounting implications are involved?
4. To determine the cost of an operational asset, how should the following items be treated: *(a)* invoice price, *(b)* freight, *(c)* discounts, *(d)* title verification costs, *(e)* installation costs, *(f)* break-in costs, and *(g)* cost of major overhaul before operational use?
5. A machine was purchased on the following terms: cash, $100,000, plus five annual payments of $5,000 each. How should the acquisition cost of the machine be determined? Explain.
6. How is asset acquisition cost determined when the consideration given is equity securities?
7. Basically, how are assets recorded when they are acquired by exchanging another asset?
8. When does the "culmination of an earnings process" occur upon exchange of assets?
9. When dissimilar assets are exchanged, what value is used as the cost of the asset acquired?
10. When several operational assets are purchased for a single lump-sum consideration, cost apportionment is usually employed. Explain the procedure. Why is apportionment necessary?
11. Should donated assets be recorded in the accounts? If so, how should they be recorded and at what value?
12. What is discovery value? If discovery value is recognized in the accounts, what is the effect on subsequent expense amounts?

Part B

13. Some businesses construct plant assets for their own use. What costs should be capitalized for these assets? Explain what to do about *(a)* general company overhead and any incremental costs incurred, and *(b)* costs of construction in excess of the purchase price from an outsider.
14. Basically, what amount of interest should be capitalized as a part of the cost of an asset?
15. For what types of assets requiring a substantial completion or processing time is interest capitalization inappropriate?
16. If interest can be capitalized on an asset requiring a substantial completion period, when must interest capitalization begin and cease?
17. XYZ Company borrowed $2 million at 10% to finance construction of a new loading pier, which turned out to cost $3 million aside from capitalized interest. XYZ owes other debt. To what extent, if any, can interest in excess of $200,000 be capitalized in any full year the pier is under construction? As to the other debt, how is the interest rate determined for capitalization purposes?
18. XY Corporation added a new wing at a cost of $300,000, plus $10,000 spent in making passageways through the walls of an old structure to the existing plant. The plant was 10 years old and was being depreciated by an equal amount each year over a 30-year life. Over what period should the new wing be depreciated?
19. Distinguish between maintenance, ordinary repairs, and extraordinary repairs.
20. Explain the accounting for *(a)* extraordinary repairs, *(b)* replacements, and *(c)* betterments.
21. Outline the accounting steps related to the disposition of an operational asset, assuming it is not traded in on another asset.

EXERCISES

Part A: Exercises 10–1 to 10–11

E 10–1 (Acquisition of Land; Noncash Considerations)

Under the cost principle, what cost should be used for recording the land acquired in each of the following independent cases? Give reasons in support of your answer.

Case A—At the middle of the current year, a check was given for $40,000 for the land and the buyer assumed the liability for unpaid taxes in arrears at the end of last year, $1,000, and those assessed for current year, $900.

Case B—Issued 14,000 shares (par $1) of capital stock with a "market value" of $6 per share (based upon a recent sale of 10 shares) for the land. The land was recently appraised at $80,000 by independent and competent appraisers.

Case C—Rejected an offer two years ago by the vendor to sell the land for $8,000 cash. Issued 1,000 shares of capital stock for the land (market value of the stock, $7.80 per share based on several recent large transactions and normal weekly stock trading volume).

Case D—Issued 1,000 shares of capital stock, par $40, for the land. The market value (stock sells daily with an average daily volume of 5,000 shares) was $60 per share at time of purchase of the land. The vendor earlier offered to sell the land for $59,000 cash. Competent appraisers valued the land at $61,000.

E 10–2 (Asset Acquisition; Note Payable)

Vee Corporation acquired equipment on credit. Terms were $14,000 cash down payment plus payments of $10,000 at the end of each of the next two years. The seller's implicit interest rate was 14%. The list price of the equipment was $34,000.

Required (round to the nearest dollar):

a. Give the entry to record the purchase.
b. Give the entry to record the last $10,000 payment.

E 10–3 (Assets Acquired; Note Payable; Discount)

The following situations are independent:

a. Delivery equipment with a list price of $30,000 was purchased; terms were 2/10, n/30. Payment was made within the discount period.
b. Delivery equipment with a list price of $20,000 was purchased; terms were 2/10, n/30. Payment was made after the discount period.
c. Delivery equipment listed at $9,000 was purchased and invoiced at 2/10, n/30. In order to take advantage of the discount, the company borrowed $8,000 of the purchase price by issuance of a 60-day, 15% note, which was paid with interest at maturity date.

Required:

Give entries in each separate situation for costs, borrowing, and any expenses involved.

E 10–4 (Acquisition of Multiple Assets for a Single Price)

Freeman Company purchased a tract of land on which were located a warehouse and an office building. The cash purchase price was $140,000 plus $10,000 in fees connected with the purchase. The following data were collected concerning the property:

	Tax assessment	Vendor's book value	Original cost
Land	$20,000	$10,000	$10,000
Warehouse	40,000	20,000	60,000
Office building	60,000	50,000	80,000

Required:

Give the entry to record the purchase; show computations.

E 10–5 (Asset Cost; Numerous Incidental Expenditures)

For each of the following numbered items, indicate, by using one of the five lettered choices listed below, which accounting treatment is correct. Explain questionable items and any assumptions that you make. Each cost, identified as a numbered item, was incurred by a corporation incident to acquisition of a new machine.

Lettered Choices:

a. Increases or decreases Machinery account.
b. Debit Prepaid Expense or Deferred Charge and amortize separately from machinery.
c. Debit an expense account for current period.
d. Debit Plant, Property, and Equipment account (other than machinery).
e. An accounting treatment other than the four choices above. Explain.

Items Affecting Machinery Cost:

1. Invoice price of the machinery, net of discount.
2. Cash discount for prompt payment of foregoing invoice not taken.

3. Cost of moving machinery into place.
4. Cost of removing old machine that this machinery replaced.
5. Cost of installing sound insulation so new machine will not disturb those who work near it.
6. Special electrical wiring required to connect new machine.
7. Enlargement of electrical system of plant to accommodate new machine and provide for some expected future needs.
8. Sales tax based on purchase price of new machinery.
9. Service contract paid in full covering first two years' operation of the machine.
10. Payment to technicians who assisted with break-in of new machine.
11. Cost of materials used while testing new machine.
12. Cost of training three employees who will operate machine.
13. Debit to machine which was offset by credit to Miscellaneous Revenue amounting to anticipated first year's savings from use of new machine.
14. Insurance premium paid covering first year of protection of new machine against hazards to which it will be exposed.
15. Repair incurred during first year of operations.

E 10–6 (Asset Acquisition; Time Payment Plan)

Wolf Company bought a machine on a time payment plan. The cash purchase price was $25,615. Terms were $7,000 cash down payment plus four equal annual payments at year-end of $6,000, which includes interest on the unpaid balance at 11% per annum.

Required:

1. Give the entry to record the purchase. Show computations (round to nearest dollar).
2. Prepare a schedule to reflect the accounting entries for each of the four installment payments. Round amounts in the schedule to the nearest dollar (see Chapter 5).

E 10–7 (Assets Exchanged; Similar and Dissimilar)

Beech Corporation has some old equipment that cost $70,000; accumulated depreciation is $40,000. This equipment was traded in on a new machine that had a list price of $80,000; however, the new machine could be purchased without a trade-in for $75,000 cash. The difference between the market value of the new asset and the market value of the old asset will be paid in cash.

Required:

Give the entry to record the acquisition of the new machine under each of the following independent cases:

Case A—The new machine was purchased for cash with no trade-in.

Case B—The equipment and the machine are dissimilar. The old equipment is traded in, and $50,000 cash is paid.

Case C—Same as Case B, except that the equipment and the machine are similar.

E 10–8 (Assets Exchanged; Five Different Cases)

On January 1, 19C, Seismographics Corporation exchanged old equipment that cost $10,000 (accumulated depreciation, $4,500) for new equipment. The market value of the new equipment was $8,000. The market value of the old equipment could not be reliably estimated.

Required:
Give the entry to record the acquisition of the new equipment under each of the following independent cases:

Case A—The assets are dissimilar. No cash was involved.

Case B—The assets are dissimilar. Cash of $3,000 was paid by Seismographics.

Case C—The assets are similar. No cash was involved.

Case D—The assets are similar. Cash of $1,000 was paid by Seismographics.

Case E—The assets are similar. Cash of $2,000 was received by Seismographics.

E 10–9 (Acquisition of Multiple Assets for a Single Price)
Brushy Machine Shop purchased the following used equipment at a special auction sale for $80,000 cash: Drill press, lathe, and a heavy-duty air compressor. The equipment was in excellent condition except for the electric motor on the lathe, which will cost $1,800 to replace with a new motor. Brushy has determined that the selling prices for the used items in local outlets are approximately as follows: Drill press, $16,800; lathe, with a good motor, $48,000, and air compressor, $21,000.

Required:
Give the entry to record *(a)* acquisition of the operational assets and *(b)* to replace the motor.

E 10–10 (Donated Assets)
The city of Akron gave New Company a building, including the land on which it is located, as an inducement to start a high technology operation in the city. The property was reliably appraised at a value of $160,000 (one fourth related to the land). The company paid transfer costs of $4,000. The building has an estimated remaining life of 25 years (no residual value).

Required:
Give the entries to record the *(a)* transfer and *(b)* depreciation expense at the end of the first year. Assume a full year of depreciation and the straight-line method.

E 10–11 (Impairment of Value; Operational Assets)
Down Manufacturing Company has a small facility, called Plant XT, that has not been used for several years due to low product demand. The company does not expect to use the facility in the foreseeable future. Efforts are being made to sell the plant for $35,000; but a realistic recovery amount is $20,000 (net of disposal costs). The accounting records show: cost, $145,000; accumulated depreciation, $80,000.

Required:
Give the entry that Down should make to record the permanent impairment of use-value.

Part B: Exercises 10–12 to 10–19

E 10–12 (Asset Constructed for Own Use)
Smith and Smith Company manufactured a new machine for its own use. The ledger account below reflects related debits and credits made during the year to the Machinery account. The machinery was ready for use at the end of the year.

Machinery (new)

Cost of dismantling old machine replaced	$ 2,400	Cash proceeds from sale of old machine	$2,000
Labor costs	18,000		
Raw materials used	24,000		
Installation cost	3,000		
Materials spoiled	800		
Profit on construction	3,000		
Spare parts	3,500		
Auxiliary tools	3,000		

An investigation revealed the following additional facts:

1. The old machine that was removed originally cost $40,000; accumulated depreciation was $38,500.
2. The manufacturing overhead account balance is $100,000; 95% of this relates to ordinary manufacture and the remainder to the self-construction.
3. Cash discounts average 2% on all raw material purchases; the entire amount of discounts taken was recorded as Purchase Discounts.
4. The installation costs was a payment to outsiders for technical assistance during the break-in period of the machine.
5. Materials spoiled is the cost of materials used during the testing and break-in period.
6. Profit on construction was credited to an account with that title. Smith and Smith estimated that it saved at least $3,000 by self-constructing the machinery instead of purchasing it.
7. The debit for spare parts is the cost of parts purchased and set aside to cover breakdowns and maintenance during the first two years of normal use of the machinery.
8. Auxiliary tools are used with the machine; they have an estimated useful life of five years. The machine is expected to last from 10 to 12 years.

Required:
Prepare journal entries to correct the machinery account and other accounts of Smith and Smith. Insofar as possible for each item, key your entries to the numbers that identify the data above. Assume the project does not qualify for interest capitalization.

E 10–13 (Capitalization of Interest; Specific Method)
Weld Corporation is constructing a plant for its own use. Weld capitalizes interest on an annual basis. The following expenditures were made during 19C: January 1, $30,000; July 1, $290,000; September 1, $800,000; and December 31, $2,110,000. The following debts were outstanding throughout the year:

Construction note, 12%	$100,000
Short-term note payable, 15%	240,000
Accounts payable (noninterest-bearing)	400,000

Weld capitalizes interest first using the interest rate on debt directly associated with the construction and then using the weighted-average interest rate of all other debt (i.e., the specific method).

Required:
1. Compute the amount of interest to be capitalized and the amount of interest to be expensed.
2. Give the entry to record the construction expenditures and interest.

E 10–14 **(Capitalization of Interest; Weighted-Average Method)**
Bullock Company is constructing a building for its own use and has been capitalizing interest based on average expenditures on a quarterly basis since development on the project began. The following expenditures were made during the first quarter:
January 1, $2,800,000; February 1, $2,550,000; and March 31, $3,650,000.

Bullock had the following debts outstanding during the quarter:

Note payable, 10% incurred specifically to finance the construction	$1,600,000
Short-term note payable, 15%	2,500,000
Mortgage note payable, 8%	1,200,000
Capitalized lease (on which the first quarter's interest amounted to $3,000)	250,000

Required:
1. Compute interest to be capitalized and interest to be expensed for the first quarter. Use the weighted-average method.
2. Give the entry to record the expenditures and the interest.
3. Explain what effect, if any, the costs of land on which the building is being erected would have on the amount of interest properly capitalizable.

E 10–15 **(Ordinary Repairs; Incurred Approach versus Allocation Approach)**
Jenkins Company operates two separate plants. In plant A, the accounting policy is to consider all ordinary (minor) repairs as expense when incurred. In contrast, in plant B, the accounting policy is to use the allocation approach that debits repair and maintenance expense equally each period. Jenkins Company has little seasonality in its production. Selected data for 19A are as follows:

	Plant A	Plant B
Estimated repair costs budgeted for year	$5,000	$5,000
Actual repair costs incurred and paid:		
First quarter	1,200	400
Second quarter	800	1,500
Third quarter	1,000	1,100
Fourth quarter	2,100	2,200

Required:
1. Give the entries in parallel columns for each plant for each of the four quarters.
2. Would you recommend any changes in the accounting policies? Explain and justify your response.

E 10–16 **(Repairs, Replacements, Betterments, and Renovations)**
The plant building of Xon Corporation is old (estimated remaining useful life, 12 years) and needs continuous maintenance and repairs. The company's accounts show that the building originally cost $600,000; accumulated depreciation was $400,000 at the beginning of the current year. During the current year, the following expenditures relating to the plant building were made:

a. Continuing, frequent, and low-cost repairs	$ 34,000
b. Added a new storage shed attached to the building, estimated useful life, eight years	72,000
c. Removed original roof; original cost, $80,000; replaced it with guaranteed, modern roof	100,000
d. Unusual and infrequent repairs due to damage from flood in desert; repairs did not increase the use value or the economic life of the asset	12,000
e. Complete overhaul of the plumbing system (old costs not known)	25,000

Required:
Give the journal entry to record each of the above items. Explain the basis for your treatment of each item.

E 10–17 (Discovery Value)
A government agency acquired by foreclosure an unprofitable coal mine that had an underground fire smoldering in it. Not wanting to be in the coal mining business, the agency offered the mine for sale during 19A. Miner Mining Company estimated the mine market value at $2.5 million and estimated that it would cost $150,000 to extinguish the fire and clear the mine of accumulated smoke and residue of the fire. On July 1, 19A, Miner offered the government agency a gross price of $1,750,000 for the mine, but specified that $450,000 would be taken off the gross price to allow for extinguishing the fire and clearing the residue. The agency accepted the offer at the end of November 19A, the deal was closed. The $1,300,000 was paid to the agency on February 1, 19B.

Required:
1. Give the entries that Miner should make to record:
   a. The purchase agreement.
   b. Payment of the $1,300,000.
   c. Incurrence of $460,000 actual costs to extinguish the fire and perform the clean-up work.
2. In view of the fact that the company bought the mine at what appears to be a bargain price, discuss the propriety of recognizing "discovery value."

E 10–18 (Disposal of Asset)
On April 1, 19E, one of the two large production machines used by Unlucky Company stripped a gear causing major internal damages. On April 10, 19E, the company decided to purchase a new machine (cost, $182,500) so that production could continue. On January 1, 19D, the accounts showed the following for the old machine: original cost, $90,000, accumulated depreciation, $63,000 (20-year life; no residual value). The company would not accept a trade-in offer of $13,500. Instead the old machine was sold on May 1, 19E, to an out-of-state company for $24,000. Unlucky spent $3,000 cleaning and moving the machine prior to shipping, which cost another $1,000. Insurance premium (prepaid) for 19E on the old machine was $45; the unused portion of the premium will be applied to the new machine.

Required:
Give all entries, by date, that Unlucky Company should make from April 1 through May 1, 19E.

E 10–19 (Asset Cost—Eight Cases)
Select the best answer for each of the following. Briefly justify your choice for each item.

1. May Company purchased certain plant assets on credit. May agreed to pay $10,000 per year for five years. The plant assets should be valued at:
   a. $50,000.
   b. $50,000 plus a charge for the market rate of interest.
   c. Present value of a $10,000 annuity for five years at the "market" interest rate.
   d. Present value of a $10,000 annuity for five years discounted at the bank prime interest rate.
2. The debit for a sales tax properly levied and paid on the purchase of machinery preferably would be to:
   a. A separate deferred charge account.
   b. Miscellaneous tax expense (which includes all taxes other than those on income).
   c. Accumulated Depreciation, Machinery.
   d. The machinery account.
3. When a closely held corporation issues preferred stock for land, the land should be recorded at the:
   a. Total par value of the stock issued.

b. Total book value of the stock issued.
c. Appraised value of the land.
d. Total liquidating value of the stock issued.

Items 4, 5, and 6 are based on the following information:

Two independent companies, Ball and Brown, are in the home building business. Each owns a tract of land held for development, but each company would prefer to build on the other's land. Accordingly, they agree to exchange their land. An appraiser was hired, and from the report and the companies' records, the following information was obtained:

	Ball Co.'s land	Brown Co.'s land
Cost (same as book value)	$ 80,000	$50,000
Market value based upon appraisal	100,000	90,000

The exchange of land was made, and based on the difference in appraised values, Brown paid $10,000 cash to Ball.

4. For financial reporting purposes, Ball would recognize a pretax gain on this exchange in the amount of:
   a. $2,000.
   b. $6,000.
   c. $10,000.
   d. $20,000.

5. For financial reporting purposes, Brown would recognize a pretax gain on this exchange in the amount of:
   a. $–0–.
   b. $10,000.
   c. $30,000.
   d. $40,000.

6. After the exchange, Ball would record its newly acquired land at:
   a. $70,000.
   b. $72,000.
   c. $80,000.
   d. $92,000.

7. Sharp Corporation acquired land, buildings, and equipment from a bankrupt company for a lump-sum price of $90,000. At the time of acquisition, Sharp paid $6,000 to

8. An improvement made to a machine increased its market value and its production capacity by 25% without extending the machine's useful life. The cost of the improvement should be:
   a. Expensed.
   b. Debited to accumulated depreciation.
   c. Capitalized in the machine account.
   d. Allocated between accumulated depreciation and the machine account.

(AICPA adapted)

PROBLEMS

Part A: Problems 10–1 to 10–11

P 10–1 (Asset Acquired; Installment Payments)

Acme Cement Company contracted to buy equipment, agreeing to make an equal annual payment of $10,832 at the end of each of the next four years. The equipment has a list price of $32,900, which is also the cash price, an estimated service life of five years, and estimated residual value of $2,000.

Required (round to nearest dollar):

1. Determine the approximate interest rate implicit in the contract and prepare a debt amortization schedule for the four-year period. Record the purchase of the equipment in conformity with GAAP. Refer to Chapter 5.
2. Assuming Acme's fiscal year coincides with the payment dates, record *(a)* the first payment and *(b)* the depreciation at the end of the first year (use straight-line depreciation).
3. Give similar entries at the end of the fourth year.

P 10–2 (Asset Acquisition; Noncash Consideration)

Machinery with a market value of $15,000 is acquired in a noncash exchange. Below are six independent assumptions (a–f) as to the consideration given in the noncash exchange:

a. Bonds held as a long-term investment, which originally cost $28,000 and had been written down 50% because of a perceived permanent loss of their value.

b. Common stock held as a short-term investment, which originally cost $14,300 included in the short-term portfolio of similar investments. The stock had a market value of $15,000 on the latest statement of financial position date.

c. Inventory carried at $9,500 on the most recent balance sheet as part of a perpetual inventory carried at LCM. When originally acquired, the goods had cost $9,900.

d. Similar used machinery with a book value of $6,000 and a market value of $6,700 plus cash of $8,300. When new, the used machinery cost $8,800.

e. Land with a book value of $7,500 and a market value of $15,000.

f. A noninterest-bearing note for $17,250 maturing in one year. Similar notes required 15% interest at the date of the exchange (refer to Chapter 5).

Required:

Give the journal entry required for each of the above independent assumptions.

P 10–3 (Acquisition Cost; Comprehensive—Five Cost Changes)

An examination of the property, plant, and equipment accounts of James Company on December 31, 19B, disclosed the following transactions:

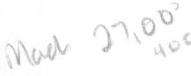

a. On January 1, 19A, purchased a new machine having a list price of $30,000. The company did not take advantage of a 1% cash discount available upon full payment of the invoice within 10 days. Shipping costs paid by the vendor was $100. Installation cost was $400, including $100 which represented 10% of the monthly salary of the factory superintendent (installation period, two days). A wall was torn out and replaced (moved two feet) at a cost of $800 to make room for the machine.

b. During January 19A, the first month of operations, the machine (see [*a*] above) became inoperative due to a defect in manufacture. The vendor repaired the machine at no cost; however, the specially trained operator was idle during the two weeks the machine was inoperative. The operator was paid the regular wages ($650) during the period, although the only work performed was to observe the repair by the factory representative.

c. On January 1, 19A, bought fixtures with a list price of $4,500; paid cash $1,500 and gave a one-year, noninterest-bearing note payable for the balance. The current interest rate for this type of note was 15%. Hint: Compute the present value of this note and round to the nearest dollar. Refer to Chapter 5.

d. On July 1, 19A, contracted for a building for $400,000. The contractor was paid by transferring $400,000 face value of 20-year 8% company bonds payable, at which time financial consultants advised that the bonds would sell at 96 (i.e., $384,000).

e. During January 19B, exchanged the electric motor on a machine for a heavier motor and paid cash, $400. The market value of the new motor was $1,250. The parts list showed a $900 cost for the original motor (estimated life, 10 years).

f. On January 1, 19A, purchased an automatic counter to be attached to a machine in use, cost $700. The estimated useful life of the counter was 7 years, and the estimated life of the machine was 10 years.

Required:

1. Prepare the journal entries to record each of the above transactions. Explain and justify your decision on questionable items.
2. Record depreciation at the end of 19A. James Company uses straight-line depreciation. None of the assets is expected to have a residual value except the fixtures (residual value is $500). Estimated useful lives: fixtures, 5 years; machinery, 10 years; and building, 40 years. Give a separate entry for each asset.

P 10–4 (Asset Acquisition; Comprehensive)

At December 31, 19A, certain accounts included in the property, plant, and equipment section of Hine Corporation's statement of financial position had the following balances:

Land	$300,000
Buildings	650,000
Leasehold improvements	400,000
Machinery and equipment	800,000

During 19B, the following transactions occurred:

a. Land site number 101 was acquired for $1.5 million. Additionally, to acquire the land, Hine paid a $90,000 commission to a real estate agent. Costs of $15,000 were incurred to clear the land. During the course of clearing the land, timber and gravel were recovered and sold for $8,000.

b. A second tract of land (site number 102) with a building was acquired for $300,000. The closing statement indicated that the land value was $200,000 and the building value was $100,000. Shortly after acquisition, the building was demolished at a cost of $20,000. A new building was constructed for $150,000 plus the following costs:

Excavation fees	$6,000
Architectural design fees	8,000
Building permit fee	2,000

The building was completed and occupied on September 30, 19B.

c. A third tract of land (site number 103) was acquired for $750,000 and was put on the market for resale.

d. Extensive work was done to a building occupied by Hine under a lease agreement that expires on December 31, 19K. The total cost of the work was $125,000, as follows:

Item	Cost	Estimated useful life (years)
Painting of ceilings	$ 5,000	1
Electrical work	45,000	10
Construction of extension to current working area	75,000	25
	$125,000	

The lessor paid half the costs incurred for the extension to the current working area.

e. During December 19B, $60,000 was spent to improve leased office space. The related lease will terminate on December 31, 19E, and is not expected to be renewed.

f. A group of new machines was purchased under a royalty agreement, which provides for payment of royalties based on units of production for the machines. The invoice price of the machines was $135,000, freight costs were $1,000, unloading costs were $1,500, and royalty payments for 19B were $22,000.

Required (disregard the related accumulated depreciation accounts):

1. Prepare a detailed analysis of the changes in each of the following statement of financial position accounts for 19B (Hint: set up a separate analysis for land, buildings, leasehold improvements, and machinery and equipment):
   a. Land.
   b. Buildings.
   c. Leasehold improvements.
   d. Machinery and equipment.
2. List the items in the fact situation which were not used to determine the answer to (1) above, and indicate where, or if, these items should be included in Hine's financial statements.

(AICPA adapted)

P 10–5 (Asset Acquired; Note Payables; Recording Errors)

FIX Company bought equipment on July 1, 19A, and made the following entries throughout the first 1½ years of ownership:

July 1, 19A:		
Equipment	30,000	
Retained earnings	2,000	
Note payable (time to maturity, 4 years)		30,000
Cash		2,000
December 31, 19A (end of the accounting period):		
Depreciation expense (½ year)	1,500	
Accumulated depreciation		1,500
June 30, 19B:		
Note payable	3,600	
Cash		3,600
December 31, 19B:		
Depreciation expense	3,000	
Accumulated depreciation		3,000

As can be inferred from the foregoing, the equipment is being depreciated on a straight-line basis with an assumed 10-year life and zero residual value. The note requires an interest payment each June 30, at 12%. The principal is to be paid on June 30, 19E.

Required (round amounts to nearest dollar):

1. Give the entries the FIX Company should have made on each of the four dates above.
2. Complete the following tabulation to show the effects of the journal entries made to each of the following items:

Item	Effects of the entries in Req. 1 — Recorded 19A	Recorded 19B	Correct 19A	Correct 19B
a. Equipment cost				
b. Note payable				
c. Retained earnings				
d. Accumulated depreciation				
e. Depreciation expense				
f. Interest expense				

3. Complete the following entry to correct the accounts at the end of 19A. The 19A accounts have been closed; also, notice that since the 19B accounts are not closed, the 19B incorrect entries can be reversed and reentered. Ignore the income tax effect.

Equipment
Prior period adjustment, error correction, 19A
  Retained earnings
  Accumulated depreciation
  Interest payable

P 10–6 (Assets Exchanged; Similar and Dissimilar Compared)

Trader Joe, Inc., has a policy of trading in equipment after one year's use. The following information is available from Trader Joe's records:

January 1, 19A—Acquired Asset A for $12,000 cash.
January 1, 19B—Exchanged Asset A for Asset B. Asset B had a market value of $14,000. Paid $3,000 in cash in the exchange.
January 1, 19C—Exchanged Asset B for Asset C. Asset C had a market value of $16,000 Paid $4,000 in cash in the exchange.
January 1, 19D—Exchanged Asset C for Asset D. Asset D had a market value of $11,000. Received $2,000 in cash in the exchange.

Assume a five-year estimated useful life and no residual value for all assets. Straight-line depreciation is used by Trader Joe.

Required:

1. Assume the assets are all similar. Give the journal entries required for each exchange.
2. Assume the assets are all dissimilar. Give the journal entries required for each exchange.

P 10–7 (Assets Exchanged; Similar and Dissimilar; No Cash versus Cash Paid)

This problem presents two independent cases—Case A similar assets and Case B dissimilar assets.

Case A—Two similar operational assets were exchanged when the accounts of the two companies involved reflected the following:

Account	Company M (designate as asset M)	Company N (designate as asset N)
Operational asset	$8,000	$8,200
Accumulated depreciation	5,500	4,800

The market value of asset M was reliably determined to be $2,800; no reliable estimate could be made of asset N.

Required (round amounts to nearest dollar):
1. Give the exchange entry for each company assuming no cash difference is involved.
2. Give the exchange entry for each company assuming a cash difference of $800 was paid by Company M to Company N.

Case B—Two dissimilar operational assets were exchanged when the accounts of the two companies involved reflected the following:

Account	Company A (designate as asset A)	Company B (designate as asset B)
Operational asset	$10,000	$14,000
Accumulated depreciation	7,000	10,500

The market value of asset A was reliably determined to be $4,500; no reliable estimate of market value could be made for asset B.

Required:
1. Give the exchange entry for each company assuming no cash difference was involved.
2. Give the exchange entry for each company assuming a cash difference of $1,200 was paid by Company A to Company B.

P 10–8 (Assets Exchanged; Cash Received versus Paid)

Part 1

Alpha Company had a used machine that originally cost $13,000 and had accumulated depreciation to date of $10,000. The used machine was exchanged for a similar machine that had a cash price of $3,700. Two independent cases are assumed:

Case A—There was a direct exchange (no cash difference was paid or received).
Case B—Alpha exchanged the old machine for the other machine and received a cash difference of $500.

Part 2

Beta Company had a used machine that originally cost $16,000 and had accumulated depreciation to date of $11,500. The used machine was exchanged for a similar machine that had a cash price of $5,000. Two independent cases are assumed:

Case C—There was a direct exchange (no cash difference was paid or received).
Case D—Beta exchanged the old machine for the other machine and paid a cash difference of $2,000.

Required (round amounts to nearest dollar):
1. Give the entries to record the exchange of similar assets in Cases A, B, C, and D.
2. Give the entries for each case assuming the assets were dissimilar.

P 10–9 (Assets Exchanged; Entries for Both Parties; Five Transactions)
In this exercise, all items of property refer to operational assets, not inventory, unless specified to the contrary. "List prices" are not necessarily market values.

Required:
Give journal entries where specified to record the following transactions:

1. Land carried on the books of A Company at $18,000 is exchanged for a computer carried on the books of B Corporation at $25,000 (cost, $35,000; accumulated depreciation, $10,000). Market value of both assets is $30,000. Give the journal entry for both A and B. The land and the computer are used in different lines of business.

2. A truck, which cost A Company $6,000, ($3,000 depreciation accumulated) has a market value of $3,400. It is traded to a dealer, plus a $5,600 cash payment, for a new truck, which has a $12,400 list price. Give the journal entry for A Company.
3. A truck which cost A Company $6,000, on which $5,000 depreciation has been accumulated, is traded to a dealer along with $6,300 cash. The new truck would have cost $7,000 if only cash had been paid; its list price is $7,500. Give the journal entry for A Company.
4. Land carried on the books of A Company at $90,000 is exchanged for land carried on the books of B Corporation at $78,000. Market value of each tract is $100,000. Give the journal entry for B Corporation.
5. Fixtures which cost A Company $15,000 (accumulated depreciation $9,000) and the market value is $8,000, are traded to B Corporation along with $500 cash. In exchange, A received fixtures from B carried by B at cost of $13,000 less $6,000 accumulated depreciation. Give the journal entry for both A and B; if necessary, round amounts to the nearest dollar.

P 10–10 (Donated Assets)

Windy City gave Hungry Company a vacant building located on city property. The building was no longer needed by the city and it was given to the company as an inducement to relocate. Hungry has relocated to Windy City. The building has a 20-year estimated useful life (no residual value) which was recognized in the donation agreement at the time that the company was guaranteed occupancy. Transfer costs of $6,000 were paid by the company. The building originally cost $150,000 ten years earlier. The building was recently appraised at $80,000 market value by the city's tax assessor. Anticipating occupancy within the next 10 days, the company spent $18,000 for repairs and internal rearrangements (good for 10 years). There are no unresolved contingencies about the building and Hungry's permanent occupancy.

Required:
Give all entries for Hungry Company related to the *(a)* donation, *(b)* renovation, and *(c)* any depreciation or amortization at the end of the first year of occupancy.

P 10–11 (Impairment of Asset Value)

Hilltop Mining Company has several mining operations in New Mexico. Plant HM–40 has property, plant, and equipment that has been idle for the past three years. Because of continuing weak prices and low demand for the output, the auditor has advised the company that, in view of the probability that the plant will not be opened in the foreseeable future, it should be written down to expected net realizable value. The property, plant, and equipment is shown in the accounts as: original cost, $800,000; accumulated depreciation, $300,000. The estimated net realizable value is $50,000. The assessed property tax for the current year of $6,000 has not been recorded.

Required:
1. Give the entries that Hilltop should make to record the decline in "use value."
2. Write an appropriate full-disclosure note.

Part B: Problems 10–12 to 10–21

P 10–12 (Asset Cost; Numerous Related Expenditures)

The following transactions related to operational assets:

a. Purchased land and buildings for $78,900 cash. The purchaser agreed to pay $900 for taxes already assessed. The purchaser borrowed $50,000 at 15% interest (principal and interest due in one year) from the bank to help make the cash payment. The property was appraised for taxes as follows: land, $25,000; and building, $50,000.

b. Prior to use of the property purchased in *(a)* above, the following expenditures were made:

Repair and renovation of building	$8,000
Installation of 220-volt electrical wiring	2,000
Removal of separate shed of no use (sold scrap lumber for $50)	300
Construction of new driveway	1,500
Repair of existing driveways	600
Deposits with utilities for connections	50
Painting company name on two sides of building	900
Installation of wire fence around property	2,500

c. Purchased a tract of land for $32,000; assumed taxes already assessed amounting to $180. Paid title fees, $50, and attorney fees of $300 in connection with the purchase. Payments were in cash.

d. The land purchased in *(c)* above was leveled and two retaining walls were built to stop erosion that had created two rather large gulleys across the property. Total cash cost of the work was $3,000. The property is being held as a future plant site.

e. Purchased a used machine at a cash cost of $8,500. Subsequent to purchase, the following expenditures were made:

General overhaul prior to use	$1,200
Installation of machine	300
Cost of moving machine	150
Cost of removing two small machines to make way for larger machine purchased	100
Cost of reinforcing floor prior to installation	400
Testing costs prior to operation	60
Cost of tool kit (new) essential to adjustment of machine for various types of work	220

Required:

Prepare journal entries to record the above transactions. Give special attention to the cost of each asset. Justify your position on doubtful items.

P 10–13 (Self-Constructed Assets; Factory Case)

Shear Corporation used its own facilities to construct a small addition to its office building. Construction began on February 1 and was completed on June 30 of the same year. Prior to the decision to construct the asset with its own facilities, Shear accepted bids from outside contractors; the lowest bid was $240,000. Detailed costs accumulated during the construction period are summarized as follows:

Materials used (including $120,000 for normal production)	$180,000
Direct labor (including $300,000 for normal production)	450,000
General supplies used on construction	6,000
Rent paid on construction machinery	5,000
Insurance premiums on construction	2,000
Supervisory salary on construction	7,000
Total general overhead for year	115,000
Total factory overhead for year:	
Fixed ($10,000 due to construction)	100,000
Variable	60,000
Direct labor-hours (including 100,000 hours for normal production)	120,000

Shear allocates factory overhead to normal production on the basis of direct labor hours.

Required:
Compute the amounts that might be capitalized:

1. Assuming the plant capacity to be 120,000 direct labor-hours and that the construction displaced production for sale to the extent indicated.
2. Assuming the plant capacity to be 200,000 direct labor-hours and that idle capacity was used for the construction.

Hint: Use fixed and variable overhead rates for factory overhead (i.e., cost ÷ direct labor-hours).

P 10–14 (Asset Cost; Allocations; Entries)

Feltham Company was incorporated on January 2, 19A, but was unable to begin manufacturing activities until July 1, 19A, because new factory facilities were not completed until that date.

The Land and Building account at December 31, 19A, was as follows:

Date		Item	Amount
19A			
Jan.	31	Land and building	$107,000
Feb.	28	Cost of removal of building	6,000
May	1	Partial payment of new construction	40,000
	1	Legal fees paid	2,000
June	1	Second payment on new construction	45,000
	1	Insurance premium	1,800
	1	Special tax assessment	2,500
	30	General expenses	18,000
July	1	Final payment on new construction	50,000
Dec.	31	Asset write-up	18,000
			290,300
	31	Depreciation—19A at 1%	2,903
		Account balance	$287,397

The following additional information is to be considered:

a. To acquire land and building, the company paid $50,000 cash and issued 500 shares of its 5% cumulative preferred stock, par value $100 per share; market value, $57,000.

b. Cost of removal of old building amounted to $6,000 with the demolition company retaining all materials of the building.

c. Legal fees covered the following:

Cost of organization	$ 500
Examination of title covering purchase of land	1,000
Legal work in connection with constr. work	500
	$2,000

d. Insurance premium covered premiums for three-year term beginning May 1, 19A.

e. The special tax assessment covered street improvements.

f. General expenses were incurred for the following from January 2, 19A, to June 30, 19A:

President's salary	$10,000
Plant superintendent covering supervision on new building	7,000
Office salaries	1,000
	$18,000

g. Because of a general increase in construction costs after entering into the building contract, the board of directors increased the value of the building $18,000, believing such an increase was justified to reflect market value at the time the building was completed. Retained Earnings was credited for this amount.

h. Estimated life of building—50 years. Write-off for 19A for ½ year—1% of asset value.

Required:

1. Prepare entries to reflect correct land, building, and accumulated depreciation accounts at December 31, 19A. Assume the 19A books have not yet been closed.
2. Show the proper presentation of land, building, and accumulated depreciation on the statement of financial position at December 31, 19A.

(AICPA adapted)

P 10–15 (Capitalization of Interest; Weighted-Average Method)

Rose Company began construction of a small building on January 1, 19B. The company's only debt during the first quarter was an unrelated long-term $300,000 note bearing interest at 11% per annum, maturity date, December 31, 19D. On May 1, 19B, the company borrowed $100,000 on a 9% construction note (interest bearing); the note matures on April 30, 19C. The company capitalizes interest on the building on the basis of average quarterly cumulative expenditures. As of the end of each quarter of the six-month construction period, construction expenditures (not including interest) were as shown below. Rose's reporting year ends on December 31. Interest is paid quarterly.

The construction expenditures were as follows:

Date, 19B	Expenditure		Date, 19B	Expenditure	
Jan. 1	Land	$ 20,000	April 30	Construction	$200,000
Jan. 31	Construction	70,000	May 31	Construction	170,000
Feb. 28	Construction	100,000	June 30	Construction	80,000
March 31	Construction	180,000			

Required:

1. Compute the amount of interest cost to be capitalized and expensed each quarter. Use the weighted-average method.
2. Give all journal entries related to the construction and interest cost.

P 10–16 (Capitalization of Interest; Weighted-Average Method)

Dobie Industries began construction of a new plant for its own use on January 1, 19A. During 19A, Dobie had the following debt outstanding (assume interest payments on December 31):

Accounts payable (noninterest bearing)	$ 80,000
Short-term note payable (14%)	500,000
Bonds payable (12%, issued at par)	1,300,000

On April 1, 19A, Dobie borrowed $500,000 on a 14%, one-year construction note to finance the plant construction. Interest on the construction note is payable annually each March 31. The weighted-average accumulated expenditures on construction for each quarter of 19A have already been computed. The payments and weighted-average accumulated expenditures are as follows:

Quarter	Payments to contractors	Weighted-average accumulated expenditures
First	$150,000	$150,000
Second	450,000	300,000
Third	750,000	675,000
Fourth	950,000	850,000

Required:

Dobie capitalizes interest using the weighted-average method (based on a weighted-average interest rate on all debt). Compute the amounts of interest to be capitalized and expensed for each quarter in 19A. Also, give the required entry in each quarter.

P 10–17 (Capitalization of Interest; Specific Method)

The problem facts to use are exactly the same as those given in P 10–16.

Required:

Assume Dobie capitalizes interest using the specific method (first applying the interest rate on loans identified with self-construction, and then applying a weighted-average interest rate based on all other debt). Compute the amounts of interest to be capitalized and expensed for each quarter in 19A and give the entry in each quarter.

P 10–18 (Extraordinary and Ordinary Repairs; Entries)

The plant asset records of Reston Company reflected the following at the beginning of the current year, January 1, 19A:

Plant building (residual value, $30,000; estimated useful life, 20 years)	$150,000
Accumulated depreciation, plant building	90,000
Machinery (residual value, $35,000; estimated useful life, 10 years)	180,000
Accumulated depreciation, machinery	90,000

During the year ending December 31, 19A, the following transactions (summarized) relating to the above accounts were completed:

a. Expenditures for nonrecurring, relatively large repairs that tend to increase economic utility but not economic lives of assets:
   Plant building $45,000
   Machinery 15,000
b. Replacement of original electrical wiring system of plant building (original cost, $18,000) 29,000
c. Additions:
   Plant building—added small wing to plant building to accommodate new equipment acquired; wing has useful life of 18 years and no residual value 54,000
   Machinery—added special protection devices to 10 machines; devices are attached to the machines and will have to be replaced every five years (no residual value) 10,000
d. Outlays for maintenance parts, labor, etc. to keep assets in normal working condition:

Quarter	Plant building	Machinery
1	$1,600	$ 1,900
2	1,800	6,100
3	1,600	1,000
4	2,000	10,000

Required:

1. Give appropriate entries to record transactions *(a)* through *(c)*. Explain the basis underlying your decisions.
2. In parallel columns, give the appropriate entries by quarter for transaction *(d)* under each of the following assumptions: (1) the accounting policy is to record all ordinary repairs as expense when incurred; and (2) the accounting policy requires use of the allocation approach. The annual budgeted amounts for repair and maintenance expense were: plant building, $7,200; and machinery, $17,000.
3. Which approach used in (2) above do you prefer? Explain.

P 10–19 (Disposal of Asset; Addition; Depreciation; Reporting)
Equipment that cost $18,000 on January 1, 19A, was sold for $10,000 on June 30, 19F. It had been depreciated over a 10-year life by the straight-line method, assuming its residual value would be $1,500.

A warehouse that cost $150,000, residual value $15,000, was being depreciated over 20 years by the straight-line method. When the structure was 15 years old, an additional wing was constructed at a cost of $90,000. The estimated life of the wing considered separately was 15 years, and its residual value is $10,000. The accounting period ends December 31.

Required:

1. Give all required entries to record:
   a. Sale of the equipment.
   b. The addition; cash was paid.
   c. Depreciation on the warehouse and its addition after the latter has been in use for one year.
2. Show how the building and attached wing would be reported on a statement of financial position prepared immediately after entry *(c)* in (1) above.

P 10–20 (Overview; Effect of Errors in Accounting for Operating Assets)
This problem deals with the effects of accounting errors on financial statements of a manufacturing company whose fiscal year is the calendar year. The company has a six-month inventory turnover. Most of its depreciable assets are depreciated over an eight-year life by the straight-line method, with zero estimated residual value. If an error makes a statement element too high, "+" should have been used for coding; if it causes the element to be too low, "−"; if the error has no effect or is completely counterbalanced, "0." There are, however, in the exhibit that follows, certain coding mistakes in reflecting the effects of the errors. You are to explain for each line the number of mistakes and identify which items are coded wrong and explain why. Answer each question independently of the others. *Hint:* Remember that depreciation of factory machinery is included in factory overhead.

	Statements for 19A			Statements for 19B		
Transactions	**Net operational assets (book value)**	**Selling or general expense**	**Cost of goods sold**	**Total assets on statement of financial position**	**Net income**	**Owners' equity**
1. Cost of rearranging Factory Machinery late in 19A was not recorded at all that year. When the invoice was received early in 19B, payment was debited to Factory Overhead.	−	0	−	0	−	−
2. Replacement of a major component of Factory Machinery early in 19A was charged to Factory Overhead. The component cost twice as much as the one replaced (the latter was 70% depreciated).	−	0	+	−	+	−
3. The company completed self-construction of an annex to the Office Building on April 1, 19A, and failed to debit any overhead to the project.	0	0	+	0	+	0

	Statements for 19A			Statements for 19B		
Transactions	Net operational assets (book value)	Selling or general expense	Cost of goods sold	Total assets on statements of financial position	Net income	Owners' equity
4. Early in 19A, the company paid legal fees of $2,000 in connection with title search for a site bought for employee parking. The fee was debited to Legal Fees (a general expense).	–	0	0	–	0	–
5. In midyear 19A, the company paid $2,000 for engineering services related to testing new factory machinery. Factory Overhead was debited.	–	0	+	–	0	+
6. Repairs which kept office fixtures in normal operating condition were made June 30, 19A, and debited to Office Fixtures.	+	+	0	+	0	+
7. Deposits paid to electric utilities early in 19A for added meters installed in the factory were debited to Factory Machinery.	+	0	+	–	–	–

P 10–21 (Measuring Asset Cost; Comprehensive Overview)

The accounts of Pall Corporation had never been audited prior to 19D. In auditing the books for the year ended December 31, 19D, the auditor found the following account for the plant:

Plant and Equipment

Debits		Credits	
19A:		19A:	
Plant purchased	$90,000	Sale of scrap	$ 300
Repairs	5,300	Depreciation (6%)	6,000
Legal	600	19B:	
Title fees	50	Depreciation (6%)	8,040
Insurance	3,000	19C:	
Taxes	1,200	Cash proceeds from old machine	1,150
19B:		Depreciation (6%)	8,160
Addition to plant	15,000	19D:	
Write-up	20,000	Depreciation (6.4%)	8,520
Interest cost related to the plant addition	1,500		
Repairs	500		
Machinery for new addition	2,000		
19C:			
New machine	3,000		
Installation	600		
19D:			
Machinery overhaul	1,350		
Replaced roof	900		
Fence	2,000		

(Balance, $114,830)

Additional data relating to plant and equipment developed during the audit follow:

a. The plant was purchased during January 19A. At that time, the tax assessment listed the plant as follows: plant site, $10,000; building, $20,000; and machinery therein, $30,000. The estimated life of the plant and machinery was 20 years.

b. During the first six months of 19A, the company expended the amounts listed in the account for the year to get the plant ready for operation; operations began July 1. The repairs relate to both the building and machinery; no detail was available. The legal fees related to the plant purchase and to all aspects of it. The $3,000 insurance premium was for a one-year policy on the plant and equipment, dated January 1, 19A ($1,000 of the premium applied to the machinery). The property tax rate for the year was 2%. The scrap was accumulated during the "repair period."

c. In 19B, a plant addition was completed for $15,000, at which time the company was paying 10% on some borrowed funds. The addition, which was not self-constructed, was under construction for four months. During the year, $1,500 was spent for ordinary repairs, of which one third was capitalized. Machinery that cost $2,000 was purchased. The asset account was written up by $20,000 to bring it in line with the bank's security allowance on loans (Contributed Capital was credited).

d. During 19C, a new machine was purchased (July 1) for $3,000 plus installation costs of $600. An old machine that cost $2,100 was sold for $1,150. The old machine was acquired when the plant was acquired.

e. During 19D, several items of equipment were completely reconditioned at a cost of $1,350. Minor repairs were debited to expense during the year. The roof was replaced on one wing of the plant. A fence was constructed around the plant to keep unauthorized personnel out; it is estimated that the fence will have 10 years of remaining life.

Required:

1. Set up a spreadsheet to compute the correct balances for the following accounts (suggested columnar captions): Land, Buildings, Machinery, and Land Improvements. (the company follows a policy of recording 6% straight-line depreciation on ending balances except for Land Improvements. Assume residual values are zero for all depreciable assets, and round amounts to nearest dollar.) Use a separate schedule to compute the balances for accumulated depreciation. Suggested line captions: list each item by year. Justify any assumptions that you make.
2. Give one compound entry to correct the accounts assuming the accounts have already been closed for 19D. Ignore income tax effects.

CASES

C 10–1 **(Acquisition Cost; Expenditures Subsequent to Acquisition)**

Kimberly-Clark

Assume that the market value of equipment acquired in a noncash transaction is not determinable by reference to a cash purchase.

Required:

1. Explain how the acquiring company should determine the capitalizable cost of equipment purchased by exchanging for it each of the following:
   a. Bonds which have an established market price.
   b. Common stock which does not have an established market price.
   c. Similar equipment which has a determinable market price.
2. Assume that the equipment was acquired and had been used by the acquiring company for three years. Expenditures related to the equipment must be made. Identify the various types of expenditures that might be involved and explain the appropriate accounting for each.

(AICPA adapted)

C 10–2 (Court Settlement; Capitalize versus Expense)

Consolidated Smelting Company, which operates in the Southwest, agreed in a court settlement to:

a. Install pollution control equipment on its smelters at an estimated cost of $18 million.
b. Pay specified medical expenses for children living near its facilities who were suffering from lead poisoning; tentatively estimated cost of $2 million to be paid as families incur expenses.
c. Pay the city and state a civil penalty of $200,000 over a four-year term in equal $50,000 installments.

Required:
1. For each item above, discuss the propriety of capitalizing versus expensing the cost.
2. What amount should be ascribed to each item immediately after the settlement (before any payments are made)?

C 10–3 (Asset Cost; Related Incidental Costs)

The invoice price of a machine is $20,000. Various other costs relating to the acquisition and installation of the machine amount to $5,000 and include such things as transportation, electrical wiring, special base, and so forth. The machine has an estimated life of 10 years and no residual value.

The owner of the business suggests that the incidental costs of $5,000 be debited to expense immediately for three reasons: (1) if the machine should be sold, these costs could not be recovered in the sales price; (2) the inclusion of the $5,000 in the machinery account will not necessarily result in a closer approximation of the market price of this asset over the years because of the possibility of changing price levels; and (3) debiting the $5,000 to expense immediately will reduce federal income taxes.

Required:
Discuss each of the points raised by the owner of the business. (AICPA adapted)

C 10–4 (Asset Cost; a Problem during Construction)

When construction was in progress on what later became a notable skyscraper and landmark in one of the nation's largest cities, construction had advanced to the point that the basement and two above-ground stories of steelwork were completed. It was then noticed that parts of the structure were sinking. This development made it necessary to remove the partial structure, reexcavate for the foundation, install pilings to prevent future sinking, and then to replicate the prior work.

Required:
1. Assume the owner of the building (i.e., not the contractor) will absorb the additional costs because the building is being erected under a cost-plus contract. Should the added costs be capitalized by the owner, or should only the costs originally incurred be capitalized as the cost of the building and the additional costs recorded and reported in some other way? If the latter, explain why and how.
2. Assume instead that the contractor, not the building owner, was required to absorb the additional costs. Should the contractor capitalize the additional costs or account for them in some other way? Explain.

C 10–5 (Asset Cost; after Acquisition But before Use)

One of your clients, a savings bank with several local branches, recently acquired ownership of a lot and building located in a historical part of the city. The building was in a dilapidated condition, unsuitable for human habitation. The bank thought at the time that it was acquiring a site for a new branch. Although a firm of architects recommended demolition, the city council, in whose discretion such activity rests, refused consent to demolish the building in view of its historical and architectural value.

In order to comply with safety requirements and to make the building suitable for use as a branch location, the bank spent $250,000 restoring and altering the old building. It had paid $90,000 for the building and lot, and had contemplated spending $200,000 on a new building after demolishing the old structure. Somewhat similar old buildings in less run-down condition could have been bought in the same area for about the same $90,000 price. It is possible, even likely, that some of these that were not so old could have been demolished without governmental intervention, and the bank could have carried out its original plan.

Now that the restoration has been completed and the bank is making final plans to open its newest branch in the restored building, the bank has been informed by the State Historical Commission that the building qualifies for and will receive a plaque designating it as a historical site. This designation will be of some value in attracting traffic to the site, probably will result in the building being pointed out when tours of the city visit the area, and so on. Under present laws, receipt of the designation may well mean that the bank can never demolish the structure and is obligated to preserve it, even if the property is later vacated.

Required:

1. Discuss the pros and cons of capitalizing the entire $250,000 spent on restoration of the building.
2. How should the $90,000 original expenditure be treated? What would have been the cost of the land if the bank had been able to carry out its original plans?
3. Sooner or later, your client is likely to seek advice as to proper accounting for subsequent costs—repairs, depreciation, possible improvements, and so on. What advice would you give?

11 OPERATIONAL ASSETS—DEPRECIATION AND DEPLETION

OVERVIEW AND PURPOSE

Chapter 10 described the characteristics of operational assets. The attribute common to all operational assets is their revenue-earning potential **through use** rather than through resale. Operational assets can be viewed as a bundle of economic service values that will be used up over time as revenues are earned. Therefore, as they are used in the earnings process, their cost must be matched with the revenues earned during each period of use to meet the requirements of the **matching principle.** Accounting methods designed to match the cost of operational assets with revenues earned focus primarily on the measurement of periodic expense and only incidentally with valuation of the related asset. These methods are broadly classified as **depreciation, depletion, and amortization.**

The purpose of this chapter is to describe the various methods used in the accounting process of allocating to expense the cost of tangible property and natural resources over their useful lives. To accomplish this purpose, the chapter is organized as follows:

Part A: Basic Concepts and Methods of Depreciation

1. Terminology.
2. Nature of depreciation.
3. Methods of depreciation.
4. Depreciation and cash flow.

Part B: Additional Cost Allocation Issues and Depletion

1. Depreciation based on investment concepts.
2. Special depreciation systems.
3. Fractional year depreciation.
4. Depletion.
5. Changes and correction of depreciation and depletion.
6. Depreciation and depletion disclosures.

Supplement 11–A: Annuity and Sinking Fund Methods of Depreciation

PART A: BASIC CONCEPTS AND METHODS OF DEPRECIATION

Terminology

The costs of the three kinds of operational assets are matched with revenue over the useful lives of the assets. The accounting terminology for the three related expenses is as follows:

1. **Depreciation**—the accounting process of allocating the periodic expiration of the cost of **tangible** property, plant, and equipment against the periodic revenue earned.
2. **Depletion**—the accounting process of allocating the periodic expiration of the cost of an asset that is a **natural resource,** such as mineral deposits and timber, against the periodic revenue earned.
3. **Amortization**—the accounting process of allocating the periodic expiration of the cost of **intangible assets** represented by **special rights** or benefits, such as prepaid insurance, patents, copyrights, and leaseholds, against the periodic revenue earned. Sometimes "amortization" is used as a general term to include all types of periodic apportionments (discussed in Chapter 12).

In each of the above three cases, for goods that are manufactured by the company, a part of the periodic cost is included in finished goods inventory; therefore, the matching for this part occurs through cost of goods sold when the goods are sold.

Accounting Terminology Bulletin 1, paragraph 56, defines depreciation accounting as follows:

> **Depreciation accounting** is a system of accounting which aims to distribute the cost or other basic value of tangible capital assets, less salvage value (if any), over the estimated useful life of the unit in a systematic and rational manner. It is a process of allocation, not of valuation.

Nature of Depreciation

Conceptually, the cost of property, plant, and equipment is a long-term prepayment of expense. The expense is prepaid in advance of use of the asset; therefore, it is recorded as an asset. As the economic service life of the asset expires, the cost of the asset is systematically allocated to operations as an expense called **depreciation.**

On the statement of income, depreciation is recognized as selling, administrative, or manufacturing expense (i.e., in cost of goods sold), depending upon the nature and use of the assets involved. Depreciation may affect the statement of income in two ways. One way is as a direct expense. For instance, depreciation on company automobiles used by salespersons is classified as a selling expense. In contrast, depreciation on machinery used in a factory is not a direct expense. It is recorded as a part of the cost of inventory; when the inventory is sold, the cost of the inventory (including an element of depreciation) is recorded as cost of goods sold. That portion of depreciation remaining in the cost of inventory on hand at the end of the period is reported as an **asset** (inventory) until the inventory is sold. Therefore, income of a given period is reduced by depreciation initially included in the cost of inventory only to the extent that such goods are sold during that period.

Causes of Depreciation

The causes of depreciation may be classified as follows:

Physical factors	Functional factors
1. Wear and tear from operation.	1. Inadequacy.
2. Action of time and other elements.	2. Obsolescence, including supersession.
3. Deterioration and decay.	

Significantly, a **change in the market value** of an operational asset is **not** recognized as one of the causes of depreciation under GAAP.[1] The three physical factors, as they affect the service life of many tangible operational assets, tend to occur continuously. The two functional factors often are less stable in occurrence. **Inadequacy** is caused by the expansion of a business that results in the inability of the operational asset to provide the increased service required, even though it still may be in good condition and capable of the service originally expected of it. **Obsolescence** may arise from inadequacy, supersession, and other causes such as no demand for the product or the service. **Supersession** occurs when new replacement assets that can provide improved service become available. In such cases, it may be desirable to dispose of the old assets.

Depreciation accounting considers all predictable factors that limit the economic usefulness of operational assets to the enterprise. The periodic apportionment of acquisition cost through depreciation should be based upon both the physical and functional causes of depreciation. Those factors that operate more or less continuously are given primary recognition in depreciation accounting. However, sudden and unexpected factors such as storms, floods, sudden change in demand, and radical disuse of assets often must be given special treatment. For example, special treatment might be applied to account for a fire, resulting in the immediate removal of an asset from the accounts and the recording of a related casualty loss.

The useful life of operational assets also is influenced by the repair and maintenance policies of the company. Inadequate maintenance and repair may reduce expense temporarily; however, the useful life of assets usually will be shortened, thereby increasing the periodic depreciation expense.

In the case of facilities temporarily idle or held pending future use, the recognition of depreciation should continue because the physical and functional causes, which tend to reduce the ultimate economic usefulness of the asset to the company, continue. Operational assets that will not be returned to service should be reduced to their estimated **net realizable value** in anticipation of disposal. Special asset accounts should be established to account for idle facilities when they are no longer classified as operational assets.

---

[1] Under current GAAP, depreciation is not caused by changes in the market value of an operational asset; however, when the book value of an asset is significantly above its use value to the entity, in terms of market value (e.g., an idle plant), the asset must be written down to reflect any permanent and significant impairment of value. The effect of such a write-down is **not** recorded as depreciation expense.

Depreciation Is an Estimate

The importance of depreciation varies with the nature of the business and the extent of its holdings of operational assets. With the possible exception of inventories, no single area of accounting offers as much variety of practice or choice as depreciation accounting. The only "accounting constant" is the starting point, which usually is historical acquisition cost; there are not many variables in measuring actual acquisition cost. Accounting for depreciation requires two estimates: (1) useful life and (2) residual value. In addition, it may be necessary to anticipate the cost of dismantling or restoration related to retirement of a plant asset. Because different companies estimate such costs differently, it is not surprising that depreciation accounting is characterized by different depreciation methods.

Factors in Determining Depreciation Expense

Periodic depreciation expense reflects an allocation of the original acquisition cost (less the estimated residual value) of the asset to operations in proportion to the economic benefits received each period from use of the asset. The variables that must be considered in computing periodic depreciation expense are as follows:

1. Actual cost (as defined in Chapter 10).
2. Estimated residual (scrap or salvage) value.
3. Estimated service life.
4. Method of depreciation.

Thus, computation of depreciation is based on one "actual" and two "estimated" factors.

The **residual value** is the amount estimated to be recoverable through sale, trade-in allowance, or by other means when the asset is retired from service by the user. To estimate residual value, allowance must be made for the costs of dismantling and disposing of the retired asset. For example, assume it is estimated that upon retirement the asset may be sold for $2,500 and that the costs of dismantling and selling are estimated to be $500. In this case, the residual value would be $2,000.

In practice, residual value often is ignored—this procedure is acceptable when the recovery and disposal amounts are expected to offset (in which case residual value is zero), or when the amounts involved are immaterial. Moreover, because residual value is estimated years in advance, conceptually, it should be discounted to present value for depreciation computations. Often the present value of estimated future residual value is negligible.

Estimating the **service life** of an asset for accounting purposes implies *(a)* use of the asset by the present owner, *(b)* use of the asset for the purpose for which it was acquired, and *(c)* a specific repair and maintenance policy over the life of the asset. The periodic amount of depreciation of an asset should be based on the use of the "economic service potentials" of the asset to the enterprise. Thus, the service life should be determined on a basis that is linked with the expiration of such values. For example, service life may be measured in terms of *(a)* definite time periods such as total months or years, *(b)* total units of output, or *(c)* total hours of operating time. Conceptually, the measure of service life should depend upon the nature of the asset involved and the primary causes of its depreciation.

Recording Depreciation

Periodic depreciation is recorded as a debit to an operating expense account or, in the case of a manufacturing company, a cost of manufacturing account (factory overhead); the credit is to a contra asset account entitled **Accumulated Depreciation.** Rather than directly crediting the related asset account, this special contra account traditionally has been credited to maintain a separation of the asset's original cost and the amount of that cost that has been matched against revenue through depreciation. The contra account should not be labeled **reserve** for depreciation because depreciation provides no "reserve."

Methods of Depreciation

A number of methods have been developed to compute depreciation expense, each of which provides a different amount of depreciation expense for each accounting period over the life of the asset. The depreciation methods may be classified as follows:

a. Based on equal allocation to each time period:
  (1) Straight line (SL).

b. Based on output:
  (2) Service hours (SH).
  (3) Productive output (PO).

c. Reducing depreciation expense each period (called accelerated depreciation):
  (4) Sum-of-the-years'-digits (SYD).
  (5) Declining balance (DB).

d. Based on investment and interest concepts (discussed in Supplement 11–A):
  (6) Annuity.
  (7) Sinking fund.

Exhibit 11–1 gives the simplified data used throughout this chapter to illustrate these methods.

Under current GAAP, the depreciation policies of a company do not have to be based upon the characteristics and uses of the company's operational assets. Thus, the selection from among the various depreciation methods is a "free" choice. Therefore, it is desirable for companies to disclose as much information as reasonably possible about why a particular depreciation method was selected.

Straight-Line Method

The straight-line method is based on the assumption that the asset loses use value as time passes. Thus, this method relates depreciation directly to the **passage of time** rather than to specific use of the asset. It is called **straight line** because it recognizes an **equal** amount of depreciation expense in each period of the service life of the asset. When graphed against time, periodic depreciation expense, accumulated depreciation, and asset book value are all represented by straight lines. The formula for computing periodic straight-line depreciation expense is:

$$D = \frac{C - R}{n_y} \quad \text{Example:} \quad D = \frac{\$6,600 - \$600}{5} = \$1,200 \text{ per period}$$

Exhibit 11–1
Data used to illustrate depreciation methods.

Item	Symbol	Illustrative amount
Acquisition cost	C	$ 6,600
Residual value	R	600
Estimated service life:		
Years	n_y	5
Service hours	n_h	20,000
Productive output in units	n_u	10,000
Depreciation rate (per year, per service hour, or per unit of productive output)	r	
Dollar amount of depreciation per period	D	

Straight-line depreciation frequently is expressed as a **percentage rate.** For example, the periodic (annual) rate *r* may be expressed as either *(a)* 20% on the net depreciable value (i.e., $1,200 ÷ $6,000 = 20%) or *(b)* 18% on cost (i.e., $1,200 ÷ $6,600 = 18%). **Exhibit 11–2** illustrates the straight-line depreciation method over the life of the asset given in Exhibit 11–1.

Evaluation. The straight-line method is simple. It meets the criterion of being "systematic and rational" (*ARB 44*, revised, par. 2). It is particularly appropriate when the following conditions prevail:

1. The decline in economic service potential of the asset is approximately the same each period; it is related to the passage of time rather than to use.
2. Use of the asset is essentially the same from period to period.
3. Repairs and maintenance expenditures are essentially the same each period.

Straight-line depreciation is deficient in that *(a)* depreciation is computed as a function of time rather than a function of use; time often is not representative of the asset's contribution to earnings; *(b)* it may not match expense with revenue; and *(c)* it causes a major distortion, relative to a pure rate-of-return concept, in certain rate-of-return computations. This distortion results because under the straight-line method, depreciation expense is a constant amount each period; therefore, the effect of depreciation on income also is a constant periodic amount. As the asset is depreciated over time, its book value (and also the book value of total assets) decreases. When net income is divided by total assets to compute the rate of return on total assets, the computed periodic rate of return increases each period and gives the appearance of an increasing rate of return on the asset. In reality, the **rate of return** probably is constant, even though the computed rate of return indicates otherwise.

In addition, when depreciable assets are used in manufacturing, the straight-line method reports depreciation as a **fixed amount per period.** However, because the same number of units are not necessarily produced each period, the straight-line method results in a **variable amount per unit** of output.

Exhibit 11–2
Depreciation schedule—straight-line method.

Year	Depreciation expense (debit)	Accumulated depreciation (credit)	Balance, Accumulated depreciation	Undepreciated asset balance (book value)
0				$6,600
1	$1,200	$1,200	$1,200	5,400
2	1,200	1,200	2,400	4,200
3	1,200	1,200	3,600	3,000
4	1,200	1,200	4,800	1,800
5	1,200	1,200	6,000	600 (residual value)
Total	$6,000	$6,000		

Service Hours Method

The service hours method is based on the assumption that the decrease in service life of the operational asset is determined primarily by the actual running time of the asset rather than by the continuing passage of time. Rather than equal periodic amounts of depreciation expense, this method results in a periodic expense that depends on the running time of the asset during each accounting period. If a machine is operated twice as much in the current period as in the prior period, the depreciation for the current period will be twice that of the last period. To use this method, the service life of the asset must be estimated in terms of total service or working hours prior to disposal; then a depreciation rate per service hour is computed.

Assuming a 20,000-hour estimated useful life, the formula for the depreciation rate per service hour would be as follows:

$$r = \frac{C - R}{n_h} \quad \text{Example:} \quad r = \frac{\$6,600 - \$600}{20,000} = \$.30 \text{ per service hour}$$

Assuming 3,800 actual hours of running time the first year, depreciation expense would be as follows:

$$D = r \times \text{Service hours, current period}$$
$$D = \$.30 \times 3,800 = \$1,140$$

Exhibit 11–3 illustrates the service hours method over the life of the asset given in Exhibit 11.1.

Evaluation. The service hours method satisfies the GAAP criterion of being rational and systematic. It also produces a logical matching of expense and revenue if the asset "uses" its service potential on the basis of running time. Under this method, the amount of depreciation varies with the productive output of the asset. However, to the extent that running time occurred without productive output, this relationship would not hold. The service hours method usually is appropriate when obsolescence is not a primary factor in depreciation and the economic service potential of the asset is used up primarily by running time. Also, wide variations in use of the asset from period to period suggest application of the service hours method. For many assets, such as buildings, furniture, and typewriters, this method would be impracticable, if not impossible,

Exhibit 11–3
Depreciation schedule—service hours method.

Year	Service hours worked*	Depreciation expense (debit)	Accumulated depreciation (credit)	Balance, Accumulated depreciation	Undepreciated asset balance (book value)
0					$6,600
1	3,800	(3,800 × $.30) = $1,140	$1,140	$1,140	5,460
2	4,000	(4,000 × $.30) = 1,200	1,200	2,340	4,260
3	4,500	(4,500 × $.30) = 1,350	1,350	3,690	2,910
4	4,200	(4,200 × $.30) = 1,260	1,260	4,950	1,650
5	3,500	(3,500 × $.30) = 1,050	1,050	6,000	600 (residual value)
Total	20,000	$6,000	$6,000		

* It is assumed that the asset was actually used in this manner and that the original estimate of the useful life was confirmed. Estimated life is 20,000 hours.

to apply. In contrast, it would be appropriate for assets such as delivery equipment, certain machines, and oil-well drilling equipment.

When depreciable assets are used in manufacturing, the service hours method of depreciation reports depreciation as a **variable amount per period** and as a **fixed amount per unit of output** when output and service hours are directly related.

Productive Output Method

The productive output and service methods are the same except for the way that output is measured. The productive output method is based on the assumption that the decrease in service life of the operational asset is determined primarily by the **number of units of output produced** (rather than service time). Thus, under this method, the service life of the asset is estimated in terms of the number of **units of output.** A proportionate part of the total cost to be depreciated (cost less residual value) is allocated to each unit of output as a cost of production; consequently, depreciation amounts fluctuate with changes in the volume of output. The cost of each unit of output includes a constant amount of depreciation, in contrast to the straight-line method where each **unit** of output is allocated a different amount of depreciation if output varies from period to period.

The cost to be depreciated over the life of the asset is divided by the estimated service life in units to derive a depreciation rate **per unit of output;** multiplication of this rate by the output for the period gives the periodic depreciation amount. Thus, computation of the rate per unit of output, assuming an estimated production life of 10,000 units of output, would be as follows:

$$r = \frac{C - R}{n_u} \quad \text{Example:} \quad r = \frac{\$6{,}600 - \$600}{10{,}000} = \$.60 \text{ per unit of output}$$

Assuming 1,800 units of actual output during the first year, depreciation expense would be computed as follows:

$$D = r \times \text{Units of output, current period}$$
$$D = \$.60 \times 1{,}800 = \$1{,}080$$

Exhibit 11–4
Depreciation schedule—productive output method.

Year	Units of output*	Depreciation expense (debit)	Accumulated depreciation (credit)	Balance, Accumulated depreciation	Undepreciated asset balance (book value)
0					$6,600
1	1,800	(1,800 × $.60) = $1,080	$1,080	$1,080	5,520
2	2,000	(2,000 × $.60) = 1,200	1,200	2,280	4,320
3	2,400	(2,400 × $.60) = 1,440	1,440	3,720	2,880
4	1,800	(1,800 × $.60) = 1,080	1,080	4,800	1,800
5	2,000	(2,000 × $.60) = 1,200	1,200	6,000	600 (residual value)
Total	10,000	$6,000	$6,000		

* It is assumed that the asset was actually used in this manner and that the original estimate of useful life was confirmed. Estimated life is 10,000 units.

Exhibit 11–4 illustrates the productive output method over the life of the asset given in Exhibit 11–1.

Evaluation. The productive output method is systematic and rational when *(a)* actual output can be measured, *(b)* the service life in units of output can be estimated reliably, and *(c)* obsolescence is not a major factor.

The differences between the periodic depreciation under the service hours method (Exhibit 11–3) and the productive output method (Exhibit 11–4) are due to a change in the efficiency of operations—the asset was used more efficiently in some periods than in others. This observation leads to the conclusion that in situations where either method could be applied the productive output method usually would be preferable.

The productive **output** method reports depreciation as a **variable amount per period** and as a **fixed amount per unit of output.** Assume an asset that cost $10,000 (no residual value) with an estimated life of five years, or 2,000 units of output, is to be depreciated. Assume further that actual output was: year 1, 350; year 2, 400; year 3, 450; year 4, 500; year 5, 300; and total, 2,000. The depreciation amounts and unit costs for the straight-line and productive output methods are compared below:

		Output depreciation		Straight-line depreciation	
Year	Units of output	Amount	Unit cost	Amount	Unit cost
1	350	$ 1,750	$5.00	$ 2,000	$5.71
2	400	2,000	5.00	2,000	5.00
3	450	2,250	5.00	2,000	4.44
4	500	2,500	5.00	2,000	4.00
5	300	1,500	5.00	2,000	6.67
Total	2,000	$10,000		$10,000	

These distinctions are important in cost analyses used for pricing, control, and other decision-making purposes.

Accelerated Depreciation Methods

The accelerated methods are designed to allocate acquisition cost so that periodic depreciation amounts are higher in the early years and lower in the later years of the life of the operational asset. The accelerated methods are based upon the assumption that new assets are more efficient than old assets; therefore, the economic service potentials "used" by the asset are greater during the early life of the asset. If the cost of this increased use of the asset is to be matched with the resulting revenue, some form of accelerated depreciation is desirable. The accelerated methods also can be defended on the basis that, as the asset gets older, maintenance and repair costs increase significantly. Therefore, the annual depreciation amount should decrease as repair expenses on the asset increase. This results in a smooth pattern of total expense (i.e., depreciation plus repairs) for the use of the operational asset. Therefore, it provides a realistic view of the **total** cost of operating an asset each year.

Numerous methods have been proposed for computing accelerated depreciation expense; however, the principal methods currently being used are the following:

1. Sum-of-the-years'-digits (SYD).
2. Declining balance (DB).

Sum-of-the-Years'-Digits (SYD) Method. This method applies a fraction, which decreases each succeeding period, to the acquisition cost of the asset (less residual value). The denominator of each fraction is the sum-of-the-years' digits for the life of the asset. The numerator, which changes each period, is the years' digits in reverse order. For example, the illustrative asset, with an estimated service life of five years, would be depreciated using the following fractions:

Denominator:
Sum-of-the-years'-digits (SYD): 1 + 2 + 3 + 4 + 5 = 15.
Numerators:
Digits in reverse order: 5, 4, 3, 2, and 1.
Fractions for each successive year of use:
First, $5/15$; second, $4/15$; third, $3/15$; fourth, $2/15$; fifth, $1/15$; total, $15/15$.

Exhibit 11–5 illustrates the SYD method over the life of the asset given in Exhibit 11–1. Notice that the decreasing fraction is multiplied by the cost to be depreciated (cost less residual value) in each period. When the life of the asset is long, it is easy to compute the SYD **denominator** using the formula:

$$\text{SYD} = n\left[\frac{n+1}{2}\right]$$

For an asset with a 25-year life, it is:

$$\text{SYD} = 25\left[\frac{25+1}{2}\right] = \underline{\underline{325}}$$

Evaluation. The SYD method satisfies the GAAP criterion of being "rational and systematic" when a declining annual depreciation amount is appropriate.

Exhibit 11–5
Depreciation schedule—SYD method.

Year	Depreciation expense (debit)*	Accumulated depreciation (credit)	Balance, Accumulated depreciation	Undepreciated asset balance (book value)
0				$6,600
1	(5/15 × $6,000) = $2,000	$2,000	$2,000	4,600
2	(4/15 × $6,000) = 1,600	1,600	3,600	3,000
3	(3/15 × $6,000) = 1,200	1,200	4,800	1,800
4	(2/15 × $6,000) = 800	800	5,600	1,000
5	(1/15 × $6,000) = 400	400	6,000	600 (residual value)
Total	$6,000	$6,000		

* Estimated life, five years.

Accelerated depreciation methods are applicable when greater economic service potentials are "used" in earlier years of the asset's life (i.e., when there is decreasing operating efficiency or revenues) or when repair and maintenance charges increase over the life of the asset.

Declining-Balance (DB) Method. The declining-balance method of depreciation was originally developed based on the then existing Internal Revenue Code. The DB rate of depreciation is determined by first computing the straight-line rate based on the net depreciable cost of the asset. The straight-line rate found in this manner then is multiplied by a **selected acceleration percentage.** This acceleration rate typically varies from a high of 200% (often called **double-declining balance**) to a low of 150%, depending on the type of property and the date of acquisition. Each year, the DB rate is multiplied by the declining book value. Based on the data given in Exhibit 11–1 and assuming a 200% acceleration rate, the DB rate would be 40% (i.e., 20% × 200%). Periodic depreciation expense would be computed as shown in **Exhibit 11–6.** If the acceleration rate had been 150%, the declining-balance depreciation rate would have been 30% (i.e., 20% × 150%), and depreciation would have been computed in a similar manner. Under this method depreciation is discontinued when the carrying value of the asset is equal to its estimated residual value. Details regarding depreciation for current income tax purposes are discussed in this chapter in the section **Depreciation and Income Taxes.**

Evaluation. The DB method is applicable to the same situations as the SYD method. Both methods are acceptable under GAAP.[2] The important conceptual

[2] A third accelerated depreciation method is the fixed-percentage-on-declining-base method. To apply this method, the book value of the asset (undepreciated asset balance) is multiplied by a constant percentage rate. Because a constant rate is applied to a **declining base,** each successive periodic depreciation amount will be less than the amount for the preceding period. The rate is computed taking into account the cost, estimated life, and residual value; consequently, the rate will automatically provide for the residual value at the end of the service life of the asset. This method is not discussed because it rarely is used.

Exhibit 11–6
Depreciation schedule—declining-balance method.

Year	Annual rate*	Depreciation expense (debit)	Accumulated depreciation (credit)	Balance, Accumulated depreciation	Undepreciated asset balance (book value)
0					$6,600
1	40%	(40% × $6,600) = $2,640	$2,640	$2,640	3,960
2	40%	(40% × $3,960) = 1,584	1,584	4,224	2,376
3	40%	(40% × $2,376) = 950	950	5,174	1,426
4	40%	(40% × $1,426) = 570	570	5,744	856
5	40%	256†	256	6,000	600
Total		$6,000	$6,000		

* Acceleration percentage, 200%; life, 5 years.
Annual rate = 20% (straight-line rate) × 200% (acceleration percentage) = 40%.
† Remaining amount needed for total depreciation of $6,000 and residual value of $600.

criterion that any depreciation method, including DB, should satisfy is an acceptable matching of periodic depreciation expense with periodic revenue.

Depreciation and Dividends

Because depreciation expense reduces reported pretax income, income tax and retained earnings also are reduced. Therefore, over the life of an operational asset, an amount equivalent to the cost of the tangible operational asset (less any residual value and income tax savings) is "held back" from retained earnings. Depreciation accounting tends to prevent the impairment of capital, which will occur if dividends are based on overstated earnings (in terms of GAAP).[3]

Depreciation and Cash Flow

Depreciation accounting measures an expense and matches it with revenue. When revenue is sufficient, depreciation, like other expenses, is recovered. However, recording depreciation has **no effect** upon the amount of assets coming into the business through the sale of its products and services. But if a business can sell its product at a price that covers all operating expenses **including depreciation,** the assets received from customers (cash and receivables) will exceed total expense outlays by at least the amount of the depreciation. Although the depreciation provision will result in holding back assets from potential dividends equivalent to the provision, it does not provide or "hold back" cash specifically. Most expenses require cash when incurred but depreciation is a noncash expense. The cash is disbursed when the operational asset is paid for. Therefore, the **cash inflow from net income may be more** than reported net income because of the noncash expenses (e.g., depreciation, depletion,

[3] Different methods of depreciation have different effects on cash flow, which is reflected in the statement of cash flows. For example, ACRS in the early years will give a higher depreciation expense amount than straight-line; consequently, income taxes would be lower. This would result in a saving of cash paid for income taxes during the early periods.

and amortization) reported on the statement of income. Recognition of depreciation does not mean that cash (or even other assets) necessarily will be available to replace those assets when their service lives expire. The assets retained in a business as a result of deducting depreciation from income are not automatically segregated into a fund for replacements. In fact, the retained funds probably will be used to pay off liabilities and to purchase new and different types of assets that also can be used to generate cash. Therefore, while such funds are not automatically segregated for asset replacement, the revenue-generating process of most companies is intended to produce the cash for replacement of old assets.

Depreciation and Income Taxes

Accelerated Cost Recovery System

The Economic Recovery Tax Act of 1981 (as amended by the Deficit Reduction Act of 1984) established a new accelerated depreciation system for income tax purposes. This mandatory system, called the **Accelerated Cost Recovery System (ACRS)**, ignores the concepts of estimated useful life and residual value. Instead, it specifies "cost recovery periods" for various classes of assets. ACRS was designed to provide for rapid recovery of the costs of operational assets with the objective of encouraging capital expenditures to modernize existing plant assets.

ACRS requires that personal property be assigned to one of the following classes:

3-year property—primarily automobiles and light trucks, machinery and equipment used in connection with research experimentation, and other ADR property with an ADR class life of four years or less.

5-year property—primarily property that does not fit into any other class of property. This includes most personal property with an ADR class life of more than four years, such as most furniture and fixtures, etc.

10-year property—public utility property with an ADR class life of more than 18 but not more than 25 years, amusement park structures, manufactured homes (including mobile homes), railroad tank cars and coal utilization property. In addition, real property with a present class life of no more than 12.5 years is included.

Generally, the recovery period for real property under ACRS depends on when the property was placed in service, such as: after 1980 and before March 16, 1984, 15 years; after March 15, 1984, and before May 9, 1985, 18 years; and after May 8, 1985, and before 1987, 19 years.

ADR stands for Asset Depreciation Range, which is a specification of the upper and lower limits of asset depreciation ranges and an "asset guideline period." This guideline is the midpoint class life used to determine in which ACRS class certain property should be included.

Under ACRS, a company may use either the accelerated cost recovery deductions or an optional straight-line method. Both methods disregard residual values for tax purposes.

The cost recovery deduction allowed under ACRS is determined by multiplying the **tax basis** of the asset by statutory recovery percentages. A partial summary of the percentages for personal property placed in service for years 1981 through 1986 is as follows:

Recovery year	3-year	5-year	10-year
1	25%	15%	8%
2	38	22	14
3	37	21	12
4		21	10
5			10
6			10
7			9
8			9
9			9
10			9
Total	100%	100%	100%

As an illustration of ACRS using statutory recovery percentages, assume that equipment in the three-year class is purchased for $10,000. The equipment has a three-year useful life and residual value of $1,000. For financial reporting purposes, the equipment is depreciated using the straight-line method. The depreciation for the equipment for tax purposes and financial reporting purposes is shown below:

	Tax depreciation	Book depreciation
Year 1 . . .	$10,000 × 25% = $ 2,500	$3,000
Year 2 . . .	$10,000 × 38% = 3,800	3,000
Year 3 . . .	$10,000 × 37% = 3,700	3,000
	$10,000	$9,000

Notice that depreciation for tax purposes is computed by multiplying the statutory recovery percentage by the tax basis of the asset, **ignoring residual value.** Depreciation for financial reporting is determined by reducing the asset's cost by its residual value and allocating the resulting depreciable cost on a straight-line basis over the asset's useful life.

If the taxpayer chooses not to use accelerated depreciation as illustrated above, straight-line depreciation can be adopted for the ACRS class life or an extended class life. For each class of property, three alternative optional recovery periods may be used with the straight-line method. They are summarized below:

Property class	Optional recovery periods
Personal property:	
3-year	3, 5, or 12 years
5-year	5, 12, or 25 years
10-year	10, 25, or 35 years
Real property:	
15-year	35 or 45 years
18-year	18, 35, or 45 years
19-year	19, 35, or 45 years

If the taxpayer elects the optional straight-line method, only one-half year's depreciation (based on the recovery period selected) may be taken in the first year. To illustrate, assume the company that acquired the $10,000 asset described above elected to use the optional straight-line method with a three-year recovery period. Annual tax depreciation is summarized below:

Year	Tax depreciation
1	$10,000 × ⅓ × ½ = $ 1,667
2	10,000 × ⅓ = 3,333
3	10,000 × ⅓ = 3,333
4	10,000 × ⅓ × ½ = 1,667
Total	$10,000

Modified Accelerated Cost Recovery System

The Modified Accelerated Cost Recovery System, known as MACRS, was enacted by the Tax Reform Act of 1986. It applies to most depreciable property placed in service after 1986. Regardless of its similarity to ACRS in name and use of classes of property, the two are intrinsically different systems for deducting the cost of tangible depreciable property. MACRS reverts back to use of ADR class lives for determining the depreciation deduction (applicable to most nonrecovery property) and, in contrast to ACRS, recognizes salvage value (but assigns it a value of zero). In addition, the cost of personal property must generally be recovered over one more taxable year under MACRS as compared to the cost of similarly named classes of property placed in service under ACRS.

MACRS defines the following classes of personal property:

3-year property—primarily horses, special tools, and assets used in research and development activities (property with an ADR midpoint life of 4 years or less).

5-year property—primarily all machinery and equipment not included in other categories, and automobiles and light trucks (property with an ADR midpoint life of more than 4 years and less than 10).

7-year property—office furniture and fixtures, agriculture equipment, equipment used on oil exploration and development, railroad track, and certain manufacturing equipment (property with an ADR midpoint life of 10 or more years and less than 16).

10-year property—certain public utility property, real estate, railroad tank cars, manufactured (mobile) homes, and coal conversion boilers and equipment (property with an ADR midpoint life of 16 or more years and less than 20).

15-year property—public utility property and certain low-income housing (property with an ADR midpoint life of at least 20 years and less than 25).

20-year property—property not depreciated using the 15-year property class (property with an ADR midpoint life of more than 25 years).

Under MACRS, most real property is 27.5-year residential rental property and 31.5-year nonresidential real property. Taxpayers are required to use the straight-line method for both of these classes of property. Also, instead of using half-year depreciation in the first year, a mid-month rule is required. This rule requires 1⁄24 of the annual depreciation in the first month and 1⁄12 each following month. The following table summarizes the percentages for personal property placed in service after 1986:

Recovery year	MACRS rate by class of property					
	3-year	5-year	7-year	10-year	15-year	20-year
1	33.33%	20.00%	14.29%	10.00%	5.00%	3.750%
2	44.45	32.00	24.49	18.00	9.50	7.219
3	14.81	19.20	17.49	14.40	8.55	6.677
4	7.41	11.52	12.49	11.52	7.70	6.177
5		11.52	8.93	9.22	6.93	5.713
6		5.76	8.92	7.37	6.23	5.285
7			8.93	6.55	5.90	4.888
8			4.46	6.55	5.90	4.522
9				6.56	5.91	4.462
10				6.55	5.90	4.461
11				3.28	5.91	4.462
12					5.90	4.461
13					5.91	4.462
14					5.90	4.461
15					5.91	4.462
16					2.95	4.461
17						4.462
18						4.461
19						4.462
20						4.461
21						2.231
Total	100.00%	100.00%	100.00%	100.00%	100.00%	100.00%

Because the ACRS and MACRS methods of recovering costs generally allocate the cost of an operational asset without considering its estimated useful life or residual value, they would be consistent with GAAP depreciation methods only by coincidence. Differences in depreciation for financial accounting purposes and income tax purposes create deferred taxes, which are discussed in Chapter 23.[4]

PART B: ADDITIONAL COST ALLOCATION ISSUES AND DEPLETION

Depreciation Based on Investment Concepts

The preceding sections discussed depreciation methods that provide (1) a **constant** depreciation amount per period (straight line), (2) a **decreasing** depreciation amount per period (SYD and DB), and (3) **varying** depreciation amounts per period (output methods). The **compound interest methods** represent a different approach; they provide an **increasing** amount of depreciation per period.

Depreciation methods other than the compound interest approaches have been criticized on a conceptual basis because they ignore the investment characteristics of the ownership of operational assets. When depreciation is based on investment concepts, an operational asset is viewed as an investment and the return on that investment as an annuity. Implicit in this view is the concept that the periodic returns on the investment in the operational asset over its

[4] At the end of 1988 the expectations are that Congress will make major income tax changes.

useful life comprise both principal and interest. Therefore, the depreciation amount each period is assumed to include two elements: (1) the recovery of the investment (i.e., principal), which is credited to accumulated depreciation and (2) the remainder, which represents **imputed interest revenue** on the investment in the operational asset.

Over the life of the asset, the imputed interest revenue decreases, and the amount of periodic depreciation expense increases. The effect of the depreciation entry each period is an increasing amount of periodic depreciation expense and a decreasing amount of income. The two methods—**annuity and sinking fund**—give the same net effect on income although they are recorded differently; they are illustrated in Supplement 11–A to this chapter.

Special Depreciation Systems

Unique features of certain depreciable assets have caused practical adaptations of the depreciation methods already discussed. The most common adaptations, referred to as **systems** (rather than methods), are discussed in this section under the following captions:

1. Inventory appraisal system.
2. Group and composite life systems.
3. Retirement and replacement systems.

Each of these systems is appropriate under GAAP (if applied properly) only in the unique situation that each one is designed to accommodate. They usually attain an acceptable level of reliability, especially when materiality is considered.

Inventory Appraisal System

Under the inventory appraisal depreciation system, the acquisition costs of depreciable assets are debited to an operational asset account in the usual manner, and depreciation usually is credited to the same account, rather than to an accumulated depreciation account. The amount recorded as depreciation expense for the period is determined by appraising the "value" of the assets on hand at the end of the reporting period in their **present condition.** The adjusting entry reduces the asset account to this appraised amount, which means that depreciation expense is debited for the difference between prior book value and the current appraised value. Residual recoveries on disposal of any of the assets are recorded as a **reduction of depreciation expense** for the period of recovery. The value of the asset on hand at the end of the period (in its present condition) is determined by an appraisal or by making an estimate of its **current acquisition cost** taking into account its present condition. The inventory appraisal system is similar to the procedures used in a periodic system of accounting for merchandise inventory (discussed in Chapter 8).

To illustrate the inventory appraisal system, assume the Hand Tools account showed a year-end balance of $1,900. An inventory of the tools on hand, valued at **current acquisition cost,** adjusted for present condition, reflected a value of $1,080 at year-end. Broken and obsolete tools were sold for $70 during the year. The entries to record the sale of old tools and periodic depreciation are as follows:

Cash	70	
Depreciation expense		70
Depreciation expense, hand tools ($1,900 − $1,080)	820	
Hand tools		820

Closing entry:

Income summary	750	
Depreciation expense, hand tools ($820 − $70)		750

The inventory appraisal system is appropriate for situations in which the asset account has **numerous items with a low unit cost,** such as hand tools, machine tools, patterns, and dies.

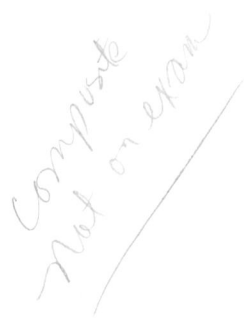

Group and Composite Systems

Many companies group certain operational assets together for depreciation purposes. For example, all of the one-ton trucks may be grouped for depreciation purposes, or an entire operating assembly, such as a plant or a refinery, may be depreciated as a single unit. In such cases, an **average depreciation** rate is applied to the group or assembly.

When an average rate of depreciation is applied to a number of **homogeneous** assets (i.e., grouped by similar characteristics and service lives), such as trucks, the procedure usually is called **group depreciation.** When an average or composite rate of depreciation is applied to a number of **heterogeneous** assets having dissimilar characteristics and service lives, such as a plant or a refinery, the procedure usually is called **composite depreciation.** The two systems are similar in the mechanical application of an average rate and in the resulting journal entries; the primary difference between them is the groups of assets to which they are applied (**homogenous** assets—**group** depreciation; **heterogeneous** assets—**composite** depreciation).[5]

Under the two systems, all of the assets in the group are recorded in one asset control account, and one accumulated depreciation account is established for the entire group. The book or carrying value, as reflected in these two accounts, applies to the entire group and not to individual assets. Subsequent acquisitions of items belonging to the group are added to the group asset account at cost.

Depreciation expense is computed by multiplying an **average depreciation rate** by the balance in the group asset account regardless of the age of each individual asset represented therein. The rate may be computed and applied to cost or to cost less residual value, as desired. The depreciation entry is made by debiting Depreciation Expense and crediting Accumulated Depreciation for the periodic amount of depreciation thus computed.

When an asset is retired from the group, the group asset account is credited for the **original cost** of the item and the Accumulated Depreciation account is debited for the **same amount less any residual recovery.** These systems, therefore, do not recognize "losses or gains" on retirement of single assets in the group.[6]

---

[5] For a full discussion of depreciation of multiple asset accounts (group and composite), see J. D. Coughlan and W. K. Strand, *Depreciation: Accounting, Taxes and Business Decisions* (New York: Ronald Press, 1969), chap. 5. Group depreciation can use the straight-line or declining-balance formulas but cannot be based on SYD or output formulas.

[6] Ibid.

Group System Illustrated. To illustrate the **group system** (i.e., homogeneous items), assume Quick Corporation purchased 10 delivery trucks at $15,000 each. Each truck has an estimated residual value of $1,500 at the end of the estimated service life of five years. The company depreciates the trucks on a group basis. Assuming depreciation is recognized on the **ending** balance in the asset account, entries under the **group system** would be as follows:

1. To record the initial purchase of 10 delivery trucks at $15,000 each:

Trucks	150,000	
Cash		150,000

2. To record group depreciation at the end of the first year:

Depreciation expense ($150,000 × 18%)	27,000	
Accumulated depreciation		27,000

Computation:

Cost (10 trucks)	$150,000
Estimated residual value	15,000
To be depreciated over five years	$135,000
Depreciation per year ($135,000 ÷ 5)	$ 27,000
Depreciation rate on asset balance ($27,000 ÷ $150,000)	18%

3. To record retirement of one truck at the end of the second year due to damage; amount received from insurance, $9,000:

Cash	9,000	
Accumulated depreciation (cost, $15,000 less residual recovery, $9,000)	6,000	
Trucks (original cost)		15,000

4. To record purchase of two additional delivery trucks at $15,500 each:

Trucks	31,000	
Cash		31,000

5. To record the retirement of a truck that has been used for 5½ years and then sold to a salvage yard for $600; original cost, $15,000:

Cash	600	
Accumulated depreciation ($15,000 − $600)	14,400	
Trucks		15,000

When the group system is used, it may be necessary to compute the **book value** of a specific asset in the group. For example, when an asset is moved from one organizational division of the company to another, it is desirable that the original acquisition cost and accumulated depreciation to date be transferred in the accounts from the prior group to the other group. In such cases, the accumulated depreciation for a specific asset may be computed as follows:

$$\frac{\text{Present age}}{\text{Service life}} \times (\text{Acquisition cost} - \text{Residual value})$$

Assume a truck is being transferred from division A to division B; the truck originally cost $15,000 and has been used for two years. Its estimated service life is five years, and the estimated residual value, $1,500. The truck has been

Exhibit 11–7
Computation of depreciation rate when a composite system is used.

Component item	Original cost	Estimated residual value	Amount to be depreciated	Estimated service life (years)	Annual depreciation*
A	$50,000	$5,000	$45,000	15	$3,000
B	20,000	4,000	16,000	10	1,600
C	7,000	600	6,400	8	800
D	3,000	-0-	3,000	3	1,000
	$80,000	$9,600	$70,400		$6,400†

* Depreciation expense in subsequent years would change if *(a)* items are added or replaced or *(b)* estimates are revised.

† Composite depreciation rate on cost: $6,400 ÷ $80,000 = 8%; composite (average) life: $70,400 ÷ $6,400 = 11 years.

Depreciation first period:

Depreciation expense ($80,000 × 8%)	6,400	
Accumulated depreciation		6,400

depreciated on a group basis; the **average** group rate being used is 18% each year. The entry to record the transfer is:

Truck—division B	15,000	
Accumulated depreciation, division A*	5,400	
Truck—division A		15,000
Accumulated depreciation, division B*		5,400

* Computation: (2 yrs. ÷ 5 yrs.) × ($15,000 − $1,500) = $5,400.

If the estimate of either the useful life or the residual value changes for assets in the group, a new average depreciation rate should be computed for the group based on the revised estimates.

Composite System Illustrated. Under the composite system, individual assets in the group may have a wide range of service lives. It is this range that has caused conceptual objections to composite life depreciation. Because of the wide range of service lives, an average depreciation rate is computed based on the **composite life** of the assets in the group. Composite life is the weighted-average life of the various units in the composite group. The composite depreciation rate is computed by dividing the total annual estimated depreciation expense for all assets in the group by the total cost of those assets, as illustrated in **Exhibit 11–7** for operating assembly X. The operating assembly, consisting of components A, B, C, and D, was acquired at a total cost of $80,000. The components have service lives ranging from 3 to 15 years.

If there are no interim changes in the asset account illustrated in Exhibit 11–7, the operating assembly will be depreciated to the residual value at the end of the 11th year (composite life: $70,400 ÷ $6,400 = 11 years). Additions and disposals of parts of the composite unit are recorded as illustrated above for the group system.

Evaluation of Group and Composite Depreciation Systems. The rationale underlying group and composite depreciation systems recognizes that realistic depreciation estimates often can be based on averages. Under both systems, additions and disposals that have different lives, residual values, or costs may necessitate a change in the group or composite depreciation rate. Moreover, an important assumption underlying their use is that gains or losses on disposition of single assets usually are not material amounts.

The main objections to the group and composite systems are that it is possible to conceal faulty estimates of useful life and residual value for long periods, and through the failure to recognize gains or losses, the systems may not correct for changes in asset usage or for other errors. These systems reduce the control over fixed assets because detailed records are not used. Also, in case individual assets become idle, depreciation on these idle assets can be computed more precisely under unit (versus group and composite) methods. In such situations, the assets involved should be **removed** from the group and accounted for separately. Small computers have significantly reduced the use of the group and composite systems.

Retirement and Replacement Systems

The retirement and replacement systems of depreciation frequently are used by public utilities because of the peculiar problems of accounting for certain assets such as line poles and other line items. These systems also are used in accounting for low-cost items such as hand tools. Under the retirement and replacement systems, no periodic adjusting entry is made for depreciation in the normal manner; instead, depreciation expense is recognized only at the **time of replacement** of the old asset.

The basic distinction between the retirement and replacement systems is that under the **retirement** system, the cost of the **old** asset (less its residual value) is debited to depreciation expense when it is replaced (i.e., a FIFO assumption). Under the **replacement** system, the cost of the **new** asset (less residual value of the **old** asset) is debited to depreciation expense when it replaces the old asset (i.e., a LIFO assumption). In applying either method, any residual recovery is recorded as a reduction of depreciation expense. To illustrate both systems, assume the Hi-Power Utility Company replaced 10 old utility poles with 10 new poles that cost $300 each. The old poles replaced originally cost $100 each and, at replacement date, each pole had a residual value (i.e., net realizable value) of $20. The entries related to the poles would be:

Basic entries (common to both systems):

1. Acquisition of old poles (on purchase date):

Pole inventory ($100 × 10)	1,000	
Cash		1,000

2. Installation of old poles (on installation date):

Transmission line ($100 × 10)	1,000	
Pole inventory		1,000

3. Purchase of new replacement poles (on purchase date):

Pole inventory ($300 × 10)	3,000	
Cash		3,000

Depreciation entries (not the same for both systems):

A. Retirement system (FIFO):

4. To remove the old poles and record depreciation expense:

Salvage inventory (net realizable value, old poles, 10 × $20)	200	
Depreciation expense		200
Depreciation expense (10 × $100; based on cost of old poles)	1,000	
Transmission line (cost of old poles)		1,000

Periodic depreciation expense: $1,000 − $200 = $800.

5. To record installation of the new poles:

Transmission line (cost of new poles, $300 × 10)	3,000	
Pole inventory (cost of new poles)		3,000

B. Replacement system (LIFO):

4. To remove the new poles from pole inventory and record depreciation expense:

Salvage inventory (net realizable value, old poles, 10 × $20)	200	
Depreciation expense		200
Depreciation expense (10 × $300; based on cost of new poles)	3,000	
Pole inventory (cost of new poles)		3,000

Periodic depreciation expense: $3,000 − $200 = $2,800.

5. To record installation of the new poles:

Entry not needed because of LIFO assumption; pole inventory was credited in entry 4.

After all of the above entries are posted the account balances are as follows for each system:

	Retirement—FIFO	Replacement—LIFO
Pole inventory	$ -0-	$ -0-
Transmission line	3,000 (new cost)	1,000 (old cost)
Depreciation expense	800	2,800

Evaluation. This example shows that the **retirement** system represents a FIFO approach, whereas the **replacement** system represents a LIFO approach in allocating the asset cost to depreciation. The retirement system provides depreciation amounts based on older costs and reports the operational asset at newer costs. The replacement system, however, provides depreciation amounts based on newer costs and reports the operational asset at older costs.

Neither system is designed to match expense with revenue because depreciation is recognized only when assets are replaced. This means that no depreciation expense is recognized between installation and retirement dates. However, when the company has reached a stable level of growth and replacement, the periodic depreciation amount may approximate the amounts that would be computed under one of the more common methods (such as straight line). Utility companies use these systems because of the difficulty in depreciating large numbers of relatively low-cost items such as poles, cross-members, brackets, and conduits. In such cases, the distinction between ordinary repairs and capitalizable replacements is difficult to establish and apply to individual assets. Although lacking in conceptual justification, the retirement system has some practical appeal, especially when retirement system depreciation closely approximates depreciation expense under one of the more common methods.

Fractional Year Depreciation

The preceding illustrations assumed that the asset year and the company's reporting year coincide. However, assets seldom are purchased on the first day of a reporting period and are seldom retired at the end of the reporting year. Therefore, depreciation often must be computed for fractional parts of a year. An accounting policy usually is established so that consistent amounts of depreciation are recorded for fractional parts of the year. Various policies which are discussed below are used to record depreciation for a fractional part of a year.[7]

Straight-Line Method. Depreciate from the first of the month all assets **acquired** on or before the 15th of the month; if **acquired** after the 15th, do not depreciate for the partial month. Assets **disposed of** on or before the 15th of the month are not depreciated for the partial month; if **disposed of** after the 15th, record a full month's depreciation. To determine the monthly depreciation amount, divide the annual amount by 12.

Accelerated Methods. Compute **annual** depreciation using the accelerated method (SYD or DB). Annual depreciation is allocated based on the number of months in which the asset is used during any partial year. Assume the asset used in Exhibit 11–5 was acquired on May 1, 19A, and was retired on April 30, 19F. The reporting year ends on December 31. Using SYD depreciation, as given in Exhibit 11–5, the computations and results would be as follows:

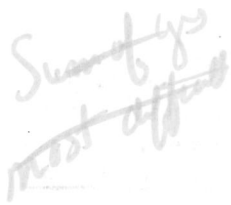

Year	Annual depreciation (Exhibit 11–5)	Months	Computation	Depreciation expense
19A	$2,000	8	(\$2,000 × $\frac{8}{12}$)	$1,333
19B	1,600	12	(\$2,000 × $\frac{4}{12}$) + (\$1,600 × $\frac{8}{12}$)	1,733
19C	1,200	12	(\$1,600 × $\frac{4}{12}$) + (\$1,200 × $\frac{8}{12}$)	1,333
19D	800	12	(\$1,200 × $\frac{4}{12}$) + (\$800 × $\frac{8}{12}$)	933
19E	400	12	(\$800 × $\frac{4}{12}$) + (\$400 × $\frac{8}{12}$)	533
19F		4	(\$400 × $\frac{4}{12}$)	135*
	$6,000	60		$6,000

* Rounded to come out even.

[7] Alternatives, in addition to those listed, include (1) depreciation computed on the balance in the asset account at the beginning of the year, (2) depreciation computed on the balance in the asset account at the end of the year, and (3) depreciation computed only on assets acquired during the first half of the year, and no depreciation on assets disposed of during the first half of the year. If these short-cut alternatives produce results that are not materially different from more precise application, they qualify under GAAP.

In the example above, depreciation for 19A is based on the first eight months (May 1, 19A–December 31, 19A) of the initial year the asset was used. Depreciation for 19B is based on the final four months (January 1, 19B–April 30, 19B) of the first year of use and the first eight months (May 1, 19B–December 31, 19B) of the second year of use. Depreciation for each of the remaining years is computed in a similar manner.

Depreciation Policy

Accounting Trends & Techniques, 1987, the AICPA annual survey of practices of 600 selected industrial corporations, shows that in 1986 annual reports, the straight-line method is used more than all other methods combined, comprising 74% of total usage. Accelerated depreciation methods account for 18% of the total, while unit-of-production methods account for over 6%. Details from the 1986 survey are presented in **Exhibit 11–8.**

The same study indicates that about 85% of the companies had material differences between depreciation reported on published financial statements and depreciation reported for income tax purposes.[8] For the most part, accelerated methods were used for tax purposes while straight line was used for financial reporting.

Companies use accelerated depreciation methods for tax purposes because of the cash flow advantage afforded by the faster tax write-offs. Differences between depreciation amounts for tax purposes and depreciation amounts for financial reporting purposes cause temporary differences, as discussed in Chapter 23. The tax advantage of accelerated depreciation methods **reverses** in later years of asset use. However, the **time value of money** still makes the accelerated methods attractive from a cash flow standpoint.

Depletion

For accounting purposes, **depletion** is the allocation of the cost of a natural resource (i.e., a wasting asset) against revenue as the resource is exploited and sold. Examples of such resources are ore, oil, coal, timber, and gravel. To account for such assets, the original cost is recorded in conformity with the **cost principle,** and that cost is allocated over the estimated total production (output) in conformity with the **matching principle.**

Accounting for Depletion

Allocation of the **cost** of the natural resource to units of inventory and cost of goods sold usually is based on a unit depletion rate which is computed by dividing *(a)* the cost of the asset (less any residual value) by *(b)* the estimated number of units that can be withdrawn economically. This approach also is used in the production (output) depreciation method. The **unit depletion rate** is multiplied by the actual units withdrawn during the period to determine the depletion amount for the reporting period. As with other tangible assets, three factors are involved: (1) actual cost, including all development costs related to the resource; (2) estimated production over the life of the resource; and (3) estimated residual value of the property after the natural resource is exhausted.

---

[8] AICPA, *Accounting Trends & Techniques, 1987* (New York, 1987), Table 3–12, p. 301.

Exhibit 11–8
Depreciation methods; frequency of use.

	Number of Companies			
	1986	1985	1984	1983
Straight line	561	563	567	564
Declining balance	49	53	54	57
Sum-of-the-years' digits	14	16	15	17
Accelerated method—not specified	77	73	76	74
Unit of production	48	54	60	65
Other	12	12	13	12

AICPA, *Accounting Trends & Techniques, 1987* (New York, 1987), Table 3–10, p. 296. The columns sum to more than 600 because some companies use different depreciation methods for different classes of depreciable assets.

The depletion amount for a period is debited to the Inventory account of the natural resource (e.g., oil, coal, or gravel) and credited to the related asset account. Then, as the inventory items are sold, the inventory cost, **including depletion,** is expensed as cost of goods sold in the usual manner. Therefore, at the end of the accounting period, part of the periodic depletion amount is included in the Inventory account, to the extent that units of the natural resource were withdrawn but not sold during the period.

To illustrate accounting for depletion, assume reserve geologists estimate that a given mineral lease has a potential production of 100,000 units. The total cost of the lease, including development costs, was $300,000 with no residual value. The estimated depletion rate per unit of mineral and its application would be computed as follows, assuming 10,000 units were extracted during the period:

Estimated depletion rate: $300,000 ÷ 100,000 units = $3.00 per mineral unit
Actual production for period: 10,000 mineral units
Depletion amount for period: 10,000 × $3.00 = $30,000

If 8,000 units were sold during the period and 2,000 remained on hand at the end of the period, the mineral inventory account would include depletion of $6,000 (i.e., 2,000 × $3.00) and cost of goods sold reported on the statement of income would include depletion of $24,000 (i.e., 8,000 × $3.00).

Acquisition costs, development costs, and tangible property costs associated with a natural resource usually are recorded in separate asset accounts and amortized on the production basis. If any of the resulting facilities, such as buildings, are likely to have a shorter life than the natural resource, their acquisition cost, less any estimated residual value, should be **depreciated** over the shorter period.

Because of the difficulties in estimating underground deposits of minerals and additional information derived through further developmental work, the depletion rate may require adjustment from time to time. The new rate is determined by dividing the unamortized mineral cost plus any additional development costs by the **remaining** estimated reserves. Past depletion amounts are **not** revised. Instead, the change in depletion rate is accounted for prospectively as a change in accounting estimate (as just described) in conformity with the provisions of *APB Opinion 20,* "Accounting Changes" (discussed in Chapter 24).

Depletion and Income Taxes

The depletion procedures discussed above are used for financial and cost accounting purposes. For federal income tax purposes, other depletion methods may be used in conformity with the Internal Revenue Code. For example, the Code permits taxpayers to use **statutory or percentage depletion** as an alternative to cost depletion illustrated above. The taxpayer usually computes both cost and statutory depletion and claims the higher amount as the depletion deduction for tax purposes. Under statutory depletion, a stated percentage of gross **income** derived from the sale of the natural resource asset may be taken as the depletion deduction on the tax return. The percentage varies from 5% on some deposits to 22% on others. Some of the more common depletion percentages are listed below:

Sulfur and uranium; if from deposits in the United States, asbestos, lead, zinc, nickel, and certain others	22%
Oil and gas	15
Gold, silver, copper, iron ore, and oil shale (from U.S. deposits)	15
Coal and sodium chloride	10
Clay and shale used for certain purposes	7½
Gravel, sand, and other items	5
Certain other minerals and metallic ores	14

Under the Code, the sum of the statutory depletion charges allowed may (and in practice frequently does) exceed the original cost of the resource. The use of cost depletion for financial reporting purposes and statutory depletion for income tax purposes causes temporary **tax differences,** as discussed in Chapter 23.

Depletion and Liquidating Dividends. Cash dividends sometimes are paid by small natural resource companies in an amount equal to accumulated income plus the accumulated amount of depletion. State laws often permit such dividends. This practice is common when the company has no plans to replace the natural resource in kind and operations are to cease when the deposit has been exhausted. In such cases, the stockholders should be informed of the portion of each dividend that represents a return of capital (i.e., the depletion amount). Assume Tex Oil Company reported the following (summarized):

Assets	$1,000,000
Accumulated depreciation	(200,000)
Accumulated depletion	(100,000)
	$ 700,000
Liabilities	$ 150,000
Capital stock	500,000
Retained earnings	50,000
	$ 700,000

If the board of directors declared and paid a cash dividend of $150,000, the journal entry would be as follows:

Retained earnings	50,000	
Return of capital to stockholders	100,000	
Cash		150,000

The return of capital to stockholders ($100,000) would be reported as a deduction in the owners' equity section of the statement of financial position.

Changes and Correction of Depreciation and Depletion

Occasionally, a business (1) changes the method of depreciation used, (2) changes estimates of service life or residual value, or (3) locates errors related to depreciation or depletion. *APB Opinion 20,* "Accounting Changes," states how each of these three different situations should be accounted for and reported. The provisions of the *Opinion* are discussed and illustrated in Chapter 24. As they relate to depreciation and depletion, they may be summarized as follows (using the term **depreciation** to refer to depletion and amortization as well):

1. **Change in accounting principle**—a change from one generally accepted method to another generally accepted method (such as from SYD to straight line). These changes require an adjustment for the differences in accumulated depreciation to date between the old and new methods. This difference is recorded as a "depreciation adjustment" and is reported on the statement of income between the captions Income Before Extraordinary Items and Net Income for the period of change.
2. **Change in estimate**—a change in the estimated useful life and/or the residual value. Changes of this type are made **prospectively.** This means that the undepreciated balance of the asset is apportioned to the new remaining life, taking into account the new estimated life and/or new residual value. No correcting entry is made.
3. **Accounting error**—Errors in depreciation made in prior years should be corrected when found. If the error affected the current period only, the incorrect entry can be reversed and the correct entry made, all during the current period. However, if the error affected one or more prior periods, the correcting entry involves making a **prior period adjustment** (reported on the statement of retained earnings) for the net effect of the error up to the **beginning** of the year during which the error is corrected. Assume a machine that cost $10,000, estimated service life of five years, no residual value, was incorrectly debited to expense when acquired. The error was discovered during the third year after acquisition. The correcting entry and the depreciation entry for the third year follow (ignoring income taxes):

   a. Correcting entry:

Machine	10,000	
Accumulated depreciation ($10,000 × ⅖)		4,000
Prior period adjustment—error correction		6,000

   b. Adjusting entry for depreciation expense, end of third year:

Depreciation expense ($10,000 ÷ 5)	2,000	
Accumulated depreciation		2,000

Depreciation and Depletion Disclosures

Because of the effects of the depreciation methods used on both financial position and the results of operations, *APB Opinion 12* reaffirmed an earlier *ARB* that the following disclosures should be made in the financial statements or accompanying notes:

a. Depreciation expense for the period.
b. Balances of major classes of depreciable assets, by nature or function, at the statement of financial position date.
c. Accumulated depreciation, either by major classes of depreciable assets or in total, at the statement of financial position date.
d. A general description of the methods used in computing depreciation on major classes of depreciable assets.

These disclosure requirements were augmented in *APB Opinion 22,* "Disclosure of Accounting Policies," which cited depreciation methods and amortization policies as examples of required disclosures; the same disclosure requirements apply to depletion.

Illustrative disclosures, shown below, are taken from the 1986 financial statements of The Standard Oil Company. The notes to the company's financial statements indicate that unit-of-throughput, unit-of-production, and straight-line methods are used. In addition, the notes describe accounting policies regarding dismantlement, restoration, and reclamation costs, capitalized interest, property disposition, and impairment of properties.

The Standard Oil Company: Notes to Financial Statements

Note A: Major Accounting and Financial Reporting Policies (in part).

Property, Plant and Equipment. Depreciation, Depletion and Amortization Costs: Depreciation of the trans-Alaska pipeline is computed by the unit-of-throughput method based on estimated applicable proved crude oil reserves. Depletion and depreciation of proved oil and gas properties and depletion of mine development costs, mineral lands and leaseholds are computed for each oil and/or gas reservoir or mine using the unit-of-production method based on applicable reserves. Other property, plant and equipment is depreciated principally by the straight-line method over estimated useful lives which are revised periodically based on experience.

Dismantlement, Restoration and Reclamation Costs: The estimated future costs of dismantling, restoring and reclaiming certain major properties and facilities, less estimated residual values, are accrued during operations.

Capitalized Interest: Interest costs incurred in connection with significant expenditures for the construction or acquisition of property, plant and equipment are capitalized.

Property Disposition: Upon disposition of property, plant and equipment, the asset cost and related accumulated depreciation are eliminated from the respective accounts. Any gain or loss is included in current operations, except those related to dispositions of pipeline property and partial dispositions of oil and gas properties which are normally recorded as adjustments to the accumulated depreciation account.

Impairment: Except for impairment of unproved oil and gas properties discussed above, reductions in the utility of major units of property, plant and equipment, which the Company intends to hold and operate, caused by obsolescence due to technological, economic or other changes are generally recognized over the remaining productive lives of the assets. However, if it is determined that the book value of property, plant and equipment exceeds future estimated cash flows (undiscounted) over the remaining productive life of the asset, such excess is charged to expense in the period of determination. Property, plant and equipment held for divestment is written down to estimated net realizable value to the extent it is less than net book value.

Summary

This chapter discussed depreciation and depletion. Depreciation is the allocation of the recognized cost of property, plant, and equipment, less any net residual value, over their estimated useful life to the current owner. The several depreciation methods—straight line, service hours, productive output, and the accelerated methods—all accomplish the same purpose. That is, each method must allocate the cost of using an asset in a systematic and rational manner to expense in conformity with the matching principle. The various depreciation methods are differentiated because each one produces a different periodic pattern of cost allocation. Currently under GAAP the selection of a method to use is a "free choice," regardless of the characteristics of the asset or how it is used. GAAP requires only that the method used is systematic and rational.

Part B discussed some additional cost allocation issues and depletion. The unique features of some depreciable assets have caused the development of adaptations of the allocation of the cost of operating assets. These practical and cost-benefit applications are called allocation systems (rather than methods). These systems have designations that suggest the approach used—inventory appraisal, group and composite life, retirement and replacement systems. These are short-cut approaches that are intended to approximate the results that would be obtained if the methods discussed in Part A were used.

Depletion is a cost allocation that relates only to natural resources. Since depletion is based on output, the productive output method is used (discussed in Part A of this chapter).

SUPPLEMENT 11–A: ANNUITY AND SINKING FUND METHODS OF DEPRECIATION

The annuity and sinking fund methods of depreciation are based on the same concepts that underlie an annuity investment. In this situation, an investment is made and returns are received, usually each period. Each periodic return includes two separate elements: *(a)* a return of principal and *(b)* investment revenue. Each period, the return of principal becomes larger (this represents depreciation) and the periodic interest element becomes smaller as the asset diminishes in value with use. The annuity and sinking fund methods yield the same overall effect on the statement of income and statement of financial position; their differences relate to the **reporting** of depreciation expense and imputed interest revenue on the income statement. In general, neither method is acceptable under current GAAP.[9]

[9] This supplement is included because it emphasizes the theoretical concept of all investments, including investments in operational assets (i.e., property, plant, and equipment).

To illustrate the annuity and sinking funds methods of depreciation, assume the following simplified data:

Investment in plant item at cost at beginning of year 1	$6,600
Estimated useful life of plant item	5 years
Residual value estimated at end of year 5	$ 600
Average cost of capital	12%
Present value of 1 for 5 periods at 12% (Table 5–2)	.56743
Present value of ordinary annuity of 5 rents at 12% (Table 5–4)	3.60478

Annuity Method of Depreciation

To apply this method, the annual depreciation amount is computed on an **annuity basis.** The amount of the estimated annual earnings from the investment (e.g., $1,736 in the example below) is assumed to represent depreciation expense; accumulated depreciation is credited for the portion that represents return of principal (e.g., column *c* below), and the difference is credited to **imputed** interest revenue (e.g., column *b* below). To illustrate, the periodic amount of depreciation expense (based on the data given above) would be computed as follows, assuming a 12% imputed interest rate:

$$\text{Depreciation expense} = \frac{C - (R \times p)}{P_0}$$

$$= \frac{\$6{,}600 - [\$600 \times p_{n=5,\,i=12\%}(.56743)]}{P_{0_{n=5;\,i=12\%}}(3.60478)}$$

$$= \$1{,}736$$

where C refers to cost, R refers to residual value, $\boldsymbol{p}$ refers to the present value of 1, and $\boldsymbol{P_0}$ refers to the present value of an ordinary annuity.

With this value, we can construct a depreciation schedule reflecting the entries for depreciation and the periodic book value of the asset from acquisition to retirement. The schedule is illustrated below.

Depreciation schedule; annuity depreciation method.

Year	*(a)* Depreciation expense dr.	*(b)* Interest revenue cr.	*(c)* Accumulated depreciation cr.	*(d)* Unamortized asset balance
0				$6,600
1	1,736	$ 792	$ 944	5,656
2	1,736	679	1,057	4,599
3	1,736	552	1,184	3,415
4	1,736	410	1,326	2,089
5	1,736	247*	1,489	600 (residual value)
	$8,680	$2,680	$6,000	

(a) Constant amount from formula as computed above.
(b) Previous unamortized asset balance multiplied by 12%.
(c) *(a)* – *(b)*.
(d) Previous balance minus current amount in *(c)*.
* Rounded to come out even.

Notice that the above schedule is identical to an annuity amortization schedule (Chapter 5) except for the column captions. Also notice the following characteristics of the annuity method, as indicated by the entries in the above schedule:

1. Depreciation Expense is debited each period for a **constant** amount, and total depreciation expense ($8,680) exceeds the total cost to be depreciated ($6,000 in the example) because depreciation expense **includes** the imputed interest (revenue).
2. Accumulated Depreciation is credited for an **increasing** amount each period, and in total it is the same as the amount to be depreciated.
3. Interest Revenue (this is imputed interest) is credited for a **decreasing** amount each period to reflect the constant rate of return on a declining investment.
4. Because of the net effect of Depreciation Expense and Interest Revenue, **periodic net expense increases** on the statement of income. It is the same as the credit to accumulated depreciation each period.
5. The carrying value of the asset decreases each period by an increasing amount.

Sinking Fund Method of Depreciation

The sinking fund method is similar to the annuity method. The primary difference is that, under the sinking fund method, imputed interest is not separately recorded and reported. In contrast, under the annuity method imputed interest is separately recognized. It should be pointed out that while a sinking fund to replace the asset being depreciated might be maintained, most companies would prefer to invest in other productive assets; formal sinking funds (asset replacement funds) are quite rare. The journal entries, assuming depreciation only and no actual sinking fund, for the two methods are as follows:

Annuity and sinking fund depreciation methods compared.

	Annuity method		Sinking fund method	
Year 1:				
Depreciation expense	1,736		944	
Accumulated depreciation		944		944
Interest revenue		792		
Year 2:				
Depreciation expense	1,736		1,057	
Accumulated depreciation		1,057		1,057
Interest revenue		679		
Year 3:				
Depreciation expense	1,736		1,184	
Accumulated depreciation		1,184		1,184
Interest revenue		552		
Year 4:				
Depreciation expense	1,736		1,326	
Accumulated depreciation		1,326		1,326
Interest revenue		410		
Year 5:				
Depreciation expense	1,736		1,489	
Accumulated depreciation		1,489		1,489
Interest revenue		247		

Notice in the illustration that the sum of the five annual amounts **credited to accumulated depreciation** under both methods is $6,000 (enough to replace the asset if its replacement cost does not rise and if the $600 estimated residual value is realized). Also, if a series of five payments of $944 [i.e., $6,000 ÷ 6.35285 ($F_{0_{n=5,\, i=12\%}}$; Table 5–3)] were made to a sinking fund earning 12%, $6,000 would accumulate at the end of five years.

The above entries reveal that the only difference between the two methods is the treatment of **imputed** interest. Both credit the same periodic amounts to accumulated depreciation; both produce the same periodic income. However, the annuity method produces a **higher** periodic depreciation expense, which is reduced by the credit to imputed interest revenue.

The compound interest methods have been criticized on the grounds that they are not "rational" because an increasing amount of periodic depreciation over the life of the asset is inconsistent with the fact that ownership costs based on value tend to decrease in later years. In addition, a part of the periodic depreciation amount under the **annuity method** is for imputed or theoretical interest, which is offset with a credit to Interest Revenue; this affects the reported income or loss of the period in which the depreciation is recorded.

For a combination of reasons, the compound interest methods have been used infrequently in practice. For reasons already cited, many companies prefer to adopt depreciation methods that result in more depreciation in earlier years and less depreciation in later years.

The limited use of these methods is confined largely to public utilities. There is some conceptual justification for their use by regulated businesses where a precalculated rate of return on investment virtually is assured by the rate-setting process. Generally, however, they do not conform to GAAP.

QUESTIONS

Part A

1. Explain and compare amortization, depletion, and depreciation.
2. What are the primary causes of depreciation? What effect do changes in the market value of the asset being depreciated have on the depreciation estimates?
3. Explain the three factors that must be considered in allocating the cost of using an operational asset.
4. What is meant by accelerated methods of depreciation? Under what circumstances would these methods generally be appropriate?
5. Considering the SYD and DB (200% rate) depreciation methods, which method will always produce the larger amount of depreciation in the first year of use of an asset? Show why.
6. In estimating the service life of an operational asset, both inadequacy and supersession should be considered. Explain these two factors.
7. Explain the effects of depreciation on *(a)* the statement of income and *(b)* the statement of financial position.
8. Explain the relationship of depreciation to *(a)* cash flow and *(b)* tangible operational assets.

9. Explain the relationship between depreciation and replacement of the assets being depreciated.
10. Compare the effect of straight line and productive output methods of depreciation on the per unit cost of output for a manufacturing company.
11. Explain what is meant by ACRS depreciation. Explain why ACRS may not conform to GAAP.

Part B

12. Explain the basic accounting policy problems that arise in respect to depreciation when the entity's reporting year and the asset year do not coincide. Consider the case of a company that closes its books on June 30 but has bought a depreciable asset on January 1.
13. Explain the inventory appraisal system of depreciation. Under what circumstances is such a system appropriate?
14. Compare the retirement and replacement depreciation systems. Explain when each of these methods would be appropriate.
15. How are composite depreciation and group depreciation similar?
16. Explain the difficulties that may arise when using group depreciation.
17. There are three categories in respect to change and correction of depreciation. Briefly explain each and outline the accounting involved as specified in *APB Opinion 20.*
18. What are the primary characteristics of depletion? Explain how depletion usually is computed for financial and cost accounting purposes.
19. Explain why percentage depletion is not acceptable under GAAP.

Supplement 11–A

20. What two depreciation methods are based on compound interest concepts? How are the methods similar? Dissimilar?
21. Explain the pattern of depreciation expense over time that occurs when the annuity and sinking fund methods of depreciation are used.

EXERCISES

Part A: Exercises 11–1 to 11–7

E 11–1 **(Depreciation Schedules, SL, SYD, DB)**
Stoner Company acquired an operational asset at a cost of $10,000 that is estimated to have a useful life of five years and residual value of $2,500.

Required:
1. Prepare a depreciation schedule for the entire life of the asset using the following methods (show computations and round to the nearest dollar):
   a. Straight-line method.
   b. SYD method.
   c. DB (200% rate) method.
2. What criteria should be considered in selecting a method?

E 11–2 **(Depreciation Computation, SL, SH, PO, SYD, DB)**

To demonstrate the computations involved in several methods of depreciating an operational asset, the following data are used:

Acquisition cost	$12,500
Residual value	$ 500
Estimated service life:	
Years	5
Service hours	10,000
Productive output (units)	24,000

Required:

Give the formula and compute the annual depreciation amount using each of the following methods (show computations and round to the nearest dollar):

1. Straight-line depreciation; compute the depreciation rate and amount for each year.
2. Service hours method; compute the depreciation rate and amount for the first year assuming 2,200 service hours of actual operation.
3. Productive output method of depreciation; compute the depreciation rate and amount for the first year assuming 4,000 units of output. Is all of the depreciation amount (computed in your answer) expensed during the current period?
4. SYD method; compute the depreciation amount for each year.
5. DB (200% acceleration rate) method; compute the depreciation amount for each year.

E 11–3 **(Depreciation, SYD, PO)**

Ace Company acquired equipment that cost $18,000, which will be depreciated on the assumption that it will last six years and have a $1,200 residual value. Several possible methods of depreciation are under consideration.

Required:

1. Prepare a schedule that shows annual depreciation expense, accumulated depreciation, and book value for the first two years assuming (show computations and round to nearest dollar):
   a. SYD method.
   b. Productive output method. Estimated output is a total of 105,000 units, of which 12,000 will be produced the first year; 18,000 for each of the next two years; 15,000 the fourth year; and 21,000 the fifth and sixth years.
2. What criteria would you consider important in selecting a method?

E 11–4 **(Identify Depreciation Methods; Depreciation Schedules)**

Veto Company bought equipment on January 1, 19X1, for $45,000. The expected life is 10 years and the residual value is $5,000. Based on three acceptable depreciation methods, the annual depreciation expense and cumulative balance of accumulated depreciation at the end of 19X1 and 19X2 are shown below.

	Case A		Case B		Case C	
Year	Annual expense	Accumulated amount	Annual expense	Accumulated amount	Annual expense	Accumulated amount
19X1	$9,000	$ 9,000	$4,000	$4,000	$7,273	$ 7,273
19X2	7,200	16,200	4,000	8,000	6,545	13,818

Required:

1. Identify the depreciation method used in each case.
2. Based on your answer to Requirement 1, prepare a depreciation schedule for each case for 19X1 through 19X4.

E 11–5 (Depreciation Schedules, SYD, PO, DB)

BAT Company acquired a machine for $10,000 that has an estimated service life of three years and a residual value of $400.

Required:

1. Prepare a depreciation schedule covering the life of the asset (19X1, 19X2, and 19X3) reflecting use of the following methods (show computations and round to the nearest dollar):
   a. SYD method.
   b. Productive output method. Total output is estimated at 30,000 units. Assume actual output for the three years was sequentially: 10,000; 9,000; and 11,000 units.
   c. DB (200% acceleration rate) method.
2. Assume same facts as in (1*c*) above except that in the second year, after 10 months, the machine was sold for $2,000 cash. Give the entry to record depreciation expense for the second year and the sale.

E 11–6 (Straight-Line Depreciation; Entries)

Opal Jewelers depreciates its display cases on a straight-line basis. Transactions relating to display cases in Store A were as follows:

a. January 2, 19A: Bought six display cases for an aggregate cash price of $9,000.
b. December 31, 19A: On the assumption that the residual value of the cases would total 10% of original cost and the cases have a useful life of five years, recorded depreciation at year-end.
c. Recorded depreciation at year-end, December 31, 19B.
d. January 2, 19C: One display case was sold for $800 cash.
e. Two additional display cases were purchased for cash on January 10, 19C, at the same unit price as the original cases. Estimated residual value and useful life are expected to be the same as for the cases originally purchased (i.e., 10% of original cost and five years, respectively).
f. Recorded depreciation at December 31, 19C, for a full year for all remaining cases.
g. Transferred one of the original display cases to Store C on January 2, 19D.

Required:

Give the entries for each transaction; show computations; closing entries are not required. Use a Fixtures account for the display cases and identify fixtures by store (e.g., Store A, Store C). Do not use the group or composite systems.

E 11–7 (Identify Three Depreciation Methods)

On January 1, 19A, Gopher Company acquired a machine for $15,000. The estimated residual value of the machine is $1,000, and the estimated useful life is five years. Gopher's year-end is December 31.

Required:

Identify the method of depreciation used by Gopher if 19B depreciation expense is: *a.* $3,600; *b.* $2,800; *c.* $3,733.

Part B: Exercises 11–8 to 11–19

E 11–8 (Application of the Inventory Appraisal System)

Mite Engineering Company acquired a large number of small tools at the beginning of operations on January 1, 19A, for $2,000. During 19A and 19B, Mite disposed of several used tools, receiving cash salvage value of $200 in 19A and $250 in 19B. During 19B,

Mite acquired additional tools at a cost of $800. Inventories of tools on hand, valued at current acquisition cost adjusted for the present condition of the tools, indicated a value of $1,400 on December 31, 19A, and $1,800 on December 31, 19B. Mite uses the inventory/appraisal system of depreciation for small tools.

Required:
Give the entries for the inventory appraisal system to record the above transactions. Include adjusting entries for depreciation and the related closing entries.

E 11–9 **(Overview; Depreciation, Depletion; Multiple Choice)**
Select the best answer for each of the following. Justify your answer to each question.

1. As generally used in accounting, what is depreciation?
   a. It is a process of asset valuation for statement of financial position purposes.
   b. It applies only to long-lived intangible assets.
   c. It is used to indicate a decline in market value of a long-lived asset.
   d. It is an accounting process that allocates long-lived asset cost to accounting periods.
2. Property, plant, and equipment should be reported at cost less accumulated depreciation on a statement of financial position dated December 31, 19C, unless:
   a. Some obsolescence is known to have occurred.
   b. An appraisal made during 19C disclosed a higher value.
   c. The amount of insurance carried on the property is well in excess of its book value.
   d. Some of the property still on hand was written down in 19A due to permanent impairment of its use value.
3. Exploitation Company acquired a tract of land containing an extractable natural resource. Exploitation Company is required by its purchase contract to restore the land to a condition suitable for recreational use after it extracts the natural resource. Geological surveys estimate the recoverable natural resource will be 3 million tons, and that the land will have a value of $600,000 after restoration. Relevant cost information follows:

Land	$6,000,000
Restoration	900,000
Geological surveys	300,000

   If Exploitation Company maintains no inventories of extracted material, what should be the debit to depletion expense per ton of material extracted?
   a. $1.80.
   b. $1.90.
   c. $2.00.
   d. $2.20.
4. Upon purchase of certain depreciable assets used in its production process, a company expects to be able to replace these assets by adopting a policy of never declaring dividends in amounts larger than net income (after deducting depreciation). If a net income is earned each year, recording depreciation will coincidentally result in sufficient assets being retained within the enterprise which, if in liquid form, could be used to replace those fully depreciated assets if—
   a. Prices remain reasonably constant during the life of the property.
   b. Prices rise throughout the life of the property.
   c. The retirement depreciation system is used.
   d. Obsolescence was an unexpected factor in bringing about retirement of the assets replaced.
5. Which of the following statements is the assumption on which straight-line depreciation is based?
   a. The operating efficiency of the asset decreases in later years.

b. Service value declines as a function of time rather than use.
c. Service value declines as a function of obsolescence rather than time.
d. Physical wear and tear are more important than economic obsolescence.

6. In 19A, Baer Company purchased a tract of land as a possible future plant site. In January 19D, valuable sulfur deposits were discovered on adjoining property and Baer Company immediately began explorations on its property. In December 19D, after incurring $100,000 in exploration costs, which were accumulated in an asset account, the company discovered sulfur deposits appraised at $1 million more than the value of the land. To record the discovery value the company should debit—
   a. $100,000 to an expense account.
   b. $100,000 to an asset account.
   c. $1,000,000 to an asset account and $100,000 to an expense account.
   d. $1,000,000 to an asset account. (AICPA adapted)

E 11–10 (Group Depreciation; Asset Torn Down, Entries)

Ohio Company owned 10 warehouses of a similar type except for varying size. The group system of depreciation is applied to the 10 warehouses, the rate is 6% each year on cost. At the end of 19G, the asset account Warehouses showed a balance of $5,300,000 (residual value $300,000), and the Accumulated Depreciation account showed a balance of $2,400,000. Shortly after the end of 19G, Warehouse No. 8, costing $400,000, was torn down. Materials salvaged from the demolition were sold for $53,000, and $15,000 was spent on demolition.

Required:
Give entries to record *(a)* depreciation for 19G, *(b)* disposal of the warehouse, and *(c)* depreciation for 19H.

E 11–11 (Composite Depreciation System Applied)

Wilson Company owned the following machines, all acquired on January 1, 19A:

Machine	Original cost	Estimated residual value	Estimated life (years)
A	$14,000	None	4
B	20,000	$2,400	8
C	36,000	4,000	10
D	38,000	2,000	12

Required:
1. Prepare a schedule based on straight-line depreciation that shows for each machine the following: cost, residual value, depreciable cost, life in years, and annual depreciation.
2. Compute the composite depreciation rate and the composite life if the machines are depreciated using the composite system.
3. Give the entry to record 19A composite depreciation.

E 11–12 (Composite Depreciation System Applied)

California Utilities owned a power plant that consisted of the following, all acquired on January 1, 19A:

	Cost	Estimated residual value	Estimated life (years)
Building	$500,000	$50,000	30
Machinery, etc.	250,000	10,000	10
Other equipment	100,000	10,000	5

Required (carry decimals to the nearest two places):

1. Compute the total straight-line depreciation for 19B on all items combined.
2. Compute the composite depreciation rate and the composite life on the plant.
3. Give the entry to record 19A composite depreciation.

E 11–13 (Replacement and Retirement Systems Compared)

Jersey Utility Company purchased 600 poles at $110 per pole, debiting the Poles Inventory account. Subsequent to the purchase, 100 of the new poles were used to replace an equal number of old poles, which were carried in the tangible operational asset account, Poles. The old poles originally cost $70 each and had an estimated residual value of $10 per pole.

Required:

1. Give all indicated entries *(a)* assuming the replacement system is employed and *(b)* assuming the retirement system is used.
2. Compare the effect of these two methods on depreciation expense and the related asset accounts.

E 11–14 (Fractional-Year Depreciation; SL and SYD Compared)

Jackson Company's records show the following property acquisitions and disposals during the first two years of operations:

Year	Acquisition cost of property	Estimated useful life (years)	Disposals: Year of acquisition	Disposals: Amount
19A	$50,000	10	—	—
19B	20,000	10	19A	$7,000

Property is depreciated for one half year in the year of acquisition. Property disposed is depreciated for one half year in its year of disposal. Assume no residual values. There are no sale proceeds upon retirement.

Required:

1. Compute depreciation expense for 19A and for 19B and the balances of the Property and related Accumulated Depreciation accounts at the end of each year under the following depreciation methods. Show computations and round to the nearest dollar. Hint: set up separate schedules for "Property" and "Accumulated Depreciation."
   a. Straight-line method.
   b. SYD method.
2. Give entries for the acquisition, periodic depreciation, and retirement of the property assuming (Hint: set up parallel columns for 19A and 19B):
   a. Straight-line method.
   b. SYD method.

(AICPA adapted)

E 11–15 (Depreciation; Asset Year and Accounting Year Different)

Maine Company acquired a computerized lathe on May 1, 19A, for $120,000. The lathe has an estimated useful life of four years and an estimated residual value of $8,000. Maine's accounting year ends on December 31.

Required:

1. Calculate depreciation expense for the years 19A and 19B, assuming Maine uses the SYD method to depreciate the lathe.
2. Calculate depreciation expense for the years 19A and 19B, assuming Maine uses the DB (200% rate) method to depreciate the lathe.

E 11–16 (Depletion of Gravel Pit, Expense and Reporting the Asset)

MJ Company's investment in a gravel quarry was $6,000,000, of which $400,000 represented land value after removal of the gravel. Geologists who were engaged to estimate the removable gravel reported originally that 5 million cubic yards (units) could be extracted. In the first year, 880,000 units were extracted and 820,000 units were sold. In the second year, 830,000 units were extracted and sales were 850,000 units.

At the start of the third year, management of MJ had the quarry examined again, at which time it was determined that the remaining removable gravel was 2 million units. Production and sales for the third year amounted to 400,000 units. In the fourth year, production was 750,000 units while sales amounted to 600,000 units.

Required:

1. Calculate the depletion expense that should be reported on MJ's statement of income for each of the four years. Assume FIFO basis and show supporting computations.
2. Show how the gravel inventory and the gravel deposit should be reported on MJ's statement of financial position at the end of the fourth year. Assume an accumulated depletion account is used.

E 11–17 (Depletion; Expense, Reporting, Entries)

Arizona Mining Company acquired property with processed ore estimated at 2 million pounds for $1,800,000. The property has an estimated value of $100,000 after the ore has been extracted. Before any ore could be removed, it was necessary to incur $500,000 of developmental costs. In the first year, 200,000 pounds were removed and 160,000 pounds of ore were sold; in the second year, 400,000 pounds were removed and 410,000 pounds were sold. In the course of the second year's production, discoveries were made that indicated that if an added $1,460,000 is spent on developmental costs during the third year, future removable ore will total 2.5 million pounds. After incurring these added costs, production for the third year amounted to 460,000 pounds and sales, 450,000 pounds.

Required:

1. Calculate the depletion expense that Arizona should report on its statement of income for each of the three years. Show supporting computations and round unit costs to the nearest three decimal places (assume FIFO).
2. Show how the resource and the inventory should be reported by Arizona on its statement of financial position at the end of the third year (FIFO basis). Assume an accumulated depletion account is used.
3. Give the journal entry to record depletion expense at the end of each of the three years.

E 11–18 (Analyze the Accounting for Depreciation, Depletion, and Donated Assets)

The accounting treatments of depreciation and depletion have both similarities and differences.

Required:

1. List *(a)* the similarities and *(b)* the differences in accounting treatments of depreciation and cost depletion.
2. Describe cost depletion and statutory depletion. Under what conditions, if any, is statutory depletion permitted?
3. Operational assets donated to corporations are placed on the books, and their depreciation or depletion is recorded. Discuss the accounting justification for recording on the books *(a)* operational assets received as a gift and *(b)* their depreciation or depletion.

(AICPA adapted)

E 11–19 (Based on Supplement 11-A; Annuity and Sinking Fund Methods)
Equipment costing $80,000 with an estimated life of four years and a residual value of $8,000 is to be depreciated by compound-interest methods.

Required (round to nearest dollar):
Using a 12% rate, prepare a depreciation schedule covering the entire life of the asset assuming the:

1. Annuity method.
2. Sinking fund method.

PROBLEMS

Part A: Problems 11–1 to 11–9

P 11–1 (Depreciation Schedule, SH; Expense, SL, SYD, DB)
Quick Producers acquired factory equipment on January 1, 19A, costing $78,000. In view of pending technological developments, it is estimated that the machine will have a resale value upon disposal in four years of $16,000 and that disposal cost will be $1,000.

Data relating to the equipment follow:

Estimated service life:	
Years	4
Service hours	20,000
Actual operations:	

Calendar year	Service hours
19A	5,700
19B	5,000
19C	4,800
19D	4,400

Required (round to the nearest dollar and show computations):
1. Prepare a depreciation schedule for the service hours method assuming the accounts are closed each December 31.
2. Compute depreciation expense for the first and second years assuming *(a)* straight line, *(b)* SYD, and *(c)* DB (200% rate).

P 11–2 (Discussion; Overview of Depreciation)
Depreciation continues to be one of the more important problem areas in accounting.

Required:
1. *a.* Explain the factors that should be considered when applying the conventional concept of depreciation to determine how the value of a newly acquired computer system should be assigned to expense for financial reporting purposes. (Ignore income tax considerations.)
   b. What depreciation methods might be used for the computer system?
2. *a.* Explain the conventional accounting concept of depreciation accounting.
   b. Discuss its conceptual merit with respect to *(i)* the value of the asset, *(ii)* periodic amounts of expense, and *(iii)* the discretion of management in selecting the method.

(AICPA adapted)

P 11–3 (Depreciation Schedules for SL, PO, SYD, and DB)

Constar Company purchased a machine that cost $145,000. It was estimated that the machine would have a net resale value at the end of its useful life of $8,000. Data relating to the machine over its service life were as follows: Estimated service life in years, 5; and output (units), 8,000. Actual operations in units of output were: year 1, 1,600; year 2, 1,900; year 3, 1,000; year 4, 1,800; and year 5, 1,700.

Required:

Prepare a depreciation schedule for the asset over the useful life for each of the following methods: *(a)* straight line, *(b)* output, *(c)* SYD, and *(d)* DB (200% rate). Show computations and round to the nearest dollar.

P 11–4 (Analysis of Three Depreciation Methods; Maximize Income; Minimize Tax)

On January 1, 19A, Vista Company, a tool manufacturer, acquired new industrial equipment for $1 million. The new equipment had a useful life of four years, and the residual value was estimated to be $100,000. Vista estimates that the new equipment can produce 14,000 tools in its first year. Production is then estimated to decline by 1,000 units per year over the remaining useful life of the equipment.

The following depreciation methods are under consideration: *(a)* DB (200% rate), *(b)* straight line, *(c)* SYD, and *(d)* units of output.

Required:

1. Which depreciation method would result in maximum income for financial statement reporting for the three-year period ending December 31, 19C? Prepare a schedule showing the amount of accumulated depreciation at December 31, 19C, under the method selected. Show supporting computations in good form. Ignore present value, income tax, and deferred income tax considerations in your answer.
2. Which depreciation method would result in minimum income for tax reporting for the three-year period ending December 31, 19C? (Assume for problem purposes that all four methods are allowable for tax purposes.) Prepare a schedule showing the amount of accumulated depreciation at December 31, 19C, under the method selected. Show supporting computations in good form. Ignore present value considerations in your answer. (AICPA adapted)

P 11–5 (Analyze Cash Flows; Depreciation, SL, DB, SYD)

Bryan Company acquired equipment on January 1, 19A, for $80,000. It is estimated that the equipment has a four-year life and a residual value of $5,000. Bryan uses the same method of depreciation for financial reporting and tax purposes and is taxed at a 30% rate. Assume there is no investment tax credit on the equipment. For purposes of this problem, ignore ACRS.

Required:

1. Calculate the cash flow effect of depreciation on income taxes for each year of the equipment's useful life assuming:
   a. Straight line.
   b. DB (200% rate).
   c. SYD.
2. Assume Bryan can invest any idle cash to yield an annual return of 12%. Which depreciation method is preferable from a tax perspective? Show computations to support your answer.

P 11–6 (Match Four Depreciation Methods with Depreciation Expense)

Equipment was acquired for $80,000 that has a six-year estimated life and a residual value of $8,000. The equipment will be depreciated by various amounts in its third full year depending on the depreciation method used.

Third-year depreciation expense under the four methods listed below (but not in the same order) amounted to (1) $12,000; (2) $11,852; (3) $13,714; and (4) $19,800. The depreciation methods used were *(a)* DB (200% rate), *(b)* productive output, *(c)* straight line, and *(d)* SYD.

The productive-output method assumed 800,000 units could be produced; in the first three years, actual output was: 200,000 units; 180,000 units; and 220,000 units, respectively.

Required:
Analyze the above data. Based on this analysis, alongside each letter *(a)* through *(d)*, which identifies the four methods, write the number (1) through (4), associated with the amount of third-year depreciation for that method. Support each answer with calculations.

P 11–7 (Analyze Asset and Accumulated Accounts; Complex)
Selected accounts included under the property, plant, and equipment caption of Abel Company's statement of financial position at December 31, 19X8, had the following balances (at original cost):

Land	$220,000
Land improvements	75,000
Buildings	600,000
Machinery and equipment (acquired 1/1/X1)	650,000

During 19X9, the following transactions occurred:

a. A plant facility consisting of land and building was acquired from Club Company in exchange for 10,000 shares of Abel's common stock. On the acquisition date, Abel's stock had a closing market price of $39 per share on a national stock exchange. The plant facility was carried on Club's accounts at $95,000 for land and $130,000 for the building at the exchange date. Current appraised values for the land and building, respectively, are $120,000 and $240,000.

b. A tract of land was acquired for $85,000 as a potential future building site.

c. Machinery was purchased at a total cost of $250,000. Additional costs were incurred as follows:

Freight and unloading	$ 5,000
Sales and use taxes	10,000
Installation	25,000

d. Expenditures totaling $90,000 were made for new parking lots, streets, and sidewalks at the corporation's various plant locations. These improvements had an estimated useful life of 15 years.

e. A machine that cost $50,000 on January 1, 19X1, was scrapped on June 30, 19X9. DB (200% rate) depreciation has been recorded on the basis of a 10-year life.

f. A machine was sold for $25,000 on July 1, 19X9. Original cost of the machine was $37,000 at January 1, 19X6, and it was depreciated on the straight-line basis over an estimated useful life of eight years and a residual value of $1,000.

Required:
1. Prepare a detailed analysis of the changes in each of the following statement of financial position accounts for 19X9 (disregard accumulated depreciation). Hint: analyze each asset separately: *(a)* land, *(b)* land improvements, *(c)* buildings, and *(d)* machinery and equipment.
2. List the items in the fact situation which were **not** used to determine the answer to (1) above, showing the relevant amounts and supporting computations for each

item. In addition, indicate where, or if, these items should be included in Abel's financial statements. Hint: set up three schedules: *(a)* loss or gain on scrapping the machine, *(b)* accumulated depreciation, DB method, and *(c)* loss or gain on sale of machine.

P 11–8 (Overview; Depreciation Schedules; SL, SYD, PO, with Changes)
Medarts Corporation has just acquired an operational asset at a cost of $80,000 that is to be depreciated over five years to a residual value of $5,000. You have been asked to develop alternate depreciation schedules based on various depreciation methods and assumptions as to usage given below.

Assumptions:

a. The straight-line method will be used. After recording depreciation three years in accordance with the original assumptions, the residual value is changed to $10,000.
b. The SYD method will be used (no revision in life or residual value).
c. The productive output method will be used. Scheduled production using the asset will be: year 1, 153,000 units; year 2, 160,000 units; year 3, 140,000 units; year 4, 100,000 units; and year 5, 72,000 units.
d. The productive output method will be used as in *(c)*; through the first two years the total expected and planned production are the same. However, at the start of year 3, the total production estimate over the service life of the asset is revised to 729,000 units, and scheduled production in years 3, 4, and 5 will be 200,000 units; 90,000 units; and 126,000 units, respectively.
e. The annuity method will be used based on a 15% imputed interest rate (optional).

Required:
Prepare a depreciation schedule for each of the assumptions given above that shows depreciation expense, accumulated depreciation, and book value. Assumption *(e)* is optional; do not solve if you have not studied Supplement 11–A.

P 11–9 (Overview; Depreciation Schedules; SL, SYD, PO)
Ginger Company bought a new machine for $60,000. It is expected to have a four-year useful life and a residual value of $6,000 at the end of that time. You have been requested to draw up schedules that will show annual depreciation for the machine each year under each of several different depreciation methods and assumptions as to how the machine will be used throughout its productive life (round to the nearest dollar).

The independent methods for which you are to supply depreciation data are as follows:

a. Straight-line method. After using the method for two years, at the start of the third year the residual value is revised downward to an estimated $4,000.
b. SYD depreciation with no revision in life estimate or residual value.
c. Productive output depreciation on the assumption that the machinery can produce 90,000 units, and production throughout the four years of use will occur as follows: year 1, 25,000 units; year 2, 32,000; year 3, 17,000; and year 4, 16,000.
d. Productive output depreciation with the same starting assumption as in *(c)* and the same production in the first two years. In the third year, however, the total production estimate over the entire service life of the machine was revised to 93,000 units, and production for years 3 and 4 were, respectively, 19,000 units and 17,000 units.
e. Use of the sinking fund method. A 14% interest rate should be assumed (optional unless you have studied Supplement 11–A).

Part B: Problems 11–10 to 11–19

P 11–10 (Depreciation; Appraisal, Retirement, and Replacement Systems Compared)
Grayson Company uses a number of small machine tools in its operations. Although there are numerous differences among the tools, they cost approximately the same and have similar useful lives. The company maintains a Machine Tools account which showed a balance of $1,800 (250 tools at $7.20) at the end of 19A. Acquisitions, retirements, and other data for 19B and 19C are given below:

	19B	19C
Acquisitions	120 at $7.50	150 at $7.80
Retirements:		
Number	150	100
Salvage proceeds	$90	$100
Ending inventory	220 at $5.50*	270 at $5.80*

* Per unit value given current condition.

Required:
1. Give the entries for each of the two years assuming (round to the nearest dollar and show computations):
   a. The inventory appraisal system is used.
   b. The retirement system is used.
   c. The replacement system is used.
2. Prepare a schedule for the two years to show the annual depreciation amount and the balance in the Machine Tools account under each system.

P 11–11 (Application of the Composite Depreciation System)
Operational assets, acquired on January 1, 19A, by Sally Company are to be depreciated using the composite system. Details regarding each asset are given in the schedule below:

Component	Cost	Estimated residual value	Estimated life (years)
A	$45,000	$5,000	10
B	15,000	-0-	6
C	38,000	8,000	15
D	6,200	200	8

Required:
1. Calculate the composite life and annual composite depreciation rate for the asset components listed above. Give the entry to record depreciation after one full year of use. Round the depreciation rate to the nearest two decimal places.
2. During 19B, it was necessary to replace component B, which was sold for $8,000. The replacement component cost $18,000 and has an estimated residual value of $1,500 at the end of its estimated six-year useful life. Record the disposal and substitution, which was a cash acquisition.
3. Record depreciation at the end of 19B.

P 11–12 (Overview; Operational Asset and Depreciation Schedule)
General Corporation, a manufacturer of steel products, began operations on October 1, 19A. The accounting department of General has started the operational asset and depreciation schedule accompanying this problem. You have been asked to assist in completing this schedule. In addition to ascertaining that the data already on the schedule are correct, you have obtained the following information from the company's records and personnel:

a. Depreciation is computed from the first of the month of acquisition to the first of the month of disposition.

b. Land A was acquired on October 2, 19A, in exchange for 3,000 newly issued shares of General's common stock. At the date of acquisition, the stock had a par value of $5 per share and a market value of $45 per share. During October 19A, General paid $26,000 to demolish an existing building on this land so it could construct a new building.

c. Construction of Building A on the newly acquired land began on October 1, 19B. By September 30, 19C, General had paid $250,000 of the estimated total construction costs of $300,000. Estimated completion and occupancy date is July 19D.

d. Land B and Building B were acquired from a predecessor corporation. General paid $890,000 for the land and building together. At the time of acquisition, the land had an appraised value of $72,000 and the building had an appraised value of $828,000.

e. Certain equipment was donated to the corporation on October 1, 19A, by a local university. An independent appraisal of the equipment when donated placed the market value at $34,000 and the residual value at $2,000.

f. Machinery A's total cost of $110,000 includes installation expense of $550 and normal repairs and maintenance of $11,000. Residual value is estimated at $5,500. Machinery A was sold on February 1, 19C.

g. On October 1, 19B, Machinery B was acquired with a down payment of $4,000 and the remaining payments to be made in 10 annual installments of $4,000 each beginning October 1, 19C. The prevailing interest rate was 18% on debts with risk characteristics similar to this debt.

GENERAL CORPORATION
Operational Asset and Depreciation Schedule
For Fiscal Years Ended September 30, 19B, and September 30, 19C

Assets	Acquisition date	Cost	Residual value	Depreciation method	Estimated life in years	Depreciation expense year ended September 30: 19B	19C
Land A	10/2/19A	$ (1)	n.a.	n.a.	n.a.	n.a.	n.a.
Building A	Under construction	250,000 (to date)	—	Straight line	30	—	$ (2)
Land B	10/1/19A	(3)	n.a.	n.a.	n.a.	n.a.	n.a.
Building B	10/1/19A	(4)	$20,000	Straight line	(5)	$19,970	(6)
Donated equipment	10/1/19A	(7)	2,000	DB (150% rate)	10	(8)	(9)
Machinery A	12/2/19A	(10)	5,500	SYD	10	(11)	(12)
Machinery B	10/1/19B	(13)	—	Straight line	10	—	(14)

n.a.—Not applicable.

Required:
Notice the 14 numbers in parenthesis in the above schedule. You are to respond about each one. Number your answer sheet from (1) to (14). For each numbered item on the schedule accompanying this problem, supply the correct amount next to the corresponding number on your answer sheet. Round each answer to the nearest dollar. Do not recopy the schedule. Show supporting computations in good form. (AICPA adapted)

P 11–13 (Retirement and Replacement Systems Compared)

Alton Company uses a large number of identical small tools in operations. On January 1, 19A, the first year of operations, 1,200 of these tools were purchased at a cost of $3 each. On December 31, 19A, 150 of the tools were sold or scrapped for $100 and were replaced at a cost of $4.20 each. On December 31, 19B, 300 of the tools were sold or scrapped for $120; they were replaced at a cost of $4.50 each. On December 31, 19C, 160 of the tools were sold or scrapped for $55, each being replaced at a cost of $3.60.

Required:

1. Give the entries to record all indicated transactions, assuming the company employed the *(a)* retirement system and *(b)* replacement system.
2. Compare the results under the two systems by showing periodic depreciation for each year and the balance in the tools account at each December 31, 19A–19C.

P 11–14 (Depreciation and Depletion; Schedule, Entries)

Colorado Mining Corporation bought mineral-bearing land for $150,000 that engineers say will yield 200,000 pounds of economically removable ore; the land will have a value of $30,000 after the ore is removed.

To work the property, Colorado built structures and sheds on the site that cost $40,000; these will last 10 years, and because their use is confined to mining and it would be expensive to dismantle and move them, they will have no residual value. Machinery that cost $29,000 was installed at the mine, and added cost for installation was $7,000. This machinery should last 15 years; like the structures, usefulness of the machinery is confined to these mining operations. Dismantling and removal costs when the property has been fully worked will approximately equal the value of the machinery at that time; therefore, Colorado does not plan to use the structures or the machinery after the minerals have been removed.

In the first year, Colorado removed only 15,000 pounds of ore; however, production was doubled in the second year. It is expected that all of the removable ore will be extracted within eight years from the start of operations.

Required:

1. Prepare a schedule showing unit and total depletion and depreciation and book value of the operational assets for the first and second year of operation.
2. Assuming that in the first year 80% of production was sold, and in the second year, the inventory carried over from the first year plus 80% of the second year's production was sold, give the entries to record accumulated depreciation and depletion. To show the effect of these costs, make the offsetting debits to cost of goods sold and inventory. Use "accumulated" accounts.

P 11–15 (Depreciation Schedule and Correcting Entry)

As of December 31, 19F, the Machinery account of Barger Company was as below:

Machinery

1/1/A	Purchase	$50,000	12/31/A	Depreciation	$5,000
7/1/B	Purchase	10,000	9/1/B	Machinery sold	1,000
11/1/C	Purchase	36,000	12/31/C	Depreciation	6,300
			12/31/D	Depreciation	7,800
			7/1/E	Machinery sold	1,000
			12/31/E	Depreciation	7,800
			12/31/F	Depreciation	9,300

Machinery sold September 1, 19B, cost $3,600 on January 1, 19A; machinery sold July 1, 19E, cost $2,500 on January 1, 19A. Machinery costing $2,000, which was purchased on July 1, 19B, was destroyed on July 1, 19F, and was a total loss. Assume the debits in the machinery account are correct.

Required:
Prepare a depreciation schedule that shows the annual depreciation and account balances. Assume a 10-year life on all items, straight-line depreciation, and no residual value. Suggested captions: Date acquired, Machinery (debit-credit), Correct depreciation by year (six columns), and Accumulated Depreciation (debit-credit).
Prepare the journal entry or entries to correct the accounts on December 31, 19F, assuming the accounts are not closed for 19F (ignore income taxes). (Hint: Prior period adjustment is debited.)

P 11–16 (Depreciation Schedule and Correcting Entry)
The accounts of Jackson Delivery Company reflected the following:

Trucks

1/1/19A	Trucks No. 1 and No. 2 (cost $3,600 each)	7,200	1/1/19C	Truck No. 1 scrapped	3,600
1/1/19C	Truck No. 3	3,900	1/1/19D	Truck No. 2 scrapped	3,600
1/1/19D	Truck No. 4	3,840			
7/1/19D	New tires, truck No. 3	400			

Accumulated Depreciation

1/1/19C	Truck No. 1 scrapped ($700 received as salvage)	2,400	12/31/19A	Depreciation	2,400
1/1/19D	Truck No. 2 scrapped ($300 received as salvage)	3,300	12/31/19B	Depreciation	2,400
			12/31/19C	Depreciation	2,500
			12/31/19D	Depreciation	2,647
			12/31/19E	Depreciation	2,713

Required:
1. Prepare a depreciation schedule showing correct account balances and depreciation by year, assuming the estimated lives of trucks No. 3 and No. 4 were changed from three to four years (other trucks have estimated service lives of three years and no estimated residual value) on January 1, 19E. Suggested captions: Date acquired, Truck no., Trucks (debit-credit*), Correct depreciation by year (five columns), and Accumulated depreciation (debit-credit*).
2. Give the journal entry or entries to correct the accounts at December 31, 19E, assuming they were not yet closed for 19E. The schedule prepared for (1) above should provide the data needed.

P 11–17 (Depreciation; SYD, SL, DB; Change in Estimate)
Machinery that cost Dutton Corporation $19,000 is expected to last 10 years and have a $1,000 residual value. Several depreciation methods in common use were applied to these data. The results in terms of annual depreciation amounts covering year 2 and year 3 are set out below:

Year	Method A	Method B	Method C
1	?	?	?
2	$2,945	$1,800	$3,040
3	2,618	1,800	2,432

Required (round to the nearest dollar):
1. Identify each method used. What is the book value of the asset at the end of year 3 for each of the three methods used to compute year 2 and year 3 depreciation given in the table above?

2. In connection with methods A and B, suppose that after the completion of year 3, it is determined that the total remaining life of the machinery is five instead of seven years. Determine the annual depreciation amount and the balance of Accumulated Depreciation at the end of year 4 and year 5.

P 11–18 (Overview; Depreciation, Depletion; Disposals)

For each of the following situations, *(a)* select the best response from those given and *(b)* explain the basis for your choice, showing computations where appropriate.

Items (1) and (2) are based on the following information: On January 2, 19A, Calcomp Manufacturing Company acquired some equipment from Silval Corporation. The sale contract requires Calcomp to make 12 annual payments of $10,800 at the end of each year. The first payment was made on December 31, 19A, and no deposit was required. The equipment has an estimated useful life of 20 years with no anticipated residual value. The prevailing interest rate for Calcomp in similar financing arrangements is 18%.

1. At what amount should Calcomp have capitalized this equipment?
   a. $51,767. *c.* $103,720.
   b. $81,390. *d.* $106,040.

2. How much interest expense should Calcomp have recorded in 19A?
   a. Zero. *c.* $7,200.
   b. $6,507. *d.* $9,318.

3. Smith Company sold an item of plant equipment. Smith received a noninterest-bearing note to be paid $1,000 per year for 10 years. The going rate of interest for this transaction is 15%. What discount from the face amount of the note (i.e., $10,000) should Smith reflect on this transaction?
   a. Zero. *c.* $4,981.
   b. $3,290. *d.* $6,710.

4. Black Company exchanged a business car for a new car. The old car had an original cost of $7,500, an undepreciated cost of $1,600, and a market value of $2,000 when exchanged. In addition, Black paid $6,200 cash for the new car. The list price of the new car was $8,300. At what amount should the new car be recorded for financial accounting purposes?
   a. $7,500. *c.* $8,200.
   b. $7,800. *d.* $8,300.

The following data pertain to questions (5) and (6) below only. On July 1, 19A, Miller Mining, a calendar-year corporation, purchased the rights to a copper mine. Of the total purchase price, $2.8 million was allocable to the copper. Estimated reserves were 800,000 tons of copper. Miller expects to extract and sell 10,000 tons of copper each month. Production began immediately. The selling price is $25 per ton. Miller uses percentage depletion (15%) for tax purposes. To aid production, Miller also purchased some new equipment on July 1, 19A. The equipment cost $76,000 and had an estimated useful life of eight years. However, after all the copper is removed from this mine, the equipment will be of no use to Miller and will be sold for an estimated $4,000. Use straight-line depreciation.

5. If sales and production conform to expectations, what is Miller's depletion expense on this mine for financial accounting purposes for the calendar year 19A?
   a. $105,000. *c.* $225,000.
   b. $210,000. *d.* $420,000.

6. If sales and production conform to expectations, what is Miller's depreciation expense on the new equipment for financial accounting purposes for the calendar year 19A?

a. $4,500. *c.* $9,000.
b. $5,400. *d.* $10,800.

7. Jones, Inc., purchased some equipment on January 2, 19A, for $24,000 (no residual value). Jones used straight-line depreciation based on a 10-year estimated life. During 19D, Jones decided that this equipment would be used only three more years and then replaced with a technologically superior model. What entry, if any, should Jones make as of January 1, 19D, to reflect this change?
   a. No entry.
   b. Debit an extraordinary item for $4,800, and credit accumulated depreciation for $4,800.
   c. Debit a prior period adjustment for $4,800, and credit accumulated depreciation for $4,800.
   d. Debit depreciation expense for $4,800, and credit accumulated depreciation for $4,800. (AICPA adapted)

P 11–19 (Supplement 11–A; Annuity and Sinking Fund Depreciation)
Equipment that cost $100,000 has an estimated three-year life and $20,000 residual value.

Required (round to the nearest dollar):
Using a 16% annual earnings rate on the equipment, prepare a depreciation schedule covering the entire life of the equipment assuming:

1. Annuity method.
2. Sinking fund method.

CASES

C 11–1 (Depreciable Tangible Assets Fully Depreciated But Still in Use)

1. Baker Corporation has certain fully depreciated tangible operational assets which are still used in the business.
   (a) Discuss the possible reasons why this could happen.
   (b) Comment on the significance of the continued use of these fully depreciated assets.
2. In the past these fully depreciated assets and their accumulated depreciation have been merged with other operational assets and related depreciation on the balance sheet. Discuss the propriety of this accounting treatment, including a consideration of other possible treatments and the circumstances in which they would be appropriate. (AICPA adapted)

C 11–2 (Depletion; What Does It Mean in Financial Statements?)
A friend of yours recently inherited capital stock in Megamining Corporation. The friend has just received the first annual financial report from the company since the inheritance. One aspect of the report in particular troubles your friend; consequently, you have been asked for an explanation of what the company seems to be saying. The excerpt reads:

> "Depletion of mines is computed on the basis of an overall unit rate applied to the pounds of principal products sold from mine production. The corporation makes no representation that the annual amount represents the depletion actually sustained or the decline, if any,

in mine values attributable to the year's operations, or that it represents anything other than a general provision for the amortization of the remaining book value of mines."

Specifically, your friend asks: (1) Is the depletion amount reported on the statement of income meaningless? (2) Are the company's mines becoming more or less valuable? (3) What is the significance of the book value of the company's mines?

Required:

Respond to your friend's questions. Identify each element of your response with the three questions your friend has asked.

C 11–3 (Depreciation and Gain or Loss on Disposal)

Some of the major car rental companies account for the gain or loss on disposal of their used cars as an adjustment to depreciation expense in the period of disposal rather than reporting gains or losses on disposal.

Required:

On what grounds, if any, can such a procedure be justified? Would your answer be different if the procedure were used by relatively few (versus most) companies in the industry?

C 11–4 (Depreciation; Single Asset Unit or Separate Subunits)

In situations where depreciable properties are treated as units rather than as part of a group of assets depreciated on a composite or group basis, the question sometimes arises as to what constitutes an appropriate property unit for accounting purposes. For example, a building as a single entity may be designated as the basic property unit. Alternatively, the elevators, escalators, heating and air-conditioning system, other mechanical equipment, plumbing, electrical system, and the basic building structure could be accounted for as separate property units.

Required:

1. What accounting problems arise if an item that could be accounted for as a single property unit is instead accounted for as a number of separate asset units?
2. Identify and explain some advantages of accounting separately for smaller property units as opposed to aggregation as a single property unit.

C 11–5 (Reporting Property and Depreciation; An Actual Case)

Kimberly-Clark

This case relates to the 1987 financial statements of Kimberly-Clark (given in the Appendix immediately following Chapter 25).

Required:

1. Give the company's accounting policies regarding property and depreciation.
2. List the kind of property and the amounts reported on the 1987 statement of financial position.
3. How much cash was spent in 1987 for "capital" assets?
4. What was the total amount of depreciation recorded in 1987?

12 INTANGIBLE ASSETS

OVERVIEW AND PURPOSE

For accounting purposes, assets are broadly classified as either tangible or intangible. **Tangible** refers to the physical substance of an asset, and **intangible** implies that the asset lacks physical substance. Intangible assets are not precisely defined in accounting. However, for accounting purposes, an intangible asset usually has the following characteristics: (1) lacks physical substance, (2) has future economic benefits (i.e., ownership rights) that often are difficult to measure, (3) has a useful life that is sometimes difficult to determine, and (4) often is acquired for operational use.

The following tabulation summarizes intangible assets that are discussed in other chapters of this textbook and the economic utility these assets provide for their owners.

Intangible asset	Economic utility
1. Cash and back deposits (Chapter 7).	Exchange value.
2. Accounts receivable (Chapter 7).	Future cash inflows.
3. Investments in equity securities (Chapter 18); investments in debt securities (Chapters 14 and 15).	Participation in *(a)* selection of management by voting shares, *(b)* dividends, *(c)* asset distributions in liquidation, and *(d)* capital appreciation.
4. Prepaid expenses (Chapter 4).	Use of goods or services already paid for, such as insurance.

The purpose of this chapter is to discuss another category of intangible assets. These assets are characterized as long-lived **operational** (or fixed) intangible assets. The primary topics discussed are intangible assets, deferred charges, and various related issues. To accomplish this purpose, the chapter is organized as follows:

1. Classification of intangible assets.
2. Basic concepts related to accounting for intangible assets.
3. Identifiable intangible assets.
4. Unidentifiable intangible assets (goodwill).
5. Some additional intangible assets.
6. Disposal of intangible assets.
7. Accounting for the cost of computer software.

Supplement 12-A: Accounting for Insured Casualty Losses and Gains

Supplement 12-B: Accounting for Life Insurance

Classification of Intangible Assets

Long-term intangible assets used in operating a business usually are classified on the statement of financial position as intangible assets. Other statement designations include intangibles, intangible operational assets, intangible fixed assets, and even other assets. The more common intangible assets are patents, copyrights, franchises, trademarks, organization costs, and goodwill.[1]

For accounting purposes, intangible operational assets are classified as follows:

1. **Identifiability:**
   a. **Identifiable**—intangible assets that have separate identities and can be sold (or purchased) individually, such as a patent.
   b. **Unidentifiable**—intangible assets that are not separable from the owning entity and cannot be sold (or purchased) separately; that is, the goodwill of a business.
2. **Manner of acquisition:**
   a. **Acquired externally**—intangible assets often are acquired from external sources by purchase, such as a franchise.
   b. **Developed internally**—intangible, assets may be developed by the company in the course of its operations, such as a patent.

Basic Concepts Related to Accounting for Intangible Assets

Valuation accounting for intangible assets involves the same accounting principles and procedures as for tangible property, plant, and equipment. These principles are: *(a)* at acquisition, application of the **cost principle,** *(b)* during the period of use, application of the **matching principle,** and *(c)* at disposition, recognition of a gain or loss on disposal equal to the difference between the consideration received and the book value of the asset.

Prior to *APB Opinion No. 17,* intangible assets were accounted for on the basis of **life expectancy.** Intangible assets with limited lives were amortized over their estimated period of future use. Intangible assets with indeterminable lives were not amortized until a realistic determination of useful life could be made. Often this determination was never made; therefore, the cost of such intangibles was never amortized. This *Opinion* stopped this practice (for assets acquired after October 1970) by providing that:[2]

> . . . the value of intangible assets at any one date eventually disappears and . . . the recorded costs of intangible assets should be amortized by systematic [debits] to income over the period estimated to be benefited. . . . The cost of each type of intangible should be amortized on the basis of the estimated life of that specific asset. . . . The period of amortization should not, however, exceed 40 years.

Intangible assets acquired prior to October 1970 do not come under the 40-year rule.

---

[1] The discussions in this chapter are in conformity with AICPA, *APN Opinion 17,* "Intangible Assets" (New York, August 1970). Intangible assets acquired before this date are accounted for in accordance with *Accounting Research Bulletin 43,* chapter 5.

[2] AICPA, *APN Opinion No. 17,* pars. 27 and 29.

Intangible assets should be recorded at acquisition at their current cash equivalent cost in conformity with the **cost principle.** Cost includes all expenditures made to acquire the asset including purchase price, transfer and legal fees, and any other expenditures related to acquisition. The acquisition cost is the current market value of all considerations given, or of the asset received, whichever is more reliably determinable. When an intangible asset is acquired for noncash considerations, in whole, or in part, its cost is any cash paid plus the current market value of the noncash consideration given. If that value cannot be determined reliably, then the market value of the right acquired is used.[3] For example, if a patent is acquired by a corporation by issuing its own capital stock as the consideration, the cost of the patent should be measured as the current market value of the shares of stock issued. If the shares issued do not have an established market value consistent with the number of shares issued for the patent, evidence of the market value of the patent itself should be used as the measure of cost of the transaction.

Amortization of the Cost of Intangible Assets

The cost of an intangible asset must be allocated to expense in a **rational and systematic manner** over the estimated useful life of the asset in conformity with the **matching principle.** This allocation process is called **amortization.** It is often difficult to estimate the economic useful life of an intangible asset. Therefore, the APB suggested that the following factors should be considered.[4]

- **a.** Legal, regulatory, or contractual provisions that may limit the maximum useful life.
- **b.** Provisions for renewal or extension that may alter a specified limit on useful life.
- **c.** Effects of obsolescence, demand, and other economic factors that may reduce useful life.
- **d.** Useful life that may parallel the service life expectancies of individuals or groups of employees.
- **e.** Expected actions of competitors and others that may restrict present competitive advantages.
- **f.** An apparently unlimited useful life that may in fact be indefinite, and benefits that cannot be reasonably projected.
- **g.** An intangible asset that may be a composite of many individual factors with varying effective useful lives.

Because of their characteristics, intangible assets seldom have a **residual value.** The acquisition cost of an intangible asset that has a reliably determinable useful life should be **systematically** amortized over that period of time. The cost of an intangible asset that does not have a determinable useful life must, nevertheless, be amortized on the basis of a reasonable estimate of useful life.

APB Opinion 17 requires that, in all instances, the period of amortization

[3] If neither the market value of the consideration given nor the intangible asset acquired can be determined with sufficient reliability, the company may have to assign a value to the intangible asset.

[4] AICPA, *APB Opinion 17*, par. 27.

need to review useful life at certain times

should not exceed 40 years. This rule is arbitrary. It was included to prevent potential abuses of the **matching principle** to manipulate reported income.

Because of the inherent difficulty in estimating the economic useful life of an intangible asset, periodic evaluations should be made to determine whether the estimate needs revision. A change in estimated useful life is a **change in accounting estimate.** When estimates are changed, the unamortized cost should be amortized over the revised useful life that remains. However, under no circumstances may the **total** amortization period exceed 40 years from acquisition date.

APB Opinion 17 states that "the straight-line method of amortization—equal annual amounts—should be applied unless a company demonstrates that another systematic method is more appropriate."

Amortization of an intangible asset usually involves a year-end adjusting entry. The amount to be amortized is recorded as a debit to expense and as a credit to either (a) the asset account (because of precedent), or (b) an accumulated amortization account (contra to the asset account).

Identifiable Intangible Assets

Identifiable intangible assets can be specifically and separately identified apart from the enterprise itself. Thus, they can be sold separately. Examples include patents, copyrights, franchises, and trademarks (but not goodwill). They may be either (a) acquired externally by purchase or (b) developed internally. In either case, they are recorded initially at cost, in conformity with the cost principle. As the economic service value of the asset declines, its cost is amortized as expense in conformity with the matching principle.

Because there is a wide variety of intangible assets, application of the foregoing principles and guidelines varies. Several identifiable intangible assets commonly encountered in business are discussed below.

Patents

successful defense only

at cost — increase value of asset if necessary

impairment loss if you don't win

A **patent** is an exclusive right recognized by law and registered with the U.S. Patent Office. A patent enables the holder to use, manufacture, sell, and control the patent without interference or infringement by others. In reality, the registration of the patent with the Patent Office is no guarantee of protection. Therefore, a patent does not become conclusive until it has been successfully defended in court. For this reason, there is general agreement that the cost of **successful** court tests should be capitalized as part of the cost of the patent. If the suit is lost, the legal cost as well as the unamortized cost of the patent is written off. The carrying amount of the patent then is reduced to its "impaired" value, which could be zero. An impairment loss should be debited for the amount of any write-down. The cost of a patent acquired **externally by purchase** is determined in conformity with the **cost principle** as discussed above.

Internally developed patents resulting from the company's own research and development (R&D) activities must be accounted for as specified as *FASB Standard* 2, which is discussed under the subsequent heading, "Research and Development (R&D) Costs." This *Standard* specifies that laboratory costs leading to the development of the patent must be **expensed as incurred.** The only costs of an internally developed patent that can be capitalized are legal fees

cost

because this is a cost to have that right.

and other costs associated with registration of the patent, such as models and drawings required for the registration.

Patents have a legal life of 17 years. The useful life of many patents is shorter because technological progress, substitute products, and other improvements cause the products or processes covered by the patents to lose their competitive advantages before the 17 years elapse. The cost of a patent should be amortized over the estimated useful life or legal life, whichever is shorter. Because the legal life of a patent is 17 years, that usually is the upper limit. Sometimes an old patent is improved or modified so that a new patent is registered. If the new patent causes the old patent to have no value, a reasonable case can be made for adding the unamortized cost of the old patent to the cost of the new patent for the new 17-year amortization period. However, most companies may rely on the conservatism constraint and immediately write off the unamortized cost of the old patent.

To illustrate the accounting for a typical patent situation, assume that early in January 19A, P Company purchased a patent that cost $27,200. The patent had a 17-year legal life. However, it was purchased one year later than the registration date. During year 2 (19B), P Company won a patent infringement suit. The cost for legal fees and court costs was $4,750. The entries are:

Beginning of 19A—Purchase of patent:

Patent	27,200	
Cash		27,200

End of 19A—Amortization:

Patent amortization expense	1,700	
Patent (or Accumulated patent amortization)		1,700
$27,200 ÷ 16 years = $1,700.		

During 19B—Patent infringement suit:

Patent	4,750	
Cash		4,750

End of 19B—Amortization:

Patent amortization expense	2,017	
Patent (or Accumulated patent amortization)		2,017
($27,200 − $1,700 + $4,750 = $30,250) ÷ 15 years = $2,017.		

Patent owners often enter into a contractual agreement with another party to let them use the patent for a stipulated amount or periodic royalties. In such cases, the amounts earned should be recognized as revenue in conformity with the revenue principle (see Chapter 6).

Copyrights

A copyright is a form of protection given by law to the authors of literary, musical, artistic, and similar works. Owners of copyrights are granted certain exclusive rights, such as *(a)* to print, reprint, and copy the work; *(b)* to sell or distribute copies; and *(c)* to perform and record the work.

Under the provisions of the 1978 copyright law, a copyright is protected for the **life of the author plus 50 more years.** Copyrights can be sold or contractually assigned to other persons.

The cost of a copyright is measured in conformity with the **cost principle.** A copyright often does not have economic value for its entire legal life. The cost of a copyright should be amortized over the period the copyrighted item is expected to produce revenue. However, copyrights should not be amortized in excess of legal life (life of the author plus 50 more years), or **in excess of the 40-year maximum** specified in *APB Opinion 17*.

The accounting entries for a copyright are similar to those for a patent.

Trademarks and Trade Names

Trademarks or trade names (such as Coca-Cola) can be registered, and renewed for 20-year periods, with the federal patent office to help substantiate ownership. Thus, names, symbols, or any other distinctive identity for a product are given legal protection. The cash equivalent amount paid for the purchase of a trademark is capitalized. Amounts directly incurred in the development, protection, expansion, registration, or defense of a trademark should be capitalized. Such capitalized amounts should be amortized over the useful life of the trademark or 40 years, whichever is shorter.

Franchises

Franchises often are granted by *(a)* governmental units for the right to use public properties or to furnish public utility services (e.g., electricity), and *(b)* business entities for the right to use a particular designation and specified services (e.g., The Container Store and Kentucky Fried Chicken). Each franchise contract specifies a period of time for which the franchise is valid and the rights and obligations of the franchisor and franchisee.

The cost of obtaining a franchise often is high. The initial cost of a franchise should be capitalized and then amortized as expense. If the franchise is for a limited period of time, its cost should be amortized over that period in a rational and systematic manner. If the time is indefinite, amortization should be based on a reliably estimated life, with periodic evaluations. These evaluations determine whether the prior estimate needs revision; however, the total amortization period may not exceed 40 years.

Annual and current payments by the franchisee to the franchisor for services, such as assistance with promotional campaigns, accounting, and organizational matters, should be expensed by the franchisee as incurred because they do not create a measurable future benefit for the franchise. If a franchise becomes worthless or is voided by law, the unamortized amount should be written off immediately as an impairment of asset value (discussed later in this chapter).

Unidentifiable Intangible Assets (Goodwill)

An **unidentifiable** intangible asset has the following characteristics: *(a)* lacks physical substance, *(b)* results from a number of concurrent economic factors, *(c)* cannot be related to specific identifiable assets (such as a patent or a machine), and *(d)* cannot be separately identified from the business entity. The only unidentifiable asset is goodwill. Goodwill has asset value because it represents expectation of "above-normal" financial performance in the future. The factors that cause goodwill for a particular business are varied. Common factors are: quality products and customer service, effective advertising, financial and social responsibility, strategic location, marketing success, established customer base, superior management, and "above-normal" financial performance in the recent past.

Goodwill can be viewed from either a conceptual view or an application view. **Conceptually** goodwill is the difference between the present value of the **estimated** (desired) future cash inflows from an investment in a business and the present value of the **normal** (usual) cash flows from a business. This conceptual view can be illustrated as follows:

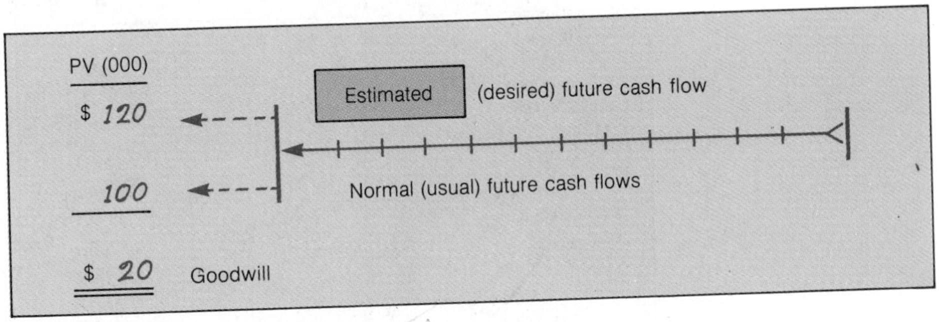

Application of the conceptual view for accounting purposes under GAAP, is as follows:

Goodwill recorded	=	Actual purchase price of the entity	−	Estimated market value of the identifiable net assets
$20 (difference)	=	$220 (negotiated)	−	$200 (estimated)

APB Opinion 16, par. 87, states that "the excess of the cost of the acquired company (i.e., actual purchase price) over the sum of the amounts assigned to identifiable assets acquired less liabilities assumed should be recorded as goodwill" (parentheses added). Under current GAAP **goodwill is given accounting recognition only when a business entity is purchased** because *(a)* goodwill cannot be separated from the entity that generated it, and *(b)* an acquisition by purchase is the only objective means of measuring the cost of goodwill so that it conforms to the **cost principle.** Goodwill may be internally developed over a period of time. However, in the absence of an arm's-length transaction, its existence and valuation cannot be objectively measured. For this reason, internally generated goodwill **should not be capitalized** by the entity that generated it.

Identifiable net assets include all tangible and intangible identifiable assets acquired less all liabilities assumed. Therefore, goodwill often is called **Excess of cost over the market value of identifiable net assets purchased.**

From an accounting perspective, goodwill poses two problems: *(a)* measuring the amount of goodwill to recognize, and *(b)* recording and amortizing the goodwill recognized.

Measuring, Recording, and Amortizing Goodwill

When an entire entity is purchased, the purchaser records the acquisition by debiting each identifiable asset and goodwill, and crediting each liability assumed in conformity with the **cost principle.** The cost principle provides that all items must be recorded at their market value as measured in the purchase transaction. Subsequent to acquisition data, depreciation, depletion, and amortization of each appropriate asset, **including goodwill,** must be recognized.

Exhibit 12–1
Statement of financial position, Company S (adapted to estimate goodwill).

	End of year 5	
	Col. 1 Book values of Company S	**Col. 2 Market values developed by Company B***
Assets:		
Cash	$ -0-	$ -0-
Receivables (net)	37,000	35,000
Inventory	61,000	60,000
Plant and equipment (net)	79,000	93,000
Patent	3,000	2,000
Total	$180,000	190,000
Liabilities:		
Current	$ 30,000	30,000
Noncurrent	60,000	60,000
Owners' equity	90,000	—
Total	$180,000	(90,000)
Estimated market value of the identifiable net assets		$100,000

* These market values were developed by Company B in advance by using price lists, appraisals, market values of similar assets, and specific price indexes.

Example. At the beginning of year 6, Company B (buyer) purchased all of the assets and liabilities of Company S (seller) for a negotiated price of $120,000 cash. Company S provided its statement of financial position (excluding cash) dated at the end of year 5 as shown in **Exhibit 12–1,** column 1, **Book values.** Company B immediately compiled the data in column 2 to reflect its best estimate of the market value of Company S.

Based on the data given in Exhibit 12–1, the amount of goodwill purchased can be computed as follows:

Purchase price for Company S	$120,000
Less: Estimated market value of the identifiable net assets purchased	100,000
Goodwill purchased by Company B	$ 20,000

Company B would make the following entries during year 6:

Beginning of year 6—To record the purchase of Company S:

Receivables (net)	35,000	
Inventory	60,000	
Plant and equipment (net)	93,000	
Patent	2,000	
Goodwill	20,000	
Current liabilities		30,000
Noncurrent liabilities		60,000
Cash		120,000

End of year 6—Adjusting entry to record annual amortization of goodwill, assuming an estimated useful life of 10 years:

Goodwill amortization expense	2,000	
Goodwill (or accumulated amortization)		2,000

$20,000 ÷ 10 years = $2,000.

Company B's financial statements at the end of year 6 would report goodwill as follows:

Statement of income:	
Operating expenses:	
Goodwill amortization expense	$ 2,000
Statement of financial position:	
Intangible assets	
Goodwill (unamortized)	18,000

In the above example, goodwill of $20,000 was recorded. Subsequent to acquisition, goodwill should be amortized as expense over its estimated useful life in conformity with *APB Opinion 17;* however, the amortization period may not exceed 40 years.[5]

Computation of the cost of goodwill was based on one **known amount**—the **purchase price** of the entity—and **one estimate**—the market value of the identifiable net assets of the entity purchased (see Exhibit 12–1, column 2). The market price of each asset and each liability must be **estimated** by the purchaser in order to properly record the acquisition. In Exhibit 12–2, notice that Company B estimated some of the Company S assets to have higher market values than book values (i.e., plant and equipment) and some of them to have lower market values (i.e., receivables, inventory, and patent). In contrast, the book values of liabilities usually approximate their current market values.[6] The differences in asset valuations can be expected because **accounting** book values do not represent current market values. When an entity is purchased, the recorded costs of the individual assets purchased are the "best estimates" of current market values in conformity with the **cost principle.**[7] This topic is discussed in more detail in Chapter 18.

Estimating Goodwill in Negotiating the Purchase Price of an Entity

As illustrated above, the amount of **goodwill** that is recognized when a business entity is purchased is the **excess** of the **actual** negotiated purchase price over the estimated market value of the identifiable net assets of the entity acquired. Acting independently, the prospective buyer and the seller will make estimates

[5] George R. Catlett and Norman O. Olson, "Accounting for Goodwill," *Accounting Research Study 10* (New York: AICPA, 1968) suggested three alternative treatments of the recorded cost of goodwill as follows: (1) deduct in full from owners' equity at the acquisition date, (2) retain goodwill indefinitely as an asset with reductions only when its value is decreased, and (3) amortize as an intangible asset over its reasonable life (this treatment was selected by the APB in *Opinion 17*). *APB Opinion 17* was effective November 1, 1970; the discussions herein assume that the goodwill was purchased on or after this effective date. Accordingly, the 40-year rule is applicable. For goodwill purchased prior to the effective date, the 40-year rule and required amortization do not apply.

[6] Refer to the discussion of liability valuations in Chapter 14.

[7] Negative goodwill (or "badwill") is suggested when the actual purchase price is **less** than the estimated market value of the identifiable net assets. *APB Opinion 17* requires that any negative goodwill be allocated to reduce proportionately the market values assigned to the noncurrent assets (except long-term investments in equity securities). The usual result is that no goodwill is recognized in such cases.

of the "value" of the business, including any goodwill. These estimates are then used as a **basis for negotiating the actual sale/purchase price** of the entity.

Computational approaches to estimate a **purchase or offer price** for negotiating purposes usually start with an estimate of future earnings. Such estimates involve uncertainties and assumptions. The following steps provide a basic framework for estimating future earnings (these steps should be adapated for each situation):

1. Select for study a series of past years' earnings that are likely to be good predictors of future earnings. The time period selected should be long enough to show the pattern of earnings fluctuations experienced by the company. Yet, the time period should be short enough to provide data relevant to the prediction. Some companies may use a 3-year time period; others may use 5 years or even 10, depending on the specific situation.
2. Adjust these past earnings for:
   a. Unusual and/or nonrecurring gains and losses.
   b. Earnings effects of changes in accounting estimates and principles.
   c. Changes that are expected to occur in expenses and revenues in the future.
3. Analyze the trend and uniformity of past earnings. Even though past earnings were above normal, any observed downward trend in the immediate past may indicate the disappearance of above-normal earning capacity. This downward trend may indicate dissipation of goodwill value.
4. On the basis of the above analysis, **project the future earnings.**

Example. Return to Exhibit 12–1 and assume that Company B developed the following projections prior to serious negotiations with Company S to set the actual purchase price (these projections were not divulged to Company S):

a. Estimated average annual earnings, $30,000, and estimated average annual net cash inflow (from earnings) for each of the next **10** years, $25,000.[8]

b. Expected annual rate of return on the total investment (i.e., the cash purchase price), 15%.

c. Estimated market value of the identifiable net assets (assumed to be unchanged at the later acquisition date), $100,000.

Based on the projections, the *(a)* negotiating price and *(b)* amount of estimated goodwill included can now be developed. These two values can be computed by using either (1) one of several rough estimate approaches (based on projected earnings) or (2) the discounted cash flow approach (based on projected cash flows).

1. **Rough estimate approaches based on earnings projections**—Two variations are (these approaches are not standardized):
   a. Arbitrary number of years' **earnings** ($30,000 for five years):

Estimated purchase price ($30,000 × 5 years)	$150,000
Estimated market value of identifiable net assets	100,000
Goodwill	$ 50,000

[8] This is a simplified projection for illustrative purposes only. Typically, the projected annual net cash inflow used would be different for each of the 10 years.

b. Arbitrary capitalization rate (22%):

Estimated purchase price ($30,000 ÷ 22%, rounded)	$136,000
Estimated market value of identifiable net assets	100,000
Goodwill	$ 36,000

2. **Discounted cash flow approach (based on cash flow projections)**—This approach is based on present value concepts (Chapter 5) applied to the estimated net cash inflow for each year. This approach is conceptually sound; the primary problem involves projection of the future cash flows.

For illustrative purposes, the estimated average annual net cash inflow of $25,000 for each of the 10 years (given above) is used. Using the expected rate of return of 15%, the PV analysis would be as follows:

Price for negotiation purposes:	
$25,000 × $P_{o_{n=10;\,i=15\%}}$ (Table 5–4, 5.01877), rounded	$125,000
Estimated market value of identifiable net assets	100,000
Estimated goodwill	$ 25,000

Refer to the acquisition entry on page 530–31.

The PV computation used a 15% discount rate. Selection of an appropriate discount rate for this purpose is subjective. The higher the discount rate the lower the estimated value of goodwill. A discount rate should take into account other investments and the risks involved. It is probable that the potential buyer and seller will use different discount rates to prepare for the negotiations.

Some Additional Intangible Assets

Statements of financial position often report captions such as "Intangibles," deferred charges, and "Other" assets. In most cases these are catchall classifications. Ideally such captions should not be used; however, the accounting profession has not provided any definitive guidance in this area. Some of these intangibles have two special characteristics: *(a)* they are long-term prepayments of expenses, and *(b)* they may not confer any "rights" to the owner.

Deferred Charges

essentially

A **deferred charge,** as it is commonly called in accounting, is a capital expenditure for a service that will contribute to the generation of future revenues; it is a **long-term prepaid expense** on the statement of financial position. **Deferred charges** are classified as noncurrent assets because their effect on revenues extends beyond the period for current assets. Deferred charges have no physical substance and can rarely be realized through their sale.[9] Examples of deferred charges include machinery rearrangement costs, long-term prepaid insurance premiums, prepaid leasehold costs, and long-term debit balances arising from interperiod income tax allocation. Research and development costs and organiza-

pr

[9] The term **charge** often is used by accountants as a synonym for **debit.**

tion costs do not fall under the purview of *APB Opinion 17*. However, when they are capitalized they usually are classified as deferred charges.[10]

Deferred charges are amortized over the future periods during which they will contribute to the generation of revenues. The 40-year maximum useful life for amortization of intangible assets specified in *APB Opinion 17* also applies to deferred charges. However, deferred charges seldom have 40-year life spans.

Leaseholds

Often a business leases property from its owner under an operating lease[11] and makes lease or rental **prepayments.** These prepayments, such as a "lease bonus" payment, cover the entire term of the lease. Such a prepayment initially should be debited to an account often entitled **Leasehold** or **Prepaid Rent Expense.** The cost of this asset should be amortized over the period benefited (which is usually the lease term) by periodically debiting rent expense and crediting the asset account.

The cost of **leasehold improvements** (under an operating lease), such as modifications of the leased property, should be debited to a Leasehold Improvement account. Leasehold improvements usually are classified as intangible assets because the leased property does not belong to the lessee. Leasehold improvements should be amortized as expense over the remaining term of the lease or the life of the improvements, whichever is shorter. Accounting for leaseholds is illustrated in Chapter 21.

Research and Development (R&D) Costs

Research and development costs, commonly called R&D costs, are among the most important expenditures made by many companies. Prior to 1975, unamortized R&D costs were a significant statement of financial position asset and were reported as a deferred charge. However, recognition and amortization of R&D costs were varied. These variations in accounting, and the potential to amortize these expenditures in various ways to manipulate income, caused the FASB to focus on the R&D issue.

This concern resulted in the issuance of *FASB Standard 2*, "Accounting for Research and Development Costs," in 1974. This *Standard* specifies accounting for R&D costs as follows:

1. All R&D costs covered by the *Standard* should be debited to expense when incurred. That is, R&D expenditures (except for item 3 below) cannot be capitalized.
2. Financial statements must disclose **total R&D** costs debited to expense in each period for which an income statement is presented.
3. Exceptions—Item 1 above does not apply to R&D costs when projects are done for outside entities by contract. Also, exceptions are made for

---

[10] *APB Opinion 17* (par. 6) states: "The provisions of this *Opinion* apply to costs of developing identifiable assets that a company defers and records as assets. Certain costs, for example, research and development costs and preoperating costs, present problems which need to be studied separately." Specific mention in *Opinion 17* of research and development (R&D) costs and preoperating (i.e., organization) costs, both of which usually are classified as deferred charges, implies that *Opinion 17* applies to deferred charges except those two which were specifically singled out for further study.

[11] An operating lease does not convey ownership; that is, it does not effectively transfer most of the rewards and risks of ownership to the lessee. A lease which transfers such rewards and risks of ownership is referred to as a capital lease. Leases are discussed in Chapter 21.

certain government-regulated entities. In these cases, any R&D costs incurred as a contractual necessity are capitalized in a work-in-process inventory. Upon completion of the contract, or specified parts of the contract, these R&D costs, along with all of the other project costs, are removed from inventory and reported as an expense (similar to cost of goods sold). Thus, the exception specifies capitalization of R&D costs related to a contract from the time incurred until the contracted project is completed (as opposed to periodic amortization).[12]

4. All unamortized R&D costs that were previously capitalized must be written off as a prior period adjustment, as of the effective date of *FASB Standard 2*.

FASB Standard 2 defined R&D costs as all of the **expenditures** for R&D activities including materials, personnel, intangibles purchased from others, contract services, and allocated indirect costs related to R&D activities. *FASB Standard 2* also specified that equipment and facilities acquired or constructed for R&D activities should be capitalized; however, depreciation on such assets constitutes R&D expense for the periods in which they are used for R&D purposes.

R&D costs, such as the following, relate to research activities:

- **a.** Laboratory research designed to discover new knowledge.
- **b.** Searching for applications of new research findings or other knowledge.
- **c.** Conceptual formulation and design of possible product or process alternatives.
- **d.** Testing in search for, or evaluation of, product or process alternatives.
- **e.** Modification of the formulation or design of a product or process.
- **f.** Design, construction, and testing of preproduction prototypes and models.
- **g.** Design of tools, molds, and dies that involve new technology.
- **h.** Design, construction, and operation of a pilot plant that does not have a scale economically feasible to the enterprise for commercial production.
- **i.** Engineering activity required to advance the design of a product so that it meets specific functional and economic requirements and is ready for manufacture.

Patent costs cannot include R&D expenditures that led to developing the patent.

FASB Standard 2 gives a practical solution to what had been a serious problem. Research studies showed it was difficult to establish criteria for identifying R&D costs that would have specific future benefits. Also, a basic issue was to stop the capitalization of many expenses under the R&D umbrella.

Capitalization of Intangibles by Development Stage Companies

A **development stage** company often incurs a wide range of **startup** costs before it has significant revenues against which such costs can be matched. Newly organized companies often capitalized such costs as intangibles and in later years amortized them when revenues materialized. **The issue is whether devel-**

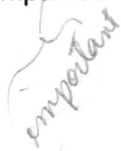

[12] FASB, *Statement of Financial Accounting Standards 68*, "Research and Development Arrangements" (Stamford, Conn., 1982), provides accounting guidelines on contract research.

Exhibit 12–2
Reporting by a development stage company.

New company was organized January 1, 19A.
Statement of financial position—December 31, 19C:

Assets (detailed)	$130,000
Liabilities (detailed)	$ 75,000
Capital stock, nopar (Note 4)	95,000
Deficit accumulated during development stage	(40,000)*
Total liabilities and stockholders' equity	$130,000

* Debit balance in retained earnings.

Note 4:

	Shares issues		Resources received		
Date	**No. shares**	**Total**	**Cash: Amt/per share**		**Noncash: Amt/per share**
19A	15,000	$75,000	$65,000/$5.00		$10,000/$5.00
19B	5,000	20,000	20,000/ 4.00		-0-
19C	None	-0-	-0-		-0-
	20,000	$95,000	$85,000		$10,000

Statement of income—years ended December 31:

	19A	19B	19C	Cumulative
Revenues (detailed)	$ 110,000	$ 145,000	$ 175,000	$ 430,000
Expenses (detailed)	(145,000)	(160,000)	(165,000)	(470,000)
Net income	$ (35,000)	$ (15,000)	$ 10,000	$ (40,000)
EPS	$ (2.33)	$ (.75)	$ .50	$ (2.00)

Statement of cash flows—not illustrated. Use the standard side captions illustrated in Chapter 19, and the same column captions shown above for the statement of income.

opment stage companies should be permitted to capitalize certain costs as intangible assets when these costs would otherwise have been expensed as incurred.

Because of the lack of guidelines and the wide variety of accounting practices, the FASB issued *Statement of Financial Accounting Standards 7,* "Accounting and Reporting by Development Stage Enterprises." The *Standard* (par. 8) defines development stage enterprises as follows (emphasis added):

> An enterprise shall be considered to be in the development stage if it is **devoting substantially all of its efforts to establishing a new business and either of the following conditions exists: *(a)* planned principal operations have not commenced or *(b)* planned principal operations have commenced but there has been no significant revenue therefrom.** A development stage enterprise will typically be devoting most of its efforts to activities such as financial planning; raising capital; exploring for natural resources; developing natural resources; research and development; establishing sources of supply; acquiring property, plant, or other operating assets, such as mineral rights; recruiting and training personnel; developing markets; and starting up production.

FASB Standard 7 requires development stage enterprises to present financial statements prepared on the **same basis as other businesses;** that is, special reporting formats are unacceptable. **Capitalization of costs is subject to the same assessment of future benefit and recoverability applicable to established businesses.** Thus, the *Standard* specifies that a development stage enterprise is required to present *(a)* on the statement of financial position the "deficit accumulated (from operations) during development stage," *(b)* a statement of income and a statement of cash flows, and *(c)* a statement of stockholders' equity. The current statements must show **information for each period** covered by the past and present statements and the cumulative amounts. Also, the statements must be **specifically identified** as those of a development stage company. Reporting by a development stage company is shown in **Exhibit 12–2.**

Prepaid Insurance Premium Cost

When liability and casualty insurance premiums are paid in advance, an intangible asset, called **prepaid insurance,** is created. If the premium provides insurance coverage for a period that extends more than one year (or the operating cycle, if longer) beyond the current statement of financial position date, the intangible asset must be apportioned between current and noncurrent assets for reporting purposes.

Example. On January 1, 19A, Company B paid a $2,500 premium for a five-year liability insurance policy. The accounting and reporting for 19A are as follows:

Entries:

January 1, 19A—insurance premium paid:		
Prepaid insurance	2,500	
Cash		2,500
December 31, 19A—adjusting entry:		
Insurance expense ($2,500 ÷ 5)	500	
Prepaid insurance		500

Reporting at December 31, 19A:

Statement of income:	
Insurance expense	$ 500
Statement of financial position:	
Current assets:	
Prepaid insurance	500
Deferred charges:	
Prepaid insurance, long term	1,500

Note: Five years was used only for illustrative purposes. Currently, most insurance premiums are paid annually.

Supplement 12–A discusses accounting for insured casualty gains and losses and Supplement 12–B discusses accounting for life insurance.

Organization Costs

Expenditures usually are incurred in organizing a business. Costs directly related to the organizing activities, such as expenditures for legal, accounting, promotional, and clerical activities may be properly capitalized as **organization costs.** Organization costs are not included in the "deficit accumulated during development stage" illustrated in Exhibit 12–2. That account relates to operating losses.

The basis for capitalization is that such costs benefit the operations of future years. To expense the total amount in the first year of operation would result in a mismatching of expense with revenue.

Because the life of a business usually is indefinite, the length of the period receiving the benefits of these costs usually is indeterminate. For this reason, and because the recognition of organization costs as an asset depends upon intangible values presumably attached to the particular business, organization costs usually are amortized over an arbitrarily selected short period of time. This conservative practice is encouraged by the tax rules. The tax rules permit the business to amortize most organization costs ratably over any period not less than five years. Organization costs generally are not amortized up to the maximum 40-year rule because of their indeterminate characteristics.

Stock Issuance Costs

Expenditures incident to the issuance of capital stock are called **stock issuance costs.** Such costs include printing stock certificates and related items, professional fees, commissions paid for selling capital stock, and the costs of filing with state agencies and the SEC. Stock issuance costs, as opposed to organizational costs, are accounted for either as *(a)* an offset to the issuance price of the capital stock to which they relate or *(b)* a deferred charge, which is amortized to expense in conformity with the matching principle (usually on a conservative basis). Stock issuance costs are excluded from the 40-year rule of *APB Opinion 17.* Stock issuance costs are discussed in Chapter 16.

Impairment of the Value of Intangible Assets

During the period an intangible asset or a deferred charge is "used," a periodic assessment of the value of future benefits associated with the asset may show that its current book value exceeds its economic utility (i.e., use value) to the enterprise. In such cases, the unamortized cost should be written down, and a loss recognized. This reflects **impairment** of value. The revised value should be amortized over the estimated remaining useful life, not to exceed 40 years from date of acquisition (*APB Opinion 17,* par. 31). When a write-down occurs due to an impairment of value, disclosure is required in notes to the financial statements (*APB Opinion 17,* par. 31). See page 500 for a disclosure of an impairment of value by the Standard Oil Company.

Disposal of Intangible Assets

When an intangible asset is sold, exchanged, or otherwise disposed of, its unamortized cost (or cost net of accumulated amortization, if separately recorded) must be removed from the accounts and a gain or loss on disposal recorded.

Because financial analysts often view intangibles as having questionable value and because of overconservatism, accounting practice in the past encouraged an arbitrary write-down of intangibles to a nominal amount (such as $100) either by lump sum in one period or over an unrealistically short estimated life. Current accounting principles do not permit this practice because it biases income and financial position downward. On this point, *APB Opinion 17* (par. 28) states that intangible assets "should not be written off in the period of acquisition" and "analysis of all factors should result in a reasonable estimate of the useful life."

Reporting Intangibles

Noncurrent assets classified as intangibles are reported under such statement of financial position (SFP) headings as **Intangibles, Deferred charges,** and **Other assets.** Although precise definitions are desirable, comparable distinctions often are not made in practice for these three captions. Therefore, there is variation in the manner in which companies report intangibles on their SFP. Often each major intangible asset reported on the SFP is described in detail in the financial statement notes.

A typical adapted example of the reporting of intangible assets follows.[13]

The Eastern Company

	1986	1985
Other assets:		
Goodwill less accumulated amortization ($57,827 in 1986 and $44,381 in 1985)	$145,617	$209,064
Patents, licenses and trademarks, less accumulated amortization ($198,026 in 1986 and $137,824 in 1985)	371,005	372,146
Prepaid pension cost	307,931	—
Sundry	120,214	114,924
Total other assets	$944,767	$696,134

Notes to Consolidated Financial Statements
Note A (in part): Summary of Significant Accounting Policies
Intangibles: Patents are amortized on a straight-line basis over the lives of the patents. Licenses are generally amortized on a straight-line basis over periods of 5 to 17 years.
Goodwill is being amortized over periods from 7 to 20 years.

Accounting for the Cost of Computer Software

The rapid development of computer technology, including personal computers, has been accompanied by the organization of computer software companies. These software companies either purchase or develop software for sale or lease. The development of a computer software package to sell or lease to external parties involves significant research and development costs. The basic accounting issue is what costs incurred in developing software packages for sale or lease should be *(a)* expensed or *(b)* capitalized. In response to requests from the Securities and Exchange Commission, American Institute of Certified Public Accountants, and the Accounting Standards Executive Committee, the FASB issued *Standard 86* (August 1985), "Accounting for the Costs of Computer Software to Be Sold, Leased, or Otherwise Marketed." The basic provisions of this *Standard* can be summarized as follows:

a. All costs incurred to establish the technological and economic feasibility of a computer software product to be marketed or leased are R&D costs and shall be expensed when incurred.

b. Costs of producing **product masters** incurred subsequent to establishing economic feasibility ([*a*] above) shall be capitalized.

c. Software production costs shall be capitalized only after all R&D activities are completed including the establishment of economic feasibility ([*a*] above).

d. Costs incurred for duplicating the product masters documentation, train-

[13] Source: AICPA, *Accounting Trends & Techniques, 1987* (New York, 1987), p. 166.

ing materials, and packaging shall be capitalized as software inventory costs on a unit-specific basis. When products are sold these unit inventory costs shall be expensed (as cost of goods sold).

e. At each statement of financial position date, the inventory of computer software must be written down to net realizable value if that value is below cost. Once written down to net realizable value the inventory cannot be subsequently written back up to cost.

This *Standard* is very precise in distinguishing between expensing intangible costs (e.g., R&D) and capitalizing inventory costs (e.g., production costs).

Summary

This chapter discussed the acquisition, amortization, and disposal of intangible operational assets. Intangible assets are characterized by *(a)* lack of physical substance and *(b)* special rights that come with ownership. Intangible assets are initially recorded at cost in conformity with the cost principle. Subsequent to acquisition the cost of an intangible asset (less any residual value, which is rare) is amortized as expense, in a rational and systematic manner, over an estimated useful life, not to exceed 40 years. Intangible operational assets are broadly classified as *(a)* identifiable (e.g., a patent) or unidentifiable (e.g., goodwill), and *(b)* acquired externally (by purchase) or internally (developed by the company). If an intangible asset unexpectedly and permanently loses value, the asset should be written down as an impairment loss to net realizable value. At disposal date, all related expenses (such as amortization) should be recorded up to the date of disposal; then the carrying value should be removed from the accounts and a disposal gain or loss recognized. Because of the diverse nature of intangibles, each asset classification may include one or more intangible assets. This chapter discussed only intangible **operational** assets.

SUPPLEMENT 12–A: ACCOUNTING FOR INSURED CASUALTY LOSSES AND GAINS

A casualty insurance policy is a contract whereby the insurance company, in consideration for a premium payment, assumes an obligation under certain circumstances to reimburse the policyholder for a loss due to storm, fire, and so forth, as stated in the policy. The reimbursement cannot legally exceed the **replacement cost** of the property (in its present condition). Under no circumstances can the indemnity collected from the insurance company exceed the **lower of replacement cost** or the amount stipulated in the contract; that is, the **face amount** of the policy.

Many casualty insurance policies carry a **coinsurance clause.** This clause provides that if the property is insured for less than a stated percentage (often 80%) of its **replacement cost** at the time of the loss, the insured is a **coinsurer** with the insurance company.[14] As a coinsurer, the insured must bear a share of losses. The share of a loss borne by the insured is determined by application

[14] The effect of coinsurance is to encourage insured parties to carry adequate insurance. In the absence of a coinsurance clause, small losses would be fully indemnified when a small amount of insurance is carried. However, if policies contain a coinsurance clause, such losses will be shared by the insured and the insurance company.

of the policy provision that the insurance company will pay the lowest of the three following amounts:

1. Face of the policy.
2. Replacement cost of the property lost.
3. Coinsurance indemnity (determined by formula).

To illustrate the effect of a coinsurance clause, assume the following for Company C:

1. Insurance policy on casualties—face, $7,000; coinsurance clause, 80%.
2. Casualty—fire; replacement cost of inventory lost at date of fire (there was a partial loss of the inventory), $5,680.
3. Total replacement cost of the insured inventory immediately prior to the fire, $10,000.

Computation of the coinsurance indemnity (by formula):

$$\frac{\text{Face of policy}}{80\% \times \text{Total replacement cost of insured property at date of casualty}} \times \begin{matrix}\text{Replacement cost}\\ \text{of the property lost}\end{matrix} = \begin{matrix}\text{Coinsurance}\\ \text{indemnity}\end{matrix}$$

$$\frac{\$7{,}000}{80\% \times \$10{,}000} \times \$5{,}680 = \underline{\underline{\$4{,}970}}$$

Thus, the insurance company would reimburse the insured (i.e., Company C) $4,970. This amount is lower than either the face of the policy ($7,000) or the replacement cost of the inventory lost ($5,680).

A **casualty loss** may result from an event such as a fire, flood, or storm. Accounting for a casualty involves *(a)* removing the asset that is lost from the accounting records, *(b)* recording any collection of indemnity from the insurance company, *(c)* adjusting any prepaid insurance affected by the loss, and *(d)* closing the net amount of the casualty gain or loss to Income Summary. Casualty **gains** result when insurance indemnities at replacement cost exceed book values at the time of the loss. In accounting for a casualty, certain procedures should be followed:

1. Determine the extent that accounting records have been damaged or destroyed. Supplement damaged records or reconstruct them, to the extent possible, if they have been destroyed.
2. Adjust the accounts for assets lost in the casualty to the date of the casualty. For example, make all necessary adjusting entries for depreciation, amortization, accrued and prepaid expense, and revenue items affected from the date of the last year-end to the date of the casualty.
3. Determine the **book value** (after the adjustments in [2] above) of all assets destroyed by the casualty, as of the date of the casualty.
4. Open a **Casualty loss account** in the general ledger. Typical entries to this account are:
   a. Debits for all assets lost (at book value), expenditures due to the casualty, and any expirations of prepaid insurance related to the casualty.
   b. Credits for the indemnity recoverable from the insurance company and any salvage recovery.
   c. Close the balance—the casualty loss or gain—to Income Summary.

Exhibit 12–3
Data to illustrate a fire loss; Fire Alarm Company.

Case Data to Date of Fire Loss (July 1):

***a.* Account balances, January 1 of current year:**	
Prepaid insurance	$ 6,400
Inventory (at cost), perpetual system	80,000
Building (at cost)	180,000
Accumulated depreciation, building (depreciation rate, 3⅓% per year on cost)	60,000
***b.* Replacement cost at date of fire (July 1):**	
Inventory, perpetual system, total loss	$ 90,000
Building—total replacement cost, net of accumulated depreciation	300,000
Building—amount of loss at replacement cost, net of accumulated depreciation, two-thirds loss ($300,000 × ⅔)	200,000
***c.* Insurance coverage:**	
Inventory	None
Building, insured—face of policy (policy includes an 80% coinsurance clause)	$250,000
Unexpired insurance on January 1 of current year (24 months unexpired)	6,400

Policy provision—After adjusting the prepaid insurance premiums for the casualty loss, the remaining premiums cover the building to the extent that the face of the policy exceeds the indemnity paid. Note: This provision is not standard in all policies; it is used here for illustrative purposes.

Accounting for a Casualty Illustrated. Fire Alarm Company had a fire loss on July 1 of the current year that involved its merchandise inventory and building. The relevant case data are given in **Exhibit 12–3.** The entries to adjust the books to the date of the fire, to record the fire loss, and to record the settlement with the insurance company are given in **Exhibit 12–4.**

The two adjusting entries given in Exhibit 12–4 (i.e., entry 1 for depreciation and entry 2 for insurance) are exactly like those at year-end, except they were recorded as of July 1, the date of the fire. Entries 3 and 4 record the casualty losses on the building and inventory (perpetual system), respectively; they are based on the respective book values on the date of the fire.[15] Entry 5 records the insurance settlement of $200,000. Entry 6 allocates a portion of the prepaid insurance at July 1 to the casualty loss. Prior to the casualty, the Prepaid Insurance account reflected a debit balance of $4,800 (i.e., $6,400 − $1,600). Under the provisions of this particular policy (Exhibit 12–3), the insurance coverage remain-

---

[15] If a periodic inventory system is used, the following entries would be made on July 1 to record the historical cost (HC) of the inventory lost:

1. Adjusting entries:

Income summary	80,000	
Inventory (beginning)		80,000
Inventory (on date of fire)	90,000*	
Income summary		90,000

* Estimated using some technique such as the gross margin method (see Chapter 9).

2. Entry to record loss on inventory destroyed:

Casualty loss	90,000	
Inventory (on date of fire)		90,000

Exhibit 12–4
Entries for fire loss; Fire Alarm Company.

July 1—To adjust asset accounts to date of fire; no "updating" entry needed for perpetual inventory system (see footnote 15 for periodic inventory system):

1. Depreciation expense, building	3,000	
Accumulated depreciation, building		3,000
January 1 to July 1: \$180,000 × 3⅓% × 6/12 = \$3,000.		
2. Insurance expense	1,600	
Prepaid insurance		1,600
Expired January 1 to July 1: \$6,400 × 6/24 = \$1,600.		

July 1—To remove book value of assets destroyed:

3. Casualty loss (building, ⅔ destroyed)	78,000	
Accumulated depreciation, building [(\$60,000 + \$3,000) × ⅔]	42,000	
Building (\$180,000 × ⅔)		120,000
4. Casualty loss (inventory)	90,000	
Inventory (perpetual; remove for total loss)		90,000

During July—To record indemnity received from the insurance company:

5. Cash	200,000	
Casualty loss		200,000

Computation by the insurance company:

Face of policy	\$250,000
Replacement cost of portion of building lost	200,000
Formula: [\$250,000 ÷ (80% × \$300,000)] × \$200,000	208,333

Use lowest amount, \$200,000. Note that in this example, the coinsurance clause did not come into play because the building was insured for more than 80% of its replacement cost.

6. To adjust the balance in the Prepaid Insurance account:

Casualty loss (insurance)	3,840	
Prepaid insurance		3,840

Analysis of prepaid insurance:

Unexpired January 1	\$6,400
Amortized to July 1	1,600
Unexpired July 1 (date of fire)	\$4,800

Amount of unexpired insurance on July 1 absorbed by indemnity:
Indemnity ÷ Face of policy (\$200,000 ÷ \$250,000) × \$4,800 . . \$3,840

December 31—To close the Casualty Loss account:

7. Casualty loss	28,160	
Income summary (a gain)		28,160

Analysis of the Prepaid Insurance and Casualty Loss accounts (entry numbers keyed to entries above):

Prepaid Insurance

Balance, January 1	6,400	2. Expired, January–July	1,600
		6. Allocated to casualty loss	3,840

Balance unexpired, \$960

Casualty Loss

3. Building	78,000	5. Indemnity	200,000
4. Inventory	90,000		
6. Absorbed insurance	3,840		
7. Gain closed to Income summary	28,160		
	200,000		200,000

ing after the indemnity is $50,000 (i.e., $250,000 face − $200,000 indemnity). Therefore, the premium "absorbed" by the fire loss is computed as: $4,800 × ($200,000 ÷ $250,000) = $3,840. Entry 6 transfers this amount from the Prepaid Insurance account to the Casualty gain (loss) account. The $960 remaining in the Prepaid Insurance account relates to the $50,000 coverage remaining. If the full amount of the policy were to continue in force (if specified in the policy), this write-down of repaid insurance would not be made. Only amortization to the date of the casualty would be recorded.

For the insured assets, the Casualty loss account reflects a credit balance (i.e., a gain) of $28,160 (before closing). The indemnity was based on replacement cost, which was more than the book value of the assets on the date they were destroyed. Because the replacement cost of many assets exceeds their book value, it is not unusual to end up with a casualty "gain." The Casualty loss account is closed to Income summary as shown in Entry 7.

SUPPLEMENT 12–B: ACCOUNTING FOR LIFE INSURANCE

Life insurance companies sell insurance policies that call for a stipulated indemnity payment to the beneficiary of the policy upon the death of the insured. In an **ordinary life** policy, the premiums are paid until the death of the insured. At that time, the stipulated benefit is paid to the beneficiary. During the period the policy is in force, it has both a cash surrender value and a loan value. In a **limited payment** policy, the premiums are paid for a stipulated period or until the death of the insured (if prior to the end of the stipulated period). The benefit is paid at death. As with the ordinary life policy, a limited payment policy also has a cash surrender value and a loan value. In **term insurance,** the premium payments are made for a stipulated period of time or until death (if prior to the end of the stipulated period); the benefit is paid only if death occurs within the stated period. Term insurance has no cash surrender or loan value. The policy must be renewed at the end of the stipulated period; otherwise it lapses. At renewal, a new premium scale is effective based on the increased age of the insured. Because there are no complexities in accounting for term insurance, this discussion will be limited to ordinary life policies.[16]

Companies have an insurable interest in certain of their **executives.** Thus, it is common for companies to insure the lives of key executives; the proceeds from the policy are payable to the company upon death of the insured executive. This payment compensates for expenditures incurred in replacing the deceased executive. In accounting for a life insurance policy of this type, premiums paid (cash paid less any dividends earned on the policy) and the related cash surrender value of the policy must be recorded and reported.[17]

The **cash surrender value** of a policy is the amount that would be refunded should the policy be terminated at the request of the insured. The **loan value**

---

[16] Accounting for a limited payment policy would be similar to accounting for an ordinary life insurance policy.

[17] Ordinary life insurance policies issued by **mutual** insurance companies usually pay dividends to policyholders. The policyholders are the "owners" of mutual insurance companies.

of a policy is the amount the insurance company will loan on a policy maintained in force. The cash surrender value is computed as of the end of the year; the loan value is computed as of the **beginning** of the year (thus, the loan value is less by interest for one year). Each policy contains a schedule that indicates the cash surrender value and the loan value for each policy year. Because a portion of the premiums that have been paid may be returned in the form of the cash surrender value when a policy is canceled, only a portion of the periodic premiums paid actually constitute expense. Thus, periodic expense is the excess of the periodic premium paid over the periodic increase in the cash surrender value.

Once a policy begins to accumulate a cash surrender value, the part of each premium payment that increases the cash surrender value represents the acquisition of an asset. Cash surrender value is reported on the statement of financial position under **Investments and Funds.**

To illustrate one sequence of entries, assume the following data were taken from an ordinary insurance policy with a face amount of $25,000:

Year	Premium (beginning of year)	Cash surrender value (end of year)
1	$720	$ -0-
2	720	-0-
3	720	210
4	720	290
5		(Etc., as specified in the policy)

Based on the above data, the indicated entries would be as follows:

Year 1:

On premium payment date:

Life insurance expense	720	
Cash		720

At year-end:

Cash surrender value of life insurance	70*	
Life insurance expense		70

* $210 ÷ 3 years = $70. Recognition of this addition to cash surrender value anticipates that the policy will be kept in force at least through the third policy year when the cash surrender value actually arises. An alternative (and more conservative) treatment would recognize the entire $210 in the third year and reduce insurance expense for that year by the same amount. Often this allocation is not made because, of the policies dropped, a large portion are dropped during the three-year period. Years 2 and 3: same as year 1.

Year 4:

On premium payment date:

Life insurance expense	720	
Cash		720

At year-end:

Cash surrender value of life insurance ($290 − $210)	80	
Life insurance expense (current)		80

The following entry would be made when the face of the policy is paid at the death of the executive whose life was insured by the company. It is assumed that (1) the cash surrender value of the policy at date of death was $3,500 and (2) that three months' premium is to be refunded in accordance with the policy provision that premiums paid beyond date of death are refunded.

Cash [$25,000 + (3/12 × $720)]	25,180*	
Life insurance expense (3/12 × $720)		180
Cash surrender value of life insurance		3,500
Gain on settlement of life insurance indemnity		21,500

* Some policies specify that this amount includes the cash surrender value (i.e., $28,680).

The gain usually would be classified as an extraordinary item on the current statement of income.

QUESTIONS

1. What distinguishes intangible assets from tangible assets? How are intangible assets reported on the statement of financial position?
2. What outlays are properly considered part of the cost of an intangible asset?
3. Cite the factors that should determine whether or not an intangible asset is amortized and, if so, over what period of time.
4. What is an identifiable intangible asset? Give some examples of such assets.
5. What is a franchise and a trademark?
6. Explain goodwill and the basis on which goodwill is amortized.
7. What is the role of the accountant in valuation of goodwill?
8. What is the maximum number of years over which a patent should be amortized? What determines this maximum? Under what circumstances, if any, should a shorter amortization period be used?
9. Define a deferred charge. Is it an intangible? Explain. How are deferred charges distinguished from prepaid expenses? Give two examples of each.
10. What items are properly debited to organization costs? Should organization costs be amortized? Explain.
11. What are the basic guidelines for accounting for research and development (R&D) costs?
12. Distinguish between trademarks and copyrights.
13. Give examples of situations in which the accounting carrying value of an intangible asset can increase. Does the accounting value of an intangible necessarily bear a close relationship to its economic value?
14. What are the primary characteristics of goodwill?
15. Under what circumstances is goodwill capitalized?
16. What is the general formula for computing goodwill? Assign values that would produce goodwill of $2 million.
17. Explain impairment of value of an intangible asset. Assume a patent that originally cost $50,000 (accumulated patent amortization, $35,000) that probably will not be

used further by the company. Its estimated current value is $1,000. Give any indicated entry; if none, explain why.

18. XT Company owns a trademark that it purchased originally for $40,000; it has been amortized to date in the amount of $26,000. The trademark has just been sold for $10,000 cash. Give any indicated entry; if none is needed, explain why.

EXERCISES (12–1 to 12–16)

E 12–1 (Overview; Characteristics of Intangible Assets)

For each of the following independent events, indicate by placing a check mark (√) in the appropriate cells: *(a)* whether the asset involved is identifiable or unidentifiable, *(b)* its manner of acquisition, and *(c)* whether it should be capitalized.

Independent event	Identifiability		Manner of acquisition		Whether capitalized	
	Identifiable	Unidentifiable	External	Internal	Yes	No
a. Purchased a patent.						
b. Purchased a trademark.						
c. After 10 years of operation, New Company's goodwill had increased considerably.						
d. Trademark developed by the company.						
e. Patent developed by the company's research program.						
f. Copyright developed by the company over a five-year period.						
g. Prepaid insurance (five-year premium).						
h. Leasehold improvements (operating lease).						
i. Purchased a company (including $1 million goodwill).						
j. Purchased a copyright.						
k. Franchise received by a public utility company.						

E 12–2 (Sale and Purchase of a Patent; No Cash)

On January 1, 19A, VO Company sold a patent to Baker Company; the patent had a net carrying value on VO's books of $20,000. As payment, Baker gave VO an $80,000 note, which was payable in five equal annual installments of $16,000, with the first payment payable on December 31, 19A. There was no established exchange price for the patent, and the note had no ready market value. The prevailing rate of interest for a note of this type at January 1, 19A, was 12%.

Required:

1. Give the entry on January 1, 19A, that VO Company should make (disregard income tax). Also, give any related entries that VO should make on December 31, 19A.
2. Give the entry that Baker Company should make on January 1, 19A.
3. Give the entries for payment of the first annual installment on the note and for patent amortization that Baker Company should make December 31, 19A (end of the annual reporting period). At January 1, 19A, 5 years of the patent's legal life of 17 years had already expired.

E 12–3 (Reporting Intangible Assets)

The adjusted trial balance of Jackson Corporation showed the following selected account balances (all debits) at December 31, 19X, end of the annual reporting period:

Cash	$ 44,000
Patent (unamortized balance)	14,000
Accounts receivable (net of allowance)	90,000
Bond sinking fund	150,000
Prepaid rent expense	1,000
Treasury stock (at cost)	60,000
Marketable equity securities, short term	50,000
Leasehold (rental prepayment)	7,000
Franchise (unamortized balance)	18,000
Investment in debt securities, long term	40,000
Rent revenue receivable (current)	3,000
Discount on bonds payable (unamortized)	4,000
Organization costs (unamortized)	9,000
Goodwill (unamortized)	70,000
Trademark (unamortized)	19,000
Prepaid insurance (two-thirds is long term)	6,000
Copyright (unamortized)	12,000
Equipment (net of accumulated depreciation)	300,000
Notes receivable, trade (short term)	10,000
Cash in closed bank (percent expected to recover, 40%)	30,000
R&D costs (not capitalizable)	39,000

Required:

Prepare the asset section of Jackson's statement of financial position at December 31, 19X. Include the proper statement of financial position classifications with separate captions for intangible operating assets, deferred charges, and other assets.

E 12–4 (Amortizing a Trademark and a Patent)

The 19A data below for Tabor Company relates to two separate intangible assets:

	Asset X (trademark)	Asset Y (patent)
Cost	$12,000	$14,000
Estimated economic life	Indefinite	14 years

Required:

1. Give the 19A entry that Tabor should make for amortization, if any, for each asset.
2. Assume Tabor Company has used asset X for eight full years prior to 19A and it is determined at the start of 19B that its remaining life will be four years. Give the appropriate adjusting entry for asset X at the end of 19B.
3. Assume asset Y, acquired on January 1, 19A, was the subject of a patent infringement suit brought by Tabor Company against another party. During 19B, the suit was settled in favor of Tabor. Tabor spent $2,000 in legal fees and court costs. Give the appropriate entries that Tabor should make during 19B.

E 12–5 (Overview; Accounting for Intangible Assets)
Select the best answer to each of the following. Briefly justify your choice.

1. Which of the following cost items would be matched with current revenues on a basis other than association of cause and effect?
   a. Goodwill.
   b. Sales commissions.
   c. Cost of goods sold.
   d. Purchases on account.
2. How should R&D costs be accounted for according to *FASB Standard 2?*
   a. Must be capitalized when incurred and then amortized over their estimated useful lives.
   b. Must be expensed in the period incurred in all but a few instances.
   c. May be either capitalized or expensed when incurred, depending upon the judgment of management.
   d. Must be expensed in the period incurred unless it can be demonstrated that the expenditure will have some future benefits.
3. The accounting for a development stage company:
   a. May be different from that of other companies in numerous ways with regard to expenditures during the development stage.
   b. Must be exactly the same as other companies in respect to accounting, reporting, and disclosure.
   c. Allows certain development stage companies to capitalize costs that other companies are not permitted to capitalize.
   d. Requires presentation of financial statements on the same basis as other companies and disclosure of certain cumulative amounts, along with the fact that the company is a development stage company.
4. H Company's R&D records contained the following information for 19C:

Materials used in R&D projects	$ 400,000
Equipment acquired that will have significant alternate future uses including future R&D projects	2,000,000
Depreciation expense for 19C on above equipment	500,000
Personnel costs involved in R&D projects	1,000,000
Consulting fees paid to outsiders for R&D projects	100,000
Indirect costs reasonably allocable to R&D projects	200,000
	$4,200,000

   The amount of R&D costs debited to expense and reported on H's 19C statement of income should be:
   a. $1,500,000.
   b. $1,700,000.
   c. $2,200,000.
   d. $3,500,000.
5. P Company has invested $40,000 in a royalty producing copyright. P's expected rate of return from the three-year project is 20%. The cash flow, net of income taxes, was $15,000 for the first year and $18,000 for the second year. Assuming the rate of return is exactly 20%, what would be the cash flow, net of income taxes, for the third year?
   a. $8,681.
   b. $11,000.
   c. $11,497.
   d. $25,920.

(AICPA adapted)

E 12–6 (Overview; Accounting for Intangible Assets)
Select the best answer to each of the following. Briefly justify your choice.

1. A copyright granted to a composer in 1988 has a legal life of:
   a. 17 years.
   b. 28 years.

c. The life of the composer plus 50 years.
d. 40 years.

2. Which of the following is not properly classified as an intangible asset:
   a. A copyright acquired by purchase.
   b. Goodwill.
   c. A patent acquired by purchase.
   d. Losses incurred by a development stage company.
3. P Corporation acquired Company A in 1969 and Company B in 1989. In both instances the acquired companies were dissolved and their assets and operations merged with other assets and activities of P. In both instances P paid more than the current market value of the identifiable net assets for its acquisitions and most of the difference was attributable to goodwill. In accounting for the goodwill:
   a. P must amortize the goodwill related to each company.
   b. P need not amortize the goodwill of either company.
   c. P need not amortize the goodwill associated with A but must amortize the goodwill associated with B.
   d. P need not amortize the goodwill associated with B but must amortize the goodwill associated with A.
4. Patents and copyrights have definite legal lives and should be amortized over:
   a. Their legal lives, but not more than 40 years.
   b. Their useful lives, but not more than 40 years.
   c. Their legal or useful life, whichever is shorter, but never in excess of 40 years.
   d. A period of 40 years.
5. X company incurred $50,000 of costs in R&D activities. These costs need not be expensed if:
   a. They give promise of a successful outcome.
   b. The projects are completed and have culminated in a profitable patent for X.
   c. X is doing contract research for another company, and the costs relate to the contract that is still in progress.
   d. The projects were begun before the issuance of *FASB Standard 2*.
6. Organizational costs:
   a. Are not covered by *APB Opinion 17* and need not be amortized.
   b. Must be amortized over a period not to exceed 40 years.
   c. Should be reported as a contra item under Owners' Equity.
   d. Should be expensed as soon as they are incurred.
7. Some intangibles are characterized as specifically identifiable, while another classification is "unidentifiable." An example of the latter is:
   a. A trademark.
   b. A perpetual franchise.
   c. A franchise for a limited term.
   d. Goodwill.
8. The legal life of a patent currently is:
   a. 28 years.
   b. 17 years.
   c. The life of the holder of the patent.
   d. 40 years.

E 12–7 (Amortization of Intangibles)

Select the best answer to each of the following. Briefly justify your choices.

1. If a company constructs a laboratory building to be used as an R&D facility, the cost of the building is matched against earnings as:
   a. R&D expense during the period(s) of construction.
   b. Depreciation deducted as part of R&D costs.
   c. Depreciation or immediate write-off, depending on company policy.
   d. An expense at such time as productive research and development has been obtained from the facility.

2. Why are certain costs of doing business capitalized when incurred and then depreciated or amortized over subsequent accounting cycles?
   a. To reduce the federal income tax liability.
   b. To aid management in the decision-making process.
   c. To match operating costs with revenues as earned.
   d. To adhere to the accounting concept of conservatism.
3. In January 19B, Idea Company purchased a patent for a new consumer product for $170,000. At the time of purchase the patent was valid for 17 years. Due to the competitive nature of the product, the patent was estimated to have a useful life of 10 years. During 19F, the product was removed from the market in response to a government order because of a potential health hazard present in the product. What amount should Idea debit to expense during 19F, assuming amortization is recorded at the end of each reporting year?
   a. $10,000. *c.* $102,000.
   b. $17,000. *d.* $130,000.
4. In conformity with GAAP, which of the following methods of amortization is almost always used for intangible assets?
   a. Sum-of-the-years'-digits (SYD). *c.* Units of production.
   b. Straight line. *d.* Declining balance (DB).
5. On January 1 of the current year, M Corporation sold a patent. M Corporation originally paid $50,000 for the patent, which now has a book value of $9,000. The terms of sale included cash payments as follows:
   $5,000 down payment.
   $5,000 per year, payable on December 31 of each of the next two years.

   The sale agreement did not specify any interest; however, 10% would be a reasonable rate for this type of transaction. M Corporation should report a gain on disposal of:
   a. $4,678. *c.* $6,000.
   b. $5,000. *d.* $5,678.

(AICPA adapted)

E 12–8 **(Goodwill; Negotiating Price; Valuation)**

Dow Corporation is negotiating with Fox Company to purchase all of Fox's assets and liabilities. You have been asked to help develop a tentative offering price in the negotiations and to evaluate "goodwill on the basis of the lastest concepts." Accordingly, you decide to use the present value approach. The following data have been assembled on Fox Company:

	Estimated current market value	Fox book value
Total identifiable assets (exclusive of goodwill)	$2,500,000	$2,400,000
Liabilities	1,000,000	1,000,000
Average annual net cash earnings expected (next five years)	520,000	

Dow expects a 16% earnings rate on this investment.

Required:

1. Compute the *(a)* tentative offering price and *(b)* amount of goodwill included in that price.
2. Assume the deal is consummated on January 1, 19A, at a $1.6 million actual cash price.
   a. Give the acquisition entry for Dow Corporation.

b. Give the December 31, 19A, adjusting entry for goodwill. Assume a 20-year estimated useful life.

E 12–9 (Goodwill; Negotiating Price; Valuation)

Big Company is considering the purchase of Small Company for cash. The following data concerning Small Company has been collected:

	Small Company book values	Estimated current market values
Total identifiable assets	$380,000	$400,000
Total liabilities	280,000	280,000
Owners' equity	$100,000	—

Cumulative total net cash earnings for the past five years, $255,000, which includes extraordinary cash gains of $45,000 and nonrecurring cash losses of $30,000.

Big Company expects a 20% earnings rate on the investment.

Required:

1. Compute *(a)* an offering price based on the information given above that Big should be willing to pay, and *(b)* the amount of goodwill included in that price.
2. Compute the amount of goodwill, assuming the negotiations resulted in an actual purchase price of $140,000 cash.
3. Give the acquisition entry for Big Company, assuming the actual purchase price given in requirement 2.

E 12–10 (Compute Goodwill; Entries)

On January 1, 19X, the statement of financial position of Nance Company (a sole proprietorship) was as follows:

Assets:		
Accounts receivable (net of allowance)		$ 60,000
Inventory		90,000
Plant and equipment (net of depreciation)		200,000
Land		30,000
Total		$380,000
Liabilities:		
Current	$38,000	
Noncurrent	80,000	$118,000
Owners' equity		262,000
Total		$380,000

On January 1, 19X, Major Corporation purchased all of the assets, and assumed all of the liabilities, listed on the above balance sheet for $290,000 cash. The assets, on date of purchase, were valued by Major as follows: Accounts receivable (net), $50,000; Inventory, $85,000; Plant and equipment (net), $200,000; and Land, $45,000. The liabilities were valued at their carrying amounts.

Required:

1. Compute the amount of goodwill included in the purchase price paid by Major Corporation.

2. Give the entry that Major Corporation should make to record the purchase of Nance Company.
3. What is the minimum amount of goodwill that Major Corporation can amortize at the end of 19X? Give the amortization entry.

E 12–11 (Compute Goodwill; Entries)

After considerable analysis, the following projections relating to BT Company were derived as a basis for estimating the potential value of goodwill in anticipation of negotiations for the purchase of BT Company by HB Company:

Average annual net cash earnings projected	$ 84,000
Market value of total identifiable assets of BT	340,000
Total liabilities	100,000

Rate of return expected on investments by prospective purchaser, 18%. Expected recovery period for the investment, five years, starting in year 1.

Required:

1. Compute the (*a*) tentative offering price by HB Company and (*b*) amount of goodwill included in that price.
2. Give the year 1 entries for HB Company, assuming negotiations resulted in an actual cash purchase price of $235,000. Any goodwill will be amortized over 20 years.

E 12–12 (Goodwill; PV; Entries)

Hotstrike Mining Company, which is available for purchase, can be expected to produce minerals for the next three years; its minerals will likely be exhausted at that time and the land will have a zero residual value due to restoration cost obligations. Best estimates place its net cash receipts at $40,000 for the first year; thereafter, annual net cash receipts will decrease each year by $10,000.

Your client is interested in this investment if an 18% rate of return is reasonably possible. An 18% rate of return is considered to be a realistic rate of return on investments of this kind.

Required (refer to chapter 5):

1. Your client has asked you to compute a cash price for negotiating purposes given the above conditions and to briefly outline any critical issues that should be considered.
2. Give the acquisition entry, assuming the negotiations resulted in an actual cash price of $70,000. Comment on your client's position.

E 12–13 (Recording a Franchise Contract)

On January 1, 19A, Shopping Center Cleaners (SCC) signed a contract with Super-Cleaners, Incorporated. The agreement provided for the payment of a franchise fee by SCC, and subsequent periodic franchise royalties based on sales. In return for these royalties, Super-Cleaners will provide specified services in the future (e.g., promotional suggestions). The franchise fee was $50,000, payable $10,000 cash and the remaining balance is payable in three equal annual installments including interest and principal, starting on December 31, 19A. The market rate of interest for such loans is 10%. The franchise fee is nonrefundable.

Required:

Give the entries that SCC should make on January 1, 19A and December 31, 19A.

E 12–14 (Based on Supplement 12-A; Fire Loss; Coinsurance)

Grife Company operates retail branches in various cities. Branches in four cities are served out of warehouse No. 16, which sustained fire damage to part of the inventory on April 10.

Between January 1 and April 10, shipments from warehouse No. 16 to its four stores were recorded as follows: Branch W, $80,500; X, $92,000; Y, $69,000; and Z, $23,000.

Shipments to branches are marked up 15% above cost, and sales prices are reflected in the foregoing amounts. The January 1 inventory at warehouse No. 16 was $48,100; purchases between January 1 and April 10 totaled $224,600; freight-in was $2,300; and purchase returns totaled $9,200.

To arrive at the total replacement cost of the April 10 inventory for insurance settlement purposes, it was agreed to deduct 10% for goods shopworn and damaged prior to the fire.

A compromise agreement between the insurance adjuster and Grife Company management set the current replacement cost of inventory lost in the fire at $21,480.

Required:

1. Estimate the total replacement cost of total inventory in the warehouse at April 10.
2. Determine the indemnity claim if the warehouse contents were insured by a single $20,000 policy having a 65% coinsurance clause. Calculate to the nearest dollar.

E 12–15 (Based on Supplement 12-A; Fire Loss; Coinsurance)

On January 1, Carson's Store had a fire insurance policy on the merchandise with a face amount of $15,000 and an 80% coinsurance clause. At that date, the company had $360 recorded in its records for unexpired insurance for one year. On January 1, the inventory was $20,000; Carson uses a perpetual inventory system. January purchases were $44,000, and January sales were $60,000. A fire on February 1 destroyed the entire stock on hand. At that time the historical cost of the inventory represented replacement cost as well.

Required:

Give journal entries to record the estimated inventory and the fire loss, assuming a 30% gross margin rate on sales.

E 12–16 (Based on Supplement 12-B; Life Insurance)

On January 1, Garfield Company purchased a $100,000 ordinary life insurance policy on its president. The following data relate to the first five years:

Year	Annual advance premium	Cash surrender value (year-end) Increase	Cash surrender value (year-end) Cumulative
1	$2,000	$ -0-	$ -0-
2	2,000	-0-	-0-
3	2,000	2,100	2,100
4	2,000	1,080	3,180
5	2,000	1,125	4,305
6	Etc.	Etc.	Etc.

Required:

1. Give all entries indicated up to (but not including) the death of the president on July 2 of the fifth year.

2. Give the entry to record insurance settlement upon death of the president. The unexpired premium at the date of death was also refunded. Assume the policy year and accounting year coincide.

PROBLEMS (12–1 to 12–10)

P 12–1 (Organization, Franchise, Trademark Costs; Goodwill)
Transactions during 19A, the first year of the newly organized Astor Corporation, included the following:

Jan.	2	Paid $6,000 attorney's fees and other related costs for assistance in securing the corporate charter, drafting bylaws, and advising on operating in other states (which the company intends). Amortize over five years.
	31	Paid $2,000 for television commercials advertising the grand opening. In addition, during the grand opening the company gave away samples of its products, which were taken from inventory; cost, $8,000 (perpetual inventory system).
Feb.	1	Paid an invoice received from the financial institution that underwrote and sold the company's $400,000 par value stock at a 10% premium. Under the contract, the underwriter charged 1% of the gross proceeds from the stock sale. The stock issuance has already been recorded.
Mar.	1	Paid $30,000 to a franchisor for the right to open a Tastee Food lunch counter on the company's premises. The initial franchise runs 10 years from March 1 and can be renewed upon payment of a second amount to be computed later on the basis of sales under the initial franchise.
May	1	Acquired for $10,200 a newly issued patent, which will be held as a long-term investment to produce royalty revenue.
July	1	Paid consultants $6,400 for services in securing a trademark enabling the company to market under the now-protected name Astor's Recipe.
Oct.	1	Obtained a license from the city to conduct operations in a newly opened department. The license, which cost $600, runs for one year and is renewable.
Nov.	1	Acquired another business and paid (among other amounts) $12,000 for its goodwill. Expected useful life, five years.
Dec.	31	Apportioned the costs of those assets subject to amortization over their indicated lives. Where no life is indicated, amortized over the longest term possible. Amortization is calculated to the nearest monthly basis; in other words, acquisition of an intangible in July would call for amortization for half of the year.

Required:

1. Give the journal entry that Astor should make for each of the above transactions. December 31 is the end of the annual accounting period; six adjusting entries are required on this date. Ignore closing entries.
2. Classify each of the intangible assets (and their amounts) for statement of financial position reporting at the end of 19A. Set deferred charges and any other appropriate items out separately from the other intangibles.

P 12–2 (Overview; Intangibles; Capitalize or Not)
For each transaction given below, enter check marks (√) in the appropriate columns to indicate how each expenditure should be recorded (as a debit). If the amount should be apportioned, check all appropriate columns. Assume that each expenditure is independent unless stated otherwise, and that it was made near the end of the annual reporting period of the entity making payment. Briefly explain the basis for each response.

No.	Transaction	(a) Debit to retained earnings	(b) Debit to current expenses	(c) Capitalize as an intangible	(d) None of the foregoing
1.	Acting on recommendations of High Technology, Inc., Y spent $60,000 rearranging its machinery. Benefits are expected to last six years.				
2.	Y paid High Technology $90,000 for R&D work the latter has done under contract for Y. The results are expected to increase Y's profits over the next seven years.				
3.	D Corporation incurred legal costs of $500,000 successfully defending one of its patents in an infringement suit. The patent runs six more years.				
4.	Assume D's suit in (3) above had turned out adversely and that D was forced to write off its patent carried at $80,000. How should the write off be treated?				
5.	Jay Company paid Zippy Corporation $50,000 for the exclusive right to repair auto transmissions in the city of Erehwon, using the Zippy name and logo in signs, ads, and the like. The franchise runs for as long as Jay is in business, but it cannot be transferred.				
6.	P Company spent $400,000 researching and developing new manufacturing equipment on which it will apply for a patent.				
7.	P incurred $10,000 legal and registration costs related to securing a patent on the equipment described in (6) above.				
8.	In 19G, Uno Company paid an author $40,000 for the copyright to the author's novel and for rights to produce a movie based on it. The copyright was issued in 19F, and the author is elderly.				
9.	As a result of an out-of-court settlement, X Company paid $14 million to another company because it had infringed on the plaintiff's patent. Most of the agreed payment relates to X's sales in prior years, the remainder to current sales.				
10.	X incurred legal costs of $750,000 in connection with the litigation described in (9) above.				

P 12–3 (Overview; Seven Different Intangibles)

Select the best answer for each of the following and indicate the basis for your choice.

1. An intangible asset (excluding R&D costs) should be—
   a. Expensed as incurred.
   b. Capitalized and not amortized until it clearly has no value.
   c. Capitalized and amortized over the estimated period benefited.
   d. Capitalized and amortized over the estimated period benefited but not exceeding 40 years.
2. Most R&D costs incurred after *FASB Standard* 2 should be—
   a. Capitalized on a selective basis and not amortized.
   b. Capitalized, then amortized over 40 years.
   c. Expensed in the year in which they are incurred.
   d. Debited directly to retained earnings.

3. Goodwill is amortized over—
   a. Its useful life if it was acquired externally.
   b. A 40-year period if it was acquired externally.
   c. Its useful life, but not to exceed 40 years, if it was acquired externally.
   d. Its useful life, but not to exceed 40 years, if it was developed internally.
4. On January 15, 19A, a corporation was granted a patent. On January 2, 19J, to protect its patent, the corporation purchased another patent that originally was issued on January 10, 19F. Because of its unique plant, the corporation does not believe the competing patent can be used in producing a product. The cost of the competing patent should be—
   a. Amortized over a maximum period of 17 years.
   b. Amortized over a maximum period of 13 years.
   c. Amortized over a maximum period of 8 years.
   d. Expensed in 19J.
5. Goodwill should be written off—
   a. As soon as possible against retained earnings.
   b. As soon as possible as an extraordinary item.
   c. By systematic debits against retained earnings over the period benefited, but not more than 40 years.
   d. By systematic debits to expense over the period benefited, but not more than 40 years.
6. A large, publicly held company registered a trademark during 19A. How should the cost of registering the trademark be accounted for?
   a. Debited to an asset account with no amortization to follow.
   b. Expensed as incurred.
   c. Amortized over 25 years if in accordance with management's evaluation.
   d. Amortized over its useful life or 17 years, whichever is shorter.
7. Unidentifiable assets include—
   a. Patents, copyrights, franchises, etc.
   b. Deferred charges only.
   c. Deferred charges and goodwill.
   d. Goodwill only.
8. Which of the following is not properly reported as a deferred charge?
   a. Stock issue costs.
   b. Discount on bonds payable.
   c. Organization costs.
   d. Deferred income taxes.
9. Prepaid expenses and deferred charges are alike in that they are both—
   a. Reported as current assets on a classified statement of financial position.
   b. Destined to be debited to expense in some subsequent period in harmony with the matching principle.
   c. Reported as other assets.
   d. Applicable to the fiscal period immediately following the statement of financial position on which they appear.
10. Inger Company bought a patent in January 19A for $6,800. For the first four years, it was amortized on the assumption that the total useful life would be eight years. At the start of the fifth year, it was determiend that six years would be the probable total life. Amortization at the end of the fifth year should be—
    a. $1,133.
    b. $1,700.
    c. $850.
    d. None of the foregoing.
11. XY Company has a lease on a site that does not expire for 25 years. With the landowner's permission, XY erected on the site a building that will last 50 years. XY should recognize expense in connection with the building's cost—
    a. One fortieth each year.
    b. One twenty-fifth each year.
    c. In totality as soon as it is completed.
    d. One fiftieth each year.

(AICPA adapted)

P 12–4 (Reporting; Patent, Franchise, R&D)

AB Company provided information on its intangible assets as follows:

a. A patent was purchased from XT Company for $1,500,000 on January 1, 19x1. AB estimated the remaining useful life of the patent to be 10 years.

b. On January 1, 19x2, a franchise was purchased from the YW Company for $500,000. In addition, 5% of revenue from the franchise must be paid to YW. Revenue from the franchise for 19x2 was $1,200,000. AB Company estimates the useful life of the franchise to be 10 years and records a full year's amortization (straight line) in the year of purchase.

c. AB incurred R&D costs in 19x2 as follows:

Materials and equipment	$120,000
Personnel	140,000
Indirect costs	60,000
	$320,000

AB estimates that these costs will be recouped by December 31, 19x5.

d. On January 1, 19x2, AB, based on new events that have occurred in the field, estimates that the remaining life of the patent purchased on January 1, 19x1, is only five years from January 1, 19x2.

Required:

1. Prepare a schedule showing the intangible assets that should be reported on AB Company's statement of financial position at December 31, 19x2.
2. Prepare a statement of income for the year ended December 31, 19x2, as a result of the above facts. Assume a 35% average income tax rate. (AICPA adapted)

P 12–5 (Comprehensive; Four Intangibles; Entries)

Brannen Corporation was incorporated on January 3, 19A. The corporation's financial statements for its first year's operations were not examined by a CPA. You have been engaged to examine the financial statements for the year ended December 31, 19B, and your examination is substantially completed. The corporation's adjusted trial balance appears on p. 559.

BRANNEN CORPORATION
Adjusted Trial Balance
December 31, 19B

	Debit	Credit
Cash	$ 11,000	
Accounts receivable	68,500	
Allowance for doubtful accounts		$ 500
Inventories	38,500	
Machinery	75,000	
Equipment	29,000	
Accumulated depreciation		10,000
Patents	102,000	
Prepaid expenses	10,500	
Organization costs	29,000	
Goodwill	24,000	
Licensing agreement no. 1	50,000	
Licensing agreement no. 2	49,000	
Accounts payable		147,500
Unearned revenue		12,500
Capital stock		317,000
Retained earnings, 1/1/19B	27,000	
Sales revenue		668,500
Cost of goods sold	454,000	
Selling and general expenses	173,000	
Interest expense	3,500	
Extraordinary loss	12,000	
Totals	$1,156,000	$1,156,000

The following information relates to accounts that may still require adjustment:

1. Patents for Brannen's manufacturing process were acquired January 2, 19B for $68,000. An additional $34,000 was spent in December 19B to improve machinery covered by the patents and was debited to the Patents account. Depreciation on operational assets has been properly recorded for 19B in accordance with Brannen's practice, which provides a full year's depreciation for property on hand June 30 and no depreciation otherwise. Brannen uses the straight-line method for all depreciation and amortization.
2. The balance in the Organization Costs account properly includes costs incurred during the organization period. Brannen has exercised its option to amortize organization costs over a five-year period beginning January 1, 19A, for federal income tax purposes and will amortize these costs for accounting purposes in the same manner. No amortization has yet been recorded.
3. On January 3, 19A, Brannen purchased licensing agreement No. 1, which was believed to have an unlimited useful life. The balance in the Licensing Agreement No. 1 account includes its purchase price of $48,000 and costs of $2,000 related to the acquisition. On January 1, 19B, Brannen bought licensing agreement No. 2, which has a life expectancy of 10 years. The balance in the Licensing Agreement No. 2 account includes the $48,000 purchase price and $2,000 in acquisition costs, but it has been reduced by a credit of $1,000 for the advance collection of 19C revenue from the agreement. No amortization on the No. 2 agreement has been recorded.

   In early 19B, an explosion caused a permanent 60% reduction in the expected revenue-producing value of licensing agreement No. 1. No entries have been made during 19A for amortization nor for the explosion in 19B.
4. The balance in the Goodwill account includes *(a)* $8,000 paid December 30, 19A, for an advertising program that management belives will assist in increasing Brannen's sales over a period of three to five years following the disbursement and *(b)* legal

expenses of $16,000 incurred for Brannen's incorporation on January 3, 19A. No amortization has ever been recorded on the goodwill.

Required:
Prepare journal entries as of December 31, 19B, as required by the information given above, in conformity with the provisions of *APB Opinion 17*. If the estimated life is not given, use the maximum. (AICPA adapted)

P 12–6 (Goodwill; Negotiation; Entries)
During 19A, Baker Corporation has been negotiating to purchase all of Charlie Company's noncash assets and to assume all of its liabilities for a single cash price. The target closing date is January 1, 19B. Baker requested, and was provided, considerable data, including the following mid-year statement of financial position (summarized for problem purposes):

CHARLIE COMPANY
Statement of Financial Position
At June 30, 19A

Assets:	
Cash	$ 19,000
Accounts receivable*	60,000
Inventory (LIFO)	140,000
Property, plant, & equipment*	300,000
Land	11,000
Franchise (unamortized balance)	20,000
Total	$550,000
Liabilities:	
Current liabilities	$ 40,000
Bonds payable	200,000
Stockholders' equity	310,000
Total	$550,000

* Net of the allowance for doubtful accounts and accumulated depreciation, respectively.

Based on appraisals, price lists, and specific price level indexes, Baker Corporation developed the following estimates of "fair" market values: cash, not to be purchased; accounts receivable, $60,000 (the allowance account is adequate); inventory (converted to FIFO), $70,000; property, plant, and equipment, $280,000; land, $40,000; and franchise, $22,000. The liabilities are appropriately valued at book value.

Based on an analysis of the statements of income and other data (and excluding all nonrecurring and extraordinary gains and losses), Baker Corporation's executives projected an average year-end annual net cash inflow from operations (i.e., from the statement of income) of $72,000 for each of the next seven years.

Requirement 1:
Compute the following: *(a)* a tentative offering price and *(b)* the amount of goodwill therein, for negotiating purposes. Assume Baker expects a 20% rate of return on this investment. Round to the nearest $1,000.

Negotiations continued throughout the remainder of 19A. During December 19A, a final purchase price of $265,000 was agreed on "to be adjusted upward (for a decrease) or downward (for an increase) for any change from the June 30, 19A, cash account balance (i.e., from $19,000)."

The December 31, 19A, statement of financial position prepared by Charlie Company is shown below in column *a* and the revised market values added later by Baker Corporation are shown in column *b*.

CHARLIE COMPANY
Statement of Financial Position
At December 31, 19A

	Col. (a) Book values of Charlie Co.	Col. (b) Market values developed by Baker Corp.
Assets:		
Cash	$ 20,000	$ —
Accounts receivable (net)	58,000	58,000
Inventory (LIFO)	160,000	90,000
Property, plant, and equipment (net)	309,000	285,000
Land	11,000	40,000
Franchise (unamortized balance)	19,000	21,000
Total	$577,000	
Liabilities:		
Current liabilities	$ 37,000	37,000
Bonds payable	200,000	200,000
Stockholders' equity	340,000	—
Total	$577,000	

Requirement 2:

a. Compute the amount of goodwill purchased by Baker Corporation.

b. Give the entry for Baker Corporation to record the purchase of Charlie Company.

c. Give the entry at the end of 19B to record the minimum amount of goodwill that can be amortized.

P 12–7 (Reclassify Accounts for Five Intangibles)

Your new client, Laser Company, is being audited for the first time on December 31, 19C, end of the accounting period. In the course of your examination, you encounter in the ledger an asset account titled Intangibles (balance, $85,224), which is presented below:

Intangibles

6/30/19A	Goodwill	9,000	12/31/19B	Amortization, 5%	2,890*
12/31/19A	R&D	10,700	12/31/19C	Amortization, 5%	4,486*
4/1/19B	Goodwill	14,600			
6/30/19B	Patent	9,600			
12/31/19B	R&D	13,900			
6/1/19C	Goodwill	12,900			
7/1/19C	Bond discount	4,800			
12/31/19C	R&D	17,100			

* Offsetting debit was to Amortization expense each year.

By tracing entries to the journal and other supporting documents, you ascertain the following facts:

a. The June 30, 19A, entry was made when the first six months' operations were profitable; although a small loss had been anticipated. At the direction of the company president, and with the approval of the board of directors, an entry was made debiting Intangibles and crediting Retained Earnings for $9,000.

b. All debit entries dated December 31 pertaining to R&D arise from the fact that the company has continuously engaged in an extensive R&D program to keep its products competitive and to develop new products. The debits represent half of the costs of the R&D program for each year and were transferred at year-end from the R&D expense account.

c. The April 1, 19B, entry was made after an extensive advertising campaign had seemingly proved particularly successful. Sales rose 8% after the campaign and never dropped again to less than a 4% increase over their former level. The debit represents the expenditures for the campaign.

d. The $9,600 debit on June 30, 19B, represents the purchase price of a patent bought because the company feared if it fell into other hands, it would damage the company's products competitively. See (*g*) for amortization information.

e. The June 1, 19C, debit was made after Laser acquired another company which will continue to operate as a 100%-owned subsidiary. The price represented an excess payment of $12,900 over the market values of identifiable net assets acquired (which were properly recorded) and was based on an expectation of continued high profitability. See (*g*) for amortization information.

f. The July 1, 19C, debit for $4,800 represents discount on a 10-year, $100,000, bond issue marketed by the company on that date. The amount is not material; therefore, straight-line amortization is appropriate.

g. The two credits to the Intangibles account represent 5% of the ending balance in the Intangibles account at the end of 19B and 19C, respectively; the offsetting debit was to "Amortization Expense." The patent and goodwill costs are to be amortized over 10 years, computed to the nearest month.

Required:

1. Give journal entries to clear out the old Intangibles account. The accounts at the end of 19C have been adjusted, but not closed. Key your entries with the letters that identify the items in the problem. Explain each entry and give the resulting account balances.
2. Give the 19C adjusting entries based on your results in requirement 1. Give the final account balances immediately prior to the 19C closing entries.

P 12–8 (Overview; Three Intangible Assets)

Select the best answer to each of the following questions:

1. Bye Corporation was organized during 19A and started operations in 19B. Expenditures during 19A and early 19B were: professional fees, $25,000; meetings and promotional activities incidental to organization, $11,000; filing and related fees, $2,000; and initial capital stock issuance costs, $3,000. If organization costs are to be amortized over a 10-year period starting in 19B, the amount of organization costs amortized in 19B would be:
   a. $2,500.
   b. $3,600.
   c. $3,800.
   d. $4,100.
   e. None of the above; explain.

2. During 19A, Starnes Corporation developed a patent. Expenditures related to the patent were: legal fees for patent registration, $7,000; tests to perfect the use of the patent for production processes, $6,000; research costs in the research laboratory, $21,000; and depreciation on equipment (that has alternative future uses) used in developing the patent, $4,000. Assuming amortization of the patent costs over the legal life of the patent, the annual patent amortization amount would be:
   a. $2,000.
   b. $1,882.
   c. $1,824.
   d. $1,000.
   e. None of the above; explain.

3. On April 1, 19X, Penn Corporation purchased all of the assets and assumed all of the liabilities of Suber Company for $140,000 cash. Suber's total identifiable asset values were: Suber's book value, $200,000; estimated market value, $230,000. Suber's total liabilities were $105,000. The amount of goodwill purchased by Penn Corporation was:

a. $75,000.
b. $45,000.
c. $30,000.
d. $15,000.
e. None of the above; explain.

5. On January 1, 19A, Kiker Company purchased a new patent for $10,200 and started amortizing it over the legal life of 17 years. At the start of 19D, Kiker estimated that the total useful life of the patent (from acquisition date) was 12 years. Kiker should record amortization on the patent at the end of 19D in the amount of:
   a. $700.
   b. $933.
   c. $600.
   d. $850.
   e. None of the above; explain.
6. On January 1, 19A, THN Company purchased a patent from the inventor, who was asking $110,000 for it. THN paid for the patent as follows: cash, $40,000; issued 1,000 shares of its own common stock, par $10 (market value, $20 per share); and a note payable due at the end of three years, face amount, $50,000, noninterest bearing. The current interest rate for this type of financing is 12%. THN Company should record the cost of the patent as:
   a. $85,589.
   b. $95,589.
   c. $98,800.
   d. $110,000.
   e. None of the above; explain.

P 12–9 (Relates to Supplement 12-A; Fire Loss; Comprehensive)

South Company operates in a leased building; it adjusts and closes books each December 31. On April 30, a fire seriously damaged its inventory and fixtures. Inventory was totally destroyed; fixtures were two-thirds destroyed. Different insurance policies cover the assets, but both have a common feature under which they are canceled for future or remaining coverage to whatever extent a portion of the total potential indemnity is collected by the insured.

The company uses a periodic inventory system, and the accounting records were saved; these reveal that in the past three years gross margin has averaged 38% of sales price. The January 1 inventory was $73,280. Between January 1 and April 30, purchases and sales were, respectively, $116,320 and $206,500. Inventory was insured by a $65,000 policy with no coinsurance clause. The latest premium payment covering a one-year period from September 1 of last year amounted to $720 on this policy.

When the books were closed last December 31, the fixtures were 2½ years old. Accounts related to the fixtures and their insurance policy are set forth below.

Fixtures		Accumulated Depreciation		Prepaid Insurance (on fixtures only)	
Balance 20,000			Year 1 900	Policy A 42	
			Year 2 1,800	Policy B 480	
			Year 3 1,800		

Policy A on the fixtures expired February 28 of the current year. Policy B was immediately put in force to replace the expired policy on the fixtures; a two-year premium was paid on it. Policy B is for $10,000 maximum coverage, provides for indemnity on the basis of replacement cost of any loss, and has an 80% coinsurance clause. It is determined that the replacement cost of the fixtures when the fire occurred was $15,000 and that the damage amounted to a loss of two-thirds of their replacement cost.

Required (round amounts to nearest dollar):
1. Adjust the books to April 30 and reflect the inventory as of that date.
2. Open a Casualty loss account; set up the indemnities collectible as a receivable due from the insurance company.
3. Transfer the net balance in Casualty loss to Income summary.

P 12–10 (Based on Supplement 12-B; Life Insurance)

On April 1, 19A, Cox Company insured the life of its president for $100,000, naming itself as beneficiary. Annual premiums paid each April 1 are $3,600. As a result of the third premium payment and at the end of the third policy year, the policy has a cash surrender value of $1,800. One year later, this amount will increase to $2,430. Allocate the third-year cash surrender value equally to each of the first three policy years.

Cox Company adjusts and closes its books on December 31 and debits premium payments to a Prepaid Life Insurance account. All premiums are paid when due. The president died on April 3, 19D. No refund of unexpired premiums as of date of death is provided for in the policy.

Required:

Make all entries related to the policy through April 3, 19D, including adjusting and closing entries at the end of each year the policy is in force.

CASES

C 12–1 (NBC Settles a Logo Problem)

The National Broadcasting Company (NBC) incurred costs of $750,000 in the development of its "N" logo shown at intervals in its TV broadcasts. Shortly after the N was announced and first used by NBC, it was discovered that an educational TV network in Nebraska had already been using a similar logo. To obtain exclusive rights to its already costly N, NBC agreed, in an out-of-court settlement, to pay $55,000 cash to Nebraska Network and to furnish it with various new and used color TV equipment without cost (NBC book value, $350,000). The equipment to be transferred was conservatively valued at $500,000 by independent appraisers. A spokesman for the Nebraska Network said the equipment to be provided by NBC would have cost $750,000 if bought new and that, for the two years preceding the settlement, efforts to get a $750,000 appropriation from the Nebraska legislature to buy such equipment had been unsuccessful. Terms of the settlement provided that $2,500 of the cash settlement was to be paid to William Korbus, who had designed the Nebraska Network's N at a cost of $100. Delivery of the equipment to the Nebraska Network was to begin approximately three months after the announced settlement and was to occur over a four-month interval.

Required:

1. How should NBC account for its original costs of $750,000 related to the logo? How should it account for the settlement with the Nebraska Network and Korbus?
2. Assuming that accounting principles for not-for-profit organizations such as the Nebraska Network were similar to those for a commercial entity, how should the Nebraska Network account for the settlement?

C 12–2 (The Directors Want to Increase Goodwill)

Blass Corporation, a retail farm implements dealer, has increased its annual sales volume to a level three times greater than the annual sales of the dealership when purchased eight years ago. At that time, a material amount of goodwill was recorded. It has never been amortized because it predated *APB Opinion 17.*

The board of directors of Blass Corporation recently received an offer to negotiate the sale of Blass Corporation to a larger competitor. As a result, the majority of the board wants to increase the current amount of goodwill on the statement of financial position because of the larger sales volume developed through intensive promotion and the current market prices of the company's products. However, a few of the company's board members would prefer to eliminate goodwill altogether from the statement of financial position in order to prevent "possible misinterpretations." Goodwill was properly recorded when the business was acquired eight years ago.

Required:

1. *a.* Discuss the meaning of the term goodwill. Do not discuss goodwill arising from consolidated statements or the conditions under which goodwill is recorded.
   b. What technique is commonly used to estimate the value of goodwill in negotiations to purchase a going concern?
2. Why are the book and market values of the goodwill of Blass Corporation different?
3. Discuss the propriety of—
   a. Increasing the stated value of goodwill prior to the negotiations.
   b. Eliminating goodwill completely from the statement of financial position prior to negotiations.

(AICPA adapted)

13 INCOME RECOGNITION

OVERVIEW AND PURPOSE

Income recognition causes many of the controversies in accounting because it necessarily also relates to recognition of *(a)* revenues and gains and *(b)* expenses and losses. **Revenue** recognition involves the recording of the resources received from selling goods and services and **expense** recognition involves the recording of resources used to earn revenues. Resources held (i.e., assets) and sources of resources (i.e., liabilities and owners' equity) are reported on the statement of financial position. Income recognition is controversial; for example, one diverse view of the controversies was stated as follows:[1]

> The balance sheet and the income statement are best regarded not as two statements but as two parts of the same statement. They are inevitably tied together. The only sensible basis for a balance sheet is to attempt to show the worth of a company at a given date. By the same token, sensible basis for a balance sheet is to attempt to show the extent to which the worth or value of a company has improved between balance sheet dates.
>
> In short, the only acceptable basis for net income determination is the "better off" view. It is not useful to anyone to claim that a company has earned a net profit of $1,000,000 unless it can be demonstrated that its value has increased by that amount.

The prior chapters included a review and discussion of quick assets, inventories, and operational assets. Now it is appropriate to supplement the discussions in Chapter 6 of the conceptual framework and implementation principles. Therefore, the main purpose of this chapter is to discuss income recognition and some related problems of implementation. Also, the discussion relates this topic to the conceptual framework and provides relevant information to support the chapters that follow. This chapter is organized as follows:

1. Fundamentals of income recognition.
2. Income recognition in special cases.
3. Revenue recognition.
4. Revenue recognition for service sales.
5. Expense recognition.
6. Recognition of gains and losses.
7. A unique problem—The oil and gas industry.

[1] Howard Ross, *The Elusive Art of Accounting: A Brash Commentary on Financial Statements* (New York: The Ronald Press, 1966), p. 191.

Fundamentals of Income Recognition

Income recognition has always been viewed as one of the most important and complex problems of accounting. For many years, income recognition has been given intensive attention by the accounting profession, often with inconclusive results. This attention is evident in the following milestones in accounting: *(a)* congressional enactment of the Securities Acts of 1933 and 1934, which gave the SEC the power to establish regulations about the content of financial statements (including income), *(b)* 1938–59, the AICPA Committee on Accounting Procedures issuance of 51 *ARBs, (c)* 1962–73, the AICPA Accounting Principles Board issuance of 31 *Opinions, (d)* from 1973 to mid-1988, the issuance of 97 statements plus the six concepts statements by the FASB, and *(e)* from the 1930s to date, the AAA issuance of various position papers most of which included major consideration of income recognition.

The main issues in income recognition are *(a)* how should income be defined and how should that definition relate to the statement of financial position elements—assets, liabilities, and owners' equity, *(b)* how should income be measured, and *(c)* how should income be identified with specific accounting periods under the **accrual accounting** concept. These income recognition problems are even more complex because of the dissimilar characteristics of different industries (e.g., manufacturing, retailing, service, and financial) and the wide range of income-producing activities (e.g., installment sales, long-term construction contracts, and the sale of services).

Income recognition sometimes is discussed as a problem separable from the statement of financial position. This cannot be done realistically because the two basic components of income, revenues and expenses, rest directly on the statement of financial position definitions of assets and liabilities. Revenues cannot be recognized unless resources in some form are increased, or a liability is decreased. Similarly, expenses cannot be recognized and measured[2] unless resources in some form are decreased, or a liability is increased. Revenues and expenses cannot be recognized[3] (without a conceptual violation) if they do not conform to the acceptable asset and liability definitions. Justifiable criticisms on this point abound because either *(a)* the definitions of revenues, expenses, assets, and liabilities are not compatible with income recognition criteria or *(b)* some or all of these definitions are so open-ended that they have no substance in determining income. Sometimes it appears that one rule-making body developed the statement of financial position definitions and a totally different group developed the statement of income definitions. A by-product of this issue has been a suggestion of nonarticulation between the statement of income and statement of financial position. The accounting model currently used and discussed in the review chapters defines the statement of financial position and statement of income as **articulated.** That is, the statement of income ties in directly to the statement of financial position through retained earnings. This means that they have an algebraic relationship (i.e., a proof of equivalence). A few accountants have proposed, with no success, that these two statements

---

[2] Measurement is the assignment of meaningful numerical values to an accounting expression, such as the components of assets, liabilities, and owners' equity.

[3] Recognized means properly measured and recorded in the accounts.

should not be directly related; that is, **nonarticulated.** This means that each statement and its elements would be defined and measured independently. However, some kind of reconciliation would be necessary for full disclosure.

At the conceptual level, Hendriksen discusses the various suggestions that have been made to define the basic nature of income, assets, and liabilities.[4] Discussion of these conceptual issues is beyond the scope of this chapter.

Definition of Income

Over the past six decades, the accounting profession has spent considerable talent, resources, and time in trying to resolve the basic problems inherent in the statement of financial position and statement of income. Based on perceived necessity, accountants tend to emphasize objective rather than subjective procedures. This explains in large part why the **transactions approach** is used to measure and record income. Basically, this approach recognizes revenues and expenses as each completed transaction occurs (e.g., remember when the journal entries were made in the prior chapters). This approach bases income recognition on completed transactions, rather than on "guess estimates," subjective valuations, and individual judgments.

The above discussion focused mainly on one controversy about income recognition. However, income recognition has involved many other controversies because it is very difficult to resolve in a conceptual, yet practical, way. Traditionally, the accounting profession has focused its attention on an accounting definition of income measured as revenues and gains minus expenses and losses. The differences of opinion during the last five decades mainly involved definitional distinctions (e.g., unusual or infrequent gains and losses, extraordinary items, and prior period adjustments) and statement of income format (e.g., current operating versus all-inclusive).

The latest definitions that directly relate to income recognition are provided by *FASB Statements of Financial Accounting Concepts No. 6* (1985). These definitions, given in Exhibit 6–4, are repeated here for instructional convenience. The impact of this statement is increasing rapidly because these definitions are being used *(a)* by the FASB in developing its recent *Statements of Financial Accounting Standards, (b)* by the accounting profession in its regular activities, and *(c)* in the accounting literature.

Statement of income:

1. Revenues are inflows or other enhancements of assets of an entity or settlements of its liabilities (or a combination of both) during a period from delivering or producing goods, rendering services, or other activities that constitute the entity's ongoing major or central operations.
2. Expenses are outflows or other using up of assets or incurrences of liabilities (or a combination of both) during a period from delivering or producing goods, rendering services, or carrying out other activities that constitute the entity's ongoing major or central operations.
3. Gains are increases in equity (net assets) from peripheral or incidental transactions of an entity and from all other transactions and other events

[4] Eldon S. Hendriksen, *Accounting Theory*, 4th Ed (Homewood, Ill.: Richard D. Irwin, 1982), chap. 7.

and circumstances affecting the entity during a period except those that result from revenues or investment by owners.

4. Losses are decreases in equity (net assets) from peripheral or incidental transactions of an entity and from all other transactions and other events and circumstances affecting the entity during a period except those that result from expenses or distributions to owners.

Statement of financial position:

5. Assets are probable future economic benefits obtained or controlled by a particular entity as a result of past transactions or events.
6. Liabilities are probable future sacrifices of economic benefits arising from present obligations of a particular entity to transfer assets or provide services to other entities in the future as a result of past transactions or events.
7. Equity (i.e., owners' equity) is the residual interest in the assets of an entity that remains after deducting its liabilities. In a business enterprise, the equity is the ownership interest.

Exhibit 13–1 shows the primary components of **net income** and their distinctive characteristics.

Accrual Basis of Accounting

Income recognition requires the use of **accrual basis accounting.** The economic effects of many business transactions involve more than one accounting period. For example, a sale of goods on credit during the 19A accounting period with collection of the related cash during 19B affects two accounting periods. Operating activities, such as these two transactions, pose a basic question about when revenues, gains, expenses, and losses should be recognized. Two different approaches are possible, *(a)* cash basis and *(b)* accrual basis. Under the cash basis, in the above example, the sale revenue would be reported in 19B, while under the accrual basis it would be reported in 19A. Notice that for a cash sale in 19A, both the cash and accrual basis would report the revenue in 19A. GAAP, for many decades, has required accrual basis accounting for all statement of income elements. This requirement was reaffirmed in *FASB Concepts 1*, par. 44, as follows:

> Information about enterprise earnings and its components measured by **accrual accounting** generally provides a better indication of enterprise performance than information about current cash receipts and payments. Accrual accounting attempts to record the financial effects on an enterprise of transactions and other events and circumstances that have cash consequences for an enterprise in the periods in which those transactions, events, and circumstances occur rather than only in the periods in which cash is received or paid by the enterprise. Accrual accounting is concerned with the process by which cash expended on resources and activities is returned as more (or perhaps less) cash to the enterprise, not just with the beginning and end of that process. It recognizes that the buying, producing, selling, and other operations of an enterprise during a period, as well as other events that affect enterprise performance, often do not coincide with the cash receipts and payments of the period.

Exhibit 13–1
Distinctive characteristics of the components of net income.

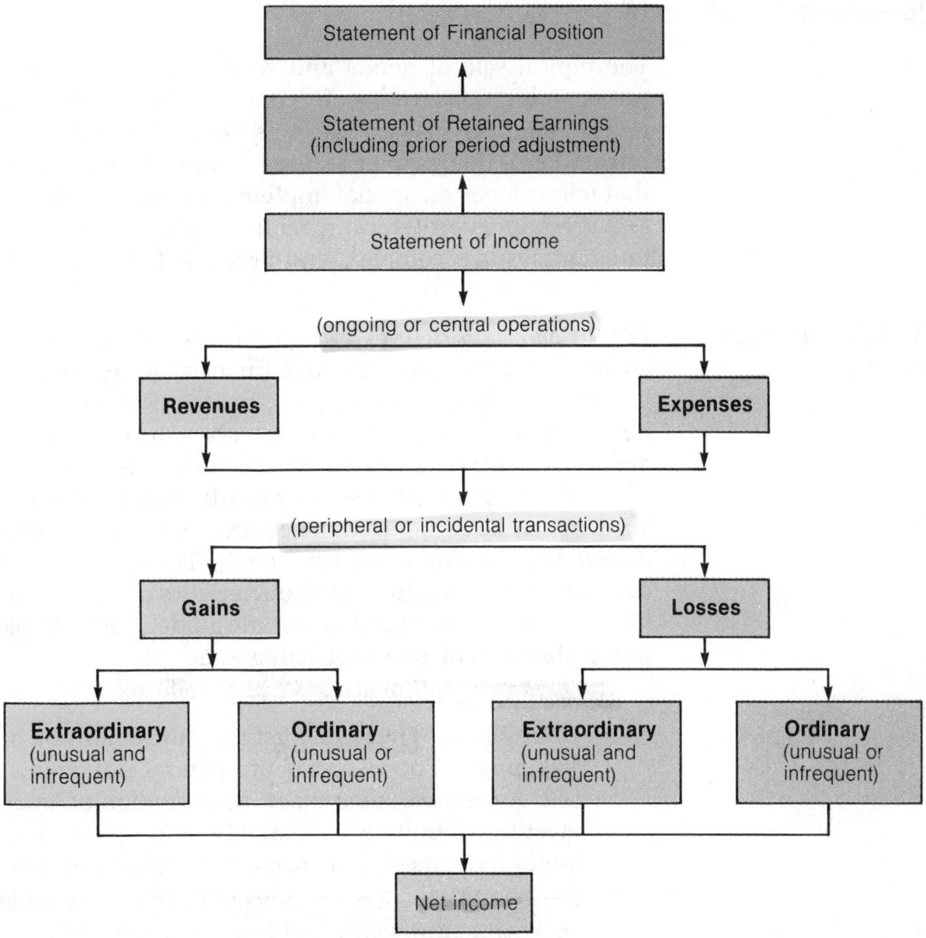

The accounting accrual process was summarized by one author as follows:[5]

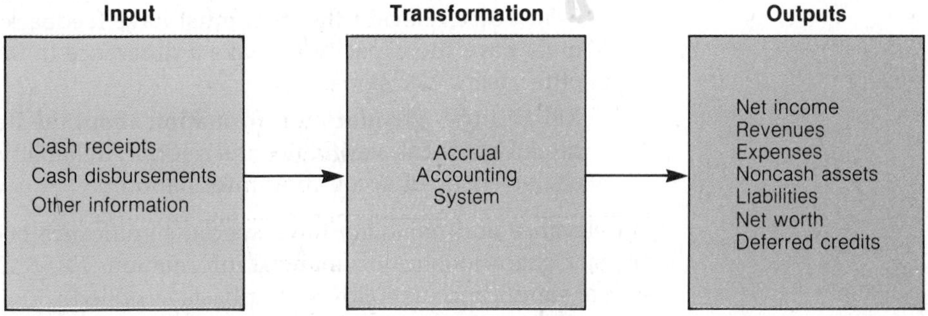

[5] William H. Beaver, *Financial Reporting: An Accounting Revolution* (Englewood Cliffs, N.J.: Prentice-Hall, 1981), p. 7.

Income Recognition in Special Cases

The typical sale of goods and services and the directly related expenses are not complex transactions. In contrast, the variety and complexity of atypical revenue and expense transactions pose difficult implementation problems. The remainder of this chapter focuses mainly on such transactions. The discussions that follow focus on special **implementation** approaches of concepts, principles, and procedures for typical revenues and expenses. You may find the adaptions to be interesting, complex, and perhaps debatable.

The Recognition Process

FASB Concepts 5 defines recognition as the process of formally incorporating an item into the accounts and financial statements of an entity as an asset, liability, revenue, expense, gain, or loss. Recognition includes depiction of an item in both words and numbers, with each amount included in the summarized amounts reported on the financial statements.

FASB Concepts 5 specified four **fundamental criteria that should be met** before an item can be recognized. They are subject to a **cost-benefit constraint** and a **materiality threshold** (see Chapter 6). The fundamental recognition criteria are derived from the **qualitative characteristics** of financial information. These recognition criteria are intended to provide guidelines for implementing the definitions of the **elements of financial statements.**

The four recognition criteria are as follows:

1. **Definitions—The item must meet the definition of an element of financial statements.** The elements of financial statements were defined on page 569. A resource must meet the definition of an asset, an obligation must meet the definition of a liability, and revenues, expenses, gains, and losses must meet their respective definitions before recognition.
2. **Measurability—The item must have a relevant attribute that is measurable with sufficient reliability.**[6] For accounting and reporting purposes, attributes are primarily quantified in units of money.
3. **Relevance—Accounting information about the item is capable of making a difference in the decisions of financial statement users.** Relevance is a primary qualitative characteristic of accounting information (see Exhibit 6–3). To be relevant the item must have feedback or predictive value. It must have the capacity to make a difference in investors', creditors', or other users' decisions.
4. **Reliability—Accounting information about the item must be representationally faithful, verifiable, and neutral.** Reliability is a primary qualitative characteristic of accounting information.

Relevance and reliability have special significance because they are the two primary characteristics of financial information. *FASB Concepts 5* explains their special significance as follows (emphasis supplied):

> Reliability may affect the **timing of recognition.** The first available information about an event that may have resulted in an asset, liability, or change therein is

---

[6] **Attribute** refers to a characteristic, trait, or aspect that is to be quantified and measured.

sometimes too uncertain to be recognized: it may not yet be clear whether the effects of the event meet one or more of the definitions or whether they are measurable, and the cost of resolving those uncertainties may be excessive. Information about some items that meet a definition may never become **sufficiently reliable** at a justifiable cost to recognize the item. For other items, those uncertainties are reduced as time passes, and reliability is increased as additional information becomes available (par. 76).

Unavailability or unreliability of information may **delay recognition** of an item, but waiting for virtually complete reliability or minimum cost may make the information so untimely that it loses its relevance. At some intermediate point, uncertainty may be reduced at a justifiable cost to a level tolerable in view of the perceived relevance of the information. If other criteria are also met, that is the appropriate point for recognition. Thus, recognition may sometimes involve a **trade-off** between relevance and reliability (par. 77).

Next, revenue recognition will be discussed followed by revenue recognition for service sales, expense recognition, and recognition of gains and losses.

Chapter 6 discussed four implementation principles—cost, revenue, matching, and full disclosure. Two of these principles, the revenue and matching principles, and the four fundamental recognition criteria provide the foundation for the process of **income recognition.**

Revenue Principle

The revenue principle applies to the sale of both **products and services.** Consistent with the four recognition criteria listed above, the revenue principle states that revenue should be recognized (i.e., recorded) when *(a)* an exchange transaction involving the transfer of goods or services has occurred and *(b)* the earning process is essentially complete. In most cases, both of these conditions are met at the time of the sale of products and/or services because the consideration received is cash and/or a receivable that will be collected. In other cases, determination of when the revenue process is essentially complete may be difficult.

The revenue principle is the implementation guideline for recognition of revenues. *FASB Concepts 5* gives further guidance in applying this principle. It states that revenues are **measured** "by the exchange values of the assets (goods and services) or liabilities involved." Two **conditions** identified by *FASB Concepts 5* are critical to revenue recognition decisions. The assets received for the products or services must be *(a)* **realized or realizable** and *(b)* the revenue must be **earned. Realization** occurs when products (goods and services) or other assets are sold for cash or noncash resources, or claims to cash are received at date of sale. **Realizabiliity** occurs when the related noncash assets received are determined to be readily convertible to known amounts of cash in conformity with the sale terms.[7] Revenues from goods and services are considered **earned** when the entity has substantially accomplished what it must do to be entitled to the benefits received, or to be received.

---

[7] *FASB Concepts 5* (par. 83) states that readily convertible assets have (i) interchangeable (fungible) units and (ii) quoted prices available in an active market that can rapidly absorb the quantity held by the entity without significantly affecting the price.

The critical issue in revenue recognition usually involves uncertainty regarding the future realizability of noncash considerations. Varying degrees of uncertainty have created alternative revenue recognition rules for different situations. These situations are discussed below.

Application of the Revenue Principle. Revenues are earned in a variety of ways, and many of them pose difficult application problems. In recognition of these problems, *FASB Concepts 5* contains a section, "Guidance in Applying Criteria to Components of Earnings," that emphasizes the following general guidelines:

- **a.** The widely acknowledged importance of earnings information leads to more stringent requirements for recognizing components of earnings than for recognizing other changes in assets or liabilities.
- **b.** Recognizing components of earnings is concerned with identifying cash-to-cash cycles that are substantially complete and with associating particular revenues, gains, expenses, and losses with those cycles.
- **c.** More stringent requirements are imposed for recognizing revenues and gains than for recognizing expenses and losses.
- **d.** Recognition of revenues and gains requires an **acceptable level of assurance** of (1) being realized or realizable and (2) being earned.

FASB Concepts 5 (par. 85) provides examples of the application of guidance criteria as follows:

- **a. Time of sale** (called the **sales method**)—The two conditions, realized (or realizable) and earned, usually are met at the **time of sale** because the product is delivered, or the services are rendered, to the customer.
- **b. Production and delivery** (called the **production method**)—When a sale, or cash receipt (or both), precedes production and delivery, as for magazine subscriptions, revenue is recognized as **delivery occurs,** not at the date of the sale or cash collection.
- **c. Percentage of completion**—If a construction contract is executed prior to production of the product, revenue is recognized as **production progresses** if reliable estimates of progress are possible.
- **d. Time basis**—If services are rendered or rights to use assets extend continuously over time (for example, interest or rent) and reliable measures based on reliable contractual prices established in advance are commonly available, revenues may be recognized as **earned as time passes.**
- **e. Completion of production**—If products or other assets are **readily realizable** because they are salable at reliably determinable prices without significant effort (for example, certain agricultural products, precious metals, and marketable securities), revenues may be recognized **at completion of production or when prices of the assets change.**
- **f. Completed transaction**—If products, services, or other assets are exchanged for nonmonetary assets that are **not readily convertible into cash,** revenues or gains or losses may be recognized on the basis that they have been earned and the **transaction is completed.** However, this requires that the timing and market value of the noncash resources received, or to be received, can be reliably estimated.

g. **Cash basis**—If the collectibility of the resources received **cannot** be reliably estimated, revenues are recognized **as the cash is collected** (called the **installment method**). If realization is unpredictable, revenue or gain is not recognized until cash is received equal to all costs (called the **cost recovery method**).

Because they have special features, the following revenue recognition methods will be discussed:

1. Percentage-of-completion and completed contract methods for long-term construction contracts.
2. Installment method of income recognition.
3. Agreements in which sales returns are permitted by the seller.
4. Cost recovery method. ———— *most usual*
5. Revenue recognition for service sales:
 a. Specific performance method.
 b. Proportional performance method.
 c. Completed performance method.
 d. Collection method.
6. A unique problem—the oil and gas industry.

Accounting for Long-Term Construction Contracts

A unique accounting problem arises in the construction industry. The problem involves (1) the amount of periodic **income to recognize** and (2) measurement of the accounting value of the **construction in process inventory** associated with extended construction period projects for items such as buildings, bridges, ships, and highways. The problem is unique because the construction period often extends over two or more annual accounting periods. Because inventory valuation affects income measurement during the construction period, the problems of inventory valuation and income measurement are interrelated. For example, assume a three-year construction period. Should income be recognized as construction progresses (i.e., each period), or should income be recognized only at the end of the three years? The answer to this income recognition question affects the accounting value of the construction in process inventory.

Under GAAP there are two acceptable methods of accounting for inventory and income on long-term construction contracts.

1. **Completed contract method**—under this method income is recognized only in the year of completion. This means that during the entire construction period all collections on the contract price and all construction expenditures are recorded in appropriately designated "holding" accounts. All construction costs are debited to an inventory account, Construction in Process. At the completion date all of the related holding accounts are closed, and the net effect is the income from the construction project.

2. **Percentage-of-completion method**—under this method an **estimated** amount of income from construction is recognized each accounting period based on percentage of completion. That is, if the project is 20 percent completed at the end of the first accounting year, that percent of the **estimated** total construction income is reported on the statement of income for that year. This means that at each year-end an estimate must be

only imp. if expends over more than 1 yr.

actually recording the inventory (bldg)

made for the **cost to complete.** This estimate is used with the *(a)* known contract price, *(b)* actual costs to date, and *(c)* income already recognized, to compute the period's estimated income from construction. At the end of each period the estimated income recognized is credited to income and debited to construction in process.

Because of their wide use and special characteristics these two methods are illustrated below.

Case data:

1. Ace Construction Company received a contract to erect a building for $1.5 million. Construction will start February 1, 19A, and is expected to be completed 2½ years from that date.
2. Progress billings (a special name for an invoice) are to be made by the contractor at the end of each month based upon a predetermined schedule, which is subject to audit by the purchaser of the building. The progress billings are payable to the contractor within 10 days after the billing.
3. The percentage of completion at the end of each accounting period during construction will be measured by the ratio of total costs incurred to date to estimated total costs to be incurred on the project (costs incurred to date plus estimated costs to complete).
4. Data for the entire construction period are shown in **Exhibit 13–2,** panel A.

Completed Contract Method Illustrated. Long-term construction contracts almost always provide for the contractor to bill the purchaser for progress payments (as agreed on in the contract). Such progress billings are debited to Accounts Receivable and credited to **Billings on Contracts.** The latter is a **contra account** to Construction in Process Inventory. If the **net** amount of Construction in Process Inventory (i.e., Construction in Process Inventory, less Billings on Contracts) is a debit, it is reported as a **current asset,** Inventory. It represents the contractor's net ownership interest in the construction inventory. If the net amount is a credit, it is reported as a **liability** because it represents the purchaser's net ownership interest.

Under the completed contract method, when the contract is completed, the **income recognized** is the difference between the accumulated credit balance in the Billings on Contracts account and the debit balance in the Construction in Process Inventory account. The accumulated **amount of Billing on Contracts** is the **amount of sales revenue.** The accumulated **amount of Construction in Process Inventory** on completion of the contract is the **amount of cost of goods sold.**[8] Therefore, the difference between the two amounts is the pretax construction income earned on the project.

Under the completed contract method, during the construction period the construction in process inventory is reported on the statement of financial position as the total accumulated costs to date, less the total progress billings to date. Income on construction contracts ($135,000 in Exhibit 13–2, panel B) is

[8] Billings on Contracts is **not** a revenue account, and Construction in Process is not a cost of goods sold account (it is an inventory account). Note the emphasis on "amount" in the referenced sentence.

Exhibit 13–2
Long-term construction contracts—income recognition compared for completed contract and percentage-of-completion methods.

Panel A—Case Data:

	19A	19B	19C	Total
Contract price				$1,500,000
Costs incurred each year	$ 350,000	$550,000	$465,000	1,365,000
Estimated costs to complete (at year-end)*	1,000,000	460,000	-0-	
Progress billings each year	300,000	575,000	625,000	1,500,000
Collections on billings each year	270,000	555,000	675,000	1,500,000

*New estimates may be made each year.

Panel B—Completed Contract Method—Income Recognition:
Year 19C:

Total contract price	$1,500,000
Total costs incurred	1,365,000
Income on construction	$ 135,000

Note: No income was recognized in 19A or 19B because contract was not completed.

Panel C—Percentage-of-Completion Method—Apportionment of Estimated Income:

	19A	19B	19C
Contract price*	$1,500,000	$1,500,000	$1,500,000
Less costs:			
Actual cost to date (cumulative)	350,000*	900,000*	1,365,000*
Estimated cost to complete	1,000,000	460,000	
Estimated total costs	1,350,000	1,360,000	1,365,000*
Estimated total income	$ 150,000	$ 140,000	$ 135,000*

Apportionment of total income (based on ratio of costs incurred to date to estimated total construction costs):

	19A	19B	19C
19A: ($350,000/$1,350,000) × $150,000	$ 38,889		
19B: ($900,000/$1,360,000) × $140,000		$ 92,647	
Less: Income recognized to date		38,889	
Income recognized in 19B		$ 53,758	
19C: Total income to be recognized (actual)			$ 135,000
Less: Income recognized to date ($38,889 + $53,758)			92,647
Income recognized in 19C			$ 42,353

*Actual.

reported **only in the year of completion** (19C in the example). The entries in the accounts of Ace Construction Company for the completed contract method are illustrated in **Exhibit 13–3.** The financial statement presentation for each year is shown in **Exhibit 13–4.**

Percentage-of-Completion Method Illustrated. Under this method, accounting for a long-term construction contract is the same as the completed contract method explained above, except that **income is recognized as earned each accounting period** during construction and **added** to the account, Construction in Process Inventory. Because the **actual** total income on the contract will not be known until completion, an estimate of it must be made each period. The estimated total amount of income then is apportioned to each period on the basis of the percentage of the total contract completed (i.e., percentage of completion) during that period.

Percentage of completion usually is determined on the basis of either *(a)* engineering and/or architectural estimates of the **work performed to date** compared to the **total work** necessary to complete the contract or *(b)* the ratio of total **costs incurred to date** on the contract to the **total costs** that are expected to be incurred on the contract. The estimated amount of income recognized

Exhibit 13–3

Long-term construction contracts—journal entries for completed contract and percentage-of-completion methods of compared.

Accounts	Method: Completed contract		Method: Percentage of completion	
Year 19A:				
1. Costs of construction:				
Construction in process inventory	350,000*		350,000	
Cash, payables, etc.		350,000		350,000
* Under the completed contract method this may include a reasonable allocation of general and administrative (G&A) expenses for periods prior to completion.				
2. Progress billings:				
Accounts receivable	300,000		300,000	
Billings on contracts		300,000		300,000
3. Collections on billings:				
Cash	270,000		270,000	
Accounts receivable		270,000		270,000
4. Recognition of income:				
Construction in process inventory	(No income recognized until completion)		38,889	
Income on construction†				38,889
† Closed to Income Summary.				
Year 19B:				
1. Costs of construction:				
Construction in process inventory	550,000		550,000	
Cash, payables, etc.		550,000		550,000
2. Progress billings:				
Accounts receivable	575,000		575,000	
Billings on contracts		575,000		575,000
3. Collections on billings:				
Cash	555,000		555,000	
Accounts receivable		555,000		555,000
4. Recognition of income:				
Construction in process inventory	(No income recognized until completion)		53,758	
Income on construction				53,758

Exhibit 13–3
(concluded)

Accounts	Completed contract		Percentage of completion	
Year 19C:				
1. Costs of construction:				
Construction in process inventory	465,000		465,000	
Cash, payables, etc.		465,000		465,000
2. Progress billings (final billing):				
Accounts receivable	625,000		625,000	
Billings on contracts		625,000		625,000
3. Collections on billings (in full):				
Cash	675,000		675,000	
Accounts receivable		675,000		675,000
4. Recognition of income (and to close the accumulated account balances):				
Construction in process inventory			42,353‡	
Billings on contracts	1,500,000		1,500,000	
Construction in process inventory		1,365,000		1,500,000
Income on construction		135,000		42,353
‡ Alternatively, this entry could be as follows (with the same results):				
Billings on contracts			1,500,000	
Construction in process inventory				1,457,647
Income on construction				42,353

Exhibit 13–4
Long-term construction contracts—financial statements for completed contract and percentage-of-completion methods compared.

	Completed contract			Percentage of completion		
	19A	19B	19C	19A	19B	19C
Statement of financial position:						
Current assets:						
Accounts receivable	$ 30,000	$ 50,000		$ 30,000	$ 50,000	
Inventory:						
Construction in process inventory	350,000	900,000		388,889*	992,647*	
Less: Billings on contracts	300,000	875,000		300,000	875,000	
Costs in excess of billings†	50,000	25,000		88,889*	117,647*	
Statement of income:						
Income on construction (detailed)	-0-	-0-	$135,000	38,889	53,758	$42,353

* These amounts exceed their counterpart amounts under the completed contract method by the amount of income recognized to date.
† Abbreviated titles are used herein for convenience. This account usually is labeled Cost of Uncompleted Contracts in Excess of Billings.

each period is accrued as a debit to Construction in Process Inventory and a credit to Income on Construction. The inventory account is debited for the income recognized because it adds to the contractor's ownership interest in the construction inventory. The income account is closed to Income Summary each period and is reported on the statement of income. Computation of the amount of estimated income to be recognized each year by the Ace Construction Company is illustrated in Exhibit 13–2, panel C.

Notice in Exhibit 13–2, panel C, that the total income on the project is apportioned to each period on the basis of the ratio of costs incurred to date to total costs to be incurred. For example, in 19A, total income of $150,000 was estimated on the project. Of that amount, $38,889 was apportioned to 19A. At the end of construction, Ace Construction Company earned $135,000 on the project, and the apportionments of income to 19A, 19B, and 19C were as shown in Exhibit 13–2.

The resulting entries in the accounts of Ace Construction Company for each method are shown in Exhibit 13–3. For each year, entries 1–3 are the same under the completed contract and percentage-of-completion methods. **Only entry 4 for recognition of income** (boxed for emphasis), **differs between the two methods.** This difference affects the carrying value of construction in process inventory (see the debit side of entry 4 under the percentage-of-completion method). The financial statement presentation for each period is shown in Exhibit 13–4 for each method.

As Exhibit 13–4 shows, both methods have the same results on the statement of financial position during the construction period, except for the amount of the ending inventory (i.e., costs in excess of billings) and retained earnings. Under the percentage-of-completion method, the inventory prior to completion of the project is greater in amount by the accumulated pretax income recognized in the current and prior periods. Thus, for Ace Construction Company the ending inventory (i.e., costs in excess of billings) is greater by $38,889 at the end of 19A and by $38,889 + $53,758 = $92,647 at the end of 19B. Recall that the estimated income recognized as earned each year was debited to Construction in Process Inventory in the percentage-of-completion method.

Projected losses—under either method, when there is a projected loss at any time, it must be recognized in full in the period in which a loss on the contract appears probable. The loss should be recognized by a debit to Loss on Construction and a credit to Construction in Process Inventory. The credit side of the entry removes from the inventory account the amount of costs in excess of expected recovery value. Also, when a loss on the contract is probable, **any income previously recognized should be "reversed" and reported as a loss** in the period that such determination is made.

For example, assume that at the end of 19B, Ace Construction Company projected a $40,000 loss on the project. Under the **completed contract method,** Ace would make the following entry at the end of 19B (in place of no entry 4 under the completed contract method in Exhibit 13–3):

Loss on construction	40,000	
Construction in process inventory		40,000

Under the **percentage-of-completion method,** the entry to recognize the loss would be as follows (in place of entry 4 for 19B under the percentage-of-completion method in Exhibit 13–3):

Loss on construction ($38,889 from 19A + $40,000)	78,889	
Construction in process inventory		78,889

The two entries given above for completed contract and percentage of completion differ by the amount of construction income recognized in 19A under the percentage-of-completion method (i.e., $38,889). This amount must be reversed in the entry to record the loss under the percentage-of-completion method.

After the above loss entries are posted, the balance in the Construction in Process Inventory account will be $860,000; that is, costs incurred to date, $900,000 (see Exhibit 13–3, entry 1 for years 19A and 19B) minus the $40,000 recognized at the end of 19B. In this case, Billings on Contracts at the end of 19B (i.e., $875,000; see Exhibit 13–4) exceeds Construction in Process Inventory (i.e., $860,000) by $15,000; this credit balance (i.e., $15,000) would be reported as a liability. In most cases, this liability would be a current liability because Ace Construction Company would reduce progress billings accordingly in the immediate future.

Therefore, **whenever a loss is probable,** construction in process inventory would be reported at **estimated net realizable value** (i.e., $860,000) under either method. Inventory and income amounts reported in prior years would not be retroactively restated in current-year comparative statements. Instead, the change in projections would be accounted for prospectively as a **change in estimate,** as illustrated above and explained in Chapters 3 and 24.

Comparison of methods—both the completed contract and percentage-of-completion methods of accounting for inventory and income on long-term construction contracts are appropriate under current GAAP. Over the entire construction period, both methods recognize the same **total** amount of pretax income.

Advocates of the **completed contract method** assert that it is more objective and more conservative because income is not recognized until all of the revenues and expenses for the completed job are known with certainty. However, this method is viewed by some accountants as deficient because income recognition does not reflect performance in each accounting period during construction. Although most of the work may be completed prior to the period in which construction is completed, all of the income is reported in the last period.

The **percentage-of-completion method** is supported on the basis that the construction company **earns** revenue as it performs the work on the contract. However, some accountants consider the percentage-of-completion method as deficient because income during the construction period is measured subjectively, on the basis of *(a)* **estimates** of work done (percentage of completion) and *(b)* **estimated** total construction cost. However, income tax considerations and a desire to shift income among accounting periods often strongly influence the choice of method. The accounting profession has sanctioned the use of either method as follows:[9]

> The committee believes that in general when estimates of costs to complete and extent of progress toward completion of long-term contracts are reasonably dependable, the percentage-of-completion method is preferable. When lack of dependable

[9] AICPA, *Accounting Research Bulletin 45,* "Long-Term Construction-Type Contracts" (New York, 1955).

estimates or inherent hazards cause forecasts to be doubtful, the completed-contract method is preferable.

Accounting for long-term construction contracts has been criticized because it sanctions a free choice between two distinctly different accounting methods for the same set of facts. Notice that the above quote merely says "preferable" (not required). Acceptance of more than one method of accounting in this case is analogous to other alternative free choices, such as inventory methods (e.g., FIFO and LIFO) and depreciation methods (e.g., straight-line and accelerated).

Installment Method of Income Recognition

Under the **installment method,** revenue is recognized as cash is collected rather than at the time of sale. **Under current GAAP, the installment method is used only when the sales method, or another GAAP method, is not appropriate because of the absence of reasonable assurance that the entire sale price will be collected, or the related expenses cannot be determined reliably in the period of sale.** These conditions indicate that the earning process is not essentially completed at the point of sale. The installment method has limited application under GAAP. For instance, it is used to account for **sales of real estate** in which the down payment is relatively low (less than approximately 25% of the total sale price) and ultimate collection of the remainder is subject to considerable uncertainty.[10] However, in most cases, the seller can estimate bad debts and other expenses (such as warranties) reliably, and thus, must apply the sales method.

To illustrate the basic accounting entries for the installment method, assume that during 19A, Tampa Company had sales of $80,000, which required use of the installment method. The cost of the items sold was $60,000, yielding a gross margin of $20,000 and a gross margin rate on sales of 25% (i.e., $20,000 ÷ $80,000). Related to these sales, Tampa collected $10,000 in 19A and $40,000 in 19B. Remaining collections were made in 19C and later. 19A and 19B journal entries for these sales are as follows.

During 19A (recognition of installment sales and related collections):

Installment accounts receivable	80,000	
Installment sales revenue		80,000
Cost of installment sales	60,000	
Inventory*		60,000

* Assuming perpetual inventory system used.

Cash	10,000	
Installment accounts receivable		10,000

December 31, 19A:

Entry to record deferred gross margin on installment sales:

Installment sales revenue	80,000	
Cost of installment sales		60,000
Deferred gross margin on installment sales		20,000

[10] *FASB Standard 66* describes the requirements for accounting for real estate sales. Paragraph 66 of *Standard 66* explicitly allows the installment method when the sale of real estate does not meet the criteria for application of the sales method.

Entry to reduce the deferred gross margin by the amount earned; 25% of the cash collected:

Deferred gross margin on installment sales	2,500	
Realized gross margin on installment sales ($10,000 × 25%)		2,500

Entry to close the recognized gross margin on installment sales:

Realized gross margin on installment sales	2,500	
Income summary		2,500

Notice that the only remaining account balances are: Installment receivable, $70,000 and deferred gross margin $17,500.

The 19A statements of income and financial position would report the following:

Sales revenue (excluding installment sales)	$300,000	
Cost of goods sold (excluding installment sales)	180,000	
Gross margin on sales	120,000	
Gross margin realized on installment sales	2,500	
Total gross margin on sales	$122,500	
Current assets:		
Installment accounts receivable	$ 70,000	
Less: Deferred gross margin on installment sales*	17,500	$52,500

* *FASB Statement of Financial Accounting Concepts No. 3*, pars. 156–58, states that "no matter how it is displayed in financial statements, deferred gross margin on installment sales is conceptually an asset valuation—that is, a reduction of an asset." In the past it has usually been reported as a current liability.

During 19B (collections on 19A installment sales):

Cash	40,000	
Installment accounts receivable		40,000

December 31, 19B (entry to reflect 19B, the realized portion of 19A installment sales):

Deferred gross margin on installment sales	10,000	
Realized gross margin on installment sales ($40,000 × 25%)		10,000

The main characteristic of the installment method, reflected in the above entries, is that the gross margin is deferred until cash related to the sales is collected. The applicable gross margin rate is applied to the total amount of cash collected for **each reporting period** to determine the amount of gross margin to be **recognized** in that period. Notice that installment sales revenue and cost of installment sales are not individually deferred, rather only the difference, gross margin, is deferred.

The entries shown above relate only to installment sales made in 19A. If additional installment sales were made in 19B, gross margin would be recognized as cash related to 19B sales was collected, **based on the 19B gross margin rate.** Thus, care must be taken to distinguish sales, costs, and cash receipts associated with each year's installment sales if the gross margin rate varies from year to year.

Repossessions are common when the installment method is used because the method is used only when reliable estimates of bad debt losses cannot be made. When a repossession is made, first assure that all accounts related to the installment sale are current as of the date of repossession. The repossession entry records the asset recovered, reduces the related installment account receivable and deferred gross margin to zero balances, and records the gain, or loss, on repossession. A typical entry is as follows:

Inventory (used item)	650	
Deferred gross margin	250	
Loss on repossession	100	
Installment accounts receivable		1,000

The inventory amount is the estimated net realizable value (discussed in Chapters 8 and 9), which is never more than current market value in present condition. Sometimes this is called **fair value,** a term which needs to be defined in each particular situation, as in this one.

The installment method has a serious conceptual flaw because sales revenues and cost of goods sold are initially recorded on the accrual basis, while gross margin and, as a result, income are deferred and later recovered as realized based on cash collections of installment receivables. Therefore, it has been characterized as part accrual and part cash basis accounting. It is inconsistent which causes many accountants, including these authors, to believe that it should be discontinued.

Agreements in Which Sales Returns Are Permitted by the Seller

FASB Standard 48, "Revenue Recognition When Right of Return Exists" (pars. 6 and 7) states the following (emphasis added):

> If an enterprise sells its product but gives the buyer the right to return the product, revenue from the sales transaction shall be **recognized at time of sale only if all of the following conditions are met:**
>
> **a.** The seller's price to the buyer is substantially fixed or determinable at the date of sale.
>
> **b.** The buyer has paid the seller, or the buyer is obligated to pay the seller and the obligation is not contingent on resale of the product.
>
> **c.** The buyer's obligation to the seller would not be changed in the event of theft or physical destruction or damage of the product.
>
> **d.** The buyer acquiring the product for resale has economic substance apart from that provided by the seller.
>
> **e.** The seller does not have significant obligations for future performance to directly bring about resale of the product by the buyer.
>
> **f.** The amount of future returns can be reasonably estimated.

When all of the above conditions are met, the realizability of the revenue is reasonably certain. Therefore, the **sales method** is appropriate because all of the revenue recognition "rules" are met. However, if one or more of the conditions are not met, the uncertainty of realizability is high; therefore, the sales method cannot be used. In this case, a variation of the installment method is used. This variation defers the sales revenue, cost of goods sold, and the gross margin to the period in which the return privilege has expired or the six conditions listed above are met.

To illustrate the accounting for sales when the purchaser has unlimited right of return and the sales method is **not** appropriate, consider the following case:

On September 30, 19A, Boston Corporation, a manufacturer, sold to retailers

50 units of a newly developed product at a unit price of $1,000. The product had a unit cost to Boston of $600; Boston used a perpetual inventory system. Because the product's marketability was uncertain, Boston sold the product for cash but gave the retailers the right to return the product for a cash refund until March 31, 19B. Boston had no basis for reliably estimating the quantity of returns. The accounting period ends December 31. On January 10, 19B, five units of the product were returned undamaged and the retailers were given credit for the returns. No other units were returned.

The entries related to this case are:

September 30, 19A, to record the initial sale:

Cash	50,000	
Sales revenue (50 units × $1,000)		50,000
Cost of goods sold	30,000	
Inventory (50 units × $600)		30,000

December 31, 19A, year-end entry to defer the gross margin:

Sales revenue	50,000	
Cost of goods sold		30,000
Deferred gross margin		20,000

Note: This method does not recognize gross margin as realized based on cash collection. This distinguishes it from the installment sales method. **Gross margin is recognized as realized under this method when *(a)* the return privilege expires or *(b)* the six conditions listed in *FASB Standard 48* are met.**

January 10, 19B, to record return of 5 units:

Inventory (5 units × $600)	3,000	
Deferred gross margin [5 units × ($1,000 − $600)]	2,000	
Cash		5,000

March 31, 19B, to record the sale on date of expiration of the return privilege:

Cost of goods sold (45 units × $600)	27,000	
Deferred gross margin ($20,000 − $2,000)	18,000	
Sales revenue (45 units × $1,000)		45,000

Note: This entry causes the income statement for 19B to show the following:

Sales revenue	$45,000
Cost of goods sold	27,000
Gross margin	$18,000

Cost Recovery Method

The **cost recovery method** sometimes is called the **sunk cost method.** All of the related costs incurred (i.e., the sunk costs) must be recovered before any revenue or gain is recognized. The cost recovery method should be used only for highly speculative transactions in which the **ultimate realization of revenue or gain** is completely unpredictable.

For example, an investor may purchase bonds for which the interest has been in default for a number of years (referred to as purchasing the bonds "flat"). Usually, the price of such bonds is a fraction of their maturity amount because of the low probability of realization of the principal and the interest revenue. Under the cost recovery method, collections of interest would not be recognized as revenue until the original investment cost is fully recovered. The amounts collected are credited to the **investment** account until its balance is zero. Collections subsequent to this point would be recognized in full as revenue or gain.

Revenue Recognition for Service Sales

This section reviews the four different methods of revenue recognition for **service sales:** (1) specific performance, (2) proportional performance, (3) completed performance, and (4) collection.

Specific Performance Method

The **specific performance method** is used to account for **service revenue** that is earned by performing a **single act.** For example, a real estate broker earns sales commission revenue on completion of a real estate transaction; a dentist earns dental service revenue on completion of surgery to remove a tooth; a laundry earns laundry service revenue on completion of the cleaning process.

FASB Standard 45, "Accounting for Franchise Fee Revenue," March 1981, deals with a particular case of service sales, franchises. It prescribes the specific performance method to account for franchise fee revenue, which the franchisor earns by selling a franchise to the franchisee. Often, it is difficult to determine the point at which the franchisor has "substantially performed" the service required to earn franchise fee revenue. In this regard, *FASB Standard 45* (par. 5) states (emphasis added):

> Franchise fee revenue from an individual franchise sale ordinarily shall be recognized, with an appropriate provision for estimated uncollectible amounts, when **all material services or conditions relating to the sale have been substantially performed or satisfied by the franchisor.** Substantial performance for the franchisor means that *(a)* the franchisor has no remaining obligation or intent . . . to refund any cash received . . . *(b)* substantially all of the initial services[11] of the franchisor required by the franchise agreement have been performed, and *(c)* no other material conditions or obligations related to the determination of substantial performance exist. . . . The commencement of operations by the franchisee shall be presumed to be the earliest point at which substantial performance has occurred.

The following example illustrates the specific performance method applied to franchise fee revenue. Assume that on April 1, 19A, Chicago Pizza Corporation

---

[11] *FASB Standard 45,* Appendix A, defines *initial service* as follows:

Common provisions of a franchise agreement in which the franchisor usually will agree to provide a variety of services and advice to the franchisee, such as the following:

a. Assistance in the selection of a site.
b. Assistance in obtaining facilities, including related financing and architectural and engineering services.
c. Assistance in advertising, either for the individual franchisee or as part of a general program.
d. Training of the franchisee's personnel.
e. Preparation and distribution of manuals and similar material concerning operations, administration, and record keeping.
f. Bookkeeping and advisory services, including setting up the franchisee's records and advising the franchisee about income, real estate, and other taxes or about local regulations affecting the franchisee's business.
g. Inspection, testing, and other quality control programs.

(franchisor) sold a franchise to Arthur Wilson (franchisee) for $20,000 cash and in addition received a note, which required five annual payments of $8,739, beginning on March 31, 19B. The note is based on an interest rate of 14% and had a present value of $30,000.

Case A—If there are no additional services to be performed by the franchisor and collectibility is reasonably assured, Chicago should make the following entry:

April 1, 19A, to record revenue:

Cash	20,000	
Note receivable	30,000	
Franchise fee revenue		50,000

Case B—If Chicago has additional services to perform for the franchisee, such as preparing the location of the new pizza restaurant, the entries for Chicago would be as follows (assuming that the costs of the services were $2,000, incurred in 19A):

April 1, 19A, to record the franchise sale and deferral of the revenue:

Cash	20,000	
Note receivable	30,000	
Deferred franchise fee revenue		50,000

During 19A, to record the cost of services provided by Chicago:

Prepaid expense, franchise services	2,000	
Cash		2,000

December 31, 19A, to accrue interest on the note receivable:

Interest receivable	3,150	
Interest revenue ($30,000 × 14% × 9/12)		3,150

February 1, 19B, to reflect the earned portion of the franchisor's fee revenue, assuming the franchise began operation on February 1, 19B:

Deferred franchise fee revenue	50,000	
Franchise service expense	2,000	
Franchise fee revenue		50,000
Prepaid expense, franchise services		2,000

In conformity with the matching principle, the 19A expenditures by the franchisor related to the franchise are deferred until the associated franchise fee revenue is recognized.

Proportional Performance Method

The **proportional performance method** is used to account for service revenue that is earned by **more than one performance act.** The proportional performance method is used only if performance of the service extends beyond one accounting period. Under this method, such revenue should be recognized based on the proportional performance of each act. The proportional performance method of accounting for service revenue is similar to the percentage-of-completion method (discussed previously). Proportional measurement of the service revenue is applied differently for different types of service transactions:

1. **Similar performance acts**—Recognize an **equal** amount of service revenue for each such act. Example: Processing of monthly mortgage payments by a mortgage banker.
2. **Dissimilar performance acts**—Recognize service revenue in proportion to the seller's direct costs to perform each act.[12] Example: Providing lessons, examinations, and grading by a correspondence school.
3. **Similar acts with a fixed period for performance**—Recognize service revenue by the **straight-line method over the fixed period** unless another method is more appropriate. Example: Providing maintenance services on equipment for a fixed periodic fee.

Completed Performance Method

The **completed performance method** is used to account for service revenue earned by performing a series of similar or dissimilar performance acts, the final act of which is so important in relation to the total service transaction that **service revenue can be considered earned only after the final act occurs.** For example, packing, loading, transporting, and delivery of freight by a trucking company earns service revenue only after delivery of the freight.

Collection Method

Under the **collection method,** revenue is recognized when **cash is collected.** The collection method is used to account for service revenue when the uncertainty is so high, or the estimates of expenses related to the revenues are so unreliable, that the requirement of reliability is not satisfied.

Expense Recognition

FASB Concepts 3 (par. 65) defines expenses as follows:

> Expenses are outflows or other using up of assets or incurrences of liabilities (or a combination of both) during a period from delivering or producing goods, rendering services, or carrying out other activities that constitute the entity's ongoing major or central operations.

After the revenue of the accounting period has been measured and recognized in conformity with the revenue principle, the **matching principle** is applied to measure and recognize the expenses of that period as the second step in the process of income recognition.

Matching Principle

The matching principle states that, for any reporting period, consistent with the recognition criteria, revenues should be determined in conformity with the revenue principle; then the expenses incurred in generating the revenue of the period should be recognized for that period.[13] The essence of the matching principle is that, as revenues are earned, certain assets are consumed (e.g.,

---

[12] If the direct cost of each act cannot be measured reliably, the total service sales revenue should be prorated to the various acts by the **relative sales value method.** If sales values cannot be identified with each act, the straight-line method to measure proportional performance should be used.

[13] Recognition of gains and losses is discussed in the section, "Recognition of Gains and Losses."

supplies) or sold (e.g., inventory) and services are used (e.g., salaries). The cost of those assets and services used up should be recognized and reported as expense of the period during which the related revenue is recognized (see Chapter 6).

FASB Concepts 5 (par. 86) categorizes expenses as follows:

a. **Direct Expenses**—Expenses, such as cost of goods sold, which are matched with revenues. These expenses are recognized based on recognition of revenues that result **directly** and **jointly** from the same transactions or other events as the expenses.
b. **Period Expenses**—Expenses such as selling and administrative salaries. These expenses are recognized **during the period** in which cash is spent or liabilities are incurred for goods and services that are used up either simultaneously with acquisition or soon after.
c. **Allocated Expenses**—Expenses such as depreciation and insurance. These expenses are **allocated** by systematic and rational procedures to the periods during which the related assets are expected to provide benefits.

Expenses Directly Related to Sales of Products or Services

Expenses Directly Related to the Sales of Products.

Expenses **directly** related to the sales of products during the period usually include the following:

1. Costs of materials and labor to manufacture, or the cost to purchase, inventory that is sold during the period (i.e., cost of goods sold).
2. Selling expenses, such as sales commissions, salaries, rent, and shipping costs.
3. Warranty expense on products sold.

Under the matching principle, expenses that are directly related to the sales of products should be recognized as expense during the reporting period in which the related sales revenue is recognized. For accounting purposes, certain expenses are difficult to classify in terms of the proximity of their relationship with sales revenue. For example, advertising and research and development (R&D) expenditures are made to enhance the marketability of a company's products. However, it is difficult to establish a direct causal link between those expenditures and specific revenues. Therefore, the allocation of such costs usually would be subjective. For this reason, GAAP requires that such costs be expensed as incurred.[14]

Expenses Directly Related to the Sales of Services.

Expenses directly related to the sales of services can be classified as follows:

1. **Initial direct costs**—costs that are directly associated with *(a)* negotiating and *(b)* consummating service transactions. These costs include commissions, legal fees, salespersons' compensation other than commissions, and nonsales employees' compensation that is applicable to negotiating and consummating service transactions.

---

[14] *FASB Standard 2* specifically requires that most R&D costs be expensed as incurred.

2. **Direct costs**—costs that have an identifiable causal effect on service sales. Examples include the cost of repair parts and service labor included as part of a service contract.

All **initial direct costs** and **direct costs** should be recognized as expense during the period in which the related service revenue is recognized under the **specific performance** and **completed performance methods** to attain an appropriate matching of revenues and expenses. Thus, initial direct costs and direct costs that are incurred prior to the recognition of revenue from performance of the service should be **deferred** as prepayments and expensed when the related service revenue is recognized.

For service revenue recognized under the **proportional performance method, initial direct costs** should be expensed as the related service revenue is recognized. However, **direct costs** should be expensed as incurred because of the high correlation between the amount of direct costs incurred and the service revenue recognized under the proportional performance method.

For service revenue recognized under the **collection method,** all initial direct costs and direct costs should be expensed as incurred.

Expenses *Not* Directly Related to Sales of Products or Services

Expenses not directly related to the sales of products or services include both **period** expenses and **allocated** expenses. Examples include: certain types of advertising expense, compensation that is applicable to the time spent in negotiating product or service transactions that are **not** consummated, general administrative expenses, depreciation expense, and amortization expense. Because no objective basis exists for relating period expenses to product or service sales revenue of the period, they should be expensed as they are incurred. Similarly, allocated expenses must be assigned to periods on a systematic and rational basis.

Recognition of Gains and Losses

Gains and losses (defined on page 569) result from peripheral or incidental transactions, events, and circumstances. Therefore, they are distinguished from revenues and expenses. **Most gains and losses are recognized when the related transaction is completed.** Thus, gains and losses from *(a)* disposal of operational assets, *(b)* sale of investments, *(c)* early extinguishment of debt, and *(d)* restructure of troubled debt are recognized in the specific entry made to record the completed transaction. For example, an entry to record the disposal of a tract of land for cash would reflect a debit to Cash, a credit to Land (for its recorded cost), and a debit to Loss (or credit to Gain) on Disposal.

Estimated losses, but **not gains,** are recognized prior to their ultimate realization. For example, **unrealized** losses on *(a)* write-downs of short-term investments to market value below cost, *(b)* disposal of a segment of the business, *(c)* pending litigation, and *(d)* expropriation of assets are recognized if they are both (1) probable and (2) can be reasonably estimated (*FASB Standard 5,* "Accounting for Contingencies," par. 8). If both conditions are not met, the nature and estimated amount of the contingent loss must be disclosed in a note to the financial statements (see the discussion on this topic in Chapter 14).

In contrast, gains usually are not recognized prior to the completion of a transaction that establishes the existence and amount of the gain [*FASB Standard 5*, par. 17(a)].[15] For example, in the case of a "probable," but as yet unrealized gain on disposal of a segment of the business, *APB Opinion 30* (par. 15) states, "If a gain is expected, it should be recognized when realized, which ordinarily is the disposal date." In some cases, potential gains may be disclosed in notes to the financial statements, provided the notes are written carefully to "avoid misleading implications as to the likelihood of realization" [*FASB Standard 5*, par. 17(b)].

A gain or loss may result from purely internal events, such as a change in accounting principle. Such gains and losses are recognized in the period when the change occurs.

In summary, accounting for gains and losses is influenced by conservatism. This often causes losses to be recognized prior to their actual incurrence, but prevents the recognition of gains prior to a completed transaction or event. *FASB Concepts 5* (par. 81) states:

> In assessing the prospect that as yet uncompleted transactions will be concluded successfully, a degree of skepticism is often warranted. Moreover, as a reaction to uncertainty, more stringent requirements historically have been imposed for recognizing revenues and gains than for recognizing expenses and losses, and those conservative reactions influence the guidance for applying the recognition criteria to components of earnings.

Because companies usually can control when to engage in transactions or events that give rise to gains or losses (e.g., disposal of investment securities, disposal of an unprofitable division of the business, early extinguishment of its debt, or a change in accounting principle), they exercise considerable latitude over the net income they report. This explains why GAAP contains relatively strict disclosure requirements for such gains and losses.

A Unique Problem—The Oil and Gas Industry

Oil and gas properties and the extraction of petroleum products present some unique accounting problems. Among these problems are *(a)* determining the cost of such properties when they are developed (not when purchased outright) and *(b)* depletion (which is complicated by statutory depletion for tax purposes). Because of the size and complexity of the industry and political influences in this industry, a wide range of accounting approaches has been used. Diversity in accounting was permitted on the basis of "industry peculiarities." Depletion was discussed in Chapter 11. The discussion to follow will focus on one aspect of accounting for depletion, that is, the cost of developing oil and gas properties. One major cost is **dry holes,** which do not produce revenue, but do involve "big-buck" expenditures for activities such as seismograph, leasing mineral rights, exploration, drilling, and abandonment. It is often said that dry holes do not produce revenue, they involve only "big-buck" expenditures. A basic

---

[15] The unrealized gain recognized on short-term investments that previously had been written down to a lower market value under the lower-of-cost-or-market (LCM) rule is limited to the amount of any previously recognized unrealized loss.

question arises about how the cost of dry holes should be accounted for—by expensing or capitalizing, or as a special loss. Two basic methods have evolved: *(a)* successful efforts and *(b)* full cost.

The basic distinction between these two methods is direct and simple. The question is how to account for the total cost of drilling a hole in the ground when a definitive determination has been made that it is a dry hole and will be abandoned. The alternative accounting methods for **total dry-hole** cost are as follows:

a. **Successful efforts**—total dry-hole cost is written off immediately as **expense.** Successful wells are not allocated any dry-hole costs. The basic argument for this method is that a known loss should not be capitalized.
b. **Full cost**—capitalize total dry-hole cost as additional cost of the successful wells, then deplete the dry-hole cost along with the other development costs of the successful wells. The basic argument for this method is that to find producing wells a search must be made; therefore, the search cost (which necessarily will involve some dry holes) is an integral part of the cost of the reserves found.

The distinction between the two methods can be illustrated with a highly simplified case as follows:

Summary accounts	Successful efforts		Full costing	
During exploration period (millions):				
Exploration cost (hole #13)*	10.0		10.0	
Cash and payable		10.0		10.0
* A "holding" cost account pending the next entry.				
Hole determined to be dry:				
Expense	10.0			
Productive properties (asset):			10.0	
Exploration costs (hole #13)		10.0		10.0
Depletion expense, year 1 (amount assumed):				
Depletion expense (hole #13)	0		.2	
Accumulated depletion		0		.2

For many years the advantages and disadvantages of these two methods were discussed, primarily within the petroleum industry. Most major companies used the successful efforts method because it was more conservative. In contrast, it is often asserted that newer and smaller companies used the full-cost method, primarily because it made both their statements of income and financial position look better regardless of their success/failure experience. The small companies argued that if they were required to use the successful efforts method, investors, looking at the companies early financial statements, would not be interested in investing. They also asserted that the major companies favored the successful efforts method because it would "shut out competition from new and small companies."

Due to increasing pressure from political and industry groups, the issue was considered by the FASB, SEC, and the Congress. The rulings have been notably inconsistent. *FASB Standard 19* (1977) specified that all companies should use the successful efforts method. The SEC procrastinated on acceptance of *Standard 19* because of fear that exploration efforts would be curtailed by the inability of the small producers to raise capital. During this period the Congress passed a bill that specifically permitted the optional use of either method. Finally, in 1978, the SEC issued three releases on the topic. These releases **proposed** a third method of accounting for all petroleum companies called **reserve recognition accounting** (RRA). This method would require each company to *(a)* **estimate** the quantity of its underground reserves, *(b)* place an estimated value on the estimated reserves, and *(c)* estimate how much the company probably will produce **each year** in the future. All of this information would be included in the annual financial statements. RRA received substantial criticism from the entire oil industry primarily on the basis that such guesswork would be neither reliable nor useful to financial statement users. As a result, in February 1981, the SEC announced that RRA was inappropriate and asked the FASB to *(a)* not reconsider the successful efforts and the full-costing methods and *(b)* develop disclosure guidelines to start in 1982. As a result, in November 1982, the FASB issued *Standard 69*, Disclosures about Oil and Gas Producing Activities. This statement requires note disclosure of the following information by publicly traded enterprises with significant oil and gas activities:

a. Proved oil and gas reserve quantities.
b. Capitalized costs relating to oil and gas producing activities.
c. Cost incurred in oil and gas property acquisition, exploration, and development activities.
d. Results of operations for oil and gas producing activities.
e. A standardized measure of discounted future net cash flows relating to proved oil and gas reserve quantities.

A company can elect to use, only on a continuing basis, either the successful efforts or full-cost method, however, under either method the company must satisfy the above disclosure requirement. A recent study about reporting in the oil and gas industry stated that:[16]

> The evidence demonstrates that the primary statements' net book value data are highly significant in explaining the market value of oil and gas properties. This measure dominates the supplementary valuation measures supplied in firms' footnotes, including the "standardized present value" measure. The evidence also clearly shows that the market distinguishes rationally between the successful efforts and the full cost accounting methods.

This brief overview of oil and gas accounting is appropriate for this book because there are critical issues about income measurement (recognition), statement of financial position reporting of oil and gas reserves, and disclosure. The above scenario presents a significant accounting issue that was neither settled by the profession (FASB), a governmental body (SEC), nor by the industry. It illustrates most emphatically the difficulty in establishing accounting "standards" when powerful interest groups, politicians, and regulatory agencies

---

[16] Travis A. Harris and James A. Ohlson, "Accounting Disclosures and the Market's Valuation of Oil and Gas Properties," *The Accounting Review*, October 1987, p. 651.

will not effectively agree on a responsible and viable position. Under these circumstances it is unlikely that a conceptual framework can have a definitive impact. However, a substantive and definitive conceptual framework of accounting should facilitate the inevitable political process in developing acceptable accounting approaches for difficult issues such as this one.

Summary

This chapter discussed income recognition which is a complex and controversial accounting issue. For many years the accounting profession has wrestled with income recognition, yet many of the controversial issues are not fully resolved. Income recognition directly involves defining and specifying how revenues, expenses, gains, and losses should be measured, recorded, and reported. This involves accrual accounting because both the amounts and timing issues must be resolved. Revenues should be recognized when there is a completed transaction and an earnings process is essentially completed. Costs should be recognized when incurred and matched as expenses with the periodic revenues recognized by measuring the assets or services used to earn those revenues. Some expenses are directly traceable to the revenues of a specific period. Other costs are indirectly related to revenues which means that costs must be allocated as expense to accounting periods (e.g., depreciation), and still others have no relationship to periodic revenues (e.g., contributions to charitable organizations). Therefore, they are recognized and reported in the period in which incurred.

Measurements of the amounts of revenues and expenses also are related to the definitions of assets and liabilities because *(a)* revenues can be earned only if assets are increased or liabilities are decreased, and *(b)* expenses are incurred only if assets are decreased or liabilities are increased.

This chapter discussed revenues and expenses that pose special measurement and recognition problems, such as long-term construction contracts, installment sales, service sales, and gains and losses. These special cases involve adaptations of the normal recognition principles.

QUESTIONS

1. Explain the relationship between income recognition and the definitions of assets and liabilities.
2. In consideration of income recognition, explain the implications of articulation and nonarticulation between the statement of income and statement of financial position.
3. Explain the cash basis and accrual basis of accounting. Explain why accounting uses the accrual basis.
4. What are the four fundamental criteria for recognition identified in *FASB Concepts 5*? What are the constraints on recognition?
5. Why may the criterion of reliability affect the timing of recognition?
6. What do the terms **realization** and **earned** mean in the context of revenue recognition?
7. Give two typical examples of revenues for which recognition occurs on the basis of the passage of time.

8. When is sales revenue recognized under the sales method?
9. A three-year $360 subscription to a business periodical is paid and delivery of the magazine starts immediately. When should the publishing company recognize this revenue?
10. Explain why accretion (i.e., a natural increase in value of a natural resource, such as growing of timber) is not accepted as a basis of recognizing revenue?
11. When is revenue first recognized, assuming the
    a. Completed contract method?
    b. Cost recovery method?
    c. Percentage-of-completion method?
12. Explain the basic differences between the two acceptable methods of accounting for long-term construction contracts.
13. Why is the ending inventory of construction in process different in amount when the percentage-of-completion method is used compared with the completed contract method? How much different will the amount be?
14. Whan a loss is projected on a long-term construction contract, in what period(s) is the loss recognized under *(a)* percentage-of-completion and *(b)* completed contract methods of accounting for long-term construction projects?
15. Under what circumstances is the installment method of recognizing revenue acceptable?
16. Describe the cost recovery method of recognizing revenue. When is it appropriate?
17. Distinguish between the specific performance method, the proportional performance method, the completed performance method, and the collection method of recognizing revenue associated with service sales.
18. Give a definition of expense. Provide three broad categories of expense.
19. What special characteristic distinguishes gains and losses from revenues and expenses?
20. Explain the three methods that have been used to report dry-holes costs by the petroleum industry. What does GAAP permit, or require, currently?

EXERCISES

Exercises 13–1 to 13–12

E 13–1 **(Revenue Principle; Special Applications)**
This exercise focuses on the revenue principle. Respond to each of the following:

a. Give a definition of revenue.
b. What should be the dollar amount of revenue recognized under the revenue principle in the case of (1) product sales and services for cash and (2) product sales and services rendered in exchange for noncash considerations?
c. How should revenue be recognized when there is a highly speculative transaction involving potential revenue that cannot be reliably estimated?
d. When should revenue be recognized in the case of long-term, low down payment sales, for which collectibility is very uncertain?
e. When should revenue be recognized for long-term construction contracts?

E 13–2 (Review of Definitions of Elements of Financial Statements)
Listed below are the seven elements of financial statements. Next are key phrases from each definition. Match the key phrases with the elements by entering one letter in each blank.

Elements: A—Revenues; B—Expenses; C—Gains; D—Losses; E—Assets; F—Liabilities; G—Equity.

Key Phrases

_____ 1. Residual interest.
_____ 2. Decreases in net assets; peripheral or incidental transactions.
_____ 3. Enhancement of assets; ongoing major or central operations.
_____ 4. Future sacrifices of economic benefits; results from past transactions or events.
_____ 5. Increases in net assets; peripheral or incidental transactions.
_____ 6. Using assets; incurring debts; ongoing major or central operations.
_____ 7. Future economic benefits; results from past transactions or events.

E 13–3 (Overview of Recognition Criteria; FASB)
Listed below are the four recognition criteria given in *FASB Concepts 5*. Next are key phrases from each definition. Match the key phrases with the criteria by entering one letter in each blank.

Criteria: A—Definitions; B—Measurability; C—Relevance; D—Reliability.

Key Phrases

_____ 1. Representationally faithful; neutral; verifiable.
_____ 2. Elements of financial statements.
_____ 3. Capable of making a difference in decisions.
_____ 4. Quantifiable; sufficient reliability.

E 13–4 (Revenue Recognition; Four Special Cases; Amounts and Explanation)
York Company has been involved in several transactions that required careful interpretation of the revenue principle. For each of the following 19B transactions: (1) specify the amount of revenue that should be recognized during 19B and (2) explain the basis for your answer.

a. Regular credit sales amounted to $250,000, of which two thirds was collected by the end of 19B; the balance will be collected in 19C.

b. Regular services were rendered on credit amounting to $190,000, of which three fourths will be collected in 19C.

c. An item that had been repossessed from the first purchaser was sold again for $5,000. A $3,000 cash down payment was received in 19B. The balance is to be paid on a quarterly basis during 19C and 19D. Repossession again would not be a surprise!

d. On January 1, 19A, the company purchased a $10,000 note as a speculative investment. Because the collectibility of the note was highly speculative, the company was able to acquire it for $1,000 cash. The note specifies 8% simple interest payable each year (disregard interest prior to 19A). The first collection on the note was $1,500 cash on December 31, 19B. Further collections are highly speculative.

E 13–5 (Revenue Recognition; Three Cases; Entries and Reporting).
Three independent cases are given below for 19A. The accounting period ends December 31.

Case A

On December 31, 19A, XT Sales Company sold a special machine (Serial No. 1713) for $100,000 and collected $40,000 cash. The remainder plus 10% interest is payable December 31, 19B. XT Company will deliver the machine on January 5, 19B. The buyer has an excellent credit rating.

Case B

On November 15, 19A, VR Company sold product X for $500. The buyer will pay for the product with two units of its own merchandise. The buyer promised to deliver the merchandise around January 31, 19B.

Case C

On January 2, 19A, RS Publishing Company collected $900 cash for a three-year subscription to a monthly *Investors Stock and Bond Advisory*. The March 19A, issue will be the first one mailed.

Required:

For each case give *(a)* any entry that should be made on the transaction date, *(b)* the revenue recognition method that should be used, and *(c)* an explanation of the reasoning for your responses to *(a)* and *(b)*.

E 13–6 (Percentage Completion; Analysis of Criteria)

It has been argued that before the percentage-of-completion method can be used properly, the following criteria must be met:

1. There is a written contract executed by buyer and seller that clearly specifies what is to be provided and received, the consideration to be exchanged, and manner and terms of settlement.
2. The buyer can satisfy obligations under the contract.
3. The seller has the ability to perform the contractual obligations.
4. The seller can estimate reliably both the cost to complete and the percentage of completion of the contract.
5. The seller has a cost accounting system that adequately accumulates and allocates cost to final cost objectives in a manner consistent with the estimating process.

Required:

1. Are the foregoing criteria adequate? What, if anything, would you add or delete?
2. Is criterion 4 concerning the ability to estimate cost to complete consistent with the quality of reliability?

E 13–7 (Completed Contract, Percentage Completion Compared; Entries)

Watson Construction Company contracted to build a plant for $500,000. Construction started in January 19A and was completed in November 19B. Data relating to the contract are summarized below:

	19A	19B
Costs incurred during year	$290,000	$120,000
Estimated additional costs to complete	125,000	
Billings during year	270,000	230,000
Cash collections during year	250,000	250,000

Required:

Give the journal entries for Watson in parallel columns, assuming *(a)* the completed contract method and *(b)* the percentage-of-completion method. Apportion on the basis of costs incurred to date to total estimated construction costs.

E 13–8 (Continuation of E 13–7; Financial Statements; Can Be Assigned Separately or Jointly)
Use the data given in E 13–7 to complete the following schedule:

	Completed contract method	Percentage-of-completion method*
Statement of income:		
Income:		
19A	$_____	$_____
19B	_____	_____
Statement of financial position:		
Receivables:		
19A	_____	_____
19B	_____	_____
Inventory—construction in process, net of billings:		
19A	_____	_____
19B	_____	_____

* Apportion on basis of costs incurred to date compared to total estimated construction costs.

E 13–9 (Percentage Completion and Completed Contract Compared; Analysis of Account Balances)
Mullen Construction Company contracted to build a municipal warehouse for the city of Dallas for $750,000. The contract specified that the city would pay Mullen each month the progress billings, less 10%, which was to be held as a "reserve." At the end of the construction, the final payment is to include the reserve. Each billing, less the 10% reserve, must be paid within 10 days after submission of a billing to the city.

Transactions relating to the contract are summarized below:

19A—Construction costs incurred during the year, $200,000; estimated costs to complete, $400,000; progress billings, $190,000; and collections per the contract.
19B—Construction costs incurred during the year, $350,000; estimated costs to complete, $115,000; progress billings, $280,000; and collections per the contract.
19C—Construction costs incurred during the year, $100,000. The remaining billings were submitted by October 1 and final collections completed on November 30.

Required:
1. Complete the following schedule:

Year	Method	Income recognized	Receivable ending balance	Construction in process inventory ending balance	Costs in excess of billings ending balance
19A	Completed contract				
	Percentage of completion*				
19B	Completed contract				
	Percentage of completion*				
19C	Completed contract				
	Percentage of completion				

* Apportion on basis of costs incurred to date compared to total estimated construction costs.

2. Explain what causes the ending balance in construction in process to be different for the two methods.
3. Which method would you recommend for this contractor? Why?

E 13–10 (Installment Sales Method; Entries)
Barr Corporation had credit sales of $55,000 in 19A that required use of the installment method. Barr's cost of the merchandise sold was $44,000. Barr collected cash of $25,000

and $30,000 related to the installment sales in 19A and 19B, respectively. The perpetual inventory system is used.

Required:
1. Give journal entries related to the installment sales for 19A and 19B.
2. Give the ending 19A balances (before the closing entries) in the following accounts: Installment Accounts Receivable; Installment Sales Revenue; Cost of Installment Sales; Deferred Gross Margin on Installment Sales; and Realized Gross Margin.

E 13–11 **(Unconditional Right of Return; Entries)**
McLaughlin Corporation developed a new product in 19A. To increase acceptance by retailers, McLaughlin sold the product to retailers with an unconditional right of return, which expires on February 1, 19B. McLaughlin has no basis for estimating returns on the new product. The following information is available regarding the product:

Sales—19A	$180,000
Cost of goods sold—19A	120,000
Returns—19A	12,000 (cost, $8,000)
Returns—January, 19B	15,000 (cost, $10,000)

All sales are on credit. Cash collections related to the sales were $40,000 in 19A and $113,000 in 19B. McLaughlin uses the perpetual inventory system.

Required:
Give journal entries for sales, returns, and collections related to the new product. The closing or reversing entries are not required. How much sales revenue should McLaughlin recognize in 19A?

E 13–12 **(Cost Recovery Method; Investment in Obsolete Inventory)**
Tony Company has an inventory of obsolete products that it formerly stocked for sale. Efforts to dispose of this inventory by selling the products at low prices have not been successful. At the end of the prior year (19A) the company reduced the value to a conservative estimate of net realizable value of $22,000. On March 1, 19B, Watson Trading Company purchased this entire inventory for $10,000 cash as a speculative investment. Watson hopes to be able to dispose of it in some foreign markets for approximately $30,000. However, prior to purchase Watson concluded that there was no reliable way to estimate the probable profitability in the venture. Therefore, Watson decided to use the cost recovery method. Subsequently, cash sales have been: 19B, $4,000; 19C, $5,000; and 19D, $8,000. Approximately 12% of the inventory remains on hand at the start of 19E.

Required:
Give the 19B, C, and D entries for Watson Trading Company.

PROBLEMS

Problems 13–1 to 13–9

P 13–1 **(LT Construction; Percentage Completion; Entries; Reporting)**
Honaker Company contracted to construct a building for $975,000. The contract provided for progress payments. Honaker's accounting year ends December 31. Work began under

the contract on July 1, 19A, and was completed on September 30, 19C. Construction activities are summarized below by year:

19A—Construction costs incurred during the year, $180,000; estimated costs to complete, $630,000; progress billings during the year, $153,000; and collections, $140,000.
19B—Construction costs incurred during the year, $450,000; estimated costs to complete, $190,000; progress billings during the year, $382,500; and collections, $380,000.
19C—Construction costs incurred during the year, $195,000. Because the contract was completed, the remaining balance was billed and later collected in full per the contract.

Required:

1. Give the contractor's entries assuming the percentage-of-completion method is used. Show computation of income apportionment on a cost basis assuming percentage of completion is measured by the ratio of costs incurred to date to total estimated construction costs.
2. Prepare statement of income and statement of financial position presentations for this contract by year assuming the percentage-of-completion method.
3. Prepare statement of income and statement of financial position presentations by year assuming the completed contract method. For each amount that is different from the corresponding amount in (2) above, explain the reason.
4. Which method would you recommend to this contractor? Why?

P 13–2 (LT Construction, Methods Compared; Entries; Reporting)
Moody Corporation contracted to construct an office building for Mitchell Company for $1 million. Construction began on January 15, 19A, and was completed on December 1, 19B. Moody's accounting year ends December 31. Transactions by Moody relating to the contract are summarized below:

	19A	19B
Costs incurred to date	$500,000	$ 850,000
Estimated costs to complete	320,000	
Progress billings to date	410,000	1,000,000
Progress collections to date	375,000	1,000,000

Required:

1. In parallel columns, give the entries on the contractor's books assuming *(a)* the completed contract method and *(b)* the percentage-of-completion method. Assume percentage of completion is measured by the ratio of costs incurred to date to total estimated construction costs.
2. For each method, prepare the statement of income and statement of financial position presentations for this contract by year.
3. What is the nature of the item "Costs in excess of billings" that appears on the statement of financial position?
4. Which method would you recommend the contractor use? Why?

P 13–3 (Accounting for Installment Sales; Entries)
Mark Corporation made a number of sales in 19A and 19B that required use of the installment method. The following information regarding the sales is available:

	19A	19B	19C
Installment sales	$200,000	$150,000	$ -0-
Cost of installment sales	160,000	112,500	-0-
Collections on 19A sales	20,000	50,000	60,000
Collections on 19B sales		30,000	75,000

Mark uses a perpetual inventory system.

Required:

1. Give journal entries relating to installment sales for the years 19A to 19C.
2. What is the year-end balance in Installment Accounts Receivable (net of any deferred gross margin) for 19A, 19B, and 19C?
3. If the sales qualified for application of the sales method, what amounts of gross margin would Mark report in 19A, 19B, and 19C?

P 13–4 (Installment Sales Method; Entries and Reporting)

Ohio Retail Company sells goods for cash, on normal credit (2/10; n/30). However, on July 1, 19A, the company sold a used computer for $2,200; the perpetual inventory carrying value was $440. The company collected $200 cash and agreed to let the customer make payments on the $2,000 whenever possible during the next 12 months. The company management stated that it has no reliable basis for estimating the probability of default. The following additional data are available: *(a)* collections on the installment receivable during 19A, $300 and during 19B, $200, and *(b)* on December 1, 19B, repossessed the computer (estimated net realizable value, $700).

Required:

1. Give the required entries for 19A and 19B assuming the installment method is used.
2. Give the balances in the following accounts that would be reported on the 19A and 19B statements of income and financial position: Realized Gross Margin on Installment Sales, Gain (loss) on Repossession, Installment Accounts Receivable, and Inventory of Used Computers.

P 13–5 (Accounting for a Franchise; Entries)

On October 1, 19A, Baker Donut Shops, Inc. (a franchisor), sold a franchise to James Johnson. Under the terms of the sale, Johnson paid $20,000 in cash and issued a note payable in four equal annual installments of $10,000 beginning on October 1, 19B. The note payments were based on a 12% interest rate. In return, Baker agreed to locate a suitable site for the franchise and assist in training personnel for the donut shop.

A site was located on December 15, 19A, at a cost to Baker of $3,000. Training of Johnson's personnel cost Baker $5,000 and was completed on February 1, 19B. The franchise began operation on February 15, 19B.

Required:

Give journal entries for Baker associated with the franchise sale for 19A and 19B.

P 13–6 (Cost Recovery Method; Obsolete Inventory)

Saxon Department Store has accumulated a stock of obsolete merchandise that it formerly sold. Routine efforts have been made to dispose of it at a low "reasonable" price. This merchandise originally cost $60,000 and was marked to sell for $132,000. The management decided to set up a special location in the basement to display and hopefully sell this stock starting in January 19B. All items will be marked to sell at a cash price which is 30% of the original marked selling price. On December 31, 19A, the company accountant transferred the purchase cost to a perpetual inventory account called, "Inventory, Obsolete Merchandise" at 30% of its purchase cost, which approximates estimated net realizable value. The management knows that a reliable estimate of the probable sales cannot be made. Therefore, the cost recovery method will be used. Subsequent sales were: 19B, $9,000; 19C, $7,000; and in 19D, the remaining merchandise was sold for $8,000.

Required:

Give the entries that Saxon should make for 19A through 19D.

P 13–7 (Revenue Recognition; Proportional Performance)

Jones and Wilson, a professional corporation, contracted to provide legal services for Brown Company. The contract specified a lump-sum payment of $60,000 on November 15, 19A. Assume that Jones and Wilson can reliably estimate future direct costs associated with the contract. The following services were performed based on the estimate by Jones and Wilson:

	Direct costs	Date completed
Research potential lawsuit	$ 5,000	December 15, 19A
Prepare and file documents	15,000	March 1, 19B
Serve as Brown's counsel during legal proceedings	15,000	October 15, 19B

Required:

1. What method of revenue recognition is appropriate for Jones and Wilson? Explain.
2. Give entries to recognize revenues related to this contract for Jones and Wilson.

P 13–8 (Recognizing and Matching Expenses with Revenue)

The general ledger of Airtime, Inc., a corporation engaged in the development and production of television programs for commercial sponsorship, contains the following asset accounts before amortization at the end of 19A:

Account	Balance (debit)
"Sealing Wax and Kings"	$75,000
"The Messenger"	36,000
"The Desperado"	19,000
"Shin Bone"	8,000
"Studio Rearrangement"	7,000

An examination of contracts and records revealed the following information:

a. The first two accounts listed above represent the total cost of completed programs that were televised during 19A. Under the terms of an existing contract, "Sealing Wax and Kings" will be rerun during 19B at a fee equal to 60% of the fee for the first televising of the program. The contract for the first run produced $300,000 of revenue. The contract with the sponsor of "The Messenger" provides that at the sponsor's option, the program can be rerun during the 19B season at a fee of 75% of the fee for the first televising of the program. There are no present indications that it will be rerun.

b. The balance in "The Desperado" account is the cost of a new program that has just been completed and is being considered by several companies for commercial sponsorship.

c. The balance in the "Shin Bone" account represents the cost of a partially completed program for a projected series that has been abandoned.

d. The balance of the "Studio Rearrangement" account consists of payments made to a firm of engineers that prepared a report relative to the more efficient utilization of existing studio space and equipment.

Required:

1. State the general principle (or principles) of accounting that are applicable to the first four accounts.
2. How would you report each of the first four accounts in the financial statements of Airtime? Explain.
3. In what way, if at all, does the "Studio Rearrangement" account differ from the first four? Explain.

(AICPA adapted)

P 13–9 (Matching Expense with Revenue)

Ogden Publishing Company prepares and publishes a monthly newsletter for an industry in which potential circulation is limited. Because information provided by the newsletter is available only on a piecemeal basis from other sources and because no advertising is carried, the subscription price for the newsletter is relatively high. Ogden recently engaged in a campaign to increase circulation that involved extensive use of person-to-person long-distance telephone calls to research directors of nonsubscriber companies in the industry. The telephone cost of the campaign was $38,000, and salary payments to persons who made the calls amounted to $51,000.

As a direct result of the campaign, new one-year subscriptions at $175 each generated revenue of $164,500. New three-year subscriptions at $450 each generated revenue of $324,000, and new five-year subscriptions at $625 generated $157,500. Cancellations are rare, but when they occur, refunds are made on a half-rate basis (e.g., if a subscriber has yet to receive $100 worth of newsletters, $50 is refunded).

Aside from the two direct costs of the campaign cited above, indirect costs, consisting of such items as allocated office space, fringe benefit costs for employees making telephone calls, and supervision amounted to $21,000.

Required:

1. Identify the specific accounting issues involved for Ogden and, for each issue, give the accounting principles that are important in resolving that issue.
2. Assume the campaign was begun and concluded in May, new subscriptions begin with the July issue of the monthly newsletter, and the company's accounting year ends December 31. How should costs of the campaign be allocated among current and future accounting years? Show calculations.

CASES

C 13–1 (Deferral of Revenue; Analysis)

On July 27, 19E, the Federal Power Commission (FPC) issued a ruling raising the ceiling price on regulated (interstate) gas, but with a "vintaging" system. Gas suppliers could charge $1.42 per thousand cubic feet on "new gas" drilled after January 1, 19C, and $1.01 on gas drilled between January 1, 19A, and December 31, 19B. The old price had been 52 cents per thousand cubic feet and remained there for all "old" gas (i.e., pre-19A gas). The FPC soon reduced the $1.01 rate to 93 cents and retained the $1.42 rate. As a result of a lawsuit against the FPC seeking a rollback to the old 52-cent rate, a Circuit Court of Appeals decided gas supplies should go ahead and collect the higher prices provided they would agree to refund the money if the final decision went against the FPC.

Required:

1. If you were part of management of a gas supplier at the time of the Circuit Court decision, what position would you take with respect to recognition of the extra amounts of revenue from the sale of "new" gas? Give reasons for whatever position you take.
2. Disregard the answer you gave to (1) above. If the revenue is deferred, how would it be accounted for until a final court decision is rendered? How would the deferred revenue be recognized if the final court decision is delayed until a new accounting year and then is favorable?

C 13–2 (Magazine Subscriptions Collected in Advance; Analysis)

At a meeting of the board of directors of Vanguard Publishing Company, where you are the controller, a new director expressed surprise that the company's statement of income reflects that an equal proportion of revenue is earned with the publication of each issue of the magazines the company publishes. This director believes that the most important event in the sale of magazines is the collection of cash on the subscriptions and expresses the view that the company's practice smooths its income and that its subscription revenue actually is earned as subscriptions are collected.

Required:

Discuss the propriety of timing the recognition of revenue on the basis of:

a. Cash collections on subscriptions.
b. Number of magazines delivered each month.
c. Both events, by recognizing part of the revenue with cash collections of subscriptions and part with delivery of the magazines to subscribers.

(AICPA adapted)

C 13–3 (Liberalism versus Conservatism in Using Accounting Practices)

Two associates, Tom, an accountant, and Jerry, an engineer, are discussing the role of accounting in managing an enterprise and reporting on its operating results. Jerry argues, "When things are so-so or are going badly, the management uses current accounting practices to portray the picture reasonably accurately, but when things are going well, these practices are applied either liberally or conservatively to the extent that a company sometimes fails to tell the true story." You join their discussion.

Required:

1. Cite some specifics that support Jerry's general line of argument.
2. How can you and Tom respond to justify current accounting practices in good times as well as bad?

14 SHORT-TERM LIABILITIES

OVERVIEW AND PURPOSE

This chapter discusses short-term liabilities. Long-term liabilities are discussed in Chapter 15. Short-term liabilities are paid with current assets. The primary issues in accounting for short-term liabilities involve (1) measurement of the amount of each such liability, (2) determination of the date that a short-term liability should be recognized, (3) measurement and recognition of interest expense and interest payable, and (4) appropriate reporting, including supplementary disclosures. Investors and creditors need information about short-term debts and the timing of the related cash flows.

The purpose of this chapter is to present the basic concepts involved in measuring, recording, and reporting of current liabilities.

To accomplish this purpose, the chapter is organized as follows:

1. Conceptual characteristics of liabilities.
2. Current liabilities defined, discussed, and illustrated.
3. Short-term obligations expected to be refinanced.
4. Contingencies and estimated liabilities.

Conceptual Characteristics of Liabilities

FASB Statements of Financial Accounting Concepts No. 6 defines liabilities as **"probable future sacrifices of economic benefits arising from present obligations of a particular entity to transfer assets or provide services to other entities in the future as a result of past transactions or events."** Liabilities do not represent an ownership interest in the debtor entity.

When a liability is incurred in conformity with the definition given above, it should be immediately recognized (i.e., recorded). The FASB definition of a liability is very important because it is specific and makes essential distinctions about what a debt really is. Prior to *FASB Concepts No. 6*, the accounting definition of a debt was vague. The amount of a liability conceptually should be **measured** as the **present value** of all future cash payments (or the cash equivalent of noncash assets and services), discounted at an interest rate consistent with the risks involved. A liability involves *(a)* a **principal** amount that is subject to interest, whether specified or not, and *(b)* **interest** on the principal amount, which is incurred as time passes (i.e., the time value of money, discussed in Chapter 5).

Accounting recognition of a liability should be on date of incurrence. The transaction that creates a liability usually identifies the date when the obligation comes into existence. However, the recognition date of a liability is not always clear cut, such as in the case of an injury to an employee, or outsider, when the final determination of whether a liability exists depends on the legal decision of a court of law.[1]

Measurement of the amount of a liability sometimes is difficult. The transaction that creates a liability usually provides the basis for measuring its amount. Measuring the amount of a liability (i.e., the amount of the credit to a liability account) is directly related to its **cause.** The cause is reflected as a debit to (1) an asset; (2) another liability; (3) retained earnings (i.e., cash or property dividends declared); (4) an expense; (5) a loss; or (6) revenue collected in advance. For example, when an asset is acquired on credit, the asset and related liability are recognized at cost under the **cost principle** because the cost of the asset received measures the amount of the liability. Sometimes, the relationship between the "cost" of the asset and the valuation of the liability is not so clear cut. Assume a company acquired a machine and promised to pay the quoted price (a single amount) of $10,000 at the end of one year from date of purchase, with no separate interest payments specified. What is the amount of the liability and the cost of the machine? The amount of the liability, and the cost of the asset, should be **measured** as the present value of the future cash payment. If the market interest rate for this level of risk is 15%, the present value (i.e., cost of the asset) would be:

$$\$10{,}000^{*} \times p_{n=1;\,i=15\%} \text{ (Table 5–2, .86957)} = \underline{\underline{\$8{,}696}} \text{ (rounded)}$$

* Includes implicit interest.

The indicated journal entries are as follows:

---

[1] From an **auditing** standpoint, **identification** of existing liabilities is a critical problem because many liabilities are easy to hide or overlook.

Purchase date:

Machine	8,696	
Note payable, 15% (face, $10,000)		8,696

Payment date:

Note payable ($10,000 − $1,304)	8,696	
Interest expense ($8,696 × 15%)	1,304	
Cash		10,000

Regarding interest on short-term liabilities (particularly those involving accrued liabilities and accounts payable of one to three months), implicit interest sometimes is not separately recognized in accounting. This is in conformity with the provisions of *APB Opinion 21* (par. 3a) that the requirement to separately account for interest does not apply to "receivables and payables arising from transactions with customers or suppliers in the normal course of business which are due in customary trade terms not exceeding approximately one year." This rule applies the materiality and cost-benefit constraints discussed in Chapter 6.

Liabilities usually are measured, recorded (i.e., recognized), and reported at their maturity amount because *(a)* the cost of the asset received and the maturity amount of the liability coincide, and *(b)* the stated interest rate on the liability is the same as its true yield or effective interest rate. This means that when the stated and effective rates are the same, the maturity amount and the present value of the liability are the same. Aside from the **materiality and cost-benefit constraints** noted above for some short-term liabilities, they should be recorded and reported at their present value at date of acquisition.

Although exchange transactions usually establish the amount and maturity date of a liability, in some situations a definite liability is known to exist, or it is probable that one exists, but the exact amount and/or the maturity date are not known precisely. Therefore, one section of this chapter discusses the recording and reporting of estimated liabilities and loss contingencies.

Current Liabilities Defined

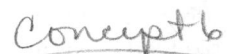

Current (i.e., short-term) liabilities are defined as "obligations whose liquidation is reasonably expected to require the use of existing resources properly classifiable as current assets, or the creation of other current liabilities."[2] Recall that current assets are those assets that are expected to be converted to cash or used in normal operations during the operating cycle of the business,[3] or one year from the balance date, whichever is longer. Because of the association between current assets and current liabilities, the time dimension that applies to current assets also applies to current liabilities. Liabilities that do not conform to this

[2] AICPA, *Accounting Research Bulletin 43,* "Restatement and Revision of Accounting Research Bulletins" (New York, 1961), chap. 3, par. 7.

[3] The normal operating cycle of a business is the average period of time between the expenditure of cash for goods and services and the time that those goods and services are converted back to cash. This cash-to-cash cycle is illustrated by the following sequence: cash expenditure, to inventory, to sale, to accounts receivable, and back to cash.

definition are called **long-term,** or noncurrent, liabilities (discussed in Chapter 15).

The usual types of current liabilities are as follows:

a. Accounts payable.
b. Short-term notes payable.
c. Cash and property dividends payable.
d. Advances and returnable deposits.
e. Accrued liabilities related to expenses.
f. Deferred revenues (i.e., revenues collected in advance).
g. Taxes (income, sales, property, and payroll).
h. Compensated-absence liabilities.
i. Current maturities of long-term debt.
j. Obligations callable on demand by the creditor.

Special accounting problems related to these current liabilities are discussed in the following sections.

Accounts Payable

Accounts payable—more descriptively, **trade accounts payable**—is a designation for recurring **trade** obligations. These obligations arise from the entity's ongoing or central operations, such as the acquisition of merchandise, materials, supplies, and services used in the production and/or sale of goods or services. Current payables not conforming to this definition should be reported separately from accounts payable (e.g., income tax payable and current payments on long-term debt).

Short-Term Notes Payable

A short-term note may be a *(a)* **trade note payable** that arises from the same source as an account payable, or *(b)* **nontrade note** payable that arises from some other source, or *(c)* current maturity of a long-term liability, which arises when the next payment on such a debt will be **made out of current assets.** A short-term note may be either *(a)* **secured,** if supported by a mortgage that specifies particular assets pledged as security or *(b)* **unsecured,** if the creditor's repayment is based on the general creditworthiness of the debtor. Disclosure for a secured note payable should include a disclosure note explaining the primary terms of the debt agreement, including the identity of any pledged assets. Finally, a note payable may be designated as either *(a)* interest-bearing or *(b)* noninterest-bearing.

From both the economic and accounting views, **all commercial debt instruments either implicitly or explicitly require the debtor to pay interest.** This is because the cost of using money over time cannot be avoided—it always represents some sacrifice. The amount of periodic interest on a debt can be calculated as follows:

$$\text{Principal amount} \times \text{Interest rate} \times \text{Time} = \text{Interest amount}$$

The **stated** rate of interest is the interest rate specified on the debt; it is used to determine the amount of **cash** interest that will be paid on the **principal** amount of the debt. In contrast, the **effective** or yield interest rate on a debt is the true (i.e., market) interest rate based on the actual cash, or cash-equivalent, amount that was borrowed. The effective rate is used to discount the future cash payments on a debt to the cash equivalent borrowed (i.e., the principal). The **principal** amount of a debt is the cash or cash equivalent amount borrowed (i.e., received by the debtor). It is also the amount that is subject to effective interest. The face amount of a debt is the amount specified on the debt instrument; it may be the same as, or different from, the principal amount. The maturity amount of a debt is the amount to be paid on the maturity date, excluding any **separate** interest payments due on that date. Maturity value is the total amount (face plus interest) payable on the due date of the note.

Interest-Bearing Notes. Interest-bearing notes specify the principal amount of the note as the face amount. In addition, the note specifies a stated rate of interest on the principal amount. For an interest-bearing note, the debtor receives cash, other assets, or services equal to the face (i.e., principal) amount and pays back that principal plus interest at the stated rate on one or more interest dates. Under these conditions, the stated and effective or yield rates are the same (this is the usual case).

To illustrate an interest-bearing note, assume that on October 1, 19A, XY Company borrowed $10,000 cash on a one-year note payable, 12% interest (payable at maturity date). XY Company received cash equal to the face amount of the note, $10,000.[4] The accounting year ends December 31, and the maturity date of the note is September 30, 19B. This transaction requires the following accounting and reporting:

Entries during 19A:

October 1, 19A—To record the interest-bearing note at its present value:

Cash	10,000	
Note payable, short term		10,000

December 31, 19A—Adjusting entry for accrued interest:

Interest expense ($10,000 × 12% × 3/12)	300	
Interest payable		300

Reporting at December 31, 19A—Interest-bearing note payable:

Statement of income:	
Interest expense	$ 300
Statement of financial position:	
Current liabilities:	
Note payable, short term	10,000
Interest payable	300

[4] It may be useful to demonstrate that under the conditions specified the present value of this interest-bearing note will be equal to the cash borrowed as well as the principal, face, and maturity amounts of the debt:

Principal: $10,000 × $p_{n=1;i=12\%}$. (Table 5–2, .89286) =	$ 8,929
Interest: $1,200 × $P_{o_{n=1;i=12\%}}$. (Table 5–4, .89286) =	1,071
Total present value	$10,000

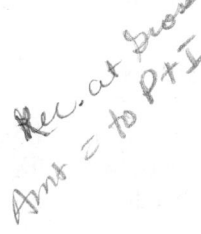

Entry at maturity date:

September 30, 19B—Payment of face amount plus interest at maturity (assuming no reversing entry was made on January 1, 19B):

Interest payable	300	
Interest expense ($10,000 × 12% × 9/12)	900	
Note payable, short term	10,000	
Cash		11,200

Noninterest-Bearing Notes. Noninterest bearing is not a descriptive designation for this type of note because such notes do, in fact, bear interest. The **face amount** of this kind of note includes **both** the principal and interest as a **single** amount to be paid back at maturity date. The borrower does not receive cash or other resources equal to the face amount of the note; rather, the borrower receives the **difference** between the face amount and the interest amount. A noninterest-bearing note does not specify either its principal amount or a stated rate of interest. The **principal** amount of a noninterest-bearing note is its future cash flows discounted at its effective interest rate (i.e., the market rate). The effective rate of interest is not specified in the note. A noninterest-bearing note sometimes is called a **discounted note** because the cash received is less than the face amount.

The effective rate on a short-term noninterest-bearing note, with a specified term, can be determined by relating the face amount of the note to the cash (or other resources) received because the amount received is the true principal amount. To illustrate, assume NB Company signed a $11,200, one-year, noninterest-bearing note and received $10,000 cash. The note was discounted at 10.714% interest (i.e., $1,200 ÷ $11,200). However, NB Company received only $10,000 cash; therefore, the effective rate of interest was 12% (i.e., $1,200 ÷ $10,000). The present value of this note is $10,000; that is:

$$\$11{,}200 \times p_{n=1;\,i=12\%} \text{ (Table 5–2, .89286)} = \underline{\underline{\$10{,}000}}$$

This debt should be recorded at its present value which can be done by recording the note on a "net" basis at its present value, or by recording it on a gross basis at its face value and offsetting this account with a discount account.

Accounting entries and reporting: (net basis):

Entries during 19A:

October 1, 19A—To record the noninterest-bearing note payable at its present value (i.e., net) amount:

Cash	10,000	
Note payable, short term (noninterest bearing)		10,000

Note: The note was recorded at its present value (i.e., principal amount) rather than at its face amount of $11,200. The interest entries will increase the $10,000 initially recorded to $11,200, which is the payment required at maturity.

December 31, 19A—Adjusting entry to record accrued interest:

Interest expense ($10,000 × 12% × 3/12)	300	
Note payable, short term		300

Note: The carrying value of the note after this entry is $10,300 (i.e., $10,000 + $300).

Reporting at December 31, 19A:

Statement of income:	
Interest expense	$ 300
Statement of financial position:	
Current liabilities:	
Note payable, short term ($10,000 + $300)	$10,300

Entries at maturity date:

September 30, 19B—To record *(a)* accrued interest to date and *(b)* payment of the face amount of the note at maturity:

(a) Interest expense ($10,000 × 12% × 9⁄12)	900	
Note payable, short term		900
(b) Note payable ($10,000 + $300 + $900)	11,200	
Cash		11,200

Entries recorded at gross basis:

October 1, 19A—To record a noninterest-bearing note payable at its gross (face) amount:[5]

Cash	10,000	
Discount on note payable	1,200	
Note payable, short term		11,200

December 31, 19A—Adjusting entry for accrued interest:

Interest expense ($1,200 × 3⁄12)	300	
Discount on note payable		300

Reporting at December 31, 19A—Noninterest-bearing note payable:

Statement of income:		
Interest expense		$ 300
Statement of financial position:		
Current liabilities:		
Note payable	$11,200	
Less: Unamortized discount	900	10,300

September 30, 19B—Payment of the face amount of the note:

Interest expense ($1,200 × 9⁄12)	900	
Note payable, short term	11,200	
Discount on note payable		900
Cash		11,200

Accounting for Short-Term Notes Payable that Have an Unrealistic Interest Rate

Chapter 7 discussed short-term notes receivable that have an unrealistic interest rate. That problem exists for notes payable and the accounting is essentially the same. That is, when a noncash asset is acquired and a note payable is given that has a stated rate of interest that is less than the current market rate of interest for the level of risk involved, the cost of the asset is the present

[5] Notice that the amount of interest expense and the liability balances are the same, regardless of whether the note is recorded at "net" or "gross."

value of the future cash payments **discounted at the current market rate of interest** rather than at the stated interest rate. Assume a machine is purchased with a one-year, $1,000, 6% interest-bearing note. The current market rate of interest for this level of risk is 12%.

1. Cost of the machine:

$$(\$1{,}000 + \$60) \times p_{n=1;\,i=12\%} \text{ (Table 5–2, .89286)} = \$946.43.$$

2. Entries:

Acquisition date:

Machine	946.43	
Note payable		946.43

Payment date:

Note payable	946.43	
Interest expense ($946.43 × 12%)	113.57	
Cash ($1,000 + $60)		1,060.00

The above example used the current market interest rate for similar notes with the same risks. This rate may be difficult to estimate reliably. Instead if the competitive cash price of the noncash asset received is known, it should be used rather than the $946.43. If the cash price is known, the true rate of interest can be readily computed (see Chapter 5).

Dividends Payable

After declaration by the board of directors, **cash or property dividends payable** should be reported as a current liability if they are to be paid within the coming year or operating cycle, whichever is longer. Cash and property dividends payable are reported as a liability between their dates of declaration and dates of payment on the legal basis that declaration is an enforceable contract that the corporation has assumed by virtue of formal declaration.[6]

Liabilities are not recognized for undeclared dividends in arrears on preferred stock or for any other dividends not yet formally declared by the board of directors. Dividends in arrears on cumulative preferred stock should be disclosed in the notes. Scrip dividends payable (liability dividends) are reported as a current liability unless there is no intention to make payment in the near future. These topics are discussed in Chapter 17.

Advances and Returnable Deposits

A special liability arises when a company receives cash deposits from customers and employees. Deposits may be received from customers as guarantees for payment of obligations that may be incurred in the future or to guarantee performance of a contract or service. For example, when an order is taken, a company may require an advance payment to cover losses that would be incurred if the order is canceled. Such advances create liabilities of the company receiving the cash until the underlying transaction is completed; therefore, they are re-

[6] Because no resources will be expended, **stock dividends issuable** are not current liabilities but are an element of stockholders' equity, as explained in Chapter 17.

corded by debiting Cash and crediting an account such as Liability, Customer Deposits.

Deposits frequently are received from customers as guarantees in case of noncollection or for possible damage to property left with the customer. For example, deposits taken from customers by gas, water, light, and other public utilities are liabilities of such companies to their customers. Also, employees may make returnable deposits to ensure the return of keys and other company property, for locker privileges, and for club memberships. Deposits should be reported as current or long-term liabilities, depending on the time involved between date of deposit and expected termination of the relationship. If the advances or deposits are interest bearing, an adjusting entry is required to accrue interest expense and to decrease the related liability.

Accrued Liabilities

Accrued liabilities were discussed in Chapter 2. Accrued liabilities are recorded in the accounts by making adjusting entries at the end of the accounting period. For example, any wages that have not yet been recorded or paid at the end of the accounting period must be recorded by debiting wage expense and crediting wages payable. Recognition of accrued liabilities is in conformity with *(a)* the definition of a liability (see Exhibit 6–4) and *(b)* the matching principle (see page 237).

Revenues Collected in Advance

Revenues collected in advance, or **unearned revenues,** arise because an entity collects cash related to a revenue transaction that does not yet qualify for recognition as revenue in conformity with the **revenue principle.** Examples of revenues collected in advance include collection of cash in advance, gift certificates, college tuition, rent, sales, magazine subscriptions, and services. Such transactions are recorded as a debit to cash and a credit to an appropriately designated current liability account. Subsequently, as the revenue is **earned,** the liability account is decreased (i.e., debited) and the appropriate revenue account is credited. This latter entry often is one of the year-end adjusting entries (see Chapter 2, adjusting entries).

To illustrate, on November 1, 19A, XT Company collected rent revenue of $6,000 for the next six months. The accounting period ends December 31. The indicated entries are:

November 1, 19A—Rent revenue collected in advance:

Cash	6,000	
Rent revenue collected in advance (or unearned rent revenue)		6,000

December 31, 19A—Adjusting entry for the portion earned:

Rent revenue collected in advance (or unearned rent revenue)	2,000	
Rent revenue ($6,000 × 2⁄6)		2,000

Unearned rent revenue of $4,000 is reported as a current liability because the lessor (XT Company) has an obligation to render future services (i.e., occupancy) during the following four months. Revenues collected in advance sometimes are called **deferred revenues,** which is not a descriptive title.

Taxes Collected for Others and Property Taxes

State and federal laws require businesses to collect taxes from customers and employees for remittance to designated governmental agencies. These include sales taxes, income taxes, property taxes, and payroll taxes. Similar collections also are made on behalf of unions, insurance companies, and employee-sponsored activities. When collections are made for others, cash and current liabilities will both increase. The collections represent liabilities that are settled when the funds are remitted to the designated parties. We will illustrate four typical situations that involve: (1) sales taxes, (2) federal income taxes withheld, (3) payroll taxes, and (4) property taxes.

Sales Taxes. Retail businesses often are required to collect a sales tax at the time of sale and to remit the tax to the taxing authority. Typical entries, assuming a 6% sales tax, are:

1. At date the tax is assessed (point of sale):

Cash and accounts receivable	530,000	
Sales revenue		500,000
Sales tax payable ($500,000 × 6%)		30,000

2. At date of remittance to taxing authority:

Sales tax payable	30,000	
Cash		30,000

Federal Income Taxes Withheld. Federal income tax law requires employers to withhold from each employee's wage or salary payment an amount representing the estimated income tax payable by the employee. The estimates are provided in tax tables available from the Internal Revenue Service (IRS). Income taxes withheld must be remitted within a certain time period to the U.S. Treasury through local depositories (banks). The amounts withheld are current liabilities of the employer until remitted.

Payroll Taxes. Companies must pay various payroll taxes in addition to the wages and salaries paid to employees. Also, companies must deduct amounts from their employees' pay for employees' federal income taxes, social security taxes, union dues, insurance premiums, and the like. The primary federal payroll taxes are commonly referred to as FICA and FUTA taxes.

FICA payroll tax is authorized by the "social security" laws; the employer must deduct tax from the pay of each employee under specified conditions. In addition to the tax paid by the employee, the employer must **match** the contribution of the employee and remit both amounts to the U.S. Treasury. The rates and amount of wages subject to this tax vary with congressional actions. For example, for 1986 employers and employees each paid a tax of 7% on the first $37,800 earned by the employee. The scheduled tax changes are:

Social security tax changes currently scheduled.

	1987	1988	1989
Tax rate	7.15%	7.51%	7.51%
Maximum taxable base	$43,800	$43,800	$43,800*
Employer's maximum tax	3,132	3,289	3,289
Employee's maximum tax	3,132	3,289	3,289

* Probably will be increased.

These payroll taxes are referred to as FICA taxes because the enabling legislation is the Federal Insurance Contributions Act. The purpose of the tax is to provide retirement pay for retirees and death benefits for the retiree's survivors.

FUTA payroll tax, also authorized by federal law, is used to finance the cost associated with the federal-state unemployment compensation program. This payroll tax is paid **only** by the employer (of one or more persons). The federal portion of this payroll tax is usually called the FUTA tax because the enabling legislation is the Federal Unemployment Tax Act. The state portion of this tax is commonly referred to as **SUTA.** The FUTA tax rate for 1987 was 6.2% on the first $7,000 in wages paid to each employee, with 5.4% maximum payable to the state (of employment) to provide the benefits when paid (if the state laws qualify), and the remaining 0.8% payable to the U.S. Treasury.

Illustration of Payroll Taxes. AB Company paid January 1988 salaries of $100,000. Income tax withholding was $20,000, and the FICA and FUTA rates applied to all salaries paid (1988 rates illustrated):

a. To record salaries and employee deductions:

Salary expense	100,000	
Federal income tax payable (from a tax table)		20,000
FICA tax payable, employees ($100,000 × 7.51%)		7,510
Cash		72,490

b. To record payroll taxes payable by the employer:

Expense, payroll taxes	13,710	
FICA tax payable, employer ($100,000 × 7.51%)		7,510
FUTA tax payable, federal ($100,000 × .8%)		800
SUTA tax payable, state ($100,000 × 5.4%)		5,400

c. To record remittance of payroll taxes:

Federal income tax payable	20,000	
FICA tax payable, employees	7,510	
FICA tax payable, employer	7,510	
FUTA tax payable, federal*	800	
SUTA tax payable, state	5,400	
Cash		41,220

*Usually paid annually.

Property Taxes. Property taxes, based on the assessed value of real and personal property, are levied at the local governing level to support school, city, county, and other designated activities. The tax assessed must be paid; if not, it constitutes a lien on the property being taxed.

Accounting for property taxes is complicated when the tax and accounting periods do not coincide. Property taxes for the current year usually are assessed near the end of the year and billed early in the next year. This means that the expense accrues **before** the actual amount of the tax is known. Therefore, estimates often must be used. In local communities, the typical sequence of assessing property taxes is as follows: by midyear, **tentative** taxable valuations are developed along with **estimated** tax rates; by year-end, each property owner receives the **actual** taxable valuation, tax rate, and the resulting property tax; and during the early part of the following year, payment is made to the taxing authority. Therefore, 1989 property taxes typically would be assessed late in 1989 and paid in 1990. Most businesses accrue property tax expense each month based on "best estimates" and handle revisions as changes in estimates. At year-end, the estimated amounts that have been recorded in the related expense and liability accounts are adjusted to agree with the actual amount assessed, which must be used for annual accounting and reporting purposes.

To illustrate accounting for property taxes, we will use a situation that involves a small company located in an expanding community during 1988. The following sequence of events occurred, with the appropriate accounting treatment illustrated:

a. January 1988—Estimate of 1988 property tax based on an expected 20% increase over the 1987 actual tax ($2,061):

($2,061 × 1.20) ÷ 12 = $206; use $200 per month as the estimate.

January 31, 1988:

Property tax expense	200		Entry made each month, January through June; total, $1,200.
Property tax payable		200	

b. July 1988—Received the following from taxing authority:

Tentative 1988 **taxable valuation,** $190,076 × Estimated 1988 tax rate per $100 valuation, $1.4470 = Estimated 1988 property tax, $2,750:

July 31, 1988 (change in estimate); ($2,750 − $1,200) ÷ six months remaining = $258; use $260 per month as the estimate.

Property tax expense	260		Entry made each month, July through November; total $1,300.
Property tax payable		260	

c. December 29, 1988—Received actual 1988 tax assessment; 1988 taxable valuation $197,076 × 1988 tax rate per $100 valuation, $1.45 = $2,858.

December 31, 1988:

Property tax expense ($2,858 − $1,200 − $1,300)	358	
Property tax payable		358

d. 1988 financial statements:

Statement of income:	
Property tax expense	$2,858
Statement of financial position:	
Current liabilities:	
Property tax payable	2,858

e. January 1989—Payment of 1988 property tax:

Property tax payable	2,858	
Cash		2,858

Regardless of the respective tax and accounting fiscal periods, this accounting approach can be adapted to conform to GAAP.

Compensated Absence Liabilities

Companies often grant employees specified periods away from work during which the regular salary or wage is continued, such as for vacations (e.g., two weeks per year) and holidays (e.g., three). When salaries and wages are paid during these "absences" from work, the expense is recognized in the current year (i.e., when earned). However, when the employees can retain and carry over unused time for these events to the next (and following) years, the question arises as to when the expense for this unused time should be recognized. Should it be recognized in the prior year in which it was **earned** or the later year(s) in which it is **taken?** Because both approaches were being used, the FASB issued *Statement 43*, "Accounting for Compensated Absences." *FASB Statement 43* **requires** that any expense that is due to compensated absences must be recognized (i.e., accrued) in the year in which it is earned, provided: *(a)* the absence from work relates to services already rendered (i.e., it was earned), *(b)* the carryover accumulates (or vests), *(c)* the "payment" is probable (i.e., the absence will occur), and *(d)* the amount (i.e., cost) can be reliably estimated.[7]

Implementing this requirement involves an adjusting entry at the end of each fiscal year to **accrue** all of the compensation cost for the vacation and holiday time that is to be carried over. This is done by recognizing an **expense and a current liability.** When the vacation or holiday time is taken, the liability account is debited at the time the employee is paid. These entries recognize the cost of compensated absences as **expense in the period earned** rather than when taken.

Compensated absences are illustrated below for a situation that involves the carryover of vacation time. CT Company has 500 employees; each employee is granted three weeks vacation time each year with full pay. Vacation time, up to a maximum accumulation of four weeks, may be carried over to subsequent years prior to termination of employment. At the end of 19A (also the end of the annual accounting period), personnel records revealed the following information concerning carryover vacation times and amounts (none from prior years):

---

[7] In the case of accumulated rights to receive nonvesting sick pay benefits (i.e., absences due to illness), accrual is not required but is permitted. A strong case can be made that the illness (when it occurs) is the major event rather than when the employee worked.

Number of employees	Weeks per employee	Carryover from 19A Total weeks	Carryover from 19A Total salaries
10	2	20	$30,000
3	1	3	6,000

Disregarding payroll taxes, the indicated entries are as follows:

December 31, 19A—Adjusting entry to accrue vacation salaries not yet taken or paid:

Salary expense	36,000	
Liability for compensated absences		36,000

Note: Although 19A salary expense has already been debited for the salaries of these employees, it is debited again for the nonproductive vacation time that will be paid in 19B. The effect is to prevent the 19A nonproductive time from being included in 19B expenses.

During 19B—Vacation time carryover is taken and the salaries paid (one person did not take two weeks of carryover, $3,000):

Liability for compensated absences	33,000	
Cash ($36,000 − $3,000)		33,000

Note: Balance remaining in the liability account, $3,000.

This illustration assumed that there was no change in the **rate of pay** from 19A to 19B (when the carryover was used) for those employees who had the carryover. If there were rate changes, the pay difference would be debited (if an increase) or credited (if a decrease) to **wage expense** during 19B as a change in estimate. For example, if the 19B wages relating to the employees who used their carryovers during 19B increased by $1,000, the 19B entry would have been as follows:

Liability for compensated absences	33,000	
Wage expense (19B)	1,000	
Cash ($36,000 + $1,000 − $3,000)		34,000

Note: Balance remaining in the liability account, $3,000.

Current Maturities of Long-Term Debt

The issue here is how to report a debt that is part current and part noncurrent. The problem arises when *(a)* periodic payments are made on a debt, and *(b)* the last payment on a long-term debt will be made in the following accounting period. In both of these cases, if the next payment is made from current assets, that portion of the debt should be reported as a **current** liability. A typical presentation is:

Current liabilities:		
Current payment on bond issue		$100,000
Long-term liabilities:		
Bonds payable	$500,000	
Less: Current payment	100,000	400,000

Classification of Obligations that Are Callable by the Creditor

FASB Statement 78 (1983) "Classification of Obligations that Are Calla the Creditor" amends *ARB No. 43*, chap. 3A, to specify that the kinds of d illustrated in the following cases must be included in the current liability classification:

> **Case A**—obligations that are payable on demand (i.e., callable), or will be due on demand within one year from the statement of financial position date, or the operating cycle, if longer, even though liquidation within that period is not expected.
>
> **Case B**—long-term obligations that are, or will be, callable by the creditor either: *(a)* because of a **violation** of the terms of the debt at the date of the statement of financial position, or *(b)* because the violation, if not cured within a specified grace period, will make the debt callable.

The concept that supports these current liability classifications is that the debtor of a long-term obligation or a callable note meeting the above specifications cannot control the payment date.

Short-Term Obligations Expected to Be Refinanced

A company may be motivated to reclassify liabilities from current to long term to improve its reported working capital position. One reason given for such reclassifications is: "because we intend to refinance the debt, we do not expect to be making any payments from current assets." *FASB Statement 6*, "Classification of Short-Term Obligations Expected to Be Refinanced," was issued to establish guidelines and to prevent abuses. It provides that current liabilities expected to be refinanced can be reclassified as long-term liabilities **only** if the debtor *(a)* fully intends to refinance the specific short-term debt and *(b)* shows an ability to refinance the debt by **actually refinancing** it on a long-term basis before the financial statements are issued, or by entering in good faith into a long-term, noncancelable **refinancing agreement** that is supported by a viable lender. The maximum amount that may be classified as long term cannot exceed the amount irrevocably refinanced less the effect of all refinancing restrictions.

Contingencies and Estimated Liabilities

The central issue here is the definition of a debt when a single specific transaction has not occurred. Liabilities often must be **estimated** because (1) a known liability exists but the ultimate amount is uncertain or (2) a loss contingency exists. A contingency is defined in *FASB Statement 5*, "Accounting for Contingencies," as "an existing condition, situation, or set of circumstances involving uncertainty as to possible gain (hereinafter, 'gain contingency') or a loss (hereinafter, 'loss contingency') to an enterprise that ultimately will be resolved when one or more future events occur or fail to occur. Resolution of the uncertainty may confirm the acquisition of an asset or the reduction of a liability or the loss or impairment of an asset or the incurrence of a liability."

FASB Statement 5 is the basic pronouncement on contingencies and estimated liabilities and is the basis for this discussion. Therefore, this section is divided into three parts: *(a)* contingent liabilities (loss contingencies) that must be accrued and reported at estimated dollar amounts in the body of the financial statements,

or contingencies.

	Amount can be reasonably estimated	Amount cannot be reasonably estimated
	LOSS CONTINGENCY	
Probable	1. Accrue **both** a loss and a liability, and report them in the body of the statements.	2. Do not accrue; report as a **note** in the financial statements.
Reasonably possible	3. Do not accrue; report as a **note** in the financial statements.	4. Do not accrue; report as a **note** in the financial statements.
Remote	5. No accrual or **note** required; however, a note is permitted.	6. No accrual or **note** required; however, a note is permitted.
	GAIN CONTINGENCY	
Probable	No accrual except in very unusual circumstances. **Note** disclosure required.	**Note** disclosure required; exercise care to avoid misleading inferences.
Reasonably possible	**Note** disclosure required; exercise care to avoid misleading inferences.	**Note** disclosure required; exercise extreme care to avoid misleading inferences.
Remote	Disclosure not recommended.	

(*b*) contingent liabilities that are reported only in the notes to the financial statements, and (*c*) gain contingencies.

FASB Statement 5 delineates contingencies and specifies particular accounting treatments on the basis of whether the contingency is:

a. Probable. The future event or events are likely to occur.

b. Reasonably possible. The chance of occurrence of the future event or events is more than remote but less than likely.

c. Remote. The chance of occurrence of the future event or events is slight.

The provisions of *FASB Statement 5* relating to contingencies may be summarized as shown in **Exhibit 14–1.**

Loss Contingencies that Must Be Accrued and a Liability Recognized

FASB Statement 5 requires that a loss contingency must be accrued as a debit to an expense or loss account and a credit to a liability account if **both** of the following conditions are met:

a. Information received prior to the issuance of the financial statements indicates that it is **probable** that an asset has been impaired or a liability has been incurred at the date of the financial statements. It must be probable that one or more future events will or will not occur confirming the fact of the loss.

b. The amount of the loss can be reasonably estimated.

This situation corresponds to Exhibit 14–1, cell 1.

FASB Standard 5 identified a number of loss contingencies that must be considered for appropriate recording, or disclosure. These include estimated losses on receivables (allowance for doubtful accounts); estimated warranty obligations; litigations, claims, and assessments; and anticipated losses on the disposal of a segment of the business (Chapter 22).

A loss contingency that meets both of the above criteria, in addition to being accrued in the accounts, must be **reported** *(a)* on the statement of financial position as a liability, and *(b)* on the statement of income as an expense (or loss) in the period in which the two criteria are first met. Three examples illustrate the **accrual of a loss contingency and recognition of a liability.**

Case A—Product Warranty Liability. R Company sold merchandise for $200,000 cash during the current period. Experience has indicated that warranty and guarantee costs will approximate .5% of sales.[8] The indicated entries are as follows:

a. In year of sale:

Cash	200,000	
Sales revenue		200,000
Warranty expense	1,000	
Estimated warranty liability ($200,000 × .5% = $1,000)		1,000

b. Subsequently, actual warranty expenditures of $987 were made during the warranty period:

Warranty liability	987	
Cash (and other resources used)		987

c. Instead, if the actual expenditure was $1,100, the entry would be:

Warranty liability	1,000	
Warranty expense	100	
Cash (and other resources used)		1,100

Case B—Liability from Premiums, Coupons, and Trading Stamps. As a promotional device, many companies offer premiums to customers who turn in coupons, box tops, and so on. At the end of each accounting period, a portion of these coupons or box tops will be outstanding (unredeemed by the customers), some of which ultimately will be turned in for redemption. These outstanding claims for premiums represent an **expense and an estimated liability** that must be recognized in the period of sale of the merchandise.

To illustrate, Baker Coffee Company offered its customers a premium—a special coffee cup free of charge (cost to Baker, 75 cents each) with the return of 20 coupons. One coupon is placed in each can of coffee when packed. The company estimated, on the basis of past experience, that only 70% of the coupons would be redeemed. The following additional data for two years are available:

---

[8] For one approach to the estimation of warranty expense, see K. R. Balachandran, R. A. Maschmeyer, and J. L. Livingstone, "Product Warranty Period: A Markovian Approach to Estimation and Analysis of Repair and Replacement Cost," *The Accounting Review*, January 1981, pp. 115–23.

	First year	Second year
Number of coffee cups purchased at $.75	6,000	4,000
Number of cans of coffee sold	100,000	200,000
Number of coupons redeemed	40,000	120,000

The indicated entries are as follows:

a. To record purchases of cups:

	First year		Second year	
Premium inventory	4,500		3,000	
Cash		4,500		3,000

b. To record the estimated liability and premium expense based on sales:

	First year		Second year	
Premium expense*	2,625		5,250	
Premium claims payable		2,625		5,250

* Computations:
Year 1: (100,000 ÷ 20) × $.75 × 70% = $2,625.
Year 2: (200,000 ÷ 20) × $.75 × 70% = $5,250.

c. To record redemption of coupons:

	First year		Second year	
Premium claims payable*	1,500		4,500	
Premium inventory		1,500		4,500

* Computations:
Year 1: (40,000 ÷ 20) × $.75 = $1,500.
Year 2: (120,000 ÷ 20) × $.75 = $4,500.

Case C—Liability from Litigation. S Company was sued during the last quarter of the current year because of an accident involving a vehicle owned and operated by the company. The plaintiff is seeking $100,000 damages. If, in the opinion of management and company counsel, it is probable that damages will be assessed and a reasonable estimate is $50,000,[9] the indicated entry is:

Estimated loss from pending lawsuit	50,000	
Estimated liability from pending lawsuit		50,000

Estimated liabilities, such as those illustrated above, may ultimately require expenditures that are more or less than the amount estimated to satisfy the actual liability. When the estimated liability is too high or too low, the difference is accounted for as a change in estimate under the provisions of *APB Opinion 20.*

Loss Contingencies that Are Disclosed Only in Notes

Potential loss contingencies, such as guarantees of indebtedness, accommodation endorsements, threat of expropriation of assets, standby letters of credit (i.e., guarantees of the credit of a third party), and risks due to fire, flood, and

[9] It is unlikely that legal counsel and management would disclose a belief that a contingent loss is probable and can be reliably estimated. This situation would suggest that it may be advisable to settle out of court. To disclose a tacit expectation of loss in advance may prejudice the outcome of the trial.

other hazards, must be assessed and accounted for in conformity with *FASB Standard 5*.

In Exhibit 14–1, cell 1, a loss contingency and the related liability are accrued and reported only when the loss is *(a)* probable and *(b)* can be reasonably estimated. In contrast, Exhibit 14–1 identifies **three** situations involving loss contingencies for which **note disclosure only** is required (accrual is not permitted): cell 2, probable but cannot be reasonably estimated; cell 3, reasonably possible and can be reasonably estimated; and cell 4, reasonably possible but cannot be reasonably estimated. The note must describe the nature of the contingency and give an estimate of the **possible** loss or range of loss, or it must state that a reasonable estimate of the **possible** loss cannot be made. For example, the financial statements of CBS, Inc., included the following note:

> Various legal actions, governmental proceedings and other claims are pending against the Company. The types of relief requested include injunctions, damages (including, in some instances, treble damages) and revocation of the Company's broadcast licenses. While the Company cannot predict the results of any litigation, it believes that it has meritorious defenses to those actions, proceedings and claims. The Company believes that the liability, if any, resulting from such litigation will not have a materially adverse effect on its consolidated operations or consolidated financial position.

Gain Contingencies

A gain contingency arises when the characteristics of a contingency are present (as defined earlier). It may result in an increase in assets or a decrease in liabilities, depending upon future events.

Contingent gains rarely are accrued; however, they are accorded note disclosure, provided the note does not give "misleading implications." The different treatment accorded gain contingencies, compared with loss contingencies, is due to application of the **conservatism constraint.**

Executory Contracts

Executory contracts or agreements occur when two parties agree to transfer resources or services but neither party has performed. They often are called **unexecuted contracts** or **agreements.** For example, a purchase agreement may have been made, but no assets have been received and no payments have been made. Other examples are lines of credit, pensions, leases, and promises of future compensation prior to any transfer of resources. When a transfer of resources occurs, the contract or agreement is no longer executory (or unexecuted). Executory contracts usually are not recorded because a transfer of assets or liabilities has not yet occurred. However, if the anticipated considerations are material, full disclosure should be made. Chapter 21 illustrates the accounting for executory and nonexecutory lease contracts.

Summary

This chapter discussed short-term liabilities. A liability, defined in conformity with *FASB Concepts 6*, should be recognized at the present value of all of its future cash payments discounted at an interest rate that is consistent with the risks involved. Short-term (i.e., current) liabilities are obligations that will be paid by using current assets for payment. There are numerous current liabilities, primarily accounts and notes payable. Current maturities of long-term liabilities usually are classified as current liabilities. Revenues collected in advance are current liabilities because there is an obligation to provide goods or services in the near future.

This chapter also discussed loss and gain contingencies. The basis for recognizing a loss contingency is whether the loss is *(a)* probable (if so, record a liability), *(b)* reasonably possible (if so, do not record a liability but disclose it in a note to the financial statements), or *(c)* remote (if so, do not record a liability; however, a disclosure note is permitted but not required).

QUESTIONS

1. Give a conceptual definition of a liability.
2. Conceptually, how should a liability be measured?
3. Relate the measurement of a liability to its cause.
4. Why are most liabilities recognized at maturity value at the beginning of the term?
5. Compute the present value of a $5,000, one-year note payable that specifies no interest, although 14% would be a realistic rate. What is the amount of the principal and the interest?
6. In evaluating a statement of financial position, some bankers say the liability section is one of the most important parts. What are the primary reasons for their position on this point?
7. Some liabilities are reported at their maturity amount. In general, when should liabilities, prior to maturity date, be reported at less than their maturity amount?
8. How is the cost principle involved in accounting for current liabilities?
9. Define a current liability.
10. Differentiate between secured and unsecured liabilities. Explain the reporting procedures for each.
11. Distinguish between the stated and effective, or yield, rate of interest on a debt.
12. Briefly define the following terms related to a note payable: principal, face, and maturity amounts.
13. Distinguish between an interest-bearing note and a noninterest-bearing note.
14. Assume $2,000 cash is borrowed on a $2,000, 10%, one-year note payable that is interest bearing and that another $2,000 cash is borrowed on a $2,200 one-year note that is noninterest bearing. For each note give the following:
    a. Face amount of the note.
    b. Principal amount.
    c. Maturity amount.
    d. Interest paid.
15. Are all declared dividends a liability between declaration and payment dates? Explain.
16. Why is a deferred revenue classified as a liability?
17. What is a compensated absence? When should the expense related to compensated absences be recognized?
18. What is the accounting definition of a contingency? What are the three characteristics of a contingency? Why is the concept important?
19. How does the accountant measure the likelihood of the outcome of a contingency? In general, how does this affect the accounting for and reporting of contingencies?
20. Briefly explain the accounting and reporting for loss contingencies.

EXERCISES

Exercises 14–1 to 14–15

E 14–1 (Interest-Bearing and Noninterest-Bearing Notes Compared)

Case A

On January 1, 19A, a heavy-duty truck was purchased that had a listed price of $28,500. Payment in full was: cash, $8,500, and a two-year, noninterest-bearing note of $20,000 (maturity date, December 31, 19B). A realistic interest rate for this level of risk was 12%. The accounting period ends December 31. Assume that this note is a current liability in this company.

Case B

On January 1, 19A, a small truck was purchased and full payment was made as follows: cash, $5,000, and a one-year, 6%, interest-bearing note of $10,000, maturity date December 31, 19A (which also is the end of the accounting period). A realistic interest rate for this level of risk was 12%.

Required (round to the nearest dollar):
Give all entries for each case from purchase date through maturity date of each note. Disregard depreciation.

E 14–2 (Interest-Bearing Note; Entries and Reporting)
On May 1, 19A, Vue Company borrowed $50,000 cash and signed a one-year, 12% interest-bearing note for that amount. Vue's accounting period ends December 31.

Required:
1. Give all of the required entries from May 1, 19A, through the maturity date of the note. Disregard reversing and closing entries.
2. Show how all amounts related to the note should be reported on the debtor's statement of financial position at December 31, 19A, and the 19A statement of income.

E 14–3 (Analysis of Two Noninterest-Bearing Notes; One Has an Unrealistic Rate)
On March 1, 19A, Bostic Company borrowed $60,000 cash from SP Bank and signed a one-year note for $70,650 (designated Note A); no interest was specified in the note. On June 1, 19A, Bostic borrowed additional cash and signed a one-year note, face amount, $17,775 (designated Note B). No interest was specified in the note; however, the going rate of interest for this level of risk was 18.5%. The accounting period ends December 31. Table 5–2; $n = 1$; $i = 18.5\% = 1.18500$.

Required:

	Note A	Note B
a. How much cash was received?	$____	$____
b. What was the face amount of the note?	$____	$____
c. What was the principal of the note?	$____	$____
d. How much interest expense should be reported in:		
19A?	$____	$____
19B?	$____	$____
e. What was the stated interest rate?	%____	%____
f. What was the yield or effective interest rate?	%____	%____

6000 x .89286

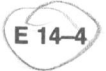

E 14–4 **(Analysis and Comparison of Interest-Bearing and Noninterest-Bearing Notes)**
On September 1, 19A, Dyer Company borrowed cash on a $6,000 note payable due in one year. Assume the going rate of interest was 12% per year for this particular level of risk. The accounting period ends December 31.

Required (round to the nearest dollar):
Complete the following tabulation:

	Assuming the note was—	
	Interest bearing	Noninterest bearing
a. Cash received	$6000	$5357.16
b. Cash paid at maturity date	$6720	$6000
c. Total interest paid (cash)	$720	$643
d. Interest expense in 19A	$240	$214
e. Interest expense in 19B	$480	$429
f. Amount of liabilities reported on 19A statement of financial position:		
Note payable (net)	$6000	$5357
Interest payable	$240	$214
g. Principal amount	$6000	$5357
h. Face amount	$6000	$6000
i. Maturity value	$6720	$6000
j. Stated interest rate	% 12	% 12
k. Yield or effective interest rate	% 12	% 12

E 14–5 **(Noninterest-Bearing Note; Entries and Reporting)**
On April 1, 19A, Reddy Company purchased a heavy machine for use in operations by paying $5,000 cash and signing a $25,000 (face amount) noninterest-bearing note due in one year (on March 31, 19B). The going rate of interest for Reddy on this type of note was 14% per year. The company uses straight-line depreciation. The accounting period ends on December 31. Assume a five-year life for the machine and 10% residual value.

Required:
1. Give all entries from April 1, 19A, through March 31, 19B (round amounts to the nearest dollar).
2. Show how all of the related items would be reported on the 19A statement of income and statement of financial position.

E 14–6 **(Current Liabilities; Original and Adjusting Entries)**
Voss Company, a large retail outlet, completed the following selected transactions during 19A and 19B:

a. At the end of 19A, accrued wages that have not yet been recorded amounted to $34,000. These accrued wages were paid in the January 15, 19B, payroll, which amounted to $173,000 (disregard payroll taxes).
b. On November 1, 19A, rent revenue for the following six months was collected, $8,400.
c. On October 1, 19A, Voss received $800 as a deposit from a customer for some special containers that are to be returned on or about March 31, 19B. Voss agreed to "give the customer credit at an annual rate of 6% interest on the deposit." The containers were returned on April 1, 19B.

Required:
Give all of the required entries (omit closing and reversing entries) during 19A and 19B for each of the above transactions. The accounting period of Voss ends on December 31.

E 14–7 (Reporting Liabilities; Dividends and Secured Notes)
The records of the Fisk Corporation provided the following information at December 31, 19A:

a. Notes payable (trade), short-term (includes a $4,000 note given on purchase of equipment that cost $20,000; assets were mortgaged in connection with purchase)	$30,000
b. Bonds payable ($30,000 due each April 1)	90,000
c. Accounts payable (including $3,000 owed to president of the company)	50,000
d. Accrued property taxes (estimated)	1,000
e. Stock dividends issuable on 3/1/19B (at par value)	26,000
f. Cash dividends declared, payable 3/1/19B	20,000
g. Long-term note payable, maturity amount (unamortized amount, $14,500)	15,000
h. Accrued interest on all bonds and notes	11,500

Required:
Assuming the fiscal year ends December 31, show how each of the above items should be reported on the statement of financial position at December 31, 19A.

E 14–8 (Entries to Record Payroll, and Related Deductions)
Pratt Company paid salaries for the month amounting to $80,000. Of this amount, $30,000 was received by employees who had already been paid the $43,800* maximum amount of annual earnings taxable in one year under FICA laws (FICA rate, 7.51%).

Of the $80,000, $14,000 was paid to employees who had already been paid the $7,000* maximum (SUTA rates: 5.4% state and .8% federal). Withholding taxes amounted to $26,000, and $1,450 was withheld from the $80,000 for investment in company stock per an agreement with certain employees.

* These amounts refer to 1987 cutoff points for wages subject to FICA and FUTA taxes.

Required:
Give entries to record the *(a)* salary payment and the liabilities for the deductions, *(b)* employer payroll expenses, and *(c)* remittance of the taxes.

E 14–9 (Recording Payroll and Related Deductions)
Cristina Corporation paid salaries and wages of $143,800. Of this amount, $3,800 was paid to employees who had already exceeded the FICA maximum. Also, $43,800 was paid to employees who had already been paid the SUTA maximum. Use the FICA and FUTA rate for 1988 given in the chapter. Income tax withholding was $35,000. Deductions for union dues (in conformity with the union agreement) was $3,000 and for insurance premiums, $12,000.

Required:
Give the entries to record liabilities for payroll deductions, payroll expenses, and remittance of the deductions.

E 14–10 (Compensated Absences; Entries and Reporting)
BV Company allows each employee to earn 15 paid vacation days each year with full pay while on vacation. Unused vacation time can be carried over to the next year; if

not taken during the next year it is lost. By the end of 19A, all but 3 of the 30 employees had taken their earned vacation time; these three carried over to 19B a total of 20 vacation days, which represented 19A salary of $4,000. During 19B, each of these three used their 19A vacation carryover; none of them had received a pay change from 19A to the time they used their carryover. Total cash wages paid were: 19A, $700,000; 19B, $721,000.

Required:

1. Give all of the entries for BV Company related to vacations during 19A and 19B. Disregard payroll taxes.
2. Compute the total amount of wage expense for 19A and 19B. How would the vacation time carried over from 19A affect the 19A statement of financial position?

E 14–11 (Estimated Warranty Expense; Recording and Reporting)
Stice, Inc., sells a line of products that carry a three-year warranty against defects. Based on industry experience, the estimated warranty costs related to dollar sales are: first year after sale—1% of sales; second year after sale—3% of sales; and third year after sale—5%. Sales and actual warranty expenditures for the first three-year period were as follows:

	Cash sales	Actual warranty expenditures
19A	$ 80,000	$ 900
19B	110,000	4,100
19C	130,000	9,800

Required:

1. Give entries for the three years for the *(a)* sales, *(b)* estimated warranty expense, and *(c)* the actual expenditures.
2. What amount should be reported as a liability on the statement of position at the end of each year?

E 14–12 (Liability for Premiums; Entries and Reporting)
Recliner Furniture Store has initiated a promotion program whereby customers are given coupons redeemable in $25 special savings certificates. Each certificate can be turned in to the savings company for its face amount at the end of the third year from its issuance to the customer. One coupon is issued for each dollar of sales. On the surrender of 750 coupons, one $25 savings certificate (cost $20) is given. It is estimated that 30% of the coupons issued will never be presented for redemption. Sales for the first period were $400,000, and the number of coupons redeemed totaled 225,000. Sales for the second period were $440,000, and the number of coupons redeemed totaled 360,000. The savings certificates are acquired as needed.

Required:
Prepare journal entries (including closing entries) relative to the premium plan for the two periods. Show amounts that should be reported in the statement of financial position and statement of income for the two periods. *Hint:* Use the following accounts: Cash, Premium Expense, Estimated Premium Claims Payable, and Income Summary.

E 14–13 (Loss Contingency; Three Cases; Entries and Explanation)
S Company is preparing the annual financial statements at December 31, 19J. During 19J, a customer fell while riding on the escalator and has filed a lawsuit for $40,000 because of a claimed back injury. The lawyer employed by the company has carefully assessed all of the implications. If the suit is lost, the lawyer's reasonable estimate is that the $40,000 will be assessed by the court.

Required:
How should the contingency be handled during 19J in each of the following cases? Give all necessary entries and/or any notes:

1. Assume that the lawyer and the management concluded that it is reasonably possible that the company will be liable, and it is reasonably estimated that the amount will be $40,000.
2. Assume instead the lawyer, the independent accountant, and management have reluctantly concluded that it is probable that the suit will be successful.
3. Assume that the conclusion of the legal counsel and management is that it is remote that there will be a contingency loss. They believe the suit is without merit.

E 14–14 (Classification of Accounts with Credit Balances; Liabilities, etc.)
The December 31, 19A, trial balance of Big Corporation provided the account titles given below (each account has a credit balance). You are to indicate to the right of each account the proper statement of financial position classification in the usual situation. Explain any questionable items.

Item (with credit balances)	Liability		Not a liability; it is—
	Short term	Long term	
1. Trade accounts payable.			
2. Stock dividend issuable.			
3. Product guarantees outstanding.			
4. Customer deposits, three-year average time.			
5. Accrued interest on note payable.			
6. Bonds payable (maturity June 1, 19H).			
7. Accrued property taxes.			
8. Long-term mortgage note (maturity November 30, 19B).			
9. Property dividend payable.			
10. Stock options outstanding.			
11. Loans from officers.			
12. Appropriation for bond sinking fund.			
13. Deferred rent revenue.			
14. Liability for compensated absences.			
15. Estimated income taxes payable.			
16. Allowance for doubtful accounts.			
17. FICA taxes, unremitted.			
18. Gain contingencies.			
19. Withholding taxes (on employee payroll).			
20. Contributed capital in excess of par.			
21. Accounts receivable.			

E 14–15 (Property Taxes; Recording)
Menlo Company is located in a relatively small town that has recently restructured its property tax procedures. During the past year (19A) the company experienced a significant increase in the property appraisal for taxes. The company paid property taxes of $12,000. However, it expects the tax for the current year, 19B, to decrease some because of citizen complaints. Both the city tax year and Menlo's accounting year end on December 31. The following events occurred during 19A:

January 20—paid the 19A property taxes.
January 30—estimated a 10 percent decrease in property taxes for 19B. The company accrues property taxes each month.
July 10—received a tentative tax notice assessment for taxes, $912,000; preliminary tax rate per $100 valuation, $1.25. The company will revise its estimate to these assessments.
December 29—received final tax notice, 19A tax assessed, $11,000, payable by January 15, 19C.
January 25, 19C—paid the 19B property tax.

Required:
Give the journal entries related to the property taxes from January 1, 19B through January 19C.

PROBLEMS

Problems 14–1 to 14–12

P 14–1 (Interest-Bearing and Noninterest-Bearing Notes Compared; Entries; Reporting)
Victor Company borrowed cash on August 1, 19A, and signed a $12,000 (face amount), one-year note payable, due on July 31, 19B. The accounting period ends December 31. Assume a going rate of interest of 16% for this company for this level of risk.

Required (round amounts to nearest dollar):
1. How much cash should Victor receive on the note assuming: Case A, an interest-bearing note, and Case B, a noninterest-bearing note?
2. Give the following entries for each case:
   a. August 1, 19A, date of the loan.
   b. December 31, 19A, adjusting entry.
   c. July 31, 19B, payment of the note, assuming no reversing entry was made.
3. What liability amounts should be shown in each case on the December 31, 19A, statement of financial position?

P 14–2 (Interest-Bearing and Noninterest-Bearing Notes Compared; Entries)
On September 1, 19A, Foster Company borrowed (received) $20,000 cash and signed a note payable due in one year. The going rate of interest for this level of risk was 12%. The accounting period ends December 31.

Required (round to the nearest dollar):
1. Complete the following tabulation:

	Assuming the note was—	
	Interest bearing	**Noninterest bearing**
a. Cash received	$20,000	$20,000
b. Cash paid at maturity date	$_____	$_____
c. Total cash interest paid	$_____	$_____
d. Interest expense, 19A	$_____	$_____
e. Interest expense, 19B	$_____	$_____
f. Amount of liabilities reported on 19A statement of financial position:		
Note payable (net)	$_____	$_____
Interest payable	$_____	$_____
g. Principal amount	$_____	$_____
h. Face amount	$_____	$_____
i. Stated interest rate	%_____	%_____
j. Yield or effective interest rate	%_____	%_____

2. Give all entries required for each note from September 1, 19A, through maturity date.

P 14–3 (Interest-Bearing and Noninterest-Bearing Notes Compared; Entries) On October 1, 19A, Kimberly Company borrowed $36,000 cash and signed a one-year note payable, due on September 30, 19B. The going rate of interest for this level of risk was 12%. The accounting period ends on December 31.

Required:

1. Compute the face amount of the note assuming:
   Case A—An interest-bearing note.
   Case B—A noninterest-bearing note.
2. Complete a tabulation as follows:

	Case A: interest bearing	Case B: noninterest bearing
a. Total cash received	$36,000	$36,000
b. Face amount of note	$____	$____
c. Total cash paid	$____	$____
d. Total interest paid	$____	$____
e. Interest expense, 19A	$____	$____
f. Interest expense, 19B	$____	$____
g. Amount of liabilities reported on the 19A statement of financial position:		
Note payable	$____	$____
Interest payable	$____	$____
h. Principal amount	$____	$____
i. Stated interest rate	%____	%____
j. Yield or effective interest rate	%____	%____
k. Time to maturity:		
October 1, 19A	Months____	Months____
December 31, 19A	Months____	Months____

3. Give entries indicated for each case from October 1, 19A, through maturity date (assume reversing entries were not made).
4. Show how the liability and expense amounts should be reflected for each case on the December 31, 19A, statement of financial position and the 19A statement of income.

P 14–4 (Noninterest-Bearing Note, Two-Year; Entries and Reporting) On January 1, 19A, Gem Company acquired a machine (an operational asset) that had a list price of $35,000. Because of a serious cash problem, Gem paid $5,000 cash and signed a two-year note with a maturity amount of $30,000 due on December 31, 19B. The note did not specify interest. Assume the going rate of interest for this company for this level of risk was 15%. The accounting period ends December 31.

Required (round amounts to nearest dollar):

1. Give the entry to record the purchase of the machine.
2. Complete the following tabulation related to the note:

a. Cash equivalent received	$______
b. Face amount	$______
c. Total interest to be paid	$______
d. Interest expense:	
19A	$______
19B	$______
e. Liabilities on the 19A statement of financial position	$______
f. Depreciation expense (on cost) (10-year estimated life; no residual value; straight line)	$______
g. Effective interest rate	%______
h. Stated interest rate	%______

3. Give all entries (exclude closing and reversing entries) from January 1, 19A, through the end of 19B.
4. Show how the liabilities and expenses would be reported on the 19A and 19B financial statements (assume the company has a two-year operating cycle).

P 14–5 (Noninterest-Bearing Note, Two-Year; Entries and Reporting)

On January 1, 19A, Lye Company purchased a large used machine for operations; the asking price was $46,000. Payment was made by $6,000 cash and a $40,000 (maturity value), two-year, noninterest-bearing note payable due on December 31, 19B. The note did not specify interest; however, for Lye, the rate for this level of risk was 14%. Assume straight-line depreciation, a five-year life, and no residual value. The accounting period ends on December 31.

Required (round amounts to nearest dollar):

1. Give the entry to record the purchase of the machine.
2. Complete the following tabulation related to the note:

a. Cash equivalent received	$______
b. Face amount of note	$______
c. Cash to be paid at maturity	$______
d. Total interest expense	$______
e. Interest expense:	
19A	$______
19B	$______
f. Depreciation expense	$______
g. Effective interest rate	%______
h. Stated interest rate	%______

3. Prepare a debt amortization schedule for this note. Use the following column headings: Date, Interest expense, and Carrying value of the liability (also refer to Chapter 5).
4. Give all entries (except closing and reversing entries) from January 1, 19A through the end of 19B.
5. Show how the liabilities and expenses should be reported on the 19A and 19B financial statements (assume the current operating cycle is two years).

P 14–6 (Property Tax; Sales Tax; Recording and Reporting)

Hudson Department Store has asked you to assist in improving its accounting for taxes. The following selected transactions that were completed during 19B have been presented to you for analysis; the accounting period ends on December 31.

a. Property taxes—Property taxes for 19A amounted to $24,000. During January 19B, Hudson estimated that the property tax would increase approximately 12% for 19B. During June 19B, the company received a tentative property tax appraisal that indicated a property valuation of $2,100,000 and an estimated 19B tax rate per $1,000 of $13.10. The final tax assessment notice was received December 19, 19B, and specified a 19B property tax of $30,000. The 19B property taxes were paid in full on January 17, 19C.

b. Sales revenue for 19B amounted to $8 million; the sales tax rate is 5%, and 97% of all sales were subject to tax. Unremitted sales tax at the end of 19B amounted to $18,000.

Required (round to the nearest dollar):

1. Give all entries indicated for *(a)* the accrual of property tax (during 19B on a monthly basis) and the payment on January 17, 19C, and *(b)* the sales tax (for 19B) transactions.
2. Show how the effects of the above tax transactions should be reported on the 19B financial statements.

P 14–7 (Compensated Absences; Entries and Reporting)

Reston Company has a personnel policy that allows each employee with at least one year's employment 20 days' vacation time and 2 holidays with regular pay. Unused days are carried over to the next year; if not taken during the next year, the vacation and holiday times are lost. Reston's accounting period ends December 31.

At the end of 19B, the personnel records showed the following:

Vacations carried over to 19C		Holidays carried over to 19C	
Total days	Total salaries	Total days	Total salaries
70	$5,600	10	$900

During 19C, all of the 19B vacation time, and eight days of the holiday time, which were carried over, were taken. Salary increases in 19C for these employees relating to the days carried over amounted to $800. Total cash wages paid were: 19B, $890,000; 19C, $920,000.

Required:

1. Give all of the entries for Reston Company related to vacations and holidays during 19B and 19C. Disregard payroll taxes.
2. Show how the effects of the above transactions should be reported on the 19B and 19C financial statements of Reston.

P 14–8 (Contingency Losses, Five Events; Explanations, Entries, Reporting)

Davis Corporation is preparing its first set of financial statements at December 31, 19A, along with the appropriate adjusting entries. Among the contingent losses under consideration are the following transactions and events:

a. Sales revenue for 19A was $960,000; unpaid credit sales at year-end amounted to $22,000; and it is probable that $1,000 of that amount will result in a loss.
b. Two of the major product lines sold during the year carry a two-year warranty for defects (both labor and parts cost). Sales of these items amounted to $40,000. On the average, warranty expenditures approximate 2% of sales price.
c. During 19A, Davis issued 5,000 "DC orange coupons." Each 10 coupons held can be turned in, within one year from the date on the coupon, for a $15 credit on any item sold by Davis that costs more than $50. Davis estimates that 40% of the coupons will be redeemed.
d. Davis was sued by a shopper for $50,000 damages due to an accident in the retail store. The shopper asserts a permanent back injury, characterized primarily by pain and stiffness. Legal counsel is of the opinion that it is probable that the plaintiff will prevail in court and that Davis will have to pay 10% of the claim; it is anticipated

that the insurance company will pay the balance. The suit, or the claim otherwise, is expected to be resolved in mid-19B.

e. Davis Corporation endorsed, and guaranteed, a $25,000, 15%, one-year mortgage note given by a local supplier (of merchandise) to Davis. The bank required a guarantor. The bank indicated that the probability of default by the supplier was reasonably possible.

f. The comprehensive liability insurance policy carried by Davis Corporation covers all claims for damages to individuals or groups due to accident, negligence, and other injuries, relating to the legitimate operations of the company. However, the insurance policy carries an escape clause that states: "When the insured is willfully negligent, as determined by an independent third party, 10% of the loss must be paid by the insured."

Required:

1. Evaluate each of the above transactions and events and recommend appropriate accounting and reporting actions. Give any entry or note required for each item.
2. Identify each liability and the amount that should be reported on the 19A statement of financial position.

P 14–9 (Redeemable Coupons; Accounting and Reporting)

For the purpose of stimulating sales, Crispy Cereal Company places a coupon in each box of cereal sold; the coupons are redeemable in chinaware. Each premium costs the company 90 cents (the cost of printing the coupons is negligible). Ten coupons must be presented by the customers to receive one premium. The following data are available:

Month	Boxes of cereal sold	Premiums purchased	Coupons redeemed
January	650,000	25,000	220,000
February	500,000	40,000	410,000
March	560,000	35,000	300,000

It is estimated that only 70% of the coupons will be presented for redemption.

Required:

1. Prepare entries for each event listed below for each of the three months:
   a. Premiums purchased.
   b. Premium expense and related liability.
   c. Coupons redeemed.
2. Complete the following schedule for each month:

Accounts	Ending account balances		
	January	February	March
Premiums—Chinaware			
Estimated premium claims payable			
Premium expense (monthly)			

P 14–10 (Estimated Warranty Costs; Entries and Reporting)

Modern Hardware, Inc., provides a product warranty for defects on two major lines of items sold since the beginning of year 1. Line A carries a two-year warranty for all labor and service (but not parts). The company contracts with a local service establishment to service the warranty (both parts and labor). The local service establishment charges a flat fee of $60 per unit payable at date of sale.

Line B carries a three-year warranty for parts and labor on service. Modern purchases the parts needed under the warranty and has service personnel who perform the work and are paid by the job. On the basis of experience, it is estimated that for line B, the three-year warranty costs are 3% of dollar sales for parts and 7% for labor and overhead. Additional data available are as follows:

	Year 1	Year 2	Year 3
Sales in units, line A	700	1,000	
Sales price per unit, line A	$ 610	$ 660	
Sales in units, line B	600	800	
Sales price per unit, line B	$ 700	$ 750	
Actual warranty outlays, line B:			
Parts	$3,000	$ 9,600	$12,000
Labor and overhead	$7,000	$22,000	$30,000

Required:

1. Give entries for annual sales and expenses for year 1 and year 2 separately by product line. Assume all sales were for cash.
2. Complete a tabulation as follows:

Accounts	Year-end amounts Year 1	Year 2	Year 3
a. Warranty expense (on statement of income)	$____	$____	
b. Estimated warranty liability (on statement of financial position)	$____	$____	$____

P 14–11 (Recording and Reporting Liabilities; Including Payroll Deductions)

The following selected transactions of MER were completed during the accounting year just ended, December 31, 19A:

a. Merchandise was purchased on account; a $10,000, one-year, 15% interest-bearing note, dated May 1, 19A, was given to the creditor. Assume a perpetual inventory system.

b. Cosigned an $8,000 note payable for another party (no entry required).

c. On June 1, the company borrowed cash; a one-year, noninterest-bearing note with a face amount of $23,200 was signed. Assume a going rate of interest of 16%.

d. Payroll records showed the following (assume amounts given are correct):

	Employee			Employer		
Gross wages	With-holding	FICA	Union dues	FICA	SUTA (state)	FUTA (federal)
$50,000	$15,000	$3,000	$500	$3,000	$1,350	$350

Remittances were: withholding taxes, $13,000; FICA, $5,800; SUTA, state, $1,200; FUTA, federal, $340; and union dues, $280.

e. The company was sued for $150,000 in damages. It appears a court judgment against the company that is reasonably estimated to be $125,000 is probable. For problem purposes, assume this is an extraordinary item.
f. On November 1, 19A, the company rented some office space in its building to XY Company and collected rent in advance for six months; total, $2,400.
g. Cash dividends declared but not yet paid, $14,000.
h. Accrued interest on the notes at December 31.

Required:

1. Give the entry or entries for each of the above transactions and events.
2. Prepare a list (title and amount) of the disclosures related to the liabilities at December 31, 19A.

P 14–12 (Overview; Liabilities; Contingency Losses; Recording and Reporting)

The following selected transactions of General Company were completed during the current accounting year ended December 31, 19A:

a. March 1, 19A, borrowed $20,000 on a two-year, 12%, interest-bearing note.
b. April 1, 19A, borrowed cash and signed an $18,838, two-year, noninterest-bearing note (no interest was specified). The market rate of interest for this level of risk was 16%.
c. June 1, 19A, purchased a special truck with a list price of $29,000. Paid $9,000 cash and signed a $20,000, one-year, noninterest-bearing note (no interest was specified). The market rate of interest for this level of risk was 16%.
d. During 19A, sold merchandise for $40,000 cash that carried a two-year warranty for parts and labor. A reasonable estimate of the cost of the warranty is 1½% of sales revenue. By December 31, 19A, actual warranty costs amounted to $250.
e. June 1, 19A, General cosigned and guaranteed payment of a $60,000, 14%, one-year note owed by a local supplier to City Bank. The bank required a cosignature; however, they believe that default by the debtor is only reasonably possible.
f. October–November 19A, in order to promote sales during these two months, General gave its customers 10,000 premium certificates based on cash sales. Each certificate turned in during December 19A and January 19B will reduce the price by 50 cents on all single items that sell above $20. A reasonable estimate is that 75% of the certificates will be redeemed. By December 31, 19A, 60% of those issued had been redeemed.
g. Year 19A, property taxes to be recorded monthly:
   1. Prior year property taxes, $2,087; expected to increase by 15% during 19A.
   2. December 10, 19A—Final tax assessment received, $2,500; paid on February 1, 19B, the latest payment date without penalty.
h. December 19A, dividends declared (not yet paid or issued):
   1. Cash, $18,000 (use payable account).
   2. Stock, $12,000 (use issuable account).
i. December 19A—Sales revenue (excluding sales taxes collected) for the month, $300,000. Sales tax 5%, applicable to 98% of the sales. No unpaid sales tax carried over from November 19A.
j. December 31, 19A, accrual of interest payable.

Required (round to the nearest dollar):

1. For each of the 10 transactions, give all entries that General should make in 19A based on the data given.
2. List each current liability (account title and the amount) that should be reported on the 19A statement of financial position of General Company.

CASES

C 14–1 (Evaluation of a Liability; Recommendations)

Howdy Equipment Company sells new and used earth-moving equipment. It uses a perpetual inventory system, and its accounting period ends December 31. On December 28, 19D, Howdy purchased a used backhoe for resale, at an agreed price of $30,000. Terms of the purchase were: cash down payment, $10,000, plus a note payable, face amount, $20,000, maturity date, December 28, 19F. The company bookkeeper entered the equipment in the perpetual inventory account at $30,000 and reported no interest expense for 19D because the note did not specify that any interest would be paid. In answer to a question by the newly engaged independent auditor, the bookkeeper said that the entry on maturity date of the note would be a debit to Notes Payable and a credit to Cash of $20,000. The transaction was recorded on January 5, 19E, because it was on that date that Howdy received the equipment and the check was drawn.

Required:

1. Evaluate the accounting treatment of the purchase of the equipment. Consider both theoretical and GAAP issues. State any assumptions that you make.
2. If you disagree with the company's accounting, give your recommendations, including reasons. As a part of your response, give the journal entries. State any factual assumptions that you make.

C 14–2 (Contingencies; Four Situations)

Unlucky Company is preparing its annual financial statements at December 31, 19A, and is concerned about application of *FASB Statement 5,* "Accounting for Contingencies." Four unrelated situations are under consideration:

1. During 19B, a shopper sued the company for $500,000 for a claimed injury that occurred on the premises owned by Unlucky. No date for the trial has been set; however, the lawyer employed by Unlucky has completed a thorough investigation. Because it can be proven that the customer did fall on the premises, the legal counsel believes it will not be difficult for the plaintiff to prove injury. There is some evidence that it was due, at least partially, to negligence by the plaintiff. The attorney believes that it is not probable, but is reasonably possible, that the suit will be successful (for the plaintiff), but for a significantly smaller amount that cannot be reasonably estimated at this time.
2. The company had a $10,000, 8%, one-year note receivable from a customer. Unlucky discounted the note, with recourse, at the bank to obtain cash before its due date (due on June 1, 19B). If the maker does not pay the bank by due date, Unlucky will have to pay it. The customer has an excellent credit rating (having never defaulted on a debt).
3. An outside party has filed a claim against Unlucky for $25,000 claiming that certain actions by Unlucky caused the party to lose a contract on which the estimated profit

was this amount. In the opinion of the legal counsel engaged by Unlucky, the probability of the claim being successful is remote. Counsel does not believe it will ever be brought to trial. If necessary, Unlucky will defend itself in court.

4. The company owns a small plant in a foreign country that has a book value of $3 million and an estimated market value of $4 million. The foreign government has clearly indicated its unalterable intention to expropriate the plant during the coming year and to reimburse Unlucky for 50% of the estimated market value.

Required:

For each situation, respond to the following:

1. What accounting recognition (i.e., journal entries), if any, should be accorded each situation at the end of 19A? Explain why.
2. Indicate how each situation should be reported on the statement of financial position.

15 ACCOUNTING FOR LONG-TERM DEBTS BY THE BORROWER AND THE LENDER

OVERVIEW AND PURPOSE

In the future as an accountant, manager, or individual entrepreneur you will have to work with debt securities, both as a borrower and as a lender. Companies seeking long-term financing and investors wanting long-term investments will consider both equity securities (i.e., capital stock) and debt securities (i.e., notes and bonds).

The purpose of this chapter is to discuss the measuring, recording, and reporting of long-term debt securities by the borrower (also called the **debtor** or **issuer**) and the lender (also called the **creditor** or **investor**).

The technical aspect of this chapter involves present value (see Chapter 5). This chapter also discusses two related issues—debt restructuring and extinguishment. To accomplish these purposes, the chapter is subdivided as follows:

Part A: Fundamentals of Accounting for Long-Term Debt Securities

1. Characteristics of long-term debt securities.
2. Long-term notes and mortgages.
3. Accounting for long-term notes by the borrower and the lender.
4. Long-term notes with an unrealistic interest rate.
5. Bonds—issuer and investor.
6. Accounting for bonds by the issuer and investor.
7. Additional issues in accounting for bonds.
8. Reporting and disclosure of long-term liabilities.

Part B: Extinguishment of Debt and Debt Restructure

1. Extinguishment of debt.
2. Troubled debt restructuring.
3. Disclosure requirements.

Supplement 15–A: Serial Bonds

PART A: FUNDAMENTALS OF ACCOUNTING FOR LONG-TERM DEBT SECURITIES

Characteristics of Long-Term Debt Securities

FASB Concepts 6 defines liabilities as "probable future sacrifices of economic benefits arising from present obligations of a particular entity to transfer assets or provide resources to other entities in the future as a result of past transactions or events." Based on this definition, the following primary characteristics of a long-term debt security can be inferred: *(a)* there is an **obligation** to transfer assets or services to specified entities at a determinable future date; *(b)* the obligation was caused by a **transaction** or event that has already occurred; *(c)* there is an enforceable contract between the parties; and *(d)* repayment of the debt principal extends beyond one year from the current statement of financial position date or the operating cycle of the debtor, whichever is longer. Typical long-term debt securities include long-term notes payable, mortgages payable, pension liabilities, lease liabilities, and bonds payable.

Investors (i.e., creditors) have no voting privileges in the issuing entity. However, the debt instrument does provide a fixed rate of interest as well as fixed cash flow dates. In addition, long-term debt agreements usually carry specified restrictions, often called **covenants.** These covenants may be disadvantageous to the borrower but afford protection to the creditor. For example, the recent financial statements of a major company included the following note:

> The 19X8 Agreement, the 19X9 Agreement, and the Note Agreement contain certain defined restrictive convenants including restrictions on dividends, working capital, total debt, tangible net worth, and investments.

The note also provided a detailed explanation and the amount of each restriction.

For practical reasons, this chapter classifies long-term debt securities as *(a)* long-term notes and mortgages and *(b)* bonds payable. Also, we discuss long-term debt securities from the viewpoints of both the debtor (borrower) and the creditor (lender).[1] This dual approach is logical and time efficient because the accounting and reporting concepts and procedures are essentially the same, except that they are inverse. That is, there is an "accounting symmetry" between the debtor and creditor. A long-term debt security represents a long-term debt for the debtor and often a long-term investment to the creditor. Both parties have the same amounts of interest and principal and the same maturity date.

Long-Term Notes and Mortgages

A long-term note is a formal document that specifies the terms of the debt. These terms are the origination and maturity dates, the principal amount, and the rate and timing of interest payments. In regard to payment, long-term notes usually specify either *(a)* periodic payment of interest (e.g., annually or semiannually) with payment in full of the principal amount at maturity date, or *(b)* **equal** periodic installment payments (e.g., monthly), each representing an interest payment and a partial payment of principal. A note that is **not**

[1] Throughout Part A, for bonds we usually use the descriptive terms **issuer** and **investor.**

supported by pledged assets (i.e., collateral) to assure payment of the debt at maturity is called an **unsecured** note payable. In case of default, the creditor has a **general claim** against the debtor's assets rather than a specific claim against a particular asset. A **secured** note payable is one that includes a mortgage document representing a pledge of specific assets as security for the debt. The pledged assets may be either tangible (e.g., land, buildings, equipment) or intangible (e.g., equity or debt securities of other entities). Secured notes payable often are called **mortgages payable** or **mortgage notes payable.**

To consider debt securities, a careful distinction must be made between the **two** interest rates commonly used in accounting for debt securities: (1) the **stated** interest rate, which is the interest rate specified in the debt instrument, and (2) the **effective** or **yield** interest rate, which is the true interest rate used to determine the actual amount of interest expense (to the issuer) and interest revenue (to the investor) **implicit** in the transaction.[2]

In any particular situation, the stated and effective interest rates may be the same or different. When the **stated** interest rate on a note is the "true market or going" rate for that particular level of risk, the stated and effective rates are the same. In this case, there is no discount or premium on the debt security to be considered. However, when these two interest rates are **different,** accounting for and reporting the debt become complex. Both situations will be discussed in this part of the chapter.

Long-term notes usually express the **stated** interest rate on an annual basis even though the **cash** interest payments may be made monthly, quarterly, or semiannually.

Special Kinds of Notes

Because of high and unstable interest rates, particularly on long-term notes, innovative debt arrangements have begun to supplement mortgage notes payable with traditional terms. These special kinds of notes include: (1) point-system mortgages, (2) shared-appreciation mortgages, and (3) variable-rate mortgages.

Point-System Mortgages. Under the point system, each point represents 1% of the face amount of the note. In a typical point-system mortgage, the lender assesses a specified number of points. This **reduces** the amount of cash the borrower receives to some amount below the face amount of the note (i.e., it is a cash holdback). Thus, each point assessed increases the effective rate of interest above the rate stated in the note. To illustrate the point system, assume you signed a $100,000, 12%, five-year mortgage note (to purchase a building). The lending institution stipulated an assessment of five points. You would receive cash of $100,000 × 95% = $95,000. Nevertheless, you would be required to pay back *(a)* the annual interest at the stated rate of 12% applied to the $100,000 face amount of the note and *(b)* the $100,000 face amount, even though you actually received only $95,000. Therefore, the effective rate of interest you actually pay approximates 14.1%, rather than the 12% stated rate specified on

[2] Throughout this chapter, we use the descriptive terms ***stated*** and ***effective*** rates. However, across industries and in the literature, the following terms are often used synonymously for the two interest rates: stated/specified/nominal/contract/coupon/cash rate and effective/yield/real/going/market rate.

the note payable. Another typical point-system mortgage requires equal periodic payments of interest and part principal (including the points), rather than payment of the entire face amount at maturity date. The computation to determine the effective rate and the entries for point-system debts are discussed on page 644 and illustrated in Exhibit 15–2.

Shared-Appreciation Mortgages (SAMs). Under the terms of this type of note, the lender specifies a stated interest rate on the note. This rate is lower than the effective rate on similar notes with the same risk. In return, the lender is granted a share of the appreciation in value, but no share of any losses, of the mortgaged assets (usually real estate). In other words, the lender "gets a piece of the action." Variations in the appreciation include a share of the earnings or a specified ownership share of a project. The appreciation provision has value; therefore, it causes the effective interest rate on the debt to be higher than the rate stated in the note. Accounting for SAMs requires estimation of the effective interest rate similar to that for a point-system mortgage. That is, to compute the unknown effective rate of interest, the best estimate of the present value of the share appreciation is subtracted from the principal of the debt (see Exhibit 15–2, panel B, computation b).

Variable-Rate Mortgages. The stated rate of interest on this type of note (also called **floating-rate,** or **adjustable-rate,** mortgages) changes periodically to correspond with changes in the prime interest rate and sometimes with changes in perceived risk.[3] The primary aim of variable-rate mortgages is to shift, from the lender to the borrower, the economic effects of changing and unstable interest rates. A **floating** interest rate on long-term notes usually is changed quarterly, semiannually, or annually; however, even three-year intervals are not uncommon. In contrast, the floating prime rate charged on short-term notes often is changed each day when the prime interest rate changes.

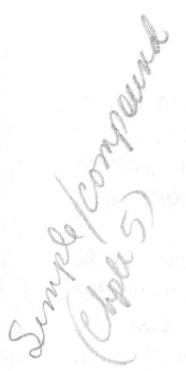

To illustrate how a typical variable-rate mortgage works, a large company reported that during July 1987, on renewal of a major long-term loan, the lending institution changed its "semiannual floating" interest rate from the "floating prime rate plus zero" to the "floating prime rate plus 1.5%." Variable-rate mortgages pose no additional accounting problems other than accruals based on the latest floating rate applicable to the note.

Accounting for Long-Term Notes by the Borrower and the Lender

Accounting for long-term notes and mortgages involves two different situations:

a. **The stated and effective interest rates are the same**—This situation does not involve any discount or premium on the debt because the stated and effective rates are the same. **Exhibit 15–1** illustrates such a situation. It also compares the entries and reporting of the issuer (i.e., borrower) and investor (i.e., lender).

[3] Typically, each bank sets its own prime interest rate. A bank's best borrowers are then charged this rate. The prime rate is changed frequently, sometimes daily.

Exhibit 15–1
Long-term note payable—entries for borrower and lender (stated and effective rates the same).

Panel A—Case Data:

On November 1, 19A, Issue Corporation borrowed cash from Investor Corporation on a $100,000, 12%, five-year note. Interest payable each October 31, 19B–19F. The principal is to be paid on October 31, 19F. The accounting period for each company ends on December 31.

Panel B—Entries for Borrower and Lender:

November 1, 19A—Debt security issued/purchased:

Borrower			Lender		
Cash	100,000		Long-term investment, note receivable	100,000	
Long-term note payable		100,000	Cash		100,000

December 31, 19A–19E—End of accounting period; interest accrual (same each year):

Borrower			Lender		
Interest expense	2,000		Interest receivable	2,000	
Interest payable		2,000	Interest revenue		2,000
$\$100,000 \times 12\% \times 2/12 = \$2,000$.					

October 31, 19B–19F—Interest payment (same each year; assumes no reversing entry on January 1):

Borrower			Lender		
Interest payable (2 months)	2,000		Cash	12,000	
Interest expense (10 months)	10,000		Interest receivable		2,000
Cash (12 months)		12,000	Interest revenue		10,000

October 31, 19F—Maturity date; payment of principal:

Borrower			Lender		
Long-term note payable	100,000		Cash	100,000	
Cash		100,000	Long-term investment, note receivable		100,000

Panel C—Reporting on Financial Statements:

Statement of income—year ended December 31, 19A:

Borrower		Lender	
Interest expense	$ 2,000	Interest revenue	$ 2,000

Statement of financial position—at December 31,19A:

Borrower		Lender	
Interest payable	$ 2,000	Interest receivable	$ 2,000
Long-term note payable	100,000	Long-term investment, note receivable	100,000

b. **The stated and effective interest rates are different**—This situation involves a discount or premium on the debt because the stated and effective rates are different. The two rates may differ because (1) the market or going rate at the level of risk involved in the debt is higher or lower than the stated rate, or (2) the note itself specifies conditions that produce this effect. In this situation the appropriate effective rate is not specified. Therefore, it must be obtained from the "money market" or must be computed by iteration (i.e., by trial and error). Notes with stated and effective rates that are different include: (1) point-system mortgage notes, (2) shared-appreciation notes, and (3) notes that are intentionally drawn with a stated interest rate that is more or less than the market or going rate of interest.

Exhibit 15–2 illustrates a point-system note that is paid in equal annual installments. Notice panel B, which presents the analysis necessary to compute the unknown effective rate. Calculators with FV and PV functions often are programmed to perform this computation directly. Panel C presents a typical **debt amortization schedule.** This schedule provides all of the data necessary to make the journal entries over the term of the note. The debt amortization schedule depicted in Exhibit 15–2 also illustrates the **interest method** of amortizing a discount (or premium). The interest method is conceptually the correct method

Exhibit 15–2
Long-term note with POINTS received by the lender—entries for issuer and investor (stated and effective interest rates are different).

Panel A—Case Data:
On November 1, 19A, BOR Corporation borrowed cash from FIN Corporation on a $100,000, 12%, five-year note, and FIN demanded (and received) 5 points on the note. Five equal annual payments (part interest and part principal) are to be made each October 31, 19B–19F. The accounting period for each company ends on December 31.

Panel B—Analysis Necessary to Account for this Note, which Includes the Economic Effects of the Points:

a. To compute the amount of the annual cash payments based on the stated rate of interest and the face of the note:

$$\$100{,}000 \div P_{o_{n=5;\,i=12\%}} \text{ (Table 5–4, 3.60478)} = \underline{\underline{\$27{,}741}} \text{ (cash).}$$

b. To compute the unknown effective interest rate (including the 5 points):

$$\$95{,}000^{*} \div P_{o_{n=5;\,i=?}} = \text{Cash payments, } \$27{,}741$$
$$P_{o_{n=5;\,i=?}} = \$95{,}000 \div \$27{,}741$$
$$P_{o_{n=5;\,i=?}} = 3.42453 \text{ (Table 5–4 value for } n = 5;\ i = ?)$$
i = Inspection of Table 5–4 for $n = 5$ indicates i to be between 14% and 15%.

$$\text{Interpolation} = 14\% + \left[\frac{3.43308\ (P_{o_{n=5;\,i=14\%}}) - 3.42453 \text{ (computed above)}}{3.43308 - 3.35216\ (P_{o_{n=5;\,i=15\%}})}\right]$$
$$= 14.1\% \text{ effective rate (rounded to the nearest tenth)}$$

Panel C—Debt/Receivable Amortization Schedule:

Date	Cash	Interest expense/revenue[(a)] (effective rate, 14.1%)	Reduction of principal	Principal balance
Nov. 1, 19A				$95,000
Oct. 31, 19B	$ 27,741	$95,000 × 14.1% = $13,395	$14,346[(b)]	80,654[(c)]
Oct. 31, 19C	27,741	80,654 × 14.1% = 11,372	16,369	64,285
Oct. 31, 19D	27,741	64,285 × 14.1% = 9,064	18,677	45,608
Oct. 31, 19E	27,741	45,608 × 14.1% = 6,431	21,310	24,298
Oct. 31, 19F	27,741	24,298 × 14.1% = 3,443[(d)]	24,298	-0-
Totals	$138,705	$43,705	$95,000	

* $100,000 − (.05 × $100,000) = $95,000.
[(a)] Rounded to nearest dollar.
[(b)] $27,741 − $13,395 = $14,346, etc.
[(c)] $95,000 − $14,346 = $80,654, etc.
[(d)] Rounded up $17 to compensate for rounding of effective interest rate.

(continued)

Exhibit 15–2
(concluded)

Panel D—Entries for Borrower and Lender:

Borrower—BOR Corporation			Lender—FIN Corporation		
November 1, 19A—Debt security issued/purchased (net of discount):[(a)]					
Cash	95,000		Long-term investment, note receivable	95,000	
Note payable (net of discount)		95,000	Cash		95,000
December 31, 19A—End of accounting period; interest accrual (see Debt Amortization Schedule):					
Interest expense ($13,395 × 2/12)	2,233		Interest receivable	2,233	
Interest payable		2,233	Investment revenue		2,233
October 31, 19B—Interest payment (assumes no reversing entry on January 1):[(b)]					
Interest payable (above)	2,233		Cash	27,741	
Interest expense ($13,395 × 10/12)	11,162		Interest receivable		2,233
Note payable	14,346		Interest revenue		11,162
Cash		27,741	Long-term investment, note receivable		14,346

Panel E—Reporting on Financial Statements:

Statement of income—year ended December 31, 19A:			
Interest expense	$ 2,233	Interest revenue	$ 2,233
Statement of financial position—at December 31, 19A:			
Interest payable	2,233	Interest receivable	2,233
Note payable	95,000	Long-term investment, note receivable	95,000

[(a)] The note could be recorded at gross ($100,000) with a "Discount on note" contra account of $5,000. This account would then be amortized in the interest entries. Each approach gives the same results (see Chapter 14, pp. 610–611 for an example of a similar situation).

[(b)] Entries during each remaining year would be calculated in the same manner, except that the amounts would be based on the figures for each respective year shown in the debt amortization schedule, panel C.

to apply and is required by *APB Opinion 21,* par. 15. However, the straight-line method can be used if its results are not materially different from those obtained by using the interest method. Notice that the periodic amounts of interest and discount amortization are quite different. That is, straight-line amortization each period is $19,000 ($95,000 ÷ 5 years) compared with interest method amortization amounts shown in Exhibit 15–2, panel C. The periodic interest expense and revenue amounts reflect similar differences.

In Exhibit 15–2 the note was recorded at its **net amount** after taking into account the five points (i.e., $100,000 × .95 = $95,000) rather than at its **gross amount** ($100,000) with a separate contra account, Discount on Note, $5,000. Either approach can be used by either the issuer or the investor because both approaches provide the same results. However, many accountants prefer the **net** approach for the following practical reasons: *(a)* the entries exactly parallel the information provided in the debt amortization schedule, and *(b)* one less account (i.e., discount or premium) is involved in accounting for and reporting the note. The gross method has a history of long usage, as well as the advantage of maintaining the discount or premium in separate accounts. The balance of these accounts always reflects the unamortized amounts.

Long-Term Notes with an Unrealistic Interest Rate

Accountants sometimes encounter a long-term note that specifies an unrealistically low or high rate of interest compared with the current market or going rate for the level of risk involved.

APB Opinion 21, "Interest on Receivables and Payables," specifies the accounting for two such situations as follows:

1. **Notes received or issued solely for cash**—The cash received or paid is assumed to be the present value of the note; therefore, discounting is not necessary.
2. **Notes issued or received for property, goods, or services**—The debtor and creditor must account for both the originating transaction and the subsequent interest payments on the basis of the present value of the note discounted at the market or going rate of interest for the level of risk involved.

To illustrate the second situation, because the client had no cash, a payment for legal services was made with a $10,000, three-year, 6% note (interest payable each year-end). The best estimate of the going or market rate of interest for this level of risk was 10% (see Chapter 5, pp. 193 and 197). Both the debtor and creditor would account for this interest-bearing note as follows:

Present value:

$10,000 × $p_{n=3;i=10\%}$ (Table 5–2, .75131)	= $7,513
($10,000 × 6% = $600) × $P_{o_{n=3;i=10\%}}$ (Table 5–4, 2.48685)	= 1,492
Present value	$9,005

Originating entry for the debtor (the amounts for the creditor are the same, but the account titles are different):

Expense (legal services)	9,005	
Note payable		9,005

Debt amortization schedule:

Date	Cash interest	Interest expense (effective rate, 10%)	Principal increase	Debt principal
Beginning year 1				$ 9,005
End year 1	$ 600	$9,005 × 10% = $ 900	$300	9,305
End year 2	600	9,305 × 10% = 931	331	9,636
End year 3	600	9,636 × 10% = 964	364	10,000
Totals	$1,800	$2,795	$995	

Entries for the debtor (the amounts for the creditor are the same, but t
account titles are different):

	Year 1		Year 2		Year 3		Maturity	
Interest expense	900		931		964			
Note payable		300		331		364	10,000	
Cash		600		600		600		10,000

Bonds—Issuer and Investor

debt securities (not owners equity)

Bonds, often called **debentures,** are debt securities **issued** by companies and government units to secure large amounts of resources. Bonds are **purchased** by investors as an important component of their long-term investment portfolios. Bonds typically are listed on a daily basis by the stock exchanges similar to the listing for equity securities. For example, *The Wall Street Journal* publishes daily information about bonds. The following is an excerpt from the bond listings in *The Wall Street Journal:*

CORPORATION BONDS
Volume, $37,300,000

Bonds	Cur Yld	Vol	High	Low	Close	Net Chg.
ANR 8 5/8 93	8.9	25	97 1/8	97 1/8	97 1/8	+ 1/4
ARX 9 3/8 05	CV	31	110 1/2	110	110	− 1 1/8
AVX 8 1/4 12	CV	1	106	106	106	− 1
Advst 9s08	CV	24	107	106 1/2	107	− 1
AetnLf 8 1/8 07	8.9	3	91	91	91	+ 1
AlaBn 6.7s99†	6.7	50	99 5/8	99 5/8	99 5/8	. . .
AlaP 7 3/4s02	9.3	25	83 3/4	83 3/4	83 3/4	+ 1/2
AlaP 9 3/4s04	9.9	45	98 1/2	98 1/2	98 1/2	+ 1/2
AlaP 10 7/8 05	10.6	18	103 1/2	102 3/4	102 3/4	− 7/8
AlaP 8 3/4 07	9.7	73	90 1/2	89 3/4	90 1/4	+ 3/8
AlaP 9 5/8 08	10.0	6	96 1/8	96	96	− 1 3/4

Bonds	Cur Yld	Vol	High	Low	Close	Net Chg.
AmMed 11 3/4 99	11.5	2	102	102	102	. . .
ATT 3 7/8s90	4.2	40	93 1/4	93 1/4	93 1/4	− 1/4
ATT 3 7/8 90r	4.2	100	93 3/8	93 1/4	93 1/4	. . .
ATT 8 3/4 00	9.2	301	96	95 1/4	95 5/8	+ 1/4
ATT 7s01	8.8	292	80 1/8	79 5/8	79 3/4	− 5/8
ATT 7 1/8s03	9.0	185	79 3/8	78 3/4	78 7/8	− 3/4
ATT 8.80s05	9.5	453	93 1/8	92 5/8	92 7/8	− 7/8
ATT 8 5/8s07	9.5	243	91	90 1/2	90 1/2	− 1/2
ATT 8 5/8 26	9.9	256	87 1/4	86 3/4	87	− 1/2
Amfac 5 1/4 94	CV	89	94	93 1/4	93 1/4	+ 1
Amoco 9.2s04	9.4	6	97 3/4	97	97 3/8	. . .

Also, valuable information about the risk of bond issues is available from Standard and Poor's Corporation and Moody's Investor Services. These service companies use the following quality designations and rating symbols:

	Rating symbols	
Quality designation	**Standard and Poor's**	**Moody's**
Prime	AAA	Aaa
Excellent	AA	Aa
Upper Medium	A	A
Lower medium	BBB	Baa
Marginally speculative	BB	Ba
Very speculative	B	B, Caa
Default	D	Ca, C

A bond is a legal document that represents a formal promise to pay: *(a)* a specified principal amount at a designated date in the future, and *(b)* periodic interest on the principal at the interest rate per period stated on the bond. The issuer prepares a formal bond agreement, often called the **bond indenture,** which specifies the terms of the bonds, including all **restrictions or covenants.** The bond indenture specifies such items as authorized amount for issuance, periodic interest (including dates), maturity date, conversion and call privileges (if any), sinking fund requirements, restrictions of retained earnings (discussed in Chapter 17), dividend restrictions on the issuer, maximum debt-to-equity ratio permitted for the borrower, and the responsibilities of an **independent trustee** appointed to protect the interests of both the issuer and the investors.

The investors receive **bond certificates.** These certificates are contractual representations that a debt is owed by one party, the issuer, to one or more other parties, the investors. A bond certificate indicates the principal amount, specified interest dates (usually semiannual), the stated rate of interest based upon the principal amount, maturity date, and any other special agreements.

When a company decides to borrow by issuing bonds, the total amount of the bonds authorized at that time usually is referred to collectively as a bond issue. A total long-term bond issue is divided into a number of small units, usually in denominations of $10,000 and $1,000, which then are sold to investors. These different denominations are used to attract a wide range of investors.

Classification of Bonds

Bonds may be classified in various ways as follows:

1. **Character of the issuing corporation**—The issuer may be a private corporation issuing **industrial** bonds. The issuer may also be a public entity issuing **municipal** or other **government** bonds.

2. **Character of the security—Secured** bonds are supported by a lien, or mortgage, on specific assets. **Unsecured** bonds have no such support. **Guaranty security bonds** are those which, in case of default, the principal and interest will be paid by a third party designated as the guarantor. For example, a parent corporation may guarantee payment of bonds issued by one or more of its subsidiary companies.

3. **Purpose of issue—Purchase money bonds** are issued in full or part payment for property. **Refunding bonds** are issued to retire existing obligations and may have the same security as the retired debt. **Consolidated bonds** replace several prior issues with a single issue and consolidate the securities for the retired issues. These types are comparatively rare.

4. **Payment of interest**—Bonds are sometimes classified according to the amount of interest that a bondholder is entitled to receive. **Ordinary** bonds entitle the investor to receive cash interest. The interest is based solely on the **stated** rate applied to the principal amount of the bond. **Income bonds** differ from **ordinary** bonds in that the payment of interest each period on income bonds depends on the issuer's earnings. **Participating bonds** have a specified minimum stated rate of interest plus a stated participation in the income of the issuer. Participation may be limited to a specified share in the issuer's earnings, or it may be unlimited.

In addition, bonds may be classified by the way that interest payments are made. **Registered bonds** are recorded in the name of the investor. The periodic interest payments are sent only to that person. Therefore, a sale or tr by the investor must be reported to the issuer, trustee, or other party designat for this purpose. In contrast, **coupon bonds** have a coupon attached for each periodic interest payment. At each coupon due date, the holder of the bond detaches the appropriate coupon, signs it, and cashes or deposits it as if it were a regular check. Sale of a coupon bond does not require **registration** of title transfer.

5. **Maturity of principal—Ordinary bonds** mature at a single specified date. In contrast, bonds maturing at a series of stated installment dates are called **serial bonds** (discussed in Supplement 15–A). **Callable bonds** give the **issuer** the option to retire them at a stated price before maturity date. In contrast, **redeemable bonds** give the **investor** the option to turn them in for a stated redemption price prior to the maturity date. **Convertible bonds** give the **investor** the option to turn them in and receive, in exchange, other specified securities of the borrower (usually common stock).

Financial Market Considerations

In the financial (i.e., money) market, a borrower needing a large sum of money must make the fundamental decision whether to use debt securities, equity securities, or a combination of the two. This decision depends on a number of factors. These factors may be peculiar to the company or based on conditions in the financial market. This topic is discussed in detail in finance textbooks.

Bonds may be marketed initially by the issuer in several ways. Typically, an entire bond issue is sold to investment bankers. Bankers **underwrite** the bond issue at a specified price and then market the bonds at a higher price to individual investors, thus realizing underwriter's compensation. Alternatively, the investment banker may agree to act as a selling agent for the borrower for an agreed commission. The selling price less the costs of selling is remitted to the issuer. However, instead of offering bonds through a public sale, some issuers sell their bonds privately to financial institutions and individual investors.

In making an investment decision, the **investor** should weigh the **guaranteed** fixed interest rate on the bonds and the bond maturity specifications against the **potential** for dividends and price appreciation on equity securities. Bonds are usually considered to be less risky as investments than equity securities. Therefore, investors often demand a higher rate of return on equity investments than on bond investments. Both interest revenue (except for tax-free municipal bonds) and dividend revenue (there are certain limited exceptions) are subject to income tax to the investor.

Bond Interest and Prices

Bonds have fixed maturity amounts, definite maturity dates, and specified cash interest payments. Because these three specifications cannot be changed, the **effective** or yield interest rate changes to reflect market forces. Therefore, **the market price of bonds fluctuates inversely with changes in the market interest rate.** When the market interest rate rises, the market price of outstanding bonds falls; when the market interest rate falls, the market price of bonds rises. Although the market price of bonds tends to move inversely with the market interest rate, the price also is influenced by changes in the issuer's financial standing and the approach of maturity (at which time the market value and maturity amount normally will coincide).

The bond indenture and the face of each bond certificate always specify the **stated** interest rate. This rate is applied to the principal amount of the bond to determine the amount of **cash interest** that will be paid each period. The **cash** interest paid each period is unaffected by the issue price of a bond (i.e., whether the issue price is at, above, or below par). To illustrate, assume each bond certificate of X Corporation specifies a **stated** rate of 7% per year. Thus, each $10,000 bond will always pay $700 cash interest each annual interest period, and a $1,000 denomination bond will always pay $70 cash each interest period.

In contrast to the stated rate of interest, the **effective** or yield interest rate is the true rate of interest incurred by the issuer and earned by the investor after taking into account the issue (or purchase) price of the bond.[4] Because the financial market may establish a rate of interest on the bonds different from the stated rate, bonds may sell at **more or less** than their **par amount.**[5]

A bond sold at **par** results in interest expense to the issuer at the stated rate of interest and interest revenue to the investor at that same rate. Only in this situation will *(a)* the stated and effective rates of interest be the same and *(b)* the bond be sold at its face (par) amount. A bond is sold at a **discount** (i.e., less than par) when the effective interest rate exceeds the stated rate. As a result, the interest expense reported by the issuer and interest revenue reported by the investor (both based on the effective rate) will be **more** than the periodic **cash** interest payments (based on the rate stated on the bond). Conversely, a bond is sold at a **premium** (i.e., more than par) when the effective interest rate is **less** than the stated rate. As a result, the interest expense reported by the issuer and interest revenue reported by the investor (both based on the effective rate) will be **less** than the periodic **cash** interest payments (based on the rate stated on the bond).[6]

Investment firms often quote bonds on a **yield basis.** A 7% bond quoted at 7–50 can be bought at a price that will earn 7½% on the price of the bond each year from date of purchase to maturity date. Thus, a $1,000 bond with a stated rate of 7%, payable 3½% **semiannually,** sold on a 7½% (yield rate) basis five years before maturity would have a price of $979.47 (computation discussed later). The $20.53 discount occurs because the effective interest rate is higher than the 7% stated rate. Bonds also may be quoted in relation to their par or maturity amount. For example, a $1,000 bond quoted at 100 is selling for $1,000 (i.e., at par); if quoted at 97, it is selling for $970 (i.e., at a discount of $30); and if quoted at 103, it is selling for $1,030 (i.e., at a premium of $30).

Determination of Bond Prices (Present Value)

The price of a bond is the present value of all of its expected net future cash flows discounted at the market (as opposed to the stated) rate of interest. Thus, the **present value** of a bond is the sum of two present value amounts: *(a)* the present value of its face (par) amount plus *(b)* the present value of the series of future **cash interest payments.** Because computation of the price of a

---

[4] See footnote 2, page 641.

[5] In the context of bonds, alternate terms for **par amount** are principal, face, and maturity amount.

[6] This discussion assumes that the issuer sells the bonds directly to the investors with no bond issue costs. Bond issue costs will be discussed in a later section.

Exhibit 15–3
Computation of bond prices.

a. PV of future principal (use the effective rate):	
$100,000 × $p_{n=5;i=8\%}$ (Table 5–2, .68058)	$68,058
b. PV of cash interest (use the effective rate):	
$7,000 × $P_{o_{n=5;i=8\%}}$ (Table 5–4, 3.99271)	27,949
Total PV—Bond price at 8% effective rate	$96,007*
Discount: $100,000 − $96,007 = $3,993.	
c. If the effective rate had been 6%, the bond price would have been $104,212, computed in the same way (a premium of $4,212).	

* Some pocket calculators are programmed to make this computation directly.

bond (i.e., its present value) is especially important for a thorough understanding of accounting for bonds, detailed illustrations are presented below. The price of a bond may be derived by computing the present value of its two future cash flows. This computation requires the following bond specifications: face (par) amount, frequency of interest payments, stated rate of interest, time to maturity (i.e., issue/purchase date to maturity date), and **effective** or market rate of interest. To illustrate, X Corporation sold a $100,000 bond with a stated rate of interest of 7% (annual payments) when the effective or market rate was 8%. The time from sale date to maturity date was five years. The sale or issue price can be computed as shown in **Exhibit 15–3.**

In summary, it is important to reemphasize that a bond sold (or purchased) at **par** has a present value **identical** to the par or maturity amount. In contrast, a bond sold (or purchased) at a **discount** has a present value at the time of issuance **lower** than face (par) amount (by the amount of the discount). A bond sold (or purchased) at a **premium** has a present value at the time of issuance **higher** than par or maturity amount (by the amount of the premium).

In the bond market, if the market price is set as a **yield rate,** then the dollar price of the bonds must be computed by using the present value computation shown above. However, if the market price is set as a **dollar amount,** then the effective interest rate must be computed as shown in Exhibit 15–2, panel B, item *(b)*.

Accounting for Bonds by the Issuer and Investor

When a bond is issued (i.e., sold), the **issuer** records the cash equivalent received for the bond as the amount of the liability—the face (par) of the bond plus any premium or minus any discount. At the date of purchase, the **investor** records the cash equivalent paid for the bond as the cost of the investment in debt securities.

Subsequent to acquisition, both the issuer and the investor must carry the bond at its par amount plus any **unamortized** bond premium or less any unamortized bond discount. Any **premium** is "amortized" against **interest expense for the issuer** and **interest revenue for the investor.** Amortization of premium has the effect of reducing the amount of periodic interest recognized as expense (to the issuer) and revenue (to the investor). This effect is consistent with the fact that, for a bond sold **above** par, the effective rate of interest is **less** than the stated rate. Conversely, the amortization of any **discount** is consistent with the fact that, for a bond sold **below** par, the effective rate is **higher** than the stated rate.

Amortization of Bond Discount and Premium

Recall that bond discount and premium occurs because the stated interest rate on the bond is different from the effective rate on the bond. The premium or discount also affects the cash-equivalent amounts recorded at the issue/purchase date by the issuer and investor. In conformity with the **matching principle,** the bond premium or discount on noncurrent debt securities must be amortized to change *(a)* the carrying values of the bonds reported by the issuer and investor and *(b)* the amount of interest expense reported by the issuer and interest revenue reported by the investor. The **amortization period** for the issuer runs from date of sale to maturity date; for the **investor,** it runs from the purchase date to maturity date (see Exhibit 15–4). Bond discount or premium usually is amortized on each interest date (a related adjusting entry will be illustrated later). Two amortization methods are used to amortize bond discount or premium. They are:

a. **Straight-line method of amortization**—Under this method, an equal dollar amount of discount or premium is amortized each interest period throughout the amortization period. The straight-line method of amortization produces a **stable dollar amount of total interest** each period rather than a **constant rate** of interest each period. It can be used under GAAP only when the interest amounts obtained are not materially different from those produced by the interest method results (*APB Opinion 21,* par. 15). Straight-line amortization is simple. However, it is conceptually deficient because a constant rate of interest is not maintained.

b. **Interest method of amortization**—Under this method, a **constant effective rate** of interest is maintained. It produces variable (as opposed to stable) dollar amounts of amortization. Because each periodic cash interest payment represents an annuity, a debt amortization schedule is needed to identify the part that is interest (based on the effective rate) and the part that causes the carrying value of the bonds to be equal to the principal amount due at maturity. In the case of a discount, the carrying value **increases** as the discount is amortized. In the case of a premium, the carrying value **decreases** as the premium is amortized.

Amortization entries can be made on either the interest dates, or at the end of the accounting period.

Accounting for Bonds by the Issuer and Investor Illustrated

To illustrate accounting for bonds in this part of the chapter, we will use the data given in **Exhibit 15–4.** Panel A presents the case data. Panel B provides a **time scale** for the bonds, which is helpful in studying bonds and in solving bond problems. The usefulness of a time scale will become more apparent when certain bond complexities are introduced.

Exhibit 15–4
Illustrative data for bonds—issuer, X Corporation; investor, Y Corporation.

Panel A—Case Data—Specifications in the Bond Indenture:

a. Maturity amount of the bonds	$100,000 (in $10,000 and $1,000 denominations).
b. Date of the bonds	January 1, 19A.
c. Maturity date	December 31, 19E (term, five years).
d. Stated interest rate	7% per year.
e. Interest payments (cash)	Annually each December 31 (amount, $100,000 × 7% = $7,000).
f. Date sold	January 1, 19A (unless otherwise stated).
g. Price or effective interest rate	As specified in the examples to follow.

Note: Accounting period for issuer and investor ends on December 31, unless otherwise stated.

Panel B—Bond Time Scale (analytical):

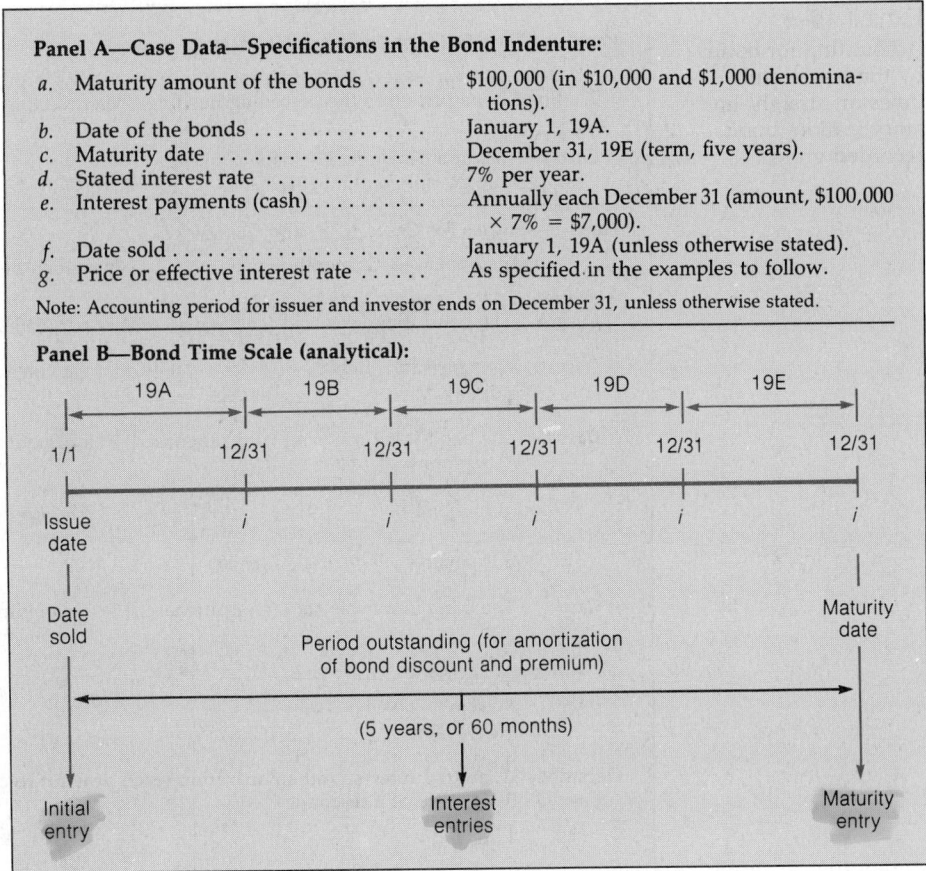

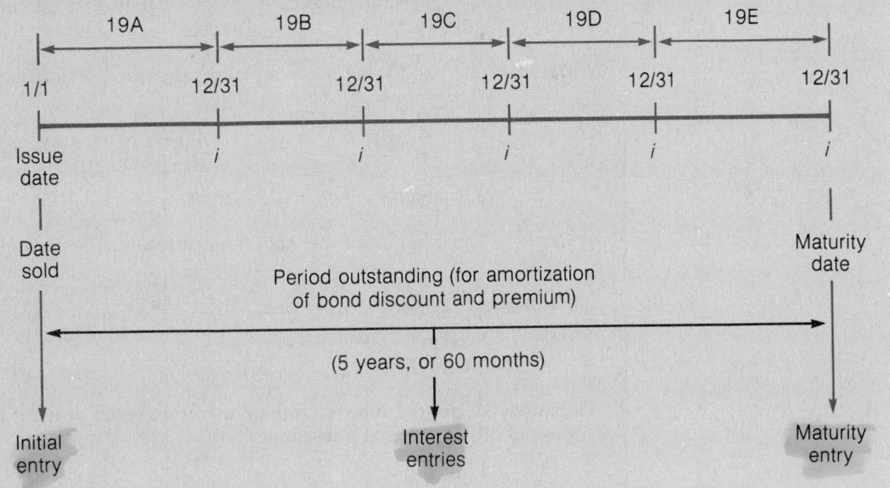

Accounting for bonds involves a choice about two issues as follows: *(a)* whether to use the straight-line or interest method of amortization (discussed above), and *(b)* whether to record the bond issue and the bond purchase **net** or **gross.** Under the net approach a bond is recorded at its issue, or purchase price; this means that any discount or premium is not separately recorded. In contrast, under the gross approach the bond account reflects the par value of a bond and the bond discount or premium is recorded in a separate account. Historically, investors have primarily used the net approach while issuers have commonly used the gross approach. The issuer and the investor each have the option of using either the net or gross approach because each gives identical results. Because of precedent, illustrations usually show the issuer using gross and the investor using net. To provide a comprehensive illustration of accounting for bonds, three exhibits are presented based on the case data analyzed in Exhibit 15–4.

Exhibit 15–5 illustrates use of the **straight-line method** of amortization recorded gross. **Exhibits 15–6** and **15–7** illustrate use of the **interest method** of amortization recorded net.

Exhibit 15–5
Accounting for bonds by the issuer and investor; straight-line amortization (bonds recorded gross).

Panel A—Case Data (given in Exhibit 15–4):

1. Basic data for issuer, X Corporation, and investor, Y Corporation.
2. Bond issue price (see the preceding heading, Determination of Bond Prices).

Case A—sold at par.
Case B—sold at a discount, $96,007.
Case C—sold at a premium, $104,212.

Panel B—Entries for Cases A, B, and C:

At issuance date, January 1, 19A:
Case A—The bond issue was sold (and purchased) at par, $100,000:

Issuer's Books—X Corporation			Investor's Books—Y Corporation		
Cash	100,000		Bond investment	100,000	
Bonds payable		100,000	Cash		100,000

Case B—The bond issue was sold (and purchased) at a discount, $96,007:

Issuer's Books—X Corporation			Investor's Books—Y Corporation		
Cash	96,007		Bond investment	100,000	
Discount on bonds payable	3,993		Discount on bond investment		3,993
Bonds payable		100,000	Cash		96,007

Case C—The bond issue was sold (and purchased) at a premium, $104,212:

Issuer's Books—X Corporation			Investor's Books—Y Corporation		
Cash	104,212		Bond investment	100,000	
Premium on bonds payable		4,212	Premium on bond investment	4,212	
Bonds payable		100,000	Cash		104,212

December 31, annual interest and amortization (each year for five years):
Case B—Bonds sold at a discount:

Issuer's Books—X Corporation			Investor's Books—Y Corporation		
Interest expense	7,799		Cash	7,000	
Discount on bonds payable ($3,993 ÷ 5 years)		799	Discount on bond investment	799	
Cash ($100,000 × 7%)		7,000	Interest revenue		7,799

Case C—Bonds sold at a premium:

Issuer's Books—X Corporation			Investor's Books—Y Corporation		
Interest expense	6,158		Cash	7,000	
Premium on bonds payable ($4,212 ÷ 5 years)	842		Premium on bond investment		842
Cash ($100,000 × 7%)		7,000	Interest revenue		6,158

Note: If the above entries were made gross for the interest method, only the amounts would change.

Panel C—Reporting (Case B, discount) December 31, 19A:

Issuer (gross)			Investor (gross)		
Statement of income:					
Interest expense		$ 7,799	Interest revenue		$ 7,799
Statement of financial position:					
Bonds payable	$100,000		Bond investment	$100,000	
Less: Unamortized discount	3,194	96,806	Less: Unamortized discount	3,194	96,806

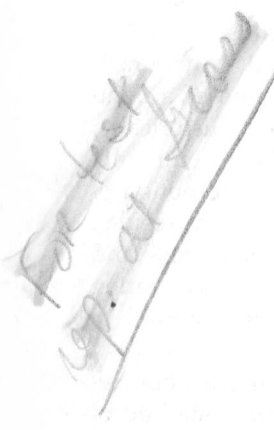

Exhibit 15–6
Accounting for bonds by issuer and investor; interest method amortization (bonds recorded net).

Panel A—Case Data (same as Exhibit 15–5 except for method of amortization):

Case A—sold at par;
Case B—sold at a discount, $96,007;
Case C—sold at a premium, $104,212

Panel B—Entries for Cases A, B and C:

At issuance date, January 1, 19A:

Case A—The bond issue was sold (and purchased) at par, $100,000:

Issuer's Books—X Corporation			Investor's Books—Y Corporation		
Cash	100,000		Bond investment	100,000	
Bonds payable		100,000	Cash		100,000

Case B—The bond issue was sold (and purchased) at a discount, $96,007:

Issuer's Books—X Corporation			Investor's Books—Y Corporation		
Cash	96,007		Bond investment	96,007	
Bonds payable		96,007	Cash		96,007

Case C—The bond issue was sold (and purchased) at a premium, $104,212:

Issuer's Books—X Corporation			Investor's Books—Y Corporation		
Cash	104,212		Bond investment	104,212	
Bonds payable		104,212	Cash		104,212

December 31, 19A, interest and amortization:

Case B—Bonds sold at a discount (see Exhibit 15–7):

Issuer's Books—X Corporation			Investor's Books—Y Corporation		
Interest expense . .	7,681		Cash	7,000	
Bonds payable .		681	Bond investment	681	
Cash ($100,000 × 7%)		7,000	Interest revenue . . .		7,681

Case C—Bonds sold at a premium (see Exhibit 15–7):

Issuer's Books—X Corporation			Investor's Books—Y Corporation		
Interest expense . .	6,253		Cash	7,000	
Bonds payable . . .	747		Bond investment . . .		747
Cash		7,000	Interest revenue . . .		6,253

Note: If the above entries were made at net for the straight-line method, only the amounts would change.

Panel C—Reporting (Case B, discount) December 31, 19A:

Issuer (net)		Investor (net)	
Statement of income:			
Interest expense	$ 7,681	Interest revenue	$ 7,681
Statement of financial position:			
Bonds payable	96,688	Bond investment	96,688

on pymt/Amt schedule
if sold at discount - bond amt increases
if sold at premium - bond amt decreases

Int Exp. 7681
Disc. Amort 681
Cash 7000

Exhibit 15–7
Amortization schedules for effective interest amortization.

Case B—Bonds sold at a discount (at $96,007):

Date	Cash interest (7% annual)	Effective interest (8% annual)	Discount amortization	Balance, unamortized discount	Carrying amount of bonds
1/1/19A starting date				$3,993	$ 96,007
12/31/19A	$7,000[a]	$7,681[b]	$681[c]	3,312[d]	96,688[e]
12/31/19B	7,000	7,735	735	2,577	97,423
12/31/19C	7,000	7,794	794	1,783	98,217
12/31/19D	7,000	7,857	857	926	99,074
12/31/19E	7,000	7,926	926	-0-	100,000

[a] $100,000 × 7% = $7,000 (based on stated rate).
[b] $96,007 × 8% = $7,681 (based on effective rate of interest).
[c] $7,681 − $7,000 = $681.
[d] $3,993 − $681 = $3,312.
[e] $96,007 + $681 = $96,688 (or $100,000 − $3,312 = $96,688).

Case C—Bonds sold at a premium (at $104,212):

Date	Cash interest (7% annual)	Effective interest (6% annual)	Premium amortization	Balance, unamortized premium	Carrying amount of bonds
1/1/19A starting date				$4,212	$104,212
12/31/19A	$7,000[a]	$6,253[b]	$747[c]	3,465[d]	103,465[e]
12/31/19B	7,000	6,208	792	2,673	102,673
12/31/19C	7,000	6,160	840	1,833	101,833
12/31/19D	7,000	6,110	890	943	100,943
12/31/19E	7,000	6,057	943	-0-	100,000

Note: When the interest method of amortization is used, an amortization schedule is needed for two reasons: *(a)* it provides the amount of bond premium or discount that should be amortized and *(b)* it shows the accounting entries in a line-by-line format.

[a] $100,000 × 7% = $7,000 (based on stated rate).
[b] $104,212 × 6% = $6,253 (based on effective rate of interest).
[c] $7,000 − $6,253 = $747.
[d] $4,212 − $747 = $3,465.
[e] $104,212 − $747 = $103,465 (or $100,000 + $3,465 = $103,465).

Additional Issues in Accounting for Bonds

This section of the chapter considers seven additional accounting issues directly related to bonds: (1) bonds that are sold **between** interest dates, (2) bonds with interest dates that do not coincide with the end of the accounting period, (3) bond issue costs, (4) nonconvertible bonds with detachable stock purchase warrants, (5) convertible bonds, and (6) induced conversions of convertible debt.

Bonds Sold (and Purchased) between Interest Dates

Bonds rarely are issued on an interest date. Therefore, when the sale/purchase transaction occurs between interest dates, the accrued interest on the bonds from the last interest date to the sale/purchase date must be recognized in the accounts of both parties. This accrued interest must be recognized on the sale date because the issuer always will pay the **full amount** of periodic **cash** interest to the holder of the bond as if it had been owned since the last interest date. Therefore, when a bond is sold/purchased between interest dates, the cash amount paid by the investor to the issuer will be *(a)* the market price of the bond plus *(b)* the accrued interest from the last interest date to the date of sale/purchase. To illustrate, on September 1, 19A, A Corporation issued Investor B a $10,000, 12% (interest payable each December 31), five-year bond dated January 1, 19A, at par plus the accrued interest. If the accounting period ends on December 31, the entries would be as follows:

Issuer A			Investor B		
September 1, 19A (issuance date):					
Cash	10,800*		Long-term investment in bonds	10,000	
Bonds payable		10,000	Interest revenue	800	
Interest expense		800†	Cash		10,800
December 13, 19A (interest date and end of accounting period):					
Interest expense	1,200		Cash	1,200	
Cash		1,200	Interest revenue		1,200

* 10,000 + ($10,000 × 12% × 8/12) = $10,800.
† ($10,000 × 12% × 8/12) = $800.

The **issuer credits** interest expense on September 1, 19A, for $800 because on December 31, 19A, interest for one full year ($1,200) will be paid to the **investor** and debited to interest expense. The resulting net debit balance of $400 in the interest expense account is the correct amount of interest expense that the issuer should report for the four-month period during 19A that the bonds were outstanding. For the same reason, the investor debits interest revenue for $800 and later credits $1,200 to the same account, which results in a credit balance of $400, representing four months of interest revenue for 19A.

Accounting for Bonds when Interest Periods and Accounting Periods Do Not Coincide

Typically, the end of the accounting period does not coincide with the interest date on bonds. In this situation, an **issuer** must **accrue** interest on a bond from the last interest date to the end of the accounting period. The investor also must accrue interest revenue on a bond investment. To illustrate, notice that the above example was simplified because the interest date and the end of the accounting period were the same and the bond was sold at par. Now, assume the same case data, except that the accounting period of each company ends on March 31. The entries would be as follows:

Issuer A			Investor B		
September 1, 19A (issuance date):					
Cash	10,800*		Long-term investment in bonds	10,000	
Bonds payable		10,000	Interest revenue	800	
Interest expense		800†	Cash		10,800

* $10,000 + ($10,000 × 12% × 8/12) = $10,800.
† ($10,000 × 12% × 8/12) = $800.

Issuer A			Investor B		
December 31, 19A (interest date):					
Interest expense	1,200		Cash	1,200	
Cash ($10,000 × 12%)		1,200	Interest revenue		1,200
March 31, 19B (end of the accounting period):					
Interest expense	300		Interest receivable	300	
Interest payable		300*	Interest revenue		300
December 31, 19B (next interest date):*					
Interest payable	300		Cash	1,200	
Interest expense	900		Interest receivable		300
Cash		1,200†	Interest revenue		900

* $10,000 × 12% × 3/12 = $300).

* Assumes no prior reversing entry.
† ($10,000 × 12% = $1,200).

The illustrations given in Exhibits 15–5 and 15–6 assumed that the bonds were sold/purchased on the origination date of the bonds, January 1, 19A, and that the interest date and the end of the accounting period coincided. The above example for Issuer A and Investor B assumed that the $10,000 bond was sold *(a)* 8 months after the date on the bonds (i.e., January 1, 19A to September 1, 19A), and *(b)* at par. Now we will add another complexity by stipulating that the bond was not sold at par. **When bonds are sold at a premium or discount the related amortization period is the time from sale to the maturity date of the bonds.** For example, a five-year bond dated January 1, 19A and sold on September 1, 19A will require that any premium or discount be amortized over 52 months (i.e., 5 years minus 8 months).

To illustrate the typical case when bonds are sold *(a)* at a premium or discount and *(b)* on a date other than the bond issue origination date or an interest date, the case immediately above relating to Issuer A and Investor B will be continued. It can be summarized as follows:

Bond: $10,000, stated interest rate, 12% payable annually each December 31. Date of the bond, January 1, 19A, five years to maturity.
Sale/purchase: September 1, 19A (remaining time to maturity, 52 months); sold to yield 10%, for $10,675; premium, $675.*

* When the sale/purchase date is between interest dates, the issue price at the effective rate (10% in this case) must be uniquely computed. This can be done by discounting to the next interest date (4 years in this case), then compute monthly discounting for the short period (4 months in this case). Instead of the monthly discounting, straight-line interpolation is used (in this case the difference is not material). The computations are as follows:

1/1/19A	Sale, 9/1/19A	12/31/19A
$10,758[(a)]	Difference, $124	$10,634[(b)]
− ($124 × 8/12 = $83) =	$10,675	= ($124 × 4/12 = $41) +

[(a)] Principal:	$10,000 × .62092 =	$ 6,209	[(b)] $10,000 × .68301 =	$ 6,830
Interest:	$1,200 × 3.79079 =	4,549	$ 1,200 × 3.16987 =	3,804
Total		$10,758		$10,634

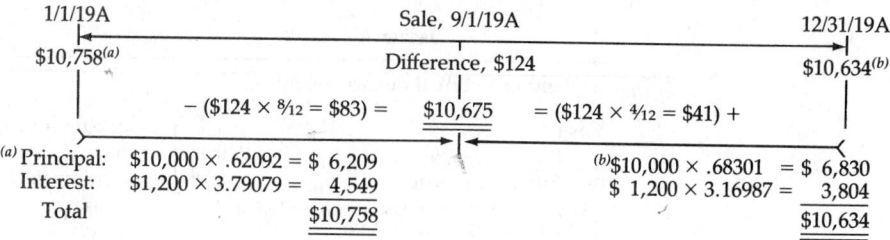

Both straight-line and interest method amortization will be illustrated. The entries would be as follows:

January 1, 19A (originating date):
No entries because no bonds were sold.

September 1, 19A (issuance date):

Issuer A			Investor B		
Cash ($10,675 + $800)	11,475		Bond investment	10,000	
Bonds payable		10,000	Premium on bond investment	675	
Premium on bonds payable		675	Interest revenue	800	
Interest expense		800*	Cash		11,475

* 10,000 × 12% × 8/12 = $800.

December 31, 19A (next interest date):

Issuer A			Investor B		
Interest expense	1,200		Cash	1,200	
Cash		1,200	Interest revenue		1,200

$10,000 × 12% = $1,200.
Note: Premium will be amortized at the end of the accounting period.

March 31, 19B (end of the accounting period):

Straight-line amortization:

Issuer A			Investor B		
Interest expense(c)	209		Interest receivable	300	
Premium on bonds payable(a)	91		Premium on bond investment		91
Interest payable(b)		300	Interest revenue		209

(a) Straight-line for Sept. 1, 19A to March 31, 19B: $675 × 7/52 = $91.
(b) $10,000 × 12% × 3/12 = $300.
(c) $300 − $91 = $209.

Interest method amortization:*

Issuer A			Investor B		
Interest expense	225		Interest receivable	300	
Premium on bonds payable(a)	75		Premium on bond investment		75
Interest payable(b)		300	Interest revenue		225

a. $41 + 1/4 ($137) = $75 (practical adaptation); a similar adjustment will have to be made each period.
b. $10,000 × 12% × 3/12 = $300.

* Amortization schedule—Interest Method; Net approach

Date	Cash interest	Interest (at yield rate)	Premium amortization	Bond carrying amount
9/1/19A				$10,675
12/31/19A	$1,200	$1,159[b]	$ 41[a]	10,634
12/31/19B	1,200	$10,634 × 10% = 1,063	137	10,497
12/31/19C	1,200	10,497 × 10% = 1,050	150	10,347
12/31/19D	1,200	10,347 × 10% = 1,035	165	10,182
12/31/19E	1,200	10,182 × 10% = 1,018	182	10,000
Total	$6,000	$5,325	$675	

a. Amortization required for the four months, $10,675 − $10,634 = $41.
b. Remainder to be amortized, $1,200 − $41 = $1,159.

if you issue inbetween dates - Amort. w/change -
won't amort. for as long

Bond Issue Costs

Typically, a number of costs are incurred in preparing and selling a bond issue. Bond issue costs include legal, accounting, underwriting, commission, engraving, printing, registration, and promotion costs. GAAP classifies these expenditures collectively as a **deferred charge** (i.e., Bond Issue Cost) rather than as an element of a bond discount or premium.[7] Therefore, bond issue costs are accounted for separately from bond premiums and bond discounts. Bond issue costs should be amortized in conformity with the matching principle over the period the bonds will be outstanding (i.e., from sale date to maturity date) because it is assumed that related future revenue benefits will flow from the proceeds of the financing. Conceptually, bond issue costs should be amortized using the interest method. However, the straight-line method is used because GAAP requires this method for deferred charges (see Chapter 12). Also, the difference between the straight-line and interest methods usually is not material in amount.

To illustrate, assume that the example in the prior section included a total bond issue cost of $300 to Issuer A. Issuer A should make the following entries (there would be none for the investor):

September 1, 19A—Bond issue cost (date of sale):

Bond issue cost	300	
Cash		300

March 31, 19B—End of accounting period; to record amortization of bond issue cost on the straight-line basis:

Bond issue expense	40	
Bond issue cost ($300 × 7/52)		40

Nonconvertible Bonds with Detachable Stock Purchase Warrants

Debt securities, usually bonds, may be issued with **stock warrants** (i.e., stock rights). A stock warrant gives the holder an option to purchase from the issuer, within a stated time period, a specified number of shares of common stock at a specified price per share. Detachable stock purchase warrants are often included with **nonconvertible** bonds to enhance the marketability of the bonds. Nonconvertible bonds with detachable stock purchase warrants usually carry a lower interest rate than they otherwise would. They tend to sell for a higher price than ordinary bonds.

Detachable stock purchase warrants can be separated from the nonconvertible bonds and traded on the market. They are **equity securities that are separable** from the debt security. Because of this separability, *APB Opinion 14,* "Accounting for Convertible Debt and Debt Issued with Stock Purchase Warrants," states that "the portion of the proceeds of debt securities issued with detachable stock purchase warrants which is allocable to the warrants should be accounted for as paid-in capital. The allocation should be based on the relative [market] values of the two securities at time of issuance." When the market value of one security (i.e., the bond or the detachable stock purchase warrant) cannot be determined, the market value of the other, if it is determinable, should be

[7] *APB Opinion 21,* par. 16.

subtracted from the total consideration to determine the value of the security with the indeterminate value.

In contrast, if the stock purchase warrants are **not detachable** no separate market for them will exist. Nondetachable stock warrants do not affect the price of the bonds nearly as much as detachable warrants. In this case, *APB Opinion 14* stipulates that the full amount of the proceeds should be recognized in the bond accounts. It also stipulates that the stock warrants should **not** be recorded as owners' equity (i.e., not as stock warrants outstanding) because there is no separate market for either the bonds standing alone or the nondetachable warrants. Thus, **there is no separate accounting on issue date for nondetachable warrants.**

To illustrate accounting for nonconvertible bonds with detachable stock purchase warrants, assume AB Corporation issued $100,000, 8%, 10-year, **nonconvertible bonds with detachable stock purchase warrants.** Each $1,000 bond carried 10 detachable stock purchase warrants. Each warrant entitled the holder to one share of common stock, par $10, at a specified option price of $15 per share. The bonds, including the detachable warrants, sold at $105,000. Shortly after issuance, the warrants were quoted on the market for $4 each. Because no market value could be determined for the bonds standing alone, the *(a)* bond issuance and *(b)* subsequent tender of the detachable stock purchase warrants would be recorded by the issuer and investor as follows:

a. Issuance of bonds with detachable stock purchase warrants:

Issuer			Investor		
Cash	105,000		Investment in bonds	100,000*	
Bonds payable, 8% (with detachable stock warrants)		100,000*	Investment, detachable stock warrants (1,000 × $4)	4,000	
Detachable stock warrants outstanding (1,000 warrants × $4)†		4,000	Premium on bond investment	1,000*	
Premium on bonds payable		1,000*	Cash		105,000

* Could be recorded using the net approach, at $101,000.
† Reported as contributed or paid-in capital.

b. Subsequent tender of the 1,000 detachable stock purchase warrants:

Issuer			Investor		
Cash (1,000 × $15)	15,000		Investment in common stock (1,000 shares)	19,000	
Detachable stock warrants outstanding (1,000 × $4)	4,000		Investment, detachable stock warrants		4,000
Common stock, par $10 (1,000 shares)		10,000	Cash		15,000
Contributed capital in excess of par, common stock		9,000			

Because of the contractual option price, the market value of the stock at the date the warrants are tendered is not recognized.

If investors allow some warrants to expire (usually because of oversight or an unfavorable stock price), the **issuer** would debit Detachable Stock Warrants

Outstanding. The issuer usually credits Premium on Bonds Payable because that was the senior security at issuance date. However, a strong argument can be made for the issuer to credit a special stockholders' equity account. In this situation, the investor should credit Investment, Detachable Stock Warrants and debit Loss on Investments.

Convertible Bonds

A **convertible bond** may be converted to capital stock (usually common stock) of the issuer at the **option of the investor.** Convertible bonds usually specify that conversion can occur only on an interest date. Typically, convertible bonds are also **callable** (usually on an interest date) at a specified redemption or call price at the **option of the issuer** and are subordinated to nonconvertible debt. Subordinated means that the convertible debt ranks below nonconvertible debt as a creditor's claim against assets in case of insolvency. Convertible bonds can be sold at an interest rate lower than that for nonconvertible bonds because investors impute a value to the conversion privilege. Convertible bonds typically are not issued with stock warrants.

Convertible bonds have a conversion ratio or a conversion price specified in the bond indenture. The **conversion ratio** is the number of shares of common stock the holder of a convertible bond will receive when it is tendered for conversion. In contrast, the **conversion price** of the stock into which the bond may be converted is the face amount of the convertible bond divided by the number of shares of common stock (per bond) to be received on conversion.

To illustrate the conversion ratio and conversion price of convertible bonds, assume AB Corporation issued 5,000, $1,000 convertible bonds, each of which can be converted to 10 shares of AB Corporation common stock. Conversion may occur at the option of the holder on any interest date after the second year from issuance. The conversion ratio for each bond would be 10 (shares of stock) to 1 (bond). Or, the conversion price of the stock would be $1,000 ÷ 10 shares = $100.

Convertible bonds offer certain advantages to both the issuer and the investor. The primary advantages to the issuer are *(a)* a lower rate of interest and *(b)* a means of securing equity (stockholder) financing in the long run. (Because the debt is not paid in cash when conversion occurs, the net effect is an increase in equity). The call option can be used by the issuer to force conversion when the aggregate price of the stock to be issued on conversion is greater than the call price of the bonds. In this case, a rational investor would take the stock in lieu of the cash.

The primary advantages of convertible bonds to the investor are: *(a)* an option to receive either the face of the bond at maturity or to convert to common stock of the issuer, *(b)* a guaranteed income flow from interest until conversion date or maturity, and *(c)* the opportunity to realize the benefits of appreciation in the price of the common stock of the issuer.

Accounting for the issuance of **convertible** bonds poses a conceptual problem—the issue (i.e., sale) price should be allocated between the bonds, as **debt,** and the conversion privilege, as **stockholders' equity.** Nevertheless, *APB Opinion 14* specifies that the issuance should be recorded as **debt only,** with no value assigned to the conversion privilege. The APB reached this conclusion on the basis that no separate market exists for either the bond standing alone or the conversion privilege.

To illustrate accounting for the **issuance** of convertible bonds, AB Corporation sold $100,000, 8%, **convertible** bonds for $106,000. The conversion feature specified that, at the option of the **investor,** each $1,000 bond was convertible to 10 shares of AB Corporation common stock, par $10, on any interest date after the end of the second year from date of issuance. The issuer and investor would record the transaction as follows:

Issuer			Investor		
Cash	106,000		Bond investment (AB Corporation, convertible bonds)	100,000	
Premium on bonds payable		6,000	Premium on bond investment	6,000	
Bonds payable, 8%, convertible		100,000	Cash		106,000

When convertible bonds are **tendered by the investor** for conversion, the issuer and investor must *(a)* update all of their respective account balances to a current status as of the date of the conversion (this updating includes recording interest accruals and discount or premium amortization) and *(b)* remove the resulting bond carrying values from the accounts. When conversion is on an interest date, and amortization has been on the interest date, all related account balances already are current.

Recording the conversion transaction poses a question as to the valuation that should be used to record the new security issued. Two methods currently are acceptable under GAAP:

1. **Book value method**—record the new security issued at the carrying value of the old security; therefore, no gain or loss is recognized on conversion.
2. **Market value method**—record the new security issued at either its current market value or the current market value of the old security converted, whichever is the more reliably determinable; therefore, a gain or loss may be recognized on conversion.

To illustrate accounting for conversion, assume that the investor in the above illustration tendered all of the convertible bonds of AB Corporation for conversion on an interest date. At conversion date, the AB common stock was selling at $110 per share. The unamortized bond premium balance was $3,000. The entries under each method would be as follows:

	Book value method		Market value method	
Issuer—AB Corporation:				
Bonds payable, convertible	100,000		100,000	
Premium on bonds payable	3,000		3,000	
Loss on conversion of convertible bonds			7,000	
Common stock (1,000 shares × $10)		10,000		10,000
Contributed capital in excess of par*		93,000		100,000
Investor:				
Investment in stock, AB Corp.	103,000		110,000	
Investment in bonds, AB Corp.		100,000		100,000
Premium on bond investment		3,000		3,000
Gain on conversion of bond investment				7,000

* $103,000 − $10,000 = $93,000; 1,000 shares × ($110 − $10) = $100,000.

The book value method appears to be widely used because many accountants view the **conversion transaction** as the culmination of a single transaction that started when the convertible bonds were issued and ended on conversion date. Because the book value method does not recognize a gain or loss on the full settlement of the debt, the stock issued in the conversion is not valued at market. The market value method is conceptually preferable because it conforms to the cost principle applied to an investment. Nevertheless, the method is deficient because the gain or loss recognized on the issuance of the capital stock usually is not recorded as stockholders' equity (conceptually it is contributed capital in excess of par).

If the conversion occurs prior to maturity, it is **not** considered to be an early extinguishment of debt (discussed in Part B). Therefore, any gain or loss recognized is not classified on the statement of income as an extraordinary item.

Induced Conversions of Convertible Debt

Convertible debt (e.g., a convertible bond) privileges sometimes are changed after the issuance date by the debtor to **induce prompt conversion** of the debt to the specified equity security (usually common stock). The inducement (called a **sweetener**) usually involves changes in the original conversion privilege, such as *(a)* an increase in the number of shares issuable on conversion, *(b)* issuance of stock rights in addition to the shares issuable on conversion, or *(c)* payment of cash or other considerations in addition to the shares issuable on conversion. The primary purpose of induced conversion is prompt settlement of the outstanding liability.

FASB Standard 84, "Induced Conversions of Convertible Debt," states that the issuer (i.e., debtor) must "recognize expense equal to the fair value of all securities and other consideration transferred in the transaction in excess of the fair value of the securities issuable pursuant to the original conversion terms. The expense shall not be reported as an extraordinary item."

To illustrate, assume the following data for the debtor:

a. Convertible bonds payable, 6%, $500,000 (500, $1,000 bonds); issued at par; conversion privilege, 10 shares of nopar common stock for each $1,000 bond.

b. Inducement (sweetener), two additional shares of the nopar common stock for each bond.

c. Market price (i.e., fair value) of the common stock on conversion date (also, this is an interest date), $100.

Entry by issuer (i.e., debtor) on conversion date:

Convertible bonds payable, 6% (500, $1,000 bonds)	500,000	
Debt conversion expense	100,000*	
Common stock, nopar (500 × 12 = 6,000 shares)		600,000

* Computation:

Shares actually issued [(500 × 12 = 6,000) × $100]	$600,000
Shares originally issuable [(500 × 10 = 5,000) × $100]	500,000
Debt conversion expense	$100,000

Entry by investor:

	Book value method		Market value method	
Investment in common stock	500,000		600,000	
Investment in bonds		500,000		500,000
Gain on investment conversion				100,000

Reporting and Disclosure of Long-Term Liabilities

Long-term liabilities usually are reported net of any unamortized discount or premium (i.e., only the net carrying value is reported). However, when the unamortized discount or premium is reported separately, the liability would appear as follows:

If a discount			If a premium		
Long-term liabilities:					
Bonds payable (Note 1)	$900,000		Bonds payable (Note 1)	$900,000	
Less: Unamortized discount	7,000		Add: Unamortized premium	7,000	
Carrying value		$893,000	Carrying value		$907,000

The investor would report the long-term investment in a similar manner.

The portion of a long-term debt that will be paid during the year following the statement of financial position date, or operating cycle if longer, should be reported as a current liability, and the remainder should be reported as a long-term debt. However, if the entire debt is to be paid from noncurrent sources (e.g., a bond sinking fund), **all** of the debt should be reported as long term. To illustrate, one company reported the following (excerpt) for 1987:

	1987	1986
Current liabilities:		
Current maturities of long-term debt	$ 522,994	$ 553,220
Long-term debt, excluding amounts included in current liabilities (Note 3)	18,976,751	18,491,889

FASB Standard 47 (par. 10b) requires disclosure of the "aggregate amount of maturities and sinking fund requirements" for all long-term debt. For example, Note 3 referred to above disclosed the following:

(3) LONG-TERM DEBT

Long-term debt at December 25, 1987 and December 26, 1986 consisted of the following:

	1987	1986
6½% mortgage bonds, due in annual installments of $333,000, through 1990	$ 1,004,000	$ 1,337,000
Unsecured notes payable to a bank under a $35,000,000 revolving credit agreement due in 1992:		
11% fixed rate through 1989	10,000,000	10,000,000
At prime rate	3,000,000	7,000,000
Unsecured note payable to a bank at 9¾%	5,000,000	—
Secured equipment notes at 8½% and 17% payable in monthly installments through 1991 and 1998, respectively	405,840	521,007
Other long-term debt	89,905	187,102
Total	19,499,745	19,045,109
Less current maturities	522,994	553,220
Total long-term debt	$18,976,751	$18,491,889

The aggregate annual principal payments for the five years subsequent to December 25, 1987 are: 1988—$523,000; 1989—$469,000; 1990—$468,000; 1991—$535,000; and 1992—$17,505,000.

Two of the loan agreements contain, among other things, provisions regarding maintenance of working capital and net worth. The Company's working capital and net worth as defined in the agreements were substantially in excess of the minimum requirements as of December 25, 1987.

To secure the 6½% mortgage bonds, the company mortgaged certain of its plant and equipment.

Under the terms of the $35,000,000 revolving credit agreement, the Company is required to pay a commitment fee of ⅜% per year on the unused portion of the commitment. The terms provide that the maximum outstanding balance is $35,000,000 through June 1990 with reductions of $5,750,000 every six months thereafter.

The Company also has a $10,000,000 line of credit at another bank which expires in May 1988. In January 1988, the Company borrowed $5,000,000 at 11% for one year under this line of credit. The proceeds repaid the 9¾% note, which was due in February 1988.

PART B: EXTINGUISHMENT OF DEBT AND DEBT RESTRUCTURE

In recent years, it has become common for debtors to pay off or otherwise settle debts before the scheduled maturity date. Also, there has been an increase in situations in which debtors have been unable to meet their scheduled debt payments (i.e., principal and/or interest) because of inadequate cash. This part of the chapter discusses these two situations. The discussions are outlined as follows:

Transaction	Basic reference	Basic accounting
1. **Extinguishment of debt**—when the creditor relieves the debtor of primary responsibility for the debt, and it is **probable** that no future payments on the debt will be required. A **reacquisition or settlement** cost is involved.	*APB Opinion 26,* "Early Extinguishment of Debt," and *FASB Standard 76,* "Extinguishment of Debt, an amendment of *APB Opinion 26.*" *FASB Standard 4,* "Reporting Gains and Losses from Extinguishment of Debt."	Record the financial statement elements used to extinguish the debt and remove the carrying value of the debt from the accounts. The difference between the reacquisition or settlement cost and the carrying value of the debt is reported as an **extraordinary** gain or loss.
2. **Troubled debt restructuring**—when the debtor encounters difficulty in making payments on debt, the creditor grants a **concession** to the debtor which relaxes the payment requirements.	*FASB Standard 15,* "Accounting by Debtors and Creditors for Troubled Debt Restructurings."	The concession by the creditor to the debtor is recorded as a reduction of the debt (including interest). In most cases the **creditor records** a loss (usually an **ordinary** loss) and the **debtor records an extraordinary gain.** In other cases, no gain or loss is recognized (however the effective interest rate must be recomputed).

Summary of Financial Statement Classifications

	Loss	Gain
1. Extinguishment of debt	Extraordinary	Extraordinary
2. Troubled debt restructuring	Ordinary	Extraordinary

The following two topics now will be discussed: (1) extinguishment of debt, and (2) in-substance defeasance.

Extinguishment of Debt

APB Opinion 26, as amended by *FASB Standards* 4 and 76, defines **extinguishment of debt** as a transaction or event in which **any** of the following occurs:

- **a.** The debtor pays the creditor and is relieved of all obligations with respect to the debt. This includes the debtor's **reacquisition of its outstanding debt securities in the open market,** whether they are subsequently canceled or held as "treasury bonds."
- **b.** The debtor is legally released from being the primary obligor under the debt, either judicially or by the creditor, and it is **probable** that the **debtor will not be required to make future payments** with respect to that debt under any guarantees.
- **c.** The debtor irrevocably **places cash or other assets in trust** to be used solely for satisfying scheduled payments of both interest and principal of a specific obligation. In addition, the possibility that the debtor will be required to make future payments must be remote.[8]

Most debts are paid according to the original terms of the debt agreement regarding both interest and principal. However, some debts are settled by extinguishment before, at, or after the maturity date of the debt.

Extinguishment of a debt is differentiated from the **normal** payment of debt in conformity with its original terms by *(a)* acquisition of the debt securities, *(b)* obtaining a release from making future payments, or *(c)* placing assets in an irrevocable trust to pay the debt.

APB Opinion 26 was issued because of the **wide diversity that existed in recording extinguishments that caused gains or losses.** Before this *Opinion* was issued some of the accounting approaches used to record and report these extinguishment gains and losses were designed to manipulate either, or both, the reported income and liability amounts. To illustrate a typical extinguishment, UT Corporation had an outstanding 6% debt of $10 million. Prior to maturity this debt could be purchased for $8 million because of the low stated interest rate. Primarily to lessen an expected net loss of $500,000 (assumed), the company borrowed $8 million at 15% interest and used the cash to purchase the old debt. The $2 million difference between the purchase price and the carrying value of the old debt was included in current pretax income as an **ordinary** gain. On the other hand, if there had been a $2 million loss, it often was reported as an extraordinary loss.

---

[8] Adapted from *FASB Standard 76*, par. 3.

As amended by *FASB Standards 4, 64, 76,* and *84*. *FASB Standard 15* specifies the accounting for troubled debt restructures. It states (par. 10) that the provisions of *APB Opinion 26* (as amended by *FASB Standard 4*) do not apply to accounting for troubled debt restructuring. Also, *APB Opinion 26* does not apply to conversions of convertible debt when conversion privileges included in terms of the debt at issuance are changed, or additional consideration is paid, to induce conversion of the debt to equity securities as described in *FASB Standard 84*, "Induced Conversions of Convertible Debt" (discussed in Part A of this chapter).

Basically, *APB Opinion 26* (as amended) requires that an extinguishment (as defined above) be recorded by *(a)* bringing all related amounts in the company's accounts up to the date of extinguishment, *(b)* removing the updated amounts from the accounts, *(c)* recording the financial statement elements (i.e., resources) used to settle the debt, and *(d)* recognizing any extinguishment gain or loss in conformity with GAAP for gains, losses, and extraordinary items. *FASB Standard 4* specifies that:

> Gains and losses from extinguishment of debt that are included in the determination of net income shall be aggregated and, if material, classified as an **extraordinary** item, net of the related income tax effect. The conclusion shall apply whether an extinguishment is early or at a scheduled maturity date or later.

Debt may be extinguished by *(a)* direct cash payments to the creditors, *(b)* exercise of a call privilege by the issuer, *(c)* purchase in the open market by the issuer, *(d)* refunding—the retirement of old debt by issuing new debt, and *(e)* in-substance defeasance. The last four types of extinguishments will be discussed and illustrated below. They pose some accounting problems that usually are not encountered with direct cash payments.

Extinguishment by Exercise of Call Privilege by Issuer

Bonds and certain other debt securities frequently carry a **call privilege.** The call privilege states that, at the option of the **issuer,** the debt may be called for payment prior to its maturity. Call time limits and call reacquisition price are specified in the bond indenture. They also are printed on each bond certificate. Extinguishment by call almost always is required to be on an interest date. Therefore, the amortization of any discount or premium and bond issue costs will be up to date and there will be no accrued interest. If the call is not on an interest date, all of those accounts must be updated with accrual and amortization entries. At the call date, all of the related **debt accounts are reduced to zero and an extraordinary gain or loss** is recognized in the amount of the difference between the **reacquisition price** and the carrying value of the bond accounts. The reacquisition price is the call price plus all costs of implementing the recall.

To illustrate the exercise of a call privilege, on January 1, 19A, corporation A issued 10-year, $100,000, 10% (payable semiannually on June 30 and December 31), **callable** bonds. The bonds can be called by the issuer at 101 on any interest date after December 31, 19C. At issuance date, the bonds were sold for $106,504 (i.e., a 9% yield rate). On June 30, 19D, corporation A called in all of the bonds and retired them. Because the amounts were not material, the company used the straight-line method of amortizing the bond premium.

Corporation A's entries at issuance and recall dates were as follows:

January 1, 19A—issuance:

Cash	106,504	
Bonds payable (callable at 101)		100,000
Premium on bonds payable		6,504

June 30, 19D—called at 101 (on interest date after the accrual and amortization entries were made):

Bonds payable (callable at 101)	100,000	
Premium on bonds payable	4,228*	
Cash		101,000
Extraordinary gain, extinguishment of debt		3,228

*Unamortized premium after June 30, 19D: $6,504 × (semiannual periods remaining, 13 ÷ total semiannual periods, 20) = $4,228.

Extinguishment by Purchase in the Open Market by Issuer

Borrowers sometimes extinguish debt early by purchasing their own debt securities in the open market. Such open-market purchases usually are not on an interest date. Therefore, prior to recording the extinguishment, any discount or premium and bond issue cost must be amortized. Also, interest must be accrued from the last interest date to the date of the open-market purchase. When the extinguishment entry is made, the difference between the **carrying amount of the debt and the reacquisition cost** is recorded as an **extraordinary item.**

To illustrate purchase in the open market, on January 1, 19A, corporation B issued 10-year, $100,000, 8% (payable semiannually on June 30 and December 31) bonds. At issuance date, the bonds were sold for $87,538 and bond issue costs were $1,000.

On March 31, 19D, corporation B purchased all of the bonds in the open market for $85,000 cash. In addition, corporation B paid reacquisition costs of $500 plus the accrued interest. Because the amounts were not material, the company used straight-line amortization of bond discount and bond issue costs. Corporation B's entries at issuance and reacquisition dates were as follows:

January 1, 19A—issuance:

Cash ($87,538 − $1,000)	86,538	
Bond issue costs (deferred charge)	1,000	
Discount on bonds ($100,000 − $87,538)	12,462	
Bonds payable, 8%		100,000

March 31, 19D—reacquisition date:

a. To update the related accounts (accruals and amortization for three months):

Bond issue expense ($1,000 × 3/120)	25	
Interest expense ($2,000 + $312)	2,312	
Bond issue cost (deferred charge)		25
Interest payable ($100,000 × 8% × 3/12)		2,000
Discount on bonds ($12,462 × 3/120)		312

b. To record the reacquisition (to reduce balances to zero):

Bonds payable, 8%	100,000	
Interest payable (from entry *a*)	2,000	
Bond issue costs, unamortized ($1,000 × 81/120)		675
Discount on bonds, unamortized ($12,462 × 81/120)		8,412
Cash ($85,000 + $2,000 + $500)		87,500
Extraordinary gain, extinguishment of debt		5,413

If corporation B used the interest method of amortization the above entries would not change except for the amounts. These amounts would be based on the schedule of debt amortization prepared for the old debt.

Extinguishment by Refunding Old Debt by Issuing New Debt

Refunding old debt by issuing new debt may involve two different situations:

1. Issuance of new debt in direct exchange for the old debt. In this situation, the old creditors become the new creditors. This situation does not occur often because of settlement agreements that must be reached between the debtor and creditors involved.
2. Issuance of new debt to obtain the cash needed to pay the creditors before maturity date. In this situation, the old creditors are paid off, and new creditors take their place.

Refunding decisions involve two important considerations: (1) the accounting impact reported on the financial statements and (2) the economic impact on each party involved. These two impacts may not be consistent. The **accounting** impact (i.e., the gain or loss on restructure) is based on historical cost. However, the **economic** impact is based on a present value analysis.

To illustrate the two situations involving refunding, assume that on January 1, 19A, CB Corporation issued $100,000 in bonds at par (10-year, 5%, payable each June 30 and December 31).

1. Refunding—by direct exchange of debt securities:
On January 1, 19E, with the agreement of the debtor and creditors, the old 5% bonds were turned in for $90,000 new bonds (six-year, 8%, payable semiannually as before). The new bonds sold at par because 8% is the current market rate for these bonds. (Note that the bondholders receive 10% less in principal but a 60% increase in the interest rate.)

Entry for the issuer:

Bonds payable, 5% (at carrying value)	100,000	
Bonds payable, 8% (at issue price)		90,000
Extraordinary gain, extinguishment of debt		10,000

Observation: For the issuer, the **accounting gain** is $10,000 (pretax). However, the issuer sustained an **economic loss** of $4,000, computed as follows:

PV of the **new** bonds (i.e., their current market price)		$90,000
PV of the **old** bonds:*		
Principal: $100,000 × $p_{n=12;\,i=4\%}$ (Table 5–2, .62460) =	$62,460	
Interest: $ 2,500 × $P_{o_{n=12;\,i=4\%}}$ (Table 5–4, 9.38507) =	23,540	86,000
Difference: Economic loss to issuer; gain to investor		$ 4,000

*Note: All amounts are discounted at 8% (4% semiannually) because that is the rate that these bonds will command for the same company.

The $4,000 was an economic loss to the issuer because a greater amount of PV was issued than was extinguished. Notice that the economic loss is not recorded.

2. Refunding—by the issuance of new debt to obtain the cash needed to purchase the old bonds in the open market:
On January 1, 19E, CB sold $86,000 in new bonds (six-year, 8%, payable semiannually as before) at par. The market price of the old bonds was 86;

therefore, only that amount of new 8% refunding bonds were sold. The entries are as follows:

a. January 1, 19E—sale of 8% bonds at par:

Cash	86,000	
Bonds payable, 8% (at issue price)		86,000

b. January 1, 19E—purchase and retirement of the 5% bonds (assuming all bondholders sell):

Bonds payable, 5% (at carrying value)	100,000	
Cash (at market value)		86,000
Extraordinary gain, extinguishment of debt		14,000

The **accounting gain** is $14,000. However, there is **no economic gain or loss** because the PV of the debt issued equals the PV of the debt extinguished.

Extinguishment by In-Substance Defeasance

In-substance defeasance results from a transaction in which the debtor irrevocably places cash or other monetary assets in a trust. In the general sense, defeasance connotes the release of a debtor from a legal liability.[9] The sole purpose of the trust is to provide the resources necessary to pay the interest and principal on a specified debt. The basic accounting issue is whether this transaction extinguishes the debt immediately. If it does, the debt need not be reported as a liability. If it does not, the debt should continue to be reported as a liability, with an asset account to record the resources that are placed in trust. *FASB Standard 76* specifies that the debt should be considered extinguished immediately **only** under the following conditions:[10]

1. The trust must be restricted to owning only monetary assets that are **essentially** risk free as to amount, timing, and collection of interest and principal.
2. The monetary assets held by the trust shall provide cash flows from interest and principal of those assets that approximately coincide, as to timing and amount, with the scheduled interest and principal payments on the debt that is being extinguished. The trust assets also must be sufficient to pay the trust administration costs.

A general description of the timing, amount, and other provisions of the debt should be disclosed for each period that the debt remains outstanding. In-substance defeasance is viewed by some accountants as a violation of the strong position GAAP takes against offsetting assets (in the trust) and liabilities (which are removed from the accounts). However, the FASB concluded that the above restrictions involve a **recognition** issue in accounting for debt, not an offsetting issue which the Board viewed as a "display issue." A display issue relates to how an item should be shown in the financial statements.

To illustrate, on January 1, year 1, SD Corporation borrowed cash on a $1 million, 4%, 10-year note payable. Interest is payable each December 31, which

---

[9] FASB, *Technical Bulletin No. 84-4*, "In-Substance Defeasance of Debt" (reference: *FASB Standard 76*, "Extinguishment of Debt," October 1984).

[10] Adapted from *FASB Standard 76*, par. 4.

also is the end of the accounting year. At the beginning of year 5 the company entered into an agreement with the creditor as follows: *(a)* increase the interest rate to 5%, *(b)* irrevocably transfer both the note and the trust assets (i.e., government securities that cost $772,000) to an independent trustee who would assume full responsibility for paying the interest at each interest date and the principal at maturity, and *(c)* value the debt securities (par value, $1 million; stated interest rate, 5%) at their current present value based on a 10% yield rate. The related entries for this debt extinguishment, assuming it satisfies the two criteria listed above, would be as follows:

January 1, year 1—Origination of the note:		
Cash	1,000,000	
Note payable, 4%, 10-Year		1,000,000
December 31, years 1–4—Interest payments:		
Interest expense ($1,000,000 × 4%)	40,000	
Cash		40,000

Beginning of year 5—To record the extinguishment:

Note payable, 4%, 10-year (principal)	1,000,000	
Investment in trust assets (cost, given)		772,000
Gain on disposal of trust assets ($782,233* − $772,000)		10,233
Extraordinary gain, extinguishment of debt†		217,767

* Computation of the present value of the debt securities:

$1,000,000 × $p_{n=6;i=10\%}$ (.56447, Table 5–2)	$564,470
$50,000 × $P_{\overline{o}n=6;i=10\%}$ (4.35526, Table 5–4)	217,763
Total present value	$782,233

† $1,000,000 − $782,233 = $217,767.

The disclosure requirements for in-substance defeasance states that a note similar to the following be included in the financial statements **each year** from the date of extinguishment to maturity date:

> *Note A:* On January 1, year 5, the company and the creditor entered into an agreement to transfer the $1,000,000, 4%, 10-year note to an independent trustee for payment of each periodic interest amount and the principal at maturity date. The interest rate on the note was increased to 5% for its six remaining years to maturity. The company also transferred government securities (current market value, $782,233) to the trustee to provide cash to pay the periodic interest and principal.

Troubled Debt Restructuring

When interest rates rise significantly and economic conditions become depressed, debtors sometimes experience severe financial strains and even bankruptcy. This occurs because they cannot generate sufficient cash to meet the required interest and principal payments on debts. Unpaid interest is a common characteristic in these cases. Foreclosures, repossessions, reorganizations, and a relaxing of contractual interest and principal payments on existing debt often occur. Creditors often agree to restructure debt so that the debtor may continue in business. Creditors realize that relaxing some terms of the debt may be economically preferable to forcing the debtor into bankruptcy.

Troubled debt restructuring is defined as a situation in which the creditor (i.e., lender), for economic or legal reasons related to the debtor's (i.e., borrower) financial difficulties, **grants a concession to the debtor** that would not otherwise be considered. The **concession** stems from an agreement between the creditor and the debtor or is imposed by law or a court. A concession means that the original terms of the debt are changed. The changes make it easier for the debtor to meet new arrangements on a debt that is, or likely will be, in default. These changes may affect the amount and/or timing of the original principal, the periodic interest payments, or some combination of the two. Because of an increasing number of troubled debt restructurings, the FASB issued *Standard 15,* which specifies accounting and reporting guidelines for both the debtor (borrower) and the creditor (lender). This Standard specifies that the critical issue in a troubled debt restructuring is the **granting of concessions by the creditor to the debtor.**

Troubled debt restructuring may occur before, at, or after the stated maturity of the debt. The **date of consummation** is the date of the restructuring (i.e., the date for accounting recognition).[11] There are two types of debt restructuring arrangements:

1. **Settlement** of debt by **transfer of assets or equity interest** of the debtor from the debtor to the creditor to satisfy a debt (fully or partially) that involves a **concession** by the creditor to the debtor. A common example of this concession is the payment of debt by the issuance of capital stock by the debtor to the creditor with a market value **less** than the carrying value of the debt owed.
2. **Continuation** of debt with **modification of terms** of the debt with respect to *(a)* interest payments and/or *(b)* the face amount that involves a **concession** by the creditor to the debtor. This type of restructuring may involve amounts only, timing only, or both. There are two important subsets to this type:
   a. The restructured **total** of the future **cash equivalent payments** (principal plus interest) is **less** than the prerestructure **carrying or book value** of the debt. **The prerestructure carrying or book value of the debt includes all principal plus all accrued interest payments and interest on these amounts up to the date of restructure.** In this situation, an entry to recognize a **gain by the debtor** and a **loss by the creditor** must be made on the date of restructure because of the concession to the debtor.
   b. The restructured **total** of the future **cash equivalent payments** (face plus interest) is **equal to, or more than,** the prerestructure **carrying or book value** of the debt. In this situation, **no entry is made on date of restructure.** However, a new effective interest rate must be computed and used (discussed below).

Troubled debt restructuring may be summarized as follows:

1. In all situations, a **troubled debt restructure** is distinguished from other debt-related transactions because of a **concession by the creditor to the**

---

[11] *FASB Standard 15* amends *APB Opinion 26,* "Early Extinguishment of Debt," to the extent needed to exclude from that *Opinion's* scope early extinguishment of debt through troubled debt restructurings.

debtor. A concession occurs when the creditor agrees to a satisfaction of the debt with less (and/or delayed) economic resources than were called for by the original debt agreement.

2. In accounting for a troubled debt restructure, the **concession** by the creditor to the debtor usually requires **recognition of a gain (extraordinary) by the debtor and a loss (ordinary) by the creditor. The gain of the debtor and the loss of the creditor, as specified by *FASB Standard 15,* is the difference between the carrying or book value of the debt immediately before restructure (called the prerestructure value) and the total future cash equivalent payments of principal and interest (undiscounted) after restructure.**
3. In accounting for a troubled debt restructure, there is an **accounting symmetry** in the entries between the debtor and creditor.

The two types of debt restructuring are discussed and illustrated in the sections that follow.

Debt Restructure by Transfer of Assets or Equity Interest

The concept underlying the transfer of assets or an equity interest by the debtor to the creditor in troubled debt restructuring is that the **assets** or **equity interest** transferred should be recorded by both parties at **current market value** (i.e., cash equivalent value) at the date of restructuring. At that time, the carrying amount of the debt is removed from the records.

Transfer of Assets to Settle Debt. In this type of restructure a concession arises only when noncash assets transferred have a market value which is **less** than the carrying value of the debt satisfied. Therefore, the debtor will realize a gain and the creditor will incur a loss on the restructure by the amount of this difference. In this type of restructure, the **debtor** must recognize **two** different "gains or losses": (1) the difference between the carrying (book) amount of the asset transferred and its market value must be recognized by the debtor as an **ordinary gain or loss on disposal;** and (2) the excess of the carrying or book value of the debt settled over the market value of the asset transferred must be recognized by the **debtor** as an **extraordinary gain** and by the **creditor** as an **ordinary,** unusual or infrequent, or extraordinary **loss** in conformity with *APB Opinion 30.* This inconsistent classification of the gain and loss was specified by *FASB Standard 15* to discourage abuses, such as a debtor restructuring debt primarily to report an ordinary gain.

Exhibit 15–8, panel B, illustrates debt restructure by transferring **noncash assets** to settle a debt. Notice the **two** gains (one ordinary and one extraordinary) recognized by the debtor and the **one** ordinary loss recognized by the creditor.

Transfer of Equity Interest of Debtor to Settle Debt. In this type of restructure, the debtor corporation transfers its **own capital stock** to the creditor to satisfy a debt. The market value of the stock transferred is **less** than the obligation satisfied. This agreement is a **concession by the creditor to the debtor,** which means that the debtor realizes a gain and the creditor incurs a loss on the restructure.

For the **debtor,** this case requires that the stock transferred be recorded when it is issued at its current market value in the normal manner, with the difference between par or stated value and the market value of the stock recorded as

Exhibit 15–8
Troubled debt restructure—settlement of debt by transferring assets or an equity interest.

Panel A—Case Data:

1. At date of restructure: Debtor Company owed Creditor Company *(a)* an overdue $1,000, five-year, 10% (payable annually) note plus *(b)* accrued interest of $50 on the note (already debited to Expense and credited to Interest Payable).
2. At date of restructure: Creditor Company, because the debtor could not make the interest payments, has agreed to a concession, which involves the transfer of **noncash** items with a market value less than the amount of the past-due debt.
3. Two different restructure situations are illustrated below.

Panel B—Transfer of Assets to Settle Debt:

Date of restructure—Debtor Company has Asset X, which has a carrying or book value of $500 and a market value of $700. Creditor Company has agreed to accept this asset in full settlement of the debt principal of $1,000 and the $50 accrued interest (this settlement represents a concession by the creditor). The prerestructure carrying value of the debt is $1,000 + $50 = $1,050.

Debtor Company[†] | **Creditor Company**

a. To recognize the gain on disposal of Asset X:

Debtor Company			Creditor Company		
Asset X ($700 − $500)	200				
Gain on disposal of Asset X		200*			

*This gain or loss must be reported separately from the gain on restructure.

b. To record settlement of the debt by transfer of Asset X:

Debtor Company			Creditor Company		
Note payable	1,000		Asset X (market value)	700	
Interest payable	50		Loss on receivable restructure .	350	
Asset X		700	Note receivable		1,000
Extraordinary gain on debt restructure ($1,050 − $700)		350	Interest receivable		50

[†] These two entries often are combined.

Panel C—Transfer of Equity Interest of the Debtor to Settle Debt:

Date of restructure—Debtor Company has some of its own unissued common stock (par $1), which has a current market value of $1.50 per share. Creditor Company has agreed to accept 600 shares of this stock in full settlement of the debt principal and the accrued interest (i.e., $1,050).

To record settlement of the debt by transfer of the unissued common stock:

Debtor Company			Creditor Company		
Note payable	1,000		Investment, common stock of Debtor Company (600 shares × $1.50)	900	
Interest payable	50		Loss on receivable restructure .	150	
Common stock, par $1 (600 shares)		600	Note receivable		1,000
Contributed capital in excess of par, 600 × ($1.50 − $1.00) . .		300	Interest receivable		50
Extraordinary gain on debt restructure ($1,050 − $900)		150			

contributed capital in excess of par. The excess of the prerestructure carrying amount of the debt over the market value of the stock issued is recorded by the debtor as an **extraordinary** gain.

The **creditor** must record the stock received as an investment at its current market value. The creditor also records a **loss** on restructure equal to the excess of the carrying or book value of the receivable over the **market value** of the stock received. The transfer of an equity interest of the debtor to satisfy a debt is illustrated in Exhibit 15–8, Panel C.

Debt Restructure by Modification of Terms

Continuation of the debt with modification of the terms of the debt in a troubled debt restructure may involve one or more of the following changes: *(a)* reduction in the interest rate, *(b)* extension of the payment date for interest, *(c)* reduction of the face amount of the debt, *(d)* extension of the payment date of the face amount, and *(e)* reduction in any accrued interest (i.e., interest accrued before the restructure date).

Modification of the terms of a debt involves one of the following two situations as prescribed by *FASB Standard 15:*

> **Situation 1**—The **total of the restructured future cash equivalent payments** is **less** than the total prerestructure **carrying or book value of the debt.** The difference is recorded by the debtor as a **gain** and by the creditor as a **loss.**
>
> **Situation 2**—The **total of the restructured future cash equivalent payments** is **more than or equal to** the total prerestructure **carrying or book value of the debt.** The cash is sufficient to pay all of the principal and some interest. Therefore, neither party records a gain or loss, but each must determine the **new effective** interest rate.

Accounting for Situation 1. The total of the restructured cash equivalent payments is **less** than the prerestructure debt carrying value.

At date of restructure, the **debtor** reduces (i.e., debits) the carrying value of the debt to an amount equal to the total future cash payments agreed to under the restructure. The debtor also recognizes an **extraordinary gain** (i.e., a credit) equal to the amount of the debt that was written off. The creditor reduces the receivable and recognizes an **ordinary loss** for that same amount.

Subsequent to date of restructure in this situation, the total of the future cash equivalents is not sufficient to permit any recognition of the prerestructure interest. Therefore, **all** cash equivalent payments are applied to reduce (i.e., debit) the carrying value of the debt by the debtor and to reduce (i.e., credit) the carrying value of the receivable by the creditor. During the period from restructure date to maturity, then, **no interest will be recognized.** At maturity date, the debt carrying values of each party will be zero. **Exhibit 15–9** illustrates this situation.

Accounting for Situation 2. The total restructured cash equivalent to be paid is **more** than or equal to the prerestructure debt carrying value.

At date of restructure, no entry is made in the accounts of either the debtor or creditor because the total of the future cash payments is sufficient to pay the carrying amount of the debt. Any **cash above that amount is construed to be payment of interest.**

In this situation, a **new effective interest rate** must be determined because *(a)* some interest will be paid and *(b) FASB Standard 15* requires that the interest method (rather than the straight-line method) must be used to allocate interest to each period subsequent to restructure. Determination of the new effective rate of interest often requires an iterative (i.e., trial and error) approach because

Exhibit 15–9
Troubled debt restructure—modification of terms; total future cash LESS than the prerestructure carrying value of the debt.

Panel A—Case Data:

1. At date of restructure: Debtor Company owes Creditor Company a $1,000, 10-year, 10% (payable annually) note. Maturity date is five years from date of restructure. There is no accrued interest.
2. At date of restructure: Creditor Company, because of a critical cash flow problem of the debtor, agreed to a concession which *(a)* defers the interest payments and *(b)* reduces the principal amount of the debt.

Panel B—Total Future Cash LESS than Prerestructure Carrying Value:

At date of restructure, Creditor Company agreed to *(a)* reduce the annual interest payments from $100 to $60 and *(b)* reduce the principal from $1,000 to $600. [Total restructured cash, $600 + ($60 × 5) = $900] − [Prerestructure carrying value of the debt, $1,000] = ($100). No interest will be recognized because all of the $900 applies to the principal.
Entries required:

Debtor Company			Creditor Company		
a. At restructure date (to record restructure gain and loss):					
Note payable	100		Loss on receivable restructure	100	
Extraordinary gain on debt restructure ($1,000 − $900)		100	Note receivable		100
b. At each interest date (years 1–5); all cash applied to principal:					
Note payable	60		Cash	60	
Cash		60	Note receivable		60
c. At maturity date (to settle the reduced principal):					
Note payable	600		Cash	600	
Cash		600	Note receivable		600

Note: After the last entry (on maturity date), the balance in the note payable and note receivable accounts, respectively, will be zero (i.e., $1,000 − $100 − ($60 × 5) − $600 = $-0-.

two present values may be involved—PV of a single amount (Table 5–2) and PV of an annuity (Table 5–4).

Subsequent to restructure, each party makes an entry (based on the **interest method**) on each interest date. This entry records the *(a)* interest for the period and *(b)* reduction of the carrying value of the debt. Therefore, a debt amortization schedule is helpful to record periodic interest and principal reduction.

Exhibit 15–10 illustrates the iteration used to determine the new effective rate of interest. The first "educated guess" involved a trial at 5% (the new rate will always be less than the original stated rate), which proved to be too high; the second trial at 3% indicated that this rate was too low; the third trial at 4% was exactly right. In most situations, the interest rate must be carried to two or three decimal places for accuracy. Also, for instructional purposes, the columns in the debt amortization schedule are captioned to indicate the periodic interest entries for both the debtor and creditor.

A Conceptual Conflict in Troubled Debt Restructuring

Many accountants do not agree with the accounting treatment of **modification of terms** of debt mandated by *FASB Standard 15* (as illustrated in Exhibits 15–9 and 15–10). They believe that the gain to the debtor and the loss to the creditor should include both *(a)* the amount of the principal concession and *(b)* the

Exhibit 15–10

Troubled debt restructure—total cash MORE than or equal to the prerestructure carrying value of the debt.

Panel A—Case Data:

1. Debt to be restructured: principal, $1,000; annual interest rate, 10% (i.e., $100) payable at each year-end. Maturity date is five years from restructure date. There is no accrued interest.
2. Restructure agreement: Reduce principal to $859 and reduce annual interest payments to $66.

Panel B—Total Future Cash MORE than Prerestructure Carrying Value:

1. Analysis of the restructure:

Total future cash payments [$859 + ($66 × 5)]	$1,189
Prerestructure carrying value of the debt	1,000
Total cash payments more than carrying value; therefore, no entry is required at restructure date	$ 189

2. Computation of new effective rate on interest (by iteration):
Objective: To find the interest rate for five periods that equates *(a)* the present value of future cash flows, after restructure (principal, $859 and interest, $66) with *(b)* the prerestructure carrying amount of the debt, $1,000.

	First Trial (5%)	Second Trial (3%)	Third Trial (4%)
Principal, $859 (Table 5–2; $n = 5$):			
1st trial at 5% (× table value, .78353)	$673		
2d trial at 3% (× table value, .86261)		$ 741	
3d trial at 4% (× table value, .82193)			$ 706
Interest, $66 (Table 5–4; $n = 5$):			
1st trial at 5% (× table value, 4.32948)	286		
2d trial at 3% (× table value, 4.57971)		302	
3d trial at 4% (× table value, 4.45182)			294
Total present value of future cash flows (to be compared with $1,000 carrying amount of the debt)	$959	$1,043	$1,000

Conclusion: The new effective rate is 4%.

Panel C—Accounting Entries (None at Date of Restructure):

a. Annual entries subsequent to restructure tabulated—debt amortization schedule, at the new effective rate:

Date	Cash interest D*—Credit cash C*—Debit cash	Interest at effective rate D—Debit interest expense C—Credit interest revenue	Reduction of principal D—Debit payable C—Credit receivable	Principal balance D—Payable balance C—Receivable balance
Start				$1,000
End year 1	$66	$1,000 × 4% = $40	$26	974
End year 2	66	974 × 4% = 39	27	947
End year 3	66	947 × 4% = 38	28	919
End year 4	66	919 × 4% = 37	29	890
End year 5	66	890 × 4% = 35†	31	859

* Explanations: D—Debtor; C—Creditor.
† Rounded to come out even.

b. Entry at maturity date (reduces the payable and receivable balance to zero):

Debtor			Creditor		
Payable	859		Cash	859	
Cash		859	Receivable		859

Note: The amounts in this illustration were kept small for practical reasons. This exhibit illustrates iteration to compute the new effective rate of interest. However, in practice straight-line allocation of the $330 interest could have been used because the amounts are not materially different. Use of straight-line would avoid the need to determine the effective rate and prepare the amortization schedule.

interest concession. That is, the gain (loss) on modification of terms should be the difference between *(a)* the prerestructure carrying amount of the debt and *(b)* the **present value** of the cash payments (i.e., principal and interest) after restructure. This treatment is consistent with the conceptual approach to valuation of receivables and payables as mandated in *APB Opinion 21,* "Interest on Receivables and Payables," because it measures the economic gain or loss of each party.

In contrast, *FASB Standard 15* mandates that the loss (gain) on modification of terms shall be measured as the difference between the *(a)* prerestructure carrying amount of the debt and *(b)* total future cash equivalent payments required after restructure. This ignores the present value of the restructured cash flows based on a realistic current interest rate.

These two opposing views can be compared by referring to Exhibit 15–9. The comparative results are as follows, assuming the going market interest rate on debts, such as the one being restructured, is 20 percent.

	FASB viewpoint		Conceptual viewpoint
Carrying amount of debt on restructure date	$1,000		$ 701*
Total cash payments after restructure ($60 × 5) + $600	900		
Present value of cash payments after restructure:			
Principal: $600 × $p_{n=5;i=20\%}$ (.40188, Table 5–2)		$241	
Interest: $60 × $P_{o_{n=5;i=20\%}}$ (2.99061, Table 5–4)		179	420
Gain (loss) on debt restructure by the **creditor**	$ (100)		$(281)

* ($1,000 × .40188 = $402) + ($100 × 2.99061 = $299) = $701.

Financial institutions (i.e., creditors) appear to strongly prefer the FASB approach. Under the FASB approach they are not required to report what, in fact, is an **economic loss.** Conceptually, the FASB position is not persuasive.

Disclosure Requirements

FASB Standard 15 (pars. 164–72) prescribes detailed disclosure requirements for both the debtor and creditor.

In substance, disclosure by the **debtor** must include: *(a)* a description of the major changes for each restructuring; *(b)* the aggregate gain on restructuring and the related income tax effect; *(c)* aggregate loss or gain on transfers of assets; *(d)* the per share amount of the aggregate gain on restructuring of payables, net of related income tax effect; and *(e)* information on any related contingent payments.

The **creditor** must disclose, for each major category of outstanding receivables, the following: *(a)* the aggregate recorded investment, *(b)* gross interest revenue that would have been recorded without restructure, *(c)* the amount of interest revenue on those receivables that was included in net income for the period, and *(d)* the amount of commitments to lend additional funds to debtors whose terms have been modified in troubled debt restructurings.

Summary

This chapter emphasized the accounting process for long-term debt securities for both parties—the borrower and lender—because the recording and reporting are essentially the same except that both the account titles and debits and credits are reversed. This means that the concepts used by each party to account for the debt security transactions are consistent.

The chapter discussed the characteristics of most long-term debt securities as follows: *(a)* an obligation to transfer assets or services in the future, *(b)* a transaction or event that has already occurred, *(c)* an enforceable contract, and *(d)* repayment extends beyond one year or the operating cycle, if longer. A long-term debt security is measured conceptually as the present (i.e., discounted) value of all of its future cash flows. This present value amount often is indicated by the sale of the security. However, it sometimes must be computed by using the market (i.e., effective) rate of interest, taking into account the related risk.

Bonds were discussed from the viewpoint of both the issuer and investor. A bond security may be sold at more than par, at par, or at less than par. When a bond security is sold or purchased above par, the premium must be amortized and, if sold below par, the discount must be amortized, over the **remaining** life of the security. Bond premiums and discounts must be amortized to interest revenue or expense using one of two methods as follows: *(a)* straight-line (acceptability depends on the materiality constraint) and *(b)* interest-method (conceptually preferable because it is based on present value concepts).

Part B of the chapter discussed two topics: *(a)* extinguishment of debt and *(b)* debt restructure. Extinguishment of debt may occur before, at, or after maturity date. Extinguishment of a debt is the settlement of a debt, other than by the payment of the debt in conformity with its original terms, by *(a)* early acquisition of the debt securities, *(b)* obtaining a release from making future payment on the debt, or *(c)* by placing assets in an irrevocable trust to pay the debt. Extinguishments of debt must be accounted for by *(a)* updating and removing from the accounts all amounts related to the debt, *(b)* recording in conformity with GAAP, all considerations used to settle the debt, and *(c)* recording ordinary and extraordinary gains and losses in conformity with GAAP.

Troubled debt restructure occurs when the *(a)* debtor cannot meet the required debt payments and *(b)* the creditor makes a favorable concession to the creditor, such as reduced or deferred interest or principal payments. These concessions by the creditor to the debtor must be recorded to show a gain for the debtor and a loss to the creditor. Accounting for troubled debt restructure involves special **rules** as discussed in the chapter.

SUPPLEMENT 15–A: SERIAL BONDS

When bonds are issued with provision for repayment of principal in a series of **installments,** the issue is called a **serial bond issue.** Serial bonds are well adapted for use by school districts and other taxing authorities that borrow money upon agreement that a special tax will be levied to pay off the obligation. As the taxes are collected, the cash is used to pay off the indebtedness.

Determining Selling Price of Serial Bonds

The selling price of serial bonds is derived by computing the selling price for each serial separately in the same way that an ordinary bond issue is valued. The prices of the various serials are then totaled. For example, serial bonds, carrying 7% interest payable 3½% semiannually, are sold to yield 5% per annum with the following maturity dates: $10,000 at the end of 12 months, $20,000 at the end of 18 months, and $30,000 at the end of 24 months.[12] The price of each serial bond and the entire issue can be computed as follows:

	Selling price	Premium
Serial No. 1 (due in 12 months—2 interest periods):		
Principal: $10,000 × .95181 (Table 5–2, n = 2; i = 2.5%)	$ 9,518	
Interest payments:		
$350 × 1.92742 (Table 5–2, n = 2; i = 2.5%)	675	
	10,193	$ 193
Serial No. 2 (due in 18 months—3 interest periods):		
Principal: $20,000 × .92860	18,572	
Interest payments: $700 × 2.85602	1,999	
	20,571	571
Serial No. 3 (due in 24 months—4 interest periods):		
Principal: $30,000 × .90595	27,179	
Interest payments: $1,050 × 3.76197	3,950	
. . . .	31,129	1,129
Total of all serials	$61,893	$1,893

Amortization of Premium and Discount on Serial Bonds

Amortization of a premium or discount on serial bonds is identical to that on ordinary bonds. However, the computations are more complicated. When the results are **not** materially different from the interest method, the straight-line method may be used. Otherwise, the interest method must be used. In both methods, the amount of periodic amortization must be related to the amount of bonds **outstanding** during the period. Therefore, the amount of periodic amortization of premium or discount will decrease as each serial is paid off at its maturity date.

Straight-line amortization of the $1,893 premium from the above example computed for each period is shown below. Notice that the premium on each serial is apportioned to the number of periods that each serial is outstanding.[13]

---

[12] Although not realistic, a short time span is used to simplify the computations.

[13] Occasionally, problems are given that fail to specify a basis for determining the amount of premium or discount applicable to each serial. In this situation, an approximation known as dollar-periods or "bonds outstanding" allocation is used. The method is straight line and should **not** be used when the interest method is mandated. The $1,893 total premium could be allocated as follows:

Serial	Par	Periods outstanding (semiannual)	Dollar periods	Allocation fraction	Allocation to serials
1	$10,000	2	$ 20,000	20/200	× $1,893 = $ 189
2	20,000	3	60,000	60/200	× $1,893 = 568
3	30,000	4	120,000	120/200	× $1,893 = 1,136
			$200,000		$1,893

The amounts in the last column are then allocated to each period on a straight-line basis, as illustrated above.

Serial no.	Total premium to be amortized	At end of 6 months	At end of 12 months	At end of 18 months	At end of 24 months
		Amortization of premium, straight line			
1	$ 193	$ 96	$ 97		
2	571	190	190	$191	
3	1,129	282	282	282	$283
	$1,893	$568	$569	$473	$283

The entries for the foregoing example are given below, with the added assumption that $5,000 par of the serial No. 3 bonds, which were to mature at the end of 24 months, were purchased for $5,100 and retired (early extinguishment) at the end of 12 months.

1. To record sale of the bonds:

Cash	61,893	
Premium on bonds payable		1,893
Bonds payable		60,000

2. To record payment of interest and straight-line amortization of premium at the end of six months:

Interest expense	1,532	
Premium on bonds payable	568	
Cash ($60,000 × 3½%)		2,100

3. To record payment of interest and amortization of premium at end of 12 months:

Interest expense	1,531	
Premium on bonds payable	569	
Cash ($60,000 × 3½%)		2,100

4. To record payment of serial No. 1 bonds at the end of 12 months:

Bonds payable (serial No. 1)	10,000	
Cash		10,000

5. To record retirement of $5,000 of serial No. 3 bonds at end of 12 months for $5,100 cash:

Bonds payable	5,000	
Bond premium	94*	
Extraordinary loss, early extinguishment of debt	6	
Cash		5,100

* ($5,000/$30,000) × ($282 + $283) = $94.

6. To pay interest, amortize premium, and pay off serial No. 2 bonds at end of 18 months:

Interest expense	1,149	
Bond premium [$191 + (5/6 × $282)]	426	
Cash ($45,000 × 3½%)		1,575
Bonds payable	20,000	
Cash		20,000

7. To pay interest, amortize premium, and pay off serial No. 3 bonds at end of 24 months:

Interest expense	639	
Bond premium (5/6 × $283)	236	
Cash ($25,000 × 3½%)		875
Bonds payable	25,000	
Cash		25,000

Interest method amortization requires knowledge of the effective rate of interest and the selling price. When serial bonds are involved, an amortization schedule should be prepared in the same manner as the amortization schedule for ordinary (nonserial) bonds. However, the maturity values of each installment must be deducted from the "carrying value" amounts when the installments are paid.

QUESTIONS

Part A

1. List and briefly explain the primary characteristics of long-term debt securities.
2. What are the primary distinctions between a debt security and an equity security?
3. Explain the difference between the stated rate of interest and the effective rate on a long-term debt security.
4. Briefly explain point-system mortgages, SAMs, and variable-rate mortgages.
5. Briefly explain the effects on interest recognized on the statement of income when the stated and effective rates of interest are different.
6. What are the primary characteristics of a bond? What distinguishes it from capital stock?
7. Contrast the following classes of bonds: *(a)* industrial versus governmental, *(b)* secured versus unsecured, *(c)* ordinary versus income, *(d)* ordinary versus serial, *(e)* callable versus convertible, and *(f)* registered versus coupon.
8. What are the principal advantages and disadvantages of bonds versus common stock for *(a)* the issuer and *(b)* the investor?
9. Distinguish between the par amount and the price of a bond. When are they the same? When different? Explain.
10. Explain the significance of bond discount and bond premium to *(a)* the issuer and *(b)* the investor.
11. Assume a $1,000, 8% (payable semiannually), 10-year bond is sold at an effective rate of 6%. Explain how to compute the price of this bond.
12. Explain why and how bond discount and bond premium affect *(a)* the statement of financial position and *(b)* the statement of income of the investor.
13. What is the primary conceptual difference between the straight-line and interest methods of amortizing bond discount and premium?
14. Under GAAP, when is it appropriate to use the *(a)* straight-line and *(b)* interest method of amortization for bond discount or premium?
15. When the end of the accounting period of the issuer is not on a bond interest date, adjusting entries must be made for *(a)* accrued interest and *(b)* discount or

premium amortization. Explain in general terms what each adjustment amount represents.

16. When bonds are sold (or purchased) between interest dates, accrued interest must be recognized. Explain why.
17. What are convertible bonds? What are the primary reasons for their use?
18. Why is the accounting different for nonconvertible bonds with detachable stock purchase warrants and nonconvertible bonds with nondetachable stock purchase warrants?

Part B

19. Define extinguishment of debt.
20. When may extinguishment of debt occur? List the various ways that extinguishment of debt occurs.
21. Explain how an accounting gain or loss to the debtor may occur when a call privilege is exercised.
22. When the issuer purchases its own debt securities in the open market to extinguish the debt, two entries usually must be made. Explain.
23. What is meant by refunding?
24. What is meant by in-substance defeasance?
25. What effect does in-substance defeasance have on the statement of financial position?
26. What is meant by troubled debt restructuring? What are some of the features of typical restructuring arrangements?
27. Explain the income classification of gains and losses from troubled debt restructuring.
28. Differentiate between a debt restructure in which debt is considered as settled and one in which it is considered as continuing.

EXERCISES

Part A: Exercises 15–1 to 15–15

E 15–1 **(LT Note; Borrower and Lender; Entries and Reporting)**
On May 1, 19A, WT Company borrowed $24,000 cash from TX Bank on a $24,000, 10%, three-year note. Interest is payable each April 30, and the principal is payable on April 30, 19D. The accounting period ends on December 31 for each party.

Required:

1. Give all current and adjusting entries through April 30, 19B, for both the borrower and the lender.
2. Show how this note and the related items would be shown on the 19A financial statements of each party.

E 15–2 **(LT Note; Borrower and Lender; Effective Rate; Amortization Schedule; Entries)**
On January 1, 19A, DK Company borrowed cash from PT Finance Company on a $30,000, 12%, two-year note. The note will be paid off in two equal installments each December 31. PT assessed DK two points. The accounting period for each company ends December 31.

Required:

1. Compute the amount of each annual payment.
2. The effective rate was computed to be 13.55%. Show how this rate was computed.
3. Prepare a debt amortization schedule for the two parties.
4. Give all entries for each party from January 1, 19A, through the maturity date.

E 15–3 **(LT Note; Borrower and Lender; Amortization Schedule; Entries)**

The following data are available: on January 1, 19A, a borrower signed a long-term note, face amount, $100,000; time to maturity, three years; stated rate of interest, 8%. The effective rate of interest of 10% determined the cash received by the borrower. The note will be paid in three equal annual installments on each December 31 (also, this is the end of the accounting period for both parties).

Required:

1. Compute the cash received by the borrower and prepare a debt amortization schedule.
2. Give the required entries for both the borrower and lender for each of the three years.

E 15–4 **(LT Note; Borrower and Lender Entries; Effective Rate; Amortization Schedule)**

The following information is known: on January 1, year 1, a borrower signed a long-term note, face amount, $100,000; time to maturity, three years; stated interest rate, 12%; and cash proceeds from the loan, $96,661. The note will be paid in equal annual installments on each December 31 (also, this is the end of the accounting period for both parties).

Required:

1. Prepare a debt amortization schedule.
2. Give the required entries for both the borrower and lender for each of the three years.

E 15–5 **(LT Note; Unrealistic Rate; Amortization Schedule; Entries, Debtor and Creditor)**

Cathy Company purchased a machine at the beginning of year 1 with a three-year, $1,000, 5% note, payable in three equal annual payments of $367 (including principal and interest) at each year-end. The current market rate of interest for this level of risk was 12%.

Required:

1. What was the cost of the machine to Cathy Company?
2. Give the entry by Cathy to record the purchase. Use the net approach.
3. Prepare the amortization schedule for the note.
4. Give the entries for both the debtor and the creditor at the end of each year (assuming the accounting year-end for the debtor and creditor coincides with the note's year-end).

E 15–6 **(Bonds; Compare Above, at, and Below Par; Effect on Effective Rates and Interest Expense)**

Rowe Corporation authorized $600,000, 8% (payable 4% semiannually), 10-year bonds payable. The bonds were dated January 1, 19A; interest dates are June 30 and December 31.

Assume four different cases with respect to the sale of the bonds: *Case A*—Sold on January 1, 19A, at par; *Case B*—Sold on January 1, 19A, at 102; *Case C*—Sold on January 1, 19A, at 98; *Case D*—Sold on March 1, 19A, at par.

Required:

1. For each case, what amount of cash interest will be paid on the first interest date, June 30, 19A?
2. In what cases will the effective rate of interest be *(a)* the same, *(b)* higher, or *(c)* lower than the stated rate?
3. After sale of the bonds, and prior to maturity date, in what cases will the carrying or book value of the bonds (as reported on the statement of financial position) be *(a)* the same, *(b)* higher, or *(c)* lower than the maturity or face amount?
4. After the sale of the bonds, in Cases A, B, and C, which case will report interest expense (on the statement of income) *(a)* the same, *(b)* higher, or *(c)* lower than the amount of cash interest paid each period?

E 15–7 **(Bonds; Compute Four Bond Prices)**
Compute the bond price for each of the following situations (show computations and round to nearest dollar):

a. A 10-year, $1,000 bond; annual interest at 7% (payable 3½% semiannually) purchased to yield 6% interest.
b. An eight-year, $1,000 bond; annual interest at 6% (payable annually) purchased to yield 7% interest.
c. A 10-year, $1,000 bond; annual interest at 6% (payable semiannually) purchased to yield 8% interest.
d. An eight-year, $1,000 bond; annual interest at 6% (payable annually) purchased to yield 6% interest.

E 15–8 **(Bonds; above, at, Below Par; Straight-Line; Issuer and Investor Entries)**
Y Corporation issued to Z Corporation a $30,000, 8% (payable 4% semiannually on June 30 and December 31), 10-year bond dated and sold on January 1, 19A. Assumptions: Case A—sold at par; Case B—sold at 103; and Case C—sold at 97.

Required:
In parallel columns for the issuer and the investor (assume a long-term investment), give the appropriate journal entries for each case on (1) January 1, 19A, and (2) June 30, 19A (use the gross method). Assume the difference between the interest method and the straight-line method of amortization is not material; therefore, use straight-line amortization.

E 15–9 **(Bond; Compute Bond Price; Interest Method; Straight-Line; Issuer and Investor Entries)**
New Corporation sold and issued to Old Corporation a $10,000, 9% (payable 4½% semiannually on June 30 and December 31), 10-year bond, dated and sold on January 1, 19A. The bond was sold at an 8% effective rate (4% semiannually).

Required:

1. Compute the price of the bond.
2. In parallel columns for the issuer and the investor (assume a long-term investment), give the appropriate journal entries on *(a)* January 1, 19A, and *(b)* June 30, 19A (use the gross method). Assume the difference between the interest method and the straight-line method of amortization is material; therefore, use the interest method.

E 15–10 **(Bond; Compute Price; Amortization Schedule; Entries—Interest Method, at Gross)**
Red Corporation sold to White Corporation a $10,000 bond, 7% interest (payable annually on December 31). The bond was sold on January 1, 19A, matures December 31, 19D, and the effective rate was 8%.

Required:

1. Compute the price of the bond.
2. Prepare a bond amortization schedule using the interest method and assuming the bonds are recorded at their gross amount.
3. In parallel columns, give entries for the issuer and the investor (a long-term investment) for the following dates, assuming the interest method of amortization: *(a)* sale of the bond, *(b)* first interest payment, and *(c)* all entries on the maturity date, December 31, 19D.
4. Show how the bond should be reported on the statements of financial position of the issuer and the investor at December 31, 19A.

E 15–11 (Bonds; Premium; Accrued Interest; Straight-Line, Gross and Net Methods)

On September 1, 19A, Golf Company sold and issued to Youngblood Company $30,000, five-year, 9% (payable semiannually) bonds for $32,320 plus accrued interest. The bonds were dated July 1, 19A, and interest is payable each June 30 and December 31. The accounting period for each company ends on December 31.

Required:

In parallel columns, give entries, using the gross method for the issuer and the net method for the investor (a long-term investment) for the following dates: September 1, 19A; December 31, 19A; January 1, 19B; and June 30, 19B. Assume the difference between the interest method and straight-line method amortization amounts is not material; therefore, use straight-line amortization.

E 15–12 (Bonds; Accrued Interest; Issuer Entries; Straight-Line, Gross)

Ryan Corporation sold and issued $150,000, three-year, 8% (payable semiannually) bonds payable for $156,400 plus accrued interest. Interest is payable each February 28 and August 31. The bonds were dated March 1, 19A, and were sold on July 1, 19A. The accounting period ends on December 31.

Required:

1. How much accrued interest should be recognized at date of sale?
2. How long is the amortization period?
3. Give entries for Ryan Corporation through February 19B (including reversing entries). Use straight-line amortization and the gross method.
4. Would the above amounts also be recorded by the investor? Explain.

E 15–13 (Bonds; Compute Price; Amortization Schedule, Interest Method, Entries, Issuer Gross, Investment)

Radian Company issued to Seivers Company $30,000, four-year, 8% bonds dated June 1, 19A. Interest is payable semiannually on May 31 and November 30. The bonds were issued on March 1, 19B, for $28,371 plus accrued interest. The bonds would have sold at the effective rate on the next interest date for $28,478. The accounting period ends December 31 for both companies. The effective interest rate was 10%.

Required (round to the nearest dollar):

1. Verify the bond price. Use straight-line interpolation between interest dates.
2. Prepare a bond amortization schedule starting on March 1, 19B, and continuing to maturity, May 31, 19E. Use interest-method amortization.
3. In parallel columns, give entries for the issuer and the investor (as a long-term investment) for the following dates: March 1, 19B, and May 31, 19B. Use interest-method amortization, and the gross method for issuer and the net method for the investor.

E 15–14 (Nonconvertible Bonds with Detachable Warrants; Entries, Issuer and Investor) Hardware Corporation issued $150,000, 6%, 10-year, nonconvertible bonds with detachable stock purchase warrants. Each $1,000 bond carried 20 detachable warrants, each of which was for one share of Hardware common stock, par $20, with a specified option price of $60. The bonds sold at 102 including the warrants (no bond price ex-warrants were available), and, immediately after date of issuance, the detachable stock purchase warrants were selling at $4 each.

The entire issue was acquired by Software Company as a long-term investment.

Required:

1. Give entries for both the issuer and the investor at date of acquisition of the bonds. Use the gross method.
2. Give the entry for the investor assuming a subsequent sale of all of the warrants to another investor at $5.50 each.
3. Disregard (2). Give the entries for the issuer and the investor assuming subsequent tender of all of the warrants by the investor for exercise at the specified option price. At this date, the stock was selling at $75 per share.

E 15–15 (Convertible Bonds; Entries, Issuer and Investor; Conversion) Stonewall Corporation issued $40,000, 5%, 10-year convertible bonds. Each $1,000 bond was convertible to 10 shares of common stock (par $50) of Stonewall Corporation at any interest date after three years from issuance. The bonds were sold at 105 to Mason Corporation as a long-term investment.

Required:

1. Give the entry for both the issuer and the investor at the date of issuance. Use the gross method.
2. Give entries for both the issuer and the investor, assuming that the conversion privilege is subsequently exercised by Mason Corporation immediately after the end of the third year. Assume 30% of any premium or discount has been amortized and that, at date of conversion, the common stock was selling at $125 per share.

Part B: Exercises 15–16 to 15–24

E 15–16 (Extinguishment by Call; Issuance and Extinguishment Entries) On January 1, 19A, RD Company issued $100,000 bonds payable with a stated interest rate of 12%, payable annually each December 31. The bonds mature in 20 years and have a call price of 103, exercisable by RD Company after the fifth year. The bonds originally sold at 105.

On December 31 of the 12th year, the company called the bonds. At that time, the bonds were quoted on the market at a price to yield 10%. RD Company uses straight-line amortization; its accounting period ends December 31.

Required:

1. Give the issuance entry for RD Company required on January 1, 19A. Use the gross method.
2. Give the entry for extinguishment of the debt.

E 15–17 (Extinguishment by Call; Update, Issuance and Extinguishment Entries) On January 1, 19A, Sty Company issued $200,000 bonds payable with a stated interest rate of 5%, payable annually each December 31. The bonds mature in 10 years and are callable after the 4th year at 101. The bonds originally sold on January 1, 19A, at 104.

On June 30 of the 6th year, the bonds were called. The company uses straight-line amortization, and the accounting period ends December 31.

Required:

1. Give the issuance entry on January 1, 19A. Use the gross method.
2. Give any entries on the extinguishment (i.e., call) date.

E 15–18 **(Extinguishment by Refunding; Issuance and Extinguishment Entries)**
On January 1, year 1, Rocket Corporation issued $500,000, 6%, 20-year bonds at 98. The interest is payable each December 31. Rocket uses straight-line amortization and the gross method. Its accounting period ends December 31.

On January 1, year 12, Rocket issued $500,000, 9%, 20-year, refunding bonds at par. On this date, the old 6% bonds could be purchased in the open market at their present value based on the current effective rate of 9%. Rocket immediately purchased all of the 6% debt.

Required (round to the nearest dollar):

1. Give the entry for issuance of the 6% bonds.
2. Give the entry for issuance of the 9% bonds.
3. Give the entry to record the extinguishment of the old debt by refunding.
4. What effect did the refunding have on the working capital of Rocket Corporation?

E 15–19 **(Extinguishment by Purchase in the Open Market; Entries)**
On January 1, 19A, Nue Corporation issued $100,000, 10%, 10-year bonds at 98. Interest is paid each December 31, which also is the end of the accounting period. The company uses straight-line amortization and the gross method. On July 1, 19F, the company purchased all of the bonds at 101 plus any accrued interest.

Required:

1. Give the issuance entry.
2. Give the interest entry on December 31, 19A.
3. Give the related entries on July 1, 19F.

E 15–20 **(Extinguishment by In-substance Defeasance)**
On January 1, 19A, Slick Corporation borrowed cash on a $900,000, 5%, seven-year, note payable. Interest is payable semiannually on each June 30 and December 31. On January 1, 19E, the company entered into an agreement with the creditors to irrevocably transfer the note to an independent trustee for payment of 10% interest each interest period and the principal at maturity. Slick transmitted to the trustee cash equal to the present value of the note so that the trustee can pay each of the six remaining interest payments and the note principal on maturity date. Cash in the amount of $704,010 was paid to the trustee to invest so that there will be sufficient cash to make the payments. Slick's accounting period ends December 31.

Required:

1. Give the entry for Slick Corporation on January 1, 19A.
2. Give the related entries on June 30 and December 31, 19A.
3. Give the extinguishment entry on January 1, 19E.
4. Show how the $704,010 was computed assuming an expected net earning rate by the trust of 10%.
5. What conditions must be met to qualify the transaction, on January 1, 19E, as an extinguishment of the $900,000 debt?

E 15–21 **(Restructure; Transfer of Noncash Asset; Entries by Each Party)**
Down Company owed Super Bank a $50,000, three-year, 10% (payable each December 31) note payable dated January 1, 19A. During 19C, Down Company experienced unusual

financial difficulties and was unable to pay the note and interest for 19C that had been accrued. On January 1, 19D, the bank agreed to settle the debt and interest (for 19C) for $2,000 cash plus some land that had a current market value of $30,000. At December 31, 19C, the records of Down Company reflected the acquisition cost of the land to be $20,000.

Required:
Give all entries required on January 1, 19D, to record this debt restructure *(a)* for Down Company and *(b)* for Super Bank.

E 15–22 **(Restructure; Transfer Cash and Noncash Assets; Entries by Each Party)**
Slow Company owed Quick Finance Company a three-year, $100,000, 10% (payable annually each December 31), note payable dated January 1, 19A. At December 31, 19C, Slow was experiencing serious financial problems and could not pay the principal and interest for 19C that had been accrued. Quick agreed to settle the debt and interest in full for $12,000 cash plus a tract of land (Slow's acquisition cost was $7,000) plus 1,000 shares of Slow common stock, par $10, that had a current market price of $35 per share. The current market value of the land on January 1, 19D, was $20,000. The agreement was accepted by both parties, and settlement was effected on January 1, 19D.

Required:
Give all entries required to record the debt restructure for *(a)* Slow Company and *(b)* Quick Finance Company.

E 15–23 **(Restructure; Modification of Terms; Compute New Interest Rate; Entries for Both Parties)**
Brown Company owed City Bank a $50,000, 10% (payable each December 31), four-year note payable dated January 1, 19A. Early in 19B, it became clear that Brown Company was experiencing difficulty in making the annual interest payment, although the company did manage to make the 19A payment. Due to expected continuing difficulties, it appeared that there was a good chance the company might default on the note (as well as other obligations). On January 2, 19C, the two parties agreed to restructure the debt by *(a)* reducing the remaining annual interest payments to $2,240 each and *(b)* reducing the principal amount (maturity amount) to $48,000. Brown paid the interest for the year 19B.

Required:
1. Compute the new yield or effective rate of interest.
2. Give all entries required on date of restructure (January 2, 19C) for each company. If no entry is required, explain the reason.
3. Give all entries required at December 31, 19C, and 19D, for each company.

E 15–24 **(Restructure, Modification of Terms; Entries by Both Parties)**
Orange Company owed National Bank a $60,000, 10% (payable each December 31), four-year note payable dated January 1, 19A. Orange Company has experienced severe financial difficulties and is likely to default on the note and interest during 19C unless some concessions are made by the bank. Consequently, on January 2, 19C, the parties agreed to restructure the debt as follows: *(a)* interest payments each year to be reduced to $1,000 per year for 19C and 19D, and *(b)* reduce the principal amount to $30,000. On December 31, 19B, Orange paid $6,000 interest for 19B.

Required:
1. Does this restructure change the yield or effective interest rate? Explain. Is a new effective rate of interest needed for accounting purposes in this situation? Explain.

2. Give all entries required for each party on the date of restructure, January 2, 19C.
3. Give all entries required for each party on December 31, 19C, and 19D.

PROBLEMS

Part A: Problems 15–1 to 15–13

P 15–1 **(LT Note; Borrower and Lender Entries; Amortization Schedule; Adjusting Entry)**
On January 1, 19A, Baker Company borrowed cash from Alter Finance Company and signed a three-year, $30,000 note. Interest is payable each December 31 at a stated interest rate of "floating prime at January 1 of each year plus 2%." The principal is due on December 31, 19C. The actual prime rates used by Alter were: January 1, 19A, 13%; January 1, 19B, 12%; and January 1, 19C, 15%. The accounting period for each company ends on December 31.

Required:
1. Compute the total amount of interest paid, by year.
2. What was the difference between the stated and effective rates? Explain.
3. Give all entries for each company through maturity date.
4. Give the 19A adjusting entry that would have been necessary had the accounting periods for each company ended on August 31 instead of December 31.

P 15–2 **(Note with Share Appreciation; Amortization Schedule; Entries and Reporting for Borrower and Lender)**
On January 1, 19A, CT Company borrowed cash from TN Financing Company on a $60,000, 14%, three-year note. Interest is payable each December 31, and the principal is payable December 31, 19C. This note is designated as Note A.

On the same date, CT Company also borrowed cash from TX Commercial Loan Company on a $200,000, 9%, five-year note. This note, designated as Note B, will be paid with five equal annual payments each December 31. TX granted a low 9% stated rate in exchange for a 10% share appreciation in an office building under construction. The current best estimate of the present value of the share appreciation at January 1, 19A, was $52,754. The accounting period for each company ends on December 31.

Required:
1. What is the amount of each annual payment on Note B?
2. For each note, what is the *(a)* stated interest rate and *(b)* effective interest rate?
3. Prepare a debt amortization schedule for Note B.
4. For each note separately, give all entries for both the borrower and the lenders through December 31, 19A.
5. Show the items and amounts that would be reported on the December 31, 19A, financial statements, by each company under the captions: revenues, expenses, assets, liabilities, and stockholders' equity (current and noncurrent classifications are not required).

P 15–3 **(Note; Points; Share Appreciation; Floating Interest; Entries)**
On January 1, 19A, A Corporation borrowed cash from B Financial Company on a $100,000, 15%, two-year note.

Case A
A Corporation received cash, $100,000. Interest only is paid each December 31; the principal is due December 31, 19B.

Case B
B Financial Company assessed A Corporation three points. The note will be paid in two equal installments each December 31.

Case C
B Financial Company agreed to a 12% stated interest rate on the note in return for a 10% share appreciation. The best estimate of the present value of the share appreciation was $14,796. The note will be paid in two equal installments each December 31.

Case D
B Financial Company specified the stated interest rate as "floating prime at the start of each semiannual period plus 1%." Interest will be paid semiannually on each June 30 and December 31. The principal is due December 31, 19B. The actual prime rates used by B Financial Company were: January 1, 19A, 14%; July 1, 19A, 13%; January 1, 19B, 13%; and July 1, 19B, 15%.

Required:
1. Complete the following schedule for B Financial Company:

Item	Case A	Case B	Case C	Case D
1. Resources loaned	$			
2. Face of note	$			
3. Stated interest rate	%			
4. Resources received	$			
5. Total interest revenue	$			
6. Effective interest rate	%			

Computations:

2. Based upon the completed schedule, give the following entries for B Financial Company for each case:
   a. January 1, 19A—To record the loan.
   b. December 31, 19A and 19B—To record interest revenue for the two years combined.
   c. December 31, 19B—To record collection at maturity date.

P 15–4 (Note with Unrealistic Interest Rate; Entries and Reporting for Both Parties, Gross Method)
Sable Company purchased merchandise for resale on January 1, 19A, for $5,000 cash plus a $20,000, two-year note payable. The principal is due on December 31, 19B; the note specified 8% interest payable each December 31.

Assume Sable's going rate of interest for this type of debt was 15%. The accounting period ends December 31.

Required:

1. Give the entry to record the purchase on January 1, 19A. Show computations (round to nearest dollar).
2. Complete a tabulation as follows:

   a. Amount of cash interest payable each December 31 . . . . $____

   b. Total interest expense for the two-year period . . . . $____

   c. Amount of interest reported on statement of income for 19A . . . . $____

   d. Amount of liability reported on statement of financial position at 12/31/19A (excluding any accrued interest) . . . . $____

3. Give the entries at each year-end for the debtor.
4. Give the entries at each year-end for the creditor.
5. Show how the debtor and creditor should report or disclose the data related to the note on the statement of income and statement of financial position at each year-end.

P 15–5 (Bonds; Compute Price; Amortization Schedule, Interest Method, Gross; Entries and Reporting)

Alpha Corporation sold and issued to Beta Corporation $200,000, 8% (payable semiannually on June 30 and December 31), three-year bonds. The bonds were dated and sold on January 1, 19A, at an effective interest rate of 10%. The accounting period for each company ends on December 31.

Required:

1. Compute the price of the bonds.
2. Prepare a debt amortization schedule for the life of the bonds (use the interest method and round to the nearest dollar).
3. Prepare, in parallel columns, entries for the issuer and the investor (as a long-term investment) through December 31, 19A. Use the gross method.
4. Show how the issuer and the investor would report the bonds on their respective statements of financial position at December 31, 19A.
5. What would be reported on the statement of income for each party for the year ended December 31, 19A?

P 15–6 (Bonds; Compute Price; Amortization Schedule, Interest Method, Gross Entries and Reporting)

Howe Corporation sold and issued to Luck Company, $40,000, 7% (payable semiannually on June 30 and December 31), four-year bonds dated January 1, 19A. The bonds were sold on January 1, 19A, at an effective rate of 6%.

Required:

1. Compute the price of the bonds.
2. Prepare a debt amortization schedule over the life of the bonds, assuming the interest method of amortization.
3. In parallel columns for the issuer and investor (as a long-term investment), give all journal entries from issuance through fiscal year-end 19A. The accounting period for Howe ends on December 31 and for Luck on November 30. Use the gross method.
4. Show how the issuer and the investor should report the bonds on their respective statements of financial position at December 31, 19A, and November 30, 19A, respectively.

5. What would be reported on the statement of income for each party for the year ended December 31, 19A, and November 30, 19A, respectively?

P 15–7 (Bonds; Accrued Interest; Entries, Straight-Line, Gross; Reporting)
Foyt Corporation sold and issued to Mears Corporation $50,000 bonds on June 1, 19A, for $51,320 plus any accrued interest. The bond indenture provided the following information:

Maturity amount	$50,000
Date of bonds	April 1, 19A
Maturity date	March 31, 19C (2 years)
Stated interest rate	6½%, payable semiannually
Interest payments	March 31 and September 30

Required:

1. In parallel columns, give entries for the issuer and investor (as a long-term investment) from date of sale to maturity. Assume the difference between the amortization amounts is not material; therefore, use straight-line amortization. Also assume the accounting period for each company ends on December 31. Use the gross method.
2. Show how the bonds would be reported on the statement of financial position of each company at December 31, 19A.
3. What would be reported on the statement of income for each company for the year ended December 31, 19A?

P 15–8 (Bonds; Comprehensive; Interest Method; Adjusting Entries)
Jones Corporation issued bonds, face amount $100,000, three-year, 8% (payable semiannually on June 30 and December 31). The bonds were dated January 1, 19A, and were sold on November 1, 19A, for $100,739 (including interest of $2,667 and a bond price of $98,072) at an effective interest rate of 9%. The bonds would have sold at the effective rate on December 31, 19A, for $98,206. The bonds mature on December 31, 19C. The bonds were purchased as a long-term investment by Smith Corporation.

Required:

1. Construct a time scale that depicts the important dates for this bond issue.
2. In parallel columns, give the entries at November 1, 19A, for the issuer and the investor.
3. Prepare a bond amortization schedule from date of sale to maturity date using the interest method.
4. In parallel columns, give the entries for both the issuer and investor for interest and amortization at the interest date, December 31, 19A. Use the interest method of amortization.
5. Compute and verify the balance in the interest accounts of the two parties to the transaction immediately after (4) above.
6. Assume the accounting period for each party ends on February 28. In parallel columns, give the adjusting entries for each party on February 28, 19B. Assume the interest method of amortization.
7. Compute the amount of amortization per month for each party, assuming straight-line amortization is used (i.e., the difference between the amortization amounts is not material).

P 15–9 (Bonds; Comprehensive; Compute Price; Interest Method; Entries for Both Parties)
Randy Corporation issued $200,000, 8% (payable each February 28 and August 31), four-year bonds. The bonds were dated March 1, 19A, and mature on February 28,

19E. The bonds were sold on August 1, 19A, to yield 8½% interest. The bonds were purchased by Voss Corporation as a long-term investment. The accounting period for each company ends on December 31. The bonds were sold for $196,967 plus accrued interest of $6,667. They would have sold on August 31, 19A for $197,027.

Required:

1. Diagram a time scale depicting the important dates for this bond issue.
2. Prepare an amortization schedule from date of sale to maturity using the interest method of amortization.
3. In parallel columns, give entries for the issuer and the investor from date of sale through February 28, 19B. Base amortization on (2) above.
4. Compute the amount of amortization per month for each party, assuming the straight-line method is used (because the difference between the amortization amounts is not material).

P 15–10 (Case A, Convertible Bonds; Entries; Case B, Detachable Stock Warrants)

This problem involves two independent cases:

Case A

On January 1, 19A, when its $30 par value common stock was selling for $80 per share, Corporation A issued $10,000,000 of 4% convertible debentures (i.e., bonds) due in 10 years. The conversion option allowed the holder of each $1,000 bond to convert the bond into five shares of the corporation's $30 par value common stock. The debentures were issued for $11,000,000. The present value of the bond payments at the time of issuance was $8,500,000, and the corporation believes the difference between the present value and the amount paid is attributable to the conversion feature. On January 1, 19B, the corporation's $30 par value common stock was split 3 for 1. On January 1, 19C, when the corporation's $10 par value common stock was selling for $90 per share, holders of 40% of the convertible debentures exercised their conversion options. For convenience, assume the corporation uses the straight-line method for amortizing any bond discount or premium.

Required:

1. Give the entry to record the original issuance of the convertible debentures.
2. Give the entry to record the exercise of the conversion option, using the book value method. Show supporting computations.

Case B

On July 1, 19C, Salem Corporation issued $2,000,000 of 7% bonds payable in 10 years. The bonds pay interest semiannually. Each $1,000 bond includes a detachable stock purchase right. Each right gives the bondholder the option to purchase for $30, one share of $1 par value common stock at any time during the next 10 years. The bonds were sold for $2,000,000. The value of the stock purchase rights at the time of issuance was $100,000.

Required:

Prepare the entry to record the issuance of the bonds. (AICPA adapted)

P 15–11 (Bonds; Detachable Stock Warrants; Entries for Issuer and Investor)

Friendly Corporation issued $500,000, 6%, nonconvertible bonds with detachable stock purchase warrants. Each $1,000 bond carried 20 detachable stock purchase warrants, each of which called for one share of Friendly common stock, par $50, at the specified option price of $60 per share. The bonds sold at 106, and the detachable stock purchase warrants were immediately quoted at $1 each on the market.

Goode Company purchased the entire issue as a long-term investment.

Required:

1. Give the following entries for Friendly Corporation (the issuer):
   a. To record the issuance of the bonds.
   b. To record the subsequent exercise by Goode of the 10,000 stock purchase warrants.
2. Assuming Goode did not exercise the 10,000 stock purchase warrants in requirement (1) above, give the following entries for Goode Company (the investor):
   a. Acquisition of the bonds (including the stock purchase warrants).
   b. Subsequent sale to another investor of half of the stock purchase warrants at $1.50 each.
   c. Subsequent exercise of the remaining half of the stock purchase warrants (by tendering them to Friendly Corporation). The market value of the stock was $62 per share.

P 15–12 (Bonds; Compute Bond Price; Straight-Line; Entries, Issuer Gross; Investor Net)
Koy Corporation sold and issued to Lott Corporation (as a long-term investment) $50,000, four-year, 11% bonds on September 1, 19A. Interest is payable semiannually on February 28 and August 31. The bonds mature on August 31, 19E, and were sold to yield 10% interest. The accounting period for both companies ends on December 31. Use the gross method for the issuer and the net method for the investor.

Required:

1. Compute the price of the bonds (show computations and round to nearest dollar).
2. In parallel columns, give all entries required through February 19B (including reversing entries) in the accounts of the issuer and the investor. Assume the difference between the interest method and the straight-line method of amortization is not material; therefore, use straight-line amortization.

P 15–13 (Analysis of a Bond Amortization Schedule)
FWS Corporation sold a $10,000, bond dated January 1, 19A. The following is the bond amortization schedule partially completed:

Date	Payment	Interest	Amortization	Carrying value
1–1–19A	—	—	—	$8,558
12–31–19A	$800	$1,027	$227	
12–31–19B				
12–31–19C				
12–31–19D				
12–31–19E				
Total				

Required:

1. Was the bond sold at a discount or at a premium? How much was the discount or premium?
2. What was *(a)* the stated rate of interest and *(b)* the effective rate of interest?
3. What was the life of the bond?
4. Which method of amortization will be used?
5. Give the issuance entries for the issuer and the investor using *(a)* the gross approach and *(b)* the net approach.
6. What were the beginning and subsequent cash flows? What does the difference represent?
7. Give the entry on December 31, 19A, for the issuer and the investor using *(a)* the gross approach and *(b)* the net approach.

8. Complete the above schedule.
9. Give the two entries for the issuer and investor that must be made on December 31, 19E, using *(a)* the gross approach and *(b)* the net approach.
10. Show what would be reported on the 19A statement of income and statement of financial position by the issuer and investor using *(a)* the gross approach and *(b)* the net approach.

Part B: Problems 15–14 to 15–24

P 15–14 (Extinguishment by Using In-substance Defeasance)

Dusty Corporation borrowed $2 million cash on a 6% note payable on January 1, 19A. This five-year note is payable in five equal annual installments of $474,793 starting on December 31, 19A. On January 1, 19C, the company entered into an agreement with the three creditors to irrevocably transfer the note and government securities (held by Dusty as a long-term investment). The trustee will make the three remaining equal interest payments on each payment date and will pay the principal on December 31, 19E. The government securities cost Dusty $1,100,000 and they will be valued at their current market value based on a 9% effective rate.

Required:
1. Give the entry that Dusty Corporation made on January 1, 19A.
2. Give the entries that Dusty Corporation made on December 31, 19A and 19B.
3. Give the extinguishment entry on January 1, 19C.
4. What conditions must be met by Dusty Company to qualify the transaction on January 1, 19C, as an extinguishment of the debt?

P 15–15 (Extinguishment; Debtor Entries; Purchase in the Open Market)

On July 1, 19A, XT Corporation issued $600,000, 5% (payable each June 30 and December 31), 10-year bonds payable. The bonds were issued at 97, and issue costs of $2,000 were paid from the proceeds. Assume straight-line amortization of discount and bond issue costs.

Due to an increase in interest rates, these bonds were selling in the market at the end of June 19D at an effective rate of 8%. Because the company had available cash, $200,000 (face amount) of the bonds were purchased in the market and retired on July 1, 19D.

Required:
1. Give the entry by XT Corporation to record issuance of the bonds on July 1, 19A.
2. Give the entry by XT Corporation to record the extinguishment of part of the debt on July 1, 19D. How should the gain or loss be reported on the 19D financial statements of XT Corporation?
3. Was the extinguishment economically favorable to the issuer, investor, or neither? Explain.

P 15–16 (Extinguishment by Refunding; Debtors Entries)

Davis Corporation issued $200,000, 4½% (payable each December 31), 10-year bonds on January 1, 19A. The issuer may call them at any time after 19D at 104. The bonds sold on January 1, 19A, at 98. Straight-line amortization is used.

Due to a large increase in interest rates, the bonds were being sold in the market at the end of 19E at 86 (i.e., at an effective rate of 8%). In view of this situation, Davis decided to issue a new series of bonds (a refunding issue) in the amount of $150,000 (8% payable annually, five-year term) on January 1, 19F; the new issue was sold at par. Davis had cash on hand sufficient for the remaining cost of retirement of the old bonds. Disregard income tax effects.

Required:

1. Give the entry for Davis Corporation to record issuance of the bonds at 98 on January 1, 19A.
2. Assume the $150,000 refunding issue was sold at par; give the required entry for Davis.
3. Assume all of the old bonds were immediately purchased in the open market at 86 on January 2, 19F. Give the required entry for Davis. How should the gain or loss be reported on the financial statements?
4. What was the economic gain or loss to the issuer and the investor?

P 15–17 (Extinguishment with Equity Securities; Call, and Refunding; Entries)
On January 1, 19x1, Grand Corporation issued $100,000, 9% (payable each June 30 and December 31), 10-year bonds payable (convertible and callable) at a 10% effective rate of interest. Each $1,000 bond is convertible, at the option of the holder, into Grand common stock (par $10) as follows: first five years—25 shares for each bond tendered; second five years—20 shares for each bond. The bonds can be called, at the option of Grand, after the fifth year at 101.

On July 1, 19x7, the market interest rate on comparable bonds is 8%, and the common stock is quoted on the market at $52 per share.

Required:

1. Give the entry to record the issuance of bonds on January 1, 19x1. Show computation of the bond issue price. Use the gross method.
2. Give the entry to record payment of bond interest and the amortization of bond premium or discount on June 30, 19x1. Assume interest method amortization.
3. Prepare the journal entries at July 1, 19x7, to record each of the following separate assumptions (use straight-line amortization):

   Assumption A—All of the bondholders converted their bonds to common stock. Use the market value method to record the conversion.

   Assumption B—Grand called all of the bonds at the stipulated call price.

   Assumption C—Grand refunded all of the outstanding 9% bonds by purchasing them in the open market at the current yield rate of interest. Cash for the refunding was obtained by issuing new 8% bonds (interest payable semiannually) at par; cash proceeds were $103,000 (face amount of bonds sold).
4. Which of the three above alternative means of retiring the old 9% bond payable was most likely to occur? Why?

P 15–18 (Three Transactions; Bonds, Detachable Warrants, Extinguishment; Entries)
This problem involves three independent situations.

1. On January 1, 1985, Hopewell Company issued its 8% bonds that had a par value of $1,000,000. Interest is payable at December 31 each year. The bonds mature on December 31, 1994. The bonds were sold to yield a rate of 10%.
2. On September 1, 19A, Junction Company issued at 104 (plus accrued interest), 4,000 of its 9%, 10-year, $1,000 par value, nonconvertible bonds with detachable stock purchase warrants. Each bond carried two detachable warrants; each warrant was for one share of common stock, at a specified option price of $15 per share. Shortly after issuance, the warrants were quoted on the market for $3 each. No market value can be determined for the bonds above. Interest is payable on December 1 and June 1. Bond issue costs of $40,000 were incurred, and deducted from the proceeds.

3. On December 1, 19x1, Cone Company issued its 7%, $2,000,000 par value bonds for $2,200,000, plus accrued interest. Interest is payable on May 1 and November 1. On July 1, 19x4, Cone purchased and retired the bonds at 98, plus accrued interest. Cone uses the straight-line method for the amortization of bond premium because the results do not materially differ from using the interest method; the total amortization period at the date of issuance was 50 months.

Required:

1. Give the entry to record the issuance of the bonds by Hopewell Company. Show supporting computations.
2. Give the entry to record the issuance of the bonds by Junction Company. Show computations.
3. Give the entries required by Cone Company:
   a. At issue date.
   b. At reacquisition date. (AICPA adapted)

P 15–19 (Restructure Entries; Assets, New Debt and Equity Securities)

DEM Company owed RUB Finance Company a $300,000, five-year, 18% (payable each year-end) mortgage note, dated January 1, 19A. DEM has experienced serious financial problems, and, as a consequence, has not paid the interest at December 31, 19C. However, each company included its accrual in the adjusting entries at that date. On January 2, 19D, a debt restructure agreement was agreed upon which provided that the principal and interest accrued will be paid in full as follows:

1. Cash, $10,000.
2. Transfer of land—original cost to DEM, $45,000, and appraised value, $137,000.
3. Transfer 20,000 shares of DEM common stock, par $1; estimated current market value, $3.00 per share.
4. Transfer of $30,000 accounts receivable; the related allowance for doubtful accounts on DEM's books is $4,000 (this appears to be realistic).
5. Transfer 5,000 shares of WIT Corporation stock held by DEM as a long-term investment; cost to DEM, $2 per share, and current market value, $10 per share.

Required:
Give all entries to record the debt restructure for each company.

P 15–20 (Restructure by Modification of Terms; Entries by Both Parties)
Baker Company owed Cox Company a $20,000, 10% (annual interest payable each December 31), four-year note payable dated January 1, 19A. Baker Company faced extreme financial difficulties. Both companies had accrued interest for the year 19B. On January 2, 19C, the parties agreed that the principal would be paid in full on maturity date and that the interest for 19B, 19C, and 19D would be settled by payment of $3,340 cash on December 31, 19D (maturity date).

Required:

1. Compute the new effective rate of interest.
2. Give all entries required on date of restructure (January 2, 19C) for each company.
3. Give all entries required on December 31, 19C, and 19D, for each company.

P 15–21 (Restructure with Modification of Terms; Entries by Both Parties)
On January 1, 19F, Day Corporation owed a $65,000 note payable to Cox Corporation that required the payment of 10% interest on each December 31; the note was due on

December 31, 19F. Because of continuing serious financial difficulties, Day informed Cox that default (and discontinuance of the business) was probable unless some concessions on terms could be negotiated. Day has paid interest through December 31, 19E. On January 1, 19F, Cox agreed to the following restructure of the debt:

a. Day will immediately transfer $15,000 of its accounts receivable to the creditor in settlement of $14,000 of the debt. The accounts of Day reflected $1,000 in the allowance for doubtful accounts that related to these receivables; thus, the current net realizable value of the receivables was reasonably stated at $14,000.
b. Day will immediately transfer its long-term investment in 800 shares of common stock (par $10) of Tye Corporation in partial settlement of the debt. Day accounts reflected a carrying value of $30,000 for the Tye stock, and its current market value was $32,000.
c. Day will pay $10,000 cash at the end of the fifth year from January 1, 19F (date of restructure) to settle the remaining $19,000 of the principal. Therefore, the restructured maturity date is December 31, 19J.
d. Day will pay $5,000 total interest over the five-year period from January 1, 19F to December 31, 19J (i.e., $1,000 cash interest per year).

Required:
1. Give any required entry of the debtor and the creditor on date of restructure, January 1, 19F. Explain how you made the decision as to *(a)* whether entries are required and *(b)* the basis for the "values" used. How would other "agreed values" produce a biased measure of restructure gain or loss?
2. Give the required entries for the debtor and the creditor on the next interest date, December 31, 19F, and on the restructured maturity date, December 31, 19J.

P 15–22 **(Restructure by Modification of Terms; Entries for Both Parties; Comprehensive)** On January 1, 19A, Overdue Corporation sold and issued to Liquid Corporation $100,000, 7% (payable annually on December 31), 10-year bonds payable to yield 8% interest. After paying interest for 19A and 19B, Overdue Corporation encountered severe financial difficulties which made it apparent that Liquid Corporation would have to make some concessions as to debt terms. Therefore, a debt restructure was agreed to on January 1, 19C, that provided *(a)* the remaining term to maturity would be 20 years from January 1, 19C, and *(b)* interest would be reduced so that the same total dollar amount of interest would be paid over the new term to maturity (20 years) as would have been paid over the old term to the old maturity date (8 years).

Required:
1. Give the entry by each party to record issuance of the bonds payable on January 1, 19A. Show computations of the original bond issuance price. Use the gross method.
2. Compute the carrying amount of the bonds by the debtor and creditor on January 1, 19C. Assume straight-line amortization.
3. Compute the new effective rate of interest (round to the nearest percent; then use straight-line interpolation to compute the approximate interest rate to two decimal places). Hint: See Chapter 5.
4. Give all entries for both the debtor and the creditor on the date of restructure, January 1, 19C. If no entry is required, explain why. Use the approximate interpolated interest rate computed in (3) above and then round to the nearest dollar.
5. Give all entries for both the debtor and the creditor on the two interest dates, December 31, 19C, and 19D.

P 15–23 (Relates to Supplement 15–A; Serial Bonds)

A serial issue of $700,000 of bonds dated April 1, 19A, was sold on that date for $707,600. The interest rate is 8%, payable semiannually on March 31 and September 30. Scheduled maturities are as follows:

Serial	Date due	Amount
B	March 31, 19B	$100,000
C	March 31, 19C	200,000
D	March 31, 19D	200,000
E	March 31, 19E	200,000

Required:

1. Prepare an amortization schedule for the issuer; use straight-line amortization and dollar-period allocation.
2. Give all entries for the issuer relating to the bonds, including reversing entries, through March 31, 19B. The issuing company adjusts and closes its books each December 31. Use straight-line amortization.

P 15–24 (Relates to Supplement 15–A; Serial Bonds)

On January 1, 19x1, Tobin Corporation sold serial bonds (dated January 1, 19x1) due as follows: serial A, $10,000, December 31, 19x5; serial B, $15,000, December 31, 19x6; and serial C, $25,000, December 31, 19x7. The bonds carried a 3% coupon (stated) interest rate per semiannual period (each June 30 and December 31) and were sold to yield 4% interest per semiannual period.

Required (round to the nearest dollar):

1. Compute the selling price of the bond issue.
2. Prepare an amortization schedule for Tobin for the life of the bond issue, assuming the interest method is used. (Hint: Discount amortization is: 6/30/x1, $306; 6/30/x6, $352.)
3. Give Tobin's entry to record retirement of half of serial C at 99½ on June 30, 19x7. Assume the accounting period ends December 31.

CASES

C 15–1 (Part A—Bonds; Analysis and Overview)

BD Corporation sold and issued to EF Corporation (as a long-term investment) a $20,000, 7%, 10-year bond. The bond was dated January 1, 19A, and interest is payable annually each December 31. Assume each company's accounting period ends December 31. Assume three different cases in respect to the sale of the bond:

Case A
Sold on January 1, 19A, at 7% yield.

Case B
Sold on January 1, 19A, at 6% yield.

Case C
Sold on January 1, 19A, at 8% yield.

Required:

1. For each case, compute the amount of interest that will be paid (i.e., cash) on the first interest date, December 31, 19A.

2. Identify which cases sold at *(a)* par, *(b)* a discount, and *(c)* a premium.
3. For each case, indicate *(a)* the stated interest rate and *(b)* the effective rate of interest.
4. Identify those cases in which the amount of cash paid and received for the bond was *(a)* the same as par, *(b)* greater than par, and *(c)* less than par.
5. Subsequent to the transaction, in which cases will the respective statements of financial position report the bonds at *(a)* par, *(b)* more than par, and *(c)* less than par?
6. Subsequent to the transaction, which cases will report interest expense and interest revenue (on the respective statement of income) at more or less than the periodic amount of interest paid in cash?
7. Identify those cases in which the maturity value of the bond liability (or bond investment) will be *(a)* the same as, *(b)* higher, or *(c)* lower than the book value.
8. Can straight-line amortization be used in each case? Explain.
9. What is the effect of periodic amortization of bond premium and discount on *(a)* interest expense (as reported on the statement of income) and *(b)* bond carrying value (as reported on the statement of financial position).
10. Compute the price of the bond for each case.
11. Explain the accounting effects of each case if the bonds were sold and issued on April 1, 19A.
12. Explain the accounting effects if bond issue costs amounted to $1,500 cash.

C 15–2 (Part A—Convertible Bonds versus Detachable Stock Warrants)

Seton Corporation is considering the issuance of $100,000, five-year bonds. Two alternatives are under consideration as follows:

Alternative A—At the beginning of year 1, issue convertible bonds which would specify that each $1,000 bond can be tendered for conversion to 15 shares of Seton's common stock, par $10, at any time after the second year from issue date of the convertible bonds. Seton's best estimate is that the convertible bonds can be sold to Investor X for $108,000 cash at the beginning of year 1, provided the common stock is selling at that time for not less than $65 per share.

Alternative B—At the beginning of year 1, issue 100 nonconvertible $1,000 bonds with 15 detachable stock purchase warrants per bond. Each warrant can be tendered at any time after year 2 for one share of Seton's common stock, par $10, at an option price of $60 per share. Seton's best estimate is that the nonconvertible bonds can be sold to Investor XX for $108,000 cash at the beginning of year 1, provided the common stock is selling at that time for not less than $65 per share. The warrants are expected to have a market value of $2 each immediately after issuance of the bonds; the bonds do not have a listed market price.

Seton's management is considering which alternative to select. The management is concerned about several issues that may influence the decision. One such issue is the comparative impact of the two alternatives on the financial statements. Your assistance in selecting an alternative has been requested.

Required:

1. Using Seton's best estimate, give the journal entries for each alternative that each party would make at the beginning of year 1. Use the gross method. Explain any differences in accounting values between the two alternatives.
2. Give the entries for each alternative that each party would make at the beginning of year 4, assuming all of the bonds in Alternative A are tendered for conversion and all of the warrants are turned in for shares in Alternative B. Seton's common

stock is selling for $75 per share. Use the market value method for Alternative A. Assume straight-line amortization.

3. Complete the schedule given below, assuming the transactions in Requirements 1 and 2 have taken place.
4. Outline your response to management's request for assistance in choosing between the two alternatives. Consider the results of Requirement 2.

	A—Convertible bonds		B—Detachable warrants	
Items	Issuer	Investor	Issuer	Investor
Gain (loss) conversion				
Investments:				
Bonds				
Common stock				
Liabilities:				
Bonds payable				
Stockholders' equity				
Common stock				
Contributed capital in excess of par				
Cash				
Inflow				
Outflow				

C 15–3 **(Analysis of Long-Term Debt; An Actual Case)**

Kimberly-Clark

This case relates to the 1987 financial statements of Kimberly-Clark (given in the Appendix immediately following Chapter 25).

Required:

1. Respond to the following:
   a. Total amount of long-term debt reported on the SFP.
   b. Total interest expense reported in 1987 and 1986.
   c. What was the amount of long-term debt called "current portion"? What does this mean?
   d. How many long-term debts were reported?
   e. What companies owed the long-term debts?
2. What did the management identify as "noteworthy" changes in long-term financing during 1987?

16 CORPORATIONS— FORMATION AND STOCKHOLDERS' EQUITY

OVERVIEW AND PURPOSE

In the United States, the dominant form of business organization is the corporation as opposed to partnerships and sole proprietorships. A **corporation** is an entity whose ownership is evidenced by shares of capital stock. For all forms of business organization, owners' equity is measured as assets minus liabilities. The total amount of the owners' **residual interest** depends on how the various assets and liabilities of the business are measured. The owners' equity of a corporation usually is called **stockholders' equity**—the term used in this text.

The primary purpose of this chapter is to discuss the fundamental concepts and distinctions applied in measuring, recording, and reporting stockholders' equity. Therefore, this chapter is organized as follows:

Part A: Contributed Capital at Formation

1. Formation of a corporation.
2. Fundamental concepts and distinctions.
3. Different kinds of equity securities.
4. Accounting for the issuance of par value stock.
5. Capital stock sold on a subscription basis.
6. Noncash sale of capital stock.
7. Assessments on capital stock.
8. Stock issue costs.
9. Unrealized capital.

Part B: Changes in Corporate Capital after Formation

1. Treasury stock.
2. Formal retirement of callable and redeemable stock.
3. Conversion of convertible preferred stock.
4. Changing par value.
5. Additional contributed capital.

PART A: CONTRIBUTED CAPITAL AT FORMATION

Formation of a Corporation

In the United States, the incorporation process is prescribed by the laws of the specific state in which a corporation is organized. State law dictates the process because there are no federal incorporation laws. Most states have adopted many of the principles recommended in the Model Business Corporation Act of 1959. Therefore, the corporate laws of the various states have many common provisions.

The laws of the various states have a significant impact on accounting for stockholders' equity. These laws specify such items as requirements for stock issuance, definition of legal capital, limitations on dividends, constraints on treasury stock, and provisions for the retirement of capital stock. It is impractical to include the legal requirements of each state. Therefore, reasonable generalizations and typical situations are used to facilitate the discussion.

For most states, the **incorporation process** can be outlined as follows:

1. The articles of incorporation are prepared by the organizers to meet the legal requirements of the state. These articles specify such items as purpose of the business, location, names of the organizers, classes and numbers of shares of capital stock authorized, and the consideration to be paid in by the organizers for their respective shares. This must be done before the corporation begins operations.
2. The articles of incorporation are filed with a designated state official (usually the secretary of state).
3. A corporate charter, if approved, is issued by the state; the charter makes the articles of incorporation operative.
4. A board of directors is selected. It meets and approves *(a)* corporate bylaws to supplement (but not change) the provisions of the charter and *(b)* corporate officers.

Classification of Corporations

The corporate form of business has both advantages and disadvantages when compared with partnerships and sole proprietorships. The primary advantages are: (1) the liability of each stockholder is limited to his or her proportionate share of total stockholders' equity, which is represented by the number of shares owned; in case of dissolution or insolvency, stockholders may lose their total investment, but, because of limited liability, not more than that amount; (2) large accumulations of funds from investors with diverse investment objectives are possible as well as access to the investment markets (e.g., stock exchanges); and (3) the continuity, transfer, expansion, and contraction of ownership interests are facilitated. The primary disadvantages include: (1) double taxation of corporate earnings (income is taxed as it is earned at the corporate level, and again after it is distributed as dividends to stockholders); and (2) the impersonal characteristics of a corporation may cause problems in stockholders' control of the corporation.

Corporations may be **classified** as follows:

A. By ownership:
1. **Public corporations**—when related to governmen operations owned by governmental units. Example Valley Authority, the Port of New York Authority transit systems.
2. **Private corporations**—when privately owned. Such ... may be either, *(a)* **nonstock**—nonprofit organizations that do not issue shares of stock (such as colleges and churches) or *(b)* **stock**—entities that issue shares of capital stock and usually are organized for profit making, such as Chrysler, Kimberly-Clark, and Exxon.

B. By availability of ownership interests:
1. **Open**—publicly held corporations with capital stock available for purchase. The shares of open corporations often are "listed" by one of the stock exchanges, such as the New York, American, or one of the regional stock exchanges.
2. **Closed**—closely held corporations with the capital stock not available for purchase and usually held by a few stockholders.

C. By state of incorporation and operating locations:
1. **Domestic**—when operating in the state in which incorporated.
2. **Foreign**—when operating in states in addition to the one in which incorporated.

Characteristics of Capital Stock

Shares of capital stock, represented by stock certificates, evidence **ownership** in a corporation. Shares may be bought, sold, or otherwise transferred by the stockholders without the consent of the corporation unless there is an enforceable agreement not to do so. Ownership of shares usually entitles the holder to certain basic rights. These rights are as follows:

1. The right to influence the **management** of the corporation through participating and voting in stockholder meetings.
2. The right to participate in the **earnings** of the corporation through dividends declared by the board of directors.
3. The right to share in the distribution of **assets** of the corporation at liquidation or through liquidating dividends.
4. The right to purchase shares of the capital stock of the corporation on a pro rata basis when new issues are offered for sale. This **preemptive** right is designed to provide each stockholder the opportunity to maintain his or her proportional ownership in the corporation. Some corporations have withheld this preemptive right because of the difficulty it creates when the corporation issues new stock.

These basic rights are shared proportionately by all stockholders of each class of stock unless the charter or bylaws (and as noted on the stock certificates) specifically provides otherwise. In the case of common stock only, all holders enjoy the basic rights. In the case of two or more classes of stock, the holders of the additional classes of stock usually have rights that are favorable or unfavorable compared with the common stock.

undamental Concepts and Distinctions

The fundamental concepts that underlie the accounting and reporting of stockholders' equity may be summarized as follows:

1. **Separate entity**—According to the law, a corporation is a nonpersonal entity that may own assets, owe debts, and conduct operations as an independent entity separate from each stockholder. Thus, it is a **separate accounting entity.**
2. **Sources of stockholders' equity**—The primary **sources** of stockholders' equity are accounted for and reported separately to provide useful data for financial statement users. Sources of stockholders' equity include the following:
   - A. **Contributed capital** (often referred to as paid-in capital):
     1. Capital stock:
        - *a.* Preferred stock.
        - *b.* Common stock.
     2. Other contributed capital or additional paid-in capital (an obsolete term, capital surplus, sometimes is used):
        - *a.* From owners:
          Contributed capital in excess of par or stated value (sometimes called **premium on capital stock**) and contributed capital from treasury stock and stock retirement transactions.
        - *b.* From outsiders:
          Contributed capital from donation of assets.
   - B. **Retained earnings:**
     1. Appropriated retained earnings (sometimes inappropriately called **reserves**).
     2. Unappropriated retained earnings.
   - C. **Unrealized capital**—Defined in a later section.

Exhibit 16–1 illustrates a typical stockholders' equity section in a statement of financial position. Notice that stockholders' equity is reported by **source;** that is, contributed capital, retained earnings, and unrealized loss on long-term investments in equity securities.

3. **Issuance of capital stock**—The issuance of capital stock is recorded in conformity with the **cost principle.** That is, the issue price recorded should be the cash consideration received plus the market value of all noncash considerations received.
4. **Sale and repurchase of shares**—Transactions of a corporation involving the sale, purchase, or resale of its own shares do not directly affect periodic net income. Any difference between the market value of the consideration received and the par or stated value of the shares sold, purchased, or resold is recorded as additional contributed (paid-in) capital.
5. **Equity versus debt**—Stockholders' equity should be clearly separated from the liabilities of the corporation.
6. **Form of business organization**—Aside from owners' equity, the accounting and reporting for a business is not affected in substance by its status as a corporation, partnership, or sole proprietorship.

Exhibit 16–1
Stockholders' equity section of a statement of financial position.

Stockholders' Equity

Contributed capital:		
Capital stock:		
Preferred stock, 6%, par $10, cumulative and nonparticipating, 20,000 shares authorized; 15,000 issued and outstanding	$150,000	
Preferred stock subscribed, 100 shares	1,000	
Total preferred stock outstanding and subscribed . .	151,000	
Common stock, nopar value, 10,000 shares authorized; 8,000 shares issued and outstanding, stated value $5	40,000	$191,000
Additional contributed capital:		
In excess of par value, preferred stock*	12,000	
In excess of stated value, common stock*	3,000	
Donation of plant site*	5,000	20,000
Total contributed capital		211,000
Retained earnings:†		
Appropriated for bond sinking fund	50,000	
Unappropriated	170,000	
Total retained earnings		220,000
Unrealized capital:		
Unrealized loss on long-term investments in marketable equity securities		(6,000)
Total stockholders' equity		$425,000

* The additional contributed capital accounts often are aggregated into a single amount on the statement of financial position with detailed disclosure in the notes or a supporting schedule (see Exhibit 16–8).
† Total retained earnings often is reported on the statement of financial position with disclosure of the appropriations in a supporting note.

7. **Terminology**—The word **capital** is used differently in accounting, finance, and the business world. For example, the word **capital** sometimes is used to mean **total** owners' equity. For precision and clarity, this text uses the word **capital** to identify that portion of stockholders' equity that relates to capital stock, including additional contributed capital. It excludes retained earnings and unrealized losses on long-term investments in equity securities. We use the generic term **contributed capital,** although paid-in capital often is used.

Prior to discussing capital stock, it may be useful to define the following terms:

1. **Authorized capital stock**—the number of shares of stock that can be issued legally, as specified in the charter of the corporation.
2. **Issued capital stock**—the number of shares of authorized capital stock that have been issued to date.
3. **Unissued capital stock**—the number of shares of authorized capital stock that have not been issued; that is, the difference between authorized and issued shares.
4. **Outstanding capital stock**—the number of shares of capital stock that have been issued and are currently owned by stockholders.
5. **Treasury stock**—shares once issued and later reacquired and which are still held by the corporation; that is, the difference between issued shares and outstanding shares.

6. **Subscribed stock**—unissued shares of stock set aside to meet subscription contracts (i.e., shares sold on credit and not yet paid for). Subscribed stock usually is not issued until the subscription price is paid in full. Subscribed shares of voting stock confer voting rights unless the subscription agreement specifies otherwise.

Different Kinds of Equity Securities

Equity securities includes all of the classifications of capital stock of corporations. Capital stock includes both common and preferred stock, which may be either par value or nopar value stock. Debt securities were discussed in Chapters 14 and 15.

Par Value Stock

The laws of each state provide for the issuance of par value stock; that is, shares of stock with a designated dollar amount per share as stated in the corporate charter and as printed on the face of the stock certificates. Par value stock may be either common or preferred. In the early history of corporations in the United States, only par value stock was authorized. Because the owners of a corporation were not personally liable to the corporation's creditors, those statutes were intended to afford a measure of protection to creditors. In this respect, the courts tended to hold that stockholders of a corporation who paid **less** than par value for their stock could be assessed an additional amount equal to the discount if it was deemed necessary to satisfy creditors' claims.

Par value stock sold initially at less than par is said to have been issued at a **discount.** Par value stock sold initially above par is said to have been issued at a **premium.** A discount liability extends to protect only creditors and **holds** the original stockholders liable unless it was contractually transferred to subsequent stockholders. Today, the issuance of par value stock at a discount is illegal in most states.[1]

Par value has no particular relationship to market value. However, par value has significance in most states because: (1) it represents the minimum stock price that must be paid at the initial sale of the stock; (2) in the case of insolvency, if the par value of all outstanding shares was fully paid in (or an equivalent amount of retained earnings was capitalized as in a stock dividend), the stockholders cannot be held personally liable to creditors; (3) it establishes the minimum amount of owners' equity the law requires to be maintained; and (4) par value often is the basis on which preferred dividends are declared. To avoid a real or implied discount, many corporations use a very low par value, such as $1 per share, and sell the stock at a much higher price.

Nopar Value Stock

True nopar stock is so designated in the charter and does not carry a stated or assigned "value" per share. However, the laws of some states authorize the issuance of nopar stock with a **stated** or **assigned** value per share. The

---

[1] Despite laws that forbid issuance of par value stock at a discount, it sometimes happens de facto when promoters and others receive shares of stock in exchange for noncash assets or services that are overvalued.

stated or assigned value is established permanently by the corporate directors and is included in the bylaws of the corporation. Most companies use a stated value for nopar stock.

The use of an assigned or stated value makes nopar stock equivalent to par value stock for accounting purposes. Both common and preferred stock may be represented by nopar shares. Nopar stock was first permitted by statute in New York in 1912. Since then, the authorization of stock without par value has become so widespread that today practically all states permit its issuance. The chief advantages **claimed** for nopar stock are: (1) it avoids a contingent liability of stockholders for stock discount, and (2) in some jurisdictions there is less tax on nopar shares. The chief disadvantage of nopar stock is that some jurisdictions levy high franchise and other taxes on nopar stock.

Legal Capital

Legal capital is that portion of stockholders' equity so specified by the laws of the state in which the corporation receives its charter. In the case of par value stock, legal capital is specified in most states as the par value of the issued or outstanding shares.[2] In the case of nopar stock, legal capital is *(a)* the full amount paid in at issuance if it is true nopar stock, or *(b)* the stated or assigned value per share as initially established by the corporate directors if it is other than true nopar stock.

Maintenance of legal capital means that a corporation must refrain from paying dividends when their effect would be to impair legal capital. In some states treasury stock cannot be purchased by the company when such cumulative expenditures would exceed the cumulative amount of retained earnings. In other states the limit is the same as for cash dividends. Legal capital also can be impaired as a result of operating losses.

Common Stock

Common stock is the primary issue of shares and normally carries all of the basic rights listed on page 707. When there is only one class of stock, all of the shares are common stock whether or not so designated.

The common stockholders are the residual owners of the corporation. As such, their position is more risky than the positions of *(a)* creditors, to whom the corporation owes legally enforceable principal and interest amounts on specified dates, and *(b)* preferred stockholders, whose shares usually specify preference dividend and liquidation amounts per share. Consequently, the common stockholders are exposed to the risks and the benefits of corporate success or failure, after creditor and preferred stockholder claims are met.

Although common stock usually is voting stock, a few corporations have issued two classes of common stock—class A, voting and class B, nonvoting. The class B stock usually is traded publicly while the class A stock is held by a small group (e.g., "the family") and traded privately. This arrangement permits control by a small group (a protection against takeovers) and, at the same time, allows access to capital markets.

---

[2] Whether legal capital at a specific date is based on shares issued or shares outstanding depends upon the laws of incorporation of the state. It appears that using outstanding shares as a basis is prevalent, particularly when there is a treasury stock restriction on retained earnings. In some states preferred stock is not included in legal capital.

Preferred Stock

Preferred stock confers **preferences,** or specifies differences, when compared with common stock. These preferences and differences related to preferred stock may involve one or more of the following:

1. Voting.
2. Dividends.
   a. Cumulative or noncumulative.
   b. Nonparticipating, partially participating, or fully participating with common stockholders in dividends in excess of the stated preferred dividend.
3. Assets in liquidation.
4. Convertibility to other securities.
5. Call features, under specified conditions.
6. Redemption.

Preferred stock usually is **par value** stock, and the dividend preference is expressed as a percentage of par. For example, 6% preferred stock has a dividend preference of 6% of the **par value** of each share. This preference does not guarantee a dividend but means that, when the corporation declares a dividend, preferred stockholders must get their 6% preferred dividend before common stockholders receive any dividends. In the case of nopar preferred stock, the dividend preference is expressed as a specific **dollar amount** per share, such as $5 per preferred share.

Voting Privileges on Preferred Stock.

Because the **right to vote** is a basic right, preferred stockholders have full voting rights unless specifically prohibited in the charter. Nonvoting specification for preferred stock represents a **negative** preference. Preferred stock usually is nonvoting because it often is used to obtain resources without diluting the voting strength of the common stock.

Cumulative Dividend Preferences on Preferred Stock.

Cumulative preferred stock provides that dividends not declared in a prior year accumulate at the preference rate on such stock. This accumulated amount must be included in full when dividends are declared in a later year before any dividends can be paid on the common stock. If dividends are not declared in a given year, they are said to have been passed, and they are called **dividends in arrears** on cumulative preferred stock. If only a part of the dividend preference is met for any year, the remainder of the cumulative preference is in arrears. Cumulative preferred stock carries the right, in dissolution of the corporation, to dividends in arrears to the extent the corporation has retained earnings. However, different provisions for dividends in arrears may be stipulated in the charter and bylaws. When the charter is silent as to the cumulative feature, most courts have ruled that preferred stock is cumulative.[3] Therefore, in this text, we assume preferred stock is cumulative unless stated otherwise. *APB Opinion 9* (par. 35) states: "When cumulative preferred dividends are in arrears, the per share and aggre-

---

[3] Rate A. Howell, John R. Allison, and Robert A. Prentice, *Business Law: Text and Cases,* 4th ed. (Hinsdale, Ill.: Dryden Press, 1988), p. 861.

gate amounts thereof should be disclosed." Dividends in arrears are not liabilities. This reporting usually is made in a note to the financial statements.

Noncumulative preferred stock provides that dividends not declared (i.e., dividends "passed") for any prior year or years are lost permanently by the preferred stockholders. As a result, the noncumulative feature has a negative effect for the investor. Noncumulative preferred stock seldom is issued.

To illustrate cumulative and noncumulative features, assume the following in cases A, B, C, D, and E, unless specified otherwise:[4]

Preferred stock, 5%, $10 par, 10,000 shares outstanding	$100,000
Common stock, $5 par, 40,000 shares outstanding	200,000
Cash dividends declared, $28,000.	

Case A. Preferred is **cumulative, nonparticipating;** dividends are in arrears for the two preceding years:*

	Preferred	Common
Step 1: Preferred, in arrears ($100,000 × 5% × 2 years)	$10,000	
Step 2: Preferred, current ($100,000 × 5%)	5,000	
Step 3: Balance, to common ($28,000 − $15,000)		$13,000
	$15,000	$13,000

* Notice in all of the cases, A–E, how the computations follow the preferred stock specifications precisely.

Case B. Preferred is **noncumulative, nonparticipating:**

Step 1: Preferred, current ($100,000 × 5%)	$ 5,000	
Step 2: Balance, to common ($28,000 − $5,000)		$23,000
	$ 5,000	$23,000

Participating Dividend Preferences on Preferred Stock. **Nonparticipating** preferred stock limits the dividends for any year to be specified dividend preference (plus any dividends in arrears). For example, 5% preferred stock, par $10, noncumulative, nonparticipating, would be limited to a $.50 dividend per share in any one year.

Partially participating preferred stock provides that the preferred stockholders participate above the preferential rate on a **pro rata basis** in dividend declarations with the common stockholders. However, this participation is only up to an additional rate, which is specified in the charter and on the stock certificate. For example, a corporation may issue 5% preferred stock, with participation up to a total of 7%. In this case, participation privileges with the common stockholders would be limited to an additional 2% above the 5% preference.

[4] Dividends are discussed substantively in Chapter 17. Cases A, B, C, D, and E are given here only to help you to understand the definition and features of preferred stock. The declaration of a dividend is much more involved than selecting a total amount.

Fully participating preferred stock means that the preferred stockholders have a preference for the current year at a stated preference rate plus any cumulative preferences that exist. The preferred stockholders also will share on a pro rata basis in any dividends declared beyond the preference rate. For example, 5% preferred stock, par $10, noncumulative, fully participating, would receive its 5% preference (i.e., $.50 per share) plus a pro rata share (based on the total par or stated value of the common and preferred stock) of any excess dividends **after** the common stockholders have received a "matching" amount (i.e., 5% of the par or stated value of the common stock in this case). Most preferred stock is not fully participating.

To illustrate the partially participating and fully participating features, assume the same capital structure that existed in Cases A and B and dividends are in arrears for the two preceding years.

Case C. Preferred is **noncumulative, partially participating** up to an additional 2%. Dividends declared, $28,000:

	Preferred	Common
Step 1: Preferred, current ($100,000 × 5%)	$ 5,000	
Step 2: Common, current matching ($200,000 × 5%)		$10,000
Step 3: Preferred, partial ($100,000 × 2%)	2,000	
Step 4: Common, matching ($200,000 × 2%)		4,000*
Step 5: Balance, to common		7,000
	$ 7,000	$21,000

* If this amount is less than $4,000 (i.e., 2% of par), steps 3 and 4 must be computed as in Case D.

Case D. Exactly the same as Case C, except total dividends declared are $16,000:

	Preferred	Common
Step 1: Preferred, current ($100,000 × 5%)	$ 5,000	
Step 2: Common, current matching ($200,000 × 5%)		$10,000
Step 3: Allocate balance based on total par value:		
Preferred, $100,000/$300,000 × $1,000	333	
Common, $200,000/$300,000 × $1,000		667
	$ 5,333	$10,667

Case E. Exactly the same as Case C, except preferred is **cumulative** and **fully participating:**

	Preferred	Common
Step 1: Preferred, in arrears ($100,000 × 5% × 2 years)	$10,000	
Step 2: Preferred, current ($100,000 × 5%)	5,000	
Step 3: Common, current matching ($200,000 × 5%)		$10,000
Step 4: Allocate balance based on total par value:		
Preferred, $100,000/$300,000 × $3,000	1,000	
Common, $200,000/$300,000 × $3,000		2,000
	$16,000	$12,000

If either the common or preferred stock is **nopar,** and the preferred has participating privileges (partial or full), a specified **dollar amount per share**

Exhibit 16–2
Dividend computations for nopar stock.

Panel A—Case Data:

a. Preferred stock, 5%, par $10, **cumulative** and **fully participating,** 10,000 shares outstanding.
b. Common stock, **nopar,** 15,000 shares outstanding; participation matching amount specified on the stock certificates, $1 per share.
c. Total dividends to be paid in 19C, $48,000; no dividends were declared or paid in 19A or 19B.

Panel B—Dividend Computations:

	Preferred	Common
Preferred, in arrears ($100,000 × 5% × 2)	$10,000	
Preferred, current ($100,000 × 5%)	5,000	
Common, to match (15,000 shares × $1)		$15,000
Participation allocation:*		
Preferred	4,500	
Common		13,500
Total	$19,500	$28,500

* Computations:

Preferred: $\frac{(10{,}000 \text{ shares} \times \$10 \times 5\% = \$5{,}000)}{(\$5{,}000 + \$15{,}000)^{\dagger}} \times \$18{,}000$ .... $ 4,500

Common: $\frac{(15{,}000 \text{ shares} \times \$1 = \$15{,}000)}{(\$5{,}000 + \$15{,}000)^{\dagger}} \times \$18{,}000$ 13,500

Total: $48,000 − $10,000 − $5,000 − $15,000 .... $18,000

† Dividend participation values. These are not par values. The par value of the preferred stock is $100,000 and the common stock is true nopar stock. These amounts on the common stock are equivalents used for dividend purposes only.

must be established in the charter to replace the missing percent and par value for the participation matching computations. **Exhibit 16–2** illustrates this case.

Asset Preference on Preferred Stock. Preferred stock that is preferred as to assets (i.e., which has a liquidation preference) provides that the preferred stockholders, in case of corporate dissolution, have a priority up to the par value or other stated amount per share over common stockholders. Often the asset preference is higher than the par or stated value. When this asset preference is satisfied, the remainder of the assets are distributed to the common stockholders. *APB Opinion 10* (par. 10) requires that "the liquidation preference of the preferred stock be disclosed in the equity section of the statement of financial position in the aggregate . . . rather than on a per share basis or by disclosure in notes."

Preferred Stock Convertible to Other Securities. Preferred stock may carry a **convertibility** provision. This provision means that, at the **option of the preferred stockholder,** the preferred shares owned may be exchanged for (converted to) other securities, usually common stock. Because the conversion privilege offers the preferred stockholder the option of holding the original preferred stock or converting it to another specified security, convertible preferred stock is favored by investors. Convertibility privileges should be disclosed in the financial statements (tabular portion or notes) of the issuing corporation.

Callable Preferred Stock. Preferred stock may be designated as **callable.** This designation means that, at the issuer's option, the preferred stock can be called in for cancellation at a specified price and date(s). All dividends in arrears on cumulative preferred stock must be paid prior to the call date. The call price usually is above par and sometimes above the original issue price. *APB Opinion 10* (par. 11) states that the corporation should disclose "on the face of the statement of financial position or in notes pertaining thereto, the aggregate or per share amounts at which preferred shares may be called."

Redeemable Preferred Stock. Preferred stock with a **redemption** privilege (i.e., redeemable stock) provides that a preferred **stockholder has the option,** under specified conditions, of returning shares to the corporation for a specified price per share within a stated time period.

Preferred Stock versus Debt. The primary characteristics of debt are that it has *(a)* no voting privileges, *(b)* a fixed maturity date and amount, and *(c)* fixed interest dates and amounts. Preferred stock that is voting, noncumulative, participating, noncallable, and nonredeemable has the primary characteristics of common stock. In contrast, preferred stock that is nonvoting, cumulative, nonparticipating, and callable at a fixed time and amount possesses more of the characteristics of debt than an equity security. Some accountants believe that preferred stock with major debt characteristics should be reported as debt rather than as stockholders' equity. Nevertheless, current GAAP does not recognize any kind of preferred stock as debt. Consequently, some corporations have issued preferred stock with major debt characteristics to avoid reporting more debt. The SEC prohibits the inclusion of such preferred stock with common stock. Therefore, for SEC purposes, preferred stock with a high level of debt characteristics sometimes is reported separately on financial statements between liabilities and stockholders' equity.

The issue of statement of financial position reporting and a related issue of whether dividends paid on such preferred stock should be reported as an expense on the statement of income are currently being considered by the FASB.

Accounting for the Issuance of Par Value Stock

Accounting for stockholders' equity emphasizes **source;** therefore, if a corporation has more than one class of stock, separate accounts should be maintained for each class. If there is only one class of stock, an account titled Capital Stock usually is used. In cases where there are two or more classes of stock, account titles such as Common Stock, Preferred Stock, 5%, and Common Stock, Nopar are used. The additional (or other) capital stock accounts represent the remaining contributed capital of the corporation. The sequence of transactions related to the issuance of stock is: *(a)* authorization of shares, *(b)* sale for cash or subscriptions (i.e., the sale of shares on credit), *(c)* collections on subscriptions (when applicable), and *(d)* issuance of the shares.

Authorization—The charter authorization to issue a specified number of shares may be recorded in the journal and in the ledger account by the following notation:[5]

Common Stock—Par Value $10 per Share
(authorized 50,000 shares)

Par Value Stock Issued for Cash. When stock is issued, a **stock certificate,** specifying the number of shares represented, is prepared for each stockholder. An entry reflecting the number of shares held by each stockholder is made in the **stockholder ledger,** a subsidiary ledger to the capital stock account.

In most cases, capital stock is sold and issued for cash rather than on a subscription (i.e., credit) basis. The issuance of 10,000 shares of common stock, par $10, for cash of $10.20 per share would be recorded as follows:

Cash	102,000	
Common stock, par $10 (10,000 shares)		100,000
Contributed capital in excess of par, common stock		2,000

The Capital Stock account is credited for the par value of the stock issued. The excess over par is credited to a descriptively named Contributed Capital account to record **source** in detail. If par value stock is sold at a discount (i.e., less than par), a **negative** stockholders' equity account, Discount on common (or preferred) stock, should be debited for the amount of the discount.

Accounting for Issuance of Nopar Stock

The statutes in various states permit either of two types of nopar stock, **true** nopar stock and **stated value** nopar stock. Therefore, some variation exists in accounting.

Authorization of nopar stock may be recorded by notation as shown for par value stock under the above caption, "Authorization." With nopar stock, most states require that the **total number of shares authorized** be shown on each stock certificate, in addition to the customary imprint of the number of shares represented by that particular stock certificate.

True nopar stock, when sold, is recorded as a credit to the capital stock account in conformity with the legal requirements of the state of incorporation. Thus, if the statutes provide that **all proceeds** represent legal capital, then the capital stock account should be credited for the full amount received. If the statutes establish a **minimum amount** per share, then at least this amount should be credited to the capital stock account, and any remainder can be credited to an "in excess of stated value" account. Without legal requirements, the total amount received should be credited to the nopar capital stock account. In this case, **no** contributed capital "in excess" is recorded.

---

[5] An alternative way of recording the authorization of capital stock is by a journal entry as follows:

Unissued common stock	500,000	
Common stock authorized, par $10 (50,000 shares)		500,000

The Unissued Common Stock account is credited when the shares are issued. The Unissued Common Stock account is a contra to the Common Stock Authorized account.

Nopar stock with a stated (or assigned) value is accounted for in the same manner as discussed for par value stock because the stated value places the nopar stock on essentially the same basis as par value stock. The amount of the sale (issue) price in **excess** of stated value should be credited to an account with a descriptive title such as Contributed (or paid in) Capital in Excess of Stated Value, Nopar Common Stock.

Capital Stock Sold on a Subscription Basis

Along with the organization of a corporation, prospective stockholders often sign a contract to purchase a specified number of shares **on credit** with payment due at one or more specified future dates. Also, a corporation may sell its capital stock on credit subsequent to incorporation. Such contractual agreements are known as **stock subscriptions.** Because a legal contract is involved, accounting recognition must be given when these transactions occur. The purchase price is debited to Stock Subscriptions Receivable. Capital Stock Subscribed is credited for the par, stated, or assigned amount per share. The difference is credited to Contributed Capital in Excess of Par (or stated value) as though the subscriber had paid for the subscribed shares in full.

To illustrate, assume 120 shares of BT Corporation common stock, par $10, are subscribed for at $12 by J. Doe. The entry by BT Corporation would be as follows:

Stock subscriptions receivable—common stock (Doe)	1,440*	
Common stock subscribed, par $10 (120 shares)		1,200
Contributed capital in excess of par, common stock		240

* Payable in three installments of $480 each.

Notice that the premium is recorded when the subscription is recorded, rather than later when all of the cash is collected. In this way, the legal claim (i.e., the stock subscription receivable) the corporation has on the subscriber is recognized.

The credit balance in **Common Stock Subscribed** reflects the corporation's obligation to issue the 120 shares on fulfillment of the terms of the agreement by the subscriber. This account is reported on the statement of financial position similar to the related capital stock account (see Exhibit 16–1). **Stock subscriptions receivable** is classified as a **current** asset if the corporation expects **current** collection. Otherwise, it is reported as a **noncurrent** asset under the category "Other assets." If there are **no plans for collection,** subscriptions receivable cannot be considered an asset. Therefore, they should be **offset** against the common stock subscribed account in the stockholders' equity section of the statement of financial position. Some accountants believe that all stock subscriptions receivable should be reported as a contra account to the related stock.

In some cases, subscription contracts call for installment payments. In such cases, separate "call" accounts may be set up for each installment. If the corporation has a number of subscriptions, it is usually desirable to maintain a **subscribers' ledger** as a subsidiary record to the stock subscriptions receivable account similar to that maintained for trade accounts receivable.

Collections on stock subscriptions receivable may be in cash, property, or services. The appropriate account is debited, and subscriptions receivable is

Exhibit 16–3
Entries for subscriptions for nopar stock.

Case data and accounts	Stated value stock*		True nopar value stock	
1. To record authorization of 10,000 shares of nopar stock:				
Notation—10,000 shares of nopar common stock authorized . . .	Stated value, $5		No stated value	
2. To record cash sale and issuance of 5,000 shares at $6:				
Cash . . .	30,000		30,000	
Common stock, nopar, stated value $5 . . .		25,000		
Common stock, nopar . . .				30,000
Contributed capital in excess of stated value, nopar common stock . . .		5,000		
3. To record subscription taken for 5,000 shares at $6; 20% collected in cash:				
Cash (5,000 × $6 × 20%) . . .	6,000		6,000	
Stock subscriptions receivable, nopar common stock . . .	24,000		24,000	
Nopar common stock subscribed (5,000 shares) . . .		25,000		30,000
Contributed capital in excess of stated value, nopar common stock . . .		5,000		
4. To record collection of subscription receivable and issuance of all of the subscribed shares:				
Cash . . .	24,000		24,000	
Stock subscriptions receivable, nopar common stock . . .		24,000		24,000
Nopar common stock subscribed . . .	25,000		30,000	
Common stock, nopar, stated value $5 (5,000 shares) . . .		25,000		
Common stock, nopar (5,000 shares) . . .				30,000

* Essentially the same as for par value stock.

credited. If a noncash asset or a service is received, the **amount** recorded would be based on the **market value** of that asset or service.

Stock certificates sometimes are not issued until the subscription price is paid in full. The last collection requires two entries. To illustrate, the third, and last, collection on the above subscription (for $1,440) was $480. The entries would be as follows:

To record the last collection:

Cash . . .	480	
Stock subscriptions receivable—common stock (Doe) . . .		480

To record issuance of the stock:

Common stock subscribed . . .	1,200	
Common stock, par $10 (120 shares) . . .		1,200

Accounting for stock subscriptions of **true nopar stock** and **stated value nopar stock** are illustrated and compared in **Exhibit 16–3.**

Default on Subscriptions

When a subscriber **defaults** after partial fulfillment of the subscription contract, certain complexities arise. In case of default, the corporation may decide to (1) return all payments received to the subscriber, or (2) issue shares equivalent to the number paid for in full, rather than the total number subscribed. These two options involve no disadvantage to the subscriber, although the corporation may incur a later economic loss if the stock prices drop. The laws of most states cover the contingency where the corporation does not elect either of these alternatives. Such laws vary considerably; two contrasting provisions are as follows:

a. The subscribed stock is **forfeited,** and all payments made by the defaulting subscriber are forfeited by the subscriber. Therefore, the forfeited amount is credited to the contributed capital of the corporation. Further, the corporation is free to resell the shares. Provisions of this type favor the corporation and seldom occur. To illustrate, refer to BT Corporation and J. Doe, page 718, assuming one $480 payment has been made by Doe prior to default. All related account balances would be removed as follows:

Common stock subscribed (120 shares)	1,200	
Contributed capital in excess of par, common stock	240	
Subscriptions receivable (Doe)		960
Contributed capital from defaulted subscriptions (amount paid in by Doe)		480

b. The stock is forfeited, and the corporation must resell the stock under a **lien** whereby the original subscriber must be reimbursed for the amount that the **net receipts** for the stock (i.e., the total cash collected from both the sale to the subscriber, and subsequent resale of the stock to another investor, less the costs incurred by the corporation in making the later sale) exceed the **original subscription price.** To avoid an incentive to default, the refund to the defaulting subscriber cannot exceed the amount paid to the date of default less resale costs. **Exhibit 16–4** illustrates the accounting for this provision.

Noncash Sale of Capital Stock

Corporations often issue capital stock for noncash assets. For example, *The Wall Street Journal* reported the following: Butterfield Equities Corporation said it privately placed 1.8 million shares of its new preferred stock and 100,000 new common shares, primarily in exchange for real estate.

When a corporation issues its capital stock for **noncash** assets or services, or to settle debt, the current market value of the stock issued or the noncash consideration received, whichever is the most **reliably determinable,** should be used to record the transaction.[6] If the current market value of either the capital stock issued or the noncash consideration received cannot be reliably determined, appraised values should be used. Further, if market values or appraisals are not reliably determinable, the values must be established by the governing authority of the company (i.e., the board of directors and management in the case of a corporation). If a reliable market value for the capital stock is established within a reasonable time after a noncash sale of the stock,

[6] AICPA, *APB Opinion 16*, "Business Combinations" (New York, 1970), par. 67; and *FASB Technical Bulletin 84–1* (Stamford, Conn., 1984), par. 7.

Exhibit 16–4
Default on stock subscriptions—shares resold under lien.

1. BT Corporation received from Subscriber Doe a subscription for 120 shares of common stock, par $10, at $12 per share:		
Stock subscription receivable, common stock (120 shares × $12)	1,440	
Common stock subscribed, par $10 (120 shares × $10)		1,200
Contributed capital in excess of par, common stock (120 shares × $2)		240
2. BT Corporation received a $480 installment on the subscription from Subscriber Doe:		
Cash	480	
Stock subscription receivable, common stock		480
3. Subscriber Doe defaults on the subscription. BT Corporation records the default under the lien provision *(b)* above:		
Common stock subscribed, par $10 (120 shares)	1,200	
Contributed capital in excess of par, common stock	240	
Stock subscription receivable, common stock ($1,440 − $480)		960
Payable to Subscriber Doe (pending resale of formerly subscribed shares)		480
4. BT Corporation resells the formerly subscribed shares for $15 per share. BT Corporation paid the cost of resale, $50, and debited this amount to the Payable to Subscriber Doe account.		
Resale of shares:		
Cash [(120 shares × $15) − $50]	1,750	
Payable to Subscriber Doe (resale costs)	50	
Common stock, par $10 (120 shares)		1,200
Contributed capital in excess of par, common stock (120 shares × $15 = $1,800) − $1,200		600
5. BT Corporation pays stipulated amount to Subscriber Doe:		
Payable to Subscriber Doe*	430	
Cash		430

* Computation:

Amount to be paid to Subscriber Doe based on lien provisions:		
Net receipts for the stock:		
Cash collected from Subscriber Doe	$ 480	
Cash collected from resale of shares	1,800	
Less: Cost of resale	(50)	
Net receipts		$2,230
Original subscription price		1,440
Remainder payable to Subscriber Doe, subject to limitation		$ 790
Limitation—total actual payments made by Subscriber Doe, less resale costs (i.e., $480 − $50)		$ 430
Therefore, pay $430 to Subscriber Doe.		

then the appraised value, or the value set by the corporation's governing authority, which was originally recorded, may be revised.

The issuance of capital stock for noncash considerations sometimes involves improper valuations. Some companies have disavowed market values and independent appraisals in order to permit the governing authority of the company to set arbitrary values in these noncash transactions. In such cases, these companies are motivated to overvalue the assets received, and, as a consequence, overvalue stockholders' equity. This condition is often referred to as **watered stock.** On the other hand, some companies are motivated to undervalue the assets received. As a consequence, they understate stockholders' equity—a condition often called **secret reserves.** Secret reserves also are created intentionally and in error by depreciating, or amortizing, a properly recorded asset over a period less than its useful life.

s of
ock

A corporation usually sells each class of its capital stock separately. However, a corporation may sell two or more classes of its capital stock for one lump-sum amount (often referred to as a **basket sale**). In addition, a corporation may issue two or more classes of its capital stock in exchange for a noncash consideration.

When two or more classes of securities are sold and issued for a single lump sum, the total proceeds must be logically allocated among the several classes of securities. Two methods used in such situations are *(a)* the **proportional method,** in which the lump sum received is allocated proportionately among the classes of stock on the basis of the relative market value of each security and *(b)* the **incremental method,** in which the market value of one security is used as a basis for that security and the remainder of the lump sum is allocated to the other class of security.

The method selected should produce the most reliable results based upon the data available at the transaction date. To illustrate, assume VW Corporation issued 1,000 shares of common stock, par $10, and 500 shares of preferred stock, par $8, in three different situations as follows:

Situation 1—Proportional Method Applied

The common stock was selling at $40 per share and the preferred at $20. The total cash received was $48,000 (a good deal for the investor). Because reliable market values are available, the proportional method is preferable as a basis for allocating the lump-sum amount as follows:

Cash	48,000		
Common stock, par $10 (1,000 shares)			10,000
Preferred stock, par $8 (500 shares)			4,000
Contributed capital in excess of par, common ($38,400 − $10,000)			28,400
Contributed capital in excess of par, preferred ($9,600 − $4,000)			5,600
* Proportional allocation:			
Market value of common (1,000 shares × $40)	$40,000	(4/5)	
Market value of preferred (500 shares × $20)	10,000	(1/5)	
Total market value	$50,000	(5/5)	

Allocation of the lump-sum sale price of $48,000:

Common stock ($48,000 × 4/5)	$38,400
Preferred stock ($48,000 × 1/5)	9,600
Total	$48,000

Situation 2—Incremental Method Applied

The common stock was selling at $40; a market for the preferred stock has not been established. Because there is no market for the preferred stock, the market value of the common must be used as a basis for the following entry:

Cash	48,000	
Common stock, par $10 (1,000 shares)		10,000
Preferred stock, par $8 (500 shares)		4,000
Contributed capital in excess of par, common [1,000 shares × ($40 − $10)]		30,000
Contributed capital in excess of par, preferred (remainder)		4,000

Situation 3—Neither the proportional method or the incremental method of allocation can be used because there is no established market for either class of stock

In this case, an arbitrary allocation is used. In the absence of any other logical basis, a **temporary** allocation may be made on the basis of relative par values. Should a market value be established for one of the securities in the near future, a correcting entry based on such value would be made. The entry to record the temporary allocation on the basis of relative par values would be similar to that shown for Situation 1, except that the apportionment of the $48,000 lump-sum amount would be based on the relative par values of the two securities as follows:

Common stock ($10,000 ÷ $14,000) × $48,000 = $34,286.

Preferred stock ($4,000 ÷ $14,000) × $48,000 = $13,714.

Assessments on Capital Stock

Some states permit the issuance of **assessable stock,** if the charter includes this provision. Also, in some states, under certain conditions, the board of directors may assess the stockholders a certain amount per share, even though the stock is not identified as assessable stock. However, such an assessment usually requires stockholder approval. A stock assessment is the collection of cash from each stockholder in proportion to the shares held without the issuance of additional stock. Stock assessments may be used when a corporation needs cash, is facing insolvency, or when the stock originally was issued at a discount. If the stock was originally issued at a discount, the assessment (up to the amount of the discount) should be credited to the discount account. If no stock discount is carried in the accounts, the credit is to a contributed capital account with an appropriate title such as "Contributed Capital from Stock Assessments." Stock assessments are not often used, except in small companies.

Stock Issue Costs

Corporations often incur large expenditures with major issues of capital stock. These expenditures include registration fees, underwriter commissions, attorney and accountant fees, printing costs, clerical costs, and promotional costs. These expenditures are called **stock issue costs.** Stock issue costs usually are not large compared with the total funds received. Two methods of accounting for stock issue costs are used:

1. **Offset method**—Under this method, stock issue costs are treated as a reduction of the amount received from the sale of the related capital

stock. The argument to support this method is that these are one-time costs that cannot be reasonably assigned to future periodic revenues and that the net cash received is the true issue price of the stock. Therefore, stock issue costs are debited to contributed capital in excess of par under this method. A practical problem arises when the stock issue costs are in excess of what would otherwise be the premium amount.

2. **Deferred charge method**—Under this method, stock issue costs are recorded as a deferred charge and then are amortized over a reasonable period. The argument for this method is that these costs create an intangible asset that contributes to the earning of future revenues and they can be allocated against future periodic revenues in conformity with the matching principle.

Although the offset method dominates, both methods are used. Subsequent to the issuance of capital stock, costs required to maintain stockholder records, transfer costs, and dividend payment costs (clerical only) are expensed when incurred. Organization costs are discussed in Chapter 12.

Unrealized Capital

Unrealized capital (see page 708) is one category of stockholders' equity. Conceptually, it may involve increments (i.e., increases) and decrements (i.e., decreases) in stockholders' equity.

Unrealized capital **increment** (i.e., a credit balance), as a category of stockholders' equity, is not widely used. It arises when assets are written up to market from cost; thus, it violates the cost principle. Because of adherence to the cost principle and conservatism, assets rarely are written up from cost to market value. GAAP exceptions can be found in the financial statements of companies in a particular industry, such as insurance and investment companies. GAAP allows these industries to account for their investments at market value and, therefore, these companies adjust their investment portfolios to market value periodically. An upward adjustment of the asset account requires an offsetting credit to either revenue, gain, or unrealized capital increment.

The write-up of operational (fixed) assets to appraisal (i.e., estimated market) value was discussed in Chapter 10 with respect to discovery value of natural resources. Except for certain specified assets such as farm products and natural resources, and investments of financial institutions, current GAAP does not permit the write-up of assets to market value. However, if such a write-up was credited to the account, **Unrealized Capital Increment,** any credit balance in this account would be reported as a separate, positive item of owners' equity, rather than as part of income.

Unrealized capital **decrement** (i.e., a debit balance) is a contra, or negative, amount in stockholders' equity. It arises when assets are written down under special circumstances. For example, *FASB Standard 12,* "Accounting for Certain Marketable Securities," requires the recording of an "unrealized loss on long-term investments in equity securities." This unrealized capital decrement on **long-term** investments must be reported as a contra item in stockholders' equity as discussed in Chapter 18, Part A.

PART B: CHANGES IN CORPORATE CAPITAL AFTER FORMATION

Treasury Stock

Accounting Trends & Techniques, 1987, page 235, reported that 392 of the 600 corporations surveyed disclosed treasury stock. These data indicate the prevalence of the purchase and sale of treasury stock, which almost always is common stock! Subsequent to the issuance of capital stock, a corporation also may purchase its own stock from stockholders or in the marketplace and hold it indefinitely, use it for special purposes, or retire it. For example, a recent annual report of Anderson, Clayton & Co., disclosed the following:

> The Company has followed the policy of using treasury common shares to fulfill its obligations under the stock option plans. When stock is issued pursuant to the stock option plans, the difference between the cost of treasury common shares issued and the option price is charged or credited to additional paid-in capital. Changes in treasury common stock were as follows:

	Shares	Amount
June 30, 1986:		
Balance at beginning of year	2,693,814	$50,457,000
Purchases	818	41,000
Issued in exercise of stock options	(101,696)	(2,626,000)
Balance at end of year	2,592,936	$47,872,000
June 30, 1985:		
Balance at beginning of year	2,761,983	$52,111,000
Purchases	7,881	264,000
Issued in exercise of stock options	(76,050)	(1,918,000)
Balance at end of year	2,693,814	$50,457,000
June 30, 1984:		
Balance at beginning of year	2,469,465	$44,307,000
Purchases	337,593	8,821,000
Issued in exercise of stock options	(45,075)	(1,017,000)
Balance at end of year	2,761,983	$52,111,000

The statutes of most states permit a corporation to purchase its own stock subject to specified limitations. **Treasury stock** is a corporation's own stock (preferred or common) that *(a)* has been issued, *(b)* is reacquired by the issuing corporation, and *(c)* has not been resold or formally retired. Thus, the purchase of treasury stock does not reduce the number of **issued** shares but does reduce the number of **outstanding** shares. Treasury shares subsequently may be resold and then reclassified as outstanding shares.

Treasury stock may be acquired for the following reasons:

1. To obtain resources when a corporation has excess cash, and the stock appears to be underpriced; therefore, the corporation attempts to augment its net assets (but not its income) by buying the shares "low" and later selling them "high."
2. To use the shares acquired for employee stock options, bonus plans, and direct sale to employees (when there are no unissued shares).
3. To establish a market for the company's stock, which is the primary reason usually cited by the company.

4. To use the shares acquired in exchange for other securities or assets.
5. To use the shares acquired for a stock dividend.
6. To increase earnings per share by reducing the shares outstanding.
7. To buy out one or more particular stockholders and to thwart takeover attempts.
8. To reduce dividend payments by reducing the shares outstanding.

Some stockholders may view the acquisition of treasury shares by a corporation as an alternative to cash dividends because it provides cash flow to the selling stockholders. Moreover, it provides a tax advantage to the selling stockholders because any long-term gain on sale of the shares to the corporation often qualifies as a capital gain for income tax, while cash and property dividends are taxed as ordinary income.

The purchase of treasury stock decreases both assets and stockholders' equity, whereas a sale of treasury stock increases both assets and stockholders' equity. Treasury stock may be obtained by purchase, by settlement of an obligation, or through donation. Treasury stock usually does not carry voting, dividend, preemptive, or liquidation rights. **Treasury stock is not an asset and it does not affect the statement of income.** Treasury stock transactions may cause retained earnings to decrease, but seldom to increase.

Companies exercise extreme care in transactions involving their own stock (including treasury stock) because of the opportunity the corporation (and its management) has to use insider information to the detriment of a stockholder from whom the corporation is acquiring, or to whom the corporation is selling, its own stock. For example, an oil company (or members of its management) with inside knowledge of a profitable oil discovery could withhold the "good" news and acquire stock at an artificially low market price. Alternatively, a company could withhold "bad" news and sell its own stock (including treasury stock) at an artificially high market price. This latter action would unfairly deprive the purchasing stockholder of the excess cash paid for the stock. For these reasons, the securities laws (particularly Rules 10b–5 and 10b–6 of the Securities and Exchange Act of 1934) prohibit corporations from engaging in deceptive conduct including acts related to transactions involving their own stock.

Why not an asset
it is contra-equity

The repurchase by a corporation of shares of its own capital stock poses a **conceptual** question about its classification. Is treasury stock an asset (i.e., an investment in equity securities) or a contraction of the stockholders' equity of the corporation? Although it has some of the attributes of an asset, it is viewed conceptually in accounting as a reduction of stockholders' equity because:

1. Even though the purchase of treasury stock involves the disbursement of assets, a corporation cannot own itself.
2. The purchase of treasury stock is a payment to the selling stockholders for their investment interest in the corporation.
3. Treasury stock essentially is the same as the unissued stock of the corporation, which is not an asset; it cannot be voted and earns no dividends.
4. Treasury stock does not change the number of shares authorized and issued; it only reduces the number of shares outstanding.
5. Treasury stock may be formally retired by the corporation.

Recording and Reporting Treasury Stock Transactions

Two methods are used to account for treasury stock:

1. Cost method (one-transaction concept).
2. Par value method (dual-transaction concept).

Both of these methods are generally accepted. However, they yield different results for individual items within the stockholders' equity section of the statement of financial position. For the same situation, the **total** amount of stockholders' equity is the same under both methods.

Cost Method.

The cost method sometimes is referred to as the one-transaction concept because the **purchase and subsequent sale** of the treasury stock are viewed as one extended transaction with two parts. First, at acquisition, the **cost** of the treasury stock is debited to a contra owners' equity account called **Treasury Stock.** Separate treasury stock accounts should be established for each class of stock with an offsetting credit to cash. At date of subsequent resale, the Treasury Stock account is credited for the **cost** of the treasury stock (in a manner similar to an inventory account). When treasury stock is acquired at different costs, specific shares may be identified. Otherwise, a FIFO or average cost per share must be used to determine the credit to the Treasury Stock account (at cost) at resale date.

When treasury stock is sold (usually a debit to cash) for **more** than its acquisition cost, the difference is credited to a contributed capital account titled, **Contributed Capital from Treasury Stock Transactions.** If treasury stock is sold for **less** than its acquisition cost, the difference is debited to the account, Contributed Capital from Treasury Stock Transactions. However, if the balance in that account is insufficient to absorb all of the debit, the excess is debited to Retained Earnings (similar to a dividend being paid to the retiring stockholder). *FASB Technical Bulletin 85–6* specifies that when treasury stock is purchased for a price significantly in excess of market price, the current market price is used as cost.

The journal entries and reporting under the cost method are illustrated in **Exhibit 16–5** (this exhibit also presents a comparison with the par value method). Under the cost method, the Treasury Stock account at the end of the accounting period is **reported as an unallocated reduction** of the total amount of contributed capital plus retained earnings, as shown in Exhibit 16–5, panel C.

Notice that under the cost method the original contributed capital accounts are unaffected. Instead, Contributed Capital from Treasury Stock Transactions is used (retained earnings may be affected upon resale).

Par Value Method.

The par value method sometimes is called the **dual-transaction concept** because it views the purchase and sale of treasury stock as two independent and separate transactions. Thus, two objectives of the par value method are:

a. At date of acquisition of treasury stock—to make a final accounting with the retiring stockholder and to adjust the capital accounts on a "constructive stock retirement" basis.

b. At date of resale of treasury stock—to record the sale in essentially the same manner as for the sale and issuance of unissued stock.

To accomplish these two purposes, the Treasury Stock account is carried at the par or stated value per share, therefore, the designation par value method. Accounting for treasury stock under the par value method is described below.

Date of Acquisition. The final accounting with the retiring stockholder is recorded as a credit to Cash for the price paid and a debit to Treasury Stock for

Exhibit 16–5
Recording and reporting treasury stock—cost and par value methods compared.

Panel A—Case Data (initial sale of stock):
To record the initial sale and issuance of 10,000 shares of common stock, par $25, at $26 per share:

	Debit	Credit
Cash (10,000 shares × $26)	260,000	
Common stock, par $25 (10,000 shares)		250,000
Contributed capital in excess of par, common stock (10,000 shares × $1)		10,000

Panel B—Entries to Record Treasury Stock Transactions:

1. Acquisition—To record the acquisition of 2,000 shares of treasury common stock at $28 per share:

Cost method

	Debit	Credit
Treasury stock, common stock (2,000 shares × $28)	56,000	
Cash		56,000

Par value method

	Debit	Credit
Treasury stock, common stock (2,000 shares × par, $25)	50,000	
Contributed capital in excess of par, common stock (at $1)	2,000	
Contributed capital from treasury stock transactions, common stock	–0–*	
Retained earnings	4,000	
Cash		56,000

* No available credit balance to absorb a debit. Alternatively, if the 2,000 shares had been acquired for $46,000, Contributed Capital from Treasury Stock Transactions would be credited for $6,000.

2. Sale—To record sale of 500 shares of the treasury stock at $30 per share (above cost and above par):

Cost method

	Debit	Credit
Cash (500 shares × $30)	15,000	
Treasury stock, common stock (500 shares × cost, $28)		14,000
Contributed capital from treasury stock transactions, common stock*		1,000

* If this sale had been at cost ($28 per share), no entry would have been made to Contributed Capital from Treasury Stock Transactions, Common Stock.

Par value method

	Debit	Credit
Cash (500 shares × $30)	15,000	
Treasury stock, common stock (500 shares × par, $25)		12,500
Contributed capital in excess of par, common stock		2,500

3. Sale—To record the sale of another 500 shares of the treasury stock at $19 per share (below cost and below par, which would be an unusual occurrence):

Cost method

	Debit	Credit
Cash (500 shares × $19)	9,500	
Contributed capital from treasury stock transactions, commons stock‡	1,000	
Retained earnings	3,500	
Treasury stock, common stock (500 shares × cost, $28)		14,000

‡ Debit limited to the credit balance in this account (entry 2); any remainder is debited to Retained Earnings.

Par value method

	Debit	Credit
Cash (500 shares × $19)	9,500	
Contributed capital from treasury stock transactions, common stock†	–0–	
Retained earnings	3,000	
Treasury stock, common stock (500 shares × par, $25)		12,500

† Debit limited to the credit balance in this account, which is zero, because there were no prior purchases of treasury stock below par value; any remainder is debited to Retained Earnings.

Exhibit 16–5
(concluded)

Panel C—Financial Statement Reporting (stockholders' equity):

Cost method

Contributed capital:	
Common stock, par $25, authorized 50,000 shares, issued 10,000 shares, of which 1,000 are held as treasury stock	$250,000
Contributed capital in excess of par, common stock	10,000
Contributed capital from treasury stock transactions, common stock	-0-
Total contributed capital	260,000
Retained earnings ($40,000* − $3,500)	36,500
Total contributed capital and retained earnings	296,500
Less: Treasury stock, 1,000 shares at cost, $28	28,000
Total stockholders' equity	$268,500

* Balance assumed.

Par value method

Contributed capital:	
Common stock, par $25, authorized 50,000 shares, issued 10,000 shares	$250,000
Less: Treasury stock, 1,000 shares at par, $25	(25,000)
Total common stock outstanding, 9,000 shares	225,000
Contributed capital in excess of par, common stock ($10,000 − $2,000 + $2,500)	10,500
Contributed capital from treasury stock transactions, common stock	-0-
Total contributed capital	235,500
Retained earnings ($40,000* − $4,000 − $3,000)	33,000
Total stockholders' equity	$268,500

* Balance assumed.

Notice that total stockholders' equity is the same under both methods.

the **par value (in the case of par value stock), stated value (in the case of nopar stock with a stated value), or average amount previously credited to the capital stock account (in the case of true nopar stock).** Also, at the date of acquisition of the treasury stock, Contributed Capital in Excess of Par must be debited for the proportionate amount of any excess over par or stated value that was paid by the stockholders when the shares originally were issued. If a debit or credit balance still remains, this excess is allocated as follows:

1. If the acquisition cost of the treasury shares is **more** than the original issue amount paid in by the retiring stockholder (i.e., there is a debit difference to be allocated):

   Step 1—Debit Contributed Capital from Treasury Stock Transactions (to the extent needed, but not in excess of any credit balance in that account from the same class of stock).

   Step 2—Allocate any remainder as a debit to Retained Earnings. The purpose of this step allocation is to maintain a distinction among the sources of contributed capital.

   In lieu of the above step allocation, *APB Opinion 6* (par. 12a) states, "the excess [debit difference] may be [debited] entirely to retained earnings in recognition of the fact that a corporation can always capitalize or allocate retained earnings for such purposes." Companies are reluctant to debit retained earnings for two reasons: *(a)* to "protect" their cumulative earnings amount and *(b)* to declare dividends in the future.

2. If the acquisition cost of the treasury stock is **less** than the original issue

amount paid in by the retiring stockholders, the excess should be credited in full to Contributed Capital from Treasury Stock Transactions.

Application of the par value method of accounting for **treasury stock** is illustrated in Exhibit 16–5.

Date of Resale. Under the par value method, the entry for resale of treasury stock is essentially the same as the entry for original sale (see exception below). Cash is debited for the amount of cash received, and Treasury Stock is credited for the par value, stated value, or average paid in (in the case of true nopar stock). If the sale price (the debit to cash) of the treasury stock is **more** than its par value, stated value, or average paid in for nopar stock originally, the full amount of the difference should be credited to Contributed Capital in Excess of Par. However, there is one exception. If the sale price (usually a debit to cash) of the treasury stock is **less** than its par value, stated value, or average paid in for nopar stock, the usual debit is to Contributed Capital from Treasury Stock Transactions. If the credit balance in that account cannot absorb the difference, the remainder is debited to retained earnings. Some accountants prefer to debit the full amount to retained earnings. Of course the company can decide to do this; it would not cause a GAAP problem. However, most companies would prefer not to debit retained earnings in this case.

The basic difference between the cost and par value methods is shown in Exhibit 16–5. Panels B and C show the different ways the two methods record and report treasury stock. The par value method is usually viewed as conceptually preferable because it maintains a "source of capital" reporting and treasury stock is reported as a negative element of contributed capital. By contrast, under the cost method, treasury stock is reported as an unallocated negative element of total stockholders' equity. Nevertheless, probably due to its relative simplicity, the cost method is used more often. For example, of the 600 companies reported in *Accounting Trends & Techniques, 1987,* 367 companies used the cost method, and only 30 companies used the par value method. However, 9 of the 367 companies using the cost method reported the cost of the treasury stock as a deduction from issued stock of the same class, which is a hybrid approach (AICPA, *Accounting Trends & Techniques, 1987,* Table 2–37, p. 235).

Accounting for Nopar Treasury Stock. Nopar stock having a **stated** or **assigned** value per share is accounted for as illustrated for par value stock under each of the two methods. The stated or assigned value per share is treated as if it were par. With **true nopar stock,** the cost method almost always is used because it can be applied exactly the same as the cost method for par value stock. If the par value method is used for nopar stock, the average paid in is substituted for par value.

Treasury Stock Received by Donation. Stockholders occasionally donate shares of a corporation's stock back to the corporation. Such donations may *(a)* be made to raise needed working capital through resale of the donated stock, or *(b)* constitute return of the stock in recognition of an overvaluation of assets originally given in exchange for the stock. Stock received by donation is classified as **treasury stock** unless it is formally retired. **Neither total assets nor total**

equity is changed by the donation of treasury stock. Three methods have been employed in recording the receipt of donated treasury stock. They are:

1. **Cost method**—When the donated stock is received, debit the Treasury Stock account for the **current market value** of the stock and credit Contributed Capital, Donated Treasury Stock for the same amount. On resale, any net asset increases or decreases that result from selling the treasury stock for amounts in excess of its carrying value would be accounted for as illustrated in Exhibit 16–5, panel B, for the cost method.
2. **Par value method**—When the donated stock is received, debit the Treasury Stock account for the par or stated value (or, in the case of true nopar stock, average paid in), debit the account that originally was credited for the premium, and credit an appropriately designated contributed capital account. Subsequent resales would be recorded as illustrated in Exhibit 16–5, panel B, for the par value method.
3. **Memo method**—When donated stock is received, a memorandum entry is made on the basis that there was no cost. Subsequent resales require a credit to Contributed Capital, Donated Treasury Stock for the resale price.

Formal Retirement of Treasury Stock

A corporation may decide to **constructively** retire treasury shares (by amending the charter) and have the shares revert to an unauthorized (i.e., not subject to resale or reissuance) status. It may also retire the treasury stock and return it to the unissued status. When treasury stock is retired, The Treasury Stock account is credited and all capital account balances **related to the treasury shares, including contributed capital from treasury stock transactions,** are reduced (i.e., debited) on a **proportionate basis.** Any difference, if a credit, is recorded in Contributed Capital from Stock Retirement; if a debit, Retained Earnings is reduced.

Exhibit 16–6 presents the journal entries for the retirement of treasury stock. The retirement of treasury stock is not unusual. For example, in 1986, UNC Corporation retired 256,258 common shares of treasury stock and AMOCO retired all of its 46,683,000 common shares of treasury stock.

Restriction of Retained Earnings for Treasury Stock

When treasury stock is purchased, assets of the corporation are disbursed to the owners of the particular shares purchased. If a corporation has a free hand, it is not difficult to perceive how creditor interests (or the interests of another class of stockholders) may be jeopardized through the distribution of corporate assets via treasury stock purchases from selected stockholders, even though legal capital may be technically correct. To prevent such situations, some states have a law that limits the cost of treasury stock that may be held at any one time to a specified amount. This limit is usually the total amount of retained earnings. This provision has the effect of requiring a restriction (often called an **appropriation**) of retained earnings equivalent to the **cost of treasury stock** held to reduce the amount of retained earnings that may be used for dividends until the treasury shares are resold.[7] The restriction is based upon the **cost** of

[7] In contrast, some states impose no limits on treasury stock if legal capital is not eroded.

Exhibit 16–6
Retirement of treasury stock.

Panel A—Case Data (from Exhibit 16–5, panel C):

	Cost method	Par value method
Common stock, par $25, 10,000 shares issued	$250,000	$250,000
Contributed capital in excess of par, common stock	10,000	10,500
Treasury stock (1,000 shares):		
At cost	(28,000)	
At par value		(25,000)
Retained earnings	36,500	33,000
Total stockholders' equity	$268,500	$268,500

Panel B—Journal Entries for Retirement of the 1,000 Shares of Treasury Stock:

	Cost method		Par value method	
Common stock, par $25 (1,000 shares)	25,000		25,000	
Contributed capital in excess of par, common stock [($10,000 ÷ 10,000 shares = $1 per share of original premium) × 1,000 shares]	1,000			
Contributed capital from treasury stock transactions	-0-		-0-	
Retained earnings*	2,000			
Treasury stock:				
At cost		28,000		
At par value				25,000

* If this is a credit, instead of a debit, the credit would be to Contributed Capital from Retirement of Common Stock.

the treasury stock held, whether the cost method or the par value method is used to account for treasury stock. Moreover, debt covenants often limit the amount of treasury stock a corporation may purchase.

Retained earnings restrictions (i.e., appropriations) related to treasury stock usually are reported by a **disclosure note** in the financial statements. Alternatively, **formal appropriation entries** may be recorded and reported as discussed in Chapter 17, Part A, under the caption, "Appropriations and Restrictions of Retained Earnings."

Formal Retirement of Callable and Redeemable Stock

Corporations often issue **callable** preferred stock, which provides that the corporation, **at its option** after a certain date, can call in the shares at a specified price for formal retirement. In contrast, **redeemable** stock provides that **at the option of the stockholder,** and under certain conditions, the shares tendered by the stockholders will be retired at a specified price per share. The exercise of the call or redemption option usually involves acquisition and formal retirement of the stock by the issuing corporation. The call or redemption price is at or above par and usually is above the original issue price. Shares called, or redeemed, are not subsequently classified as treasury stock.

When callable or redeemable stock is acquired and formally retired, cash is credited and all capital balances relating to the specific shares are removed from the accounts. Any remaining debit difference is debited to Retained Earnings as a de facto dividend, and any credit difference is credited to a contributed capital account such as Contributed Capital from Retirement of Stock. If the preferred stock is cumulative and there are dividends in arrears, such dividends must be paid and debited to Retained Earnings at the time of the call or redemption.

In respect to disclosure of callable and redeemable stock, *APB Opinion 10* (par. 10), states that "any liquidation preference of the stock be disclosed in the equity section of the statement of financial position in the aggregate, either parenthetically or 'in short' rather than on a per share basis or by disclosure in notes." Amounts of cumulative preferred dividends in arrears also should be disclosed. Also, *FASB Standard 47* (par. 10), states that the statement of financial position should disclose "the amount of redemption requirements for all issues of capital stock that are redeemable at fixed or determinable prices on fixed or determinable dates, separately by issue or combined."

To illustrate, assume a corporation had 2,500 shares of callable preferred stock (par value $100) outstanding, $250,000; contributed capital in excess of par, preferred stock, $10,000; and retained earnings, $45,000. Assume the corporation called and formally retired all of the preferred stock. Three different assumptions as to the **call and retirement** are illustrated below:

Assumption 1: The preferred stock is noncumulative and callable at the original issue price of $104 per share.

Preferred stock (2,500 shares at par, $100)	250,000	
Contributed capital in excess of par, preferred stock ($4 per share)	10,000	
Cash (2,500 shares × $104)		260,000

Note: In the case that only half of the shares are called, each amount would be half of the above.

Assumption 2: The preferred stock is noncumulative and callable at $110 per share—$6 per share above the original issue price of $104.

Preferred stock (2,500 shares at par, $100)	250,000	
Contributed capital in excess of par, preferred stock ($4 per share)	10,000	
Retained earnings	15,000	
Cash (2,500 shares × $110)		275,000

Assumption 3: The preferred stock is 5% cumulative; three years' dividends are in arrears. The stock is callable at $101 plus the dividends in arrears, which must be paid.

Retained earnings ($250,000 × 5% × 3 years)	37,500	
Cash		37,500

Note: If half of the shares were called, the above entry would record $18,750, and the cumulative dividends on the remaining shares of preferred stock also would have to be paid and recorded.

Preferred stock (2,500 shares at par, $100)	250,000	
Contributed capital in excess of par, preferred stock ($4 per share)	10,000	
Contributed capital from retirement of preferred stock		7,500
Cash (2,500 shares × $101)		252,500

If **true nopar stock** is formally retired, the average price per share originally credited to the stock account is removed from the capital stock account, Cash is credited, and any net debit or credit is accounted for as illustrated above. If nopar stock with a stated or assigned value is retired, the procedures illustrated above for par value stock are followed.

Conversion of Convertible Preferred Stock

Corporations sometimes issue **convertible** preferred stock. This stock gives the stockholder an option, within a specified time period, to exchange the convertible preferred shares currently held for other classes of capital stock, usually common, at a specified rate. The converted shares usually are formally retired when received by the corporation. Conversion privileges require the issuing corporation to set aside a sufficient number of units of the other security to fulfill the conversion privileges until they are exercised or expire. If the preferred stock is cumulative, any dividends in arrears at date of conversion must be paid.

At date of conversion, all account balances related to the converted shares are removed and the new shares issued are recorded at their par or stated value. Any difference, if a credit, is recorded in an appropriately designated contributed capital account (e.g., Contributed Capital from Conversion of Preferred Stock); if a debit, Retained Earnings is reduced. To illustrate three typical cases, assume the following data and that the converted stock is formally retired:

Preferred stock, convertible, noncumulative, par $2, shares outstanding, 100,000	$200,000
Contributed capital in excess of par, preferred stock	20,000
Common stock, par $1, shares authorized, 500,000; shares outstanding, 150,000	150,000
Contributed capital in excess of par, common stock	50,000

Case 1. The conversion privilege specifies the issuance of one share of common stock for each share of preferred stock turned in for conversion. Stockholders turn in 10,000 shares of preferred stock for conversion.

Preferred stock (10,000 shares at par, $2)	20,000	
Contributed capital in excess of par, preferred stock ($.20 per share)	2,000	
Common stock (10,000 shares at par, $1)		10,000
Contributed capital from conversion of preferred stock		12,000

Case 2. The conversion privilege specifies the issuance of two shares of common stock for each share of preferred stock converted. Stockholders turn in 10,000 shares of preferred stock for conversion.

Preferred stock (10,000 shares at par, $2)	20,000	
Contributed capital in excess of par, preferred stock ($.20 per share)	2,000	
Common stock (20,000 shares at par, $1)		20,000
Contributed capital from conversion of preferred stock		2,000

Case 3. The conversion privilege specifies the issuance of three shares of common stock for each share of preferred stock converted. Stockholders turn in 10,000 shares of preferred stock of conversion.

Preferred stock (10,000 shares at par, $2)	20,000	
Contributed capital in excess of par, preferred stock ($.20 per share)	2,000	
Retained earnings	8,000	
Common stock (30,000 shares at par, $1)		30,000

Conversion of bonds for capital stock was discussed in Chapter 15.

Changing Par Value

Companies sometimes desire to increase the number of shares outstanding. One reason is to reduce the market price per share. This often increases the market activity of the shares. One way to do this is to reduce the par value per share and yet keep total legal capital the same. A corporation, if it conforms with the applicable state laws, may amend the charter and bylaws to change the par value (and/or the number of authorized shares) of one or more classes of authorized stock. Par value stock may be called in, formally retired, and replaced with nopar stock or stock of a different par value; conversely, nopar stock may be replaced with par value stock.

To record changes in par value, all capital account balances that relate to the old stock retired are removed from the accounts and the new stock issued is recorded. If an additional credit is needed, an appropriately designated contributed capital account is credited; if an additional debit is needed, Retained Earnings is debited. The entries are similar to those illustrated above for recording the conversion of convertible preferred stock.

A stock split is a special case involving a change in par value. In a stock split, the par value per share is reduced and the number of shares outstanding is increased proportionately. Therefore, the balance in the capital stock account is unchanged. Only a memorandum entry in the original stock account is needed to reflect the new par value per share and the number of shares outstanding after the split (see Chapter 17, Part A).

Additional Contributed Capital

Legal capital (defined on page 711) is recorded in the capital stock accounts—common stock and preferred stock. All contributed capital (often called paid-in capital), **except legal capital,** is recorded in appropriately designated additional (or other) contributed capital accounts.

Contributed capital **does not** include retained earnings nor unrealized capital. No operating or extraordinary gains and losses or prior period adjustments may be recorded as contributed capital. Additional contributed capital is created by a number of events that involve the corporation and its stockholders. Several accounts for additional contributed (paid-in) capital were introduced in this chapter (such as premium and discount on stock issuances). **Exhibit 16–7** summarizes some of the transactions that may cause increases or decreases in additional contributed capital.

Corporations report numerous increases and decreases in additional contributed capital accounts. For example, numerous changes reported by one company over a three-year period are shown below in **Exhibit 16–8.**

Exhibit 16–7
Some transactions that may affect additional contributed capital.

Decreases additional contributed capital	Increases additional contributed capital
1. Issuance of stock below par or stated value (Chapter 16).	1. Issuance of stock above par or stated value (Chapter 16).
2. Sale of treasury stock below cost, cost method (Chapter 16).	2. Sale of treasury stock above cost, cost method (Chapter 16).
3. Acquisition and/or sale of treasury stock below par and/or average paid in originally, par value method (Chapter 16).	3. Acquisition and/or sale of treasury stock below par and/or average paid in originally, par value method (Chapter 16).
4. Conversion of convertible preferred stock (Chapter 16).	4. Receipt of donated treasury stock or donated assets (Chapter 16).
5. Retirement of callable or redeemable preferred stock (Chapter 16).	5. Conversion of convertible preferred stock (Chapter 16).
6. Payment of a liquidating dividend (Chapter 17).	6. Retirement of callable or redeemable preferred stock (Chapter 16).
7. Quasi-reorganizations (Supplement 17–A).	7. Conversion of convertible bonds (Chapter 15).
	8. Distribution of a stock dividend (Chapter 17).

Exhibit 16–8
Disclosure schedule; reporting the details of stockholders' equity—an actual case.

THE INTERLAKE CORPORATION
Consolidated Statement of Shareholders' Equity
For the Years Ended December 28, 1986, December 29, 1985 and December 30, 1984

	Common stock and paid-in capital		Common stock held in treasury				
	Shares	Amount	Shares	Amount (in thousands)	Retained earnings	Foreign currency translation	Total
Balance December 25, 1983	14,317	$122,331	(2,649)	$(31,414)	$268,966	$(32,482)	$327,401
Net income					36,551		36,551
Cash dividends					(14,095)		(14,095)
Dividend reinvestment		988	114	1,532			2,520
Shares purchased			(1,000)	(21,625)			(21,625)
Stock incentive plans		946	152	1,712			2,658
Translation (loss)						(12,483)	(12,483)
Divestiture						2,337	2,337
Balance December 30, 1984	14,317	124,265	(3,383)	(49,795)	291,422	(42,628)	323,264
Net income					28,181		28,181
Cash dividends					(14,470)		(14,470)
Dividend reinvestment		957	119	1,758			2,715
Stock incentive plans		1,007	143	1,889			2,896
Translation gain						9,167	9,167
Balance December 29, 1985	14,317	126,229	(3,121)	(46,148)	305,133	(33,461)	351,753
Net income					32,555		32,555
Cash dividends					(14,873)		(14,873)
Dividend reinvestment		879	62	926			1,805
Stock incentive plans	78	4,486	176	1,830			6,316
Translation gain						4,283	4,283
Cancel treasury stock	(2,883)	(43,392)	2,883	43,392			—
Acme Steel Company spin-off					(131,477)		(131,477)
Balance December 28, 1986	11,512	$ 88,202	—	—	$191,338	$(29,178)	$250,362

Summary

The corporate form of business organization is dominant (primarily in terms of size and diversity) in the United States. A corporation is formed by meeting the legal requirements of a selected state. Ownership is evidenced by shares of capital stock. The basic voting stock is called **common stock** (regular and special) and other classes of stock are called **preferred stock.** The latter class usually is characterized by specified preferences. Both classes can be par or nopar value stock.

The primary sources of financing a corporation are owners, creditors, and profitable operations. The classifications of stockholders' equity for a corporation emphasize the primary sources of stockholders' equity—contributed (or paid-in) capital from the owners and retained earnings of the company. Capital stock may be sold (i.e., issued) at or above par value for cash, noncash assets, or on credit (called **subscriptions**).

Companies often purchase their own shares of stock from stockholders. These purchased shares are called **treasury stock** until they are resold. A purchase of treasury stock decreases both assets (e.g., cash) and stockholders' equity. A sale of treasury stock (and of unissued stock) has the opposite effect.

QUESTIONS

Part A

1. Define public, private, open, closed, domestic, and foreign corporations.
2. What are the four basic rights of all stockholders? How may one or more of these rights be withheld from the stockholder?
3. Explain each of the following: authorized capital stock; issued capital stock; unissued capital stock; outstanding capital stock; subscribed stock; and treasury stock.
4. In accounting for corporate capital, explain what it means to report by source, and the significance of doing so.
5. Explain how the cost principle relates to the issuance of capital stock.
6. Define the term capital as it is usually applied in accounting.
7. Define legal capital in the general sense.
8. Distinguish between par and nopar stock.
9. Distinguish between common and preferred stock.
10. Explain the difference between cumulative and noncumulative preferred stock.
11. Explain the difference between nonparticipating, partially participating, and fully participating preferred stock.
12. Explain the asset preference related to preferred stock.
13. Distinguish between callable and redeemable preferred stock.
14. Under what circumstances should stock subscriptions receivable be reported *(a)* as a current asset, *(b)* as a noncurrent asset, and *(c)* as a deduction in the stockholders' equity section of the statement of financial position?
15. Explain secret reserves and watered stock.
16. How should premium and discount on capital stock be accounted for and reported?
17. How are assets valued when shares of stock are given in payment for these assets?

18. Briefly explain the two methods of accounting for stock issue costs.
19. What is the difference between unrealized capital increment and unrealized capital decrement?

Part B

20. Define treasury stock.
21. What is the effect on assets, liabilities, and stockholders' equity of the *(a)* purchase of treasury stock and *(b)* sale of treasury stock?
22. Explain the theoretical difference between the one-transaction concept and the dual-transaction concept in accounting for treasury stock.
23. Under both the cost and par value methods of accounting for treasury stock, total stockholders' equity is unaffected; yet some components of stockholders' equity are affected. Is this statement correct? Explain.
24. Why have many states limited purchases of treasury stock to the amount reported as retained earnings? How may the restriction on retained earnings be removed?
25. In recording treasury stock transactions, why are "gains" recorded in a contributed capital account, whereas "losses" may involve a debit to retained earnings?
26. How is treasury stock reported on the statement of financial position: *(a)* under the cost method and *(b)* under the par value method?
27. How is stock donated back to the corporation recorded?
28. When treasury stock is formally retired, retained earnings may be affected. Explain when this situation may exist.

EXERCISES

Part A: Exercises 16–1 to 16–13

E 16–1 (Stock Issuance; Effects on the Statement of Financial Position)

NIC Corporation received a charter authorizing 100,000 shares of $10 par value stock. During the first year, 60,000 shares were sold at $16 per share. Five hundred additional shares were issued in payment for legal fees. At the end of the first year, reported net income was $23,000. Dividends of $10,000 were paid on the last day of the year. Liabilities at the year-end amounted to $60,000.

Required:

Complete the following tabulation (show calculations); state any assumptions that you make.

Item	Amount	Assumptions
a. Total assets	$	
b. Owners' equity	$	
c. Contributed capital	$	
d. Issued capital stock	$	
e. Outstanding capital stock	$	
f. Unissued capital stock	$	
g. Treasury stock	$	

E 16–2 (Prepare Stockholders' Equity; Two Classes of Stock; Subscribed Stock)

The charter of RAE Corporation authorized 100,000 shares of nopar common stock and 20,000 shares of 6%, cumulative and nonparticipating preferred stock, par value $10 per share. Stock issued to date: 40,000 shares of common sold at $220,000 and 10,000 shares of preferred stock sold at $21 per share. In addition, subscriptions for 2,000 shares of preferred have been taken, and 30% of the purchase price of $21 has been collected. The stock will be issued upon collection in full. The Retained Earnings balance is $288,000. At year-end there was a $10,000 unrealized loss on long-term investments in equity securities.

Required:
Prepare the stockholders' equity section of the statement of financial position.

E 16–3 (Prepare Stockholders' Equity; Subscriptions; Donation; Unrealized Loss)
Prepare, in good form, the stockholders' equity section of the statement of financial position for Warren Corporation.

Retained earnings	$ 390,000
Premium on common stock	40,000
Preferred stock subscribed, but not yet issued (3,000 shares)	30,000
Preferred stock, 6%, par $10, authorized 25,000 shares (15,000 shares issued)	150,000
Common stock, par $20, authorized 500,000 shares (110,000 shares issued)	2,200,000
Stock subscriptions receivable, preferred	4,000
Donation of plant site	50,000
Premium on preferred stock	30,000
Unrealized loss on long-term investment in equity securities	10,000

E 16–4 (Analysis of Stockholders' Equity; Prepare Statement)
The following data were provided by the accounts of Mitar Corporation at December 31, 19C:

Subscriptions receivable (noncurrent)	$ 5,000
Retained earnings, 1/1/19C	450,000
Capital stock, par ?, authorized 100,000 shares	500,000
Future site for office (donated to Mitar)	15,000
Capital stock subscribed, 1,000 shares (to be issued upon collection in full)	10,000
Premium on capital stock	200,000
Subscriptions receivable, capital stock (due in three months)	2,000
Bonds payable	100,000
Net income for 19C (not included in retained earnings above)	95,000
Dividends declared and paid during 19C	40,000

Required:

1. Respond to the following (state any assumptions that you made):
   a. Total retained earnings at end of 19C is . . . . $______
   b. Retained earnings on 1/1/19C was . . . . $______
   c. Number of shares outstanding is . . . . $______
   d. Legal capital is . . . . $______
   e. Total stockholders' equity is . . . . $______
   f. Number of shares issued is . . . . ______
   g. Average selling price per share including any shares subscribed was . . . . $______
   h. Number of shares sold including any shares subscribed was . . . . ______
   i. Par value per share is . . . . $______
2. Prepare the stockholders' equity section of the statement of financial position at December 31, 19C. Use good form, complete with respect to details.

E 16–5 (Compute Dividends; Preferred Stock, Cumulative and Partially Participating)
Darby Corporation has the following stock outstanding:

Preferred, 6%, par $10, cumulative and partially participating up to an additional 2%; outstanding, 5,000 shares. No dividends were declared during the prior two years.

Common stock, nopar, outstanding, 10,000 shares; participating matching dividend, $1.50 per share.

The board of directors has just declared a cash dividend of $33,000.

Required:
You have been requested to complete the following journal entry to record the dividend declaration (show computations):

Dividends declared, preferred stock*	_____	
Dividends declared, common stock*	_____	
Dividends payable		_____

* Closed to retained earnings.

E 16–6 (Compute Dividends; Preferred Stock, Comprehensive Six Cases)
AB Corporation has the following stock outstanding:

Common, $50 par value—6,000 shares.
Preferred, 6%, $100 par value—1,000 shares.

Required:
Compute the amount of dividends payable in total and per share on the common and preferred stock for each separate case:

Case A
Preferred is noncumulative and nonparticipating; dividends declared, $20,000.

Case B
Preferred is cumulative and nonparticipating; two years in arrears; dividends declared, $34,000.

Case C
Preferred is noncumulative and fully participating; dividends declared, $24,000.

Case D
Preferred is noncumulative and fully participating; dividends declared, $40,000.

Case E
Preferred is cumulative and partially participating up to an additional 3%; three years in arrears; dividends declared, $60,000.

Case F
Preferred is cumulative and fully participating; three years in arrears; dividends declared, $50,000.

E 16–7 (Compute Dividends; Preferred Stock; Four Cases)
Davis Corporation reported net income during four successive years as follows: $1,000; $2,000; $1,000; and $23,000.

The capital stock outstanding consisted of $70,000 common (par $20 per share) and $30,000 of 5% preferred (par $10 per share).

Required:
If net income in full were declared and paid as dividends each year, determine the amount to be paid on each class of stock for each of the four years, assuming:

Case A
Preferred is noncumulative and nonparticipating.

Case B
Preferred is cumulative and nonparticipating.

Case C
Preferred is noncumulative and fully participating.

Case D
Preferred is cumulative and fully participating.

E 16–8 **(Compute Dividends; Preferred Stock; A Legal Constraint)**
PT Corporation has the following account balances:

Common stock, par $5, 40,000 shares outstanding	$200,000
Preferred stock, par $20, 9%, cumulative and nonparticipating, 5,000 shares outstanding	100,000
Contributed capital in excess of par:	
Common	80,000
Preferred	15,000
Retained earnings (total cash dividends limited to the balance in retained earnings; no dividends were paid during the two prior years)	220,000

Required (show computations):

1. The average issue price per share for: *(a)* common was $_____, and *(b)* preferred was $_____.
2. Compute dividends for each class of stock under each of the following proposals:
   a. The dividend declaration is $50,000.
   b. The dividend declaration specifies that (1) the same amount of dividends per share will be paid for each class of stock, and (2) all preferences of the preferred stock are met. Does this situation pose a problem? Explain.

E 16–9 **(Stock Issuance; Par Value and Nopar Value; Subscriptions)**
New Corporation received a charter authorizing the issuance of 200,000 shares of common stock. Give the journal entries in parallel columns for the following transactions during the first year, assuming: Case A—true no par stock; and Case B—par value of $5 per share.

a. To record authorization (memorandum).
b. Sold 100,000 shares at $7; collected in full and issued the shares.
c. Received subscriptions for 10,000 shares at $7 per share; collected 60% of the subscription price. The stock will not be issued until collection is in full.
d. Issued 200 shares to an attorney in payment for legal fees related to the charter. Use the deferred charge method.
e. Issued 10,000 shares and in addition paid $190,000 cash in total payment for a building.
f. Collected balance on subscriptions receivable in *(c)*.

State and justify any assumptions you make. Assume all transactions occurred within a short time span.

E 16–10 **(Stock Issuance; Nopar with Stated Value versus True Nopar; Subscriptions)**
The charter of Voss Corporation authorized the issuance of 400,000 shares of nopar common stock. Give journal entries for the following transactions, assuming: Case A—the board of directors set a stated value of $1 per share; and Case B—the stock is true nopar. Set up two pairs of columns so that Case A is to the left and Case B is to the right. Explain and justify any assumptions that you made. Assume all transactions occurred within a short time span.

a. Authorization recognized (memorandum).
b. Sold 150,000 shares at $5 and collected in full; the shares were issued.
c. Received subscriptions for 12,000 shares at $5 per share; collected 40% of the subscription price. The shares will be issued upon collection in full.
d. Issued 500 shares for legal services related to the charter. Use the deferred charge method.
e. Issued 2,000 shares and in addition paid $80,000 cash for some used machinery.
f. Collected balance of subscriptions in *(c)*.

E 16–11 **(Stock Issuance; Subscriptions; Default)**
The charter of Maly Corporation authorized 100,000 shares of $10 par value common stock. A. B. Cook subscribed for 500 shares at $25 per share, paying $2,500 down, the balance to be paid $1,000 per month. The stock will not be issued until collection in full. After paying for three months, Cook defaulted. Six months later, the corporation sold the stock for $33 per share.

Required:
1. Give all journal entries related to the 500 shares originally subscribed for by Cook, assuming Maly refunded all collections made to date of default.
2. Give the journal entry for the default, assuming shares equivalent to the collections were issued to Cook (at $25 per share). Also give the entry for the sale of the remaining shares at $33 six months later.
3. Give the journal entries, assuming:
   a. The stock is true nopar.
   b. The subscriber paid in full as scheduled over the 10-month period.

E 16–12 **(Noncash Sale of Stock; Three Cases)**
The charter for Kay Manufacturing Corporation authorized 100,000 shares of common stock ($10 par value) and 10,000 shares of preferred stock ($50 par value). The company issued 600 shares of its common and 100 shares of its preferred stock for used machinery.

Required:
For each separate situation, give the entry to record the purchase of the machinery, assuming: Case A—the common stock currently is selling at $70 and the preferred at $80; Case B—the common stock has been selling at $70, and there have been no recent sales of the preferred stock, and no reliable value can be placed on the used machinery; and Case C—there is no current market price for either class of stock (however, the machinery has been independently appraised at $44,000).
State and justify any assumptions made.

E 16–13 **(Common and Preferred Stock Issued; Four Transactions)**
The charter of VET Company authorized 10,000 shares of common stock, par $20, and 10,000 shares of preferred stock, par $10. The following transactions were completed. Assume each is completely independent.

a. Sold 200 shares of common and 100 shares of preferred stock for a lump sum amounting to $6,150. The common had been selling during the current week at $25, and the preferred at $12.
b. Issued 90 shares of preferred stock for some used equipment. The equipment had been appraised at $1,200; the book value shown by the seller was $600. A reliable market value on the preferred stock has not been established.
c. A 10% assessment on par value was voted on both the common and preferred when 6,000 shares of common and 4,000 shares of preferred were outstanding. The assessment was collected in full.

d. Sold 300 shares of common and 200 shares of preferred stock to one person for a total cash price of $10,000. The common recently had been selling at $26; there were no recent sales of the preferred.

Required:
Give the journal entry for each transaction. State and justify any assumptions that you make.

Part B: Exercises 16–14 to 16–20

E 16–14 **(Changes in Stockholders' Equity; and Overview)**
Each numbered item in the tabulation given below changes the amount of owners' equity. Some affect retained earnings *(a)* directly and appear on the retained earnings statement, *(b)* others affect retained earnings indirectly because they are reported on the statement of income, and *(c)* others are not reported on either statement.

Item	(a)	(b)	(c)
1. Donation of a plant site to the company			
2. Purchased treasury stock (cost method)			
3. Declaration of cash dividend payable next period			
4. Unrealized loss on marketable securities			
5. Sale of additional common stock of the corporation			
6. Sold the company's capital stock on credit.			
7. Corrected an accounting error (expense) from a prior period			
8. Default on a stock subscription			
9. Collected a stock assessment.			
10. Restricted retained earnings by making an entry equal to the cost of treasury stock purchased			
11. Exchanged the corporation's capital stock for land			
12. Investors tendered their convertible preferred stock for the common stock of the corporation			

Required:
Indicate with a check mark where each of the numbered items should be reported. Be prepared to discuss any questionable items.

E 16–15 **(Treasury Stock, Cost Method; Entries and Reporting)**
Fisher Corporation had outstanding 10,000 shares of preferred stock, par value $10, and 10,000 shares of nopar common stock sold initially for $20 per share. Contributed capital in excess of par on the preferred stock amounted to $40,000; the Retained Earnings balance was $81,600. The corporation purchased 200 shares of its preferred at $25 per

share and 500 shares of its common at $30 per share. Subsequently, 100 shares of the common treasury stock were sold for $26 per share.

Required:

1. Give entries to record the treasury stock transactions, assuming the cost method is used.
2. Prepare the resulting stockholders' equity section of the statement of financial position subsequent to the above transactions.

E 16–16 (Treasury Stock, Par Value Method; Entries and Account Balances)
Minnesota Corporation had the following stock outstanding:

Common stock, nopar, 20,000 shares (originally sold at $15)	$300,000
Preferred stock, par $10, 6,000 shares (originally sold at $25)	60,000

The following treasury stock transactions were completed:

a. Purchased 50 shares of the common stock at $17 per share.
b. Purchased 20 shares of the preferred stock at $27.
c. Sold 30 shares of the common stock at $14.
d. Sold 10 shares of the preferred stock at $35.

Required:

1. Give entries for all of the above stock transactions, assuming the par value method is used for treasury stock.
2. Give resulting balances in each stockholders' equity account; assume a beginning balance in Retained Earnings of $80,000.

E 16–17 (Treasury Stock; Cost and Par Value Methods Compared; Entries and Account Balances)
On January 1, 19A, Simon Corporation issued 10,000 shares of $20 par value common stock at $50 per share. On January 15, 19D, Simon purchased 50 shares of its own common stock at $55 per share. On March 1, 19D, 20 of the treasury shares were resold at $58. The balance in Retained Earnings was $25,000 prior to these transactions.

Required:

1. Give all entries indicated in parallel columns, assuming application of *(a)* the cost method and *(b)* the par value method.
2. Give the resulting balance in each one of the stockholders' equity accounts for each method.

E 16–18 (Treasury Stock; Analysis; Entries)
During year 19B, Veech Corporation had several changes in stockholders' equity. The comparative statements of financial position for 19A and 19B reflected the following amounts in stockholders' equity:

	Balances December 31	
	19A	**19B**
Common stock, par $10, issued	$600,000*	$700,000†
Contributed capital in excess of par	180,000	230,000
Contributed capital, sale of treasury stock		1,000
Retained earnings	120,000	146,000
Treasury stock	18,000	1,400

* Includes 1,000 shares of treasury stock.
† Includes 100 shares of treasury stock (the 1,000 shares held at the end of 19A were sold, and the 100 shares held at the end of 19B were purchased during 19B).

Required:

1. What method was used to account for treasury stock? Explain the basis for your conclusion.
2. Give the required entry for each transaction that affected stockholders' equity during 19B. Show how you determined the amounts used in each entry.

E 16–19 (Treasury Stock; Reporting; Restrictions; Cost and Par Value Methods Compared)

The records of Pincoff Corporation at December 31, 19A, showed the following, assuming the cost method was used for treasury stock:

Assets	$139,000
Liabilities	32,000
Stockholders' equity:	
Common stock, par $10, 7,000 shares	70,000
Treasury stock, 1,000 shares (at cost)	17,000
Contributed capital in excess of par	14,000
Retained earnings	40,000

Required:

Prepare statements of financial position (including any disclosure notes) for the corporation with special emphasis on the stockholders' equity section if the state law places a restriction on retained earnings equal to the cost of treasury stock held. Also assume the following:

1. The cost method is used.
2. The par value method is used. *Hint:* Certain of the above account balances must be modified for the par value method.

E 16–20 (Preferred Stock Converted to Common Stock; Five Cases)

The records of Lawrence Corporation reflected the following:

Preferred stock, 1,000 shares outstanding, par $100	$100,000
Common stock, 1,000 shares outstanding, par $50	50,000
Contributed capital in excess of par, preferred stock	5,000
Contributed capital in excess of par, common stock	2,000
Retained earnings	50,000

The preferred stock is convertible into common stock. Give the entry, or entries, required in each of the following cases:

Case A

The preferred shares are converted to common stock share for share.

Case B

The preferred shares are converted to common stock on a one-for-three basis; that is, three shares of common are issued for each share of preferred.

Case C

The preferred shares are converted, on a share-for-share basis, for a new class of stock known as Common Class B, nopar.

Case D

The preferred shares are converted, to common stock on a one-for-five basis (i.e., five shares of common are issued for each share of preferred) plus a cash payment by the holders of the preferred in the amount of $35 per share of common received.

Case E

The preferred shares are converted to common stock on a par-for-par basis; that is, two shares of common are issued for each share of preferred.

PROBLEMS

Part A: Problems 16–1 to 16–10

P 16–1 (Stockholders' Equity; Donation; Appropriation; Unrealized Capital)
Use appropriate data from the information given below to prepare the stockholders' equity section of a statement of financial position for CT Corporation.

Stock subscriptions receivable, preferred stock	$ 8,000
Retained earnings appropriated for bond sinking fund	40,000
Unrealized capital increment per appraisal of natural resources (discovery value)	44,000
Preferred stock, 6%, authorized 1,000 shares, par $100 per share, cumulative and fully participating	90,000
Bonds payable, 7%	200,000
Common stock, nopar, 5,000 shares authorized and outstanding	250,000
Donation of future plant site (to CT)	6,000
Premium on preferred stock	15,000
Discount on bonds payable	1,000
Retained earnings, unappropriated	250,000
Preferred stock subscribed (to be issued upon collection in full)	10,000
Unrealized loss on long-term investments in equity securities	5,000

P 16–2 (Entries and Reporting; Par and Nopar; Subscriptions; Unrealized Loss)
Don Corporation was granted a charter that authorized 10,000 shares of 6% preferred stock, par value $10 per share, and 100,000 shares of common stock, nopar value. No stated or assigned value was identified with the common stock. During the first year, the following transactions occurred:

a. 20,000 shares of common stock were sold for cash at $12 per share.
b. 2,000 shares of preferred stock were sold for cash at $25 per share.
c. Subscriptions were received for 2,000 shares of preferred stock at $25 per share; 20% was received as a down payment, and the balance was payable in two equal installments. The shares will be issued upon collection in full.
d. 5,000 shares of common stock, 500 shares of preferred stock, and $37,500 cash were given as payment for a small plant that the company needed. This plant originally cost $40,000 and had a depreciated value on the books of the selling company of $20,000. Assume the prior market price per share did not change.
e. The first installment on the preferred subscriptions was collected.

Required:
1. Give journal entries to record the above transactions. State and justify any assumptions you made.
2. Prepare the stockholders' equity section of the statement of financial position at year-end. Retained earnings at the end of the year amounted to $121,500. There was a $10,000 balance in the account, "Unrealized Loss on Long-Term Investments in Equity Securities."

P 16–3 (Entries; Subscriptions; Default, Two Assumptions)
Ace Corporation was issued a charter that authorized 500,000 shares of $5 par value common stock. A. B. Rye subscribed for 10,000 shares at $20 per share and paid a 30% cash down payment. The remaining 70% was payable in four equal quarterly amounts. After paying the first quarterly amount, Rye defaulted. The stock is issuable at date of full payment.

Required:

1. Give the journal entries to record *(a)* the subscription and *(b)* collection of the first quarterly payment.
2. Assumption A—Give the journal entries to record *(a)* the default by Rye and the issuance to Rye of shares equivalent to the cash paid by Rye and *(b)* sale one month later of the remaining subscribed shares to another party for cash at $22 per share (the cost of reselling was 40 cents per share).
3. Assumption B—Give the journal entries to record *(a)* the default by Rye and *(b)* resale one month later under lien of all of the subscribed shares to another party for cash at $22 per share (the cost of reselling was 40 cents per share), including any cash refunded to Rye.

P 16–4 (Entries and Reporting; Subscriptions; Noncash Sale)

The charter of Day Corporation, to operate a manufacturing business, authorized 300,000 shares of common stock, nopar value, and 50,000 shares of 6% preferred stock, which is cumulative and nonparticipating with par value per share of $10. During the early part of the first year, the following transactions occurred:

a. Each of the six incorporators of Day Corporation subscribed to 1,000 shares of the common at $18 per share and 500 shares of the preferred at $12 per share. Half the subscription price was paid, and half the subscribed shares issued.
b. Another individual purchased 500 shares of Day common and 100 shares of preferred stock, paying $9,280 cash.
c. One of the incorporators purchased a used machine for $40,000 and immediately transferred it to the corporation for 2,000 shares of common stock, 200 shares of preferred stock, and a one-year, 15% interest-bearing note for $8,000.
d. The investors paid the subscriptions, and the remaining stock was issued.

Required:

1. Give all journal entries indicated for Day Corporation.
2. Prepare the stockholders' equity section of the statement of financial position. Assume retained earnings of $53,320 at year-end.

P 16–5 (Entries and Reporting; Subscriptions; Noncash Sale; Par, Nopar, Stated Value Compared)

Vance Corporation received a charter that authorized 100,000 shares of common stock. During the first year, the following transactions affecting stockholders' equity were completed:

a. Immediately after incorporation sold 80,000 shares at $25 per share for cash.
b. Near year-end received a subscription for 1,000 shares at $25 per share, collected 60% in cash, balance due in two equal installments within one year. The stock will be issued upon collection in full.
c. Near year-end issued 500 shares for a used machine that would be used in operations. The machine cost $20,000 new and was carried by the seller at a book value of $11,000. It was appraised at $15,000 six months previously by an independent appraiser.
d. Collected half of the unpaid subscriptions in *(b)*.

Required:

1. Give the journal entries for each of the above transactions, assuming: Case A—the stock has a par value of $10 per share; Case B—the stock is true nopar value; and Case C—the stock is nopar; however, it is assigned a stated value of $5 per share.

Set up parallel amount columns for each case. State and justify any assumptions you make.

2. Prepare the stockholders' equity section of the balance sheet at the end of the first year for each case. Assume a balance in Retained Earnings of $462,500 at year-end.

P 16–6 **(Entries and Reporting; Subscriptions; Noncash Sale; Par, Nopar, and Stated Value Compared)**

The charter for WK Corporation authorized 500,000 shares of common stock. During the first year of operations, the following transactions affected stockholders' equity:

a. Immediately after incorporation, the corporation sold 400,000 shares of its capital stock at $10 per share; collected cash.
b. Immediately after incorporation, received a subscription for 10,000 shares of capital stock from one individual at $10 per share. Collected 40% of the subscription, and the balance is due at the end of one year. The shares will be issued upon collection in full.
c. Near year-end, exchanged 6,000 shares of capital stock for a plant site. The site was carried on the books of the seller at $25,000, and it had been independently appraised within the past month at $70,000. The market value of the stock is $10 per share.
d. Collected $12,000 on the subscription in *(b)*.

Required:

1. Give journal entries for the above transactions, assuming:

Case A
Par value stock; $4 par value per share.

Case B
True nopar value stock.

Case C
Nopar value stock with a stated value of $2 per share.

Set up parallel amount columns for each case. State and justify any assumptions you made.

2. Prepare the stockholders' equity section of the statement of financial position at the end of the first year for each case. Assume a $94,000 ending balance in the Unappropriated Retained Earnings account, a reserve for bond sinking fund of $27,000, and unrealized loss on long-term equity investments of $11,000.

P 16–7 **(Entries and Reporting; Par and Nopar; Subscriptions, Deferred Change)**

The charter of Koke Corporation authorized the issuance of 20,000 shares of 6% cumulative, nonparticipating preferred stock, par $10 per share, and 100,000 shares of common stock, nopar value. During the first year of operations, the following transactions affecting stockholders' equity were completed:

a. The company sold 9,000 shares of the preferred stock at $25 per share for cash; the stock was issued.
b. Subscriptions were received for an additional 1,000 shares of preferred stock at $25 per share; 20% was collected, the balance is to be paid in four equal installments; the stock will be issued upon collection in full.
c. Each of the three promoters was issued 1,000 shares of common stock (only the common stock has voting privileges) at $20 per share; each paid one fifth in cash. The remainder was considered to be appropriate reimbursement for promotional activities; the shares were issued. Use the deferred charge method.

d. An individual purchased 100 shares of preferred and 100 shares of common stock and paid a single sum of $4,400. The stock was issued. Assume a current market price of $25 for the preferred stock and that, at this date, no current market price for the common was established.
e. Collected cash from the subscribers [*(b)* above] for the first installment.
f. Issued 5,000 shares of common stock for a used plant. The plant had been independently appraised during the past month at $110,000 and was reported by the seller at a book value of $60,000. Assume that, at this date, no current market price for the common was established.

Required:
1. Prepare journal entries to record the foregoing transactions. State and justify any assumptions you make.
2. Prepare the stockholders' equity section of the statement of financial position, assuming retained earnings at year-end of $32,200 and an unrealized loss on long-term investment in equity securities of $6,600.

P 16–8 (Reconstruct Entries Based on Stockholders' Equity)
The stockholders' equity section of the statement of financial position for the Star Corporation at the end of its first accounting year was reported as follows:

Contributed capital:		
Capital stock:		
Preferred, 6%, cumulative, nonparticipating, $100 par value, redeemable at $125 per share, authorized 5,000 shares; issued and outstanding 4,185 shares	$ 418,500	
Preferred stock subscribed, 465 shares (J. Doe)	46,500	$ 465,000
Common stock, stated value $8 per share, authorized 1,500,000 shares; issued and outstanding 954,000 shares	7,632,000	
Common stock subscribed, 106,000 shares	848,000	8,480,000
Other contributed capital:		
In excess of par, preferred	15,000	
In excess of stated value, common	21,200	36,200
Retained earnings		110,000
Total stockholders' equity		$9,091,200

Required:
Prepare journal entries during the first year as indicated by the above report. Use the memorandum approach to record the authorization and assume that all stock was purchased through subscriptions under terms of 30% cash down payment and 70% payable six months later. Also assume that of the 70%, all but 10% of the subscribers had paid in full by year-end. Shares are not issued until collection in full from the subscriber.

Test

P 16–9 (Compute Dividends; Preferred Stock, Three Cases)
Zapata Corporation reported net income during five successive years as follows: $20,000; $30,000; $9,000; $5,000; and $48,000. The capital stock consisted of $300,000, $20 par value common, and $200,000, $10 par value, 6% preferred.

Required:
For each separate case, prepare a tabulation showing the amount (and computations) each class of stock would receive in dividends if: (1) the entire net income was distributed each year and (2) 60% of each year's earnings were distributed that year.

Case A
Preferred stock is noncumulative and nonparticipating.

Case B
Preferred stock is cumulative and nonparticipating.

Case C
Preferred stock is cumulative and fully participating.

P 16–10 **(Compute Dividends; Comprehensive, Five Cases)**
The charter of Ace Corporation authorized 5,000 shares of 6% preferred stock, par value $20 per share, and 8,000 shares of common stock, par value $50 per share. All of the authorized shares have been issued. In a five-year period, annual dividends paid were: $4,000; $40,000; $32,000; $5,000; and $36,000, respectively.

Required:
Prepare a tabulation (including computations) of the amount of dividends that would be paid to each class of stock for each year under the following separate cases:

Case A
Preferred stock is noncumulative and nonparticipating.

Case B
Preferred stock is cumulative and nonparticipating.

Case C
Preferred stock is noncumulative and fully participating.

Case D
Preferred stock is cumulative and fully participating.

Case E
Preferred stock is cumulative and partially participating up to an additional 2%; assume the dividend for year 5 was $42,000 instead of $36,000.

Part B: Problems 16–11 to 16–16

P 16–11 **(Treasury Stock; Cost and Par Value Methods Compared; Entries and Account Balances)**
At January 1, 19A, the records of Frazer Corporation provided the following:

Capital stock, par $10, 60,000 shares outstanding	$600,000
Contributed capital in excess of par	240,000
Retained earnings	160,000

During the year, the following transactions affecting stockholders' equity were recorded:

a. Purchased 500 shares of treasury stock at $20 per share.
b. Purchased 500 shares of treasury stock at $22 per share.
c. Sold 600 shares of treasury stock at $25.
d. Net income for 19A was $45,000.

The state law places a restriction on retained earnings equal to the cost of treasury stock held.

Required:
1. Give entries for the initial issuance of stock and for each of the above transactions, in parallel columns, assuming application of *(a)* the cost method and *(b)* the par value method. Assume FIFO flow for treasury stock.

2. Give the resulting balances in each capital account. Include any required disclosure note related to the treasury stock.

P 16–12 (Treasury and Donated Stock; Cost Method; Entries and Stockholders' Equity)
Monet Corporation had 30,000 shares of $10 par value capital stock authorized, of which 20,000 shares were issued three years ago at $15 per share. During the current year, the corporation received 500 shares of the capital stock as a bequest from a deceased stockholder; in addition (at approximately the same date), 1,000 shares were purchased at $14 per share. State law places a restriction on retained earnings equal to the cost of treasury stock held. At the end of the year, a cash dividend of 85 cents per share was paid; prior to the dividend, retained earnings amounted to $40,000.

Required:

1. Prepare entries to record all of the transactions, assuming the cost method for recording treasury stock is used. Record the donated stock at its market value.
2. Prepare the stockholders' equity section of the statement of financial position at year-end and include any required disclosure notes related to the treasury stock.

P 16–13 (Treasury Stock Retired; Entries, Cost and Par Value Compared)
The records for Maryville, Inc., provided the following data on stockholders' equity:

a. Preferred stock, par $50, issued 2,000 shares.
b. Preferred treasury stock, 200 shares (cost $54 per share).
c. Premium on preferred stock at original issue, $2 per share.
d. Common stock, par $100, issued 3,000 shares.
e. Common treasury stock, 300 shares (cost $98 per share).
f. Premium on common stock at original issue, $3 per share.

The stockholders voted to retire all of the treasury stock immediately and to purchase for retirement another 400 shares of common stock that could be purchased currently at $125 per share.

Required:
Give entries in parallel columns for the following transactions, assuming application of the (1) cost method and (2) par value method:

a. Purchase of the 400 shares of outstanding common stock and their immediate retirement. This transaction does not affect treasury stock.
b. Retirement of all of the treasury shares. Give separate entries for the preferred and common stock.

P 16–14 (Treasury Stock; Entries and Reporting; Cost and Par Value Methods Compared)
Fibber Corporation reported the following summarized data prior to the transactions given below:

Assets	$660,000
Less: Liabilities	100,000
	$560,000

Stockholders' equity:	
Preferred stock, $10 par	$300,000
Common stock, $5 par	150,000
Contributed capital in excess of par, preferred stock	30,000
Retained earnings	80,000
	$560,000

The state law places a restriction on the retained earnings equal to the cost of treasury stock held.

The following transactions affecting stockholders' equity were recorded:

a. Purchased preferred as treasury stock, 600 shares at $15.
b. Purchased common as treasury stock, 1,000 shares at $20.
c. Sold preferred treasury stock, 100 shares at $17.
d. Sold common treasury stock, 400 shares at $14.

Required:

1. Give entries in parallel columns for the treasury stock transactions *(a)* through *(d)*, assuming application of the (1) cost method and (2) par value method.
2. Prepare the resulting statement of financial position for each method with emphasis on stockholders' equity. Include any required note disclosure.

P 16–15 (Exchange of Old Shares for New Shares; Entries for Seven Cases)

Rather Corporation had authorized and outstanding 100,000 shares of capital stock, par value $2 per share. The stockholders approved the exchange of two new shares for each share of the old stock.

Required:

Give the journal entries to record the change under each of the following independent cases (assume a sufficient balance in retained earnings):

Case A

The old stock was sold at par, and the new stock was nopar value stock with no stated or assigned value.

Case B

The old stock was sold at a premium of $3 per share, and the new stock was nopar value stock with a stated value of $2 per share.

Case C

The old stock was sold at a premium of $1.50 per share, and the new stock was nopar value stock with a stated value of $2 per share.

Case D

The old stock was sold at par, and the new stock was nopar value stock with a stated value of $1.50 per share.

Case E

The old stock originally was sold at a premium of $1.50 per share, and the new stock was $1 par value.

Case F

The old stock was sold at a premium of $3 per share, and the new stock was nopar value stock with no stated or assigned value.

Case G

The old stock was sold at a premium of $1 per share, and the new stock was nopar value stock with no stated or assigned value.

P 16–16 (Overview; Stock Issuance; Treasury Stock)

At the end of 19B, the comparative statements of financial position for Sandford Corporation reported the following stockholders' equity amounts:

	Balances December 31	
	19A	**19B**
Preferred stock, par $10, shares authorized 20,000	$150,000	$200,000
Common stock, nopar, shares authorized 100,000; issued near the end of 19A, 30,000; 19B, 31,000	210,000	218,000
Contributed capital in excess of par, preferred stock	74,000	155,600
Treasury stock, preferred	2,000	1,000
Treasury stock, common	2,100	3,500*
Retained earnings	60,074	97,974†

Restriction on retained earnings at the end of 19A equal to the cost of treasury shares held: Preferred stock, $5,124; common stock, $1,950 (300 shares).

* Increased by 200 shares during 19B at $8 per share.
† No dividends were declared during 19B.

Required:

1. What method is being used to account for the treasury stock? Explain.
2. At the end of 19A, what had been the average selling price per share (by the corporation) of the *(a)* preferred and *(b)* common shares?
3. Complete the following tabulation for the treasury stock held at December 31, 19A (show computations):

	Number of treasury shares held	Average cost per share
Preferred	____	____
Common	____	____

4. How many shares were outstanding at December 31, 19A, for *(a)* preferred and *(b)* common?
5. What was the total amount of stockholders' equity at December 31, 19A?
6. Give the required entry for each transaction that affected stockholders' equity during 19B (exclude consideration of net income). The preferred stock sold for $26 per share in 19B.
7. Explain the reasons for a possible disclosure concerning treasury stock sometimes required by state laws.

CASES

C 16–1 (Conceptual; Classification of Treasury Stock)

Arguments are made that treasury stock is an asset because it is purchased, owned, and paid for in cash like any other asset. Further, as with other assets, it can be sold for cash at any time in an established market. Conclusion: because treasury stock has the overriding attributes of an asset, it should be reported and classified on the statement of financial position as an asset.

Required:

1. Assuming you have no GAAP constraints to consider, how do you think treasury stock should be classified, with assets or with stockholders' equity, on the statement of financial position?
2. Justify your position indicated in (1) above (do not use current GAAP as a reason).
3. Assume the issuing company has a bond sinking fund being accumulated to retire outstanding bonds payable at maturity date. It is administered by an independent

outside trustee in accordance with the bond agreement. Assume the sinking fund investments include stock of the issuing company. How should that particular stock be classified? Explain the basis for your conclusions.

C 16–2 (Issuance of Capital Stock to Organizers; Valuation)

C. Banfield, an engineer, developed a special safety device to be installed in backyard swimming pools that, when turned on, would set off an alarm should anything (e.g., a child) fall into the water. Over a two-year period, Banfield's spare time was spent developing and testing the device. After receiving a patent, three of Banfield's friends, including a lawyer, considered plans to produce and market the device. Accordingly, a charter was obtained, which authorized 200,000 shares of $10 par value stock. Each of the four organizers contributed $20,000, and each received in return 2,000 shares of stock. They also agreed that, for other considerations, each would receive 5,000 additional shares. The remaining shares were to be held as unissued stock. Each organizer made a proposal as to how his additional 5,000 shares would be paid for. These individual proposals were made independently; then the group considered them as a package. The four proposals were as follows:

Banfield: The patent would be turned over to the corporation as payment for the 5,000 shares. An independent appraisal of the patent could not be obtained.

Lawyer: 1,000 shares would be received for legal services already rendered during organization, 1,000 shares would be received as advance payment for legal retainer fees for the next three years, and the balance would be paid for in cash at par.

Friend No. 2: A small building, suitable for operations, would be given to the corporation for the 5,000 shares of stock. It was estimated that $20,000 would be needed for renovation prior to use. The owner estimates that the market value of the building is $750,000 and there is a $580,000 loan on it to be assumed by the corporation.

Friend No. 3: To pay $10,000 cash on the stock and to give a 12% (the going rate) interest-bearing note for $40,000 (subscriptions receivable) to be paid out of dividends over the next five years.

Required:

You have been engaged as in independent CPA to advise the group. Specifically, you have been asked the following questions:

1. How would the above proposals be recorded in the accounts? Assess the valuation basis for each, including alternatives.
2. What are your recommendations for an agreement that would be equitable to each organizer? Explain the basis for such recommendations.

C 16–3 (A Reporting Issue Concerning Preferred Stock; Equity versus Debt)

Onray Corporation reported the following items on its statement of financial position dated December 31, 1987:

Liabilities:	
Long-term note payable, 12% interest payable each June 30 and December 31 (maturity date December 31, 1992)	$ 500,000
Stockholders' equity:	
Common stock, nopar	6,000,000
Preferred stock, par $100, nonvoting, 9% cumulative, nonparticipating, and mandatory redemption at par no later than December 31, 1992, 4,000 shares authorized and outstanding	400,000
Retained earnings	800,000

Required:

1. Critically evaluate the reporting classifications applied by Onray. Did Onray violate current GAAP? Explain.
2. Disregarding all current accounting "rules," how do you think Onray should report the four items shown above? Explain why.

C 16–4 (Equity versus Debt Agreements; Asset Purchased)

Ellis Corporation purchased equipment with a cash price of $144,000, for $107,000 cash and a promise to deliver an indeterminate number of shares of its $5 par common stock, with a market value of $15,000 on January 1 of each year for the next four years. Hence, $60,000 in "market value" of shares will be required to discharge the $37,000 balance due on the equipment.

The corporation then acquired 5,000 shares of its own stock (which became treasury shares) in the expectation that the market value of the stock would increase substantially before the delivery date.

Required:

1. Discuss the propriety of recording the equipment at—
   a. $107,000 (the cash payment).
   b. $144,000 (the cash price of the equipment).
   c. $167,000 (the $107,000 cash payment + the $60,000 market value of treasury stock that must be transferred to the vendor in order to settle the obligation according to the terms of the agreement). Assume an ordinary annuity.
2. Discuss the arguments for treating the balance due as—
   a. A liability.
   b. Treasury stock subscribed.
3. Assuming that legal requirements do not affect the decisions, discuss the arguments for treating the corporation's treasury shares as—
   a. An asset awaiting ultimate disposition.
   b. A capital element awaiting ultimate disposition. (AICPA adapted)

C 16–5 (Conceptual; Debt versus Equity Securities Used to Purchase an Asset)

On January 1, 19A, CPZ Corporation purchased a tract of land for long-term use as a possible future plant site in exchange for $50,000 cash plus a five-year note with no interest, even though the current interest for similar debt is 15%. The note is to be paid in $20,000 annual amounts; the first $20,000 is due one year from the date of the land purchase and the last $20,000 is due at the end of five years. The note also specifies (quite unusually) that instead of being payable in cash, each $20,000 annual amount is to be settled by issuance of 20,000 shares of CPZ common stock, par $1, to the holder of the note. On the date land was purchased, the market value of the stock set aside to be issued on the five dates by CPZ Corporation was $180,000.

Required:

1. Develop and explain the basis for the journal entry that CPZ should make on January 1, 19A.
2. Give, and explain the basis for, the entry(s) that CPZ should make on December 31, 19A.
3. Explain how the following items should be reported on the 19A financial statements of CPZ Corporation: *(a)* interest expense, *(b)* land, *(c)* debt, and *(d)* contributed capital.

C 16–6 **(Reporting Stockholders' Equity; an Actual Case)**

Kimberly-Clark

The 1987 annual report of Kimberly-Clark is shown in an Appendix immediately following Chapter 25. You are to respond to the following questions related to 1987 unless stated otherwise:

1. What types of capital stock does the company use? Give the par value per share.
2. At the end of 1987, how many shares were *(a)* authorized, *(b)* issued, *(c)* held as treasury stock, *(d)* unissued, and *(e)* outstanding.
3. What is the average amount paid in above par value for the shares outstanding at the end of 1987?
4. What percent of total assets was provided by the stockholders overall at the end of 1987?
5. What percent of the shares of common stock issued was held as treasury stock at the end of 1987?
6. What was the percent of 1987 earnings to the 1987 dividends declared?
7. Explain the changes in authorized capital stock in 1987.
8. Explain the changes in treasury stock during 1987.
9. Explain why no preferred stock is reported on the 1987 statement of financial position.
10. What was the percentage change in the balance of retained earnings from December 31, 1984, through December 31, 1987?

17 CORPORATIONS— RETAINED EARNINGS, STOCK RIGHTS, AND OPTIONS

Don't make a lot of entries to Retained earnings

OVERVIEW AND PURPOSE

Should some shares of stock of a corporation be acquired, the profit or loss on the investment could include cash from (a) dividend revenues and (b) a market value increase or decrease at resale date above or below the original investment. Cash dividends basically depend on the cumulative income earned by the corporation and available cash. Also, cash dividends likely would have a major impact on the future market price of your shares.

Chapter 16 discussed the recording and reporting of stockholders' equity by source, application of the cost principle in capital stock transactions, and recognition of treasury stock transactions. The increases and decreases from these transactions are not reported on the statement of income because they arise from transactions between the corporation and its stockholders.

The purpose of this chapter is to conclude the discussion of corporate capital. This is done by presenting the application of the concepts and procedures used in measuring, recording, and reporting retained earnings and stock rights and options. To accomplish this purpose, the chapter is organized as follows:

Part A: Retained Earnings

1. Characteristics of retained earnings.
2. Nature of dividends.
3. Special stock dividends.
4. Legality of dividends.
5. Stock splits.
6. Appropriations and restrictions of retained earnings.
7. Reporting retained earnings.

Part B: Stock Rights and Options.

1. Stock rights and warrants.
2. Accounting for stock rights.
3. Stock option incentive plans for employees.
4. Stock appreciation rights.
5. Additional disclosures required for stock option plans (noncompensatory and compensatory).
6. Overview of accounting for stock issued to employees.

Supplement 17–A: Quasi-Reorganizations

PART A: RETAINED EARNINGS

Characteristics of Retained Earnings

Retained earnings represent accumulated net income (or net loss), gains and losses, and prior period adjustments of a corporation, less its cash dividends, property dividends, stock dividends, and other amounts transferred to the contributed capital accounts. If the accumulated losses and distributions of retained earnings exceed the accumulated gains, a **deficit** will exist (i.e., a debit balance) in retained earnings. All income (net of any losses) of the corporation that is not distributed as dividends increases total stockholders' equity.

Some variation in terminology with respect to retained earnings exists. The terms **surplus, earned surplus,** and **earned capital** were once used to denote what is now called **retained earnings.** More descriptive terminology was needed to provide statement users with a clear description of the nature of each item reported. Also, the older terms are misleading because no "surplus" exists. As explained in Chapter 16, a distinction is maintained between **contributed** or **paid-in capital** and **retained earnings** to delineate the primary sources of total stockholders' equity.

Total retained earnings may include two categories: appropriated or restricted retained earnings and unappropriated retained earnings. When these two categories are recorded separately in the accounts, the Retained Earnings account (if not designated otherwise) represents the **unappropriated** portion of retained earnings (i.e., it has not been set aside, appropriated, or restricted for specific reasons). The second category, **appropriated** retained earnings, includes specially designated amounts in separate accounts, such as Retained Earnings Appropriated for Bond Sinking Fund or Retained Earnings Appropriated for the Cost of Treasury Stock. The reporting of appropriated and unappropriated retained earnings is discussed later in this chapter.

Increases and decreases in total retained earnings can be summarized as follows:

Retained Earnings

Decreases (debits)	Increases (credits)
• Net loss (including extraordinary losses) • Prior period adjustments (primarily correction of accounting errors of prior periods) • Cash dividends • Property dividends • Scrip dividends • Stock dividends • Treasury stock and stock retirement transactions	• Net income (including extraordinary gains) • Prior period adjustments (primarily correction of accounting errors of prior periods) • Removal of deficit by quasi-reorganization

Nature of Dividends

Dividends are distributions of cash, noncash assets, or the corporation's own stock to the stockholders in proportion to the number of outstanding shares of each class of stock held by each stockholder. A dividend requires a credit to the account that represents the item distributed (i.e., cash, noncash asset, or capital stock) and a debit to Retained Earnings (some exceptions are explained later). The types of dividends encountered frequently are:

Usual:

1. Cash dividends (cash disbursed).
2. Property dividends (noncash assets disbursed).
3. Stock dividends (corporation's own stock issued).

Special:

4. Liquidating dividends (return of contributed capital).
5. Scrip dividend (long-term liability).

Corporations rarely distribute all of their earnings as cash or property dividends for a number of economic, legal, and contractual reasons. The corporation may want to *(a)* conserve cash for other immediate uses, *(b)* expand, grow, and modernize by investing the assets received when income was earned, and *(c)* provide a cushion of resources to minimize the effect of recessions and other unforeseen contingencies. Some state laws and bond covenants place restrictions on the amount of retained earnings that may be used for cash and property dividends. These constraints recognize the effects of cash and property dividends; that is, such dividends require (1) a disbursement of assets, and (2) a reduction in retained earnings by the same amount. Cash and property dividends cannot be paid without this dual effect. Aside from this effect, there is no particular relationship between retained earnings and any asset.

Relevant Dividend Dates

Prior to payment, dividends must be formally **declared** by the board of directors of the corporation. Four dates are important in accounting for dividends: (1) date of declaration, (2) date of record, (3) ex-dividend date, and (4) date of payment.

Date of Declaration. On this date, the corporation's board of directors formally announces the dividend declaration. In the case of a **cash or property dividend,** the declaration is recorded on this date as a debit to Retained Earnings and a credit to Dividends Payable. In the absence of fraud or illegality, the courts have held that formal declaration of a cash, property, or liability (i.e., scrip) dividend constitutes an enforceable contract between the corporation and the stockholders. Therefore, on the dividend declaration date such dividends are recorded and a liability (i.e., dividends payable) is recognized.

In the case of a **stock dividend,** no corporate assets are involved, directly or indirectly. Therefore, the courts have held that a stock dividend declaration is revocable up to the date of issuance. Because there is no liability, an entry is not required on declaration date. However, accountants sometimes prefer to make an entry on declaration date to recognize the **intention** to issue additional stock (i.e., credit Stock Dividends Issuable, which is reported as a positive item under stockholders' equity since it is not a liability).[1]

---

[1] See the subsequent section on stock dividends. Also, in the case of cash dividends, if the declaration date and payment date are in the same accounting period, there would be no essential reason to make an entry in the accounts on the declaration date.

Date of Record. This date is selected by the board of directors and is stated in the declaration. Usually it follows the declaration date by two to three weeks. The date of record is the date on which the list of **stockholders of record** is prepared. Individuals holding stock at this date, as shown in the corporation stockholders' record, receive the dividend, regardless of sales or purchases of stock after this date. **No dividend entry is made in the accounts on this date.** The time between the declaration and record dates is provided so that all changes in share ownership can be registered with the transfer agents.

Ex-Dividend Date. Technically, the ex-dividend date is the day after the date of record. However, to provide time for transfer of the stock, the stock exchanges advance the effective ex-dividend date by three or four days. Thus, one who holds the stock on the day prior to the stipulated ex-dividend date receives the dividend.

Between the declaration date and the ex-dividend date, the market price of the stock includes the dividend. On the stipulated ex-dividend date, the price of the stock usually drops because the recipient of the dividend already has been identified, and succeeding owners of the stock will not receive that particular dividend. Thus, **under the revenue principle, dividend revenue is earned on the declaration date** and not on the date of record, the ex-dividend date, or the date of payment. The importance of the ex-dividend date is evidenced by a continuing topic, "Dividend News," in *The Wall Street Journal.* For example, the issue of September 9, 1987 reported the following:

Stocks Ex-Dividend September 10

Company	Amount	Company	Amount
Ametek Inc	.25	Mark Controls Corp	.08
Carolina Pw&lt $5pf	1.25	North Amer Phillips	.25
Charter Medical clA	.06	Northeast Sav F.A. pfA	.56¼
Charter Medical clB	.06	North'nlndPubSv adjpfA	.75
Chemical Waste Mgmt	.02	North'nlndPbSv 4¼ % pf	1.06¼
Chris Craft Ind $1 pf	.25	O'Sullivan Corp	.08
Chris Craft Ind $1.40pf	.70	Skyline Corp	.12
GATX Corp	.37½	Stanhome Inc	.23
General Housewares	.06	Starrett (LS) Co	.29
Green Mountain Power	.46½	TCW Conv Sec Fund	.13
Holly Sugar Corp	.25	Triangle Corp	.05
Kerr Glass Mfg pfB	.42½	Waste Management	.09

Date of Payment. This date also is determined by the board of directors and usually is stated in the declaration. The date of payment typically follows the declaration date by four to six weeks. At the date of payment of cash or property dividends, the liability recorded at date of declaration is debited and the appropriate asset account is credited.[2] A stock dividend distribution usually is recorded on the date of its issuance as illustrated in a subsequent section.

Types of Dividends

Cash Dividends. Cash dividends are the usual form of distributions to stockholders. The declaration must meet the preferences of the preferred stock and then may extend to the common stock.

To illustrate a cash dividend, assume the following announcement is made: The board of directors of Bass Company, at their meeting on January 20, 19A, declared a dividend of 50 cents per share, payable March 20, 19A, to stockholders of record on March 1, 19A. Assume that 10,000 shares of nopar capital stock are outstanding.

At date of declaration (January 20, 19A):

Retained earnings* (10,000 shares × $.50)	5,000	
Cash dividends payable		5,000

* Or Cash Dividends declared, which is later closed to Retained Earnings.

At date of record (March 1, 19A):

No entry. The list of dividend recipients is prepared as of this date. At date of payment (March 20, 19A):

Cash dividends payable	5,000	
Cash		5,000

Cash Dividends Payable is reported on the statement of financial position as a current liability if the duration of the dividend liability fits the definition of a current asset; otherwise, it is a long-term liability.

Property Dividends. Corporations occasionally pay dividends with noncash assets. Such dividends are called **property dividends.** The property may be investments in the securities of other companies held by the corporation, real estate, merchandise, or any other noncash asset designated by the board of directors. A property dividend is recorded at the current **market value** of the assets transferred in conformity with *APB Opinion 29*, "Accounting for Nonmonetary Transactions." Therefore, when the corporation's book value of the property to be distributed as the dividend is different from its market value on the declaration date, the corporation should recognize a gain or loss on disposal of the asset as of the declaration date. Most property dividends are paid with the securities of other companies that the dividend-issuing corporation has held as an investment. This kind of "property" avoids the problem of indivisibility of units that would occur with most noncash assets.

The following excerpt from the disclosure notes in the 1986 financial report of Interlake Corporation illustrates a property dividend (also called a dividend in kind):

---

[2] A cash or property dividend is a nonreciprocal transfer, which is defined as a transfer of assets or services in one direction. That is, either from an enterprise to its owners or another enterprise or from owners or another entity to the enterprise, with no assets or services coming from the other direction. Also, cash and property dividends are not paid on treasury stock.

> On June 23, 1986 The Interlake Corporation made a tax-free distribution (the Spin-Off) of shares in the Acme Steel Company, a wholly-owned subsidiary. Shareholders received one share in Acme Steel Company for each share of the Interlake Corporation common stock owned of record on June 9, 1986. No gain or loss was recorded arising from the Spin-Off. Retained earnings were charged \$131,477,000 for the book value of assets distributed, which comprised working capital of \$36,406,000, investments in associated companies and other long-term assets of \$26,940,000, property, plant and equipment of \$91,379,000 less long-term liabilities of \$23,248,000. Future adjustments relating to the Spin-Off amounts may occur, but are not expected to be material.

Assume for discussion purposes that Interlake *(a)* had 5,000 shares of its own common shares outstanding, *(b)* had paid \$100 for each share of Acme Steel Company it held as an investment (1,000 shares), and *(c)* carried the investment shares at cost (i.e., \$100,000). The market value of each Acme Steel Company share was \$150 on declaration date. The dividend transactions of Interlake would be recorded as follows:

At declaration date:

Investment in stock of Acme Steel [1,000 shares × (\$150 − \$100)]	50,000	
Gain on disposal of investment		50,000
Retained earnings (1,000 shares × \$150)	150,000	
Property dividend payable		150,000

At payment date:

Property dividend payable	150,000	
Investment in stock of Acme Steel		150,000

Liquidating Dividends. Distributions that are a **return of the amount received when stock was issued** rather than assets acquired through earnings are called **liquidating dividends.** Owners' equity accounts other than Retained Earnings are debited. Any dividend that is not based on retained earnings is a liquidating dividend to the extent that it is not debited to Retained Earnings. Liquidating dividends may be either **intentional** or **unintentional.**

Intentional liquidating dividends occur when the board of directors knowingly declares dividends that will, in effect, represent a return of investment, in whole or in part, to the stockholders, as when a corporation is reducing its permanent capital.

Mining companies sometimes pay dividends on the basis of earnings computed prior to the deduction for depletion. This would be an intentional liquidating dividend equal to the amount of depletion. A mining company might pay such a liquidating dividend when it is exploiting a nonreplaceable asset that no longer exists after it is fully exploited. Stockholders should be informed of the portion of any dividend that represents a return of capital. Such dividends are not investor-income and usually are not taxable to stockholders as income. Rather, they reduce the **cost basis** of the stock investment.

In accounting for liquidating dividends, an additional contributed capital account rather than Retained Earnings is debited because a portion of contributed capital is returned. Rather than debiting the capital stock accounts, as would be done if shares were being retired, other contributed capital accounts such as the "in excess of par" accounts may be debited. In some cases, it may be desirable to set up a special account, Capital Repayment, which would be reported as a deduction (contra account) in the contributed capital section of the statement of financial position. For example, assume Dako Corporation declared a cash dividend of $40,000 and informed the stockholders that 75% of it was a liquidating dividend. The entries would be:

At declaration date:

Retained earnings ($40,000 × 25%)	10,000	
Capital repayment ($40,000 × 75%)	30,000	
Dividends payable		40,000

At payment date:

Dividends payable	40,000	
Cash		40,000

Unintentional liquidating dividends may occur when the balance of retained earnings is overstated because of overstatement of income or other inappropriate accounting. For example, any error that overstated revenue or understated expense would cause retained earnings to be overstated. In such cases, if reported retained earnings (prior to correction) were used in full for dividends, part of the dividend would be a liquidating dividend. Unintentional liquidating dividends paid, and later discovered, would require an error-correcting entry to correct the Retained Earnings account and the other accounts that were affected.

The following excerpt from the *The Wall Street Journal* illustrates an actual liquidating dividend:

> Canal-Randolph Corp. directors authorized a second liquidating dividend of $33 a share, payable July 17 to stock of record July 12.
>
> Under the liquidation plan approved in April, the real estate and stockyard concern distributed its first liquidating dividend of $22 a share June 1.

Scrip Dividends. Sometimes a corporation that has a temporary cash shortage will declare a dividend to maintain its continuing dividend policy by issuing a scrip dividend. A scrip dividend (also called a **liability dividend**) occurs when the board of directors declares a dividend and issues promissory notes, called **scrip,** to the stockholders. This declaration means that a **comparatively long time** (e.g., six months or one year) will elapse between the declaration and payment dates. In most cases, scrip dividends are declared when a corporation has sufficient retained earnings as a basis for dividends but is short of cash. A stockholder may hold the scrip until due date and collect the dividend, or sell (i.e., discount) the scrip to a financial institution to obtain immediate cash. When scrip is used the due date and rate of interest are specified. Scrip usually is payable at a specified future date. The interest period usually is specified as the time from the declaration date to the payment date. However, if the dividend is payable part cash and part scrip, the interest period usually starts on the dividend payment date. A scrip or liability dividend is recorded as a debit to Retained Earnings and a credit to a liability account such as Scrip Dividends Payable or Notes Payable to Stockholders. On payment, the liability account is debited and the cash account is credited. Because interest paid on a liability dividend is not a part of the dividend, any interest payments should be debited to Interest Expense rather than directly to Retained Earnings as a part of the dividend. In other respects, accounting for a liability dividend is the same as for a cash dividend.

Assume DV Corporation declared a 19X dividend of $.25 per share on its 200,000 outstanding shares of nopar capital stock. Scrip was issued in full for the dividend that specified a 10% interest rate and a maturity date six months after declaration date.

At declaration date:

Retained earnings (200,000 shares × $.25)	50,000	
Scrip dividends payable (or notes payable to stockholders)		50,000

At scrip payment date:

Scrip dividends payable	50,000	
Interest expense ($50,000 × 10% × 6/12)	2,500	
Cash		52,500

Stock Dividends

A stock dividend is a **proportional** distribution to stockholders of **additional shares of common or preferred stock** of the corporation. **A stock dividend does not change the assets, liabilities, or total stockholders' equity of the issuing corporation. It does not change the proportionate ownership of any stockholder.** Rather, it usually causes the transfer of an amount from Retained Earnings to the contributed (permanent) capital accounts (e.g., capital stock and contributed capital in excess of par). Therefore, it only changes the **internal content** of stockholders' equity between contributed capital and retained earnings. If additional contributed capital accounts are debited in full for a stock dividend, retained earnings is unaffected.

A stock dividend may be issued from treasury stock or unissued stock. When a stock dividend is of the same class as that held by the recipients, it is called an **ordinary** stock dividend. When a class of stock other than the one already held by the recipients is issued, such a dividend is called a **special** stock dividend (e.g., preferred shares issued to the common stockholders).

Numerous reasons exist for a company to issue a stock dividend, such as the following:

1. To permanently retain earnings in the business by **capitalizing** a portion of the retained earnings. The effect of a stock dividend, through a debit to Retained Earnings and offsetting credits to permanent capital accounts, is to raise the contributed (and legal) capital and thereby "shelter" the new legal capital from future declaration of cash or property dividends.
2. To continue dividend distributions without disbursing assets (usually cash) that may be needed for operations. This action may be motivated by a desire to pacify stockholders; they may be willing to accept a stock dividend representing accumulated earnings because the stockholder can sell these additional shares. Ordinary stock dividends are not subject to income tax to stockholders. Instead, they reduce the investment cost **per share** to the investor.

3. To increase the number of shares outstanding, which reduces the market price per share and which, in turn, tends to increase trading of shares in the market. More small investors can afford investments in equity securities if the unit cost is low. Stock dividends also reduce earnings per share.

The three primary issues in accounting for stock dividends are the values that should be recognized, the accounts and dates that should be used, and the manner of disclosure in the financial statements.

Accounting Issues Related to Ordinary Stock Dividends. There is considerable disagreement among accountants about the values that should be recognized for stock dividends. The basic issue, aside from the availability of retained earnings and amounts of unissued stock and treasury stock, is whether the stock issued for the dividend should be recorded at market value, at par or stated value, or at some other value.

A stock dividend usually is based on the availability of retained earnings. Therefore, the question arises as to the amount of retained earnings to capitalize (i.e., transfer to contributed capital). First, state laws and GAAP do not establish a maximum. Therefore, the board of directors has the authority to capitalize whatever amount it desires, subject to certain specified legal and contractual constraints (e.g., the retained earnings restriction for the cost of treasury stock held). Second, state laws vary as to *(a)* the availability of additional contributed capital as a basis for stock dividends and *(b)* the **minimum** amount of retained earnings that must be capitalized for a stock dividend. With respect to the availability of **additional contributed capital** as a basis for a stock dividend, a few states permit any type of additional contributed capital to be used, other states prohibit its use, while still others only permit the use of additional contributed capital in excess of the par or stated value of the stock. Regarding the **minimum** amount of retained earnings that must be capitalized, the statutory minimum in most states is par or stated value. If the stock is true nopar, the minimum amount is the average per share originally paid in.

Because of the lack of agreement about the validity of market value versus par value and the resulting diversity in recording stock dividends, the AICPA Committee on Accounting Procedures issued *ARB 43*, which reaffirmed two distinct situations affecting the amount of retained earnings for an **ordinary** stock dividend:

Situation 1—Small Stock Dividend; Market Value Method. When the proportion of the additional shares issued is **small** in relation to the total shares **previously outstanding** (i.e., less than 20–25% of the outstanding shares), the **current market value** of the additional shares should be capitalized. The market value of the stock dividend is measured on the basis of the market price per share **immediately after** the stock dividend is **issued.** The Committee on Accounting Procedure of the AICPA rationalized this position as follows:

> . . . many recipients of stock dividends look upon them as distributions of corporate earnings and usually in an amount equivalent to the [market] value of the additional shares received. Furthermore, it is to be presumed that such views of

> recipients are materially strengthened in those instances, which are by far the most numerous, where the issuances are so small in comparison with the shares previously outstanding that they do not have any apparent effect upon the share market price and, consequently, the market value of the shares previously held remains substantially unchanged. The committee therefore believes that where these circumstances exist the corporation should in the public interest account for the transaction by transferring from [retained earnings] to the category of permanent capitalization . . . an amount equal to the [market] value of the additional shares issued [i.e., the market value immediately after issuance].[3]

Use of **market value immediately after issuance** is further suggested because the market price per share, in the case of a small stock dividend, may not drop proportionately to the increased number of shares outstanding after the dividend. When market price per share does not drop proportionately, the stockholders receive a real value increase in their holdings.

Situation 2—Large Stock Dividend; Par Value Method. When the proportion of the additional shares issued is **large** in relation to the total shares previously outstanding (i.e., more than 20–25%), no less than the legal minimum (usually par, or stated value, or average paid in for nopar stock) should be capitalized. If the dividends is in the 20–25% range, a judgment call is available based on the situation. The committee, giving the appearance of a political compromise, continued the rationalization as follows:

> Where the number of additional shares issued as a stock dividend is so great that it has, or may reasonably be expected to have, the effect of materially reducing the share market value, the committee believes that the implications and possible constructions discussed in the [above quotation] are not likely to exist. . . . Consequently, the committee considers that under such circumstances there is no need to capitalize [retained earnings], other than to the extent occasioned by legal requirements.[4]

Although *ARB 43* was intended to settle the issue for current GAAP purposes, the disagreement continues. Strong arguments are made for the par value method, as a minimum, because *(a)* legal capital is preserved, *(b)* the corporation's assets, liabilities, and total stockholders' equity are not changed, and *(c)* the stockholders' proportionate ownership is not changed. Arguments based on market value changes lack persuasive validity because of measurement problems. However, it is generally recognized that if a company doubles its number of shares outstanding by issuing a stock dividend, the competitive market price necessarily will reduce by one half, absent any other market variables.

Recording a Stock Dividend. Fundamentally, a stock dividend is recorded as a debit to retained earnings and a credit to the capital stock issued. In addition to the "large and small" dividend distinction discussed above, there are disagreements about whether market price (when used) should be determined at declaration or issuance date. When market value is used, any excess of that price

---

[3] AICPA, *Accounting Research Bulletin 43*, "Restatement and Revision of Accounting Research Bulletins" (New York, 1953), chap. 7, sec. B, par. 10.

[4] Ibid.

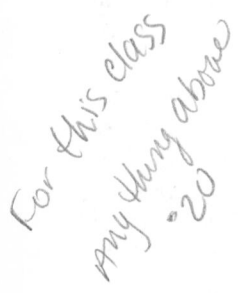

above par or stated value must be measured. Clearly this excess cannot be measured prior to the market value date. *ARB 43*, ch. 7, par. 10, specifies that for a small stock dividend market value at issuance date must be used. Since that source uses the word **issuance** exclusively throughout (declaration is never mentioned), many accountants believe that market value at issuance date (if used) also applies to a large stock dividend. However, such a belief is not supported by subsequent interpretations.

As already explained, the declaration of a stock dividend is revocable prior to issuance date. Given this contingency and the market-price problem discussed above, many accountants do not make an originating journal entry on declaration date, rather they make the originating journal entry on issuance date. Moreover, whether or not the originating entry is made on the declaration or issuance date, a disclosure note is needed for financial statements prepared **between** these two dates. Given these considerations, either recording approach can be used with precisely the same results as follows:

Declaration date—declared a 10% common stock dividend; issued 10,000 shares, par $1; market value immediately after **issuance,** $5 per share.

	Originating entry date at			
	Declaration		**Issuance**	
Declaration date (market price not known):				
Retained earnings	10,000		None	
Stock dividends issuable*		10,000		
* Reported as a credit under stockholders' equity until issuance.	Also use disclosure note		Use disclosure note	
Issuance date (market price known):				
Retained earnings	40,000		50,000	
Stock dividends issuable	10,000			
Common stock		10,000		10,000
Contributed capital in excess of par (or stated) value		40,000		40,000

Clearly, the differences between these two approaches are trivial; either one satisfies GAAP in all respects.

treasury stock does part. in stock split

Special Stock Dividends

In the case of **special** stock dividends, such as a stock dividend in preferred stock issued to common stockholders, the market value of the dividend (i.e., the preferred) shares should be capitalized by the issuing corporation. Issuance of the dividend shares usually would not be expected to have much impact on the market value of the other (i.e., the common) stock. In this instance, stockholders would appear to receive a dividend equal to the market value of the dividend shares received.

Exhibit 17–1 provides a comprehensive example of the issuance of:

Case A—a small stock dividend, market value method; **Case B**—a large stock dividend, par value method; **Case C**—a large stock dividend, average paid in method, and **Case D**—a special stock dividend.

Exhibit 17–1
Stock dividend entries—AZ Corporation.

Panel A—Case Data Prior to the Dividend:

Preferred stock, par value $20, 10,000 shares authorized, 5,000 shares outstanding	$100,000
Common stock, par value $10, 20,000 shares authorized, 10,000 shares outstanding	100,000
Contributed capital in excess of par, preferred stock	10,000
Contributed capital in excess of par, common stock	15,000
Retained earnings	150,000
Total stockholders' equity	$375,000

Market price per share immediately **before** issuance of dividend shares: Preferred, $25; Common, $24.

Panel B—Stock Dividend Entry at Date of Issuance of Dividend Shares (each situation is independent):

Case A—a small stock dividend; market value method: A 10% common stock dividend (i.e., one additional common share is issued for each 10 shares already held) is declared on the common stock. The market price remains $24 per share. Management elected to capitalize market value.

Retained earnings (1,000 shares at market, $24)	24,000	
Common stock, par $10 (1,000 shares)		10,000
Contributed capital in excess of par, common stock		14,000

Case B—A large stock dividend; par value method: A 50% common stock dividend (i.e., one additional common share for each two shares already held) is declared on the common stock. The market value per share drops immediately to $16. Management decides to capitalize par value.

Retained earnings (5,000 shares at par, $10)	50,000	
Common stock, par $10 (5,000 shares)		50,000

Case C—A large stock dividend; average paid-in method: A 50% common stock dividend is declared on the common stock. The market value drops immediately to $16 per share. Management decides to capitalize on the basis of the average paid in (more than par).

Retained earnings (5,000 shares at $11.50*)	57,500	
Common stock, par $10 (5,000 shares)		50,000
Contributed capital in excess of par, common stock		7,500

* Computation: ($100,000 + $15,000) ÷ 10,000 shares = $11.50.

Case D—A special stock dividend: A 20% common stock dividend (i.e., one additional share for each five shares already held) is issued to both common and preferred stockholders. The market price per share does not change appreciably after issuance from $24.

Retained earnings, (3,000 shares* at $24)	72,000	
Common stock, par $10 (3,000 shares)		30,000
Contributed capital in excess of par, common stock		42,000

* Computation: (10,000 + 5,000 shares) × 20% = 3,000 shares.

To conclude the discussion of **stock dividends,** it is appropriate to reemphasize that an important aspect of such dividends is that an amount of the retained earnings often is transferred to contributed (permanent) capital (i.e., "capitalized"). This transfer shows that the company has "grown through earnings" by permanently removing such earnings from dividend availability. For many corporations, a large amount of their contributed capital came from this source.

Therefore, the reported retained earnings of many companies is much less than their total accumulated earnings, minus cash and property dividends paid, over the life of the corporation.

Dividends and Treasury Stock

Dividends are not paid on treasury stock because it would involve recording by a corporation of a transaction with itself. However, treasury stock may be used for the issuance of a stock dividend. If treasury stock is used for this purpose, the stock dividend should be recorded as a debit to Retained Earnings (or other appropriate account) for the **market value** of the treasury stock issued and a credit to Treasury Stock for the **book value** of the treasury stock issued. Any difference is debited or credited to an appropriate additional contributed capital account. If additional contributed capital is insufficient to make up the debit difference, the excess should be debited to retained earnings.

In respect to treasury stock, a stock dividend usually is not deemed to increase the number of shares of treasury stock held.

Fractional Share Rights

Fractional share rights usually must be issued with a stock dividend when the stock dividend is not on a one-for-one (i.e., 100%) basis. For example, if stockholder A owned 150 shares of AZ Corporation's common stock, and the corporation issued a 15% stock dividend, stockholder A should receive 150 shares × 15% = 22½ shares. Because parts of a share cannot be issued, the corporation would issue 22 full shares and one fractional share **right** equivalent to half of a share of common stock. Soon after issuance, such stock rights usually are traded on the market. Stockholder A could purchase one of these rights from another stockholder, and then turn in the two rights for another share of stock.

To illustrate the accounting for fractional share rights related to a stock dividend, **Exhibit 17–2** extends the stock dividend case of AZ Corporation given in Exhibit 17–1. Panel A restates the illustrative data; panel B gives the entries to record the stock dividend, including fractional share rights, under varying specifications; and panel C presents the effects on the financial statements. In Exhibit 17–2, panel C, notice that stock rights outstanding are reported along with the related capital stock account. Also notice that the sum of all fractional share rights (1,350) represents a lower number of full shares (270 shares in this instance).

Legality of Dividends

Retained earnings and certain elements of contributed capital as a basis for dividends has already been mentioned. Precise identification of the elements of stockholders' equity that are available for cash, property, and stock dividends, respectively, would require study of the laws of each state. However, at least two provisions appear to be uniform: (1) dividends may not be paid from **legal capital** (usually represented in the capital stock accounts—par value, stated value, and average paid in on nopar stock); and (2) retained earnings are available for dividends unless there is a contractual or statutory restriction (e.g., cost of

Exhibit 17–2
Fractional share rights in a stock dividend—AZ Corporation.

Stock dividends Par does not change.
Stock split – par value changes.

Panel A—Case Data:

1. AZ Corporation declared a 20% (i.e., 1 for 5) stock dividend on the 10,000 shares outstanding of its common stock, par $10 (i.e., a stock dividend of 2,000 common shares).
2. The market value of the common shares before the stock dividend was $24.
3. Of the 2,000 dividend shares, 1,730 full shares were issued, in addition to 1,350 fractional share rights for the remaining 270 shares. Each fractional share right represented one fifth of a share of stock (i.e., 1,350 fractional share rights × ⅕ share each = 270 shares). These fractional share rights were issued to stockholders that held numbers of shares not evenly divisible by five (e.g., a holder of nine shares would receive one additional share plus four fractional share rights of ⅕ share each). Thus, to obtain one common share, five such rights must be presented to AZ Corporation.

Panel B—Stock Dividend Entries:

1. Date of issuance of dividend shares, including fractional share rights (dividend assumed to be "small" therefore, market value is capitalized); the market price did not change:

Retained earnings, (2,000 shares at market, $24)	48,000	
Common stock, par $10 (1,730 shares × $10)		17,300
Common stock rights outstanding (1,350 rights for 270 shares at par $10)		2,700
Contributed capital in excess of par, common stock (2,000 shares × $14*)		28,000

* Market value, $24 − Par value, $10 = Premium, $14.

2. Date of disposition of fractional share rights under three different cases:

Case A—All fractional share rights are turned in to AZ Corporation, and the 270 shares are issued.

Common stock rights outstanding (1,350 rights)	2,700	
Common stock, par $10 (270 shares)		2,700

Case B—Only 90% of the rights are turned in for 243 shares (i.e., 270 × 90%), and the remainder lapse.

Common stock rights outstanding	2,700	
Common stock, par $10 (243 shares)		2,430
Contributed capital, lapse of stock rights (135 rights for 27 shares, par $10)		270

Case C—Assume AZ Corporation did not issue fractional share rights (entry 1). Instead, it paid stockholders the market value of $4.80 (i.e., $24 ÷ 5) for each fractional share right. The issuance of the stock dividend would be recorded as follows (instead of entry 1):

Retained earnings (2,000 shares at market, $24)	48,000	
Common stock, par $10 (1,730 shares × $10)		17,300
Contributed capital in excess of par, common stock (1,730 shares × $14)		24,220
Cash (1,350 fractional share rights × $4.80)		6,480

Exhibit 17–2
(concluded)

Panel C—Financial Statement Presentation of Effects of Stock Dividend:
Including fractional share rights, between date of issuance (entry 1 above) and date of disposition of fractional share rights (entry 2). For basic data, see Exhibit 17–1, panel A.

AZ CORPORATION
Stockholders' Equity

Contributed capital:		
Capital stock:		
Preferred stock, $20 par value, 10,000 shares authorized, 5,000 shares outstanding		$100,000
Common stock, $10 par value, 20,000 shares authorized, 11,730 shares outstanding	$117,300	
Common stock fractional share rights outstanding (for 270 shares)	**2,700**	120,000
Total capital stock		220,000
Other contributed capital:		
Contributed capital in excess of par, preferred stock	10,000	
Contributed capital in excess of par, common stock [$15,000 (Exhibit 17–1) + $28,000 (entry 1 above)]	43,000	53,000
Total contributed capital		273,000
Retained earnings:		
Unappropriated [$150,000 (Exhibit 17–1) – $48,000 (entry 1 above)]		102,000
Total stockholders' equity		$375,000

treasury stock held). With these two provisions, numerous variations exist, depending upon the state statutes and the type of dividend, such as the following:

1. All contributed capital, other than legal capital, is available for dividends.
2. Specified items of contributed capital, other than legal capital, are available for dividends.
3. Contributed capital, other than legal capital, is available for dividends on preferred stock but not on common stock.
4. Unrealized capital is not available for any kind of dividends.
5. Unrealized capital is available for stock dividends only.
6. Debits in the additional contributed capital accounts and a deficit in retained earnings must be restored before payment of any dividends.
7. Dividends from retained earnings must not reduce the retained earnings balance below the cost of treasury stock held.

The accountant has a responsibility when the legality or accounting treatment of dividends is at issue to *(a)* ensure that such matters are referred to an attorney and *(b)* ascertain that the financial statements disclose all material facts concerning such dividends.

Stock Splits

A stock split is a change in the number of shares outstanding accompanied by an offsetting change in the par or stated value per share. A stock split is implemented by either calling in all of the old shares and concurrently issuing the split shares, or by issuing the additional split shares with notification to the stockholder of the change in par or stated value per share of all shares.

The primary purpose of a stock split often is explained on the basis that the resulting increase in shares outstanding will decrease the market price per share. In turn, this will increase the market activity of the stocks and prices will rise. A stock split also reduces earnings per share. In a **pure** (i.e., typical or normal) stock split, no accounting entry is needed because there is no change in the dollar amounts in the capital stock account (i.e., legal capital), additional contributed capital, or retained earnings. Instead, the increase in the number of shares is exactly counterbalanced by a proportional reduction in the par or stated value per share (after the split). Therefore, in a pure stock split, the following dollar amounts are **not changed:** (1) capital stock account (i.e., legal capital), (2) additional contributed capital accounts, (3) retained earnings, and (4) total stockholders' equity. The following items are **changed:** (1) par or stated value per share and (2) shares issued, outstanding, in treasury, and subscribed.

To illustrate a 200% (two new shares for each old share called in) pure stock split, and to compare it with a 100% stock dividend (one additional share for each share already outstanding), assume Split Corporation is authorized to issue 200,000 shares of common stock, par $10, of which 40,000 shares were issued initially at par, and retained earnings has a current balance of $450,000. The different effects of a 100% stock dividend and a 200% pure stock split may be contrasted as shown below:

Split Corporation—Stock dividend and stock split compared.

Shares outstanding		Par per share		Prior to stock dividend or stock split	100% stock dividend	200% stock split
40,000	×	$10	=	$400,000		
80,000	×	10	=		$800,000*	
80,000	×	5	=			$400,000
Total contributed capital				400,000	800,000	400,000
Retained earnings				450,000	50,000*	450,000
Total stockholders' equity				$850,000	$850,000	$850,000

* Retained earnings capitalized: 40,000 shares × $10 = $400,000; entry: Debit retained earnings $400,000, credit contributed capital accounts, $400,000.

Notice that the stock dividend changed both contributed capital and retained earnings. The stock split, however, changed neither of these amounts. Total stockholders' equity was unchanged by either the stock dividend or the stock split. The word **pure** is used because a typical or normal stock split was described. During the past several years, some stock splits have been issued that did not exactly maintain the offsetting relationship between the split shares and the change in the par or stated value per share, such as a 2 for 1 stock on $10 par value stock and a reduction of par value per share to $6. Also, some financial statements inappropriately refer to a **stock dividend** as a stock split. A reverse stock split decreases the number of shares. It also involves a proportional **increase** in the par or stated value per share.

Appropriations and Restrictions of Retained Earnings

From time to time, retained earnings may be **appropriated** as a result of management action or **restricted** by contract or law. An appropriation and a restriction of retained earnings involve a constraint on a specified portion of accumulated earnings for a specific purpose. Such specific appropriations and restrictions nevertheless represent a part of **total** retained earnings. Thus, retained earnings is comprised of two subcategories: (1) appropriated and restricted retained earnings, and (2) unappropriated retained earnings.[5]

Appropriations and restrictions of retained earnings usually are recorded as debits to the Retained Earnings account (i.e., unappropriated retained earnings) and credits to descriptively designated **appropriation or restriction of retained earnings** accounts. This is a convenient way to provide information for reporting and/or disclosing appropriations and restrictions. Some companies still inappropriately use the word **reserve** in the titles of appropriation and restriction accounts, such as "Reserve for Retained Earnings Invested in the Business." For **reporting purposes** on the financial statements, the appropriations and restrictions may be reported by any one of three approaches:

1. Report each appropriation and restriction as a separate item on the statement of retained earnings.
2. Report appropriations and restrictions parenthetically on the statement of retained earnings.
3. Disclose appropriations and restrictions in the notes to the financial statements.

When the need for an appropriation or restriction no longer exists, or management decides it is not needed, the appropriated balance is returned to the unappropriated retained earnings account. This is done by making an entry reversing the one that initially set up the appropriation.

Retained earnings are appropriated and restricted primarily to protect the **cash position** of the corporation by reducing the amount of cash dividends that otherwise might be paid. Appropriations and restrictions of retained earnings arise in the following situations:

1. To fulfill a **legal requirement,** as in the case of a restriction by state law on retained earnings equivalent to the cost of treasury stock held.
2. To fulfill a **contractual agreement,** as in the case of a debt covenant that stipulates a restriction on the use of retained earnings for dividends that require the disbursement of assets.
3. To report a discretionary appropriation by the board of directors to constrain a specified portion of retained earnings as an aspect of **financial planning.**
4. To report a discretionary appropriation by the board of directors of a specified portion of retained earnings in anticipation of **possible future losses.**

The appropriation or restriction of retained earnings by transferring an amount from retained earnings to an **appropriated** retained earnings account has no effect on assets. An appropriation is a "clerical" identification. It does not set aside specific assets such as cash. This effect would occur only if as a separate action, cash also is set aside in a separate fund, such as a bond sinking fund.

[5] Accountants traditionally use the term **appropriation of retained earnings** to include both appropriations and restrictions, but not the other way around; only the source is different. We use these terms in the traditional way.

Types of Appropriations and Restrictions Illustrated

Restriction Required by Law. To protect creditors and others, the laws of some states place a restriction on retained earnings equal to the cost of treasury stock held. This legal restriction could be recorded as follows:

End of year 19A—treasury stock held, cost, $20,000:

Retained earnings	20,000	
Retained earnings restricted for cost of treasury stock		20,000
Report the $20,000 restriction in the financial statements by one of the three approaches listed above.		

End of year 19B—one fourth of the treasury stock is still held:

Retained earnings restricted for cost of treasury stock	15,000	
Retained earnings		15,000
Report the remaining $5,000 restriction in the financial statements.		

Restriction Required by Contract. To offer security to lenders, credit agreements often include various provisions restricting payment of cash and property dividends. One type of provision calls for the periodic **restriction** of a specific amount of retained earnings similar to the restriction illustrated above. Another common provision called **funding** requires *(a)* the periodic deposit of a specific amount of **cash** in a fund, held by a trustee, and *(b)* a restriction of retained earnings to match the funding.

To illustrate the latter situation, assume that Y Corporation issued $500,000 bonds payable, and the bond indenture required the issuer to restrict $10,000 of retained earnings annually, in addition to depositing the same amount of cash each year in a bond sinking fund. The entries at the start would be:

To establish the restriction:

Retained earnings	10,000	
Retained earnings restricted for bonds payable		10,000

To establish the bond sinking fund:

Bond sinking fund	10,000	
Cash		10,000

The next statement of financial position would report the bond sinking fund as an asset under "Investments and funds." It would also report the $10,000 restriction using one of the three approaches listed above. When the bonds mature, the cash accumulated in the bond sinking fund would be used to pay the maturity amount. The restriction account balance then would be returned to the unrestricted retained earnings account.

Appropriated Retained Earnings for Financial Planning. Many corporations that begin with a small initial capital investment grow by retaining a large portion of their earnings in the business. In such cases, it may be desirable to capitalize a portion of accumulated earnings by issuing stock dividends. The board of directors also may disclose their intention not to use a specific amount of retained earnings for cash or property dividends by establishing discretionary appropriation accounts such as the following:

Retained Earnings Appropriated for Investment in Plant.

Retained Earnings Appropriated for Working Capital.

Some companies also establish a fund, such as a building fund, to accumulate cash needed to acquire additional operational assets.

Appropriation for Possible Future Losses. In case of possible future losses, the board of directors will sometimes direct that a portion of retained earnings be appropriated and identified with titles such as the following:

Retained Earnings Appropriated for Possible Future Inventory Cost Declines.[6]
Retained Earnings Appropriated for Possible Loss in Pending Lawsuit.
Retained Earnings Appropriated for Self-Insurance.

Even if the event does happen, any actual loss arising therefrom should be recorded as an ordinary, unusual or infrequent, or extraordinary item. This would be done whether or not there is a related appropriation account. Such **losses should not be debited to the appropriation account.** After the loss is recognized as a deduction to derive net income, the appropriation should be returned to unappropriated retained earnings. Thus, the effect of having reported the appropriation prior to the loss was to *(a)* hold back an equivalent amount of retained earnings from dividends and treasury stock transactions, and *(b)* report unappropriated retained earnings at the same balance that would exist if the event occurred during the current year and was reported on the statement of income. The primary purpose of appropriations is communication to statement users since dividends are issued at the discretion of the board of directors.

For all types of appropriations and restrictions the purpose during the relevant period is to protect cash by removing specific amounts from availability to be paid as current dividends. Once an appropriation or restriction is returned to unappropriated retained earnings, the full amount once again becomes available for dividends.

Reporting Retained Earnings

Under GAAP, the statement of retained earnings may include the following:

1. Beginning balance of retained earnings.
2. Restatement of beginning balance for prior period adjustments.
3. Restatement of beginning balance for retroactive-type accounting changes.
4. Net income or loss for the period.
5. Dividends.
6. Appropriations and restrictions of retained earnings.
7. Adjustments made pursuant to a quasi-reorganization.
8. Ending balance of retained earnings (the result).

Exhibit 17–3 illustrates the reporting of the above items (except for item 7 above, quasi-reorganization). Supplement 17–A discusses quasi-reorganizations.

[6] An appropriation for possible future inventory cost decline is not the same account discussed in Chapter 9 with respect to the valuation of inventory at LCM (Allowance to Reduce Inventory to Lower-of-Cost-or-Market). That account was related to a cost decline that had **already** materialized. The appropriation account relates to a **possible** cost decline in the **future.**

Exhibit 17–3
Statement of retained earnings; reporting prior period adjustments and appropriations.

Panel A—Basic Case Data (RST Corporation):

1. For the year ended December 31, 19K, RST Corporation reported the following:
   a. Retained earnings balance, December 31, 19J, $158,000.
   b. Net income, $52,000.
   c. Dividends declared and paid, $30,000.
2. During 19K, it was discovered that 19J depreciation expense was understated by $20,000 (the applicable tax rate during 19J was 30%). An amended tax return was submitted for 19J.

Panel B—Reporting Retained Earnings:

RST CORPORATION
Statement of Retained Earnings
For Year Ended December 31, 19K

Balance in retained earnings, 1/1/19K	$158,000
Adjustments applicable to prior periods (a debit):	
Correction of accounting error in 19J, net of $6,000 income tax saving (see Note 4)	(14,000)
Balance in retained earnings, 1/1/19K, as corrected	144,000
Add: Net income for 19K	52,000
Total	196,000
Deduct: Dividends for 19K	(30,000)
Balance in retained earnings, 12/31/19K (see Note 5)	$166,000

(reconcile order)

Note 4: During 19J, the company inadvertently understated depreciation expense by $20,000. This accounting error caused an overstatement of the reported income of 19J, and of the balance in retained earnings at December 31, 19J (January 1, 19K), by $14,000, which reflects the $6,000 tax effect of the error. The error was detected and corrected during 19K by debiting Retained Earnings for a Prior Period Adjustment in the aftertax amount of $14,000. To correct other affected accounts, an income tax receivable was set up for the $6,000 tax saving and Accumulated Depreciation was increased by $20,000.

Note 5: Appropriations and restrictions:

Appropriation for investment in plant	$ 35,000
Restriction for cost of treasury stock	25,000
Unappropriated retained earnings	106,000
Total retained earnings	$166,000

PART B: STOCK RIGHTS AND OPTIONS

Stock Rights and Warrants

Corporations often issue **stock rights** that provide the holder with an option to acquire a specified number of shares of capital stock in the corporation under prescribed conditions and within a stated future time period. When rights are issued to **current stockholders,** the corporation issues **one stock right for each share of stock owned.** However, it may take more than one right to acquire an additional share of stock.

Evidence of ownership of one or more stock rights is a certificate called a **stock warrant.**[7] A stock warrant typically specifies *(a)* the number of rights represented by the warrant, *(b)* the option price (which may be zero) per share of the specified stock, *(c)* the number of rights required to obtain a share of

[7] Stock rights sometimes are referred to as stock warrants.

the stock, *(d)* the expiration date of the rights, and *(e)* instructions for exercising the rights. When more than one right is required to obtain one share of stock in the future, the rights represent fractional shares and they are called **fractional share rights.**

Three dates are important regarding stock rights: (1) **announcement date** of the rights offering, (2) **issuance date** of the rights, and (3) **expiration date** of the rights. Between the announcement date and the issuance date of the rights, the related stock will sell **rights on.** That is, the price of the stock will be increased by the value of the rights because the stock and the rights are not separable during that period of time. After the issuance date of the rights and until expiration of the rights, the shares and rights sell **separately.** That is, the **shares** sell **ex rights** during this period of time and the **rights** have a separate price.

Stock rights received by a stockholder may be: (1) **exercised** by purchasing additional shares of the specified stock from the corporation, (2) **sold** at the market value of the rights, or (3) allowed to **lapse** on the expiration date.

Cases in which corporations often issue stock rights and options include the following:

1. To give **existing stockholders** the first chance to buy additional shares when the corporation decides to raise additional equity capital by selling a large amount of **unissued shares.**
2. As **compensation to outsiders** (such as underwriters, promoters, and professionals) for services provided to the corporation.
3. To represent fractional shares when a **stock dividend** is declared and issued (illustrated in Exhibit 17–2).
4. As additional **compensation to officers** and other employees of the corporation. These rights often are referred to as **stock options or stock incentive plans.**
5. To enhance the **marketability of other securities** issued by the corporation. These include issuing common stock rights with convertible bonds payable (discussed and illustrated in Chapter 15).

Accounting for Stock Rights

The issuance of stock rights causes accounting problems for **both** the recipient (i.e., the investor) and the issuing corporation. Stock rights received on corporate stock held by an **investor** have no additional cost. Therefore, the current carrying value of the shares already owned is **allocated** by the **investor** between the original shares and the rights received, based on the then-current market values. Accounting for rights received by investors is discussed in Chapter 18.

Accounting for stock rights by the **issuing corporation** involves either a memorandum entry or a regular journal entry on each of the three relevant dates defined above: (1) announcement date, (2) issuance date, and (3) expiration date. Cases 1 through 4 (listed above) are discussed below. Case 5 was discussed in Chapter 15.

Case 1—issuance of stock rights related to a planned sale (primarily to existing stockholders) of unissued stock. In this case, stock rights may be issued ir advance of the planned sale date to give current stockholders the "first chance" to purchase the new shares being offered for sale.

Case data:

	Amount
X Corporation account balances prior to the decision to issue rights:	
Common stock, par $10, authorized 100,000 shares, issued and outstanding 30,000 shares	$300,000
Contributed capital in excess of par, common stock	150,000
Retained earnings	70,000

Decision of X Corporation:

- To increase the outstanding shares by 50% (i.e., to issue 15,000 additional shares).
- Issue price per share to current stockholders—$30 plus two stock rights.
- Announcement date: January 1, 19J.
- Issue date for rights: March 1, 19J.
- Expiration date for rights: September 1, 19J.

Market prices:

Rights—Between issuance and expiration dates, average $5 per right.
Stock —At announcement date, $30 per share.
—At issue date, $30 per share.
—At expiration date, $34 per share.

Journal entries by X Corporation:

January 1, 19J—Announcement date—no entry (because it is not a completed transaction).

March 1, 19J—Issuance date—memorandum only (because there is no flow of resources; the option price and the market price are the same ($30). There is only a commitment to issue shares contingent upon the future actions of the other party. The memo expresses that commitment):

Memo—Issued 30,000 stock rights to current stockholders for 15,000 shares of stock to be sold. Each share will be sold for $30 cash plus the receipt of two stock rights. After September 1, 19J, all outstanding rights will expire and the remaining shares will be sold in the market at the then-current market price.

July 1, 19J—Exercise date—1,000 stock rights exercised by one stockholder (a completed transaction with resource flows):

Cash (1,000 rights ÷ 2 = 500 shares) × $30	15,000	
Common stock, par $10 (500 shares)		5,000
Contributed capital in excess of par, common stock		10,000
(Remaining rights outstanding, 29,000 for 14,500 shares of common stock.)		

Case 2—compensation to outsiders. A corporation sometimes needs to conserve cash during the early part of its life. Therefore, it may issue some of its own shares for professional services rendered. In some instances, **stock rights** rather than shares are issued.

Assume the same data as in Case 1. In addition, a decision was made to issue Attorney Brown 100 stock rights that specified a $30 option price. The rights were issued as payment for legal services. The rights were issued on March 1, 19J, expire on December 31, 19J, and were exercised by Brown on July 1, 19J. At that time the market value of the stock was $35. The required journal entries are:

March 1, 19J—Issue date (payment of a liability is a completed transaction):

Expense (legal services)	250	
Stock rights outstanding (100 rights ÷ 2 = 50 shares × $5)		250

July 1, 19J—Exercise date:

Cash (50 shares × $30)	1,500	
Stock rights outstanding (for 50 shares × $5)	250	
Common stock, par $10 (50 shares)		500
Contributed capital in excess of par, common stock ($35 − $10) × 50 shares		1,250

During the period the stock rights are outstanding, the item "Stock rights outstanding (for 50 shares), $250" should be reported under stockholders' equity as a positive item along with the capital stock account to which it relates.

Case 3—stock rights issued with a stock dividend. This case was illustrated in Exhibit 17–2.

Case 4—stock rights issued with employee incentive compensation plans. This is a complex case; it is discussed under the next caption.

Stock Option Incentive Plans for Employees

The discussion of corporations is concluded with stock option plans because they usually involve the issuance of capital stock. Corporations often establish stock option plans whereby shares of stock in the company are issued to employees over a period of time. For example, 542 of the 600 companies reported in *Accounting Trends & Techniques, 1987*, disclosed stock option plans. The purposes of stock option plans are varied. They may be used to help recruit and retain outstanding employees, to encourage ownership in the company by employees, and to obtain additional resources from equity owners. Often **stock options** (represented by stock rights) are granted to a particular group of employees to purchase common stock over an extended period of time as a form of additional compensation to encourage superior performance.

Plans for the issuance of capital stock to employees are designated with a variety of terms, none of which has been accorded standard usage. For instance, Hewlett-Packard Company refers to its plan simply as a "stock option plan." Fairchild Industries, Inc., refers to its plan as a "stock incentive plan." Interlake, Inc., has a "stock incentive program" consisting of a "stock appreciation rights plan," a "stock awards plan," and a restricted "stock purchase plan." In stock option plans, the issuing corporation is designated as the **grantor,** and the employee recipient is designated as the **grantee.**

The most important characteristic of a stock option plan from an accounting

[handwritten margin notes:]
ⓐ Employees pay on full / (grantor to employee) — no cost to company + no compensation to employee
ⓑ Option price is above market price of the stock at date of grant
If not both of these then it is

Equals all employees everyone eligible approx market price limited time

perspective is whether the plan causes **additional expense to the company.** Thus, for accounting purposes, the distinction is between the following two basic categories of stock option incentive plans for employees:

1. **Noncompensatory plans**—These plans specify the issuance of company stock to employees at a price that is **not significantly less** than the **market price.** Thus, (a) **no additional cost** to the company and (b) **no additional compensation** to the employee are recognized. An example of a noncompensatory plan is the employee stock purchase plan of Kaman Corporation. Kaman disclosed the following in the notes to its 1986 annual report:

Stock Purchase Plan

The Kaman Corporation Employees Stock Purchase Plan allows employees to purchase Class A common stock of the Company, through payroll deductions, at 85% of the average market value of the shares at the time of purchase. The original plan was extended in 1984 and provides for the granting of rights to employees to purchase a maximum of 750,000 shares of Class A common stock of the Company through five consecutive offering periods of one year each, commencing on July 1, 1984. There are no charges or credits to income in connection with the plan.

2. **Compensatory plans**—These plans involve both (a) **compensation expense** to the grantor and (b) **compensation income** to the grantee. Such plans usually specify the issuance of company stock to designated employees at a set price per share (to be paid by the employee) that is **significantly less** than the current market price of the stock at measurement date (defined later). In some cases, the employee receives the stock under specified conditions at no cost.

Accounting for stock options granted to employees is governed by *Accounting Research Bulletin (ARB) 43* (chap. 13B), as amended and supplemented by *APB Opinion 25,* "Accounting for Stock Issued to Employees" and *FASB Interpretation 28,* "Accounting for Stock Appreciation Rights and Other Variable Stock Option or Award Plans." The discussions to follow are based on these pronouncements.[8]

Accounting for Noncompensatory Stock Option Plans for Employees

Noncompensatory stock options involve no expense to the company and no compensation to the employees. Therefore, they cause no special accounting problems. *APB Opinion 25* (par. 7) defines a noncompensatory stock plan as one that possesses at least the following four characteristics:

1. Substantially all full-time employees meeting limited employment criteria are included.
2. The stock is offered to eligible employees equally, or is based on a uniform percentage of salary or wages.
3. The time permitted for exercise of an option or purchase right is limited to a reasonable period.

[8] Currently, the FASB is considering changes in these pronouncements to specify more uniform accounting standards for stock option incentive plans. An exposure draft of "Postemployment Benefits Other Than Pensions" is expected during 1988.

4. The discount from the market price of the stock is no greater than would be reasonable in an offer of stock to stockholders or others. Discounts up to 15% are currently being permitted in actual practice.

Accounting for a noncompensatory stock option plan involves recording the issuance (i.e., sale) of the stock in conformity with the **cost principle.** The option price per share is the issue price. To illustrate accounting for noncompensatory stock options, Company Y has a **stock purchase plan.** The employees may acquire stock from the company at a discount of 4% from the market price through payroll deductions. Typical entries for a noncompensatory plan, including $7,200 of voluntary payroll deductions for **employee stock purchases,** would be (amounts assumed):

Look at this

1. To record the monthly payroll of $90,000 and related deductions:

Salary and wage expense	90,000	
Withholding income tax payable		18,400
Payroll taxes payable		6,500
Liability—employee stock purchase plan*		7,200
Cash (or salary and wages payable)		57,900

* Per payroll deductions authorized in advance by employees.

2. To record issuance of the required number of shares to employees (market price per share, $18.75):

Liability—employee stock purchase plan	7,200	
Capital stock, par $15 (400 shares*)		6,000
Contributed capital in excess of par		1,200

* $7,200 ÷ ($18.75 × 96%) = 400 shares.

Accounting for Compensatory Stock Option Incentive Plans for Employees

A stock option plan for employees that does not meet all four of the characteristics of a noncompensatory plan must be classified and accounted for as a **compensatory** stock option incentive plan. Therefore, a compensatory stock option incentive plan for employees involves: *(a)* an **expense** to the grantor corporation **in addition** to the regular wage and salary expense, and *(b)* additional compensation income to the grantee.

Accounting for compensatory stock option plans requires: *(a)* application of the **cost principle** to measure and record the **total amount of compensation cost** during the relevant service period, and *(b)* application of the **matching principle** to allocate the total compensation cost as periodic expense throughout the **service period** of the grantee (from date of grant).

There is a wide range of diverse and complex specifications included in the numerous types of compensatory stock option plans that exist in industry. Therefore, measurement, recording, and reporting are complex. For this reason, the related APB and FASB pronouncements are often detailed (also somewhat vague and controversial). The discussions and illustrations that follow present the **basic distinctions** and **recording requirements** that must be used for all plans. For practical reasons, we do not comprehensively discuss each plan in the wide range of compensatory plans.

The various stock option incentive plans may be classified as:

1. **Stock options**—These options give the grantee (i.e., the employee) the right to buy a specified number of **shares** of the common stock of the grantor (i.e., the issuing company) at a specified price per share.
2. **Stock appreciation rights (SARs)**—These rights provide a **cash** bonus to the employee (grantee) based upon the change in the market value of specified shares of capital stock from the date of grant to the exercise date.
3. **Combination plans**—Typically these plans give the grantee the option to select one alternative from among two or more alternatives, such as to select either stock options or cash (SARs).

To account for any stock option plan, five basic questions must be resolved. To illustrate resolution of these basic questions, a simplified stock option plan for AB Corporation is presented in **Exhibit 17–4.**

Question 1: Is the plan compensatory?

To be classified as compensatory, the plan must **fail** to meet any one of the four characteristics of a noncompensatory plan (see page 780).

- AB Corporation's plan is compensatory because, according to the data given in Exhibit 17–4, it does **not** meet all four of the criteria for a **noncompensatory** plan. That is, *(a)* it is limited to only 10 executives (not substantially all of the full-time employees), and *(b)* the discount from the market price of the stock is 33⅓% [i.e., ($30 − $20) ÷ $30]. Discounts associated with noncompensatory plans range no higher than 15%. Either factor makes the plan compensatory.

Question 2: When should the total compensation cost be measured?

Conceptually, total compensation cost should be measured when the **grantor** foregoes alternate uses (e.g., sale) of the optioned shares. This date is called the **measurement date** under GAAP, as specified by *APB Opinion 25* (par. 10). It is **"the first date on which are known both (1) the number of shares that an individual employee is entitled to receive and (2) the option price . . . if any."** Both of these specifications are necessary to measure **total** compensation cost. The measurement date is usually the **date of grant.** However, a compensation plan may have provisions that cause the measurement date to be **later** than the date of grant (which introduces accounting complexities).

- For AB Corporation, the measurement date is the date of grant. On that date, January 1, 19B, both (1) the number of optioned shares (5,000) and (2) the option price per share ($20) are known (see Exhibit 17–4).

Question 3: What is the amount of total compensation cost?

Total compensation cost for executive Z is determined on the measurement date. It is the difference between the market value of the stock on that date and the option price per share, multiplied by the number of optioned shares.[9]

---

[9] Conceptually, compensation cost should be the market value of stock rights (not the shares themselves). Because the value of the stock rights cannot be known (there is no market in the options), the difference between the market price and the option price per share is used as a surrogate valuation.

Exhibit 17–4
Data for compensatory stock option plan—AB Corporation.

Plan Specifications and Actual Data for Stock Option Transactions of Executive Z:

1. AB Corporation—plan specifications—executive stock options:
   a. Options approved for each of 10 designated executives.
   b. 5,000 shares of common stock, par $5, for each executive.
   c. Nontransferable, exercisable (i.e., it vests) 5 years after grant and prior to expiration date, which is 10 years from date of grant. Exercisc of option requires continuing employment to date exercised.
   d. Option price, $20 per share.
2. On January 1, 19B, executive Z was granted an option for 5,000 shares:
   a. For services to be performed from date of grant to first exercise date (i.e., vesting date) at December 31, 19F (approximately equal services each year).*
   b. At January 1, 19B, the quoted market price was $30 per share.
   c. The option was exercised by executive Z on December 31, 19F, when the quoted market price per share was $60 (a steady increase during 19B through 19F).

* The vesting date is important because on that date the employee can exercise the option to acquire the stock with no constraints as to continued employment or disposition of the shares.

If the market value of the stock is less than its option price on the measurement date, no compensation cost is recorded. *APB Opinion 25* states that "if the quoted market price is unavailable, the best estimate of the market value of the stock should be used to measure compensation."

- For AB Corporation (Exhibit 17–4), total compensation cost on the measurement date (date of grant, January 1, 19B) was $50,000. That is, MV of the stock on measurement date, $30, minus option price, $20, times optioned shares, 5,000, equals $50,000.

Question 4: To what service period should total compensation cost be assigned as periodic expense?

Under the matching principle, total compensation cost should be allocated as **periodic expense** over a **service period** that extends from the date of grant to the date on which the employee has no further service obligations or constraints imposed by the stock option incentive plan. Usually the service period will end at the first date that the option is exercisable (i.e., the vesting date). From that date forward, if the option is exercised, the employee controls the disposition of the shares. Sometimes the compensation plan specifies the service period. If the termination of the service period is not known at the date of grant, the grantor must use a "best estimate." The assignment of total compensation cost to periodic expense must begin in the first year and extend through the end of the service period. The service period is not reduced in length by early exercise of the options. When estimates of the service period are used, revisions are accounted for as a "change in accounting estimate." Another complexity occurs when the measurement date is after the date of grant (discussed later).

- For AB Corporation, the total compensation cost of $50,000 should be allocated as expense equally to each year of the five-year service period from date of grant (January 1, 19B) to the first exercise date (December 31, 19F). Executive Z is required to work full time for the company during that period.

Question 5: What journal entries should be made by the grantor?

The journal entries to record the effects of a compensatory stock option plan will vary depending upon whether the:

1. Measurement date is **on** the date of grant.
2. Measurement date is **after** the date of grant.

Measurement Date on Date of Grant. If the measurement date is on the **date of grant,** the number of optioned shares, the option price, and the market price of the stock are known. Therefore, total compensation cost can be computed. **Total compensation cost is recorded on the date of grant as a debit to Deferred Compensation Cost and a credit to Executive Stock Options Outstanding.** These two accounts are reported on the statement of financial position under stockholders' equity as follows:

Contributed capital:		
Executive stock options outstanding	$XXX	
Less: Deferred compensation cost	XX	$X

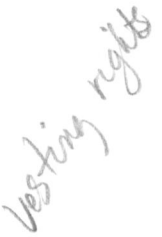

Deferred compensation cost is subtracted from executive stock options outstanding because the stock options have been issued to the employee and the stock has not been issued. However, the employee has not yet earned the stock options; and consequently, no owners' equity has been created for the unearned stock options.[10]

For each subsequent period in the employee's service period, total compensation cost is allocated on a straight-line basis. Straight-line allocation is used because it is reasonable to assume that the employee will provide equal service each period.

Exhibit 17–5 illustrates accounting for AB Corporation when the measurement date is on the grant date. Panel A restates the case data. Panel B gives the entries required *(a)* on the measurement date, *(b)* at each year-end to record the assignment of periodic expense, and *(c)* on the exercise date. Panel C shows the related reporting. This exhibit should be studied carefully. Notice that it is coordinated with the above discussion.

Note in Exhibit 17–5 that the "actual incentive compensation earned" by the grantee, Executive Z, was ($60 − $20) × 5,000 shares = $200,000. The total additional compensation expense reported by the grantor, AB Corporation, was ($30 − $20) × 5,000 shares = $50,000. This comparison shows a primary reason for the popularity of stock option incentive plans.

Measurement Date after Date of Grant. **If on the date of grant either the number of optioned shares or option price is not known, or if the appropriate market price is not known, total compensation expense cannot be computed.** This means that the measurement date must be **after** the date of grant. Nevertheless,

---

[10] *APB Opinion 25* (par. 14) also states, "If stock is issued in a plan before some or all of the services are performed, part of the consideration recorded for the stock issued is unearned compensation and should be shown as a **separate reduction of stockholders' equity.** The unearned compensation should be accounted for as expense of the period or periods in which the employee performs service."

Exhibit 17–5

Accounting for compensatory stock options, AB Corporation—measurement date is date of grant.

Panel A—Case Data:

1. AB Corporation—executive stock option incentive plan:
   Options approved for each of 10 designated executives under the following terms:
   a. 5,000 shares of common stock, par $5.
   b. Nontransferable, exercisable 5 years after grant and prior to expiration date, which is 10 years from date of grant; exercise of options requires continuing employment to first exercise (i.e., vesting) date.
   c. Option price, $20 per share.
2. On January 1, 19B (i.e., the date of grant), executive Z was granted an option for 5,000 shares:
   a. For services to be performed from date of grant to first exercise (vesting) date, December 31, 19F.
   b. At January 1, 19B, the quoted market price was $30 per share.
   c. The option was exercised by executive Z on December 31, 19F, when the quoted market price per share was $60 (a steady increase during 19B–19F).

Panel B—Entries of AB Corporation for Stock Option Transactions of executive Z:

1. January 1, 19B—date of grant; to record total deferred compensation cost and the issuance of stock options to executive Z:

Deferred compensation cost [($30 − $20) × 5,000 shares]	50,000	
Executive stock options outstanding (for 5,000 shares of common stock)		50,000

2. December 31, 19B, through 19F—to record the annual allocation of deferred compensation cost to compensation expense (equal amount for each of the five years):

Compensation expense	10,000	
Deferred compensation cost		10,000

$50,000 ÷ 5 years = $10,000 per year (straight line because approximately equal services each year).

3. December 31, 19F—exercise date, to record the stock rights tendered by executive Z and issuance of the 5,000 shares:

Cash (5,000 shares × $20 option price)	100,000	
Executive stock options outstanding (for 5,000 shares)	50,000	
Common stock, par $5 (5,000 shares)		25,000
Contributed capital in excess of par, common stock		125,000

Panel C—Reporting on the Financial Statements of 19B:

Statement of income:

Compensation expense		$ 10,000

Statement of financial position:

Stockholder's Equity

Contributed capital:		
Common stock, par $5, authorized 500,000 shares, issued and outstanding 200,000 shares (assumed)		$1,000,000
Executive stock options outstanding (for 5,000 shares of common stock)	$50,000	
Less: Deferred compensation cost	40,000	10,000
Other contributed capital (etc.)	(not illustrated)	

Note: For additional disclosures required, see the last section of the chapter.

periodic compensation expense must be recorded for each service year from the date of grant. Therefore, between the date of grant and the later measurement date, "best estimates" of total compensation cost must be used for accounting purposes. At the end of each service year from the date of grant to the later measurement date, the "best estimate" must be revised. This is done by using the latest year-end price of the stock because this stock price is considered to be the new best estimate.[11] Also, new estimates may have to be made for either the number of optioned shares or the option price or both. These changes in estimates represent the new "best estimate." Although changes in accounting estimates are spread prospectively over the current and future periods. *FASB Interpretation 28,* Appendix B, illustrates use of the "catch-up" method. Application of this method means that when the estimated stock price changes, the amount recorded in the prior year must be updated in full in the current year with a catch-up amount.

Exhibit 17–6 illustrates the accounting for AB Corporation when **the measurement date is later than the date of grant.** Panel A gives the changes assumed in the option plan. Panel B shows the entries at: *(a)* date of grant, January 1, 19B, *(b)* year-end to record periodic expense (for the periods of service between the grant date and the later measurement date for which the estimates were made), and *(c)* exercise date. The **measurement date** is the first date that the options can be exercised, December 31, 19D. Panel C shows the related reporting. Notice that AB Corporation had to estimate **total compensation cost** at the end of 19B and 19C, and subsequently determined the actual amount at the end of 19D (the measurement date). To compute estimated total compensation expense at the end of 19B and 19C, the grantor had to use *(a)* the year-end market price of the stock as the best estimate and *(b)* a best estimate for the option price. The expense amounts for 19C and 19D were computed using the catch-up method. Study Exhibit 17–6 carefully to understand the use of **estimates** to record periodic compensation expense.

Lapse of Stock Options

Employee stock options outstanding may be allowed to **lapse** due to:

1. **Failure of an employee to fulfill the option obligations** due to severance, disability, or death (i.e., the options now are not exercisable). Such situations should be accounted for as a change in accounting estimates in conformity with *APB Opinion 20.* The **credit** balance relating to the particular lapsed option carried in the stock options outstanding account, and any related **debit** balance carried in the deferred compensation cost account, should be removed. The difference should be accounted for as a reduction of **compensation expense** in the period of forfeiture (*APB Opinion 25,* par. 15).
2. **Failure to exercise because the option price of the stock is higher than the quoted market price of the stock** (i.e., it would not be rational to exercise the options). In this situation the employee has fulfilled the obligations (i.e., services) of the option plan. However, the options lapsed on December 31, 19K. For example, assume Executive K (Exhibit 17–6, panel

[11] *FASB Interpretation 28,* "Accounting for Stock Appreciation Rights and Other Variable Stock Option or Award Plans" (Stamford, Conn., December 1978). There is some misunderstanding of this interpretation because in par. 18 it prescribes "prospective application" (which is how a change in estimate is treated), but in Appendix B the catch-up (retroactive approach) is illustrated. The change in estimate approach spreads the catch-up amounts over the remaining periods on a straight-line basis. The change in estimate approach appears to be conceptually and practically preferable, especially when significant increases followed by significant decreases in market prices occur.

If net income goes down — option price goes up

Exhibit 17–6
Accounting for compensatory stock options, AB Corporation—measurement date subsequent to date of grant.

measurement date

Panel A—Case Data:
1. Basic data as given in Exhibit 17–5, except the option price is unspecified.
2. Date of grant to Executive K—January 1, 19B:
 a. A stock option for 5,000 shares of common stock, par $5, is granted to Executive K, exercisable after 5 years from date of grant and within 10 years from date of grant at which time the option expires.
 b. Option price—to be established on December 31, 19D, by reducing the basic option price of $20 by the percentage increase in net income for 19B through 19D (a three-year period).
 c. Additional compensation will be for services to be rendered from date of grant, January 1, 19B, to the first exercise date, December 31, 19F, assuming approximately equal services each year.
 d. Market price per share of stock on date of grant, $20.
3. Estimates made on December 31, 19B, and December 31, 19C, of the amounts for December 31, 19D, measurement date:
 a. Estimated percentage increase in net income for 19B through December 31, 19D: 15%.
 b. Resulting estimated option price on Decembe 31, 19D, measurement date: $20 × (1 − .15) = $17 per share.
 c. Market price estimated for December 31, 19D, measurement date: for 19B, use the actual market price on December 31, 19B—$22 per share; for 19C, use the actual market price on December 31, 19C—$24 per share.
4. Actual amounts on December 31, 19D, the measurement date:
 a. Percentage increase in net income for 19B through December 31, 19D: 10%.
 b. Resulting actual option price: $20 × (1 − .10) = $18 per share.
 c. Market price per share of stock quoted on December 31, 19D: $28.
5. December 31, 19F—Executive K exercised the option on December 31, 19F, when the quoted price per share was $60.

Panel B—Entries of AB Corporation for Stock Option Transactions of Executive K:
1. January 1, 19B (date of grant to Executive K):
 No entry—measurement and recording of compensation expense will begin on December 31, 19B, and will be based on estimated amounts until the measurement date.
2. December 31, 19B—end of period; to record stock options and compensation earned by Executive K during 19B—based on estimated future market price (use actual current market price, $22) and estimated future option price (i.e., $17):

Deferred compensation cost, estimated[($22 − $17) × 5,000 shares]	25,000	
Executive stock options outstanding		25,000
Compensation expense [straight-line ($25,000 ÷ 5 years) = $5,000 per year]	5,000	
Deferred compensation cost		5,000

3. December 31, 19C—end of period; to record stock options and compensation earned by Executive K during 19C—based on estimated future market price (use actual current market price, $24) and estimated future option price (i.e., $17):

Deferred compensation cost		
[($24 − $17) × 5,000 shares = $35,000] − $25,000	10,000	
Executive stock options outstanding		10,000
Compensation exense[a]	9,000	
Deferred compensation cost		9,000

	Per year
[a] [($24 − $17 = $7) × (5,000 shares) = $35,000] ÷ 5 years =	$7,000
Add catch-up for 19B ($7,000 − $5,000) =	2,000
Total	$9,000

Exhibit 17–6
(concluded)

Panel B (concluded):

4. December 31, 19D—**measurement date;** to record stock options and compensation earned by Executive K during
 19D—based on actual current market price (i.e., $28) and actual option price (i.e., $18) on the measurement date:

Deferred compensation cost ..	15,000	
Executive stock options outstanding ([($28 − $18) × 5,000 = $50,000]		
− $25,000 − $10,000).....................................		15,000
Compensation expense[b].....................................	16,000	
Deferred compensation cost		16,000

	Per year
[b] [($28 − $18 = $10) × (5,000 shares) = $50,000] ÷ 5 years	$10,000
Add catch-up for 19B ($10,000 − $5,000)	5,000
Add catch-up for 19C ($10,000 − $9,000)	1,000
Total	$16,000

5. December 31, 19E, and 19F—end of period; to record compensation earned by Executive K during 19E and 19F:

Compensation expense[c].....................................	10,000	
Deferred compensation cost		10,000

[c] [($28 − $18 = $10) × 5,000 shares = $50,000] ÷ 5 years = $10,000.

6. December 31, 19F—exercise date; to record the stock rights tendered by Executive K and the issuance of the
 5,000 shares:

Cash ($18 × 5,000 shares) ...	90,000	
Executive stock options outstanding (for 5,000 shares)..................................	50,000	
Common stock, par $5 (5,000 shares)..		25,000
Contributed capital in excess of par, common stock		115,000

Panel C—Reporting on 19C and 19D Financial Statements:

	19C		19D	
Statement of income:				
Compensation expense		$9,000		$ 16,000
Statement of financial position:				
Contributed capital:				
Common stock, par $5, authorized 500,000 shares;				
issued and outstanding 80,000 shares (assumed)		$400,000		$400,000
Executive stock options outstanding (for 5,000				
shares); see Note X	$ 35,000*		$50,000‡	
Less: Deferred compensation expense........................	(21,000)†	14,000	(20,000)§	30,000
Other contributed capital, etc. (not illustrated)				

* $25,000 + $10,000 = $35,000.
† ($25,000 − $5,000) + ($10,000 − $9,000) = $21,000.
‡ $35,000 + $15,000 = $50,000.
§ $21,000 (from 19C) + $15,000 − $16,000 = $20,000.
Note X: For additional disclosures required, see a later section of the chapter.

B) did not exercise the stock rights by December 31, 19K. All compensation
expense has been recorded. However, there is a remaining credit balance
of $50,000 in Executive Stock Options Outstanding. What should be the
disposition of this balance on the date of lapse, December 31, 19K? *APB
Opinion 25* and *FASB Interpretation 28* are silent on this specific situation.

Be able to evaluate if comp for non compensatory

Two approaches are used:

✓ a. Transfer the credit balance of Executive Stock Options Outstanding to an appropriately designated account such as "Contributed Capital from Lapsed Stock Options." This approach increases permanent capital by the amount of compensation expense on the basis that the employee made a contribution of permanent capital.

✓ b. Allocate the credit balance of Executive Stock Options Outstanding to compensation expense of the current period and a reasonable number of future periods as a **change in estimate.** This approach does not assume that the employee made a contribution to permanent capital. Rather, it assumes that the prior debits to compensation expense (which decreased retained earnings) should be "corrected" as a change in estimate. This method increases retained earnings rather than permanent capital. Also, some accountants believe that *FASB Interpretation 28* (par. 5) applies: "If all parts of the grant or award are forfeited or cancelled, accrued compensation expense shall be adjusted by decreasing compensation expense in that period." This approach is conceptually preferable.

Stock Appreciation Rights

Stock appreciation rights (defined on page 782) were developed primarily to provide cash incentives to employees and to take advantage of favorable income tax provisions. These plans involve the issuance of **stock appreciation rights** (SARs) that, upon exercise, require the grantor to pay cash (in some cases, either cash or common stock) to the grantee. The amount of cash to be paid is based on the difference between the **grant price** and the market price of the company's common stock on exercise date. SAR plans involve dates similar to stock option incentive plans—grant date, measurement date, exercise date, and year-ends during the service period. Total compensation cost must be allocated to years within the service period (from date of grant). Neither the market price nor the exercise date is known in advance so estimates must be used each year to record annual compensation expense. Also, because **cash** will be paid, the account, "Stock Appreciation Plan Liability" replaces the "Executive Stock Options Outstanding" account that usually is used with stock incentive plans.[12]

To illustrate SARs, the following simplified case is presented:

On January 1, 19A, Soker Corporation began a stock appreciation rights plan. It specifies that, for each stock appreciation right (SAR), the grantee will receive cash for the difference between the market value per share of the company's common stock and $10 per share on the measurement date. The rights require continuing employment and may be exercised at any time between the end of year 4 and the expiration date. The rights expire at the end of six years from grant date or when employment is terminated, if earlier. The service

[12] The entries used for stock option incentive plans usually are set up on the deferral basis (see Exhibit 17–6). In contrast, SARs usually are set up on the accrual basis as illustrated here. Either approach may be used in either situation because the entries can be made so that their **net** effects (but not detailed effects) are the same.

period is from the grant date to the earliest exercise date (because this is the vesting date).

On January 1, 19B, Executive May was granted 5,000 SARs under the above incentive plan. Executive May exercised the SARs on December 31, 19E. Relevant year-end market prices of Soker's common stock (par $1) were: 19A, $10; 19B, $11; 19C, $13; 19D, $13; 19E, $14; and 19F, $12. The accounting period ends December 31.

Questions:

1. Is this a compensatory plan? Explain.
2. What is the measurement date? Explain.
3. What is total compensation cost?
4. What is the service period? Explain.
5. Explain how total compensation expense should be allocated to periodic expense.
6. Give all entries related to the SARs granted to Executive May.
7. Compute the following amounts:
   a. Total compensation expense reported by the grantor.
   b. Total cash received by the grantee.

Responses:

1. The plan is compensatory because it does not apply to all employees. It creates compensation expense for the grantor and additional compensation income to the grantee.
2. The measurement date is the exercise date, December 31, 19E (one year prior to expiration).
3. Total compensation cost is: ($14 − $10) × 5,000 SARs = $20,000 (not known until the end of 19E).
4. The service period extends from date of grant, January 1, 19B, to the earliest exercise date, December 31, 19E; a service period of four years.
5. A part of total compensation expense is allocated to each year within the service period. The allocation, therefore, must be based on estimates because the actual stock price at exercise date is not known in advance. Thus, to compute total compensation cost at the end of each year, the year-end market prices are successively used as the best estimate of the stock price on the exercise date. Total estimated compensation expense then is allocated on the straight-line basis, using the service period of four years.
6. Entries:

   January 1, 19B—date of grant:

Memo entry only given details of the grant.

December 31, 19B—record estimated compensation expense using latest stock price as the best estimate of the stock price at exercise date:

Compensation expense	1,250	
Stock appreciation plan liability		1,250

[($11 − $10) × 5,000 SARs = $5,000] ÷ 4 years = $1,250.

December 31, 19C—record the revised estimate of compensation expense:*

Compensation expense	4,583	
Stock appreciation plan liability		4,583

Computations:

($13 − $10) × 5,000 SARs = $15,000 total.
$15,000 − (19B, $1,250) = $13,750 to be amortized.
$13,750 ÷ 3 years = $4,583.

* In this situation, the current market price exceeded last year's estimate (as well as market value at date of grant). Had the current market price decreased to an amount below last year's market price (but not below market price at date of grant), the accounting would follow that for a change in estimate; i.e., the effect should be spread over the current and future periods. In the event that the current market price fell below the market value at grant date, the liability account would be reduced to zero (i.e., a debit) with a resulting credit to expense.

December 31, 19D—same as 19C because stock price did not change, $4,583.
December 31, 19E—record **actual** compensation expense:

Compensation expense	9,584	
Stock appreciation plan liability		9,584

Computations:

($14 − $10) × 5,000 SARs = $20,000 total.
$20,000 − (19B, $1,250 + 19C, $4,583 + 19D, $4,583) = $9,584 remainder to expense.

December 31, 19E—to record exercise of SARs:

Stock appreciation plan liability ($1,250 + $4,583 + $4,583 + $9,584)	20,000	
Cash [($14 − $10) × 5,000 SARs]		20,000

7. Total compensation expense reported by the grantor (Soker) and the cash paid to the grantee (May) are the same, $20,000.

The method of accounting prescribed by the authoritative pronouncements for stock option incentive plans versus stock appreciation rights plans are inconsistent. With essentially the same economic effects, the company may report significantly different *(a)* total compensation cost, *(b)* patterns of compensation expense for each year in the service period, and *(c)* amounts and items on the statement of financial position.

Additional Disclosures Required for Stock Option Plans (Noncompensatory and Compensatory)

ARB 43 (chap. 13B, par. 15) requires grantor companies to disclose certain information about their stock option plans. The purpose of these disclosures is to inform existing and potential investors and creditors of the company's obligation to make such shares available to employees under existing option plans. This information would be important, for example, to an investor contemplating the purchase of a controlling interest in the company. Based on the **full-disclosure principle,** the required disclosures are:

a. The status of the option plan at the end of the period.
b. The number of shares under option.
c. The option price.
d. The number of shares into which options are exercisable.
e. The number of shares exercised during the period and the option price thereof.

Read for exam
Excellent flow chart

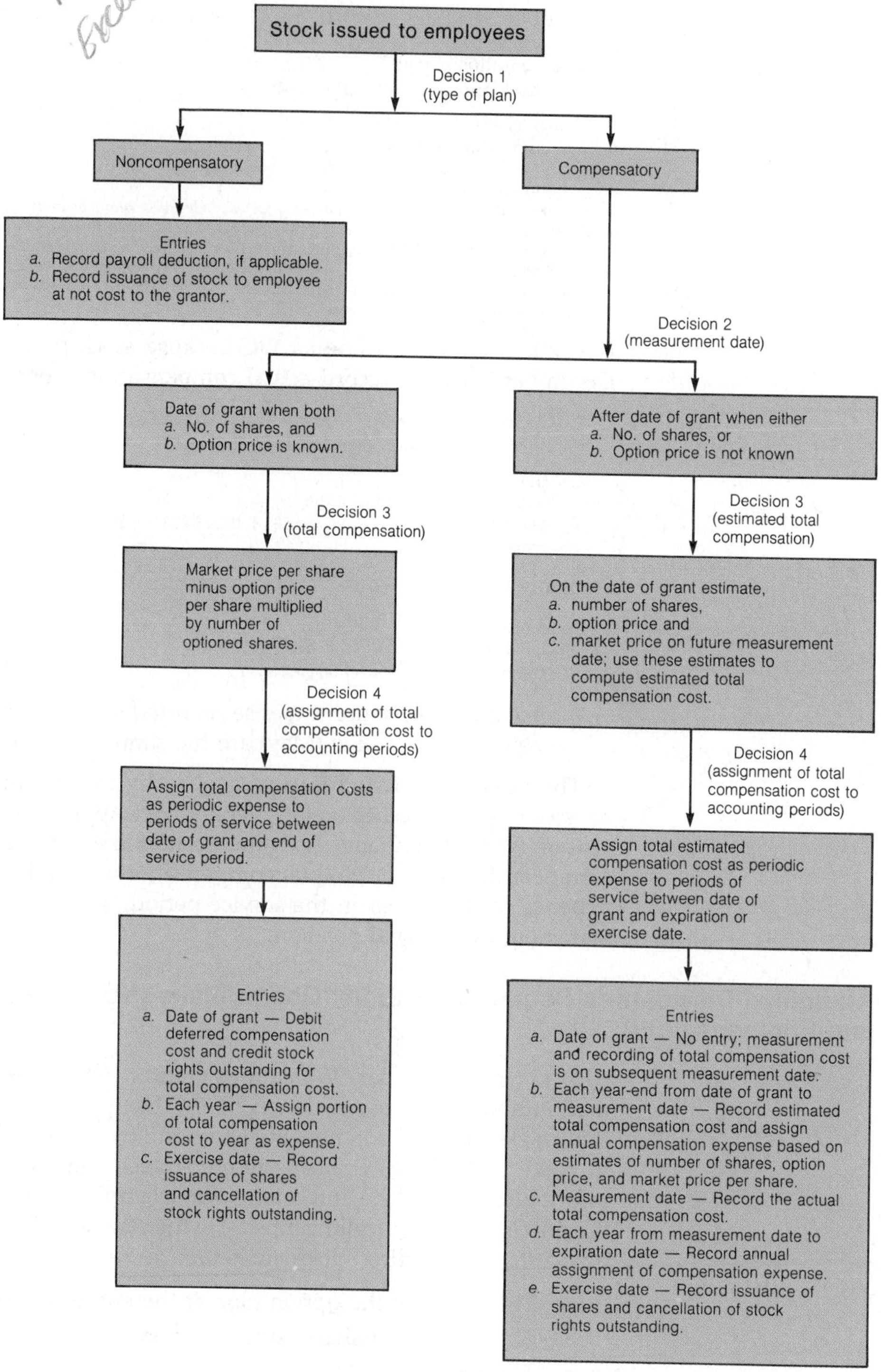

Exhibit 17–7
Stock options issued to
employees—summarized.

Overview of Accounting for Stock Issued to Employees

Exhibit 17–7 summarizes the decisions and sequence of entries for:

1. Noncompensatory stock option plans.
2. Compensatory stock option plans:
   a. Measurement date on date of grant.
   b. Measurement date subsequent to date of grant.

Summary

This chapter discussed retained earnings, which is an important element of stockholders' equity. Retained earnings usually is defined as accumulated earnings minus dividends. However, there are other "uses" of retained earnings, such as in some treasury stock transactions and other changes in contributed capital. Investors are very interested in the amount of retained earnings, which is needed to support cash and property dividends. This chapter also discussed the different kinds of dividends: cash dividends, property dividends (i.e., paid with noncash assets), liquidation dividends (i.e., a return of some contributed capital), scrip dividends (i.e., a debt instrument given to stockholders), and stock dividends (i.e., payable in the corporation's shares).

Total retained earnings is represented by two amounts: (1) appropriated (and restricted) amounts which are not available to support dividends, and (2) the unappropriated amount (i.e., the remainder). Restricted retained earnings reflect limitations variously applied by law, contract, and a corporation itself. The primary purposes of appropriations and restrictions are to communicate certain information to statement users and to protect the company's cash position.

This chapter also discussed a related topic that involves the issuance of capital stock to employees—stock rights and options. Stock **incentive** plans for employees may be noncompensatory (i.e., no cost to the corporation and no compensation to the employee) or compensatory (i.e., a cost to the corporation and compensation to the employee). This chapter discussed the different accounting methods required for each of these cases.

SUPPLEMENT 17–A: QUASI-REORGANIZATIONS

If a corporation has sustained heavy losses over an extended period of time that cause a significant **deficit** in Retained Earnings, and there are unrealistic carrying values for the assets, a quasi-reorganization may be desirable from both the management and accounting points of view.

Quasi-reorganization is a procedure whereby a corporation, without **formal** court proceedings of dissolution, can establish a new basis for accounting for assets, liabilities, and stockholders' equity. In effect, a quasi-reorganization is an accounting reorganization in which a "fresh start" is reflected in the accounts with respect to certain assets, liabilities, legal capital, and retained earnings.

The Committee on Accounting Procedure of the AICPA recognized the procedure, provided it is properly safeguarded.[13] The Securities and Exchange Commission also recognized quasi-reorganization and listed certain associated safeguards or conditions. These conditions are:

1. Retained earnings immediately after the quasi-reorganization must be zero.
2. Upon completion of the quasi-reorganization no deficit shall remain in any corporate capital account.
3. The effects of the whole procedure shall be made known to all stockholders entitled to vote and appropriate approval in advance obtained from them.
4. A fair and conservative statement of financial position shall be presented as of the date of the reorganization, and the readjustment of values should be reasonably complete, in order to obviate as far as possible future readjustments of like nature.[14]

The accounting guidelines to record a quasi-reorganization are: *(a)* the recorded values relating to appropriately selected assets are restated; *(b)* the capital accounts (and occasionally the liabilities) are restated, and the Retained Earnings account is restated to a zero balance; and *(c)* the corporate entity itself is unchanged.[15] Subsequent to a quasi-reorganization there must be full disclosure on the financial statements for the year of reorganization of (1) the reorganization procedure and (2) its effects. Also, the retained earnings amount must be "dated" for a period of 3 to 10 years after the reorganization date, as illustrated in Note 1 of panel B in Exhibit 17–8.

In the case data presented in **Exhibit 17–8,** panel A, the company could consider two alternatives (note the $400,000 debit balance in Retained Earnings). First, the corporation could be **dissolved,** pay creditors, and then form a new corporation. The new corporation would receive the remaining assets and report their total amount as the stockholders' equity of the new corporation.

Alternatively, the corporation may undergo a **quasi-reorganization** (without dissolution). This would be less cumbersome and less expensive than legal reorganization. By complying with the conditions set forth above, including creditor and stockholder approval, the quasi-reorganization may be effected without paying off the creditors at this time. The **entries** needed are reflected in Exhibit 17–8, panel B. That exhibit also shows the restated statement of financial position amounts immediately after the quasi-reorganization. The quasi-reorganization restatements of specific account balances are transferred to retained earnings. Retained earnings then is restated to a zero balance, and legal capital is reduced accordingly.

In general, a quasi-reorganization is justified when *(a)* a large deficit from operations exists, *(b)* it is approved by the stockholders and creditors, *(c)* the cost basis of accounting for operational assets becomes unrealistic in terms of

---

[13] *ARB 43*, chap. 7, sec. A.

[14] Securities and Exchange Commission, *Accounting Series Release 25*.

[15] For a detailed treatment of quasi-reorganization, see J. S. Schindler, *Quasi-Reorganization* (Michigan Business Studies, vol. 13, no. 5) (Ann Arbor: Bureau of Business Research, University of Michigan, 1958).

Exhibit 17–8
Accounting for a quasi-reorganization.

Panel A—Case Data:

1. Statement of financial position at January 1, 19J, immediately prior to quasi-reorganization:

Current assets	$ 200,000
Operational assets	1,300,000
	$1,500,000
Liabilities	$ 300,000
Capital stock	1,500,000
Contributed capital in excess of par	100,000
Retained earnings	(400,000)
	$1,500,000

2. The inventories are overvalued by $50,000, and the carrying value of the operational assets should be reduced by $350,000.

Panel B—Entries and Balances:

Accounts	Balances before quasi-reorganization	Entries to record quasi-reorganization*		Balances after quasi-reorganization
Current assets	$ 200,000		*(a)* $ 50,000	$ 150,000
Operational assets	1,300,000		*(b)* 350,000	950,000
Total assets	$1,500,000			$1,100,000
Liabilities	$ 300,000			$ 300,000
Capital stock	1,500,000	*(d)* $700,000		800,000
Contributed capital in excess of par	100,000	*(c)* 100,000		-0-
Retained earnings	(400,000)	*(a)* 50,000 *(b)* 350,000	*(c)* 100,000 *(d)* 700,000	(Note 1)
Total liabilities and stockholders' equity	$1,500,000			$1,100,000

Note 1 (on statement of financial position): Retained earnings represents accumulations since January 1, 19J, at which time a $400,000 deficit was eliminated as a result of a quasi-reorganization.

* Explanation of entries:

(a) To write down a current asset (inventory) by $50,000.
(b) To write down an operational asset by $350,000.
(c) To write off contributed capital in excess of par as a partial offset to the deficit in retained earnings, $100,000.
(d) To bring retained earnings up to a zero balance and to restate legal capital by the same amount (i.e., $400,000 + $50,000 + $350,000 − $100,000 = $700,000). This leaves legal capital at $800,000, the amount necessary to reconcile the basic accounting model after quasi-reorganization. Legal capital can be restated by (1) reducing par value per share (requires a charter change) or (2) reducing the shares outstanding (no charter change required).

going-concern values,[16] *(d)* a break in continuity of the historical cost basis clearly is needed so that realistic financial reporting is possible, *(e)* the retained

[16] The AICPA *Technical Aids* (CCH, sec. 4220.01) state: "Thus, the official statements of the SEC and the APB can be interpreted as indicating that a quasi-reorganization, if otherwise appropriate, could result in a write-up as well as a write-down of assets." *APB Opinion 6,* (par. 17) states: "The Board is of the opinion that property, plant and equipment should not be written up by an entity to reflect appraisal, market or current values which are above cost. This statement is not intended to change the accounting practice followed in connection with quasi-reorganizations or reorganizations."

Also, restructure of debt that sometimes occurs in a quasi-reorganization does not come under the provisions of *APB Opinion 26* or *FASB Standard 15* (debt restructure is discussed in Chap. 15, part B).

earnings balance is totally inadequate to absorb an obvious decrease in going-concern asset values, and *(f)* a "fresh start," in the accounting sense, appears to be desirable or advantageous to all parties who are concerned with the corporation. A quasi-reorganization, by approval of the creditors and stockholders, usually is supervised by a court to assure adequate protection of the interests of all parties. Because legal capital, as measured in the accounts, is reduced in a quasi-reorganization, all concerned parties seek equity through court supervision to avoid future litigation.

QUESTIONS

Part A

1. Explain how an appropriation of retained earnings can save cash.
2. What are the principal sources and uses of retained earnings?
3. Differentiate between total retained earnings and the balance of the Retained Earnings account.
4. What are the four important dates relative to dividends? Explain the significance of each.
5. Distinguish between cash dividends, property dividends, and liability or scrip dividends.
6. What is a liquidating dividend? What are the responsibilities of the accountant with respect to such dividends?
7. Explain the difference between intentional and unintentional liquidating dividends.
8. Basically what is the difference between a cash or property dividend and a stock dividend?
9. When property dividends are declared and paid, a loss or gain often must be reported. Explain this statement.
10. Explain how interest paid on a liability or scrip dividend is recorded.
11. Contrast the effects of a stock dividend (declared and issued) versus a cash dividend (declared and paid) on assets, liabilities, and total stockholders' equity.
12. Contrast the effects of a typical small stock dividend (declared and issued) versus a typical cash dividend (declared and paid) on the components of stockholders' equity.
13. Explain why the total amount of retained earnings reported on the statement of financial position often is not the net amount of all accumulated earnings (and losses) less all accumulated cash and property dividends.
14. Distinguish between a stock dividend and a pure stock split.
15. What are the primary reasons for appropriating and restricting retained earnings?
16. Explain the distinction between *(a)* a bond sinking fund and *(b)* an appropriation of retained earnings for bond sinking fund.
17. What items are properly reported on the statement of retained earnings?
18. Is the following statement correct? "Retained earnings was reduced by the $10,000 appropriated for plant expansion." Explain.
19. Does a bond sinking fund cause a restriction on retained earnings? Explain.

Part B

20. What is the difference between stock rights and stock warrants?
21. Can stock rights usually be bought and sold? Explain.
22. List the three important dates with respect to stock rights. When will the related stock sell *(a)* rights on and *(b)* ex rights?
23. List the five primary situations when stock rights are used.
24. Explain how the following account should be reported: "Stock rights outstanding (for 100 shares), $3,000."
25. Stock option incentive plans for employees may be either noncompensatory or compensatory. Briefly explain each.
26. Give the two primary accounting principles that underlie the accounting for compensatory stock option incentive plans for employees. Also, identify their application.
27. What is the measurement date for a compensatory stock option incentive plan? Why is it sometimes later than the date of grant?
28. What is the amount of total compensation expense in a stock option plan?
29. Why are estimates necessary when the measurement date is later than the date of grant of a compensatory stock option?
30. What are stock appreciation rights?

EXERCISES

Part A: Exercises 17–1 to 17–11

E 17–1 (Overview; Subclassifications of Stockholders' Equity)
Stockholders' equity has the following subclassifications:

A. Capital stock.
B. Additional contributed capital (excluding donated capital).
C. Donated capital.
D. Retained earnings.
E. Retained earnings appropriated.
F. Unrealized capital.
G. Unallocated deduction.

Match each item below with the letter above that corresponds to its proper classification within stockholders' equity. Use NA if the above classifications are not applicable (give explanations if needed):

1. ______ Net loss.
2. ______ Restriction on retained earnings.
3. ______ Goodwill.
4. ______ Extraordinary item.
5. ______ Cash dividends declared; not paid.
6. ______ Bond sinking fund.
7. ______ Treasury stock, cost method.
8. ______ Plant site given by Twin City.
9. ______ Net income.
10. ______ Correction of accounting error.
11. ______ Legal capital.
12. ______ Premium on capital stock.
13. ______ Subscribed stock.
14. ______ Stock dividends declared; not issued.
15. ______ Prior period adjustment.

E 17–2 **(Property Dividend Recorded; Common and Preferred Stock)**
The records of Frost Corporation showed the following at the end of 19C:

Preferred stock, 6% cumulative, nonparticipating, par $20	$200,000
Common stock, nopar value (50,000 shares issued and outstanding)	240,000
Contributed capital in excess of par, preferred stock	30,000
Retained earnings	125,000
Investment in stock of Ace Corporation (500 shares at cost)	10,000

The preferred stock has dividends in arrears for 19A and 19B. On January 15, 19C, the board of directors approved the following resolution: "The 19C dividend, to stockholders of record on February 1, 19C, shall be 6% on the preferred stock and $1.00 per share on the common stock; the dividends in arrears are to be paid on March 1, 19C, by issuing a property dividend using the requisite amount of Ace Corporation stock. All current dividends for 19C are to be paid in cash on March 1, 19C." On January 15, 19C, the stock of Ace Corporation was selling at $60 per share and at $62 on March 1, 19C.

not relevant to corp.

Required:

1. Compute the amount of the dividends to be paid to each class of stockholders, including the number of shares of Ace Corporation stock and the amount of cash required by the declaration. Assume that divisibility of the shares of Ace Corporation poses no problem.
2. Give journal entries to record all aspects of the dividend declaration and its subsequent payment.

E 17–3 **(Cash Dividend Recorded; Error in Retained Earnings)**
On November 1, 19G, Toni Corporation declared the 19G cash dividend of $1.50 per share on its 20,000 outstanding shares of common stock (par $1, originally sold at $10 per share). The dividend is payable on January 5, 19H, to its stockholders of record as of December 30, 19G. On declaration date, the balance in the retained earnings account was $23,000; this balance had not been corrected for a $3,000 overstatement of the 19F net income (caused by an understatement of 19F depreciation expense). The annual accounting period ends December 31.

Required:

1. Give all entries required for the declaration and payment in full of the dividend as declared. Include any additional disclosure notes.
2. Were any problems posed by this cash dividend? Explain.

E 17–4 **(Cash Dividend Recorded; Return of Capital; Entries)**
On December 1, 19B, the board of directors of Jax Mining Company declared a maximum cash dividend permitted by the state law. The company had never declared a dividend prior to this time. There were 100 stockholders, each holding 200 shares of stock with a par value of $5 per share. The laws of the state provide that "dividends may be paid equal to all accumulated profits prior to the depletion amount." Retained Earnings showed a correct balance of $60,000; depletion for the year amounted to $12,000 (accumulated depletion was $20,000). The dividend was payable 60 days after declaration date.

Required:

1. Give all entries related to the dividend through the payment date.
2. What special notification, if any, should be given the stockholders?
3. What items related to the dividend declaration would be reported on a statement of financial position dated December 31, 19B, assuming net income for 19B of $15,000

(included in the $60,000 balance of retained earnings given above)? Write any note that may be needed to fully disclose the dividend.

E 17–5 (Cash and Scrip Dividend; Entries)

On September 1, 19D, Fox Corporation declared a cash dividend of $1 per share on its 400,000 outstanding shares of common stock (par $1). The dividend is payable on December 1, 19D, to stockholders of record as of October 1, 19D, as follows: one-fourth cash and the balance with scrip, which will be paid on June 30, 19E, plus 12% annual interest starting on payment date of cash. The annual accounting period ends December 31. The amount in the retained earnings account is adequate for payment of the dividend.

Required:

Give all required journal entries, through final payment, directly related to this dividend.

E 17–6 (Stock Dividend Recorded; Dates Cross Two Periods)

The records of Round Corporation showed the following balances on November 1, 19B:

Capital stock, par $10	$300,000
Contributed capital in excess of par . .	102,000
Retained earnings	200,000

On November 5, 19B, the board of directors declared a stock dividend to the stockholders of record as of December 20, 19B, of one additional share for each five shares already outstanding; issue date, January 10, 19C. The market value of the stock immediately after the issuance was $18 per share. The annual accounting period ends December 31.

Required:

1. Give entries in parallel columns for the stock dividend assuming, for problem purposes, *Case A*—market value is capitalized, *Case B*—par value is capitalized, and *Case C*—average paid in is capitalized.
2. Explain when each value should be used.
3. In respect to the stock dividend, what should be reported on the statement of financial position at December 31, 19B, assuming no intervening dividend transactions?

E 17–7 (Stock Dividend with Fractional Share Rights; Entries and Reporting)

The accounts of WP Corporation provide the following data at December 31, 19C:

Capital stock, par $5, authorized shares 100,000; issued and outstanding 20,000 shares	$100,000
Contributed capital in excess of par	80,000
Retained earnings	150,000

On May 1, 19D, the board of directors of WP Corporation declared a 50% stock dividend (i.e., for each two shares already outstanding one additional share is to be issued) to be issued on June 1, 19D. The stock dividend is to be capitalized at the average of contributed capital per share at December 31, 19C.

On June 1, 19D, all of the required shares were issued for the stock dividend, except for those required by 1,300 fractional share rights (representing 650 full shares) issued.

On December 1, 19D, the company honored 900 of the fractional share rights by issuing the requisite number of shares. The remaining fractional share rights were still outstanding at the end of 19D.

Required:

1. Give the required entries by WP Corporation at each of the following dates:
   a. May 1, 19D.
   b. June 1, 19D.
   c. December 1, 19D.

2. Prepare the stockholders' equity section of the statement of financial position at December 31, 19D, assuming net income for 19D was $30,000.
3. Assume instead that the fractional share rights specified that *(a)* two such rights could be turned in for one share of stock without cost, or *(b)* each right could be turned in for $2.50 cash. As a result, 900 rights were turned in for shares, 200 rights for cash, and the remainder lapsed. Give the entry to record the ultimate disposition of all the fractional share rights.

E 17–8 (Stock Dividend and Stock Split; Effects Compared)

Uncertain Corporation has the following stockholders' equity:

Capital stock, par $12, 20,000 shares outstanding . .	$240,000
Contributed capital in excess of par	70,000
Retained earnings	500,000
Total stockholders' equity	$810,000

The corporation decided to triple the number of shares currently outstanding (to 60,000 shares) by taking one of the following alternative and independent actions:

a. Issue a (2 for 1) stock dividend (40,000 additional shares) and capitalize retained earnings on the basis of par value.
b. Issue a pure (3 for 1; that is, 3 new shares issued for each old share replaced) stock split by changing par value per share proportionately.
c. Issue a (3 for 1) stock split and change the par value per share to $5.

Required:

1. Give the journal entry that should be made for each alternative action. If none is necessary, explain why. On the stock splits, the old shares are called in, and the new shares are issued to replace them.
2. For each alternative, prepare a schedule that reflects the stockholders' equity immediately after the change. For this requirement, complete the following schedule, which is designed to compare the effects of the three alternative actions:

Item	Before change	Stock dividend	Pure stock split (par $4)	Stock split (par $5)
Shares/par value				
Capital stock	$	$	$	$
Contributed capital in excess of par				
Total contributed capital				
Retained earnings				
Total stockholders' equity	$	$	$	$

Be prepared to explain and compare the effects among the four columns in the above schedule.

E 17–9 (Appropriations and Restrictions of Retained Earnings; Entries)

TV Corporation carries separate accounts for appropriations and restrictions of retained earnings. One such account is entitled Reserve for Profits Invested in Operational Assets, $420,000. Capital stock outstanding, par value $20, amounted to $400,000.

The company had bonds payable outstanding of $200,000. The following accounts were also carried: Bond Sinking Fund, $100,000; and Bond Sinking Fund Reserve, $100,000.

The board of directors voted a 10% stock dividend and directed that the market value of the stock, $130 per share, be capitalized, using as a basis "the reserves for profits invested in operational assets" to the extent possible.

Required:

Give entries for the following, using preferable titles:

a. To originally establish the reserve related to fixed (operational) assets.
b. To record the issuance of the stock dividend.
c. To originally establish the bond sinking fund.
d. To originally establish the reserve for the bond sinking fund.
e. To record payment of the bonds, assuming the bond sinking fund and the reserve each have a $180,000 balance at retirement date.

E 17–10 (Prepare a Statement of Income and Statement of Retained Earnings)

Using the simplified data below for the year ended December 31, 19X, prepare (1) a single-step statement of income and (2) a statement of retained earnings. Assume all amounts are material and are annual data.

Current items (pretax):	
a. Sales revenue	$400,000
b. Cost of goods sold	160,000
c. Expenses	120,000
d. Extraordinary loss (pretax)	20,000
e. Prior period adjustment—correction of error in recording income taxes of a prior year; income tax was understated	2,100
f. Restriction for bond sinking fund	10,000
g. Dividends declared and paid	30,000
Balances—beginning of period:	
h. Retained earnings (unappropriated)	130,000
i. Restriction for bond sinking fund	60,000
Income taxes—assume a 40% average rate.	

Average number of common shares outstanding during the year, 40,000.

E 17–11 (Prepare Comparative Statements of Income and Retained Earnings)

Using the simplified data below, construct comparative statements of (1) income (single step) and (2) retained earnings for 19A and 19B. Assume all amounts are material, annual data, and an average tax rate of 40% on all items. Disregard EPS.

	19A	19B
Current items (pretax):		
a. Sales	$110,000	$120,000
b. Cost of goods sold	45,000	50,000
c. Expenses	25,000	29,000
d. Extraordinary gain	3,000	
e. Extraordinary loss		6,000
f. Dividends declared and paid	12,000	10,000
g. Appropriation for profits invested in operational assets	10,000	
h. Prior period adjustment—correction of accounting error made in prior period; income tax was understated and no additional tax effect	2,200	
Beginning balances:		
Unappropriated retained earnings	130,000	?
Appropriation for profits invested in operational assets	–0–	?

Part B: Exercises 17–12 to 17–18

E 17–12 (Stock Sale; Stock Rights Issued; Some Lapses; Entries)

Lytle Corporation has outstanding 50,000 shares of common stock, par $5. On January 15, 19A, the company announced its decision to sell an additional 25,000 shares of unissued common stock at $15 per share and to give the current stockholders first chance to buy shares proportionally equivalent to the number now held. To facilitate this plan, on February 1, 19A, each stockholder was issued one right for each common share currently held. Two rights must be submitted to acquire one additional share for $15. Rights not exercised lapse on June 30, 19A.

Required:
Give any entry or memorandum that should be made in the accounts of Lytle Corporation on each of the following dates:

January 15, 19A, the date of the announcement.

February 1, 19A, issuance of all the rights. At this date, the stock of Lytle Corporation was quoted on the market at $12.50 per share.

June 27, 19A, exercise by current stockholders of 98% of the rights issued.

June 30, 19A, the remaining rights outstanding lapsed because of the deadline.

E 17–13 (Employee Stock Purchase Plan; Compensatory?; Entries)

Davis Corporation has a stock purchase plan with the following provisions:

Each full-time employee, with a minimum of one year's service, may acquire, from Davis Corporation, its common stock, par $10, through payroll deductions at 10% below the market price on the date selected by the employee for a stock purchase (i.e., the exercise date). The exercise decision must be made within one year from the payroll deduction date.

Employee Adam signed a payroll deduction form on January 1, 19C, for $60 per month. At that date, the market price of the stock was $27. Assume a monthly salary of $2,000 and other payroll deductions in the aggregate of 18%. At the end of 19C, Adam requested that stock be purchased equal to the amount accumulated to Adam's credit. At that date, the market price of the stock was $25.

Required:

1. Is this a compensatory plan? If yes, how much should be recorded as additional compensation for Adam? Explain.
2. How many shares will Adam acquire for the 19C deductions? Show computations.
3. Give entries to record *(a)* one monthly payroll and *(b)* issuance of the shares for the year, assuming unissued shares are used.

E 17–14 (Stock Incentive Plan; Compensatory?; Analysis; Entries)

Victor Corporation has a stock option plan that was announced on January 1, 19B, with the following provisions:

Each vice president will receive stock options during 19B–19C (if still employed by the company) to purchase 5,000 shares of Victor common stock, par $1 (100,000 shares authorized, 30,000 shares outstanding). The rights are nontransferable and expire immediately after December 31, 19F. The option price is $40 per share. The service period is from date of grant to the expiration date.

On January 1, 19C, Vice President Moe was granted an option for 5,000 shares when the current market price was $36. On December 31, 19F, Moe exercised all of the options; at that date, the Victor stock was selling at $61 per share.

Required:

1. Is this a compensatory plan? How much is total compensation cost? Explain.
2. What is the service period? How much compensation cost should be allocated to each year as expense? Explain.
3. Give all entries related to the stock options granted to, and exercised by, Vice President Moe.
4. How much actual "incentive pay" did Moe receive? How much additional compensation expense did Victor Corporation report?

E 17–15 (Stock Incentive Plan; Compensatory?; Analysis; Entries)

Rex Corporation is authorized to issue 300,000 shares of common stock, par $1, of which 140,000 shares have been issued. The corporation initiated a stock bonus plan during 19A for designated managers. Each manager will receive stock options to purchase 1,000 shares of Rex common stock, if still employed by the company, any time after two years from date of grant, January 1, 19A. The rights are nontransferable and expire immediately after December 31, 19E. The option price is $20 per share; the market price on date of grant was $24. The services will be rendered approximately equally over the five-year period ending December 31, 19E.

Required:

1. Is this a noncompensatory plan? Explain.
2. What is the measurement date? Explain.
3. What is the amount of total compensation cost for each manager (e.g., manager Roe)?
4. Over what period should this compensation cost (for manager Roe) be assigned as expense? How much should be assigned to 19A and 19B? Explain.
5. What entry should be made on the date of grant (for manager Roe)?
6. What entry should be made on December 31, 19A (for manager Roe)?
7. Give the entry to record the exercise of the option by manager Roe on December 31, 19E, when the market price of the common stock was $80 per share.
8. How much actual "incentive pay" did manager Roe receive? How much additional compensation expense did Rex Corporation report?

E 17–16 (Performance Option Plan; Measurement Date?; Analysis; Entries)

In October 19A, Meno Corporation announced a stock option incentive plan for its six top executives. The plan provided each executive 3,000 stock options for Meno's common stock, par $1, at a standard option price of $36 per share reduced by the percentage increase in EPS from December 31, 19A, to December 31, 19C. The rights are nontransferable and are exercisable three years after grant date and prior to five years from date of grant. Continuing employment is required through exercise date, and the service period ends on the first possible exercise date.

On January 1, 19B, Executive Smith was granted 3,000 options when the market price was $30 per share. On December 31, 19B, Meno's management believed that the EPS increase would be met and that Executive Smith would exercise his options at the first exercise date. By December 31, 19C, Meno's EPS had increased by 20%. On December 31, 19C, Meno's stock was selling at $40. For simplification, assume total compensation cost at the end of 19B was estimated to be $24,000.

Executive Smith exercised his option on December 31, 19D, when the market price of the stock was $60 per share.

Required

1. Is this a compensatory plan? Explain.
2. What date is the measurement date? Explain.
3. What is total compensation cost?

4. What is the service period? Explain.
5. Explain how total compensation cost is allocated to periodic expense in this situation.
6. Give all entries related to Executive Smith's stock option.
7. How much actual "incentive pay" did Executive Smith receive? How much additional compensation expense did Meno Corporation report?

E 17–17 **(Stock Appreciation Rights; Analysis; Estimates; Entries)**

On January 1, 19A, TP Corporation established a stock appreciation rights plan that offers rights (SARs) to selected executives that can be redeemed for cash equal to the difference between the market price of the company's common stock at grant date and market price at the first exercise date. The rights can be exercised three years from grant date and expire four years from grant date or when employment is terminated, if earlier. The service period is considered to be three years because exercise is expected (highly probable) to occur on December 31, 19C.

Executive Brown was granted 1,000 SARs on January 1, 19A (when the common stock price was $20) and exercised the rights on December 31, 19C. Relevant market prices at year-end on TP common stock were: 19A, $23; 19B, $27; 19C, $30; and 19D, $26.

Required:

1. Answer the following questions:
   a. Is this plan compensatory? ______ Yes ______ No
   b. The measurement date is ______
   c. The service period is ______
   d. Total compensation cost is $______
   e. Total cash paid by grantor to grantee is $______
2. Give the appropriate journal entries from January 1, 19A, through December 31, 19C.

E 17–18 **(Stock Incentive Plan; Lapse of Rights; Analysis; Entries)**

Stacy Corporation offers a stock option incentive plan that it granted to six of its top executives. During the second year from date of grant, but prior to the permissible exercise date, one of the six executives resigned and accepted employment with a competitor. In accordance with the provisions of the incentive plan, the stock option for the resigned executive lapsed. At the date of lapse, the relevant account balances for all six executives combined were: Deferred Compensation Expense, $225,000; and Executive Stock Options Outstanding, $300,000. The service period extends for three more years including the second year.

Required:

1. Briefly explain what accounting treatment should be accorded the one-sixth of these balances that relate to the one resigned executive.
2. Give all journal entries directly related to the lapsed options.

PROBLEMS

Part A: Problems 17–1 to 17–9

P 17–1 **(Analysis and Correction of Stockholders' Equity; Entries)**

Careless Corporation was organized on January 1, 19A, and began operations immediately. Unfortunately, the company hired an incompetent bookkeeper. For the years 19A through 19C, the bookkeeper presented an annual statement of financial position that reported only one amount for stockholders' equity: 19A, $137,700; 19B, $156,600; and 19C, $185,000. Also, the condensed statement of income reported: 19A, net loss, $17,500; 19B, net profit, $12,000; and 19C, net profit, $40,930 (cumulative earnings of $35,430). Based on the $35,430, the president has recommended to the board of directors that a cash dividend of $35,000 be declared and paid during January 19D. The outside director on the board has objected on the basis that the company's financial statements contain major errors (there has never been an audit). You have been engaged to clarify the situation. The single stockholders' equity account, provided by the bookkeeper, appeared as follows:

Stockholders' Equity

19A Stock issue costs	1,300	19A Common stock, par $5, 20,000 shares issued	160,000
19A Net loss	17,500	19B Net profit (including $10,000 land write-up to appraisal)	22,000
19B Bought 100 shares of company stock from unhappy stockholder Doe	700	19B Common stock, 200 shares issued	1,800
Depreciation expense* (19A, $1,500; 19B, $1,700; 19C, $2,300)	5,500	19C Sold 30 of the Doe shares	270
Cash shortages* (19A, $2,000; 19B, $2,500; 19C, $500)	5,000	19C Net profit	40,930
19C Cash loan to the company president	10,000		
	40,000		225,000

* Recorded but not shown on the statements of income as expense.

Based upon the concerns of the board of directors, three of the major questions you must address are:

Requirement 1:
What amount of retained earnings would be available to support a cash dividend (assume the above figures have been found to be arithmetically accurate and that there is no change in income tax)?

Requirement 2:
Based on your calculations in requirement 1, what journal entries should be made for declaration, and later payment, of the full amount available as a cash dividend?

Requirement 3:
What entry, prior to the dividend entries in requirement 2, is necessary *(a)* to close the above single stockholders' equity account, and *(b)* to record the various components of stockholders' equity in separate accounts? Use the cost method for treasury stock and the offset method for stock issue costs.

P 17–2 (Dividend; Property and Scrip; Entries)
On June 1, 19G, Ward Corporation had outstanding 10,000 shares of capital stock, par value $10 per share. The shares were held by 10 stockholders, each having an equal number of shares. The Retained Earnings account showed a credit balance of $60,000, although the company was short of cash. The company owned 20,000 shares (2%) of the stock of Carson Corporation that had been purchased as a long-term investment for $20,000. The current market value is $1.25 per share. On June 1, 19G, the board of directors of Ward Corporation declared a dividend of $4 per share "to be paid with the Carson stock 30 days after declaration date and scrip to be issued for the difference.

The scrip will be payable at the end of 12 months from payment date of the property dividend and will earn 12% interest per annum." The accounting period ends December 31.

Required:

1. Give all entries related to the dividends through date of payment of the scrip.
2. Illustrate how all items related to the dividend declaration should be reported by Ward on *(a)* the statement of financial position and *(b)* the statement of income at the end of 19G, including any notes needed for full disclosure (i.e., write the notes as they should appear in the statements).

P 17–3 (Dividends; Common and Preferred; Property and Scrip)

The summarized statement of financial position at December 31, 19D, for Saxon Corporation is shown below.

Cash	$ 28,000
Receivables	36,000
Inventory	110,000
Long-term investment, 4,000 shares (4%) of Mita Corporation stock at cost	6,000
Operational assets (net)	80,000
Other assets	10,000
Total	$270,000
Current liabilities	$ 26,000
Bonds payable	50,000
Preferred stock, 6%, par $100, cumulative	20,000
Common stock, nopar (5,000 shares)	100,000
Contributed capital in excess of par, preferred	5,000
Retained earnings	69,000
Total	$270,000

The dividends on preferred stock are three years in arrears (excluding the current year, 19E). On November 1, 19E, the board of directors of Saxon declared dividends, payment date December 1, as follows:

a. Preferred stock, all dividends in arrears plus the current year dividend; payment to be made by transferring the requisite number of shares of Mita stock at its current market value of $5 per share.

b. Common stock, $4 per share for the current year, payment to be made by transferring the remainder of the Mita stock and issuing a scrip dividend for the balance. The scrip will earn 10% annual interest. The scrip, including interest, will be paid at the end of five months from date of declaration.

Required:

1. Compute the amount of dividends payable on each class of stock and the amount of the scrip dividend.
2. Give entries to record the transfer of the Mita stock and the issuance of the scrip dividend. Use separate accounts for the common and preferred stock.
3. Give the adjusting entry at December 31, 19E, for the interest on the scrip dividend.
4. Give the entry to record payment of the scrip dividend and interest on April 30, 19F.
5. Prepare the stockholders' equity section of the statement of financial position as of December 31, 19E. Assume reported net income of $26,000 for 19E (does not yet include the interest on the scrip dividend and gain on disposal of Mita stock; assume no change in income tax expense for these items).

P 17–4 (Dividends: Cash and Stock; Fractional Shares; Entries)

On November 5, 19A, the board of directors of Evers Corporation declared *(a)* a 40% common stock dividend on the common stock (i.e., two additional shares of common for each five shares already held), and *(b)* a cash dividend on the preferred stock for the one year in arrears and for the current year. The board of directors specified that the average originally paid in per share of common will be capitalized for the stock dividend. For problem purposes only, assume the declaration and issue (or payment) dates are the same. At November 1, 19A, the records of the corporation showed:

Stockholders' Equity

Preferred stock, 7%, $10 par value, authorized 20,000 shares, issued 10,000 shares	$100,000
Common stock, nopar, stated value $5, authorized 50,000, issued 15,000 shares	75,000
Contributed capital in excess of par, preferred	20,000
Contributed capital in excess of stated value, common	30,000
Retained earnings	160,000

Upon issuance of the stock dividend, 5,000 fractional share rights (for 2,000 shares) were distributed to stockholders. On December 30, 19A, 4,500 fractional share rights were exercised for 1,800 shares. The remaining rights are outstanding to date.

Required:

1. Give entries to record *(a)* issuance of the stock dividend, *(b)* payment of the cash dividend, and *(c)* exercise of the rights.
2. Prepare the stockholders' equity section of the 19A statement of financial position after giving effect to the entries in (1) above and assuming net income for 19A was $18,000.
3. Give the entry required assuming lapse of the remaining rights on October 30, 19B.

P 17–5 (Dividends; Cash and Stock; Fractional Shares; Entries and Reporting)

On December 31, 19A, the accounts for Akers Corporation showed the following balances:

Stockholders' Equity

Preferred stock, 7%, par value $25, noncumulative, authorized 10,000 shares, outstanding 8,000 shares	$200,000
Common stock, nopar, stated value $10, authorized 20,000 shares, outstanding 12,000 shares	120,000
Contributed capital in excess of par, preferred	15,000
Contributed capital in excess of stated value, common	30,000
Retained earnings	175,000

During 19B, the following transactions, in order of date, were recorded relating to the capital accounts:

a. Apr. 1 A stock dividend was issued whereby (1) each holder of 10 preferred shares received 1 share of common stock and (2) each holder of 6 shares of common stock received 1 additional share of common. The market price of the common stock was $15 per share immediately after issuance of the stock dividend. In issuing the stock dividend, 2,700 shares of common stock and 1,000 fractional share rights were issued. Each fractional share right represents one-tenth of a share of stock.

b. Nov. 1 All of the rights were redeemed except 100, which remained outstanding.

c. Dec. 15 A 7% cash dividend on the preferred shares and a $1.00 per share dividend on the common shares were declared and paid.

d. Dec. 31 Reported net income was $70,000.

Required:

1. Give the journal entries for each of the above transactions during 19B.
2. Prepare the stockholders' equity section of the statement of financial position at December 31, 19B.
3. Assume Akers paid cash to the stockholders in lieu of issuing fractional share rights. The cash distribution was based on the market value of $15 per common share. Give the entry on April 1, 19B, to record the dividend transaction. What would be the total stockholders' equity of Akers Corporation on December 31, 19B, in this situation if all other factors remain as they were given above?

P 17–6 **(Dividends; Property, Scrip; Fractional Shares; Entries and Reporting)** Dawn Corporation records reflect the following data at the end of 19A:

Current assets	$ 167,000
Operational assets (net)	960,000
Other assets	300,000
Long-term investment in AC Corp. stock (5,000 shares at cost)	5,000
	$1,432,000
Current liabilities	$ 60,000
Long-term liabilities	100,000
Preferred stock, 6%, par $100	300,000
Common stock, nopar, 100,000 shares outstanding	800,000
Contributed capital in excess of par, preferred	12,000
Retained earnings	160,000
	$1,432,000

To date, 3,000 shares of the preferred stock (6%, $100 par value, cumulative, nonparticipating) have been issued. Authorized shares were: common, 200,000; and preferred, 3,000. No dividends were declared or paid for 19A. During the subsequent two years, the following transactions affected stockholders' equity:

Year 19B:

a. Feb. 1 Declared and immediately issued one share of the AC Corporation stock for each share of preferred stock as a property dividend to pay the dividends in arrears from 19A to date. The current market value of the AC stock was $3.50 per share. In addition, a cash dividend was paid to complete payment of the dividends in arrears.

b. Oct. 1 Declared and immediately issued scrip dividends amounting to 6% on the preferred and $1.00 per share on the common stock. Interest on the scrip is 7% per year (maturity date, September 30, 19C).

c. Dec. 31 Reported 19B net income was $150,000, including all effects of the above transactions.

Year 19C

d. Sept. 30 Paid the scrip dividends including 7% per annum interest for 12 months.

e. Nov. 1 Declared and issued a stock dividend, payable in common stock to holders of both preferred and common stock. The preferred holders are to receive "value" equivalent to 6%, and the common holders are to receive one share for each five shares held. The "value" and the amount to be capitalized per share as a debit to Retained Earnings is the market value. The price per share of the common stock immediately after the stock dividend was $1.50. Issued the stock dividend in full to the preferred. Fractional share rights for 500 shares (i.e., 2,500 rights) were issued to common stockholders.

f. Dec. 1 The fractional share rights specified that five such rights could be turned in for one share of common stock. On this basis, 1,800 of the outstanding fractional share rights were turned in. The remaining 700 rights remain outstanding.

g. Dec. 31 Reported 19B net income was $95,000, including all effects of the above transactions.

Required:
1. Give the journal entries for each of the above transactions (round to the nearest dollar).
2. Prepare the stockholders' equity section of the statement of financial position at December 31, 19C, after recognition of the above transactions.

P 17–7 **(Retained Earnings; Appropriations and Restrictions; Reporting)**
The following annual data were taken from the records of Yen Corporation at December 31, 19X (assume all amounts are material; the items in parentheses are credit balances):

Current items (pretax):	
a. Sales revenue	$(450,000)
b. Cost of goods sold	230,000
c. Expenses	85,000
d. Extraordinary	30,000
e. Stock dividend issued	80,000
f. Cash dividend declared and paid	25,000
g. Correction of accounting error involving understatement of income tax expense from prior period (not subject to income tax)	8,000
h. Current restriction for bond sinking fund	10,000
i. Current appropriation for plant expansion	40,000

Income taxes:
Assume an average income tax rate of 40% on all items except the prior period adjustment.

Balances, January 1, 19X:	
j. Unappropriated retained earnings	$(120,000)
k. Restriction for bond sinking fund	(20,000)
l. Appropriation for plant expansion	(60,000)

Required:
1. Prepare a single-step statement of income for the year ended December 31, 19X. Disregard EPS.
2. Prepare a statement of retained earnings for the year ended December 31, 19X that separately discloses each restriction on total retained earnings.
3. Give any entries related to the appropriations and restrictions that would have been made, assuming subdivisions of retained earnings are recorded in separate accounts.
4. Assume Yen Corporation set up a bond sinking fund to pay off the bonds payable at maturity. Also assume the bonds ($200,000 principal) mature when the bond sinking fund has a balance of $194,000 and the restriction for bond sinking fund has a balance of $190,000. Give all related entries to record the bond payment at maturity data (assume all interest has already been paid).

P 17–8 **(Comparative Retained Earnings; Appropriations; Reporting)**
Fumer Corporation records provided the following annual data at December 31, 19B, and 19C (assume all amounts are material):

	19B	19C
Current items (pretax):		
a. Sales revenue	$240,000	$260,000
b. Cost of goods sold	134,000	143,000
c. Expenses	71,000	77,000
d. Extraordinary loss	7,000	2,000
e. Cash dividend declared and paid	20,000	
f. Stock dividend issued		30,000
g. Restriction for bond sinking fund	10,000	10,000
h. Increase in bond sinking fund	10,000	10,000
i. Prior period adjustment—error correction, salary expense understated	6,000	
j. Income taxes—assume an average rate of 45% on all items including extraordinary items and prior period adjustments.		
Balances, January 1, 19B:		
k. Restriction for bond sinking fund	70,000	?
l. Unappropriated retained earnings	160,000	?
m. Appropriation for plant expansion	65,000	?
n. Bond sinking fund	75,000	?
o. Bonds payable	100,000	?

Required:

1. Prepare a single-step comparative statement of income for years 19B and 19C. Common stock outstanding, 10,000 shares.
2. Prepare a comparative statement of retained earnings for the years 19B and 19C that sets out separately each of the restrictions and appropriations of retained earnings.

P 17–9 (CPA; Analysis and Correction of Retained Earnings Account)

Perkins Corporation is undergoing an audit. The books show an account entitled Surplus, which is reproduced below covering a five-year period, January 1, 19B, to December 31, 19F.

Credits

19B–19E	Net income carried to surplus	$ 800,000
19B	Offset with debit to goodwill—authorized by management	50,000
12/31/19C	Contributed capital in excess of par	6,000
1/1/19D	Correction of prior accounting error*	2,000
1/1/19D	Donation to company—operational asset	5,000
3/31/19D	Refund of prior years' income taxes due to carryback of a 19C net operating loss to 19B	9,000
7/1/19E	Reduction in capital stock from par value, $100, to par value, $50, with no change in number of shares outstanding (10,000); approved by stockholders	500,000
12/31/19F	Net income, 19F	170,000
		$1,542,000

* Not included in net income 19B–19E.

Debits

19B–19E	Cash dividends declared	$ 520,000
12/31/19B	To reserve for bond sinking fund (required annually 19A–19E)	20,000
12/31/19D	Reserve for bond sinking fund	20,000
12/31/19E	Reserve for bond sinking fund	20,000
9/1/19F	Fifty percent stock dividend	250,000
		$ 830,000

Required:

1. The above account is to be closed and replaced with appropriate accounts. Complete a worksheet analysis of the above account to reflect the correct account balances and the corrections needed. It is suggested that the worksheet carry the following

columns: *(a)* surplus account per books; *(b)* net income, 19F; *(c)* corrected unappropriated retained earnings, December 31, 19F; and *(d)* columns for debits and credits to any other specific accounts needed.

2. Give the entry or entries to close this account as of December 31, 19F, and to set up appropriate accounts in its place. (AICPA adapted)

Part B: Problems 17–10 to 17–17

P 17–10 (Incentive Stock Plan; Comprehensive Overview; No Complexities; Entries and Reporting)

WT Corporation is authorized to issue 400,000 shares of common stock, par $5, of which 160,000 are outstanding; issue price $8 per share. On January 1, 19A, the company initiated a stock incentive plan for certain executives. The plan provides for each qualified executive to receive an option for 4,000 shares of the common stock. Subject to continued employment, the option is exercisable at any time after four years and prior to expiration, which is five years from the date of grant. The options are nontransferable, and the specified option price is $60 per share. The option is considered to be additional compensation, prorated equally for the period from the date of grant to the first exercise (i.e., vesting) date, which is four years. On January 1, 19A, J. Doe, the company president, was granted an option under the plan when the market price of the stock was $71. Doe exercised the option on December 28, 19E, when the market price of the stock was $90 per share.

Required:

1. Is this a compensatory plan? Explain.
2. What is the measurement date? Explain?
3. What is the amount of the total compensation to Doe?
4. Over what period should Doe's compensation be assigned as expense? How much should be assigned to 19A? to 19B? Explain.
5. Give appropriate entries on the following dates for Doe's option (if none, explain why):
   a. Date of grant.
   b. Measurement date.
   c. End of each year, starting on December 31, 19A.
   d. Exercise date
6. Show how Doe's option would affect the statements of income and financial position at the end of 19A and 19B.
7. What were the amounts of *(a)* actual incentive pay "earned" by Doe and *(b)* the total additional compensation expense reported by WT Corporation?

P 17–11 (Incentive Stock Plan; Comprehensive Overview; No Complexities; Entries and Reporting)

Rye Corporation has a stock option incentive plan for its top managers that includes the following provisions:

a. Each manager that qualifies will receive an option to acquire 10,000 shares of Rye common stock, par $2, at an option price of $12 per share.
b. The option is nontransferable and, if not exercised, expires after five years from date of grant.
c. The option cannot be exercised prior to the end of two years from date of grant and requires continued employment in the company.

d. The stock option is for additional compensation for the year of the grant and the following four years; approximately equal services each of the five years.

An option was granted to the president on January 1, 19A, at which time the common stock was selling for $20 per share. Assume the option is exercised on December 31, 19E, when the stock is quoted at $45 per share.

At January 1, 19A, 90,000 shares of common stock, par $2 (authorized 200,000 shares) were outstanding (issued at par).

Required:

1. Is this a compensatory plan? Explain.
2. What is the measurement date? Explain.
3. Compute the total compensation cost for the option granted to the president.
4. Over what period of time should this total compensation be assigned as expense? Explain.
5. Give the appropriate entries for the option granted to the president at the following dates (if none, explain why):
   a. Date of grant.
   b. Measurement date.
   c. End of each year, starting on December 31, 19A.
   d. Exercise date.
6. Illustrate how the option granted to the president would affect the statements of income and statements of financial position at the end of 19A and 19B.
7. What were the amounts of *(a)* total compensation expense recorded, and *(b)* incentive pay "earned" by the president?

P 17–12 (Stock Incentive Plan; Measurement and Grant Dates Different; Comprehensive; Entries and Reporting)

Manford Corporation has 100,000 shares of common stock, par $20, authorized, of which 40,000 shares are outstanding. The company has a stock option plan that provides the following:

a. Each qualified manager shall receive on January 1, an option for a computed number of shares of common stock at a computed option price per share. The computation of the number of option shares and the option price shall be made three years after the option is granted and will be related to the increase in net income over the three-year period. The plan provides additional compensation for qualified managers for services to be performed approximately equally during the years 19x1–x5.

b. The options are nontransferable and must be exercised not earlier than three years and not later than five years from date of grant. Employment with the company is required through the exercise date.

On January 1, 19x1, an option was granted to J. Dean, the controller. At that date, the common stock was quoted on the market at $50 per share. Assume Dean exercised the option near the end of 19x5 when the price of the stock was $90. The following additional information is available:

	Estimates made 12/31/x1 of what the amount would be on 12/31/x3*	Actual amount on 12/31/x3
Number of shares optioned	500	510
Option price	$60	$62
Market price per share	$67 †	$71

* Estimate at 12/31/x2 same as estimate at 12/31/x1.

† Estimate of future market price, based on actual market price on 12/31/x1.

Required:

1. Is this a compensatory plan? Explain.
2. When is the measurement date? Explain.
3. Over what period should total compensation expense for Dean be assigned?
4. Give appropriate entries (related to Dean) for the following dates (if none, explain why):
   a. Date of grant.
   b. End of 19x1 and 19x2.
   c. Measurement date.
   d. End of 19x3, 19x4, and 19x5.
   e. Exercise date.
5. Show how Dean's option would affect the statements of income and financial position for 19x2 and 19x3.
6. How much actual incentive compensation did Dean "earn"? How much additional compensation expense did Manford Corporation report?

P 17–13 (Stock Incentive Plan; Comprehensive; Dates of Grant and Measurement Different; Entries and Reporting)

Huber Corporation is authorized to issue 200,000 shares of common stock, par $10, of which 75,000 shares have been issued. On January 1, 19x2, the corporation initiated a stock option plan for its three top managers. The plan provides that each manager will receive an option to purchase, no later than December 31, 19x6, 2,000 shares of the common stock at a base option price of $48, which will be adjusted for changes in earnings per share (EPS), and requiring continued employment through actual exercise date. The option price is to be established on December 31, 19x4, and will be based on changes in EPS. EPS for 19x1 was $2. The option price will be established at the end of 19x4 as follows:

> The option price per share will be the basic option price of $48 multiplied by the additive inverse of the percentage change (i.e., 1 minus the % of change) in EPS from December 31, 19x1 through 19x4.

The options are nontransferable and expire on December 31, 19x6. The stock was quoted at $45 per share on the market on January 1, 19x2. On December 31, 19x2, the management made what they consider to be realistic estimates that EPS would increase steadily to $3.20 at December 31, 19x4, and that the stock price would be $46 per share on that date; this latter estimate was based upon the actual market price of the stock on December 31, 19x2, which was $46. These estimates were not revised in 19x3 because the actual market price of the stock was very close to $46 on December 31, 19x3, and EPS expectations remained the same. EPS on December 31, 19x4, actually turned out to be $3, and the actual market price of the stock was $47.

The president received the options with the option price unknown on January 1, 19x2. The service period was established to be 5 years (i.e., x2 through x6). Assume the president exercised the option on December 31, 19x6, when the market price of the stock was $64.

Required:

1. Is this a compensatory plan? Explain.
2. What is the measurement date? Explain.
3. Over what period should total compensation cost for the president be assigned?
4. Give appropriate entries (related to the president) on the following dates (if none, explain why):
   a. Date of grant.
   b. End of 19x2 and 19x3.

c. Measurement date.
d. End of 19x4, 19x5, and 19x6.
e. Exercise date.

5. Show how the president's option would affect the statements of income and financial position for 19x3 and 19x4.
6. What were the amounts of *(a)* additional compensation expense reported by the grantor and *(b)* the actual incentive compensation "earned" by the grantee?

P 17–14 (Stock Appreciation Rights; Analysis; Entries)

Delphi Corporation has just employed a new president with the following compensation package: (1) salary, $200,000 per year (minimum employment period, three years), (2) an annual bonus of 10% of the dollar increase in accrual basis income before extraordinary items, and (3) 10,000 stock appreciation rights (SARs) tied to the market price of Delphi's common stock. This problem focuses on the SARs granted to the new president on January 1, 19A, when the market price per share was $30. Four other executives also participate in this SAR plan.

The SAR plan specifies that each SAR will earn for the grantee cash equal to the difference between the market price of Delphi's common stock on grant date and on exercise date. The SARs may be exercised at any time after the end of the fourth year from the grant date, and they expire at the end of the fifth year from grant date, or at date of termination of employment, if before the end of the fifth year. The service period is from grant date to expected (a high probability) exercise (i.e., vesting) date, December 31, 19D.

The president exercised the SARs on January 4, 19E, when the market price per share was $40. Relevant year-end market prices of Delphi's common stock are: 19A, $33; 19B, $38; 19C, $35; 19D, $40; and January 4, 19E, $40. The accounting period ends December 31.

Required:

1. Respond to the following questions:
   a. Is this plan compensatory? Why?
   b. What is the measurement date? Explain.
   c. What is total compensation cost?
   d. What is the service period? Explain.
   e. How is total compensation expense allocated to annual periodic expense?
2. Give all entries related to the SARs granted to the president from the grant date through the exercise date.

P 17–15 (An Overview of Chapters 16 and 17)

Howard Corporation is a publicly owned company whose shares are traded on a national stock exchange. At December 31, 19B, Howard had 25,000,000 shares of $10 par value common stock authorized, of which 15,000,000 shares were issued and 14,000,000 shares were outstanding.

The stockholders' equity accounts at December 31, 19B, had the following balances:

Common stock	$150,000,000
Contributed capital in excess of par	80,000,000
Retained earnings	50,000,000
Treasury stock (at cost)	18,000,000

During 19C, Howard had the following transactions:

a. On February 1, 19C, a secondary distribution of 2,000,000 shares of $10 par value common stock was completed. The stock was sold to the public at $18 per share, net of issue costs.

b. On February 15, 19C, Howard issued, at $110 per share, 100,000 shares of $100 par value, 8% cumulative preferred stock with 100,000 detachable warrants. Each warrant contained one right, which with $20 could be exchanged for one share of $10 par value common stock. On February 15, 10C, the market price for one stock right was $1.
c. On March 1, 19C, Howard reacquired 20,000 shares of its common stock for $18.50 per share. Howard uses the cost method to account for treasury stock.
d. On March 15, 19C, when the common stock was trading for $21 per share, a major stockholder donated 10,000 shares, which are appropriately recorded as treasury stock.
e. On March 31, 19C, Howard declared a semiannual cash dividend on common stock of 10 cents per share, payable on April 30, 19C, to stockholders of record on April 10, 19C. The appropriate state law prohibits cash dividends on treasury stock.
f. On April 15, 19C, when the market price of the stock rights was $2 each and the market price of the common stock was $22 per share, 30,000 stock rights were exercised. Howard issued new shares to settle the transaction.
g. On April 30, 19C, employees exercised 100,000 options that were granted in 19A under a noncompensatory stock option plan. When the options were granted, each option had a preemptive right and entitled the employee to purchase one share of common stock for $20 per share. On April 30, 19C, the market price of the common stock was $23 per share. Howard issued new shares to settle the transaction.
h. On May 31, 19C, when the market price of the common stock was $23 per share, Howard declared a 5% stock dividend distributable on July 1, 19C, to stockholders of record on June 1, 19C. The appropriate state law prohibits stock dividends on treasury stock. On July 1, 19C, immediately after issuance of the dividend shares, the market price of the common stock was $20.
i. On June 30, 19C, Howard sold the 20,000 treasury shares reacquired on March 1, 19C, and an additional 280,000 treasury shares costing $5,600,000 that were on hand at the beginning of the year. The selling price was $25 per share.
j. On September 30, 19C, Howard declared a semiannual cash dividend on common stock of 10 cents per share and the yearly dividend on preferred stock, both payable on October 30, 19C, to stockholders of record on October 10, 19C. The appropriate state law prohibits cash dividends on treasury stock.
k. On December 31, 19C, the remaining outstanding rights expired.
l. Net income for 19C was $25,000,000.

Required:
Prepare a schedule to be used to summarize, for each transaction, the changes in Howard's stockholders' equity accounts for 19C. The columns on this schedule should have the following 11 headings:

Date of transaction (or beginning date); Common Stock—number of shares; Common stock—amount; Preferred stock—number of shares; Preferred stock—amount; Common stock warrants—number of rights; Common stock warrants—amount; Additional contributed capital (including contributed capital in excess of par, etc.); Retained earnings; Treasury stock—number of shares; and Treasury stock—cost amount.

(AICPA adapted)

17–16 (Relates to Supplement 17–A; Quasi-Reorganization, Entries and Reporting)

The following account balances were shown on the books of Overton Corporation at December 31, 19D:

Noncumulative preferred stock, 5% par $100, 2000 shares outstanding	$200,000
Common stock, par $50, 5,000 shares outstanding	250,000
Retained earnings (deficit)	(45,000)

At a stockholders' meeting (including holders of preferred shares) the following actions related to a quasi-reorganization were decided upon:

a. Amendment to the charter shall be obtained authorizing a total of 5,000 shares of preferred stock, 6%, par $100 per share, cumulative, and 40,000 shares of nopar common stock.

b. All outstanding stock shall be returned in exchange for the new stock as follows:
   (1) For each share of the old preferred stock, one share of new preferred. Purchased for cash at par 20 shares of old preferred stock from a dissatisfied stockholder and the remainder exchanged.
   (2) For each share of the old common stock, two shares of the new common stock; the credit to the nopar stock account shall be at an amount that creates a credit balance in contributed capital from conversion sufficient to exactly eliminate the deficit in retained earnings. All of the old common shares were exchanged.

c. The retained earnings deficit shall be written off against the credit created by the conversion of the common stock. The above actions were subsequently approved by Overton's creditors.

During the ensuing year, 19E, the following additional transactions and events were completed.

d. Sold 200 shares of the new preferred stock at $112 per share.

e. The company issued 1,200 shares of nopar common stock in payment for a patent tentatively valued by the seller at $20,000. (The current market value of a share of the common stock was $15.)

f. The company sold 50 shares of nopar common stock at $19 per share, receiving cash. Overton also issued 100, $1,000 bonds at 102; one share of common stock, as a bonus, was given with each bond.

g. At the end of 19E, the board of directors met and was informed that the net income before deductions for bonuses to officers was $100,000. The directors approved the following actions:
   (1) 500 shares of nopar common stock (from authorized but unissued shares) shall be issued to the officers as a bonus (at no cost to the officers). The market price of a nopar common share on this date was $16.
   (2) Declared and paid cash dividends (for one year) on the preferred stock outstanding.

Required:

1. Prepare journal entries to record the above transactions, including the quasi-reorganization.
2. Prepare the stockholders' equity section of the statement of financial position after all of the above transactions were recorded.

P 17–17 **(Relates to Supplement 17–A; Quasi-Reorganization; Entries and Reporting)** During the last five years, Norwood Corporation experienced severe losses. A new president has been tentatively employed who is confident the company can be saved from bankruptcy (and dissolution). Working with an independent CPA, the new president has proposed a quasi-reorganization with the constraints that *(a)* the capital structure must be changed to eliminate the deficit in retained earnings and *(b)* it must be approved by the stockholders and creditors. The Norwood board of directors approved the proposal and submitted it to a vote to the stockholders and obtained approval of the creditors.

Prior to quasi-reorganization, Norwood's statement of financial position (summarized) reflected the following:

Cash	$ 20,000
Accounts receivable	94,000
Allowance for doubtful accounts	(4,000)
Inventory	150,000
Operational assets	800,000
Accumulated depreciation	(300,000)
Deferred charges	40,000
	$ 800,000
Current liabilities	$ 150,000
Long-term liabilities	240,000
Common stock, par $50	500,000
Preferred stock, par $100	100,000
Contributed capital in excess of par, preferred stock	30,000
Retained earnings, deficit	(220,000)
	$ 800,000

The quasi-reorganization proposal, as approved by the stockholders and creditors, provided the following:

a. To adequately provide for probable losses on accounts receivable, increase the allowance to $6,000.
b. Write down the inventory to $100,000 because of obsolete and damaged goods.
c. Reduce the book value of the operational assets to $400,000 by increasing accumulated depreciation.
d. With the agreement of the creditors, reduce all liabilities by 5%.
e. Reduce the par value of the preferred shares to $60.
f. Eliminate the contributed capital in excess of par on the preferred stock.
g. Call in the old common stock and issue a new common stock, nopar. Set up a new nopar common stock account reduced by the amount needed to adjust retained earnings to zero.

Required:
1. Give a separate entry for each of the above changes.
2. Prepare a statement of financial position immediately after the quasi-reorganization.

CASES

C 17–1 (Recommendations about Dividends)
Tranor Corporation's accounts on January 1 showed the following balances (summarized):

Cash	$ 35,000
Other current assets	25,000
Operational assets (net)	235,000
Other assets	55,000
	$350,000
Current liabilities	$ 30,000
Long-term liabilities	60,000
Capital stock, par $10 (20,000 shares)	200,000
Contributed capital in excess of par	10,000
Retained earnings	50,000
	$350,000

The board of directors is considering a cash dividend, and you have been requested to provide assistance as an independent CPA. The following questions have been referred to you:

1. What is the maximum amount of cash dividends that can be paid on January 1? Explain.
2. Approximately what amount of dividends would you recommend based upon the data from the accounts? Explain.
3. Give the entries that should be made assuming a $26,000 cash dividend is declared with the following dates specified: *(a)* declaration date, *(b)* record date, and *(c)* payment date.
4. Assuming a statement of financial position is prepared between declaration date and payment date, how should the dividend declaration be reported?

C 17–2 (Financial Shares; Analysis)

Tudor Corporation made the following entry to record the final disposition of all fractional share rights issued in connection with a "small" stock dividend:

Fractional share rights outstanding	3,750	
Common stock, par $10		2,000
Contributed capital, lapsed stock rights		1,250
Cash		500

Required:

1. What dispositions were made of the total of the fractional share rights, as evidenced by the above entry? State specifically what the stockholders did with their fractional share rights to dispose of them.
2. On what date would Tudor have known the number of fractional share rights it would have to issue as a part of the stock dividend distribution?
3. How would the above entry be altered if the stock dividend had been "large" instead of "small"?

C 17–3 (Should the Board of Directors Declare a Dividend?)

Drake Company was started in 1975 to manufacture a wide range of plastic products from three basic components. The company was originally owned by 23 stockholders; however, five years after formation, the capital structure was expanded considerably, at which time preferred stock was issued. The preferred is nonvoting, cumulative, nonparticipating, 6% stock. The company has experienced a substantial growth in business over the years. This growth was due to two principal factors: *(a)* the dynamic management and *(b)* geographic location. The firm served a rapidly expanding area with relatively few regionally situated competitors.

The December 31,1987 audited statement of financial position showed the following (summarized):

Cash	$ 11,000	Current liabilities	$ 38,000
Other current assets	76,000	Long-term notes payable	60,000
Investment in K Co. stock (at cost)	30,000	Preferred stock, par $100 (500 shares)*	50,000
Plant and equipment (net)	310,000	Common stock, $15 par value (10,000 shares)*	150,000
Intangible assets	15,000	Premium on preferred stock	2,000
Other assets	8,000	Retained earnings	25,000
	$450,000	Profits invested in plant	125,000
			$450,000

* Authorized shares—preferred, 2,000; common, 20,000.

The board of directors has not declared a dividend since organization; instead, the profits are used to expand the company. This decision was based on the facts that the original capital was small and there was a decision to limit the number of stockholders. At the present time, the common stock is held by slightly fewer than 50 individuals. Each of these individuals also owns preferred shares; their total holdings approximate 46% of the outstanding preferred. The preferred was issued at the time of the expansion of capital.

The board of directors has been planning to declare a dividend during the early part of 1988, payable June 30. However, the cash position as shown by the statement of financial position has raised serious doubts as to the advisability of a dividend in 1988. The president has explained that most of the cash will be needed shortly to pay for inventory already purchased.

The company has a chief accountant but no controller. The board relies on an outside CPA for advice concerning financial management. The CPA was asked to advise about the contemplated dividend declaration. Four of the seven members of the board felt very strongly that some kind of dividend must be declared and paid, and that all stockholders "should get something."

Required:
You have been asked to analyze the situation and make whatever dividend proposals that appear to be worthy of consideration by the board. Present amounts to support your recommendations in a form suitable for consideration by the board in reaching a decision. Provide the basis for your proposals, and indicate any preferences that you may have.

C 17–4 (Relates to Supplement 17–A; Quasi-Reorganization)
Marks Corporation, a medium-sized manufacturer, has experienced operating losses for the past five years. Although operations for the current year ended also resulted in a loss, several important changes made the fourth quarter a profitable one; as a result, future operations of the company are expected to be profitable.

The treasurer suggested a quasi-reorganization to *(a)* eliminate the accumulated deficit of $325,000 in retained earnings, *(b)* write up the $600,000 cost of operating land and buildings to their current market value, and *(c)* set up an asset of $175,000 representing the estimated future tax benefit of the losses accumulated to date.

Required:
1. What are the characteristics of a quasi-reorganization? (That is, of what does it consist?)
2. List the conditions under which a quasi-reorganization generally would be justified.
3. Discuss the propriety of the treasurer's proposals to—
   a. Eliminate the deficit of $325,000.
   b. Write up the value of the operating land and buildings of $600,000 to their current market value.
   c. Set up an asset of $175,000 representing the future tax benefit of the losses accumulated to date. (AICPA adapted)

18 INVESTMENTS IN SECURITIES AND CONSOLIDATED FINANCIAL STATEMENTS

OVERVIEW AND PURPOSE

If $100,000 cash is to be invested, numerous investments would come to mind including real estate, debt securities (e.g., bonds), and equity securities (e.g., common stock). Also, consideration should be given to whether short-term, long-term, or a mix of these investments should be made. An investor would soon realize some of the needs of a **user** of financial statements. Chapter 15 discussed long-term debt securities by the issuer (i.e., debtor or borrower) and the investor (i.e., the creditor or lender). This chapter discusses short-term investments in debt and equity securities and long-term investments in equity securities.

To accomplish this purpose the chapter is subdivided as follows:

Part A: Investments in Securities

1. Characteristics of investment securities.
2. Acquisition of short-term and long-term investment securities.
3. Realized and unrealized gains and losses.
4. Accounting for short-term investments in debt securities.
5. Accounting for long-term investments in equity securities.
6. Equity method of accounting for long-term investments in equity securities.
7. Disclosure of investments in equity securities.
8. Market value method for equity securities.
9. Some special problems in accounting for equity investments.

Part B: Consolidated Financial Statements

1. Concept of a controlling interest.
2. Acquiring a controlling interest.
3. Accounting and reporting problems.
4. Consolidation of financial statements subsequent to acquisition.
5. Push-down accounting.
6. Accounting for futures contracts—an investment.

PART A: INVESTMENTS IN SECURITIES

Characteristics of Investment Securities

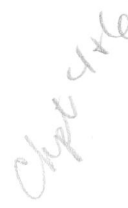

Investment securities may be classified as either short- or long-term, and each group may include both equity and debt securities. Chapter 15 discussed long-term **debt securities** and Chapters 16 and 17 discussed accounting for **equity securities** primarily by the issuer. Equity securities represent ownership interests whereas debt securities represent creditor interests.

For accounting purposes **short-term** investments in equity and debt securities must satisfy the following criteria:

a. **Current asset**—the security must meet the requirements of the definition of a current asset.

b. **Readily marketable**—the security must be regularly traded on a security exchange or some other regularly established market.[1]

c. **Investor's conversion intention**—the investor's intention must be to convert the security to cash within one year from the statement of financial position date, or the operating cycle, if longer.

Short-term investments in securities often include common stock, preferred stock, short-term debt securities such as certificates of deposits, Treasury bills and similar commercial paper, and corporate and government bonds that have a ready market.

Long-term investments in securities must satisfy the following criteria:

a. The investment includes all securities that do not meet the three requirements listed above for short-term investments.

b. The investment must satisfy all of the criteria for inclusion in the statement of financial position caption, "Investments and Funds" (see Chapter 4).

Long-term investments in securities often include common stock, preferred stock, bonds, long-term notes, and other debt securities.

This chapter discusses four different methods of accounting for short-term debt and equity securities and long-term investments in equity securities. To enhance understanding of each method, the following designations are used:

1. **Cost**—original cost (non-LCM).
2. **Cost, LCM**—lower of original cost or current market.
3. **Market value**—current market value at the end of the reporting period.
4. **Equity method**—a special method for long-term equity securities.

Acquisition of Short-Term and Long-Term Investment Securities

Investment securities may be purchased directly from the issuing company or from individual investors. They also may be purchased indirectly through stockbrokers and dealers, through the stock exchanges, or over the counter.

---

[1] *FASB Interpretation No. 16*, "Clarification of Definitions and Accounting for Marketable Equity Securities that Become Nonmarketable" (Stamford, Conn., February 1977), provides some detailed rules pertaining to marketability.

At date of acquisition of an investment security an appropriately designated investment account is debited for the cost of the investment in conformity with the **cost principle.** Cost includes the basic cost of the security plus brokerage fees, excise taxes, and any other transfer costs incurred by the purchaser. Capital stock may be purchased for cash, "on margin," or on a subscription basis. When stock is purchased on margin, only part of the purchase price is paid initially. The balance is borrowed (usually through a brokerage firm). The stock investment should be recorded at its cost, including the portion financed with borrowed funds.

An investment in capital stock sometimes is made on a **subscription basis** involving a down payment and a liability for the balance. In this case, the investor debits the investment account for cost, credits cash for the down payment, and credits a liability for the balance. **Interest** specified on a subscription contract, or on funds borrowed to purchase the investment, should be recorded as periodic interest expense in the same manner as interest on any other debt. It should **not** be capitalized as part of the cost of the investment.

When **noncash considerations** (property or services) are given for an investment, the cost assigned to the securities should be measured by *(a)* the **market value** of the consideration given, or *(b)* the market value of the securities received, whichever can be more reliably determined. Inability to reliably determine either one of these market values in an exchange of unlisted or closely held securities for property for which no established market value exists will require the use of appraisals or estimates.

Securities frequently are purchased between **regular** interest or dividend dates. For such purchases accrued interest is recorded on debt securities because interest is a legal obligation. **Cash** or **property dividends are not accrued** on equity securities because the earnings process is not completed until the dividends are actually declared.

A purchase of two or more classes of securities for a **single lump sum** (called a **lump-sum** or **basket purchase**) necessitates allocation of the total cost to each class of securities based upon available market value information. When the market value of each class is available, the **proportional method** is used to allocate the lump-sum price based on relative market values. Alternatively, if the market prices of all but one class of securities are known, the **incremental method** is applied. This method allocates total cost first to the class(es) of securities with the known market value(s), and then assigns the remainder of the lump-sum price to the class of stock that does not have a market price (see Chapter 16, page 732).

Two cases are used to illustrate the purchase of an equity investment.

Case A—Cash Purchase. On October 1, 19C, Blue Corporation purchased 5,000 shares of Clear Corporation's common stock, par $5, at $20 per share. Commissions incurred by Blue Corporation were $500. The annual dividend date for the stock is usually July 1. The last dividend was $.50 per share. The investment is recorded as follows:

Long-term (or short-term) investment, common stock, Clear Corp. [(5,000 shares × $20) + $500]	100,500	
Cash		100,500

(Note that dividends are not accrued in this entry.)

Case B—Noncash Purchase. Same facts as in Case A except Blue Corporation transferred a tract of vacant land (carried in Blue's accounts at $35,000) plus $5,500 cash as a payment in full for the common stock. The common stock of Clear Corporation is regularly selling at $20 per share. The disposal of the land and the purchase of the stock are recorded as follows:

Long-term (or short-term) investment, common stock, Clear Corp. (5,000 shares × $20) + $500	100,500	
Land		35,000
Gain on disposal of land		60,000
Cash		5,500

Accounting for investments is facilitated if a consistent system of security-cost identification is used. A record of each individual security should be maintained. This record documents units purchased (by certificate number), dates, and unit cost. These details are important when a security is subsequently sold because it should be "costed out" on a systematic basis. Otherwise, errors and manipulation of gains and losses may occur.

Usually identification of securities sold is not difficult. However, identification is difficult when there is a large number of transactions, when blocks of securities have been transferred through an estate, or when the issuer has exchanged substitute securities for those originally purchased. Income tax law requires use of "first-in, first-out" when specific identification cannot be made. Use of specific identification, FIFO, or average (but not LIFO) cost procedures is acceptable for financial accounting purposes. However, most companies use the same approach for tax and accounting purposes to avoid recording deferred income taxes (see Chapter 23).

The choice of a particular "cost flow" method may affect the gain or loss reported. To illustrate, if 10 shares of X Corporation stock were purchased at $150 per share and later an additional 30 shares were purchased at $200 per share, the subsequent sale of 5 shares at $180 per share would pose a cost identification problem. If the five shares can be identified by certificate number as a part of the first purchase, a **gain** of $30 per share should be recognized. Alternatively, if they are identified with the second purchase, a **loss** of $20 per share should be recognized. The averaging procedure would report a **loss** of $7.50 per share computed as follows:

First purchase	10 shares × $150 =	$1,500
Second purchase	30 shares × 200 =	6,000
Total	40	$7,500
Average cost per share, $7,500 ÷ 40 shares		$187.50
Sale price per share		180.00
Loss per share		$ 7.50

Accounting for Investment Securities after Acquisition

After acquisition the accounting for investment securities is somewhat different for short-term investments than for long-term investments. These differences can be summarized as follows:

a. **Short-term investments in debt and equity securities**—Depending on the type of security, short-term investments may be accounted for after acquisition date on the basis of: (1) cost, LCM (2), cost, or (3) market. For example, *Accounting Trends & Techniques, 1987* (p. 113), presented the following data concerning the methods used:

	Number of companies			
	1986	**1985**	**1984**	**1983**
Cost:				
Approximates market	259	253	252	255
No reference to market	18	15	17	21
Market value disclosed	2	6	6	3
Lower of cost or market	43	40	40	34
Market value	3	5	5	3

b. **Long-term investments in equity securities**—Depending on the level of ownership (i.e., proportion of the voting shares owned) long-term investments may be accounted for using the *(a)* Cost, LCM, *(b)* equity method, or *(c)* market value method. Also, when the investor has a controlling interest in the investee corporation, consolidated financial statements must be presented.

Accounting for Short-Term Investments in Securities

Accounting for short-term investments in securities traditionally has been characterized by a wide diversity of practice, both in recording and reporting. Part of this problem has been because of the different characteristics of short-term debt and equity securities. Because of the numerous ways that were being used to measure, record, and report investments in marketable securities, many of which were grossly misleading, the FASB issued *FASB Standard 12,* "Accounting for Certain Marketable Securities." This *Standard* improved the accounting for equity securities by specifying measurement and reporting rules, but did not resolve the accounting for debt securities, therefore, accounting for debt securities continues to be guided by *ARB No. 43,* chap. 3A, par. 9.

Accounting for Short-Term Investments in Equity Securities

FASB Standard 12 requires that both short-term (and long-term) investments in marketable equity securities be valued at each statement of financial position date on a portfolio lower-of-cost-or-market basis as follows:[2]

> The carrying amount of a marketable equity securities portfolio shall be the lower of its aggregate cost or market value, determined at balance sheet date. The amount by which aggregate cost of the **portfolio** exceeds market value shall be accounted for as the valuation allowance.
>
> Marketable equity securities owned by an entity shall . . . be grouped into separate portfolios according to the current or noncurrent classification of the securities for the purpose of comparing aggregate cost and market value to determine carrying amount.

For instructional clarity, we refer to this as the **Cost, LCM method.**

The above requirements involve application of the portfolio basis and the distinction between realized and unrealized gains and losses.

---

[2] *FASB Standard 12* specifically relates only to equity securities (not to debt securities). However, *FASB Standard 12* makes one exception as follows: The term [equity securities] ". . . does not encompass preferred stock that by its terms either must be redeemed by the issuing enterprise or is redeemable at the option of the investor, nor does it include treasury stock or convertible bonds." The exception recognizes that the specified redemption requirement makes such preferred stock almost like a debt security, and *FASB Standard 12* does not consider debt securities. Also, *FASB Standard 12* is not applicable to mutual life insurance companies because of specified practices.

Portfolio Basis Defined. At the end of each reporting period, the short-term equity investments are grouped into one aggregate **portfolio** to determine total (i.e., aggregate) original cost and total market value. Short-term debt securities usually are grouped in a separate portfolio. Similarly, long-term investments are grouped in separate portfolios.

Realized and Unrealized Gains and Losses

To account for both short- and long-term investments in **equity** securities, *FASB Standard 12* makes a careful distinction between **realized** and **unrealized** gains and losses. **Realized** gains and losses usually relate to the **sale** of equity securities. **Unrealized** gains and losses **do not** relate to the sale of securities, rather they relate to the application of the **lower-of-cost-or-market** rule to the total investment portfolio (of equity securities) at the **end** of each annual accounting period. In this context, the following definitions are applied in accounting for investments in equity securities:

1. **Realized gain**—At date of sale, the net amount received is more than the original cost (i.e., purchase cost) on an individual equity security basis.
2. **Realized loss**—A realized loss is recognized when:
   a. At date of sale, there is an **excess** of the original cost of an individual equity security over the net proceeds received by the investor.
   b. An individual equity security is **transferred** between the long- and short-term portfolios and its market value at date of transfer is below its original cost.
   c. An individual security is written down due to a **permanent** decline in its market value below its original cost.
3. **Unrealized loss**—An unrealized loss occurs when the end-of-period current market value of a portfolio of investments in equity securities is less than the total cost of that portfolio. An unrealized loss is recognized only at the end of an accounting period in an adjusting entry. If the portfolio is a short-term investment; the unrealized loss is recorded, and then reported on the statement of income. However, if the portfolio is a long-term investment, the unrealized loss is reported as a **negative** element of stockholders' equity (discussed later). For short-term investments the year-end adjusting entry debits an **unrealized loss** account (e.g., Unrealized Loss on Short-Term Equity Investments), and credits an allowance account (e.g., Allowance to Reduce Short-Term Equity Investments to LCM). The unrealized loss amount is reported on the current statement of income. The allowance account is reported on the statement of financial position as a contra account (i.e., deduction) to the related investment account.
4. **Unrealized gain**—An unrealized gain occurs when the current market value of the **portfolio** of investments in equity securities is above the total portfolio valued at LCM at the end of the prior period. The resulting unrealized gain can only be recorded to the extent of the write-downs for unrealized losses. For this reason it often is called an **unrealized loss recovery.** That is, under the Cost, LCM method, the valuation of the investment portfolio can never exceed the original cost of the total portfolio

cost. An unrealized gain (i.e., reduction of prior unrealized losses) is recorded in an adjusting entry only at the end of an accounting period, and then is reported on the statement of income. However, if a long-term investment is involved, the unrealized gain is reported as an element of stockholders' equity (discussed later). For short-term investments this unrealized gain (or loss recovery) is recorded as a debit to the previously established allowance account and a credit to an unrealized gain (or loss recovery account). Application of Cost, LCM method in this manner can be summarized as: **write down for unrealized losses, write back up for unrealized loss recoveries, but do not write up above original cost.**

The sale of a short-term equity investment is recorded as a debit for the resources received, a credit to the investment account for its original cost, and the difference is recorded as a **realized** gain or loss.

Cost, LCM Method for Short-Term Equity Securities Illustrated. To illustrate the Cost, LCM method for short-term investments in equity securities, Zero Corporation invested temporarily idle cash in two short-term investments and made the following entry:

March 1, 19A—to record acquisition:

Investment in equity securities, short term	16,200*	
Cash		16,200

* Apex common, nopar (50 shares × $104) + Rye preferred, par $50 (200 shares × $55).

November 1, 19A—received a cash dividend of $1 per share on the Rye preferred stock:

Cash (200 shares × $1)	200	
Investment revenue		200

December 31, 19A—Quoted market prices, Apex common, $96; Rye preferred, $56.25:
To record the unrealized loss:

Unrealized loss on short-term investments	150*	
Allowance to reduce short-term investments to market		150

*** Computation:**

Stock	Shares	Cost		Market	
Apex common	50	× $104 = $ 5,200		× $96.00 = $ 4,800	
Rye preferred	200	× 55 = 11,000		× 56.25 = 11,250	
Total		$16,200	−	$16,050	= $150†

† Balance needed in the allowance account.

Reporting for 19A:

Statement of income:		
Investment revenue		$ 200
Unrealized loss on short-term investments*		(150)
Statement of financial position:		
Current assets:		
Investment in equity securities, short term	$16,200	
Less: Allowance to reduce to market	150	$16,050

* Some accountants prefer a title similar to the following: Unrealized loss on marketable securities.

When a short-term equity security is sold, any amount in the **allowance** account is **disregarded** because that balance relates to the **total** portfolio and not to any single part of it. **The allowance account is adjusted only at each year-end.**

To illustrate, on January 26, 19B, Zero sold all of its short-term investments in equity securities for cash as follows: Apex common, $98 per share, and Rye preferred, $54 per share. This transaction would be recorded as follows:

January 26, 19B:

Cash (50 shares × $98) + (200 shares × $54)	15,700	
Loss (realized) on sale of investments	500	
Investment in equity securities, short term (50 shares × $104) + (200 shares × $55)		16,200

To conclude this example, assume the following for 19B:

a. Zero Corporation purchased a short-term equity investment and made the following entry:

June 6, 19B:

Investment in equity securities, short term. AB Corporation, common stock, par $5 (100 shares × $70)	7,000	
Cash		7,000

b. At the end of 19B, the AB Corporation stock was selling at $71. At the end of 19B the portfolio consists of only AB stock—portfolio cost, $7,000 and portfolio market, $7,100 (higher than cost). Therefore, the allowance account must be reduced to a zero balance. However, it has a balance carried over from 19A of $150. Therefore, the following entry must be made to reduce the allowance account balance to zero:

December 31, 19B:

Allowance to reduce short-term investments to market	150	
Unrealized loss recovery on short-term investments		150

As a result of the 19B transactions, Zero Corporation would report the following on its 19B financial statements:

Statement of income (for 19B):	
Loss on sale of short-term investments	$ 500
Unrealized loss recovery on short-term investments*	(150)
Statement of financial position (end of 19B):	
Current assets:	
Investment in equity securities, short term, at cost (approximate market, $7,100)	$7,000

* Some accountants prefer a title similar to the following: Unrealized gain on marketable securities.

Consider the effect of recording the LCM loss (of $150 in 19A). First, for 19A it **reduced** 19A current assets and income by the amount of the unrealized loss. Second, in the next year (19B) the unrealized loss is "reversed" to prevent it from being **double counted.** This procedure does not affect the amount of **realized** gain or loss on sale of the investment. The net effect is to shift any unrealized loss to the earlier year when it occurred, and thus, better conform to the matching principle.

Accounting for Short-Term Investments in Debt Securities

Short-term investments in **debt** securities are recorded in the investment account at **cost** in conformity with the cost principle. Any discount or premium caused by a difference between the maturity value (or par) of the debt security and the acquisition price usually is not separately recorded. Also, because of the short holding period, this discount or premium usually is not amortized; thus, the investment account continues to carry the cost amount until the investment is sold.

As noted above, *FASB Standard 12* superseded *ARB No. 43* only with regard to equity securities. Therefore, *ARB No. 43* continues as the "official" basis for accounting for short-term investments in debt securities. It specifies the cost (not LCM) method for short-term investments in debt securities. Under this method they are carried at **acquisition cost** except when (1) their current market value is less than cost by a **substantial** amount and (2) the market value decline is **not** due to **temporary** conditions. When both of these conditions exist, *ARB No. 43* requires that the short-term debt security be written down to market value to recognize the **permanent** impairment of the assets value. Subsequent to this write-down, which would not occur often, any recovery in market value is not recognized in the accounts. This is not the LCM rule illustrated above for equity securities. The reduced carrying value then is used as **cost** for future accounting purposes. Therefore, a permanent decline usually is recorded as a direct credit to the investment account and a debit to a loss (realized) account, such as "Impairment Loss on Investments in Marketable Securities."

Application of the cost (not LCM) method to short-term investments in debt securities is not complex. However, when a debt security is purchased or sold between interest dates, the interest accrued since the last interest date must be computed and recorded separately from cost because on the next interest date the new owner of the debt security will receive the full cash amount of interest for the interest period just ended. On the transaction date, the buyer and the seller of the debt actually will "offset cash" for the amount of interest accrued from the prior interest date to the date of purchase/sale. The amount of accrued interest at transaction date is separately identified because it does not affect the cost or sale price of the security. Rather, it affects the amount of investment revenue earned.

Transfers of a debt security from the short-term portfolio to the long-term portfolio (and vice versa) are made at the carrying value at the date of transfer.

Cost Method for Short-Term Debt Securities Illustrated. To illustrate application of the **cost method** (not LCM) in accounting for and reporting short-term investments in debt securities, we will consider transactions from acquisition date through sale date. The accounting period ends December 31.

June 30, 19A—Purchased a $10,000 bond of KD Corporation at 98 (i.e., $9,800 cash) plus accrued interest. The bond pays 9% interest each March 31.

Investment in debt securities, short term	9,800	
Interest receivable* ($10,000 × 9% × 3/12; April–June)	225	
Cash ($9,800 + $225)		10,025

* Interest Receivable is debited because this amount will be included in the interest collected during the next reporting period (i.e., on March 31, 19B). If the collection is to be made in the current period, it would be more convenient to debit Interest Revenue.

December 31, 19A (end of the accounting period):

a. To accrue interest for June 30–December 31:

Interest receivable ($10,000 × 9% × 6/12)	450	
Interest revenue		450

b. KD bonds are quoted at 97.5:

No entry is required to record the lower market value because (1) there is no indication that the market value decline is significant, and (2) there is no indication of a permanent impairment of asset value.

Reporting for 19A (cost method):

Statement of income:	
Interest revenue	$ 450
Statement of financial position:	
Current assets:	
Investments in debt securities, short term, at cost (market value, $9,750)	9,800
Interest receivable ($225 + $450)	675

March 31, 19B—interest date:

Cash ($10,000 × 9%)	900	
Interest receivable ($225 + $450)		675
Interest revenue ($10,000 × 9% × 3/12; January–March)		225

October 1, 19B—Sold the bond investment for $9,850 cash plus accrued interest:

Cash [$9,850 + ($10,000 × 9% × 6/12 = $450)]	10,300	
Investment in debt securities, short term		9,800
Interest revenue ($10,000 × 9% × 6/12; April–Sept.)		450
Gain (realized) on sale of short-term investment		50

Many companies use the Cost, LCM method, rather than the cost method, for short-term investments in debt securities because: *(a) FASB Standard 12* does not specifically forbid such use, *(b)* it is easier to use the same method for both equity and debt securities, *(c)* the Cost, LCM valuation is as logical for short-term investments in debt securities as for equity securities, and *(d)* for comparative purposes (it is more widely used than the cost method). Usually a separate portfolio is set up for debt securities and the Cost, LCM method is applied to those securities in exactly the same way as illustrated earlier for equity securities.

Long-term investments in **debt** securities are accounted for by using the cost method. This topic was discussed in Chapter 15.

Accounting for Long-Term Investments in Equity Securities

Four different methods are used to account for a long-term equity investment: (1) cost, (2) Cost, LCM, (3) equity, and (4) market value. The investor is **not** given a "free choice" in selecting which of these methods to apply. Based on specified conditions, only one of these methods is appropriate for each kind of investment. In addition, when one company owns a **controlling interest** in the outstanding voting stock of another company, the controlling company usually must prepare **consolidated financial statements** (discussed in Part B of this chapter).

To account for long-term investments in the voting capital stock of another company, *APB Opinion 18* defined two important factors, "significant influence" and "control," as follows:

1. **Significant influence**—The ability of the **investor** company to affect, to an important degree, the operating and financial policies of another company through ownership of a sufficient portion of its **voting** stock. The ability to exercise significant influence also may be shown in several other ways. These ways include representation on the board of directors, interchange of managerial personnel, material intercompany transactions, and technological dependency. To attain a reasonable degree of uniformity, the APB provided an operational rule. This rule states that an investment of **20% or more of the outstanding voting stock** should lead to the presumption that, in the absence of evidence to the contrary, an investor has the ability to exercise **significant influence** over the other company.[3]
2. **Controlling interest**—A controlling interest exists when the investor company owns enough of the **voting** stock of the other company to determine its operating and financial policies. Ownership of **over 50%** of the outstanding voting stock usually would assure **control;** however, in some cases, this percent may not be sufficient (discussed in Part B). In still other cases, ownership of less than 50% of the outstanding voting stock may create a controlling interest. Factors such as the number of stockholders and the extent of stockholder participation in voting have some bearing on the point at which a controlling interest is attained. Operationally, the APB presumption is that a controlling interest is represented by **over 50% of the voting stock,** absent other compelling factors.

Cost, LCM Method of Accounting for Long-Term Investments in Equity Securities

The Cost, LCM method of accounting used for short-term equity investments (see page 827) also is used for long-term investments in equity securities. In conformity with *FASB Standard 12* it must be used for long-term investments in equity securities **except** when the investor has stock holdings that confer **significant influence** or **control.**[4] Cost, LCM would be used when *(a)* nonvoting stock is held and *(b)* when the number of voting shares held is small (arbitrarily defined as less than 20%).

---

[3] An investor may be **unable** to exercise significant influence over the investee's policies when:

a. Opposition by the investee, such as litigation or complaints to governmental regulatory authorities, challenges the investor's ability to exercise significant influence.
b. The investor and investee sign an agreement under which the investor surrenders significant rights as a stockholder.
c. Majority ownership of the investee is concentrated among a small group of stockholders who operate the investee without regard to the views of the investor.
d. The investor tries and fails to obtain representation on the investee's board of directors.

The above list, from *FASB Interpretation 35,* "Criteria for Applying the Equity Method of Accounting for Investments in Common Stock" (Stamford, Conn., May 1981), is intended to be illustrative and not all-inclusive.

[4] *FASB Standard 12,* par. 6, provides this exception by stating that: "Investments accounted for by the equity method, as described in *APB Opinion No. 18,* are beyond the scope of this Statement except for the provisions of paragraph 18."

The Cost, LCM method is applied to **long-term** investments in equity securities in the same way as for short-term investments in equity securities (see page 827), **except for one major difference**—that is, how the **unrealized loss** (and loss recovery) is reported. For short-term investments the unrealized loss is reported as a **deduction on the statement of income** on the basis that it is a current loss (i.e., the investment will be sold within the next year, or operating cycle, if longer). In contrast, when the investment is long term, the unrealized loss is debited to a **stockholders' equity account.** This is a negative (i.e., contra) stockholders' account. The credit to the allowance account (e.g., Allowance to Reduce Long-Term Equity Investments to LCM) is essentially the same as for short-term investments. This account is reported, as before, on the statement of financial position as a contra account to the related investment account.

For illustrative purposes refer to the prior case for Zero Corporation (page 827), and compare the entries and reporting under two assumptions as follows:

Cost, LCM method (account titles abbreviated for practical reasons)

Short-term equity securities			Long-term equity securities		
March 1, 19A—acquisition:					
Investment in equity securities, ST	16,200		Investment in equity securities, LT	16,200	
Cash		16,200	Cash		16,200
November 1, 19A—dividend:					
Cash	200		Cash	200	
Investment revenue		200	Investment revenue		200
December 31, 19A—unrealized loss (boxed for emphasis):					
Unrealized loss on ST investment*	150		Unrealized loss on LT investment†	150	
Allowance to reduce ST investments to LCM		150	Allowance to reduce LT investments to LCM		150
* Reported on the statement of income.			† Reported on the statement of financial position.		

Cost (LCM) Method Illustrated. **Exhibit 18–1** illustrates the application of the Cost, LCM method applied to long-term investments in equity securities. Panel A gives the case data. Notice the following in panel B:

1. On December 31, 19A and 19B (entries 2 and 5), **LCM** is applied to the aggregate long-term investment portfolio, **not** to individual securities.
2. The April 14, 19B, realized loss due to the **permanent** decline in the market value of Y Corporation stock ($25,000), and the August 10, 19B, **realized gain** on the sale of Z Corporation stock ($4,000) are both closed to Income Summary and reported on the statement of income, as shown in panel C.
3. On August 10, 19B, when 1,000 shares of Z Corporation stock were **sold,** a **realized gain** was recognized for the difference between the selling

price and the **original cost.** Also, a proportionate part of the balance in Allowance to Reduce Long-Term Investments in Equity Securities to Market **was not removed** for the securities sold. Instead, the allowance account for the entire portfolio is adjusted **only** at the end of the period.

4. On December 31, 19B, the $4,500 **credit** to Unrealized Loss on Long-Term Investments in Equity Securities is in the nature of a **loss recovery.** It represents a recovery of the prior write-down of the aggregate portfolio to its market value (i.e., $6,000 − $1,500 = $4,500).

The following example illustrates actual reporting under the cost (LCM) method:

MASCO CORPORATION

	1986	**1985**
Current assets:		
Cash and cash investments	$ 71,410,000	$ 94,530,000
Marketable securities	142,000,000	218,900,000

Notes to Consolidated Financial Statements

Marketable Securities

Marketable securities (principally equity securities and U.S. Government securities) are carried at the lower of cost or market. At December 31, 1986, the cost was $142 million with a market value of $150 million; at December 31, 1985, cost approximated market value.

Included in marketable securities are equity securities, including preferred stocks, with a cost and a market value of $119.7 million and $126.3 million, respectively, at December 31, 1986, and a cost which approximates market value of $164 million at December 31, 1985. At December 31, 1986, unrealized gains approximated $9.8 million, and unrealized losses approximated $3.2 million.

Realized gains and losses on sales of marketable securities are determined on a specific-identification basis. Sales of marketable securities resulted in net realized gains of $14.1 million in 1986, $18.6 million in 1985 and $3.3 million in 1984.

Equity Method of Accounting for Long-Term Investments in Equity Securities

The equity method of accounting for long-term investments is not appropriate for the equity investments discussed above because in those cases the investor did not have enough voting shares to be able to exercise either significant influence or control. **The equity method is used only when the investor has significant influence or control.**[5]

Conceptual Basis of the Equity Method

For the investor, the Cost, LCM, and equity methods are different because they are based on dissimilar concepts of *(a)* investment revenue and *(b)* investment valuation. The conceptual difference is that the Cost, LCM method views the investor and investee as **two** separate entities. In contrast, the equity method views the investor and investee companies as a specially related entity (i.e., significant influence but not control) for investment valuation and income recog-

[5] *APB Opinion No. 18,* "The Equity Method of Accounting for Investments in Common Stock (March 1971).

Exhibit 18–1
Cost, LCM method for long-term investments in equity securities.

Panel A—Case Data:

1. January 5, 19A—ABC Company purchased the following equity securities as a long-term investment (less than 20% of the outstanding voting shares in each case):
   Y Corporation, common stock, par \$5, 5,000 shares at \$12.
   Z Corporation, preferred stock, par \$10, 4,000 shares at \$20.
2. December 31, 19A—Market values: Y stock, \$10; and Z stock, \$21 (temporary).
3. April 14, 19B—Market value of Y Corporation stock decreased to \$7; for purposes of this illustration, the decrease was considered to be permanent.
4. August 10, 19B—Unexpectedly sold 1,000 shares of the Z Corporation stock for cash, \$24 per share.
5. December 31, 19B—Market values: Y stock, \$5.50; and Z stock, \$22 (any increase or decrease from previous market values is considered to be temporary).

Panel B—Entries:

1. January 5, 19A—Purchase date:

Long-term investments in equity securities	140,000	
Cash [(5,000 × \$12) + (4,000 × \$20)]		140,000

2. December 31, 19A—Adjusting entry to LCM:

Unrealized loss on long-term investments in equity securities (stockholders' equity)	6,000	
Allowance to reduce long-term investments in equity securities to market		6,000

Computation:

Security	Shares	Cost	Market	Unrealized gain (loss)
Y	5,000	× \$12 = \$ 60,000	× \$10 = \$ 50,000	
Z	4,000	× 20 = 80,000	× 21 = 84,000	
Total		\$140,000 −	\$134,000 =	\$(6,000)

3. April 14, 19B—Permanent decline (impairment) in value of Y Corporation stock:

Loss in market value of long-term investment [5,000 × (\$12 − \$7)] (realized)	25,000	
Long-term investments in equity securities		25,000

4. August 10, 19B—Sale of 1,000 shares of Z Corporation stock:

Cash (1,000 × \$24)	24,000	
Long-term investments in equity securities (1,000 × \$20)		20,000
Gain on sale of equity securities (realized)		4,000

5. December 31, 19B—Adjusting entry to LCM:

Allowance to reduce long-term investments in equity securities to market	4,500	
Unrealized loss on long-term investments in equity securities		4,500

nition. *APB Opinion No. 18* gives the accounting guidelines for the equity method.[6] The guidelines are as follows:

1. **Single entity concept**—The equity method requires that the **investor's investment** after acquisition be measured as:

$$\left\{\begin{matrix}\text{Investment}\\ \text{cost}\end{matrix}\right\} + \left\{\begin{matrix}\text{Proportionate}\\ \text{share of}\\ \text{investee's}\\ \text{income}\end{matrix}\right\} - \left\{\begin{matrix}\text{Proportionate}\\ \text{share of}\\ \text{investee's}\\ \text{dividends}\end{matrix}\right\} - \left\{\begin{matrix}\text{Adjustments}\\ \text{of investee's}\\ \text{reported}\\ \text{income}\end{matrix}\right\} = \begin{matrix}\text{Investor's}\\ \text{investment}\\ \text{after acquisition}\end{matrix}$$

[6] This *Opinion* states that income and owners' equity amounts should be the same whether a subsidiary is consolidated or accounted for by the equity method (see Part B of this chapter). Also, *FASB Standards 34* and *58* specify the extent that interest capitalized by the investee can be included in the investor's amounts under the equity method. The issue of capitalizing interest costs is beyond the scope of this chapter.

Exhibit 18–1
(concluded)

Computation:

Security	Shares	Cost	Market	Unrealized gain (loss)
Y	5,000	× $ 7 = $35,000	× $ 5.50 = $27,500	
Z	3,000	× 20 = 60,000	× 22.00 = 66,000	
Total		$95,000	− $93,500 =	$(1,500)

Credit balance in allowance account (before December 31, 19B, adjustment)	$6,000
Credit balance needed in allowance account	1,500
Adjustment needed (debit)	$4,500

Panel C—Financial Statements of ABC Company:

	19A		19B	
Statement of income:				
Loss in market value of long-term investments (impairment)		—		$25,000
Gain on sale of long-term investments		—		4,000
Statement of financial position:				
Investments and funds:				
Investments in equity securities, at cost	$140,000		$95,000	
Less: Allowance to reduce equity investments to market	(6,000)		(1,500)	
Investment portfolio at LCM		$134,000		$93,500
Stockholders' equity:				
Unrealized capital:				
Unrealized loss on long-term investments in equity securities		(6,000)		(1,500)

2. **Investment revenue** is measured as:

$$\left.\begin{matrix}\text{Proportionate}\\ \text{share of}\\ \text{investee's}\\ \text{reported income}\end{matrix}\right\} - \left\{\begin{matrix}\text{Adjustments}\\ \text{of investee's}\\ \text{reported}\\ \text{income}\end{matrix}\right. = \begin{matrix}\text{Investment}\\ \text{revenue}\end{matrix}$$

Measurement of the investor's investment and revenue can best be understood in terms of journal entries (amounts assumed):

a. To record purchase of 20% of investee's common stock:

	Debit	Credit
Investment account (20% ownership)	100,000	
Cash		100,000

b. To record proportionate share of investee's reported income ($60,000):

	Debit	Credit
Investment account ($60,000 × 20%)	12,000	
Investment revenue		12,000

c. To record dividends declared by investee ($40,000):

	Debit	Credit
Dividends receivable ($40,000 × 20%)	8,000	
Investment account		8,000

d. To record additional expenses related to income of investee ($1,000, explained later):

Investment revenue ($1,000 × 20%)	200	
Investment account		200

Resulting cumulative balances:

Investment account	$103,800
Investment revenue account	11,800

Under the cost method, the investment account would show a balance of $100,000 and investment revenue would be $8,000. From this it can be seen that under the equity method, the investment and revenue accounts of the **investor** are influenced by income, dividend, and expense changes that are proportionate to those reported by the investee. This is because the equity method views the investor and investee companies as a single economic entity.

The distinction **between voting and nonvoting shares** is important in the case of equity securities because the investor who owns voting shares can exercise some influence (or control) over the financial policies of the issuing corporation. The proportion of the voting shares owned determines the extent or degree of influence (or control) that the investor has over the policies of the issuing corporation. For example, if the investor owns more than 50% of the outstanding voting shares, that investor usually can exercise control because of the level of ownership held (represented only by voting shares).

APB Opinion 18 sets forth procedures for applying the equity method. Among them are the following:

a. The investment in common stock should be shown in the statement of financial position of the investor as a single amount, and the investor's share of the investee's earnings or losses should be shown in the statement of income of the investor as a single amount except for the extraordinary items as specified in *(b)* below.

b. The investor's share of the investee's extraordinary items and prior period adjustments should be reported by the investor in conformity with *APB Opinion 30* and *FASB Standard 16*, respectively. That is, the investor should classify such items in a manner similar to its own extraordinary items and prior period adjustments.

c. Sales of stock of the investee by the investor should be accounted for as gains or losses equal to the difference at the time of sale between selling price and carrying amount of the stock sold.

d. Intercompany profits and losses should be eliminated.

e. A difference between the cost of an investment and the amount of underlying equity in net assets of an investee (i.e., assets, including **goodwill**) should be accounted for as if the investee were a consolidated subsidiary.

Equity Method Illustrated

The above application procedures are illustrated in **Exhibit 18–2.** This exhibit has three panels: panel A, case data; panel B, journal entries; and panel C, financial statements. Refer to that exhibit as you study the following six types of **journal entries that the investor must make under the equity method:**

1. **Record the proportionate share of the investee's reported income** by debiting Investment in Equity Securities and crediting Investment Revenue. In case of a loss, the investment account is credited and Investment Loss is debited. If the investee reports extraordinary items, they must

be separately recorded in this entry. Thus, the investor's investment account increases and decreases with the gains and losses of the investee company. When the investee earns income, the investor is presumed to **earn** a proportionate part of that income, with a consequent increase in asset value, and vice versa for losses (see Exhibit 18–2, panel B, entry *(b)*).

2. **Record dividends** declared as a debit to Dividends Receivable (or Cash if received by the investor) and a credit to Investment in Equity Securities. In effect, dividends declared and paid by the investee company to the investor are viewed as a conversion of part of the investment account balance to Cash. It is thus a liquidation of that part of the investment. See Exhibit 18–2, panel B, entry *(c)*.

3. **Record the proportionate share of additional expense** if the investor's cost (i.e., market value of the investee's assets) on date of acquisition was in excess of the investee's book value at that date.
   Examples of additional expenses that must be recorded are:

   a. **Depreciation expense:** Investor Company acquired 20% of the outstanding voting shares (i.e., a 20% interest in the net assets) of Investee Company. At date of acquisition, depreciable assets owned by Investee Company were carried at $500,000. However, the market value was $700,000 (a difference of $200,000). Assuming straight-line depreciation, a 10-year remaining life, and no residual value, Investor Company would recognize additional annual depreciation of $4,000 [i.e., ($200,000 × 20%) ÷ 10 years].

   The additional depreciation amount is debited to Investment Revenue and credited to Investment in Equity Securities. It would not be appropriate for Investor Company to record this additional depreciation by debiting Depreciation Expense and crediting Accumulated Depreciation because Investor Company reports the market value of depreciable assets (as of the date of acquisition) of Investee Company as an implicit part of the cost in the investment account rather than in a separate operational asset account. A similar example would be the amortization of patents (or other intangibles) owned by Investee Company. See Exhibit 18–2, panel A, item 3*b*, and panel B, entry *(d)*.

   b. **Short-term investments purchased:** Assets such as **short-term** investments held by the Investee Company at date of acquisition of the long-term investment in equity securities may necessitate recognition of additional expense similar to depreciation expense. For example, if at date of acquisition of the long-term investment, the Investee's carrying value for the short-term investments is less than their market value (cost to the Investor), additional expense for a proportionate share of this difference would have to be recognized as a credit to Investment in Equity Securities and a debit to Investment Revenue when the short-term investment is sold. This entry usually is made in the year following acquisition of the long-term investment. The disposal of current assets usually will occur during the next period. The investee's inventory would be handled in the same manner; that

Exhibit 18–2
Accounting for long-term investments using the equity method.

Panel A—Case Data:

1. On January 1, 19A, Investor Company purchased 3,600 shares (representing 20%) of the outstanding voting common stock of Investee Company for $300,000 cash. Investor Company can exercise significant influence over Investee Company's operating and financial policies. Therefore, Investor Company must apply the equity method.
2. Data on Investee Company at acquisition date, January 1, 19A:

		Book value	Market value
Assets not subject to depreciation:			
Inventory (FIFO basis)		$ 400,000	$ 405,000
Land		150,000	165,000
Total		550,000	570,000
Assets subject to depreciation (net of accumulated depreciation; remaining life, 10 years)		500,000	700,000
Total assets		$1,050,000	$1,270,000
Liabilities		$ 50,000	$ 50,000
Common stock (18,000 shares, par $50)	$900,000		
Retained earnings	100,000	1,000,000	1,220,000
Total liabilities and stockholders' equity		$1,050,000	$1,270,000

3. Analysis of the acquisition:

a. Computation of the proportionate part of goodwill purchased by Investor Company:

Purchase price for 20% interest in Investee Company		$ 300,000
Market value of 20% of identifiable net assets purchased:		
Total market value of assets of Investee Company	$1,270,000	
Less: Total liabilities of Investee Company	(50,000)	
Total market value of identifiable net assets of Investee Company	1,220,000	
Percentage purchased by Investor Company	×20%	
Market value of 20% of the identifiable net assets purchased		244,000
Goodwill purchased (20%)		$ 56,000*

* Amortization of goodwill over 40 years (maximum period permitted): $56,000 ÷ 40 = $1,400 per year.

b. Computation of percent of investee's individual asset values purchased by Investor (proportionate part of each asset of Investee Company adjusted to market value on January 1, 19A):

	Market value	Book value	Proportionate part of market value over book value
Inventory	$405,000 –	$400,000	(×20%) = $ 1,000†
Land	165,000 –	150,000	(×20%) = 3,000
Depreciable assets	700,000 –	500,000	(×20%) = 40,000‡

† Additional cost of goods sold in 19A based on the assumption that the beginning inventory is sold during 19A: $1,000.

‡ Additional depreciation over 10 years (no residual value): $40,000 ÷ 10 = $4,000 per year.

4. On December 31, 19A (end of the accounting year), Investee Company reported the following data:

a. Income before extraordinary items	$ 80,000
Extraordinary gain (net of tax)	30,000
Net income	$110,000
b. Total cash dividends declared and paid on December 31, 19A	$ 50,000

Exhibit 18–2
(continued)

Panel B—Investor Company's Entries and Related T-Accounts:

a. January 1, 19A—To record acquisition of investment:

Investment, Investee Company common stock (3,600 shares)	300,000	
Cash		300,000

b. December 31, 19A—To recognize investment revenue and an increase in the investment account, based on the proportionate share of income reported by Investee Company (panel A, item 4*a*):

Investment, Investee Company common stock ($110,000 × 20%)	22,000	
Investment revenue ($80,000 × 20%)		16,000
Extraordinary gain (appropriately described) ($30,000 × 20%)		6,000

c. December 31, 19A—To record cash dividend received on Investee Company shares (panel A, item 4*b*):

Cash ($50,000 × 20%)	10,000	
Investment, Investee Company common stock		10,000

d. December 31, 19A—To record depreciation on the $40,000 increase in depreciable assets implicit in the purchase price paid for the investment (panel A, item 3*b*):

Investment revenue ($40,000 ÷ 10 years)	4,000	
Investment, Investee Company common stock		4,000

e. December 31, 19A—To record additional cost of goods sold associated with excess of market value over book value of inventory of Investee Company (panel A, 3*b*), assuming the goods were sold during 19A:

Investment revenue [($405,000 − $400,000) × 20%]	1,000	
Investment, Investee Company common stock		1,000

f. December 31, 19A—To record periodic amortization of the $56,000 goodwill purchased (panel A, 3*a*):

Investment revenue ($56,000 ÷ 40 years)	1,400	
Investment, Investee Company common stock*		1,400

* Notice that goodwill was included in the investment account entry on January 1, 19A.

Investor's T-accounts (entry references are for entry letters above):

Investment, Investee Company Common Stock (3,600 shares; 20%)

a.	Acquisition (cost)	300,000	*c.*	Dividends received	10,000
b.	Proportionate share of net income of investee	22,000	*d.*	Additional depreciation	4,000
			e.	Additional cost of goods sold	1,000
			f.	Amortization of goodwill	1,400
	Balance	305,600			

Investment Revenue (ordinary)

d.	Additional depreciation	4,000	*b.*	Reported income	16,000
e.	Additional cost of goods sold	1,000			
f.	Amortization of goodwill	1,400			
				Balance	9,600

Extraordinary Gain (appropriately described)

			b.	Reported gain	6,000
				Balance	6,000

Exhibit 18–2
(concluded)

Panel C—Investor Company's Financial Statement Presentation, December 31, 19A:

Statement of financial position:	
Investment, Investee Company common stock, at equity (cost $300,000)	$305,600
Statement of income:	
Investment revenue (on investment accounted for by the equity method)	9,600
Extraordinary gain (appropriately described)	6,000

is, as a credit to Investment in Equity Securities and a debit to Investment revenue (when the inventory is sold).[7] This entry is illustrated in Exhibit 18–2, panel B, entry *(e)*.

Similarly, when a **long-term** asset is disposed of by the Investee Company subsequent to the acquisition date of the long-term investment in equity securities, any gain or loss reported by the Investee Company must be adjusted for a proportionate part of any "accounting difference" between the carrying value of the Investee and its market-value that the investor "purchased" at acquisition date.

4. **Record amortization each year of any purchased goodwill** resulting from the acquisition transaction. As explained in Chapter 12, goodwill is measured as the excess of the cost of the investment to the investor over the market value of the identifiable **net** assets of the investee. Identifiable assets exclude goodwill. Goodwill is not physically identifiable or separately recorded in the accounts of the Investee Company in any form. For example, the proportionate part of the goodwill purchased was computed to be $56,000 at acquisition date. If a 40-year amortization period is used, additional expense of $1,400 (i.e., $56,000 ÷ 40) would be recognized each year by the investor as a debit to Investment Revenue and a credit to Investment in Equity Securities. Goodwill is amortized against Investment Revenue in the manner described in (3*a*) immediately above because it reduces investment revenue (or increases investment loss). This amortization amount is credited to Investment in Equity Securities. The cost of goodwill was included in that investment account as an implicit element of the investor's acquisition cost. See Exhibit 18–2, panel A, item 3*a*, and panel B, entry *(f)*.
5. **Record any gain or loss on the sale** of all or a part of the investment in equity securities. This amount is equal to the difference between the sale price and the then carrying value of that investment (as reflected in the investment account). Typically, this entry would involve a debit to Cash for the selling price, a credit to Investment in Equity Securities for

[7] For Investee's inventory costed by the LIFO method, the difference between book value and market value of a LIFO base layer would not be adjusted in the manner described above as long as that LIFO base layer is not liquidated.

the carrying value of the securities sold (on the equity basis), and a debit to a Loss on Disposal or a credit to Gain on Disposal for the difference.

6. **Eliminate any intercompany gains and losses** (discussed in Part B).

In Exhibit 18–2, the ending balance in the investment account represents the adjusted 20% ownership interest of Investor Company in the net assets of Investee Company. The $305,600 ending balance is reported on the statement of financial position of Investor Company, as shown in panel C. The revenue and gain accounts represent the proportionate share of the income (as adjusted) of Investee Company that is recognized in the accounts of Investor Company, as shown in panel C.

Note that the equity method is **not** a cost-basis method; therefore, the LCM concept does not appear to be applicable. Nevertheless, some companies indicate that their investments using the equity basis are at LCM.

A typical accounting policy provided by the 1986 annual report of ADDSCO Industries, Inc. concerning the equity method is shown below. This is an example of the company's policy for affiliates when the company does not own more than 50% of the outstanding voting stock.

> *Principles of consolidation:*
> The accompanying consolidated financial statements include the accounts of ADDSCO Industries, Inc. and all majority owned subsidiaries. Investment in an unconsolidated 50% owned affiliate is accounted for by the equity method. All material intercompany transactions and accounts are eliminated in consolidation.

Disclosure of Investments in Equity Securities

Disclosure requirements specified by *FASB Standard 12* for Investments in equity securities are:

a. As of the date of each statement of financial position presented, aggregate cost and market value with identification as to which is the carrying amount.

b. As of the date of the latest statement of financial position presented, the following:

  i. Gross unrealized gains representing the excess of market value over cost for all marketable equity securities in the portfolio having such an excess.

  ii. Gross unrealized losses representing the excess of cost over market value for all marketable equity securities in the portfolio having such an excess.

c. For each period for which a statement of income is presented:

  i. Net realized gain or loss included in the determination of net income.

  ii. The basis on which cost was determined in computing realized gain or loss (i.e., average cost or other method used).

  iii. The change in the valuation allowance(s) that has been included in the determination of net income.

The following excerpt from the 1986 annual report of Bowne & Co., Inc., included the information required by *FASB Standard 12* as follows:

BOWNE & CO., INC.

	1986	1985
Current assets:		
Cash and temporary cash investments	$29,009,000	$15,306,000
Marketable securities	4,464,000	4,210,000

Notes to Consolidated Financial Statements

Note 3: Cash and Temporary Cash Investments

The Company's policy is to invest cash in excess of operating requirements in income producing investments. Investments of $22,689,000 (1986) and $6,912,000 (1985) include certificates of deposit, commercial paper and money market accounts stated at cost which approximates market.

Note 4: Marketable Securities

Marketable securities include equity securities, notes and bonds. Securities which the company intends to hold for a limited period are classified as current marketable securities. These securities are held primarily for their interest or dividend yields and carried at the lower of cost or market. Realized and unrealized gains and losses were immaterial in each year. Realized gains and losses are determined on a specific identification basis.

Market Value Method for Equity Securities

The market value method of accounting for long-term investments in equity securities is fundamentally different from the cost and equity methods. The market value method is based upon the concept of **current market value accounting.** Under this method each individual investment is revalued at each statement of financial position date to the current market value of the securities held. The LCM concept is **not** applied with the market value method.

Currently, the market value method is **not in conformity with GAAP** except for the portfolios of certain specialized industries. These include insurance companies, pension funds, and mutual funds. The method is only applied to securities that are readily marketable. The cost method is used for "nonmarketable" securities.

The market value method may be outlined as follows:

1. At date of acquisition, investments are recorded at cost in conformity with the **cost principle.**
2. Subsequent to acquisition, each individual investment account balance is adjusted at the end of the accounting year to the current market value of the securities held. The adjusted amount then becomes the new "carrying value" for subsequent accounting.
3. Cash and property dividends declared and paid are recognized by the investor as "Investment Revenue (dividends)."
4. Increases or decreases in the market value of the equity securities are recognized at the end of each accounting period using either of two approaches as follows:
   a. **Current approach**—The price change during the current period is recognized as "Investment Revenue, or Loss (market value change)" in the accounts and in the **current statement of income.**
   b. **Deferral approach**—The price change during the current period is recorded as a deferred item in **owners' equity,** "Unrealized Market

Gain, or Loss." When a security is subsequently **sold,** the difference between its **carrying value** in the investment account and its **original cost** must be removed from its deferred status in the unrealized account and recognized as "Investment Revenue, Market Value Change." Any additional difference is recognized as "Gain or Loss on Sale of Investments."

5. At disposition of the investment, the difference between the carrying value at that date and its sale price is recognized as a gain or loss on disposal.

Exhibit 18–3 illustrates application of the market value method (for both of the above approaches).

Many accountants believe that all marketable equity securities, whether short term or long term, should be accounted for using the market value method. They contend that market value data *(a)* report the economic consequences of holding the investment, *(b)* are more useful to decision makers than cost or equity data in projecting future cash flows, *(c)* are objectively determinable for many stocks *(d)* avoid the LCM asymmetric treatment for market when it is above cost, and *(e)* prevent the opportunity to "manage earnings" through the sale of selected investments acquired at a low original cost with a high current market value, followed a few months later by a repurchase.[8]

Many arguments have been advanced against the valuation of marketable equity securities at market value. The principal arguments cited against the market value method are: *(a)* it violates the **cost principle** and places on the statement of financial position values that may not be objectively determined and may be temporary; *(b)* it violates the traditional **revenue principle** because revenue recognition is based on market changes rather than on sale; and *(c)* because of the volatility of some stock prices, it introduces a vacillating effect in the statement of financial position and on reported net income.

Some Special Problems in Accounting for Equity Investments

Several special problems relating to the acquisition, holding, and sale of equity investments are discussed below under the following headings:

1. Investment revenue—cash dividends and interest revenue.
2. Stock split of investment shares.
3. Stock rights on investment shares.
4. Special-purpose funds as long-term investments.

Investment Revenue

Cash dividends on short-term investments in **capital stock** of other companies are recognized as earned at the time of the **declaration of the cash dividend.** Cash dividends on capital stock held as an investment are not accrued prior

[8] Variants of this view are presented by W. J. Morris and B. A. Coda, "Valuation of Equity Securities," *Journal of Accountancy*, January 1973, pp. 48–54; and W. H. Beaver, "Accounting for Marketable Equity Securities," *Journal of Accountancy*, December 1973, pp. 58–64.

Exhibit 18–3
Accounting for long-term investments—market value method.

Panel A—Case Data:

1. On January 1, 19A, Intel Company purchased, as a long-term investment, 1,000 of the 50,000 outstanding shares of common stock, par $1, of Decca Corporation at $20 per share.
2. At December 31, 19A, the market price of the Decca stock was $25, and Decca's reported net income was $80,000.
3. During October 19B, Decca declared and paid a $1 per share cash dividend.
4. At Dec. 31, 19B, market price of Decca stock was $22, and Decca's reported net income was $65,000.
5. On November 1, 19C, Intel sold 400 of the Decca shares at $26.
6. Intel's accounting period ends December 31; it will use the market value method.

Panel B—Entries—Current versus Deferral Approaches:

Accounts and computations	Market change reported: Current approach		Deferral approach	
1. January 1, 19A—Acquisition of long-term investment:				
Long-term investment, Decca stock (1,000 shares × $20)	20,000		20,000	
Cash		20,000		20,000
2. December 31, 19A—Record market value change:				
Long-term investment, Decca stock [($25 − $20) × 1,000 shares]	5,000		5,000	
Investment revenue, market gain on investments		5,000		
Unrealized market gain/loss on investments				5,000
3. October 19B—Record $1 per share cash dividend:				
Cash (1,000 shares × $1)	1,000		1,000	
Investment revenue, dividends		1,000		1,000
4. December 31, 19B—Record market value change:				
Investment loss, market loss on investments	3,000			
Unrealized market gain/loss on investments			3,000	
Long-term investment, Decca stock [($25 − $22) × 1,000 shares]		3,000		3,000
5. November 1, 19C—Sale of 400 Decca shares at $26:				
Cash (400 shares × $26)	10,400		10,400	
Unrealized market gain/loss on investments (carrying value, $22 − original cost, $20) × 400 shares*			800	
Investment revenue, market value change				800
Long-term investment, Decca stock (carrying value, $22 × 400 shares)		8,800		8,800
Gain on sale of investments (sale price, $26 − carrying value, $22) × 400 shares		1,600		1,600

* Because 400 Decca shares were sold, the amount in the unrealized account associated with those shares must be removed. The per share amount removed is based on the difference between the "current carrying value" ($22) and their original cost ($20) = $2 per share. Therefore, the total amount removed is, $2 × 400 shares = $800. The reason is that (1) the balance in the unrealized account relates only to the unsold shares and (2) the market gain is separated from the gain on sale ($1,600), which is the same as the current approach recognizes.

to declaration. Stock dividends are not accounted for as investment revenue.

Cash dividends on short-term investments in **capital stock** of other companies are recognized as earned at the time of the **declaration of the cash dividend.** Cash dividends on capital stock held as an investment are not accrued prior to declaration. Stock dividends are not accounted for as investment revenue.

To conserve cash and yet make a distribution to stockholders, a corporation may issue a **stock dividend.** When a stock dividend is issued, the distributing corporation debits Retained Earnings and credits the appropriate capital stock

Exhibit 18–3
(concluded)

Panel C—Reporting:

	Market change reported					
	Current approach			Deferral approach		
Financial statements	**19A**	**19B**	**19C**	**19A**	**19B**	**19C**
Statement of income:						
Investment revenue, dividends:						
19B (1,000 shares × $1)		$ 1,000			$ 1,000	
Investment revenue (loss), market value:						
19A [1,000 shares × ($25 – $20)]	$ 5,000					
19B [1,000 shares × ($25 – $22)]		(3,000)				
19C [400 shares × ($22 – $20)]						$ 800
Gain (loss) on sale of investments:						
19C [400 shares × ($26 – $22)]			$1,600			1,600
Statement of financial position:						
Assets:						
Long-term investment, Decca Corp.:						
19A (1,000 shares × $25)	25,000			$25,000		
19B (1,000 shares × $22)		22,000			22,000	
Owners' equity:						
Unrealized gain (loss) on long-term investment in equity securities:						
19A [1,000 shares × ($25 – $20)]				5,000		
19B [1,000 shares × ($22 – $20)] (or $5,000 – $3,000)					2,000	

accounts. The effect of a stock dividend from the **issuing corporation's** view is to "capitalize" a part of retained earnings. Significantly, a stock dividend does not decrease the assets of the issuing corporation (see Chapter 17).

From the **investor's** point of view, the nature of a stock dividend is suggested by the effect on the issuing corporation. The investor neither receives assets from the corporation nor owns more of the issuing corporation. The investor merely has more shares to represent the same prior proportional ownership. Thus, the receipt of a stock dividend in the **same class of stock** as already owned results, from the investor's viewpoint, in more shares but no increase in the cost (carrying value) of the holdings.

The investor should make no entry for revenue nor change the investment account other than to record a **memorandum entry** for the number of shares received. In case of a sale of any of the shares, a new cost per share is computed by adding the new shares to the old and dividing this sum into the carrying value.

Assume Investor X purchased 1,000 shares of common stock, par $5, of ABC Corporation at $90 per share. Subsequently, Investor X received a 50% common stock dividend. The investor later sold 200 of the common shares at $75 per share. The cost method entries would be:

At acquisition date:

Long-term investment in equity securities, ABC Corp. (1,000 shares × $90)	90,000	
Cash		90,000

At date of stock dividend:

Memorandum entry only—Received 50% common stock dividend of 500 shares from ABC Corporation; revised cost per share: $90,000 ÷ (1,000 + 500 = 1,500 shares) = $60.

At date of sale of 200 common shares:

Cash (200 shares X $75)	15,000	
Long-term investment in equity securities, ABC Corp. (200 shares X $60)		12,000
Gain on sale of investments		3,000
(Remaining shares: 1,300 at $60 cost per share).		

These procedures would be **followed for the cost, equity, and market value methods;** the only difference in application would be the total carrying value (i.e., cost, market, or equity amount). For all three methods, the appropriate total carrying value would be divided by the new total number of shares owned to determine the carrying value per share after the stock dividend.

If the stock dividend is of a **different class of stock** than that on which the dividend was declared, such as preferred stock received as a dividend on common stock, or vice versa, three methods of accounting for the dividend have been suggested:

1. **Allocation method**—Record the new stock at an amount determined by allocating the carrying value of the old stock between the new stock and the old stock on the basis of the relative market values of the different classes of stock after issuance of the dividend.
2. **Noncost method**—Record the new stock in terms of shares only (as a memorandum entry). When it is sold, recognize the total sale price as a gain.
3. **Market value method**—Do not change the carrying value of the old stock. Instead, record the new stock at its **market value** upon receipt with an offsetting credit to dividend revenue. This method is based on the assumption that stock of a different class received as a dividend is similar to a property dividend.

The **allocation method** is the most consistent with GAAP; the noncost method is the most conservative; and the market value method is seldom used.

Exhibit 18–4 shows the application of the **allocation method,** which assigns the original cost to the two classes of stock. This method would be followed for the **cost, equity, and market value methods,** with the appropriate carrying value allocated.

Interest receivable and interest revenue on investments in debt securities (e.g., bonds) are accrued at the end of the accounting period with an adjusting entry. Bonds and similar debt securities purchased at a price above par are acquired at a premium; if acquired below par, at a discount. Premium or discount on a long-term investment is amortized. However, on a **short-term** bond invest-

Exhibit 18–4
Investor accounting for a stock dividend in a different class of stock.

Panel A—Case Data:

1. Investor X purchased 100 shares of JKL Company common stock at $75 per share (total cost, $7,500).
2. When the market value of the common stock was $10,000, Investor X received a stock dividend of 40 shares of JKL preferred stock with a market value of $2,500. Using the allocation method, the cost may be apportioned as follows:

$$\text{Cost allocated to common} = \$7,500 \times \frac{\$10,000}{\$12,500} = \$6,000 \text{ (\$60 per share)}$$

$$\text{Cost allocated to preferred} = \$7,500 \times \frac{\$2,500}{\$12,500} = 1,500 \text{ (\$37.50 per share)}$$

Total cost allocated $7,500

Panel B—Indicated Entry to Record Receipt of Stock Dividend by Investor X:

Investment in preferred stock of JKL Company (40 shares × $37.50)	1,500	
Investment in common stock of JKL Company		1,500

ment it is not amortized because, by definition, the investment will be converted to cash in the near future instead of being held to maturity (also see Chapter 15).

Stock Split of Investment Shares

Although a stock split is different from a stock dividend from the point of view of the **issuer,** the two are virtually identical from the point of view of the **investor.** In both cases, the investor has more shares than before the split or dividend, but with the same total cost as before.[9] To the **investor,** the accounting for a stock split is the same as for a stock dividend of the same class as already owned. Only a **memorandum entry** is made to record the number of new shares received and the cost (or carrying value) per share is recomputed.

Stock Rights on Investment Shares

The privilege given stockholders (investors) of purchasing additional shares of stock from the issuing corporation at a specific price and by a specified future date is commonly known as a **stock right.** The certificate evidencing one or more rights often is called a **stock warrant.**

The term **stock right** is usually interpreted as **one right for each share of old stock.** For example, a holder of two shares of stock who receives rights to subscribe for one new share is said to own two stock rights rather than one.

There is one right per old share regardless of the "new" share arrangement. In this case two rights call for one share only. Rights have value when the holder can buy additional shares through **exercise** of the rights at a lower **option price** per share than on the open market without rights. As the spread between the option price and the market price changes subsequent to issuance of the rights, the value of the rights will change.

When the intention to issue stock rights is declared, the stock will start

[9] In a reverse split, such as a two-for-three split, the number of outstanding shares is reduced rather than increased. Reverse stock splits are rare.

Exhibit 18–5
Accounting for stock rights by the investor.

Panel A—Case Data:

1. AB Company purchased 500 shares of stock in XY Corporation at $93 per share.
2. At a later date, AB Company received 500 stock rights entitling AB Company to subscribe to 100 additional shares at $100 per share. Thus, each stock right represents one-fifth of a full share of XY stock.
3. Upon receipt of the rights, each share of stock on which the rights were issued had a market value of $120 (ex rights), and the rights had a market value of $4 each at the time they were received.

Panel B—Entries:

Case A—Assume that instead of subscribing for the additional shares, the investor later sold the rights at $4.50 each. The investor's entries are:

1. To record acquisition of stock investment:

Investment—stock of XY Corporation (500 shares × $93)	46,500	
Cash		46,500

2. To record receipt of 500 rights on XY Corporation stock investment:

Investment—stock rights of XY Corporation*	1,500	
Investment—stock of XY Corporation		1,500

* Allocation of investment cost to stock rights on basis of relative market values:

Shares: $\frac{\$120}{\$124} \times \$46,500 = \$45,000$ (i.e., $90 per share)

Rights: $\frac{\$4}{\$124} \times \$46,500 = \underline{1,500}$ (i.e., $3 per right)

Total cost $46,500

3. To record sale of the 500 stock rights of XY Corporation at $4.50 each:

Cash (500 rights × $4.50)	2,250	
Investment—stock rights of XY Corporation (500 rights × $3)		1,500
Gain on sale of stock rights		750

Case B—Assume that the investor exercised the rights to subscribe to the additional shares and later sold one of the new shares for $140. The investor's entries are:

1. To record acquisition of stock investment—Same as entry 1 above.
2. To record receipt of stock rights—Same as entry 2 above.
3. To record exercise of the 500 rights and receipt of 100 new shares of stock of XY Corporation:

Investment—stock of XY Corporation [100 shares × $115 (i.e., $100 cash + 5 rights × $3 = $15 cash)]	11,500	
Investment—stock rights of XY Corporation (500 rights × $3)		1,500
Cash (100 shares × $100)		10,000

4. To record sale of one of the new shares for $140 cash:

Cash (1 share × $140)	140	
Investment—stock of XY Corporation (1 share × $115)		115
Gain on sale of stock investment		25

If the rights are not sold or exercised, they will lapse. In this situation, theoretically, a loss equivalent to the allocated cost of the rights should be recognized by the investor. However, as a practical matter, the allocation entry (entry 2 in both cases above) usually is reversed for the portion that lapses.

selling in the market "rights on." The market price of a share selling "rights on" includes the value of a share and the value of a right. After the rights are issued, the shares will sell in the market "ex rights." Also, after issuance, rights usually have a separate market from that of the related stock. Thus, they will be separately quoted at a specific market price. After rights are received, the investor has shares of stock and stock rights. Both arise out of the original cost.

To determine the gain or loss on the sale of either the stock or the rights, it is necessary to allocate the total cost of the investment between the stock and the rights. This allocation usually is based on relative market values; that is, the total cost of the old shares is allocated between the old stock and the rights in proportion to their relative market values at the time the rights are issued.

Exhibit 18–5 shows the accounting for stock rights by the investor under two independent cases.

Special-Purpose Funds as Long-Term Investments

Special-purpose funds often are long-term investments. They usually are reported on the statement of financial position under the noncurrent caption, "Investments and Funds."

Companies often set aside cash, and sometimes other assets, in special funds to be used in the future for a given purpose. Funds may be set aside *(a)* by contract, as in the case of a bond sinking fund, *(b)* by law, as in the case of rent deposits, or *(c)* voluntarily, as in the case of a plant expansion fund.

A special-purpose fund sometimes is a current asset, as in the case of a short-term savings account, or more commonly a noncurrent asset, when it is not directly related to current operations. The following are typical examples of long-term funds:

1. Funds set aside to retire a specific long-term liability, such as bonds payable, mortgages payable, long-term notes payable (see Chapter 5, page 191, case B and Chapter 15, liabilities).
2. Funds set aside to retire preferred stock (see Chapter 17, appropriations of retained earnings).
3. Funds set aside to purchase major assets, such as land, buildings, and plant (see Chapter 5, page 182, and Chapter 10).

Typically, special-purpose funds are deposited with an independent trustee, such as a financial institution. In this case, arrangements often are agreed upon whereby a specific rate of interest will be earned each period on the balance in the fund. Usually, the earnings (normally interest) on the fund each period are added to the fund balance. A typical fund is illustrated in **Exhibit 18–6.**

Summary

Part A of this chapter focused on investments in equity securities, which may be held for short- or long-term purposes, and short-term debt securities. Investments in securities that *(a)* are marketable and *(b)* are intended by the management to be converted to cash within the time period used for current assets are called **short-term investments** (i.e., a current asset). The remaining investments in marketable securities are classified as long term and are reported under the statement of financial position caption, "Investments and funds."

Short-term investments in equity securities are accounted for by valuing them using the Cost, LCM method. Under this method the cost and market value of the investment portfolio are compared. If market is below cost, an entry is

Exhibit 18–6
Accounting for a special-purpose fund.

Panel A—Case Data:

1. WT Corporation has plans to build a new office building five years hence. The plans estimate the total construction cost to be $1,300,000 and a six-month construction period.
2. The company decided to make five $200,000 cash deposits to a special construction fund each July 1, starting on July 1, 19A. The fund will be administered by an **independent trustee.** The trustee will increase the fund each June 30 at a 10% interest rate on the fund balance at that date.
3. WT Corporation's accounting period ends December 31.
4. The office building was completed on schedule, and the contractor was paid $1,300,000 on July 2, 19F, and the fund was closed.

Panel B—Fund Accumulation Schedule (annuity due basis):

Date	Cash deposits	Interest revenue earned	Fund increases	Fund balance
7/1/19A	$ 200,000		$ 200,000	$ 200,000
6/30/19B		$ 200,000 × 10% = $ 20,000	20,000	220,000
7/1/19B	200,000		200,000	420,000
6/30/19C		420,000 × 10% = 42,000	42,000	462,000
7/1/19C	200,000		200,000	662,000
6/30/19D		662,000 × 10% = 66,200	66,200	728,200
7/1/19D	200,000		200,000	928,200
6/30/19E		928,200 × 10% = 92,820	92,820	1,021,020
7/1/19E	200,000		200,000	1,221,020
6/30/19F		1,221,020 × 10% = 122,102	122,102	1,343,122
	$1,000,000	$343,122	$1,343,122	

Panel C—Selected Journal Entries:

		Debit	Credit
7/1/19A:	Special building fund	200,000	
	Cash		200,000
12/31/19A:	Receivable on building fund	10,000	
	Interest revenue ($20,000 × 6/12)		10,000
6/30/19B:	Special building fund	20,000	
	Receivable on building fund		10,000
	Interest revenue		10,000
7/1/19B:	Special building fund	200,000	
	Cash		200,000
7/2/19F:	Cash	43,122	
	Office building	1,300,000	
	Special building fund		1,343,122

made that debits an unrealized loss account (reported on the statement of income) and credits an allowance account to reduce cost to LCM (reported on the statement of financial position as a contra account to the investment account). The portfolio of investments in debt securities is reported *(a)* under short-term provisions of *ARB No. 43* at cost (not LCM) or *(b)* the same as short-term equity securities (based on consistency).

Long-term investments in debt securities are accounted for at cost (discussed in Chapter 15). Long-term equity investments (except those that qualify for the equity method) are accounted for at Cost, LCM similarly to short-term investments, except that in the LCM entry a stockholders' equity unrealized **capital** loss account is debited rather than a statement of income unrealized loss account. The equity method is used when the investor has enough voting shares to have significant influence (20% of the shares up to 50%). This method views the companies as a specially related economic unit for accounting purposes.

PART B: CONSOLIDATED FINANCIAL STATEMENTS

Part B presents the fundamental concepts of **consolidated** financial statements. The complexities involved are deferred to advanced texts that develop this topic. *APB Opinion 16,* "Business Combinations," provides the basic accounting guidelines for consolidated financial statements.[10] **Consolidation of the financial statements of a parent company and a subsidiary is a reporting procedure only; therefore, it does not affect the accounts of either the parent company or the subsidiary. Consolidated financial statements are prepared only by the parent company, not by the subsidiary.**

Concept of a Controlling Interest

When an investor company owns over 50% of the outstanding voting stock of another company, in the absence of overriding constraints, a controlling interest exists. The investor company is called the **parent** company. The other company is called a **subsidiary** company. In a parent-subsidiary relationship, both corporations **continue as separate legal entities;** therefore, they are separate accounting entities (refer to separate entity assumption, Chapter 6). **As separate entities, they have separate accounting systems and separate financial statements.** However, because of the controlling ownership relationship, the **parent** company (but not the subsidiary) may be required to prepare **consolidated financial statements.** In consolidated financial statements the parent and the subsidiary (or subsidiaries) are viewed by accountants as a **single economic entity.** Thus, the parent company may prepare two sets of financial statements: one set as a separate entity and another set as a consolidated entity, which is required. To prepare consolidated financial statements, the **separate** financial statements of the parent and subsidiary are combined each period by the parent company into one overall (i.e., consolidated) set of financial statements as if they were one single entity. The statement of income, statement of financial position, and statement of cash flows (SCF) are consolidated in this manner.

Consolidated financial statements are not always prepared when over 50% of the stock of another corporation is owned because certain constraints may preclude the exercise of a controlling interest. Consolidation as a single economic entity is required as follows (*FASB Standard 94,* "Consolidation of All Majority Owned Subsidiaries," October 1987):

---

[10] This part of the chapter often is used when the class has numerous accounting and finance majors who will not enroll in an advanced accounting course on consolidations. It also is a helpful background for that course. However, it can be omitted without affecting subsequent chapters.

1. **Control of voting rights**—Control is presumed to exist when more than 50% of the **outstanding voting stock** of another entity is owned by the investor. Nonvoting stock is excluded from consideration because control without vote is not possible. However, there is one exception which is explained below. A subsidiary that is more than 50% owned in certain circumstances and does not qualify for consolidation is called an **unconsolidated subsidiary.** In this exception the investment is reported using the **equity method,** if there is significant influence; and using the **cost method,** if there is neither control nor significant influence (see Part A of this chapter).
2. **Exception to the general rule**—*FASB Standard 94* states that "a majority-owned subsidiary shall not be consolidated if control is likely to be temporary or if it does not rest with the majority owner (as, for instance, if the subsidiary is in legal reorganization or in bankruptcy or operates under foreign exchange restrictions, controls, or other governmentally imposed uncertainties so severe that they cast significant doubt on the parent's ability to control the subsidiary)." All other majority-owned subsidiaries must be consolidated.

Acquiring a Controlling Interest

A company may acquire a controlling interest in the voting stock of another company in two ways:

1. **Pooling of interests**—The parent company acquires the voting stock of an existing corporation by exchanging shares of its own capital stock for shares of the subsidiary. In this case, the parent disburses relatively little cash or other assets and incurs no liabilities in the acquisition. For example, the 1986 financial statements of Dean Foods Company included the following note (partial):

Business Combinations:
Shareholders of the Company and The Larsen Company (Larsen), a processor and marketer of canned and frozen vegetables, approved a merger agreement on April 28, 1986, whereby Larsen became a wholly-owned subsidiary. The Company exchanged 5,965,752 shares of the Company's common stock (adjusted for the stock split on May 28, 1986) for all outstanding shares of Larsen. The merger has been accounted for as a pooling-of-interests and, accordingly, the accompanying financial statements for all years presented have been restated to include the financial position and results of operations of the combined companies.

2. **Purchase**—The parent company acquires the voting stock of an existing corportion primarily by paying cash, transferring noncash assets, or incurring debt. In this situation, the parent disburses a significant amount of resources. For example, the 1987 financial statements of Gerber Products Company included the following note (partial):

On July 31, 1986, the Company, through a subsidiary, Soft Care Apparel, Inc., purchased certain assets of the Baby Products Division of The Kendall Company, a subsidiary of the Colgate-Palmolive Company for $58,403,000 in cash. The acquired assets include the manufacturing and marketing operations for infantwear, bedding, sleepers and cloth diapers sold under the Curity label. In fiscal 1987, the Company also acquired six children's centers for cash.

All of the acquisitions have been accounted for as purchases and, accordingly, the consolidated statements of operations include the acquired businesses from their respective dates of acquisition.

Accounting and Reporting Problems

GAAP requires that each subsidiary prepare its own financial statements. However, the parent company is required to prepare **consolidated** financial statements. These statements include all subsidiaries, except those designated as **unconsolidated** subsidiaries, as described above. It is the **parent company,** and not the subsidiary company, that prepares the consolidated statements. Consolidated financial statements include an **item-by-item combination (aggregation) of the parent and subsidiary statements.** For example, the amount of cash shown on a consolidated statement is the sum of the amounts of cash shown on the separate statements of the parent and the subsidiaries.

Consolidated financial statements are the means by which a controlling interest is **reported.** However, the parent company **records** the investment in its subsidiaries using either the cost or equity method. The cost method is often used in the accounts because the parent company does not desire to formally enter into its accounts the income, dividend offset, additional depreciation, amortization of goodwill, and so on, required by the equity method.[11] Also, the accounting periods of the parent and the subsidiary may be different. Changes in percentage of ownership complicate the equity method. Not infrequently, a company, when it moves from the equity method range (i.e., 20–50%) to a controlling interest range (over 50%), will adjust the accounts from the equity basis to the cost basis. For practical reasons, the illustrations in this chapter use the cost method of accounting for the investment.

The consolidated statements are developed by using a **consolidation worksheet.** The consolidation procedures can be adapted on the consolidation worksheet so that the consolidation results are the same whether the cost or equity method is used in the accounts of the parent company. It is from these worksheets that the consolidated financial statements are prepared.

This section will focus on the **preparation of consolidated financial statements.** When preparing consolidated financial statements, the **method of acquisition—pooling of interests versus purchase**—has a significant impact both on the parent company and on the consolidated statements.

Before discussing the pooling of interests and purchase methods, the steps necessary to prepare the consolidation worksheet will be discussed. It is important to remember that these steps refer to worksheet entries and the resulting consolidated financial statements, and **not** to the journals and ledgers of the separate legal entities involved. These steps can be summarized as follows:

1. Enter the separate financial statements of the parent and each subsidiary on the worksheet, using one column for each entity. Additional column headings are provided for "Eliminations" and "Consolidated Statements."

---

[11] The equity method often is called **one-line consolidation.** Instead of a line-by-line consolidation of the individual account balances, the equity method does all of this in the single account "investment."

2. The assets and liabilities of the subsidiary are substituted for the investment account reflected on the books of the parent. This substitution is accomplished on the worksheet by "eliminating" the owners' equity accounts of the subsidiary against the investment account of the parent.
3. Intercompany receivables are eliminated.
4. Intercompany revenues, expenses, gains, and losses are eliminated.
5. Any other intercompany items are eliminated.
6. Adjustments are made on the worksheet to reflect certain acquisition effects that differ from the book values, such as **goodwill** purchased by the parent as part of the cost of the investment in the subsidiary.
7. The remaining revenues and expenses of the parent and subsidiary are combined on the worksheet to derive a consolidated statement of income.
8. The assets and liabilities of the parent and subsidiary are combined to derive a consolidated statement of financial position.
9. The resource inflows and outflows of the parent and subsidiary are combined on a separate worksheet to derive a consolidated statement of cash flows (SCF).

Consolidated financial statements usually are prepared *(a)* at the date of acquisition of a controlling interest (statement of financial position only) and *(b)* for each accounting period subsequent to acquisition (statements of income, financial position, and cash flows). The consolidation worksheet and resulting financial statements are influenced by the way the stock of the subsidiary was acquired; that is, by *(a)* pooling of interests or *(b)* purchase.

Combination by Pooling of Interests

The acquisition of a controlling interest by the parent company in the stock of a subsidiary company by an exchange of shares of stock often occurs because the combination can be effected without the disbursement of cash or other resources by the parent company. The exchange of shares is viewed as the **uniting of ownership interests** (and not as a purchase/sale transaction) between the parent company and the stockholders of the subsidiary company. Therefore, the recorded assets, liabilities, revenues, expenses, and so forth, for both entities are **combined for consolidated statement purposes at their recorded book values.** The incomes of the parent and its subsidiaries are combined and restated as consolidated income. Because a purchase/sale transaction is **not** presumed when shares of stock are exchanged, market values of the assets of the subsidiary are not used in consolidation on the **pooling of interests basis.**

APB Opinion 16, "Business Combinations" (par. 47), states, "the combining of existing voting common stock interests by the exchange of stock is the essence of . . . [a] pooling of interests." However, the *Opinion* specifies 12 conditions that must be met in order for the pooling of interests method to be appropriate. If they are met, the pooling of interests method **must be used.** All combinations **not** meeting all 12 specifications **must** use the purchase method. Because of these 12 conditions, not all stock exchanges will meet the criteria for pooling of interests.

The **general** characteristics of the **pooling of interests** method of preparing consolidated statements may be summarized as follows:

1. The parent company must own 90% or more of the voting shares of the subsidiary.
2. The assets and liabilities of the combining companies are reported at the previously established **book values** of **both** the parent and the subsidiary. Although adjustments may be made to reflect consistent applications of accounting principles, the **current market values of the assets of the subsidiary** at the time of the combination are **not used** as a substitute for their book values at that date.
3. No purchased goodwill results from the combination.
4. The retained earnings balances of the combining companies are added to determine the retained earnings balance of the combined companies at date of acquisition.
5. After combination, comparative financial statements which pertain to pre-combination periods must be restated on the combined basis "as if" the companies were consolidated throughout those periods.

Preparing a Consolidated Statement of Financial Position Immediately after Acquisition, Pooling of Interests Method. **Exhibit 18–7** shows the preparation of a consolidated statement of financial position immediately after acquisition. In this case, there was an exchange of shares of a 90% voting interest that qualifies as a **pooling of interests.** Panel A gives the case data. Panel B illustrates the worksheet used to prepare the consolidated statement of financial position immediately after the combination.

In Exhibit 18–7, panel B, the worksheet is begun by entering the two separate statements of financial position, using **book values** for each company immediately **after** the acquisition entry. Notice that two account balances on the Company P statement of financial position (i.e., the investment and parent common stock accounts) reflect the acquisition entry. The worksheet is designed to provide an orderly procedure for combining the two separate statements of financial position into a consolidated statement (the last column). The pair of columns for **eliminations** is used to **prevent double counting of reciprocal items;** that is, transactions that are strictly between the two companies must be eliminated because there is now only one entity. In this instance, two reciprocal items must be eliminated:

a. The investment account balance reflected on the statement of financial position of Company P ($90,000) must be eliminated. In its place, the various assets and liabilities of Company S will be added to those of the parent. Similarly, 90% of the common stock reported by Company S must be offset. It now is owned by the parent company. Thus, elimination entry *(a)* on the worksheet offsets the investment account balance on the statement of financial position of the parent against the capital stock account reflected on the statement of financial position of the subsidiary.

b. Intercompany debt—Current liabilities of Company S include a $5,000 account payable owed to Company P; therefore, accounts receivable on the statement of financial position of Company P also includes this

Exhibit 18–7
Consolidated statement of financial position, Company P (parent) and Company S (subsidiary), pooling of interests method, immediately after acquisition of a 90% controlling interest by Company P.

Panel A—Case Data:

1. Company P issued 900 shares of its $100 par common stock to the stockholders of Company S for 900 of the 1,000 outstanding shares of Company S common stock, par $100. This is an exchange of shares (a continuity of the previously existing ownership), and we will assume that it meets the 12 conditions (specified in *APB Opinion 16*) for pooling of interests (including the criterion which requires at least 90% ownership). Company S will continue as a separate legal entity and as a 90% subsidiary of Company P. As a result of this transaction, Company P immediately made the following acquisition entry:

Investment in Company S common stock (90% ownership)*	90,000	
Common stock (900 shares at $100 par)		90,000

* Because the acquisition under the pooling of interests concept is not viewed as a purchase/sale transaction, it is variously recorded at: *(a)* par value of the stock issued, *(b)* the proportionate share acquired of the subsidiary's contributed capital, or *(c)* the proportionate book value of the subsidiary acquired. Some accountants prefer to use average contributed capital per share. This is a minor, but unsettled issue; however, in any case, the elimination entry is adapted to attain the pooling of interests results.

2. Immediately **after** the exchange, the respective statement of financial position reflected the following:

Assets	Company P book value	Company S Book value	Company S Market value	Liabilities and Owners' Equity	Company P book value	Company S book value
Cash	$610,000	$ 20,000	$ 20,000	Current liabilities	$ 10,000	$ 20,000†
Accounts receivable (net)	10,000†	40,000	40,000	Long-term liabilities	50,000	40,000
Inventories	20,000	30,000	25,000	Common stock (par $100)	690,000	100,000
Investment in Co. S	90,000			Retained earnings	200,000	50,000
Plant and equipment (net)	200,000	110,000	151,000			
Patents (net)	20,000	10,000	14,000			
	$950,000	$210,000	$250,000		$950,000	$210,000

† At date of acquisition, Company S owed Company P $5,000 accounts payable. Carrying and market value are assumed to be the same for receivables and payables.

amount. When the two statements of financial position are combined, this **intercompany debt** must be eliminated, because it is not a payable or receivable involving the combined entity and outsiders. Elimination entry *(b)* on the worksheet accomplishes this offset.

After the elimination entries for all intercompany items are reflected on the worksheet, the two statements of financial position are aggregated line by line. The 10% interest of the **minority stockholders** of Company S represented by their proportionate share of the stockholders' equity of the subsidiary company is set out separately (denoted by M). The last column of the worksheet provides all the data needed to prepare a formal consolidated statement of financial position. Notice that the **book values** of Company S are added to the **book values** of Company P, and that the **market values given in the data above do not affect the reporting for a combination by pooling of interests.**

Combination by Purchase

The acquisition of a controlling interest by purchase occurs when the combination does not meet all of the 12 conditions specified by *APB Opinion 16* for a pooling of interests. Typically, an acquisition by purchase occurs when the parent com-

Exhibit 18–7
(concluded)

Panel B—Worksheet to Develop Consolidated Statement of Financial Position, Pooling of Interests Method:
COMPANY P AND ITS SUBSIDIARY, COMPANY S (90% OWNERSHIP)
Pooling of Interests Method; Immediately after Acquisition

Account	Statement of financial position per books		Eliminations		Consolidated statement of financial position
	Company P	Company S	Debit	Credit	
Cash	610,000	20,000			630,000
Accounts receivable (net)	10,000	40,000		(b) 5,000	45,000
Inventories	20,000	30,000			50,000
Investment in Company S	90,000*			(a) 90,000	
Plant and equipment (net)	200,000	110,000			310,000
Patents (net)	20,000	10,000			30,000
	950,000	210,000			1,065,000
Current liabilities	10,000	20,000	(b) 5,000		25,000
Long-term liabilities	50,000	40,000			90,000
Common stock (par $100):					
Company P	690,000*				690,000
Company S		100,000	(a) 90,000		10,000M
Retained earnings:					
Company P	200,000				−245,000
Company S		50,000			5,000M
	950,000	210,000			1,065,000

M—minority stockholders' 10% interest in Company S.
* Includes effect of acquisition entry of $90,000 given in panel A, 1.
Eliminations:
(a) To eliminate the investment account balance against the stockholders' equity (90%) of the subsidiary.
(b) To eliminate the intercompany debt of $5,000.

pany acquires a controlling interest in the subsidiary company by purchasing the voting stock from the subsidiary's stockholders primarily with cash and noncash assets. This situation is viewed as a **purchase/sale transaction.** Therefore, **market values** related to the **subsidiary** must be introduced into the consolidation procedures in conformity with the **cost principle.** *APB Opinion 16* (par. 66) states: "Accounting for a business combination by the purchase method follows the principles normally applicable under historical cost accounting to recording acquisitions of assets and issuances of stock and to accounting for assets and liabilities after acquisition." This citation means that, at acquisition date, the parent company must debit the investment account for the **market value** of the shares of the subsidiary acquired. The parent company presumably paid market value for the investment. The significant implication of this requirement is that in preparing consolidated statements, the assets of the **subsidiary** (including any purchased goodwill) must be valued by the parent company at their **market values at date of acquisition** before being aggregated with the **book values** of the assets of the parent company.[12]

[12] Recall that in a pooling of interests, book values rather than market values of the subsidiary are used in consolidation.

Exhibit 18–8

Consolidated statement of financial position, Company P (parent) and Company S (subsidiary), purchase method; immediately after acquisition of a 90% controlling interest by Company P.

Panel A—Case Data:

1. Company P purchased, in the open market, 90% of the 1,000 shares of outstanding voting stock of Company S for $211,000 cash. Company P recorded the acquisition as follows:

Investment in Company S common stock (90% ownership)	211,000	
Cash		211,000

2. The statements of financial position of Company P and Company S immediately after the above entry were as given below in panel B (first 2 columns). Notice that this is exactly the same data given in Exhibit 18–7, panel A, item 2, except for the effects of the above acquisition entry.
3. Analysis of the purchase:
   a. Computation of goodwill purchased by Company P:

Purchase price for 90% interest in Company S		$211,000
Market value of 90% of the identifiable **net** assets purchased:		
Total market value of identifiable assets of Company S (Exhibit 18–7, panel A, item 2)	$250,000	
Less: total liabilities of Company S (Exhibit 18–7, panel A, item 2)	(60,000)	
Total market value of identifiable net assets of Company S	190,000	
Proportional part purchased by Company P	×90%	
Market value of 90% of the identifiable **net** assets purchased		171,000
Goodwill purchased (90%)		$ 40,000

   b. Proportionate part of each asset of Company S adjusted to market value (i.e., parent's cost) as of date of combination:

	Parent's cost (market value)		**Subsidiary's book value**		**Proportionate part of excess of cost (market) over book value**
Inventory	$ 25,000	–	$ 30,000	× 90% =	$ (4,500)†
Plant and equipment	151,000	–	110,000	× 90% =	36,900
Patents	14,000	–	10,000	× 90% =	3,600
Goodwill (per above)	40,000	–	-0-		40,000
Total (see worksheet entry [*a*] below)					$76,000

† Parent's cost (i.e., market value) is less than subsidiary's book value.

Although there are numerous additional complexities in application of the **purchase method, the general characteristics may** be outlined as follows:

1. On the consolidated statement of financial position, the assets and liabilities of the subsidiary are reported by the parent company at **cost** on the date of acquisition in conformity with the cost principle. Thus, it is not only the **market value of the stock acquired at that date;** it is also the cost of the net assets of the subsidiary purchased by the parent.
2. Individual assets of the subsidiary are reported at their individual market values as of the date of acquisition. These include all identifiable tangible and intangible assets (receivables, inventory, land, equipment, patents, etc.). Liabilities of the subsidiary usually are reported at their book values (because these usually are their equivalent market values).
3. At acquisition date, the **difference** between the total purchase cost and the market value of the **identifiable** tangible and intangible assets acquired (less the subsidiary's liabilities) represents an unidentifiable asset. This

Exhibit 18–8
(concluded)

Panel B—Worksheet to Develop Consolidated Statement of Financial Position, Purchase Method:

COMPANY P AND ITS SUBSIDIARY, COMPANY S (90% OWNERSHIP)
Purchase Method; Immediately after Acquisition

Account	Statement of financial position from accounts		Eliminations and restatements		Consolidated statement of financial position
	Company P	Company S	Debit	Credit	
Cash	399,000*	20,000			419,000
Accounts receivable (net)	10,000	40,000		*(c)* 5,000	45,000
Inventories	20,000	30,000		*(a)* 4,500	45,500
Investment in Company S	211,000*			*(a)* 76,000 *(b)* 135,000	
Plant and equipment (net)	200,000	110,000	*(a)* 36,900		346,900
Patents (net)	20,000	10,000	*(a)* 3,600		33,600
Goodwill			*(a)* 40,000		40,000
	860,000	210,000			930,000
Current liabilities	10,000	20,000	*(c)* 5,000		25,000
Long-term liabilities	50,000	40,000			90,000
Common stock:					
Company P	600,000				600,000
Company S		100,000	*(b)* 90,000		10,000M
Retained earnings:					
Company P	200,000				200,000
Company S		50,000	*(b)* 45,000		5,000M
	860,000	210,000			930,000

M—minority stockholders' 10% interest in Company S.
* Includes effects of the acquisition entry ($610,000 − $211,000 = $399,000).
Eliminations and restatements:
(a) To record the restatement of assets to market value and to eliminate the net effect from the investment account (panel A, item 3*b*).
(b) To eliminate the proportionate part of the stockholders' equity of the subsidiary (90%) and to eliminate an equal amount from the investment account (which now must be zero). Entries *(a)* and *(b)* may be combined.
(c) To eliminate the intercompany payable/receivable of $5,000.

difference is reported as **"goodwill from acquisition."** Goodwill from acquisition is subsequently amortized as an expense on the parent's consolidated statements of income.

4. Immediately after acquisition by purchase, the retained earnings balance of the **combined entity** is defined as the retained earnings balance of the parent company only. Thus, the retained earnings balance of the subsidiary is eliminated and, as a consequence, is not reported on the consolidated statement of financial position.
5. After combination by purchase, comparative financial statements of precombination periods must be reported on a consolidated basis.

Preparation of Consolidated Statement of Financial Position Immediately after Acquisition, Purchase Method. **Exhibit 18–8** shows preparation of a consolidated statement of financial position on the **purchase basis** immediately after acquisition. Except for the method of acquisition, Exhibit 18–8 is based upon the situation for Company P and Company S in Exhibit 18–7, panel A.

In order to prepare the worksheet, the amount of **goodwill purchased** must be determined. Goodwill is computed as the difference between the purchase price paid by the parent and the market values of the identifiable **net** assets of the subsidiary. Also, notice that in Exhibit 18–8, panel A, items in 3*b* have market values different from their book values.

The worksheet shown in Exhibit 18–8, panel B, is started by entering the two statements of financial position, using amounts immediately **after** the acquisition entry. Notice that two accounts (i.e., Cash and Investments) on Company P statements of financial position reflect the acquisition entry. Also, the middle pair of columns are called Eliminations and Restatements because *(a)* restatement entries must be made to change the assets of Company S from book value to market value for the **proportionate** part of the market value purchased by Company P (entry [*a*] on the worksheet) and *(b)* elimination entries must be made for intercompany items (entries [*b*] and [*c*] on the worksheet). The computations of these amounts are given in Exhibit 18–8, panel A, items 3*a* and 3*b*. They indicate that inventories must be reduced by $4,500; plant and equipment increased by $36,900; patents increased by $3,600; and goodwill recorded in the amount of $40,000. This amount reflects the proportionate part of the excess of market value over book value of each of these items acquired by Company P.[13] The net offset for these amounts is recorded in the **investment account** as an elimination because that account was debited at acquisition for the market value of the net assets acquired (90%).

The worksheet is completed by extending each item horizontally, considering the eliminations and restatements. The last column gives all of the data needed to prepare a formal consolidated statement of financial position on the purchase basis.

A comparison of Exhibit 18–7 (pooling of interests) with Exhibit 18–8 (purchase) reflects three underlying conceptual differences. The first difference is that in a pooling of interests the book values of the subsidiary are added to the book values of the parent, whereas in a purchase the market values of the subsidiary at acquisition are added to the book values of the parent. The second difference is that goodwill is not recognized in a pooling of interests; in contrast, goodwill usually is recognized in a purchase. The third difference is the treatment of retained earnings in the consolidation. In a pooling of interests all owners before the acquisition transaction continue as owners after the transaction; therefore, the retained earnings of both companies are combined to derive consolidated retained earnings. In a purchase acquisition the parent company buys the subsidiary shares and the prior owners do not continue as owners; therefore, the consolidated retained earnings are limited to the parent company's retained earnings. This can be observed in Exhibit 18–7 (retained earnings, $245,000) and Exhibit 18–8 ($200,000). These three basic differences will be maintained in the consolidated financial statements of all subsequent periods.

---

[13] In computing goodwill (see Exhibit 18–8, panel A, 3*a*), if the total purchase cost is **less** than the summed market values of the individual assets of the subsidiary less liabilities, "negative goodwill" occurs. Negative goodwill should not be recognized. The difference should be allocated to **reduce** the purchase cost (i.e., market estimates) of the **identifiable** tangible and intangible assets.

Consolidation of Financial Statements Subsequent to Acquisition

At the end of each accounting period subsequent to acquisition of a controlling interest in another company, the parent company (but not the subsidiary company) will prepare a consolidated statement of financial position, a consolidated statement of income, and a consolidated SCF. The worksheets shown in Exhibits 18–7 and 18–8 can be expanded to develop both a consolidated statement of financial position and a statement of income. A separate worksheet usually is needed to develop a consolidated statement of cash flows. That statement is discussed in Chapter 19.

In this section, an expanded worksheet to develop a consolidated statement of financial position and statement of income subsequent to acquisition will be illustrated for both *(a)* pooling of interests and *(b)* purchase. The same data will be used for both illustrations. The section will end with an illustration of the formal consolidated statements on a purchase basis.

Preparation of Consolidated Statements Subsequent to Acquisition, Pooling of Interests Method

Exhibit 18–9 shows the preparation of a consolidated statement of financial position and statement of income under the pooling of interests method, one year after acquisition. The case data given in Exhibit 18–7 (pooling of interests) is continued here. Exhibit 18–9, panel A, gives the separate financial statements of companies P and S **one year after** the January 1, 19A, acquisition by **pooling of interests.** Panel B shows the worksheet that will be used to consolidate the separate financial statements for the year ended December 31, 19A.

The consolidation worksheet shown in Exhibit 18–9 for the **pooling of interests method** is similar to the worksheet shown in Exhibit 18–7 (consolidated statement of financial position at acquisition) but expanded to include the statement of income. The reported amounts from the separate statements are entered directly in the first two columns of the worksheet. For convenience and to faciliate understanding, common stock, retained earnings at date of acquisition, and income subsequent to acquisition are set out separately. The expanded worksheet involves only one "elimination" not previously discussed—the $7,000 **intercompany sales.** During the year, Company S transferred goods to Company P that cost Company S $7,000. Company S recorded this as a sale, and Company P recorded it as a purchase. This is an intercompany transaction that must be eliminated to prevent double counting of sales revenue and cost of goods sold. When Company P sold the goods to outsiders, a sale was recorded at that time.[14] If the goods have not yet been sold by Company P, the credit would be to inventory instead of cost of goods sold. The eliminations are explained at the bottom of the worksheet. Because the consolidated statements are prepared on a pooling of interests basis, the **book values** of the two companies are aggregated item by item. Notice that **combined income,** $72,000, is the sum of the net income amounts reported by the companies separately. Of this $72,000, 10% of the **subsidiary's** net income ($12,000) is assigned to the minority interest

[14] The elimination of intercompany sales of $7,000 assumed the goods were transferred at cost. However, if *(a)* the transfer price had included an element of profit for the selling entity and *(b)* the goods were still held by the purchasing entity, the difference (unrealized intercompany inventory profit) would be eliminated by debiting Sales Revenue for the selling price, crediting Cost of Goods Sold for the cost, and crediting Ending Inventory for the difference.

Exhibit 18–9
Consolidated financial statements, Company P (parent) and Company S (subsidiary), 90% ownership, pooling of interests method.

Panel A—Case Data:
Reported amounts at December 31, 19A (end of first year)—pooling of interests method:

	At December 31, 19A	
	Company P	Company S
Statement of income:		
Sales revenue	$520,000	$105,000*
Cost of goods sold	300,000*	53,000
Depreciation expense	20,000	4,000
Patent amortization expense	2,000	1,000
Other expenses	138,000	35,000
Total expenses	460,000	93,000
Net income	$ 60,000	$ 12,000
Statement of financial position:		
Cash	$639,000	$ 24,000
Accounts receivable (net)	15,000†	45,000
Inventories (LIFO)	30,000	29,000
Investment in Company S (pooling basis)	90,000‡	
Plant and equipment (net)	180,000	106,000
Patents (net)	18,000	9,000
Total assets	$972,000	$213,000
Current liabilities	$ 12,000	$ 21,000†
Long-term liabilities	40,000	30,000
Common stock (par $100)	690,000	100,000
Retained earnings	230,000§	62,000
Total equities	$972,000	$213,000

* Includes a sale by Company S to Company P, $7,000 (cost to Company S); Company P resold the items during 19A.
† Includes a $3,000 debt that Company S owes to Company P.
‡ Must be carried forward at the amount recorded at date of acquisition.
§ During 19A, Company P declared and paid a $30,000 cash dividend to all stockholders.

($1,200). The remainder ($70,800) represents the consolidated net income to be reported by the parent. A similar allocation is made for retained earnings.

Preparation of Consolidated Statements Subsequent to Acquisition, Purchase Method

Exhibit 18–10 shows preparation of a consolidated statement of financial position and statement of income under the **purchase method** one year after acquisition. It continues the situation given for Companies P and S in Exhibit 18–9, panel A. However, because that information assumes pooling of interests, it must be adapted to reflect a combination by purchase. Exhibit 18–10, panel A, presents the adapted situation (statements of income and financial position at the end of the first year). Panel B presents the consolidation worksheet.

The worksheet prepared immediately after acquisition (Exhibit 18–8) is expanded to include the statement of income (on the purchase basis). Because of the restatement (i.e., write-up) of plant and equipment and patents and recognition of purchased goodwill, the expanded worksheet must include *(a)* additional depreciation expense, *(b)* additional patent amortization expense,

Exhibit 18–9
(concluded)

Panel B—Worksheet to Develop Consolidated Statement of Income and Statement of Financial Position, Pooling of Interests Method:

COMPANY P AND ITS SUBSIDIARY, COMPANY S (90% OWNERSHIP)
At December 31, 19A

Items	Reported amounts		Eliminations		Consolidated statements
	Company P	Company S	Debit	Credit	
Statement of income:					
Sales revenue	520,000	105,000	(*c*) 7,000		618,000
Cost of goods sold	300,000	53,000		(*c*) 7,000	346,000
Depreciation expense	20,000	4,000			24,000
Patent amortization expense	2,000	1,000			3,000
Other expenses	138,000	35,000			173,000
	460,000	93,000			546,000
Income (to statement of financial position)	60,000	12,000			72,000
Apportioned for consolidation:					
Minority interest (10% × $12,000)					1,200M
Parent interest (remainder)					70,800
Statement of financial position:					
Cash	639,000	24,000			663,000
Accounts receivable (net)	15,000	45,000		(*b*) 3,000	57,000
Inventories	30,000	29,000			59,000
Investment in Company S	90,000			(*a*) 90,000	–0–
Plant and equipment (net)	180,000	106,000			286,000
Patents (net)	18,000	9,000			27,000
	972,000	213,000			1,092,000
Current liabilities	12,000	21,000	(*b*) 3,000		30,000
Long-term liabilities	40,000	30,000			70,000
Common stock:					
Company P	690,000*				690,000
Company S		100,000	(*a*) 90,000		10,000M
Retained earnings:					
Company P ($200,000 at acquisition less $30,000 dividends)	170,000				215,000
Company S (at acquisition)		50,000			5,000M
Income (from statement of income)	60,000	12,000			70,800 1,200M
	972,000	213,000			1,092,000

M—Minority stockholders' interest of 10% in Company S.
* Includes effects of the acquisition entry (i.e., $600,000 + $90,000 = $690,000; see Exhibit 18–7).
Eliminations:
(*a*) To eliminate investment account balance against stockholders' equity (90% ownership) of the subsidiary.
(*b*) To eliminate intercompany debt of $3,000.
(*c*) To eliminate intercompany sales of $7,000 (at cost from Company S to Company P); the items were resold by Company P during 19A.

and (*c*) goodwill amortization expense. These, and all other eliminations and restatements, are explained in Exhibit 18–10. The restatement of assets to market value (including goodwill) subsequent to the date of acquisition is based upon the amounts determined at acquisition date (see Exhibit 18–10, panel B, entry *a*).

Exhibit 18–10
Consolidated financial statements, Company P (parent) and Company S (subsidiary), 90% ownership, purchase method.

Panel A—Case Data:

1. Reported amounts at December 31, 19A (end of first year)—purchase method:

	At December 31, 19A	
	Company P	**Company S**
Statement of income:		
Sales revenue	$520,000	$105,000*
Cost of goods sold	300,000*	53,000
Depreciation expense	20,000	4,000
Patent amortization expense	2,000	1,000
Other expenses	138,000	35,000
Total expenses	460,000	93,000
Net income	$ 60,000	$ 12,000
Statement of financial position:		
Cash	$428,000	$ 24,000
Accounts receivable (net)	15,000†	45,000
Inventories	30,000	29,000
Investment in Company S (purchase method)	211,000‡	
Plant and equipment (net)	180,000	106,000
Patents (net)	18,000	9,000
Total assets	$882,000	$213,000
Current liabilities	$ 12,000	$ 21,000†
Long-term liabilities	40,000	30,000
Common stock (par $100)	600,000	100,000
Retained earnings	230,000§	62,000
Total equities	$882,000	$213,000

2. The goodwill and related asset values computed **at date of acquisition** (Exhibit 18–8, panel A, items 3*a* and 3*b*) are used **without change** for consolidation purposes in subsequent years. Recall the following amounts; goodwill, $40,000; inventory decrease, $4,500; plant and equipment increase, $36,900; and patents increase, $3,600.

* Includes a sale by Company S to Company P, $7,000 (cost to Company S); Company P resold the items during 19A.
† Includes a $3,000 debt that Company S owes to Company P.
‡ Must be carried forward at amount recorded (cost) at date of acquisition.
§ During 19A, Company P declared and paid a $30,000 cash dividend to all stockholders.

Although GAAP requires that goodwill (recognized in the purchase method only) must be amortized, income tax laws and regulations do not permit a deduction in the income tax return. This is a controversial issue; for example, the following is quoted from *The Wall Street Journal*, March 24, 1988, page 26:

> Of the major industrial nations, only the U.S. requires its companies to amortize, or write off, good will against earnings but doesn't allow any tax deductions. In other words, there are both earnings effects and no tax benefits. In most European countries, including Britain, good will is treated entirely on the balance sheet and has no earnings effects. . . . Canada, Japan and West Germany require good will to be amortized against earnings. However, the good-will charges are in large measure tax deductible, which gives companies from these countries a cash-flow advantage over a U.S. purchaser. In effect, the governments of Japan, Germany and Canada provide a subsidy for the purchase of U.S. companies.

The cash advantage results from the income tax difference.

Exhibit 18–10
(*concluded*)

Panel B—Worksheet to Develop Consolidated Statement of Income and Statement of Financial Position, Purchase Method:

COMPANY P AND ITS SUBSIDIARY, COMPANY S (90% OWNERSHIP)
At December 31, 19A

Items	Reported Amounts Company P	Reported Amounts Company S	Eliminations and Restatements Debit	Eliminations and Restatements Credit	Consolidated Statements
Statement of income:					
Sales revenue	520,000	105,000	(e) 7,000		618,000
Cost of goods sold	300,000	53,000		(e) 7,000	346,000
Depreciation expense	20,000	4,000	(d) 3,690		27,690
Patent amortization expense	2,000	1,000	(d) 360		3,360
Goodwill amortization expense			(d) 1,000		1,000
Other expenses	138,000	35,000			173,000
	460,000	93,000			551,050
Income (to balance sheet)	60,000	12,000			66,950
Apportioned for consolidation:					
Minority interest (10% × $12,000)					1,200M
Parent interest (remainder)					65,750
Statement of financial position:					
Cash	428,000*	24,000			452,000
Accounts receivable (net)	15,000	45,000		(c) 3,000	57,000
Inventories	30,000	29,000		(a) 4,500†	54,500
Investment in Company S	211,000*			(a) 76,000	
				(b) 135,000	–0–
Plant and equipment (net)	180,000	106,000	(a) 36,900	(d) 3,690	319,210
Patents (net)	18,000	9,000	(a) 3,600	(d) 360	30,240
Goodwill (net)			(a) 40,000	(d) 1,000	39,000
	882,000	213,000			951,950
Current liabilities	12,000	21,000	(c) 3,000		30,000
Long-term liabilities	40,000	30,000			70,000
Common stock:					
Company P	600,000				600,000
Company S		100,000	(b) 90,000		10,000M
Retained earnings:					
Company P ($200,000 at acquisition less $30,000 dividend)	170,000				170,000
Company S (at acquisition)		50,000	(b) 45,000		5,000M
Income (from statement of income)	60,000	12,000			65,750
					1,200M
	882,000	213,000			951,950

M—Minority stockholders' 10% interest in Company S.
* Includes effects of the acquisition entry.
† LIFO assumed. When this cost flows out of inventory, the credit will be to cost of goods sold; subsequently it will be credited to Company P retained earnings.

Restatements and eliminations:

(a) To restate the assets of Company S to market and to eliminate the net effect from the investment account (from goodwill computations, Exhibit 18–8, panel A, items 3a and 3b). It is especially important to understand that the market value restatements for assets each period subsequent to acquisition are always determined at date of acquisition. This explains why the data here are exactly the same as that in Exhibit 18–8 for plant and equipment, patents, and goodwill.

(b) To eliminate the proportionate part of stockholders' equity of the subsidiary owned by the parent (90%) and to eliminate an equal amount from the investment account (which now must be zero).

(c) To eliminate the intercompany debt, $3,000.

(d) To recognize additional market value expenses: depreciation, $36,900 ÷ 10 years = $3,690; patent amortization, $3,600 ÷ 10 years = $360; and goodwill amortization, $40,000 ÷ 40 years = $1,000.

(e) To eliminate intercompany sales, $7,000 (at cost).

Consolidated Financial Statements Illustrated

The consolidated statement of income and statement of financial position (purchase method) for Company P are shown in **Exhibit 18–11.** Notice the manner of presenting the minority interest and the more descriptive caption for goodwill, "Cost of investment in excess of market value of identifiable net assets of subsidiary." Goodwill is identified by various titles in statements of financial position. For example, the 1986 Annual Report of Crane Company used "Cost in Excess of Net Assets Acquired." Illinois Tool Works Inc. (1986) used the single word, "Goodwill." The exhibit also shows two formats that are widely used for presentation of the minority interest on the statement of financial position. These items are boxed in Exhibit 18–11 for emphasis.

Comparison of the Pooling of Interests and Purchase Methods

The results of the *(a)* pooling of interest and *(b)* purchase methods are compared in **Exhibit 18–12.** The comparison reveals that **net income** is lower (by $5,050) under the purchase method. This approach requires *(a)* restatement of the subsidiary's assets to market value and *(b)* recognition of goodwill. Each of these must be allocated on an annual basis to **expense** ($3,690 + $360 + $1,000 = $5,050). **Cash and common stock** are lower under the purchase method. At acquisition, cash rather than common stock was used to acquire the controlling interest. The purchase method requires recognition of market values (for the subsidiary's assets; i.e., inventories, patents, and plant and equipment) and purchased goodwill. This caused goodwill of $39,000 to be reported under the purchase method. **Retained earnings** is higher under pooling of interests. Retained earnings is the sum of the parent and subsidiary amounts. In contrast, when the purchase method is used, retained earnings of the subsidiary at acquisition is eliminated along with the subsidiary's other owners' equity accounts. This is because they represent the parent company's investment. The **minority interest** is net income and retained earnings is the same under both methods.

Mainly because of *(a)* the effect on **cash** and *(b)* the accounting effects on **net income and retained earnings,** companies usually prefer pooling of interests. Also, because the pooling of interests method retains the book value basis of accounting for subsidiary assets, pooling provides the parent company with the **opportunity to report later gains** on the sale of subsidiary assets with market values in excess of cost. This opportunity is not likely under the purchase method, because with this method, the assets of the subsidiary are recorded at market value when they are acquired by the parent. Another reason companies may prefer pooling of interests is that the parent company will report a higher income. Pooling transactions were fairly common during the mid-1960s, prior to the issuance of *APB Opinion 16.*

In contrast to the preference of the acquiring company, the stockholders of the acquired company often prefer to receive cash rather than stock of the parent company. In respect to the accounting aspects and the opportunity to manipulate reported earnings, *APB Opinion 16* placed severe restrictions on use of the pooling of interests approach. This is evidenced by the requirement that a business combination must satisfy all of 12 criteria for it to be accounted for as a pooling of interests.

Finally, we emphasize that **none** of the entries reflected on a consolidated worksheet (e.g., Exhibit 18–10) are recorded in the accounts of the parent or subsidiary companies. They are merely worksheet entries used to derive the consolidated financial statements **reported** by the parent company.

Exhibit 18–11
Consolidated statement of income and statement of financial position (purchase method).

COMPANY P AND SUBSIDIARY, COMPANY S
Consolidated Statement of Income (purchase method)
For the Year Ended December 31, 19A

Sales revenue		$618,000
Expenses:		
Cost of goods sold	$346,000	
Depreciation expense	27,690	
Patent amortization expense	3,360	
Goodwill amortization expense	1,000	
Other expenses	173,000	551,050
Combined net income, including minority interest		66,950
Minority interest in net income of subsidiary (10%)		1,200
Consolidated net income		$ 65,750

Consolidated Statement of Financial Position (purchase method)
At December 31, 19A

Assets

Cash	$452,000
Accounts receivable (net)	57,000
Inventories	54,500
Plant and equipment (net)	319,210
Patents (net)	30,240
Cost of investment in excess of market value of identifiable net assets of subsidiary	39,000
Total assets	$951,950

Liabilities

Current liabilities	$ 30,000	
Long-term liabilities	70,000	$100,000
*Interest of Minority Stockholders in Subsidiary**		
Common stock	10,000	
Retained earnings	6,200	16,200
*Stockholders' Equity**		
Common stock, par $100, 6,000 shares outstanding	600,000	
Retained earnings ($170,000 + $65,750)	235,750	835,750
Total liabilities and stockholders' equity		$951,950

* Alternate presentation of minority interest:

Stockholders' Equity

Common stock, par $100, 6,000 shares outstanding		$600,000
Retained earnings		235,750
Total interest of parent company		835,750
Interest of minority stockholders in subsidiary:		
Common stock	$10,000	
Retained earnings	6,200	16,200
Total stockholders' interest, including interest of minority stockholders		$851,950

FASB Standard 79, "Elimination of Certain Disclosures for Business Combinations by Nonpublic Enterprises," amended *APB Opinion 16*. *FASB Standard 79* eliminated the requirement for nonpublic companies (usually small companies) to present pro forma results of operations when the purchase method is used. These pro forma results relate to restatement of the results of operations for the year prior to the combination.

Exhibit 18–12
Comparison of pooling of interests and purchase methods (based on Exhibits 18–9 and 18–10).

For year ended December 31, 19A	Method: Pooling (Exhibit 18–9)	Method: Purchase (Exhibit 18–10)	Difference—pooling over purchase
Net income:			
Parent interest	$ 70,800	$ 65,750	$ 5,050
Minority interest	1,200	1,200	-0-
Cash	663,000	452,000	211,000
Inventories	59,000	54,500	4,500
Investment in Company S	-0-	-0-	-0-
Plant and equipment (net)	286,000	319,210	(33,210)
Patents (net)	27,000	30,240	(3,240)
Goodwill	-0-	39,000	(39,000)
Liabilities	100,000	100,000	-0-
Common stock, Company P	690,000	600,000	90,000
Retained earnings:			
Parent interest	285,800	235,750	50,050
Minority interest	6,200	6,200	-0-

Push-Down Accounting

When the purchase method is used to effect a business combination, the parent company includes the subsidiary's assets in the consolidated financial statements at their market values (as of the acquisition date). However, when the financial statements of the subsidiary are **separately** presented in the **parent company's** financial statements as supplemental information, they are not restated to market value. The subsidiary's statements report cost-basis amounts, or book values. This reporting situation introduces an inconsistency regarding the subsidiary's reported values in the parent's financial report.[15]

Some accountants have proposed that this inconsistency be resolved by restating the subsidiary's financial statements to **market values** when they are included in the parent's statements as supplemental information. This reporting proposal has become known as **push-down accounting.** In push-down accounting, the parent company's purchase cost (i.e., the market values of the subsidiary's assets included in the parent company's consolidated statements) is "pushed down" into the subsidiary's separate financial statements when they are included as supplemental information in the parent's financial statements.[16]

Accounting for Futures Contracts—An Investment

Business entities and other investors often purchase a **futures contract** as an investment or as a hedge to offset the risks of future price changes. A futures contract is between a buyer or seller of a **commodity or a financial instrument**

[15] AICPA, Accounting Standards Executive Committee, Issues Paper, "Push-Down Accounting" (New York; October 30, 1979).

[16] See Michael E. Cunningham, "Push-Down Accounting: Pros and Cons," *Journal of Accountancy*, June 1984, pp. 72–77, for an excellent analysis of the issue.

and the **clearinghouse** of a **futures exchange.** Futures contracts are varied; however, such contracts have three common characteristics:[17]

- **a.** They obligate the buyer, or seller, to accept or make delivery of a commodity or financial instrument at a specified time or they provide for **cash settlement** periodically rather than delivery.
- **b.** They can be effectively canceled before the specified time by entering into an offsetting contract for the same commodity or financial instrument.
- **c.** All changes in the market value of **open contracts** are settled on a regular basis, **usually daily.**

Two accounting approaches are used to record and report a futures contract. They are called the **market-value** approach and the **hedge-deferral** approach. The primary issue in accounting for a futures contract is whether changes in the market value of a futures contract should be recognized as a gain or loss in the reporting period that the market price changes or whether the gain or loss should be deferred to a later date.

FASB Standard 80 specifies two criteria for determining the accounting approach for futures contracts that should be used:

1. The item to be hedged exposes the company to market price or interest rate risk.
2. The futures contract reduces that risk and is designated as a hedge.

The **market-value approach** must be used if **both** of these criteria are not met. The market-value approach requires that all gains and losses due to market price changes be **recognized in the reporting period that the market prices change.**

The **hedge-deferral approach** must be used when either of the two, or both, criteria are met. The hedge-deferral approach requires that all gains and losses due to market price changes be deferred and recognized at the **termination** of the futures contract as an adjustment to the cost (or price) in the subsequent terminating transaction.

A simplified futures contract case is used to illustrate these approaches:
Case A—Market-value approach, and **Case B**—Hedge-deferral approach.
Data—MD Company is a producer of a grain-based product.

October 19A—The company determined that it will need 10,000 bushels of grain near the end of February 19B. The company expects the current $3 price per bushel of grain to change. It does not want to assume the risk of such market changes.

November 1, 19A—The company decided to purchase a futures contract from Chicago Clearing House, Inc., to hedge (i.e., shift) the risk of market price changes of grain. This futures contract, which cost $800, provides that the company will purchase the grain at the date it is needed at the then market price (or pay the equivalent amount of cash if it is not purchased). However, between the date the futures contract is purchased (November 1, 19A) and the termination date (when the grain is purchased), Chicago Clearing

[17] *FASB Statement of Financial Accounting Standards 80,* "Accounting for Futures Contracts" (Stamford, Conn., August 1984).

House, Inc., will **pay** the company cash for all market price **increases** (from the $3 beginning hedge price), and **collect** cash from the company for all market price decreases (from the hedge price of $3). Thus, for the $800 fee, the company shifted the risk of market price changes to the clearinghouse. Changes in the market price of the grain are settled every day, and the cash offset is payable or collectible each weekend.

December 31, 19A—end of the reporting period:
The market price of the grain changed to $2.80.

February 24, 19B—the following events occur:

a. The market price of the grain is $3.30.

b. Purchased the 10,000 bushels of grain, which are needed for production, at $3.30 cash.

c. Termination of the futures contract.

Required Entries:

Case A—Market-value approach (used if the two criteria are not met)			Case B—Hedge-deferral approach (used if either, or both, criteria are met)		
November 1, 19A—To record the futures contract:					
Prepaid expense, futures contract	800		Prepaid expense, futures contract	800	
Cash		800	Cash		800
December 31, 19A—To record the market price drop in futures commodity:					
Loss on futures contract	2,000[(a)]		Inventory cost adjustment, futures contract	2,000[(b)]	
Cash		2,000	Cash		2,000
10,000 bushels × ($3 − $2.80) = $2,000.					
(a) Reported as a loss on 19A statement of income.			*(b)* Reported as a deferred charge on the 19A statement of financial position.		
February 24, 19B—To record the market price increase in futures commodity:					
Cash	5,000		Cash	5,000	
Gain on futures contract		5,000[(c)]	Inventory cost adjustment, futures contract		5,000[(d)]
10,000 bushels × ($3.30 − $2.80) = $5,000.			*(d)* Net offset to cost of grain, $5,000 − $2,000 = $3,000.		
(c) Reported as a gain on 19B statement of income.					
To record purchase of the grain:					
Grain inventory	33,000		Grain inventory	30,000	
Cash		33,000	Inventory cost adjustment, futures contract	3,000	
10,000 bushels × $3.30.			Cash		33,000
To record termination of futures contract:					
To adjust 19A prepaid expense (from first entry):					
Expense, futures contract	800		Expense, futures contract	800	
Prepaid expense, futures contract . .		800	Prepaid expense, futures contract		800
To reconcile futures contract results:					
Cash inflow		$5,000	Cash inflow		$5,000
Cash outflow		2,000	Cash outflow		2,000
Net gain on futures contract		$3,000	Decrease in inventory cost		$3,000

Summary

Part B of this chapter gives an introduction to consolidated financial statements. This discussion is important for accounting and finance majors who may not take the advanced accounting course on consolidated statements.

Consolidated statements are prepared (by only the parent company) when the parent company has a controlling interest in another company (called a **subsidiary**). A controlling interest exists for accounting purposes when the parent company owns more than 50% of the outstanding voting stock of the subsidiary; the only exception to this basic rule is when control is likely to be temporary or if it does not rest with the majority owner.

Consolidated statements basically involve aggregation on a line-by-line basis of the assets, liabilities, equity, revenues and gains, and expenses and losses of the parent and subsidiary. The manner of acquisition—by pooling (an exchange of shares), or by purchase (using assets to acquire the subsidiary's shares) has a significant impact on the consolidated statements. Consolidation of the financial statements of a parent company and a subsidiary is a reporting procedure only; therefore, it does not affect the accounts of either the parent or the subsidiary. Consolidated statements are prepared only by the parent company and not by the subsidiary. This chapter shows typical consolidation worksheets used to prepare the consolidated statement of financial position and statement of income.

QUESTIONS

Part A

1. Distinguish between debt and equity securities; also between short-term and long-term investments.
2. What accounting principle is applied in recording the acquisition of an investment? Explain its application in cash and noncash acquisitions.
3. Briefly explain the accounting for short-term investments in equity securities.
4. An investor purchased 100 shares of PQ common stock at $20 per share on March 15, 19A. At the end of the 19A accounting period, December 31, 19A, the stock was quoted at $19 per share. On June 5, 19B, the investor sold the stock for $22 per share. Assuming a short-term investment, provide answers to the following:
   a. March 15, 19A—Debit to the investment account, $____ .
   b. December 31, 19A—Unrealized loss, $____ .
   c. June 5, 19B—Gain or loss on sale of the investment, $____ .
5. On June 15, 19A, Baker Company purchased 500 shares of preferred stock, par $10, at $30 per share. The market value of these shares at the end of the accounting period, December 31, 19A, was $28 per share. Show how this short-term investment should be reported on the 19A statement of financial position.
6. Briefly explain the accounting for short-term investments in debt securities.
7. What is meant by an impairment loss?
8. Explain why interest revenue is accrued on investments but dividend revenue is not accrued.
9. Under the cost, LCM method for investments in equity securities no distinction is

made between voting and nonvoting stock, but the distinction is important with respect to the equity and consolidation methods. Explain why.

10. Explain when the cost, LCM method of accounting for equity investments is applicable.
11. Explain how the LCM concept is applied to long-term investments in equity securities. How is "cost" determined when an investment is reclassified from short term to long term or vice versa?
12. Explain the basic features of the equity method of accounting for long-term investments. When is the equity method applicable?
13. Assume Company R acquired, as a long-term investment, 30% of the outstanding voting common stock of Company S at a cash cost of $100,000. At date of acquisition, the SFP of Company S showed total stockholders' equity of $250,000. The market value of the assets of Company S was $20,000 greater than their book value at date of acquisition. Compute goodwill purchased, if any. What accounting method should be used in this situation? Explain why.
14. Assume the same facts as given in question 13, with the additional data that the net assets have a remaining estimated life of 10 years and goodwill will be amortized over 20 years (assume no residual values and straight-line depreciation). How much additional depreciation and amortization expense should be reported by the investor, Company R, each year in accounting for this long-term investment? Give the entries to record additional depreciation and amortization of goodwill.
15. The equity method of accounting for a long-term investment in equity securities usually will reflect a greater amount of investment revenue than the cost method in the same circumstances. Explain why.
16. Explain the basic features of the market value method of accounting for investments in securities. Is it a generally accepted method? Explain.
17. How would the market value method of accounting for investments in securities, in contrast to the cost method, tend to prevent "managed" earnings?
18. Basically, the investor accounts for an ordinary stock dividend and a stock split in the same way. Briefly, explain the accounting that should be followed by the investor in these situations.
19. What is a convertible security? Assume an investor has a convertible security with a carrying value of $200,000, which is turned in to the issuer for conversion. The investor receives, through the conversion, common stock with a current market value of $225,000. Explain how the investor should account for the conversion of this long-term investment.
20. What is a stock right (or warrant)? If stock rights have a market value, how would the investor account for the receipt of stock rights?

Part B

21. Explain the characteristics of acquisition of a long-term investment accounted for by the *(a)* pooling of interests method and *(b)* purchase method.
22. Contrast the primary effects on the statement of financial position and statement of income of a pooling of interests versus a purchase. Why are the effects different?
23. Explain why market values are used in the purchase method but not in the pooling of interests method.
24. Explain why goodwill is recognized in a purchase but not in a pooling of interests.
25. What are intercompany items in respect to consolidated financial statements? Why must they be eliminated in preparing consolidated financial statements?

26. What is meant by minority interest in consolidated statements? How is this interest reported on *(a)* the statement of income and *(b)* the statement of financial position?
27. Explain the basic reasons why many companies, other things being equal, would prefer the pooling of interests method over the purchase method of accounting for parent/subsidiary relationships.

EXERCISES

Part A: Exercises 18–1 to 18–16

E 18–1 **(Classification of Investments in Securities)**
Match the different securities listed below with their usual classification as investments by entering the appropriate letter in each blank space. Usual classification as investments: A—Short-term equity investment; B—Short-term debt security; C—Long-term equity security; D—Long-term debt security; E—None of the above.

Typical securities

____ 1. Abbott common stock, nopar; acquired to use temporarily idle cash.
____ 2. Land acquired for short-term speculation.
____ 3. U.S. Treasury bills; mature in six months.
____ 4. GE preferred stock, par $100, mandatory redemption within next 12 months.
____ 5. Staufer common stock, par $5; acquired to attain a continuing controlling interests.
____ 6. Frazer bonds, 9%, mature at the end of 10 years; acquired for indefinite holding period.
____ 7. Foreign Corporation, common stock; difficulties encountered in withdrawing cash earned.
____ 8. Certificates of deposit (CDs); mature at end of one year.
____ 9. Savings certificate at local Savings and Loan Association; has been active for the past five years.
____ 10. Acorn common stock, par $1; acquired as a short-term investment, but now so profitable that it is not reasonable to sell it.

E 18–2 **(ST Equity Investments; Entries and Reporting, Cost, LCM)**
On November 1, 19A, Decker Company acquired the following short-term investments in marketable equity securities:

Corporation X—500 shares common stock (nopar) at $60 cash per share.

Corporation Y—300 shares preferred stock (par $10, nonredeemable) at $20 cash per share.

The annual reporting period ends December 31. On December 31, 19A, the quoted market prices were: Corporation X stock, $52; and Corporation Y stock, $24.

Data for 19B:

3/2/19B	Received cash dividends per share as follows: X stock, $1; and Y stock, 50 cents.
10/1/19B	Sold 100 of the Y shares at $25 per share.
12/31/19B	Market values: X stock, $46; and Y stock, $26.

Required:

1. Give the entry for Decker Company to record the purchase of the securities.
2. Give any adjusting entry needed at the end of 19A.
3. Give the items and amounts that should be reported on the 19A statement of income and statement of financial position.
4. Give all of the entries for 19B.
5. Give the items and amounts that should be reported on the 19B statement of income and statement of financial position.

E 18–3 (ST Equity Investments; Purchase, Sale, Transfer; Entries and Reporting; Cost, LCM) At December 31, 19A, the short-term equity investments of Vista Company were as follows:

Security	Shares	Unit cost	Unit market price
Preferred stock, 8%, par $10, Knight Corp	600	$90	$88
Common stock, nopar, Dyer Corp	200	30	31

The transactions below relate to the above short-term equity investments and those bought and sold during 19B. The reporting year ends December 31.

Feb. 2 Received the annual 8% cash dividend from Knight Corporation.
Mar. 1 Sold 150 shares of the Dyer stock at $34 per share.
May 1 Sold 400 shares of Knight stock at $89.50 per share.
June 1 Received a cash dividend on Dyer stock of $3.50 per share.
Aug. 1 Purchased 4,000 shares of Rote Corporation's common stock at $45 per share.
Sept. 1 Transferred all shares of Dyer common stock from the short-term portfolio to the long-term portfolio. At this date the Dyer stock was quoted at $28 per share.

At December 31, 19B, the quoted market prices were as follows: Knight preferred, $98; Dyer common, $28; and Rote common, $44.50.

Required:

1. Give the entry that Vista Company should have made on December 31, 19A, to record the equity investments at cost, LCM.
2. Give the entries for 19B through September 1.
3. Give the entry(s) required at December 31, 19B.
4. List the items and amounts that should be reported on Vista's 19B statement of income and statement of financial position.

E 18–4 (ST Debt Security; Cost (not LCM) Method; Comprehensive; Entries and Reporting) On September 1, 19A, New Company purchased 10, $1,000, 6%, bonds of Vue Corporation as a short-term investment at 96 plus accrued interest. The bonds pay annual interest each July 1. New paid cash, including any accrued interest. The annual reporting period ends December 31. At December 31, 19A, the Vue bonds were quoted at 95¾.

Required:

1. Give the journal entry for New Company to record the purchase of the bonds assuming the cost (not LCM) method will be used.
2. Give any adjusting entries required at December 31, 19A.
3. Give the items and amounts that should be reported on the 19A statement of income and statement of financial position.
4. Give the required entry on July 1, 19B.
5. On August 1, 19B, New Company sold four of the bonds at 96.5 plus any accrued

interest. The remaining six bonds were transferred to the long-term portfolio of debt securities. Give the required entry(s).

6. There were no additional transactions during 19B. List the short-term investment items and amounts that would be reported on the 19B statement of income and statement of financial position.

E 18–5 (ST Debt Security; Cost, LCM Method; Entries and Reporting)

On August 1, 19A, West Company purchased for cash four $10,000 bonds of Moe Corporation at 98 plus accrued interest. The bonds pay 9% interest, payable on a semiannual basis each May 1 and November 1. The annual reporting period ends December 31.

Required:

1. Give the following entries for West Company, assuming the cost, LCM method will be used:

8/1/19A	Paid $40,100 cash for the bonds including any accrued interest.
11/1/19A	Collected interest on the bonds.
12/31/19A	Adjusting entries (if any). The bonds were quoted on the market on this date at 96 excluding any accrued interest.
12/31/19A	Market value, $38,400.

2. Show how the effects of this short-term investment should be reported on the 19A statements of income and financial position.
3. On February 1, 19B, two of the bonds were sold for $19,950 cash including any accrued interest. Give the required entry. Assume no reversing entries were made on January 1, 19B.
4. Give the entry for the collection of interest on May 1, 19B.

E 18–6 (Basket Purchase of Securities; Allocation; Entry)

Voss Company purchased stock in the three different companies listed below, for a lump sum of $113,400, to be held as a long-term investment:

N Corporation, common stock (par, $10), 300 shares; O Corporation, preferred stock (par $100), 400 shares; P Corporation common stock (nopar) 500 shares.

In addition, Voss paid transfer fees and other costs related to the acquisition amounting to $600. At the time of purchase, the stocks were quoted on the local market at the following prices per share: N common, $100; O preferred, $120; and P common, $84.

Required:

Give the entry to record the purchase of these long-term investments and payment of the transfer fees and other costs. Record each stock in a separate account and show the cost per share.

E 18–7 (LT Equity Investments; Cost, LCM; Entries and Reporting)

During 19A, Shale Company purchased shares in two corporations with the intention of holding them as long-term investments. Transactions were in the following order:

a. Purchased 200 of the 10,000 shares outstanding of common stock of T Corporation at $31 per share plus a 4% brokerage fee and a transfer cost of $52.
b. Purchased 300 of 4,000 outstanding shares of preferred stock (nonvoting) of P Corporation at $78 per share plus a 3% brokerage fee and a transfer cost of $198.
c. Purchased an additional 20 shares of common stock of T Corporation at $35 per share plus a 4% brokerage fee and a transfer cost of $4.

d. Received $4 per share cash dividend on the P Corporation stock (from earnings since acquisition).

Required:

1. Give the entry in the accounts of Shale Company for each transaction, applying the cost, LCM method.
2. The market value of the shares held at the end of 19A were: T stock, $34; and P stock, $75. Give the appropriate adjusting entry for Shale Company.
3. The market values of the shares held at the end of 19B were: T stock, $36; and P stock, $77. Give the appropriate adjusting entry.
4. Show how the statement of income and statement of financial position for Shale Company would report relevant data concerning the long-term investments for 19A and 19B.

E 18–8 (LT Equity Investment; Equity Method; Compute Goodwill; Entries)

On January 1, 19A, JR Company purchased 400 of the 1,000 outstanding shares of common stock of RV Corporation for $30,000. At that date, the statement of financial position of RV showed the following book values:

Assets not subject to depreciation, $40,000*; Assets subject to depreciation (net), $26,000†; Liabilities, $6,000; Common stock (par $50), $50,000; Retained earnings, $10,000.

* Same as market value.
† Market value $30,000; the assets have a 10-year remaining life (straight-line depreciation).

Required:

1. Assuming the equity method is appropriate, give the entry by JR Company to record the acquisition at a cost of $30,000. Assume a long-term investment.
2. Show the computation of goodwill purchased at acquisition.
3. Assume at December 31, 19A (end of the accounting period), RV Corporation reported a net income of $12,000. Assume goodwill amortization over a 10-year period. Give all entries indicated on the records of JR Company.
4. In February 19B, RV Corporation declared and paid a $2 per share cash dividend. Give the necessary entry for JR Company.

E 18–9 (LT Equity Investment; Equity Method; Compute Goodwill; Entries in T-Accounts)

On January 1, 19A, Case Corporation purchased 3,000 of the 10,000 outstanding shares of common stock of Dow Corporation for $28,000 cash. At that date, Dow's statement of financial position reflected the following book values:

Assets not subject to depreciation, $25,000*; Assets subject to depreciation (net), $30,000†; Liabilities, $5,000; Common stock (par $4), $40,000; Retained earnings, $10,000.

* Same as market value.
† Market value $38,000; estimated remaining life of 10 years (straight-line depreciation).

Required:

1. If goodwill is relevant to this investment, show the computation of goodwill purchased at acquisition.
2. At the end of 19A, Dow reported income before extraordinary items, $20,000; extraordinary loss, $2,000; and net income, $18,000. In December 19A, Dow Corporation paid a $1 per share cash dividend. Reconstruct the following accounts (use T-account format) for Case Corporation: Cash, Investment in Dow Corporation Stock, Investment Revenue—Ordinary, and Extraordinary Loss. Apply the appropriate method of accounting for long-term investments in equity securities, and assume straight-line

amortization of any goodwill is over 10 years. Date and identify all amounts entered in the accounts.

E 18–10 **(LT Equity Investment; Cost, LCM and Equity Methods Compared; Entries)** On January 3, 19A, TA Company purchased 2,000 shares of the 10,000 outstanding shares of common stock of UK Corporation for $14,600 cash. At that date, the statement of financial position of UK Corporation reflected the following: nondepreciable assets, $50,000 (same as market value); depreciable assets (net), $30,000 (market value, $33,000); total liabilities, $20,000; and stockholders' equity, $60,000. Assume a 10-year remaining life (straight-line depreciation) on the depreciable assets and amortization of goodwill over 10 years.

Required:
Complete a tabulation similar to the one given below for each item *(a)* through *(g)*. Provide the Investor's entries and other information assuming: Case A—the cost, LCM method is appropriate, and Case B—the equity method is appropriate.

Entries required and other information	Case A: Cost, LCM method appropriate		Case B: Equity method appropriate	
a. Entry at date of acquisition.				
b. Goodwill purchased—computation only.				
c. Entry on 12/31/19A to record $15,000 net income reported by UK.				
d. Entry on 12/31/19A for additional depreciation expense.				
e. Entry on 12/31/19A for amortization of goodwill.				
f. Entry on 12/31/19A to recognize decrease in market value of UK stock, quoted market price, $7 per share. Assume this is the only long-term equity investment held.				
g. Entry on 3/31/19B for a cash dividend of $1 per share declared and paid by UK.				

E 18–11 **(Equity Securities; Market Value Method; Entries and Reporting)** On January 10, 19A, BT Company purchased as a long-term investment 15% of the 10,000 shares of the outstanding common stock of N Company (par value, $10 per share) at $50 per share. During 19A, 19B, and 19C, the following additional data were available:

	19A	19B
Reported net income of N Co. at year-end	$30,000	$35,000
Cash dividends paid by N Co. at year-end	10,000	15,000
Quoted market price per share of N Co. stock at year-end	57	55

On January 2, 19C, BT Company sold 100 of N Co. shares at $56 per share.

Required:
1. Assuming the market value method is used, give all entries indicated in the accounts of BT Company, assuming the company uses the current approach.
2. Prepare a tabulation to show the investment revenue for 19A, 19B, and 19C of BT Company and the balance in the investment account at year-end 19A, 19B, and 19C. Assume no cash dividends were paid by N Co. during 19C and that the quoted market price of N Co. common stock was $56 per share at December 31, 19C.

E 18–12 **(LT Equity Investment; Stock Dividend; Investor's Entries)**
Each of the following situations is completely independent; however, each relates to the receipt of a stock dividend by an investor.

Case A
Doe Corporation had 20,000 shares of $50 par value stock outstanding when the board of directors voted to issue a 25% stock dividend (i.e., one additional share for each four shares owned).

Required:
Van Company owns 2,000 shares of the Doe Corporation stock (a long-term investment) acquired at a cost of $65 per share. After receiving the stock dividend, Van Company sold 200 shares of the additional stock for $70 per share. Give the entries for Van Company to record (1) acquisition of the 2,000 shares, (2) receipt of the stock dividend, and (3) sale of the 200 shares. Assume the cost, LCM method is appropriate for the investor.

Case B
During the course of an audit, you find two accounts of the investor, May Company, as follows:

Investments in Stock of Yew Company ($100 par value)

	Debits	
Jan. 1	Cost of 100 shares	$17,500
Feb. 1	50 shares received as a stock dividend (at par $100)	5,000
	Credits	
July 1	25 shares of dividend stock sold at $125	3,125

Income summary

	Credits	
Feb. 1	Stock dividend on Yew Company stock	$ 5,000
Aug. 1	Cash dividend on Yew Company stock	3,000

Required:
Assuming the cost, LCM method is appropriate for the investor, restate these accounts on a correct basis. Give reasons for each change.

E 18–13 **(LT Equity Investment; Cash and Stock Dividends; Stock Split; Entries)**
PA Company purchased common stock (par value $10; 50,000 shares outstanding) of SU Corporation as a long-term investment. Transactions (which occurred in the order given) related to this investment were as follows:

a. Purchased 600 shares of SU common stock at $90 per share (designated as lot No. 1).
b. Purchased 2,000 shares of SU common stock at $96 per share (designated as lot No. 2).
c. At the end of the first year, SU Corporation reported net income of $52,000.
d. SU Corporation paid a cash dividend of $2 per share on the common stock.
e. After reporting net income of $5,000 for the second year, SU Corporation issued a stock dividend whereby each stockholder received one additional share for each two shares owned. At the time of the stock dividend, the stock was selling at $85.
f. SU Corporation revised its charter to provide for a stock split. The par value was reduced to $5. The "old" common stock was turned in, and the holders received in exchange two shares of the new stock for each old share turned in.

Required:
Give the entries for each transaction as they should be made in the accounts of PA Company. Show computations. Assume the cost, LCM method is appropriate because less than 20% of SU's voting stock is held by PA.

E 18–14 **(LT Equity Investment; Stock Rights; Entries)**
Corporation M issued one stock right for each share of common stock owned by investors. The rights provided that for each six rights held, a share of preferred stock could be purchased for $80 cash (par of the preferred was $50 per share). When the rights were issued, they had a market value of $7 each and the common stock was selling at $142 per share (ex rights). Taylor Company owned 300 shares of Corporation M common stock, acquired as a long-term investment at a cost of $22,350. Assume the cost, LCM method.

Required:
1. How many rights did Taylor Company receive?
2. Determine the carrying value of the stock rights received by Taylor Company, and give any entry that should be made upon receipt of the rights.
3. Assume Taylor Company exercised the rights when the market value of the preferred stock of Corporation M was $130. Determine the cost of the new stock and give the entry to record the exercise of the rights.
4. Assume instead that Taylor Company sold its rights for $7.40 each. Give the entry to record the sale.

E 18–15 **(LT Equity Investment; Stock Dividend; Stock Rights; Entries)**
Give entries in the accounts of Cisco Corporation under the cost, LCM method for the following transactions, which occurred over a period of time and in the chronological order shown:

a. Cisco Corporation purchased 100 shares of Bell Corporation common stock at $99 per share as a long-term investment.
b. Bell Corporation issued a 10% stock dividend in additional common shares.
c. Bell Corporation issued rights to current common stockholders entitling each holder of five old shares to buy one additional share of new common stock at $96. At the time, the rights sold for $4 per right and the shares outstanding sold for $116 each (ex rights). Make an allocation to the rights.
d. Cisco Corporation exercised all of its rights and bought new shares.
e. Cisco Corporation sold 120 shares of Bell stock for $100 per share, failing to identify the specific shares disposed of (use FIFO procedures). What is the status of the investment account after this sale (shares, cost per share, and total investment amount)?

E 18–16 **(Special-Purpose Fund; Accumulation Schedule; Entries)**
On January 1, 19A, Koke Company decided to create a special-purpose fund to be identified as the "Special Contingency Fund." The resources in the fund will be used to reimburse employees injured while on the job. The company desires to accumulate a $150,000 fund balance by the end of 19C by making equal annual deposits starting on January 1, 19A. The independent trustee handling the fund will increase the fund by 9% compound interest each December 31.

Required:
1. Compute the amount of the annual deposits, and prepare a fund accumulation schedule.

2. Give the entries relating to the fund that Koke Company should make each year.
3. Assume that on January 2, 19D, the trustee made the first payment from the fund in the amount of $1,000. Give the entry, if any, that Koke Company should make.

Part B: Exercises 18–17 to 18–22

E 18–17 **(Pooling; 100% Ownership; Consolidation Worksheet)**
On January 1, 19A, Company A acquired all of the outstanding shares of Company B common stock by exchanging, on a share-for-share basis, 4,000 shares of its own stock. The acquisition qualifies as a pooling of interests. The statements of financial position reflected the following summarized data immediately before acquisition:

	Company A	Company B
Assets not subject to depreciation	$200,000	$50,000*
Assets subject to depreciation (net and 10-year remaining life)	120,000	25,000
	$320,000	$75,000
Liabilities	$ 40,000*	$ 5,000
Common stock (par $10)	200,000	40,000
Retained earnings	80,000	30,000
	$320,000	$75,000

* Includes a $5,000 debt owed by Company A to Company B.

Required:
1. Give the entry in the accounts of Company A for the acquisition of this long-term investment.
2. Prepare a consolidation worksheet immediately after acquisition.

E 18–18 **(Pooling; 90% Ownership; Consolidation Worksheet)**
On January 1, 19A, Company W acquired 90% of the outstanding shares of Company X common stock by exchanging, on a share-for-share basis, 3,600 shares of its own stock. The acquisition qualifies as a pooling of interests. The statements of financial position reflected the following summarized data immediately before acquisition:

	Company W	Company X
Assets not subject to depreciation	$180,000	$40,000*
Assets subject to depreciation (net and 10-year remaining life)	120,000	25,000
	$300,000	$65,000
Liabilities	$ 20,000*	$ 5,000
Common stock (par $10)	200,000	40,000
Retained earnings	80,000	20,000
	$300,000	$65,000

* Includes a $4,000 debt owed by Company W to Company X.

Required:
1. Give the entry in the accounts of Company W for the acquisition of this long-term investment.
2. Prepare a consolidation worksheet immediately after acquisition.

E 18–19 (Purchase; 100% Ownership; Goodwill; Worksheet)

In January 19A, Company P purchased, for $149,000 cash, all of the 10,000 outstanding voting shares of the common stock of Company S. The acquisition qualifies as a purchase. Immediately before acquisition, the following additional summarized data were available:

		Company S	
	Company P book value	Book value	Market value
Assets not subject to depreciation	$410,000	$ 80,000*	$ 85,000†
Assets subject to depreciation (net)	200,000	60,000	67,000‡
Total	$610,000	$140,000	$152,000
Liabilities	$ 40,000*	$ 10,000	
Common stock (par $10)	500,000	100,000	
Retained earnings	70,000	30,000	
Total	$610,000	$140,000	

* Includes a $12,000 debt owed by Company P to Company S.
† Entire market value excess over cost is on short-term investments.
‡ Estimated remaining life, 10 years (straight-line depreciation).

Required:

1. Give the entry in the accounts of Company P to record acquisition of this long-term investment.
2. Compute the amount of any goodwill purchased.
3. Prepare a consolidation worksheet immediately after acquisition.

E 18–20 (Purchase; 60% Ownership; Goodwill; Worksheet)

In January 19A, Company P purchased, for $96,200 cash, 60% of the 10,000 outstanding voting shares of the common stock of Company S. The acquisition qualifies as a purchase. Immediately before acquisition, the following additional summarized data were available:

		Company S	
	Company P book value	Book value	Market value
Assets not subject to depreciation	$410,000	$ 80,000*	$ 85,000†
Assets subject to depreciation (net)	200,000	60,000	67,000‡
Total	$610,000	$140,000	$152,000
Liabilities	$ 40,000*	$ 10,000	
Common stock (par $10)	500,000	100,000	
Retained earnings	70,000	30,000	
Total	$610,000	$140,000	

* Includes a $12,000 debt owed by Company P to Company S.
† Entire market value excess over cost is on short-term investments.
‡ Estimated remaining life, 10 years (straight-line depreciation).

Required:

1. Give the entry in the accounts of Company P to record acquisition of this long-term investment.
2. Compute the amount of any goodwill purchased.
3. Prepare a consolidation worksheet immediately after acquisition.

E 18–21 (Purchase, 80%; Worksheet for Statement of Income and SFP)

On January 1, 19A, Company J purchased an 80% interest in Company K for $116,400. The acquisition qualifies as a purchase. At acquisition, the goodwill purchased was computed as follows:

Purchase price for 80% interest in Company K		$116,400
Market value of identifiable assets	$153,000*	
Less: Liabilities	20,000	
Market value of identifiable net assets	133,000	
Proportion purchased	×80%	
Market value of identifiable net assets purchased		106,400
Goodwill purchased (80%)		$ 10,000

* Includes $5,000 excess over book value of operational assets.

At the end of 19A, the financial statements reflected the following (summarized):

	Reported at end of 19A	
	Company J	Company K
Statement of income:		
Sales revenue	$360,000	$ 80,000
Interest revenue		400
	360,000	80,400
Cost of goods sold	150,000	42,000
Other operating expenses	109,600	26,300
Interest expense	400	100
	260,000	68,400
Net income	$100,000	$ 12,000
Statement of financial position:		
Current assets	$172,000	$ 80,000
Investment in Company K	116,400	
Operational assets (net)	400,000	90,000
	$688,400	$170,000
Current liabilities	$ 50,000	$ 30,000
Common stock	500,000	100,000
Retained earnings	138,400	40,000*
	$688,400	$170,000

* At acquisition, the balance was $28,000.

Intercompany items at year-end were as follows:

a. Company J sold Company K inventory (goods at cost) during the year amounting to $5,000; Company K resold the goods during 19A.
b. Company J paid Company K $400 interest during the year. The related liability was recognized and paid off during 19A.
c. Company J owed Company K $3,000 at the end of the year.

Required:
Prepare a worksheet to develop consolidated statements of income and financial position at the end of 19A. Assume straight-line depreciation is used, the operational assets have a 10-year remaining life, and goodwill will be amortized over 20 years.

E 18–22 (Purchase, 80%; Worksheet; Statement of Income and SFP)

On January 1, 19A, X Company purchased 80% of the outstanding common stock of Y Company at a cost of $137,200. The acquisition qualifies as a purchase. At acquisition, the goodwill purchased was computed as follows:

Purchase price for 80% interest in Y Co.		$137,200
Market value of identifiable assets	$191,500*	
Less: Liabilities	25,000	
Market value of identifiable net assets	166,500	
Proportion purchased	×80%	
Market value of identifiable net assets purchased		133,200
Goodwill purchased (80%)		$ 4,000

* Includes excess over book value of inventory, $1,250 (assume LIFO flow); and operational assets, $6,250.

After one year of operations, each company prepared a statement of financial position and statement of income as follows (summarized):

	Reported at end of 19A	
	X Company	**Y Company**
Statement of income:		
Sales revenue	$340,000	$ 90,000
Cost of goods sold	190,000	46,000
Depreciation expense	32,000	15,000
Other operating expenses	72,000	17,000
Interest expense	2,000	1,000
	296,000	79,000
Net income	$ 44,000	$ 11,000
Statement of financial position:		
Current assets	$170,800	$ 40,000
Investment in Y Company	137,200	
Operational assets (net)	330,000	160,000
	$638,000	$200,000
Liabilities	$138,000	$ 30,000
Common stock	400,000	150,000
Retained earnings	100,000	20,000*
	$638,000	$200,000

* Balance at date of acquisition, $9,000.

Additional data:

a. Sales of X Company to Y Company during the year were $15,000 (at cost); the items were resold by Y Company during 19A.

b. Depreciation on operational assets—assume a 10-year remaining life and straight-line method.

c. Amortization of goodwill—assume a 20-year amortization period.

Required:
Prepare a worksheet to develop consolidated statements of income and financial position at the end of 19A.

PROBLEMS

Part A: Problems 18–1 to 18–12

P 18–1 **(ST Equity Investment; Cost, LCM Method; Entries)**
On January 1, 19A, Joy Company acquired the following short-term investments in equity securities:

Co.	Stock	No. of shares	Cost per share
T	Common (nopar)	1,000	$20
U	Common (par $10)	600	15
V	Preferred (par $20, nonconvertible)	400	30

Per share data subsequent to the acquisition are as follows:

12/31/19A	Market values: T stock, $16; U stock, $15; and V stock, $34.
2/10/19B	Cash dividends received: T stock, $1.50; U stock, $1; and V stock, 50 cents.
11/1/19B	Sold the shares of V stock at $38.
12/31/19B	Market values: T stock, $12; U stock, $17; and V stock, $33.

Required:

1. Give all entries indicated for Joy Company for 19A and 19B. Use the cost, LCM basis. There was no balance in the allowance account on January 1, 19A.
2. Show how the statement of income and statement of financial position for Joy Company would reflect the short-term investments for 19A and 19B.

P 18–2 (ST Equity Investment; Cost, LCM; Entries and Reporting)

On December 31, 19A, Raven Company's portfolio of short-term investments in equity securities was as follows (purchased on September 1, 19A):

Security	Shares	Unit cost	Unit market
BC Corp., common stock, nopar	50	$186	$187
CD Corp., preferred stock, 6%, par $40	200	40	35

Transactions relating to this portfolio during 19B were as follows:

Jan. 25	Received a 6% dividend check on the CD shares.
Apr. 15	Sold 30 shares of BC Corporation stock at $151 per share.
July 25	Received a $45 dividend check on the BC shares.
Oct. 1	Sold the remaining shares of BC Corporation at $149.50 per share.
Dec. 1	Purchased 100 shares of EF Corporation common stock at $47 per share plus a $30 brokerage fee.
Dec. 5	Purchased 400 shares of GH Corporation common stock, par $1, at $15 per share.
Dec. 31	Transferred the CD shares to the long-term investment portfolio of equity securities.

On December 31, 19B, the following unit market prices were available: BC stock, $140; CD stock, $38; EF stock, $51; and GH stock, $14.

Required:

1. Give the entries that Raven Company should make on *(a)* September 1, 19A, and *(b)* December 31, 19A. Use the cost, LCM method.
2. Give the short-term investment items and amounts that should be reported on the 19A statement of income and statement of financial position.
3. Give the journal entries for 19B related to the short-term investments.
4. Give the short-term investment items and amounts that should be reported on the 19B statement of income and statement of financial position.

P 18–3 (ST Investment, Debt Securities; Cost, LCM Basis; Entries and Reporting)

On April 1, 19A, Lyn Company purchased for cash eight $1,000, 9% bonds of Star Corporation at 102 plus any accrued interest. The bond interest is paid semiannually on each May 1 and November 1. Lyn Company's annual reporting period ends on December 31. Lyn Company will use the cost, LCM basis to account for this short-term investment.

On December 1, 19A, six of these bonds were sold for cash at 101½ plus any accrued interest. At December 31, 19A, the Star Corporation bonds were quoted at 97.

Required:

1. Give the entry for Lyn Company to record the purchase of the bonds on April 1, 19A.
2. Give the entry for interest collected during 19A.
3. Give the entry on December 1, 19A.
4. Give any adjusting entry(s) required on December 31, 19A.
5. Show what items and amounts should be reported on the 19A statement of income and statement of financial position.

P 18–4 (ST Debt Investment; Cost, Not LCM; Entries and Reporting)

At December 31, 19A, the portfolio of short-term investments in debt securities held by Dow Company was as follows:

Security	Par value	Interest Rate	Interest Payable	Cash cost*	Date purchased
X Corp. bonds	$10,000	6%	Nov. 1	$ 9,800	Sept. 1, 19A
Y Corp. bonds	20,000	9%	Dec. 31	20,400	Dec. 31, 19A

* Excluding any accrued interest.

Dow's annual reporting period ends on December 31; the company will use the cost (not LCM) method in conformity with GAAP as specified in *ARB No. 43*.

Transactions relating to the portfolio of short-term investments in debt securities during 19B were as follows:

June 1	Sold the Y Corp. bonds at 103 (cash), plus any accrued interest.
Nov. 1	Collected interest on the X Corp. bonds.
Dec. 1	Purchased $30,000 of Z Corp. bonds at 99½ plus accrued interest. These bonds pay 8% interest, payable on a semiannual basis each March 1 and September 1.
Dec. 31	Transferred the X Corp. bonds to the portfolio of long-term debt securities.

Required:

1. Give the 19A entries for Dow Company to record the purchase of the debt securities, collections of interest, and all related adjusting entries.
2. Give all of the 19B entries, including interest collections and any adjusting entries.
3. List the items and amounts that would be reported on the 19B statement of income and the current section of the statement of financial position. The Z Corp. bonds were quoted at 99 on December 31, 19B.

P 18–5 (ST Equity Investments and Debt Securities; Cost, LCM; Entries and Reporting)

At December 31, 19A, Piper Company held two short-term investment portfolios as follows:

Description	Quantity	Total cost	Unit market prices
1. Equity securities:			
Damon common stock	50 shares	$2,300	$ 47
Martin common stock	100 shares	2,100	19
2. Debt security:			
Hydro Corp., $1,000 bonds, 9% payable annually on June 1	10 bonds	10,400	103.5

Transactions relating to short-term investments during 19B were as follows (the annual reporting period ends December 31):

3/1/19B	Sold 30 shares of the Damon common stock at $50 per share.
4/1/19B	Sold 70 shares of the Martin common stock at $20 per share.
6/1/19B	Collected interest on the Hydro bonds.
6/2/19B	The Hydro bonds were transferred to long-term debt investments; the market price at this date was 103.
9/1/19B	Received a cash dividend of $1 per share on the Damon common stock.
12/1/19B	Purchased 300 shares of ATX common stock at $26 cash per share.

Piper Company accounts for its equity and debt securities at cost, LCM.

Quoted market prices at December 31, 19B, were as follows: Damon common stock, $45; Martin common stock, $21; ATX common stock, $28; and Hydro Corp. bonds, $1,010 per bond (i.e., 101).

Required:

1. Show how the two short-term investment portfolios should be reported on the 19A statement of financial position. Show computations.
2. Give the entries for the 19B transactions through December 1, 19B.
3. Give the entry(s) to record LCM on the short-term equity securities at December 31, 19B.
4. Give the items and amounts that must be reported on the 19B statement of income and the current section of the statement of financial position.

P 18–6 (LT Equity Investment; Entries and Reporting for Two Years)

On January 1, 19A, Rae Company purchased 4,000 of the 40,000 shares outstanding of common stock (par $10) of DB Corporation for $80,000 cash, and 3,000 of the 100,000 shares outstanding of common stock (nopar) of CX Corporation for $7 per share cash as long-term investments. These are the only long-term equity investments held. The accounting periods for all of the companies end on December 31.

Subsequent information was as follows:

	DB	CX
December 31, 19A:		
Income reported for 19A	$40,000	$20,000
Cash dividend per share declared and paid during 19A	1.00	None
Market price per share of stock	15	8
October 20, 19B:		
Sold 1,000 shares of CX stock at $11 per share.		
December 31, 19B:		
Income reported for 19B	50,000	26,000
Cash dividend per share declared and paid during 19B	1.00	.60
Market price per share of stock	17	6
Reclassified the CX stock as a current asset (short-term investment).		

Required:

1. Give all of the entries indicated for Rae Company for 19A and 19B.
2. Show how the long-term investments in equity securities and the related investment revenue would be reported on the financial statements of Rae Company at the end of each year.

P 18–7 (LT Equity Investment; Cost, LCM; Entries and Reporting for Three Years)

During January 19A, Poe Company purchased 5,000 of the 50,000 outstanding shares of common stock (par $1) of Styp Corporation at $15 per share cash as a long-term investment (the only long-term equity investment held). The accounting period for both companies ends December 31. During 19A, 19B, and 19C, the following additional data were available:

1. Styp Corporation:

	19A	19B
Net income reported by Styp at year-end	$15,000	$20,000
Cash dividends declared and paid by Styp during the year (total)	6,000	12,000
Market price per share (Styp stock)	6	5

2. On December 31, 19B, Poe determined that the drop in market price was permanent (not temporary) due to unusual circumstances.
3. On January 2, 19C, Poe sold 1,000 shares of the Styp stock at $5.20 per share.
4. On December 31, 19C, Styp shares were selling at $4.75.

Required:

1. Give all of the entries indicated in the accounts of Poe Company, assuming the cost, LCM method of accounting for long-term investments in equity securities is used.
2. Show how all of the related accounts and amounts would be reported on Poe's 19A, 19B, and 19C statement of income and statement of financial position.

P 18–8 **(LT Equity Investment; Goodwill; Entries and Reporting for Three Years)** On January 1, 19A, Parr Company purchased 30% of the 30,000 outstanding common shares, par $10, of Stub Corporation at $17 per share as a long-term investment (the only long-term equity investment held). The following data in respect to Stub Corporation had been assembled by Parr Company:

1. At acquisition date, January 1, 19A:

	Valued at	
	Book	Market
Assets not subject to depreciation	$250,000	$260,000*
Assets subject to depreciation, net (10-year remaining life; straight line)	200,000	220,000
	$450,000	
Liabilities	$ 50,000	50,000
Common stock (par $10)	300,000	
Retained earnings	100,000	
	$450,000	

* Difference due to inventory (FIFO), sold during 19A.

2. Selected data available at December 31, 19A, and 19B:

	19A	19B
Cash dividends declared and paid by Stub Corporation during the year	$ 8,000	$ 5,000
Income reported by Stub:		
Income before extraordinary items	24,000	(10,000) loss
Extraordinary loss	(2,000)	
Quoted market price per share, Stub Corporation stock (December 31)	20	18

3. On January 2, 19C, Parr Company sold 500 of the Stub shares at $18 per share.

Required:

1. Give all of the appropriate entries for Parr Company during 19A and 19B. Use straight-line amortization of goodwill over a 30-year period.
2. Give the entry required on January 2, 19C.
3. Show what items and amounts based on requirements 1 and 2 will be reported on the 19A, 19B, and 19C statements of income, and 19A and 19B statements of financial position.

P 18–9 **(LT Equity Investment, Cost, LCM and Equity Methods Compared; Entries and Reporting)**

On January 1, 19B, AV Company purchased 3,000 of the 15,000 outstanding shares of common stock of DC Corporation for $80,000 cash as a long-term investment (the only long-term equity investment held). At that date, the statement of financial position of DC Corporation showed the following book values (summarized):

Assets not subject to depreciation	$140,000*
Assets subject to depreciation (net)	100,000†
Liabilities	40,000
Common stock (par $10)	150,000
Retained earnings	50,000

* Market value, $150,000; difference relates to short-term investments.
† Market value, $140,000, estimated remaining life, 10 years. Use straight-line depreciation with no residual value and amortization of goodwill over 20 years.

Additional subsequent data on DC Corporation:

	19B	19C
Income before extraordinary items	$25,000	$26,000
Extraordinary item—gain		5,000
Cash dividends declared and paid	10,000	12,000
Market value per share	25	26

Required:

1. For Cases A (assume the cost, LCM method is appropriate) and B (assume the equity method is appropriate), provide the investor's entries or give the required information for items *(a)* through *(d)* in a tabulation similar to the one below.

Entries required and other information	Case A: Cost, LCM method is appropriate		Case B: Equity method is appropriate	
a. Entry at date of acquisition. *b.* Amount of goodwill purchased. *c.* Entries at 12/31/19B: (1) Investment revenue and dividends. (2) Additional depreciation expense. (3) Amortization of goodwill. (4) Additional expense associated with short-term investments (held by DC) for which market value (i.e., purchase price to AV) exceeded book value; these investments were sold during 19B (5) Recognition of change in market value of DC stock. *d.* Entries at 12/31/19C: (1) Investment revenue and dividends. (2) Additional depreciation expense. (3) Amortization of goodwill. (4) Recognition of change in market value of DC stock.				

2. For each case, reconstruct the investment, the allowance, and the unrealized capital accounts.
3. Explain why the investment account balance is different between the cost, LCM and equity methods.

P 18–10 (LT Equity Investment; Cost, LCM; Cash and Stock Dividends; Split; Entries and Reporting)

Allen Corporation completed the following transactions, in the order given, relative to the portfolio of stocks held as long-term investments:

Year 19A:

a. Purchased 200 shares of MC Corporation common stock (par value $10) at $70 per share plus a brokerage commission of 4% and transfer costs of $20.
b. Purchased, for a lump sum of $96,000, the following stocks of NP Corporation:

	Number of shares	Market price at date of purchase
Class A, common, par value $20	200	$ 50
Preferred, noncumulative, par value $50	300	100
Class B, nopar common stock (stated value $100)	400	150

Year 19B:

c. Purchased 300 shares of MC Corporation common stock at $80 per share plus a brokerage commission of 4% and transfer costs of $60.
d. Received a stock dividend on the MC Corporation stock; for each share held, an additional share was received.
e. Sold 100 shares of MC Corporation stock at $45 per share (from lot 1).

Year 19C:

f. Received a two-for-one stock split on the class A common stock of NP Corporation (the number of shares doubled).
g. Cash dividends declared and paid:

MC Corporation common stock—$10 per share.
NP, class A, common stock—$5 per share.
NP, preferred—6%.
NP, class B, nopar common stock—$15 per share.

	Year-end stock prices		
	19A	19B	19C
MC, common stock	$ 70	$ 40	$ 39.95
NP, class A, common	51	47	24
NP, preferred stock	98	95	96
NP, class B, common	140	144	144

Required:

1. Give entries for Allen Corporation for the above transactions assuming the cost, LCM method is appropriate. Show calculations and assume FIFO order when shares are sold.
2. What items and amounts would be shown on the 19A, 19B, and 19C statements of income and statements of financial position by Allen Corporation in respect to the long-term investments?

P 18–11 **(LT Equity Investment; Market Value Method; Current verus Deferral Approaches; Entries and Reporting)**

On January 1, 19A, Taft Company purchased, as a long-term investment, 6% of the 50,000 (par $10) shares of the outstanding common stock of Company S at $11 per share during the years 19A, 19B, and 19C. The following additional company data were available:

End of 19A: Reported net income, $30,000; Cash dividends declared and paid, $20,000; Market value per share, $15.

End of 19B: Reported net income, $25,000; Cash dividends declared and paid, $15,000; Market value per share, $14.

December 10, 19C: Taft Company sold 200 shares of Company S stock at $17.50 per share.

Required:

1. Assuming the market value method is used, give the entries for Taft Company for each transaction related to the investment, assuming:

   a. Current approach—market changes are reported on the statement of income.
   b. Deferral approach—market changes are reported on the statement of financial position as a separate element of owners' equity.

2. In parallel columns for each of the above assumptions, show, at the end of 19A, 19B, and 19C, the following:

   a. Balance of the investment account.
   b. Balance in the unrealized owners' equity each year-end.
   c. Revenue from the investment for each period.

   For this requirement, assume there were no additional investment transactions during 19C and the market value of Company S stock was $17.50 per share on December 31, 19C.

P 18–12 **(Special-Purpose Fund; Accumulation Schedule; Entries and Reporting)**

On January 1, 19A, Case Corporation created a special building fund by depositing a single sum of $100,000 with an independent trustee. The purpose of the fund is to provide resources to build an addition to the older office building during the latter part of 19E. The company anticipates a total construction cost of $500,000 and completion by January 1, 19F. The company plans to make equal annual deposits each December 31, 19A through 19E, to accumulate the $500,000. The independent trustee will increase the fund each December 31, at an interest rate of 10%. The accounting periods of the company and the fund end on December 31.

Required:

1. Compute the amount of the equal annual deposits that will be needed, and prepare a fund accumulation schedule through December 31, 19E, for Case Corporation.
2. The total cash outlay by Case will be $________
   Total interest revenue will be $________
   The effective interest rate will be ________ %
3. Give the entries for Case on: (*a*) January 1, 19A and (*b*) December 31, 19A.
4. Give the entries for Case on January 3, 19F—Addition completed and the actual cost of $525,000 paid in full. The trustee paid interest on the fund for two extra days at the fund rate.
5. Show what the 19B Case statements of income, financial position, and cash flows should report.

6. Assume the accounting period of Case Corporation ends on October 31 (instead of December 31) and the fund year-end is unchanged. Give any adjusting entry(s) that Case should make at its 19C year-end.

Part B: Problems 18–13 to 18–16

P 18–13 **(Pooling, 90%; Worksheet for Statement of Income and SFP)**

On January 1, 19A, Company A acquired 90% of the common stock of Company B by issuing 13,500 shares of its own common stock to the stockholders of Company B for an equal number of Company B shares. The acquisition qualifies as a pooling of interests.

After one year of operations, each company prepared a statement of income and statement of financial position as follows (summarized):

	Reported at end of 19A	
	Company A	Company B
Statement of income:		
Sales revenue	$620,000	$140,000
Interest revenue	700	
	620,700	140,000
Cost of goods sold	370,000	75,000
Depreciation expense	40,000	15,000
Other operating expenses	132,700	36,300
Interest expense	1,000	700
	543,700	127,000
Net income	$ 77,000	$ 13,000
Statement of financial position:		
Current assets	$335,000	$101,000
Investment in Company B	135,000	
Operational assets (net—remaining life, 10 years)	330,000	149,000
	$800,000	$250,000
Liabilities	$ 80,000	$ 40,000
Common stock (par $10)	600,000	150,000
Retained earnings	120,000	60,000*
	$800,000	$250,000

* Balance at acquisition date, $47,000.

Intercompany items and adjustments for 19A:

a. Company B sold $17,000 worth of goods (at cost) to Company A during the year; these goods were resold by Company A during 19A.
b. Company B paid Company A $700 interest during the year.
c. At the end of 19A, Company B owed Company A $20,000.

Required:

1. Prepare a worksheet at the end of 19A to develop a consolidated statement of income and statement of financial position. Assume straight-line depreciation.
2. Prepare a consolidated statement of income and statement of financial position clearly identifying the minority interest.

P 18–14 **(Pooling, 90%; Worksheet for Statement of Financial Position and Statement of Income.)**

On January 1, 19A, Company C acquired 90% of the outstanding common stock of Company D by exchanging 18,000 shares of its own common stock for an equal number of shares of Company D. The acquisition qualifies as a pooling of interests.

After one year of operations, each company prepared a statement of income and a statement of financial position as follows (summarized):

	Reported at end of 19A	
	Company C	Company D
Statement of income:		
Sales revenue	$ 630,000	$180,000
Interest revenue	1,000	
	631,000	180,000
Cost of goods sold	370,000	98,000
Depreciation expense	37,000	16,000
Other operating expenses	140,000	45,000
Interest expense	4,000	1,000
	551,000	160,000
Net income	$ 80,000	$ 20,000
Statement of financial position:		
Current assets	$ 560,000	$110,000
Investment in Company D (at cost)	180,000	
Operational assets (net)	360,000	160,000
Total	$1,100,000	$270,000
Current liabilities	$ 70,000	$ 30,000
Common stock (par $10)	940,000	200,000
Retained earnings	90,000	40,000
Total	$1,100,000	$270,000

* Company D retained earnings balance at acquisition date was $20,000.

Data relating to 19A eliminations:

a. During the year, Company C sold merchandise to Company D for $35,000 (at cost); Company D resold the merchandise during 19A.

b. During 19A, Company D paid Company C $1,000 interest on loans.

c. At the end of 19A, Company D owed Company C $20,000.

Required:

1. Prepare a worksheet at the end of 19A to develop a consolidated statement of income and statement of financial position.
2. Prepare a consolidated statement of income and statement of financial position clearly identifying the minority interest.

P 18–15 (Purchase, 90%; Goodwill; Worksheet for Statement of Income and Statement of Financial Position)

On January 1, 19A, Company P acquired 90% of the common stock of Company S by paying $226,000 cash. The acquisition qualifies as a purchase. After one year of operations, each company prepared the statement of income and statement of financial position that follow (summarized):

	Reported at end of 19A	
	Company P	Company S
Statement of income:		
Sales revenue	$620,000	$140,000
Interest revenue	700	
	620,700	140,000
Cost of goods sold	370,000	75,000
Depreciation expense	40,000	15,000
Other operating expenses	132,700	36,300
Interest expense	1,000	700
	543,700	127,000
Net income	$ 77,000	$ 13,000
Statement of financial position:		
Current assets	$109,000	$101,000
Investment in Company S	226,000	
Operational assets (net—remaining life, 10 years)	330,000	149,000
	$665,000	$250,000
Liabilities	$ 80,000	$ 40,000
Common stock (par $10)	465,000	150,000
Retained earnings	120,000	60,000
	$665,000	$250,000

The following Company S data were available at acquisition date:

	Book value	Market value
Current assets	$130,000	$130,000
Operational assets (net)	107,000	150,000
Liabilities	40,000	40,000
Retained earnings	47,000	

Intercompany items for 19A:

a. Company S sold $17,000 worth of goods (at cost) to Company P during the year; Company P resold the goods during 19A.

b. Company S paid Company P $700 interest during the year.

c. At the end of 19A, Company S owed Company P $20,000.

Required:

1. Compute the purchased goodwill, if any, at date of acquisition.
2. Prepare a worksheet at the end of 19A to develop a consolidated statement of income and statement of financial position. Use straight-line depreciation and amortize goodwill over 20 years.

P 18–16 (Purchase 80%; Goodwill; Worksheet for Consolidated Statement of Income and Statement of Financial Position)

On January 1, 19A, Company X purchased for cash, in the open market, 80% of the outstanding common stock of Company Y at a cost of $188,000. The acquisition qualifies as a purchase. At date of acquisition, the following Company Y data were available:

	Book value	Market value
Current assets	$120,000	$112,500
Operational assets	140,000	150,000
Liabilities	40,000	40,000

After one year of operations, each company prepared a statement of income and a statement of financial position as follows (summarized):

	Reported at end of 19A	
	Company X	Company Y
Statement of income:		
Sales revenue	$630,000	$180,000
Interest revenue	1,000	
	631,000	180,000
Cost of goods sold	370,000	98,000
Depreciation expense	37,000	16,000
Other operating expenses	140,000	45,000
Interest expense	4,000	1,000
	551,000	160,000
Net income	$ 80,000	$ 20,000
Statement of financial position:		
Current assets	$372,000	$110,000
Investment in Co. Y (at cost)	188,000	
Operational assets (net)	360,000	160,000
Total	$920,000	$270,000
Liabilities	$ 70,000	$ 30,000
Common stock (par $10)	760,000	200,000
Retained earnings	90,000	40,000*
Total	$920,000	$270,000

* Balance at date of acquisition, $20,000.

Data relating to 19A eliminations and restatements:

a. During the year, Company X sold merchandise to Company Y for $35,000 (at cost); Company Y resold the merchandise during 19A.
b. During 19A, Company Y paid Company X $1,000 interest on loans.
c. At the end of 19A, Company Y owed Company X $20,000.
d. The depreciable assets of Company Y have an estimated remaining life of 10 years (no residual value, straight-line depreciation).
e. Goodwill is to be amortized over a 20-year life.

Required:

1. Compute the goodwill purchased, if any, at date of acquisition.
2. Prepare a worksheet to develop a consolidated statement of income and statement of financial position.

CASES

C 18–1 (Relates to Part A; Market Value Method; a Decision, Current versus Deferral)

ACE Investors Company buys and sells various equity securities. Approximately 90% of their total assets are composed of these securities. Because ACE operates in one of the specialized industries permitted to use the market value method, ACE accounts for, and reports, its long-term investments on that basis. Currently, ACE uses the deferral approach to account for, and report, the market value changes in this investment portfolio. The company has decided to reconsider its use of the deferral approach because some major competitors use the current approach, and some of ACE's executives are concerned about its effects on their retirement pay. You have been asked to consult with ACE on this proposed change. Accordingly, you have assembled the following data taken from their records:

a. January 1, 19A, purchased long-term equity securities, cost $50 million.
b. December 31—market value (millions of dollars):

   19A, $56.0; 19B, $52.0; 19C, $49.5.

c. Cash dividends received (millions of dollars):

   19A, $4.0; 19B, $4.2; 19C, $4.1.

d. December 1, 19C, sold for $6.0 million, 10% of the securities from the portfolio that originally cost $5.0 million; carrying value, $5.2 million.

ACE's accounting period ends December 31.

Required:

1. Briefly explain the differences between the two approaches under consideration by ACE.
2. Give possible reasons why some of the ACE executives are concerned about their retirement pay.
3. *(a)* Which approach would you recommend for ACE? To support your recommendations, you have been requested to provide comparative accounting entries under each approach and to complete the schedule given below.
   (b) After completing the schedule, what general conclusions can be drawn from it in regard to financial statement effects?
4. What is the fundamental distinction between the two approaches?

Schedule of Comparative Effects on the Statement of Financial Position and Statement of Income

	19A		19B		19C	
Items	Current	Deferral	Current	Deferral	Current	Deferral
Statement of Financial Position:						
Assets						
Liabilities						
Stockholders' equity						
Statement of Income:						
Revenues						
Expenses						
Income						

C 18–2 **(Relates to Part B; Analytical, Challenging; Should the Acquisition Be Purchase or Pooling?)**

Lee Corporation is currently negotiating to acquire Rudd Corporation, a successful enterprise that would complement the operations of Lee. An important factor in the negotiations has been the potential effects of the acquisition on Lee's financial statements. Accordingly, Lee's management has requested that you prepare pro forma (i.e., "as if") statements of financial position for the year just ended, under two assumptions—(1) pooling of interests and (2) purchase.

The statements of financial position and statements of income for the two corporations for the year just ended (prior to acquisition) are as follows:

	Lee Corp.	Rudd Corp. Book value	Rudd Corp. Appraised
Statement of financial position:			
Cash	$ 485,000	$ 15,000	$ 15,000
Receivables (net)	30,000	65,000	50,000
Inventories	85,000	70,000	70,000
Land	50,000		
Plant (net)	600,000	100,000	230,000
Patents (net)	10,000	30,000	40,000
	$1,260,000	$ 280,000	
Current liabilities	$ 40,000	$ 15,000	15,000
Long-term liabilities	110,000	25,000	25,000
Common stock (par $10)	1,000,000	200,000	
Retained earnings	110,000	40,000	
	$1,260,000	$ 280,000	
Statement of income:			
Sales revenue	$6,000,000	$1,000,000	
Costs and expenses (excluding depreciation and amortization)	5,754,000	967,000	
Depreciation	65,000	10,000	
Amortization of patents	1,000	3,000	
Net income	$ 180,000	$ 20,000	
Market price per share (average shares sold per trading day, 650)	$24.00	Not quoted	

At year-end, Rudd Corporation owed a $10,000 current liability to Lee Corporation. For case purposes, assume that all depreciable assets and intangible assets have a remaining useful life of 10 years from date of acquisition (and straight-line).

Required:

1. Assumption No. 1—At the start of the new year, Lee will acquire all of the outstanding shares of Rudd by exchanging stock on a share-for-share basis so that the acquisition would qualify as a pooling of interests.
   a. Give the pro forma entry that Lee would make to record the exchange.
   b. Prepare a pro forma consolidation worksheet immediately after acquisition.
2. Assumption No. 2—At the start of the new year, Lee will purchase all of the outstanding stock of Rudd for $460,000 cash so that the acquisition would qualify as a purchase.
   a. Give the pro forma entry that Lee would make to record the investment.
   b. Prepare a pro forma consolidation worksheet immediately after acquisition.
3. Which course of action would you recommend to Lee's management? Discuss the primary advantages and disadvantages of your recommendation. Use appropriate data developed for the two assumptions.

C 18–3 (Analysis of Subsidiaries; an Actual Case)

Kimberly-Clark

The annual report of Kimberly-Clark is given in the appendix after Chapter 25. You are to respond to the following questions about the 1987 financial statements.

1. What were the accounting policies related to subsidiaries?
2. How many (a) "consolidated subsidiaries" and (b) "equity companies" are affiliated with Kimberly-Clark? Also, how many are foreign locations?

3. Complete the following schedule for 1987:

Location	Kimberly-Clark's Income Amount	%
United States		
Canada		
Europe		
Latin/South America		
Far East		
Consolidated		

4. How are sales between locations (i.e., geographical areas) priced?

19 STATEMENT OF CASH FLOWS

OVERVIEW AND PURPOSE

Not infrequently most of us experience cash flow problems, that is, maintaining a sufficient stream of cash inflows (i.e., cash receipts) to meet our required cash outflows (i.e., cash payments) on a timely basis. Most businesses have this same problem from time to time. For example, a new business almost always starts with a cash flow problem which usually continues intermittently during the first five to seven years. These cash flow problems arise because the timing of cash inflows often lag the timing of cash needs. During periods of depressed economic activities, or due to ineffective planning, large businesses can also experience similar cash flow problems.

A major problem for investors, creditors, and other interested parties is that they need to realistically project the prospective (i.e., the future) cash flows of the business and hence project their own prospective cash flows. In Chapter 6, we quoted *FASB Concepts No. 1* on this point as follows: "Since investors' and creditors' cash flows are related to enterprise cash flows, financial reporting should provide information to help investors, creditors, and others assess the amounts, timing, and uncertainty of prospective net cash inflows to the related enterprise."

The purpose of this chapter is to discuss *FASB Standard 95* (November 1987) which requires a statement of cash flows designed to help investors, creditors, and others to project a company's cash flows and thus their own prospective net cash flows from investments in, and loans to, that company. In this context, the chapter is organized as follows:

1. Background.
2. Fundamental concepts of the statement of cash flows (SCF).
3. Characteristics of the statement of cash flows.
4. Comparison of the direct and indirect methods.
5. Additional issues in preparing a statement of cash flows, direct method.
6. Application of the SCF, indirect method.
7. Disclosure requirements under the indirect method.

Background

This chapter discusses *FASB Statement of Financial Accounting Standards No. 95,* "Statement of Cash Flows." A required statement of cash flows was long overdue, but it was practically assured when *FASB Concepts 5* (December 1984) was issued because par. 13 stated that a full set of financial statements for a reporting period should show (emphasis supplied):[1]

a. Financial position at the end of the period.
b. Earnings (net income) for the period.
c. Comprehensive income (total nonowner changes in equity) for the period.
d. **Cash flows during the period.**
e. Investments by and distributions to owners during the period.

Given this relatively recent recognition of the usefulness of a statement of cash flows, its long evolution is interesting. In the 1890s, and continuing into the 1930s, the accounting profession emphasized accrual accounting because, during that time period, cash basis accounting was widely used by medium-sized and small companies. Cash basis accounting was viewed by the accounting profession as an impediment to improving accounting. Consequently, there was a determined effort by the accounting profession to suppress the various cash basis financial statements being used because they did not appropriately measure income, assets, and liabilities. Perhaps as a result of the suppression of cash basis reports during that era, the "statement of funds, sources and uses," which was based on working capital, evolved. It was often included (but never required) in the financial reports. As might be expected during the 1930s and through the 1940s, there was considerable variation in the title, format, content, and terminology of the "funds flow" statement. Due to increasing criticisms of this situation, the AICPA commissioned a research study and the results were published in *Accounting Research Study No. 2* (1961), "Cash Flow Analysis and the Funds Statement," by Perry Mason. This study recommended that the required financial statements include a "funds" statement. Next, in 1963 *APB Opinion 3,* "The Statement of Source and Application of Funds" was issued. This *Opinion* stated that a source and application of funds statement should be presented as supplementary information (but it was not required). The statement vaguely defined "funds" as working capital and cautioned that certain terms such as cash flow, cash earnings, and cash earnings per share should be avoided because they "may be misleading and might downgrade the significance of earnings per share."

Eight years later, *APB Opinion 19,* "Reporting Changes in Financial Position" (March 1971) was issued in response to increasing interest in, and use of, a "statement of sources and applications of funds" by the business community, stock exchanges, and regulatory agencies. This *Opinion* redesigned the old "funds statement" and specified a new title as statement of changes in financial position, and made it mandatory. *APB Opinion 19* was a significant milestone because it defined **funds** as either working capital or cash. It stated that (emphasis supplied):

---

[1] Throughout the seven prior editions of this book cash flow statements were emphasized.

> The statement may be in balanced form or in a form expressing the changes in financial position in terms of **cash or cash and [short-term] investments combined,** of all quick assets, or of working capital.
>
> If the format shows the flow of cash, changes in other elements of working capital (e.g., in receivables, inventories, and payables) constitute sources and uses of cash and should accordingly be disclosed in appropriate detail in the body of the statement.

The cash basis statement was not widely used until the Financial Executives Institute strongly recommended it for use by their member companies. The following survey of 600 leading companies shows the significant increases that then occurred in use of the cash basis report:

Basis	**1986**		**1985**		**1984**		**1983**		**1982**		**1981**		**1980**	
Cash	398	66%	372	62%	356	59%	314	52%	254	42%	134	22%	59	10%
Working capital	202	34	228	38	244	41	286	48	346	58	466	78	541	90

Source: AICPA, *Accounting Trends Techniques 1987* (New York, 1987), p. 109.

The FASB initiated its work on cash flows in December 1980 when it issued a discussion memorandum "Reporting Fund Flows, Liquidity, and Financial Flexibility." This was followed by numerous releases and two exposure drafts. All of this activity culminated approximately seven years later (November 1987) with the issuance of *FASB Standard 95*.

Thus, we can characterize the change to requiring a statement of cash flows as long overdue, but certainly not sudden, as evidenced above. The long delay was due to three main factors: (1) aversion by the accounting profession to required cash basis reporting, (2) the strong influence of lack of precedent, and (3) the reluctance of companies (like most people) to communicate detailed information about their cash position. The recent change to required cash flow reporting has been due to five main factors: *(a)* realization of the particular usefulness of cash flow information for investors and creditors, *(b)* recognition given to its importance in *FASB Concepts 5*, *(c)* concern about the economic effects of inflation on cash held, *(d)* understanding of the technical difficulties involved for investors trying to convert accrual data to cash data, and *(e)* recognition of the importance of information about the liquidity and financial flexibility of an enterprise.

The remainder of this chapter will discuss the statement of cash flows as specified in *FASB Standard 95*.

Fundamental Concepts of the Statement of Cash Flows (SCF)

Purposes of the Statement of Cash Flows

The fundamental purpose of the new statement of cash flows (SCF) is to help investors, creditors, and other decision makers in two important ways:

a. To assess the **past performance** of the entity in generating, planning, and controlling the actual cash inflows and outflows.

b. To assess the entity's **probable future cash inflows, outflows, and net cash flows,** including its ability to meet future obligations and to pay dividends. This assessment should help the investor, or creditor, project a return on resources committed to the entity.

Consistent with the fundamental purpose, the statement of cash flows should be designed for use by investors, creditors, and other decision makers as follows:

a. To provide information about the cash inflows (receipts) and cash outflows (payments) of an entity for each specific reporting period.
b. To report cash inflows and outflows of an entity, classified as cash flows from (1) operating activities, (2) investing activities and (3) financing activities. Also, related disclosures to the statement should report any related investing and financing transactions that do not directly affect cash.
c. To use a basic format and consistent terminology that are understandable and helpful to investors, creditors, and other decision makers to assess (1) the entity's future ability to generate net cash inflows, (2) the entity's ability to meet its future obligations (including dividends), and (3) the causes of the difference between net income and cash flow from operating activities.

To meet these objectives *FASB Standard 95* gives detailed reporting guidelines for the statement of cash flows.

Characteristics of the Statement of Cash Flows

Basic Format

FASB Standard 95 specifies and illustrates the basic format for the statement of cash flows that is consistent with the purposes given above. The required format with illustrative amounts is outlined in **Exhibit 19–1.**

Classifications on the Statement of Cash Flows

FASB Standard 95 noted the diversity and ambiguity of cash flow terminology in past practice. The term **funds** was variously used to mean working capital, cash, cash plus temporary investments, and net income plus depreciation expense. To assure consistent terminology and comparability *FASB Standard 95* carefully defines the six categories (A–F) included on the required SCF. These definitions (with explanations) are as follows:

A. **Cash flows from operating activities.** This includes all transactions and events not defined as investing or operating activities. This classification reports **both** the cash inflows and cash outflows that are directly related to items reported on the statement of income. The usual cash flows under this classification are:

Inflows—cash received from:	Outflows—cash paid for:
Customers.	Purchase of goods for resale.
Interest on receivables.	Interest on liabilities.
Dividends from investments.	Income taxes, duties, fines, etc.
Gains on discontinued operations.	Losses on discontinued operations.
Refunds from suppliers.	Salaries and wages.

A gain or loss on an extraordinary item or a discontinued operations gain or loss may be "removed" from operating activities. The full cash effect is included in investing or financing activities, whichever is the dominant source.

The difference between the above inflows and outflows is called the **net cash inflow (outflow) from operating activities.** Typically, the net

Exhibit 19–1
The basic format of a statement of cash flows.

SIMPLE COMPANY

A.	**Cash flows from operating activities:**		
	Cash inflows (detailed)	$ 58	
	Cash outflows (detailed)	(38)	
	Net cash inflow (outflow) from operating activities		$20
B.	**Cash flows from investing activities:**		
	Cash inflows (detailed)	21	
	Cash outflows (detailed)	(30)	
	Net cash inflow (outflow) from investing activities		(9)
C.	**Cash flows from financing activities:**		
	Cash inflows (detailed)	88	
	Cash outflows (detailed)	(65)	
	Net cash inflow (outflow) from financing activities		23
D.	**Effect of foreign exchange rates**		-0-
E.	**Reconciliation with statement of financial position:**		
	Net increase (decrease) in cash during the period		34
	Add: Beginning cash balance		42
	Ending cash balance		$76
F.	**Noncash investing and financing activities**—must be disclosed in a separate schedule.		

amount will be an inflow because in the long term, revenues necessarily must exceed expenses.

B. **Cash flows from investing activities.** This major classification on the SCF reports both cash inflows and outflows that are related to the use of cash for obtaining the productive facilities used by the company and other noncash assets. The **cash outflows** under this classification represent the "investments" of cash by the entity to acquire its noncash assets. The **cash inflows** under this classification occur only when cash is received from the prior investments. The typical cash flows under this classification are:

Outflows—cash paid for:	Inflows—cash received from:
Property, plant and equipment.	Disposal of property and plant equipment.
Investment in debt and equity securities	Disposal of investments in securities.
Lending to other parties.	Collection of a loan (excluding interest, which is an operating activity).
Other assets used in productive activities, such as a patent (excluding inventories, which are operating activities).	Disposal of other assets used in productive activities (excluding inventories).

The difference between the above cash inflows and outflows is called **net cash inflow (outflow) from investing activities.**

C. **Cash flows from financing activities.** This major classification on the SCF represents **both** cash inflows and outflows that are related to **how cash was obtained** to finance the enterprise (including its operations). The **cash inflows** under this classification represent the financing activities used to obtain cash for the entity. The **cash outflows** occur only when cash is paid back to the owners and creditors for their prior cash-providing activities. The usual cash flows under this classification are:

Inflows—cash received from:	Outflows—cash paid to:
Owners—issuing equity securities.	Owners for dividends and other distributions.
Creditors—borrowing on notes, mortgages, bonds, etc.	Owners for treasury stock purchased.
	Payment of principal amounts borrowed (excluding interest, which is an operating activity).

The difference between the above cash inflows and outflows is called **net cash inflow (outflow) from financing activities.**

D. **Effect of foreign exchange rates.** This classification applies only to companies that have foreign operations or foreign currency transactions. This classification reports the effect of exchange rate changes on cash balances held in foreign currencies. These changes affect the amount of cash reported on the statement of financial position.

E. **Reconciling balances.** *FASB Standard 95* requires reporting of the three related amounts: (1) net increase (decrease) in cash, (2) beginning cash balance, and (3) ending cash balance, as shown in Exhibit 19–1.

F. **Noncash investing and financing activities.** These are the investing and financing transactions that involve some noncash effects. There are two types: (1) no cash is received or paid (such as settling a debt in full by issuing the company's capital stock to the creditor) and (2) part cash and part noncash (such as settling a debt with 30 percent cash and 70 percent capital stock (the noncash activity is 70 percent)). These noncash activities must be reported in a separate schedule or set out separately in the disclosure notes.

FASB Standard 95 states that "Financial statements shall not report an amount of cash flow per share. Neither cash flow nor any component of it is an alternative to net income as an indicator of an enterprise's performance, as reporting per share amounts might imply."

Cash and Cash Equivalents

FASB Standard 95 requires that a statement of cash flows explain the change during the period in **cash and cash equivalents** (rather than ambiguous terms such as **funds**). Cash equivalents are defined as "short-term, highly liquid investments" that are both:

a. Readily convertible to known amounts of cash.
b. So near their maturity that they present insignificant risk of changes in value because of changes in interest rates.

Generally, only investments with original maturities of less than three months qualify as a cash equivalent under this definition.[2] Examples of cash equivalents are Treasury bills, money market funds, and commercial paper. Any accounting gains or losses from cash purchases and sales will change the cash balance by

[2] **Original maturity** means original maturity to the entity holding the investment. For example, both a three-month U.S. Treasury bill and a three-year Treasury note purchased three months from maturity qualify as cash equivalents. However, a Treasury note purchased three years ago does not become a cash equivalent when its remaining maturity is three months.

those amounts. A company must set a policy concerning which short-term, highly liquid investments shall be treated as cash equivalents and a change in that policy must be treated as a change in accounting principle (i.e., retroactive application as discussed in Chapter 24).

FASB Standard 95, par. 7, states that "The total amounts of cash and cash equivalents at the beginning and end of the period shown in the statement of cash flows shall be the same amounts as similarly titled line items or subtotals shown in the statement of financial position as of those dates." This means that the statement of financial position must report "cash and cash equivalents" instead of only "cash" (see Chapter 4).

In our discussions, for illustrations of the SCF we use the term **cash** and when cash equivalents are present we use the term **cash and cash equivalents.**

Comparison of the Direct and Indirect Methods

This section discusses and illustrates **application** of the fundamental concepts of the SCF. The FASB considered two primary approaches for the SCF as follows:

1. **Direct** (or gross) **method** which reports the **components** of cash flows from operating activities as gross receipts and gross payments. This method starts with **revenues and expenses** to compute net cash inflow (outflow) from operating activities. A special disclosure note is required.
2. **Indirect** (or reconciliation, or net) **method** which reports only net changes in the cash flows from operating activities. This method starts with **net income** to compute net cash inflow (outflow) from operating activities.

At the outset the FASB appeared to favor the direct method. However, after considerable time and controversy the Board issued *FASB Standard 95* which permits the use of either method. **However, this standard strongly recommends the direct method.**

Exhibit 19–2 shows a statement of cash flows based on the **direct** method and **Exhibit 19–3** shows the statement based on the **indirect method.** These statements are located on facing pages to emphasize the differences between them.

A simplified case, Simple Company, is used to focus on the differences between the two methods. Notice in Part A that the basic difference between the two methods is the way that cash **flows from operating activities** is reported (boxed for emphasis). The two methods report the same net cash flow from each of the five classifications (A–E). Therefore, the basic difference is in the **detailed amounts that are shown within the classification, cash flows from operating activities.**

Notice in Part A that the **direct method** reports the gross cash flow amount for each revenue and expense. It is called the **direct method** because the accrual basis revenues and expenses amounts reported on the statement of income are directly converted to the cash basis amounts reported on the SCF.

In contrast, the **indirect method** starts with accrual basis net income and converts that amount to a cash basis. This means that under operating activities it reports only net income, changes in certain statement of financial position accounts, and net cash flow from operating activities. It is called the **reconciliation** or **net method** because it starts with net income (which is a difference) and

Exhibit 19–2
Statement of cash flows, direct method.

SIMPLE COMPANY
Statement of Cash Flows—Direct Method
For the Year Ended, December 31, 19B
(in thousands)

A. Cash flows from operating activities:		
Cash inflows:		
Cash received from customers	$58	
Cash outflows:		
Payments to employees	(26)	
Payments for administrative and selling expenses	(12)	
Net cash inflow from operating activities		$20
B. Cash flows from investing activities:		
Cash inflows:		
Cash received from sale of plant assets	21	
Cash outflows:		
Cash paid for acquisition of plant assets	(30)	
Net cash outflow from investment activities		(9)
C. Cash flows from financing activities:		
Cash inflows:		
Cash received from sale of common stock	48	
Cash received from long-term debt	40	
Cash outflows:		
Cash paid on long-term debt (principal only)	(46)	
Cash paid for treasury stock purchased	(8)	
Cash paid for dividends	(11)	
Net cash inflow from financing activities		23
D. Effect of foreign exchange rates on cash		-0-
E. Net increase (decrease) in cash plus cash equivalents during 19B		34
Cash balance, January 1, 19B		42
Cash balance at December 31, 19B		$76*

* Agrees with the statement of financial position. *FASB Standard 95* **requires** Part E.

reconciles net income with net cash flow from operations by using another set of differences. The significant issue is which method reports cash flow information about operating activities that is more useful to investors, creditors, and other interested parties. It is also significant that *FASB Standard 95* requires that a reconciliation of net income to net cash flow from operating activities shall be provided in a separate schedule when the direct method is used.

The remainder of this chapter discusses the direct and indirect methods. The **direct method** is discussed first because it is preferable for the following reasons:

1. It has much greater relevance for investors and creditors because it reports gross cash amounts for revenues and expenses rather than net conversion amounts.
2. It reports operations, investment, and financing activities consistently; that is, cash inflows and outflows by source under all three activities. The indirect method shows the inflows and outflows under investing and financing activities but not under operating activities.
3. It emphasizes the primary long-term source of cash operating **activities.**

Exhibit 19–3
Statement of cash flows, indirect method.

SIMPLE COMPANY
Statement of Cash Flows—Indirect Method
For the Year Ended, December 31, 19B
(in thousands)

A. Cash flows from operating activities:		
Net income (from the statement of income)	$22	
Add (deduct) to reconcile net income to net cash inflow:		
Accounts receivable increase	(8)	
Depreciation expense	4	
Salaries payable increase	2	
Net cash inflow from operating activities		$20
B. Cash flows from investing activities:		
Cash inflows:		
Cash received from sale of plant assets	21	
Cash outflows:		
Cash paid for acquisition of plant assets	(30)	
Net cash outflow from investment activities		(9)
C. Cash flows from financing activities:		
Cash inflows:		
Cash received from sale of common stock	48	
Cash received from long-term debt	40	
Cash outflows:		
Cash paid on long-term debt (principal only)	(46)	
Cash paid for treasury stock purchased	(8)	
Cash paid for dividends	(11)	
Net cash inflow from financing activities		23
D. Effect of foreign exchange rates on cash		-0-
E. Net increase (decrease) in cash plus cash equivalents during 19B		34
Cash balance, January 1, 19B		42
Cash balance at December 31, 19B		$76*

* Agrees with the statement of financial position. *FASB Standard 95* **requires** Part E.

4. Its computational procedures are not as complex as the indirect method although industry has had more experience with the indirect method. However, this is offset to some extent because a reconciliation of net income and net cash flow must be disclosed.
5. It is easier to explain and understand.
6. It is strongly recommended in *FASB Standard 95.*

Preparation of the Statement of Cash Flows, Direct Method

The statement of cash flows (SCF) cannot be prepared by using a trial balance nor the spreadsheet often used to prepare the statements of income, financial position, and retained earnings. However, the application problems are similar because both the accrual basis statements and the statement of cash flows can be prepared with or without a spreadsheet. Therefore the following two approaches to develop the SCF are discussed:[3]

[3] Sometimes a T-account approach is used for instructional purposes only. In essence it shows the spreadsheet data and analysis in individual T-accounts.

a. **Schedule approach**—this approach involves a series of computations to "build up" a statement of cash flows, piece by piece (sometimes called the **pick and choose** approach). This approach is useful primarily for very simple cases.

b. **Spreadsheet approach**—this approach uses a specially designed spreadsheet that incorporates (1) summary cash flow entries for analytical purposes, (2) a complete SCF, and (3) numerous internal checks of accuracy. This approach necessarily predominates in industry and public accounting.

Two illustrative cases are used in this chapter. The first is Simple Company, shown in Exhibits 19–2 and 19–3. The other is an expanded case designated Complex Company. The case data for Simple Company are given in **Exhibit 19–4.** The data needed to prepare a statement of cash flows are as follows:

1. A complete statement of income—used primarily in preparing the cash flows from operating activities.
2. Comparative statements of financial position and retained earnings—used in preparing the cash flows from all activities—operating, investing, and financing.
3. Analyses of selected accounts that reflect several different kinds of transactions and events. These selected individual account analyses usually are necessary because the total change amount in an account balance during the year often does not reveal the underlying nature of the cash flows.

Schedule Approach to Develop a SCF, Direct Method

Assume that the SCF, Direct Method for Simple Company (Exhibit 19–2) was developed using the schedule approach. This approach involves the following three steps:

Step 1. Obtain a statement of income and the comparative statement of financial position as shown in Exhibit 19–4. Notice the key check amount, which is the net increase, or decrease, in the cash balance (e.g., $34).

Step 2. Prepare three schedules to compute:
A—Net cash flow from operating activities.
B—Net cash flow from investing activities.
C—Net cash flow from financing activities.
Often the most demanding problem is developing Schedule A—net cash flows from operating activities. Developing Schedule B (investing activities) and Schedule C (financing activities) primarily rest on an analysis of the change in each individual asset, liability, and equity account to sort out the investing and financing cash inflows and outflows. The results of the analysis of individual accounts are shown in Exhibit 19–4, item 3. In actual cases this aspect is time consuming. However, in textbook problems the results of such an account analysis necessarily are given; therefore, completion of these are relatively straight-forward.

Step 3. Use the three schedules to prepare the formal SCF (Exhibit 19–2).

Exhibit 19–4
Simple Company, current statements of income and financial position (in thousands).

1. Statement of Income, for the Year Ended 12/31/19B:

Sales revenue	$66
Salaries expense	(28)
Depreciation expense	(4)
Administrative and selling expenses (excluding salaries)	(12)
Net income	$22

2. Comparative Statement of Financial Position, 12/31/19B:

Items	12/31/19A*	12/31/19B	Increase (decrease)
Cash (no cash equivalents)	$ 42	$ 76	$34
Accounts receivable	31	39	8
Plant assets	82	81	(1)
Accumulated depreciation	(20)	(14)	6 Cr.
Total assets	$135	$182	$47
Salaries payable	$ 3	$ 5	$ 2
Notes payable, long-term	46	40	(6)
Common stock, par $10	61	101	40
Contributed capital in excess of par	9	17	8
Treasury stock	0	(8)	8 Dr.
Retained earnings	16	27	11
Total liabilities and stockholders' equity	$135	$182	$47

3. Analysis of Individual Accounts to Identify Cash Flows (source: accounting records):
   a. Cash account—Increase during 19B, $34.
   b. Plant assets account:
      (1) Purchased plant assets for cash, $30.
      (2) Sold old plant assets for cash $21; recorded as follows (at book value):

Cash	21	
Accumulated depreciation	10	
Plant assets		31

   c. Long-term notes payable account:
      Borrowed cash, $40.
      Payments on note principal, $46.
   d. Treasury stock account—Purchased treasury stock for $8 cash.
   e. Statement of retained earnings:

Balance, 1/1/19B	$16
Net income for 19B	22
Cash dividend paid in cash at end of 19B	(11)
Balance, 12/31/19B	$27

   f. Issued common stock for $48 cash.

* Arranged in order of date to facilitate discussions to follow.

The three schedules needed for Simple Company are shown, with explanations, in **Exhibit 19–5.** Let us see how they were developed for each primary classification on the SCF—operating, investing, and financing activities.

Computing Net Cash Flow from Operating Activities. This discussion refers to Step 2 which uses the data given in Exhibit 19–4. Under the direct method each major category—revenues, gains, expenses, and losses—must be converted to a cash basis as shown in Exhibit 19–5, Schedule A. Accrual basis revenues and expenses reported on the statement of income often will include **noncash**

Exhibit 19–5

Schedules to prepare the SCF, direct method; Simple Company.

Schedule A—Computation of Net Cash Flow from Operating Activities (conversion of statement of income from accrual to cash basis):

Items from SI and Comparative SFP	Accrual basis	Cash Basis: Change	Cash Basis: Amount	Explanation
Sales revenue	$66			Accounts receivable increase, $8; subtracted because sales includes this amount of credit sales.
Accounts receivable—increase (−); decrease (+)		−8	$58	
Deduct expenses:				
Salaries expense	28			Salaries payable increase, $2; subtracted because less cash was paid for salaries than was reported as salary expense in the statement of income.
Salaries payable—increase (−); decrease (+)		−2	26	
Administrative and selling expense	12			No addition or subtraction because there were no accruals; all of this expense was paid in cash this period.
Accrued expense payable—increase (−); decrease (+)		0	12	
Depreciation expense (only a −)	4	−4	0	Depreciation expense, $4; always subtracted because it is always a noncash expense.
Net income:				
Accrual basis	$22			
Cash basis			$20	Reported on the SCF (Exhibit 19–2).

Schedule B—Direct Method—Computation of Net Cash Flows from Investing Activities (analysis of comparative SFP and individual accounts):

Items from comparative SFP and account analysis	Cash inflows cash (outflows)	Explanation
Purchase of plant assets	$(30)	Payment in full for noncash asset.
Sale of plant assets	21	Total cash received from sale of noncash asset.
Net cash inflow (outflow) from investing activities	$ (9)	Reported on the SCF (Exhibit 19–2).

Schedule C—Direct Method—Computation of Net Cash Flows from Financing Activities:

Items from comparative SFP and account analysis	Cash inflows cash (outflows)	Explanation
Issuance of common stock	$ 48	From common stock account and cash records.
Borrowing on long-term note	40	From note payable account and cash records.
Payments on long-term note	(46)	Same as above.
Purchase of treasury stock	(8)	From treasury stock account and cash records.
Paid cash dividend	(11)	From statement of retained earnings and cash records.
Net cash inflow (outflow) from financing activities	$ 23	Reported on the SCF (Exhibit 19–2).

amounts which are reflected as a change in the balances of accounts receivable, inventories, and accounts payable. When accounts receivable (or any other trade receivable) decrease during the period, more cash is collected than the amount of revenue recognized on the accrual basis. Alternatively, when accounts receivable (or any other trade receivable) increase, less cash is collected than the revenue recognized on the accrual basis. Therefore, the formula under the direct method to convert amounts from the accrual basis to the cash basis for **all revenues** is:

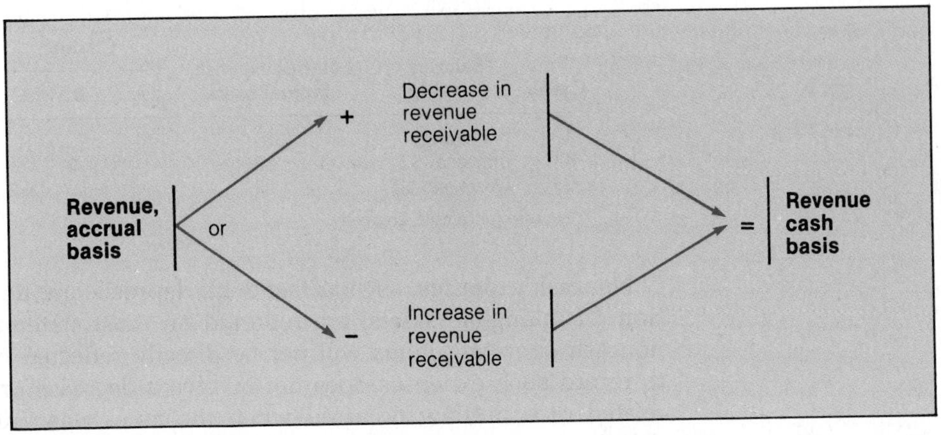

This formula applies to all revenues—service, interest, dividends, royalty, rent, and so on. Notice application of this formula to sales revenue in Exhibit 19–5, Schedule A. The following cases illustrate application of this formula:

Case	Accounts receivable	Revenue, accrual basis	Change A	Change B	Change C	Revenue, cash basis (inflow)
A.	No change	$66	-0-			$66
B.	Increase, $8*	66		−8		58
C.	Decrease, $8	66			+8	74

* The case for Simple Company.

When **accrued** expense, such as salaries, wages, interest, rent, income tax, or a trade payable decreases during the period, more cash is paid than the amount of the accrual basis expense. Alternatively, when an accrued expense increases, less cash is paid than the accrual basis expense. Therefore, the formula, under the direct method, to convert from the accrual basis to the cash basis for **all such expenses** is:

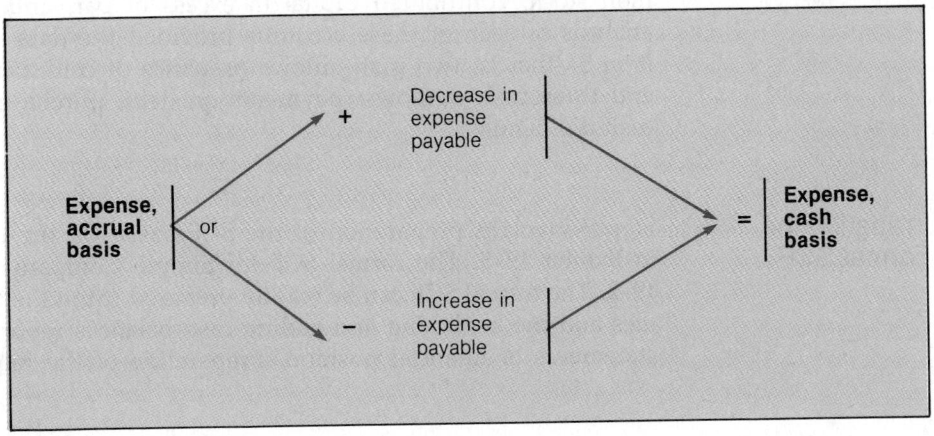

Notice application of this formula to salaries payable in Exhibit 19–5, Schedule A. The following cases illustrate application of this formula:

Case	Salaries payable	Salaries expense, accrual basis	Change A	Change B	Change C	Salaries expense, cash basis (outflow)
A.	No change	$28	-0-			$28
B.	Increase, $2*	28		−2		26
C.	Decrease, $2	28			+2	30

* The case for Simple Company.

Noncash expenses, such as bad debt, depreciation, **depletion,** and **amortization** (of intangible assets) are reported on most statements of income. These noncash operating items will not be directly reflected on the SCF. The entry to record such expenses does not involve a decrease or increase to cash. The related cash outflow occurred when the asset was purchased, or when the debt incurred to buy it was paid. If these guidelines are followed, Schedule A can be readily and accurately prepared.

Computing Net Cash Flow From Investing Activities. This discussion refers to Step 2 which uses the data given in Exhibit 19–4, item 2. The analysis of individual accounts given in Exhibit 19–4, item 3 provides the case data needed to prepare this schedule. An analysis of the changes during 19B in the balances of the accounts listed on the statement of financial position (Exhibit 19–4, item 2) was done to obtain data that involved investing activities. In the case of Simple Company, the analysis found that the only account in investing activities was plant assets. Notice that the purchase of a plant asset and its subsequent sale both are **investing** activities; the former is a cash outflow and the latter is a cash inflow.

Computing Net Cash Flows from Financing Activities. This discussion refers to Step 2 which uses the data given in Exhibit 19–4. An analysis of the accounts shown in the comparative statements of financial position indicated that the "financing" type of accounts for Simple Company included notes payable, common stock, contributed capital in excess of par, and retained earnings. An analysis of each of these accounts provided the data shown in Exhibit 19–4, item 3—that is, two cash inflows (issuance of common stock and borrowing) and three cash outflows (payments on debt, purchase of treasury stock and cash dividends).

Preparing the Formal SCF

Step 3 involves preparation of the SCF based on the three schedules shown in Exhibit 19–5. The formal SCF for Simple Company was shown in Exhibit 19–2. The formal SCF can be readily prepared using the three completed schedules and the beginning and ending cash balances reported in the comparative statements of financial position. Preparation of the required reconciliation of net income to net cash flow from operating activities is discussed later in this chapter.

Spreadsheet Approach to Developing a SCF (Direct Method)

The spreadsheet approach to develop the SCF usually is more efficient than the schedule approach, particularly in complex cases and in all cases when the data available are not complete. The primary advantages of the spreadsheet approach are that it *(a)* brings together and synthesizes all of the data used, *(b)* is an organized approach that ties together all of the five classifications on the SCF, *(c)* starts simultaneously with the statements of income and financial position, *(d)* develops the analysis in a debit = credit format, and *(e)* provides continuing proofs of accuracy. Sometimes it is viewed as cumbersome compared with the schedule approach, but this comparison usually overlooks the advantages of using a spreadsheet when complex data must be analyzed.[4]

Exhibit 19–6 shows a completed spreadsheet for Simple Company (based on the data given in Exhibit 19–4). Notice the following features: *(a)* it starts with the statements of income and financial position, *(b)* it analyzes all changes between the beginning and ending balances by using a series of straightforward debit = credit entries, *(c)* it provides all of the information for the SCF, and *(d)* it balances throughout.

How to Prepare a Direct-Method Spreadsheet for the SCF.

The SCF spreadsheet is easy to prepare by using an organized approach as follows:

Step 1. Set up the four money columns with the standard headings shown in Exhibit 19–6.

Step 2. Enter the statement of income (amounts in the two middle columns) and the comparative statement of financial position (amounts in the first and last money columns) exactly as shown in Exhibit 19–6.

Step 3. Immediately below Step 2 data copy the following side captions (leaving adequate space below each of the "cash flow" captions): statement of cash inflows (outflows); cash flows from operating activities; cash flows from investing activities; cash flows from financing activities; net increase (decrease) during the year; and totals (to verify).

Step 4. Enter debit = credit entries under the two "analysis of changes" columns. **The spreadsheet is complete when the changes between the beginning and ending balances on each line in Phases A and B are accounted for by the analytical entries.**

Explanation of Spreadsheet Entries.

It is preferable to start with the first item on the statement of income and then continue in order until all entries are made. The rationale for each entry is given below. For instructional convenience the following abbreviations are used: OA = operating activities, IA = investing activities, FA = financing activities, and SFP = comparative statement of financial position. Also, entries on the worksheet are coded as a, b, c, etc., for reference

[4] The book of forms prepared for this text provides the full SCF format for the solutions.

Exhibit 19–6

Spreadsheet to prepare the SCF, direct method; Simple Company, December 31, 19B (in thousands).

Items from statements of income and financial position	Beginning balance 1/1/19B	Analysis of changes: Debit	Analysis of changes: Credit	Ending balance 12/31/19B
Phase A—Analysis of Statement of Income:				
Revenues:				
Sales	-0-		a 66	-0-
Expenses:				
Salaries	-0-	b 28		-0-
Depreciation	-0-	c 4		-0-
Administration and selling (including interest)	-0-	d 12		-0-
Net income (to retained earnings)	-0-	e 22		-0-
Phase B—Analysis of Financial Position:				
Cash	42	o 34		76
Accounts receivable	31	f 8		39
Plant assets (analysis needed)	82	h 30	g 31	81
Accumulated depreciation	(20)	g 10	c 4	(14)
Total assets	135			182
Salaries payable	3		i 2	5
Notes payable, long-term (analysis needed)	46	j 46	k 40	40
Common stock, par $10	61		l 40	101
Contributed capital in excess of par	9		l 8	17
Treasury stock	0	m 8		(8)
Retained earnings (see statement of retained earnings)	16	n 11	e 22	27
Total liabilities and stockholders' equity	135			182

	Inflows	Outflows	Subtotals
Statement of Cash Inflows and (Outflows):			
Cash flows from operating activities:			
From customers—sales	a 66		
Accounts receivable increase		f 8	$58
Paid to employees—salaries		b 28	
Salaries payable increase	i 2		(38)
Administrative and selling expense		d 12	20
Cash flows from investing activities:			
Sale of plant assets	g 21		
Purchase of plant assets		h 30	(9)
Cash flows from financing activities:			
Issuance of common stock	l 48		
Borrowing on long-term notes	k 40		
Payments on long-term notes		j 46	23
Purchase of treasury stock		m 8	
Paid cash dividend		n 11	
Net increase (decrease) in cash during the year*		o 34	
Totals (to verify)	390	390	$34

* Must agree with statement of financial position.

purposes. Notice that the spreadsheet entries track the original journal entries. Entries a–e "enter" the statement of income as follows:

Entry a—for revenues; a major source of cash:

OA—From customers (a debit to cash inflow)*	66	
Sales (to record)		66

* This amount is adjusted in entry f, for the effects of changes in accounts receivable.

Entry b—for expenses that require cash:

Salaries expense (to record)	28	
OA—Paid to employees (a credit to cash outflow)*		28

* This amount is adjusted in entry *i*, salaries payable.

Entry c—for noncash expenses; no effect on cash flows:

Depreciation expense (to record)	4	
Accumulated depreciation (on SFP)*		4

* Noncash expenses are not reported on the SCF; no OA, IA, or FA effects.

Entry d—for expenses that require cash:

Administration and selling expenses (to record)	12	
OA—Paid to providers (a credit to cash outflow)*		12

* This amount is all cash because there were no related accruals or deferrals.

Entry e—to transfer net income to retained earnings:

Net income (i.e., income summary)	22	
Retained earnings*		22

* A noncash transfer; no OA, IA, or FA effects.

After the above entries are made **all** of the statement of income accounts and **some** of the statement of financial position accounts have been reconciled. Those reconciled can be "checked off" because no additional entries will be made to them. Spreadsheet entries f–o "account" for the remaining changes in the account balances reported during the period in the statement of financial position. Each entry which follows also classifies cash receipts and payments as either OA, IA, or FA. These spreadsheet entries can be made in any order; however, for instructional convenience they follow the spreadsheet order. Therefore, we start with accounts receivable, then operational assets, and so on.

Entry f—to record the increase in accounts receivable:

Accounts receivable (check off; this account is now reconciled)	8	
OA—From customers* (effect on cash flow)		8

* This adjusts the $66 sales revenue amount to the cash basis, $58. Notice that entry *a* could have been made to include the entry as follows:

OA—From customers ($66 − $8)	58	
Accounts receivable	8	
Sales		66

Entry g—for the sale of old plant assets:

IA—Sale of plant assets* (effect on cash flow)	21	
Accumulated depreciation (to remove)	10	
Plant assets (to remove)		31

* This is the cash inflow; see analysis of plant assets, Exhibit 19–4.

Entry h—for the purchase of plant assets:

Plant assets	30	
IA—Purchase of plant assets* (effect on cash flow)		30

* This is the cash outflow for this transaction; see analysis of plant assets.
Note: After spreadsheet entries g and h are made plant assets and accumulated depreciation are fully reconciled.

Entry i—for increase in salaries payable:

OA—Paid to employees* (effect on cash flow)	2	
Salaries payable (increase during year)		2

* This is an adjustment of salaries expense entry b, from the accrual to cash basis. Check off this account because it is reconciled. Notice that entry b could have been made to include this entry.

Entry j—for payment of long-term note payable:

Notes payable	46	
FA—Payment on note* (effect on cash flow)		46

* This is the cash outflow; see analysis of notes payable.

Entry k—for borrowing on note payable:

FA—Borrowing on note payable* (effect on cash flow)	40	
Notes payable		40

* This is the cash inflow; see analysis of notes payable; check off notes payable because it is now reconciled.

Entry l—for issuance of common stock:

FA—Issuance of common stock (effect on cash flow)	48	
Common stock, par $10*		40
Contributed capital in excess of par*		8

* Check off these two accounts because they are reconciled.

Entry m—for purchase treasury stock:

Treasury stock*	8	
FA—Purchase of treasury stock (effect on cash flow).		8

* Check off treasury stock because it is reconciled.

Entry n—for cash dividend paid:

Retained earnings*	11	
FA—Payment of dividend (effect on cash flow)		11

* Check off retained earning because it is reconciled (i.e., $16 + $22 − $11 = $27).

Entry o—to enter, for balancing purposes only, the key check figure which is the change in cash during the period as shown on the SFP:

Cash	34	
Net increase during the year (to balance)		34

* This fully reconciles the beginning and ending cash balances ($42 + $34 = $76). Therefore, we can check off the cash account because no additional spreadsheet entries will be made to it. This is an optional entry on the spreadsheet.

The above entries complete the spreadsheet analysis because all accounts are reconciled. Finally, sum the two analysis columns to verify that debits = credits. Prepare the SCF by using only the bottom part of the spreadsheet (see Exhibit 19–2). Notice that the subtotals in the lower right column of the spreadsheet tie directly with the subtotals on the SCF.

Additional Issues in Preparing a Statement of Cash Flows, Direct Method

The preceding discussion established the basic concepts and applications used to develop a statement of cash flows (SCF). This section expands on those basics to incorporate the additional issues usually encountered in developing a SCF. These issues add some complexity, but they can be resolved logically if the dominant objective is kept in mind—**on the SCF include all cash inflows and cash outflows and exclude all accrual amounts.** However, for most transactions the accrual and cash amounts are the same, such as cash sales and expenses, investments of cash, cash borrowing and repayment, and cash dividends. The additional issues involve only transactions when the accrual basis and cash basis amounts are different. Among these issues, the two more involved issues are (1) accounts receivable with the allowance for doubtful accounts and (2) cost of goods sold, with inventory and accounts payable.

This section discusses the following topics in order:

a. An expanded SCF case—Complex Company

b. Additional SCF issues:

1. Accounts receivable and the allowance for doubtful accounts.
2. Converting cost of goods sold to a cash basis.
3. Noncash expenses and certain equity transactions.
4. Income taxes and interest paid or received.
5. Noncash investing and financing activities.
6. Foreign currency cash flows.

An Expanded SCF Case—Complex Company

The expanded case for Complex Company is used to illustrate some of the above topics. Prior to discussing the issues listed above, familiarization with this case will be helpful. **Exhibit 19–7** gives the case data and **Exhibit 19–8** shows the SCF, direct method. Complex Company developed the SCF by following the three steps given on page 908.

For instructional purposes **both the schedule approach and the spreadsheet approaches using the direct method are shown** for Complex Company. The schedule approach is shown in **Exhibit 19–9** and the spreadsheet approach in **Exhibit 19–10.**

Now for a quick overview of the SCF for Complex Company—notice, in Exhibit 19–7, the three data sets on Complex Company—statement of income, comparative statement of financial position (the key check figure is the cash plus cash equivalents change, $31), and the extensive analysis of individual accounts. Notice in Exhibit 19–8 how the cash-flow data are reported in the SCF. The three major classifications of activities stand out—operating, investing, and financing. Finally, notice the disclosure note, which relates to a transaction that was part **noncash** and part cash (discussed later). The discussion of each issue in this section will be directly related to the schedule and spreadsheet approaches because these show **how** the analysis is done. To illustrate, examine

Exhibit 19–7

Complex Company, case data for year 19X (in thousands).

A. Statement of Income, Year 19X:

Revenues:	
Sales and services	$96
Dividends (X Corp.)	1
Gain on sale of operational assets	3
Gain on sale of cash equivalents	2
Expenses:	
Cost of goods sold	(42)
Depreciation expense	(8)
Bad debt expense	(3)
Interest expense (on bonds)	(4)
Amortization of bond discount	(1)
Remaining expenses	(13)
Income tax expense*	(9)
Income before extraordinary items and discontinued operations	22
Extraordinary loss, land condemnation $20 (tax saving, $6)	(14)
Discontinued operations, gain $10 (tax expense, $3)	7
Net income (to retained earnings)	$15

* Total income taxes paid, $9 − $6 + $3 = $6.

B. Comparative Statement of Financial Position, December 31, 19X:

Items	12/31/19W	12/31/19X	Increase* (decrease)
Cash	$ 30	$ 67	$37
Cash equivalents	6	0	(6)
Total	36	67	31
Investment, short term (stock of X Corp.)	12	12	0
Accounts receivable	32	29	(3)
Allowance for doubtful accounts	(2)	(5)	(3)
Inventory (perpetual system)	30	37	7
Prepaid insurance	4	2	(2)
Land	60	40	(20)
Operational assets	80	96	16
Accumulated depreciation	(20)	(26)	(6)
Other assets (includes discontinued operations, $13)	35	22	(13)
Total assets	$267	$274	7
Accounts payable	$ 26	$ 30	4
Interest payable	2	1	(1)
Income tax payable	11	4	(7)
Notes payable, longterm	0	10	10
Bonds payable	80	60	(20)
Unamortized bond discount	(3)	(2)	1
Common stock, nopar	100	130	30
Retained earnings	51	41	(10)
Total liabilities and stockholders' equity	$267	$274	$ 7

* For contra accounts, the algebraic signs must be strictly applied.

Exhibit 19–7
(concluded)

C. Analysis of Individual Accounts to Identify Cash Flows (source, accounting records):

a. Cash and cash equivalents increase during 19X, $37.
b. Sold cash equivalents in January 19X for $8 cash; none held at end of 19X.
c. Insurance expense is included in the remaining expenses account.
d. Cash borrowed on long-term note at the end of 19X, $10.
e. Statement of Retained Earnings, Year Ended December 31, 19X:

Beginning balance	$51
Net income for 19X	15
Cash dividend declared and paid in 19X	(15)
Stock dividend issued in 19X	(10)
Ending balance	$41

f. Operational Asset account:

	Asset	Accumulated depreciation
Beginning balance	$80	$20 credit
Disposal of asset (for cash, $15)	(14)	(2)
Acquisition of new asset (machine)*	30	
Depreciation		8
Ending balance	$96	$26

* Paid cash $10 and issued common stock in full settlement, $20 (market value).

g. Bonds Payable account:

	Bonds	Unamortized balance
Beginning balance	$80	$3 debit
Discount amortization for 19X		(1)
Bonds retired at end of 19X	(20)	
Ending balance	$60	$2

h. Land account:

Beginning balance	$60
Sale due to condemnation (extraordinary loss); cash received in full payment, $40	(60)
Land acquisition (paid cash, $40)	40
Ending balance	$40

i. Discontinued operations:
Closed out completely by selling the remaining assets for cash $23. The $13 cost of these assets is included in the account Other Assets.

j. Income Tax Payable account:

Beginning balance		$11
Additions for current income taxes (source: statement of income):		
Tax on continuing operations	$9	
Extraordinary loss ($20), tax saving	(6)	
Discontinued operations ($10), tax expense	3	
Increase in payable (net)		6
Cash payments made during 19X		(13)
Ending balance		$ 4

Exhibit 19–8
Direct method, SCF—Complex Company.

COMPLEX COMPANY
Statement of Cash Flows
For the Year Ended December 31, 19X
(in thousands)

Cash flows from operating activities:		
Cash inflows:		
From customers	$99	
From gain on cash equivalents sold	2	
From dividends received on short-term investments	1	
Cash outflows:		
Paid to suppliers (for cost of goods sold)	(45)	
Paid for interest	(5)	
Paid for income taxes	(11)	
Paid for remaining expenses	(13)	
Net cash inflow from operating activities		$28
Cash flows from investing activities:		
Cash inflows:		
From sale of operational assets	15	
From sale of land (condemnation)	40	
From discontinued operations	23	
Cash outflows:		
Paid for purchase of land	(40)	
Paid for operational assets (Note A)	(10)	
Net cash outflow for investing activities		28
Cash flows from financing activities:		
Cash inflows:		
Borrowing on long-term note	10	
Cash outflows:		
Payment on bond principal	(20)	
Paid cash dividend	(15)	
Net cash outflow for financing activities		(25)
Net increase in cash plus cash equivalents during 19X		31
Cash plus cash equivalents, January 1, 19X		36
Cash plus cash equivalents, December 31, 19X		67

Note A—The company purchased an operational asset (machine); payment was part cash and part the company's unissued common stock as follows:

Cash paid	$10
Common stock issued	20
Total asset cost recorded	$30

application of the **schedule approach** in Exhibit 19–9, to compute net cash flow from: Schedule A, operating activities; Schedule B, investing activities, and Schedule C, financing activities. Next, examine the **spreadsheet approach** in Exhibit 19–10 which is used to develop the same three net cash flow amounts. You will find the "Explanation of Spreadsheet Entries" that start on page 915 very helpful to clarify certain issues.

Explanation of Spreadsheet Entries. In this more complex case some combined entries are made. For instructional convenience the following abbreviations are used: OA = operating activities, IA = investing activities, FA = financing activities, and SFP = comparative statement of financial position. The references below to analysis *a* through *j* relate to data given in Exhibit 19–7. Explanatory notes also are given.

Exhibit 19–9
Schedules to prepare the SCF, direct method—Complex Company (in thousands).

Schedule A—Computation of Net Cash Flow from Operating Activities (conversion of statement of income from accrual to cash basis):

Items from SI and Comparative SFP	Accrual basis	Cash basis: Change	Cash basis: Amount	Explanation
Sales and service revenue	$96			Accounts receivable decrease, $3; added because more cash was collected than accrual revenue.
1.* Accounts receivable—increase (−); decrease, $3 (+)		+ 3[a]	$99	
Dividend revenue	1		1	Collected in full; no accruals or deferrals.
2. Gain on sale of operational assets	3	− 3	0	Deduct because this is an investing activity; included under that caption.
Gain on sale of cash equivalents	2		2	Collected cash in full.
Deduct expenses:				
Cost of goods sold	42			Add inventory increase because cash was required to increase inventory; however, a change in accounts payable affects this. The increase in accounts payable was subtracted because this amount was purchased on credit.
3. Inventory increase, $7 (+); decrease (−)		+ 7[b]		
4. Accounts payable increase, $4 (−); decrease (+)		− 4[b]		
Cash paid to suppliers for purchases			45	
5. Depreciation expense (only a −)	8	− 8	0	A noncash expense.
6. Bad debt expense (only a −)	3	− 3	0	A noncash expense.
7. { Interest expense	4			Add the $1 decrease in the payable because cash in excess of the accrued interest was paid.
Interest payable increase (−); decrease, $1 (+) }		+ 1	5	
8. Amortization of bond discount (only a −)	1	− 1	0	A noncash expense.
9. { Remaining expenses (includes insurance expense)	13			Deduct the decrease of $2 in the prepaid account because no cash was paid for insurance this period.
Prepaid insurance increase (+); decrease, $2 (−) }		− 2	11	
10. { Income tax expense ($9 − $6 + $3)	6			Add the $7 decrease because more cash was required to decrease this liability.
Income tax payable increase (−); decrease, $7 (+) }		+ 7	13	
Add gains, deduct losses:				
11. Extraordinary loss (pretax)	20	−20	0	Condemnation of land is an investing activity; income tax is included in the prior item because it is an operating activity.
12. Discontinued operations, gain	10	−10	0	This also is an investing activity.
Net income: Accrual basis	$15			
Cash basis			$28	Reported on SCF (Exhibit 19–8).

* Numbered only for instructional convenience.
[a] Allowance for doubtful accounts is a noncash account (in a manner similar to accumulated depreciation). Since it does not affect either cash or net income, it is not included. Notice that bad debt expense, like depreciation expense, is shown below as a noncash expense.
[b] The net effect of these two adjustments is to convert cost of goods sold (accrual basis) to a cash basis. The cash amount is the same as actual cash paid for purchases during the accounting period.

Exhibit 19–9
(concluded)

Schedule B—Computation of Net Cash Flows from Investing Activities analysis of comparative SFP and individual accounts):

Items	Cash inflows (+) Cash outflows (−)	Explanation
Sale of operating assets	+$15	From examination of operating asset accounts and cash account.
Disposal of land; condemnation	+ 40	From examination of land and cash accounts.
Discontinued operations, assets	+ 23	Examination of statement of income, cash account, and other assets.
Purchase of land	− 40	Examination of land and cash accounts.
Purchase of operational asset (machine)	− 10*	From examination of operational asset, cash, and capital stock accounts. Also, income tax records are used.
Net cash inflow (outflow) from investing activities	$28	Reported on the SCF (Exhibit 19–8).

Schedule C—Computation of Net Cash Flows from Financing Activities:

Items	Cash inflows (+) Cash outflows (−)	Explanation
Borrowing on long-term note payable	+$ 10	From examination of note payable account and SFP.
Payment of bonds (principal)	− 20	Examination of bond payable account and cash records.
Payment of cash dividend	− 15	From statement of retained earnings.
Net cash inflow (outflow) from financing activities	$(25)	Reported on the SCF (Exhibit 19–8).

* Report in separate schedule—Noncash transactions:

Cash paid	$10
Common stock	20
Total	$30

Exhibit 19–10

Spreadsheet to prepare SCF, direct method—Complex Company, December 31, 19X (in thousands).

Items from statements of income and financial position	Beginning balance 1/1/19X	Analysis of changes: Debit	Analysis of changes: Credit	Ending balance 12/31/19X
Phase A—Analysis of Statement of Income:				
Revenues:				
Sales and services			a 96	
Dividend (X Corp.)			b 1	
Gain on sale of operational assets			c 3	
Gain on sale of cash equivalents			d 2	
Expenses:				
Cost of goods sold		e 42		
Depreciation expense		f 8		
Bad debt expense		g 3		
Interest expense (on bonds)		h 4		
Amortization of bond discount		i 1		
Remaining expenses (including insurance expense)		j 13		
Income tax expense		k 9		
Income before extraordinary items and discontinued operations		22		
Extraordinary loss, land condemnation (tax saving, $6)		k & l 14		
Discontinued operations, gain $10 (tax, $3)		k & m	m 7	
Net income (to retained earnings)		t 15		
Phase B—Analysis of Financial Position:				
Cash	30			67
Cash equivalents	6			0
Total	36	u 31		67
Investment, short-term (stock of X Corp.)	12			12
Accounts receivable	32		a 3	29
Allowance for doubtful accounts	(2)		g 3	(5)
Inventory	30	e 7		37
Prepaid insurance	4		j 2	2
Land	60	r 40	l 60	40
Operational assets	80	s 30	c 14	96
Accumulated depreciation	(20)	c 2	f 8	(26)
Other—assets (includes discontinued operations, $13)	35		m 13	22
Total assets	267			274
Accounts payable	26		e 4	30
Interest payable	2	h 1		1
Income tax payable	11	k 7		4
Notes payable, long term	0		n 10	10
Bonds payable	80	o 20		60
Unamortized bond discount	(3)		i 1	(2)
Common stock, nopar	100		s 20	
			q 10	130
Retained earnings	51	p 15	t 15	
		q 10		41
Total liabilities and retained earnings	267			274
Subtotal		272	272	

Exhibit 19–10
(concluded)

	Analysis of changes Debit		Analysis of changes Credit		
Statement of Cash Flows:	Inflows		Outflows		
Cash flows from operating activities:					
From customers—sales and services	a	99			
From dividends on short-term investments	b	1			$102
From sale of cash equivalents	d	2			
Paid to suppliers (for purchases)			e	45	
Paid for interest			h	5	
Paid for remaining expenses			j	11	(74)
Paid for income taxes			k	13	
					28
Cash flows from investing activities:					
From sale of operational asset	c	15			
From sale of land (condemnation)	l	40			
From discontinued operations	m	23			28
Paid for land purchase			r	40	
Paid for operational assets*			s	10	
Cash flows from financing activities:					
Borrowing on long-term note	n	10			
Payment on bonds (principal)			o	20	(25)
Paid cash dividend			p	15	
Net increase (decrease) in cash during the period			u	31	31
Totals		462		462	
Beginning cash plus cash equivalents balance					36
Ending cash plus cash equivalents balance					$ 67

* Report in separate schedule—noncash transactions:

Cash paid	$10
Common stock	20
Total	$30

Entries a through m, "enter" the statement of income amounts in the two analysis columns as follows:

Entry a—for sales and service revenue and accounts receivable:

OA—From customers (cash inflow)	99	
Accounts receivable decrease ($32 – $29)		3
Sales and services (already on the spreadsheet)		96

This spreadsheet entry converts sales revenue to a cash basis. The decrease in accounts reeivable is added to accrual basis sales because cash inflow was more than accrual sales.

Entry b—for dividend revenue (stock of X Corp.):

OA—From short-term investments	1	
Dividend (X Corp., already on the spreadsheet)		1

This spreadsheet entry reflects a cash inflow; accrual basis and cash flow were equal.

Entry c—sale of operational assets (combined entry):

IA—Cash from sale of operational assets	15	
Accumulated depreciation	2	
Operational assets		14
Gain on disposal (already on the spreadsheet)		3

This spreadsheet entry removes the gain from operating activities and reflects the cash inflow as an investing activity.

Entry d—sale of cash equivalents (see analysis *b*):

OA—Cash from sale of cash equivalents	2	
Gain on sale of cash equivalents (already on spreadsheet)		2

This spreadsheet entry reflects the gain in cash which is an operating activity.

Entry e—to determine cash flow related to cost of goods sold:

Cost of goods sold (accrual; already on spreadsheet)	42	
Inventory increase ($37 − $30)	7	
Accounts payable increase ($30 − $26)		4
OA—Cash paid for purchases to suppliers		45

This spreadsheet entry reflects the increase in inventory which requires **more** cash and the increase in accounts payable which requires **less** cash than the accrual basis. The net effect is to restate cost of goods sold on a cash basis ($42).

Entry f—for depreciation expense (no cash effect):

Depreciation expense (already on spreadsheet)	8	
Accumulated depreciation		8

This spreadsheet entry reconciles the expense and accumulated accounts but cash flows are not affected (i.e., depreciation is a noncash expense).

Entry g—for bad debt expense (no cash effect):

Bad debt expense (already on the spreadsheet)	3	
Allowance for doubtful accounts		3

This entry reflects bad debt expense as a noncash expense; like depreciation expense.

Entry h—to determine cash flow related to interest expense (combined):

Interest expense (already on spreadsheet)	4	
Interest payable decrease ($2 − $1)	1	
OA—Cash paid for interest		5

This spreadsheet entry reflects a decrease in interest payable because cash outflow is more than accrual basis expense.

Entry i—for amortization of bond discount (noncash):

Expense—amortization of bond discount (already on the statement of income)	1	
Unamortized bond discount (see analysis *g*)		1

This spreadsheet entry reflects a noncash expense; like depreciation expense.

Entry j—to determine cash flow related to remaining expenses:

Remaining expenses (already on the spreadsheet)	13	
Prepaid insurance decrease ($4 − $2)		2
OA—Cash paid for remaining expenses		11

This spreadsheet entry reflects a decrease in prepaid insurance. This means that cash outflow is less than the accrual basis expense.

Entry k—for income tax (see analysis *j*):

Income tax payable decrease ($11 − $4)	7	
Income tax expense (already on spreadsheet	9	
Income tax on discontinued operations (already on the spreadsheet)	3	
Income tax saving, EO item (already on the spreadsheet)		6
OA—Cash paid for income tax		13

This spreadsheet entry restates accrual basis expense to a cash basis. The decrease in income tax payable caused cash outflow to be **more** than accrual basis expense.

Entry l—for extraordinary loss (pretax because the tax is in entry k) for land sold under condemnation; (see analysis *h*).

IA—Cash from sale of land	40	
Extraordinary loss on land condemnation (pretax, already on spreadsheet)	20	
Land		60

This spreadsheet entry removes the extraordinary loss from operating activities and reflects the full cash inflow as an investing activity.

Entry m—for discontinued operations (pretax because the tax is in entry k; (see analysis *i*):

IA—Cash from discontinued operations	23	
Other assets, discontinued operations		13
Gain on discontinued operations (pretax, already on the spreadsheet)		10

This spreadsheet entry removes the gain from operating activities and reflects the full cash received as an investing activity.

Entry n—for borrowing on note payable (see analysis *d*):

FA—Cash from borrowing (notes payable)	10	
Notes payable (from examination of bond account)		10

This spreadsheet entry reflects a cash inflow from borrowing; a financing activity.

Entry o—for bond retirement, year-end (see analysis *g*):

Bonds payable (principal)	20	
FA—Paid cash to retire bonds		20

This spreadsheet entry reflects the payment of debt; a financing activity.

Entry p—for cash dividend (see analysis *e*):

Retained earnings	15	
FA—Paid cash dividend		15

This spreadsheet entry reflects the payment of a cash dividend (outflow); a financing activity.

Entry q—for stock dividend, noncash (see analysis *e*):

Retained earnings	10	
Common stock		10

This spreadsheet entry reflects the issuance of a stock dividend; a noncash item in stockholder equity.

Entry r—for land acquisition (see analysis *h*):

Land	40	
IA—Paid for land		40

This spreadsheet entry reflects a cash outflow for land; an investing activity.

Entry s—for purchase of operational asset (see analysis *f*):

Operational asset	30	
IA—Cash, purchased operational asset		10
Common stock, nopar		20

This spreadsheet entry reflects a part cash, part noncash transaction. The cash part is an investing activity and the noncash part is not (for SCF purposes). The noncash part must be reported as a separate disclosure schedule.

Entry t—for net income to retained earnings (see statement of income and analysis *e*):

Net income (already on spreadsheet)	15	
Retained earnings		15

This spreadsheet entry does not reflect a SCF activity. It is made for balancing purposes.

Entry u—optional for balancing (see cash account):

Cash	31	
Increase in cash during 19X		31

This optional spreadsheet entry is made only for balancing and checking purposes.

Accounts Receivable and the Allowance for Doubtful Accounts. The first item on the statement of cash flows, direct method, is cash inflow from revenues as shown in Exhibit 19–2 for Simple Company (i.e., $58). This case assumed that an Allowance for Doubtful Accounts was not needed. The problem of converting accrual basis revenue amounts reported on the statement of income to a cash basis has been introduced (page 909). In that discussion the effect of increases and decreases in accounts receivable on cash flow from sales revenue was computed as follows:

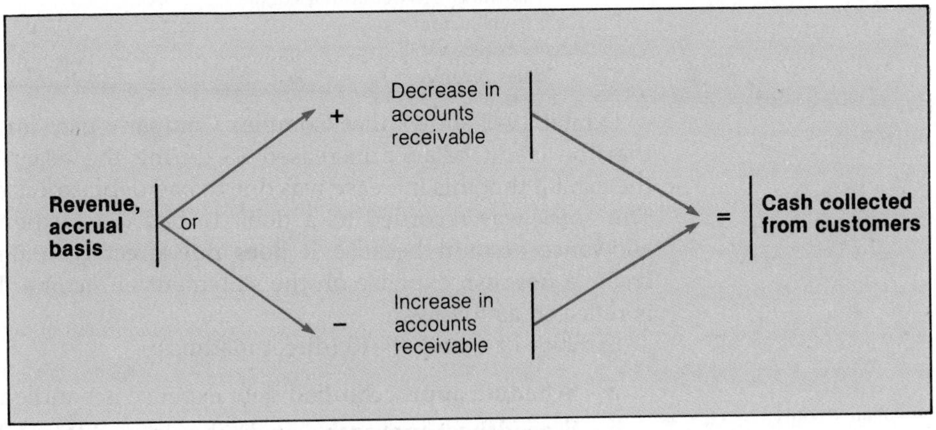

However, that discussion did not consider the case when an **Allowance for Doubtful Accounts** is needed, which is the usual case when some sales are on credit. The Allowance for Doubtful Accounts is more complex because *(a)* it is a contra account to accounts receivable, *(b)* it is increased for bad debt expense reported on the statement of income, and *(c)* it is decreased when an uncollectible account is written off (and accounts receivable is credited for the same amount).

The Accounts Receivable and Allowance for Doubtful Accounts involve three different items (entries) as follows: *(a)* the difference between total sales for the period and cash collected for sales (a cash entry), *(b)* recognition of bad debt expense (a noncash entry), and *(c)* the write-off of an uncollectible account (a noncash entry). A cash flow analysis must recognize changes due to each of these three items. This analysis can be made on the basis of net accounts receivable or gross amounts. Gross amounts are preferable to avoid algebraic complications.

To illustrate, assume that X Company's financial statements showed the following for 19B (in thousands):

Statement of income:			
Sales revenue	$60		
Bad debt expense	1		

	Balance		
	12/31/19A	12/31/19B	Increase (decrease)*
Comparative statement of financial position:			
Accounts receivable	+ $10	+ $12	+ $2
Allowance for doubtful accounts	− 6	− 7	− 1
Net	+ $ 4	+ $ 5	+ $1

* Notice the algebraic implications.

Analysis—Since the Allowance for Doubtful Accounts contains only noncash amounts, it is clear that cash flow from sales revenue is computed as: $60 minus the $2 increase in accounts receivable = $58. This is the computation using the schedule approach. If the spreadsheet approach is used, two analysis entries would be made as follows:

1. Bad debt expense (as shown above for X Company)	1	
Allowance for doubtful accounts		1
2. Cash from customers	58	
Accounts receivable	2	
Sales revenue		60

Exhibit 19–7 shows that Complex Company uses an allowance account and that the credit balance increased $3 during the year. We can readily see on the exhibit that this increase was due to bad debt expense (statement of income). The entry was recorded as a debit to bad debt expense and a credit to the allowance account because **it does not affect cash flows.** However, it does create a **noncash** expense on the statement of income. Notice that this change is reflected as follows:

Exhibits 19–9 and 19–10 (direct method):

a. Schedule approach—bad debt expense is handled as a noncash expense.

b. Spreadsheet approach—analysis entry debits bad debt expense and credits allowance for doubtful accounts ($3).

Now let's go one step further—what is the effect of a **bad debt write-off?** A write-off decreases (debits) the allowance account and reduces (credits) accounts receivable, which clearly indicates that it **does not affect cash flows.** It reduces each account by the same amount and the difference between them remains the same as before. Nevertheless, the write-off must be considered because it changes the ending balance of accounts receivable. This poses a problem because the change from the beginning to the ending balance of accounts receivable is used to compute cash flows. This problem can be resolved very simply as follows:

Schedule approach—remove the write-off from the ending balance of accounts receivable and use the restated balance to compute the cash flow effects of accounts receivable.

Spreadsheet approach—simply reverse the write-off entry and proceed as if it did not exist.

Converting Cost of Goods Sold to a Cash Basis. This issue often appears to be complex; however, it is simple and straightforward. The statement of income reports cost of goods sold on the accrual basis, while the SCF must report cash paid to suppliers. The cash paid to suppliers is the amount of cash paid for purchases (past and current) during the current period. This means that the **conversion must consider two directly related accounts—inventory and accounts payable.** The conversion recognizes that it requires cash to increase inventory and to reduce accounts payable. Conversely, a decrease in inventory and an increase in accounts payable both reduce cash requirements. Consider the following cases:

Case	Cost of goods sold (accrual basis)	Inventory change Increase (decrease)	Accounts payable change Increase (decrease)	Cost of goods sold (cash basis)
A	42	0	0	$42
B	42	7 more cash paid	0	49
C	42	(7) less cash paid	0	35
D	42	0	(4) less cash paid	38
E	42	0	4 more cash paid	46
F*	42	7 more cash paid	(4) less cash paid	45
G	42	(7) less cash paid	4 more cash paid	39

* Case F is the case for Complex Company—for the schedule approach refer to Exhibit 19–9 and for the spreadsheet approach see Exhibit 19–10.

Noncash Expenses and Certain Equity Transactions. Analysis of the statement of income to develop cash flows from operating activities requires that the **noncash expenses** be identified and **excluded** from cash flows. These noncash expenses are internally recognized but they do not reduce (i.e., credit) cash. Common noncash expenses are depreciation, bad debts, depletion and amortization of intangibles (e.g., patents, copyrights, franchises, and bond discount or premium). Under both the schedule (Exhibit 19–9) and spreadsheet (Exhibit 19–10) approaches the noncash expenses are excluded.

Also, noncash **equity** transactions such as stock dividends, stock splits, changes in par value, and appropriations and restrictions of retained earnings are not reported on the SCF because they do not create cash inflows or outflows.

Gains and Losses. The statement of income reports three kind of gains and losses:

1. Gains and losses that are included on a pretax basis in the operating activities part of the statement, such as the gain or loss on the disposal of an operational asset.
2. Extraordinary gains and losses which are separately reported on a net of tax basis.
3. A gain or a loss from the disposal of a segment of a business which is separately reported on a net of tax basis similar to, but separate from, an extraordinary item.

These gains and losses pose two issues. First, a critical issue for the statement of cash flows is whether the transactions that cause a gain or loss should be classified as an operating, investing, or financing activity. The provisions of *FASB Standard 95* specify that these transactions should be classified as operating, investing, or financing activities depending on their dominant characteristics, and not on the fact that their gain or loss was reported on the statement of income. In cases when the classification is not clear, *FASB Standard 95*, par. 87, states that "—the appropriate classification generally should depend on the nature of the activity that is likely to be the predominate source of cash flows for the item. For example, the presumption is that the acquisition or production of productive assets is an investing activity."

The second issue, after the classification is determined, is how to reflect these gains and losses in the SCF. The important point is that a gain or loss, standing alone, does not represent a cash flow. For example, consider the following entry to record the disposal of an operational asset (e.g., a machine) by Complex Company:

Cash	15,000	
Accumulated depreciation	2,000	
Operational assets		14,000
Gain on disposal of operational assets		3,000

The cash inflow was $15,000 although the gain reported on the statement of income was only $3,000. This transaction is properly classified as an **investing activity** with a cash inflow of $15,000. To develop the SCF the gain must be removed from operating activities (i.e., the statement of income) and the full $15,000 must be included as a cash inflow under investing activities. This simple application procedure is illustrated for Complex Company as follows:

Schedule Method—Exhibit 19–9. First, notice in Schedule A (operating activities) that the $3,000 gain is excluded from the cash basis. Second, in Schedule B (investing activities) the full $15,000 is included as a cash inflow.

Spreadsheet Method—Exhibit 19–10. Notice that spreadsheet entry c is exactly like the original entry given above; it removes the gain and records the $15,000 cash inflow as an investing activity.

The **extraordinary loss** and the gain from **discontinued operations** reported on the statement of income by Complex Company were analyzed in exactly the same manner as the gain on disposal of operational assets (above).

The analysis of gains and losses excludes the individual income tax effects. The reason for using gross (i.e., pretax) amounts is discussed in the next subsection.

Income Taxes and Interest Paid or Received. A basic issue in the SCF is whether income tax, interest expense, and interest revenue should be classified as: *(a)* only operating activities or *(b)* an operating, investing, or financing activity depending on the classification of the item that caused the tax or interest. *FASB Standard 95,* par. 23, specifies that cash payments for taxes, duties and fines, and interest should be classified as cash payments for taxes, duties and fines, and interest should be classified as cash outflows and inflows from operating activities. The reasons given in *FASB Standard 95,* par. 92, were as follows: For income tax—"The Board decided that allocation of income taxes paid to operating, investing, and financing activities would be so complex and arbitrary that the benefits, if any, would not justify the costs involved." And for interest—"The Board perceived widespread support for the notion that operating cash flows should, insofar as possible, include items whose effects are included in determining net income to facilitate an understanding of the reasons for differences between net income and net cash flow from operating activities."

Noncash Investing and Financing Activities. The basic SCF issue for noncash transactions is whether they should be reported (or disclosed) on the SCF. Consider the case of the settlement of a $50,000 debt in full by issuing the creditor 10,000 shares of the debtor company's common stock with a fair market value of $50,000. In this case no cash was involved. However, the essence of this exchange can be viewed "as if" two events happened as follows: (1) a financing activity represented by the sale of the stock for $50,000 cash and (2) simultaneously, another financing activity represented by payment of debt principal. Some accountants argue that these two "as if" effects should be reported in the SCF (financing activities) as a simultaneous cash inflow and cash outflow. *FASB Standard 95,* par. 32, did not accept this argument, rather the Board specified a disclosure only, as follows:

> Information about all investing and financing activities of an enterprise during a period that affect recognized assets or liabilities but that do not result in cash receipts or cash payments in the period shall be reported in related disclosures. Those disclosures may be either narrative or summarized in a schedule, and they shall clearly relate the cash and noncash aspects of transactions involving similar items.

The last sentence in this quotation includes the words "cash and noncash aspects" which is often misunderstood. Although *FASB Standard 95* uses the term **noncash investing and financing activities** it also includes transactions that are **part cash and part noncash.** Consider the following entry by Complex Company for the purchase of an operational asset (e.g., a machine):

Operational assets, machine	30,000	
Cash		10,000
Common stock issued (market value)		20,000

Clearly, this investing activity is one-third cash and two-thirds noncash (*FASB Standard 95* calls it a **noncash transaction**). In any event, part cash and part noncash transactions must be reported as follows:

a. **Cash part**—must be reported in the SCF. For an analysis of such transactions refer to Exhibits 19–9 (schedule method) and 19–10 (spreadsheet method) and notice the $10,000 cash outflow under investing activities.
b. **Noncash part**—must be shown in a **separate disclosure schedule** which **must provide** an explanation and show both the cash and noncash amounts as illustrated in Note A in Exhibit 19–8 for Complex Company.

Foreign Currency Cash Flows. The **effects of foreign exchange rates** is a special classification on the SCF specified by *FASB Standard 95*. This classification was reflected in Exhibits 19–1, 19–2, and 19–3. This separate classification was deemed necessary by the FASB because it is a unique cash inflow, or outflow, that does not precisely fit the other three classifications. However, some accountants argue that it should be included in operating activities. This classification relates to *FASB Standard 52*, "Foreign Currency Translation." The special classification applies the provisions of *FASB Standard 52* to cash receipts and payments. *FASB Standard 95*, par. 25, specifies this SCF classification as follows:

> A statement of cash flows of an enterprise with foreign currency transactions or foreign operations shall report the reporting currency equivalent of foreign currency cash flows using the exchange rates in effect at the time of the cash flows. An appropriately weighted average exchange rate for the period may be used for translation if the result is substantially the same as if the rates at the dates of the cash flows were used. The statement shall report the effect of exchange rate changes on cash balances held in foreign currencies as a separate part of the reconciliation of the change in cash and cash equivalents during the period.

Determination of the amount that must be reported for this classification is beyond the scope of intermediate accounting.

Disclosure Requirements under the Direct Method

The SCF, direct method, has three disclosure requirements as follows (*FASB Standard 95*; paragraph number is given in parenthesis):[5]

1. Separately disclose the noncash investing and financing activities (par. 32) as shown in Exhibit 19–8.
2. Disclose the policy for determining which items are treated as cash equivalents (par. 10).
3. Reconciliation of net income with net cash inflow (outflow) from operating activities (par. 29). This reconciliation schedule for Complex Company is as follows:

[5] In contrast the indirect method requires seven disclosures; see page 941.

COMPLEX COMPANY
Reconciliation of Net Income to Net Cash Inflow (Outflow) from Operating Activities
For the Year 19X
(in thousands)

Net income (accrual basis, from statement of income)	$15
Add (deduct) to reconcile net income to net cash flow from operating activities:	
1.* Accounts receivable decrease	3
2. Gain on sale of operational assets	(3)
3. Inventory increase	(7)
4. Accounts payable increase	4
5. Depreciation expense	8
6. Bad debt expense	3
7. Interest payable decrease	(1)
8. Amortization of bond discount	1
9. Prepaid insurance decrease	2
10. Income tax payable decrease	(7)
11. Extraordinary loss (pretax)	20
12. Discontinued operations, gain	(10)
Net cash inflow from operating activities	$28

* Numbered only for instructional convenience.

Preparing the Reconciliation Schedule, Direct Method

The reconciliation schedule for the direct method is prepared in exactly the same way as shown in Exhibit 19–9, Schedule A (for Complex Company). Notice that it starts in column 1 with the **accrual** basis amounts taken directly from the statement of income, Exhibit 19–7. Notice that the net income of $15 is the last amount in column 1. The middle column converts accrual basis income ($15) to a cash basis ($28) as shown and explained in Exhibit 19–9, Schedule A. Next, the **reconciliation schedule** was copied by assigning the same sign as before for all changes related to all revenues and gains, and **reverse the signs** for all changes related to expenses and losses, because here we are adjusting income instead of adjusting expenses (which are deductions to compute net income). The algebraic sum will be "net cash inflow (outflow) from operating activities." Notice that there are 12 such changes in Exhibit 19–9, Schedule A. The reconciliation shown above reflects the same 12 changes and it is correct. The reasons that this direct conversion will always be correct is obvious in Exhibit 19–9, Schedule A because the total of the first column is net income (accrual basis), $15, and the 12 changes shown in the schedule result in net income converted to a cash flow amount, $28 (called **net cash inflow from operating activities** on the SCF). Also, see Exhibit 19–11, Schedule A, and the related discussion.

This concludes our discussion of the SCF, direct method, which is clearly preferable because it is *(a)* more useful in projecting future cash flows, *(b)* easier to understand and prepare, and *(c)* strongly recommended by the FASB. The next section discusses the traditional indirect method.

Application of the SCF, Indirect Method

The indirect method of reporting cash flows has been used to some extent for more than four decades. As we indicated in Part A it was reluctantly continued in *FASB Standard 95.* Recall from Exhibits 19–2 and 19–3 that it differs from the direct method in one very important way. That is, for **operating activities,** instead of reporting cash inflows from individual revenues and outflows for individual expenses, it **starts with net income** and reconciles net income with net cash flows from operating activities. For this reason the indirect method is often called the **reconciliation method.** This means that operating activities are reported under the indirect method exactly like the reconciliation disclosure shown on page 933 for Complex Company. However, when the indirect method is used, the reconciliation schedule is more difficult to prepare because the direct method schedule (Exhibit 19–9, Schedule A) is not available; therefore, the indirect reconciliation of net income has to be made. Also, it is important to note that *FASB Standard 95*, par. 30, specifically condones a one-line presentation in the SCF of net cash flow from operating activities as follows (which may well be its usual application in the future):

> If the indirect method is used, the reconciliation may be either reported within the statement of cash flows or provided in a separate schedule, with the statement of cash flows reporting only the net cash flow from operating activities. If the reconciliation is presented in the statement of cash flows, all adjustments to net income to determine net cash flow from operating activities shall be clearly identified as reconciling items.

Compared to the direct method, the indirect method involves only an **application** and reporting difference. Therefore, the discussion which follows will illustrate its application using the *(a)* schedule approach and *(b)* spreadsheet approach.

The direct and indirect methods require the same basic data. Therefore, Exhibit 19–7 provides the case data needed—statement of income, comparative statement of financial position, and the analysis of individual accounts.

Schedule Approach—SCF, Indirect Method

This approach involves the development of three schedules to compute net cash flow from operating, investing, and financing activities. **Exhibit 19–11** shows the three schedules with explanations. Notice that Schedules B and C are identical with those prepared using the direct method (Exhibit 19–9).[6]

[6] The adjustments to convert accrual income to cash flow from operations are varied. Although careful analysis is needed, the following table (adapted from Welsch and Short, *Fundamentals of Financial Accounting*, 5th ed. [Homewood, Ill.: Richard D. Irwin, 1987], p. 765), may be useful for checking purposes with the indirect method and when preparing reconciliation **disclosure schedules** for the direct method.

	Plus and minus adjustments to reconcile net income with net cash flow from operating activities	
Item	**When item increases**	**When item decreases**
Accounts receivable (trade)	–	+
Accounts payable (trade)	+	–
Accrued liability and unearned revenue	+	–
Prepaid asset and accrued revenue	–	+
Inventory	–	+
Depreciation, depletion, and amortization	+	
Amortization of discount and bonds payable	+	
Amortization of premium on bonds payable	–	
Amortization of discount on bond investment	–	
Amortization of premium on bond investment	+	
Losses on the statement of income	+	
Gains on the statement of income	–	

Exhibit 19–11
Schedules to prepare the SCF, indirect method; Complex Company.

Schedule A—Computation of Net Cash Flows from Operating Activities:

Items (see Exhibit 19–7)	Amount	Explanation
Net income, accrual basis	$15	From statement of income.
Add (subtract) to convert to cash basis:		
Accounts receivable increase, (−); decrease, $3 (+)	+ 3[a]	Add because cash inflow from sales transactions is **more** than accrual basis sales.
Gain on sale of operational assets, $3	− 3	Subtract because this gain is included in net income but this entire transaction is an investing activity.
Inventory increase, $7 (−); decrease (+)	− 7[b]	Subtract because cash outflow for inventory is **more** than accrual basis inventory cost included in cost of good sold.
Accounts payable increase, $4 (+); decrease (−)	+ 4[b]	Add because cash outflow for purchases (and hence cost of goods sold) is **less** than accrual basis cost of purchases.
Depreciation expense, $8 (only *a* +)	+ 8	Add because this is a noncash expense; cash flow is not affected.
Bad debt expense, $3 (only *a* +)	+ 3	Add because this is a noncash expense; exactly like depreciation expense.
Amortization of bonds payable discount, $1 (only *a* +)	+ 1	Add because this is a noncash expense; exactly like depreciation expense.
Interest payable increase, (+); decrease, $1 (−)	− 1	Subtract because cash outflow for interest is **more** than accrual basis interest expense.
Prepaid expense (insurance) increase (−); decrease, $2 (+)	+ 2	Add because the cash outflow this period was zero; the cash outflow for this expense (remaining expenses) was **less** than the accrual basis expense.
Income tax payable increase (+) decrease, $7 (−); this includes all income taxes	− 7	Subtract because cash outflow for income tax expense was **more** than accrual basis expense.
Extraordinary loss (+)	+20	Add because this loss on land condemnation is an investment activity. The income tax amount ($6 tax saving) is included above in operating activities.
Discontinued operations, gain (−)	−10	Deduct because this is an investment activity; the income tax amount ($3) is included above in operating activities.
Net cash inflow from operating activities	$28	Reported on the SCF (Exhibit 19–12).

Exhibit 19–11
(concluded)

Schedule B—Computation of Net Cash Flows from Investing Activities (analysis of comparative SFP and individual accounts):

Items	Cash inflows (+) cash outflows (−)	Explanation
Sale of operating assets	+ $15	From examination of operating asset accounts and cash account.
Disposal of land; condemnation	+ 40	From examination of land and cash accounts.
Discontinued operations, assets	+ 23	Examination of statement of income, cash account, and other assets.
Purchase of land	− 40	Examination of land and cash accounts.
Purchase of operational assets	− 10†	From examination of operational asset, cash, and capital stock accounts. Also, income tax records are involved.
Net cash inflow (outflow) from investing activities	$28	Reported on the SCF (Exhibit 19–12).

Schedule C—Computation of Net Cash Flows from Financing Activities:

Items	Cash inflows (+) cash outflows (−)	Explanation
Borrowing on long-term note payable	+ $10	From examination of note payable account and SFP.
Payment of bonds (principal)	− 20	Examination of bond payable accounts and cash records.
Payment of cash dividend	− 15	From statement of retained earnings.
Net cash inflow (outflow)	$(25)	Reported on the SCF (Exhibit 19–12).

[a] Allowance for doubtful accounts is a noncash account (in a manner similar to accumulated depreciation). Since it does not affect either cash or net income, it is not included. Notice that bad debt expense, like depreciation expense, is shown below as a noncash expense.
[b] The net effect of these two adjustments is to convert cost of goods sold (accrual basis) to a cash basis. The cash amount is the same as actual cash paid for purchases during the accounting period.
† Report in separate schedule—Noncash transactions:

Cash paid	$10
Common stock	20
Total	$30

The SCF, indirect method, prepared from these three schedules is shown in **Exhibit 19–12.** Notice that one-line reporting of cash flows from operating activities could have been used, in which case the related disclosure reconciliation schedule would be separately reported.

Spreadsheet Approach—SCF, Indirect Method

When the indirect method is used the spreadsheet does not include the statement of income because the individual revenues and expenses are not analyzed to determine their respective cash flows. Instead net income is reconciled with net cash flow from operating activities. This means that the first analysis on the spreadsheet starts with net income and computes the changes in the various

Exhibit 19–12
Statement of cash flows, indirect method; Complex Company.

COMPLEX COMPANY
Statement of Cash Flows
For the Year Ended December 31, 19X
(in thousands)

Cash flow from operating activities:		
Net income (accrual basis; from statement of income)	$15	
Add (deduct) to reconcile net income to net cash flow:		
Accounts receivable decrease	3	
Gain on sale of operational assets	(3)	
Inventory increase	(7)	
Accounts payable increase	4	
Depreciation expense	8	
Bad debt expense	3	
Interest payable decrease	(1)	
Amortization of bond discount	1	
Prepaid insurance decrease	2	
Income tax payable decrease	(7)	
Extraordinary loss (pretax)	20	
Discontinued operations, gain	(10)	
Net cash inflow from operating activities		$28
Cash flows from investing activities:		
Cash inflows:		
From sale of operational assets	15	
From sale of land (condemnation)	40	
From discontinued operations	23	
Cash outflows:		
Paid for purchase of land	(40)	
Paid for operational assets (Note A)	(10)	
Net cash outflow for investing activities		28
Cash flows from financing activities:		
Cash inflows:		
Borrowing on long-term note	10	
Cash outflows:		
Payment on bond principal	(20)	
Paid cash dividend	(15)	
Net cash outflow for financing activities		(25)
Net increase in cash plus cash equivalents during 19X		31
Cash plus cash equivalents, January 1, 19X		36
Cash plus cash equivalents, December 31, 19X		$67

Note A: The company purchased an operational asset; payment was part cash and part the company's unissued common stock as follows:

Cash paid (25%)	$10
Common stock issued	20
Total asset cost recorded	$30

accounts (from the comparative statement of financial position) that reconcile net income and cash flows from operating activities. It follows the pattern shown in the schedule approach (Exhibit 19–11, Schedule A). **Exhibit 19–13** shows the spreadsheet for the indirect method. The remaining parts of the analysis—cash flows from investing and financing activities—are the same as when the direct method is used (Exhibit 19–6).

Explanation of spreadsheet entries—the entries shown on the spreadsheet,

Exhibit 19–13

Spreadsheet to prepare SCF, indirect method, Complex Company.

Items	Balance 1/1/19X	Analysis: Debit	Analysis: Credit	Balance 12/31/19X
Cash	30			67
Cash equivalents	6			0
Total	36	t 31		67
Noncash accounts:				
Investment, short term (stock of X Corp.)	12			12
Accounts receivable	32		b 3	29
Allowance for doubtful accounts	(2)		c 3	(5)
Inventory	30	d 7		37
Prepaid insurance	4		f 2	2
Land	60	n 40	k 60	40
Operational assets	80	o 30	j 14	96
Accumulated depreciation	(20)	j 2	m 8	(26)
Other assets (includes discontinued operations, $13)	35		l 13	22
Total assets	267			274
Accounts payable	26		e 4	30
Interest payable	2	h 1		1
Income tax payable	11	i 7		4
Notes payable, long term	0		p 10	10
Bonds payable	80	q 20		60
Unamortized bond discount	(3)		g 1	(2)
Common stock, nopar	100		o 20	130
			s 10	
Retained earnings	51	s 10	a 15	41
		r 15		
Total liabilities and retained earnings	267	163	163	274
Statement of Cash Inflows and (Outflows)				
Reconciliation of net income to cash flow from operating activities:				
Net income (from statement of income)		a 15		
Changes to reconcile net income with net cash flow:				
Accounts receivable decrease		b 3		
Gain on sale of operational assets			j 3	
Inventory increase			d 7	
Accounts payable increase		e 4		
Depreciation expense		m 8		
Bad debt expense		c 3		$ 28
Interest payable decrease			h 1	
Amortization of bond discount		g 1		
Prepaid insurance decrease		f 2		
Income tax payable decrease			i 7	
Extraordinary loss (pretax)		k 20		
Discontinued operations, gain			l 10	
Cash flows from investing activities:				
From sale of operational asset		j 15		
From sale, land condemnation		k 40		
From discontinued operations		l 23		28
Paid for land purchase			n 40	
Paid for operational assets			o 10	
Cash flows from financing activities:				
Borrowing on long-term note		p 10		
Payment on bonds (principal)			q 20	(25)
Paid cash dividend			r 15	
Net increase (decrease) in cash during the period			t 31	$ 31
Totals		307	307	

Exhibit 19–13, using the indirect method with explanations are given below. Spreadsheet entries **a through m** are called **reconciling** entries. They reconcile for all **noncash changes** that affected net income.

Entry a—for net income; $15:

Net income	15	
Retained earnings		15

This entry is used to start the reconciliation; net income is shown as an inflow to be reconciled by the noncash reconciling entries. The credit to retained earnings reflects the effects of the original closing entry.

Entry b—for the decrease in accounts receivable:

Reconciling amount (add to net income)	3	
Accounts receivable		3

This account reconciles for the difference between the beginning and ending balances of accounts receivable with net income. It is added to net income because cash inflow from sales transactions was **more** than sales revenue.

Entry c—for bad debt expense:

Reconciling amount (add to net income)	3	
Allowance for doubtful accounts		3

This entry reconciles for this noncash item that was included in computing net income. Add because this is a noncash item.

Entry d—for the inventory increase:

Inventory	7	
Reconciling amount (subtract from net income)		7

Deduct because cash outflow for inventory was **more** than accrual basis inventory included in cost of goods sold.

Entry e—for accounts payable increase:

Reconciling amount (add to net income)	4	
Accounts payable		4

This entry reconciles the difference between the beginning and ending balance of accounts payable with net income. Add because cash outflow for purchases (and hence, cost of goods sold) is **less** than accrual purchases.

Entry f—for prepaid (unexpired) insurance decrease:

Reconciling amount (add to net income)	2	
Prepaid insurance		2

This is a noncash expense; add because cash outflow was less than accrual expense (i.e., remaining expenses in this case).

Entry g—for amortization of bond discount:

Reconciling amount (add to net income)	1	
Unamortized bond discount		1

This is the same type of effect as depreciation expense. Add because this is a noncash item like depreciation.

Entry h—for interest payable decrease:

Interest payable	1	
Reconciling amount (subtract from net income)		1

This entry reconciles the beginning and ending balance of interest payable with net income. Subtract because cash outflow was **more** than accrual expense.

Entry i—for income tax payable decrease:

Income tax payable	7	
Reconciling amount (subtract from net income)		7

This entry reconciles the beginning and ending balance of income tax payable with net income. Subtract because cash outflow was more than accrual expense.

Entry j—for sale of operational asset:

Investing activities, sale of operational asset	15	
Accumulated depreciation	2	
Operational assets		14
Reconciling amount (subtract from net income)		3

This entry removes the gain on sale of an operational asset from operating activities because it is an investing activity. Add to net income because it was noncash addition in computing net income.

Entry k—for extraordinary loss (pretax because entry i included the income tax):

Extraordinary loss (add to net income)	20	
Investing activities, sale of land	40	
Land		60

This entry removes the extraordinary loss because it is an investing activity rather than an operating activity. Add to operating activities because it was a noncash deduction in computing net income. Notice that the full cash effect ($40) is included under investing activities.

Entry l—for restructure gain (pretax because entry i included the tax):

Investing activities, discontinued operations	23	
Reconciling amount (subtract from net income)		10
Other assets (discontinued)		13

This entry removes the extraordinary gain from operating activities because it is an investing activity. Subtract because it was a noncash addition in computing net income. Notice that the full cash effect is included under investing activities.

Entry m—for depreciation expense:

Reconciling amount (add to net income)	8	
Accumulated depreciation		8

This entry reconciles for this noncash item that was included in computing net income. Add because this is a noncash item.

Entry n—for land purchase:

Land	40	
Investing activity (cash paid)		40

This spreadsheet entry recognizes a cash investing activity.

Entry o—for purchase of an operational asset for part cash and part noncash:

Operational assets	30	
Common stock (issued in part payment)		20
Investing activity (cash paid)		10

This spreadsheet entry recognizes an investing activity of $10 (cash). This entry requires a disclosure schedule that includes the following:

Cash	$10
Common stock	20
Total asset cost	$30

Entry p—for borrowing on note payable:

Financing activities (cash)	10	
Note payable, long-term		10

This entry recognizes a financing activity (cash inflow).

Entry q—for payment on bond principal:

Bonds payable (principal)	20	
Financing activity (cash paid)		20

This entry recognizes a financing activity (cash outflow).

Entry r—for payment of a cash dividend:

Retained earnings	15	
Financing activity (cash paid)		15

Entry s—for reconciling purposes only; stock dividends and stock splits do **not** directly or indirectly affect cash flows.

Retained earnings	10	
Common stock, nopar		10

Entry t—optional balancing entry for net cash inflow during the period:

Cash	31	
Net increase in cash during the period		31

Disclosure Requirements under the Indirect Method

The SCF, indirect method has seven disclosure requirements as follows (*FASB Standard 95* paragraphs are given in parentheses):

1. Separately disclose the noncash investing and financing activities (par. 32) as shown in Exhibit 19–8.
2. Disclose the policy for determining which items are treated as cash equivalents (par. 10).
3. Reconciliation of net income with net cash inflow (outflow) from operating activities (par. 29) unless included in the SCF.
4. The amount of cash paid for interest (par. 29).
5. The amount of cash paid for income tax (par. 29).
6. Changes during the period in receivables, inventory, and accounts payable (par. 29).
7. Clear identification of all reconciling items (par. 30).

Summary

The statement of cash flows is one of the three required financial statements. Although it has been used to some extent for several decades *(a)* its format has been varied, *(b)* it was seldom presented in financial statements, and *(c)* little concern was given to it by authoritative standards-setting groups. *FASB*

Standard 95 (November 1987) changed the situation because it *(a)* exclusively requires a SCF, *(b)* proscribes a detailed format, and *(c)* gives detailed guidelines for content.

The primary purpose of the new SCF is to provide cash flow information in a manner that maximizes its usefulness to investors, creditors, and others in projecting future cash flows related to the enterprise.

FASB Standard 95 permits two different methods for reporting cash flows, called the direct and indirect methods. These alternative methods differ only in respect to cash flows from **operating activities**—investing and financing activities are reported in exactly the same way under both methods. The direct method reports the cash inflows from the main classifications of revenues and cash outflows for the main classifications of expenses. In contrast, the indirect method reports operating activities by showing a reconciliation of net income with net cash flow from operating activities. *FASB Standard 95* strongly recommends the direct method because it is more relevant for investors, creditors, and other interested parties.

Two approaches are available for developing the SCF—the schedule approach and the spreadsheet approach. Both approaches are efficient; however the spreadsheet approach is preferable in complex cases because it is a coordinated and self-checking approach.

QUESTIONS

Part A

1. Compare the purposes of the statement of financial position, statement of income, and statement of cash flows.
2. Explain the basic difference between the three activities reported on the SCF—operating, investing, financing.
3. List three major cash inflows and three major cash outflows under *(a)* operating activities, *(b)* investing activities, and *(c)* financing activities.
4. Define a noncash investing activity. Give an example of the two possible cases.
5. Define a noncash financing activity. Give an example of each of the two possible cases.
6. Define a cash equivalent for SCF purposes.
7. What policy must a company adopt about cash equivalents? What accounting concept must the company follow if the policy is changed?
8. Explain the basic difference between the direct and indirect methods of reporting on the SCF. Use net income $5,000, sales revenue, $100,000 and an increase of accounts receivable, $10,000 to illustrate the basic difference. Which method provides the most relevant information to investors and creditors?
9. Explain why cash paid during the period for purchases and for salaries is not specifically reported on the SCF, indirect method, as cash outflows.
10. Explain why a $50,000 increase in inventory during the year must be included in developing cash flows for operating activities under both the direct and indirect methods.
11. What are the three reconciling amounts that must be reported at the bottom of

the SCF? Which one must agree with a key amount in another financial statement. Use assumed amounts for illustrative purposes.

12. One of the criticisms of the SCF, indirect method is that it does not report each of the three activities consistently. Explain the basis for this argument.
13. Explain why an adjustment must be made to compute cash flow from operating activities for depreciation expense, bad debt expense, and amortization of intangibles (e.g., patents, copyrights, franchises, goodwill, and bond discount or premium).
14. Explain why gains and losses reported on the statement of income usually must be omitted (or removed) from operating activities to compute cash flow from operating activities.
15. X Corporation's records showed the following: Sales, $80,000 and accounts receivable decrease $10,000, after the write-off of a $3,000 bad debt. Assuming the direct method, compute the cash inflow from customers.
16. Explain the two ways that the SCF, indirect method, can be designed to report cash flows from operating activities.

EXERCISES

Exercises 19–1 to 19–15

E 19–1 (SCF; Terminology; Format; Requirements)

Two lists are given below—key terms and brief descriptions. You are to match the descriptions with the terms by entering one letter in each blank to the left.

	Key terms		Brief description
____	1. Fundamental purpose of the SCF.	A.	Net cash increase (decrease), beginning balance, and ending balance.
____	2. Basic components of the SCF.	B.	Cash flows related to obtaining cash for the enterprise.
____	3. Three reconciling lines at the bottom of the SCF.	C.	Cash flows primarily related to the income statement.
____	4. Must be disclosed in a separate SCF schedule.	D.	Financial statements shall not report this ratio.
____	5. Cash flows from operating activities.	E.	Includes highly liquid investments, but not all short-term investments.
____	6. Cash flow per share.	F.	Cash flows from three activities: operating, investing, and financing.
____	7. SCF, direct method.	G.	Add (deduct) to adjust net income to net cash flows.
____	8. This amount must agree with the change in cash.	H.	Noncash investing and financing activities.
____	9. Cash flows from investing activities.	I.	The two usual approaches to develop the SCF.
____	10. This is a special item on the SCF.	J.	To help investors, creditors, etc., to assess future cash flows.
____	11. SCF, indirect method.	K.	Cash flows related to obtaining productive facilities and other noncash assets.
____	12. Schedule and spreadsheet.	L.	Reports cash flows for each major revenue and expense.
____	13. Cash equivalents.	M.	Effect of foreign exchange rates on cash.
____	14. Cash flows from financing activities.	N.	Net increse (decrease) in cash during the period.
____	15. This item on the SCF, indirect method, must be clearly identified as a reconciliation.	O.	Does not report cash flows for revenues and expenses, but reconciles net income with cash flows.

E 19–2 (SCF; Examples of Cash Inflows and Outflows; Compare the Direct and Indirect Methods)

A format overview of the SCF, direct method is given below with three numbered blank spaces under each cash inflow and outflow—

Operating activities:
  Cash inflows:
    1.
    2.
    3.
  Cash outflows:
    1.
    2.
    3.
Investing activities:
  Cash inflows:
    1.
    2.
    3.
  Cash outflows:
    1.
    2.
    3.
Financing activities:
  Cash inflows:
    1.
    2.
    3.
  Cash outflows:
    1.
    2.
    3.

Required:

1. Give major examples in the blank spaces.
2. Assume the indirect method is used instead. Give the format, with three examples, that would be used for operating activities. Be prepared to discuss your examples.

E 19–3 (SCF Reporting; Direct and Indirect Methods Compared)

To compare SCF reporting using the direct and indirect methods, enter check marks on each line to indicate *(a)* which items are reported under the direct and indirect methods and *(b)* which items are reported on the statements of income and/or financial position. Explain any major difference between the two methods.

Cash flows (and related changes)	(a) SCF method		(b) Statement of:	
	Direct	Indirect	Income	Financial position
1. Revenues from customers				
2. Accounts receivable increase or decrease				
3. Payments to suppliers				
4. Inventory increase or decrease				
5. Accounts payable increase or decrease				
6. Payments to employees				
7. Wages payable, increase or decrease				
8. Depreciation expense				
9. Net income				
10. Cash flows from operating activities				
11. Investing activities				
12. Financing activities				
13. Net increase or decrease in cash during the period				

E 19–4 (SCF; Cash Flow Analysis of Sales)

The records of ZZ Company showed sales revenue of $100,000 (on the statement of income) and a change in the balance of accounts receivable. To demonstrate the effect of changes in accounts receivable on cash inflows from customers, five independent cases are used. Complete the following tabulation for each independent case:

Case	Sales revenue (from statement (of income)	Accounts Receivable increase (decrease)	Computations	Amount inflow
A	$100,000	$ –0–		
B	100,000	10,000		
C	100,000	(10,000)		
D	100,000	9,000*		
E	100,000	(9,000)*		

* Includes the effect of a $1,000 write-off of an uncollectible account.

E 19–5 (SCF; Cash Flow Analysis of Cost of Goods Sold)

The records of Atlas Company showed cost of goods sold (on the statement of income) of $60,000 and a change in the inventory and accounts payable balances. To demonstrate the effect of these changes on cash outflow for cost of goods sold (i.e., payments to suppliers) eight independent cases are used. Complete the following tabulation for each case:

Case	Cost of goods sold	Inventory increase (decrease)	Accounts Payable increase (decrease)	Computations	Amount outflow*
A	$60,000	$ -0-	$ -0-		
B	60,000	6,000	-0-		
C	60,000	(6,000)	-0-		
D	60,000	-0-	4,000		
E	60,000	-0-	(4,000)		
F	60,000	6,000	4,000		
G	60,000	(6,000)	(4,000)		
H	60,000	(6,000)	(6,000)		

* This is the amount of cash paid during the current period for past and current purchases.

E 19–6 (SCF, Direct Method; Analysis of Cash Inflows and Outflows)
The records of Easie Company provided the following data:

a. Sales revenue, $95,000 (statement of income); accounts receivable decreased, $5,000.
b. Cost of goods sold, $42,000 (statement of income); inventory decreased, $3,000; accounts payable, no change.
c. Wage expense, $16,000 (statement of income); wages payable decreased, $1,500.
d. Depreciation expense (statement of income), $4,000.
e. Purchased productive asset for $18,000; paid one-third down and gave a two-year, interest-bearing note for the balance.
f. Borrowed $20,000 cash on a note payable.
g. Sold an old operational asset for $3,000 cash; original cost, $10,000, accumulated depreciation, $9,000.
h. Paid a $2,500 note payable (principal).
i. Paid a cash dividend, $4,000.

Required:
For each of the above transactions give *(a)* its SCF activity and *(b)* the SCF (direct method) inflow, or outflow amount. Also, give any disclosure schedules required.

E 19–7 (SCF, Direct Method; Prepare Using Schedule Approach)
The following data were provided by the accounting records of SM Company at year-end, December 31, 19B:

Statement of income:

Sales	$70,000
Cost of goods sold	(42,000)
Depreciation expense	(5,000)
Remaining expenses	(18,000)
Gain on sale of investments	3,000
Loss on sale of operational assets	(1,000)
Net income	$ 7,000

Comparative statement of financial position:

	December 31 19A	December 31 19B	Increase (decrease)
Debits			
Cash	$ 34,000	$ 33,500	$ (500)
Accounts receivable (net)	12,000	17,000	5,000
Inventory	16,000	14,000	(2,000)
Long-term investments	6,000		(6,000)
Operational assets	80,000	98,000	18,000
Treasury stock		11,500	11,500
Total debits	$148,000	$174,000	$26,000
Credits			
Accumulated depreciation	$ 48,000	$ 39,000	$ (9,000)
Accounts payable	19,000	12,000	(7,000)
Bonds payable	10,000	30,000	20,000
Common stock, nopar	50,000	65,000	15,000
Retained earnings	21,000	28,000	7,000
Total credits	$148,000	$174,000	$26,000

Analysis of selected accounts and transactions:

a. Sold operational assets for $6,000 cash; cost, $21,000, and two-thirds depreciated (the loss or gain is not an extraordinary item).
b. Purchased operational assets for cash, $9,000.
c. Purchased operational assets: exchanged unissued bonds payable of $30,000 in payment.
d. Sold the long-term investments for $9,000 cash, net of tax (assume the gain or loss is an extraordinary item).
e. Purchased treasury stock for cash, $11,500.
f. Retired bonds payable at maturity date by issuing common stock, $10,000.
g. Sold unissued common stock for cash, $5,000.

Required:
Prepare a SCF, direct method (use the schedule approach).

E 19–8 **(SCF, Direct Method; Use Schedule Approach)**
The accounting records of Sympel Company provided the following data:
Statement of income for year ended December 31, 19B:

Sales	$150,000
Cost of goods sold	(90,000)
Depreciation expense	(2,000)
Remaining expenses	(32,000)
Net income	$ 26,000

Comparative statement of financial position amounts:

	December 31		
Debits	**19A**	**19B**	**Increase (decrease)**
Cash	$ 4,000	$17,000	$13,000
Accounts receivable (net)	5,000	9,000	4,000
Inventory	10,000	12,000	2,000
Investment, long term	2,000		(2,000)
Operational assets	30,000	47,000	17,000
Total debits	$51,000	$85,000	$34,000
Credits			
Accumulated depreciation	$ 5,000	$ 7,000	$ 2,000
Accounts payable	3,000	5,000	2,000
Notes payable, short term (nontrade)	4,000	3,000	(1,000)
Notes payable, long term	10,000	18,000	8,000
Common stock, nopar	25,000	40,000	15,000
Retained earnings	4,000	12,000	8,000
Total credits	$51,000	$85,000	$34,000

Analysis of selected accounts and transactions:

a. Sold the long-term investment at cost, for cash.
b. Declared and paid a cash dividend of $7,000.
c. Purchased operational assets that cost $17,000; gave a $12,000 long-term note payable and paid $5,000 cash.
d. Paid a $4,000 long-term note payable by issuing common stock; market value, $4,000.
e. Issued a stock dividend, $11,000.

Required:
Prepare a SCF, direct method (use the schedule approach).

E 19–9 **(SCF, Indirect Method; Prepare the Reconciliation for Operating Activities)** The data given below were provided by the accounting records of Darby Company. Prepare the reconciliation of net income with cash flow from operations for inclusion in the SCF, indirect method.

Net income (accrual basis), $40,000.
Depreciation expense, $8,000.
Decrease in wages payable, $1,200.
Decrease in trade accounts receivable, $1,800.
Increase in merchandise inventory, $2,500.
Amortization of patent, $100.
Increase in long-term liabilities, $10,000.
Sale of capital stock for cash, $25,000.
Amortization of premium on bonds payable, $200.
Accounts payable increase, $4,000.
Stock dividend issued, $10,000.

E 19–10 **(SCF, Indirect Method; Prepare the Reconciliation for Operating Activities)** The data given below were provided by the accounting records of Sileo Company. Prepare the reconciliation of net income with cash flow from operating activities for inclusion in the SCF, indirect method.

Net income (accrual basis), $50,000.
Depreciation expense, $6,000.
Increase in wages payable, $1,000.
Increase in trade accounts receivable, $1,800.
Decrease in merchandise inventory, $2,300.
Amortization of patent, $200.
Decrease in long-term liabilities, $10,000.
Sale of capital stock for cash, $25,000.
Amortization of discount on bonds payable, $300.

E 19–11 (SCF, Direct and Indirect Methods; Use Schedule Approach to Prepare the Statement)
Randy Company was organized on January 1, 19A. During the year ended December 31, 19A, the company provided the following data:

Statement of income:	
Sales revenue	$75,000
Cost of goods sold	(30,000)
Depreciation expense	(2,000)
Remaining expenses	(27,000)
Net income	$16,000

Statement of financial position:	
Cash	$ 58,000
Accounts receivable (net)	$20,000
Merchandise inventory (perpetual)	10,000
Machinery (net)	23,000
Total	$111,000
Accounts payable	$ 10,000
Accrued expenses payable	17,000
Dividends payable	4,000
Notes payable, short term (cash)	10,000
Notes payable, short term (equipment)	20,000
Common stock	40,000
Retained earnings	10,000
Total	$111,000

Analysis of selected accounts and transactions:

a. Sold 2,000 shares of common stock, par $10, at $20 per share; collected cash.
b. Borrowed $10,000 on a one-year, 9%, interest-bearing note; the note was dated June 1, 19A.
c. During 19A, purchased machinery that cost $25,000; paid $5,000 cash and signed a $20,000, one-year, 10%, interest-bearing note.
d. Purchased merchandise for resale at a cost of $40,000 (debited Inventory because the perpetual system is used); paid $30,000 cash, balance credited to Accounts Payable.
e. At December 31, 19A, declared a cash dividend of $6,000; paid $2,000 in December 19A; the balance will be paid March 1, 19B.

Required:
1. Prepare a SCF, direct method (schedule approach).
2. Prepare a SCF, indirect method (schedule approach).

E 19–12 (SCF, Direct Method; Complete Spreadsheet)
Analysis of accounts: *(a)* purchased an operational asset, $30,000, issued capital stock in full payment, *(b)* purchased a long-term investment for cash, $10,000, *(c)* paid cash

dividend, $10,000, *(c)* sold operational asset for $5,000 cash (cost, $18,000, accumulated depreciation, $16,000), and *(d)* sold capital stock, 500 shares at $11 per share cash. Complete the spreadsheet for SCF, direct method.

Item	Balances 12/31/19A	Analysis		Balances 12/31/19B
		Debit	Credit	
Analysis of income:				
Sales			120,000	
Cost of goods sold		48,000		
Depreciation		6,000		
Amortization of bond premium			300	
Wage expense		22,000		
Income tax expense		10,000		
Interest expense		7,000		
Remaining expenses		2,300		
Gain on sale of operational asset			3,000	
Net income		28,000		
Analysis of financial position:				
Cash	19,500			32,200
Accounts receivable (net)	34,000			34,000
Merchandise inventory	78,000			85,000
Investments, long term				10,000
Operational assets	168,500			180,500
Total	300,000			341,700
Accumulated depreciation	44,000			34,000
Accounts payable	21,000			19,000
Wages payable	1,500			500
Income taxes payable	2,000			3,500
Bonds payable	100,000			100,000
Premium on bonds payable	4,000			3,700
Common stock, nopar	120,000			155,500
Retained earnings	7,500			25,500
Total	300,000			341,700
Statement of cash inflows and (outflows)		*Inflows*	*Outflows*	
Cash flows from operating activities:				
Cash flows from investing activities:				
Cash flows from financing activities:				
Net increase (decrease) in cash				
Totals				

E 19–13 **(SCF, Direct Method; Complete Spreadsheet)**
Analysis of accounts: *(a)* Retired bonds, paid $20,000 cash, *(b)* bought long-term investment, $10,000 cash, *(c)* purchased operational asset, $7,000 cash, *(d)* purchased short-term investment, $3,000 cash, *(e)* paid cash dividend, $4,000, and *(f)* issued capital stock, 500 shares at $19 cash per share. Complete the spreadsheet for SCF, direct method.

Item	Balances 12/31/19A	Analysis		Balances 12/31/19B
		Debit	Credit	
Analysis of income:				
Sales			104,000	
Cost of goods sold		55,000		
Depreciation expense		8,000		
Patent amortization		300		
Remaining expenses		17,700		
Net income		23,000		
Analysis of financial position:				
Cash	15,000			21,500
Investment, short term				3,000
Accounts receivable	17,000			21,000
Inventory (perpetual)	10,000			15,000
Investments, long term				10,000
Operational assets (net)	60,000			59,000
Patent (net)	3,000			2,700
Other assets	7,000			7,000
Total	112,000			139,200
Accounts payable	12,000			22,000
Accrued expenses payable				8,700
Bonds payable	40,000			20,000
Common stock, par $10	35,000			40,000
Contributed capital in excess of par				4,500
Retained earnings	25,000			44,000
Total	112,000			139,200
Statement of cash inflows (outflows)		*Inflows*	*Outflows*	
Cash flows from operating activities:				
Cash flows from investing activities:				
Cash flows from financing activities:				
Net increase (decrease) in cash				
Totals				

E 19–14 **(SCF, Indirect Method; Complete Spreadsheet)**
The data used in this exercise are given in Exercise 19–12.

Required:
Complete the SCF, indirect method spreadsheet given below.

Item	Balances 12/31/19A	Analysis: Debit	Analysis: Credit	Balances 12/31/19B
Cash plus short-term investments	19,500			32,200
Noncash accounts:				
Accounts receivable (net)	34,000			34,000
Merchandise inventory	78,000			85,000
Investments, long term				10,000
Operational assets	168,500			180,500
Total	300,000			341,700
Accumulated depreciation	44,000			34,000
Accounts payable	21,000			19,000
Wages payable	1,500			500
Income taxes payable	2,000			3,500
Bonds payable	100,000			100,000
Premium on bonds payable	4,000			3,700
Common stock, nopar	120,000			155,500
Retained earnings	7,500			25,500
Total	300,000			341,700
Statement of cash inflows (outflows):				
Conversion of net income to cash flow from operating activities:				
Cash flows from investing activities:				
Cash flows from financing activities:				
Net increase (decrease) in cash				
Totals				

E 19–15 (SCF, Indirect Method; Complete Spreadsheet)
The data used in this exercise are given in Exercise 19–13.

Required:
Complete the SCF, indirect method spreadsheet given below.

Item	Balances 12/31/19A	Analysis Debit	Analysis Credit	Balances 12/31/19B
Cash	15,000			21,500
Investment, short term				3,000
Accounts receivable	17,000			21,000
Inventory (perpetual)	10,000			15,000
Investments, long term				10,000
Operational assets (net)	60,000			59,000
Patent (net)	3,000			2,700
Other assets	7,000			7,000
Total	112,000			139,200
Accounts payable	12,000			22,000
Accrued expenses payable				8,700
Bonds payable	40,000			20,000
Common stock, par $10	35,000			40,000
Contributed capital in excess of par				4,500
Retained earnings	25,000			44,000
Total	112,000			139,200
Statement of cash inflows (outflows):				
Conversion of net income to cash flow from operating activities:				
Cash flows from investing activities:				
Cash flows from financing activities:				
Net increase (decrease) in cash				
Totals				

PROBLEMS

Problems 19–1 to 19–12

P 19–1 (SCF, Direct Method; Analysis of Cash Flows and Reporting)
Some selected transactions from the records of Dever Company are given below. The annual reporting period ends December 31, 19B. The company uses the SCF, direct method. Analyze each transaction and give the following:

a. Classification of the transaction on the SCF (operating, investing, financing, or none of these)
b. Whether a cash inflow or outflow and the amount reported on the SCF.
c. Any required disclosure; give the disclosure note or schedule with amount(s).

Example:
Declared and paid a cash dividend, $10,000.

Response:

a. Financing activity.
b. Cash outflow, $10,000.
c. No separate disclosure or schedule.

1. Purchased operational asset (machine) for $30,000; gave a one-year interest-bearing note for $20,000 and paid cash for the difference.
2. Issued 1,000 shares of capital stock, par $10, at $25 per share. Received cash $12,000 and a three-year interest-bearing note for $13,000.
3. Cost of goods sold on the statement of income, $40,000; inventory increased, $10,000 and all purchases are on a strict cash basis.
4. Declared a cash dividend of $8,000 and set up a short-term dividends payable account for $5,000 (to be paid in 19C).
5. Purchased treasury stock for $12,000; gave a one-year interest-bearing note for $2,000.
6. Sales revenue, $120,000; accounts receivable decreased, $8,000 (assumes no allowance account).
7. Salary and wage expense, $30,000; salaries and wages payable increased by $1,000.
8. Depreciation expense, $9,000 (shown on the statement of income).
9. Paid a note payable in full, $5,000.
10. Sold an old operational asset for $7,000 cash; original recorded cost, $20,000, accumulated depreciation to date, $18,000.
11. Issued a stock dividend which was debited to retained earnings, $15,000.
12. Sold an investment in land for $35,000; received cash $10,000 and a one-year interest-bearing note for the remainder. The land was originally recorded in the accounts at $13,000; therefore, a $22,000 gain on sale of land investment was recorded.
13. Received a cash dividend of $3,000 on a long-term investment in the common stock of Z Corporation.
14. Cost of goods sold on the statement of income, $62,000; inventory decreased by $9,000 and accounts payable increased by $4,000.
15. Received a $11,000 stock dividend on a long-term investment in the capital stock of XB Corporation.
16. Income taxes at end of year:

Statement of financial position: Income taxes payable increase, $4,000.

Statement of income:	
Taxable income	$100,000
Income tax expense	35,000
Income aftertax	65,000
Extraordinary loss (debt restructure), net of $7,000 (income tax savings)	13,000
Net income	$52,000

17. Interest expense, $9,000; interest payable increased, $2,000.
18. Income tax expense, $13,000; income taxes payable decreased, $4,000.
19. Interest revenue, $11,000; interest receivable decreased, $1,500.
20. Insurance expense, $5,000; prepaid (unexpired) insurance decreased, $3,000.

P 19–2 (SCF; Direct Method; Schedule Approach)

The statements of income and financial position and an analysis are given below for Supreme Company.

Comparative statement of financial position:

	12/31/19A	12/31/19B	Increase (decrease)
Debits			
Cash	$ 40,000	$ 44,900	$ 4,900
Accounts receivable (net, no write-offs)	60,000	52,500	(7,500)
Merchandise inventory	180,000	141,600	(38,400)
Prepaid insurance	2,400	1,200	(1,200)
Investments, long term	30,000		(30,000)
Land	10,000	38,400	28,400
Operational assets	250,000	259,000	9,000
Patent (net)	1,600	1,400	(200)
	$574,000	$539,000	$(35,000)
Credits			
Accumulated depreciation	$ 65,000	$ 79,000	$ 14,000
Accounts payable	50,000	53,000	3,000
Wages payable	2,000	1,500	(500)
Income taxes payable	9,000	13,400	4,400
Bonds payable	100,000	50,000	(50,000)
Premium on bonds payable	5,000	1,700	(3,300)
Common stock, par $10	300,000	306,000	6,000
Contributed capital in excess of par	15,000	18,000	3,000
Retained earnings	28,000	16,400	(11,600)
	$574,000	$539,000	$(35,000)

Statement of income:

Sales revenue	$399,100
Cost of goods sold	(224,400)
Depreciation expense	(14,000)
Patent amortization	(200)
Bond premium amortization	3,300
Salary expense	(80,000)
Income tax expense	(18,000)
Interest expense	(7,700)
Remaining expense (includes insurance expense)	(44,000)
Interest revenue	900
Extraordinary gain	10,000
Net income	$ 25,000

Analysis of selected accounts and transactions:

a. Purchased operational asset, cost $9,000; payment by issuing 600 shares of stock.
b. Payment at maturity date to retire bonds payable, $50,000.
c. Sold the long-term investments for $40,000, net of tax.
d. Error in recording prior years' income taxes; paid during 19B (a prior period adjustment), $6,600.
e. Purchased land, $28,400; paid cash.
f. Cash dividends declared and paid, $30,000.

Required:

Prepare a SCF, direct method (schedule approach).

P 19–3 (SCF, Direct Method; Schedule Approach)

The records of Easy Trading Company provided the following information: and the year ended December 31, 19B:

Statement of income, 19B:

Sales revenue	$80,000
Cost of goods sold	(35,000)
Depreciation expense	(5,000)
Bad debts expense	(1,000)
Insurance expense	(1,000)
Interest expense	(2,000)
Salaries and wages expense	(12,000)
Income tax expense	(3,000)
Remaining expenses	(13,000)
Loss on sale of operational assets	(2,000)
Net income	$ 6,000

Statement of financial position:

	1/1/19B	12/31/19B
Cash	$ 15,000	$ 31,000
Accounts receivable	30,000	28,500
Allowance for doubtful accounts	(1,500)	(2,000)
Inventory	10,000	15,000
Prepaid insurance	2,400	1,400
Operational assets	80,000	81,000
Accumulated depreciation	(20,000)	(16,000)
Land	40,100	81,100
Total	$156,000	$220,000
Accounts payable	$ 10,000	$ 11,000
Wages payable	2,000	1,000
Interest payable		1,000
Notes payable, long term	20,000	46,000
Common stock, nopar	100,000	136,000
Retained earnings	24,000	25,000
Total	$156,000	$220,000

a. Wrote off $500 accounts receivable as uncollectible.

b. Sold operational asset for $4,000 cash (cost, $15,000; accumulated depreciation, $9,000).

c. Issued common stock for $5,000 cash.

d. Declared and paid a cash dividend, $5,000.

e. Purchased land, $20,000 cash.

f. Acquired land for $21,000 and issued common stock as payment in full.

g. Acquired operational assets, cost $16,000; issued a $16,000, three-year, interest-bearing note payable.

h. Paid a $10,000 long-term maturity by issuing common stock to the creditor.

i. Borrowed cash on long-term note, $20,000.

Required:

Prepare a SCF, direct method (schedule approach).

P 19–4 (SCF, Indirect Method; Schedule Approach)

This problem uses the data given in Problem 19–3. No additional information is needed.

Required:
Prepare a SCF, indirect basis using the schedule approach. Indicate sources of data and computations.

P 19–5 (SCF, Indirect Method: Schedule Approach)
The statements of income and financial position of Kenwood Company and a related analysis are given below.

KENWOOD COMPANY
Statement of Income
For the Year Ended December 31, 19B

Sales revenue	$1,000,000
Expenses and losses:	
Cost of goods sold	560,000
Salaries and wages	190,000
Depreciation	20,000
Patent amortization	3,000
Loss on sale of equipment	4,000
Interest expense	16,000
Miscellaneous expenses	8,000
Total expenses	801,000
Income before income taxes and extraordinary item	199,000
Income tax expense (including tax on the EO gain)*	90,000
Income before extraordinary item	109,000
Extraordinary item—gain on early extinguishment of long-term bonds payable ($10,000* income tax)	12,000
Net income	$121,000

* Total income tax, $90,000.

The SFP is shown on p. 958.

Analysis of selected accounts and transactions:

a. On February 2, 19B, Kenwood issued a 10% stock dividend to stockholders of record on January 15, 19B. The market price per share of the common stock on February 2, 19B, was $15.

b. On March 1, 19B, Kenwood issued 3,800 shares of common stock for land. The common stock had a current market value of approximately $40,000 on March 1, 19B.

c. On April 15, 19B, Kenwood repurchased its long-term bonds payable with a face value of $50,000 for cash. The gain of $22,000 was correctly reported as an extraordinary item on the income statement because this early extinguishment of the bonds payable occurred prior to their maturity date (12/15/19K).

d. On June 30, 19B, Kenwood sold equipment that cost $53,000, with a book value of $23,000, for $19,000 cash.

e. On September 30, 19B, Kenwood declared and paid a 4 cents per share cash dividend to stockholders of record on August 1, 19B.

f. On October 10, 19B, Kenwood purchased land for $85,000 cash.

Required:
Prepare the SCF schedules, indirect method (i.e., use the schedule approach).
(AICPA adapted)

KENWOOD COMPANY
Comparative Statement of Financial Position

Assets	**December 31 19B**	**19A**
Current assets:		
Cash	$ 100,000	$ 90,000
Accounts receivable (net of allowance for doubtful accounts of $10,000 and $8,000, respectively)	210,000	140,000
Inventory	260,000	220,000
Total current assets	570,000	450,000
Land	325,000	200,000
Plant and equipment	580,000	633,000
Less: Accumulated depreciation	(90,000)	(100,000)
Patents	30,000	33,000
Total assets	$1,415,000	$1,216,000

Liabilities and Stockholders' Equity	**December 31 19B**	**19A**
Liabilities:		
Curent liabilities:		
Accounts payable	$ 260,000	$ 200,000
Salaries and wages payable	200,000	210,000
Income tax payable	140,000	100,000
Total current liabilities	600,000	510,000
Bonds payable (due 12/15/19K)	130,000	180,000
Total liabilities	730,000	690,000
Stockholders' equity:		
Common stock, par value $5, authorized 100,000 shares, issued and outstanding 50,000 and 42,000 shares, respectively	250,000	210,000
Additional paid-in capital	233,000	170,000
Retained earnings	202,000	146,000
Total stockholders' equity	685,000	526,000
Total liabilities and stockholders' equity	$1,415,000	$1,216,000

P 19–6 **(SCF, Direct Method)**

This problem uses the data given in Problem 19–5. No additional information is needed.

Required:

Prepare the SCF schedules, direct method (i.e., use the schedule approach). Indicate sources of data and computations.

P 19–7 **(SCF, Direct Method; Prepare Spreadsheet)**

At December 31, 19A, the following data for Lincoln Company were available:

Statement of financial position:

	December 31		Increase
	19A	**19B**	**(decrease)**
Debits			
Cash	$ 4,000	$ 11,000	$ 7,000
Accounts receivable (net)	9,000	12,000	3,000
Inventory	8,000	5,000	(3,000)
Long-term investments	2,000		(2,000)
Plant	30,000	30,000	
Equipment	20,000	22,000	2,000
Land	10,000	40,000	30,000
Patents	8,000	7,000	(1,000)
	$91,000	$127,000	$36,000
Credits			
Accumulated depreciation—plant	$ 7,000	$ 10,000	$ 3,000
Accumulated depreciation—equipment	10,000	8,000	(2,000)
Accounts payable	8,000	2,000	(6,000)
Wages payable	1,000		(1,000)
Notes payable, long term	10,000	19,000	9,000
Common stock, nopar	50,000	75,000	25,000
Retained earnings	5,000	13,000	8,000
	$91,000	$127,000	$36,000

Statement of income:

Sales revenue	$90,000
Cost of goods sold	(55,000)
Depreciation expense, plant	(3,000)
Depreciation expense, equipment	(2,000)
Patent amortization	(1,000)
Remaining expenses	(20,000)
Loss on sale of equipment	(1,000)
Income tax expense (including tax on EO gain)	(4,000)
Income from continuing operations	4,000
Extraordinary item: Gain on sale of long-term investment (net of $2,000 tax)	8,000
Net income	$12,000

Analysis of selected accounts and entries:

a. At the end of the year, sold equipment that cost $8,000 (50% depreciated) for $3,000 cash (this was not an extraordinary item).

b. Purchased land that cost $10,000; paid $2,000 cash, gave long-term note for the balance.

c. Paid $4,000 to retire long-term note payable at maturity.

d. Sold $10,000 common stock at par.
e. Purchased equipment costing $10,000; paid half in cash, balance due in three years (interest-bearing note).
f. Issued 1,500 shares of common stock, market value $15,000, for land that cost $20,000, the balance paid in cash.
g. Sold the long-term investments for $10,000 cash.
h. Declared and paid dividends, $4,000.

Required:
1. Prepare a SCF, direct method spreadsheet,
2. Prepare the SCF.

P 19–8 **(SCF, Indirect Method, Schedule Approach)**
This problem uses the data given in Problem 19–7. No additional information is needed.

Required:
Prepare the SCF schedules, indirect method (i.e., use the schedule approach). Indicate sources and computations.

P 19–9 **(SCF, Direct Method; Spreadsheet)**
The records of ABE Company provided the following data for the accounting year ended December 31, 19B:

Comparative statement of financial position, December 31, 19B:

	12/31/19A	12/31/19B	Increase (decrease)
Debits			
Cash	$ 30,000	$ 69,000	$39,000
Investment, short term (X Co. stock)	10,000	8,000	(2,000)
Accounts receivable	56,000	86,000	30,000
Inventory	20,000	30,000	10,000
Prepaid interest (expense)		2,000	2,000
Land	60,000	25,000	(35,000)
Machinery	80,000	90,000	10,000
Other assets	29,000	39,000	10,000
Discount on bonds payable	1,000	900	(100)
Total debits	$286,000	$349,900	$63,900
Credits			
Allowance for doubtful accounts	$ 6,000	$ 7,000	$ 1,000
Accumulated depreciation	20,000	26,900	6,900
Accounts payable	33,000	45,000	12,000
Salaries payable	5,000	2,000	(3,000)
Income taxes payable	2,000	8,000	6,000
Bonds payable	70,000	55,000	(15,000)
Common stock, nopar	100,000	131,000	31,000
Preferred stock, nopar	20,000	30,000	10,000
Retained earnings	30,000	45,000	15,000
Total credits	$286,000	$349,900	$63,900

Statement of income:

Sales revenue	$180,000
Cost of goods sold	(90,000)
Depreciation expense	(6,900)
Amortization of bond discount	(100)
Bad debt expense	(1,000)
Salaries	(32,900)
Interest expense	(6,000)
Remaining expenses	(4,000)
Income tax expense*	(12,100)
Gain on sale of land, condemnation (income tax, $5,400)	18,000
Loss on bond retirement (tax saving, $300)	(1,000)
Net income	$ 44,000

* Total income tax, $12,100, including the effects of additional tax on the gain and the tax saving on the loss.

Analysis of selected accounts and transaction:

1. Issued bonds payable for cash, $5,000.
2. Sold land due to condemnation for $53,000 cash; book value, $35,000; extraordinary item, net of tax.
3. Purchased machinery for cash, $10,000.
4. Purchased short-term investments for cash, $2,000.
5. Declared a property dividend on the preferred stock and paid it with a short-term investment (X Company stock); market value and carrying value are the same, $4,000.
6. Prior to maturity date, retired $20,000 bonds payable by issuing common stock; the common stock had a market value of $21,000.
7. Acquired other assets by issuing preferred stock with a market value of $10,000.
8. Statement of retained earnings:

Balance, January 1, 19B	$30,000
Net income for 19B	44,000
Dividends paid, cash	(15,000)
Stock dividend issued, common stock	(10,000)
Property dividend, X Company stock	(4,000)
Balance, December 31, 19B	$45,000

Required:

1. Prepare a spreadsheet to develop a SCF, direct method.
2. Prepare the SCF, direct method.

P 19–10 (SCF, Indirect Method; Schedule Approach)

This problem uses the data given in Problem 19–9. No additional information is needed.

Required:

Prepare a SCF, indirect method using the schedule approach. Indicate sources and computations.

P 19–11 **(SCF, Indirect Method; Complete Spreadsheet)**
The statements of income and financial position and analysis of selected accounts of Summer Company are given below.

Statement of financial position:

	12/31/19A	12/31/19B	Increase (decrease)
Debits			
Cash plus short-term investments	$ 40,000	$ 44,900	$ 4,900
Accounts receivable (net)	60,000	52,500	(7,500)
Merchandise inventory (perpetual)	180,000	141,600	(38,400)
Prepaid insurance	2,400	1,200	(1,200)
Investments, long term	30,000		(30,000)
Land	10,000	38,400	28,400
Operational assets	250,000	259,000	9,000
Patent (net)	1,600	1,400	(200)
	$574,000	$539,000	$(35,000)
Credits			
Accumulated depreciation	$ 65,000	$ 79,000	$ 14,000
Accounts payable	50,000	53,000	3,000
Wages payable	2,000	1,500	(500)
Income taxes payable	9,000	13,400	4,400
Bonds payable	100,000	50,000	(50,000)
Premium on bonds payable	5,000	1,700	(3,300)
Common stock, par $10	300,000	306,000	6,000
Contributed capital in excess of par	15,000	18,000	3,000
Retained earnings	28,000	16,400	(11,600)
	$574,000	$539,000	$(35,000)

Statement of income:

Sales revenue	$400,000
Cost of goods sold	(224,400)
Depreciation expense	(14,000)
Patent amortization	(200)
Bond premium amortization	3,300
Remaining expenses (including interest)	(149,700)
Extraordinary gain	10,000
Net income	$ 25,000

Analysis of selected accounts and entries:

a. Purchased operational asset, cost $9,000; payment by issuing 600 shares of stock.
b. Payment at maturity date to retire bonds payable, $50,000.
c. Sold the long-term investments for $40,000.
d. Purchased land, $28,400; paid cash.
e. Retained earnings, beginning balance

Retained earnings, beginning balance	$28,000
Prior period adjustment, income tax, paid in 19B	(6,600)
Net income, 19B	25,000
Cash dividend paid	(30,000)
Ending balance	$16,400

Required:
1. Prepare a SCF, indirect method spreadsheet.
2. Prepare the SCF.

P 19–12 (SCF, Indirect Method, Spreadsheet Approach; an Adapted Actual Case; Complex and Challenging)

The following data relating to Acres Company were available on December 31, 19C:

Comparative Statement of Financial Position

	19B		19C	
Cash		$ 8,000		$ 9,000
Accounts receivable	$19,000		$16,000	
Less: Allowance for doubtful accounts	1,000	18,000	1,000	15,000
Inventory at lower of cost or market		45,000		44,000
Long-term investment, Jones, Inc. (equity method)				15,000
Long-term investment, Campbell Company:				
Common stock, at cost	14,000		12,000	
Less: Allowance to reduce to market	2,000	12,000	-0-	12,000
Property, plant, and equipment	60,000		74,000	
Less: Accumulated depreciation	18,000	42,000	19,000	55,000
Total assets		$125,000		$150,000
Accounts payable		$ 6,000		$ 11,300
Income taxes payable		2,000		4,000
Deferred income taxes payable, current		2,000		3,000
Current maturity on serial bonds payable		1,000		1,000
Deferred income taxes payable, long term				1,000
Serial bonds payable, 5%, maturing in $1,000 annual serials beginning 1/1/19A		22,000		21,000
Premium on serial bonds payable		1,100		1,050
Notes payable, long term				4,000
Common stock, par $10		45,000		50,000
Contributed capital in excess of par		3,900		5,000
Retained earnings		44,000		48,650
Unrealized loss on long-term investments		(2,000)		
Total equities		$125,000		$150,000

Statement of Income
Year Ended December 31, 19C

Sales revenue		$100,000
Cost of goods sold		65,000
Gross margin		35,000
Operating expenses:		
Depreciation	$ 4,000	
Interest	1,050	
Income taxes:		
Current payable	8,000	
Deferred, current	3,000	
Deferred, long term	1,000	17,050
Operating income		17,950
Investment revenue (Jones, Inc.)		2,700
Income before extraordinary items		20,650
Extraordinary items (assumed extraordinary for problem purposes only):		
Realized gain on sale of investments (net of tax)	3,000	
Loss on sale of machinery (net of tax)	1,000	2,000
Net income		$ 22,650

Analysis of selected accounts and transactions:

1. During 19C, part of the long-term investment in the common stock of Campbell Company was sold for $5,000 cash, which is net of tax. The acquisition cost of these shares was $2,000. Assume extraordinary gain or loss (for problem purposes only).

2. During 19C, machinery was sold for $1,000 cash which is net of tax; the cost of this machinery was $5,000; accumulated depreciation to date of disposal was $3,000. Assume extraordinary gain or loss (for problem purposes only).
3. During 19C, Acres Company purchased machinery for $19,000. The total cost was paid in cash except for $4,000 which was financed by a long-term note payable.
4. Dividends declared and paid during 19C amounted to $18,000.
5. During 19C, Acres Company issued 500 shares of common stock at $12.20 per share.
6. As a matter of accounting policy, due to the immateriality of the amounts involved, Acres Company amortizes the premium on the serial bonds payable each year on a straight-line basis (an equal amount each year).
7. Acres' investment in Jones, Inc., is 30% of the outstanding voting common stock of Jones, Inc. The investment was made on January 1, 19C, with a cash outlay of $12,900. This was at book value; therefore, no additional depreciation or amortization will be involved. Acres will account for it using the equity method (no consolidated statements are anticipated).
8. At the end of 19C, Acres recorded $2,700 as its 30% share of Jones; reported net income (debit long-term investment account; credit, investment revenue).
9. During 19C, Jones, Inc., declared and paid cash dividends of $2,000 (entry made by Acres: Debit cash $600; credit long-term investment, Jones, $600).

Required:
1. Prepare a SCF, indirect method, spreadsheet.
2. Prepare the SCF, indirect method.

CASE

C 19–1 (SCF: Direct or Indirect?)

During the FASB considerations there was considerable debate, disagreement, and voting about the direct and indirect methods of reporting operational activities on the SCF. There was considerable pressure on the Board from various groups with no clear preference. The following quotations from *FASB Standard 95,* suggests the diversity of views:

> 107. The principal advantage of the direct method is that it shows operating cash receipts and payments. Knowledge of the specific sources of operating cash receipts and the purposes for which operating cash payments were made in past periods may be useful in estimating future operating cash flows. The relative amounts of major classes of revenues and expenses and their relationship to other items in the financial statements are presumed to be more useful than information only about their arithmetic sum—net income—in assessing enterprise performance.
>
> 108. The principal advantage of the indirect method is that it focuses on the differences between net income and net cash flow from operating activities.
>
> 109. Many providers of financial statements have said that it would be costly for their companies to report gross operating cash receipts and payments. They said that they do not presently collect information in a manner that will allow them to determine amounts such as cash received from customers or cash paid to suppliers directly from their accounting systems.
>
> 111. A majority of respondents to the Exposure Draft asked the Board to require use of the direct method. Those respondents, most of whom were commercial lenders, generally said that amounts of operating cash receipts and payments are particularly important in assessing an enterprise's external borrowing needs and its ability to repay borrowings. They indicated that creditors are more exposed to fluctuations in net cash flow from operating activities than to fluctuations in net income and that information on the amounts of operating cash receipts and payments is important in assessing those fluctuations in net cash flow from

operating activities. They also pointed out that the direct method is more consistent with the objective of a statement of cash flows—to provide information about cash receipts and cash payments—than the indirect method, which does not report operating cash receipts and payments.

As a basis for your analysis of the two methods, make appropriate check marks on each line in the following overview.

Cash inflows and outflows (and related changes)	**Reported on**		
	SCF method		**Comparative statement of financial position**
	Direct	**Indirect**	
1. Cash inflow from sales			
2. Cash inflow from services			
3. Cash inflow from interest			
4. Cash inflow from dividend received			
5. Accounts receivable increase or decrease			
6. Interest receivable increase or decrease			
7. Payments to suppliers (cash purchases)			
8. Inventory increase or decrease			
9. Accounts payable increase or decrease			
10. Payments for salaries and wages			
11. Wages and salaries payable increase or decrease			
12. Payments for income tax			
13. Income taxes payable increase or decrease			
14. Net income			
15. Net cash flow from operating activities			
16. Investing activities			
17. Financing activities			
18. Net increase or decrease in cash during the period			
19. Cash, beginning balance			
20. Cash, ending balance			

Required:

Consider the above comments and your checkoff responses above. *(a)* Prepare an outline of the advantages of each method and *(b)* be prepared to discuss both your outline and your responses in the checkoff overview.

20 ACCOUNTING FOR PENSION PLANS BY EMPLOYERS

OVERVIEW AND PURPOSE

Most people are concerned about their future retirement benefits. Since the early 1900s these concerns have resulted in numerous public and private retirement programs—social security, company retirement programs for employees, and private programs including tax-sheltered savings plans. If a person is knowledgeable about these opportunities, and consistently takes advantage of them, financial security after actual retirement is assured. In this chapter you will learn about company (employer) pension plans. Often these plans provide the major source of retirement dollars. These plans have experienced tremendous growth in the number of employees involved and the amount of resources set aside to pay the retirement benefits earned. For example, in 1975 the approximate data were: persons covered, 28 million; resources set aside to pay the promised retirement benefits, $215 billion; and retirement benefits paid, $15.8 billion. In contrast, recent projections for 1995 are: 48 million persons, $3.0 trillion resources, and $50 billion in benefits. A recent survey of 600 major companies found that 560 of them reported pension and retirement plans.[1] For many companies, pension expense is a large part of total expenses. Companies establish pension plans and pay for the employees' future pension benefits because they believe that this will motivate the employees to be more productive during the service years when the benefits are "earned."

The purpose of this chapter is to discuss company (i.e., employer) spònsored pension plans. Emphasis is on the characteristics of these plans and how the employer should record, report, and disclose their economic effects on the company. Financial reporting is needed to inform investors, management, and employees of the status of **their** retirement program. To accomplish this purpose, the chapter is subdivided as follows:

Part A: Fundamentals of Accounting for Pension Plans

1. Characteristics of employer pension plans.
2. Application of *FASB Statement of Financial Accounting Standard 87*, "Employers' Accounting for Pensions."
3. Special procedures used in pension accounting.
4. Employer's comprehensive spreadsheet to determine pension entries and reporting.

Part B: Additional Pension Plan Issues

Amortization of losses and gains—more details.
2. Additional minimum pension liability.
3. Reporting, including note disclosures.
4. Comprehensive three-year demonstration case.
5. Curtailments and settlements of pension plans, and termination benefits.

Supplement 20-A: Alternative Methods of Amortizing Unrecognized Pension Costs

[1] AICPA, *Accounting Trends & Techniques,* Annual Survey of Accounting Practices Followed in 600 Stockholders' Reports (New York, 1987), p. 274.

PART A: FUNDAMENTALS OF ACCOUNTING FOR PENSION PLANS

The importance of pension plans involves two issues: *(a)* the pension costs and liabilities reported by the employer and *(b)* the pension funds accumulated to pay retirement benefits to retired employees. Concerning the latter issue, an article appeared in *The Wall Street Journal* (November 2, 1987) entitled "Pension Funds: New Power, New Responsibility." The first two paragraphs stated:

> Pension funds, long the most staid and quiet of shareholders, have suddenly awakened to the tremendous power they command. Public and private pension systems now own close to half the stock of all companies listed in the S&P 500. (Even after "black Monday," most funds, looking to the long term, did not sell.) New York state's pension fund alone can vote up to 2% of most major U.S. corporations. On the verge of becoming majority shareholders in corporate America, pension funds are beginning to flex their muscles.
>
> It used to be that resolutions introduced by shareholders at annual meetings, even the most publicized, typically attracted no more than 3% of the vote. But in the past 18 months, pension funds have initiated resolutions that tallied 15% to 40% of the vote. That a movement so powerful could emerge so suddenly has taken everyone by surprise—not least of all the pension funds themselves. It is the result of three converging trends: mounting social pressures, takeover-generated battles for corporate control, and the sheer size of pension funds.

This chapter recognizes these broad economic impacts by focusing on the accounting and reporting of pension plan assets, funds, liabilities, and costs (or expenses).

Characteristics of Employer Pension Plans

In simple terms an employer pension plan involves promises to make retirement payments to employees starting after a specified retirement date. To accomplish this objective, the company (employer) pension plan typically includes the following phases:

- **a.** Establish a formal (i.e., written) **pension plan** which specifies such **policies** as: employee eligibility requirements, basis for computing retirement benefits that will be paid, how the assets needed to support the retirement benefits will be accumulated (called **funding**) and how those assets will be administered.
- **b.** During the employment period record **pension expense** and the pension liability, and make **cash payments** to the designated pension fund. The pension fund usually is administered by an outside independent entity (called the **trustee**).
- **c.** During the employee's retirement period assure that the retiree is paid the promised retirement benefit from the pension fund.

The Pension Plan. A company may set up either a defined benefit or a defined contribution pension plan. **A defined benefit** pension plan involves a promise by the employer to each employee to provide retirement benefits at retirement based on a specified formula. The primary variables in the formula are: *(a)* years of qualified service (employment), *(b)* average annual compensation as an employee (often the annual average for the last three years prior to retirement), and *(c)* age.[2] Under these plans the formula for computing future resources to be expended is specified. The retirement benefits can be realistically estimated, but the amount of cash funding is uncertain. Therefore, the cash that must be paid to the pension fund each year during the employment period requires numerous estimates and **a present value** computation (discussed later).

A **defined contribution** pension plan involves a promise by the employer to each employee to pay a specified amount of cash each period into a pension fund (such as 5% of the employee's salary). No promise is made about the amount of the retirement benefits; the employees will receive only what the pension fund can "afford" during the retirement period. The payments to the fund are certain but retirement benefits are uncertain.

Notice that the risk of pension plan performance (i.e., earnings) is borne by the employer in a defined benefit plan and by the employees in a defined contribution plan. Most company pension plans are defined benefit plans because of their *(a)* higher motivational impact on the employees, *(b)* income tax advantage (discussed below), and *(c)* recognition in ERISA (discussed below).

The employer's accounting for a defined contribution plan is simple because the **only entry** made in the accounts is a debit to pension expense, and a credit to cash, for each payment to the pension fund. In contrast, accounting for a defined benefit plan is both complex and controversial because the future retirement benefits (a liability for the company) must be translated (using present value concepts) to current payments to the pension fund and pension expense.

Another distinction among pension plans is whether they are contributory or noncontributory. A **contributory pension plan** specifies that *(a)* the employees must pay a part of the funding needed to provide the specified benefits, or *(b)* they may voluntarily pay additional cash to the pension fund to increase their retirement benefits. A **noncontributory pension plan** means that the employer will provide all of the funding.

There are a number of tax, legal, and accounting considerations involved in designing an appropriate pension plan for a particular company.

Income Tax Considerations. Most pension plans are established formally by the employer to meet Internal Revenue Code qualifications so that:

1. Cash paid by the employer into the pension plan is deductible by the employer for income tax purposes when contributed.
2. Earnings of the pension fund are not subject to income tax.
3. Employer contributions on behalf of employees are not taxable to employees when the contributions are made.
4. Retirement benefits are taxable to retirees; this defers income tax, which is favorable to employees because they are usually in lower income tax brackets when they retire than during their employment period.

[2] *FASB Statement of Financial Accounting Standards No. 87* "Employers' Accounting for Pensions," (Stamford, Conn.: December 1985), par. 11.

Legal Considerations. Federal legislation, entitled The Employees Retirement Income Security Act of 1974 (ERISA), has had a substantial impact on the funding and administration of pension plans. It requires employers with **defined benefit plans** to fund the future benefits (i.e., set aside cash in a pension fund). Prior to this act, employers had the option of funding or not funding in advance. ERISA created the Pension Benefit Guaranty Corporation (PBGC), which has as its primary purpose the administration of terminated plans. Also, the PBGC must monitor all private pension plans to determine the risks of ultimate nonpayment of pension benefits. ERISA provided incentives for certain companies to withdraw from multiemployer pension plans, which are maintained jointly by two or more unrelated employers (i.e., not under common control). Congress later passed the Multiemployer Pension Plan Amendment Act of 1980. This legislation provides for increased employer obligations (especially for unfunded vested benefits) for multiemployer plans and made PBGC coverage of multiemployer plans mandatory. In combination, these two acts restricted the flexibility of private pension plan arrangements and made funding mandatory.

Accounting Considerations. Accounting for pensions involves two entities: (1) the **employer** whose employees are covered by the pension plan and (2) the **funding agency** (i.e., a trustee). Accounting by the employer involves the recognition of pension expense and the payment of cash into a pension fund administered by the funding agency.

In contrast, accounting by the funding agency relates to investment of the pension fund assets and pension payments to retirees. *FASB Standard 35,* "Accounting and Reporting by Defined Benefit Plans" (March 1980), addresses financial reporting by "pension plans" as separate entities. *FASB Standard 35* is not concerned with issues relating to financial statement disclosures by employers regarding the plans they initiate. This chapter does not discuss accounting by the funding agency.

The discussions and illustrations in this chapter primarily focus on accounting, funding, and reporting for **defined benefit pension plans by the employer.** This topic has five primary phases:

1. Estimating the pension benefits that will be paid to each employee after retirement.
2. Estimating the amount of the employer's required cash contribution to the pension fund. This amount, plus the fund's earnings, will be used to pay the retirement benefits to retired employees.
3. Allocating the employer's pension cost, in a rational and systematic manner, as expense to the accounting periods during which the employer receives the productive benefits from the qualified employees.
4. Estimating the amount of the employer's pension liability.
5. Monitoring and adjusting cash contributions and pension expense for changes in expectations concerning the pension plan and the factors that affect it. These include factors such as earnings on the pension fund, changes in pension benefits, and revisions of mortality rates.

The accounting and reporting for pension plans discused in this chapter are based on *FASB Standards 87* and *88*.[3]

Concepts that Underlie Pension Accounting

The basic concepts that underlie pension accounting are as follows:

a. **Accounting entities**—the employer and the funding agency (i.e., the trustee) are separate and independent entities. Each one maintains its own accounting system. The employer records cash contributions to the pension fund, periodic pension expense, and pension liabilities.

b. **Actuary**—typically, the employer engages an outside **actuary** to provide professional actuarial estimates each year about the economics of the pension plan. Each year the actuary, in consultation with the company's executives, provides the company with a detailed report, which gives the basic data about *(a)* pension expense and *(b)* pension obligations (i.e., pension liabilities). A defined benefit pension plan specifies the pension benefit promised to each employee on retirement. The amount of the benefit is determined by the pension plan formula which is based on the pension policies specified in the pension plan. **Actuarial factors** are the data used by the actuary to determine the present value of pension funding needed, pension expense, and pension liabilities. Actuarial determinations and estimates provided by the actuary are an integral part of accounting for pension costs because such costs are future oriented. Therefore, measures of pension costs are uncertain. Actuarial factors which pension actuaries must estimate include retirement age, mortality (the life expectancies of employees), employee turnover, interest rates, administrative requirements, future salary levels, pension benefits, and vesting provisions. **Vesting** (or vested benefits) refers to an employee's right to receive a pension benefit even though that person does not remain an employee of the company until retirement. Vesting benefits are specified in the pension plan because they are important to employees and they have a major effect on the actuary's estimates. Since vesting is an add-on benefit it increases both pension expense and pension funding. The pension plan may not specify any vesting benefits, or it may specify full vesting as pension credits are earned. Partial vesting sometimes is specified, such as, no vesting for the first 5 years, 50% during the next 5 years, and 100% after 10 years.

c. **Funding**—in noncontributory pension plans all of the funding is provided by *(a)* the employer and *(b)* the earnings on the pension fund. Funding refers to the cash payments to a pension fund and the accumulated earnings. Funding may be handled in three ways:

   1. Internal pension fund—cash is set aside and invested by the company in a pension fund administered internally by the company.

---

[3] *FASB Standard 87* supercedes *APB Opinion 8* (as amended), *FASB Standard 36*, and *FASB Interpretation 3*. In addition, paragraphs 70 and 75 of *FASB Standard 87* amend *FASB Standard 5* and *APB Opinion 16* (*FASB Standard 87*, par. 9).

2. Independent pension fund—cash is paid to an independent pension funding agency that invests and administers the pension fund and makes the payments to the retirees.
3. Purchase of a retirement annuity—cash is paid to an insurance company to purchase retirement annuities for the retirees. The insurance company then accepts the responsibility for paying the pension benefits to the retirees.

Approaches 1 and 3 are used primarily for defined contribution pension plans. Approach 2 usually is used for defined benefit pension plans. Under this approach an independent funding agency (i.e., the trustee), such as a bank or pension fund company, administers the funding plan. Under this arrangement, the employer gives cash to the funding agency. The funding agency invests the cash in securities and other assets, receives revenue from pension plan investments to increase the fund, and on retirement of employees, pays cash (i.e., pension benefits) to retirees. The funding agency also is paid an administrative fee from the fund. Since a pension fund earns a return on the assets of the fund, the employer will disburse less cash into the fund than is paid out to the retirees. The assets held by the fund at any point in time have a carrying value equal to the cumulative payments received from the employer plus the cumulative net earnings on the fund assets minus the cumulative retirement benefits paid to retirees.

The two critical problems in a pension plan usually are *(a)* the periodic cash payments to the fund by the employer and *(b)* reporting the full amount of the pension liability. Because cash shortages are common in many companies and for other reasons, there is a strong tendency to make minimum payments, or to defer payments, to a pension fund. As a consequence, pension plans often are underfunded; that is, the resources of the pension plan are inadequate to support the future pension benefits.

d. **Basic accounting entries**—accounting for a pension plan by the employer (not the funding agency) involves three distinct phases during the employment period:
   1. Determination of the amount of pension expense that must be recognized each year and reported in the current statement of income.
   2. Determination of the amount of cash that will be paid into the pension fund each year.
   3. Determination of the accrued (prepaid) pension obligations. Amounts 1 and 2 may be the same in a given year (i.e., when the expense amount is fully funded during the year) or different (i.e., when the expense is either underfunded or overfunded during the year).

To illustrate the basic accounting entries, assume the correct amount of pension expense in 19A is $40,000 (computation discussed later). The basic entry for each of the three cases (fully funded, underfunded, and overfunded) is:

1. **Fully funded** (cash paid into pension fund is $40,000):

Pension expense	40,000	
Cash		40,000

2. **Underfunded** (cash paid into pension fund is $35,000). The underfunding causes an **accrued pension cost** (a **liability**):

Pension expense	40,000	
Accrued pension cost*		5,000
Cash		35,000

3. **Overfunded** (cash paid into pension fund is $45,000). The overfunding creates a **prepaid pension cost** (an **asset**):

Pension expense	40,000	
Prepaid pension cost*	5,000	
Cash		45,000

* *FASB Standard 87* uses "Accrued/prepaid" in journal entries. This chapter also uses this designation.

e. **Application of present value concepts**—implementation of the above phases requires the application of present value concepts, **primarily by the actuary.** For a defined benefit pension plan, the future retirement benefits promised by the employer, as specified in the pension plan formula, must be computed by the actuary. With this information available the next step is to compute the present value (PV) of these future benefits. This PV is called the **projected benefit obligation** (PBO) because it is the current liability of the employer to fund the pension plan. Both funding and pension expense are related to this amount.

To adequately comprehend pension plan accounting it is helpful to understand the way that present values are used in a pension plan. To accomplish this instructional purpose a hypothetical case is used (i.e., Hypo Company). Basically, this case is designed *(a)* to show how pension expense and cash funding are computed and *(b)* to illustrate the distinction between the accounting by the employer and the funding agency. To avoid complexities at this time we assume one employee (J. Doe) and a very specific retirement benefit, $10,000 per year for 12 years. **Exhibit 20–1** gives the simplified case data. Panel B shows a diagram application of the basic concepts applied by the actuary, and panel C shows the basic entries by the employer and the pension fund agency. The entries by the agency are not discussed further in this chapter.

In studying this background case notice the following:

1. **Actuary**—based on the promised benefits specified in the pension plan, and an agreement with the company about the applicable interest rates and actuarial estimates, the actuary computes the projected benefit obligation (PBO). Basically, this computation involves three steps: *(a)* compute the PV of the future benefits as of the expected retirement date (e.g., in the Hypo case, at a 9% interest rate, $71,607), *(b)* compute the PV of the amount derived in *(a)* at the current date (at an 8% discount rate in this case); this amount ($22,573) is called the **projected benefit obligation** (PBO), and *(c)* using the PBO amount and the discount rate, compute the annual pension expense and funding amounts needed ($2,637). These two amounts are the same in this case because the pension cost is fully funded, and certain complexities in computing pension expense did not apply (discussed later).
2. **Employer and funding agency**—the basic entries for each of these independent entities are compared in panel C.

Exhibit 20–1

Pension fund accumulation and disbursement, Hypo Company (for a single employee).

Panel A—Case Data:

Hypo Company adopted a noncontributory, defined benefit pension plan on January 1, 19C, which covered all employees. Under the plan, J. Doe, an employee since January 1, 19C, is to receive pension benefits. The plan specifies that at the end of 15 years, Doe will retire, whereupon Doe will receive retirement benefits of $10,000, at each year-end, for a period of 12 years.

It is estimated that the fund will earn a net 8% interest rate during the accumulation (funding) period, and 9% during the disbursement (retirement) period.

Required:

Assuming full funding (i.e., cash payments to a pension fund) each year-end by Hypo Company and no change in Doe's promised benefits, compute the following: *(a)* the present value (PV) of the benefits on Doe's retirement date, *(b)* the PV of the promised benefits on Doe's employment date (called the **projected benefit obligation,** or PBO), and *(c)* the annual year-end funding payments to be made by Hypo Company.

Panel B—Response Diagrammed and Computed for One Employee, J. Doe:

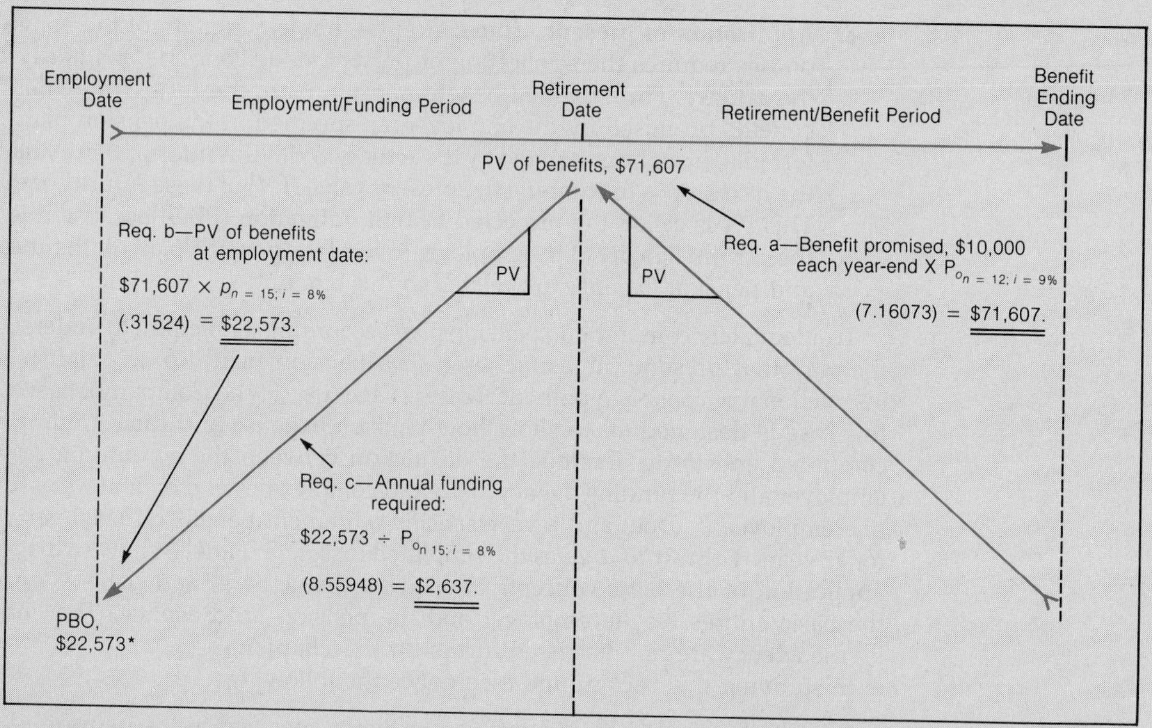

Panel C—Basic Entries:

By employer each year during period of employment (the subject of this chapter):*

Pension expense	2,637	
Cash (to fund trustee)		2,637

By funding agency each year during period of employment (not discussed in this chapter):

Cash (from Hypo Company)	2,637	
Pension liability		2,637

By funding agency each year during period of retirement (not discussed in this chapter):†

Pension liability	10,000	
Cash		10,000

* In conformity with *FASB Standard 87* (discussed later), this pension expense amount is provided each year by the actuary in the projected benefit obligation (PBO). Changes in the pension plan and fund earnings may cause these amounts to vary in later years.

† Also, numerous entries are made to record the operations of the pension fund.

This concludes the overview of how the pension accounting by the employer relates to the activities of the actuary and the funding agency. The remainder of this chapter will focus on *(a)* how the **employer** uses the projected benefit obligation (PBO) and data about the pension plan assets, and *(b)* the recording, reporting, and note disclosures for a defined benefit pension plan. This overview will significantly help you to understand the complexities, and the FASB guidelines, which follow.

Application of *FASB Statement of Financial Accounting Standard 87*, "Employers' Accounting for Pensions"

Objectives of *FASB Standard 87*. *FASB Standard 87* was issued in December 1985. It superceded *APB Opinion 8*, "Accounting for the Cost of Pension Plans," which was issued in November 1966. Recognizing that *APB Opinion 8* was controversial and technically burdensome, *FASB Standard 87* (par. 6) states that its objectives are (emphasis supplied):

a. To provide a measure of net periodic pension cost* that is more **representationally faithful** than those used in past practice because it reflects the terms of the underlying plan and because it better approximates the recognition of the cost of an employee's pension over that employee's service period.
b. To provide a measure of net periodic pension cost that is more **understandable and comparable** and is, therefore, more useful than those in past practice.
c. To provide **disclosures** that will allow users to understand better the extent and effect of an employer's undertaking to provide employee pensions and related financial arrangements.
d. To **improve reporting** of financial positions.

* *FASB Standard 87* states that it uses the term net periodic pension *cost* rather than net pension *expense* because part of the cost recognized in a period may be capitalized along with other costs as part of an asset such as inventory.

FASB Standard 87 (par. 5) states that pension accounting is in a transitional stage, and therefore, the statement is evolutionary and not likely to be the final step in pension accounting.

Effective Dates of *FASB Standard 87*. In an effort to mitigate the impact of the accounting changes, *FASB Standard 87* established a **phased transition** as follows:

1. *FASB Standard 87* is effective for reporting years beginning after December 15, 1986 (i.e., statements dated December 15, 1987, or later).
2. Certain pension related liabilities do not have to be accrued prior to reporting years beginning after December 15, 1988. These liabilities are discussed under the heading **Additional Minimum Pension Liability** on page 996.
3. For pension plans *(a)* outside the United States or *(b)* for nonpublic enterprises that have no plan with more than 100 employees, the effective date is for reporting years beginning after December 15, 1988.
4. In all cases, earlier application is encouraged.

Scope of *FASB Standard 87.* *FASB Standard 87* is directed primarily to single-employer defined benefit pension plans. However, its provisions apply to all pension plans regardless of the manner of financing the plan or whether the plan is written or implied. *FASB Standard 87* **does not** apply to *(a)* life and health benefits during employment or *(b)* postemployment life and health care benefits.[4]

Accounting Specifications in *FASB Standard 87.* Pension accounting requires recognition of periodic pension expense and cash funding before the actual payment of benefits to the retirees. Therefore, pension accounting requires the use of:

1. **Assumptions** (i.e., estimates) about *(a)* future events that will determine the amount and timing of the benefit payments and *(b)* factors that affect the current cost (i.e., the present value) of the future benefit payments.
2. An accounting approach to **attribute** (allocate) the cost of pension benefits as **expense** to the individual years of service of the qualified employees.

FASB Standard 87 provides guidelines for using the pension benefit formula to determine information about pension plan assets, pension obligations, and periodic pension expense. *FASB Standard 87* specifies that the **measurement dates** for plan assets and obligations are "as of the date of the financial statements or, if used consistently from year to year, as of a date not more than three months prior to that date." This provision gives flexibility in assembling the various estimates needed for year-end accounting purposes. For example, most companies whose annual accounting period ends on December 31 will request that the actuary's report be received and dated September 30 of the current year. Often the three-month period is needed for the company to assimilate the contents of the actuary's report into the year-end adjusting and closing procedures. For a large company the actuary's annual report is a large and complex document.

Prior to an illustration of pension plan accounting by the employer a discussion of the unique characteristics and terminology of defined benefit pension plans is necessary. The next section discusses these topics.

Assumptions Related to Pension Plan. Accounting for pension plans is significantly affected by **assumptions** about future events. Both pension expense and cash funding are determined by the future uncertain retirement benefits that will be paid to retired employees. These future benefit payments must be estimated in current accounting periods, based on current assumptions about future events that will affect pension costs. These assumptions include estimates of mortality rates, interest rates, employee withdrawals and retirements, changes in compensation, and pension benefits set by law. Pension estimates are of direct concern to four parties—the company management, the independent actuary, the company accountants, and the independent auditors.

Pension-related estimates, in large part, are provided by an independent

---

[4] *FASB Standard 87*, pars. 7–9. Throughout this chapter, frequent references are made to specific paragraphs of *FASB Standard 87*. These references are designed to facilitate your use of the *Standard*.

actuary. The actuary provides estimates of *(a)* the funding requirements for a pension plan, *(b)* the present value of the employer's pension-related obligations, and *(c)* the amount of the periodic change in the employer's obligations. Each of these estimates is based on the **present value** of the future employee benefits specified by the **pension benefit formula** in the employer's pension plan. Determining the present value of future benefits requires the use of an estimated interest (i.e., discount) rate. As conditions related to the pension plan change, the actuary reviews and revises the pension estimates used.

The actuary develops the pension estimates by working closely with the company. The detailed personnel records of the company are necessary to provide data about each employee—length of employment, age, and so on. Similarly, the company accountants provide basic financial data about the employees; for example, turnover rates, and wage and salary data needed by the actuary. At the same time the actuary must work with the executive management to attain agreement on the interest discount rates, anticipated changes in the compensation structure, and other variables that may affect the actuary's report. Clearly, it would be impractical for the actuary to work in isolation from the company. Finally, the company accountants record, report, and disclose the financial effects of the pension plan. The external independent auditors request significant amounts of data from the actuary to support the audit process.

Attribution—Allocation of Pension Costs. **Attribution** is used in *FASB Standard 87* to refer to the process of **allocating** or assigning pension costs to the accounting periods in which the employees earn the rights to future pension benefits. The employees earn those rights by providing services to (i.e., working for) the employer. **Attribution is an application of the matching principle—each accounting period, pension costs are matched with the productivity benefits received by the employer from the employees.** *FASB Standard 87* gives the accounting guidelines for allocating each kind of pension cost to the accounting periods in which the employees render productivity benefits to the employer. Later sections will discuss and illustrate attribution of pension costs.

Special Procedures Used in Pension Accounting

FASB Standard 87 states that **accrual accounting** should be applied to pensions. However, three **special characteristics** of past pension accounting are specified even though they are inconsistent with certain features of accrual accounting. These characteristics are: (1) delaying recognition of certain pension-related events, (2) reporting net cost (i.e., net expense), and (3) offsetting liabilities and assets.

Delayed (or deferred) recognition means that certain changes in the employer's pension obligations and changes in the value of pension plan assets are not recorded when they occur. Instead, the changes are recognized systematically over subsequent periods.

The **net cost** characteristic means that various components of periodic pension expense are combined into a single "net" expense amount. For example, *FASB Standard 87* specifies that periodic pension expense should contain the cost of benefits earned by employees during the period, interest cost on the employer's pension obligations, and revenues earned by the pension plan assets. These expenses and revenues along with other pension-related expenses **are netted** to determine net periodic pension expense.

Offsetting allows the reporting of certain recognized pension assets (i.e., prepaid pension cost) and liabilities (accrued pension cost) as net amounts on the employer's statement of financial position. The application of these special characteristics of pension accounting will be discussed in later sections.

Accounting for Defined Benefit Pension Plans

FASB Standard 87 emphasizes the accounting requirements for defined benefit pension plans because such plans are more complex than defined contribution plans. The following basic elements are required by *FASB Standard 87* to account for defined benefit pension plans:

1. Pension benefit obligations of the employer.
2. Pension plan assets.
3. Net periodic pension expense.
4. Accrued/prepaid pension cost.

In the following sections, we discuss each of these elements and illustrate how they are used. In addition, we discuss underfunded or overfunded pension benefit obligation and emphasize how the special characteristics of pension accounting (i.e., delayed recognition, net costs, and offsetting) affect the amounts reported on the employer's financial statements.

Pension Benefit Obligations of the Employer

The **pension benefit obligations** represent the liability side of pension accounting. The obligations are related to the **actuarial present value** of promised future pension benefits payable to employees for services rendered up to the measurement date. *FASB Standard 87* defines three different pension obligations; each one is used for a different purpose. The three obligations, developed by the actuary, are designated as follows:

1. Projected benefit obligation (PBO).
2. Accumulated benefit obligation (ABO).
3. Vested benefit obligation (VBO).

Projected Benefit Obligation (PBO).

The **projected benefit obligation** is the full pension liability on the specified measurement date (i.e., the end of the accounting year). It is the actuary's estimate of the present value of the total benefits earned by employees. It is based on actuarial determinations, information about the covered employees, and **assumed future compensation levels of the employees.** The PBO provides details about the various components of pension expense. This estimate of the pension liability is based explicitly on the **pension benefit formula.**[5] The projected benefit obligation assumes that (1) **the plan will continue in effect** and (2) specific actuarial estimates will not change. The PBO and the status of pension plan assets (discussed later) are the two basic data sources used in pension accounting.

---

[5] Plans for which the pension benefit formula is based on future compensation are sometimes called **pay-related, final-pay, final-average-pay,** or **career-average-pay plans.**

Exhibit 20–2
Actuary's report—projected benefit obligation and related data, DB Company.

Date submitted: October 19B, for annual reporting period ending December 31, 19B

Items (all at PV) and brief explanations*	Amount
a. PBO, beginning balance (prior years ending balance)	$ 900
b. Service cost (PV of pension benefits earned during 19B)	80
c. Interest cost ($900 + $60) × 8%, to include interest on the obligation from the prior year [see *(e)* below] and the prior service cost recognized on January 1, 19B	77
d. Transition cost, $90, which the actuary included in the $900 beginning PBO balance from the prior year. It arises only as a result of the change from *APB Opinion 8* to *FASB Standard 87*. This cost is discussed later	-0-
e. Prior service cost on January 1, 19B (for employee services prior to establishment of the pension plan)	60
f. Actuarial losses (gains) made by the actuary for changes in actuarial assumptions (Also, there is a $10 loss included in the $900 PBO, as a carryover from the prior year.)	6
g. Pension benefits paid to employees (from trustee's report, Exhibit 20–3)	(30)
h. PBO, ending balance (carried forward as beginning balance in 19C)	$1,093
i. Accumulated benefit obligation (ABO)	$ 920
j. Vested benefit obligation (VBO)	$ 800
k. Discount (interest) rate used by actuary	8%
l. Average remaining service period of employees (to be used for straight-line amortization of unrecognized pension costs)	10 years

* Explanations included for instructional purposes.

The PBO is provided annually by the actuary. **Exhibit 20–2** shows an actual PBO report adapted for instructional purposes. Notice that this report prepared by the actuary starts with the ending PBO balance from the prior period, gives five pension expenses (*b* through *f*), shows the ending PBO balance, provides the accumulated benefit obligation and the vested benefit obligation, and gives additional data needed by the employer (*k* and *l*).

To complete the PBO, the actuary obtains from the trustee of the pension plan three amounts as follows: *(a)* pension benefits paid to the employees during the year, *(b)* the actual return on plan assets, and *(c)* the expected return on plan assets (see trustee's report, Exhibit 20–3).

Also, it is important to note that the detailed components in the PBO reflect the **pension plan formula** specified in the pension plan. This PBO report will be referred to later to illustrate how it is used by the employer, DB Company.

Accumulated Benefit Obligation (ABO). The accumulated benefit obligation also is computed by the **actuary.** It is calculated in the same manner as the PBO except that it is less because it is based on current and past compensation levels, rather than on expected higher future compensation levels. Therefore, it would be the employer's current obligation if the pension plan was discontinued as of the measurement date. If the pension benefit formula does not specify that pension benefits are to be based on future compensation levels, the accumulated benefit obligation and the projected benefit obligation would be equal.[6] Otherwise, the projected benefit obligation will be higher than the accumulated benefit obligation. The reason can be demonstrated by referring to the example given in Exhibit 20–1 (Hypo Company). Notice that the PBO was computed to be $22,573 assuming that estimated future compensation levels would increase. This PBO computation is shown below and compared with the ABO. Notice that the ABO is less only because the actuary's estimate of future benefits necessarily will be lower (since no future pay increases are included).

Today	← PV —	**Retirement**	← PV —	**Benefits**
↓ PBO (PV)		↓		(Compensation with the increase)
*$22,573	←(× .31524*)←	$71,607	←(× 7.16073†)←—	$10,000
↓ ABO (PV)		↓		↓ (Compensation without the increase)
*$20,316	←(× .31524*)←	$64,477	←(× 7.16073†)←—	$9,000 (Assumed)

* $p_{n=15; i=8\%}$.
† $P0_{n=12; i=9\%}$.

As will be explained later, the accumulated benefit obligation is used for only one purpose, that is to compute an additional minimum pension liability (pages 996–97).

Vested Benefit Obligation (VBO). The **vested benefit obligation** is the present value of the employer's obligation for pension benefits for which the employee's right to receive a present or future pension benefit is not contingent on remaining an employee of the employer. The actuary computes this obligation separately and then includes it in both the projected and accumulated benefit obligations because it is an add-on benefit and cost. The actuary's report, Exhibit 20–2, shows that the vested benefit obligation is $800. The relationships among the three pension obligations given in the actuary's report are as follows:

1. Vested benefit obligation (VBO)	$ 800
Add nonvested benefit obligation	120
2. Accumulated benefit obligation (includes VBO)	920
Add: Effect of estimated future compensation levels	173
3. Projected benefit obligation (PBO)	$1,093

The vested benefit obligation is not used in the usual accounting for pension plans. However, when the company is involved in curtailments, settlements, and termination benefits, the vested benefit obligation for each covered employee must be honored. These special situations are discussed in Part B of this chapter.

Pension Plan Assets

Pension plan assets are the resources that have been segregated and restricted, in a pension fund administered by the funding trustee, to provide future benefits

[6] Plans for which the pension benefit formula is not based on future compensation levels are also called **nonpay-related** or **flat-pay plans.**

for retirees. Plan assets include *(a)* investments (primarily stocks, bonds, and other securities) and *(b)* operational assets used in the operations of the pension fund (i.e., building, equipment, and fixtures). Plan assets must be in a trust or otherwise restricted from other uses and must have been actually paid in to, or earned by, the pension fund. Receivables from the employer company cannot be included in the fund assets. Pension plan assets, as of any measurement date, include the cumulative:

a. Contributions by the employer, plus
b. Net earnings on the pension fund, minus
c. Pension benefits paid to retirees.

Pension plan assets are valued on measurement date at either fair market value or "market-related value," depending upon the purpose for which they are used. The fair market value of pension plan assets is the amount that could be received in a current sale between a willing buyer and a willing seller (i.e., not a forced or liquidation sale). Market-related value is either *(a)* fair market value or *(b)* a calculated value that recognizes changes in fair market value of the plan investments by allocating them in a systematic and rational manner using a five-year average (*FASB Standard 87*, par. 30). The only purpose of this allocation, which permits the use of a market-related value that is different from fair market value, is to reduce the volatility of periodic pension expense by using a long-term average.

Pension plan **operational assets used in operations** of the pension fund are valued as of each measurement date at their carrying (book) value as shown in the records of the fund trustee. The sum of the plan investments (at fair market value or market-related value) and plan operational assets used in operations (at carrying value) is called (in *FASB Standard 87*) **"plan assets at fair value."** The FASB decided to use book value of the plan operational assets, rather than fair market value, to compute "plan assets at fair value" because the "value" of the operational assets is not available for paying pension benefits. The trustee of the funding agency prepares an annual report that uses these definitions. The report is dated to agree with the PBO for use by both the actuary and the employer company. **Exhibit 20–3** shows an actual trustee's report adapted for instructional purposes.

Underfunded/Overfunded Projected Benefit Obligation. *FASB Standard 87* carefully defines the projected benefit obligation (provided by the actuary) and the pension plan assets at fair value (provided by the fund trustee). These terms and their definitions are critical because they are used by the employer to measure any **underfunding or overfunding** of pension obligations at each measurement date.

An **underfunded projected benefit obligation,** on any measurement date, is the excess of the projected benefit obligation over the pension plan assets at fair value.[7] If plan assets at fair value exceed the projected benefit obligation,

[7] Underfunded sometimes is called **unfunded.** Since unfunded can be read to mean zero funding, we use the more precise terms **underfunded** and **overfunded.**

Exhibit 20–3
Trustee's report—status of pension plan assets and related data, DB Company.*

Date submitted: For the annual reporting period ending December 31, 19B

	Items	Amount
a.	Plan assets, beginning balance (prior year's ending balance at fair value)	$780
b.	Actual return on plan assets during 19B (reinvested in the fund)	76†
c.	Cash received from employer during 19B (DB Company)	85
d.	Pension benefits paid to current retirees during 19B	(30)
e.	Plan assets, ending balance (at fair value, carried forward as beginning balance in 19C)	$911
f.	Expected rate of return (five-year average) on plan assets held at the beginning of 19B is 10%. For 19B, the computation is $780 × 10%	$ 78†

* Explanations included for instructional purposes.
† Difference: $2 loss on plan assets compared with expected.

the employer has **overfunded** its pension obligation. This relationship is summarized in **Exhibit 20–4.**

We emphasize the **underfunded** or **overfunded** projected benefit obligation because *(a)* it is the amount of the pension liability (or asset) of the employer on the measurement date, as described in *FASB Standard 87* (par. 98) and *(b)* its amount must be disclosed in the notes to the financial statements.

To illustrate underfunding and overfunding, assume that on the measurement date, December 31, 19X1, Ace Company has a projected benefit obligation of $1,000 and plan assets at fair value of: Case A, $800, and Case B, $1,100. The underfunded (overfunded) projected benefit obligations for Ace Company and DB Company:

	Ace Company		DB Company
	Case A	Case B	Exhibits 20–2 & 20–3
Projected benefit obligation (PBO)	$1,000	$1,000	$1,093
Plan assets at fair value	(800)	(1,100)	(911)
Underfunded (overfunded) projected benefit obligation	$ 200	$ (100)	$ 182

Overfunding and underfunding of pension liabilities are of great concern to the covered employees, the employer company, the fund managers, and those concerned about the general economy. Pension funds tend to be invested approximately equally in debt securities (e.g., bonds) and equity securities (e.g., common stock). For example, on October 27, 1987, *The Wall Street Journal* reported that "The stock market's biggest players—the pension funds that own about 25% of all U.S. equities—seem relatively unscathed by the carnage so far, particularly compared with smaller investors forced to sell stock by margin calls." This report refers to October 19, 1987, called **"Black Monday,"** because on that day the Dow Jones average incurred the largest drop in stock prices in

Exhibit 20–4
Relationship of the projected benefit obligation to the pension plan assets.

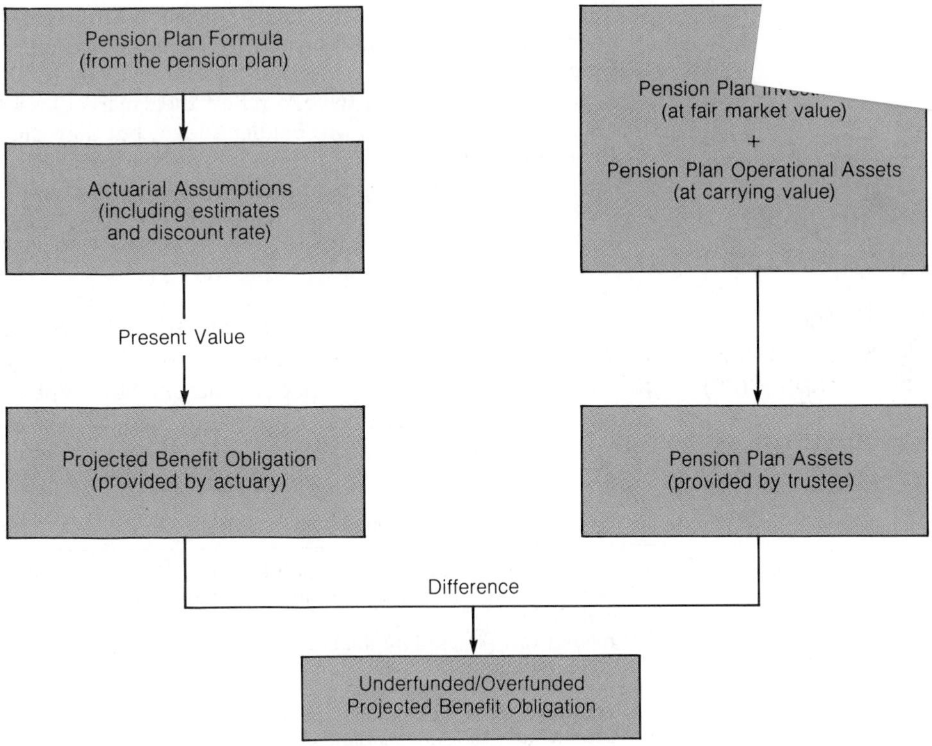

the history of the market. Prior to that drop most pension plans were significantly overfunded, but the next day many were significantly underfunded. For example the above report stated that "At American Telephone & Telegraph, for example, the stock drop sliced $4 billion from the retirement funds' assets, which totaled $31 billion at the end of September. Although that cut the stocks' fraction of the assets from about 55% to 50%, AT&T pension chief David Feldman says the fund still has a surplus, and he doesn't plan any changes." And how did the other pension funds react? On November 2, 1987 *The Wall Street Journal* again reported:

> Black Monday reinforced three lessons for fund managers, says Dallas Salisbury, president of the Employee Benefit Research Institute: Diversify, focus on the long-term and don't panic. Funds that followed the rules generally have fared well during the market's tribulations. Inland Steel Industries Inc.'s pension coffers are still so overfunded because of its balanced-investment strategy that it doesn't expect to make any contribution through 1989, says Theodore Myers, chief financial officer.
>
> George Reagan, equity manager of the $17.5 billion Teacher Retirement System of Texas, confides he worried he was being "too conservative" when he built up the fund's cash reserves. The stock market dive, though, "validated our investment philosophy 100%," he says. Wilson Foods Corp. says it also learned it was investing its fund just right.

At the same time delayed expense recognition made the news as follows:

> Even though a new accounting standard forces companies to acknowledge pension obligations in their balance sheets and earnings, some analysts don't believe it will have much of an impact on corporate profits anytime soon.

Accounting specialist Lee J. Seidler of Bear Stearns sent clients a report yesterday saying 1987 earnings won't be affected because pension expenses for this year were determined by asset levels at the end of 1986.

Some companies may have to reflect their market losses in calculating next year's pension expenses, Mr. Seidler added, but they can stretch them out over 10 or 15 years for reporting purposes. The companies don't have to start showing liabilities in excess of assets on their balance sheets until 1989.

"It will be a long time before the impacts of Black Monday show up in pension expenses," Mr. Seidler said.

Net Periodic Pension Expense (Six Components)

Net periodic pension expense, as defined in *FASB Standard 87*, is the amount reported in an employer's statement of income as the cost of the pension plan for an accounting period. Net periodic pension expense is the sum of six cost components in a defined benefit pension plan.[8] These six components, basically measured at present value, are as follows:

Component	Source	Amount for DB Company
1. **Service cost**—the present value of the pension benefits earned by covered employees during the current reporting period.	PBO by actuary (Exhibit 20–2)	$80
2. **Interest cost**—interest on the beginning PBO to bring it up to present value.	PBO by actuary (Exhibit 20–2)	77
3. **Transition cost amortization**—changeover cost from *APB Opinion No. 8* to *FASB Standard 87.*	Company (Exhibit 20–6)	9
4. **Prior service cost amortization**—cost of retroactive benefits based on compensation earned before the pension plan was initiated.	Company (Exhibit 20–6)	6
5. **Losses and gains amortization**—from plan assets and changes in actuarial assumptions. Amortization of unrecognized pension costs for (3), (4), and (5) is discussed later.	Company (Exhibit 20–6)	1
6. Expected return on plan assets—the expected earnings of the pension plan for the current year.	Fund status by trustee (Exhibit 20–3)	(78)*
Total—net periodic pension expense		$95

* Notice the offsetting (or netting) of expense and revenue; discussed on page 977. The reason for using expected rather than actual is discussed later.

Exhibit 20–5 gives an overview of the development of net periodic pension expense. Next we discuss each of these six components in numbered order.

Service Cost (Component 1). The service cost component of net periodic pension expense for **each annual reporting** period is the **actuarial present value** of the pension benefits earned by qualified employees in that period based on the **pension** benefit formula (from the pension plan). This component of net periodic pension expense is currently incurred by the employer based on pension credits earned by the covered employees. Each year, the service cost component

[8] *FASB Standard 87* uses the terms **net periodic pension cost, service cost,** and **interest cost,** instead of "expense." The Board explains that this *Standard* "uses the term **net periodic pension cost** rather than net periodic pension expense because part of the cost recognized may be capitalized along with other costs as part of an asset such as inventory." This same problem exists for depreciation expense. We use the terms **net periodic pension expense, service cost,** and **interest cost** for instructional convenience.

Exhibit 20–5
Relationships of pension benefit formula, projected benefit obligation, pension plan assets and net periodic pension expense.

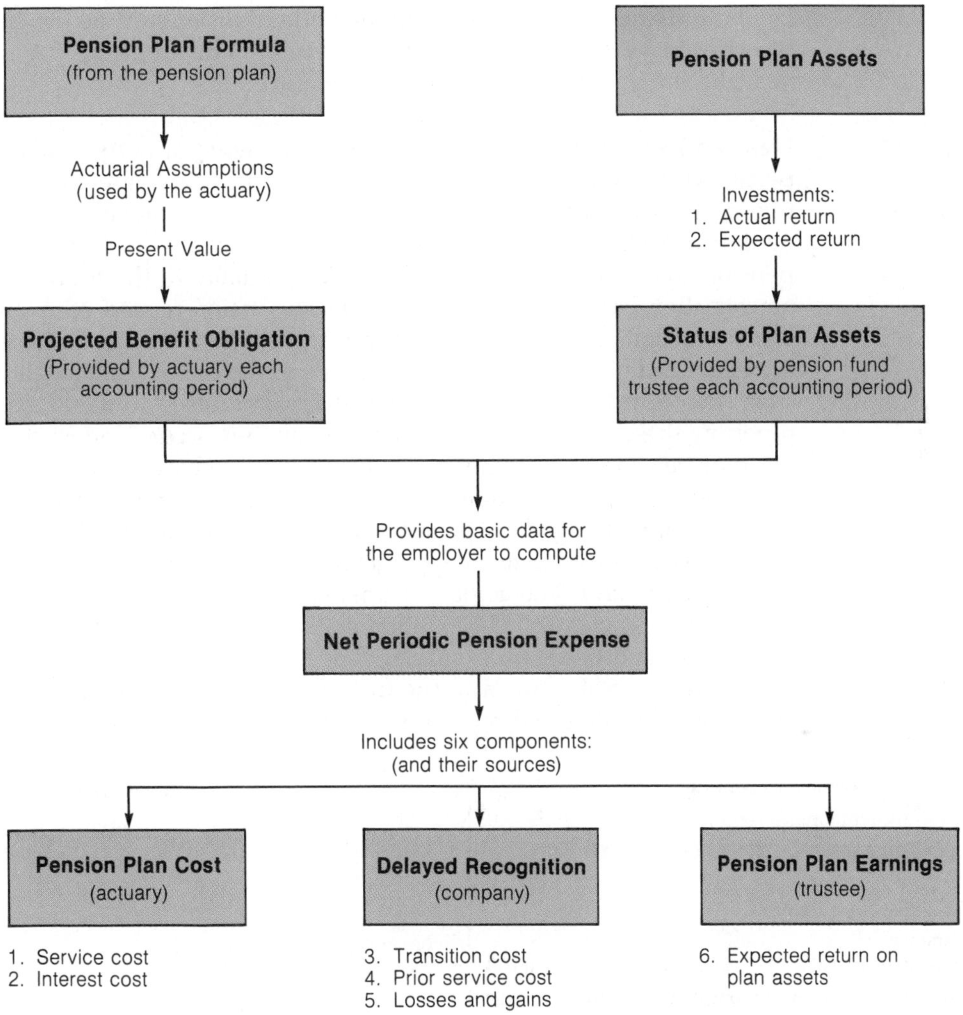

increases the **projected benefit obligation.** Service cost incorporates **assumed future compensation levels** of the qualified employees. Thus, it measures the period's service cost and the increase in pension liability, as the actuarial present value of the pension credits earned by the employees. Service cost is computed each period on the assumption that the pension plan will continue indefinitely.

Interest Cost (Component 2). This is the interest cost component of net periodic pension expense for each annual reporting period. It exists because there was a pension obligation carried over from the prior year (the projected benefit obligation) and interest on that obligation must be recognized for the current year. Interest cost arises on the PBO because the estimated pension benefits will be paid in the future, whereas pension expense is based on the change in the present value of those benefits during the curent accounting period. Therefore, current pension expense is increased by the periodic interest cost, and the beginning PBO is increased by the same amount to a present value at the end of the current reporting period.

The interest cost component of net periodic pension expense is computed by multiplying the **projected benefit obligation amount at the beginning of the current year,** plus any other PBO amounts dated at the beginning of the year, by the actuary's interest (i.e., discount) rate.

Amortization of Unrecognized Pension Costs

Delayed Recognition. The next three components of net periodic pension expense—transition, prior service, and losses and gains—are accounted for, and reported, in a unique way. They are pension cost/liability amounts that are neither recorded nor reported when they are initially incurred. Instead, these pension costs are recorded and reported gradually in the future on a periodic amortization basis. This means that these pension-related costs and liabilities are not recognized as liabilities. As a result, these three components are called **unrecognized** pension costs and the accounting process is called **delayed recognition.** The primary purpose of delayed recognition is to avoid recording and reporting these three pension liabilities when they occur. Under accrual accounting (not pension accounting) they would have to be recorded when incurred. To illustrate delayed recognition applied to prior service cost (PSC), assume DB Company changed its pension plan (effective January 1, 19B) to give its employees increased pension benefits for service prior to the date of the change (i.e., retroactively). The actuary estimated that the PV of the prior service cost of this change was $60,000. Under pension accounting this $60,000 pension cost can be amortized, for example, over 10 years and this new pension liability can be paid in cash now or in the future. The results under **accrual** accounting and **delayed** or deferred recognition can be illustrated as follows:

Accrual accounting			Delayed recognition†		
January 1, 19B—recognition:					
Deferred pension cost, PSC*	60,000		No entry is made because recognition is delayed (or deferred).		
Pension liability, PSC		60,000			
December 31, 19B—amortization:					
Pension expense	6,000		Pension expense	6,000	
Deferred pension cost, PSC		6,000	Pension liability, PSC		6,000
December 31, 19B—funding by the company (amount assumed):					
Pension liability, PSC	4,000		Pension liability, PSC	4,000	
Cash		4,000	Cash		4,000
Amounts reported in the 19B financial statements:					
Statement of income:					
Pension expense, PSC		$ 6,000	Same as accrual		$6,000
Statement of financial position:					
Assets:					
Deferred pension cost, PSC		54,000	None (understated by $54,000)		
Liabilities:					
Pension liability, PSC		56,000	(Understated by $54,000)		2,000

Conclusion: Under delayed or deferred recognition the statement of income is correct, but the statement of financial position is grossly understated. This example is shown (in 000s) in another format in Exhibit 20–6. This FASB decision has been forcefully criticized on conceptual grounds.

* A deferred charge.

† This is similar to the case of an operational asset (such as a machine) purchased on credit, but the asset and the related liability are not recorded. However, periodic depreciation is nevertheless recorded as a debit to expense and a credit to a liability account.

Delayed recognition in this manner has been widely criticized on the basis that it materially understates both assets and liabilities over a long period of time. Pension accounting has always used, and *FASB Standard 87* continues to use, delayed recognition. The *Standard* (Summary, page 4) justifies continuation of delayed recognition as follows:

> The Board believes that an employer with an unfunded pension obligation has a liability and an employer with an overfunded pension obligation has an asset. The most relevant and reliable information available about that liability or asset is based on the fair value of plan assets and a measure of the present value of the obligation using current, explicit assumptions. The Board concluded, however, that recognition in financial statements of those amounts in their entirety would be far too great a change from past practice. Some Board members were also influenced by concerns about the reliability of measures of the obligation.
>
> The delayed recognition included in the *Statement* results in excluding the most current and most relevant information from the statement of financial position. That information, however, is included in the required disclosures.

Accounting Recognition. Under *FASB Standard 87,* delayed recognition means that an unrecognized loss or gain will **not** be recorded in the accounts nor **reported** on the financial statements when incurred. However, this unrecognized amount will be shown on the actuary's PBO report only once as a decrease or increase—see Exhibit 20–2 for transition cost, prior service cost, and loss(gain). However, the employer does not record the initial unrecognized amounts in the accounting system, but must maintain a **separate informal amortization record.**

Amortization of Unrecognized Pension Costs. *FASB Standard 87* specifies that amortization of the unrecognized pension costs must be rational and systematic. This means that straight-line amortization often is used based on the average remaining service period of employees (this computation is discussed in Supplement 20–A). Also, an unrecognized pension cost or gain that *(a)* first occurs at the **beginning** of the current accounting year or *(b)* is carried forward from the prior year, must be amortized starting **in the current year.** An unrecognized pension cost or gain that first occurs at the **end** of the current year must be amortized **starting in the following accounting year.**[9] Now, we will discuss amortization of each of the three unrecognized pension costs.

Transition Cost (Component 3). The transition cost component of net periodic pension cost is the changeover cost from *APB Opinion 8* to *FASB Standard 87.* Therefore, it can initially occur only once; that is, at the beginning of the changeover year. The latest date for the changeover is for years beginning after December 31, 1988. However, its amortization may continue for many years (see page 1018). *FASB Standard 87*, par. 76, states that transition cost is measured on the changeover date as the difference between *(a)* the PBO and *(b)* the fair value of the pension fund assets plus any previously recognized underfunded pension

[9] This procedure is the same as depreciation on an operational asset (e.g., equipment). If acquired at the beginning of the current period, a full period of depreciation is recorded in the current period. If acquired at the end of the current period, depreciation is not recorded for the current period.

cost. The amount, thus determined, must be amortized over the average service periods remaining for employees expected to receive the related benefits. If the periods are less than 15 the employer may still use a 15-year period. Notice in Exhibit 20–2 that the actuary's report shows transition cost (item *d*) of $90 included in the 19B PBO for the changeover that year only (it could have been shown separately). Employer company does not record the $90 transition cost in its accounts but amortizes it starting at the end of the year of change. Straight-line amortization is used, based on the average remaining service period of the qualified employees at January 1, 19B (the changeover date). For DB Company if the 19B average is 10 years, the amortization would be computed as follows:

Unrecognized transition cost (L means loss):

Unamortized balance, January 1, 19B	L $ 90
Increase (decrease) during 19B	–0–
Total unrecognized	L 90
Amortized at December 31, 19B ($90 ÷ 10 years)	L 9*
Unrecognized, December 31, 19B	L $81

* Increases 19B net periodic pension expense.

The unrecognized transition cost would be fully amortized at the end of year 10 assuming the average remaining service period remains the same. The average remaining service period usually is recomputed at the beginning of each year and the new estimate is used.[10] The PBO is not affected in any way by the amortization amounts computed by DB Company.

Prior Service Cost (Component 4). The prior service cost component of net periodic pension expense is the cost of **retroactive** pension benefits caused by:

1. A pension plan amendment to give pension benefits to employees for services rendered **before** the pension plan was **initiated.**
2. Later plan **amendments** that give increased pension benefits based on employee services rendered during periods prior to the amendments.

FASB Standard 87, pars. 25, 26, and 27, specifies that prior service cost will increase the PBO on each amendment date. The new balance must be amortized *(a)* by assigning an equal amount for each employee that will benefit from the amendment date to retirement date, or *(b)* by using the straight-line method to reduce the detailed computations. The straight-line method may be used based on the average remaining service periods of all employees that will receive the benefit.

To illustrate, Exhibit 20–2 shows that prior service cost of $60 was added to the PBO liability on January 1, 19B. DB Company, using the group method and a group average remaining service period of 10 years would compute the amortization on December 31, 19B as follows: $60 ÷ 10 years = $6. This increases 19B **net periodic pension expense.**

[10] *FASB Standard 87*, par. 77, provides an exception "*(a)* if the average remaining service period is less than 15 years, the employer may elect to use a 15-year period, and *(b)* if all or almost all of a plan's participants are inactive, the employer shall use the inactive participants' average remaining life expectancy period. That same amortization shall also be used to recognize any unrecognized net obligation related to a defined contribution plan."

Losses and Gains (Component 5). This component of net periodic pension expense is the most difficult to understand because it is a residual amount that includes data from the reports of both the actuary and the fund trustee.

Pension accounting is based on estimates. As time passes, actual experience (i.e., actual results) will be different from the prior estimates. The losses and gains component of net periodic pension expense is used to accumulate and amortize differences between actual and estimated results. If actual results are higher than expected results there is a gain; if the opposite occurs there is a loss. These differences, for an accounting period, come from two sources:

1. **Projected benefit obligation**—increases or decreases in the amount of the projected benefit obligation due to changes in actuarial assumptions.
2. **Plan assets**—the difference between the actual return on plan assets and the expected return on plan assets.

The **gain or loss due to actuarial changes** shown in the projected benefit obligation is provided by the actuary each accounting period (see Exhibit 20–2, item *f*). The actuarial gain or loss is the net effect of changes in actuarial assumptions, such as the assumed discount rate, retirement estimates, compensation rates, turnover, and mortality rates. The employer amortizes this gain or loss to periodic pension expense using a systematic and rational approach (often straight line). This topic is discussed later in Part B. The gain or loss due to **plan assets** is the difference between the actual and the expected return on plan assets as shown on the trustee's report (see Exhibit 20–3).[11]

The employer must follow special procedures to account for the return on plan assets. These procedures are as follows:

1. The **expected** return (rather than actual return on plan assets is used as component 6 of net periodic pension expense discussed later).
2. The second **source** of gains and losses (listed above) is the **difference** between the expected return and the actual return on plan assets. This difference, which must be accounted for, is **allocated** along with the gains and losses from the PBO.

Therefore, at the end of an accounting period the total amount unamortized (i.e., the unrecognized gain or loss) is the sum of the following:

a. Unrecognized (i.e., unamortized) gain or loss from prior periods (the beginning balance).
b. Gain (loss) from changes in the actuarial assumptions included in the projected benefit obligation (in the actuary's report).
c. Gain (loss) from plan assets (from the trustee's report).

The **unrecognized** net gain or loss is amortized as a component of net periodic pension expense over future periods on a systematic and rational basis. *FASB Standard 87*, pars. 33, 34, and 35, specifies a test for amortization, and uses two alternative methods called the *(a)* **minimum method** and *(b)* **systematic method** (discussed on page 996). For instructional convenience, we assume

[11] The trustee computes the expected return on plan assets by multiplying the fair value of plan assets as of the **beginning** of the period by the **expected long-term rate of return** on plan assets. The fair value of plan assets is a calculated value that recognizes changes in fair value in a systematic and rational manner over not more than five years (see page 980).

for DB Company that the straight-line method, based on the average remaining service period, is used. For example, the amortization of the $10 loss (Exhibit 20–2, item *f*, unamortized balance on January 1, 19B) is amortized as: $10 ÷ 10 years = $1.

Actual and Expected Returns (Component 6) on Pension Plan Assets. As explained above, pension accounting uses both the actual return and the expected return on plan assets. Plan assets consist of *(a)* fund investments and *(b)* all of the operational assets owned and used in plan operations, such as property, plant, and equipment.

Actual Return on Plan Assets. This amount is the sum of the *(a)* actual return on plan **investments** plus *(b)* change in the carrying (book) value of the plan assets used in **operations** as of the **end** of the current year. The **actual return on plan investments** is provided by the trustee as the change in the **fair value** of plan investments, net of pension contributions and benefit payments, during the current accounting period. The actual return on plan investments may be positive or negative.

Expected Return on Plan Assets. This is a projected amount which is computed by multiplying the **market-related** value of plan assets, provided by the trustee, as of the **beginning** of the period by the **expected long-term rate of return** on plan assets. The market-related value of plan assets is either (1) fair value or (2) a "calculated value that recognizes changes in fair value in a systematic and rational manner over not more than five years" (see page 981). The long-term **rate** of return (i.e., an interest rate percentage) on plan assets is estimated by the **trustee,** based on the average rate of earnings expected on funds invested in the pension fund and an assessment of future probabilities. It is a five-year average rate, but can be revised at any time. **The expected return on plan assets is the sixth component of net periodic pension expense.**

Deferred Gain or Loss on Plan Assets. This amount is the current period's unrecognized gain or loss on plan assets. It is computed by the **employer** as follows:

Actual return on plan assets − **Expected return on plan assets** = **Deferred gain or loss on plan assets**

This gain or loss must be accounted for; it is recognized as it is amortized by the employer company in the component of net periodic pension expense called **Unrecognized Gains and Losses.**

To illustrate, using DB Company, the net periodic pension expense for 19B would be as follows:

Component	Source	Amount
1. Service cost	PBO (Exhibit 20–2)	$80
2. Interest cost	PBO (Exhibit 20–2)	77
3. Transition cost	Amortization (page 988)	9
4. Prior service cost	Amortization (page 988)	6
5. Losses and gains	Amortization (above)	1
6. Expected return on plan assets	Trustee's report (Exhibit 20–3)	(78)
Net periodic pension expense		$95

* Includes gains and losses from *(a)* actuarial changes and *(b)* plan assets.

The FASB specified the above rules and their application for plan assets to provide a "smoothing" effect on net periodic pension expense, and hence on net income. Since the return on plan assets is significantly affected from year to year by market changes in stock prices (usually the major investment) pension expense will similarly be affected. The rules ameliorate these effects by *(a)* using the expected return (rather than the actual return), and *(b)* prescribing a projected five-year average **rate** of return to compute the expected return in dollars.

Accrued/Prepaid Pension Cost

At the end of each accounting period, the employer prepares a journal entry to record: *(a)* pension expense (a debit), *(b)* cash payments (a credit) made to the pension fund during the year, and *(c)* any difference between *(a)* and *(b)*. This difference may require either a debit or a credit to accrued/prepaid pension cost. If pension expense is greater than the cash payments during the year, a credit is made to the accrued/prepaid pension cost. Alternatively, if pension expense is less than the cash payments during the year, a debit is made to the accrued/prepaid account.

FASB Standard 87 uses the designation **Accrued/prepaid pension cost** to record this difference. Therefore, a credit **balance** in this account is an accrued liability and a debit **balance** is an asset (prepaid pension cost).

The Board does not specify the exact account titles that must be used. If the accrued (or prepaid) pension cost is a liability it should be so designated in conformity with *FASB Concepts No. 5.* Alternatively, if it is a prepaid cost it should be designated as an asset for the same reason.

The 19C journal entry for DB Company would be as follows (with sources):

Pension expense (page 984)	95	
Cash (trustee's report, Exhibit 20–2)		85
Accrued/prepaid pension cost ($96 − $85)		10

Employer's Comprehensive Spreadsheet to Determine Pension Entries and Reporting

The prior discussions explained and illustrated the following:

a. The actuary's report on the PBO (Exhibit 20–2).
b. The trustee's report on plan assets (Exhibit 20–3).
c. The six components of net periodic pension expense and their relationships to *(a)* and *(b)* above.
d. The distinction between the formal accounting (e.g., journal entries) and the supplemental records needed for pension reporting.

This section presents a spreadsheet (usually computerized) used by some employer companies. It brings together the reports of the actuary, the trustee, and the amortization of the three unrecognized pension costs, to compute net periodic pension expense and accrued/prepaid pension cost in an organized and verifiable way. These latter two amounts, and cash contributions by the employer company to the pension fund, provide data for the pension entry that the company must record in the accounts and report in the financial statements.

The prior illustrations of DB Company are continued in the comprehensive spreadsheet, which is instructionally convenient because it provides an integrated overview of the preceding illustrations for the company. The completed

Exhibit 20–6

Pension plan spreadsheet for DB Company, 19B. To compute (1) unrecognized pension costs, (2) periodic pension expense, and (3) accrued (prepaid) pension cost. (Refer to Exhibit 20–2 for the basic PBO report and to Exhibit 20–3 for the trustee's report.)

Items	PBO (actuary)	Pension plan assets (trustee)	Unrecognized pension cost (by company)	Net periodic pension expense (by company)	(Accrued)/prepaid cost (by company)
Beginning Balances 19B:	$ 900	$780	$100	$-0-	$(20)
Changes in PBO during 19B:					
Service cost	80			(1) 80	
Interest cost ($900 + $60) × 8%	77[a]			(2) 77	
Unrecognized costs (delayed):					
Transition cost:					
Unrecognized at beginning 19B			L $ 90[b]		
Increase (decrease) in 19B			-0-		
Total unrecognized			L 90		
Amortized in 19B ($90 ÷ 10)			L 9	(3) 9	
Unrecognized balance at end 19B			L $ 81		
Prior service cost:					
Unrecognized at beginning 19B			$-0-		
Increase (decrease) Jan. 1, 19B	60		L 60		
Total unrecognized			L 60		
Amortized in 19B ($60 ÷ 10)			L 6	(4) 6	
Unrecognized balance at end 19B			$ 54		
Loss (gain):					
Unrecognized, beginning 19B			L $ 10[c]		
Change from PBO, 19B	6		L 6		
Change from plan assets, 19B			L 2		
Total unrecognized			L 18		
Amortized in 19B ($10 ÷ 10 years)			1	(5) 1	
Unrecognized at end of 19B			L $ 17		
Changes in plan assets during 19B:					
Expected return ($780 × 10%) = $78			$2	(6) (78)	
Actual return on plan assets		76			
Cash received from company		85			85
Pension benefits paid to retirees	(30)	(30)			
Ending Balances, 19B:					
PBO	$1,093				
Plan assets		$911			
Under (over) funded PBO		$182			
Unrecognized pension costs			$152		
Net periodic pension expense for 19B				$95	(95)
(Accrued)/prepaid pension cost					$(30)

Proof: Beginning $900 − $780 − $100 = $20, accrued; Ending $1,093 − $911 − $152 = $30, accrued

Accounting entry:			
Pension expense	95	or	
Accrued/prepaid pension cost ($20 − $30)			10
Cash			85

[a] The $60 PSC must be included because it was recognized on January 1, 19B.
[b] This amount is included in the $900 PBO carried over from the prior year.
[c] This amount is included in the $900 PBO carried over from the prior year.

comprehensive spreadsheet is shown in **Exhibit 20–6.** Before continuing, it is helpful to review Exhibits 20–2 and 20–3. The spreadsheet is easily prepared as follows:

Step 1. Set up the six standardized captions at the top of the spreadsheet.

Step 2. Set up side captions under the "Items" caption. Next, in the second column, "PBO," enter all amounts, including the beginning balance from the report of the actuary (without changes or omissions). Next, enter the amounts from the trustee's report in the third column (i.e., beginning balance, actual return on plan assets, cash received from employer company, pension benefits paid by the pension fund to current retirees, and ending balance of plan assets).

Step 3. (Very important.) In the column "Unrecognized pension costs (company)" analyze each of the three unrecognized items—transition cost, prior service cost, and loss (gain)—using vertically for each cost this formula: Beginning unrecognized balance + Increase (decrease) during the current period = Total unrecognized − Amortization for the current period = Ending unrecognized balance. Also, notice that the loss (gain) for the difference between the expected return and actual return on plan assets (i.e., the $2 loss) is accounted for by including it under the "Loss (gain)" caption for subsequent amortization.

Step 4. Extend the six components of pension expense to the column "Net periodic pension expense" and compute the algebraic total. Notice the six components are numbered for instructional convenience.

Step 5 Complete the column "Accrued (prepaid) pension cost" by entering the beginning balance (carried over from the prior period), cash paid to the pension fund (a deduction of the liability), net periodic pension expense (an addition to the liability), and then compute and enter the ending balance.

Step 6. Check accuracy:

a. Beginning balance: PBO − Plan assets − Unrecognized pension costs = Accrued (prepaid) pension cost. Notice that the beginning balance of net periodic pension expense will always be zero because it was closed at the end of the prior period.

b. Ending balances: Same formula as in *(a)* above.

Step 7. Prepare the journal entry for employer company as follows:

Pension expense	____	
Accrued/prepaid pension cost, or*	____	
Accrued/prepaid pension cost*		____
Cash		____

* Each period this account will be debited or credited, but not both.
Also, use the appropriate data (as adjusted) from this spreadsheet for note disclosure.

Notice that the salient features of this spreadsheet are as follows:

1. It starts with the reports of the actuary and the trustee and ends with the entry required for the employer company.

2. It is internally consistent because the beginning and ending totals have equality and each column is summed algebraically.
3. Details are provided about the PBO, plan assets, amortization, net pension expense, and the accrued/prepaid pension cost. These details are consistent horizontally line by line.
4. Aside from the reports of the actuary and trustee, additional schedules are not needed to complete the spreadsheet.
5. Ending totals of each column, and the totals of each of the three unrecognized pension costs, are used to start a spreadsheet for the next reporting period.

A Critical Issue—The Actuary's Discount Rate

The prior discussions illustrated the use by the actuary of an estimated discount (interest) rate, which may be revised each year to measure **at present value** the projected, accumulated, and vested benefit obligations. The amounts of these present values are significantly affected by the estimated rate and are very sensitive to rate changes. This means that the employer's net periodic pension expense and the accrued/prepaid pension liability are sensitive to small changes in the discount rate. For example, one article explained the significance of this problem as follows:[12]

> The principal drawback of the new pension cost will be its meaningless volatility—its almost certain tendency to change from year to year for no substantive reason. Its volatility will be due primarily to the new requirements for choosing the interest rate for discounting purposes. Since an important part of pension cost is the discounted value of future benefit payments, the choice of the discount rate has a major effect on the cost calculation. And since the discounted payments extend many years into the future, the cost calculation is very sensitive to changes in the discount rate. A 1-percentage-point change in the discount rate, for example, can change important components of pension cost by as much as 15 to 20 percent.

The primary criticisms are *(a)* that changes in the estimated interest rate will cause considerable volatility in pension expense and pension liability and *(b)* small changes in the rate can be used to manipulate both reported income and pension liability. To ameliorate these criticisms, *FASB Standard 87* states that:

> Assumed discount rates shall reflect the rates at which the pension benefits could be effectively settled. It is appropriate in estimating those rates to look to available information about rates implicit in current prices of annuity contracts that could be used to effect settlement of the obligation (including information about available annuity rates currently published by the Pension Benefit Guaranty Corporation). In making those estimates, employers may also look to rates of return on high-quality fixed-income investments currently available and expected to be available during the period to maturity of the pension benefits.

---

[12] Barnet N. Berin and Dale Gerboth, "Is FASB 87 Workable?" *Financial Executive Magazine*, Financial Executive Institute, October 1987, p. 18.

PART B: ADDITIONAL PENSION PLAN ISSUES

The remainder of this chapter will discuss the following topics: *(1)* amortization methods for unrecognized pension costs, *(2)* additional minimum pension liability, *(3)* reporting, including note disclosures, *(4)* a three-year comprehensive case, and *(5)* curtailments, settlements, and terminations.

Amortization of Losses and Gains—More Details

The losses/gains component of net periodic pension expense was discussed above on page 989 and illustrated in Exhibit 20–6. For instructional convenience, the straight-line method of amortization was used based on the average remaining service period, which is recomputed each year. *FASB Standard 87* specifies two different methods that can be used to amortize the unrecognized losses/gains amount, called the **minimum method** and the **systematic method.** The reason for special amortization procedures is that this component, in contrast to transition cost and prior service cost, comes from several different sources. Also, it usually is large in amount due to differences between actual and estimated amounts.

FASB Standard 87, pars. 32–35, specifies detailed **amortization rules** for losses/gains: Rule 1, test to determine whether any amortization is required; Rule 2, only if the answer is positive, compute the minimum amortization required; and Rule 3, apply either the minimum method or the straight-line method. If the answer is negative, no amortization is required. The FASB specified these technical rules because of a concern that the unrecognized loss/gain amount may become excessive due to inadequate amortization in the early years. These rules often are referred to as **corridor amortization** because an arbitrary 10% (i.e., 10-year) basis is specified.[13]

For example, *FASB Standard 87* (page 92) provides the following case (adapted):

Data needed (beginning of year):*

Projected benefit obligation (actuary's report)	$1,200
Plan assets at fair value (same as market-related value) (trustee's report)	$ 880
Unrecognized loss (gain) (from company records)	$ 140
Average remaining service period	10 years

* *FASB Standard 87* states that: "The amortization must always reduce the beginning-of-the-year balance. Amortization of a net unrecognized gain results in a decrease in net periodic pension cost; amortization of a net unrecognized loss results in an increase in net periodic pension cost."

[13] *FASB Standard 87,* par. 32, describes this method as follows: "As a minimum, amortization of an **unrecognized net gain or loss** (excluding asset gains and losses not yet reflected in market-related value) shall be included as a component of net pension cost for a year if, as of the beginning of the year, that unrecognized net gain or loss exceeds 10 percent of the greater of the projected benefit obligation or the market-related value of plan assets. If amortization is required, the minimum amortization shall be that excess divided by the average remaining service period of active employees expected to receive benefits under the plan. If all or almost all of a plan's participants are inactive, the average remaining life expectancy of the inactive participants shall be used instead of average remaining service."

Minimum Method of Amortization

Rule 1. Test to determine whether any amortization is required:

a. The beginning PBO balance ($1,200) must be used because it is higher than the beginning plan assets balance ($880).

b. Test as follows:

Unrecognized loss (gain)	$140
Projected benefit obligation (10% × $1,200)	120
Excess (positive)	$ 20

Conclusion: Amortization is required.

Rule 2. Compute the minimum amortization that must be recorded:

a. Unrecognized loss (gain) at beginning of the period subject to amortization	$140
b. Corridor = 10% of the greater of the PBO ($1,200), or the fair value of plan assets ($880)	120
c. Unrecognized loss (gain) outside the corridor	$ 20
d. Amortization using the minimum method ($20 ÷ 10 years)	$ 2

Notice that the minimum amortization of $2 is slightly more than 1% of the unrecognized amount, $140. This is typical, which means that minimum amortization will seldom affect the amortization by a material amount. Because of this many accountants believe that the rules are for naught aside from the cost-benefit constraint (see Chapter 6).

Systematic Method of Amortization

Rule 3 allows any systematic method of amortizing the unrecognized beginning balance of the loss/gain amount to be used instead of the minimum method, providing *(a)* it is greater than the minimum (rule 2), *(b)* the method is used systematically, and *(c)* the method used is disclosed. To illustrate using the above example, assuming the average remaining service period will be used, the amortization would be as follows:

Amortization assuming the company decides to use a 10% rate: $140 × 10%	$14*

* Can be used because it is above the minimum of $2 and it is systematic and rational.

Additional Minimum Pension Liability

FASB Standard 87 specifies that an additional minimum pension liability must be recorded under prescribed guidelines. The word **additional** means that it increases the recognized liability above the amount **already shown** in the account, Accrued/Prepaid Pension Cost. The purpose of this requirement is to increase the recognized pension liability when a pension plan is grossly underfunded and to reduce the volatility (i.e., wide fluctuations) in the pension liability account. It is a smoothing procedure "invented" by the FASB to ameliorate some of the problems caused by delayed recognition of [illegible] pension costs—transition cost, prior service cost, and los[illegible] additional minimum liability requires a **separate entry to record [illegible] ity, in addition to the pension entry already discussed.** It does [illegible] amortization of the unrecognized pension costs; rather it focuses o[illegible] amount of the recognized pension liability.

FASB Standard 87, par. 36, requires that the total recognized pension liab[illegible] be at least equal to any excess of the employer's **accumulated** benefit obligatio[illegible] over the fair value of the pension plan assets.[14]

If the accumulated benefit obligation is **more** than the pension plan assets at fair value, an additional minimum pension liability may have to be recorded (see below). In contrast, if the accumulated benefit obligation is less than the pension plan assets at fair value, an additional minimum pension liability will **not** be recorded. Therefore, the additional minimum computation uses three different **end of period** values: (1) the accumulated benefit obligation (ABO), (2) pension plan assets at fair value, and (3) the balance in the Accrued/Prepaid Pension Cost account. The formula is as follows (dr. = debit and cr. = credit):

	Case X	Case Y
a. Accumulated benefit obligation (actuary's report)	$500cr.	$500cr.
b. Less: Pension plan assets at fair value (trustee's report)	300dr.	300dr.
Difference—total recognized pension liability required (also called under-funded or overfunded PBO)	200cr.	200cr.
c. Adjustment for pension liability already recorded (balance in accrued/prepaid pension cost):		
Case X—credit, accrued balance	150cr.	
Case Y—debit, prepaid balance		150dr.
d. Additional minimum pension liability required	$ 50cr.	$350cr.

In Case X the $50 additional liability increases the **total** pension liability to the amount required ($200). In Case Y, to report the $200 minimum liability, the accrued/prepaid **debit** balance of $150 must be adjusted to a $200 credit balance. This requires an additional liability of $350; that is, the difference between a $200 credit balance and a $150 debit balance is a $350 credit. For each case the results would be as follows:

	Case X	Case Y
Additional pension liability to be recorded	$ 50cr.	$350cr.
Accrued (prepaid) pension liability already recorded	150cr.	150dr.
Total recognized pension liability	$200cr.	$200cr.

These computations and the related entry are further illustrated for four other cases as follows, using debit = dr. and credit = cr.:

[14] This is the only case in which the accumulated benefit obligation is used to implement *FASB Standard 87.*

19B	Over-funded Case A	Underfunded Case B	Case C	Case D
enefit obligation	$100cr.	$100cr.	$100cr.	$100cr.
air value	110dr.	80dr.	80dr.	80dr.
er-) funded ABO—Total uired	$ 10dr.	$ 20cr.	$ 20cr.	$ 20cr.
or the 19B ending the accrued/prepaid ccount:				
d (credit balance)	-0-	-0-	15cr.	-0-
d (debit balance)	-0-	-0-	-0-	15dr.
minimum pension to record (19B entry)	$-0-	$ 20cr.	$ 5cr.	$ 35cr.*
ized prior service cost of 19B (maximum asset debit)	$ 8	$ 8	$ 8	$ 8

* … he net effect is a total recognized pension liability of $20 recorded in all underfunded cases. Case D should be studied carefully; it shows that the difference between a credit of $20 and a debit of $15 is a credit of $35 (not $5).

Next, the separate entry to record the **additional** minimum pension liability is unique as specified by *FASB Standard 87*. This statement specifies that a separate liability should be credited for the computed amount (as above) to an account such as "Additional Minimum Pension Liability." The offsetting debit must be to a new account, "Intangible pension asset," but **this debit cannot exceed the amount of the unrecognized prior service cost at the end of the current year.** Any difference between the additional liability amount and the unrecognized prior service cost must be debited to a **contra equity** account such as "Unrealized Pension Cost." *FASB Standard 87*, par. 37, explains this rule as follows:

> If an additional minimum liability is recognized pursuant to paragraph 36, an equal amount shall be recognized as an intangible asset, provided that the asset recognized shall not exceed the amount of unrecognized prior service cost. If an additional liability required to be recognized exceeds unrecognized prior service cost, the excess (which would represent a net loss not yet recognized as net periodic pension cost) shall be reported as a separate component (that is, a reduction) of equity, net of any tax benefits that result from considering such losses as timing differences for purposes of applying the provisions of *APB Opinion No. 11*, "Accounting for Income Taxes."

In conformity with these rules, the data given above for the four cases would be recorded in the first year (i.e., end of 19B) as follows:

Accounts (end of 19B)	Case A	Case B		Case C		Case D	
Intangible pension asset[a]	(no entry)	8		5		8	
Unrealized pension cost[b]		12				27	
Additional minimum pension liability[c]			20		5		35

Explanation:
a. Cannot exceed the 19B ending amount of unrecognized prior service cost, $8.
b. Report on the statement of financial position, stockholders' equity, under a subcaption "Unrealized capital."
c. For reporting on the statement of financial position net this with the balance of Accrued/Prepaid Pension Cost.

In **subsequent** years, the balance in the three accounts (recorded above) must be continually adjusted. *FASB Standard 87*, par. 38, explains the adjustment as follows: "When a new determination of the amount of additional liability is made to prepare a statement of financial position, the related intangible asset and separate component of equity shall be eliminated or adjusted as necessary."

In making the adjustment, three rules must be followed: *(a)* the additional minimum liability account must be adjusted from its prior balance to its new balance, *(b)* the balance in the intangible asset account never can exceed the unamortized balance of prior service cost at the end of the current year, and *(c)* the unrealized capital account is changed for the difference (*FASB Standard 87*, page 109).

To illustrate the adjustments for the next year, 19C, refer to the above illustration and assume that *(a)* the new additional minimum liability is $3 and *(b)* unamortized prior service cost is $8 in each year for all cases. The following entries for 19C would be made to adjust the account balances of the prior year.

Items	Case B		Case C		Case D	
Balances from 19B:						
Intangible pension asset	$ 8dr.		$5dr.		$ 8dr.	
Unrealized pension cost	12dr.				27dr.	
Additional minimum pension liability	20cr.		5cr.		35cr.	
Additional minimum liability, for 19C	3		3		3	
Unamortized prior service cost, for 19C	8		8		8	
19C entry to adjust the 19B balances:						
Additional minimum pension liability	17[a]		2[b]		32[c]	
Intangible pension asset		8		2		8
Unrealized pension cost		9				24

[a] $20 − $3 = $17.
[b] $5 − $3 = $2.
[c] $35 − $3 = $32.

Adjusted balances in the accounts at the end of 19C:	Case B	Case C	Case D
Intangible pension asset	$0*	$3	$0
Unrealized pension cost	3	0	3
Additional minimum pension liability	3	3	3

* Computations: $8 − $8 = $0; $12 − $9 = $3; $20 − $17 = $3; etc.

The above reductions of the intangible asset and unrealized equity account followed a FIFO pattern which is consistent with the FASB objective to minimize the asset amount (sometimes called **pension goodwill**) by imposing the PSC constraint. *FASB Standard 87* is silent on this point. As a result, companies often use a LIFO pattern which causes the intangible asset to be higher than when the FIFO pattern is used. Either approach inconsistently appears to be acceptable.

The additional minimum pension liability has received considerable criticism because *(a)* it does not resolve the delayed recognition/pension liability problem, *(b)* unique computations are used, and *(c)* no reason was given for many of

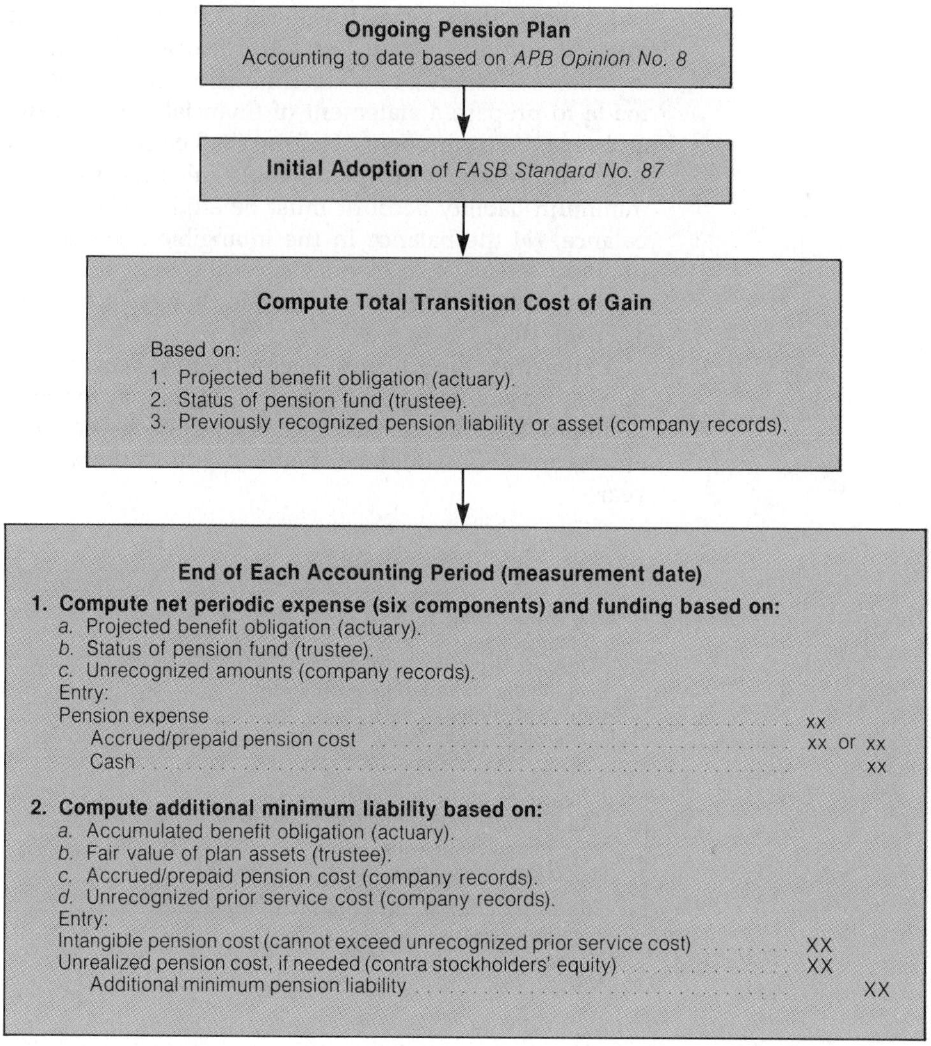
Ongoing Pension Plan
Accounting to date based on *APB Opinion No. 8*
Initial Adoption of *FASB Standard No. 87*
Compute Total Transition Cost of Gain
Based on:
1. Projected benefit obligation (actuary).
2. Status of pension fund (trustee).
3. Previously recognized pension liability or asset (company records).
End of Each Accounting Period (measurement date)
1. Compute net periodic expense (six components) and funding based on:
a. Projected benefit obligation (actuary).
b. Status of pension fund (trustee).
c. Unrecognized amounts (company records).
Entry:
Pension expense XX
Accrued/prepaid pension cost . . . . . XX or XX
Cash XX
2. Compute additional minimum liability based on:
a. Accumulated benefit obligation (actuary).
b. Fair value of plan assets (trustee).
c. Accrued/prepaid pension cost (company records).
d. Unrecognized prior service cost (company records).
Entry:
Intangible pension cost (cannot exceed unrecognized prior service cost) XX
Unrealized pension cost, if needed (contra stockholders' equity) XX
Additional minimum pension liability XX

Exhibit 20–7
Overview of accounting for pensions with emphasis on the minimum pension liability.

the rules specified. The following comments by Miller are indicative of these problems:[15]

> The additional liability balance merely goes up and down from year to year as needed to achieve the desired result. It does not accrue interest, is not amortized and is not paid off. In short, its balance is simply plugged at the end of each period.
>
> *The offsetting debit.* If there is a plugged credit balance for the additional liability, there also must be a plugged debit. *Statement No. 87* requires the employer to set up an on-balance sheet "pension intangible" that goes up and down in tandem with the additional liability. The FASB limits the balance of the intangible to no greater than the balance of the unrecognized prior service cost, which corresponds to pension goodwill.

[15] Paul B. W. Miller, "The New Pension Accounting," *Journal of Accountancy*, American Institute of CPAs, February 1987, pp. 86–94.

FASB Standard 87 gives two interesting and informative dissents as follows:

> Mr. Sprouse objects, however, to the unique recognition practices this *Statement* establishes for an "intangible asset." In certain situations, this *Statement* calls for an employer to recognize an intangible asset to offset the result of a loss on plan assets or to eliminate an intangible asset to offset the result of a gain on plan assets. Similar recognition or elimination of an intangible asset is required to offset the effects of changes in actuarial assumptions related to the accumulated benefit obligation. Those features are unacceptable to him. In his view, those recognition practices can be neither reconciled with the Board's conceptual framework nor readily understood by financial statement users. He believes they seriously diminish the credibility of employers' accounting for pension costs.
>
> Mr. Brown believes that an employer has an obligation under a defined benefit plan and that information about that obligation and the resources accumulated to meet it should be included in financial reports. In his view, however, the nature of point-in-time value measures of plan assets and of plan obligations (whether measured in terms of vested benefits, accumulated benefits, or projected benefit obligations) is such that they do not fall meaningfully and readily within the present structure of financial statements. Delayed recognition of price changes and of actuarial gains and losses is embodied in the methodology of this *Statement* for pension cost determination. To require balance sheet recognition of selected point-in-time market values and actuarial liability estimates—and this only when liabilities exceed assets—is inconsistent both internally and with expense recognition methodology. It would also, in Mr. Brown's view, be confusing to users. He does not believe that the proposed intangible assets and separate components of equity that would be recorded in tandem with additional liability recognition would add meaningful or understandable information. For these reasons, he believes that plan asset and pension obligation information is better presented in disclosures to financial statements.

An overview of accounting for pensions, with an emphasis on the minimum pension liability, is given in **Exhibit 20–7.**

Reporting, Including Note Disclosures

The financial effects of a pension plan often are reported on the statement of income and under **each** of the statement of financial position captions—assets, liabilities, and stockholders' equity—as follows:

Statement of income:

Net periodic pension expense

Statement of financial position:

- Assets:
  - Prepaid pension cost
  - Intangible pension asset (related to the additional minimum liability)
- Liabilities:
  - Accrued pension cost
  - Additional minimum pension liability*
- Owners' equity:
  - Unrealized capital:
    - Unrealized pension cost (debit—related to the additional minimum liability)

* Additional pension liability is combined with accrued/prepaid pension cost for reporting purposes.

Detailed **note disclosures** are specified by *FASB Standard 87*, par. 54. Note disclosures provide information not recorded in the accounts or reported in the statement of income or statement of financial position under the provisions of *FASB Standard 87*. This information is not recognized or recorded in the accounts because of the three special characteristics of pension accounting—delayed recognition, net cost, and offsetting (see page 977). The *Standard* explains that note disclosures are to "provide more complete and more current information that can be practically incorporated in financial statements at the present time" (*FASB Standard 87*, Summary, page 3).

The **required note disclosures** are (par. 54):

a. A description of the plan including employee groups covered, type of benefit formula, **funding policy,** types of assets held and significant nonbenefit liabilities, if any, and the nature and effect of significant matters affecting comparability of information for all periods presented.
b. The amount of net periodic pension expense for the period showing separately the service cost component, the interest cost component, the actual return on assets for the period, and the net total of other components.*
c. A schedule reconciling the funded status of the plan with amounts reported in the employer's statement of financial position, showing separately:
   (1) The fair value of plan assets.
   (2) The projected benefit obligation identifying the accumulated benefit obligation and the vested benefit obligation.
   (3) The amount of unrecognized prior service cost.
   (4) The amount of unrecognized net gain or loss (including asset gains and losses not yet reflected in market-related value).
   (5) The amount of remaining unrecognized net obligation or net asset existing at the date of initial application of this *Standard.*
   (6) The amount of any additional minimum pension liability.
   (7) The amount of net pension asset or liability recognized in the statement of financial position (which is the net result of combining the preceding six items).
d. The estimated weighted-average discount rate and rate of compensation increase (if applicable) used to measure the projected benefit obligation and the weighted-average expected long-term rate of return on plan assets.
e. If applicable, the amounts and types of securities of the employer and related parties included in plan assets, and the approximate amount of annual benefits of employees and retirees covered by annuity contracts issued by the employer and related parties. Also, if applicable, the alternative amortization methods used.

* The net total of other components is the net effect during the period of certain delayed recognition provisions of *FASB Standard 87*. This net total includes:
a. The net asset gain or loss during the period deferred for later recognition (in effect, an offset or a supplement to the actual return on assets).
b. Amortization of unrecognized prior service cost.
c. Amortization of the unrecognized net gain or loss from earlier periods.
d. Amortization of the unrecognized net obligation or net asset existing at the date of initial application of this Standard (transition cost).

Note disclosures are illustrated on page 1003.

Pension note disclosures, Dun & Bradstreet Corporation.

THE DUN & BRADSTREET CORPORATION
NOTES TO CONSOLIDATED FINANCIAL STATEMENTS

Note 4. Retirement Plans

The Company has defined benefit pension plans which provide benefits to substantially all employees in the United States. Effective January 1, 1986, the Company adopted Statement of Financial Accounting Standards (SFAS) No. 87 "Employers' Accounting for Pensions" for all of these plans. Adoption of SFAS No. 87 reduced 1986 pension costs by approximately $22,932,000. Pension cost (benefit) for 1986 is summarized as follows:

Service Cost	$17,546,000
Interest Cost	38,122,000
Actual Return on Plan Assets	(99,025,000)
Net Amortization and Deferral	27,886,000
Foreign Plans	8,314,000
Total Pension Benefit	$(7,157,000)

During the fourth quarter of 1986, the Company offered a voluntary early retirement opportunity, enabling certain employees to elect early retirement. The early retirement opportunity, which was accounted for under SFAS No. 88, "Employers' Accounting for Settlements and Curtailments of Defined Benefit Pension Plans and for Termination Benefits," resulted in a charge to 1986 expense of $100 million.

Additionally a curtailment and settlement gain of $7,649,000 was included in the determination of the gain on the sale of Technical Publishing Company.

The Company's pension cost was $21,556,000 in 1985 and $29,984,000 in 1984.

The status of the defined benefit plans covering employees in the United States at December 31, 1986, was as follows:

	Funded	Unfunded
Fair Value of Plan Assets	$701,925,000	—
Actuarial Present Value of Benefit Obligations:		
Vested Benefits	(412,375,000)	$(7,163,000)
Non-vested Benefits	(31,523,000)	(417,000)
Accumulated Benefit Obligation	(443,898,000)	(7,580,000)
Effect of Projected Future Salary Increases	(86,363,000)	(8,214,000)
Projected Benefit Obligation	(530,261,000)	(15,794,000)
Plan Assets in Excess of (Less than) Projected Benefit Obligation	171,664,000	(15,794,000)
Unrecognized Net (Gain) Loss	(5,588,000)	1,563,000
Unrecognized Prior Service Cost	1,800,000	1,077,000
Unrecognized Net (Asset) Obligation at December 31, 1986	(197,627,000)	5,774,000
Accrued Pension Cost	$(29,751,000)	$(7,380,000)

The expected long-term rate of return on plan assets was 9.0% for 1986 and 7.5% for 1985. The discount rate and rate of increase in future compensation levels used in determining the actuarial present value of accumulated benefit obligations at December 31; 1986, were 8% and 5.9%, respectively. Plan assets are invested in a diversified portfolio that primarily consists of equity and debt securities.

The actuarial present value of vested and non-vested accumulated plan benefits as of January 1, 1985, for funded plans was $322,350,000 and $35,207,000, respectively; net assets available for plan benefits amounted to $524,222,000.

In addition to providing pension benefits, the Company provides various health care and life insurance benefits for retired employees. Substantially all of the Company's domestic employees become eligible for these benefits if they reach normal retirement age while working for the Company. The costs of providing such benefits were not material to the Company's results of operations for 1986, 1985 and 1984.

Comprehensive Three-Year Demonstration Case

Part A discussed the basic characteristics of a defined benefit pension plan and the related accounting. For instructional convenience the illustration of Hypo Company showed one year only. Now we illustrate a comprehensive three-year case for Employer Company. Employer Company is a scaled-down version of a major company. The purpose of this three-year illustration is to provide an overview that continues the same case throughout. It shows the relationships and continuity of the PBO, fund assets, amortization of the unrecognized costs, and the pension liability.

Employer Company started a noncontributory defined benefit pension plan on January 1, 19A. During 19A, the company accounted for the pension plan in conformity with *APB Opinion 8*. The company decided to start the initial application of *FASB Standard 87* on January 1, 19B. This case illustrates the *(a)* **transition** to apply *FASB Standard 87* and *(b)* pension accounting for the 19B, 19C, and 19D accounting periods in conformity with *FASB Standard 87*. The case emphasizes the (1) basic amount provided each year-end by the actuary, the **projected benefit obligation (PBO),** (2) **fund status** provided by the fund trustee, and (3) computation of **net periodic pension expense** and the **accrued/prepaid pension cost** by the employer. For each year, data are given about the changes in the PBO and the pension plan assets. Based on these data, the employer's accounting entries and disclosures are given. (All amounts are in thousands.)

First, examine **Exhibit 20–8** and notice the three consecutive reports (19B, 19C, and 19D) provided by the actuary (PBO) and the pension fund trustee (pension plan assets). Notice that on each report **the ending balance for each period is carried forward as the beginning balance for the next period.**

Using the data provided by the actuary and the trustee (Exhibit 20–8), Employer Company can prepare an analytical spreadsheet each period to readily compute the information needed for recording and reporting purposes. These three spreadsheets for 19A, 19B, and 19C are shown in **Exhibit 20–9A, 20–9B,** and **20–9C.** Notice that the first three columns are taken directly from the reports of the actuary and fund trustee. The fourth column is used to analyze the three unrecognized items to compute the amounts on a delayed recognition basis. As this column is completed each item is concurrently extended to one of the last two columns—net periodic pension expense and accrued/prepaid cost. The last column reflects only changes in the accrued (prepaid) pension liability.

Important characteristics of this spreadsheet are: (1) it incorporates proofs of accuracy (beginning and ending balances), (2) it sets out the beginning and ending balances of the unrecognized pension costs, (3) it provides separate amounts for each of the six components of periodic pension expense, (4) it maintains a cumulative record of the accrued (prepaid) pension liability, and (5) it specifically provides the data for the entry that must be made in the company's accounts. Finally, it directly provides information for two required note disclosures—funding status and reconciliation of the recognized and unrecognized net obligations with the accrued (prepaid) pension cost. These two disclosures taken directly from the spreadsheet are shown on page 1009.

Finally, a test must be done to determine whether an entry should be made

Exhibit 20–8
Three annual reports—provided by the actuary and fund trustee for Employer Company.

A. Actuary's Report—Projected Benefit Obligation and Related Data:

Items	19A	19B	19C	19D
1. PBO, beginning balance	(not applicable—*APB Opinion No. 8*)	$1,000[a]	$1,120	$1,344
2. Service cost (PV of pension credits)		110	120	130
3. Interest cost (9% based on beginning balance)[b]		90	101	139
Unrecognized pension costs:				
4. Transition cost		[a]		
5. Prior service cost (PSC) (Jan. 1, 19D; start amortization at the end of 19D)				200
6. Loss (gain): from plan assets changes in actuarial assumptions			111[c]	0
7. Pension benefits paid to retirees		(80)	(108)	(139)
8. PBO, ending balance	$1,000	$1,120	$1,344	$1,674
9. Accumulated benefit obligation		$ 800	$ 950	$1,260
10. Discount interest rate used by actuary		9%	9%	9%
11. Average remaining service period of employees[d]		10	9	8

B. Pension Plan Trustee's Report—Pension Plan Assets and Related Data:

Items	19A	19B	19C	19D
1. Plan assets, beginning balance		$ 800	$ 925	$1,032
2. Actual return on plan assets at fair value		100	90	99
3. Cash received from Employer Company		105	125	240
4. Pension benefits paid to retirees		(80)	(108)	(139)
5. Plan assets, ending balance	$ 800	$ 925	$1,032	$1,232
6. Expected return on plan assets:				
a. Rate		10%	9.7%	9.6%
b. Amount (line 1 × line 6a; assumed to be the same as market-related value)		$ 80	$ 90	$ 99
7. Unrecognized gain (loss) on plan assets (line 2 − line 6b)		$ 20	$ -0-	$ -0-

a. PBO includes $200 transition cost.
b. $1,000 × 9% = $90; $1,120 × 9% = $101; ($1,344 + PSC, $200) × 9% = $139.
c. 19C, due to actuary's changes in actuarial assumptions.
d. See Supplement 20–A for computation methods.

for an additional minimum pension liability. The test and its results are as follows:

a. Test based on accumulated benefit obligation and plan assets (see below and p. 1009):

Computation of additional minimum liability (based on December 31, 19D balances):

Accumulated benefit obligation	$1,260
Less: Plan assets at fair value	(1,232)
Underfunded accumulated benefit obligation (minimum total pension liability required)	28
Accrued pension liability (balance from above)	(22)
Additional minimum liability	$ 6

Exhibit 20–9A

Pension plan spreadsheet analysis for Employer Company, 19B; to compute: (1) unrecognized pension costs, (2) net periodic pension expense, and (3) accrued (prepaid) pension cost.

Items	PBO (actuary)	Pension plan assets (trustee)	Unrecognized pension cost (by company)	Net periodic pension expense (by company)	(Accrued)/prepaid cost (by company)
Beginning Balances 19B:	$1,000	$800	$200	$-0-	$-0-
Changes in PBO during 19B:					
Service cost	110			(1) 110	
Interest cost ($1,000 × 9%)	90			(2) 90	
Unrecognized costs (delayed):					
Transition cost:					
Unrecognized at beginning 19B			L $200		
Increase (decrease) in 19B			-0-		
Total unrecognized			L 200		
Amortized in 19B ($200 ÷ 10)			L 20	(3) 20	
Unrecognized balance at end 19B			L $180		
Prior service cost:					
Unrecognized at beginning 19B			$-0-		
Increase (decrease) in 19B			-0-		
Total unrecognized			-0-		
Amortized in 19B (none)			-0-	(4) -0-	
Unrecognized balance at end 19B			$-0-		
Loss (gain):					
Unrecognized, at beginning 19B			$-0-		
Change from PBO 19B			-0-		
Change from plan assets, 19B			G (20)*		
Total unrecognized			G (20)		
Amortized in 19B (none)			-0-	(5) -0-	
Unrecognized at end 19B			G $(20)		
Changes in plan assets during 19B:					
Expected return $800 × 10% = $80			$20	(6) (80)	
Actual return on plan assets		100			
Cash received from company		105			105
Pension benefits paid to retirees	(80)	(80)			
Ending Balances, 19B:					
PBO	$1,120				
Plan assets		$925			
Under (over) funded PBO		$195			
Unrecognized pension costs			$160		
Net periodic pension expense for 19B				$140	(140)
(Accrued)/prepaid pension cost					$(35)

* Amortization starts next period.

Proof: Beginning $1,000 − $800 − $200 = $-0-; Ending $1,120 − $925 − $160 = $35 (accrued)

Accounting entry: Pension expense	140	
Accrued/prepaid pension cost ($0 − $35)	or	35
Cash		105

Exhibit 20–9B

Pension plan spreadsheet analysis for Employer Company, 19C (continued from Exhibit 20–9A).

Items	PBO (actuary)	Pension plan assets (trustee)	Unrecognized pension cost (by company)	Net periodic pension expense (by company)	(Accrued)/ prepaid cost (by company)
Beginning Balances 19C:	$1,120	$ 925	$160	$-0-	$(35)
Changes in PBO during 19C:					
Service cost	120			(1) 120	
Interest cost ($1,120 × 9%)	101			(2) 101	
Unrecognized costs (delayed):					
Transition cost:					
Unrecognized at beginning 19C			L $180		
Increase (decrease) in 19C			L -0-		
Total unrecognized			L 180		
Amortized in 19C ($180 ÷ 9)			L 20	(3) 20	
Unrecognized balance at end 19C			L $160		
Prior service cost:					
Unrecognized at beginning 19C			$-0-		
Increase (decrease) in 19C			-0-		
Total unrecognized			-0-		
Amortized in 19C			-0-	(4) -0-	
Unrecognized balance at end 19C			-0-		
Loss (gain):					
Unrecognized, beginning 19C			G $ 20		
Change from PBO 19C	111*		L 111†		
Change from plan assets, 19C			-0-		
Total unrecognized			L 91		
Amortized in 19C ($20 ÷ 10)			G 2	(5) (2)	
Unrecognized at end 19C			L $ 93		
Changes in plan assets during 19C:					
Expected return $925 × 9.7% = $90 →			$-0-	(6) (90)	
Actual return on plan assets		90			
Cash received from company		125			(125)
Pension benefits paid to retirees	(108)	(108)			
Ending Balances, 19C:					
PBO	$1,344				
Plan assets		$1,032			
Under (over) funded PBO	$312				
Unrecognized pension costs			$253		
Net periodic pension expense for 19C				$149	(149)
(Accrued)/prepaid pension cost					$(59)

* Changes in actuarial assumptions.

† Minimum amortization check: Compare beginning PBO, $1,120; with plan assets, $925. Use the larger: $1,120 × 10% = $112 (rounded). This amount is greater than the unrecognized gain as of January 1, 19C, $20; therefore, no amortization is required. The company elected to amortize unrecognized gains and losses based on the nine-year average employee service period (see page 995).

Proof: Beginning $1,120 − $925 − $160 = $35; Ending $1,344 − $1,032 − $253 = $59

Accounting entry:		
Pension expense	149	
Accrued/prepaid pension cost ($35 − $59)		24
Cash		125

Exhibit 20–9C

Pension plan spreadsheet analysis for Employer Company, 19D (continued from Exhibits 20–9A and 20–9B).

Items	PBO (actuary)	Pension plan assets (trustee)	Unrecognized pension cost (by company)	Net periodic pension expense (by company)	(Accrued)/ prepaid cost (by company)
Beginning Balances 19D:	$1,344	$1,032	$253	$-0-	$ (59)
Changes in PBO during 19D:					
Service cost	130			(1) 130	
Interest cost ($1,344 + PSC, $200) × 9%	139*			(2) 139	
Unrecognized costs (delayed):					
Transition cost:					
Unrecognized at beginning 19D			L $160		
Increase (decrease) in 19D			-0-		
Total unrecognized			L 160		
Amortized in 19D ($160 ÷ 8)			L 20	(3) 20	
Unrecognized balance at end 19D			L 140		
Prior service cost:					
Unrecognized at beginning			$-0-		
Increase (decrease) Jan. 1, 19D	200		L 200†		
Total unrecognized			L 200		
Amortized in 19D ($200 ÷ 8)			L 25	(4) 25	
Unrecognized balance at end 19D			L $175		
Loss (gain):					
Unrecognized, beginning 19B			L $ 93		
Change from PBO 19B			-0-		
Change from plan assets 19B			-0-		
Total unrecognized			L 93		
Amortized in 19B ($93 ÷ 8)			L 12	(5) 12	
Unrecognized at end 19B			L $ 81		
Changes in plan assets during 19B:					
Expected return $1,032 × 9.6% = $99			$-0-	(6) (99)	
Actual return on plan assets		99			
Cash received from company		240			240
Pension benefits paid to retirees	(139)	(139)			
Ending Balances, 19D:					
PBO	$1,674				
Plan assets		$1,232			
Under (over) funded PBO	$442				
Unrecognized pension costs			$396		
Net periodic pension expense for				$227	(227)
(Accrued)/prepaid pension cost					$ (46)

* This amount is included PSC, $200 because it was started on January 1, 19D.
† Amortization starts next period.
Note: Computation and entry for additional minimum pension liability is shown on page 997.

Proof: Beginning $1,344 − $1,032 − $253 = $59, Ending $1,674 − $1,232 − $396 = $46

Accounting entry:

Pension expense	227	
Accrued/prepaid pension cost ($46 − $59)	13 or	
Cash		240

b. Entry to record the additional minimum pension liability on December 31, 19D:

Intangible pension asset*	6	
Additional minimum pension liability		6

* Cannot exceed unrecognized prior service cost.

Disclosures Required

FASB Standard 87, par. 54, specifies five categories of disclosures that are required. These disclosures for Employer Company are shown below. Notice that **all of the amounts** are directly provided by the spreadsheets by year (i.e., Exhibits 20–9A, 20–9B, and 20–9C).

a. Description of the pension plan:
1. Employees covered—all employees with more than two years of employment in the company.
2. Type of formula: Defined benefit plan.
3. Funding—Annual payments approximating the amount of the projected benefit obligation. Funding is by an external financial institution; basic investment policy—55% equity securities, 30% debt securities, and 15% other investments.

b. Components of net periodic pension expense:

	19B	19C	19D
Service cost	$110	$120	$130
Interest cost	90	101	139
Recognized (amount amortized):			
Transition cost	20	20	20
Prior service cost	-0-	-0-	25
Losses (gains)	-0-	2	12
Expected return on plan assets	(80)	(90)	(99)
Net periodic pension expense	$140	$149	$227

c. Reconciliation of funding with the accrued/prepaid balance (which is reported on the statement of financial position):

	19B	19C	19D
Disclosure notes:			
Projected benefit obligation (ending)	$1,100	$1,322	$1,650
Plan assets at fair value	925	1,032	1,232
Under (over) funding (delayed recognition basis)	175	290	418
Add: Unrecognized pension costs	160	253	396
Total under (over) funding on full recognition basis	$ 335	$ 543	$ 814
Projected benefit obligation (PBO)	$1,120	1,344	$1,674
Less: Plan assets at fair value	925	1,032	1,232
Under (over) funding of PBO (delayed recognition basis)	195	312	442
Add (deduct):			
Unrecognized transition cost	180	160	140
Unrecognized prior service cost	-0-	-0-	175
Unrecognized gain (loss) on plan asset and changes in actual assumptions	(20)	93	81
Subtotal	160	253	396
(Accrued)/prepaid pension cost recognized	$ (35)	$ (59)	$ (46)

d. Interest rates:			
Used by the actuary for discounting	9%	9%	9%
Used by the trustee for expected long-term rate on plan assets	10%	9.7%	9.6%
e. Employee Company's securities held in the pension plan	None	None	None
Amortization methods used to amortize unrecognized pension costs (SL = straight-line)	SL	SL	SL

Curtailments and Settlements of Pension Plans, and Termination Benefits

Defined benefit pension plans sometimes are changed in special ways that may affect the *(a)* employer's projected benefit obligation, *(b)* payment of the vested benefit obligation of each employee affected, and *(c)* plan assets required. *FASB Standard 88* provides accounting guidelines for such changes.

FASB Standard 88 is directly related to *FASB Standard 87*. First, the statements have the **same transition dates** and second, the accounting implications are consistent.

FASB Standard 88 defines the events that "require certain previously **unrecognized** amounts to be recognized in earnings and as adjustments to liabilities and assets" and specifies that "settlement of all or part of the pension benefit obligation should be the event that requires recognition of all or part of the previously unrecognized gain or loss" (par. 27). Therefore, **the requirements of *FASB Standard 88* focus on the effects of changes on the projected, accumulated, and vested benefit obligations, and the three unrecognized pension amounts**—transition cost, prior service cost, and gains and losses. *FASB Standard 88* classifies the changes as *(a)* pension plan curtailments, *(b)* pension plan settlements, and *(c)* terminations.

Pension Plan Curtailments

FASB Standard 88, par. 6, defines a pension plan **curtailment** as an event that either:

a. Reduces the expected years of future service of present employees, or

b. Eliminates, for a significant number of employees, the accrual of defined benefits for some or all of their future services.

These special events may cause a decrease (resulting in a gain) or an increase (resulting in a loss) of the **projected benefit obligation.**

Accounting for Curtailments. When a curtailment occurs, any **unrecognized prior service cost** and **unrecognized transition cost** related to years of service no longer expected to be rendered due to the curtailment should be **recognized** as a **loss.** However, any unrecognized transition amount in the case of an **overfunded** projected benefit obligation (i.e., an asset) is **not** immediately recognized. For example, if a curtailment eliminates half of the estimated remaining future years of service related to the prior service cost and transition cost, then the loss is half of the remaining unrecognized prior service and transition cost. We will call this loss the **prior service and transition loss.**

In addition to the prior service and transition loss, a curtailment may **decrease** (a **gain**) or **increase** (a **loss**) the **projected benefit obligation.** We will call this gain or loss the **PBO gain or loss.**

FASB Standard 88, par. 13, specifies the following:

a. Any **PBO gain** (as defined above) should be **recognized** to the extent that the **PBO gain exceeds any unrecognized net loss.** If there is an **unrecognized net gain, all** of the PBO gain should be recognized as a curtailment gain.
b. Any **PBO loss** (as defined above) should be **recognized** to the extent that the **PBO loss exceeds any unrecognized net gain.** If there is an **unrecognized net loss, all** of the PBO loss should be recognized as a curtailment loss.

For this calculation, **unrecognized net gain or loss includes** any unrecognized transition asset (i.e., **overfunded.** PBO at date of transition). Several cases are possible, including the following (amounts, in thousands, assumed):

	Case A	Case B	Case C	Case D	Case E	Case F
PBO gain (loss)	$100	$100	$ 100	$(100)	$(100)	$(100)
Unrecognized net gain (loss)	$ 50	$ (50)	$(120)	$ 50	$ (50)	$ 120
Curtailment gain (loss)	$100	$ 50	$ -0-	$ (50)	$(100)	$ -0-

If the net sum of the **prior service and transition loss and the curtailment gain or loss** is a **loss,** it should be **recognized** when it is **probable** that a curtailment will occur and the effects can be **reasonably** estimated. If the net sum is a **gain,** it should be **recognized** when the related employees **terminate** or the **curtailment occurs.** The corresponding credit (if a loss) or debit (if a gain) is to accrued/prepaid pension cost.

Illustration of a Curtailment. CURT Corporation significantly reduced its operations for one line of its products. Although no facilities were closed, a significant number of employees were terminated. At date of termination, the portion of the actuary's projected benefit obligation related to the terminated employees was $110. There were no unrecognized losses or gains *(a)* at transition or *(b)* after transition to *FASB Standard 87.*

The entry to record the **reduction** in the projected benefit obligation due to the curtailment of pension benefits (i.e., reduction of the employer's pension obligations) is:

Accrued/**prepaid** pension cost	110	
Gain from curtailment		110

A comprehensive illustration of accounting for curtailments is presented in **Exhibit 20–10,** which emphasizes the following points:

1. In Case A (panel B), unrecognized transition **gain** is **not** recognized at date of curtailment. The net gain recognized due to the curtailment is the difference between prior service and transition loss, $20, and PBO gain, $500. This net curtailment gain is recognized in full because there is an unrecognized net **gain** of $150.
2. In Case B (panel B), unrecognized transition **cost** and unrecognized prior service cost are recognized to the extent that future service is reduced

Exhibit 20–10
Accounting for pension curtailments.

Panel A—Case Data (all amounts in thousands):

1. On January 1, 19C, Wilson Company significantly reduced its operations and terminated a number of employees.
2. The impact of the curtailment was to reduce Wilson's projected benefit obligation by $500 and the expected future years of employee service by 50%.
3. Two independent cases are considered based on the following pension obligations and plan assets as of January 1, 19C:

	Case A	Case B
Projected benefit obligation	$ 1,000	$1,000
Plan assets at fair value	(1,100)	(900)
Under (over) funded PBO	(100)	100
Add (deduct) unamortized items:		
Unrecognized transition (cost) gain	100	(90)
Unrecognized net gain (loss)	150	(150)
Unrecognized prior service cost	(40)	(40)
Accrued (prepaid) pension cost	$ 110	$ (180)

Panel B—Analysis of Effects of Curtailment:

Case A—Unrecognized transition gain not recognized at curtailment date:

	Before curtailment	Effects of curtailment (gain) loss	After curtailment
PBO	$ 1,000	$(500) *(a)*	$ 500
Plan assets at fair value	(1,100)		(1,100)
Under (over) funded PBO	(100)		(600)
Add (deduct) unamortized items:			
Unrecognized transition gain	100	−0− *(b)*	100
Unrecognized net gain	150		150
Unrecognized prior service cost	(40)	20 *(c)*	(20)
Accrued (prepaid) pension cost	$ 110	$(480)	$ (370)

(a) PBO gain is $500, the amount of the reduction in the PBO. The $500 is recognized in full because there is an unrecognized net gain of $150 at date of curtailment.
(b) Unrecognized transition gain is not immediately recognized.
(c) Prior service and transition loss is $20 (i.e., $40 × 50% = $20).

Entry to reflect curtailment, January 1, 19C:

Accrued/**prepaid** pension cost	480	
Gain from curtailment		480

(i.e., 50 percent). The PBO gain, $500, is recognized only to the extent that it exceeds unrecognized net loss, $150.

Pension Plan Settlements

FASB Standard 88, par. 3, defines a pension plan **settlement** as a transaction that meets **all** of the following criteria:

a. The transaction is an irrevocable action.

b. It relieves the employer (or the plan) of primary responsibility for a pension plan obligation. This means that, as a minimum, the **vested benefit obligation** must be paid.

c. It eliminates significant risk related to the obligation and assets used to effect the settlement.

Exhibit 20–10
(concluded)

Case B—Unrecognized transition cost recognized at curtailment date:

	Before curtailment	Effects of curtailment (gain) loss	After curtailment
PBO	$ 1,000	$(500) *(a)*	$ 500
Plan assets at fair value	(900)		(900)
Under (over funded) PBO	100		(400)
Add (deduct) unamortized items:			
Unrecognized transition cost	(90)	45 *(b)*	(45)
Unrecognized net loss	(150)	150 *(a)*	-0-
Unrecognized prior service cost	(40)	20 *(b)*	(20)
Accrued (prepaid) pension cost	$ (180)	$(285)	$(465)

(a) PBO gain is $500, the amount of reduction in the PBO due to curtailment. However, only $350 of this gain is recognized (i.e., the excess PBO gain over unrecognized net loss: $500 − $150 = $350).
(b) Prior service and transition loss is $65 [i.e., ($90 × 50% = $45) + ($40 × 50% = $20) = $65].

Entry to reflect curtailment, January 1, 19C:

Accrued/**prepaid** pension cost	285	
Gain from curtailment		285

Examples are *(a)* lump-sum cash payments to replace future pension benefits, and *(b)* the purchase of an annuity to cover vested benefits.[16] Each of these events clearly meets all three of the above criteria.

Accounting for Settlements. *FASB Standard 88,* par. 9, specifies that the **maximum gain or loss** that can be recognized for a settlement is the **net of any unrecognized gain or loss and any unrecognized net asset at transition date** (i.e., the unrecognized net asset related to an overfunded projected benefit obligation when *FASB Standard 87* is first applied).[17] The maximum gain or loss is recognized in **full** if the **entire** projected benefit obligation is settled. If only part of the projected benefit obligation is settled, a pro rata portion of the maximum amount is recognized. The pro rata portion is equal to the percentage reduction in the projected benefit obligation. For example, if 25 percent of the projected benefit obligation is settled, 25 percent of the maximum gain or loss should be recognized.

---

[16] *FASB Standard 88,* par. 5, states: "An **annuity contract** is a contract in which an insurance company unconditionally undertakes a legal obligation to provide specified benefits to specific individuals in return for a fixed consideration or premium. An annuity contract is irrevocable and involves the transfer of significant risk from the employer to the insurance company. Some annuity contracts (participation annuity contracts) provide that the purchaser (either the plan or the employer) may participate in the experience of the insurance company. Under those contracts, the insurance company ordinarily pays dividends to the purchaser. If the substance of a participation annuity contract is such that the employer remains subject to all or most of the risks and and rewards associated with the benefit obligation covered or the assets transferred to the insurance company, the purchase of the contract does not constitute a settlement."

[17] *FASB Standard 88,* par. 10, states that if the purchase of a participating annuity contract (see footnote 16) constitutes a settlement, the maximum gain (but not the maximum loss) should be reduced by the cost of the participation right before determining the amount to be recognized in earnings.

If the cost of all settlements in a period is less than or equal to the sum of the service cost and interest cost components of net periodic pension expense, gain or loss recognition is permitted but not required for the settlements (*FASB Standard 88*, par. 11).

When a settlement gain or loss is recognized, the corresponding debit (if a gain) or credit (if a loss) is to **accrued/prepaid pension cost.**

Illustration of a Settlement. Settle Corporation has a defined benefit pension plan. On December 31, 19E, the company settled the **vested benefit obligation** of $1,200 by purchasing with pension plan assets nonparticipating annuity contracts. A summary of Settle's pension plan obligations and a reconciliation of recognized and unrecognized amounts prior to the settlement is given below:

Projected benefit obligation	$2,000
Plan assets at fair value	(2,100)
Overfunded projected benefit obligation	(100)
Unrecognized net gain (i.e., asset) at transition (at adoption of *FASB Standard 87*)	200
Unrecognized net gain subsequent to transition	200
Accrued (prepaid) pension cost	$ 300
Vested benefit obligation	$1,200

The **maximum** gain Settle Company can recognize is $400 (i.e., $200, unrecognized transition gain, plus $200, unrecognized net gain). Because Settle is only settling 60 percent of its projected benefit obligation (i.e., $1,200 ÷ $2,000 = 60%), the gain to be recognized is:

$400 × 60% = $240 gain.

The projected benefit obligation, plan assets, and recognized and unrecognized amounts following the settlement are as follows:

Analysis of the Effects of a Pension Plan Settlement

	Before settlement	Effects of settlement	After settlement
Projected benefit obligation	$ 2,000	$(1,200)*	$ 800
Plan assets at fair value	(2,100)	1,200	(900)
Overfunded projected benefit obligation	(100)	-0-	(100)
Unrecognized transition asset (gain)	200	(120)†	80
Unrecognized net gain	200	$ (120)†	80
Accrued (prepaid) pension cost	$ 300	$ (240)	$ 60

* Settlement of the **vested** benefit obligation of $1,200.
† $200 × ($1,200 ÷ $2,000 = 60%) = $120.

The entry to record the settlement gain is:

Accrued/prepaid pension cost	240	
Settlement gain		240

Termination Benefits

Termination benefits may be provided to employees when their employment is terminated before their expected retirement dates. Termination benefits may be lump-sum payments, periodic future payments, or both. *FASB Standard 88*, par. 15, discusses termination benefits and gives the related accounting guidelines. Termination benefits may be either:

a. **Special termination benefits** offered for only a short period of time.
b. **Contractual termination benefits** required by the pension plan only if a special event, such as a plant closing, occurs.

The cost of termination benefits must include any lump-sum payments and the **present value** of any expected future payments. Termination benefits may be paid from company assets and/or pension plan assets.

Employers who offer **special** termination benefits must recognize a loss and a related liability when *(a)* the employees accept the offer, and *(b)* termination benefits can be reasonably estimated. Employers who provide **contractual** termination benefits must recognize a loss and a related liability when *(a)* it is **probable** that employees will be entitled to benefits and *(b)* the amount can be **reasonably estimated.**

Illustration of Termination Benefits. On January 1, 19E (start of the accounting year), TB Corporation significantly reduced its operations related to Product A. The company terminated 100 employees effective immediately. Each employee was given a special $5,000 termination benefit, payable as follows: January 1, 19E, $3,000 and December 31, 19E, $2,000 (plus 10% interest). These payments exceeded the **vested** benefits of each employee affected. A curtailment was not involved.

The entries related to the termination benefits only are (000s):

January 1, 19E:

Loss, termination benefits	500	
Cash		300
Liability for termination benefits		200

December 31, 19E:

Liability for termination benefits	200	
Interest expense ($200 × 10%)	20	
Cash		220

Termination benefits often are paid even though there is no pension plan as in the above example. However, if there is an ongoing pension plan that is affected the above entries would be made and, in addition, a pension curtailment would also be accounted for as previously illustrated (*FASB Standard 88*, par. 15).

Summary

After reading this chapter you probably will have some empathy with this quotation:[18] "Most companies are struggling to understand the new requirements of *Financial Accounting Standard No. 87*. Difficult as that may be, more

[18] Paul B. W. Miller, "The New Pension Accounting," *Journal of Accountancy*, AICPA, February 1987, pp. 86–94.

problems lie ahead, as management begins to focus on the long-term implications of the new requirements." Nevertheless, at the outset the chapter shows that the basic issues in accounting for a pension are to: *(a)* measure the future pension benefits, *(b)* determine the present value of those benefits, and *(c)* use that present value to determine funding requirements, pension expense, and any recognized pension liability. Fundamentally, recognized pension liability is the excess of pension expense over the funding set aside to pay the future benefits. A significant part of the funding is interest earned on the pension fund from the time cash is set aside for this purpose to the time the retired employee receives the benefits. To attribute (i.e., allocate) pension costs the matching principle is applied; that is, the pension costs are allocated to expense each reporting period on the basis of periodic pension credits earned by the employees.

Accounting for, and reporting of, pension plans rests primarily on two externally generated reports: *(a)* the actuary's report called the **Projected benefit obligation (PBO),** which is a debt to the employer company and *(b)* the pension fund trustee's report, called the **Status of pension fund assets.** *FASB Standard 87* specifies the measurement of pension expense, called **net periodic pension expense.** This expense is the sum of six components (some are costs and others are gains) as follows: service cost, interest cost, transition cost, prior service cost, losses and gains, and expected return on plan assets. Three of these costs—transition cost, prior service costs, and gains and losses—are called **unrecognized pension costs** because their total amounts are not recorded in the statements of income and financial position. Rather, these components are amortized and the amortizations only are recorded. These components are measured by the *(a)* actuary—service cost and interest cost, fund trustee—*(b)* return on plan assets, and *(c)* by the company—transition cost, prior service cost, and losses and gains.

The chapter presents a comprehensive spreadsheet for the employer that brings together determination of the PBO, pension plan assets, net periodic pension expense, accrued/prepaid pension cost, and the employer's pension entry. For summary purposes we recommend that you review this spreadsheet in Exhibits 20–6, 20–9A, 20–9B, and 20–9C.

SUPPLEMENT 20-A: ALTERNATIVE METHODS OF AMORTIZING UNRECOGNIZED PENSION COSTS

FASB Standard 87 specifies amortization methods for the three unrecognized pension costs—prior service, transition, and losses and gains. This supplement discusses the alternative amortization methods.

Prior Service Cost

FASB Standard 87, pars. 25–26, specifies two alternative methods for amortizing unrecognized prior service cost. The first method is based on total employee service rendered in each period; we call it the **service method.** The service method usually results in a **declining** amortization amount over time due to the retirement of employees who are affected by the plan amendment which created the prior service cost. An alternative method, **straight-line,** is allowed based on the average remaining service period of qualified employees. The straight-line method amortizes unrecognized prior service cost more rapidly than the service method and results in **equal** amortization amounts in each period.

To illustrate, assume that Small Company amended its pension plan on January 1, 19D. The amendment caused an unrecognized prior service cost of $48 (in thousands). Employees affected by the amendment are labeled A, B, C, D, and E. Each employee is scheduled to retire as follows:

Employee	Date of retirement	Remaining service years (as of January 1, 19D)
A	December 31, 19D	1
B.	December 31, 19E	2
C	December 31, 19E	2
D	December 31, 19F	3
E.	December 31, 19G	4

The following schedule for 19D provides a convenient method to determine total future service years and service years rendered in **each** accounting year. This schedule would be revised each year.

Schedule of future service years and service years rendered in each accounting year.

Employee	Future service years	19D	19E	19F	19G
A	1	1			
B	2	1	1		
C	2	1	1		
D	3	1	1	1	
E	4	1	1	1	1
Total future service years	12				
Service years rendered		5	4	2	1

Service Method. The service method of amortizing prior service cost is based on the ratio of service years rendered in an accounting year to total future service years. For example, in 19D, 5/12 of the total prior service cost is amortized. Periodic amortization of prior service cost using the service method is shown in the following schedule.

Schedule of service method amortization of unrecognized prior service cost (PSC).

Year	Prior service cost		Amortization rate	Amortization of unrecognized PSC	Balance unrecognized PSC*
19D	$48	×	5/12	$20	$28
19E	48	×	4/12	16	12
19F	48	×	2/12	8	4
19G	48	×	1/12	4	-0-
				$48	

* These values typically change each year because of changes in the denominator.

Notice the typical **declining** amortization amount over time in the schedule given above. Declining amortization is caused by the retirement of employees affected by the plan amendment.

Straight-Line Method. The straight-line method of amortizing prior service cost is based on the **average remaining service period of qualified employees** (i.e., those affected by the pension plan amendment). The average remaining service period for Small Company is computed as:

$$\frac{\text{Total future service years, 12}}{\text{Number of qualified employees, 5}} = 2.4 \text{ years}$$

Annual amortization for 19D is: \$48 ÷ 2.4 years = \$20. The following schedule shows periodic amortization amounts for the straight-line method.

Schedule of straight-line amortization of unrecognized prior service cost.

Year-end	Amortization	Balance, unrecognized prior service cost
January 1, 19D		$48
19D	$20	28
19E	20	8
19F	8*	-0-
	$48	

* Requires 2.4 years to fully amortize on a straight-line basis, assuming no future change in the average remaining service period.

Transition Cost

FASB Standard 87, par. 77, specifies that the straight-line method illustrated above must be used. However, it provides an exception—if the average remaining period is less than 15 years, the employer may still use a 15-year period to amortize transition cost.

Gains and Losses

FASB Standard 87, pars. 32–34, specify technical rules for amortizing gains and losses. These rules were discussed on page 989. The rules use the average remaining service period computed as shown above.

QUESTIONS

Part A

1. Distinguish between a defined contribution pension plan and a defined benefit pension plan.
2. Distinguish between the three parties involved in accounting and reporting for a pension plan.

3. What are the primary actuarial factors related to a pension plan?
4. Explain the three funding approaches that the employer can use for pension plans.
5. Distinguish between a contributory pension plan and a noncontributory pension plan.
6. Employer X has a defined benefit pension plan. The estimated pension expense for 19W is $100,000. Explain and give the 19W journal entry for each of the following cases: Case A—X pays 100% of the pension expense; Case B—X pays 80% of the expense; Case C—X pays 120% of the expense.
7. Employee X will receive an annual pension benefit of $12,000 for five years, starting on December 31, 1990. Assuming an interest rate of 8%, how much must be in the pension fund on January 1, 1990? Explain why the answer is not $60,000.
8. Employer W must build a pension fund of $50,000 by December 31, 19X5. Five equal annual payments are made into the fund starting on December 31, 19X1. The fund will earn 8%. What is the amount of each payment? Explain why it is not $10,000.
9. Explain why pension accounting must be based on assumptions and estimates.
10. What is the pension benefit formula?
11. Explain the application of the matching principle in accounting for pensions.
12. What does attribution mean in pension accounting?
13. Three special features of pension accounting are *(a)* delayed recognition, *(b)* net cost, and *(c)* offsetting. Explain each feature.
14. What is the vested benefit obligation?
15. List and define the six components of net periodic pension expense.
16. Explain the additional minimum pension liability.
17. VW Company recorded an additional minimum liability as follows (000s):

Intangible pension asset	15	
Unrealized pension cost	3	
Additional minimum pension liability		18

Explain each line in the above entry.

18. Define and explain the projected benefit obligation (PBO).
19. Define and explain the report on the status of pension plan assets.
20. Explain what is meant by the "under (over) funded PBO."
21. Explain the difference between the projected benefit obligation and the accumulated benefit obligation.

Part B

22. Explain the primary approaches (i.e., rules) for amortizing unrecognized pension costs.
23. Explain the purpose and application of the additional minimum pension liability. Illustrate its computation with the following data: Prepaid pension cost, $10; accumulated benefit obligation, $300; and plan assets at fair value $240.
24. In the case of the unrecognized pension costs, such as prior service cost, which are first incurred during 19B, amortization may or may not be appropriate at the end of 19B. Explain why.
25. Explain a pension plan curtailment.
26. Explain a pension plan settlement.
27. Explain termination benefits.

EXERCISES

Part A: Exercises 20–1 to 20–13

E 20–1 **(Understanding Special Pension Terminology)**
Match the brief definitions with the terms by entering one letter in each space provided.

Terms

_____ 1. Defined benefit pension plan
_____ 2. Funding agency (trustee)
_____ 3. Contributory pension plan
_____ 4. *FASB Standard 87*, "Employers' Accounting for Pensions"
_____ 5. Noncontributory pension plan
_____ 6. Defined contribution pension plan
_____ 7. Attribution (of pension plan costs)
_____ 8. Actuary
_____ 9. Measurement date
_____ 10. Pension plan assumptions
_____ 11. Pension plan assets
_____ 12. Pension benefit formula

Brief definition

A. The employer provides all of the funding required
B. *APB Opinion 8* was superceded by this pronouncement
C. Resources administered by the trustee
D. Allocation (assignment) of pension costs to accounting periods
E. Pension benefit computations are specified, which determine funding required
F. Special estimates about future events that affect pension costs
G. The date that pension plan assets and obligations are measured
H. Pension contributions are defined, which determine the pension benefits
I. Specifies the retirement benefits in conformity with the pension plan
J. The employees provide some or all of the funding required
K. Administers, invests, and pays from the pension plan assets
L. A professional person qualified to provide actuarial estimates of pension funding requirements

E 20–2 **(Understanding Special Pension Terminology)**
Match the brief definitions with the terms by entering one letter in each space provided.

Terms

_____ 1. Projected benefit obligation
_____ 2. Expected return on plan assets
_____ 3. Amortization of gains and losses
_____ 4. Pension plan assets
_____ 5. Net periodic pension expense
_____ 6. Fair market value (of plan assets)
_____ 7. Amortization of prior service costs
_____ 8. ERISA (1974)
_____ 9. Prepaid pension cost
_____ 10. Accumulated benefit obligation

Brief definition

A. Amount reported as total pension expense for the period; comprised of six components
B. Allocation to periodic expense of the cost of retroactive pension benefits
C. Actuarial present value of all future pension benefits excluding the effects of expected future compensation levels
D. Employee Retirement Income Security Act of 1974
E. Cost of future pension benefits earned during the current accounting period

Terms		Brief definition
_____ 11.	Interest cost	F. The interest rate used by the actuary to adjust for the time value of money
_____ 12.	Discount rate	G. Present value of the employee's benefits not contingent on remaining an employee
_____ 13.	Service cost (pensions)	H. Allocation to periodic expense of the difference between expected and actual return on plan assets and changes in actuarial assumptions.
_____ 14.	Amortization of transition cost	I. Cumulative fund assets plus unrecognized pension costs in excess of the PBO.
_____ 15.	Vested benefit obligation	J. Difference between plan assets at fair market value at the beginning and ending of the period minus contributions and plus distributions during the accounting period
_____ 16.	Actual return on plan assets	K. The value of plan assets between a willing buyer and a willing seller (not a forced sale)
		L. Attribution (allocation) to accounting periods of the costs recognized when *FASB Standard 87* is first applied
		M. Actuarial present value of all future pension benefits including the effects of current and future compensation levels
		N. Projected benefit obligation at the beginning of the current accounting period multiplied by the actuary's discount rate
		O. Resources set aside to provide future pension benefits to retirees
		P. Beginning market-related value of pension plan assets multiplied by the expected rate of return on plan assets

E 20–3 **(Pension Plan; One Employee; Compute PBO and Funding Payments; Entries)** Fisher Company initiated a noncontributory, defined benefit pension plan on January 1, 1988. The accounting period ends December 31. This exercise relates to one employee, V. R. Able. The pension formula specifies that Able will receive five annual retirement benefits of $50,000 at the end of each year, starting on December 31, 1998. Fisher Company will fully fund the pension plan by contributing 10 equal annual amounts starting on December 31, 1988. The pension fund will earn 8% annual interest during Able's service period and 7% during the retirement (payment) period.

Required (round to the nearest $1):

1. Compute the *(a)* projected benefit obligation and *(b)* equal annual funding payment that must be made by Fisher Company.
2. Give the 1988 and 1989 pension entries for Fisher.
3. Give the entry for the funding agency on December 31, 1998 to record payment of the first benefit to Able.

E 20–4 (Pension Plan; Five Employees; Compute PBO and Funding Payments, Entries)
Plans are being made to fund the prospective pension benefits of a group of employees of Farr Company due to retire in nine years and to be paid amounts from one to five years after retirement as below:

End of year 1	$ 90,000
End of year 2	50,000
End of year 3	30,000
End of year 4	15,000
End of year 5	5,000
Thereafter	-0-
Total of pension payments	$190,000

Funds deposited with the pension fund trustee will earn 6% per annum. The pension plan contract calls for deposit of an amount sufficient to fund all of the expected payments from the fund by the date the employees retire.

Required (round amounts to nearest dollar):

1. *(a)* Compute the amount required by the trustee on the employees' retirement date, assuming the first pension payment is one year after retirement, and *(b)* prepare a proof schedule reflecting the 6% earnings on unused funds and pension payout by the trustee.
2. Using the funding amount computed in (1) above, compute *(a)* the projected benefit obligation and *(b)* the amount of each of the eight equal annual payments required to fully fund the pensions, assuming a 6% interest rate. The payments into the pension fund will be made the last eight years of employment preceding retirement, and the last payment into the fund will coincide with the retirement date of the employees. Hint: A diagram may be helpful.

E 20–5 (Understanding the PBO, Plan Assets, and Under- or Overfunding)
BV Company has a noncontributory, defined benefit pension plan. Data available for 19C were:

Projected benefit obligation (PBO):	
Balance, January 1, 19C	$ 82,000
Balance, December 31, 19C	107,000
Plant assets (at fair value):	
Balance, January 1, 19C	$ 40,000
Balance, December 31, 19C	70,000

Required:

1. How much did the PBO increase during 19C? Give six items that could have caused the PBO to change.
2. How much did the pension plan assets change during 19C? Give three items that could have caused the change in plan assets.
3. Compute the amount of the under (over) funded PBO at *(a)* January 1, 19C, and *(b)* December 31, 19C. Explain what these amounts mean.

E 20–6 (Understanding the Relationships between the Actuary's Report and the Trustee's Report)
Below are listed items that are shown on the 19B PBO, **actuary's report** (AR) or the trustee's report, status of plan asset (TR). Enter one check mark to the left for each item to indicate the report on which each one would appear. However, if a single item appears in both reports enter two check marks. If the item does not appear on either report do not enter a check mark on that line.

AR	TR	Items (19B unless stated otherwise)
____	____	1. December 31, 19A, ending pension obligation
____	____	2. Interest cost
____	____	3. Loss (gain) related to changes in actuarial assumptions
____	____	4. Unrecognized pension costs
____	____	5. Cash funding by the employer
____	____	6. Prior service cost (increase)
____	____	7. Net periodic pension expense
____	____	8. Actual return on plan assets
____	____	9. Accrued/prepaid pension costs
____	____	10. Under (over) funded PBO
____	____	11. December 31, 19A, balance of pension plan asset
____	____	12. Pension benefits paid to retirees
____	____	13. Transition cost (increase or decrease)
____	____	14. PBO balance, January 1, 19C
____	____	15. Expected return on plan assets
____	____	16. Pension plan assets, January 1, 19C
____	____	17. Service cost
____	____	18. Accumulated benefit obligation

E 20–7 (Understanding the Distinctions and Relationships between the PBO and Plan Assets)
Below are listed the items that appear on either (or both) the PBO and the status of pension plan assets (PPA). Enter one check mark on each line to indicate which one would appear. However, if an item appears on both enter two check marks on that line.

PBO	PPA	Items (19B unless stated otherwise)
____	____	1. Actual return on plan assets
____	____	2. Transition cost
____	____	3. End balance of pension plan assets
____	____	4. Interest cost
____	____	5. Pension benefits paid to retirees
____	____	6. Service cost
____	____	7. Loss (gain) related to changes in actuarial assumptions
____	____	8. Plan assets on December 31, 19A
____	____	9. Ending BPO balance
____	____	10. Prior service cost
____	____	11. Cash payments by employer
____	____	12. Expected return on plan assets

E 20–8 (Prepare Trustee's Report; Analysis; Prepare Employer's Entries)
Mason Company has a noncontributory, defined benefit pension plan. On December 31, 19C (end of the accounting period and the measurement date), information about the pension plan included the following:

a. Projected benefit obligation (actuary):

January 1, 19C	$ 40,000
Service cost	60,000
Interest cost	3,600
Pension benefits paid	(–0–)
December 31, 19C	$103,600

[Interest (discount) rate used by actuary, 9%.]

b. The trustee's report on plan assets showed a beginning balance of $50,000, cash received from the employer, $37,000, and an actual return and expected return on plan assets of $10,000.

c. Unamortized prior service cost, gains and losses, transition costs, and additional minimum liability—none (from company records).

Required:
1. Prepare the trustee's report on the status of the plan assets.
2. Compute the amount of the under (over) funding of the PBO on the beginning and ending dates.
3. Give the 19C entry for Mason Company to record net periodic pension expense.
4. Give the same entry, assuming cash funding of $55,000 (instead of $37,000).
5. Show how the interest of $3,600 was computed.

E 20–9 (Compute Net Periodic Pension Expense and Under- or Overfunded PBO; Entries)
The 19B records of Jax Company provided the following data related to its noncontributory, defined benefit pension plan (amounts in 000s):

a. Projected benefit obligation (report of actuary):

Balance, January 1, 19B	$ 750
Service cost	300
Interest cost	60
Pension benefits paid	(100)
Balance, December 31, 19B	$1,010

Discount rate used by actuary, 8%.

b. Plan assets at fair value (report of trustee):

Balance, January 1, 19B	$ 602
Actual return on plan assets	42
Contributions, 19B	254
Pension benefits paid, 19B	(100)
Balance, December 31, 19B	$ 798

Expected long-term rate of return on plan assets, 7%.

c. January 1, 19B, balance of unrecognized prior service cost, gains and losses, and transition cost, zero.

Required:
1. Compute 19B net periodic pension expense. Show the correct amount for each of the six components.
2. Give the 19B entry(s) for Jax Company to record pension expense and funding.
3. Compute the under (over) funded PBO at the beginning and end of 19B.

E 20–10 (Compute Net Periodic Pension Expense and Under- or Overfunding of the PBO; Entries)
Fox Company has a noncontributory, defined benefit pension plan. On December 31, 19B (end of the accounting period and measurement date), the following data were available:

a. Projected benefit obligation (actuary's report):

Balance, December 31, 19A	$ 90,000
Prior service cost (due to plan amendment on January 1, 19B)	10,000
Balance, January 1, 19B	100,000
Service cost	65,000
Interest cost	8,000
Pension benefits paid	(-0-)
Balance, December 31, 19B	$173,000

Interest (discount) rate used by actuary, 8%.

b. Funding report of the trustee:

Balance, January 1, 19B	$105,000
Actual return on plan assets*	5,000
Cash received from employer	50,000
Pension benefits paid to retirees	(–0–)
Balance, December 31, 19B	$160,000

* Same as the expected return.

Required:

1. Show how the interest cost was computed.
2. Compute net periodic pension expense. Assume prior service cost will be amortized over a 10-year average remaining service period. Show the correct amounts for each component.
3. Give the 19B entry for Fox Company to record net periodic pension expense.
4. Give the same entry assuming cash funding from the employer of $71,000, and no other changes.
5. Compute the under (over) funding of the PBO for requirements 3 and 4.

E 20–11 **(Compute Net Periodic Pension Expense and Under- or Overfunded PBO; Entries)** New Company started a noncontributory, defined benefit pension plan on January 1, 19A. Data available for 19B were:

a. Projected benefit obligation, 19B (actuary's report):

Balance, January 1, 19B	$60,000
Service cost	20,000
Interest cost (interest rate, 10%)	6,000
Prior service cost	–0–
Losses (gains) due to change in actuarial assumptions (amortization to start in 19C)	(4,000)
Pension benefits paid	(1,000)
Balance, December 31, 19B	$81,000

b. Status of fund assets (trustee's report):

Balance, January 1, 19B	$55,000
Actual earnings on plan assets (same as expected return)	5,000
Payments received from employer during 19B	30,000
Pension benefits paid	(1,000)
Balance, December 31, 19B	$89,000

c. Company records: Unamortized gain from 19A due to changes in asumptions, $3,000 (this amount was included in the 19A PBO). There are no gains or losses on plan assets. Unamortized (unrecognized) prior service cost and transition cost from 19A are zero.

Required:

1. Compute net periodic pension expense for 19B assuming the 19A losses (gains) are amortized for 19B over a 15-year average remaining service period.
2. Give the 19B pension expense and funding entry for New Company.
3. Give the same entry assuming the 19B cash payment by employer was $18,000 instead of $30,000.
4. Compute the under (over) funded PBO for requirements 2 and 3.

E 20–12 **(Pension Spreadsheet; Underfunded and Accrued Pension Cost; Entries)**
GEE Company has a defined benefit pension plan. At the end of the current reporting period, December 31, 19X5, the following information was available:

a. Projected benefit obligation (actuary's report):

Balance, January 1, 19X5	$600
Service cost	78
Interest cost ($600 × 7%, actuary's rate)	42
Loss (gain) change in actuarial assumptions*	18
Pension benefits paid	(40)
Balance, December 31, 19X5	$698

* Amortization to start in 19X6.

b. Status of fund assets (trustee's report):

Balance, January 1, 19X5	$500
Actual return on plan assets (same as expected)	30
Cash received from employer company	70
Pension benefits paid to retirees	(40)
Balance, December 31, 19X5	$560

c. From company records, unamortized pension from prior years (amortize over a 9-year average remaining service period):

Transition cost	$ 18
Prior service cost	27
Losses (gains)	36
Total	$ 81

Required:

1. Set up and complete a comprehensive spreadsheet to develop the pension data required at the end of 19X5.
2. Give the employer's pension entry at December 31, 19X5.

E 20–13 **(Pension Spreadsheet; Underfunded and Accrued Pension Cost; Entry)**
Avis Company has a defined benefit pension plan. At the end of the current reporting period, December 31, 19B, the following information was available:

a. Projected benefit obligation (actuary's report):

Balance, January 1, 19B	$750
Service cost	80
Interest cost ($750 × 10%, actuary's rate)	75
Loss (gain) change in actuarial assumptions*	(7)
Pension benefits paid	(34)
Balance, December 31, 19B	$864

* Amortization to start in 19X6.

b. Status of fund assets (trustee's report):

Balance, January 1, 19B	$600
Actual return on plan assets (same as expected)	54
Cash received from employer company	150
Pension benefits paid to retirees	(34)
Balance, December 31, 19B	$770

c. From company records, unamortized pension from prior years (amortize over a 10-year average remaining service period):

Transition cost	$100
Prior service cost	30
Losses (gains)	(20)
Total	$110

Required:
1. Set up and complete a comprehensive spreadsheet to develop the pension data required at the end of 19B.
2. Give the employer's pension entry at December 31, 19B.

Part B: Exercises 20–14 to 20–25

E 20–14 **(Understanding Pension Accounting Terminology)**
Match the following brief descriptions with the terminology by entering the appropriate letter in each blank.

Terminology

_____ 1. Unrecognized gain/loss on pension plan assets
_____ 2. Report on the pension fund
_____ 3. Projected benefit obligation
_____ 4. Actual return on plan assets
_____ 5. Accrued/prepaid pension cost
_____ 6. Pension expense
_____ 7. Expected return on plan assets
_____ 8. Unrecognized pension cost (e.g., prior service cost)
_____ 9. *FASB Standard 87*
_____ 10. Additional minimum pension liability

Brief description

A. Present value of all pension obligations; provided by actuary
B. Beginning amount of plan assets at market-related value times expected long-term rate of return
C. The account debited to record periodic pension expense
D. *FASB Standard 87* that completely supercedes *APB Opinion 8*
E. Pension fund balances at fair value adjusted for contributions provided by the trustee and benefits
F. Difference between expected and actual return on plan assets
G. A pension liability that is not included in accrued/prepaid pension cost
H. Ending balance of plan assets at fair value minus contribution plus pension benefits minus beginning balance of plan assets at fair value
I. A statement of financial position account that may be either an asset or a liability
J. An amount that is not recorded when incurred because of delayed recognition; it is recognized through periodic amortization.

E 20–15 **(Understanding Pension Accounting Terminology)**
Match the following items with the financial statements by entering the appropriate letter in each blank.

Items	Reported on the financial statements
_____ 1. Accumulated benefit obligation	A. Statement of income, expense
_____ 2. Unrealized pension cost	B. Statement of income, gains and losses
_____ 3. Unrecognized gains (losses)	C. Statement of financial position, assets
_____ 4. Additional minimum pension liability	D. Statement of financial position, liabilities
_____ 5. Unrecognized prior service cost	E. Statement of financial position, owners' equity
_____ 6. Pension benefits paid	F. None of the above
_____ 7. Expected return on pension plan assets	
_____ 8. Unrecognized transition cost	
_____ 9. Accrued pension cost	
_____ 10. Net periodic pension expense	
_____ 11. Vested benefit obligation	
_____ 12. Unfunded accumulated benefit obligation	
_____ 13. Pension plan assets at fair value	
_____ 14. Prepaid pension cost	
_____ 15. Pension plan assets used in operations of the plan (i.e., furniture and fixtures)	

E 20–16 **(Understanding Pension Accounting Terminology)**

Match the following brief descriptions with the terminology by entering appropriate letters in the blanks.

Terminology

_____ 1. Curtailment
_____ 2. Accrued/prepaid pension cost
_____ 3. Termination benefits
_____ 4. Settlement
_____ 5. *FASB Standard 87*
_____ 6. Interest expense
_____ 7. Loss, termination benefits
_____ 8. None of the above

Brief description

A. *FASB Standard 88* has the same transitory date as this earlier statement
B. An irrevocable event (or transaction) that (1) relieves the employer of a primary pension obligation and (2) reduces the employer's risks
C. The effects of a curtailment gain or loss are recorded in this account
D. Special or contractual benefits paid to employees who retire early
E. An event that either (1) reduces expected years of future service or (2) reduces the number of employees
F. This account is debited when it is probable that early retirees will be entitled to special benefits and the amount can be reasonably estimated
G. When termination benefits are paid over an extended time, this account must be periodically debited
H. Vested benefit obligation—for pension benefits retained regardless of employment to retirement date

E 20–17 **(Minimum Amortization of Unrecognized Losses or Gains)**

TV Company is preparing the 19X2 entry to record pension expense, funding, and the change in accrued/prepaid pension cost. The company has a noncontributory, defined benefit plan. This date is the end of the annual accounting year. The company has the reports of the actuary and the fund trustee. This is the second year after changing from *APB Opinion 8* to *FASB Standards 87* and *88*. The company is preparing a comprehensive spreadsheet similar to Exhibit 20–6.

Concern has been expressed about the three unrecognized pension costs—transition, prior service, and gains and losses. The first two costs will be properly amortized based on the average remaining service period (currently 10 years). The concern in this exercise is about the amortization of losses and gains. Separate data maintained in the company showed the following at December 31, 19X2:

Company record of unrecognized losses (gains):

	Case A	Case B
a. Losses (gains):		
Balance loss (gain) Jan. 1, 19X2	$ 15,000	$ 8,000
Increase (decreases) during 19X2	–0–	–0–
Total	15,000	8,000
Amortization during 19X2*	?	?
Balance, December 31, 19X2	$?	$?

* Included in pension expense.

	Case A	Case B
b. Additional data on January 1, 19X2:		
Projected benefit obligation (actuary)	100,000	80,000
Plan assets at market-related value	80,000	100,000
Average remaining service years	10	10

Required:

For each case complete the above schedule using the minimum method. Show computations.

E 20–18 (Apply Minimum Amortization of Unrecognized Losses or Gains)

West Corporation initiated a noncontributory, defined benefit pension plan on January 1, 19C, and applied the provisions of *FASB Standard 87*. Information is available for the reporting year ended December 31, 19E, for the following independent cases (amounts in thousands):

	Case A	Case B
Projected benefit obligation, January 1, 19E	$500	$700
Plan assets at fair value, January 1, 19E*	400	800
Unrecognized (gain) or loss	(50)	30
Average remaining service period of active employees	10 years	15 years

* Same as market-related value.

Required (round all amounts to nearest thousand):

West uses the straight-line method, based on the average remaining service period of active employees, to amortize unrecognized gain or loss (subject to required minimum amortization).

a. Compute the amount of straight-line amortization of unrecognized gain or loss in each case.
b. Verify that the amortization computed in *(a)* meets the minimum required amortization.

E 20–19 (Minimum Pension Liability; Four Years; Entries)

Goode Corporation established a noncontributory, defined benefit pension plan for its employees in 19A. On January 1, 19D, Goode initially applied the provisions of *FASB Standard 87* related to the recognition of an additional minimum pension liability to its pension accounting. The following information is available for the reporting years ended December 31, 19G (in 000s):

Items	19D	19E	19F	19G
Projected benefit obligation	$1,100	$1,500	$2,000	$2,500
Accumulated benefit obligation	900	1,050	1,400	1,900
Plan assets at fair value	800	1,100	1,300	1,400
(Accrued)/prepaid pension cost	100	25	(90)	(180)
Unrecognized prior service cost	150	180	160	200

Required:

1. Compute the required additional minimum liability for each year, 19D through 19G.
2. Give the entry to recognize the additional minimum liability for each year, 19D through 19G. Ignore deferred income taxes.

E 20–20 (Minimum Liability; Three Cases; Entries)

XY Company has a noncontributory, defined benefit pension plan. It is December 31, 19X, end of the accounting year and measurement date for the pension plan. The following data for three separate cases, as of the measurement dates, are (in 000s):

Items (at December 31, 19X)	Case A	Case B	Case C
a. Projected benefit obligation	$500	$500	$500
b. Accumulated benefit obligation	400	400	400
c. Vested benefit obligation	180	180	180
d. Pension plan assets at book value	275	275	275
e. Pension plan assets at fair value	300	420	300
f. (Accrued)/prepaid pension cost	0	40	(10)
g. Unrecognized prior service cost	110	90	75

Required:

1. For each case, compute the "additional minimum pension liability" that should be reported.
2. For each case *(a)* explain whether a minimum liability must be reported and why, and *(b)* if yes, give the entry. Ignore deferred income taxes.

E 20–21 (Prepare Pension Spreadsheet; Additional Minimum Pension Liability; Entries)

Fox Company has a noncontributory, defined benefit pension plan. The following data are available at December 31, 19B, which is the end of the accounting period and the measurement date:

a. Projected benefit obligation (actuary):

Balance, January 1, 19B	$223,000
Service cost	80,000
Interest cost	?
Prior service cost	-0-
Losses (gains) due to changes in assumptions	8,000
Pension benefits paid	(30,000)
Balance, December 31, 19B	$?

Average remaining service period, 10 years.
Actuary's discount rate, 8%
Accumulated benefit obligation, $292,000.

b. Pension plan assets (trustee):

Balance, January 1, 19B, at fair value	$200,000
Contributions to the pension plan by Fox	70,000
Actual return on plan assets	10,000
Benefits paid to retirees	(30,000)
Balance, December 31, 19B, at fair value	$250,000

Long-term expected rate of return on plan assets, 7%.
Market-related value = Fair value.

c. Other balances at December 31, 19A: Unrecognized pension costs (total), $3,000, only prior service has a balance; accrued pension cost, $20,000.

Required:

1. Prepare a comprehensive spreadsheet as shown in Exhibit 20–6.
2. Give the annual pension entry for Fox.
3. Compute the additional minimum pension liability and give the related entry.
4. Give the entry for the next year assuming additional minimum pension liability is $10,000.

E 20–22 **(Prepare Comprehensive Spreadsheet; Additional Minimum Pension Liability; Entries)**

Saxon Company has a noncontributory, defined benefit pension plan. The accounting period ends December 31, 19C (also the pension measurement date). Pension plan data for 19C are as follows:

a. Projected benefit obligation:	
Balance, January 1, 19C	$5,000
Service cost	3,000
Interest cost	400
Loss (gain) due to change in actuarial assumptions	25
Pension benefits paid	(60)
Balance, December 31, 19C	$8,365
Accumulated benefit obligation, $8,365.	
Actuary's discount rate, 8%.	
Average remaining service period, 10 years.	
b. Pension plan assets:	
Balance, January 1, 19C, at fair value	$4,000
Actual return; gain (expected return $160; 4%)	150
Contribution to the pension fund by Saxon	3,200
Benefits paid to retirees	(60)
Balance, December 31, 19C	$7,290
c. Company records:	
(1) January 1, 19C, Unamortized amounts:	
Unrecognized prior service cost	$ 500
Unrecognized gain/loss	300 (gain)
Unrecognized transition cost	200
(2) December 31, 19C changes:	
Unrecognized prior service cost	no change
Unrecognized (gain)/loss ($175–$150)	25
Unrecognized transition cost	no change
(3) (Accrued)/prepaid pension cost at January 1, 19C	(600) cr.

Amortize all unrecognized items over the average service period (for problem purposes).

Required:

1. Prepare a schedule of relationships similar to Exhibit 20–6 in the chapter.
2. Based on requirement 1, give the December 31, 19C entry to record pension expense and funding for Saxon.
3. Test to determine whether additional minimum pension liability is required. Show computations and give the related entry.
4. Give the related entry for the next year assuming the additional minimum liability is $200.

E 20–23 **(Pension Curtailment; Analysis; Entry)**

CT Company has a noncontributory, defined benefit pension plan. On June 1, 19D, the company reduced its operations and, as a consequence, terminated 150 of its regular employees. As of that date the actuary provided the following information (000s):

	Total	Related to terminations
Projected benefit obligation	$1,000	$100
Composed of the following:		
Accumulated benefit obligation:*		
Vested benefits	$ 700	$ 75
Noninvested benefits	200	15
Total	900	
Effect of projected future compensation levels	100	10
Total	$1,000	$100

* Excludes effect of projected future compensation levels.

There were no unrecognized losses or gains *(a)* at transition date or *(b)* after transition date.

Required:

1. Complete the following schedule:

Items	Curtailment Before	Curtailment Effects	Curtailment After
PBO			
Composed of the following:			
Accumulated benefit obligation			
Vested benefits			
Nonvested benefits			
Total			
Effect of projected future compensation levels			
Total			

2. Give the entry to record the curtailment.

E 20–24 (Pension Settlement; Analysis; Entry)

Stacy Company has a non-contributory, defined benefit pension plan. On December 31, 19E (end of the accounting period and pension measurement date), the company settled its vested benefit obligation of $248. Settlement was made by purchasing, with pension plan assets, nonparticipating annuity contracts that cost $248. Relevant pension plan data on this date were (all amounts in 000s):

a.	Actuary's report, December 31, 19E (before the settlement):	
	Projected benefit obligation	$400
	Accumulated benefit obligation	300
	Vested benefit obligation	248
	Effects of projected future compensation levels.	100
b.	Trustee's report (before settlement):	
	Pension plans assets at fair value	$415
c.	Company records (before the settlement):	
	Unrecognized net assets at transition	$ 50
	Unrecognized net gain subsequent to acquisition	60
	Accrued/prepaid pension cost (a credit)	95

Required:
1. What percent of the PBO was settled?
2. Complete an analysis of the pension plan settlement to determine its effects (similar to the one shown in the chapter).
3. Give the entry to record the settlement.

E 20–25 **(Pension Termination; Entries)**
On January 1, 19G (accounting period ends December 31), Fox Company reduced its payroll by terminating 40 employees. Each terminated employee was given *(a)* a lump-sum payment of $1,000, on January 1, 19G, and *(b)* six monthly payments of $100 starting on January 31, 19G. The payments were made from company assets. All of the terminated employees accepted the termination benefits as of January 1, 19G.

Required:
1. Compute the cost of the termination benefits as of January 1, 19G. Use a 2% interest rate, compounded monthly.
2. Give the following entries for Fox Company:
   (a) January 1, 19G—to record the termination.
   (b) January 1, 19G—to record the lump-sum cash payment.
   (c) January 31, 19G—to record the first monthly payment.

PROBLEMS

Part A: Problems 20–1 to 20–5

P 20–1 **(Prepare the Actuary's and Trustee's Reports; Compute Pension Expense; Give Employer's Entry; All from Scrambled Data)**
On January 1, 19A, Mesa Company adopted a noncontributory, defined benefit pension plan for its employees. The following scrambled information related to the plan is available for the years 19C, 19D, and 19E:

	19C	19D	19E
a. Service cost	$100	$ 120	$ 125
b. Interest cost (discount rate, 10%)	100	116	134
c. Actual return on plan assets	81	98	115
d. Contributions to the fund (by Mesa)	150	150	150
e. Pension benefits paid	40	56	69
f. Accumulated benefit obligation, December 31	800	1,000	1,200

g. Expected return on plan assets is the same as actual return *(c)* for each year, 19C–19E.
h. Accrued pension cost, January 1, 19C, $100.
i. Projected benefit obligation, January 1, 19C, $1,000.
j. Plan assets at fair value, January 1, 19C, $900 (same as market-related value).
k. Mesa had no unrecognized transition amount or unrecognized prior service cost during the three years, 19C–19E.
l. There were no changes in actuarial assumptions during the three years, 19C–19E.

Mesa applied the provisions of *FASB Standard 87* for reporting pension-related amounts. Mesa's reporting period ends on December 31.

Required:

1. Prepare a schedule showing the amount of projected benefit obligation, plan assets at fair value, and unfunded or overfunded projected benefit obligation as of December 31, 19C, 19D, and 19E.
2. Prepare a schedule to determine net periodic pension expense for each year, 19C, 19D, and 19E.
3. Give the entry to record net periodic pension expense and funding for each year, 19C, 19D, and 19E.

P 20–2 (Pension Spreadsheet; Overfunded and a Prepaid Pension Cost; Entry)

Waters Company has a defined benefit pension plan. At the end of the current reporting period, December 31, 19B, the following information was available:

a. Projected benefit obligation (actuary's report):	
Balance January 1, 19B	$75,000
Service cost	20,000
Interest cost ($75,000 × 10%, actuary's rate)	7,500
Loss (gain) change in actuarial assumptions*	(200)
Pension benefits paid	(21,000)
Balance, December 31, 19B	$81,300
Accumulated benefit obligation	$60,000
Vested benefit obligation	$20,000
Average remaining service period, 10 years.†	

* At December 31, 19B.
† Assume this is appropriate for all amortizations.

b. Status of fund assets (trustee's report):	
Balance, January 1, 19B	$80,000
Actual return on plan assets (same as expected)	8,000
Cash received from employer company	15,000
Pension benefits paid to retirees	(21,000)
Balance, December 31, 19B	$82,000
c. From company records—Unrecognized pension costs:	
Transition cost	$ 5,000
Prior service cost	10,000
Losses (gains)	(1,000)
Total	$14,000
Accrued (prepaid) pension cost	($19,000)

Required:

1. Set up and complete a comprehensive worksheet to develop the pension data required at the end of 19B.
2. Give the employer's pension entry at December 31, 19B.

P 20–3 (Prepare the Actuary's and Trustee's Reports from Scrambled Data; Then Prepare a Pension Spreadsheet)

VIK Company first applied the provisions of *FASB Standard 87* to its noncontributory defined benefit pension plan on January 1, 19A. It is now December 31, 19B, end of the current accounting period and the following scrambled data have been copied from the actuary's report, trustee's report and company records:

Items (at December 31, 19B unless otherwise stated)	Amount
a. Service cost	$14,700
b. Actuary's discount rate, 7%	
c. Pension benefits paid to retirees	1,000
d. Expected return on plan assets	1,600
e. Pension plan assets at fair value, December 31, 19A	7,500

f. Average remaining service period, 12 years	
g. Accumulated benefit obligation	10,000
h. Transaction cost, unamortized, January 1, 19B	1,200
i. Actual return on plan assets (expected return, $1,600)	1,500
j. Projected benefit obligation, December 31, 19A	15,000
k. Losses (gains) unamortized on December 31, 19A	3,600
l. Vested benefit obligation	3,000
m. Contribution by VIK to the pension fund	14,000
n. Prior service costs, unamortized, January 1, 19B	3,000
o. Increase in pension costs during 19B due to change in actuarial assumptions	1,100

Required:

1. Prepare the report of the *(a)* actuary and *(b)* fund trustee.
2. Prepare a comprehensive spreadsheet and give VIK's pension entry at December 31, 19B.

P 20–4 (Prepare a Comprehensive Spreadsheet and Respond to a Query about the Use of Cash)

Stoney Company first applied the provisions of *FASB Standard 87* to its noncontributory, defined-benefit program on January 1, 19C. The annual accounting period ends on December 31. Data about the pension plan for 19D are given below.

a. Projected benefit obligation (actuary's report):	
Balance January 1, 19D	$8,000
Service cost	960
Interest cost ($8,000 × 8% actuary's rate)	640
Loss (gain) change in actuarial assumptions*	330
Pension benefit paid to retirees	(800)
Balance, December 31, 19D	$9,130

* At December 31, 19D.

Accumulated benefit obligation	$8,000
Vested benefit obligation	3,000
Actuary's estimated discount rate	8%
Average remaining service period (assumed appropriate for all amortizations)	11 years
b. Status of fund assets (trustee's report):	
Balance, January 1, 19D	$6,300
Actual return on plan assets	500
Cash received from employer company	1,500
Pension benefits paid to retirees	(800)
Balance, December 31, 19D	$7,500
Expected return on plan assets	$ 500
c. Company data of January 1, 19D:	
Unrecognized transaction cost	$ 330
Unrecognized prior service cost	990
Unrecognized losses (gains)	(220)
Total unrecognized	$1,100
(Accrued)/prepaid pension cost	$ (600)

Required:

1. Prepare a comprehensive pension spreadsheet and give Stoney's 19D journal entry for the pension plan.
2. The company president asked the following question: We paid $1,500 cash to the pension fund but the pension liability was reduced by only $300. Why? Prepare your response with data and explanation.

P 20–5 (Comparative Cases; Prepare Two Comprehensive Spreadsheets; Employer's Entry) Art Company first applied the provisions of *FASB Standard 87* to its noncontributory, defined pension plan in 19B. The annual accounting period ends December 31. Data about the pension plan for 19C are given below for two comparative cases to emphasize how losses versus gains affect the results.

	Case A	Case B
a. Actuary's PBO Report at December 31, 19C:		
Projected benefit obligation (actuary's report):		
Balance, January 1, 19C	$500	$500
Service cost	100	100
Interest cost ($500 × 10%), actuary's rate)	50	50
Loss (gain) change in actuarial assumptions*	8	(8)
Pension benefits paid to retirees	(10)	(15)
Balance, December 31, 19C	$648	$627

* At December 31, 19C; amortizations start in 19D.

	Case A	Case B
Accumulated benefit obligation	$500	$484
Vested benefit obligation	$200	$184
Actuary's estimated interest rate	10%	10%
Average remaining service period†	8 years	8 years
b. Status of fund assets (trustee's report):		
Balance, January 1, 19C	$450	$450
Actual return on plan assets	20	20
Cash received from employer company	150	120
Pension benefits paid to retirees	(10)	(15)
Balance, December 31, 19C	$610	$575
Expected return on plan assets	$ 24	$ 25

† Assume eight years is appropriate for all amortizations.

	Case A	Case B
c. Company data on January 1, 19C:		
Unrecognized transition cost	$ 8	$ 8
Unrecognized prior service cost	16	16
Unrecognized losses (gains)*	24	(24)
Total unrecognized	$ 48	$-0-
(Accrued)/prepaid pension cost	$ (2)	$ (50)

* Due only to changes in actuarial assumptions.

Required:

Prepare a comprehensive spreadsheet and give the employer's journal entry for the pension plan for Case A and Case B. When preparing these two spreadsheets focus on the effects of losses versus gains.

Part B: Problems 20–6 to 20–13

P 20–6 (Comprehensive Spreadsheet; Additional Minimum Liability; Entries) Frazier Company has a noncontributory, defined benefit pension plan. The company must record its pension expense for the year ended December 31, 19E. The following data are available (in 000s):

a. Actuary's report:	
Balance, January 1, 19E	$300
Service cost	30
Interest cost (at 8%)	24
Loss (gain) actuarial changes	10
Pension benefits paid to retirees	(100)
Balance, December 31, 19E	$264
Accumulated benefit obligation, end of 19E	$247

b. Fund trustee's report:

Balance, January 1, 19E (at fair value)*	$200
Actual return on plan assets	18
Expected return on plan assets, 10%	
Payments received from Frazier	60
Pension benefits paid	(100)
Balance, December 31, 19E	$178

* Same as market-related value.

Data from company records:

Unrecognized transition cost (January 1, 19E)	$ 27
Unrecognized prior service cost (January 1, 19E)	36
Unrecognized loss (January 1, 19E)	4
Total unrecognized	$ 67

Amortization periods, for problem purposes only:
Transition cost 9 years; prior service cost, 10 years; and losses (gains), 4 years.
(Accrued)/prepaid pension cost, January 1, 19E, $(33).

Required:

1. Prepare a pension spreadsheet and give the 19E entry for Frazier Company.
2. Compute any additional minimum pension liability to be recorded for 19E and give the related entry.
3. Give the related entry for 19F assuming the additional minimum liability for 19F is $10.

P 20–7 (Comprehensive Spreadsheet; Additional Minimum Liability; Entries)

Jacks Company has a noncontributory, defined benefit pension plan. The company must record its pension expense for the year ended December 31, 19H. The following data are available (in 000s):

a. Actuary's report:

Balance, January 1, 19H	$300
Service cost	50
Interest cost (at 8%)	24
Loss (gain) actuarial changes (December 31, 19H)	(10)
Pension benefits paid to retirees	(124)
Balance, December 31, 19H	$240
Accumulated benefit obligation, end of 19H	$243

b. Fund trustee's report:

Balance, January 1, 19H (at fair value)*	$170
Actual return on plan assets	27
Expected return on plan assets, 12%	
Payments received from Jacks	110
Pension benefits paid	(124)
Balance, December 31, 19H	$183

* Same as market-related value.

c. Data from company records:

Unrecognized transition cost (January 1, 19H)	$ 60
Unrecognized prior service cost (January 1, 19H)	40
Unrecognized loss (gain) (January 1, 19H)	–0–
Total unrecognized	$100

Average remaining service period is 10 years (for problem purposes use this for amortizing each of the three unrecognized pension costs).
Accrued/prepaid pension cost, January 1, 19H, $30 accrued.

Required:

1. Prepare a pension spreadsheet and give the 19H entry for Jacks Company.
2. Compute any additional pension liability for 19H and give the related entry.
3. Give the related entry for the next period, 19I, assuming the additional minimum liability required for 19I is $40 and the unamortized PSC does not change.

P 20–8 (Prepare Pension Spreadsheet and Additional Minimum Liability for Two Consecutive Years)

AAP Company has a noncontributory, defined benefit pension plan. This case focuses on the accounting required at December 31, 19C and 19D, with emphasis on the PBO, plan assets, unrecognized pension costs, net periodic pension expense, accrued/prepaid pension cost and the additional minimum pension liability. The data for the two years are as follows (in 000s):

	19C	19D
a. Actuary's (PBO):		
Projected benefit obligation, beginning	$1,700	$2,196
Service cost	180	210
Interest cost	136	198
Prior service cost	240	
Loss (gain), actuarial changes	20	5
Loss (gain), plan assets		
Pension benefits paid	(80)	(125)
Projected benefit obligation, ending	$2,196	$2,484
Accumulated benefit obligation	$1,775	$2,109
Average remaining service period*	10 years	9 years
Actuary's interest rate	8%	9%

* For problem purposes assume minimum amortization of unrecognized loss/gain does not apply; therefore, use these periods for all amortization.

	19C	19D
b. Trustee's report (plan assets at fair value):†		
Balance at beginning	$1,000	$1,210
Actual return on plan assets	90	110
Contributions from employer	200	440
Pension benefits paid to retirees	(80)	(125)
Balance at ending	$1,210	$1,635
Expected return on plan assets	10%	10%

† Same as market-related value.

	19C	19D
c. AAP Company records:		
Unrecognized cost at beginning:		
Prior service cost	$ -0-	$ 216
Transition cost	300	270
Loss (gain)	150	165
Total	$ 450	$ 651

Required:

1. Prepare a comprehensive pension spreadsheet and give the related pension entry for AAP Company for *(a)* 19C and *(b)* 19D.
2. Compute the additional minimum pension liability for 19C and 19D and give any related entry for *(a)* 19C and *(b)* 19D. Also, give the 19D ending balances in the three related accounts.

P 20–9 (Prepare Pension Spreadsheet for Two Years with Corridor (Minimum) Amortization Test; Entries)

Voss Company has a noncontributory, defined benefit pension plan for its employees. The data available at year-end for December 31, 19X1 and 19X2 are as follows (000s):

	19X1	19X2
a. Actuary's report (PBO):		
Projected benefit obligation, beginning	$1,520	$1,752
Service cost	200	238
Interest cost	152	140
Prior service cost	20	13
Loss (gain), plan assets	10	6
Pension benefits paid	(150)	(170)
Projected benefit obligation, ending	$1,752	$1,979
Accumulated benefit obligation	$ 920	$1,000
Average remaining service period*	10 years	10 years

* For problem purposes use this for all unrecognized pension costs except losses (gains).

	19X1	19X2
b. Trustee's report (plan assets at fair value):		
Balance at beginning	$ 940	$1,084
Actual return on plan assets	84	92
Contributions from employer	210	320
Pension benefits paid to retirees	(150)	(170)
Balance at ending	$1,084	$1,326
Expected return on plan assets	10%	10%

† Same as market-related value.

	19X1	19X2
c. Voss Company records:		
Unrecognized costs at beginning:		
Prior service cost	$ 100	$ 110
Transition cost	40	36
Loss (gain)	182	174
Total	$ 322	$ 320

Required:

1. Prepare a comprehensive pension spreadsheet (see Exhibit 20–9) and give the related pension entry for Voss Company for *(a)* 19X1 and *(b)* 19X2. Show how you computed the amortization amount for unrecognized loss/gain, using the straight-line method. Also compute the minimum amortization to test against the straight-line method.
2. Explain why additional minimum pension liability does not apply in this situation.

P 20–10 **(Pension Curtailment; Analysis and Entry)**

Hardy Company experienced financial difficulties in 19D. In response, one action taken by Hardy's management was to offer special termination benefits to certain employees. Each employee was offered $10,000 in a lump-sum cash payment to resign. One hundred employees accepted the offer. The special termination benefits were paid from Hardy's assets, not from pension plan assets.

In addition, Hardy's pension plan obligation was curtailed. The amount of the reduction in Hardy's projected benefit obligation due to the curtailment was $500,000. None of this amount was vested, and therefore, Hardy did not reduce pension plan assets. Expected future years of employee service was reduced by 25 percent due to the curtailment. Details of Hardy's pension plan obligation, assets, and recognized and unrecognized amounts as of December 31, 19D (termination date) are given below (amounts in thousands):

Projected benefit obligation (PBO)	$2,800
Plan assets at fair value	(2,000)
	800
Add (deduct) unamortized items:	
Unrecognized transition cost	(400)
Unrecognized net gain	200
Unrecognized prior service cost	(100)
Accrued (prepaid) pension cost	$ 500

Required:

1. Prepare an analysis of the effects of the curtailment (similar to Exhibit 20–11). Show computations.
2. Give the entry to reflect the curtailment and special termination benefits.

P 20–11 **(Pension Curtailment; Analysis and Entries)**

Casey Company has a noncontributory, defined benefit pension plan for its employees since 19A. Faced with declining demand for its products, Casey reduced its operations in 19E. Because of the reduced level of operations, a number of employees were terminated, and Casey's pension obligations were curtailed. The impact of the curtailment was to reduce Casey's projected benefit obligation by $200,000 and the expected future years of employee service by 20 percent, as of January 1, 19E. The following pension plan information is based on two independent cases as of January 1, 19E (amounts in thousands):

	Case A	Case B
Projected benefit obligation (PBO)	$1,200	$1,500
Plan assets at fair value	(1,000)	(2,000)
	200	(500)
Add (deduct) unamortized items:		
Unrecognized transition (cost) gain	(50)	80
Unrecognized net gain (loss)	(100)	120
Unrecognized prior service cost	(30)	(40)
Accrued (prepaid) pension cost	$ 20	$ (340)

Required:

1. Prepare an analysis of the effects of the curtailment for each case (similar to Exhibit 20–11). Show computations.
2. Give the entry to reflect the curtailment for each case.

P 20–12 **(Pension Settlement; Analysis and Entries)**

On December 31, 19E, Watson Corporation reduced its pension obligations by purchasing nonparticipating annuity contracts with pension plan assets. The annuity contracts were designed to provide Watson's employees with future pension benefits in return for a fixed payment of $500,000 by Watson. A summary of Watson's pension plan obligation, assets, and recognized and unrecognized components immediately before the settlement is given below for two independent cases (amounts in thousands):

	Case A	Case B
Projected benefit obligation (PBO)	$2,500	$2,000
Plan assets at fair value	(2,200)	(2,200)
	300	(200)
Add (deduct) unamortized items:		
Unrecognized transition (cost) gain	(50)	70
Unrecognized net gain (loss)	(120)	130
Unrecognized prior service cost	(40)	(40)
Accrued (prepaid) pension cost	$ 90	$ (40)

Required (round to the nearest thousand):

1. Prepare an analysis of the effects of the settlement for each case. Show computations. The analysis should have column headings as follows:

Item	Before settlement	Effects of settlement	After settlement

2. Give the entry to reflect the settlement for each case.

P 20–13 (Supplement 20–A—Pension Plan Amendment; Amortization of Prior Service Cost)
On January 1, 1989, Toycar Company amended its noncontributory, defined benefit pension plan. The amendment caused an unrecognized prior service cost of $290,000. Thirty employees were affected by the amendment. For purposes of determining remaining service years, these employees could be divided into several groups:

Group	Employees in group	Years to retirement (remaining service years)
1	5	3
2	5	4
3	10	5
4	10	6

Toycar's accounting year ends on December 31.

Required:

1. Compute the total future service years and the service years rendered in each accounting year associated with employees affected by the pension plan amendment.
2. Assume that Toycar uses the service method to amortize prior service cost. Prepare a schedule to determine the amount of prior service cost amortization to be included in net periodic pension expense in each accounting year in which service is received by affected employees.
3. Assume that Toycar uses the straight-line method to amortize prior service cost (round to one decimal):
   a. Compute the average remaining service period at January 1, 1989.
   b. Compute the amount of annual amortization of unrecognized prior service cost.

CASES

C 20–1 (Is *FASB Standard* 87 Workable? No! Yes!)
FASB Standard 87, "Employers' Accounting for Pensions," was one of the most controversial standards issued by the FASB, as illustrated by the following excerpts from an article in *The Wall Street Journal* about the *Standard* shortly before its release ("Accounting Proposal Troubles Firms," *The Wall Street Journal*, December 6, 1985, p. 6):

> Corporate financial executives are fuming about a controversial pension-accounting rule that the Financial Accounting Standards Board is expected to issue soon.
>
> They say the proposed rule is vexing on two counts: It would burden corporate balance sheets by placing a hefty new liability on the books, and it would make bottom-line financial results more volatile.
>
> The FASB set the four-year phase-in period to cushion the rule's effects. But some financial executives in depressed smoke-stack industries argue that boosting liabilities simply by a bookkeeping change is like kicking them when they're down.

This debate continues unabated. For example, an interesting article in the *Financial Executive Magazine* (September/October 1987) contained an interesting dialogue in "Is FASB '87 Workable?" The dialogue was summarized as follows:

No!

1. The rule-making body of the accounting profession has issued the Statement despite objections by the overwhelming majority of their own profession, clients, and related professions. This is either admirable or foolish. Only time will tell.
2. The Statement is much too complex. Simpler solutions exist.
3. It does not accomplish its objectives of presenting a more meaningful measure of pension expense and introducing balance sheet items helpful to readers of financial statements.

4. The FASB based its decisions on conceptualizations, rather than user needs.

The authors of the article continue with comments to support these statements.

Yes!

The four myths concerning the Statement are as follows:

1. FASB 87 represents bad accounting.
2. The new standards eliminate management's ability to tailor financial reporting to individual facts and circumstances.
3. The accounting and disclosure requirements do not provide the information that users need.
4. As a result of all of the above, corporate financial managers are badly served.

The authors of the article continue with comments to deflate these myths.

Required:

1. Discuss the requirements of *FASB Standard 87* that cause concern to companies affected by the standard. Give reasons why companies might be upset.
2. Be prepared to discuss this controversy, even including your opinion. Also, focus on delayed recognition and its implications.

C 20–2 **(Analysis of Pensions; An Actual Case)**

Kimberly-Clark

The annual report of Kimberly-Clark is given in the Appendix at the end of Chapter 25. Respond to the following questions related to the 1987 financial statements.

1. Does the company have a defined benefit retirement plan?
2. Give the items and amounts that comprise net periodic pension expense.
3. Is the pension plan contributory or noncontributory?
4. Basically, how are retirement benefits determined?
5. Basically, how is pension funding handled?
6. Give the following amounts related to the pension plan at December 31, 1987.
   a. Projected benefit obligation.
   b. Accumulated benefit obligation.
   c. Plan assets at fair value.
   d. Expected return on plan assets.
   e. Actual return on plan assets.
   f. Net periodic pension expense.
7. How is the transition adjustment being amortized?
8. What discount and interest rates are being used or realized?

21 ACCOUNTING FOR LEASES

OVERVIEW AND PURPOSE

What would the owner of a small, newly organized automobile business do in the case of a shortage of cash? One alternative would be to diversify in a profitable area only if the 10 special automotive vehicles that would be needed could be obtained. The vehicles would cost approximately $300,000 including all attachments. Of course, the owner could consider borrowing the 20% down payment required and financing the remainder, which would be 100% financing. A preliminary inquiry among potential lenders indicated that such financing is not available. But then, a leasing company offered what they called a **noncash deal.** They proposed to buy the vehicles for the company to use and only charge rent; the first rental would not be due until the end of the first month of use. This would give the company time to render services and collect cash before the first payment is due. Besides, they said, the full amount of each rent payment would be deductible for income tax purposes and that the company would not have to "mess with depreciation." Sounds like a great deal—yes? This chapter would help the owner assess the leasing offer because it discusses the characteristics, uses, and accounting for leases.

The purpose of this chapter is to discuss the fundamentals of accounting for leases. To accomplish this, Part A emphasizes the underlying principles of lease accounting under simplifying assumptions. Part B analyzes the accounting implications of more complex lease provisions. The chapter is organized as follows:

Part A: Fundamentals of Accounting for Leases by Lessors and Lessees

1. Historical background of accounting for leases
2. Basic accounting for leases.
3. Accounting for operating leases.
4. Recognizing capital leases.

Part B: Additional Issues in Accounting for Leases

1. Bargain purchase options in capital leases.
2. Residual value in capital leases.
3. Depreciation of a leased asset by the lessee.
4. Executory and initial direct costs.
5. Sale-leaseback arrangements.
6. Classification of lease receivables and payables.
7. Lease disclosure requirements.

Supplement 21–A: Operating Leases—Interest Method of Amortizing Unearned Rent Revenue/Leasehold

Supplement 21–B: Leveraged Leases

PART A: FUNDAMENTALS OF ACCOUNTING FOR LEASES BY LESSORS AND LESSEES

The acquisition and use of property often is facilitated through leasing arrangements. A lease contract involves at least two parties and an asset that is being leased. The **lessor** owns the asset and receives periodic rents in exchange for allowing a second party to use it. The **lessee** is obligated to pay these periodic rents and has the contractual right to use the lessor's asset.

Leasing has increased rapidly during the past three decades. Today it is used in practically all industries and it involves a wide range of assets leased for varying time periods. Leases by businesses of all sizes vary from the daily rental of an automobile or monthly rental of an office to long-term leases of copiers, computers, health service equipment, heavy duty trucks, railroad cars, airplanes, ships, and buildings. Of the 600 companies surveyed in *Accounting Trends & Techniques, 1987,* 555 disclosed the use of some type of leasing arrangement.[1] Because of the increasing use and diversity of lease contracts, much attention has been given to accounting for these agreements. A number of studies also have been conducted to determine the effect of accounting alternatives proposed and adopted by the FASB.[2]

Historical Background of Accounting for Leases

Accounting for leases has, and continues to be, controversial. Historically, leases were accounted for as executory contracts; that is, the lease was not recorded—only the rentals were recorded (see Chapter 14, page 623, discussion of executory contracts).

Difficulties in accounting for leases arise because of the wide range of lease terms. Some are designed exclusively as financing arrangements; others are used to facilitate short-term use of assets. A major challenge to accountants is to recognize the **economic substance** of a lease arrangement rather than focusing exclusively on its **legal** characteristics. For example, many lease agreements are similar to the acquisition of an asset financed by the issuance of debt. Accounting for these transactions consistently requires that companies in similar economic positions be treated in a similar manner. Implementing this objective has been difficult and has resulted in a number of arbitrary criteria being used to determine the accounting for a lease.

Current standards of financial accounting and reporting for leases have been evolving since 1949 when *ARB No. 38* was issued. The latest of the accounting profession's major efforts to set standards for lease accounting are: *FASB Standard No. 13,* "Accounting for Leases," May 1976; *FASB Standard No. 23,* "Inception of the Lease," August 1978; *FASB Standard No. 91,* "Accounting for Nonrefundable Fees and Costs Associated with Originating or Acquiring Loans and Initial Direct Costs of Leases," December 1986, as amended; and *FASB Standard No. 98,* "Accounting for Leases: Sale-Leaseback Involving Real Estate, Sales-Type Leases of Real Estate, Definition of the Lease Term, and Initial Direct Costs of

---

[1] AICPA, *Accounting Trends & Techniques, 1987* (New York, 1987), Table 2–28.

[2] For example, see A. Rashad Abdel-khalik, "The Economic Effects on Lessees of *FASB Statement 13, 'Accounting for Leases,'" Research Report* (Stamford, Conn., FASB, 1981).

handwritten margin note: definition of lease

Direct Financing Leases," May 1988.[3] Many of the amendments and interpretations deal with specific issues which are beyond the scope of this textbook. Nevertheless, *FASB Standards 13, 23,* and *91,* as amended and interpreted, are the primary sources for this chapter.

At one time, lease agreements were fairly standard. However, in recent years they have become complex, due largely to the creative drafting of contracts to take advantage of favorable income tax provisions. Today leases vary considerably, from operating leases (such as the short-term rental of a truck) to leveraged capital leases (such as a three-party long-term rental of a large computer). Lessors usually are large leasing companies, individual investors, or manufacturers; lessees are from practically all industries. The primary advantages attributed to leasing include the following:

1. Leasing may help a manufacturer increase sales of its products (i.e., by using lease/buy financing contracts as a secondary means of selling products).

2. Leasing may resolve a critical cash problem for the lessee by making available 100% financing for the leased asset.[4]

3. In the case of certain short-term leases, the lessee's debt-to-equity ratio is not increased. If the lessee has other debt contracts that restrict the amount of debt the lessee may incur, use of short-term leasing arrangements to obtain the assets needed may be desirable if the terms are set such that the lessee is not required to record an additional liability. This is often called **off-balance-sheet financing.**

4. Leasing makes immediately available, to the lessee, needed equipment that is not obsolete and is in new or good condition.

5. Leasing may help the lessee avoid the risk and cost of idle equipment.

6. Leasing may provide income tax advantages for all parties to the lease agreement. These tax advantages stem from the investment tax credit (when available), accelerated depreciation, and tax deductibility of the full amount of certain lease payments. **Lease agreements often are drawn to shift most of the tax advantages to the party that is in the higher tax bracket** (see Supplement 21–B).

7. When the requirements of the income tax regulations are met the lessee can deduct the full amount of each rental for income tax purposes.

Basic Accounting for Leases

FASB Standard 13, par. 1, defines a lease as "an agreement conveying the right to use property, plant, or equipment (land and/or depreciable assets) usually for a stated period of time."[5]

[3] In May 1976, the FASB combined *FASB Standards 17, 22, 23,* and *26–29,* and *FASB Interpretations 19, 21, 23, 24, 26* and *27,* in a revised version: *FASB Statement of Financial Accounting Standards No. 13,* "Accounting for Leases" (Stamford, Conn., 1976).

[4] An important issue to the lessee is determination of whether to lease or buy the needed asset. Certain finance texts consider this issue in greater detail.

[5] This definition does not include [a] "agreements that are contracts for services that do not transfer the right to use property, plant, or equipment from one contracting party to the other . . . , [b] lease agreements concerning the rights to explore for or to exploit natural resources such as oil, gas, minerals, and timber . . . , nor [c] licensing agreements for items such as motion picture films, plays, manuscripts, patents, and copyrights."

For accounting purposes, leases are classifed broadly as *(a)* **operating** leases and *(b)* **capital** leases. The basic distinction made is that an operating lease is viewed as an **executory** contract and capital leases are **executed** contracts (see Chapter 14, page 623). Therefore, an operating lease is not recorded—only the rentals are recorded. In contrast, a capital lease is recorded at the inception of the lease. In leasing the distinction between an executory contract and an executed contract is made on a **material ownership** test. The specific provisions of the lease contract between the lessor and lessee, rather than the characteristics of the leased asset, determine the lease classification. **An operating lease does not transfer a material ownership interest** from the lessor to the lessee. In contrast, **a capital lease specifies the transfer of a material ownership interest** in the leased asset from the lessor to the lessee. An example of a **lease provision** that indicates the transfer of a material ownership interest in the leased asset is the transfer of title to the leased asset from the lessor to the lessee at the end of the lease term. The transfer of a **material ownership interest** (not legal ownership) often is described as a transfer of "most of the risks and rewards of ownership" of the leased asset. Risks involve such disadvantages as casualty loss, wear and tear, obsolescence, and maintenance. Rewards often involve such benefits as the right to use, periodic rents rather than a costly purchase, increase in the value of the leased asset, and transfer of legal ownership of the leased asset at the end of the lease term. *FASB Standard 13* gives specific criteria for identifying a capital lease; all leases not meeting those criteria are operating leases.

To illustrate the characteristics of an **operating** lease, assume Lessor Company leased a computer to Lessee Company on a monthly basis. Lessor Company is responsible for ownership (i.e., executory) costs, such as maintenance, property taxes, and insurance. In this lease the lessee incurred only one risk—the payment of the rentals—and obtained only one benefit—temporary use of the asset. Thus, no material ownership interest was transferred. In contrast, assume Lessor Company leased an identical computer to Lessee Company on a long-term, noncancelable lease. The lease specified that, at the end of the lease term, Lessee Company would own the leased asset with no additional payments. In this case, the **lessee** assumed almost all of the risks and rewards of ownership from the date of the lease agreement; therefore, it is a **capital** lease.

Operating leases pose no significant accounting problems. In contrast, capital leases raise difficult accounting issues because they effectively transfer a **material ownership interest.** That is, **most of the risks and rewards of ownership** are assumed by the lessee even though the lessor does not formally transfer ownership of the leased asset. This transfer of a material ownership interest strongly suggests a **sale/purchase transaction** wherein the *(a)* lessor should record a sale and *(b)* lessee should record a purchase of the leased asset when the lease is initiated. However, in accounting for leases, a **lessee** may want to avoid reporting the lease liability (and capitalizing the leased asset) because recording the lease liability would increase the debt-to-equity ratio. Therefore, one objective of *FASB Standard 13* is to define cases in which a material ownership interest is transferred and, as a consequence, to require the lessee to record the leased item as an asset and record the related lease liability.

This objective is consistent with the **full-disclosure principle,** which requires that an entity report all of its assets and liabilities. In cases in which no capitalization is necessary, *FASB Standard 13* requires substantial disclosures of future lease payments in notes to the financial statements. In respect to income measurement, the **matching principle** governs the amount and timing of expense to be reported for leases, and the **cost principle** governs the determination of the cost of any leased assets capitalized. In turn, asset cost affects the future amount of expense recognized.

A **lessor** may be motivated to record a lease as a sale of the leased asset, thus recognizing revenue on the sale at the date the lease is initiated. Therefore, a fundamental accounting issue for lessors is the timing of revenue recognition. Consequently, a basic objective of *FASB Standard 13* is to provide guidelines for the recognition of lease revenue by the lessor. This is accomplished by defining the circumstances when the leased asset should be treated as sold. Thus, the **revenue principle** is of primary importance to the lessor, as is the **full-disclosure principle,** which governs the disclosures of lease revenue and any lease receivables created by the lease.

In view of these issues, *FASB Standard 13* basically provides the following recording and reporting guidelines:

Summary of accounting entries for leases.

Lessor	**Lessee**
OPERATING LEASES	

No recognition of a sale at inception of the lease.
Recognize periodic collection as rent revenue:
Cash xx
    Rent revenue xx
Recognize depreciation as with other depreciable assets.
	No capitalization of cost of leased asset at inception of the lease.
	Recognize periodic payment as rent expense:
	Rent expense xx
	    Cash xx

CAPITAL LEASES	

Recognize transfer (similar to a sale) of the leased asset at inception of the lease:
Lease receivable xx
    Asset leased* xx
* See Exhibit 21–4 for a sales-type lease.
	Recognize acquisition (similar to a purchase) of the leased asset at inception of the lease:
	Leased asset xx
	    Lease liability xx

Recognize periodic collection as part interest revenue and as part reduction of the principal of the receivable:
Cash xx
    Interest revenue xx
    Lease receivable xx
	Recognize periodic payment as part interest expense and as part reduction of the principal of the liability:
	Interest expense xx
	Lease liability xx
	    Cash xx
	Recognize depreciation expense as with other depreciable assets.

Because each lease involves both a lessor and a lessee, an "accounting symmetry" theoretically exits. That is, the two parties usually record opposite and symmetrical entries. This symmetry is shown in the above summary. Such symmetry is prevalent in many kinds of transactions, such as a credit sale (i.e., between the seller and buyer) and bonds (i.e., between the borrower and lender). In Part A of this chapter, this symmetry is maintained for instructional purposes.[6] *FASB Standard 13* broadly classifies leases for the lessor and lessee as follows:

1. **Capital leases**—broadly defined as a lease that transfers a material ownership interest in the leased asset from the lessor to the lessee.
2. **Operating leases**—all other leases.

The next sections discuss and illustrate accounting by the lessor and lessee for the above lease classifications (leveraged leases are discussed in Supplement 21–B). Operating leases are discussed first because they pose no new substantive accounting issues.

Accounting for Operating Leases

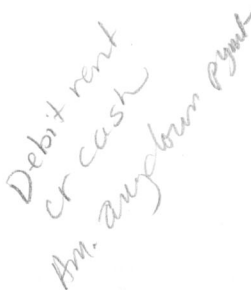

An operating lease does not transfer a material ownership interest in the leased asset from the lessor to the lessee. It does not meet the criteria for classification as a capital lease. Accounting for an operating lease is illustrated in **Exhibit 21–1.** Panel A gives the case data, and panel B gives the entries.

In some cases, an operating lease provides that, in addition to the periodic rent, a nonrefundable down payment is made at the inception of the lease agreement. In this case the lessor debits Cash and credits Unearned Rent Revenue when the down payment is received. The **lessee** debits an asset account called Leasehold (or Prepaid Rent Expense) and credits Cash. Each party must amortize the prepayment over the life of the lease on a systematic and rational basis. This case is illustrated in Exhibit 21–1, panel C. Alternative amortization methods, for operating leases, commonly used by the lessor (for Unearned Rent Revenue) and the lessees (for Leaseholds) are as follows:

1. **Straight-line method—A constant dollar amount** of the prepayment is allocated as revenue (lessor) or expense (lessee) to each accounting period covered by the lease.
2. **Interest (present value) method—A constant rate** of revenue/expense allocation is used each period by applying the annuity concept to the prepayment. Supplement 21–A discusses this method.

The straight-line method usually is used because of its simplicity and because the results are not materially different from the interest method.

Recognizing Capital Leases

Prior to the issuance of *FASB Standard 13,* most lessees accounted for all leases as operating leases, which were discussed in the preceding section. Proponents of lease capitalization contended that in many cases the operating lease approach was improper because it results in **off-balance-sheet financing;** that is, obtaining financing without recording the contractual debt. In their view, a lease that transfers a material ownership interest in the leased property creates an asset

[6] However, in some cases a lease may be classified differently (i.e., as an operating or as a capital lease) by the lessor and lessee. In such cases, the "accounting symmetry" does not exist. (See, for example, residual value guarantees by third parties in Part B of this chapter.)

Exhibit 21–1
Operating lease—accounting by lessor and lessee.

Panel A—Case Data (annual rentals are used only for instructional purposes):

1. Lessor rents an office to Lessee for an annual rental of $4,800, payable in advance each March 1.
2. The accounting years of each party end on December 31.

Panel B—Entries:

Lessor			Lessee		
March 1, 19A:					
To record annual rental:					
Cash	4,800		Rent expense	4,800	
Rent revenue		4,800	Cash		4,800
December 10, 19A:					
To record payment of property taxes on the entire building:					
Expense	6,000		No entry.		
Cash		6,000			
December 31, 19A (etc.):					
To record payment of monthly telephone bill incurred by the lessee:					
No entry.			Expense	65	
			Cash		65
December 31, 19A (end of accounting year):*					
To record adjusting entry (two months' rent unearned by lessor and prepaid by lessee):					
Rent revenue ($4,800 × 2/12)	800		Prepaid rent expense	800	
Unearned rent revenue		800	Rent expense		800

* In addition to the accrual entry illustrated, the lessor records depreciation expense on the building for the year.

Panel C—Nonrefundable Down Payment of $720 for a Two-Year Operating Lease:

Lessor			Lessee		
March 1, 19A:					
Cash	720		Prepaid rent expense (or Leasehold)	720	
Unearned rent revenue		720	Cash		720
December 31, 19A (straight-line amortization):					
Unearned rent revenue	300		Rent expense	300	
Rent revenue		300	Prepaid rent expense (or Leasehold)		300

for the **lessee** that is more than a temporary right to use the leased property. They contended that the lessee should recognize this material interest by capitalizing as an **asset** the present value of the future lease rentals. Further, they reasoned that such a **lease creates a liability** equal to the present value of the future rents, which also should be recognized by the lessee. Similar reasoning led to the conclusion that, where material ownership is transferred, the **lessor** should recognize a sale of the asset. Thus, the lessor would record a receivable and remove the cost of the asset from the lessor's records. Therefore, the material ownership interest (i.e., the asset) should be **depreciated** by the lessee (rather than by the lessor). Moreover, the lease rental payments should be accounted for by both parties in the same manner as periodic payments on a long-term liability; that is, each rental is a combination of interest and reduction of debt.

Proponents of lease capitalization also pointed out that recognition of an asset and a liability on lessee's financial statements would make their statements comparable with those of entities that purchased their operational assets and financed the purchase price with long-term debt. They argued that a lessee company that leased properties under long-term leases and a company that owned similar properties financed by long-term debt were in the same economic position. Both companies were committed to a series of regular payments over a long term; lessees paid "rents," while owners paid interest and principal on the debt. Both had exclusive rights to use similar assets over most or all of the useful lives of the assets. In many long-term lease contracts, the lessee is committed to pay repairs and maintenance, taxes and insurance, and similar **executory** costs associated with assets over their useful lives. If lessees could avoid recognition of assets and liabilities while owners could not, their financial statements would not be comparable even though they were in similar economic and, to some extent, similar legal positions.

Opposition to the capitalization of lease rentals arose because lessees were reluctant to recognize a lease-related liability. They pointed out that various other long-term **executory contracts** are not recognized under GAAP, and that lease contracts should not be singled out for different treatment.[7] Lessees argued that sudden recognition of large, previously unrecorded long-term lease liabilities could cause some lessees to be in technical default on other long-term debt covenants, which limited their indebtedness to a certain amount or required a certain ratio of assets to debt. These ratio agreements often did not consider the possible recognition of liabilities related to lease contracts because at that time GAAP did not require such recognition. In effect, altering accounting rules for leases caused some companies to change existing debt agreements. The FASB moved ahead because it did not accept the opposition's arguments as persuasive. Also, it decided to consider other executory contracts separately (e.g., pensions).

Accounting for Capital Leases

Part A of this chapter discusses and illustrates accounting by the lessor and lessee in situations that are not complicated by special conditions and complex lease contract provisions. Thus, in Part A, we assume that: (1) the lessor and lessee use the same interest, or discount, rate in the lease calculations, (2) the leased asset has no residual value, (3) there is no bargain purchase option or guaranteed residual value, and (4) the lessor owns the leased asset at the end of the lease term. Part B will discuss special lease situations, at which time the related technical definitions will be introduced.

Capital leases were broadly defined in the prior sections. Because of the significant differences between accounting for operating and capital leases and the difficulty in defining a **material ownership interest,** *FASB Standard 13* specifies detailed criteria which qualify a lease contract as a capital lease. These criteria are outlined in **Exhibit 21–2.** Notice that **four criteria apply to both lessors and lessees; if any one of these four criteria is met by the lessee, the lease qualifies as a capital lease for the lessee. In contrast lessors must meet any one of the four criteria plus two additional criteria (which do not apply to**

---

[7] Employment contracts whereby employers agree to pay certain salaries for future services, purchase commitments that do not involve probable losses, and pensions are but a few of the types of executory contracts for which an asset and corresponding liability are not recognized under GAAP.

Exhibit 21–2

Criteria for identifying capital leases—lessor and lessee.

Capital lease for lessor	Capital lease for lessee
The lease must meet **any one** of the following four criteria:*	The lease must meet **any one** of the following four criteria:*
1. The lease transfers ownership of the leased asset to the lessee by the end of the lease term.	1. Same.
2. The lease contains a bargain purchase option.	2. Same.
3. The lease term is equal to 75% or more of the total estimated economic life of the leased asset.	3. Same.
4. The present value of the minimum lease payments at the inception of the lease is at least 90% of the market value of the leased asset at that time.†	4. Same.
In addition, the lease must meet **both** of the following criteria:	
5. Collectibility of the minimum lease payments is reasonably assured.	5. Not applicable.
6. No important uncertainties surround the amount of unreimbursable costs yet to be incurred by the lessor under the lease.‡	6. Not applicable.

* Criteria 3 and 4 do not apply if *(a)* the beginning of the lease term falls within the last 25% of the total economic life of the leased asset, *(b)* land is the only asset leased, or *(c)* the lease involves both land and building(s).

† The rent payment required in a capital lease often is called the periodic lease rent, periodic rent, or simply rent. However, the term used in FASB pronouncements on leases is **minimum lease payments.** The term **minimum** is used because, as is discussed in Part B of this chapter, various lease provisions require the application of certain offsets in computing the periodic lease rents. The technical definitions of minimum lease payments and other selected terms that are used in lease accounting are given in Exhibit 21–5.

‡ Important uncertainties might include commitments by the lessor to guarantee performance of the leased asset in a manner more extensive than the typical product warranty or to protect the lessee from obsolescence of the leased asset. However, the necessity of estimating executory costs such as insurance, maintenance, and taxes to be paid by the lessor does not by itself constitute an important uncertainty under this provision.

lessees). Because of these two additional criteria for the lessor, not all leases that qualify as capital leases for the lessee also qualify as capital leases for the lessor. Thus, a capital lease to the lessee could be an operating lease to the lessor. These criteria constitute the transfer of ownership tests. They were carefully drawn to identify situations in which a material ownership interest transferred by the provisions of the contract will be appropriately accounted for by the lessor and lessee.

In Exhibit 21–2, criterion 1 specifically requires a provision in the lease contract that legal ownership will be transferred. Criterion 2 is a provision that gives the lessee the right (an option) to buy the leased asset at a price that is significantly lower than the expected market value at the option date. Criterion 3 specifies a lease term equal to at least 75% of the life of the asset. The test assumes that this period of time is sufficient for a material ownership interest to be recognized. Criterion 4 assumes that if the present value of the lease payments is at least 90% of the market value of the leased asset at the lease inception date, a material ownership interest has been transferred. Criteria 5 and 6 provide for risks that might make the first four criteria inoperative (and to prevent abuse of those criteria).

In addition to making a careful distinction between operating and capital leases, *FASB Standard 13* further defines capital leases for the lessor as either direct financing leases or sales-type leases. Based on these distinctions the subclassifications of leases can be outlined as follows:

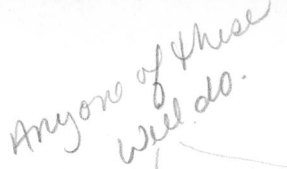

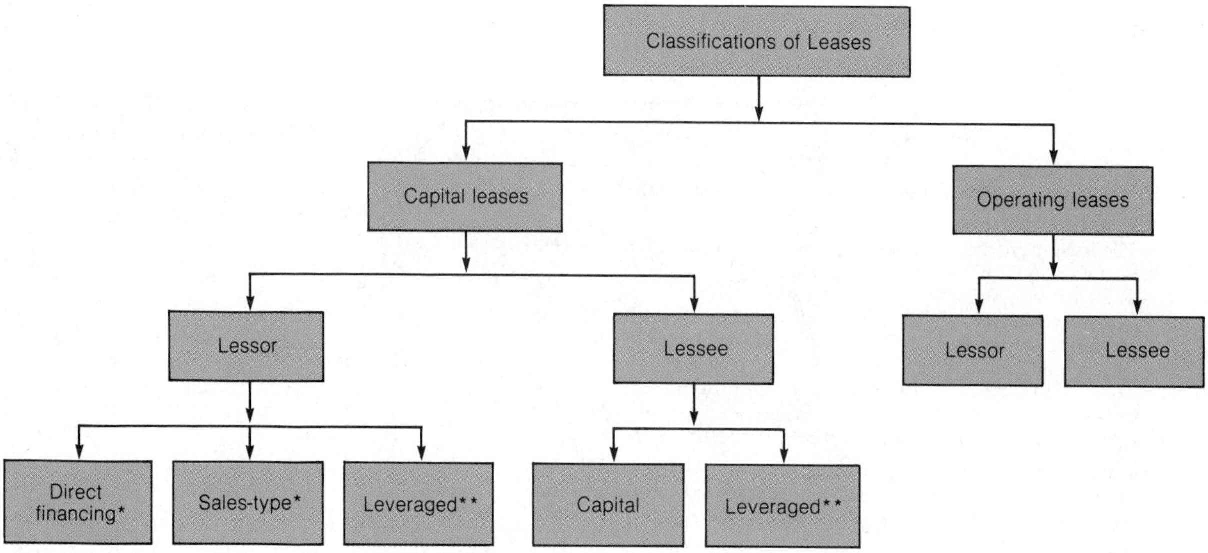

*Discussed below. **Discussed in Supplement 21-B.

a. Direct financing lease—For this type of capital lease, the only revenue the **lessor** recognizes is **interest revenue on the lease receivable.** There is no profit margin at inception of the lease because the cost (or carrying value) of the leased asset is the same as its selling price. **For a direct financing lease, the rental payments are computed based upon the lessor's cost of the leased asset plus interest at the market rate.** At the inception date of the lease, the lessor records a "sale" of the leased asset by debiting a lease receivable and removing the cost of the leased asset from the records. As each rental payment is collected, the lessor recognizes **interest revenue** on the lease receivable.[8] Such leases are called **direct financing** leases because the lessor is engaged in leasing (i.e., not selling) assets only as a way to earn interest (i.e., financing revenue) on available funds. Similarly, the **lessee** views the lease as a means of financing the acquisition of a needed asset.

b. Sales-type lease—For this type of lease, the **lessor** recognizes **two kinds of revenue.** First, at inception of the lease, **sales revenue** and **cost of goods sold** are recognized, resulting in a **"manufacturer's or dealers' profit or loss."** This profit represents the difference between the normal selling price of the leased asset and its cost to the lessor. Second, as each rental payment is collected, **interest revenue** on the lease receivable is recognized. This kind of lease is called a **sales-type** lease because the lessor recognizes revenue at lease inception in the same manner as for a regular sale. This type of lease typically is used by a dealer rather than a leasing company. The main objective is to recognize the gross profit on the sale at the inception of the lease.

The lessee makes no distinction between direct financing leases and sales-type leases. At inception date of the lease, the leased property is recorded as

[8] Accrual entries are used if the accounting period differs from the lease payment period.

an asset at its **cost to the lessee.** The lessee subsequently makes the required rental payments and recognizes interest expense at each interest date whether or not the lease is a direct financing or sales-type lease. Therefore, for the lessee, all such leases are called **capital leases.** In summary, for all capital leases, the lessee: *(a)* records the cost of the leased asset and the related lease liability at lease inception date, *(b)* records interest expense and a reduction of the lease liability at each rental payment date, *(c)* records executory costs, such as taxes, maintenance, and insurance, during each accounting period, and *(d)* records normal depreciation on the leased asset at the end of each accounting period.

The remainder of this part of the chapter focuses on accounting for capital leases by the lessor and lessee. First, we discuss a direct financing lease and next a sales-type lease. For each situation, we use a common illustration and present symmetrical entries for the lessor and lessee because we assume both parties use the same interest or discount rate.[9]

Exhibit 21–3 illustrates the accounting for a **direct financing** lease to the lessor and for a **capital** lease to the lessee. Panel A gives the case data that qualifies as a capital lease to both parties. For comparative purposes, panel B gives the entries for both the lessor and the lessee. Panel C illustrates the lease amounts that would be reported on the 19A statements of income and financial position of the lessor and the lessee.

Lessee Accounting for Capital Leases. The lessee records a capital lease, at date of inception, as a debit to an asset account, with a title such as Leased Property, and a credit to Lease Liability for the **present value** of all future rents required in the lease agreement. Thus, the **lessee's basic approach** to lease valuation can be expressed as follows:

$$\begin{array}{c}\text{Valuation of leased asset and}\\ \text{related liability at lease inception*}\end{array} = \begin{array}{c}\text{Periodic lease}\\ \text{payments}\end{array} \times \begin{array}{c}\text{Present value of annuity of}\\ n \text{ rents at } i \text{ rate of interest}\end{array}$$

* Part B discusses bargain purchase options and residual value; they will affect this computation. For instructional purposes we assume in Part A that these two factors are zero.

In Exhibit 21–3, the lessee's computation of the valuation of the leased asset and the related lease liability is:[10]

$$\text{Leased asset valuation} = \$36{,}556 \times P_{d_{n=3;\,i=10\%}} \text{ (Table 5–6, 2.73554)} = \underline{\underline{\$100{,}000}}$$

Exhibit 21–3 next shows the lessee's journal entries and reporting based on the rentals specified in the lease contract and the $100,000 cost of the asset as computed above.

Lessee's Interest Rate. Determining the appropriate interest rate to use in the present value discounting by the **lessee** is important. It directly affects the valuation of the leased asset and the related lease liability recorded at inception

[9] For simplicity, throughout Part A, the lessee is assumed to know and use the lessor's implicit interest rate used in the lease. More complex situations are discussed in Part B.

[10] Throughout this section, lease payments are assumed to be made on the first day of each period; thus, present value of an **annuity due** is used.

Exhibit 21–3

Accounting for a capital lease—direct financing; lessor and lessee accounting.

Panel A—Case Data (simplified by assuming a common interest rate, no bargain purchase option, and zero residual value):

1. On January 1, 19A, lessor and lessee signed a three-year lease; the estimated useful life of the leased property is three years (there are no collection or cost uncertainties, and the present value of the rentals equals the cost of the leased asset, $100,000). Thus, the lease qualifies as a direct financing lease.
2. Lessor retains ownership of the leased asset, and the estimated residual value is zero.
3. The lease requires three annual rentals of $36,556 each, payable each January 1, beginning January 1, 19A (an annuity due). Lessor had a 10% target rate of return (i.e., implicit rate of interest) on the cost of the asset; therefore, the lessor computed the periodic rentals as follows: $100,000 ÷ $P_{d_{n=3;i=10\%}}$ (Table 5–6, 2.73554) = $36,556.
4. The accounting year of each party ends on December 31.

Panel B—Entries:

Lessor			Lessee		
January 1, 19A (inception of lease):*					
Lease receivable	100,000		Leased property†	100,000	
Asset (on direct financing lease)		100,000	Lease liability (on capital lease)		100,000
January 1, 19A (first rental):					
Cash	36,556		Lease liability	36,556	
Lease receivable		36,556	Cash		36,556
December 31, 19A (accrual of 19A interest):					
Lease receivable (see schedule below)	6,344		Interest expense	6,344	
Interest revenue		6,344	Lease liability		6,344
December 31, 19A (depreciation expense for one year):					
Not applicable.			Depreciation expense (straight line, $100,000 × ⅓)	33,333	
			Accumulated depreciation		33,333

* See footnote 13.

† Lessee's computation of cost of leased asset: $36,556 × $P_{d_{n=3;i=10\%}}$ (Table 5–6, 2.73554) = $100,000.

Lease Amortization Schedule (annuity due basis):

Date	Annual lease payments	Annual interest at 10%	Decrease (increase) in lease receivable/liability	Lease receivable/liability balance
1/1/19A	Initial value			$100,000[a]
1/1/19A	$ 36,556	—	$ 36,556	63,444
12/31/19A	—	$6,344[b]	(6,344)	69,788
1/1/19B	36,556	—	36,556	33,232
12/31/19B	—	3,324†	(3,324)	36,556
1/1/19C	36,556	—	36,556	-0-
	$109,668	$9,668	$100,000	

[a] Known by lessor; computed as shown by lessee.

[b] $63,444 × 10% = $6,344.

† Rounded to come out even.

Panel C—Financial Statements, 19A:

Lessor:

Statement of income:

Interest revenue, $6,344.

Statement of financial position:

Lease receivable, $69,788 (from lease amortization schedule above).

Lessee:

Statement of income:

Interest expense, $6,344; and depreciation expense, $33,333.

Statement of financial position:

Leased property (cost $100,000 less accumulated depreciation, $33,333, from Panel B entries for Lessee), $66,667.

Lease Liability, $69,788 (from lease amortization schedule above).

(Detailed disclosures are discussed in Part B of this chapter under "Lease Disclosure Requirements.")

of the lease. The higher the interest rate the lower the amount capitalized for the asset and recorded for the liability, and vice versa.

The lessee must compute the valuation of the asset leased and the lease liability by discounting the lease payments using the lower of the *(a)* lessee's incremental borrowing rate, or *(b)* the discount rate used by the lessor (also called the **lessor's implicit interest rate**). If the lessor's implicit interest rate is not known, or cannot be reliably estimated, the lessee's incremental borrowing rate must be used. This is defined in *FASB Standard 13* as "The rate that, at lease inception date, the lessee would have incurred to borrow (over a similar term) the funds necessary to purchase the leased asset." Also refer to the technical definitions given in Exhibit 21–5.[11]

The basic accounting for leases by lessees and lessors, as shown in this chapter, is the same whether the two parties use the same or different interest rates. Use of different interest rates causes asymmetry in the recorded amounts; however, the symmetry in the account titles usually remains intact.[12] Note that the choice of a specific interst rate by the **lessee** does not affect total expenses (i.e., interest expense plus depreciation expense). However, the timing of the recognition of each of these two expenses is affected.

Lessee's Depreciation. *FASB Standard 13* states that the **lessee** should depreciate the asset cost ($100,000 in Exhibit 21–3) in a manner consistent with the lessee's normal depreciation policy. In Part A, we assume that there is no residual value. However, residual value, bargain purchase options, and guaranteed residual value may affect depreciation by the lessee. These topics are discussed in Part B.

The account titles used in Exhibit 21–3 may vary. For example, instead of using an accumulated depreciation (or amortization) account, credits in the depreciation entries could be made directly to the asset account (which parallels the procedures outlined in *FASB Standard 13*). The "depreciation" also can be viewed as the amortization of an intangible (i.e., a right to use the leased property). Also, the debit could be to Expense—Amortization of Leased Property Rights, instead of Depreciation Expense.

The lessee's entries given in Exhibit 21–3, panel B, parallel those that would be recorded for an actual purchase on a credit basis involving periodic payments that are part principal and part interest. Also, notice the lessee's depreciation entry for the leased asset.

---

[11] *FASB Standard 13* requires that the recorded value of the leased asset may not exceed its market value; that is, if the present value of the lease payments is greater than the market value of the leased asset at the lease inception date, both the asset and liability must be recorded at the market value of the leased asset. In this case the implied interest would have to be computed. For example, if the market value of the lease asset in Exhibit 21–3 was $95,985, the implicit interest rate would be computed as: $95,985 ÷ $36,556 = 2.6257; reference to Table 5–6, for $n = 3$, shows that the implicit interest rate is almost exactly 15%. The entries for the lessee (only) would change with respect to amounts.

[12] It is possible that use of different interest rates by lessor and lessee will cause criterion 4 (Exhibit 21–2) for a capital lease (i.e., the present value of the lease payments must be greater than 90% of the market value of the leased asset) to be met by one party (lessor or lessee) and not by the other. If this occurs, and if criteria 1 through 3 are not met by a lease arrangement, one party may account for the lease as a capital lease while the other accounts for it as an operating lease.

Lessor Accounting for Capital Leases—Direct Financing. For comparative purposes, Exhibit 21–3 illustrates accounting by both the lessor and the lessee for one type of capital lease—**direct financing. Lessor** accounting (but not lessee accounting) for capital type leases is different for *(a)* **direct financing leases** versus *(b)* **sales-type leases.** This section discusses lessor accounting for **direct financing leases.**

Recall that the lessor classifies a lease as a **direct financing** lease if there is no "manufacturer's or dealer's profit or loss." In this situation, the lessor's cost (or carrying amount, if different) of the leased asset is assumed to equal its market value at the inception date; therefore, it is used by the lessor to compute the lease rentals. Typically, leasing companies (as opposed to manufacturers and dealers) have only direct financing leases, rather than sales-type leases, because they purchase property for lease and not for resale. The lessor's profit objective is to set the periodic lease rentals at a level sufficiently high to yield the target (expected) rate of return (i.e., interest) on the lessor's investment in the leased asset. Expressed as a formula, the **lessor's basic approach** to compute the amount of the periodic lease rentals is as follows:

$$\text{Periodic lease rental}^{*} = \frac{\text{Lessor's investment (i.e., cost or carrying amount, if different) in leased asset}}{\text{Present value of annuity of } n \text{ rents at } i \text{ rate of interest}}$$

* Part B discusses bargain purchase option and residual value; they will affect this computation. For instructional purposes we assume in this part that these two factors are zero.

In Exhibit 21–3, the lessor's computation of the periodic lease rental is:

$$\text{Rent} = \$100{,}000 \div P_{d_{n=3;\,i=10\%}} \text{ (Table 5–6, 2.73554)}$$
$$= \underline{\underline{\$36{,}556}}$$

The interest rate used by the lessor in the above present value computation is the lessor's target rate of return on the investment.

For comparative purposes, Exhibit 21–3, panel B, illustrates the basic accounting symmetry between the lessor and lessee. Notice that the lessor's equation given above is simply a rearrangement of the **lessee's** formula (see preceding heading, "Lessee Accounting for Capital Leases").[13]

[13] In Exhibit 21–3, panel B, the entry at date of inception of the lease was recorded at "net"; alternatively, it could have been recorded at "gross" as follows, which gives the same results for each party:

Lessor

January 1, 19A (inception of lease):		
Lease receivable	109,668	
Asset (on lease)		100,000
Unearned interest revenue		9,668
January 1, 19A (1st rental):		
Cash	36,556	
Lease receivable		36,556
December 31, 19A (adjusting entry):		
Unearned interest revenue	6,344	
Interest revenue		6,344

Lessor Accounting for Capital Leases—Sales-Type. **The basic distinction between direct financing leases and sales-type leases is that in a sales-type lease, a "manufacturer's or dealer's profit or loss" is recognized by the lessor at inception of the lease.** This means that in a sales-type lease the market value of the leased asset at the inception of the lease is greater or less than the lessor's cost (or carrying amount, if different).

Sales-type leases typically arise when a manufacturer or dealer uses a leasing arrangement as a secondary means of marketing its products. The objectives of a company that either sells or leases its products are to earn a profit on the sale of the leased asset and also to earn interest on the related lease receivable. Thus, for a sales-type lease, two different "profits" are recognized during the lease term:

1. **Manufacturer's or dealers' profit** (gross margin or gross profit) is recognized in full **at date of inception** of the lease. It is computed as follows:

Normal sales price (market value) of the leased asset	−	Cost (or carrying amount, if different) of the leased asset	=	Manufacturer's or dealer's profit or loss

2. **Interest revenue** on the lease receivable is recognized **over the term of the lease.** The total amount of interest is computed as follows:

Gross lease receivable (includes the interest charge)	−	Normal sales price (market value) of the leased asset	=	Total interest revenue

Exhibit 21–4 illustrates accounting for a sales-type lease by Lessor X and Lessee Y. Panel A gives the case data. Panel B gives the lessor's and lessee's entries, and panel C shows the amounts reported on the statements of income and financial position for the first year. The lessee's entries are presented to show that they are not affected by whether the lease is direct financing or sales-type to the lessor.

It is important to emphasize that for a **sales-type** lease the lessor's lease

Lessee

January 1, 19A (inception of lease):		
Leased property	100,000	
Discount on lease liability	9,668	
Lease liability		109,668
January 1, 19A (1st rental):		
Lease liability	36,556	
Cash		36,556
December 31, 19A (adjusting entry):		
Interest expense	6,344	
Discount on lease liability		6,344

FASB Standard 13 (pars. 17 and 18) implies to some people that the lessor, but not the lessee, must record a capital lease at "gross." However, because either approach can be adapted easily to conform the company's financial statement disclosures to *FASB Standard 13*, either approach can be used for the **recording** phase of accounting for leases, as indicated by inquiry of the FASB. Moreover, this general principle holds: **The FASB was concerned with the information a company discloses and only incidentally with the specific journal entries it makes.**

Exhibit 21–4
Accounting for a capital lease—sales type; lessor and lessee accounting.

Panel A—Case Data (simplified by assuming a common interest rate, no bargain purchase option, and zero residual value):

1. On January 1, 19A, Lessor X and Lessee Y signed a three-year lease, which qualified as a capital lease to both parties. The annual rental is payable each January 1, beginning January 1, 19A (i.e., an annuity due).
2. The leased asset had a cash-equivalent sales price (i.e., market value) of $120,000 and cost Lessor X $100,000, which indicates a gross margin of $20,000. The asset had an estimated useful life of three years and zero estimated residual value.
3. Lessor X retains title to the leased asset and, based upon a 10% target (expected) return on the receivable, computed the annual rentals as: $120,000 ÷ $P_{d_{n=3;i=10\%}}$ (Table 5–6, 2.73554) = $43,867.
4. The accounting year ends on December 31 for both parties.

Panel B—Entries:

Lessor			Lessee		
January 1, 19A (inception of lease):					
Lease receivable	120,000		Leased property	120,000*	
Cost of goods sold	100,000		Lease liability		120,000
Sales revenue		120,000	* Lessee's computation: $43,867 × (2.48685 × 1.10) = $120,000.		
Asset (on sales-type lease)		100,000			
January 1, 19A (first rental):					
Cash	43,867		Lease liability	43,867	
Lease receivable		43,867	Cash		43,867
December 31, 19A (accrual of 19A interest):					
Lease receivable	7,613		Interest expense	7,613	
Interest revenue		7,613	Lease liability		7,613
December 31, 19A (depreciation expense for one year):					
Not applicable.			Depreciation expense ($120,000 × ⅓)	40,000	
			Accumulated depreciation		40,000

Lease Amortization Schedule (annuity due basis):

Date	Annual lease payments	Annual interest at 10%	Decrease (increase) in lease receivable/liability	Lease receivable/liability balance
1/1/19A	Initial value			$120,000[a]
1/1/19A	$ 43,867	—	$ 43,867	76,133
12/32/19A	—	$ 7,613[b]	(7,613)	83,746
1/1/19B	43,867	—	43,867	39,879
12/31/19B	—	3,988	(3,988)	43,867
1/1/19C	43,867	—	43,867	-0-
	$131,601	$11,601	$120,000	

[a] Known by lessor; computed by lessee as shown above.
[b] $76,133 × 10% = $7,613.

payments are based on selling price. Therefore, the **lessee** capitalizes the leased asset on the basis of the lessor's normal **selling price** (which is considered to be the market valuation) rather than on the lessor's cost. For a direct financing lease the lessor computes the periodic rental based on the cost of the asset rather than on selling price.

In Exhibit 21–4, the lessor's entry at the date of inception of a sales-type

Exhibit 21–4
(concluded)

Panel C—Financial Statements, December 31, 19A:

Lessor:
Statement of income:
Sales revenue, $120,000; cost of goods sold, $100,000; and interest revenue, $7,613.
Statement of financial position:
Lease receivable, $83,746 (from lease amortization schedule above).

Lessee:
Statement of income:
Interest expense, $7,613; and depreciation expense, $40,000.
Statement of financial position:
Leased property (cost, $120,000 less accumulated depreciation, $40,000, from panel B entries for lessee), $80,000.
Lease liability $83,746 (from lease amortization schedule above).
(Detailed disclosures are discussed in Part B of this chapter under "Lease Disclosure Requirements.")

lease is similar to the entry that would be made if the leased asset had been sold outright on credit. That is, the lessor debits the Lease Receivable and credits Sales Revenue for the sale price of the leased asset ($120,000). This amount is the same as the present value of the rents to be received. At the same time, the lessor debits Cost of Goods Sold and credits the leased asset for its cost or carrying amount (as inventory), $100,000. The difference of $20,000 (i.e., $120,000 − $100,000) measures the lessor's "manufacturer's or dealer's profit" on the "sale." The subsequent entries by the lessor to record collections of periodic rent, interest revenue, and reduction of the lease receivable are the same, except for amounts, as the lessor's entries under a direct financing lease (Exhibit 21–3).

Termination of Lease Agreements. A capital lease agreement may terminate due to *(a)* a change of provisions in the lease, *(b)* renewal or extension of the original lease, or *(c)* expiration of the lease term. *FASB Standard 13* specifies the accounting for termination by the lessee and lessor as follows:

By lessor: On termination, the net carrying value of the lease receivable is removed from the accounts, and the leased asset is recorded at the lower of its original cost or present market value. Any difference is recognized as gain or loss in the period of termination.

By lessee: On termination, both the net carrying value of the leased asset and the lease liability are removed from the accounts. A gain or loss is recognized in the period of termination for any difference.

Example: Assume the lease illustrated in Exhibit 21–4 is terminated on January 1, 19B. The fair market value of the leased asset on this date is $81,000. The entries are:

Lessor

Asset	81,000	
Loss on lease termination	2,746	
Lease receivable		83,746

Lessee

Lease liability	83,746	
Accumulated depreciation	40,000	
Leased property		120,000
Gain on lease termination		3,746

In conclusion, Part A of this chapter discussed and illustrated the basic fundamentals of accounting and reporting for operating and capital leases by the lessee and operating, direct financing, and sales-type leases by the lessor. Complexities were excluded for instructional purposes.

PART B: ADDITIONAL ISSUES IN ACCOUNTING FOR LEASES

Part A discussed and illustrated the fundamentals of accounting and reporting for leases by lessees and lessors. Part B considers the following additional issues in accounting for leases:

1. Bargain purchase options in capital leases.
2. Residual value in capital leases.
3. Depreciation of a leased asset by the lessee.
4. Executory and initial direct costs.
5. Sale-leaseback arrangements.
6. Classification of lease receivables and payables.
7. Lease disclosure requirements.

Exhibit 21–5 presents a list of technical lease terms and their definitions as set forth in *FASB Standard 13.* These terms will be referred to throughout Part B.

Bargain Purchase Options in Capital Leases

A **bargain purchase option** (BPO) permits a lessee to purchase leased property, during a specified period of the lease term, at a "bargain" price. This price is sufficiently low to **reasonably assure** that the lessee will take advantage of the "bargain." In effect, a BPO is viewed as a sale and transfer of ownership of the leased asset, which is represented by the "residual value" of the leased property by the lessor to the lessee at the specified "bargain" price. Refer to Exhibit 21–5 for the technical definition of a BPO. Notice that the definition of **minimum lease payments in Exhibit 21–5 states: "If the lease contains a BPO, only the rental payments over the lease term and the BPO payment are included in the minimum lease payments."** This means that when there is a BPO, all residual values are disregarded when computing the lease rent amount. In this case residual value is used only to determine whether the purchase option is a "bargain."

Including a BPO in a capital lease contract means that there are **two** cash flows to the lessor from the lessee: one is from the periodic rentals and the other is from the BPO price. Thus, a BPO affects *(a)* the amount of the annual rentals required to meet the lessor's target rate of return and *(b)* the lessee's capitalizable cost of the leased asset. Compared with the cases in Part A which assumed zero residual value of the leased asset and no BPO, the **annual rental in a lease with a BPO is less than without a BPO** because the lessor recovers part of the investments in the leased asset through the BPO price. This recovery reduces the amount that must be received from the periodic rentals. Therefore, the **lessor** includes the BPO amount in computing the amount of each annual

clue Know for reading purposes + general info

Exhibit 21–5
Technical lease definitions.

Lease term—The fixed noncancelable term of the lease plus periods covered by **bargain renewal options** and plus all periods covered by renewal options during which there will be a loan outstanding from the lessor to the lessee, before the exercise date of a **bargain purchase option.** However, the lease term cannot extend beyond the exercise date of a bargain purchase option. In other words, the lease term is the period during which the lessee can reasonably be expected to continue leasing (due, in some cases, to a bargain renewal option or a bargain purchase option).*

Bargain renewal option—An option allowing the lessee to renew the lease for a rental that is sufficiently lower than the expected market rental of the property at the exercise date of the option that exercise of the option appears (at the lease inception date) to be reasonably assured.

Bargain purchase option (BPO)—An option allowing the lessee to purchase the leased property for a price that is sufficiently lower than the expected market value of the property at the exercise date of the option that exercise appears (at the lease inception date) to be reasonably assured.

Minimum lease payments—lessee—The rental payments that the lessee is obligated (or can be required) to make in connection with the leased property, excluding executory costs (e.g., insurance, maintenance, and taxes) that the lessee is required to pay. If the lease contains a BPO, only the minimum rental payments over the lease term and the BPO payment are included in the minimum lease payments. If the lease does not contain a BPO, minimum lease payments include: *(i)* the minimum rental payments called for by the lease over the lease term; *(ii)* any residual value guarantee by the lessee at the expiration of the lease term; and *(iii)* any penalty payment the lessee can be required to make if the lease is not renewed or extended at the expiration of the lease term.

Minimum lease payments—lessor—Same as the payments described for the lessee plus any residual value guarantee by a third party unrelated to either the lessee or the lessor. (Note: When there is a BPO, residual value is of no future concern to the lessor because the leased asset will be retained by the lessee at the end of the lease term.)

Estimated residual value of the leased asset—The estimated market value of the leased asset at the end of the lease term. The **unguaranteed residual value** is the estimated residual value less any portion guaranteed by the lessee or by a third-party guarantor.

Interest rate implicit in the lease—The interest rate that, at the lease inception date, causes the present value of *(i)* the minimum lease payments (excluding any executory costs to be paid by the lessor) and *(ii)* the **unguaranteed** residual value to be equal to the market value of the leased property (less any investment tax credit retained by the lessor).

Lessee's incremental borrowing rate—The rate that, at lease inception date, the lessee would have incurred to borrow (over a similar term) the funds necessary to purchase the leased asset.

* As amended by *FASB Standard 88,* par. 22, May 1988.

rental. The **lessee** includes the BPO in computing the cost of the leased asset to be capitalized (i.e., the present value of the minimum lease payments).

Exhibit 21–6 illustrates lessor and lessee accounting for a BPO case. The case, used initially in Exhibit 21–3, is adapted to include a BPO of $10,000 exercisable at the end of the three-year lease term. The estimated residual value at the exercise date is $15,000. This case involves a **direct financing lease** to the lessor and a **capital lease** to the lessee.

Exhibit 21–6, panel A, shows the **lessor's** computation of the annual rentals in which the BPO amount of $10,000 is deducted. Notice that the lessor must consider two different cash inflows in the computation: *(1)* the cash to be received when the BPO is exercised and *(2)* the annual rentals. This two-stage computation by the lessor is based on the *(a)* lease specifications; *(b)* lessor's recorded cost (or carrying value, if different) of the leased asset because the lease is a direct financing lease; and *(c)* lessor's target rate of return (i.e., the implicit interest

Exhibit 21–6

Accounting for a direct financing lease with a bargain purchase option.

Panel A—Case Data (adapted from Exhibit 21–3):

1. On January 1, 19A, lessor and lessee signed a three-year lease that qualifies as a direct financing lease to the lessor and a capital lease to the lessee. The leased asset cost the lessor $100,000; the estimated total life of the asset is four years; and the estimated residual value at the end of that time is zero.
2. The lessee has an option to purchase the asset for $10,000 on December 31, 19C. At that date (i.e., end of the third year), the estimated residual value is $15,000 (a bargain).
3. The lease requires three annual rentals of $33,809, payable each January 1. Lessor had a target rate (i.e., the implicit interest rate) of 10% on the cost of the asset. Therefore, the lessor computed the periodic rentals as follows:

Cost (or carrying value, if different) of leased asset (total PV of the lease)	$100,000
Deduct: PV of BPO; $10,000 × $p_{n=3;i=10\%}$ (Table 5–2, .75131)	7,513
Net asset cost to be recovered through rentals (PV of the asset excluding BPO)	$ 92,487
Annual rental $92,487 ÷ $P_{d_{n=3;i=10\%}}$ (Table 5–6, 2.73554)	$ 33,809

4. The accounting year of each party ends on December 31.

Panel B—Entries:

Lessor			Lessee		
January 1, 19A (inception of lease):*					
Cash	33,809		Leased property†	100,000	
Lease receivable**	66,191		Lease liability		66,191
Asset		100,000	Cash		33,809

* This entry records the $10,000 BPO in the receivable account. Alternatively, the entry could be made to record the BPO amount in the asset account, Leased Property.

Lessor			Lessee		
December 31, 19A (adjusting entries):					
Lease receivable	6,619		Interest expense**	6,619	
Interest revenue**		6,619	Lease liability		6,619
** Computation: See schedule below.			Depreciation expense	25,000	
			Accumulated depreciation ($100,000 ÷ 4 years = $25,000).		25,000
December 31, 19C (exercise of BPO):					
Cash	10,000		Lease liability	10,000	
Lease receivable		10,000	Cash		10,000

† Lessee's computation of cost of leased asset (the lessee capitalizes the BPO):

PV of rentals: $33,809 × $P_{d_{n=3;i=10\%}}$ (Table 5–6, 2.73554)	$ 92,487
PV of BPO: $10,000 × $p_{n=3,i=10\%}$ (Table 5–2, .75131)	7,513
Valuation of leased asset to be capitalized (rentals plus BPO)	$100,000

Lease Amortization Schedule with Bargain Purchase Option (annuity due basis):

Date	Annual lease payments	Annual interest at 10%	Decrease (increase) in lease receivable/liability	Lease receivable/liability balance
1/1/19A	Initial value			$100,000[a]
1/1/19A	$ 33,809	—	$ 33,809	66,191
12/31/19A	—	$ 6,619[b]	(6,619)	72,810
1/1/19B	33,809	—	33,809	39,001
12/31/19B	—	3,900	(3,900)	42,901
1/1/19C	33,809	—	33,809	9,092
12/31/19C	—	908‡	(908)	10,000
12/31/19C	10,000[c]	—	10,000	-0-
	$111,427	$11,427	$100,000	

‡ Rounded to come out even.
[a] Known by lessor; computed by lessee as shown above.
[b] $66,191 × 10% = $6,619.
[c] BPO price.

rate) on the investment. The BPO is discounted from the first exercise data of the BPO to the lease inception date. Often this period of time is less than the lease term. See Exhibit 21–5 for the technical definition of the implicit interest rate.

The **lessee** knows the lease specifications (which include the annual rental amount of $33,809) and the BPO (at end of third year, $10,000). We assume that the lessee has been informed by the lessor that the implicit rate of interest in the lease is 10%.[14] With these data, the lessee computes the capitalizable **cost** of the leased asset. The lessee's computations are given in Exhibit 21–6, panel B.

Exhibit 21–6, panel B, also presents representative entries for the lessor and lessee. Notice that only the **lessee** records **depreciation** expense on the leased asset because under a capital lease a purchase of the leased asset by the lessee is assumed. **When there is a BPO, the lessee depreciates the leased asset over its total expected useful life** (less any estimated residual value at the end of that time) rather than the lease term of three years. It always is **assumed** that the BPO will be exercised which causes the lessee to receive title and permanent ownership of the leased asset.

If, on December 31, 19C (the BPO date), the lessee let the bargain purchase option **lapse,** the lessor and the lessee would remove from their respective accounts all remaining balances related to the lease contract and recognize a loss. If that had occurred (assuming the December 31, 19C, accrual entry has been made), the **lessor's** and the **lessee's** December 31, 19C, entries to record lapse of the BPO would be as follows (assume the **new** estimate of residual value of the leased asset on that date was $8,000 instead of the original estimate of $15,000, and the lease was not renewed):[15]

Lessor:

Asset (new residual value)	8,000	
Loss on lapse of lease purchase option	2,000	
Lease receivable (Exhibit 21–6, panel B)		10,000

Lessee:

Lease liability (Exhibit 21–6, panel B)	10,000	
Loss on lapse of lease purchase option	15,000	
Accumulated depreciation ($25,000 × 3)	75,000	
Leased property		100,000

[14] Assumed to be less than the incremental borrowing rate of the lessee.

[15] The **lessor** has a loss of $2,000 because the estimated $8,000 residual value on the BPO date, December 31, 19C, was less than the balance in the Lease Receivable account of $10,000. Had there been no change in the original estimate of residual value of $15,000, the lessor would record a gain of $5,000. Alternate computation of the **lessee's** loss is:

Cash disbursed from 1/1/19A through 12/31/19C ($33,809 × 3)		$101,427
Expenses recognized through 12/31/C:		
Interest (Exhibit 21–6, panel C)	$11,427	
Depreciation ($25,000 × 3)	75,000	
Total expenses recognized		86,427
Excess of payments over amounts debited for the lease (i.e., the loss)		$ 15,000

ıe in Capital Leases

Residual value is a complex issue in accounting for capital leases. Residual value often exists at the termination date of a capital lease, especially when the lease term is less than the total estimated economic life of the leased property. In such cases, two different estimated residual values may have to be considered, one at the end of the lease term, and the other at the end of the total estimated useful life of the leased property. For example, in Exhibit 21–6, panel A, item 2, the **estimated** residual value at the end of the three-year lease term was $15,000, and at the end of the asset's four-year total estimated life, the estimate was zero. The discussion in this section explains how residual value affects the computation of the **minimum lease payments** by the lessor and the cost to be capitalized by the lessee (see Exhibit 21–5 for technical definitions). **Residual value is not recognized when there is a BPO; it is used only to determine whether the option is a "bargain."**

When the leased asset has **economic value** at the end of the lease term, that residual value must be incorporated into the accounting for the lease. Therefore, it is necessary to determine which party (i.e., lessor or lessee) the lease agreement specifies shall own the leased asset (and therefore the RV) at the end of the lease term.

The accounting impact of an estimated residual value (at the end of the lease term) in a capital lease can be summarized as follows:[16]

Lessee gets the residual value:

1. The leased property and its residual value at the end of the lease term belong to the **lessee at no additional cost** (above the annual lease rentals). In this situation, the residual value does not affect *(a)* the **lessor's** computation of the periodic lease payments nor the lessor's accounting, or *(b)* the **lessee's** cost to be capitalized. However, the **lessee** should depreciate the asset over its **total** useful life less any estimated residual value at the end of that total life.
2. The estimated residual value at the end of the lease term is "sold" by the lessor and "purchased" by the lessee through a BPO. In this situation, the BPO amount is included in the lease accounting by **both** the **lessor** and **lessee** as discussed above and illustrated in Exhibit 21–6.

Lessor retains the residual value:

3. When the lessor retains the residual value (i.e., the lessor gets the leased assets back at the end of the lease term) there is a risk that the lessee will not properly maintain the leased asset, in which case the RV is low or zero. To minimize this risk, the lease agreement may require the lessee to guarantee all or part of the estimated residual value. Thus, the estimated residual value retained by the lessor at the end of the lease term may be *(a)* **unguaranteed** by the lessee, *(b)* **guaranteed in full** by the lessee,

[16] If the estimated residual value at the end of the lease term is zero, the accounting and related lease computations are as illustrated in Part A of this chapter. A zero residual value was assumed throughout those discussions.

(c) **guaranteed** in part by the lessee, or *(d)* **guaranteed by a third party** for a fee depending upon the provisions of the lease agreement. These four cases are discussed below.

Unguaranteed Residual Value Retained by Lessor

When the lease agreement provides that the **lessor** retains the leased asset at the end of the lease term, any residual value is owned by the **lessor.** When that residual value is **unguaranteed** by the lessee, the **lessor** should compute the periodic rentals by deducting the present value of the estimated residual value from the total amount to be recovered under the lease agreement because the RV is not "sold." The **lessee** capitalizes only the lease payments, which **excludes any amount for residual value** because the lessee does not "buy" the RV. This means that the **lessee does not** capitalize the unguaranteed residual value retained by the lessor (thus creating a situation in which entries by lessee and lessor are **not** symmetrical).

Exhibit 21–7 (adapted from Exhibit 21–3) illustrates a direct financing lease with a $10,000 **unguaranteed** residual value at the end of the lease term. The **lessor's** computation of the annual rentals in which the PV of the unguaranteed residual value is deducted as shown in panel A. Panel B gives selected entries for the lessor and lessee and the lessee's computation of the cost of the leased asset, which **does not include** the unguaranteed residual value because it is "owned" by the lessor. Thus, the entries (and the amortization schedules) of the lessor and lessee differ (even though they use the same implicit interest rate) because the estimated unguaranteed residual value is retained in the lessor's accounts but is not capitalized in the lessee's accounts. The lessor's entry on January 1, 19A, the date of inception of the lease, removes the cost of the leased asset and records the receivable which includes the $10,000 residual value. The **last entry,** made at the termination of the lease, removes the residual value ($10,000) from the receivable account and returns it to its original asset account.[17]

The separate **amortization schedules** for the lessor and lessee given in Exhibit 21–7 should be compared. The **lessor's** amortization schedule, as shown, leaves an ending asset balance of $10,000 (the residual value) in the lessor's Lease Receivable account. The initial value in the Lease Receivable account for the lessor is the lessor's cost of the leased asset (i.e., $100,000) because the lessor plans to recover the total cost from the lessee's payments and the asset is returned to the lessor at the end of the lease term. In contrast, the **lessee's** amortization schedule starts with the lease liability amount (i.e., $92,487), which excludes the PV of the RV and ends with a zero balance. Notice that the **lessee** depreciates the leased asset over the lease term and disregards the unguaranteed residual value.

At the end of the lease term, the residual value of the leased asset (i.e.,

---

[17] Some accountants prefer to leave the PV of the residual value in its original asset account for amortization during the lease term because it will not be "collected for" during that term. Both approaches produce the same end results. *FASB Standard 13*, par. 18a, states that "the unguaranteed residual value accuring to the benefit of the lessor" should be "recorded as [included in] the gross investment in the lease." This specification relates more fundamentally to computation of the lease payments by the lessor and not to the details of a specific journal entry (see last sentence of footnote 13).

Exhibit 21–7
Accounting for a direct financing with unguaranteed residual value.

Panel A—Case Data (adapted from Exhibit 21–3):

1. On January 1, 19A, lessor and lessee signed a three-year direct financing lease. Lessor's cost (or carrying value, if different) was $100,000.
2. Lessor retains ownership of the leased asset at the termination of the lease term. At that time, the estimated residual value (RV) is $10,000, which is **unguaranteed** by the lessee because the contract did not impose a residual value guarantee on the lessee.
3. The lease requires three annual rentals of $33,809, payable each January 1. The lessor's target rate of return is 10%; therefore, the lessor computed the periodic rentals, on an annuity due basis, as follows:

Cost of the leased asset (PV of the asset)	$100,000
Deduct: PV of the estimated RV, $10,000 × $p_{n=3;i=10\%}$ (Table 5–2, .75131)	7,513
Net asset cost to be recovered through rentals (PV of the asset net of PV)	$ 92,487
Annual rental: $92,487 ÷ $P_{d_{n=3;i=10\%}}$ (Table 5–6, 2.73554)	$ 33,809

4. The accounting year of each party ends on December 31.

Panel B—Entries:

Lessor			Lessee		
Lease receivable	100,000*		Leased property	92,487†	
Asset		100,000	Lease liability		92,487

* This entry records the $10,000 RV in the lease receivable account. The entry could have been made to record the RV in an asset account, Leased Property.

† Lessee's computation of cost of leased asset (the unguaranteed residual value is **not capitalized** by the lessee): $33,809 × $P_{d_{n=3;i=10\%}}$ (Table 5–6, 2.73554) = $92,487.

January 1, 19A (first rental):

Lessor			Lessee		
Cash	33,809		Lease liability	33,809	
Lease receivable		33,809	Cash		33,809

December 31, 19A (adjusting entries):

Lessor			Lessee		
Lease receivable	6,619		Interest expense	5,868	
Interest revenue		6,619	Lease liability		5,868
See lessor's amortization schedule below.			See lessee's amortization schedule below.		
			Depreciation expense	30,829	
			Accumulated depreciation		30,829
			($92,487 ÷ 3 years = $30,829).		

December 31, 19C (end of lease term—to remove the RV from the Lease receivable account) / (—to remove the asset from the accounts):

Lessor			Lessee		
Asset	10,000		Accumulated depreciation	92,487	
Lease receivable		10,000	Leased property		92,487

Lease Amortization schedule (annuity due basis):

		Lessor				Lessee	
Date	Lease payments	Interest at 10%	Receivable decrease (increase)	Receivable balance	Interest at 10%	Liability decrease (increase)	Liability balance
1/1/19A	Initial value			$100,000			$92,487
1/1/19A	$33,809	—	$33,809	66,191	—	$33,809	58,678
12/31/19A	—	$6,619	(6,619)	72,810	$5,868	(5,868)	64,546
1/1/19B	33,809	—	33,809	39,001	—	33,809	30,737
12/31/19B	—	3,900	(3,900)	42,901	3,072*	(3,072)	33,809
1/1/19C	33,809	—	33,809	9,092	—	33,809	-0-
12/31/19C	—	908*	(908)	10,000 (RV)			

* Rounded to come out even.

$10,000), which is retained by the lessor in this case, is transferred by the **lessor** from the Lease Receivable account, which then will have a zero balance, to the original asset account (see December 31, 19C, entry). In contrast, all of the **lessee's** lease account balances will be zero already.

For a **sales-type lease** with an unguaranteed residual value, *FASB Standard 13* **requires that the lessor deduct the present value of the unguaranteed residual value from both sales revenue and cost of goods sold.** The main purpose of this rule is to avoid overstating sales revenue. Notice that this does not affect the manufacturer's or dealer's profit, lease receivable, or annual interest revenue. **Exhibit 21–8** (adapted from Exhibit 21–4 to include $10,000 residual value at the end of the lease term) shows the case of a sales-type lease with an unguaranteed residual value. Notice in Exhibit 21–8 that both sales revenue ($112,487) and cost of goods sold ($92,487) are computed by deducting the present value of the unguaranteed residual value [$10,000 × $p_{n=3;i=10\%}$ (Table 5–2, .75131) = $7,513] from the cash equivalent price ($120,000) and carrying value ($100,000), respectively. This approach results in the same manufacturer's or dealer's profit as when residual value is guaranteed. However, both sales revenue and cost of goods sold are reduced because the residual value is not "sold" (it reverts to the lessor).

Residual Value Guaranteed by Lessee and Retained by Lessor

When the lessor retains the residual value of the leased asset, the lease agreement may require the **lessee to guarantee all or part of the estimated residual value** at the end of the lease term. Such guarantees are made to motivate the lessee to take better care of the leased asset.

Residual Value Fully Guaranteed by the Lessee. In this case, the residual value estimated at the inception of the lease is fully guaranteed by the lessee, which means that the lessee must pay cash equivalent to make up any residual value deficiency. The deficiency is based on an appraisal (usually by an independent party) at the end of the lease term. To continue the example of Exhibit 21–7, assume the actual residual value at the end of the lease term determined in accordance with the lease contract is $9,000, rather than the previously estimated $10,000. Assuming a fully guaranteed residual value, the lessee must pay the lessor $1,000 cash.

To compute the periodic lease payments when the RV is fully guaranteed, the lessor **deducts the present value of the total residual value** from the total amount to be recovered under the lease agreement because at the inception of the lease the lessor expects to realize the full amount of the residual value at the end of the lease term (i.e., the RV was not "sold").

To illustrate a capital lease with a **RV fully guaranteed** by the lessee, Exhibit 21–7 is adapted. **Exhibit 21–9** gives the adapted case. Panel A restates the case data to incorporate a **fully guaranteed residual value of $10,000** and shows that the lessor deducts the PV of the guaranteed residual value to compute the periodic rentals. Notice that the **lessee** capitalizes $100,000 (i.e., the same amount recognized by the lessor), which is the "net cost to be recovered through rentals" of $92,487 (as computed in panel A, item 3) **plus the present value of the fully guaranteed residual value** of $7,513. The **lessee** capitalizes the sum of these two amounts (i.e., $100,000) because the lease liability is the total

Exhibit 21–8
Accounting for a sales-type lease with unguaranteed residual value.

Panel A—Case Data (adapted from Exhibit 21–4):

1. On January 1, 19A, lessor and lessee signed a three-year lease, which qualified as a capital lease to both parties. The annual rental is payable each January 1.
2. The leased asset had a cash-equivalent sales price of $120,000 and cost the lessor $100,000. The asset had an estimated useful life of four years. The residual value was expected to be $10,000 at the end of the lease term (December 31, 19C).
3. The lessor retained title to the leased asset and, based upon a 10% target (expected) return on the receivable computed the annual rentals as:

Selling price of the leased asset	$120,000
Deduct: PV of estimated RV, $10,000 × $p_{n=3;i=10\%}$ (Table 5–2, .75131)	7,513
Net asset value to be recovered through rentals	$112,487
Annual rental: $112,487 ÷ $P_{d_{n=3;i=10\%}}$ (Table 5–6, 2.73554)	$ 41,121

4. The accounting year ends on December 31 for both parties.

Panel B—Entries:

Lessor

January 1, 19A (inception of lease):		
Lease receivable	120,000	
Cost of goods sold	92,487*	
Sales revenue		112,487**
Asset		100,000

* Lessor's cost of goods sold is the carrying value of the asset less the PV of the unguaranteed residual value ($100,000 − $7,513 = $92,487), because the residual value was not sold.
** Lessor's sales revenue: $120,000 − $7,513 = $112,487.

January 1, 19A (first rental):		
Cash	41,121	
Lease receivable		41,121
December 31, 19A (adjusting entries):		
Lease receivable	7,888	
Interest revenue		7,888

See lessor's amortization schedule below.

December 31, 19C (end of lease term—to remove the RV):		
Asset (RV)	10,000	
Lease receivable		10,000

Lessee

Leased asset	112,487†	
Lease liability		112,487

† Lessee's computation of leased asset cost excluding the unguaranteed RV is: $41,121 × $P_{d_{n=3;i=10\%}}$ (Table 5–6, 2.73554) = $112,487.

Lease liability	41,121	
Cash		41,121
Interest expense	7,137	
Lease liability		7,137

See lessee's amortization schedule below.

Depreciation expense	37,496	
Accumulated depreciation ($112,487 ÷ 3 years = $37,496).		37,496
(—to remove the asset from the accounts):		
Accumulated depreciation	112,487	
Leased asset		112,487

present value guaranteed to be transferred from the lessee to the lessor (see panel B, Lease Amortization Schedule, last column). Notice that a guaranteed RV is added by the lessee; in contrast, an unguaranteed RV is excluded (see Exhibit 21–7).

At termination of the lease on December 31, 19C, the **actual** residual value is determined (independently as specified in the lease agreement). This residual value then is compared with the guaranteed RV to determine whether the lessee owes the lessor additional consideration. In Exhibit 21–9, the "actual" residual value at the end of 19C was determined independently to be $9,000.

Exhibit 21–8
(concluded)

Lease Amortization Schedule (annuity due basis):

Date	Lease payments	Lessor: Interest at 10%	Lessor: Receivable decrease (increase)	Lessor: Receivable balance	Lessee: Interest at 10%	Lessee: Liability decrease (increase)	Lessee: Liability balance
1/1/19A	Initial value			$120,000			$112,487
1/1/19A	$ 41,121	—	$ 41,121	78,879	—	$ 41,121	71,366
12/31/19A	—	$ 7,888[(a)]	(7,888)	86,767	$ 7,137[(b)]	(7,137)	78,503
1/1/19B	41,121	—	41,121	45,646	—	41,121	37,382
12/31/19B	—	4,565	(4,565)	50,211	3,739‡	(3,739)	41,121
1/1/19C	41,121	—	41,121	9,090	—	41,121	-0-
12/31/19C	—	910*	(910)	10,000 (RV)			
	$123,363	$13,363	$110,000		$10,876	$112,487	

‡ Rounded to come out even.
(a) $78,879 × 10% = $7,888.
(b) $71,366 × 10% = $7,137.

Therefore, the lessee is obligated to pay the lessor $1,000 cash (i.e., $10,000 − $9,000). If the guaranteed value had been **less** than the **actual** value, the lessor would have no obligation to make a refund to the lessee.

The estimated residual value on a capital lease should be evaluated periodically to determine whether it is realistic. If the estimate is revised by a material amount, a change in estimate should be recognized and the subsequent lease entries (and schedules) revised accordingly (see *FASB Standard 13,* par. 17d). Fully guaranteed residual value is accounted for in the same way for direct and sale-type leases.

Residual Value Partially Guaranteed by the Lessee. When the **lessee guarantees only a part of the estimated residual value** of the leased asset, the **lessor** bases the computation of the periodic lease payments (and the related amortization schedule) on the estimated residual value (similar to Exhibit 21–7). In contrast, to compute the amount to be capitalized, the lessee adds to the lessor's lease payments only the partially guaranteed amount (as illustrated in Exhibit 21–9). Therefore, the amounts recorded by the lessor and lessee would not be the same. This guideline is the same for direct and sales-type leases.

Residual Value Guaranteed by Third Party and Retained by Lessor

The residual value of a leased asset may be **guaranteed** in full or in part by a **third party guarantor,** usually retained by the lessor for a fee. In this case, the lessor would deduct the amount of the guarantee to compute the lease payments because the cash for any residual value deficiency will come from a different source. The lease receivable includes both sources, the present value of **both** the rental payments and the guaranteed RV. The **lessee** does not include the present value of the guaranteed RV in the cost of the leased asset because the RV is guaranteed by a third party (not the lessee). This results in asymmetrical entries between the lessor and lessee.

Exhibit 21–9
Accounting for a direct financing lease with fully guaranteed residual value.

Panel A—Case Data (adapted from Exhibit 21–7):

1. On January 1, 19A, Lessor A and Lessee B signed a three-year direct financing lease. Lessor's cost (or carrying value, if different) was $100,000.
2. Lessor retains ownership of the leased asset at termination of the lease; on January 1, 19A, lessor and lessee estimated a residual value of $10,000. Also, the terms of the lease agreement specify that the lessee will **guarantee** a minimum residual value of $10,000. If the actual residual value determined at the end of the lease term is less than $10,000, the lessee must pay the difference in cash at lease termination date.
3. The lease requires three annual rentals of $33,809, payable each January 1, beginning on January 1, 19A. The lessor's target rate of return is 10%; therefore, the lessor computed the periodic rentals, on an annuity due basis, as follows:

Cost of the leased asset	$100,000
Deduct the PV of the guaranteed residual value:	
$10,000 × $p_{n=3;i=10\%}$ (Table 5–2; .75131)	7,513
Net asset cost to be recovered through rentals	$ 92,487
Annual rental: $92,487 ÷ $P_{d_{n=3;i=10\%}}$ (Table 5–6, 2.73554)	$ 33,809

4. The actual residual value at December 31, 19C, was determined independently to be $9,000.
5. The accounting year of each party ends December 31.

Panel B—Entries:

Lessor			**Lessee**		
January 1, 19A (inception of lease):					
Lease receivable	100,000		Leased property*	100,000	
Asset		100,000	Lease liability		100,000
January 1, 19A (first rental):					
Cash	33,809		Lease liability	33,809	
Lease receivable		33,809	Cash		33,809
December 31, 19A (adjusting entries):					
Lease receivable	6,619		Interest expense	6,619	
Interest revenue		6,619	Lease liability		6,619
			Depreciation expense	30,000	
			Accumulated depreciation		30,000
			[($100,000 − $10,000) ÷ 3 years = $30,000].		
December 31, 19C (lease termination; assuming an actual residual value of $9,000):					
			Accumulated depreciation	90,000	
Asset (market value)	9,000		Lease liability	10,000	
Cash ($10,000 − $9,000)	1,000		Loss on lease contract	1,000	
Lease receivable		10,000 (RV)	Leased property		100,000
			Cash		1,000

* Lessee's computation of cost of leased asset (the guaranteed residual value is capitalized):

Lease payments: $33,809 × $P_{d_{n=3;i=10\%}}$ (Table 5–6, 2.73554)	$ 92,487
Guaranteed RV: $10,000 × $p_{n=3;i=10\%}$ (Table 5–2, .75131)	7,513
Total cost of leased asset to be capitalized	$100,000

Consider the data given in **Exhibit 21–10.** The lessor retains the estimated residual value of $20,000, which is fully guaranteed by a third party (not the lessee). The **lessor includes** the present value of the residual value as part of the lease payment, resulting in a lease receivable of $84,974 + $15,026 = $100,000. This amount is greater than 90% of the leased asset's market value (i.e., $100,000 × 90% = $90,000) at the inception of the lease. Therefore, for the **lessor,** the lease satisfies criterion 4 (Exhibit 21–2) for a **capital lease** in this case.

In contrast, in this case the **lessee excludes** consideration of the guarantee

Exhibit 21–9
(concluded)

Lease Amortization Schedule (annuity due basis):

Date	Lease payments	Interest at 10%	Decrease (increase) in receivable/liability	Lease receivable/liability balance
1/1/19A	Initial value			$100,000
1/1/19A	$ 33,809	—	$33,809	66,191
12/31/19A	—	$ 6,619	(6,619)	72,810
1/1/19B	33,809	—	33,809	39,001
12/31/19B	—	3,900	(3,900)	42,901
1/1/19C	33,809	—	33,809	9,092
12/31/19C	—	908**	(908)	10,000 (guaranteed RV)
	$101,427	$11,427	$90,000	

** Rounded to come out even.

from the minimum lease payments (it is not a part of the payments that the lessee must make). The lessee computes the present value of the lease payments of $84,974 (Exhibit 21–10, panel A, item 5). This amount is less than 90% of the market value of the asset at lease inception (i.e., 90% × $100,000 = $90,000). Because of this, and the fact that no other requirement for a capital lease is met in this case (no transfer of ownership at the end of the lease term, no bargain purchase option, and a lease term that is less than 75% of the leased asset's life) the **lessee** treats the lease as an **operating lease.**

Thus, by using a third-party guarantor, a lessor may be able to record a lease as a capital lease while the lessee may record the lease as an operating lease, thereby circumventing the FASB's attempt to ensure accounting symmetry between lessor and lessee (equivalent accounting treatment of a lease contract between contracting parties).

Exhibit 21–11 summarizes the complex implications of residual values in lease accounting when the lessor and lessee use the same implicit interest rate.

Depreciation of a Leased Asset by the Lessee

The depreciable life and estimated residual value used by the lessee in computing periodic depreciation expense on a leased asset in a capital lease arrangement depend on the terms of the lease contract. If the lease does not contain a BPO or transfer ownership to the lessee at the end of the lease term, the period of depreciation must be the **lease term** rather than the total useful life of the leased property. In this case, the **residual value** must be ignored by the lessee if no residual value is guaranteed by the lessee. However, if the lessee does guarantee a residual value amount (either in total or in part), the guaranteed amount must be used by the lessee as the residual value.

If ownership of the leased asset is **transferred from the lessor to the lessee** at the end of the lease term or the lease contains a BPO, the **lessee** depreciates the capitalized cost over the **total useful life** of the leased asset to the lessee (rather than over the term of the lease). In this case, the lessee uses the estimated

Exhibit 21–10

Accounting for a direct financing lease with residual value guaranteed by a third party.

Panel A—Case Data:

1. On January 1, 19A, lessor and lessee signed a three-year lease. The lessor's cost (or carrying value, if different) was $100,000.
2. Lessor retains the residual value (i.e., ownership) of the leased asset at the termination of the lease; on January 1, 19A, lessor estimates a residual value at the end of the lease term (December 31, 19C) of $20,000, which is fully guaranteed by a third party (not by the lessee). The useful life of the asset is five years.
3. The lease does not contain a BPO.
4. The lease requires three annual rentals of $31,063, payable each January 1, beginning January 1, 19A. The lessor's target rate of return is 10%. Therefore the lessor computed the periodic rentals, on an annuity due basis, as follows:

Cost of the leased asset	$100,000
Deduct: PV of the guaranteed residual value:	
$20,000 × $p_{n=3;i=10\%}$ (Table 5–2, .75131)........	15,026
Net asset cost to be recovered through rentals	$ 84,974
Annual rental: $84,974 ÷ $P_{d_{n=3;i=10\%}}$ (Table 5–6, 2.73554)	$ 31,063

5. The lessee computes the present value of minimum lease payments as: $31,063 × $P_{d_{n=3;i=10\%}}$ (Table 5–6, 2.73554) = $84,974.

Panel B—Entries:

Lessor (direct financing lease)

January 1, 19A (inception of lease):		
Lease receivable	100,000	
Asset		100,000
January 1, 19A (first rental):		
Cash	31,063	
Lease receivable		31,063
December 31, 19A (adjusting entries):		
Lease receivable	6,894	
Interest revenue		6,894

See lessor amortization schedule below.

Lessee (operating lease)

No entry.

Rent expense*	31,063	
Cash		31,063

* Or Prepaid rent.

No entry.†

† Or, alternatively:

Rent expense	31,063	
Prepaid rent		31,063

Lessor's Lease Amortization Schedule (Annuity Due Basis):

Date	Lease payments	Interest at 10%	Decrease (increase) in receivable	Lease receivable balance
1/1/19A	Initial value			$100,000
1/1/19A	$31,063	—	$31,063	68,937
12/31/19A	—	$ 6,894[(a)]	(6,894)	75,831
1/1/19B	31,063	—	31,063	44,768
12/31/19B	—	4,477	(4,477)	49,245
1/1/19C	31,063	—	31,063	18,182
12/31/19C	—	1,818	(1,818)	20,000 (RV)
	$93,189	$13,189	$80,000	

(a) $68,937 × 10% = $6,894.

Exhibit 21–11
Summary of residual value (RV) accounting (assuming the lessor and lessee use the same interest rate).

Situation	Symmetrical entries and schedules?	Reason
1. No RV.	Yes	No RV effect on either party.
2. Unguaranteed RV (Exhibits 21–7 and 21–8).	No	Lessor **includes** (i.e., deducts) the PV of the RV in lease rental computation. Lessee **excludes** (i.e., does not add) RV in cost computation.
3. RV fully guaranteed by lessee (Exhibit 21–9).	Yes	Lessor **includes** (i.e., deducts) **total** RV in lease rental computations. Lessee **includes** (i.e., adds) **fully** guaranteed RV in cost computation.
4. RV partially guaranteed by lessee (page 1069).	No	Lessor **includes** (i.e., deducts) **total** RV in lease rental computations. Lessee **includes** (i.e., adds) the portion of RV that is **partially** guaranteed in cost computation.
5. Full or part RV guarantee by third party (Exhibit 21–10).	No	Lessor **includes** (i.e., deducts) RV guarantee in lease rental computations. Lessee **excludes** (i.e., does not add) RV in cost computation (because the RV is guaranteed by a third party).

residual value as of the end of the asset's useful life (rather than as of the end of the lease term). The longer useful life and lower residual value are used in such cases because it is assumed that the lessee will retain the asset after the end of the lease term. This assumption is required by *FASB Standard 13* when the lease *(a)* contains a BPO or *(b)* transfers ownership of the leased asset from the lessor to the lessee at the end of the lease term.

Executory and Initial Direct Costs

Two kinds of lease costs incurred by the **lessor** are given special accounting treatment. They are *(a)* executory costs and *(b)* initial direct costs.

Executory Costs

Executory costs are expenses of ownership and use that include insurance, property taxes, and maintenance. In the case of an **operating** lease, the executory costs typically are paid by the lessor and are recovered by the lessor in the periodic lease rentals. In the case of a **capital** lease, a major part, if not all, of the executory costs usually are shifted by the lease contract for direct payment by the lessee. Therefore, they are not included in the periodic rentals. However, to the extent that the executory costs are incurred by the lessor and then added each year to the current lease payment, they should be excluded by the **lessee** in computing the present value of the periodic rentals for capitalization purposes. Instead, they should be reported by the lessee as an expense when incurred as an addition to the current lease payment. If such executory costs are not known by the lessee at the time the current lease payment is made, they should be estimated.

Assume in Exhibit 21–3 that the **lessor** agreed to insure the leased asset at a cost of $1,000 per year and then to bill the lessee. The current lease payment should then be $37,556. This amount is equal to the minimum lease rentals required to yield a 10% rate of return to the lessor ($36,556) **plus** the annual executory costs ($1,000). The reason for this is that the lease receivable (lessor) and payable (lessee) are shown **net** of the executory costs as shown in Exhibit 21–3. That is, the executory costs are excluded by the lessee in computing the amount capitalized. Interest revenue (lessor) and interest expense (lessee) are unaffected by the inclusion of executory costs since the $1,000 is paid directly to the insurer; thus, discounting would be inappropriate. Journal entries to reflect the annual executory costs incurred by the lessor on the date of the first rental are as follows:

January 1, 19A (first rental received):

Lessor:

Cash	37,556	
Lease receivable		36,556
Insurance payable (or prepaid insurance)		1,000

Lessee:

Lease liability	36,556	
Insurance expense	1,000	
Cash		37,556

Initial Direct Costs

Initial direct costs are incremental costs incurred by the **lessor** in negotiating and consummating a lease agreement. They include legal fees, cost of credit and other investigations, commissions and employees' compensation directly related to initiating the lease, and clerical costs of preparing and processing the lease documents. These costs have no effect on the lessee's accounting.

In the case of an **operating lease,** the initial direct costs should be apportioned by the lessor over the lease term on a reasonable basis (usually straight line) in order to match them with revenues that they helped earn. In the case of a **direct financing lease,** initial direct costs must be included in the gross investment in the lease. This means that these costs must be added to the cost of the leased asset to compute the annual rentals. On this point *FASB Standard 91*, par. 23, states that "Lessors shall account for initial direct costs as part of the investment in a direct financing lease. The practice of recognizing a portion of the unearned income at inception of the lease to offset initial direct costs shall no longer be acceptable." The effect of this is to spread the indirect costs over the term of the lease. In the case of a **sales-type lease,** the initial direct costs should be **expensed** by the lessor in the year in which the lease is initiated (i.e., as an offset to manufacturer's or dealer's profit) because they are considered to be a "selling" expense in the year in which the manufacturer's or dealer's margin is recognized.

Sale-Leaseback Arrangements

When the owner of an asset sells it and immediately leases it back from the buyer, the transaction is called **sale-leaseback.** The use of the property continues without interruption. These transactions are subject to the provisions of paragraphs 32–34 of *FASB Standard 13,* as amended by *FASB Standard 28.* The characteristics of a typical sale-leaseback arrangement may be diagrammed for the seller-lessee and the buyer-lessor as follows:

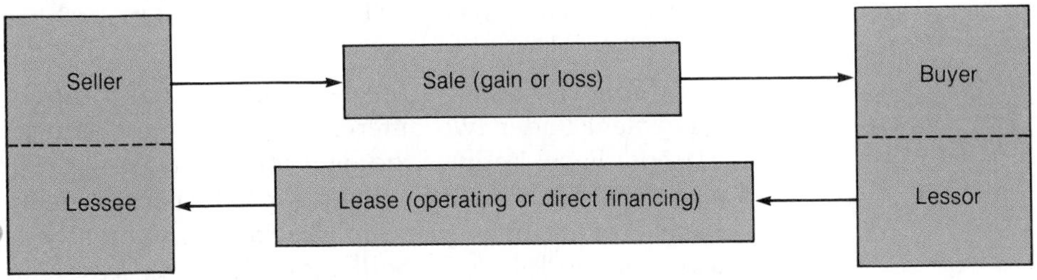

Typically, a sale-leaseback transaction involves a sale of the property at approximate current market value and a long-term lease. The periodic rents are set to earn a realistic rate of interest on the sale price. The seller/lessee usually pays the executory costs (i.e., insurance, taxes, maintenance, etc.).

One advantage offered by a sale with a leaseback arrangement is that it allows the lessee to take a tax deduction for lease payments on leased assets. The inducements to lessors also are tax related, due to the investment tax credit (if provided in the income tax regulations) and early tax deductions for accelerated depreciation and interest expense on any debt used to finance the purchase of the asset for leasing.

Under the provisions of *FASB Standards 13* and *28,* the lessor and lessee in a sale with a leaseback arrangement identify the lease as an operating or capital lease by applying the criteria listed in Exhibit 21–2. If the lease provisions satisfy one of the four criteria, the lease must be classified as a direct financing lease (a sales-type lease is not permitted by *FASB Standard 13*). All other leases are classified as operating leases. Once the determination is made that the leaseback is an operating lease or a direct financing lease, the accounting by the lessor is the same as illustrated earlier in this chapter. Sale with a leaseback arrangement poses a problem for the **seller-lessee** (they pose no special problem for the buyer-lessor) in accounting for any **gain or loss on the sale of the asset to the buyer-lessor.** The problem arises because there is a high probability that the sale transaction and the leaseback transaction are not independent because the same two parties structure the two transactions. Without constraints, the seller-lessee could sell the asset to the buyer-lessor for an unrealistically high (or low) price purposely to report a gain (or loss) on the sale. The seller-lessee could then lease the asset back under an agreement with a present value equal to the sale price of the asset. Upon completion of both transactions, the seller-lessee would be in the same economic position as if neither the sale nor the leaseback had occurred. However, a "phantom" gain or loss on the sale would have been reported. Because of these and other possibilities, the FASB specified detailed guidelines for seller-lessees.

FASB Standard 13 treats sale-leaseback arrangements as though the two transactions were a single financing transaction in which any gain or loss on the sale is deferred and amortized by the seller-lessee.[18] In this regard, *FASB Standard 13* (par. 33) as amended by *FASB Standard 28* (par. 3c) states:

> Any profit or loss on the sale shall be deferred and amortized [by the lessee] in proportion to the amortization of the leased asset, if a capital lease, or in proportion to the related gross rental [debited] to expense over the lease term, if an operating lease, unless . . . the fair [market] value of the property at the time of the transaction is less than its undepreciated cost, in which case a loss shall be recognized immediately up to the amount of the difference between undepreciated cost and fair [market] value.

Exhibit 21–12 shows the seller-lessee's basic entries for a sale-leaseback arrangement under two different cases. A short-term lease is used for practical reasons. Panel A gives the data for the two cases. Panel B gives the analysis and panel C shows the entries for both parties assuming an operating lease. Panel D gives the entries and lease amortization schedule for a direct financing lease for the lessor. In both cases the seller-lessee must defer recognition of the $15,000 unearned gain on the sale of the asset. The gain is amortized with a year-end adjusting entry. Under Case A, operating lease, the seller-lessee credits rent expense (or revenue) for the amortized portion of the unearned gain (i.e., $15,000 ÷ 5 years = $3,000). Under Case B, direct financing lease, the seller-lessee records the periodic amortization as a credit to depreciation expense or revenue. A credit to an expense or revenue account, rather than to a gain account, is consistent with the FASB's view that a sale-leaseback transaction essentially is a single transaction. Thus, deferral and amortization of the unearned gain usually is viewed as an adjustment to the seller-lessee's expense or revenue associated with the leased asset. Aside from these entries, the lessee accounts for the lease in the same way as previously illustrated.

Under Case B (direct financing lease), if there is a loss on the sale, the seller-lessee must recognize the loss on the date of sale. The loss is recognized immediately because the market value of the leased asset was less than the seller-lessee's carrying value, which is considered compelling evidence that the seller-lessee sustained a loss in value. The lessee's entries for the direct financing lease are the same as previously illustrated.[19]

---

[18] *FASB Standard 28,* "Accounting for Sales with Leasebacks: An Amendment of *FASB Standard 13*" (Stamford, Conn., May 1979) provides accounting guidelines for exceptions to the more general situation covered by *FASB Standard 13.*

[19] *FASB Standard 98,* "Accounting for Leases," was issued in May 1988. It relates primarily to leasing real estate with the following topics:

1. Sale-leaseback transactions involving real estate—this includes land with equipment such as manufacturing facilities and office buildings with furniture and fixtures.
2. Sales-type leases with real estate.
3. Definition of lease term (see Exhibit 21–5).
4. Indirect costs of direct financing leases.

This standard also amends *FASB Standards 13, 66, and 91,* and rescinds *FASB Standard 26* and *Technical Bulletin No. 79–11.*

Classification of Lease Receivables and Payables

When a lessor has lease receivables (and the lessee has lease payables) extending beyond one year (or the operating cycle of the business, if longer), there is a problem in classifying the balances as **current** or **noncurrent.** The lessor's lease receivable, as well as the lessee's payable, should be reported net of any interest included in the lease payment amounts, or stated differently, at present value using the interest rate applied to the lease.

To illustrate the classification of lease receivables (payables) for reporting purposes involving an annuity due, refer to the amortization schedule in Exhibit 21–3, panel B. The lease classification is illustrated from the perspective of the lessor's lease receivable. The same conclusions also apply to classification of the lessee's lease payable.

At December 31, 19A, assuming the operating cycle is one year or less, the lessor has an upcoming lease receivable of $36,556, collectible on January 1, 19B. The last receivable of $36,556 is collectible on January 1, 19C. These amounts must be reduced by any **unearned interest** included therein because it will not be earned until the next period. For example, in 19B, $3,324 of interest revenue will be recognized and this amount must be deducted from the current portion of the 19A lease receivable. The net **lease receivable (current portion)** after deducting unearned interest at December 31, 19A, is $33,232 (i.e., $36,556 – $3,324). The last rent of $36,556, due on January 1, 19C, is classified as a **noncurrent asset;** there is **no** unearned interest in the last installment.[20] Partial statements of financial position of the lessor at December 31 would show the following (for this annuity due case):

	19B		19A	
Current assets:				
Lease receivable	$36,556		$36,556	
Less: Unearned interest	-0-		3,324	
Principal amount		$36,556		$33,232*
Noncurrent assets:				
Lease receivable		-0-		36,556†
Total lease receivable		$36,556		$69,788‡

* Excludes unearned interest at December 31, 19A.
† Includes all unearned interest on or after December 31, 19A.
‡ See Exhibit 21–3, panel B, last column of amortization schedule.

[20] An alternative to the classification shown here is to discount the next period's rental payment at the interest rate implicit in the lease for the time prior to receipt of the payment. Because, in Exhibit 21–3 the payments are on the first day of the year, the current receivable would be $36,556 and the noncurrent receivable (discounted for one period) would be $33,232 (i.e., $36,556 × $p_{n=1;i=10\%}$ [Table 5–2, .90909]). This technique is not widely used in practice. One problem with discounting the current payment by only one period is that the sum of the current portions over the life of the lease will exceed the total principal amount of the lease receivable. However, the correct method of classifying lease receivables and payables between current and noncurrent is unresolved. For a discussion of these issues, see Robert J. Swieringa, "When Current Is Noncurrent and Vice Versa!" *The Accounting Review*, January 1984, pp. 123–30, and A. W. Richardson, "The Measurement of the Current Portion of Long-Term Lease Obligations—Some Evidence from Practice," *The Accounting Review*, October 1985, pp. 744–52.

Exhibit 21–12
Accounting for sale-leaseback; operating lease and direct financing lease.

Panel A—Case Data:
On January 1, 19A, Seller/Lessee sold a warehouse to Buyer/Lessor for \$95,000 that had a carrying value of \$80,000, estimated remaining life, five years, and no residual value (use straight-line depreciation). Simultaneously, the two parties signed a five-year lease with a 12% implicit interest rate; annual lease rents start on January 1, 19A. Two cases will be illustrated: Case A, the lease qualifies as an operating lease, and Case B, the lease qualifies as a direct financing lease for the lessor.

Panel B—Analysis:
1. Unearned gain by seller: \$95,000 − \$80,000 = \$15,000.
2. Lease payments: \$95,000 ÷ $P_{d_{n=5;\,i=12\%}}$ (Table 5–6, 4.03735) = \$23,530.

Panel C—Case A: Operating Lease:

Seller/Lessee			Buyer/Lessor		
Jan. 1, 19A—Sale/purchase of warehouse:					
Cash	95,000		Warehouse	95,000	
Warehouse (net)		80,000	Cash		95,000
Unearned gain on SLB sale		15,000			
Jan. 1, 19A—To record the operating lease:			(no entry)		
(no entry)					
Jan. 1, 19A—To record first lease payment:					
Rent expense	23,530		Cash	23,530	
Cash		23,530	Rent revenue		23,530
Dec. 31, 19A—Adjusting entries, to record depreciation expense:			Depreciation expense	19,000	
			Accumulated depreciation		19,000
(no entry)			\$95,000 ÷ 5 years − \$19,000.		
To record amortization of unrecognized gain:*					
Unearned gain on SLB sale	3,000				
Rent expense		3,000	(no entry)		
\$15,000 ÷ 5 years = \$3,000.					

* Straight-line method is used because equal payments are made each year.

Lease Disclosure Requirements

FASB Standard 13 requires disclosure of many details concerning leasing arrangements in the financial statements or their accompanying notes. The primary lease disclosures may be summarized as follows:

Lessee disclosures:

1. For capital leases, disclose:
   a. The gross amount of assets recorded under capital leases presented by major classes according to nature or function.
   b. Future minimum lease payments in the aggregate and for each of the five succeeding fiscal years, with separate deductions from the total for *(a)* executory costs (including any profit thereon) included

Exhibit 21–12
(concluded)

Panel D—Case B: Direct financing lease for the lessor and a capital lease for the lessee

Seller/Lessee			Buyer/Lessor		
Jan. 1, 19A—Sale of warehouse:					
Cash	95,000		Warehouse	95,000	
Warehouse		80,000	Cash		95,000
Unearned gain on SLB sale		15,000			
Jan. 1, 19A—To record the direct financing lease:					
Leased asset	95,000		Lease receivable	95,000	
Lease liability		95,000	Warehouse (on lease)		95,000
Jan. 1, 19A—First lease payment (see amortization schedule below):					
Lease liability	23,530		Cash	23,530	
Cash		23,530	Lease receivable		23,530
Dec. 31, 19A—Adjusting entries:					
To record depreciation expense:					
Depreciation expense	19,000		(no entry)		
Accumulated depreciation ($95,000 ÷ 5)		19,000			
To record amortization of unrecognized gain:					
Unearned gain on SLB sale	3,000				
Depreciation expense		3,000	(no entry)		
$15,000 ÷ 5 = $3,000.					
To record accrued interest on lease receivable/liability:†					
Interest expense	8,576		Lease receivable	8,576	
Lease liability		8,576	Interest revenue		8,576

† Lease Amortization Schedule (annuity due basis):

Date	Annual lease payment	Annual interest at 12%	Lease receivable/liability decrease (increase)	Receivable/liability balance
1/1/19A				$95,000
1/1/19A	$ 23,530		$23,530	71,470
12/31/19A		$ 8,576	(8,576)	80,046
1/1/19B	23,530		23,530	56,516
12/31/19B		6,782	(6,782)	63,298
1/1/19C	23,530		23,530	39,768
12/31/19C		4,772	(4,772)	44,540
1/1/19D	23,530		23,530	21,010
12/31/19D		2,520	(2,520)	23,530
1/1/19E	23,530		23,530	-0-
	$117,650	$22,650	$95,000	

in the minimum lease payments and *(b)* the amount of the imputed interest necessary to reduce the net minimum lease payments to present value.

   c. The total of minimum sublease rentals to be received in the future under noncancelable subleases.
   d. Total contingent rentals (the amounts are dependent on some factor other than the passage of time) actually incurred.

2. For operating leases having initial or remaining noncancelable lease terms in excess of one year, disclose:
   a. Future minimum rental payments required in the aggregate and for each of the five succeeding fiscal years.
   b. The total of minimum rentals to be received in the future under noncancelable subleases.

3. For all operating leases, disclose rental expense, with separate amounts for minimum rentals, contingent rentals, and sublease rentals.

4. Provide a general description of the lessee's leasing arrangements including, but not limited to, the following:
   a. The basis on which contingent rental payments are determined.
   b. The existence and terms of renewal or purchase options and escalation clauses.
   c. Restrictions imposed by lease agreements, such as those concerning dividends, additional debt, and further leasing.

Lessor disclosures:

1. For sales-type and direct financing leases, disclose:
   a. The components of the net investment in sales-type and direct financing leases:
      (1) Future minimum lease payments to be received, with separate deductions for *(i)* amounts representing executory costs (including any profit thereon) included in the minimum lease payments and *(ii)* the accumulated allowance for **uncollectible** minimum lease payments receivable.
      (2) The unguaranteed residual values accruing to the benefit of the lessor.
      (3) Unearned interest revenue.
   b. Future minimum lease payments to be received for each of the five succeeding fiscal years.
   c. Total contingent rentals included in income.

2. For operating leases, disclose:
   a. The cost and carrying amount, if different, of property on lease or held for leasing by major classes of property according to nature or function, and the amount of accumulated depreciation in total.
   b. Minimum future rentals on noncancelable leases in the aggregate and for each of the five succeeding fiscal years.
   c. Total contingent rentals included in income.

3. Provide a general description of the lessor's leasing arrangements.

The following excerpt from the 1987 annual report of Hughes Supply Inc. shows typical lease disclosures. Note that Hughes has both operating and capital leases. The details given in the disclosure notes are necessary to meet the *FASB Standards* on leases.

HUGHES SUPPLY, INC.

	1987	1986
	(in thousands)	
Property, plant and equipment, at cost:		
Land	$ 9,462	$ 4,411
Buildings and improvements	17,074	15,856
Transportation equipment	14,602	13,483
Furniture, fixtures and equipment	12,193	10,217
Leased property under capital leases	6,902	6,383
Total	60,233	50,350
Less accumulated depreciation and amortization	23,014	20,079
Net property, plant and equipment	37,219	30,281
Current Liabilities:		
Short-term debt	$ 1,857	$ —
Current portion of long-term notes	1,371	1,147
Current portion of capital lease obligations	552	427
Accounts payable	31,925	29,893
Accrued compensation and benefits	4,458	3,709
Other current liabilities	6,702	4,410
Total current liabilities	46,865	39,586
Long-Term Debt, less current portion:		
Notes and subordinated debentures	33,458	17,306
Capital lease obligations	3,179	3,236
Total long-term debt	36,637	20,542

NOTES TO CONSOLIDATED FINANCIAL STATEMENTS

Note 8: Lease Commitments

Fourteen of the Company's branch facilities are leased under capital leases from a corporation which is owned by three of the directors of Hughes Supply, Inc. The leases generally provide that all expenses related to the properties are to be paid by the lessee. The leases provide for rental adjustments every five years based on appraised fair market values discounted ten percent. The leases were last adjusted effective April 1, 1983. The leases all expire within ten years; however, it is expected that they will be renewed. Rents under these agreements amounted to $831,000, $801,000 and $798,000 for the fiscal years ended in 1987, 1986 and 1985, respectively. In addition, the Company made aircraft rental payments aggregating $141,000, $125,000 and $123,000 in fiscal 1987, 1986 and 1985, respectively, to the related corporation. The balances related to properties under capital leases are included in the balance sheets as follows (in thousands):

	January 30, 1987	January 31, 1986
Leased property under capital leases (consisting of land and buildings)	$6,902	$6,383
Accumulated amortization	4,155	3,713
	$2,747	$2,670

Substantially all of the facilities of USCO Incorporated and Paine Supply Companies (see Note 2) are leased from former shareholders of the companies or their affiliates, under operating leases expiring from 1988 to 1995. The leases contain renewal options and purchase options at fair value. The expense under these leases was $41,000 subsequent to the business acquisitions in December, 1986.

Future minimum payments, by year and in the aggregate, under the aforementioned leases and other noncancelable operating leases with initial or remaining terms in excess of one year as of January 30, 1987, are as follows (in thousands):

Hughes Supply, Inc.
(concluded)

Fiscal years ending	Capital leases	Operating leases
1988	$ 920	$ 847
1989	574	649
1990	543	397
1991	543	85
1992	534	—
Later years	3,233	—
Total minimum lease payments	6,347	$1,978
Less amount representing interest	2,616	
Present value of net minimum lease payments	3,731	
Less Less current portion of obligations under capital leases	552	
Long-term obligations under capital leases	$3,179	

Lease-related expenses deducted from income are as follows (in thousands):

	Fiscal years ended		
	January 30, 1987	January 31, 1986	January 25, 1985
Capital lease amortization	$441	$415	$413
Capital lease interest expenses	$381	$407	$435
Operating lease rentals (excluding month-to-month rents)	$561	$399	$461

Summary

Accounting for leases is controversial.[21] Lessees may want to avoid recognition on their statements of financial position of lease liabilities and capitalization of the related assets. In contrast, lessors may want to classify leases as sales-type so they can recognize a manufacturer's or dealer's profit at the date of inception of the lease. These opposite motivations have spawned many "creative" lease agreements. These agreements usually are structured to satisfy these motivations through lease specifications that qualify the lease as a capital lease to the lessor but as an operating lease to the lessee.

Based on the criteria for capital leases (Exhibit 21–2), it appears that a lease that qualifies as a capital lease to a lessor would also qualify as a capital lease to the lessee because the lessor must satisfy two additional criteria not applicable to the lessee. However, this is not the case. Often lease terms are structured to provide a sales-type lease to the lessor and an operating lease to the lessee. Avoiding this accounting symmetry requires creativity by company lawyers. For example, the lease agreement can avoid satisfying criteria 1 through 3 for a capital lease (Exhibit 21–2), while criterion 4 can be satisfied by the lessor but not by the lessee. This effect can be accomplished by including in the lease agreement a residual value guarantee that causes the present value of the minimum lease payments to be more than 90% of the market value of the leased asset. Thus, the lease qualifies as a capital lease (i.e., direct financing or sales-type) to the lessor. The lessee can avoid satisfying criterion 4 by engaging, for a fee, a third-party guarantor to guarantee the residual value demanded by the lessor (see Exhibit 21–10). Thus, the lease is classified as an operating

[21] For criticisms of *FASB Standard 13*, see John W. Coughlan, "Regulation, Rents, and Residuals," *The Journal of Accountancy*, February 1980, pp. 58–66, and Kathryn M. Means and Paul M. Kazenski, "SFAS 91: New Dilemmas," *Accounting Horizons*, December 1987, pp. 63–66.

lease to the lessee. Another way for the lessee to avoid satisfying criterion 4 is to use a higher incremental borrowing rate in the present value discounting while avoiding learning of the lower implicit rate used by the lessor. These kinds of issues ensure that lease accounting will continue to be a challenge to the accounting profession in the future.

SUPPLEMENT 21–A: OPERATING LEASES—INTEREST METHOD OF AMORTIZING UNEARNED RENT REVENUE/LEASEHOLD

When a **nonrefundable down payment** is made in advance on an **operating lease,** the prepayment may be amortized by lessor and lessee using either the straight-line method or the interest (present value) method. The **straight-line method** (shown in Exhibit 21–1) allocates a **constant dollar** amount of the prepayment to revenue (lessor) or expense (lessee) in each accounting period covered by the lease. In contrast, the **interest method** allocates a **constant rate** of revenue or expense per period, thus giving effect to the interest element of the advance rental. Recording by the lessor and lessee for a prepayment using the interest method is shown in **Exhibit 21–13.** Panel A gives the case data and panel B gives the entries.

In Exhibit 21–13, each party amortizes an increasing amount of the prepayment each year, from $1,778 in 19A to $2,231 in 19C, as shown in column (3). The amount increases because annual interest [column (2)] is computed on a declining unamortized advance rental balance [column (4)]. The interest method is conceptually preferred by some because it gives effect to the interest element of the advance rental. That is, the lessor receives cash in advance and "incurs" interest expense on the unearned rent revenue (a liability). The lessee pays cash in advance and "earns" interest revenue on the asset, leasehold (to emphasize this point, see the alternative set of entries given in Exhibit 21–13). Disregarding the conceptual aspect, the straight-line method usually is used because *(a)* it is less complex, *(b)* the amortization amounts produced by the two methods often are not materially different, and *(c)* many accountants interpret *FASB Standard 13* to specify straight-line amortization for most situations.

SUPPLEMENT 21–B: LEVERAGED LEASES

Fundamental Characteristics

A **leveraged lease** is a complex form of a capital lease that involves one or more parties in addition to the lessor and lessee. Debt is a key element of a leveraged lease arrangement; the lender (loan participant) is an added party. Instead of providing 100% of the cost of **depreciable** property to be leased, the lessor usually provides from 20% to 40%. The lender furnishes the remaining funds needed with a nonrecourse loan. Nonrecourse in this context means that the lender cannot take assets other than the leased property in the event the lessor defaults on payments to the lender.

A lessor with taxable income from other sources can benefit from leveraged

Exhibit 21–13
Operating lease with interest method amortization of advance rental—accounting by lessor and lessee.

Panel A—Case Data:

Lessor rents an office to lessee under the following lease terms:

a. Lease term, three years, beginning January 1, 19A.
b. Annual rental, $4,800 payable in advance each January 1.
c. Advance rental (i.e., a down payment in addition to annual rentals), $6,000, payable January 1, 19A.
d. Interest rate applicable to the advance rental, 12%.
e. Accounting years of each party end on December 31.

Panel B—Entries:

Lessor			Lessee		
January 1, 19A:					
To record advance rental:					
Cash	6,000		Leasehold (prepaid rent expense)	6,000	
Unearned rent revenue		6,000	Cash		6,000
To record annual rental:					
Cash	4,800		Rent expense	4,800	
Rent revenue		4,800	Cash		4,800
December 31, 19A (end of the accounting period):					
To record amortization of advance rental (for 12 months):*					
Unearned rent revenue	1,778		Rent expense	1,778	
Rent revenue		1,778	Leasehold		1,778

* An alternate set of entries could be made to recognize separately the interest on the advance rental, as follows:

Unearned rent revenue	1,778		Rent expense	2,498	
Interest expense	720		Interest revenue		720
Rent revenue		2,498	Leasehold		1,778

Computations: Schedule of Amortization of Advance Rental Payment—Interest Method

Period	(1) Periodic rent	(2) Interest (12%)	(3) Amortization of advance rental	(4) Unamortized balance of advance rental
1/1/19A				$6,000
12/31/19A	$2,498[(a)]	$ 720[(b)]	$1,778[(c)]	4,222[(d)]
12/31/19B	2,498	507	1,991	2,231
12/31/19C	2,498	267*	2,231	-0-
	$7,494	$1,494	$6,000	

* Rounded to come out even.

[(a)] Implied annual rent = $6,000 \div P_{0_{n=3;\,i=12\%}}$.
= $6,000 ÷ 2.40183 (Table 5–4)
= $2,498

[(b)] $6,000 × 12% = $720.

[(c)] $2,498 − $720 = $1,778.

[(d)] $6,000 − $1,778 = $4,222.

Note: An ordinary annuity is assumed; that is, the advance payment represents the present value of three equal year-end amounts of $2,498 each. Alternatively, an **annuity due** could have been assumed, that is, that the three payments would be at the **beginning** of each period.

leasing because, for **tax** purposes, the lessor can deduct from taxable income depreciation expense on the leased property. The lessor can then use the investment tax credit (if available in the income tax code) to further reduce income taxes—even though the lease would qualify otherwise as a capital lease for **financial accounting** purposes. Although the lessor may put up only 20% of the cost of depreciable property to be leased, 100% of the investment tax credit (if available) and depreciation can be used by the lessor to reduce income taxes.

The lender's loan is secured by a first lien on the leased property, by assignment of the lease, and by assignment of the lease rentals. This means that the lender has first priority on the leased property and the lease receivables under the lease agreement in the event the leveraged lessor fails to pay the lender the amount owed on the debt incurred to purchase the leased property. Creditworthiness of the lessee is important. Conditional title to the leased property is vested in an **owner trustee** who issues trust certificates evidencing each participant's equity interest. An **indenture trustee** holds the security interest in the leased property for the benefit of the lender. The trustee receives rental payments from the lessee, which then are distributed to the lender and to the lessor through the owner trustee.

Because the contractual arrangements are complex and costly, it is seldom feasible to apply leveraged leasing to low-cost assets. It would cost as much to arrange a leveraged lease on a $50,000 asset as on a $1,000,000 one, and because the "front-end" costs are high, rentals from the less costly asset typically would not justify the costs involved.

There are two distinct but interrelated elements of leveraged leases: cash flows and the accounting for those cash flows. **Exhibit 21–14** shows these elements. Panel A gives the case data, panel B shows the various schedules related to leveraged leases, and panel C gives the journal entries for the lessor.

The diagram below shows (with data from Exhibit 21–14) the typical relationships in a leveraged lease.

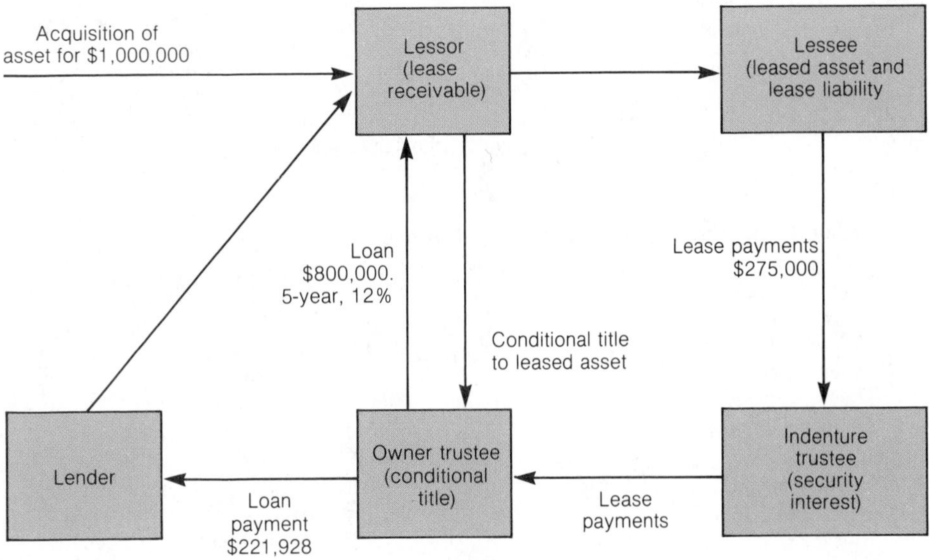

Exhibit 21–14

Panel A—Case Data:

1. On January 1, 19A, Lessor acquired an asset with a five-year useful life, no residual value, for $1,000,000.
2. Lessor financed the asset acquisition by borrowing $800,000 at an interest rate of 12%, to be repaid in five equal payments of $221,928 on each December 31.
3. Lessor received a 10% investment tax credit (realized at the end of 19A and assumed for instructional purposes) on the cost of the asset and uses sum-of-the-years'-digits method of depreciation. Lessor's average tax rate is 40%.
4. Lessor leased the asset on January 1, 19A, for five years to Lessee for an annual lease payment of $275,000, payable on each December 31.

Panel B—Debt Amortization Schedule, Schedule of Cash Flows, and Allocation of Cash Flows:

Schedule 1—Debt Amortization Schedule:

Year-end	(a) Cash payment (given)	(b) Interest expense (12% of [d])	(c) Reduction of principal (a) − (b)	(d) Unamortized principal (d) − (c)
Jan. 1, 19A				$800,000
19A	$ 221,928	$ 96,000	$125,928	674,072
19B	221,928	80,889	141,039	533,033
19C	221,928	63,964	157,964	375,069
19D	221,928	45,008	176,920	198,149
19E	221,928	23,779*	198,149	-0-
	$1,109,640	$309,640	$800,000	

*Rounded to come out even.

Schedule 2—Cash Flow Schedule:

Year-end	(a) Annual cash rentals (per lease)	(b) Annual depreciation expense (SYD)	(c) Annual cash interest paid (Sch. 1)	(d) Principal reduction (Sch. 1)	(e) Total expense (b) + (c)	(f) Taxable income (loss) (a) − (e)	(g) Tax-saving (expense) 40% of (f)	(h) Net Annual cash flow [(a) + (g)] −[(c) + (d)]
Jan. 1, 19A	Initial investment							$(200,000)
Jan. 1, 19A	Investment tax credit							100,000
19A	$ 275,000	$ 333,333	$ 96,000	$125,928	$ 429,333	$(154,333)	$ 61,733	114,805
19B	275,000	266,667	80,889	141,039	347,556	(72,556)	29,022	82,094
19C	275,000	200,000	63,964	157,964	263,964	11,036	(4,414)	48,658
19D	275,000	133,333	45,008	176,920	178,341	96,659	(38,664)	14,408
19E	275,000	66,667	23,779	198,149	90,446	184,554	(73,822)	(20,750)
	$1,375,000	$1,000,000	$309,640	$800,000	$1,309,640	$ 65,360	$(26,145)	$ 139,215

Schedule 3—Proof of Cash Flows and Proof of Income:

Cash inflows:	
Rents (5 × $275,000)	$1,375,000
Investment tax credit	100,000
Total inflows	1,475,000
Cash outflows:	
Down payment	200,000
Payments (5 × $221,928)	1,109,640
Income taxes	26,145
Total outflows	1,335,785
Cumulative cash flow	$ 139,215

Revenue:	
Rents	$1,375,000
Expenses:	
Depreciation	1,000,000
Interest	309,640
Total expenses	1,309,640
Income before taxes	65,360
Taxes	(26,145)
Income	39,215
Add: Investment tax credit	100,000
Net income	$ 139,215

Exhibit 21–14
(concluded)

Schedule 4—Allocation of Annual Cash Flows to Investment and Income:

Year	Lessor's net investment at beginning of year (a)	Annual cash flow: Total (b)	Annual cash flow: Allocated to investment (c)	Annual cash flow: Allocated to income (d)	Components of income: Pretax income (e)	Components of income: Tax effect of pretax income (f)	Components of income: Investment tax credit (g)
19A	$200,000	$214,805(1)	$123,643(3)	$ 91,162(2)	$42,800(5)	$17,121(5)	$ 65,483(5)
19B	76,357(4)	82,094	47,290	34,804	16,340	6,536	25,000
19C	29,067	48,658	35,409	13,249	6,220	2,488	9,517
19D	(6,342)	14,408	14,408	—	—	—	—
19E	(20,750)	(20,750)	(20,750)	—	—	—	—
		$339,215	$200,000	$139,215	$65,360	$26,145	$100,000

(1) See Schedule 2, column *(h)*. However, 19A cash flow excludes the $200,000 investment in the leased asset.
(2) If Lessor's "net investment at beginning of year" is positive, cash flow allocated to income equals 45.58% × Net investment at beginning of year. If "Net investment at beginning of year" is negative, cash flow allocated to income equals zero. This allocation rate (45.58%) is solved iteratively until a rate is found that fully amortizes the Lessor's net investment.
(3) Cash flow allocated to investment = Total cash flow − Cash flow allocated to income.
(4) Lessor's net investment at beginning of 19B = Lessor's net investment at beginning of 19A − Cash flow allocated to investment in 19A.
(5) The allocation of cash flows to pretax income in 19A is:

$65,360 × ($91,162/$139,215) = $42,800

This technique recognizes income proportionate to the total cash flows in 19A relative to total cash flows over all years. Allocations in the "tax effect" and "Investment tax credit" columns are similar.

Panel C—Lessor Journal Entries in 19A:

January 1, 19A (inception of the lease):

Lease receivable (net)	265,360	
Investment tax credit receivable	100,000	
Unearned lease revenue		165,360
Cash		200,000

Computations:
Gross lease receivable, $1,375,000 − Gross liability, $1,109,640 = Net lease receivable, $265,360.

Total pretax income, $65,360 + ITC, $100,000 = Unearned lease revenue, $165,360.

December 31, 19A (collection of 19A **net** rent):

Cash (net rent)	53,072	
Lease receivable		53,072

Computation:
Lease rental, $275,000 − Debt payment, $221,928 = $53,072, net rent.

December 31, 19A (realization of investment tax credit):

Income tax payable	100,000	
Investment tax credit receivable		100,000

December 31, 19A (recognition of 19A's pretax income and investment tax credit benefit):

Unearned lease revenue ($42,800 + $65,483)	108,283	
Income from leveraged lease (panel B, Sch. 4, col. [*e*])		42,800
Investment tax credit recognized (panel B, Sch. 4, col. [*g*])		65,483

December 31, 19A (recognition of tax effect of leveraged lease):

Income tax payable (panel B, Sch. 2, col. [*g*])	61,733	
Income tax expense (panel B, Sch. 4, col. [*f*])	17,121	
Deferred income tax liability		78,854*

* Computation of deferred income tax:

Tax loss (Sch. 2, col. [*f*])	$154,333
Pretax accounting income (Sch. 4, col. [*e*])	42,800
Temporary difference	$197,133
Deferred taxes ($197,133 × 40%)	$ 78,854

Cash Flows under Leveraged Leases

In a typical leveraged lease, the **lessor** has a net cash inflow during the early years of the lease, a net cash outflow in the later years, and a final receipt of cash if the leased asset has a residual value and is sold after the lease terminates. Early tax-deductible expenses are high because interest on the unpaid debt is high in the early years and because of accelerated depreciation. This combination, plus the investment tax credit (if available), causes tax benefits in the early years of the lease. These benefits create net cash inflows because of the reduction of tax that otherwise would be paid on income **from other sources.** In the later years, a reverse effect is experienced: lower interest and depreciation amounts cause taxable income to rise and tax payments to increase. However, due to the time value of money, the early cash inflows create a distinct advantage in favor of leveraged leasing.

Exhibit 21–14, panel A, presents the data on a leveraged lease. The lessor acquired an asset (for leasing purposes) at a cost of $1,000,000, of which a $200,000 down payment was made. The balance of $800,000 was to be paid in equal installments over the next five years (January 1, 19A–December 31, 19E).

Panel B presents four schedules. Schedule 1 is the debt amortization schedule, assuming an interest rate of 12% and five equal annual payments at each year-end. Schedule 2 presents the cash flows. The lessor rents the asset for five annual year-end rents of $275,000 each, as reflected in column *(a)*. As shown in column *(b)*, the lessor depreciates the asset over a five-year life using an accelerated method with no estimated residual value. Thus, the first year's depreciation is $333,333. The lessor receives an investment tax credit of $100,000 (i.e., $1,000,000 × 10%) due to the acquisition of the qualifying asset, which is reflected on the second line of Schedule 2. The lessor's total annual expense related to the lease is reflected in Schedule 2, panel B, column *(e)*. It is composed of the annual depreciation and interest. Taxable income, consisting of annual rentals minus annual expenses, is reflected in column *(f)*, and the related tax saving (expense) is shown in column *(g)*. When the total in column *(f)* is a loss, the lessor experiences a tax saving of 40% of the amount of the loss because losses on the leveraged lease activities are used to offset income that otherwise would be taxable at 40%. Finally, the lessor's annual cash flow is shown in column *(h)*. Some elements of the cash flow are fixed. For example, the debt payments cause a fixed annual outflow of $221,928, and the lease rents cause a fixed periodic inflow of $275,000. Column *(h)* shows the typical pattern of cash flows for a leveraged lease, positive in early years and negative in later years. Schedule 3 presents a proof of cash flows and income, and Schedule 4 illustrates the allocation of total income to each period.

Accounting for Leveraged Leases

Leveraged leases create no special accounting problems for the **lessee.** The lessee accounts for a leveraged lease in a manner similar to nonleveraged leases, as operating or capital leases, depending on which is appropriate.

However, leveraged lease accounting for the **lessor** is unique and complex. Under *FASB Standard 13,* annual income of the lessor from a leveraged lease is measured in such a way that annual income differs from aftertax income. The allocation of income in a particular year depends on the **net lease investment** during that year.

FASB Standard 13 defines the **net lease investment** of the lessor as (1) rentals receivable under the leveraged lease, plus (2) any receivable for an investment tax credit to be realized, plus (3) any residual value of the leased property, minus (4) lessor's nonrecourse debt on borrowing to acquire the leased property, minus (5) unearned lease revenue, minus (6) any investment tax credit deferred for recognition in future periods. Thus, in Exhibit 21–14, the net lease investment on January 1, 19A, is $200,000. That is, total rentals receivable ($275,000 × 5 years = $1,375,000), plus investment tax credit receivable ($1,000,000 × 10% = $100,000), plus residual value of the property (0), minus lessor's total debt on the asset ($221,928 × 5 years = $1,109,640), minus unearned lease revenue ($165,360), minus investment tax credit deferred to future periods (0).

FASB Standard 13 requires that a rate of return be computed on the net investment in years in which net investment is positive such that, when applied to the net investment in those years, it will fully distribute income and amortize net investment. In each year, the difference between the net cash flow and the amount of income recognized, if any, increases or decreases the net investment balance. Computation of this rate of return requires the use of a computer due to the number of iterative attempts needed to derive a rate that fully amortizes the net investment. This allocation is shown in panel B, Schedule 4. The rate of return is 45.58% (computed iteratively). Annual cash flows [column *(b)*] are allocated, based on this rate, between (1) amortization of net investment and (2) income. For example, the 19A allocation to income [column *(d)*] is $91,162 ($200,000 × 45.58%). The remaining cash flow is assumed to reduce the net investment balance ($214,805 − $91,162 = $123,643 reduction). The net investment balance at the beginning of 19B then is $76,357 ($200,000 − $123,643 = $76,357), as shown in column *(a)*. In years in which the net investment balance is negative, such as 19D, the entire cash flow for that year is allocated to the net investment balance and no income is recognized. Notice that the total cash flow allocated to investment must sum to the initial net investment; thus, the sum of column *(c)* is $200,000. Similarly, the sum of column *(d)*, allocation to income, must equal total net income plus investment tax credit.

The remaining accounting problem is allocation of annual income to its component parts; that is, pretax income, tax expense, and any investment tax credit. This allocation is done on a proportionate basis; for example, in 19A, pretax income [column *(e)*] is allocated $42,800 [total pretax income times 19A allocation to income divided by total allocation to income (i.e., $65,360 × ($91,162 ÷ $139,215) = $42,800)]. Tax expense [column *(f)* is allocated a proportionate amount, ensuring a 40% tax rate. Investment tax credit [column *(g)*] in 19A also is recognized on a proportionate basis: $100,000 × ($91,,162 ÷ $139,215) = $65,483. Journal entries reflecting these 19A allocations are shown in panel C. Notice that the Lease Receivable beginning balance is recorded net of the corresponding liability of the lessor (i.e., $1,375,000 − $1,109,640 = $265,360).

Additional details of the FASB approach are provided in Appendix E of *FASB Standard 13*.

QUESTIONS

Part A

1. Match the lettered items immediately below with the statements numbered (in parentheses) that follow by entering one letter in each blank space.

   A. Lessor; B. Capital lease; C. Operating lease; D. Lessee.

   _____ (1) Contract in which lessor finances property leased.
   _____ (2) Lender in a lease contract transaction.
   _____ (3) Tenant in a lease contract transaction.
   _____ (4) Type of lease that requires capitalization.
   _____ (5) Type of lease that does not require capitalization.
   _____ (6) Property owner in a lease contract transaction during the lease term.

   Questions (2) and (3) below are based on the following information (briefly explain your choices):

   Marne Company purchased a machine for leasing purposes on January 1, 19A, for $900,000. The machine has a five-year life, no residual value, and will be depreciated on a straight-line basis. On March 1, 19A, Marne leased the machine to Dal Company for $390,000 a year for four-year period ending February 28, 19E. During the year ended December 31, 19A, Marne incurred normal maintenance and other related expenses of $15,000 under the provisions of this assumed operating lease. Dal paid $390,000 to Marne on March 1, 19A.

2. Assuming an operating lease, what was the income before income taxes derived by Marne from this lease for the year ended December 31, 19A?

   a. $55,000. *c.* $115,000.
   b. $70,000. *d.* $160,000.

3. What was rent expense for Dal from this lease for the year ended December 31, 19A?

   a. $70,000. *c.* $250,000.
   b. $120,000. *d.* $325,000.

4. Give the primary GAAP concepts of accounting for an operating lease by lessors and lessees.
5. Advance rental payments often are received under operating lease contracts that extend well beyond a single fiscal year. Give the acceptable accounting procedures that should be used for advance rentals. (Also see Supplement 21–A.).
6. What is meant by capitalization of a lease from the view of the lessee?
7. From a lessee's standpoint, leases are classified as capital or operating leases. What criteria are used to identify a capital lease?
8. From a lessor's view, a capital lease involves two types of leases. Identify the types and distinguish between them.

Part B

9. Briefly define the following terms related to capital leases (refer to the technical definitions):

   a. Lease term.
   b. Bargain purchase option.
   c. Bargain renewal option.
   d. Minimum lease payments from the standpoint of the lessee.
   e. Minimum lease payments from the standpoint of the lessor.
   f. Interest rate implicit in the lease.

10. How does a lessee determine what interest rate is appropriate for capitalization of a lease?
11. How does unguaranteed residual value in a sales-type lease affect the lessor's accounting in recording the entries at date of inception of the lease?
12. Briefly explain how inclusion of a provision of residual value guaranteed by a third party in a capital lease can result in asymmetric accounting by lessor and lessee.
13. Define initial direct costs.
14. Define executory costs.
15. When computing annual depreciation, what residual value should the lessee use for a leased asset under a capital lease? Briefly explain each alternative.
16. What distinguishes leveraged leases from other leases? What pattern of cash flows can normally be expected in a leveraged lease? (Supplement 21–B)

EXERCISES

Part A: Exercises 21–1 to 21–7

E 21–1 **(Operating Lease; Leasehold Costs; Entries)**

Arrow Company signed an operating lease contract effective for five years from January 1, 19A. Arrow is to pay $20,000 at the start of the lease plus $5,000 monthly rentals throughout the lease term. During January 19A, Arrow spent $10,000 renovating the property leased and also built an addition to the leased property with the lessor's consent at a cost of $80,000. The estimated life of the addition is 15 years, and its residual value is zero. The lease contract does not contain a renewal option and may be terminated by the lessee with six months notice.

Required:
Give all entries on Arrow's books to reflect the renovation outlays, leasehold, and rental payments for 19A and entries at the end of 19A, assuming Arrow's accounting year is the calendar year. The straight-line method of amortization is to be used.

E 21–2 **(Explain Distinctions; Capital versus Operating, and Financing versus Sales-Type Leases)**

Part A
Capital leases and operating leases are the two classifications of leases described in FASB pronouncements, from the standpoint of the lessee.

Required:
1. Describe how a capital lease would be accounted for by the lessee both at the inception of the lease and during the first year of the lease, assuming the lease transfers ownership of the property to the lessee by the end of the lease term.
2. Describe how an operating lease would be accounted for by the lessee both at the inception of the lease and during the first year of the lease, assuming equal monthly payments are made by the lessee at the beginning of each month of the lease. Do not discuss the criteria for distinguishing between capital leases and operating leases.

Part B
Sales-type leases and direct financing leases are two of the classifications of leases described in FASB pronouncements, from the standpoint of the lessor.

Required:
Compare and contrast a sales-type lease with a direct financing lease as follows:

1. Net investment in the lease.
2. Recognition of interest revenue.
3. Manufacturer's or dealer's profit.

Do not discuss the criteria for distinguishing between the leases described above and operating leases.

E 21–3 (Lease: Apply Lease Criteria; Entries for Lessor and Lessee)
Kim Leasing Company agreed with Lee Corporation to provide the latter with equipment under lease for a three-year period. The equipment cost Kim $20,000 and will have no residual value when the lease term ends. Kim expects to collect all rentals from Lee and has no material cost uncertainties. The carrying value of the equipment was $20,000 at the inception of the lease. The three equal annual rents (amount to be determined) are to be paid each January 1, starting January 1, 19A, at which time the equipment was delivered. Lee has agreed to pay taxes, maintenance, and insurance throughout the lease term as well as any other "ownership" costs. Kim expects a 14% return (known to Lee). The accounting year of both companies ends December 31.

Required (round to the nearest dollar):
1. What kind of lease is this to Lee? To Kim?
2. Compute the annual rentals and prepare an amortization schedule reflecting the interest and principal elements of Lee's payments over the three-year term of the lease. Give all journal entries relating to the lease for Lee Corporation for 19A including year-end adjusting entries.
3. Give all journal entries for Kim Leasing Company relating to the lease for 19A including year-end adjusting entries.

E 21–4 (Lease: Financing or Sales Type; Schedule; Entries for Lessor)
Brown Company uses leases as a secondary means of selling its products. The company contracted with Blue Corporation to lease a machine to be used by Blue as an operational asset. The retail market value of the asset at the inception of the lease was $50,000; it cost Brown $40,000 and is carried in its inventory at that value. Payments of $11,231 are to be made by Blue at the end of each of the five quarters following inception of the lease. Brown's implicit interest rate is 4% per quarter, which is known by Blue. The lease qualified as a capital lease for both parties.

Required (round to the nearest dollar):
1. Classify the lease and show how the $11,231 rental payment was computed and prepare an amortization schedule for use by Brown covering the five-quarter term of the lease.
2. Give Brown's journal entries at the inception of the lease and upon receipt of the first payment. Assume the first receipt coincides with the end of Brown's accounting year.

E 21–5 (Lease Classification; Schedule and Entries)
On January 1, 19A, Ellen Company entered into a four-year lease agreement with Mae Company, whereby Ellen agreed to provide Mae with specified equipment. The equipment cost Ellen $25,000 and will have no residual value at the end of the lease term. At the lease inception date, the equipment had a retail market value of $25,000. Ellen's target rate of return (implicit interest rate on cost) is 12% (known to Mae). Lease rental payments are to be made on each December 31. Both Ellen's and Mae's accounting year-end is December 31. Ellen expects to collect all rentals from Mae and there are no material cost uncertainties. Straight-line depreciation is used by Mae.

Required (round to the nearest dollar):

1. What kind of lease is this to Ellen? To Mae?
2. Compute the annual lease rentals and prepare an amortization schedule for Mae.
3. Give Mae's journal entries at the lease inception date and cash payment date, and adjusting entries at December 31, 19A.

E 21–6 **(Lease: Financing or Sales Type; Schedule and Entries; Lessor and Lessee)**
MPI Corporation (lessor) and JRD Company (lessee) agreed to a noncancelable lease. The following information is available regarding the lease terms and the leased asset:

a. MPI's cost of the leased asset, $40,000. The asset was new at lease inception date.
b. Lease term, three years, beginning January 1, 19A. Lease rental payments are made each January 1, beginning January 1, 19A.
c. Estimated useful life of leased asset, three years. Estimated residual value at end of lease, zero.
d. Sales price of leased asset on January 1, 19A, $45,000.
e. MPI's implicit interest rate, 15% on retail price (known to JRD).
f. MPI expects to collect all rentals from JRD, and there are no material cost uncertainties.

Required:

1. What kind of lease is this to MPI? To JRD?
2. Compute the annual lease rentals.
3. Prepare an amortization schedule for the lease.
4. Give the journal entries for both parties on January 1, 19A, and December 31, 19A. Do not make closing entries.

E 21–7 **(Lease; Analysis of Dealer's Profit or Loss)**
Hardin Company is an equipment dealer who sometimes uses leasing as a means to sell its products. On January 1, 19A, Hardin leased equipment to Wesley Corporation. The lease term was four years, with annual lease payments of $6,769 to be paid on each December 31. The equipment has an estimated zero residual value at the end of the lease term. The equipment was carried on Hardin's accounts at a cost of $24,000. Hardin expects to collect all rentals from Wesley, and there were no material cost uncertainties at inception of the lease. The implicit interest rate on the lease was 11% on the selling price (known to Wesley).

Required:

1. What kind of lease is this to Hardin? To Wesley?
2. What is the cost of the equipment to Wesley?
3. What is the dealer's profit or loss recognized by Hardin?
4. Assume the implicit interest rate is 4% (not 11%). What is the dealer's profit or loss recognized by Hardin?
5. Give the entries (based on the 11%) at date of inception of the lease for each party.

Part B: Exercises 21–8 to 21–18

E 21–8 **(Overview of Special Lease Cases; Provide Explanations)**
Select the best answer in each of the following. Justify each choice that you make.

1. On the first day of its accounting year, Lessor, Inc., leased certain property at an annual rental of $100,000 receivable at the beginning of each year for 10 years. The first payment was received immediately. The leased property, which is new, cost $550,000 and has an estimated useful life of 12 years and no residual value. Lessor's

implicit rate is 12%. Lessor had no other costs associated with this lease. Lessor should have accounted for this lease as a sales-type lease but it mistakenly treated the lease as an operating lease. What was the effect on net income during the first year of the lease by having treated this lease as an operating lease rather than as a sales-type lease?

a. No effect.
b. Overstated.
c. Understated.
d. The effect depends on the method selected for income tax purposes.

2. The appropriate valuation of leased assets under an operating lease on the statement of financial position of a lessee is as follows:
   a. Zero.
   b. The absolute sum of the lease payments.
   c. The sum of the present values of the lease payments discounted at an appropriate rate.
   d. The market value of the asset at the date of the inception of the lease.
3. What are the three types of expenses that a lessee experiences with capital leases?
   a. Lease expense, interest expense, amortization expense.
   b. Interest expense, amortization expense, executory costs.
   c. Amortization expense, executory costs, lease expense.
   d. Executory costs, interest expense, lease expense.
4. When measuring the present value of future rentals to be capitalized in connection with a capital lease, identifiable payments to cover taxes, insurance, and maintenance should be accounted for as follows:
   a. Included with the future rentals to be capitalized.
   b. Excluded from future rentals to be capitalized.
   c. Capitalized, but at a different rate and recorded in a different account than future rentals.
   d. Capitalized, but at a different rate and during a different period from the rate and period used for the future rental payments.
5. GAAP requires that certain lease agreements be accounted for as purchases. The theoretical basis for this treatment is that a lease of this type:
   a. Effectively conveys most of the benefits and risks incident to the ownership of property.
   b. Is an example of form over substance.
   c. Provides the use of the leased asset to the lessee for a limited period of time.
   d. Must be recorded in accordance with the concept of cause and effect.
6. Your client constructed an office building at a cost of $500,000 and then sold this building to Jones for a large gain. The client leased it back from Jones for a stipulated annual rental. How should this gain be treated?
   a. Recognized in full as an ordinary item in the year of the transaction.
   b. Recognized in full as an extraordinary item in the year of the transaction.
   c. Amortized as an adjustment of the rental cost, an ordinary item, over the life of the lease.
   d. Amortized as an extraordinary item over the life of lease.

(AICPA adapted)

E 21–9 (Direct Financing Lease with BPO; Schedule; Entries for Lessor)

Lessor Y and Lessee Z contract for the lease of a machine for six rentals of $6,000 each. The first $6,000 rental is to be paid at the inception of the lease, and $6,000 is to be paid at the start of each of five quarters thereafter. They also agree that at the time of the sixth payment, for an added $6,930 bargain purchase option payment, Z can buy the property. The interest rate is 2.5% per quarter. The lease qualifies as a direct financing lease.

Required (round to the nearest dollar):
1. Calculate the lease payments and prepare an amortization schedule for the lease covering the six-quarter term.
2. Give the lessor's entries at the inception of the lease and at the time of the sixth payment if the lessee exercises the purchase option. Assume a direct financing lease.

E 21–10 **(Direct Financing Lease with BPO)**

Harris Company leased a computer to Land Company for a five-year period. Harris paid $46,965 for the computer (estimated useful life five years, no residual value). The lease started on January 1, 19A, and qualifies as a direct financing lease to the lessor and a capital lease to the lessee. Harris uses a target rate of return of 14% in all lease contracts. The first rental payment was on January 1, 19A, and the accounting periods end on December 31.

Required:
1. Compute the annual rental for the lessor and the amount to be capitalized for the lessee. The computer reverts to the lessor at the end of the lease term.
2. Now assume instead, that the lease contract contains a BPO, which states that Land Company can purchase the computer on December 31, 19D, for $14,000, at which time its estimated residual value is $17,500. Compute the annual rental for the lessor and the amount to be capitalized for the lessee. Show whether the BPO is really a bargain.
3. Give the entries at inception date under requirements 1 and 2 for the lessor and lessee.

E 21–11 **(Financing Lease; Unguaranteed RV; Schedules; Ordinary and Annuity Due)**

The present value to a lessor of a lease on which the lessee is obligated to make a $20,000 payment at the end of each of the next three years and on which there is an unguaranteed residual value of $4,000 at the end of the lease term is $49,133 if the lessor's implicit interest rate is 14%. The lease qualifies as a direct financing lease.

Required (round amounts to the nearest dollar):
1. Prepare an amortization schedule for the lessor covering the three-year lease term.
2. Compute the present value of a similar lease, assuming the lessor's implicit rate is 12%. Prepare an amortization schedule similar to the one required in (1) above.
3. Assume instead that each of the three $20,000 annual payments is paid at the beginning of each year, in advance, and that the $4,000 residual value is expected at end of the lease term of three years. What is the present value of the lease payments at 14%? Prepare the lessor's amortization schedule for this lease.

E 21–12 **(Sales-Type Lease; Unguaranteed RV; Inception Entries)**

On January 1, 19A, ABC Company signed a lease contract with Abel Company. The leased asset cost ABC $45,000 and had a normal selling price of $55,000. Three annual rentals, based on the selling price, are payable by Abel on January 1, beginning in 19A. The asset reverts to ABC at the end of the lease term, December 31, 19C, and is estimated to have an unguaranteed residual value on that date of $3,000. ABC's implicit interest rate is 12%, which is known to Abel.

Required:
1. What type of lease is this for ABC?
2. Compute the annual lease rentals.

3. Give the lessor's entry on January 1, 19A.
4. Give the lessee's entry on January 1, 19A.

E 21–13 (Guaranteed RV by Third Party; Lessor, Direct Financing; Lessee, Operating) Mark Leasing Company (lessor) and Ash Corporation (lessee) signed a four-year lease on January 1, 19A. The leased property cost Mark $50,000, which was also its carrying value at inception of the lease. The leased asset had an estimated useful life of six years and the property reverts to Mark at the end of the lease term. Lease payments of $12,830 are payable on January 1 of each year and were set to yield Mark a return of 12%, which was known to Ash. The estimated residual value at the end of the lease term is $10,000 and is guaranteed by a third party. The lease contains no bargain purchase option, and Mark is reasonably certain of the collectibility of lease rentals and there are no additional costs to be incurred. The lease qualifies as a direct financing lease to the lessor, but an operating lease to the lessee.

Required:

1. What evidence supports this as a direct financing lease for the lessor? Give Mark's journal entries at inception of the lease and to record the first lease payment.
2. What evidence supports this as an operating lease for Ash? Explain. Give Ash's journal entries at inception of the lease and to record the first lease payment.

E 21–14 (Direct Financing Lease; RV Partially Guaranteed by the Lessee) Davis Company leased a large copier to Gore Company for a three-year period. Davis paid $15,000 for the copier and immediately placed it on this lease on January 1, 19A (estimated useful life four years and an estimated residual value at the end of the lease term of $3,000). Davis used an expected rate of return of 16% on cost (known by Gore). Because of inadequate maintenance the lessee agreed to guarantee two thirds (i.e., $2,000) of the residual value. The lease qualifies as a direct financing lease for the lessor and a capital lease for the lessee. The lessee uses straight-line depreciation. The first lease payment is on January 1, 19A; the accounting periods for both parties end on December 31. At the lease termination date, an independent appraiser provided an estimated residual value of $1,500. The lessee immediately paid the difference of $500 (i.e., $2,000 guaranteed RV minus $1,500, the actual RV).

Required:

1. Compute the minimum lease payment for the lessor and the amount to be capitalized by the lessee.
2. Give the entries for the lessor and lessee on January 1, 19A.
3. Give the entries for the lessor and lessee to record the lease termination.

E 21–15 (Accounting for Executory Costs) On January 1, 19A, Lessor A leased a machine to Lessee B on a three-year direct financing lease to the lessor and a capital lease to the lessee. The machine cost the lessor $30,000 and was immediately placed on lease at a 12% target rate of return (known by both parties). The lease did not contain a BPO and there is no residual value. The rentals are payable each year starting on January 1, 19A. The accounting periods end December 31. All executory costs are to be paid by the lessee. However, insurance coverage was provided, at a cost of $50 per year, under the lessor's blanket policy. This amount is billed each year along with the lease rental.

Required:

1. Compute the annual lease rental.

2. Give the entry for the lessor and lessee to record the inception of the lease (do not include the first rent payment).
3. Give the entry for the lessor and lessee to record the first rent payment.

E 21–16 (Sale-Leaseback; Direct Financing Lease)

Green Grocery owns the building it uses; it has current carrying value on January 1, 19A of $90,000, a 10-year remaining life and no residual value. On this date it was sold to Investor Brown for cash for $100,000. Simultaneously, the two parties executed a 10-year direct financing lease with a 12% implicit interest rate; each annual rent is payable on December 31 (end of the accounting periods).

Required:
1. Compute the annual rents to be paid by Green to Brown.
2. Give the entries for the seller/lessee (Green Grocery) for 19A. Use straight-line depreciation.

E 21–17 (Supplement 21–A; Operating Lease; Amortization, Interest Method)

Dee Company paid $5,000 on January 1, 19A, to Hill Properties as an advance lease bonus to secure a three-year lease on premises it will occupy starting from that date. Additionally, $6,000 will be paid as rent on each December 31 throughout the term of the lease. The lease contains no specific renewal agreement. Dee's accounting period ends December 31. Hill will maintain the property and pay taxes and other ownership costs.

Required (round to the nearest dollar):
1. What type of lease contract is involved? Explain.
2. What are Dee's alternatives as to treatment of the $5,000? Develop an interest method amortization schedule using a 14% rate (assume an ordinary annuity).
3. What is Dee's total occupancy cost for 19A under each alternative given in your response to (2) above?
4. What lease-related items should Dee's financial statements report as of December 31, 19A, if the amortization schedule developed in (2) above is used?

E 21–18 (Supplement 21–B; Leveraged Lease; Comprehensive)

Lansing Leasing, Inc., leased a machine with a five-year useful life to Blue Company for a five-year period beginning January 1, 19A. Lansing acquired the machine at a cost of $250,000, paid $50,000 cash, and borrowed the remainder at 8% per annum. The loan agreement provides for four equal annual payments starting on December 31, 19A.

Blue agreed to pay five equal annual year-end rents of $64,273. Lansing will realize a 10% investment credit the first year and will depreciate the machine (which has no residual value) by using the DB (200% acceleration) method. Lansing has extensive income from other sources and pays income tax at an average rate of 40%; any losses on a single phase of its operations result in a 40% income tax saving.

Required (round amounts to the nearest dollar):
1. Prepare a debt amortization schedule for this leveraged lease similar to Exhibit 21–14, panel B, Schedule 1.
2. Prepare a cash flow analysis similar to Exhibit 21–14, panel B, Schedule 2.
3. Give ABC's journal entries at date of inception of the lease.
4. Give Abel's journal entries at date of inception of the lease.

PROBLEMS

Part A: Problems 21–1 to 21–7

P 21–1 (Lease: Determine Type; Entries for Lessor and Lessee)
Lessor X and Lessee Y enter into a four-year lease agreement on January 1, 19A, which requires equal annual payments on each January 1, and, in addition, a single lump-sum prepayment of $3,000. The leased asset, recently purchased new, cost the lessor $37,290.

The annual lease payments were computed to yield Lessor X a 12% yield (the implicit interest rate after considering residual value; known to Lessee Y). The leased asset has an eight-year life with zero residual value at the end of year 8. There is no bargain purchase option, and the asset is retained by Lessor X at the end of the lease term. Depreciation will be on the straight-line basis. The accounting period for both lessor and lessee ends December 31.

Required:
1. Compute the annual lease payment.
2. What type of lease is this? Explain.
3. In parallel columns for the lessor and lessee, give the following:
   a. Entries at the inception of the lease, including the initial advance payment.
   b. Adjusting and closing entries for the year ended December 31, 19A. Use straight-line amortization for the prepayment.

P 21–2 (Operating Lease; Down Payment; Entries for Both Parties)
On July 1, 19A, Staley Company leased a small building and its site to West Company on a five-year contract. The lease provides for an advance rental at $5,000 plus an annual rental of $18,000 payable each January 1 starting in 19A. The lease can be terminated at any year end by the lessee with a six-month advance notice. There is no renewal agreement. On July 8, 19A, West Company spent $8,000 on internal changes and painting. Staley's accounts showed the following data on January 1, 19A: Undepreciated cost of the building, $125,000 (accumulated depreciation, $30,000), estimated remaining life, 15 years, and estimated residual value, $5,000. The accounting period for each company ends December 31.

Required:
1. Give the entries for the lessor and lessee for 19A, 19B, and through July 1, 19C. Both companies will use straight-line depreciation and amortization of the advance rental. Use reversing entries; closing entries not required.
2. Give the amounts that each party should report on the 19A and 19B statements of income and financial position.

P 21–3 (Direct Financing Lease; Ordinary versus Annuity Due; Schedules; Entries for Both Parties)
On January 1, 19A, Armor Leasing Company leased to Hogg Service Company a new machine that cost $20,000. The lease is a direct financing lease to Armor and a capital lease to Hogg, who agreed to pay all executory costs and assume other risks and costs of ownership. Armor computed the periodic rents at an amount that will yield an annual return on cost of 10%, and the lessee, being aware of this rate, also uses it to record the lease and calculate interest expense. The property is expected to have no residual value at the end of the four-year lease term. There are no collection or cost uncertainties. Both lessor and lessee have accounting years ending December 31.

Required (round all amounts to the nearest dollar):

1. If the annual rents are payable at the end of each year, provide the following: *(a)* the amount of the periodic rental payments and *(b)* an amortization schedule for the lessor reflecting interest and recovery of investment throughout the four-year lease term.
2. Assume instead that the annual rentals are payable at the start of the lease and annually thereafter. Provide the answers to *(a)* and *(b)* that were required in (1) above.
3. Hogg depreciates all assets using the straight-line method. Give entries under (1) above for both lessor and lessee relating to the lease for 19A, including adjusting and closing entries.

P 21–4 (Direct and Sales-Type Compared; Schedules; Entries Both Parties)

On January 1, 19A, Gem Corporation leased to Anderson Company new equipment that cost Gem $50,000. The lease agreement specified that Anderson is to make four equal annual lease payments (each January 1, beginning January 1, 19A) to yield Gem a 12% return. The equipment has a four-year useful life with no residual value. Straight-line depreciation will be used. Ownership of the leased asset automatically transfers to Anderson at the end of the lease term. Gem informed Anderson of the interest rate implicit in the lease. Gem expects to collect all rentals from Anderson, and there are no material cost uncertainties at inception of the lease. The accounting period for both Gem and Anderson ends December 31.

Required:

1. If the equipment has a cost or carrying value of $50,000 on January 1, 19A, and the lease rentals are based on this amount, what type of lease is this to the lessor? To the lessee? Explain. Compute the annual rental payments and prepare an amortization schedule for the lessor and the lessee. Prepare all journal entries associated with the lease for the lessor and the lessee for the years ended December 31, 19A and December 31, 19B, including adjusting and closing entries.
2. If the equipment has a normal cash selling price of $60,000 on January 1, 19A, and the lease rentals are based on this amount, what type of lease is this to the lessor? To the lessee? Explain. Compute the annual rental payments and prepare an amortization schedule for the lessor and lessee. Prepare all journal entries associated with this lease for the lessor and the lessee for the years ended December 31, 19A, and December 31, 19B, including adjusting and closing entries.

P 21–5 (Amortization Schedules; Sales-Type Lease; Entries for Both Parties)

Key Company uses leases as a secondary means of selling its products. On January 1, 19A, it contracted with Lock Corporation to lease machinery for six years that had a sales price of $90,000 and that cost Key $60,000 (its carrying value in inventory). Equal annual lease payments of $18,786 are to be made each January 1, starting on January 1, 19A. Key's implicit interest rate is 10% based on sales price (known to Lock). This lease qualifies as a capital lease for both parties. The accounting period for both companies ends on December 31.

Required (round to the nearest dollar):

1. Prepare an amortization schedule for Key and Lock covering the six-year lease term.
2. Give the lessor's and lessee's entries at the inception of the lease. The lessee uses straight-line depreciation and zero residual value of the asset after six years. Also, give the adjusting and closing entries for both parties at December 31, 19A.

P 21–6 **(Direct Financing and Sales-Type Leases Compared; Entries for Both Parties)** On January 1, 19A, Sun Company leased to Marfa Corporation new equipment. The equipment cost Sun $38,000. The lease agreement specified that Marfa is to make five equal annual lease payments (on December 31, beginning December 31, 19A) to yield Sun a 14% return. The equipment has a five-year useful life with no residual value. Ownership of the leased asset transfers to Marfa at the end of the lease term. Marfa is aware of the implicit interest rate used by Sun. Straight-line depreciation will be used. Sun expects to collect all rentals from Marfa, and there are no material cost uncertainties at inception of the lease. The accounting period for both Sun and Marfa ends December 31.

Required:

1. If the equipment has a sales price of $42,000 on January 1, 19A, and the lease rentals are based on this amount, what type of lease is this to the lessor? To the lessee? Explain. Compute the annual rental payments and prepare an amortization schedule for the lessor and lessee. Give all journal entries associated with this lease for the lessor and the lessee for the year ended December 31, 19A, including adjusting and closing entries.
2. If the equipment has a cost or carrying value of $38,000 on January 1, 19A, and the lease rentals are based on this amount, what type of lease is this to the lessor? To the lessee? Explain. Compute the annual rental payments and prepare an amortization schedule for the lessor and the lessee. Give all journal entries associated with this lease for the lessor and the lessee for the year ended December 31, 19A, including adjusting and closing entries.

P 21–7 **(Direct Financing Lease; Different Interest Rates Used by Lessor and Lessee; Entries)** On January 1, 19A, Lessor Able leased a machine to Lessee Baker on a three-year lease that qualifies as a direct financing lease. The machine cost Able $80,000 immediately prior to the lease. The machine has a three-year estimated useful life and no residual value. The lessor used a 11% target rate of return. The three annual lease payments start on January 1, 19A. The lessee uses straight-line depreciation, will retain the machine at the end of the lease term, and has a borrowing rate of 10%. The lessee must use the lower of the two interest rates. The accounting period for each company ends on December 31.

Required:

1. Compute the equal annual rentals that the lessor will receive.
2. Prepare an amortization schedule for the lessor and give the related entries through December 31, 19A.
3. Compute the lease capitalization amount and prepare an amortization schedule for the lessee and give the related entries through December 31, 19A.
4. Complete the following 19A comparative tabulation for the lessor and lessee and explain any differences:

Items	Lessor	Lessee
Statement of income:		
Interest revenue		
Interest expense		
Depreciation expense		
Statement of financial position:		
Lease receivable		
Lease liability		
Leased property		
Accumulated depreciation		

Part B: Problems 21–8 to 21–22

P 21–8 **(Sales-Type Lease; BPO; Entries for Both Parties)**

On January 1, 19A, Lessor Ray and Lessee Evans signed a four-year lease that qualifies as a sales-type lease. The equipment cost Ray $90,000 and the cash sale price is $140,000. The equipment has a six-year estimated useful life. Estimated residual values were: end of year 4, $20,000, and end of year 6, $8,000. The lease gives Evans an option to buy the equipment at the end of year 4 for $15,000 cash. The lease requires four equal annual rents starting on January 1, 19A. Ray's expected rate of return on the lease is 15% and the incremental borrowing rate of Evans is 16%. On December 31, 19D, the lessee exercised the purchase option, at which time a new estimate of residual value was $18,000.

Required:

1. Compute the annual rent and the amount the lessee should capitalize.
2. Prepare a lease amortization schedule for the lessor and lessee.
3. Give the entries for the lessor and lessee from the date of inception through the lease termination date.

P 21–9 **(Analysis to Classify Lease; Capital versus Operating; Unguaranteed RV; Entries for Both Parties)**

Lessor Sales Company and Lessee Manufacturing Company agreed to a noncancelable lease. The following information is available regarding the lease terms and the leased asset:

a. Lessor's cost of the leased asset, $30,000. The asset was new at the inception of the lease term.
b. Lease term, four years starting January 1, 19B.
c. Estimated useful life of the leased asset, six years. Estimated residual value at end of six years, zero.
d. On January 1, 19B, estimated unguaranteed residual value of the leased asset one day after the end of the lease term is $4,000.
e. Depreciation method for the leased asset, straight line.
f. Lessee's incremental borrowing rate on January 1, 19B, 18%. The lessee is considered a high-risk borrower.
g. Bank prime rate of interest on January 1, 19B, 10%.
h. Purchase option price of leased asset exercisable one day after the end of the lease term, $4,500.
i. Title to the leased asset retained by the lessor unless the purchase option is exercised.
j. Sales price of leased asset on January 1, 19B, $40,000.
k. Lessor's unreimbursable cost uncertainties, none.
l. Four annual lease rentals due on January 1 of each year during the lease term, with the first payment due at inception of the lease term, $11,643.
m. The accounting period for the lessor and lessee ends on December 31.

Both the lessor and lessee knew all of the above information.

Required (round to the nearest dollar):

1. What was the lessor's implicit interest rate in this lease?
2. What type of lease was this to the lessee? To the lessor? Explain.
3. In parallel columns for the lessor and lessee, record the following:

a. Entry, or entries, at inception of the lease on January 1, 19B, if appropriate.
b. Adjusting and closing entries on December 31, 19B.

P 21–10 (Lease Classification; Entries for Lessor and Lessee)

The following data are available about a noncancelable lease that involves a leased asset that was new at inception date of lease term:

Lease term	6 years
Interest rate implicit in the lease	12%
Lessee's incremental borrowing rate	14%
Amount of each lease payment	$ 3,648
Lessor's cost of asset (market value)	$15,000
Lessee has no way of knowing the interest rate implicit in the lease.	
Each lease payment occurs at the end of each period, (i.e., an ordinary annuity).	
Unreimbursable cost uncertainties of lessor	None
Credit standing of lessee	Excellent
Depreciation method, if needed	Straight line
Estimated useful life of asset	6 years
Estimated residual value at end of lease term	$–0–
Accounting period for both parties ends on December 31.	

Required (round to the nearest dollar):

1. What type of lease is this to the lessee? To the lessor? Explain.
2. Give entries in parallel columns for lessor and lessee to record:
   a. The inception of the lease on January 1, 19A.
   b. All entries needed at year-end, December 31, 19A, for both parties to record lease payment (receipt), interest, depreciation, and so forth, including closing entries.

P 21–11 (Direct Financing Lease; Unguaranteed RV; Entries for Both Parties)

Jinx, Incorporated, purchased a machine (for leasing purposes) on January 1, 19A, for $270,000. By prior agreement the machine was delivered to Pine Company (lessee) under a direct financing lease whereby Pine paid the first lease rental of $73,516 on January 1, 19A, and agreed to pay three more such annual rentals.

At the end of the four-year lease term, the machine will revert to the lessor, at which time it is expected to have a residual value of $20,000 (none of which was guaranteed by the lessee). The lessor's implicit interest rate was 10% on cost.

Required (round amounts to the nearest dollar):

1. Show how the lessor computed the annual rental.
2. Prepare a lease amortization schedule for the lessor.
3. Give all of the entries for the lessor on the following dates:
   January 1, 19A—Purchase and other transactions.
   December 31, 19A—End of the accounting period.
   Year 19D—Return of the machine by the lessee at the termination of the lease. At this date the machine has an actual market value of $14,000 (instead of the $20,000 estimated residual value).
4. How would the lessor's entries differ at the end of the lease term if the actual market value of the machine turned out to be $23,000 (instead of the estimated residual value of $20,000)?

P 21–12 (Capital Lease; RV, Third-Party Guarantee; Schedules and Entries for Both Parties)
The following data are available regarding a noncancelable lease:

a. Lease term, five years, beginning January 1, 19A.
b. The leased property cost the lessor $400,000 on January 1, 19A.
c. Estimated useful life of the asset, six years; residual value at the end of the six-year useful life, $20,000.
d. On January 1, 19A, the estimated residual value of the leased asset at the end of the lease term, $50,000. This residual value is guaranteed in full by a third-party guarantor (not the lessee).
e. Depreciation method for the leased asset, straight line.
f. No bargain purchase option available to the lessee. Ownership retained by lessor at the end of lease term.
g. Five annual lease payments are payable on January 1 of each year (starting January 1, 19A) to yield the lessor a 14% return (implicit interest rate). Lessee does not know, and cannot reliably estimate, the lessor's yield rate. Lessee's incremental borrowing rate is 16%.
h. Lessor's unreimbursable cost uncertainties, none. Lessee's credit rating, excellent.
i. Lessor and lessee accounting year-end, December 31.

Required (round to the nearest dollar):
1. Compute the annual rentals by the lessor.
2. What type of lease is this to the lessor? To the lessee? Explain.
3. Prepare an amortization schedule for the lessor. Give the following entries for the lessor:
   a. At the inception of the lease and for the initial lease rental on January 1, 19A.
   b. Adjusting and closing on December 31, 19A.
4. Prepare an amortization schedule for the lessee. Give the following entries for the lessee:
   a. At the inception of the lease and for the initial lease rental on January 1, 19A.
   b. Adjusting and closing on December 31, 19A.

P 21–13 (Direct Financing Lease; Change in RV; Amortization Schedule)
On January 1, 19A, Ray Leasing Company leased equipment to a lessee for an eight-year term whereby $45,000 rents are payable each January 1, starting on January 1, 19A. The unguaranteed residual value of the equipment at the end of the lease term is $20,000. The interest rate implicit in the lease is 15%. The accounting period for both the lessor and lessee ends on December 31. The lease qualifies as a direct financing lease.

Required (round to the nearest dollar):
1. Compute the initial investment value (i.e., cost to the lessor) of the leased property and the total amount of interest to be earned by Ray over the lease term.
2. Immediately after the fifth annual payment, the lease amortization schedule shows a lease receivable balance of $114,181. Prepare the amortization schedule for the lessor, using the value determined in (1) above to prove the correctness of that amount. For problem purposes stop the amortization schedule after the January 1, 19E payment.
3. Immediately after the fifth payment, Ray determined that the expected unguaranteed residual value of $20,000 probably will be zero. This change in accounting estimate will decrease the unrecovered investment value by the present value of the previously

estimated residual value. Prepare the journal entry to record this change. After adjusting the January 1, 19E receivable balance, complete the lease amortization schedule developed in (2) above from the $114,181 value in view of this new determination.

P 21–14 (Sales-Type Lease; Schedule; Entries for Both Parties)

On December 31, 19A, a lessor leased a machine that cost $70,000. The machine was leased on January 1, 19B, for five years under a sales-type lease, which required annual payments of $28,199 at the end of each year. At inception of the lease, the sales value of the leased asset was $110,000. At the end of the lease term, the machine will revert to the lessor, at which time the estimated residual value will be $5,000 (none of which is guaranteed by the lessee). The lessor's implicit rate of interest was 10% on the investment.

Required (round amounts to the nearest dollar):

1. Show how the lessor computed the annual rental of $28,199.
2. Prepare a lease amortization schedule for the lessor.
3. Give the following entries for the lessor:
   a. To record acquisition of the machine on December 31, 19A.
   b. To record the inception of the lease on January 1, 19B.
   c. To record collection of the first rental and recognition of interest revenue on December 31, 19B (end of the accounting period).
   d. To record, at termination of the lease on December 31, 19F, the last rental, interest revenue, and return of the asset, assuming the estimate of residual value is confirmed.
4. How would the lessor's entries differ at the end of the lease term, assuming the market value of the returned machine was $4,000 (instead of the $5,000 estimated residual value)?

P 21–15 (Sales-Type Lease; Amortization Schedules; Entries for Both Parties)

Lessor Company entered into a lease with Lessee Company on January 1, 19D. The following data relate to the leased asset and the lease agreement:

a. Asset leased—large construction crane.
b. Cost to Lessor, $150,000.
c. Estimated useful life, 10 years.
d. Estimated residual value at end of useful life, $10,000.
e. Lessor's normal selling price, $200,000.
f. Lease provisions:
   (1) Noncancelable; the asset will revert to Lessor at the end of the lease term.
   (2) Estimated residual value at end of lease term, $20,000 (none guaranteed).
   (3) Ownership does not transfer to Lessee by the end of the lease term.
   (4) No bargain purchase option is included.
   (5) Lease term, six years starting January 1, 19D.
   (6) Lease payment at each year-end, starting December 31, 19D, $43,329.
g. Lessor's implicit rate of return, 10% (assume Lessee knows this rate).
h. Lessee's incremental borrowing rate, 12% (assume this is evidence of a good credit rating).
i. Lessor has no material cost uncertainties.

Required (show computations and round to the nearest dollar):

1. What kind of lease was this to Lessee Company? Give the basis for your response.
2. What kind of lease was this to Lessor Company? Give the basis for your response.

3. For Lessor Company, give the entries to record *(a)* the lease at inception date and *(b)* the first rental.
4. For Lessee Company, give the entries to record *(a)* the lease at inception date and *(b)* the first rental.

P 21–16 (Determine the Kind of Lease; Schedule; Entries for Both Parties)
Lessor and lessee agreed to a noncancelable lease for which the following information is available:

a. Lessor's cost of the asset leased, $25,000. The asset was new at the inception of the lease term.
b. Lease term, four years starting January 1, 19C.
c. Estimated useful life of the leased asset, six years.
d. On January 1, 19C, lessor and lessee estimated that the residual value of the leased asset on the purchase option date (see h below) will be $6,000 and zero at the end of its useful life. The residual value is not guaranteed.
e. Depreciation method for the leased asset, straight line.
f. Lessee's incremental borrowing rate, 10%. Lessee has an excellent credit rating.
g. Lessor's interest rate implicit in the lease, 10%.
h. Purchase option price of leased asset exercisable on January 2, 19F, $5,000.
i. Title to the leased asset retained by the lessor unless the purchase option is exercised.
j. Sale value of leased asset on January 1, 19C, $30,000.
k. Lessor's unreimbursable cost uncertainties, none.
l. Four annual lease rentals payable each January 1 during the lease term, with the first payment due at inception of the lease term, $7,526.

Required (round to the nearest dollar):
1. Show how the annual rental was computed.
2. Is this an operating lease or a capital lease to the lessee? Explain. Compute the lessee's capitalizable cost of the leased asset.
3. What type of lease is this to the lessor? Explain.
4. Prepare an amortization schedule. In parallel columns for the lessee and lessor, record the inception of the lease on January 1, 19C (if appropriate), and the adjusting and closing entries on December 31, 19C.
5. Prepare the financial statement presentation of all lease-related accounts as they would appear in the financial statements of the lessee at December 31, 19C, for the year then ended. Note disclosures are not required.

P 21–17 (Direct Financing Lease; Executory Cost; Partially Guaranteed RV; Entries)
Stockton Leasing Company (lessor) entered into a four-year noncancelable, direct financing lease with Acme Corporation (lessee) on January 1, 19A. The leased asset has a six-year life, with zero residual value at the end of the six years. On January 1, 19A, both lessor and lessee estimated the residual value of the asset at the end of the lease term to be $30,000, of which Acme guaranteed $20,000. The leased asset cost $500,000 (same as its market value). Lease payments are to be made on December 31 of each year, starting December 31, 19A, and are set to yield 16% to Stockton (implicit interest rate). This interest rate is known to Acme, who has an 18% incremental borrowing rate. Straight-line depreciation is used. Stockton agreed to pay annual executory costs of $3,000 and included this amount in the lease rentals. There is no bargain purchase option, and ownership is retained by Stockton at the end of the lease term. The accounting period for both companies ends on December 31.

Required (round to the nearest dollar):

1. Compute the annual lease rentals.
2. Prepare amortization schedules for the lessor and lessee.
3. Record the following for the lessor and lessee:
   a. Entry at the inception of the lease.
   b. Adjusting and closing entries at December 31, 19A.
4. Assuming that the actual residual value of the leased asset on December 31, 19D (end of lease term) was $15,000, prepare entries for lessor and lessee on December 31, 19D, to record the return of the asset to the lessor.
5. Ignore requirement 4. Assuming that the actual residual value of the leased asset on December 31, 19D was $25,000, prepare entries for lessor and lessee on December 31, 19D, to record the return of the asset to the lessor.

P 21–18 (Accounting for Initial Direct Lease Costs)

On January 1, 19A, Lessor Smith leased equipment to Lessee Thomas. The equipment cost the lessor $40,000 and the lessor's expected rate of return was 15%. The three annual payments are to start on December 31, 19A. The lease has no BPO and there is no residual value. The lessor incurred, and paid, initial indirect costs of $600 in consummating the lease. The lessor recorded these costs as a credit to cash and a debit to a temporary holding account called Initial Direct Leasing Costs. The rent payments were indirectly set to cover such costs.

Required:

1. Compute the annual rent (ordinary annuity basis) set by the lessor assuming the following cases:

   Case A
   An operating lease (including the initial direct leasing costs).
   Case B
   A direct financing lease (including the initial direct leasing costs).
   Case C

   A sales-type lease (including the direct leasing costs). The normal or regular selling price of the leased asset is $60,000.
2. Give the lessor's entries for *(a)* the inception of the lease and *(b)* the payments related to the lease at the end of the first year, for each case.
3. Give any entry needed for each case that the lessor should make during the first year for the initial direct costs.
   Note: The lessee's entries are unaffected.

P 21–19 (Sale-Leaseback; Operating and Direct Financing Leases Compared)

On January 1, 19A, Supergrocery, Inc., sold the building currently used to Diversified Investors for $9,000,000; which is its current market value. Prior to the sale the carrying value of the building was $7,000,000. The estimated remaining useful life of the building is 10 years and no residual value at that time; straight-line depreciation is used.

On January 1, 19A, Supergrocery signed a 10-year noncancelable leaseback agreement that has a 15% implicit rate of return for the lessor. The lessee's incremental borrowing rate also is 15%. The annual rent payments start on January 1, 19A. During 19A, Supergrocery would pay $10,000 for executory costs (e.g., insurance, taxes, maintenance), if this transaction qualifies as a direct financing lease. Alternatively, if this qualifies as an operating lease, this $10,000 would be paid by the buyer/lessor. For problem purposes only, two cases are assumed about the lease: Case A—an operating lease; Case B—a direct financing lease.

Required (for practical reasons give all amounts in 000s):

1. Compute the annual lease payments and the gain or loss on the sale of the building.
2. Give the 19A entries for the seller/lessee and the buyer/lessor in parallel columns for Case A—operating lease.
3. (*a*) Prepare the lease amortization schedule through 19B for Case B—direct financing lease.
   (*b*) Give the 19A entries for the seller/lessee and the buyer/lessor in parallel columns for Case B—direct financing lease.

P 21–20 **(Supplement 21–A; Operating Lease; Advance Payment; Ordinary Annuity Basis)**
In lieu of making four $10,000 rent payments spaced at one-year intervals with the first payment due at the end of the first year of the lease term, the lessee and lessor agree that the lessee can make a lump-sum initial payment, the amount to be computed, at the start of the four-year lease term. This amount was calculated on the basis of an agreed 16% annual interest rate.

Required (round all amounts to the nearest dollar):

1. Compute the lump-sum initial payment amount.
2. Prepare an amortization schedule for the lessor covering the entire lease term. Show the lessor's entries to reflect receipt of the initial payment and adjusting entries at the end of the first, second, and last years if the lease year and accounting year of the lessor coincide. Entries are to be based on the amortization schedule.
3. On the assumption that the lessee amortizes the prepayment on a straight-line basis, give the lessee's entries to record the initial payment and year-end adjustments if the lease year and lessee accounting year coincide.
4. Has the lessor or lessee adopted a more realistic approach to recognition of the periodic effects of the lease? Explain.

P 21–21 **(Supplement 21–A; Operating Lease; Advance Payment; Annuity Due Basis)**
A lessor and a lessee began negotiations that would have provided that the lessee pay six semiannual $8,000 rents for the use of property with the first payment to be at the beginning of the lease term. However, after agreeing that money was worth 14% per year at the time, the parties finally agreed that the lessee would instead pay $? at the outset and that this single advance payment would be in lieu of all other rents for the three-year term. Assume an operating lease.

Required (round to the nearest dollar):

1. Show how the advance payment was calculated and prepare an amortization schedule covering the entire term of the lease.
2. Give journal entries for both the lessor and lessee, based on the amortization schedule, which reflect the advance payment and adjusting entries (assuming the lease year and accounting year of the parties coincide) at the end of years 1 and 3. Lessor and lessee use the interest method of amortization.
3. Instead of using the interest method of amortization as in (2) above, assume that the lessor and lessee amortize the advance payment computed in requirement (1) above by the straight-line method. Give entries for both parties to record amortization at the end of the year if the lease year and accounting year of the parties coincide.

P 21–22 **(Supplement 21–B; Leveraged Lease; Debt Amortization; Cash Flow; Entries)**
A lessor arranged financing of property to be leased to a lessee under a leveraged lease contract. The property cost the lessor $700,000 and is expected to have a five-year life and zero residual value. It will be depreciated by the lessor using the SYD

method. The 10% investment tax credit will be realized by the lessor in the first year (assumed for instructional purposes). The lessor has other income in addition to this lease; all income will be taxed at a rate of 40%, and any losses result in a 40% tax saving. The parties agreed on five annual rental payments of $175,000 at the end of each year for the use of the property.

The lessor paid $200,000 of the purchase price of the property and borrowed the remaining $500,000 at an annual interest rate of 10%. Five annual payments of $131,899 at the end of each year will fully amortize the debt and pay all interest.

Required (round all amounts to the nearest dollar):

1. Prepare a debt amortization schedule, a cash flow schedule, and a schedule of allocation of cash flow to income and investment (similar to Exhibit 21–14) covering the entire lease term.
2. Prepare journal entries for the lessor for the first year of the lease.

(*Hint:* The rate of return required to fully amortize the lessor's net investment is 22.824%).

CASES

C 21–1 (Off-Balance-Sheet Financing)

The corporation where you are employed as controller is contemplating leasing (as a lessee) a larger proportion of its operational assets than in the past. As assets become fully depreciated and/or are retired, many of them would be replaced by leased assets. You have been asked by the board of directors to advise about certain specific financial accounting issues.

Item 1: The company is heavily in debt, and one director is concerned about becoming a lessee under a capital lease because, as the director said, "we do not want all that debt on the balance sheet." Can you offer any comments that might relieve this anxiety?

Item 2: Having learned that interest must be recognized in connection with lease obligations and that within modest limits there may be some discretion as to the interest rates selected, some board members want to use the lowest possible rate while others want to use the highest possible rate. Specifically, you are asked what would be the difference insofar as the financial statements are concerned between the two alternatives.

Item 3: If some of the lease contracts contemplated could be drawn so as to avoid the lease capitalization requirements of *FASB Standard 13*, what would be the effect on the financial statements of using such lease contracts?

C 21–2 (Implementing *FASB Standard 13*—Interest Rate)

Pertinent provisions of *FASB Standard 13* concerning the interest rate to be used in capitalizing leases are cited below:

> "A lessor shall compute the present value of the minimum lease payments using the *interest rate implicit in the lease*. . . . A lessee shall compute the present value of the minimum lease payments using his incremental borrowing rate . . . unless *(i)* it is practicable for him to learn the implicit rate computed by the lessor, and *(ii)* the implicit rate computed by the lessor is less than the lessee's incremental borrowing rate. If both of these conditions are met, the lessee shall use the implicit rate."

Interest rate implicit in the lease is defined as the discount rate which, when applied to the minimum lease payments (excluding executory costs) and to the unguaranteed residual value of the property to the lessor, causes the present value at the start of the lease term to equal the [market] value of the property to the lessor at the inception of the lease.*

APB Opinion 21, which deals with the imputation of interest to receivables and payables, indicates that the choice of an interest rate "may be affected by the credit standing of the issuer, restrictive covenants, the collateral, payment and other terms pertaining to the debt, and, if appropriate, the tax consequences to the buyer and seller."

* There are some qualifications to this abstracted definition, but they are not important for present purposes. Italics supplied in the first quotation.

Required:
Evaluate the foregoing criteria in light of the following assertions:

1. Asking a lessor what interest rate is inherent in a lease transaction would be similar to asking a farmer what rate is implicit in the price the farmer can expect *now* for next fall's corn crop. There are varying degrees of risk in any operation having a distant future; the higher the farmer's future risks are thought to be, the higher the farmer will set his or her rate and, likewise, for the lessor.
2. The assumption that a lease has an implicit interest rate, in many cases, represents circular reasoning in that the market value of the leased asset itself (i.e., the benchmark value used in determining the implicit rate) is determined by market forces. The value of the property stems from the rentals it will command rather than the rentals stemming from the value of the property.
3. One determinant of the implicit interest rate in a lease is the residual value of the property to be leased. This is a subjective judgment, which, depending on the property, can be substantially in error. Lessors will not disclose what this guess is.

C 21–3 (Concern about Debt-Equity Ratio and Third-Party RV Guarantees)

Software Corporation has entered into a debt agreement that restricts its debt-to-owners'-equity ratio to less than two to one. The corporation is planning to expand its facilities, which creates a need for additional financing. The board of directors is considering leasing the additional facilities but is concerned that leasing may violate its existing debt agreement, which would place the corporation in default. The potential lessor insists that the lease be structured such that it can be accounted for as a capital lease by the lessor (the lessor is a dealer and wants to recognize the dealer's profit on the transaction immediately). In addition, the lessor requires that the residual value of the leased asset be guaranteed when it reverts to the lessor at the end of the lease term. Software's board has asked you to analyze the following alternatives:

Alternative A—Software would enter into a lease that qualifies as a capital lease (to Software). If this alternative is selected, Software's reported debt-to-owners'-equity ratio would be 1.9, and its ability to issue debt in the future would be seriously constrained.

Alternative B—Software would enter into a lease and pay a third party to guarantee the residual value of the leased property. The lease would be structured such that it would qualify as an operating lease to Software and a capital lease to the lessor. In this case, Software's reported debt-to-owners-'equity ratio would be unaffected by the lease contract.

Required:
Analyze and explain the consequences of each of the above alternatives.

22 EARNINGS PER SHARE AND FINANCIAL STATEMENT ANALYSIS

OVERVIEW AND PURPOSE

If a rational investor has $100,000 to invest in the near future, a primary objective would be to maximize the present value of the probable future cash returns. An investor often considers a wide range of investments such as real estate, equipment purchased for leasing, government securities or mutual funds, or investment in a going business by purchasing its debt (e.g., bonds) or equity securities (e.g., common stock). In respect to a going business, both investors and creditors have a common problem; that is, the difficulty in estimating the future success of the target company in terms of probable future cash flows. To do this each party should assess many sources of information including the relatively recent financial statements of the company. Although these statements provide historical data, such data are important in making future cash flow predictions. Assessing financial statements is not an easy task because they contain highly summarized information. One phase involves evaluating the data presented in the financial statements. This includes earnings per share and financial statement analysis, which are the topics of this chapter. This chapter is organized as follows:

Part A: Earnings per Share (EPS)

1. Fundamentals of earnings per share.
2. Types of capital structure for EPS purposes.
3. Computing EPS with a simple capital structure.
4. Computing EPS with a complex capital structure.
5. Reporting earnings per share.
6. Additional issues in EPS computations.

Part B: Financial Statement Analysis

1. Overview of financial statement analysis.
2. Comparative financial statements and percentage analysis.
3. Ratio analysis.
4. Interpretation and Use of Ratio Analysis.
5. Interim and segment reporting.

Supplement 22–A: Dilution/Antidilution D/A Test—Combinations Approach

Supplement 22–B: Segment (or Line of Business) Reporting and Discontinued Operations

PART A: EARNINGS PER SHARE (EPS)

Fundamentals of Earnings per Share

From a long-term perspective the four most important financial measures of the success of a company are return on investment, cash flows, debt-equity, and earnings per share. First, we consider earnings per share (EPS) because *(a)* it is specifically required by GAAP, and *(b)* it is perceived as the single most important **ratio** by many users of financial statements. It is viewed by investors as a broad indicator of probable future cash flows and can be used as a basis for comparison among companies.

Earnings per share (EPS) applies only to common stock.[1] For many years EPS amounts were computed and reported in various ways on an optional basis. *APB Opinion 9,* "Reporting the Results of Operations" (1966), recommended, but did not require, that EPS be disclosed in the statement of income. *APB Opinion 15,* "Earnings per Share," issued in 1969, changed the recommendation to a requirement. This complex *Opinion* is supplemented by a 186-page *Interpretation.*[2] The discussions and illustrations that follow focus on *APB Opinion 15* and the *Interpretation.*[3]

Earnings per share, in conformity with *APB Opinion 15,* is reported in the statement of income as follows:

Earnings per common share:	
Income before extraordinary items	$5.00
Extraordinary gain (loss)	(.50)
Net income	$4.50

The sale of common stock creates assets (almost always cash) that can be used by the enterprise, and essentially earnings per share is a measure of how well management uses those assets during the specified reporting periods. The basic equation for computing EPS is:

$$\frac{\text{Income} - \text{Dividend claim of preferred stock}}{\text{Average number of common shares outstanding}} = \text{EPS}$$

The income amount is net of income tax. The numerator in the equation applies only to common stock. Therefore, dividends on preferred stock must be subtracted because the preferred stockholders have a dividend preference before dividends can be paid to the common stockholders. This means that preferred dividends must be deducted if:

a. Dividends on **noncumulative** preferred stock have been declared on the preferred stock (if not declared they are lost to those stockholders), or

---

[1] For an evaluation of EPS in terms of the qualitative characteristics described in *FASB Statement of Financial Accounting Concepts No. 2,* see Lola Woodward Dudley, "A Critical Look at EPS," *Journal of Accountancy,* August 1985, pp. 102–11.

[2] J. T. Ball, *Computing Earnings per Share,* AICPA, *Unofficial Accounting Interpretations of APB Opinion 15.*

[3] *FASB Standard No. 21,* "Suspension of the Reporting of Earnings per Share and Segment Information by Nonpublic Enterprises" (Stamford, Conn., April 1978), suspended the EPS reporting requirement for most closely held corporations.

b. Dividends have or have not been declared on **cumulative** preferred stock (these dividends are not lost by those stockholders). Regardless of the number of years for which cumulative preferred dividends are in arrears, **only the current year's preferred dividend is subtracted from income** (in the numerator of the EPS computation) because EPS relates to the income of only one year (the dividends of prior years were considered in computing the EPS of those prior years). When the year shows a **loss,** the preferred dividend requirement for that year is **added** to the loss in the EPS computation.

To maintain consistency with the numerator (i.e., income is earned throughout the year) the denominator in the equation must be the weighted-average number of common shares outstanding during the period when the income was earned. The average must be computed for each year in which the number of shares outstanding changes. Changes in the number of shares outstanding are caused by the *(a)* issuance of additional common shares, *(b)* purchase of treasury stock, *(c)* stock dividends, and *(d)* stock splits.

To illustrate how the average number of shares outstanding is computed, consider a simple case for a corporation that had the following changes in common shares outstanding:

	Shares
January 1, 19A, outstanding	10,000
July 1, 19A, issued additional shares	5,000
October 1, 19A, purchased treasury stock	(2,000)
December 31, 19A, outstanding	13,000

The average number of shares outstanding for 19A is computed as follows:

Inclusive dates	**Shares outstanding**	**Months outstanding**	**Weighted shares outstanding**
Jan. 1–June 30	10,000	6	60,000
July 1–Sept. 30	15,000	3	45,000
Oct. 1–Dec. 31	13,000	3	39,000
		12	144,000

Average number of shares outstanding: 144,000 ÷ 12 = 12,000.

Stock dividends, stock splits, and reverse splits are given special treatment in EPS computations. The new shares of stock they create are subdivisions of previously outstanding stock. Therefore, when stock dividends, stock splits, or reverse splits increase or decrease shares outstanding during the period, computation of the average number of shares of common stock outstanding should give **retroactive** restatement to the change in capital structure. The computation should not weight the additional shares of common stock created by the fraction of the period they were outstanding. Instead, the computed average number of shares outstanding is based on the assumption that the additional shares of common stock created by the stock dividend or split were **outstanding throughout the reporting period** regardless of when the stock dividend or split occurred.

Therefore, all actual shares outstanding prior to the issuance of any common

Exhibit 22–1

Computation of weighted-average number of shares of common stock outstanding when stock dividends and stock splits occur.

Case A—Stock Dividend:

1. Illustrative data for year, 19X:

	Shares
Common shares outstanding, January 1–March 31	10,000
April 1, 19X, sold and issued common shares	1,000
Shares outstanding, April 1–May 31	11,000
June 1, 19X, issued a 100% stock dividend	11,000
Shares outstanding, June 1–August 31	22,000
September 1, 19X, sold and issued common shares	2,000
Shares outstanding, September 1–December 31	24,000

2. Computation of the weighted-average common shares outstanding (including a stock dividend):

Inclusive dates	Actual shares outstanding	Retroactive restatement for stock dividend on June 1		Equivalent shares outstanding	Months outstanding		Weighted shares outstanding
Jan. 1–March 31	10,000	× 2	=	20,000	× 3	=	60,000
April 1–May 31	11,000	× 2	=	22,000	× 2	=	44,000
June 1–August 31	22,000*		=	22,000	× 3	=	66,000
Sept. 1–Dec. 31	24,000*		=	24,000	× 4	=	96,000
Totals					12		266,000

Weighted-average number of shares outstanding: 266,000 ÷ 12 = 22,167.

* These numbers already include the stock dividend.

Case B—Stock Dividend, Treasury Stock, and Stock Split:†

1. Illustrative data for year, 19X:

	Shares
Common shares outstanding, January 1–February 24	100,000
February 25, 19X, issued a 5% stock dividend	5,000
Shares outstanding, February 25–March 20	105,000
March 21, 19X, purchased treasury stock	(525)
Shares outstanding, March 21–October 8	104,475
October 9, 19X, sold and issued common shares	10,000
Shares outstanding, October 9–November 20	114,475
November 21, 19X, split the common stock—2 shares issued for each share turned in	114,475
Shares outstanding, November 21–December 31	228,950

† Adapted from J. T. Ball, *Computing Earnings per Share*, AICPA, *Unofficial Interpretations of APB Opinion 15*, p. 114.

shares in a stock dividend or split are restated retroactively, for the effect of any stock dividends or splits, to **year-end equivalent shares outstanding.** Then the year-end equivalent shares are weighted by the fraction of the period they were outstanding. Stock dividends and stock splits have the same effect on EPS computations. Therefore, no distinction is made between them for this purpose.

Similarly, in reporting EPS for **comparative financial statements,** prior years' EPS amounts are recomputed based on the most recent year's capital structure. In other words, all stock dividends or splits are restated retroactively for all

210
12
420
210
2500
16500
2500
14000

Exhibit 22–1
(concluded)

2. Computation of the weighted-average common shares outstanding (including a stock dividend, treasury stock, and a stock split):

Inclusive dates	Actual shares outstanding	Retroactive restatement: Stock dividend	Retroactive restatement: Stock split	Equivalent shares outstanding	Days outstanding	Weighted shares outstanding
January 1–February 24	100,000	× 1.05	× 2 =	210,000	× 55	= 11,550,000
February 25–March 20............	105,000*		× 2 =	210,000	× 24	= 5,040,000
March 21–October 8	104,475*		× 2 =	208,950	× 202	= 42,207,900
October 9–November 20	114,475*		× 2 =	228,950	× 43	= 9,844,850
November 21–December 31	228,950‡				× 41	= 9,386,950
Totals					365	78,029,700

Weighted-average number of common shares outstanding: 78,029,700 ÷ 365 = 213,780.

‡ Already includes effect of stock dividend and stock split.
* Already includes effect of stock dividend.

prior years reported as though they were outstanding throughout all the periods reported.

Two cases are presented in **Exhibit 22–1** to illustrate computation of the average number of common shares outstanding when stock dividends (Case A) or splits (Case B) occur.

In Exhibit 22–1, Case A, the 100% stock dividend occurred on June 1. Therefore, each share outstanding **before** that date is restated retroactively to two shares. This restatement enables the corporation to relate its earnings for the year to the current capital structure at the year-end date. The shares outstanding **after** the June 1 stock dividend are **not** retroactively restated because shares outstanding subsequent to that date **already reflect the stock dividend.**

In Case B, the February 25 stock dividend requires restatement of actual shares outstanding from January 1 through February 24. The November 21 stock split requires restatement of all actual shares outstanding before that date (but not after the date), including the shares restated for the February 25 stock dividend.

Now that you have an understanding of the fundamentals of EPS computations, the more complex issues will be discussed.

Types of Capital Structure for EPS Purposes

APB Opinion 15 identifies two different types of capital structures and prescribes different EPS presentations for each. A capital structure's classification depends on the existence of **potentially dilutive securities. Dilution** occurs when EPS is **reduced** on the **assumption** that convertible securities, such as convertible preferred stock or convertible bonds, have been converted to common stock, or that options and warrants have been exercised. **Antidilution** is the opposite effect; that is, an **increase** in EPS. Antidilutive securities are **excluded** from all earnings per share computations. In contrast, all dilutive securities are **included.**

The two types of capital structure are as follows:

1. **Simple capital structure**—The stockholders' equity either *(a)* consists **only of common stock** or *(b)* **includes no potentially dilutive securities** that on their conversion or exercise could in the aggregate **dilute** (i.e., **decrease**) earnings per common share. For **simple capital structures,** the *Opinion* prescribes a single EPS presentation as follows (amounts assumed):[4]

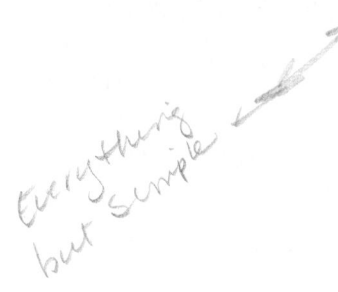

Earnings per common share:	
Income before extraordinary items	$1.50
Extraordinary loss	(.11)
Net income	$1.39

2. **Complex capital structure**—Complex capital structures include **all** capital structures except those described above as simple. A capital structure is complex if the corporation has outstanding convertible securities or rights that are **potentially dilutive** to EPS. Dilutive securities that may increase the outstanding shares of common stock include: *(a)* convertible preferred stock; *(b)* convertible bonds payable; and *(c)* stock rights, stock options, stock warrants, and other securities that provide for the conversion into or purchase of common stock. For **complex capital structures,** *APB Opinion 15* prescribes a **dual EPS presentation** that reports the dilutive effects in two sets of EPS amounts as follows (amounts assumed):

	Primary EPS	Fully diluted EPS
Income before extraordinary items	$1.40	$1.25
Extraordinary loss	(.10)	(.09)
Net income	$1.30	$1.16

Basically, EPS is computed by dividing periodic income associated with common stock by the average number of common shares outstanding during the period. However, depending on the corporation's capital structure, income (i.e., the numerator) and average number of shares (i.e., the denominator) often must be adjusted for certain items. *APB Opinion 15* provides specific guidelines concerning these items. **The basic guideline is that when either the denominator or numerator is changed the other one must also be changed if there are any related effects.**

Computing EPS with a Simple Capital Structure

A simple capital structure may include (1) only common stock (including fully paid subscribed common stock) or (2) common stock and **nonconvertible** preferred stock. The illustrations given in Chapter 3 involved simple capital struc-

[4] *APB Opinion 15* does not require EPS amounts for extraordinary items. These amounts may be deduced by taking the difference between EPS for income before extraordinary items and EPS for net income. We present EPS for all three income amounts because the *Opinion* recommends their presentation as a convenience to statement users, and companies usually report all three EPS amounts when they have extraordinary gains and losses. When there has been discontinued operations another line is added.

Exhibit 22–2
EPS computations for a simple capital structure with nonconvertible preferred stock.

Panel A—Case Data for Jade Corporation, 19C:

1. Capital stock:

Common stock, par $1, outstanding on January 1, 19C	90,000 shares
Common stock sold and issued on May 1, 19C	6,000 shares
Preferred stock, par $20, 6%, cumulative, nonconvertible, nonparticipating; outstanding throughout 19C	2,500 shares

2. Income data for the year ended December 31, 19C:

Income before extraordinary items	$124,000
Extraordinary gain (net of income tax)	10,000
Net income	134,000
Average income tax rate for 19C, 40%.	

Panel B—EPS Preliminary Computations:

1. For numerator (income):
   Preferred dividend claim, for current year only, 19C:
   $50,000 (total par value; 2,500 shares × $20) × 6% (dividend preference rate) = $3,000.

2. For denominator (shares):
   Computation of weighted-average number of common shares outstanding during 19C:

Inclusive dates	Actual shares outstanding	Months outstanding	Weighted shares outstanding
January 1–April 30, shares outstanding	90,000	× 4	360,000
May 1, sold additional shares	6,000		
May 1–December 31, shares outstanding	96,000	× 8	768,000
December 31, shares outstanding	96,000		
Totals		12	1,128,000

Weighted-average number of shares outstanding during 19C, 1,128,000 ÷ 12 = 94,000.

Panel C—Earnings per Common Share (for a simple capital structure):

Earnings per common share outstanding:

Income before extraordinary items: ($124,000 − $3,000* = $121,000) ÷ 94,000 shares*	$1.29
Extraordinary gain: $10,000 ÷ 94,000 shares	.11
Net income: ($134,000 − $3,000* = $131,000) ÷ 94,000 shares	$1.39

*Panel B, 1. Notice that the nonconvertible preferred stock effects were excluded from both the numerator and the denominator.

tures. **Exhibit 22–2** shows the computation of EPS for a simple capital structure that has **nonconvertible** preferred stock.

Computing EPS with a Complex Capital Structure

Corporations with **complex capital structures,** that is, those that do not meet the definition of a simple capital structure, must present two sets of EPS data with equal prominence on the statement of income. *APB Opinion 15* describes these two sets as follows:

1. **Primary EPS** is based on the outstanding common shares plus dilutive common stock equivalents (CSEs), which are securities that *(a)* have a dilutive effect and *(b)* are, in substance, equivalent to common shares.[5]

[5] Any reduction of EPS from dilutive securities of **less than 3%** in the aggregate may, but need not, be considered as dilution in the computation and presentation of EPS discussed throughout

2. **Fully diluted EPS** reflects the **maximum dilution** of EPS that would have occurred if all contingent issuances of common stock, that would individually reduce EPS, had taken place at the beginning of the period (or time of issuance of the convertible security, if later). Therefore, it includes the effects of common shares, CSEs, and all other dilutive securities.

The EPS relationships among simple and complex capital structures are shown below:

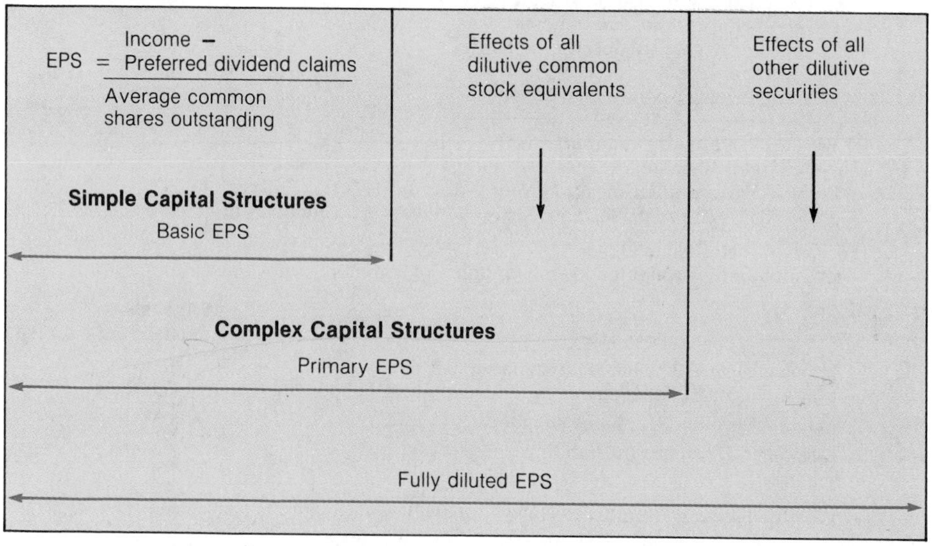

Notice in the above diagram that primary EPS is an extension of basic EPS, and fully diluted EPS is an extension of primary EPS.

The computations of primary and fully diluted EPS are extensive. As an advance guideline these computations are outlined in **Exhibit 22–3.** Frequent reference to this overview will be helpful.

To determine whether a security or a stock right is a CSE and to compute the number of equivalent shares for EPS purposes, separate consideration must be given to the following two categories that may increase the number of shares in the denominator:

a. **Equity contracts**—common stock rights, options, warrants, and other common stock purchase contracts, and subscribed common stock, if not fully paid.
b. **Convertible securities**—securities convertible to common shares such as convertible preferred stock and convertible bonds payable.

---

the *Opinion*. This optional test is based on materiality. It is applied in practice on the "net income" line for EPS. There are two independent tests: (1) the difference between *(a)* EPS ignoring all dilutive securities and *(b)* primary EPS, and (2) the difference between *(a)* EPS ignoring all dilutive securities and *(b)* fully diluted EPS. Example: EPS ignoring all dilutive securities, $1; and primary EPS, 98 cents; because the difference is less than 3%, the corporation may report either 98 cents or $1 as primary EPS. Fully diluted EPS, 97 cents; difference 3%, must report fully diluted EPS of 97 cents.

Exhibit 22–3 Overview of EPS computations (discussion to follow).

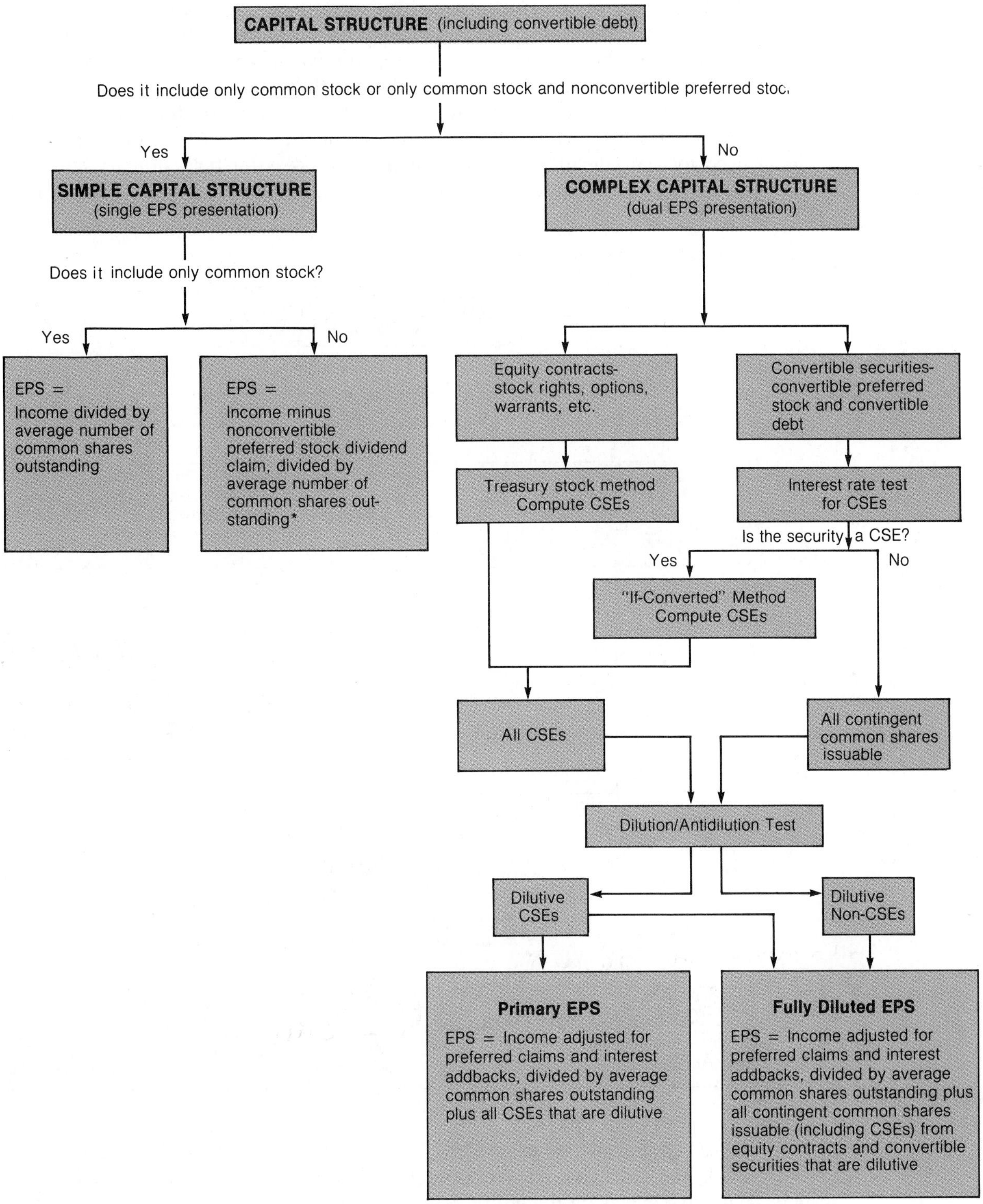

* If the preferred stock is cumulative, deduct the dividends for the current year whether declared or not; if noncumulative, deduct for current year only if declared during the current year.

If either an equity contract or a contract for a convertible security is classified as a dilutive CSE, it **is assumed to have been converted to common stock at the beginning of the current reporting period** (or at its issuance date during this period, if later) and will be included in computing both primary and fully diluted EPS. These two categories (i.e., equity contracts and convertible securities) must be considered separately because they have different characteristics. As a result, their effects on the computation of EPS are different. However, either category may result in an increase in the number of common shares used to compute EPS. The computational process for both primary and fully diluted EPS is outlined below based on the case data given in **Exhibit 22–4.**

EPS computations summarized.

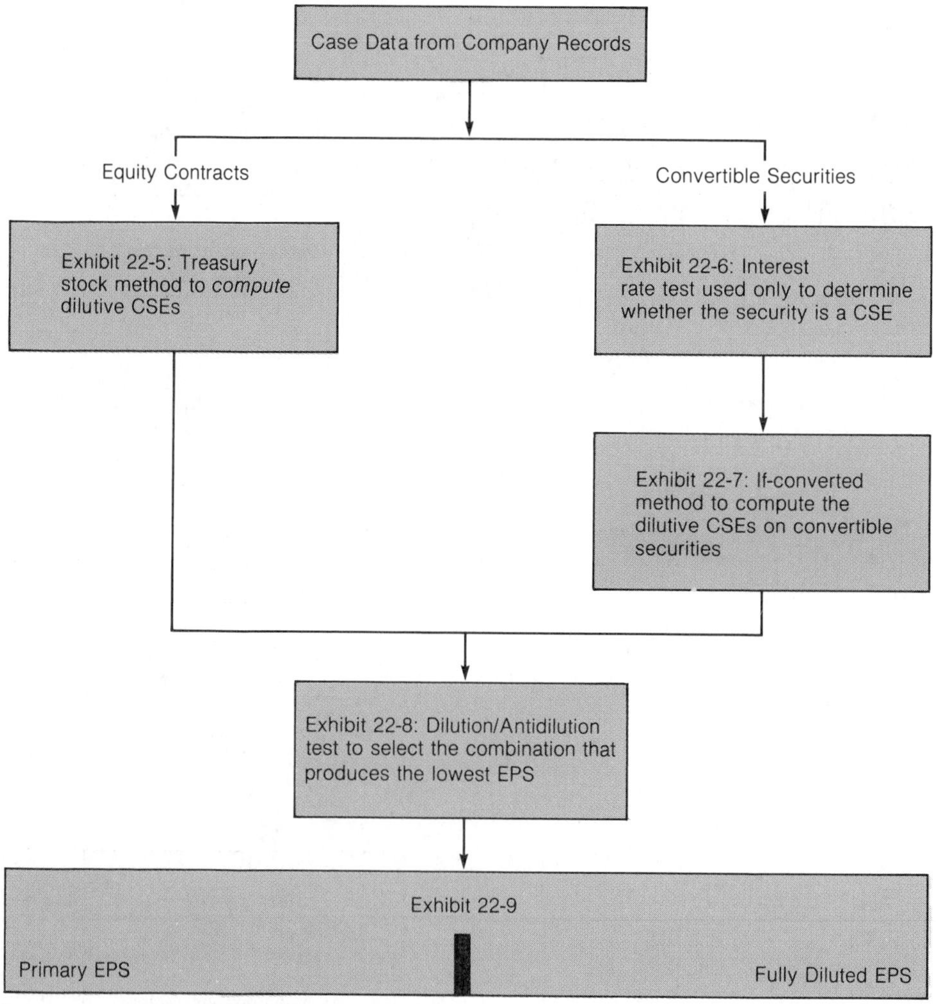

Equity Contracts—Treasury Stock Method. Common stock rights, subscribed stock, and other common stock purchase contracts, if exercise is assumed, would have two effects on the entity: *(a)* an increase in the number of common shares

Exhibit 22–4
Case data for computing EPS for a complex capital structure—Jade Corporation, 19C.

Panel A—Case Data (repeated for convenience from Exhibit 22–2):

1. Capitals stock:	
Common stock, par $1, outstanding on January 1, 19C	90,000 shares
Common stock sold and issued on May 1, 19C	6,000 shares
Nonconvertible preferred stock, par $20, 6%, cumulative, nonparticipating; outstanding throughout 19C	2,500 shares
2. Income data for the year ended December 31, 19C:	
Income before extraordinary items	$124,000
Extraordinary gain (net of income tax)	10,000
Net income	134,000
Average income tax rate for 19C, 40%.	

Panel B—Additional Case Data (for a complex capital structure):

1. Stock rights:	
a. Outstanding for common shares	2,000 shares
b. Exercise (option) price per share of common stock	$ 20
c. Average market price per share of common stock during the reporting period, 19C	25
d. Market price per share of common stock at end of the reporting period, 19C	25
2. Convertible securities (in addition to the nonconvertible securities listed in panel A):	
a. Convertible preferred stock, nopar, $7 annual dividend per share, cumulative, nonparticipating; each preferred share is convertible to 8 shares of common stock; outstanding throughout the year, 1,000 shares; issue price, $108 per share ..	$108,000
b. Series A convertible bonds payable, $200,000, 8% payable anually; each $1,000 bond is convertible to 30 shares of common stock; issue price at par*	200,000
c. Series B convertible bonds payable, $500,000, 10% payable annually; each $1,000 bond is convertible to 50 shares of common stock; issue price at par*	500,000
As a corporate bond interest rate at dates of issuance of all convertible securities	12.6%

* The bonds were assumed to have been sold at par for instructional convenience.

outstanding, and *(b)* usually an increase in the cash of the corporation because their exercise usually requires a cash payment by the investor. Therefore, to be consistent with the **assumed** exercise of the equity contracts, an assumption also must be made regarding the concurrent use of the **assumed** cash inflow. That is, the corporation could use the cash inflow to acquire additional income-generating assets, to retire debt, or to acquire treasury stock. *APB Opinion 15* selected the latter; therefore, it specifies an assumption called the **treasury stock method.** To compute the increase in the number of common shares caused by the "as if" exercise of the equity contracts, the treasury stock method **assumes that the corporation would apply any cash proceeds from exercise of the stock rights to purchase treasury common stock** (see exception discussed below).

The treasury stock method can be explained by an example. If outstanding stock rights entitle their owners to purchase 2,000 common shares for $20 per share, exercise of these stock rights would result in a $40,000 (i.e., 2,000 × $20) cash inflow. If the market value of the company's common stock is $25 per share (indicating that exercise is likely because the option price is less than the market price), the company could use the proceeds to purchase 1,600 (i.e., $40,000 ÷ $25) of its own common shares (i.e., treasury stock). Under the treasury stock method, the net increase of 400 shares (i.e., 2,000 − 1,600) is the number of CSE shares **added** to the average number of common shares

Exhibit 22–5
Equity contracts—Treasury stock method to compute common stock equivalents (CSEs)—Jade Corporation, 19C.

	Shares
Shares that would be issued upon exercise of rights (Exhibit 22–4, panel B)	2,000
Cash proceeds if rights were exercised, 2,000 rights × $20 (option price) = $40,000.	
Treasury stock shares that could be purchased, $40,000 ÷ $25 (average market price)	(1,600)
Common stock equivalent (i.e., incremental number of common shares that would be outstanding	400 CSEs

outstanding in the **denominator** of the EPS calculation, thereby decreasing EPS. This **application of the treasury stock method** to the stock rights of Jade Corporation, based on the data given in Exhibit 22–4, is illustrated in **Exhibit 22–5.**

The stock rights were **dilutive** because they increased the number of "as if" shares outstanding by 400 and no dollar amount to "match" those shares was added to income in the numerator.

In contrast, if the average market price of the common stock during the reporting period had been **less** than the option price, the above computation, if made, would have **reduced** the number of shares outstanding and the effect on the computed EPS amount would have been **antidilutive** (i.e., it would have caused EPS to increase). In that case, the stock rights would have been excluded because *Opinion 15* does not permit the use of CSEs in EPS computations if the CSEs have an **antidilutive effect.**[6] **Therefore, the treasury stock method automatically excludes antidilutive equity contracts.**

The *Opinion* specifies a variation of the treasury stock method when the number of shares of common stock that can be purchased as treasury stock, due to exercise of outstanding stock rights, **exceeds 20%** of the number of common shares outstanding at the end of the period. In these situations, the assumed cash inflow would be applied in two steps:

1. First, apply the cash to an "as if" repurchase of common shares at the average market price, but not in excess of 20% of the outstanding shares.
2. Apply the balance of the cash to *(a)* an "as if" reduction of any short-term or long-term debt outstanding, and then, to *(b)* an "as if" purchase of investments in U.S. government securities or commercial paper (i.e., debt securities). In these situations, the "as if" **net-of-tax interest** effect, which would accompany the reduction of debt and/or purchase of interest-bearing securities, must be added back to income in the **numerator** of the EPS computation.

In Exhibit 22–5 the 2,000 additional common shares that would be issued on exercise of the rights are less than 20% of the 96,000 common shares outstand-

[6] *APB Opinion 15*, par. 36, recommends that assumption of exercise not be reflected in EPS data until the market price of the common stock has exceeded the exercise or option price for substantially all of three consecutive months ending with the last month of the period to which EPS data relate.

ing at the end of the period (i.e., less than 19,200 shares). Therefore, the full amount of the assumed proceeds from exercise of the rights in this example is applied to the "as if" purchase of treasury stock.

Convertible Securities—Interest Rate Test. **Convertible preferred stock and convertible debt securities** usually provide that the holder, under specified conditions, may convert them to common shares. Thus, they may constitute CSEs when issued. *FASB Standard 85* specifies that convertible securities are considered common stock equivalents if the **effective yield** interest rate to the holder **at time of issuance** is significantly below what would be a comparable rate for a similar security of the issuer without the conversion option. To illustrate a convertible security that is a CSE, assume a corporation can sell a new issue of nonconvertible bonds at a 13% annual interest rate. However, the same bonds, **if convertible** to common stock, would be marketable at an 8% annual interest rate. The 5% difference in interest rates measures the value of the conversion privilege. In this example, the convertible bonds probably would qualify as CSEs.

In actual cases, the interest rate without the conversion privilege (e.g., 13% in the above example) would not be known. Therefore, the average **"Aa" corporate bond interest rate** is used for the benchmark to determine whether a convertible security is a CSE.[7] This is called the **interest rate test,** and it is used **only** to determine whether a convertible security is a CSE.

Under the **interest rate test,** a convertible security should be considered as a CSE at the time of issuance if, based on its market price, it has an **effective yield interest rate** which is **less than two-thirds of the then current Aa corporate bond interest rate.**[8] The "effective yield" interest rate is based on the security's stated annual interest rate or dividend payments and any original issuance premium or discount.[9] If the security does not have a stated maturity date, effective yield is the security's stated annual interest or dividend payment divided by its market price at issuance. The effective interest rate for bonds issued at a premium or discount can be computed as shown in Exhibit 15–10 (page 678). If bonds or preferred stock are issued at par, the effective interest rate and the stated interest rate are the same. If issued at a discount, the effective rate is higher than the stated rate, and if issued at a premium, the effective rate is lower than the stated rate.

---

[7] *FASB Standard 85,* "Determining Whether a Convertible Security Is a Common Stock Equivalent" (an amendment of *APB Opinion 15,* February 1982, par. 5), states that "In recent years, the bank prime interest rate has been more volatile than it was in years preceding the issuance of *Opinion 15,*" and in par. 7 that "The phrase 'bank prime interest rate' in paragraph 33 of *Opinion 15* is deleted and replaced by 'average Aa corporate bond yield.' " The **average** bond yield is based on bond yields for a brief period of time, such as one week, including or immediately preceding the date of issuance of the security being tested. *FASB Standard 85* became effective for issues after February 28, 1982.

[8] If no market price of the convertible security is available, this test should be based on the "fair" value of the security. If there is a scheduled change in the interest rate or dividend rate during the first five years after issuance, the lowest scheduled rate should be used (*APB Opinion 15,* par. 33).

[9] Any call premium or discount must also be included in the computation of the effective yield. The effective yield is the lowest of yield to maturity and the yields to all call dates (*FASB Standard 85,* par. 3).

Exhibit 22–6
Convertible securities—interest rate test to identify CSEs—Jade Corporation, 19C.

	Effective rate	Decision
1. Aa bond interest rate for comparison (Exhibit 22–4, panel B), 12.6% × ⅔	8.4%	
2. Effective yield on convertible securities (Exhibit 22–4, panel B):		
a. Convertible preferred stock, issued at $108: (Dividend, 1,000 shares × $7) ÷ (Issue price, $108,000)	6.5%	Lower, CSE
b. Series A convertible bonds payable, issued at par:* (Interest, $200,000 × 8%) ÷ (Issue price, $200,000) . . .	8.0%	Lower, CSE
c. Series B convertible bonds payable, issued at par:* (Interest, $500,000 × 10%) ÷ (Issue price, $500,000) . .	10.0%	Higher, not CSE

* Debt securities issued at a premium or discount are illustrated in a later section.

The **interest rate test** to determine whether a convertible security is a CSE is illustrated in **Exhibit 22–6** (based on the data given in Exhibit 22–4, panel B).

In Exhibit 22–6, application of the interest rate test shows that the convertible preferred stock and the series A convertible bonds payable are CSEs. It also shows that the series B convertible bonds are **not** CSEs. The interest rate test is a pragmatic solution to the problem of defining a CSE for **convertible securities.** A convertible security bought to yield less than two thirds of the Aa corporate bond interest rate may well have been acquired more for the potential appreciation of the underlying common stock than for its debt features (e.g., annual yield).[10] Therefore, its conversion feature was an important factor in the total consideration paid for it. If the security was purchased primarily for this conversion feature, then it is reasonable to assume that (at least at the date of its issuance) the security is "likely" to be converted to common stock.

Convertible Securities—If-Converted Method. The interest rate test is used **only** to determine whether a convertible security is a CSE. It does not measure the **number** of CSEs represented by the security. **If the interest rate test is met, the number of common stock equivalents related to the convertible security is computed using the if-converted method.** This method assumes the following:

a. The CSE convertible security is converted to common shares at the beginning of the reporting period (or at time of issuance, if later); **the CSE shares are added to the denominator** in the EPS computation.

b. The "as if" reduction in a **convertible debt** security would cause a reduction in interest expense because reported income was reduced by the amount of aftertax interest expense on the debt. Therefore, the conversion assumption requires that the interest, net of income tax, be added back to income (i.e., **added to the numerator** in the EPS computation).

c. In the case of CSE **convertible preferred stock,** the CSE shares are added to the denominator. In addition, preferred dividend claims are **not** de-

[10] Note that the effective yield is based on **pretax yield** because the Aa bond interest rate is pretax.

Exhibit 22–7
Convertible securities—If-converted method to compute CSEs—Jade Corporation, 19C.

	Shares
1. Convertible securities that qualify as CSEs (Exhibit 22–6):	
a. Convertible preferred stock (Exhibit 22–4, panel B), (1,000 × 8)	8,000
b. Series A convertible bonds payable (Exhibit 22–4, panel B): ($200,000 ÷ $1,000) × 30	6,000
2. Convertible securities that did not qualify as CSEs (Exhibit 22–9):	
c. Series B convertible bonds payable (Exhibit 22–4, panel B): ($500,000 ÷ $1,000) × 50	25,000

Note: CSEs from the convertible preferred stock and series A convertible bonds will be used to compute primary and fully diluted EPS. Series B convertible bonds (if-converted shares, 25,000) will be used only in fully diluted EPS. All are subject to the D/A test shown in Exhibit 22–8.

ducted from the numerator because if conversion is assumed at the beginning of the current period, the preferred stock would have no such claim.

In **Exhibit 22–7,** the if-converted method is illustrated for the convertible securities of Jade Corporation.

Fully Diluted EPS

APB Opinion 15 requires companies to present **fully diluted EPS,** which is the lowest amount of EPS the company would report if **all its dilutive outstanding equity contracts** (e.g., stock rights, options, warrants, etc.) **and convertible securities were assumed to be converted to common stock.** Thus, **in addition** to CSE securities whose conversion to common stock was assumed for computation of primary EPS, computation of fully diluted EPS also must consider convertible securities that were not classified as CSEs. The purpose of this consideration is to show the lowest possible EPS amount. Determination of this "lowest possible" EPS amount is related to the concept of dilution/antidilution (D/A).

Most of the methods involved in the computation of fully diluted EPS, including such computations as the number of if-converted shares and the amount of interest (net of tax) to add back to the numerator of the EPS computation, are the same in the computation of fully diluted EPS as in the computation of primary EPS. However, in applying the **treasury stock method** to equity securities to compute fully diluted EPS, the **ending market price** per share of stock is substituted for the average market price used for primary EPS if the ending market price is higher. Thus, when the ending market price is higher, fully diluted EPS is reduced below primary EPS by use of the treasury stock method because less "treasury stock" would be purchased.

In the illustration of EPS calculations for Jade Corporation, the average market price and the ending market price of Jades' common stock are assumed to be equal for instructional convenience (Exhibit 22–4, panel B). Therefore, the treasury stock method gives identical results for both primary and fully diluted EPS. Application of the treasury stock method with fully diluted EPS is discussed later.

Dilution/Antidilution (D/A)

Dilution/antidilution (D/A) must be considered **only with complex capital structures;** that is, for primary and fully diluted EPS. **Dilution** means a **decrease** in EPS amounts resulting from **equity contracts or convertible securities.** The equity contracts and convertible securities that cause this effect are called **dilutive**

Exhibit 22–8
Dilution/antidilution (D/A) test—short-cut approach—Jade Corporation, 19C.

Panel A—Six Implementation Steps

1. Determine net income to **common stockholders** (i.e., net income minus all preferred dividend claims).
2. Determine whether equity contracts (e.g., stock rights, options, warrants) are dilutive.
3. Compute Tentative EPS, that is, EPS based upon net income to common stockholders and assuming the conversion of all **dilutive equity contracts** to common stock.* "Income to common stockholders" used in this computation should be the higher of *(a)* income before extraordinary items or *(b)* net income. Use of the higher amount increases the probability of identifying a dilutive security.
4. Compute the D/A ratio amount for each convertible security. Then rank the respective D/A ratio amounts from lowest to highest.
   The D/A ratio amount for each convertible security is computed as follows:

$$\text{D/A ratio} = \frac{\text{Effect of assumed conversion on numerator of EPS}}{\text{Effect of assumed conversion on denominator of EPS}} = \frac{\text{Interest expense (net of tax) or preferred dividend amount}}{\text{Number of common shares into which the security can be converted}}$$

5. For **primary EPS,** consider **only** convertible securities which are **CSEs.**
   a. Compare the lowest D/A ratio amount to Tentative EPS (computed in step 3). This comparison determines whether this first convertible security is dilutive or antidilutive. The security is dilutive if its D/A ratio amount is less than Tentative EPS. It is antidilutive if its D/A ratio amount is greater than Tentative EPS. If **dilutive,** assume conversion of the security to common stock, and compute a new Tentative EPS. Compare this new Tentative EPS with the next larger D/A ratio amount. Repeat this process until an antidilutive security is found or until the list of convertible securities is exhausted.
   b. If the security is antidilutive, the D/A test for primary EPS is complete. All remaining convertible securities have higher D/A ratio amounts and, hence, are antidilutive.
   c. Primary EPS is the last Tentative EPS amount computed in step 5*a* above.
6. For **fully diluted EPS,** again perform step 4, starting with the same beginning Tentative EPS amount computed in step 3. This time, however, the comparison of D/A ratio amounts and Tentative EPS amounts involves all convertible securities (i.e., CSEs and nonCSEs). The D/A test for fully diluted EPS is complete when an antidilutive security is found. Fully diluted EPS is the last Tentative EPS amount computed.

* Equity contracts are treated differently from convertible securities in the D/A test. The common shares associated with dilutive equity contracts are included in the computation of Tentative EPS because equity contracts usually directly affect only the denominator of the EPS computation. In contrast, the assumed conversion of convertible securities affects both the numerator and the denominator.

securities. Antidilution means an **increase** in EPS amounts caused by **antidilutive** equity contracts or convertible securities. **To attain the maximum dilutive effect on EPS (a goal based on conservatism), *APB Opinion 15* requires that all antidilutive securities be excluded and all dilutive securities be included in computing both primary (if a CSE) and fully diluted EPS amounts** (also see Supplement 22–A).

Footnote 8 of *APB Opinion 15* identifies one exception to this general rule; it states:

> The presence of a common stock equivalent or other dilutive securities together with income from continuing operations and extraordinary items may result in diluting one of the per share amounts which are required to be disclosed on the face of the income statement—i.e., . . . income before extraordinary items, . . . and net income—while increasing another. In such a case, the common stock equivalent or other dilutive securities should be recognized for all computations even though they have an antidilutive effect on one of the per share amounts.

Because of this provision, the D/A test should be made on the **higher** of *(a)* income before extraordinary items or *(b)* net income. If the lower amount were

Exhibit 22–8
(concluded)

Panel B—Implementation of the Dilution/Antidilution (D/A) Test

1. Net income to common stockholders [$134,000 − ($50,000 × 6%) − (1,000 shares × $7)] = $124,000.
2. Stock rights are dilutive because they increase the number of shares of common stock (denominator) used to compute EPS by 400 shares (Exhibit 22–5).
3. Tentative EPS [$124,000 ÷ 94,400 shares (94,000 shares, Exhibit 22–2, panel B + 400 shares)] = $1.31.
4. D/A ratios of all convertible securities for ranking:

	Ratio amount	Rank order for later use
a. Convertible preferred stock [(1,000 shares × $7) ÷ 8,000 shares]	$ .88	1
b. Series A convertible bonds [($200,000 × 8% × .60*) ÷ 6,000 shares]	1.60	3
c. Series B convertible bonds [($500,000 × 10% × .60*) ÷ 25,000 shares]	1.20	2

5. Primary EPS—Comparison of D/A ratio amounts to tentative EPS amounts considering CSEs only (Exhibit 22–6):
   a. Convertible preferred stock dilutive because D/A ratio amount ($0.88) is less than Tentative EPS ($1.31); new Tentative EPS [$124,000 + (1,000 × $7)] ÷ (94,000 + 8,000 shares) = $1.28.
   b. Series A convertible bonds antidilutive because D/A ratio amount ($1.60) is more than the new Tentative EPS ($1.28).
   c. Therefore, the primary EPS for net income is $1.28
6. Fully diluted EPS—Comparison of D/A ratio amounts to tentative EPS amounts, considering all convertible securities:
   a. Convertible preferred stock dilutive because D/A ratio amount ($0.88) is less than Tentative EPS ($1.31); new Tentative EPS is same as 5*a* above, $1.28.
   b. Series B convertible bonds dilutive because D/A ratio amount ($1.20) is less than new Tentative EPS ($1.28); new Tentative EPS is [$124,000 + (1,000 × $7) + ($500,000 × 10% × .60* = $161,000)] ÷ (94,000 + 400 + 8,000 + 25,000 shares = 127,400 shares) = $1.26.
   c. Series A convertible bonds antidilutive because D/A ratio amount ($1.60) is more than new tentative EPS ($1.26).
   d. Therefore, fully diluted EPS for net income is $1.26

* (1 − tax rate).

used, a security could be labeled incorrectly as antidilutive. D/A must be considered at two levels in EPS computations as follows:

1. **For primary EPS**—A test based on **CSEs only.**
2. **For fully diluted EPS**—A test based on **all** potentially dilutive securities (i.e., all CSEs and non-CSEs).

D/A Test for Primary EPS. Exhibits 22–5 and 22–6 show that three securities qualify as CSEs: the stock rights, convertible preferred stock, and series A convertible bonds payable.

When there is more than one CSE security (as in this case), the D/A effect of a security often depends on the **order** in which the securities are tested for D/A. As a result all possible combinations of the securities should be tested for D/A. The combination yielding the lowest EPS amount should be selected for use in computing primary EPS.

D/A Test for Fully Diluted EPS. Exhibit 22–6 shows that only one potentially dilutive security (i.e., the series B convertible bonds payable) does **not** qualify as a CSE. Therefore, in conducting the D/A test for fully diluted EPS, the series B convertible bonds payable, in addition to the three CSE securities, also must be considered. For fully diluted EPS, the D/A test must **reconsider** the two convertible securities classified as CSEs for computing primary EPS because a security that was dilutive for primary EPS may be antidilutive for fully diluted EPS.

The D/A test for the computation of the EPS of Jade Corporation is presented in **Exhibit 22–8.** Notice that (1) the series A convertible bonds are **antidilutive** for both primary and fully diluted EPS, and (2) the stock rights are included in each computation because they are always dilutive when the common stock price exceeds the option price. The lowest EPS amount is selected for both primary and fully diluted EPS (boxed for emphasis in Exhibit 22–8).

The D/A test can be done by using either the *(a)* short-cut approach or *(b)* combinations approach. The combinations approach involves burdensome calculations that pose cost-benefit and materiality constraints. In contrast, the short-cut approach usually provides reasonable results.[11] The aim of this method is to identify the lowest (i.e., the most dilutive) amounts for primary EPS and fully diluted EPS. The method involves the six steps given in Exhibit 22–8, panel A; panel B shows the implementation of these six steps by Jade Corporation. Supplement 22–A provides a comprehensive illustration of the combinations approach.

Exhibit 22–9 shows how the amounts computed in the prior schedules are brought together to compute primary and fully diluted EPS. Notice the consistency between the denominator and numerator maintained throughout as follows:

Primary EPS (on net income):

	Net income	Nonconvertible preferred dividend	Stock rights	Convertible preferred CSE		
	$134,000 − $3,000 −	$7,000	+ $0 +	$7,000	$\dfrac{\$131,000}{102,400}$	= $1.28 †
	94,000		+ 400 +	8,000		

Fully diluted EPS (on net income):

	From primary EPS	Stock rights	Convertible preferred CSE	Series B convertible bond (non-CSE)		
	$134,000* − $3,000 − $7,000 +	$0 +	$7,000	+ $30,000	$\dfrac{\$161,000}{127,400}$	= $1.26 †
	94,000	400 +	8,000	+ 25,000		

* Includes extraordinary gain of $10,000.
† Agrees with Exhibit 22–8, panel B.

[11] Without this short-cut method, a company with n convertible securities would need to make 2^n calculations to identify the lowest EPS amount. With the short-cut method, only n calculations are needed. See S. Davidson and R. L. Weil, "A Shortcut in Computing Earnings per Share," *Journal of Accountancy*, December 1975, pp. 45–47.

Exhibit 22–9
Computation of primary and fully diluted EPS (complex capital structure)—Jade Corporation, 19C.

Panel A—Primary EPS:

$$\frac{\text{Numerator}}{\text{Denominator}} = \text{EPS}$$

Income before extraordinary items:

$$\frac{\$124{,}000^{(a)} - \$3{,}000^{(b)}}{94{,}000^{(c)} + 400^{(d)} + 8{,}000^{(c)}} = \frac{\$121{,}000}{102{,}400} = \$1.18$$

Extraordinary gain:

$$\frac{\$10{,}000^{(f)}}{102{,}400} = .10$$

Net income:

$$\frac{\$134{,}000^{(g)} - \$3{,}000^{(b)}}{102{,}400} = \frac{\$131{,}000}{102{,}400} = \$1.28$$

Explanation:
(a) Income before extraordinary items (Exhibit 22–4, panel A).
(b) Dividend claim of nonconvertible preferred stock ($50,000 × 6%).
(c) Average number of common shares actually outstanding during the year (Exhibit 22–2, panel B).
(d) CSE shares from stock rights (Exhibit 22–5).
(e) CSE shares from convertible preferred stock (Exhibit 22–7).
(f) Extraordinary gain (Exhibit 22–4, panel A).
(g) Net income (Exhibit 22–4, panel A).
Note: Series B convertible bonds were excluded because they were not CSEs based on the interest rate test (Exhibit 22–6). Series A convertible bonds were excluded because they were antidilutive (Exhibit 22–8).

Panel B—Fully Diluted EPS:

Income before extraordinary items:

$$\frac{\$124{,}000^{(a)} - \$3{,}000^{(a)} = \$30{,}000^{(b)}}{94{,}000^{(a)} + 400^{(a)} + 8{,}000^{(a)} + 25{,}000^{(c)}} = \frac{\$151{,}000}{127{,}400} = \$1.18$$

Extraordinary gain:

$$\frac{\$10{,}000}{127{,}400} = .08$$

Net income:

$$\frac{\$161{,}000}{127{,}400} = \$1.26$$

Explanation:
(a) Panel A. In this example, the CSE securities which were dilutive for primary EPS and also were dilutive for fully diluted EPS.
(b) Interest expense (net of income tax) on series B convertible bonds, Exhibit 22–4 ($500,000 × 10% × .60 = $30,000); added back because it was deducted to compute net income.
(c) If-converted shares from series B convertible bonds; not CSE but dilutive (Exhibits 22–7 and 22–8).
Note: Fully diluted EPS includes *(a)* average common shares actually outstanding, *(b)* all dilutive CSEs, and *(c)* all other common shares that could be issued from dilutive securities (i.e., series B convertible bonds; not CSEs, but dilutive; Exhibits 22–7 and 22–8).

Reporting Earnings per Share

APB Opinion 15, as amended by *FASB Standard 21,* requires that EPS data be "shown on the face of the income statement" for all periods presented by "publicly held" corporations. In addition, the following should be disclosed (paraphrased from *APB Opinion 15,* pars. 19–21):

a. A description, in summary form, that explains the rights and privileges of the various securities outstanding.

b. A schedule or note to explain the bases upon which both primary and fully diluted EPS are calculated.

Exhibit 22–10
Reporting EPS for a complex capital structure.

JADE CORPORATION
Statement of Income (partial)
For the Year Ended December 31, 19C

Income before extraordinary items		$124,000
Extraordinary gain (net of income taxes of $6,667)		10,000
Net income		$134,000
Earnings per share (Note *X*):		
	Primary	**Fully diluted**
Income before extraordinary items	$1.18	$1.18
Extraordinary gain (net of tax)	.10	.08
Net income	$1.28	$1.26

Notes to the financial statements:

Note *X*. EPS amounts were computed in conformity with the provisions of *APB Opinion 15*. Primary EPS includes all dilutive common stock equivalents, based on stock rights and options outstanding (using the treasury stock method) plus those based on convertible securities (using the "if-converted" method). Fully diluted EPS includes all additional contingent common shares that would be issued for all convertible securities that are dilutive; thus, it represents maximum dilution.

The outstanding stock rights, convertible preferred stock, and series A convertible bonds payable were determined to be common stock equivalents; however, the series A convertible bonds had antidilutive effects on both primary and fully diluted EPS and, accordingly, were excluded from consideration as common stock in all EPS computations. The series B convertible bonds, although not common stock equivalents, were included in the computation of fully diluted amounts. The income amounts were adjusted for the interest (net of income taxes) effects of these securities.

The rights and privileges of the stock rights and the convertible securities are explained in the notes related to those items (refer to the statement of financial position).

No shares were issued during the past two years for exercise of stock rights or conversion of convertible securities.

c. All assumptions and any resulting adjustments used in calculating the EPS data.
d. The number of shares issued upon conversion, exercise, or satisfaction of equity contracts during at least the most recent annual accounting period and any subsequent interim period presented.
e. Computations and/or reconciliations as needed to provide a clear understanding of the manner in which the EPS amounts were computed.

The statement of income presentation of the EPS of Jade Corporation for 19C is shown in **Exhibit 22–10.**

Additional Issues in EPS Computations

Effect of Stock Dividends and Stock Splits with Stock Rights and Convertible Securities

When a company issues additional shares of common stock in a stock dividend or a stock split at the time it has stock rights or convertible securities outstanding, the number of shares of common stock represented by the stock rights or convertible securities, as used in EPS computations, must be adjusted for the effect of the stock dividend or split. For example, assume Jade Corporation (Exhibit 22–4, panel A) had split its common stock 2 for 1 during 19C. In this case, the numbers of shares of common stock represented by the outstanding stock rights and convertible securities of Jade would be doubled as shown on p. 1131:

Security	Number of common shares used in EPS computations without 2-for-1 stock split (Exhibits 22–5 and 22–7)	Effect of 2-for-1 stock split		Number of common shares used in EPS computations with 2-for-1 stock split
1. Common stock (Exhibit 22–2, panel B)	94,000	× 2	=	188,000
2. Stock rights	400	× 2	=	800
3. Convertible preferred stock	8,000	× 2	=	16,000
4. Series A convertible bonds payable	6,000	× 2	=	12,000
5. Series B convertible bonds payable	25,000	× 2	=	50,000

The numbers of shares of common stock, given above, would be used in all EPS-related computations.

Application of the Treasury Stock Method to Fully Diluted EPS

In applying the treasury stock method to compute primary EPS, the **average market price** of the stock **always** is used. In contrast, for computing fully diluted EPS, the **ending market price** per share of stock is substituted for the average market price per share if the ending market price is **higher.** This reduces fully diluted EPS below primary EPS by use of the treasury stock method.

To show the effect of a higher end-of-period (versus average) price of common stock subject to stock rights or other stock purchase contracts, assume the price of the common stock of Jade Corporation at December 31, 19C, was $40 per share (average for the year was $25; Exhibit 22–4, panel B). This change would not affect primary EPS. However, it would decrease fully diluted EPS because it would increase the number of shares of common stock added to the denominator in the fully diluted EPS computation, as shown below:

Number of CSE shares represented by stock rights for primary EPS (Exhibit 22–5)	400
Number of shares represented by stock rights for fully diluted EPS	1,000*

* Computation:

Shares that would be issued upon exercise of rights (Exhibit 22–4, panel B)	2,000
Cash proceeds if rights were exercised: 2,000 rights × $20 (option price) = $40,000.	
Less: Treasury stock that could be purchased at year-end: $40,000 ÷ $40 (market price)	(1,000)
Common shares added to denominator in fully diluted EPS computation	1,000

With the above change, Jade Corporation's fully diluted EPS would be computed using 1,000 common stock equivalent shares added to the denominator of the EPS computation (instead of the 400 shares used for computing primary EPS).

Application of Interest Rate Test and If-Converted Method to Convertible Debt Securities Issued at a Premium or Discount

Debt securities, including those that are convertible, usually are issued at a **premium** or a **discount.** When there is a premium or discount, the effective yield on the debt securities is different from their stated interest rate. Therefore, the interest rate test used to determine whether convertible debt securities are CSEs must be based on their **effective yield,** taking into account the premium or discount on issue of the convertible debt. Also, the D/A ratio used to identify dilutive securities must be based on the net-of-tax interest expense on the convertible debt, including any related **amortization** of premium or discount recorded as part of the interest expense on the bonds. Finally, if the convertible debt is dilutive, the net-of-tax interest addback to the numerator in the EPS computation must include the effect of amortization of the premium or discount.

To show the effect of premium or discount amortization on EPS computations, assume the series B convertible bonds payable of Jade Corporation (Exhibit 22–4, panel B) were 20-year bonds and were issued to yield 9% instead of 10% (stated interest rate). The total issue price would then be $545,643 instead of par.[12] Because the effective yield of 9% is greater than two-thirds of the Aa bond rate (i.e., 12.6% = ⅔ = 8.4%), the series B convertible bonds are not CSEs. The interest effect of the bonds on EPS would be computed based on the effective interest rate applied to the net carrying value of the bonds each period if the interest method of amortization is used. If the straight-line method of amortization is used, the interest effect would be:

Cash interest ($500,000 × 10%)	$50,000
Amortization of premium (straight-line):	
Issue price $545,643 − par, $500,000 = $45,643 premium	
Premium amortization ($45,643 ÷ 20 years)	2,282
Pretax interest effect	47,718
Multiply by the effect of the tax rate (1 − .40 = .60)	x 60%
Interest effect	$28,631

The interest effect would be included in the numerator of fully diluted EPS computations, assuming series B convertible bonds are dilutive.

Summary of Earnings per Share

When a corporation has a simple capital structure, it presents only one set of EPS amounts. In contrast, a corporation with a complex capital structure presents both primary and fully diluted EPS amounts for (1) income before extraordinary items, (2) extraordinary items, and (3) net income. Primary EPS relates the three categories of income (or loss) to the basic capital structure of the corporation, that is, *(a)* its outstanding common stock and *(b)* all dilutive CSEs. On the other hand, fully diluted EPS reflects the maximum possible dilution. Therefore, the number of shares in the denominator of the fully diluted EPS computation includes *(a)* the weighted average number of common shares outstanding, plus *(b)* all dilutive CSEs (i.e., those used in computing primary EPS), plus *(c)* all other contingent issuances of common stock that would reduce EPS. If *(c)* is zero, primary and fully diluted EPS are the same.

Exhibit 22–3 presents an overview of EPS computations for both simple and complex capital structures. This exhibit is an excellent review of this part of the chapter.

PART B: FINANCIAL STATEMENT ANALYSIS

FASB Concepts Statement 1 states that the primary objectives of financial statements are to help users of financial statements to (1) make rational investment, credit, and similar decisions, (2) assess the amounts, timing, and uncertainty

[12] [$500,000 × $p_{n=20, i=9\%}$ (Table 5–2, .17843)] + [$50,000 × $P_{o_{n=20, i=9\%}}$ (Table 5–4, 9.12855)] = $545,643.

of future cash receipts, and (3) evaluate the resources, claims to those resources, and the related changes (see also, Chapter 6). Financial statement analysis is an evaluative and interpretative process that helps the user make economic decisions.[13]

Overview of Financial Statement Analysis

Analysis of financial statements focuses on the data presented in external financial reports, supplemented with information from other sources such as company management, investment advisors, trade associations, business periodicals, government agencies, and other materials distributed by the company. These latter sources often are important because they may disclose useful information on a more timely basis than the published financial statements. For example, unreported litigation may threaten the profit potential of a company, and sources such as *The Wall Street Journal* may provide timely disclosure of such events.

One of the primary objectives of financial statement analysis is to identify and assess **major changes** in trends, amounts, and relationships. Investigation and evaluation of the **reasons underlying those changes** are particularly important. Recognition of a **turning point** may provide an early warning of a significant change in the future success or failure of the business.

Financial statements are **organized summaries** of the extensive activities of a business. For example, the published financial statements of a large corporation, such as General Motors, Exxon, or IBM, usually contain from 10 to 15 printed pages, including the supporting notes. It is difficult to imagine the number of transactions, the critical accounting decisions, and the details summarized in these few pages. Summarization causes communication problems. On the other hand, excessive detail is undesirable because statement users experience time constraints in analyzing a mass of data (often called **information overload**).

Investors, lenders, and others have many variables to consider when making decisions. Decisions relating to businesses are particularly influenced by economic considerations, with earnings, financial position, and cash flows being especially significant factors. An entity's financial statements that span several reporting periods and include selected long-term trend data are important sources of economic information. However, this may not necessarily be the most important source in all cases.

Understanding, analyzing, and interpreting financial statements can be enhanced if the purpose of the statements is understood. As *FASB Concepts Statement 1* states: "The information should be comprehensible to those who have a reasonable understanding of business and economic activities and are willing to study the information with reasonable diligence."

Analysis of financial statements is an organized approach to pull out information from the financial statements that is relevant to the particular decision. Thus, the thrust of financial statement analysis in a particular situation should be determined in terms of the decision(s) being contemplated. In this chapter, the discussions are based on selected analytical and interpretative approaches that are widely used by decision makers.

---

[13] Leopold A. Bernstein, *Financial Statement Analysis: Theory, Application, and Interpretation*, 4th ed. (Homewood, Ill.: Richard D. Irwin, 1988).

Typically, analysis and interpretation of financial statements should involve most of the following phases, which are usually done in this sequential order:

1. Examine the auditors' report.
2. Analyze the statement of accounting policies included in the notes to the financial statements.
3. Examine the financial statements as a whole, including notes and supporting schedules.
4. Apply analytical approaches such as—
   a. Comparative statements.
   b. Horizontal and vertical percentage analyses.
   c. Ratio (proportionate) analyses.
5. Search for important supplemental information.

Each of these phases is discussed in the sections that follow.

Examine the Auditors' Report

Expert financial analysts often suggest that in evaluating a financial statement, the first basic step is careful examination of the auditors' report (also called the Report of the Independent Certified Public Accountants). This presumes that the financial statements are audited. If they are not, one should first ascertain their credibility. The auditors' report is important because it provides the analyst with an independent and professional opinion about the "fairness" of the representations in the financial statements. Also, it calls attention to all major concerns the auditors had as a result of the auditors' intensive examination.

The auditors' report was discussed in Chapter 4. It would be advisable to restudy that discussion. **An unqualified auditors' opinion for Kimberly-Clark Corporation is given in the Appendix following Chapter 25.**

Instead of an **unqualified opinion,** the auditor may give *(a)* a qualified opinion, *(b)* an adverse opinion, or *(c)* a disclaimer of opinion about the financial statements. Each of these unfavorable opinions must include an explanation by the auditor of the factors underlying the decision for this opinion. These unfavorable opinions alert the statement user to major problem areas in the company that should be investigated. An unfavorable auditors' opinion may cause the SEC or the stock exchanges to stop the public trading of the company's stock, which can have a serious effect on the financial interests of investors.

Below is an example of a qualified opinion (and related notes) that shows the kind of information often cited by an auditor. **Notice the "subject to" opinion in the second and third paragraphs below of the Report of the Independent Certified Public Accountants.** This may have been the most important item of information in the 1986 financial statements of this company.

The Shareholders and the Board of Directors
Allegheny International, Inc.:

We have examined the consolidated balance sheets of Allegheny International, Inc. and consolidated subsidiaries as of December 28, 1986 and December 29, 1985 and related consolidated statements of operations, additional paid-in capital, retained earnings (accumulated deficit), accumulated foreign currency translation adjustments, and changes in financial position for each of the years in the three-year period ended December 28, 1986. Our examinations were made in accordance with generally accepted auditing standards and, accordingly, included such tests of the accounting records and such other auditing procedures as we considered necessary in the circumstances.

As described in Note 6 to the consolidated financial statements, the Company has received waivers from lending institutions suspending the applicability of certain debt covenants while it arranges to keep its current financing in place to the consummation of the merger described in Note 2. The Company's ability to continue as a going concern is contingent upon its ability to maintain adequate financing and attain profitable operations. The consolidated financial statements do not include any adjustments relating to the recoverability or classification of recorded asset amounts or the amounts and classification of liabilities that might be necessary should the Company be unable to continue as a going concern.

In our opinion, subject to the effects on the 1986 consolidated financial statements of such adjustments, if any, as might have been required had the outcome of the matters referred to in the preceding paragraph been known, the aforementioned consolidated financial statements present fairly the financial position of Allegheny International, Inc. and consolidated subsidiaries as of December 28, 1986 and December 29, 1985 and results of their operations and changes in their financial position for each of the years in the three-year period ended December 28, 1986 in conformity with generally accepted accounting principles applied on a consistent basis.

Analyze the Statement of Accounting Policies

Accounting must accommodate a wide variety of circumstances. Although accounting principles and their implementation are prescribed primarily by the *ARBs, APB Opinions, FASB Statements* and by precedent, there is considerable room for judgment by the reporting entity and by the independent accountant about the accounting treatment given many transactions.

In response to the **full disclosure principle,** *APB Opinion 22,* "Disclosure of Accounting Policies," states that "information about the accounting policies adopted by a reporting entity is essential for financial statement users." Accounting policies are the specific policies and methods that have been adopted by a company for preparation of its financial statements. The *Opinion* requires that a statement of these policies be stated either in the notes, or preferably **"in a separate Summary of Significant Accounting Policies preceding the notes to the financial statements or as the initial note."** The summary must disclose all important accounting policies. These include *(a)* selections from acceptable alternatives, *(b)* accounting policies used that are peculiar to the industry, and *(c)* unusual or innovative applications of generally accepted accounting principles (GAAP). Examples include the basis for consolidated statements, depreciation and amortization methods, inventory costing and valuation (e.g., LCM), translation of foreign currencies, revenue recognition on long-term construction contracts, franchising, and leasing. A statement of accounting policies is shown in the Appendix (following Chapter 25). It should be examined at this time.

The information in the statement of accounting policies is fundamental to understanding, interpreting, and evaluating the information reported in the financial statements. It is particularly useful in evaluating the **credibility of the statements and the reliability of the reported earnings,** and in comparing data among companies, industries, and reporting periods.

Integrative Examination of Financial Statements

After the auditors' opinion has been examined and the summary of accounting policies used by the company has been analyzed, the evaluation and interpretive process should continue with a careful study of the financial statements in their entirety. This phase of the analysis involves an integrative study of each statement to gain overall perspective and to identify major strengths and weaknesses. This study also identifies unusual changes, such as **turning points** (up or down) in the trends of sales revenue, expenses, income, asset structure, liabilities, capital structure, and cash flow.

The overall examination should include careful study of all of the statements included and the **notes** referred to in those statements. Each note should be read and evaluated. Consideration of the notes as a separate activity is not particularly fruitful because a specific note usually is informative only in the context of the specific statement item to which it is referenced. **The position of the accounting profession is that the disclosure notes are an integral part of the financial statements.**

Concurrent with, or subsequent to, the overall examination of the financial statements under review, the analyst may find it helpful to apply some of the analytical techniques discussed in the next section.

Comparative Financial Statements and Percentage Analysis

Various approaches are used to enhance communication through financial statements, such as ratio analysis, graphic presentations, special tabulations, subclassifications of information on the statements, comparative financial statements, and supplementary information in separate schedules and notes to the statements.

Comparative Financial Statements

Comparative financial statements present financial information for the current and one or more past periods in a way that facilitates comparison by the statement user among several reporting periods. Basically, comparative financial statements involve two perspectives:

1. **Short-term comparative statements**—This perspective involves reporting financial information covering the *(a)* current reporting period and *(b)* one or two immediately preceding reporting periods. A strong movement is currently under way in the accounting profession to require that comparative financial statements present data for three, rather than two, years.
2. **Long-term comparative data**—This perspective involves reporting selected financial data from a series of prior years' financial statements for 5, 10, 15, or 20 prior reporting periods.

The **long-term summaries** of selected financial information included in the annual financial report provide data on the long-term financial performance of a company. The data are particularly relevant for financial statement analysis. The annual financial statements for one year give only a limited view of the successes and failures of a company. In contrast, the long-term summary provides a broad overview of where the company has been (financially) in the past. Also, it provides clues as to where it may go in the future. In this regard, the results of one or even two years may give a limited view of the potential of the company.

Notice the financial statements of Kimberly-Clark Corporation, presented in the Appendix following Chapter 25. That report includes *(a)* current statements of income covering a **three-year** period, 1985–87, and *(b)* a long-term summary that reports selected data for a **five-year** period (1983–87). These reports are in conformity with the **quality of comparability** discussed in *FASB Concepts Statement 2* (see Chapter 6).

Percentage Analysis of Financial Statements

Financial information expressed in absolute dollar amounts is the accepted means of conveying accounting information. Conversion of these absolute amounts to percentages, or ratios, reveals proportionate relationships that often are difficult to perceive from dollar amounts only. Conversion of dollar amounts involves dividing one amount by another amount; the result is expressed as a percent or as a ratio.

First, we will consider the use of percentage analysis on comparative financial statements. Then we will discuss some specific applications of percentages and ratios to individual items.

Percentage analysis (in any form) seldom is part of the "published" body of financial statements. When needed, it is viewed as supplementary information. Analysts and other users typically rely on two variations of percentage analysis called *(a)* **vertical percentage analysis** and *(b)* **horizontal percentage analysis.**

Vertical analysis is the expression of each item on a particular financial statement as a percent of one specific item, called the base amount. The base amount is always equal to 100%. When the base amount is zero, meaningful percentage or ratio analysis cannot be computed. For example, on the statement of financial position, the **base amount** (the denominator) used is total assets, and each individual asset (the numerator) is expressed as a percent of total assets. On the statement of income, the base amount used is net revenue, and on the statement of cash flows, the base amount could be the net increase in cash during the period.

Exhibit 22–11 illustrates vertical percentage analysis on statements of financial position and income of ACE Corporation. Notice the vertical analysis format: the current year results are in the first column, and single underscores for dollar amount subtotals facilitate the presentation in a single column for each period. Placing the various items for the two periods side by side in the two columns is preferable to separate statements to permit more convenient comparison. Both the dollar amounts and vertical percents are developed for each reporting year. The vertical percents on the statement of financial position were derived by dividing the total asset amount into each individual account balance. Vertical analysis emphasizes proportional relationships within each reporting period, rather than between reporting periods.

To illustrate the usefulness of the percentages, notice for example, that cash was 11% of total assets in 19A, but 19% in 19B (the current year), and total debt in 19A was 39% of total assets and 34% in 19B. We can see from vertical analysis that the composition of items on the statement of financial position changed materially. Also, notice the vertical percentage analysis on the statement of income. The base amount is total revenues (net of any returns and discounts). The vertical percentages for the individual items do not appear to have changed materially from 19A to 19B.

Exhibit 22–11
Comparative financial statements with vertical percentage analysis.

ACE CORPORATION
Comparative Statement of Financial Position with Vertical Percentage Analysis
Years Ended December 31, 19B, and 19A

	19B		19A	
	Amount	**Percent**	**Amount**	**Percent**
Assets				
Current assets:				
Cash	$ 42,250	19	$ 23,400	11
Investments, short term (at LCM)	2,000	1	5,000	3
Accounts receivable (net of allowance)	20,000	9	25,000	12
Inventory (FIFO, LCM)	22,000	10	20,000	10
Prepaid insurance	300	0	600	0
Total current assets	86,550	39	74,000	36
Funds and investments (at cost)	39,100	18	39,100	19
Property, plant, and equipment	140,000	64	125,000	61
Accumulated depreciation	(50,000)	(23)	(37,500)	18
Remaining assets	3,600	2	3,400	2
Total assets	$219,250	100	$204,000	100
Liabilities				
Current liabilities:				
Accounts payable	$ 25,000	11	$ 24,700	12
Notes payable	5,000	2	10,000	5
Accrued liabilities	450	0	300*	0
Total current liabilities	30,450	13	35,000	17
Bonds payable, 10%	45,000	21	45,000	22
Total liabilities	75,450	34	80,000	39
Stockholders' Equity				
Common stock, nopar (20,000 shares)	74,000	34	74,000	36
Preferred stock, 8%, par $1; cumulative, nonconvertible (10,000 shares)	10,000	5	10,000	5
Contributed capital in excess of par, preferred	4,000	2	4,000	2
Retained earnings	55,800*	25	36,000	18
Total stockholders' equity	143,800	66	124,000	61
Total liabilities and stockholders' equity	$219,250	100	$204,000	100

* Cash dividends declared and paid:

Preferred stock: 8% × $10,000 =	$ 800
Common stock: $.72 × 20,000 shares =	14,400
Total	$15,200

Horizontal analysis involves the use of percentages, or ratios, to measure the extent that each item changes from one year (the base amount) to one or more following years. For example, the ACE statement of financial position shown in Exhibit 22–11 would indicate that the cash balance increased by 81% from 19A to 19B [i.e., ($42,250 − $23,400) ÷ $23,400 = 81%].

Exhibit 22–12 illustrates the use of horizontal percentage analysis on the statement of income of ACE Corporation. Notice that the change is calculated by dividing the amount of increase or decrease for each item by the base year amount, which is the amount reported in the earlier reporting period. Horizontal

Exhibit 22–11
(concluded)

ACE CORPORATION
Comparative Statement of Income with Vertical Percentage Analysis
For the Years Ended December 31, 19B and 19A

Items	19B Amount	19B Percent	19A Amount	19A Percent
Revenues:				
Sales (net of returns and discounts)	$384,382*	99	$357,372*	99
Investment revenue	2,800	1	3,128	1
Gain on sale of investments	200		500	
Total revenues	387,382	100	361,000	100
Expenses:				
Cost of goods sold	230,000	60	220,000	61
Distribution expense	55,500	14	54,000	15
Administrative expense	46,382	12	45,000	12
Interest expense	5,500	1	6,500	1
Loss on disposal of assets			500	0
Income tax expense (30%)	15,000	4	10,500	3
Total expenses	352,382	91	336,500	92
Income before extraordinary items	35,000	9	24,500	7
Extraordinary gain (net of $1,500 tax)			3,500	1
Net income	$ 35,000	9	$ 28,000	8
Earnings per share (20,000 shares):				
Income before extraordinary items		$1.71†		$1.185‡
Extraordinary gain		-0-		.175
Net income		$1.71		$1.36

* Approximately 60% on credit.
† [$35,000 − (preferred dividend claim, $10,000 × 8% = $800) = $34,200] ÷ 20,000 shares = $1.71.
‡ [$24,500 − $800 (see †) = $23,700] ÷ 20,000 shares = 1.185.

analysis is applied to the statements of financial position and cash flows in exactly the same manner.

The results of horizontal analysis should be used to focus on those items that involve relatively large dollar amounts. That is, sales revenue for ACE Corporation involves hundreds of thousands of dollars while the gain on sales of investments involves only a few hundred dollars. The small change of 8% in sales revenue (when the large dollar amounts are involved) will usually be more significant than a larger change in an item that does not involve a large dollar amount (e.g., gain on sale of investments, 60%). In other words, the analysis should involve scrutiny of not only the resulting percentages but also the relative importance of the item being analyzed.

Ratio Analysis

Ratio analysis involves measuring the proportional relationship between two single amounts. These amounts may be selected from one financial statement, such as the statements of income or from two statements, such as the statements of income and financial position. The amounts may represent the balances of two different accounts, the balance of one account and a classification total (such as total assets), or two classification totals.

Exhibit 22–12
Comparative statement of income with horizontal percentage analysis.

ACE CORPORATION
Comparative Statement of Income with Horizontal Percentage Analysis
for the Years Ended December 31, 19B, and 19A

Items	19B	19A	Change from 19A to 19B: Amount	Percent
Revenues:				
Sales (net of returns and allowances)	$384,382	$357,372	$27,010	8
Investment revenue	2,800	3,128	(328)	(10)
Gain on sale of investments	200	500	(300)	(60)
Total revenues	387,382	361,000	26,382	7
Expenses:				
Cost of goods sold	230,000	220,000	10,000	5
Distribution expense	55,500	54,000	1,500	3
Administrative expense	46,382	45,000	1,382	3
Interest expense	5,500	6,500	(1,000)	(15)
Loss on disposal of assets		500	(500)	(100)
Income tax expense	15,000	10,500	4,500	43
Total expenses	352,382	336,500	15,882	5
Income before extraordinary items	35,000	24,500	10,500	43
Extraordinary gain (net of tax)		3,500	(3,500)	(100)
Net income	$ 35,000	$ 28,000	$ 7,000	25
Earnings per share (20,000 shares):				
Income before extraordinary items	$1.71	$1.185	$.525	44
Extraordinary gain	-0-	.175	(.175)	(100)
Net income	$1.71	$1.36	$.35	26

Ratio analysis can be expressed in a variety of ways. As an example, working capital has been discussed and referred to in several prior chapters. The **current ratio,** which expresses the relationship between current assets and current liabilities, is one way of analyzing a company's working capital position. To illustrate, assume the following data are taken from a statement of financial position:

Total current assets	$5,000,000
Total current liabilities	2,000,000
Difference—working capital	$3,000,000

The amount of working capital, $3,000,000, standing alone, is a useful figure; however, expression as a ratio adds insight to this relationship. The current ratio based on the above amounts is 2.5.

Current ratio = $5,000,000 ÷ $2,000,000 = 2.5 (a ratio).

Also, this ratio may be expressed as 250%; 2.5 to 1; or that there is $2.50 of current assets for each $1 of current liabilities.

Ratio analysis is helpful only when the proportional relationship between the selected factors sheds additional light on the interpretation of the individual absolute amounts. In view of the large number of ratios that could be computed, it is important for analysis purposes to select those amounts that *(a)* involve relevant relationships and *(b)* are functionally related. For example, the relationship between bad debt expense and credit sales is more meaningful than the relationship between bad debt expense and total sales (including cash sales). In evaluating significance, consideration must be given to the **purposes** for which the ratios are to be used. Investors, managers, and creditors encounter different kinds of problems and decisions. Therefore, different ratios often are meaningful to each group of users within the context of specific decisions that are to be made. Because a complete study of ratio analysis is beyond the scope of this text, only representative ratios having general application are discussed. The analyses selected for discussion will be explained under the following headings:

1. Ratios that measure **current position.**
2. Ratios that measure **equity position.**
3. Ratios that measure **operating results.**

The discussions that follow illustrate ratio analysis by using the financial statement data for ACE Corporation given in Exhibit 22–11.

Ratios that Measure Current Position

Ratio measurements in this category focus on working capital; they are supplementary to the statements of income and cash flows. Seven ratios often used to measure current position are summarized in **Exhibit 22–13.** Notice that they are expressed variously as a percent, decimal, fraction, or turnover figure. The analysis of current position involves measures of *(a)* ability to pay short-term obligations and *(b)* movement of current assets.[14]

Ratios that Measure Ability to Pay Short-Term Obligations. The three ratios often used for this purpose are discussed below (numbered to correspond to Exhibit 22–13).

1. Current ratio—This ratio (also called the **working capital ratio**) has long been used as an index of short-term liquidity; that is, the ability of the business to meet the maturing claims of its creditors from the current operating assets. The amount of working capital and the related ratio have a direct impact on the amount of short-term credit that may be obtained. The working capital ratio is unique to the industry in which the business operates, and even to the business itself in the light of its operating and financial characteristics. For example, a ratio of 2.11 to 1 may be realistic in one situation, but it may be too low or too high in another situation. The peculiarities of the industry in which the firm operates and other factors, such as methods of financing and seasonal fluctuations, also should be considered in evaluating a particular current ratio.

The current ratio is only one measure or index of ability to meet short-term obligations, and it has certain weaknesses. A high current ratio may be the result of overstocking of inventory, and it is influenced by the inventory cost

[14] There is no single "generally accepted" method of computing specific ratios or of determining the values to be used in their computations. The computation should be determined by (1) the data available and (2) the use and interpretation expected in the particular situation. The formulas presented in this chapter reflect one approach.

Exhibit 22–13
Ratios that measure current position.

Ratio	Formula for computation	Summary of significance
A. Ratios that measure ability to pay short-term obligations:		
1. Current (or working capital) ratio.	Current assets / Current liabilities	Test of short-term liquidity. Indicates ability to meet current obligations from current assets as a going concern. Measure of adequacy of working capital.
2. Acid-test (or quick) ratio.	Quick assets / Current liabilities	A more severe test of immediate liquidity than the current ratio. Tests ability to meet sudden demands upon liquid current assets, particularly cash.
3. Working capital to total assets.	Working capital / Total assets	Indicates relative liquidity of total assets and distribution of resources employed as to liquidity.
B. Ratios that measure movement of selected current assets (turnover):		
4. *a.* Receivable turnover.	Net credit sales / Average trade receivables (net)	Credit and collection efficiency of trade accounts and notes.
b. Age of accounts receivables.	365 (days) / Receivable turnover (computed per [*a*] above)	Average number of days to collect trade receivables.
5. Inventory turnover. *a.* Merchandise turnover (retail firm).	Cost of goods sold / Average merchandise inventory	Indicates liquidity of inventory. Average number of times inventory "turned over" or was sold during the period. Indicates possible over- or understocking.
b. Finished goods turnover (manufacturing firm).	Cost of goods sold / Average finished goods inventory	Same as 5*a*.
c. Raw material turnover.	Cost of raw materials used / Average raw materials inventory	Number of times raw material inventory was "used" on the average during the period.
d. Days' supply in inventory.	365 (days) / Inventory turnover (computed per [*a*], [*b*], or [*c*] above)	Number of days' supply in the average inventory. Indicates general condition of over- or understocking.
6. Working capital turnover.	Net sales / Average working capital	Indicates the effectiveness with which average working capital was used to generate sales.
7. Percent of each current asset to total current assets.	Each current asset / Total current assets	Indicates relative investment in each current asset to total current assets.

flow method used. A business may have a high current ratio even though it has a cash deficit. Furthermore, a high current ratio may indicate excess funds that should be invested or used for other purposes.

To illustrate, the current ratios for ACE Corporation (data from Exhibit 22–11) are:

19A: \$74,000 ÷ \$35,000 = 2.11 (to 1)

19B: \$86,550 ÷ \$30,450 = 2.84 (to 1)

2. **Acid-test ratio**—Cash, accounts receivable, short-term notes receivable, and short-term investments in marketable securities generally represent funds that are readily available for paying current obligations. They are collectively called **quick assets.** Inventories, on the other hand, must be sold and collection made before cash is available for paying obligations. In many cases, particularly where there are raw materials and work in process inventories, the marketability of the inventory involves considerable uncertainty as to when the inventory can be ultimately converted to cash. In view of these considerations, the **acid-test or quick ratio** (quick assets divided by current liabilities) is used as a test of **immediate liquidity.** Traditionally, an acid-test ratio of 1 to 1 (a rule of thumb standard) has been considered desirable. As with the current ratio, the acid-test ratio for a particular company must be evaluated in terms of industry characteristics and other factors.

To illustrate, the acid-test ratios for ACE Corporation (data from Exhibit 22–11) are:

19A: (Quick assets, \$23,400 + \$5,000 + \$25,000 = \$53,400)
÷ (Total current liabilities, \$35,000) = 1.53 (to 1)

19B: (\$42,250 + \$2,000 + \$20,000 = \$64,250) ÷ \$30,450 = 2.11 (to 1)

3. **Working capital to total assets**—The ratio of working capital to total assets is a generalized expression of the distribution and liquidity of the assets employed after current liabilities have been deducted from current assets. An excessively high ratio might indicate excess cash, inability to collect receivables, and/or over-stocking of inventory, whereas a low ratio may indicate a weakness in the current position.

To illustrate, the working capital to total assets ratios for ACE Corporation (data from Exhibit 22–11) are:

19A: (Working capital, \$74,000 − \$35,000 = \$39,000)
÷ (Total assets, \$204,000) = .19 (or 19%)

19B: (\$86,550 − \$30,450 = \$56,100) ÷ (\$219,250) = .26 (or 26%)

Ratios that Measure the Movement of Current Assets (Turnover). The four categories of ratios in this group relate primarily to accounts receivable, inventory, and overall working capital (see Exhibit 22–13).

4. **Accounts receivable turnover**—In some businesses, cash sales predominate, whereas in others credit sales predominate. In either case, the amount of trade receivables on the average should bear some relationship to the credit sales for the period and the credit terms. Because the balance of accounts receivable indicates a cash lag which reduces current cash otherwise available for productive purposes, a measure of the efficiency of credit and collections in a company is useful. The two accounts receivable ratios provide important insights into a company's efficiency relative to its credit and collection activities. The two most commonly used measures are accounts receivable turnover and age

of accounts receivable. The basic relationship measured is between credit sales and accounts receivable.

To illustrate these two ratios, the data for ACE Corporation (given in Exhibit 22–11) will be used for 19B:

a. Accounts receivable turnover $= \dfrac{\text{Net credit sales}}{\text{Average accounts receivable}}$

19B: $= \dfrac{\$384{,}382 \times 60\% = \$230{,}629}{(\$20{,}000 + \$25{,}000) \div 2 = \$22{,}500}$

$= 10.25$ (turnover)

b. Age of accounts receivable $= \dfrac{365 \text{ days}}{10.25}$

$= 35.6$ (average number of days to collect)

Assuming the credit terms are 1/10, n/30, it appears that collections lagged terms by about six days on the average—a suggestion of possible laxity in *(a)* granting credit and/or *(b)* making collections.

The above illustration also points out several technical aspects of the computation:

a. Should the total of cash and credit sales, or credit sales only, be used in the computation? Because only credit sales cause accounts receivable, a more stable and meaningful ratio will result if credit sales only are used. Otherwise a shift in the proportion of cash to credit sales will affect the ratio, even though collection experience is unchanged. Therefore, total credit sales should be used if it is available or may be reconstructed.

b. Should the ending balance of receivables or average receivables be used? The **average monthly** receivables balance should be used in order to smooth out seasonal influences. Ideally, the average should be determined by adding the 13 monthly balances (January 1 and January 31 through December 31) of trade accounts and trade notes receivable and then dividing by 13. In the absence of monthly balances, the average of the annual beginning and ending balance or only the ending balance may be used (with a potentially significant loss of information).

c. Receivables should be net of the allowance for doubtful accounts.

d. Trade notes receivable should be included in averaging receivables.

Whether to express the receivable movement as a "turnover" or as "number of days to collect" is a matter of preference.[15]

5. Inventory turnover—The inventory turnover ratio expresses the relationship between the **cost of goods sold (or used) and the average inventory balance.** The procedure for determining the average inventory balance is similar to that discussed above for average receivables. Basically, to compute this ratio, average

---

[15] Some analysts prefer to use 250 (5-day workweek) or 300 (6-day workweek) days, as the case may be, as an approximation of the number of business days in the year.

inventory is divided into cost of goods sold. To illustrate, inventory turnover and days' supply in inventory for ACE Corporation (based on data given in Exhibit 22–11) would be:

$$\text{Inventory turnover} = \frac{\text{Cost of goods sold}}{\text{Average balance of merchandise inventory}}$$

$$\text{19B:} \quad = \frac{\$230{,}000}{(\$20{,}000 + \$22{,}000) \div 2 = \$21{,}000} = \begin{matrix}\text{11 times}\\ \text{(turnover)}\end{matrix}$$

$$\text{Days' supply in inventory} = \frac{\text{365 days}}{11} = \text{33 (days supply)*}$$

* One way to measure the operating cycle of a business is to sum the age of the accounts receivable and the days supply of inventory. For ACE Corporation this would be, 35.6 + 33 = 68.6 days.

Merchandise inventory turnover may be expressed as a "turnover" or as "days' supply"; the latter, as illustrated above, appears more often in current usage. The turnover or days' supply figure has significance because the amount of inventory on hand normally should have a close relationship to cost of goods sold. The relationship will vary among industries and businesses; for example, a grocery store normally would expect a high inventory turnover, whereas an antique dealer may expect a low turnover. Also, the ratio represents an average—a generalization that does not reflect the rate for individual items but rather the average rate for all items. For example, a grocery store may have an average turnover of 20, yet it may have items on the shelves that have not turned over at all for a three-month period. Furthermore, this ratio is influenced by the inventory cost flow method used, which may affect comparison among companies. For example, when inventory prices are rising, companies using LIFO will tend to have higher computed turnover rates than those using other cost flow methods.

Profitability is also directly related to inventory turnover. To illustrate, assume that the inventory turnover is 12 (cost of goods sold, $1,200,000 ÷ average inventory, $100,000) and that the company realizes a "profit" of $1,000 each time the $100,000 investment in inventory turns over. A $12,000 profit is indicated. Now assume another company is identical in every respect except that its inventory turnover is 6, indicating a $6,000 profit on a similar $100,000 inventory investment.

Work in process inventory turnover is computed by dividing cost of goods manufactured by the average work in process inventory. With respect to all inventories, turnover computations based on appropriate **unit** data, when practicable, will provide more reliable results than when based only on dollar amounts.

The accounts receivable and inventory turnover computations illustrated above used one value from the statement of income (i.e., credit sales and cost of goods sold, respectively) and one value from the statement of financial position (i.e., average accounts receivable and average inventory, respectively). In such cases, the single statement of income amount encompasses the entire reporting period, whereas a statement of financial position figure represents a specific end-of-period amount. **Therefore, to attain reasonable consistency for all ratios**

that relate a statement of income amount to a statement of financial position amount, the latter amount should be an average.

6. **Working capital turnover**—Working capital has a functional relationship to sales revenue through accounts receivable, inventory, and cash. Therefore, the ratio of sales revenue to working capital is often used as a measure of the effectiveness of a company's "use" of working capital to generate revenue. To illustrate, the working capital for ACE Corporation would be computed as follows (data from Exhibit 22–11):

$$\text{Working capital turnover} = \frac{\text{Net sales revenue}}{\text{Average working capital}}$$

$$\text{19B turnover:} \quad = \frac{\$384{,}382}{[(\$74{,}000 - \$35{,}000) + (\$86{,}550 - \$30{,}450)] \div 2} = 8$$

7. **Percent of each current asset to total current assets**—A **vertical** percentage analysis of current assets that uses **total current assets** as the base (100%) often is used. This analysis may have significance in that *(a)* the relative composition of the current asset structure is revealed, and *(b)* when compared with similar data from prior periods, important trends may be revealed. An analysis of current assets applied to ACE Corporation would be as follows (i.e., a vertical analysis):

	19B		19A	
	Amount	**Percent**	**Amount**	**Percent**
Current assets:				
Cash	$42,250	49	$23,400	32
Investments, short term	2,000	2	5,000	7
Accounts receivable (net)	20,000	23	25,000	34
Inventory	22,000	26	20,000	27
Prepaid insurance	300	—	600	—
Total current assets	$86,550	100	$74,000	100

The newly required statement of cash flows (Chapter 19) probably will reduce the significance (and use) of several of the working capital ratios.

Ratios that Measure Equity Position

The statement of financial position reports the two basic sources of funds used by a business: *(a)* owners' equity and *(b)* creditors' equity. The relationships between these two different types of equities often are measured because they reflect certain financial strengths and weaknesses of the business; in other words, the long-term solvency of a business and its potential capacity to generate and obtain investment resources. **Exhibit 22–14** summarizes four ratios that commonly are used to measure equity relationships when compared to various financial statement amounts.

Equity ratios 1 through 3 focus on the amount of resources provided by creditors as opposed to the amount provided by owners (including retained earnings). Because debt and capital have significantly different characteristics, the relationship between debt and owners' equity is important. Debt requires the payment of interest at specific intervals; in addition, at maturity the principal must be paid regardless of whether the company earned income or incurred a

Exhibit 22–14
Ratios that measure equity position.

Ratio	Formula for computation	Summary of significance
Equity ratios:		
1. Debt to equity.	Total liabilities / Owners' equity	Measures the balance between resources provided by creditors and resources provided by owners (including retained earnings).
2. Owners' equity to total assets.*	Owners' equity / Total assets	Proportion of assets provided by owners. Reflects financial strength and cushion for creditors.
3. Creditors' equity to total assets.	Total liabilities / Total assets	Proportion of assets provided by creditors. Extent of leverage.
4. Book value per share of common stock outstanding at year-end.	Common stock equity / Number of outstanding common shares	Number of dollars of common equity (at book value) per share of common stock.

* Total assets are represented by the statement of financial position totals (i.e., total assets or liabilities plus owners' equity). Total assets sometimes are called **total equities.**

loss. Interest on debt is an expense and is tax deductible. In contrast to debt, owners' equity does not have a maturity date. Dividends are paid only if *(a)* earnings have accumulated and *(b)* the dividends are declared. A dividend is not an expense and is not tax deductible. Because of these differences, the equity ratios are often closely monitored by interested parties.

The three equity ratios basically measure the same relationship; that is, the relationship of debt to owners' equity. The three equity ratios for ACE Corporation are illustrated below (based on data provided in Exhibit 22–11).

1. **Debt to equity ratio**—This equity ratio is the most widely used of the three because it provides a direct reading of the relationship between debt and owners' equity. The 19B debt to equity ratio for ACE Corporation is as follows:

$$\frac{\text{Total debt}}{\text{Total owners' equity}} = \frac{\$75,450}{\$143,800} = 52\% \text{ (or .52)}$$

Interpretation: Debt is 52% of owners' equity; therefore, the owners are providing more resources than the creditors.

2. **Owners' equity to total assets**—This ratio measures the relationship between owners' equity and total assets. Therefore, it represents the percent of total resources (i.e., assets) provided by owners (including retained earnings). The 19B ratio for ACE Corporation is:

$$\frac{\text{Owners' equity}}{\text{Total assets}} = \frac{\$143,800}{\$219,250} = 66\% \text{ (or .66)}$$

Interpretation: The owners provided 66% of the total assets, and the creditors provided the remaining 34%.

3. Creditors' equity to total assets—This ratio is the same as 2 above except that the numerator is now total debt. For ACE Corporation this 19B ratio is:

$$\frac{\text{Total debt}}{\text{Total assets}} = \frac{\$75{,}450}{\$219{,}250} = 34\% \text{ (or .34)}$$

Based on the above illustrations, it should be clear why only one of these three approaches is necessary in any given situation.

4. Book value per share of common stock—Book value per share of common stock is computed by dividing total **common stockholders' equity** by the number of **common shares outstanding.** When more than one class of stock is outstanding, total stockholders' equity must be **allocated** among the various classes in conformity with the legal and statutory claims that would be effective in case of liquidation of the company. Because additional classes of stock typically are preferred stock, the usual case requires an allocation based on the preferential rights of the preferred stockholders. Liquidation, cumulative, and participating preferences must be included in the computation.

To illustrate, refer to Exhibit 22–11 and notice that ACE's preferred stock is cumulative. Now assume that it has a **liquidation preference** of $3 per share, and at December 31, 19B, preferred dividends were in arrears for two years (including 19B). Computation of book value per common share at December 31, 19B, would be as follows:

Total stockholders' equity		$143,800
Allocation to preferred stock:		
Liquidation value (10,000 shares × $3)	$30,000	
Cumulative dividends in arrears ($10,000 × 8% × 2 years)	1,600	
Total allocated to preferred stock equity		31,600
Balance applicable to common stock equity		$112,200
Book value per share of common stock ($112,000 ÷ 20,000 shares)		$5.61

Although often computed, book value per share of common stock has limited usefulness. It has little, if any, correlation to the market value per share of common stock. Some investors view with interest a stock that has a book value significantly in excess of its market price because this may suggest a "good" buy. Under the cost and matching principles and because of conservatism, the total assets of a business, particularly during a period of rising prices, are apt to have book values considerably below market values.

Ratios that Measure Operating Results

Many investors are more interested in a company's statement of income than in its statement of financial position. This is because a company can continue to expand, develop financial position, generate high cash inflows, and pay attractive dividends when its long-term earnings record has been good and it appears likely to be favorable in the future. Consequently, ratio analysis related to **operating results** is given considerable attention by both investors and creditors.

Exhibit 22–15
Ratios that measure operating results.

Ratio	Formula for computation	Summary of significance
1. Profit margin.	Income* / Net sales	Indicates net profitability of each dollar of sales revenue.
2. Return on investment: *a.* On total assets.	Income plus interest expense (after tax) / Average total assets†	Rate earned on **all resources** used. Measures earnings on all investments provided by owners and creditors.
b. On owners' equity.	Income / Average owners' equity	Rate earned on resources provided by owners (excludes creditors). Measures earnings accruing to the owners.
c. Financial leverage.	Rate of return on owners' equity minus rate of return on total assets.	Reflects the advantage gained by borrowing at an interest rate that is lower than the rate earned on total assets.
3. Investment turnover.	Net sales / Average total assets†	Indicates efficiency with which total resources are utilized.
4. Earnings per share on common stock (EPS).	Income associated with common stock / Common shares outstanding	Income earned on each share of common stock. Indicates ability to pay dividends and to grow from within. Discussed in Part A.
5. Price-earnings ratio.	Market price per share / Earnings per share	Reflects the relationship between the latest earnings per share amount and the current market price per share; provides a rough measure of how the market values one share of stock.
6. Dividend-income payout ratio.	Cash dividends per share / Earnings per share	Measures the percent of income that is represented by cash dividends.
7. Dividend-market value payout ratio.	Cash dividends per common share / Market price per share	Provides a rough estimate of the expected rate of return per share of stock.

* Income before extraordinary items, rather than net income, usually is preferable. The inclusion of extraordinary gains and losses may be misleading because they are unusual and infrequent.
† Average total assets as used here is also called total liabilities plus owners' equity, total equities, and total investment. These three terms usually refer to the same statement of financial position amount.

Exhibit 22–15 summarizes seven ratios that are widely used to help assess the earnings and cash flow strengths of a business.

1. **Profit margin**—The ratio of income to net sales usually is called the **profit (gross) margin** because it is the ratio of net sales revenue to cost of goods sold. It is widely used as an index of profitability. However, one significant factor related to profitability—the total assets used to earn the income—is given no consideration in the ratio. To illustrate, assume the accounts of Company X showed the following data: income, $20,000; net sales, $200,000, and total assets, $1,000,000. In this case the profit margin appears to be very high at 10% (i.e. $20,000 ÷ $200,000). However, when profit performance is measured by the 2% return on total assets (i.e., $20,000 ÷ $1,000,000), it appears to be

very low. Thus, profit margin ratio has value primarily for evaluation of trends and for comparison with industry and competitor statistics.

2. **Return on investment**—Many accountants consider return on total assets to be the single most important ratio because it incorporates both earnings and investment (i.e., total assets) when measuring profitability. Fundamentally, return on any investment is computed by **dividing the income earned from that investment by the investment that was at risk to earn the income.** When return on investment is computed for a business, total investment is measured as total assets (from the statement of financial position).

The broad concept of return on investment has two important applications for a single business entity:

a. Evaluating proposed capital additions and other investment decisions on the basis of projected cash flows (not discussed herein).[16]
b. Measuring the annual rate of return earned on the total assets employed during the period; this analysis is based on accrual accounting results (i.e., book values) for each accounting period standing alone.

The discussions in this section relate to the latter application. With income as the numerator, return on assets employed for a business may be computed on the basis of either (or both):

a. **Total assets**—income divided by average total assets.
b. **Owners' equity**—income divided by average total owners' equity.

Financial analysts also use the two return ratios together to measure **financial leverage** (also called **trading on the equity**). **Financial leverage is the effect of borrowing at a rate of interest (net of income tax) that is higher, or lower, than the rate of return (net of income tax) earned on total assets.** To illustrate, if a business can borow at 8% and earns 12% on the funds borrowed, the financial leverage is **positive.** In contrast, if the borrowing rate is 12% and the earning rate is 8%, the financial leverage is **negative.** Businesses borrow in anticipation of positive financial leverage. We have defined financial leverage precisely because the term is used differently in another context.

To illustrate computation of *(a)* return on total assets, *(b)* return on owners' equity, and *(c)* financial leverage, the following data for ACE Corporation is restated for convenience (from Exhibit 22–11):

	19B	19A
Statement of financial position:		
Total assets	$219,250	$204,000
Total liabilities	$ 75,450	$ 80,000
Total stockholders' equity (no preferred stock)	143,800	124,000
Total investment (book value)	$219,250	$204,000

[16] For a fundamental discussion, see Harold Bierman, Jr., and Seymour Smidt, *The Capital Budgeting Decision* (New York: Macmillan); or James C. Van Horne, *Financial Management and Policy* (Englewood Cliffs, N.J.: Prentice-Hall, 1987).

	19B	19A
Statement of income:		
Total revenues (pretax)	$387,382	$361,000
Total expenses (pretax and before interest expense)	(331,882)	(319,500)
Interest expense (pretax)	(5,500)	(6,500)
Pretax income	50,000	35,000
Income tax (30%)	(15,000)	(10,500)
Income before extraordinary items	35,000	24,500
Extraordinary gain (loss), net of tax	—	3,500
Net income	$ 35,000	$ 28,000

Computation of the 19B ratios illustrated for ACE Corporation:

a. Return on total assets:

$$\frac{\text{Income + Interest expense, net of tax}}{\text{Average total assets}} = \text{Return on total assets}$$

$$\text{19B:} \quad \frac{\$35{,}000 + (\$5{,}500 \times 70\%) = \$\ 38{,}850}{(\$204{,}000 + \$219{,}250) \div 2 = \$211{,}625} = 18\%$$

To compute return on total assets, interest expense (net of income tax) is added back to net income because the interest was paid to creditors of the entity. Because the denominator includes the resources provided by both creditors and owners, the numerator must include the return on both types of equities. Income before extraordinary items usually should be used to avoid any distortion due to nonrecurring and unusual items.

Return on total assets measures the profitability of the total assets available to the business. It indicates the efficiency with which management used the **total** available resources to earn income.

b. Return on owners' equity:

$$\frac{\text{Income}}{\text{Average stockholders' equity}} = \text{Return on owners' equity}$$

$$\text{19B:} \quad \frac{\$35{,}000}{(\$124{,}000 + \$143{,}800) \div 2 = \$133{,}900} = 26\%$$

Return on owners' equity measures the return that accrues to the stockholders **after** the interest paid to the creditors is deducted. It does not measure the efficiency with which total resources were used, but rather the **residual return** to the owners on their investment in the business.

c. Financial leverage:

Return on owners' equity	−	Return on total assets	=	Financial leverage
19B: 26%	−	18%	=	8% (positive)

Financial leverage is measured as the difference between return on owners' equity and return on total assets. The only difference between these two percentages is the effect of debt. The financial leverage for

ACE Corporation was a positive 8%. The 8% positive effect in favor of owners' equity resulted because the company earned a higher rate of return on total assets than the after-tax rate of interest paid for borrowed resources. Had there been no debt, the rate on total assets and the rate on owners' equity would have been the same.

3. **Investment turnover**—This ratio, also called the **asset turnover,** is computed by dividing net sales by average total assets for the year. It is used as a measure of the effectiveness with which management used the total resources at their disposal to earn revenue. It is similar in concept to inventory turnover. A company may have high investment turnover, viewed as a favorable condition, in the face of a net loss.

The investment turnover for ACE Corporation for 19B was:

$$\frac{\text{Net sales}}{\text{Average total assets}} = \frac{\$384{,}382}{(\$204{,}000) + (\$219{,}250) \div 2 = \$211{,}625} = 1.82 \text{ (times)}$$

4. **Earnings per share on common stock**—This ratio relates income to the average number of common shares outstanding. It reduces income (or loss) to a per share basis (discussed in detail in Part A).

5. **Price-earnings ratio**—This ratio, sometimes called the **multiple,** is frequently used by analysts and investors for evaluating stock prices because it relates the earnings of the business to the **current market price** of the stock. This ratio changes each time the market price of the stock changes. Several years ago, multiples of 20 or more were not unusual; however, multiples in the range of 5 to 10 currently are more common. The multiple usually should be computed on the basis of EPS before extraordinary items.

To illustrate, the 19B price-earnings ratio for ACE Corporation is (assuming a current market price per share of common stock of $11.75):

$$\frac{\text{Market price per share}}{\text{Earnings per share}} = \frac{\$11.75}{\$1.71 \text{ (Exhibit 22–11)}} = 7 \text{ (times)}$$

The primary weakness of this ratio is the timing mismatch between the numerator (i.e., the market price date) and the denominator (i.e., the end of the reporting period).

6. **Dividend-income payout ratio**—This ratio relates cash dividends declared on common stock during the reporting period to the income available to common stockholders for that period. It measures the percent of income that is represented by cash dividends. It can be computed for ACE Corporation as follows (19B):

$$\frac{\text{Cash dividends*}}{\text{Income†}} = \frac{\$14{,}400 \text{ (Exhibit 22–11)}}{\$34{,}200 \text{ (Exhibit 22–11)}} = 42\% \text{ (or .42)}$$

* Related to common stock. However, this ratio also is computed on the total of cash dividends to common shares plus preferred dividends.
† After deducting current preferred dividends, $35,000 − $800 = $34,200.

The primary weakness of this ratio is the timing mismatch between the numerator (i.e., the dividend declaration date) and the denominator (i.e., the end of the reporting period).

7. **Dividend-market value payout ratio**—This ratio relates cash dividends per share for the reporting period to the ending **market price** per share of stock. The ratio gives investors a rough estimate of the return per share on a stock investment based on the market price of the stock that existed at the end of the current reporting period. To illustrate, the 19B common stock dividend-market value payout ratio for ACE Corporation common stock would be computed as follows:

$$\frac{\text{Cash dividends per share}}{\text{Market price of the stock per share}} = \frac{\$.72 \text{ (Exhibit 22–11)}}{\$11.75 \text{ (given in item 5 above)}} = 6\% \text{ (or .06)}$$

The primary disadvantage of this ratio is the timing mismatch between the numerator (i.e., the dividend declaration date) and the denominator (i.e., the market price date).

Interpretation and Use of Ratio Analysis

Ratio analysis of financial statements is used widely along with more sophisticated techniques for making investment and credit decisions. Ratios communicate some aspects of the economic situation of an entity better than the absolute amounts reported on the financial statements. **The overriding disadvantage of ratio analyses, based on financial statement data, is that book values rather than market values are used in the computations.** Nevertheless, empirical studies have demonstrated that the traditional financial ratios are closely associated with the process by which stock prices are formed.[17] Financial ratios have been used successfully in prediction models to project whether a business would fail.[18] Thus, it is not surprising that financial and bank lending officers make wide use of ratio analysis in evaluating the future economic prospects of individual companies.

Ratios covering a period of years (as they must to be very useful) represent average conditions. Therefore, they must be interpreted in light of the "smoothing" effect inherent in any average. However, when viewed over an extended period of time, ratios may signal important **turning points,** either favorable or unfavorable, with respect to the future economic prospects for the business. One writer has compared effective use of ratios to the interpretation of a thermometer reading—beyond a certain range the fever reading indicates **something** is wrong with the patient, but does not indicate exactly what the problem is. An unfavorable ratio can similarly be thought of as a red flag—the matter

---

[17] W. H. Beaver, P. Kettler, and M. Scholes, "The Association between Market Determined and Accounting Determined Risk Measures," *The Accounting Review,* October 1970, pp. 654–82. For an extension of this work, see W. H. Beaver and J. Manegold, "The Association between Market-Determined and Accounting-Determined Measures of Systematic Risk: Some Further Evidence," *Journal of Financial and Quantitative Analysis,* June 1975, pp. 231–84.

[18] W. H. Beaver, "Financial Ratios as Predictors of Failure," *Empirical Research in Accounting: Selected Studies, 1966.* Supplement to *Journal of Accounting Research,* pp. 71–111; E. I. Altman, "Financial Ratios, Discriminant Analysis, and the Prediction of Corporate Bankruptcy," *Journal of Finance,* September 1968, pp. 589–609; and E. B. Deakin, "A Discriminant Analysis of Predictors of Business Failure," *Journal of Accounting Research,* Spring 1972, pp. 167–79.

should be investigated. However, one ratio or even several ratios, whatever their values, may not convey a clear message.

Consequently, a primary problem confronting the statement user relates to the evaluation of a ratio. For example, is it good or bad that the inventory turnover for a company is 12? In determining what constitutes an unfavorable or favorable ratio for a particular business, the following comparisons are suggested:

1. Comparison of the actual ratios for the current year with those of preceding years for the company. Comparisons of selected ratios for the company over a period of 5 to 10 years often are included in the published financial statements.
2. Comparison of the actual ratios for the company with budgeted or standard ratios developed internally by the company. However, this kind of comparison seldom is available to external statement users.
3. Comparison of the company's ratios with those of its competitors. The published financial reports of competitors provide information that may make this comparison feasible.
4. Comparison of the company's ratios with ratios for the industry in which the company operates. Industry statistics may be obtained from the following sources:
   a. Industry trade associations—Major industries support one or more trade associations that collect and publish financial statistics about the industry.
   b. Bureaus of business research at universities—Many major universities collect, analyze, and publish a wide range of regional statistics on local industries and businesses.
   c. Governmental agencies—Agencies that deal directly with business often publish, or have available as a matter of public record, financial information about industries and individual companies. The more prominent ones are the U.S. Department of Commerce, the U.S. Department of the Treasury, and the Securities and Exchange Commission, Washington, D.C.
   d. Commercial sources such as:
      (1) Robert Morris Associates.
      (2) Dun & Bradstreet.

Despite the wide use of ratio analysis, this technique has a number of limitations. Because of these limitations, ratios must be interpreted with some skepticism. Some of the important limitations are:

1. Ratios represent average conditions that existed in the **past;** they are based on historical data that incorporate all of the peculiarities of the past.
2. When the data on which ratios are based are historical book values, they do not reflect either *(a)* price-level effects or *(b)* current market values.
3. The method of computing each ratio is not standardized. Therefore, the computations (and hence, the results) can be influenced by data selection choices. Except for the EPS ratio, they are not subject to audit.

4. The use of alternative accounting methods may have an effect on ratios. For example, the previous chapters have indicated the significant effects on financial statement amounts of such alternatives as FIFO versus LIFO and straight-line versus accelerated depreciation.
5. Changes in accounting estimates and principles (such as a change from FIFO to LIFO) may affect the ratios for the year of change. Also, to develop data for long-term trends, it may be necessary to adjust the data for the effects of unusual or nonrecurring items and extraordinary items.
6. Comparisons among companies are difficult. Each company has different operating characteristics such as product lines, methods of operation, size, methods of financing, and geographical location. Also, the use of different accounting methods obscures interfirm comparisons.
7. All other investors have the same data available and can also compute the same ratios. Studies have shown that the market very quickly absorbs this information. As a result, it is extremely difficult to consistently earn above-average returns on stock investments by relying on publicly available information.[19] Thus, **excessive reliance** on ratio analysis, or any analysis based upon publicly available information, should consider this limitation.

Although the limitations are significant, ratio analysis is an important technique for financial statement interpretation because ratios reflect fundamental relationships in an entity. However, the results must be used with care.

Search for Additional Information

An investor should search for information to supplement that provided by the financial statements. Hearsay is hazardous; one should seek objective data concerning the company—its operations, policies, competitive position, the quality of the management, and other nonquantitative information. Brokerage firms and security analysts typically gather and disseminate this type of information. Periodic reports, by listed companies, filed with the SEC are available. They provide considerable information not included in the annual financial statements.

The financial press is a timely source of financial information. Examples of financial publications include *Fortune, Barrons, The Wall Street Journal, Business Week, Forbes,* and various industry publications. These publications are available in most libraries.

Interim and Segment Reporting

Interpretation and analysis of financial statements also involve a careful study of the notes and supplementary schedules that are integral parts of those statements. Major supplementary information that is required to be disclosed includes (1) interim reporting and (2) segment (line of business) reporting. The remaining sections of this chapter will discuss these two topics.

---

[19] For a summary of this evidence, see E. F. Fama, *Foundations of Finance* (New York: Basic Books, 1976), chap. 5.

Interim Reporting

Annual financial statements often are not timely because investors cannot wait until after the end of each annual reporting period to make all their investment decisions. Therefore, interim data, usually on a quarterly basis, often are presented by companies to provide timely information. Moreover, empirical research has demonstrated that stock prices reflect the impact of quarterly accounting information.[20]

Because of the wide diversity that had developed in applying GAAP to interim reports, *APB Opinion 28,* "Interim Financial Reporting," was issued in May 1973. That *Opinion* **does not require interim financial statements; rather, its primary purpose is to provide guidelines for their preparation.** Interim reports may be monthly, quarterly, or semiannual (usually they are quarterly) and may take the form of either complete financial statements or only summarized financial data. They may be prepared for each interim period or on a cumulative year-to-date basis, or both.

Underlying Concepts of Interim Reporting. Preparing interim reports presents difficulties because of a number of unavoidable factors. These include seasonality of revenues, major costs that occur only in one interim period but benefit other interim periods within the same reporting year, seasonality of production activities, extraordinary items and accounting changes that occur in one interim period but not others, selection of appropriate income tax rates for each interim period, and LIFO inventory liquidation during one or more interim periods but which are restored before the end of the reporting year. Because of these inherent problems, two opposing views of the nature of an interim period exist.

1. **Discrete view**—each interim period is viewed as a basic reporting period, which stands separate and alone without considering it as a part of a longer (i.e., the annual) reporting period. Under this view, revenue and expense recognition, accruals, and deferrals for the interim period follow the same principles and procedures as for an annual period, and there would be no "interim-period" allocations. Thus, an expense incurred in one interim period usually would not be allocated to the other interim periods.
2. **Integral-part view**—each interim period is viewed as an inseparable part of the annual reporting period. Under this view, revenue and expense recognition, deferrals, and accruals are affected by judgments made at the end of each interim period about the results of operations for the remainder of the reporting year. Thus, an expense incurred in one interim period may be **allocated** among other interim periods within the reporting year.

---

[20] R. G. May, "The Influence of Quarterly Earnings Announcements on Investor Decisions as Reflected in Common Stock Price Changes," *Empirical Research in Accounting: Selected Studies, 1971.* Supplement to *Journal of Accounting Research,* pp. 119–63; P. Brown and J. W. Kennelly, "The Information Content of Quarterly Earnings: An Extension and Some Further Evidence," *Journal of Business,* July 1972, pp. 403–15; and G. J. Foster, "Quarterly Accounting Data: Time Series Properties and Predictive-Ability Results," *The Accounting Review,* January 1977, pp. 1–21.

APB Opinion 28 **states that "each interim period should be viewed primarily as an integral part of the annual period."** However, the *Opinion* makes some practical concessions on this point.

Guidelines for Preparing Interim Financial Reports. *APB Opinion 28* gives the following guidelines for preparing interim reports:

1. In general, the accounting principles and practices used by the company in preparing its annual financial statements should be used for interim reports, with certain modifications (discussed below).
2. Revenue from products and services sold should be recognized as earned during the interim period on the same basis as followed for the annual period.
3. Costs and expenses for interim periods are classified as:
   a. Costs that are **directly associated** with interim revenue are reported in the interim period.
   b. Costs and expenses that are **not directly associated** with interim revenue must be allocated to interim periods on a reasonable basis.

Costs Directly Associated with Revenue. Costs directly associated with revenue, such as cost of goods sold, wages, salaries, fringe benefits, and warranties, should be expensed in the interim period in which the related revenue is recognized, with the following exceptions or disclosures:

a. Use of the gross margin method (discussed in Chapter 9) for computing cost of goods sold must be disclosed.

b. If LIFO is used and LIFO inventory is liquidated during an interim period and it is expected to be restored by year-end, cost of goods sold for the interim period should be debited for the anticipated replacement cost of the number of units liquidated and an estimated liability should be credited.

c. Inventory declines, unless temporary, should not be deferred to future interim periods; recovery in later interim periods should be recognized as gains, but not in excess of the previously recognized losses.

Costs Not Directly Associated with Revenue. All costs not directly associated with revenue should be accounted and reported for interim periods as follows:

a. Recognize as expense in the interim period in which incurred, or allocate among interim periods based on an estimate of time expired, benefit received, or activity associated with the periods.

b. Arbitrary allocation of such costs should not be made. If any costs cannot be reasonably allocated, they should be assigned to the interim period in which incurred.

c. Gains and losses that arise in any interim period, similar to those that would not be deferred at year-end, should be recognized in the interim period in which they arise.

d. Income tax expense for each interim period should be based on an estimate of the annual rate as made at the end of each quarter. Revision of the rate for subsequent interim periods is treated as a change in estimate.

Unusual or nonrecurring items and extraordinary items should be recognized in the interim period in which they occur. Similarly, contingent losses not directly associated with revenue and the related liabilities should be recognized in the interim period in which they occur. Accounting changes are accounted for and reported in essentially the same manner as discussed in Chapter 24 for annual reporting periods.

Disclosure of Summarized Interim Financial Data. When a company reports summarized interim information, the following data should be reported, as a minimum:

a. Sales, income taxes, and net income.
b. Disposal of a segment of a business and extraordinary, unusual or infrequently occurring items.
c. Primary and fully diluted earnings per share (EPS).
d. Seasonal revenue, costs, or expenses.
e. Significant changes in estimates or provisions for income taxes.
f. Changes in accounting principles or estimates.
g. Significant changes in financial position.

Interim Reporting Illustrated. To illustrate interim reporting, the following data were selected from the first quarter operations (ended March 31, 19H) of Interim Corporation:

Selected items	Amount
Sales of products and services	$500,000
Interest revenue	1,000
Extraordinary loss	15,000
Correction of 19G accounting error (credit)	6,000
Cost of goods sold	241,000
Operational assets, cost (10-year remaining life, no residual value, straight line)	480,000
Salary and wage expense	89,000
Inventory allowance change, LCM (temporary)	4,000
Advertising expense (benefits first and second quarters equally)	18,000
Annual property tax for 19H (estimated)	12,000
Contribution to United Fund for 19H	6,000
Shipping supplies expense	7,000
Unusual loss	4,000
Estimated average income tax rate, 30%; reporting period ends December 31; 30,000 common shares outstanding.	

Exhibit 22–16 illustrates the quarterly interim statement amounts needed to meet the reporting requirements of *APB Opinion 28.* Notice in the exhibit that careful distinctions were maintained between costs directly related to interim revenue and all other costs not directly related to interim revenue.

Exhibit 22–16
Interim (quarterly) statements of income and retained earnings, Interim Corporation.

INTERIM CORPORATION
Statement of Income
For Quarter Ending March 31, 19H

	Explanation	Amount
Revenues:		
Sales of products and services	Direct: recognize in full as earned	$500,000
Interest revenue	Direct: recognize as earned on accrual basis	1,000
Total revenues		501,000
Expenses:		
Cost of goods sold	Directly related to interim revenue	241,000
Salaries and wages	Directly related to interim operations, accrual basis	89,000
Depreciation expense	Allocate on time basis, $480,000 × 3/120	12,000
Inventory decline, LCM	Not recognized because deemed temporary	–0–
Advertising expense	Allocate on benefit basis, $18,000 ÷ 2 (defer half to next interim period)	9,000
Contributions	Recognize when incurred, not related to operations nor allocable reasonably	6,000
Property tax expense	Accrual basis, $12,000 × 1/4 (time basis)	3,000
Shipping expense	Accrual basis	7,000
Unusual loss	Recognized when it occurred, not allocated	4,000
Income tax expense	Accrue on basis of estimated average tax rate ($501,000 − $371,000) × 30%	39,000
Total expenses		410,000
Income before extraordinary item		91,000
Extraordinary loss (net of $4,500 income tax)		10,500
Net income		$ 80,500
Earnings per share (30,000 common shares outstanding):		
Income before extraordinary items ($91,000 ÷ 30,000 shares)	$3.03	
Extraordinary loss ($10,500 ÷ 30,000 shares)	(.35)	
Net income ($80,500 ÷ 30,000 shares)	$2.68	

Statement of Retained Earnings
For Quarter Ending March 31, 19H

Beginning balance (assumed)	$100,000
Prior period adjustment, error correction ($6,000 × 70%)	4,200*
Balance as adjusted	104,200
Net income	80,500
Ending balance	$184,700

* Error corrections during interim periods are assumed at the beginning of the reporting year.

The Appendix following Chapter 25 illustrates the interim (quarterly) financial data reported by Kimberly-Clark Corporation.

Segment (or Line of Business) Reporting

Many large corporations engage in more than one line of business. Also, many smaller corporations have diversified their operations into more than one industry. In the past, investors seeking to assess the relative attractiveness of the capital stock of a diversified company were faced with the difficult task of analyzing and interpreting company financial reports that reported aggregated data with no information on the performance of its various "lines of business."

To better understand the problem, suppose you are an investor analyzing General Electric Company (GE). GE produces and sells products ranging from light bulbs to household appliances to aircraft engines. Supply and demand for these three product groups (consumer nondurables, consumer durables, and heavy machinery) react differently during good and bad economic times. For example, consumers will continue to buy light bulbs during recessions as well as during prosperous times. To a lesser extent, consumers also must have kitchen ranges to prepare their meals during hard times. However, they probably will continue to use their old ranges longer than during prosperous times. Thus, price changes affect the demand for kitchen ranges more than the demand for light bulbs. The demand for air travel and the related demand for aircraft engines is even more responsive to price changes than the demand for light bulbs. Stated differently, each of these three industrial groups possesses different **risk characteristics.** Investors who know the relative proportions of company resources committed to operations in these (and other) specific industries likely can make more informed decisions than investors who only know the aggregate data of the company.

This line of reasoning is the basis for *FASB Standard 14*, "Financial Reporting for Segments of a Business Enterprise." A segment of a business is a subdivision in the business that derives revenues from **individual** products or services that are significant parts of the business. In addition, segment reporting applies to each major customer that provides 10% or more of the company revenue, and foreign operations (if they provide 10% or more of total revenues or identifiable assets). Supplement 22–B provides a comprehensive discussion of segment (or line of business) reporting.

Summary of Financial Statement Analysis

Financial statements present highly summarized data in a standard format and in dollars. To provide additional insights in understanding numerous relationships within and among the statements of income, financial position, and cash flows, analytical techniques often are used. In addition to earnings per share data, these important relationships often are examined to help statement users assess and evaluate the dollar amounts as a basis for *(a)* evaluating management performance and *(b)* projecting future cash flows.

The techniques of financial statement analysis involve a comprehensive examination of the financial statements, which includes the following: examination of the auditor's report, a study of the accounting policies, and application of certain widely used techniques. The techniques include percentage analysis of the individual statements (horizontal and vertical) and ratio analysis. Ratio analysis is used primarily to measure *(a)* current position, *(b)* equity position, and *(c)* operating results. Also, interim and segment reporting are provided to help users to better evaluate and interpret the financial statements.

Interpretation and use of the results of ratio analysis must be done with care because misleading inferences are possible. A decision about whether a particular ratio is too high or too low often is judgmental, however, comparisons with realistic standards is helpful. Also, ratios are based on averages which may include wide variations in the data used to compute them. Nevertheless, ratios can be useful for comparative purposes and for identifying turning points.

SUPPLEMENT 22–A: DILUTION/ANTIDILUTION D/A TEST—COMBINATIONS APPROACH

This is the conceptual way to apply the D/A test to attain maximum dilution in complex capital structures. It involves testing all possible combinations of the dilutive contracts and securities. Application of this approach is illustrated in **Exhibit 22–17** for Jade Corporation. Panel A gives the case data needed, panel B shows the D/A test of the four possible combinations for primary EPS, and panel C illustrates the D/A test of the eight possible combinations for fully diluted EPS.

SUPPLEMENT 22–B: SEGMENT (OR LINE OF BUSINESS) REPORTING AND DISCONTINUED OPERATIONS

Segment Reporting

Segment reporting is required for large companies because financial statement users need information about the major revenue generating activities of a company to help them assess and project the various risks, prospects, and cash flows.

This reasoning is the basis for the requirement that companies must report **segment data.** The basis is supported by the results of a number of empirical research studies that have indicated that hypothetical investment decisions based on segment data turn out better than decisions based on aggregated data.[21]

In recognition of these circumstances, the FASB first issued *FASB Standard 14,* "Financial Reporting for Segments of a Business Enterprise," December 1976, which set out the general principles described earlier in Part B. In November 1977, *FASB Standard 18* was issued; it provided that segment information was not required in statements for **interim periods.** *FASB Standard 21,* issued in April 1978, suspended the requirement of reporting segment information by **nonpublic companies.** A nonpublic company is one whose debt or equity securities do not trade in a public market, or is not required to file financial statements with the SEC.[22] Finally, *FASB Standard 30* (1979) amended *FASB Standard 14* in respect to certain required disclosures.

---

[21] For example, see D. W. Collins, "SEC Product-Line Reporting and Market Efficiency," *Journal of Financial Economics,* June 1975, pp. 125–64. Also, D. W. Collins and R. Simonds, "SEC Line-of-Business Disclosure and Market Risk Adjustments," *Journal of Accounting Research,* Autumn 1979, pp. 352–83; and R. Simonds and D. W. Collins, "Line of Business Reporting and Security Prices: An Analysis of an SEC Disclosure Rule: Comment," *The Bell Journal of Economics,* Autumn 1978, pp. 646–58.

[22] *FASB Standard 21* also eliminated the requirement that EPS must be reported by such companies.

Exhibit 22–17
Dilution/antidilution (D/A) test—Jade Corporation, 19C.

Panel A—Case Data:

1. Net income, $134,000 (Exhibit 22–2).
2. Average common shares outstanding, 94,000 shares (Exhibit 22–2).
3. Dividend claims of nonconvertible preferred stock, 2,500 shares × $20 × 6% = $3,000.
4. Stock rights—400 CSE shares (Exhibit 22–5).
5. Convertible preferred stock—Dividends, 1,000 shares × $7 = $7,000.
   —8,000 CSE shares (Exhibit 22–7).
6. Series A convertible bonds —Interest effect, $200,000 × 8% × .60 = $9,600.
   —6,000 CSE shares (Exhibit 22–7).
7. Series B convertible bonds*—Interest effect, $500,000 × 10% × .60 = $30,000.
   —Common shares if converted, 25,000 shares (Exhibit 22–7).

* For fully diluted only.

Panel B—D/A Test for Primary EPS:

Items included	Numerator / Denominator	EPS
1. Common stock and stock rights.	$\frac{\$134{,}000^{(a)} - \$3{,}000^{(b)} - \$7{,}000^{(c)}}{94{,}000^{(d)} + 400^{(e)}}$	= $1.31
2. Common stock, stock rights, and convertible preferred stock.	$\frac{\$134{,}000^{(a)} - \$3{,}000^{(b)}}{94{,}000^{(d)} + 400^{(c)} + 8{,}000^{(f)}}$	= **[$1.28]**
3. Common stock, stock rights, and series A convertible bonds.	$\frac{\$134{,}000^{(a)} - \$3{,}000^{(b)} - \$7{,}000^{(c)} + \$9{,}600^{(g)}}{94{,}000^{(d)} + 400^{(c)} + 6{,}000^{(h)}}$	= $1.33
4. Common stock, stock rights, convertible preferred stock, and series A convertible bonds.	$\frac{\$134{,}000^{(a)} - \$3{,}000^{(b)} + 9{,}600^{(g)}}{94{,}000^{(d)} + 400^{(c)} + 8{,}000^{(f)} + 6{,}000^{(h)}}$	= $1.30

Note: Footnotes given at end of panel C.

Reportable Segment Defined. In the context of *FASB Standard 14,* a **reportable segment** is defined by "(a) identifying the individual products or services from which the enterprise derives its revenue, (b) grouping those products and services by industry lines into industry segments . . . , and (c) selecting those industry segments that are significant with respect to the enterprise as a whole."

The three reportable segments are: *(a)* industry, *(b)* foreign, and *(c)* major customers.

Industry Segments. An industry segment is one which meets **any one** of the following criteria:

a. Its revenue is 10% or more of the combined revenue of all segments of the entity.

b. The absolute amount of its operating profit or loss is 10% or more of the greater, in absolute amount, of—
   (1) The combined operating **profit** of all industry segments of the entity that **did not** incur an operating loss, or
   (2) The combined operating **loss** of all industry segments of the entity that **did incur** an operating loss.

c. Its identifiable assets are 10% or more of the combined identifiable assets of all industry segments (of the entity).

Exhibit 22–17
(continued)

Panel C—D/A Test for Fully Diluted EPS:

Items included	Computation	EPS
1. Common stock and stock rights.	See panel A	\$1.31
2. Common stock, stock rights, and convertible preferred stock.	See panel A	\$1.28
3. Common stock, stock rights, and series A convertible bonds.	See panel A	\$1.33
4. Common stock, stock rights, convertible preferred stock, and series A convertible bonds.	See panel A	\$1.30
5. Common stock, stock rights, and series B convertible bonds.	$\frac{\$134{,}000^{(a)} - \$3{,}000^{(b)} - \$7{,}000^{(c)} + \$30{,}000^{(i)}}{94{,}000^{(d)} + 400^{(e)} + 25{,}000^{(j)}}$	= \$1.29
6. Common stock, stock rights, convertible preferred stock, and series B convertible bonds.	$\frac{\$134{,}000^{(a)} - \$3{,}000^{(b)} + \$30{,}000^{(i)}}{94{,}000^{(d)} + 400^{(e)} + 8{,}000^{(f)} + 25{,}000^{(j)}}$	= **\$1.26**
7. Common stock, stock rights, series A convertible bonds, and series B convertible bonds.	$\frac{\$134{,}000^{(a)} - \$3{,}000^{(b)} - \$7{,}000^{(c)} + \$9{,}600^{(g)} + \$30{,}000^{(i)}}{94{,}000^{(d)} + 400^{(e)} + 6{,}000^{(h)} + 25{,}000^{(j)}}$	= \$1.30
8. Common stock, stock rights, convertible preferred stock, series A convertible bonds, and series B convertible bonds.	$\frac{\$134{,}000^{(a)} - \$3{,}000^{(b)} + \$9{,}600^{(g)} + \$30{,}000^{(i)}}{94{,}000^{(d)} + 400^{(e)} + 8{,}000^{(f)} + 6{,}000^{(h)} + 25{,}000^{(j)}}$	= \$1.28

Explanation:
[a] Net income.
[b] Dividend claims of nonconvertible preferred stock.
[c] Dividend claims of convertible preferred stock.
[d] Average common shares outstanding.
[e] CSEs represented by stock rights.
[f] CSEs represented by convertible preferred stock.
[g] Interest effect of series A convertible bonds.
[h] CSEs represented by series A convertible bonds.
[i] Interest effect of series B convertible bonds.
[j] Common shares represented by series B convertible bonds if converted.

FASB Standard 14, as amended by *FASB Standards 18, 21*, and *30*, requires that for **each reportable industry segment** the company report the following:

a. Segment revenue.
b. Segment operating income or loss.
c. Identifiable segment assets.
d. Other related disclosures.

Segment revenue includes all product and service sales to unaffiliated customers (i.e., customers from outside the enterprise), intersegment sales, and interest on segment trade receivables. It does **not** include interest revenue on loans to other segments.

Segment operating gain or loss is segment revenue (as defined above) less all segment operating expenses. Operating expenses for a segment include *(a)* operating expenses that are **directly** related to a segment's revenue and *(b)* operating expenses incurred by the company that can be "allocated on a reasonable basis" to a segment(s) for whose benefit those expenses were incurred. **None** of the following can be added or deducted in computing the operating income or loss of a segment: (1) company revenues not derived from the segment,

(2) general company expenses, (3) interest expense, (4) income tax, (5) equity in income of unconsolidated subsidiaries or other equity investees, (6) extraordinary items, (7) minority interests in income, and (8) cumulative effect of an accounting change.

Identifiable segment assets include the tangible and intangible identifiable assets of the segment that are used (1) exclusively by the segment or (2) jointly by two or more segments (allocated on a "reasonable" basis). Asset valuation accounts, such as Allowance for Doubtful Accounts and Accumulated Depreciation, also must be included. Assets that cannot be included are (1) those used for general company purposes and (2) loans or advances to other segments.

Other related disclosures for a segment include: (1) the aggregate amount of depreciation, depletion, and amortization expense; (2) the amount of capital expenditures during the period (i.e., additions to property, plant, and equipment); (3) the company's equity in the net income and investment in unconsolidated subsidiaries and other equity investees whose operations are vertically integrated with the segment (including disclosure of the geographic area in which that investee operates); and (4) the effect on the segment of all changes in accounting principle.[23]

Foreign Operations. In addition, *FASB Standard 14* requires companies to report the following three items for each **foreign operation,** if either (1) revenue from foreign operations is 10% or more of the combined revenue of all segments of the entity, or (2) identifiable assets of the entity's foreign operations are 10% or more of the combined identifiable assets of the entity:

- **a.** Revenues.
- **b.** Operating income or loss.
- **c.** Identifiable assets.

Major Customers. *FASB Standard 30* (par. 6) states that "If 10 percent or more of the combined revenue of an enterprise is derived from sales to any **single customer,** that fact and the amount of revenue from each such customer shall be disclosed . . . but the identity of the customer need not be disclosed. . . ." A group of entities under common control, the federal government, a state government, or a local government each is considered as a single customer. The industry segments making the sales, rather than the identity of the customer, must be disclosed.

Basic Reporting by Segments. Data on these three segment groups—**reportable industry segments, foreign operations, and major customers**—are intended to provide investors with the data needed to assess the relative risks of diversified companies.

All of the required information about a segment may be reported in any of the following ways: (1) within the body of the financial statements (with appropri-

[23] Vertical integration refers to the complementary nature of a parent and its subsidiaries' product lines whereby one supplies inputs to the other. An example of vertical integration would be General Motors and Libbey-Owens-Ford or Fisher Body. Another example would be American Telephone and Telegraph and Western Electric (which builds the telephones).

ate note disclosure); (2) entirely in notes to the financial statements; or (3) in a separate schedule. Whichever way is selected, the segment disclosures must be an integral part of the financial statements.

Segment Reporting Illustrated. To illustrate segment reporting, the following pretax data were selected from the 19A accounts of SG Corporation, which has two identifiable segments (Segment A—Lumber Division, and Segment B—Allied Products Division):

	Segment	
Selected items	**A**	**B**
Sales revenue	$480,000	$320,000
Interest revenue	3,000	2,000
Investment revenue on equity securities (cost method), $6,000.		
Operating expenses	240,000	75,000
Operating expenses, company, $100,000; allocation	½	½
Depreciation expense	48,000	19,000
Depreciation expense, joint, $18,000; allocation	⅔	⅓
Depreciation expense, general, $4,000.		
Interest expense, general, $3,000.		
Expenses, general, $150,000.		
Extraordinary gain, $20,000.		
Cumulative effect of change in accounting principle, $10,000 (debit).		
Assets (tangible and intangible), net; at year-end	200,000	100,000
Assets (tangible and intangible), net; used jointly, $90,000; allocation	⅔	⅓
Assets, general company, net; at year-end, $60,000.		
Income tax rate, 30%; accounting period ends December 31.		

Exhibit 22–18 illustrates the computation of segment information for reporting purposes. Notice that a careful distinction was maintained among: (1) direct segment information; (2) indirect segment information; and (3) general company revenues, expenses, and identifiable assets. The allocations used in the exhibit for indirect segment information were simplified; on this point *FASB Standard 14* merely states that such indirect segment data be identified with reportable segments "on a reasonable basis."

The Appendix following Chapter 25 illustrates an actual segment report by one well-known company.

Discontinued Operations (Disposal of a Segment of a Business)

The disposal by a company of a segment of its business is an important accounting and reporting issue. *APB Opinion 30,* "Reporting the Results of Operations," provides reporting guidelines for discontinuance of a **segment** of a business that is sold, abandoned, spun off, or otherwise disposed. The guidelines for **discontinued operations require that any loss or gain on disposal, less the applicable income tax effect, be reported separately as a component of income before extraordinary items.** For this purpose the *Opinion* defines **segment of a business** as "a component of an entity whose activities represent a separate major line of business or class of customer." A segment may be a subsidiary division, department, or other part of the entity provided that its assets, results of operations, and activities can be clearly distinguished physically and operationally, for financial reporting purposes, from the other operations of the entity.

Exhibit 22–18
Segment reporting, SG Corporation.

SG CORPORATION
Segment Data for Year 19A

		Segment A		Segment B	Company
Statement of income:					
Net revenues:					
Sales (direct)		$480,000		$320,000	$800,000
Interest revenue (direct)		3,000		2,000	5,000
Investment revenue (company)					6,000
Total segment revenue		483,000		322,000	
Total company revenue					811,000
Expenses:					
Operating expenses (direct)		240,000		75,000	315,000
Operating expenses (indirect)	$100,000 × ½	50,000	$100,000 × ½	50,000	100,000
Depreciation expense (direct)		48,000		19,000	67,000
Depreciation expense (joint)	$ 18,000 × ⅔	12,000	$ 18,000 × ⅓	6,000	18,000
Depreciation expense (company)					4,000
Interest expense (company)					3,000
General company expense					150,000
Total segment expense (pretax)		350,000		150,000	
Total company expense (pretax)					657,000
Segment operating income (pretax)		$133,000		$172,000	
Total company income (pretax)					154,000
Income tax expense ($154,000 × 30%)					46,200
Income before extraordinary items and accounting changes					107,800
Extraordinary gain (net of $6,000 income tax)					14,000
Change in accounting principle (net of $3,000 income tax saving)					(7,000)
Net income					$114,800
Statement of financial position:					
Assets:					
Used directly		$200,000		$100,000	$300,000
Used jointly	$ 90,000 × ⅔	60,000	$ 90,000 × ⅓	30,000	90,000
General company assets					60,000
Total assets at 12/31/19A					$450,000

Note: The company operates in two industries: A, which involves lumber, and B, which involves paper and allied products. Revenue by segment includes sales to unaffiliated customers and intersegment sales. Segment operating income is revenue less operating expenses but does not include general company expenses, interest expense, income tax expense, extraordinary items, and accounting change effects. Total company revenue ($811,000) is more than total segment revenue, by $6,000, because of general company revenue on equity investments (cost method) of $6,000. Total company expense of $718,600 was more than total segment expense of $500,000, because of general company expenses (depreciation, $4,000, interest expense, $3,000, general corporate expense, $150,000, and income tax expense, $61,600). There were no foreign sales nor sales to a single unaffiliated customer or government agency in excess of 10% of total revenue.

The *Opinion* does **not** apply to the disposal of assets related to the evolution of the entity's business, such as the disposal of a machine, **part** of a division, subsidiary, line of business, or the phasing out of product lines, changes in services, the disposal of one or more unrelated assets, or changes due to technological improvements.

To account for the discontinuance of a segment, two dates must be carefully identified. The **measurement date** is the date on which the entity **formally contracts** with a buyer to sell a specific segment. The **disposal date** is the **closing** date of sale of the assets (i.e., when the segment is transferred) or the date that operations cease if the disposal is by abandonment.

The measurement and disposal dates may be the same. However, in most cases, disposal date follows the measurement date. In situations where the two dates differ, the selling entity typically agrees to continue the **usual operations** of the segment being discontinued until the disposal date. Therefore, any gains or losses from segment operations during that period of time are considered to be those of the seller.

Measurement and Disposal Dates the Same. If the measurement and disposal dates are the same, a single journal entry is made to record the full consideration received and to remove the carrying (i.e., book) values of all segment assets sold. The difference between these two amounts is the pretax "gain or loss on sale of segment." When comparative statements include the year of disposal, the **gain or loss on disposal, net of tax,** must be reported on the statement of income immediately preceding "Income from operations before extraordinary items."

To illustrate the situation in which the measurement and disposal dates are the same, assume that on September 1, 19B, XT Corporation sold and transferred its specialty products division for $200,000 cash. The carrying value of the segment's assets was $230,000. The accounting year ends December 31, and the applicable income tax rate was 30%. The summary entry and appropriate reporting would be as follows for XT Corporation:

September 1, 19B (measurement and disposal date):

Cash	200,000	
Loss on disposal of segment (pretax)	30,000*	
Assets, Specialty Products Division		230,000

* Income tax saving $30,000 × 30% = 9,000 (reflected in income tax entry).

Comparative statement of income, 19B and 19A:

	19B	19A
Income from continuing operations (assumed)	$265,000	$262,000
Discontinued operations (Note 6):		
Income from discontinued operations*		9,000
Gain (loss) from disposal of discontinued operations, net of income tax ($9,000)	(21,000)	
	$244,000	$271,000

* Income from operations of the unit, from the measurement date of the discontinuation decision and the disposable date.

Note 6. Discontinued operations—on September 1, 19B, the company sold its Specialty Products Division. The measurement and disposal dates were September 1, 19B. The company received $200,000 cash for the sale of the division; a disposal loss of $30,000 (less an income tax saving of $9,000) was recognized.

Measurement and Disposal Dates Different—but in the Same Reporting Period. **When the measurement and disposal dates are different** and the selling entity continues the segment operations, the accounting and reporting is more complex. In this situation, the accounting and reporting are influenced by whether these two dates are in *(a)* the **same** accounting period or *(b)* **different** accounting periods. **When the measurement and disposal dates are different (the usual case) but both are in the same accounting period,** the accounting and reporting would be as follows:

Same as above for XT Corporation, except that the measurement date is September 1, 19B, and the disposal date is December 31, 19B.

1. September 1, 19B—measurement date:
   The disposal entry may be made at this date. However, because the disposal date is also in this year, the entry usually is deferred to the later date within the current year to accommodate any subsequent changes agreed on by the parties.
2. September 1–December 31, 19B—account for the operations of the discontinued segment separately.
3. December 31, 19B—end of accounting period and disposal date:
   a. Record disposal of the Specialty Products Division:

Cash	200,000	
Loss on disposal of segment (pretax)	30,000*	
Assets, Specialty Products Division		230,000

* Income tax saving, $30,000 × 30% = $9,000 (reflected in income tax entry).

   b. At December 31, 19B, the accounting records provided the following data for the Specialty Products Division: income (pretax), 19A, $15,000; January 1, 19B, to August 31, 19B, $8,000; September 1, 19B, to December 31, 19B, $4,000. The $4,000 income from segment operations during the **run-down period** from September 1, 19B, through December 31, 19B, and the $30,000 loss on disposal of the segment are closed to Income Summary at year-end. The income tax effect on each of these amounts is included in the 19B income tax entry.

Comparative statement of income:

		19B	19A
Income from operations, net of tax (assumed 30%)		$265,000	$262,000
Discontinued operations (Note 6):			
Income from discontinued operations, net of tax:			
19A: ($15,000 × 70%)			10,500
19B: From January 1, to August 31, 19B ($8,000 × 70%)		5,600	
Gain (loss) on disposal of discontinued operations, net of tax:			
Income from operations of discontinued operations, September 1 to December 31, 19B ($4,000 × 70%)	$ 2,800		
Loss on disposal ($30,000 × 70%)	(21,000)	(18,200)	
Net income		$252,400	$272,500

Note 6. Discontinued operations. In 19B, the company decided to sell its Specialty Products Division. The measurement date was September 1, 19B, and the disposal date was December 31, 19B. The company received $200,000 cash for the assets of the discontinued segment; a disposal loss of $30,000 (less an income tax saving of $9,000) was recognized. Incomes from the discontinued segment were: 19A, $15,000 (less income tax effect, $4,500), and 19B, $8,000 (less income tax saving, 2,400). Total loss on disposal recognized in 19B was $26,000 (i.e., $30,000 − $4,000) less the income tax effect of $6,200 (i.e., $9,000 − $2,800).

Measurement and Disposal Dates Different—in Different Reporting Periods. **When the measurement and disposal dates are in different reporting periods, the contract to sell a segment must be recorded on measurement date.** Because of the continuing operation of the segment by the selling company until disposal date and the additional requirement that the contract of sale must be recorded on measurement date, an **estimate** must be made of any expected loss (but not a gain) from the segment operations up to the **disposal date.** A gain is recognized only when it is earned. An **estimated loss must be accrued on measurement date.** The accounting and reporting are illustrated below.

Situation. On September 1, 19B, XT Corporation concluded an agreement to sell its Specialty Products Division to another party for $200,000 cash, payable on the closing date, March 1, 19C. XT Corporation will continue to operate the division between the measurement date, September 1, 19B, and disposal date, March 1, 19C. The accounting period ends December 31. The carrying (or book) value of the Division's net assets on measurement date was $230,000; the income tax rate is 30%. Recall from the prior page that the incomes from discontinued operations were: 19A, $15,000 and for 19B (to August 31), $8,000.

At the end of 19B, the accounting records reflected a $6,000 pretax loss from the Specialty Division's operations for the period September 1, 19B, to December 31, 19B. An estimated pretax loss of $9,000 is expected for the period January 1, 19C, to disposal date, March 1, 19C. However, on the latter date, the accounting records reflected an actual pretax loss from the division's operations of $12,000.

The accounting and reporting for this situation are as follows:

September 1, 19B—measurement date:

a. To record the loss on disposal:

Special receivable	200,000	
Loss on disposal of segment (pretax)	30,000*	
Assets, Specialty Products Division		230,000

* Income tax saving, $30,000 × 30% = $9,000.

December 31, 19B—end of the accounting period:

b. To accrue the estimated loss from operations of the segment:

Estimated loss on segment operations (pretax)	9,000*	
Accrued loss on segment operations (a liability)		9,000

* Income tax saving, $9,000 × 30% = $2,700.
Note: This entry may be made on the measurement date; however, it often is not made until the end of the accounting period because a better estimate may be made.

Reporting at end of 19B:

Comparative Statement of Income, 19A and 19B	19B	19A
Income from continuing operations, after tax (assumed)	$265,000	$262,000
Discontinued operations (Note 6):		
Income (loss) from discontinued operations, net of tax:		
19A: ($15,000 × 70%)		10,500[a]
19B: From January 1 to August 31, 19B ($8,000 × 70%)	5,600	
From September 1 to December 31, 19B [($9,000 + $6,000) × 70%]	(10,500)[b]	
Gain (loss) on disposal of segment, net of tax ($30,000 × 70%)	(21,000)[c]	
Net income	$239,100	$272,500

[a] Income (loss) prior to measurement date. [b] Actual 19B loss plus estimated 19C loss; estimated income (loss)—estimated (unrealized) gains cannot exceed estimated (unrealized) loss. [c] Actual gain or loss on sale of disposed segment.

Note 6. Discontinued operations. During 19B, the company decided to sell the Specialty Products Division for $200,000 cash. The measurement date was September 1, 19B, and the disposal date will be March 1, 19C, during which time the company has agreed to continue the normal operations of the Division. Loss from the discontinued segment operations during 19B was $15,000, less a $4,500 income tax saving; net loss, $10,500.

January 1, 19B to March 1, 19C—The accounting records reflected a $12,000 actual loss from the discontinued segment, of which $9,000 was offset against the credit balance in the account "Accrued loss on segment operations" (see December 31, 19B, entry above, which reduces the accrued loss account balance to zero). Therefore, the accounting records pertaining to the discontinued segment reflected the following on March 1, 19C:

Loss on segment operations, pretax ($12,000 − $9,000)	$3,000
Income tax saving (reflected in the income tax entry), $3,000 × 30%	900
Loss on 19C segment operations, net of tax	$2,100

March 1, 19C—entry on disposal date:

Cash	200,000	
Special receivable		200,000

Comparative statement of income, 19C and 19B

	19C	19B
Income from continuing operations, after tax (assumed)	$279,000	$265,000
Discontinued operations (Note 6):		
Income (loss) from discontinued operations (net of income tax) (19B, $10,500 loss − $5,600 gain)	(2,100)	(4,900)
Gain (loss) on disposal of segment (net of income tax)		(21,000)
Net income	$276,900	$239,100

Note 6. Discontinued operations. In 19B, the company decided to sell the Specialty Products Division for $200,000 cash, collectible on the disposal date, March 1, 19C. The company continued to operate the division until this disposal date. Loss from discontinued operations from January 1, 19C, to March 1, 19C, was $3,000 more than originally estimated, less a $900 income tax saving. A loss of $30,000 (less a $9,000 income tax saving) on the sale of the assets of the division was reported as of the measurement date, September 1, 19B.

QUESTIONS

Part A

1. What is the basic difference in EPS computations and reporting between a simple capital structure and a complex capital structure?
2. What is a common stock equivalent? How do common stock equivalents affect EPS computations?
3. What is the 3% materiality rule in EPS computations and how is it used?
4. Contrast primary EPS and fully diluted EPS.
5. Explain the treasury stock method.
6. What is the interest rate test and when is it used?
7. What is the difference between a dilutive security and an antidilutive security? Why is the distinction important in EPS considerations?
8. A company split its common stock 2 for 1 on June 30 of its accounting year ended December 31. Before the split, there were 4,000 shares of common stock outstanding.

How many shares of common stock should be used in computing EPS? How many shares of common stock should be used in computing a comparative EPS amount for the preceding year?

9. Explain why nonconvertible securities do not cause a complex capital structure while convertible securities do cause a complex capital structure.
10. Explain why and when dividends on nonconvertible preferred stock must be subtracted from income to compute EPS in both simple and complex capital structures.

Part B

11. Why is the past financial record of a company important to statement users? What is meant by a turning point?
12. Explain why financial analysts and others, in analyzing financial statements, examine the auditors' report and the summary of accounting policies.
13. Explain why the notes to the financial statements should be read carefully when analyzing financial statements. Why are long-term summaries considered important to statement users?
14. Distinguish between vertical and horizontal analyses. Briefly explain the importance of each.
15. What is meant by ratio analysis? Why is it important in the analysis of financial statements?
16. Distinguish between the current ratio and the quick ratio. What purpose does each serve?
17. Current assets and current liabilities for two companies with the same amount of working capital are summarized below. Evaluate their relative liquidity positions.

	X Company	Y Company
Current assets	$200,000	$900,000
Current liabilities	100,000	800,000
Working capital	$100,000	$100,000

18. X Corporation has an accounts receivable turnover of 15; interpret this figure. What is the age of the receivables? What does it reveal?
19. Y Corporation has an inventory turnover of 9; interpret this figure. What is the average number of days of supply?
20. Explain and illustrate the effect of financial leverage.
21. Compute and explain the meaning of the book value per share of common stock of the Craft Manufacturing Company, assuming the following data are available:

Preferred stock, par $100, 6%, cumulative, nonparticipating, 200 shares issued and outstanding, liquidation value is par	$ 20,000
Common stock, par value $10, 10,000 shares issued and outstanding	100,000
Retained earnings	7,000
(Three years' dividends in arrears on preferred stock including current year.)	

22. Explain the circumstances where a company has debt financing and the leverage factor is *(a)* positive, *(b)* negative, and *(c)* zero.
23. Explain the return on assets employed. Why is it a fundamental measure of profitability?
24. What is meant by the multiple? Why is it considered important?
25. What are the principal limitations in using ratios?

EXERCISES

Part A: Exercises 22–1 to 22–8

E 22–1 **(Analyze the Capital Structure; Average Shares; Compute EPS)**
At the end of 19A the records of Bose Corporation reflected the following:

Common stock, par $5, authorized 500,000 shares:	
Outstanding 1/1/19A, 300,000 shares	$1,500,000
Sold and issued 4/1/19A, 2,000 shares	10,000
Issued 10% stock dividend, 9/30/19A, 30,200 shares	151,000
Preferred stock, 6%, par $10, nonconvertible, noncumulative, authorized 50,000 shares, outstanding during year, 20,000 shares	200,000
Contributed capital in excess of par, common stock	180,000
Contributed capital in excess of par, preferred stock	100,000
Retained earnings (after the effects of current preferred dividends declared during 19A)	640,000
Bonds payable, 6½%, nonconvertible	1,000,000
Income before extraordinary items	182,000
Extraordinary loss (net of tax)	(18,000)
Net income	164,000
Average income tax rate, 40%.	

Required:

1. Is this a simple or complex capital structure? Explain.
2. What kind of EPS presentation is required? Explain.
3. Compute the required EPS amounts (show computations).
4. Compute the required EPS amounts, assuming the preferred is cumulative.

E 22–2 **(Analyze the Capital Structure; Average Shares; Compute EPS)**
The records for Arkin Corporation, at the end of 19A, reflected the following:

Common stock, nopar, authorized 500,000 shares:	
Outstanding at beginning of year, 100,000 shares	$200,000
Sold and issued during the year, September 1, 3,000 shares	8,000
Preferred stock, 9%, par $10, nonconvertible, cumulative, authorized 20,000 shares:	
Outstanding during the year, 6,000 shares	60,000
Contributed capital in excess of par, preferred stock	5,000
Retained earnings	150,000
Bonds payable, 6½%, nonconvertible	400,000
Income before extraordinary items	130,000
Extraordinary gain (net of tax)	20,000
Net income	150,000

Required:

1. Is this a simple or complex capital structure? Explain.
2. What kind of EPS presentation is required? Explain.
3. Compute the required EPS amounts (show computations).
4. Compute the required EPS amounts, assuming the preferred stock is noncumulative and the current year's dividend has not been declared and that the preceding year's dividend was passed (i.e., not declared).

E 22–3 **(Compute EPS for Three Years; Stock Dividend and Split)**
Huxley Corporation's accounting year ends on December 31. During the three most recent years, its common shares outstanding changed as follows:

	19C	19B	19A
Shares outstanding, January 1	150,000	120,000	100,000
Sale of shares, 4/1/19A			20,000
25% stock dividend, 7/1/19B		30,000	
2-for-1 stock split, 7/1/19C	150,000*		
Shares sold, 10/1/19C	50,000		
Shares outstanding, December 31	350,000	150,000	120,000

* For each share turned in two new shares were issued so that the shares doubled.

Net income	$375,000	$330,000	$299,000

Required:

1. For purposes of calculating EPS at the end of each year, for each year independently, determine the number of shares outstanding.
2. For purposes of calculating EPS at the end of 19C, when comparative statements are being prepared on a three-year basis, determine the number of shares outstanding for each year.
3. Compute EPS for each year based on year computations in (2).

E 22–4 (Analyze the Capital Structure; Stock Dividend; Compute EPS)

At the end of 19A the records of Alert Corporation showed the following:

Common stock, nopar, authorized 250,000 shares:	
Outstanding 1/1/19A, 52,000 shares	$595,000
Purchased treasury shares 4/1/19A, 2,000 shares (at cost)	(46,000)
Issued a 100% stock dividend on 12/1/19A on outstanding shares (50,000 additional shares).	
Preferred stock, par $10:	
Class A, 6%, nonconvertible, noncumulative, outstanding 10,000 shares	100,000
Class B, 7%, nonconvertible, cumulative, outstanding 20,000 shares	200,000
Contributed capital in excess of par, preferred stock	100,000
Retained earnings (no dividends declared in 19A)	570,000
Bonds payable, 7%, nonconvertible	120,000
Income before extraordinary items	180,500
Extraordinary gain (net of tax)	10,000
Net income	190,500
Average income tax rate, 40%.	

Required:

1. Is this a simple or complex capital structure? Explain.
2. What kind of EPS presentation is required? Explain.
3. Compute the required EPS amounts (show computations).

E 22–5 (Compute Complex EPS; Three Kinds of Gains and Losses)

To illustrate EPS reporting for various combinations of gains and losses, assume 1,000 weighted-average shares of common stock for primary EPS are outstanding for the five cases given below.

Items	Case A (all gains)	Case B (all losses)	Case C (mixed)	Case D (mixed)	Case E (mixed)
Income (loss)	$10,000	$(10,000)	$10,000	$(10,000)	$(10,000)
Extraordinary items (loss)	6,000	(6,000)	(6,000)	6,000	6,000
Discontinued operations (loss)	3,000	(3,000)	(3,000)	3,000	(3,000)
Net income (loss)	$19,000	$(19,000)	$ 1,000	$ (1,000)	$ (7,000)

Assume a complex capital structure and *(a)* that for fully diluted EPS the weighted-average number of shares outstanding is 1,500 and *(b)* that income (loss) amounts on line 1 above, are $12,000.

Required:

1. Compute primary EPS for each case.
2. Compute fully diluted EPS for each case.
3. Give a proof of your answer to requirement 2.

E 22–6 **(Analyze Capital Structure; Stock Split; Convertible Securities; Compute EPS)** At the end of 19A, the records of Rust Corporation reflected the following:

Common stock, nopar, authorized 250,000 shares; issued and outstanding throughout the period to 12/1/19A, 60,000 shares. A stock split issued 12/1/19A doubled outstanding shares	$840,000
Preferred stock, 5%, par $10, nonconvertible, cumulative, nonparticipating, shares authorized, issued, and outstanding during year, 10,000 shares	100,000
Contributed capital in excess of par, preferred stock	30,000
Retained earnings (no cash or property dividends declared during year)	570,000
Bonds payable, 8%, issued 1/1/19A; each $1,000 bond is convertible to 60 shares of common stock after the stock split on 12/1/19A (bonds initially sold at par)	200,000
Income before extraordinary items	86,000
Extraordinary loss	(14,000)
Net income	72,000
Average income tax rate, 30%.	
Aa bond interest rate (at date of issuance of bonds), 15%.	

Required:

1. Is this a simple or complex capital structure? Explain.
2. What kind of EPS presentation is required? Explain.
3. Compute the required EPS amounts (show computations, rounded to two decimal places, and assume all amounts are material).

E 22–7 **(Analyze Capital Structure; Nonconvertible Preferred; Stock Rights; Compute EPS)** The records of Dean Corporation showed the following as of December 31, 19A:

Common stock, par $10, authorized 400,000 shares, issued and outstanding during 19A, 200,000 shares	$2,000,000
Contributed capital in excess of par, common stock	300,000
Common stock rights outstanding (for 20,000 shares of common stock)	200,000
Preferred stock, 8%, par $100, nonconvertible, cumulative, authorized 40,000 shares, outstanding during 19A, 10,000 shares	1,000,000
Contributed capital in excess of par, preferred stock	400,000
Retained earnings	7,000,000
Net income (no extraordinary items)	2,000,000

Additional data:

Common stock rights issued on April 1, 19A: option price, $15 per share; average market price of common stock during the period (i.e., 4/1/19A–12/31/19A) the rights were outstanding, $25; market price of common stock on 12/31/19A, $28.

Required:

1. Is this a simple or complex capital structure? Explain.
2. Prepare the required EPS presentation for 19A. Show all computations. Disregard the optional 3% materiality test.

E 22–8 (Analyze Capital Structure; Stock Rights; Preferred Stock; Compute EPS)

At the end of 19A the records of Badger Corporation reflected the following:

Common stock, par $10, authorized 100,000 shares; issued and outstanding throughout the year, 50,000 shares	$500,000
Stock rights outstanding (all year for 10,000 shares of common stock at $15 per share)	100,000
Preferred stock, par $50, 7%, cumulative, convertible into common stock share for share, authorized 10,000 shares; issued and outstanding throughout year, 2,000 shares	100,000
Contributed capital in excess of par, common stock	80,000
Retained earnings (no dividends declared during the year)	470,000
Bonds payable, 10%, nonconvertible	150,000
Income before extraordinary items	85,000
Extraordinary gain (net of tax)	35,000
Net income	120,000

Average income tax rate, 30%.
Average market price of the common stock during 19A, $25 per share.
Market price of common stock on 12/31/19A, $22 per share.
Aa bond interest rate at date of issuance of preferred stock, 10%.

Required:

1. Is this a simple or complex capital structure? Explain.
2. What kind of EPS presentation is required? Explain.
3. Compute the required EPS amounts (show computations and assume all amounts are material).

Part B: Exercises 22–9 to 22–18

E 22–9 (Horizontal and Vertical Analysis, Statement of Income)

Fox Trading Company's statements of income (condensed) for two years are shown below.

	December 31	
	19A	19B
Gross sales	$221,000	$242,000
Returns	(1,000)	(2,000)
	220,000	240,000
Cost of goods sold	(110,000)	(130,000)
Gross margin	110,000	110,000
Expenses:		
Selling	(62,000)	(63,000)
Administrative (including income taxes)	(30,000)	(31,000)
Interest (net of interest revenue)	(3,000)	2,000
Net income before extraordinary items	15,000	18,000
Extraordinary gain (loss), net of tax	5,000	(3,000)
Net income	$ 20,000	$ 15,000
Shares of common stock outstanding	10,000	10,000

Required:

1. Prepare a multiple-step comparative statement of income including a vertical percentage analysis. Round to the nearest percent.
2. Prepare a single-step statement of income including horizontal percentage analysis. Round to the nearest percent.

E 22–10 (Horizontal and Vertical Analysis, Statement of Financial Position)

Goode Company's statement of financial position (condensed and unclassified) for two years is shown below.

	December 31	
	19A	19B
Cash	$ 11,000	$ 26,000
Accounts receivable (net)	17,000	19,000
Inventory (FIFO, LCM)	31,000	40,000
Prepaid expenses	2,000	1,000
Funds and investments (at cost)	15,000	22,000
Operational assets	110,000	126,000
Accumulated depreciation	(30,000)	(45,000)
Intangible assets	4,000	11,000
Total	$160,000	$200,000
Accounts payable	$ 19,000	$ 15,000
Remaining current liabilities	8,000	10,000
Long-term mortgage payable	33,000	33,000
Common stock, par $5	50,000	60,000
Contributed capital in excess of par	20,000	40,000
Retained earnings	30,000	42,000
Total	$160,000	$200,000

Required:

1. Prepare a comparative statement of financial position in good form including a vertical percentage analysis. Round to the nearest percent.
2. Prepare a comparative statement of financial position in good form, including a horizontal percentage analysis. Round to the nearest percent.

E 22–11 (Analysis of Working Capital)

The following data were taken from the financial statements of Walker Company.

	19A	19B
Current assets		
Cash	$ 30,000	$ 40,000
Short-term investments	10,000	10,000
Trade accounts receivable (net)	60,000	70,000
Notes receivable	6,000	2,000
Inventory	150,000	170,000
Prepaid expenses	4,000	2,000
Current liabilities	90,000	120,000

Required:

Based on the above data, compute the *(a)* amount of working capital, *(b)* current ratio, and *(c)* acid-test ratio for each year. Evaluate each ratio and compare the results of the two reporting periods. Round to the nearest percent.

E 22–12 (Ratio Analysis of Current Assets; Significance)

The condensed financial data given below were taken from the annual financial statements of Tatum Corporation:

	19A	19B	19C
Current assets (including inventory)	$ 200,000	$ 250,000	$ 270,000
Current liabilities	150,000	180,000	130,000
Cash sales	800,000	780,000	820,000
Credit sales	200,000	280,000	250,000
Cost of goods sold	560,000	600,000	600,000

	19A	19B	19C
Inventory (ending)	120,000	140,000	100,000
Quick assets	80,000	90,000	85,000
Accounts receivable (net)	60,000	58,000	64,000
Total assets (net)	1,000,000	1,200,000	1,400,000

Required:

1. Based on the above data, calculate the following ratios for 19B and 19C; use 365 days for computation purposes. Round to one decimal point (e.g., ratios, 5.2 and percents, 8.4%). Also, briefly explain the significance of each ratio listed. Use the following format:

Ratio	19B	19C	Significance
a. Current ratio.			
b. Acid-test ratio.			
c. Working capital to total assets.			
d. Accounts receivable turnover.			
e. Age of accounts receivable.			
f. Merchandise inventory turnover.			
g. Days' supply in inventory.			
h. Working capital turnover.			

2. Evaluate the overall results of the computations including trends.

E 22–13 (Ratio Analysis; Inventory and Receivables; Assess Results)

The following data were taken from the financial statements of Boston Company:

	19A	19B	19C
Sales—cash	$190,000	$200,000	$220,000
Sales—credit	100,000	120,000	130,000
Average receivables	25,000	34,000	50,000
Average inventory	60,000	70,000	80,000
Cost of goods sold	180,000	190,000	200,000

Required:

1. Prepare a ratio analysis (including turnover and days) of *(a)* inventory and *(b)* receivables. Use 365 days. Credit terms are 2/10, n/30. Round to one decimal place and even days. Also, briefly explain the significance of each ratio. Use the following format:

Year	Turnover ratio	Days	Significance

2. Assess possible impacts of any trends that your analysis indicates relative to *(a)* inventory and *(b)* receivables.

E 22–14 (Compute Book Value per Share; Common and Preferred Stock)

Supreme Manufacturing Corporation's statement of financial position showed the following as of December 31, 19A:

Total liabilities	$100,000
Preferred stock, 7%, par value $50 per share	200,000
Common stock, nopar, 30,000 shares outstanding	360,000
Contributed capital in excess of par, preferred stock	40,000
Retained earnings	80,000

Required:

Compute the book value per share of common stock assuming:

1. None of the preferred shares have been issued.
2. Preferred is noncumulative and nonparticipating; liquidation preference value of preferred is par.

3. Preferred is cumulative and nonparticipating (three years' dividends in arrears including current year); liquidation value of preferred is par.
4. Preferred has a liquidation value of $60 per share and is noncumulative and nonparticipating.
5. Preferred has a liquidation value of $60 per share and is noncumulative and nonparticipating, and the Retained Earnings account shows a deficit of $30,000, instead of the $80,000 credit balance shown above.

E 22–15 (Compute and Explain Profitability Ratios)

The 19C comparative financial statements for Kellog Corporation reported the following data:

	19A	19B	19C
Sales revenue	$12,000,000	$13,000,000	$14,000,000
Net income	100,000	120,000	100,000
Interest expense, net of income tax	10,000	12,000	9,000
Stockholders' equity	1,400,000	1,450,000	1,460,000
Total assets	3,500,000	3,500,000	3,700,000
Market value per share	$66	$72	$45
Shares of common stock outstanding	20,000	20,000	24,000

Required:

1. Based on the above financial data, compute the following ratios for 19B and 19C: *(a)* profit margin; *(b)* return on total assets; *(c)* return on owners' equity; *(d)* the leverage factor; *(e)* simple EPS; and *(f)* price-earnings ratio. Carry computations to two decimal places (e.g., ratios, 5.22 and percents 8.43%.)
2. As an investor in the common stock of Kellog, which ratio would you prefer as a single measure of profitability? Why?
3. Explain any significant trends that appear to be developing.

E 12–16 (Compute and Assess Profitability Ratios for Five Years)

The following data relate to the Fast Printing Company:

	19A	19B	19C	19D	19E
Net income	$ 12,000	$ 15,000	$ 25,000	$ 30,000	$ 40,000
Interest expense (net of tax)	1,000	1,200	2,000	2,200	3,000
Sales revenue	120,000	140,000	180,000	230,000	260,000
Total assets	50,000	72,000	110,000	160,000	190,000
Total liabilities	25,000	30,000	40,000	70,000	80,000

Required:

1. For each of the five years, compute the *(a)* profit margin, *(b)* return on owners' equity, *(c)* return on total assets, and *(d)* financial leverage factor. Round to the nearest percentage.
2. Based on Requirement 1, assess the five-year trend of earnings reflected in the statement of income.

E 22–17 (Compute and Summarize Significance of Ratios of Current Position, Equity Position, and Operating Results)

Simpel Corporation's 19A and 19B statements of financial positions and 19B statement of income are as follows (in thousands):

	December 31			
	19A		19B	
Statement of financial position:				
Cash	$ 10		$ 19	
Investments (short term)	2		3	
Accounts receivable (net of allowance)	21		17	
Inventory (FIFO, LCM)	30		36	
Prepaid expenses	3		2	
Funds and investments	30		30	
Operational assets (net of accumulated depreciation)	80		80	
Accounts payable		$ 20		$ 18
Accrued liabilities		1		2
Note payable, long term		40		40
Common stock, par $1		60		60
Contributed capital in excess of par		15		15
Retained earnings (including 19B income)		40		52
Totals	$176	$176	$187	$187

Statement of income (19B):	
Sales revenue (⅓ on credit)	$153
Investment revenue	6
Cost of goods sold	(70)
Distribution expense	(20)
Administrative expense	(15)
Interest expense	(4)
Income tax expense (40%)	(20)
Net income	$ 30
Dividends declared and paid ($.30 per share)	$ 18
Market price per common share	$ 8

Required:
For each requirement, use a format similar to the following (example given):

Ratio	Formula	Computation	Significance—key words
1. Current ratio	Current assets ÷ current liabilities	$\frac{\$77}{\$20} = 3.9$	Short-term liquidity; adequacy of working capital

Note: Round ratios to one decimal place (3.5); round percentages to the nearest percent (35%).

1. Compute the 19B ratios that measure current position (as given in Exhibit 22–13 and in the same order).
2. Compute the 19B ratios that measure equity position (as given in Exhibit 22–14 and in the same order).
3. Compute the 19B ratios that measure operating results (as given in Exhibit 22–15 and in the same order).

E 22–18 (Interim Reporting; Application of Guidelines)
In the context of interim reporting, items may be *(a)* recognized in the interim statements of the current interim period, *(b)* recognized in the current interim period but require special disclosure, *(c)* deferred in their entirety (i.e., not recognized until some later interim period, or not at all), or *(d)* amortized or accrued (i.e., recognized partly in the current interim period and partly in subsequent interim periods). A number of items

are listed below that require a decision as to how they should be incorporated on interim statements. You are to match the letters given above with the numbered items given below to indicate how each item should be incorporated on the interim statements.

1. Salaries allocable to services rendered during the current period.
2. Inventories estimated by use of the gross margin method.
3. Temporary declines in market value of inventories.
4. Short-term stock investment gains from recoveries of market value (not in excess of previously recognized market declines).
5. Materials and wages allocable to products sold this period.
6. Costs benefiting two or more interim periods.
7. Increase in gross margin due to liquidation of a layer of LIFO base inventory expected to be replenished by year-end.
8. Quantity discounts allowed to customers based upon annual volume of their purchases.
9. Contingencies and other uncertainties which may affect fairness of presentation.
10. Income tax on income of first quarter where total income for the first quarter only puts company in "normal tax" bracket; subsequent operations are expected to be sufficiently profitable that by end of second quarter and thereafter taxable income of company will be in a higher bracket.

E 22–19 **(Supplement 22-B—Identify Reporting Segments; Give Basis)**
ACR Corporation has expanded rapidly, and segment reporting has become an accounting issue. The following situations are under consideration (in millions):

Situation	Revenues	Operating profit	Identifiable assets
1. Product Group A	$28	$5	$15
2. Foreign Operation—SA	27	4	14
3. Single Customer X	30	5	13
4. Foreign Operation—ME	28	6	16
5. Product Group B	29	4	15
6. Single Customer Y	28	6	17
7. Product Group C	30	7	13

Additional data:

	In millions
a. Combined operating profit of all industry segments (no operating losses)	$ 50
b. Combined identifiable assets of all industry segments	160
c. Combined revenue of all segments of the entity	300

Required:
Select those segments that ACR Corporation should report as identifiable segments. Explain the basis for your decision in each situation.

E 22–20 **(Supplement 22-B—Segments; Prepare Statements of Income and Financial Position)**
Big Company has two segments of its operations that qualify as identifiable segments. The revenues of the specialty products segment approximate 11% of total revenues, and the identifiable net assets of the services segment approximate 17% of total identifiable assets.

Relevant pretax data for 19X are as follows (in thousands):

	Specialty	Services	Company*
Revenues	$1,350	$ 975	$9,760
Direct expenses	800	400	6,000
Companywide expenses (allocable)			1,800†
General company expenses (not allocable)			1,385
Identifiable assets‡ (net of depreciation)	250	1,200	5,600
Income tax rate, 40%.			

* Excludes the segment amounts.
† Allocate on the basis of direct expense ratios.
‡ None used jointly.

Required:

1. Prepare the statement of income for the company. Use three columns: Speciality segment; Services segment; and Total company. Show computations.
2. Show what amounts should be reported on the statement of financial position for Identifiable assets for each segment and total company.

E 22–21 **(Supplement 22–B—Discontinued Operations; Recording and Reporting)**
On August 1, 19X, Fischer Company decided to discontinue the operations of its Services Division, which qualifies as an identifiable segment. An agreement was formalized to sell this segment for $156,000 cash. The book value of the assets of the Services Division was $180,000. The disposal (i.e., closing) date also was on August 1, 19X. The income tax rate is 35%, and the accounting period ends December 31. On December 31, 19X, the aftertax income from continuing operations, including all operating losses and gains associated with the Services Division prior to August 1, 19X, was $400,000.

Required:

1. Give the entry(s) to record the sale of the Services Division.
2. Complete the 19X statement of income, starting with income from continuing operations.

PROBLEMS

Part A: Problems 22–1 to 22–7

P 22–1 **(Analyze Capital Structure; Stock Dividend; Convertible Securities; Compute EPS)**
At the end of 19A, the records of Ecru Corporation showed the following:

Common stock, nopar, authorized 400,000 shares:	
Outstanding 1/1/19A, 200,000 shares	$1,650,000
Treasury shares acquired 6/1/19A, 1,000 shares (at cost)	(15,000)
Stock dividend issued, 11/1/19A, 19,900 shares (10%, one additional share to reach 10 shares outstanding)	398,000
Preferred stock, 5%, par $20, noncumulative, nonconvertible, authorized, issued and outstanding throughout the year, 10,000 shares	200,000
Contributed capital in excess of par, preferred stock	75,000
Retained earnings (no cash or property dividends declared during 19A)	942,000
Bonds payable, series A, 7%, each $1,000 bond is convertible to 20 shares of common stock after stock dividend (bonds issued at par)	50,000
Bonds payable, series B, 6%, each $1,000 bond is convertible to 57 shares of common stock after stock dividend (bonds issued at par)	400,000

Income before extraordinary gain	400,000
Extraordinary gain (net of tax)	20,000
Net income	420,000

Average income tax rate for 19A, 30%.
Aa bond interest rate at date of issuance of: 7% bonds, 12%; 6% bonds, 8%.
Both bond series were issued prior to January 1, 19A.

Required:

1. Is this a simple or complex capital structure? Explain.
2. Prepare the EPS presentation with all supporting computations.

P 22–2 **(Analyze Capital Structure; Stock Rights and Convertible Securities; Compute EPS)** Racer Corporation is developing its EPS presentation at December 31, 19A. The records of the company provide the following information:

Liabilities	
Convertible bonds payable, 7% (each $1,000 bond is convertible to 100 shares of common stock)	$150,000
Stockholders' Equity	
Common stock, nopar, authorized 100,000 shares:	
Outstanding 1/1/19A, 59,000 shares	214,000
Sold and issued 10,000 shares on 4/1/19A	40,000
Common stock rights outstanding (all year for 4,000 shares of common stock)	16,000
Preferred stock, par $10, 6%, cumulative, convertible (each share is convertible into ½ of 1 share of common stock), authorized 10,000 shares, outstanding during 19A, 5,000 shares	50,000
Contributed capital in excess of par, preferred stock	15,000
Retained earnings	452,000
Income before extraordinary items	110,000
Extraordinary gain (net of tax)	20,000
Net income	130,000

Additional data:

a. Stock rights—option price, $4 per share; average market price of the common stock during 19A, $6; market price of common stock on 12/31/19A, $7.
b. Convertible bonds—issue price, par.
c. Aa bond interest rate on dates of issuance of all convertible securities, 8%.
d. Average income tax rate, 30%.

Required:

1. Is this a simple or complex capital structure? Explain.
2. What kind of EPS presentation is required? Explain.
3. Prepare the required EPS presentation for 19A. Show all computations.
4. Were there any antidilutive securities? How was this determined?
5. How should antidilutive securities be treated in the computations of EPS? Why?

P 22–3 **(Actual Case Adapted; Complex Capital Structure; Compute EPS for Two Alternatives)** Bird Company has a compensatory stock option plan under which options to buy 255,000 common shares were issued in 19A. These options are exercisable during 19B and 19C at $16 per share. In 19B, Bird reported net income of $500,000; the company's capital structure remained unchanged that year.

Outstanding stock consists of 1 million common shares, which traded at an average price of $20 per share throughout 19B. The company's long-term debt consists of a $2,500,000 bond issue sold at par, which pays 12% annual interest and was outstanding throughout 19B. Bird had no other indebtedness. Bird's average income tax rate is 30%.

Required:

1. Compute primary EPS for 19B.
2. Suppose the facts given above are modified as follows: Bird issued the stock options on July 1, 19B. Per share market price of Bird's stock averages $20 throughout the last quarter of 19B. Compute primary EPS for 19B. Ignore the 3% materiality rule.

P 22–4 **(Analyze Capital Structure; Convertible Bonds Sold at a Premium; Compute EPS)**
At the end of 19A, the records of Mo Corporation reflected the following information:

Common stock, nopar, authorized 500,000 shares:	
Outstanding 1/1/19A, 125,000 shares	256,000
Sold and issued on 8/1/19A, 15,000 shares	30,000
Bonds payable, 6%, convertible	100,000
Premium on bonds payable	9,200
Retained earnings	900,000
Net income (no extraordinary items)	350,000

The convertible bonds were issued on July 1, 19A to yield 4.03%. The Aa corporate bond interest rate was 12%. Each $1,000 bond is convertible to 30 shares of common stock. Premium amortization related to the bonds during 19A was $800. Mo's average income tax rate during 19A was 30%.

Required:

1. Is this a simple or complex capital structure? Explain.
2. Prepare the required EPS presentation for 19A. Show all computations. Disregard the optional 3% materiality test.

P 22–5 **(Analyze Capital Structure; Stock Warrants; Nonconvertible Securities; Compute EPS)**
The records of Moak Corporation reflected the following data at the end of 19A:

Liabilities	
Bonds payable, 5%, convertible (each $1,000 bond is convertible to 40 shares of common stock)	$150,000
Stockholders' Equity	
Common stock, par $2, authorized 400,000 shares:	
Outstanding 1/1/19A, 150,000 shares	300,000
Sold and issued on 10/1/19A, 20,000 shares	40,000
Common stock warrants outstanding (all year for 6,000 shares)	12,000
Preferred stock, 6%, par $5, nonconvertible, cumulative, authorized 100,000 shares, outstanding during 19A, 20,000 shares	100,000
Contributed capital in excess of par, common stock	375,000
Contributed capital in excess of par, preferred stock	45,000
Retained earnings	280,000
Income before extraordinary items	170,000
Extraordinary loss (net of tax)	(20,000)
Net income	150,000

Additional data:

a. Stock warrants—option price, $3 per share; average market price of common stock during 19A, $3.60 per share; market price of common stock on 12/31/19A, $3.50 per share.
b. Convertible bonds—issue price, par; Aa bond interest rate at date of issuance of the bonds was 9%.
c. Average income tax rate, 30%.

Required:

1. Is this a simple or complex capital structure? Explain.
2. What kind of EPS presentation is required? Explain.
3. Prepare the required EPS presentation for 19A. Show all computations. Disregard the optional 3% materiality test.
4. Were there any antidilutive securities? How was this determined?
5. How should antidilutive securities be treated in EPS computations? Why?

P 22–6 (Analyze Capital Structure; Stock Dividend; Convertible Securities; Compute EPS)
At the end of 19A the records of Magenta Corporation reflected the following:

Common stock, nopar, authorized 500,000 shares; issued and outstanding throughout period, 100,000 shares	$680,000
Stock dividend issued, 12/31/19A, 50,000 shares (not included in the 100,000 shares above)	340,000
Retained earnings (aftereffect of dividends on all shares)	500,000
Bonds payable, 4½%, each $1,000 bond is convertible to 80 shares of common stock after the stock dividend (bonds issued at par)	100,000
Bonds payable, 6½%, each $1,000 bond is convertible to 90 shares of common stock after the stock dividend (bonds issued at par)	300,000
Income before extraordinary items	210,000
Extraordinary gain	12,000
Net income	222,000
Average income tax rate, 30%.	
Aa bond interest rate at date of issuance: 4½% bonds, 7%; 6½% bonds, 8%.	

Required:

1. Is this a simple or complex capital structure? Explain.
2. What kind of EPS presentation is required? Explain. Disregard the optional 3% materiality test.
3. Compute the required EPS amounts (show computations, rounded to two decimal places, and assume all amounts are material).

P 22–7 (Computing a Loss per Share)
Granville Corporation's statement of financial position at December 31, 19D, reported the following:

Accrued interest payable	$ 1,000
Long-term notes payable, 10%, due in 19G	50,000
Bonds payable, 7%, each $1,000 of face value is convertible into 90 shares of common stock; bonds mature in 19M	800,000
Preferred stock, 5%, nonconvertible, cumulative, par value $100	250,000
Common stock, par value $5	700,000
Common stock rights outstanding all year entitling holders to acquire 40,000 shares of common stock at $9 per share	200,000
Net loss for 19D	125,000

Additional data:

a. During 19D, 1,000 shares of preferred stock were issued at par on July 1. Dividends are paid semiannually, on May 31 and November 30. Declaration precedes payment by three weeks. On newly issued shares, dividends are prorated from issue date.
b. Aa bond rate of interest was 8% when the convertible bonds were issued at par.
c. Average market price of common stock during 19D was $10; market price per share of common stock on 12/31/19D was $10.

d. Income tax rate of Granville is 30%.
e. Granville earned taxable income of $400,000 during 19A–19C.

Required:
Compute the EPS amount that Granville should report on the statement of income for 19D. Show all computations.

Part B: Problems 22–8 to 22–15

P 22–8 (Overview of All Ratios)
Below are columns listing commonly used ratios (column 3), ratio formulas (column 4), and significance—key words (last column). For each commonly used ratio, identify its formula by entering the appropriate letter in the first column and identify its significance by entering the appropriate number in the second column.

The current ratio is given as an example. Use each letter and number only once.

Matching		Commonly used ratio	Basic formula	Significance—key words
Formula	Significance			
F	3	Current ratio	A. $\frac{\text{Income}}{\text{Average owners' equity}}$	1. Profitability of each sales dollar.
		Book value per common share	B. $\frac{\text{365 days}}{\text{Receivable turnover}}$	2. Proportion of assets provided by owners.
		Profit margin	C. $\frac{\text{Net sales}}{\text{Average total assets}}$	3. Test of current liquidity.
		Dividend-income payout ratio	D. $\frac{\text{Market price per share}}{\text{Earnings per share}}$	4. Rate of return on all resources used.
		Age of accounts receivable	E. $\frac{\text{Cost of goods sold}}{\text{Average inventory}}$	5. Rough estimate of the expected rate of return per share of stock.
		Creditors' equity to total assets	F. $\frac{\text{Current assets}}{\text{Current liabilities}}$	6. Credit and collection efficiency.
		Inventory turnover	G. $\frac{\text{Cash dividends per share}}{\text{Market price per share}}$	7. Relative investment in each current asset to total current assets.
		Accounts receivable turnover	H. $\frac{\text{365 days}}{\text{Inventory turnover}}$	8. Efficiency in use of total assets.
		Working capital turnover	I. $\frac{\text{Income}}{\text{Net sales}}$	9. Percent of income that is paid out in cash dividends.

Matching		Commonly used ratio	Basic formula	Significance—key words
Formula	Significance			
		Return on owners' equity	J. $\frac{\text{Net credit sales}}{\text{Average trade receivables}}$	10. Effectiveness of use of working capital to generate sales.
		Days supply in inventory	K. $\frac{\text{Each current asset}}{\text{Total current assets}}$	11. Proportion of assets provided by creditors.
		Financial leverage	L. $\frac{\text{Cash dividends per share}}{\text{Earnings per share}}$	12. Severe test of immediate liquidity.
		Debt to equity	M. Return on owners' equity minus return on total assets	13. Number of dollars of common stock equity per share of common stock.
		Earnings per share	N. $\frac{\text{Total liabilities}}{\text{Total assets}}$	14. Relationship between earnings per share and market price.
		Acid-test ratio	O. $\frac{\text{Working capital}}{\text{Total assets}}$	15. Times average inventory was sold.
		Dividend-market value payout ratio	P. $\frac{\text{Income plus interest expense net of tax}}{\text{Average total assets}}$	16. Relationship between debt and resources provided by owners.
		Return on total assets	Q. $\frac{\text{Net sales}}{\text{Average working capital}}$	17. Number of days' supply in inventory.
		Working capital to total assets	R. $\frac{\text{Owners' equity}}{\text{Total assets}}$	18. Liquidity of total assets and distribution of resources.
		Investment turnover	S. $\frac{\text{Income associated with common stock}}{\text{Common shares outstanding}}$	19. Average number of days to collect trade receivables.
		Price-earnings ratio	T. $\frac{\text{Quick assets}}{\text{Current liabilities}}$	20. Rate of return on resources provided by owners.
		Percent of each current asset to total current assets	U. $\frac{\text{Total liabilities}}{\text{Owners' equity}}$	21. Income earned on each share of common stock.
		Owners' equity to total assets	V. $\frac{\text{Common stock equity}}{\text{Outstanding shares of common stock}}$	22. Advantage of borrowing at a rate of interest that is lower than rate earned on total assets.

P 22–9 **(Compute and Assess Current Position Ratios for Three Years)**
The following data were taken from the annual financial statements of Lynch Corporation:

	19A	19B	19C
Current assets:			
Cash	$ 10,000	$ 5,000	$ 8,000
Short-term investments	45,000	30,000	20,000
Trade receivables	180,000	170,000	190,000
Less: Allowance for doubtful accounts	(5,000)	(6,000)	(8,000)
Notes receivable (nontrade)	110,000	125,000	100,000
Inventory	298,000	355,000	387,000
Prepaid expenses	12,000	11,000	13,000
Total	$ 650,000	$ 690,000	$ 710,000
Current liabilities:			
Trade payables	$ 70,000	$ 158,000	$ 196,000
Notes payables	90,000	72,000	60,000
Accrued wages payable	72,000	46,000	52,000
Income taxes payable	19,000	23,000	24,000
Deferred rent revenue	2,000	2,000	2,000
Accrued liabilities	17,000	19,000	16,000
Total	$ 270,000	$ 320,000	$ 350,000
Additional data:			
Cash sales	$3,300,000	$3,500,000	$3,200,000
Credit sales	1,500,000	1,700,000	1,800,000
Cost of goods sold	2,500,000	2,900,000	2,800,000
Total assets (net)	6,600,000	7,200,000	7,200,000

Required:

1. Compute each of the seven ratios that measure current position for 19A, 19B, and 19C. Round to one decimal place (e.g., ratios, 5.2; and percents, 8.4%).
2. Set up and complete a tabulation similar to the following to indicate the usefulness of the results derived in Requirement 1 (an example is provided for the current ratio):

Ratio	Computed ratio			Significance and assessment
	19A	19B	19C	
1. Current ratio.	2.4	2.2	2.0	Test of adequacy of working capital. Consistent decrease—unfavorable
2. Etc.				

P 22–10 **(Compute and Evaluate Ratios; Current Position, Equity Position and Operating Results for Three Years)**
The financial statements of Davis Manufacturing Company for a three-year period reported the following:

	19A	19B	19C
Total assets	$2,000,000	$2,040,000	$1,940,000
Total current assets	368,000	450,000	480,000
Total current liabilities	230,000	150,000	150,000
Operational assets (net)	1,248,000	1,257,600	1,260,000
Total liabilities	1,090,000	1,110,000	900,000
Common stock (par value $100)	600,000	600,000	700,000
Retained earnings	310,000	330,000	340,000
Sales revenue (net)	6,600,000	7,000,000	7,100,000
Net income (after tax)	50,000	70,000	40,000
Interest expense (net of tax)	34,000	38,000	30,000

Required (round to nearest percent, or if a decimal, to two places):

1. Based on the above data, compute the following ratios to measure the current position for each year.
   a. Current ratio.
   b. Working capital turnover.

   Evaluate the current position. What additional information do you need to adequately evaluate the current position? Explain.
2. Based on the above data, compute the following ratios to measure the equity position:
   a. Debt to equity.
   b. Creditors' equity to total assets.
   c. Book value per share of common stock.

   Evaluate the equity position. What additional information do you need to adequately evaluate the equity position? Explain.
3. Based on the above data, compute the following ratios to measure operating results and leverage:
   a. Profit margin.
   b. Return on total average assets.
   c. Return on average owners' equity.
   d. Financial leverage.

   Evaluate the operating results and financial leverage.

P 22–11 (Compute, Interpret, and Evaluate Three Equity Ratios, and Average)

The statements of financial position for two similar companies reflected the following:

	Company A	Company B
Current liabilities	$ 30,000	$100,000
Long-term liabilities	70,000	300,000
Stockholders' equity:		
Common stock, par $5	220,000	46,000
Preferred stock, par $10	100,000	20,000
Contributed capital in excess of par, common	20,000	4,000
Retained earnings	60,000	30,000
Net income, included in the above retained earnings amount (less taxes, 45%)	49,500	13,000

Required:

1. Compute the three equity ratios listed in the chapter that measure equity position. Interpret the results.
2. Compute the leverage factor for each company. The average interest rate on total liabilities is 10% for both companies.
3. Interpret and evaluate the situation for each company.

P 22–12 (Ratios to Measure Operating Results; Evaluate Implications)

The following annual data were taken from the records of Tricky Trading Corporation:

	19A	19B	19C	19D	19E
Sales revenue	$400,000	$420,000	$450,000	$440,000	$490,000
Net income	15,000	16,000	20,000	5,000	40,000
Total assets	200,000*	220,000	230,000	240,000	250,000
Owners' equity	100,000*	110,000	120,000	115,000	140,000
Market price per common share	20	20	33	14	60
Dividends per common share	4	4	4	1	5
Capital stock outstanding (shares)	4,000	4,000	4,000	3,900	3,800
Interest expense (net of tax)	4,000	4,500	4,600	5,000	4,100

* The beginning balance was the same as this year-end balance.

Required:
Compute each of the seven ratios to measure operating results and leverage for the years 19B, C, D, and E. Immediately following each ratio, evaluate and comment on the results (e.g., trends, problems, and favorable/unfavorable implications).

P 22–13 (Leverage; Sell Capital Stock versus Debt; Analytical)
Alabama Corporation is considering building a second plant at a cost of $600,000. The management is considering two alternatives to obtain the funds: *(a)* sell additional common stock or *(b)* issue $600,000, five-year bonds payable at 8% interest. The management believes that the bonds can be sold at par (for $600,000) and the stock at $10 per share.

The balance sheet (before the new financing) reflected the following:

Liabilities	None
Common stock, nopar	$300,000
Retained earnings	120,000
Average income for past several years (net of tax)	30,000

The average income tax rate is 35%. Average dividends per share have been 50 cents per share per year. Expected increase in pretax income (excluding interest expense) from the new plant, $100,000 per year.

Required:
1. Prepare an analysis to show *(a)* expected income after the addition, *(b)* cash flows from the company to prospective owners of the new capital, and *(c)* the leverage advantage or disadvantage to the present stockholders of issuing the bonds to obtain the financing.
2. What are the principal arguments for and against issuing the bonds (as opposed to selling the common stock)?

P 22–14 (Based on Supplement 22–B—Discontinued Segment)
Century Company, a diversified manufacturing company, had four separate operating divisions engaged in the manufacture of products in each of the following areas: food products, health aids, textiles, and office equipment.

Pretax data for the two years ended December 31, 19B, and 19A, are presented below:

	Net sales		Cost of goods sold		Operating expenses	
	19B	19A	19B	19A	19B	19A
Food products	$3,500,000	$3,000,000	$2,400,000	$1,800,000	$ 550,000	$ 275,000
Health aids	2,000,000	1,270,000	1,100,000	700,000	300,000	125,000
Textiles	1,580,000	1,400,000	500,000	900,000	200,000	150,000
Office equipment	920,000	1,330,000	800,000	1,000,000	650,000	750,000
	$8,000,000	$7,000,000	$4,800,000	$4,400,000	$1,700,000	$1,300,000

Additional pretax data:
On January 1, 19B, Century adopted a plan to sell the assets and product line of the office equipment division and expected to realize a gain on this disposal. On September 1, 19B, the division's assets and product line were sold for $2,100,000 (two-thirds cash collected on this date), resulting in a gain of $640,000 (exclusive of operations during the phaseout period).

The company's textiles division had six manufacturing plants that produced a variety of textile products. In April 19B, the company sold one of these plants and realized a gain of $130,000 (carrying value, $200,000). After the sale, the operations at the plant that was sold were transferred to the remaining five textile plants that the company continued to operate.

In August 19B, the main warehouse of the food products division, located on the banks of the Bayer River, was flooded when the river overflowed. The resulting damage of $420,000 is not included in the financial data given above. Historical records indicate that the Bayer River normally overflows every four to five years causing flood damage to adjacent property; this loss was not covered by insurance.

For the two years ended December 31, 19B, and 19A, the company had interest revenue earned on investments of $70,000 and $40,000, respectively.

For the two years ended December 31, 19B, and 19A, the company's net income (after income tax) was $1,152,000 and $804,000, respectively.

Income tax expense for each of the two years should be computed at a rate of 40%.

Required:

1. Prepare in proper form a comparative statement of income of Century Company for the two years ended December 31, 19B, and December 31, 19A.
2. Give or explain the entries related to the discontinued segment on *(a)* measurement date and *(b)* disposal date.

(AICPA adapted)

P 22–15 **(Supplement 22–B—Discontinued Segment)**

On April 1, 19X, Carter Company signed a contract to sell its Teck Products Division to Baker Company for $300,000 cash; one-third on April 1, 19X, and the remainder on closing date, July 1, 19X. Carter will continue to operate the Division until the disposal date. The book (i.e., carrying) value of the net assets of the Teck Division on June 30, 19X, is $280,000. The income tax rate is 40%, and the annual reporting period ends December 31. The estimated income (pretax) of the Teck Division, for the period January 1–June 30, 19X, was $13,000; however, the actual pretax income amount turned out to be $15,000.

At December 31, 19X, the accounting records provide the following data for Teck Products Division: Pretax income from operations: 19W, $16,500; 19X, $15,000. Carter's aftertax income from operations (excluding income from Teck Products Division) was $600,000 for 19W and $630,000 for 19X.

Required:

1. Give the entries by Carter Company for 19X related to the sale of the Teck Products Division, including explanations.
2. Prepare the comparative statement of income dated December 31, 19X, including an appropriate disclosure note.

CASES

C 22–1 **(Recommend Which Company's Stock Should Be Purchased; Ratio Analysis)**

Investor Doe is considering investing $100,000 cash in the common stock of either Company A or Company B. The two companies are in the same industry, but in different regions of the country. The following summarized data were taken from the annual audited financial statements (in thousands):

	Company A	Company B
Statement of income:		
Sales revenue	$3,500	$ 9,400
Cost of goods sold	(1,910)	(5,640)
Operating expenses	(400)	(1,710)
Interest expense	(90)	(350)
Income tax expense	(462)	(680)
Extraordinary gain (loss), net of tax	(22)	350
Net income	$ 616	$ 1,370
Statement of financial position:		
Current assets	$1,000	$ 4,000
Operational assets	4,500	19,000
Accumulated depreciation	(1,500)	(7,000)
Investments, long term (cost)	400	100
Other assets	600	7,900
Total	$5,000	$24,000
Current liabilities	$ 900	$ 2,000
Long-term liabilities	100	1,800
Capital stock, par $1	3,000	18,000
Retained earnings	1,000	2,200
Total	$5,000	$24,000
Additional data for current year:		
Quick assets	$ 400	$ 500
Average income tax rate	42%	40%
Market price—none, sold only in local market.		

After examining the data given above, Investor Doe has tentatively expressed a strong preference for Company B because it *(a)* is larger, *(b)* has almost five times as much in total assets, and *(c)* earned more than twice as much. Doe has asked you to confirm the soundness of his tentative decision by analyzing the data available.

Because the only information now available to you is given above, a comparative analysis of the current position, equity position, operating results, and financial leverage seems appropriate as a start.

Required:

1. Prepare your analysis and support it with comments related to each value.
2. Based only upon your analysis, prepare your recommendation to Doe, which is limited to consideration of these two companies. Give a brief to-the-point summary of the basis for your recommendation.

C 22–2 (What Investors Want from the Annual Report)

This case is adapted from a special article by Ned Reynolds in *The Wall Street Journal*, January 18, 1988. The article posed a provocative issue as follows:*

> "American companies spend an estimated $2 billion a year on annual reports to shareholders. But their message often falls on deaf ears, research suggests.
>
> A survey conducted by Hill & Knowlton Inc. asked a sample of individual investors where they got their best investment information. Only 3% named the annual report—1% less than those who cited friends and relatives."

The author correctly states that companies traditionally view the annual report as an opportunity to radiate optimism, not to report failings. The author then posed a very relevant issue:

> "But since the October market crash, which dealt investor confidence a severe blow, companies need to think seriously about enlisting the annual report as a natural way of getting investors to trust them."

* Mr. Reynolds is senior vice president in the financial relations division of Hill & Knowlton Inc.

The Hill & Knowlton survey asked questions about how credible do investors find annual reports. Comments received, such as the following, presented a bleak view:

- "Annual reports hide too much. They don't tell the entire truth." (California investor.)
- "They are not dependable." (New York investor.)
- "The annual report is little more than a piece of advertising." (St. Louis securities analyst.)
- "I think annuals are much too biased." (Los Angeles investor.)
- "I believe they lie in these reports." (Wisconsin investor.)

Author Reynolds then states that:

> "Nonetheless, the annual report is the best shot a publicly held company has all year to speak directly to investors. The report is a powerful platform for management to persuade investors to buy or hold the company's stock. That's exactly what an annual report should be doing if it is earning its keep.
>
> "To succeed, an annual report must answer the investor's gut question: 'What's in it for me?'—a question that ought to be displayed on the wall of every preparer of annual reports."

The research findings pinpointed the investors' complaints about annual reports:

a. **Credibility.** Investors complain that annual reports are too promotional. The reports play down negatives, investors say, and present only management's viewpoint. Some investors distrust what they read in annual reports.
b. **Business segments.** Annual reports often fail to adequately show or explain information about a company's various business segments, investors say.
c. **Detail.** Contrary to a common view, the majority of investors do not believe annual reports are too detailed. In fact, investors are eager for more facts in annuals—provided they are relevant.
d. **The Future.** Investors believe annual reports fail to tell them what management is doing to build the shareholder's investment.
e. **Clarity.** Investors criticize companies for using stilted wording and "technicalese" in their annual reports. They want to hear from companies in clear, straightforward language.

The author concludes the article as follows:

> "It is unlikely that during the October market debacle investors cooly scrutinized company annual reports before calling their brokers. But perhaps many investors might think twice about unloading their positions if management seizes the opportunity in its next annual report to foster an underlying sense of confidence by credibly answering that essential question: 'What's in it for me?' "

Required:

1. Be prepared to suggest ways that might be used by companies to resolve each of the five complaints.
2. Prepare notes to support your suggestions.

C 22–3 (Analysis of Segment Reporting; An Actual Case)
The annual report of Kimberly-Clark is given in the Appendix following Chapter 25. Respond to the following questions related to 1987:

1. Complete the following schedule for 1987 (millions):

	Sales		Operating profit		Assets	
Product class	**Amount**	**%**	**Amount**	**%**	**Amount**	**%**
Class I						
Class II						
Class III						
Combined						
Interclass						
Unallocated expenses						
Consolidated		100%		100%		100%

2. Explain what Product Classes I, II, and III include.
3. Complete the following schedule for 1987 (millions):

	Sales		KC's share of net income	
	Amount	**%**	**Amount**	**%**
United States				
Canada				
Europe				
Latin/South America				
Far East				
Combined				
Intergeographical sales				
Consolidated		100%		100%

4. (a) Have the operations been profitable at Terrace Bay, Ont., and Longlac, Ont.?
   (b) What management action was taken?

23 ACCOUNTING FOR INCOME TAXES

OVERVIEW AND PURPOSE

Corporations are required to pay federal income taxes; and most states impose state income taxes on corporations. Income tax expense usually is a significant amount on the statement of income and income taxes payable usually is a significant short-term liability on the statement of financial position. Cash paid during the reporting period to settle income taxes payable is reported on the statement of cash flows under operating activities.

This chapter discusses **income tax allocation,** which applies the matching principle to compute periodic income tax expense. The objective is to match income tax expense on the statement of income with the transactions that caused related income tax consequences. Allocation is necessary because some of these income tax consequences are reported for accounting purposes and for income tax purposes in different accounting periods. This chapter is organized as follows:[1]

1. Background
2. Basic objective and principles of income tax allocation.
3. Temporary income tax differences.
4. Deferred income tax liabilities and assets.
5. Annual computation and recognition of income taxes.
6. A limitation on deferred tax assets.
7. Application of the enacted tax laws or rates.
8. Initial adoption of the provisions of *FASB Standard 96*.
9. Additional issues related to income tax allocation.
10. Net operating tax loss carrybacks and carryforwards (NOLs).
11. Application of carryback and carryforward procedures in interperiod income tax allocation.
12. Analysis of net operating loss carrybacks and carryforwards (NOLS) for income tax allocation.
13. Interperiod tax-planning strategies.
14. Intraperiod income tax allocation.
15. Income tax effects of prior period adjustments.
16. Financial statement presentation and disclosure of deferred income taxes.
17. Investment tax credit (ITC).

[1] This chapter was written two months after *FASB Standard No. 96,* "Accounting for Income Taxes," was distributed. At this time many questions and interpretations of the provisions of this standard are unanswered. This chapter provides generalizations and applications based on realistic assumptions about the unanswered questions and interpretations of this complex standard. One well-known accountant recently made this point as follows: "To paraphrase a folk expression, *FASB 96* contains so much medicine we're going to be sick a long time after we get well. The statement is an indigestible collection of some of the most complex rules ever devised. While the rules may fit the FASB's conceptual model, they are going to be enormously difficult to comprehend and apply." (Dale L. Gerboth, "Commentary—On the Profession," *Accounting Horizons,* June 1988, American Accounting Association, Sarasota, FL, p. 95).

Background

On January 11, 1988, the following "Business Bulletin" appeared on the front page of *The Wall Street Journal:*

> **BIG ONE-TIME GAINS from accounting changes will boost company profits.** Earnings increases, some over 50%, are expected as companies begin adopting the Financial Accounting Standards Board's new rule on deferred taxes. It requires that by 1989 balance sheets be adjusted to reflect reduced top tax rates of 34%, down from 46% in 1986. Changes could show up as early as 1987's fourth quarter results.
>
> If the change had been in effect in 1986, earnings of Standard & Poor's 400 companies would have been 23% higher, says Oppenheimer & Co. Using estimated earnings, Bear, Stearns & Co. extrapolates that adoption for 1987 would mean a 51.6% increase in AMR Corp.'s earnings, a 38% gain for Briggs & Stratton Corp. and an 18% rise for American Telephone & Telegraph Co. The gain is a one-time adjustment, so companies adopting the rule will show a big drop in earnings the next year. "For the next three years earnings won't be comparable," says Pat McConnell of Bear, Stearns.
>
> That could confuse the stock market, says Charles Kulp of Feely & Willcox, noting that footnotes get overlooked.

The thrust of this news item is income tax allocation which directly affects reported net income. The income of corporations is subject to income tax; therefore, corporations must prepare both periodic financial statements and income tax returns. The statement of income reports income tax expense based on **pretax accounting income** (defined by GAAP) and the tax return shows income tax payable based on **taxable income.** Since GAAP and income tax requirements are different, accounting income and taxable income usually will differ. The difference between net income and taxable income is caused by permanent and temporary income tax differences. Permanent differences arise from transactions that are reported on either the statement of income or tax return, but not both.[2] Income tax allocation is used to determine the effects (i.e., the tax consequences) of only **temporary differences** and net operating losses (NOLs) on reported income, assets, and liabilities.

Income tax is a major expense and a short-term liability for most corporations. Partnerships and sole proprietorships do not pay income taxes; instead, the owners must include their respective shares of company income on their personal income tax returns. Chapter 3 defined two kinds of income tax allocation that must be reflected in the financial statements:

1. **Interperiod income tax allocation**—the allocation of income taxes **among** accounting periods to determine income tax expense for each period.
2. **Intraperiod income tax allocation**—the allocation of total income tax expense for a period [determined in (1) above] to various elements on the current financial statements. Interperiod allocation necessarily must precede intraperiod allocation each period.

This chapter discusses both interperiod and intraperiod income tax allocation; intraperiod tax allocation was discussed briefly in Chapter 3. **Interperiod** income

---

[2] These were called **permanent differences** in *APB Opinion 11.* They are not discussed further because they never are involved in interperiod income tax allocation.

tax allocation is necessary when there are **temporary differences** (discussed later); that is, when **taxable income** for an accounting period shown in the income tax return (computed in conformity with income tax laws and regulations) is different from **pretax accounting income** reported for the same accounting period in the statement of income (computed in conformity with GAAP).

The discussions in this chapter are in conformity with *FASB Standard 96,* "Accounting for Income Taxes." Prior to this standard, accounting for income taxes was in conformity with *APB Opinion No. 11,* "Accounting for Income Taxes." *APB Opinion 11* specified the **deferred approach.** In contrast, *FASB Standard 96,* par. 117, specifies an **"asset and liability approach."**[3]

Overview of Changes Specified by *FASB Standard 96*

FASB Standard 96 was issued in response to criticisms of *APB Opinion 11* that *(a)* the deferred method was deficient, *(b)* the provisions of *APB Opinion 11* were too vague, *(c)* the implementation required too much time, and *(d)* the resulting deferred tax amounts reported on the statement of financial position were excessive, confusing, and meaningless. *FASB Standard 96* requires use of the **asset and liability** method, gives detailed guidelines, and introduces new terminology. The changes made by *FASB Standard 96* are significant and complex. The primary changes, discussed in this chapter can be summarized and compared to *APB Opinion 11* as follows:

Item	Asset-liability method (*FASB Standard 96*)	Deferred method (*APB Opinion 11*)
1. Basic concept of deferred income tax amounts: Debits Credits	 Asset Liability	 Deferred charge Deferred credit
2. Conforms to accrual basis	Fully	Partially
3. Measurement approach used	Starts with INCOME TAX PAYABLE Income tax payable plus net deferred income tax equals income tax expense	Starts with INCOME TAX EXPENSE Income tax expense minus income tax payable equals deferred income tax
Computations required: *a.* Income tax expense *b.* Deferred income tax *c.* Income tax payable	 Sum of *c* plus *b* Computed independently From income tax return	 Computed independently Difference between *a* and *c* From income tax return
4. Reversing (turn around) directly related to	Asset recovery (life) and liability settlement (to payment date)	Future revenues, gains, expenses and losses
5. Future enacted tax rate changes	Recognized	Not recognized
6. Discounting of future income tax differences	No	No

[3] The computation of income tax payable for corporations is a technical subject. Our purpose in this textbook is not to emphasize these technical computations because they are taught in various income tax courses. Rather, this chapter discussses the reporting of income taxes on the statements of income and financial position. Therefore, for our purposes average income tax rates usually are used.

FASB Standard 96 is effective for fiscal years beginning after December 15, 1988, although earlier application is encouraged. The cumulative effect when *FASB Standard 96* is first applied must be included in the first year shown in comparative statements, or in the first year applied if comparative statements are not reported.

Basic Objective and Principles of Income Tax Allocation

FASB Standard 96 states the following:[4]

> The objective in accounting for income taxes on an accrual basis is to recognize the amount of current and deferred taxes payable or refundable at the date of the financial statements *(a)* as a result of all events that have been recognized in the financial statements and *(b)* as measured by the provisions of enacted tax laws. . . .
>
> To implement that objective, all of the following basic principles are applied in accounting for income taxes at the date of the financial statements:
>
> a. A current or deferred tax liability or asset is recognized for the current or deferred tax consequences of all events that have been recognized in the financial statements;
>
> b. The current or deferred tax consequences of an event are measured by applying the provisions of enacted tax laws to determine the amount of taxes payable or refundable currently or in future years; and
>
> c. The tax consequences of earning income or incurring losses or expenses in future years or the future enactment of a change in tax laws or rates are not anticipated for purposes of recognition and measurement of a deferred tax liability or asset.

Implementation of this objective and the three principles requires the following computations each accounting period:

1. Computation of **income tax payable** on the income tax return in conformity with income tax laws and regulations. This liability is reported on the statement of financial position until paid.
2. Computation of **deferred income tax** based on temporary differences (discussed later). This computation may involve both a **deferred tax liability** for future taxable amounts and a **deferred tax asset** for future tax deductible amounts. These liability/asset amounts are reported on the statement of financial position.
3. Computation of **income tax expense** (which is the algebraic **sum** of 1 and 2 above). This expense is reported in the statement of income. It is important to notice that income tax expense is a residual amount—it is **not** independently computed.

Interperiod Income Tax Allocation—What and Why

Prior to the issuance of *APB Opinion 11* in 1967, which required interperiod income tax allocation, most companies simply reported the amount of income taxes payable shown on the income tax return as the amount of income tax **expense** on the statement of income. During the earlier period some accountants

[4] This is an overview; the terminology and computations are explained and illustrated in the sections that follow.

criticized this current-basis method arguing that it did not properly match income tax expense with the items that caused the tax. Also, the Internal Revenue Regulations of 1954, which first permitted use of accelerated depreciation for income tax purposes, increased the concerns of many accountants about the current-basis method. In response to these concerns, *APB Opinion 11* was issued. Next, the Economic Recovery Tax Act of 1981 specified ACRS accelerated depreciation, which was continued in the Tax Reform Act of 1986. ACRS guidelines allow depreciation periods as short as three years on certain kinds of property. The "best" estimates made by companies (in conformity with GAAP) for computing straight-line depreciation often involve much longer estimated useful lives than the ACRS lives. This means that a longer depreciation life often is used for financial accounting purposes than for income tax purposes. In response to these events and criticisms of *APB Opinion 11*, the FASB issued *Standard 96*. The basic concept of this *Standard* is that income tax expense should be matched with the transaction or event that caused the tax in the first place. Interperiod income tax allocation focuses on what income tax effects should be reported on the statement of income (i.e., income tax expense) and the statement of financial position (i.e., income tax payable).

Now consider why interperiod income tax allocation is required. For example, examine the following case related to an operational asset owned and used in producing revenues by Simple Company. The annual depreciation on this asset has income tax consequences on net income and liabilities.[5] Information relevant to this asset's income tax consequences is shown below. Sales revenue and expenses, but not income taxes, are held constant in this case in order to focus on the income tax consequences.

	Amounts per year (000s)
Sales revenue	$1,200
Expenses before depreciation and income tax	920
Income before depreciation and income tax	$ 280
Depreciation expense on plant:*	
For accounting purposes ($450 ÷ 5 years) = $90 ⎤ → TEMPORARY DIFFERENCE, $60.	
For income tax purposes ($450 ÷ 3 years) = $150 ⎦	
Income tax rate, 30%	

* Plant cost $450; estimated useful life for accounting purposes, five years; for tax return purposes, three years (straight-line; no residual value).

Exhibit 23–1 shows a five-year comparative analysis of the income tax consequences of the above data for two cases: Case A, with no income tax allocation and Case B, with income tax allocation. The Simple Company case is not presented to illustrate application of the specific provisions of *FASB Standard 96*. Rather, it is a hypothetical illustration designed **only** to show the effects on the statement of income over an allocation period of time by comparing "no allocation" (Case A) and "with allocation" (Case B). The comparative focus is on **income tax expense and net income.** Examine these two lines in Exhibit

[5] *FASB Standard 96* defines "income tax consequence" essentially as the effects on income taxes—current or deferred—of a transaction or event. Also, this *Standard* uses the term **financial income;** this chapter uses the more descriptive term **pretax accounting income.**

Exhibit 23–1

Five-year comparative analysis of a statement of income with: Case A, no tax allocation and Case B, with tax allocation.

	Statement of income					
	19X1	19X2	19X3	19X4	19X5	Total
Case A—No income tax allocation (income tax expense and payable are the same):						
Income before depreciation and income taxes	$280	$280	$280	$280	$280	$1,400
Depreciation expense	90	90	90	90	90	450
Pretax accounting income	190	190	190	190	190	950
Income tax expense (30% rate)*	39	39	39	84	84	285
Net income	$151	$151	$151	$106	$106	$ 665
Case B—With income tax allocation:						
Income before depreciation and income taxes	$280	$280	$280	$280	$280	$1,400
Depreciation expense	90	90	90	90	90	450
Pretax accounting income	190	190	190	190	190	950
Income tax expense (30% rate)†	57	57	57	57	57	285
Net income	$133	$133	$133	$133	$133	$ 665

* Computation on the tax return:

	19X1–19X3	19X4–19X5
Income before depreciation and income taxes	$280	$280
Less depreciation for income tax purposes ($450 ÷ 3 yrs.)	150	-0-
Taxable income	130	280
Multiply by tax rate	× 30%	× 30%
Income tax payable	$ 39	$ 84

† Based on income tax allocation: ($190 × 30% = $57).

23–1. Income tax allocation **never** changes income tax payable because this amount is determined only in the income tax return in conformity with the enacted tax laws and the related tax regulations (discussed later).

Notice the following in the comparative analysis given in Exhibit 23–1:

1. The **total** column is the same for Case A (no tax allocation) and Case B (with tax allocation). This indicates that interperiod income tax allocation only affects reporting **within** a determinable period of time (called the **reversing period;** discussed later).
2. The only **lines** that are different between Case A (no tax allocation) and Case B (with tax allocation) are *(a)* income tax expense and *(b)* as a direct result, net income. This indicates that interperiod income tax allocation directly affects periodic net income by allocating total income tax expense for financial accounting purposes for the five-year period in a different way than it is reported on the several tax returns.
3. In Case A (no income tax allocation) income tax **expense** was $39 for the first three years and $84 for the last two years (total, $285). In contrast, Case B (with income tax allocation) income tax expense ($57) was the same for each year of the five years (total, $285). Also, these differences are reflected in net income.

The analysis shows the rationale for interperiod income tax allocation because it matches total income tax expense (i.e., $285) with revenues that the asset helped earn over its five-year life, rather than over the arbitrary three-year period reflected in Case A (i.e., the income tax period).

Overview of the Application of Interperiod Income Tax Allocation

Exhibit 23–1, Case B for Simple Company shows that **with income tax allocation:**

a. Income tax expense is the same each year due to allocation (in Case A it is different).

b. Income tax payable is unaffected by tax allocation.

c. Income tax allocation involves a total amount (the $450 amount to be depreciated by Simple Company) that is the same for accounting and income tax purposes, but there are temporary differences between accounting (five years) and income tax (three years) recognition.

The amount of income tax expense shown each year in Exhibit 23–1, Case B (with allocation) required interperiod income tax allocation, which is recorded in the accounts of the corporation. This requires accounting recognition of a deferred income tax asset (a debit) or deferred income tax liability (a credit)—in the Simple case only a liability was recognized. The deferred income tax liability for Simple Company is computed as follows:

Schedule for temporary differences to compute deferred income tax

	19X1	19X2	19X3	19X4	19X5	Total
Depreciation expense for:						
Statement of income	$ 90	$ 90	$ 90	$ 90	$ 90	$450
Income tax return	(150)	(150)	(150)	–0–	–0–	(450)
Temporary difference*	(60)[o]	(60)[o]	(60)[o]	90[r]	90[r]	–0–
Multiply by tax rate	×30%	×30%	×30%	×30%	×30%	×30%
Deferred income tax (liability)	$ (18)	$ (18)	$ (18)	$ 27	$ 27	$–0–

FASB Standard 96 calls the difference between the amount of depreciation shown on the statement of income and income tax return a **temporary difference.** The next section discusses temporary differences in detail.

[o] = These are called **originating differences** because the tax deferral is increased.

[r] = These are called **reversing** or **turnaround** differences because the tax deferral is reduced to zero by the end of the deferral period.

Now the data needed to **record income taxes** for each year are available as follows: *(a)* income taxes payable for each year (Exhibit 23–1), and *(b)* the deferred income tax liability or asset for each year (immediately above). Therefore, the annual entries to record income taxes can be made as follows:

Account	19X1		19X2		19X3		19X4		19X5	
Income tax expense[a]	57		57		57		57		57	
Deferred income tax liability		18		18		18	27[b]		27[b]	
Income tax payable[c]		39		39		39		84		84

[a] Income taxes payable plus deferred income tax liability minus any deferred income tax asset $39 + $18 = $57).

[b] These are debits because of the reversing or turnaround that always occurs (computed above).

[c] These liability amounts are paid on an essentially current basis (from the tax return).

The cumulative balance in the deferred income tax liability account is:

	19X1	19X2	19X3	19X4	19X5
Deferred income tax liability (a credit balance)*	$18	$36	$54	$27	$-0-

* Reported in the statement of financial position as a liability.

Notice that the deferred income tax liability account balance increases for the origination amounts then decreases by the reversal amounts, and always ends with a zero balance at the end of the reversal period.

The schedule of temporary differences given above to compute deferred income tax is the key computation because *(a)* income tax payable is computed on the income tax return and *(b)* income tax expense is the sum of income tax payable and deferred income tax. This schedule is a continuing computation of the status of the deferred tax account. The basic computation is shown in this schedule because it involves computation of the **temporary difference,** which is then multiplied by the current tax rate(s) to determine the increases and decreases in deferred **income tax.** If this account has a credit balance it is called a **deferred income tax liability;** if it has a debit balance it is called a **deferred income tax asset.**

A significant aspect of interperiod income tax allocation is illustrated in the journal entries given above for the five years. The deferred tax liability account increased during the first three years to a $54 cumulative credit balance. Then during the next two years the debits reduced the account to a zero balance. In this way the total tax is allocated over the useful life of the asset. Notice that income tax expense is equal each of the five years (i.e., $57). The accumulation of the $54 and the subsequent reduction of it to zero is called the **reversing, or turnaround, characteristic** of interperiod income tax allocation. **It will always occur.** Now return to Exhibit 23–1 and compare the two net income lines. These amounts differ for one reason only; that is, how income tax expense was allocated to each year. In Case A the "allocation" was based only on the tax return. In Case B total income tax expense was allocated equally to each year. This illustrates the basic concept of interperiod income tax allocation.

Be sure you understand the basic principles and their application shown in this case before continuing your study because the following discussions will use these concepts and procedures to illustrate the complexities of interperiod income tax allocation.

Temporary Income Tax Differences

Temporary income tax differences[6] were briefly defined on page 1201. This section expands that definition. *FASB Standard 96,* par. 9, identifies two sources of temporary differences. Temporary differences occur only because accounting standards and income tax laws differ as to when they recognize assets, liabilities, owners' equity, revenues, gains, expenses, and losses. Temporary differences used for income tax allocation are based on the same total amounts, but the **timing** of recognition differs. All temporary differences originate in one or more

[6] A similar category was called timing differences in *APB Opinion 11.*

years and reverse or turn around in one or more other years. The two basic sources of temporary differences are:

1. The amount of taxable income (in the tax return) is different than the pretax accounting income (related to the statement of income) for two or more years.
2. Assets or liabilities have different recovery or settlement timing dates during the respective "holding" periods.

Most transactions and events recognized in the financial statements are also included in the income tax return for the same year; therefore, they do not create temporary differences. As a result, *FASB Standard 96* (pars. 9 and 13) lists only 10 kinds of temporary differences. However, they are classified in four basic categories as follows:

Deferred tax liabilities (credits):

1. **Revenues and gains that are included in the tax return AFTER they are included in pretax accounting income.** This case causes income tax expense for the originating period to be **more** than income tax payable for that period. A deferred income tax liability (a credit) is recorded in the originating period because there is a taxable amount that will be paid in the future. Examples are:
   a. Gross margin on installment sales is recognized for accounting purposes before it is included in taxable income in the income tax return (Chapter 13).
   b. Income on long-term construction contracts when percentage of completion is used for accounting purposes and completed contract is used for tax purposes (Chapter 13).
   c. Short-term investments when a LCM unrealized gain (i.e., loss recovery) is recognized for accounting purposes during the holding period while the actual gain on date of disposal is used for tax purposes (Chapter 18).
2. **Expenses and losses that are included in the tax return BEFORE they are included in pretax accounting income.** This case causes income tax expense for the originating period to be **more** than income tax payable for that period. Therefore, a deferred tax liability (a credit) is recorded in the originating period(s). Examples are:
   a. Use of straight-line depreciation for accounting purposes and an accelerated rate for income tax purposes.
   b. Use of a longer depreciation period for accounting purposes than is used for income tax purposes.

Deferred tax assets (debits):

3. **Revenues and gains that are included in the tax return BEFORE they are included in pretax accounting income.** This case causes income tax expense in the originating period to be **less** than income tax payable for that period. Therefore, a deferred income tax asset (a debit) is recorded in the originating period because the income tax is already paid. Examples are:

a. Rent revenue collected in advance when included in taxable income before it is included in pretax accounting income.
b. Gain on disposal of an asset when included in taxable income before it is included in pretax accounting income.

4. **Expenses and losses that are included in the tax return AFTER they are included in accounting pretax income.** This case causes income tax expense for the originating period to be **less** than income tax payable for that period. Therefore, a deferred tax asset (a debit) is recorded. Examples are:
   a. Estimated loss on disposal of a segment of a business recognized for accounting purposes but reported on the income tax return later on the basis of the actual loss (Chapter 22).
   b. Employee compensation expense recognized for accounting purposes on the basis of estimates but included later on the tax return on the basis of actual expense incurred.
   c. Short-term investment when a LCM unrealized loss is recognized for accounting purposes during the holding period while the actual loss on date of disposal is used for tax purposes (Chapter 18).
   d. Allowance for doubtful accounts is used for accounting purposes while direct write-off is required for tax purposes.

The discussions which follow will explain and illustrate these four types of temporary differences.

To emphasize, temporary differences *(a)* relate only to items that will be recognized on both the statement of income and the tax return, but in different reporting periods, *(b)* always cause a deferred income tax liability (a credit), or asset (a debit) be recorded, and *(c)* always reverse (i.e., turn around) in one or more future reporting periods.

An overview of the prior discussions is presented in **Exhibit 23–2**. The discussions which follow will expand this overview to include the complexities and guidelines given in *FASB Standard 96*.

Deferred Income Tax Liabilities and Assets

In accounting for deferred income tax a careful terminology distinction must be made between *(a)* temporary differences and *(b)* the deferred income tax liability or asset. Temporary differences, as previously defined, are **pretax** amounts due to (1) a difference between taxable income and pretax accounting income in an accounting period and (2) a difference in the timing basis when the tax consequences of an asset or liability are included in accounting income versus taxable income. In contrast, **a deferred income tax liability (a credit and future taxable amount) or asset (a debit and future deductible amount) is the result of multiplying a temporary difference by the current income tax rate(s).**

Temporary differences ordinarily cause future taxable amounts or future tax deductible amounts when (or as) the related asset is recovered, or when (or as) the related liability is settled. **Future taxable amount** relates to a deferred tax liability (a credit) because the liability will be paid, or offset, in the future. **Future deductible amount** relates to a deferred tax asset because the asset is either *(a)* **deductible** in the future from a deferred tax liability or *(b)* **refundable**

Exhibit 23–2
Overview of income tax allocation.

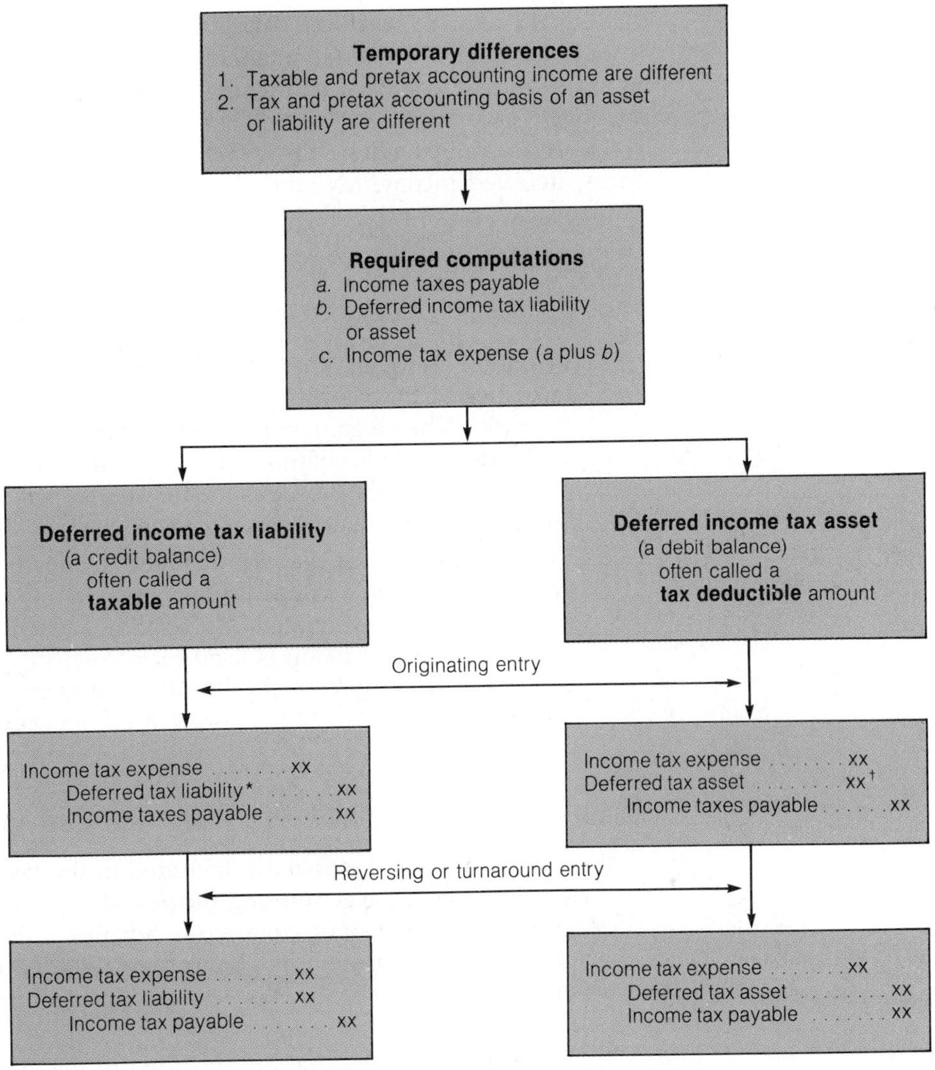

in the future (the tax is already paid). Future taxable and deductible amounts usually are simply called **taxable and deductible amounts.** A deferred tax liability or asset is determined each accounting period. This determination must include the **tax consequences** of all temporary differences; that is, the amount of taxes payable or refundable in the future and any additional tax liabilities or assets of the current accounting year. The **net change** during the accounting year in the deferred income tax liability and asset accounts is recognized as a deferred tax liability or a deferred tax asset. In this regard, it is convenient to think of a single account called **deferred income tax.** If it has a net credit balance there is a net tax liability. If it has a net debit balance there is a net tax asset.[7] *FASB*

[7] *FASB Standard 96*, par. 17e, specifies a limit or cap on a **net deferred tax asset;** discussed on page 1211.

Standard 96, par. 16, specifically states that this **net algebraic change** in deferred income tax liability or asset plus income taxes payable as shown in the tax return shall be recognized as **income tax expense** on the current statement of income.[8]

The relationships among taxable and deductible amounts, temporary differences, deferred income tax, and the related terminology, can be summarized as follows:

Taxable Amounts (a deferred tax liability and a credit):

1. **Revenues and gains that are included in the tax return AFTER they are recognized for accounting purposes.**
   Example: When a gain on installment sales is recognized for tax purposes as the receivable is collected, but was earlier recognized for accounting purposes when the sale was made. The tax will be paid in the future; therefore, future taxes will be higher.
2. **Expenses and losses that are included in the tax return BEFORE they are recognized for accounting purposes.**
   Example: When accelerated depreciation is used for tax purposes but straight-line depreciation is used for accounting purposes. The expense will not be tax deductible in the future; therefore, future taxes will be higher.

Deductible Amounts (a deferred tax asset and a debit):

1. **Revenues and gains that are included in the tax return BEFORE they are recognized for accounting purposes.**
   Example: Rent revenue collected in advance which was recognized for tax purposes when collected but recognized for accounting purposes later on the accrual basis. The tax is already paid; therefore, future taxes will be lower.
2. **Expenses and losses that are included in the tax return AFTER they are recognized for accounting purposes.**
   Example: Product warranty costs recognized for tax purposes as the warranty conditions are met but recognized for accounting purposes earlier on the accrual basis. The expense will be tax deductible in the future; therefore, future taxes will be lower.

The terms **pretax accounting income** (also called **financial income**) and **taxable income** are used extensively in *FASB Standard 96* and in this chapter. Precise definitions of these terms are essential because the difference between them is the sum of all of the temporary differences. Therefore,

---

[8] This is a major distinction between the old requirements *(APB Opinion 11)* and the new *FASB Standard 96* requirements referenced on page 1197. That is, Payable + Deferred = Expense; under *APB Opinion 11* it was: Payable − Expense = Deferred.

		Temporary Differences				
Taxable income	+	Taxable amounts*	−	Deductible amounts†	=	Pretax accounting income
Example: $500	+	$400	−	$200	=	$700

or, inversely

Pretax accounting income	−	Taxable amounts	+	Deductible amounts	=	Taxable income
Example: $700	−	$400	+	$200	=	$500

* Deferred tax liabilities.
† Deferred tax assets.

There are two practical problems in implementing these two definitions: (1) taxable income comes from the income tax return, which typically is prepared some time after the end of the accounting period, and (2) pretax accounting income is included in the statement of income but is not reported as a separate amount. For instructional purposes one, or both, of these amounts are provided. Pretax accounting income does appear as a separate caption or number on the statement of income. However, it is not unusual in preparing the tax return to start with **net income** from the statement of income and then make "adjustments" to convert that amount to **taxable income.** In this process **taxable accounting income** is identified and computed; when this is done this amount will be available when tax allocations are analyzed.

Annual Computation and Recognition of Income Taxes

The prior discussions emphasized the objectives and principles of income tax allocation. A hypothetical case was used to illustrate the reasons for interperiod income tax allocation. Those discussions will be concluded by indicating a coordinated approach that is used to compute the *(a)* deferred income tax amount(s) and *(b)* the journal entry required for income taxes at each year-end. This approach involves the following steps at each year-end (these steps are expanded later):

1. Collect the essential accounting and income tax data for the year and focus on identification of temporary differences.
2. Develop a reconciliation between pretax accounting income (i.e., the accounting amount that would be subject to tax) and taxable income (i.e., the amount subject to tax on the income tax return). Compute income taxes payable for the year.
3. Develop a schedule of temporary differences (between pretax accounting income and taxable income).
4. Convert the temporary differences to tax amounts and compute the balance in the deferred tax account at the end of each period.
5. Prepare the entry at the end of the accounting period to record income taxes.

Exhibit 23–3
Spreadsheet application of interperiod income tax allocation; Simple Company (a deferred tax liability; depreciation).

Step 1—Basic accounting and income tax data:

	Amounts per year (000s)
Sales revenue	$1,200
Expenses before depreciation and income tax	920
Income before depreciation and income tax	$ 280

Depreciation expense on plant:*
For accounting purposes ($450 ÷ 5 years) = $90 ⎤
For income tax purposes ($450 ÷ 3 years) = $150 ⎦ → TEMPORARY DIFFERENCE, $60.
Income tax rate, 30%

* Plant cost $450; estimated useful life for accounting purposes, five years; for tax return purposes, three years (straight line; no residual value).
Note: Simplifying assumptions: *(a)* no changes in the temporary difference, *(b)* no carrybacks and carryforwards, and *(c)* no changes in tax rates. These topics are discussed later in the chapter.

Step 2—Reconciliation of accounting income and taxable income:

	19X1	19X2	19X3	19X4	19X5
Accounting income before depreciation and tax	$280	$280	$280	$280	$280
Depreciation expense for accounting purposes	90	90	90	90	90
Pretax accounting income (as defined in *FASB Statement 96*)	190	190	190	190	190
Temporary difference (depreciation) (step 3)	$(60)^{o}$	$(60)^{o}$	$(60)^{o}$	90^{r}	90^{r}
Taxable income	$130	$130	$130	$280	$280
Income tax rate	×30%	×30%	×30%	×30%	×30%
Income tax payable (shown on tax return)	$ 39	$ 39	$ 39	$ 84	$ 84

Step 3—Schedule of temporary differences between pretax accounting and taxable income:

	19X1	19X2	19X3	19X4	19X5
Temporary differences:					
Depreciation (in statement of income)	$ 90	$ 90	$ 90	$ 90	$ 90
Deduct depreciation (in tax return)	(150)	(150)	(150)	–0–	–0–
Temporary difference	$ $(60)^{o}$	$ $(60)^{o}$	$ $(60)^{o}$	$ 90^{r}	$ 90^{r}

Step 4—Conversion of temporary differences to tax amounts and to compute the balance in the deferred tax liability account each period:

	19X1	19X2	19X3	19X4	19X5
Temporary difference (from step 3 × 30%, deferred tax liability)	$ $(18)^{o}$	$ $(18)^{o}$	$ $(18)^{o}$	$ 27^{r}	$ 27^{r}
Add beginning balance (credit)	0	→ (18)	(36)	(54)	(27)
Total, ending balance (credit)	$(18)	$(36)	$(54)	$(27)	$ 0

Step 5—Journal entry to record income taxes at end of year:

	19X1 Dr.	19X1 Cr.	19X2 Dr.	19X2 Cr.	19X3 Dr.	19X3 Cr.	19X4 Dr.	19X4 Cr.	19X5 Dr.	19X5 Cr.
Income tax expense (payable plus deferred)*	57		57		57		57		57	
Deferred income tax liability (from step 4)		18°		18°		18°	27^{r}†		27^{r}†	
Income tax payable (from step 2)		39		39		39		84		84

* Proof, $190, step 2, × 30% = $57.
† The debits to the deferred income tax liability account for the last two years (the reversing periods) reduce the account balance to zero.
^{o} = Originating difference.
^{r} = Reversing difference.

Spreadsheet for a Deferred Income Tax Liability. Rather than presenting an array of disconnected illustrations, a comprehensive and efficient spreadsheet is demonstrated in **Exhibit 23–3.** For this purpose, the hypothetical case for Simple Company is used. Because of the simplifying assumptions, the spreadsheet can include each of the five allocation periods (i.e., 19X1 through 19X5).

Therefore, the spreadsheet provides a broad view of how interperiod income tax allocation is applied.

This hypothetical illustration does not include three pervasive problems usually encountered in interperiod income tax allocation as follows: *(a)* changes in temporary differences which are common each year, *(b)* application of carryback and carryforward procedures (prescribed by *FASB Standard 96*), and *(c)* changes in enacted income tax rates. Typically, the five steps listed above would have to be **redone each year-end** to consider changes in temporary differences, income tax rates, and reversing periods. These topics are discussed later.

The spreadsheet is designed to provide the data needed, step by step, to prepare the year-end journal entry to record income taxes for the period. Each step provides data needed for the next step. **Step 1** provides the basic data about the temporary income tax differences. In this case the data indicates that depreciation for tax purposes (over three years) is faster than for accounting purposes (over five years). This causes a temporary difference ($60 per year for the first three years). **Step 2** is important because it reconciles pretax accounting income and taxable income and analyzes the temporary differences related to depreciation in this case. Notice that the temporary differences throughout are identified as originating (o) and reversing (r) differences for instructional convenience. There are three originating differences ($60 each) and two reversing differences ($90 each) and they algebraically sum to zero. This step flows from step 1 and it provides assurance that the temporary differences are properly identified. It also includes computation of income tax payable at each year-end as reflected on the income tax return. **Step 3** supplements the data in step 2; it is an important schedule because it shows how temporary differences are computed. In fact, this is how the temporary difference amounts in step 2 were computed. This schedule becomes much more important when carrybacks and carryforwards are discussed later. **Step 4** provides a conversion of the temporary differences shown in step 3 to **income tax amounts** by applying the currently enacted income tax rate(s). It also provides the year-end balance in the deferred tax liability account, which is reported on the statement of financial position. **Step 5** is the objective of all of the prior steps—step 2 provides the income tax payable amount and step 4 gives the deferred income tax amount. And finally, income tax expense is computed as the residual or balancing amount.

To reemphasize, this spreadsheet illustrates the following basic characteristics of interperiod income tax allocation:

1. All temporary differences are related to differences in the **timing** of accounting recognition compared with income tax recognition.
2. All temporary differences originate, then reverse, and eventually end with a net zero effect. Reversals also are called "dispositions of temporary differences."
3. Income tax expense is identified (i.e., matched) on the statement of income of the periods in which the tax was incurred rather than with the periods in which the item was recognized in the income tax returns.
4. A deferred tax liability has a credit balance (because there is a future tax liability to be settled.)
5. The balance in a deferred tax liability account is reported each period under liabilities on the statement of financial position. Similarly, a deferred

Exhibit 23–4

Spreadsheet application of interperiod income tax allocation; Simple Company (a deferred tax asset; rent revenue).

Step 1—Basic accounting and income tax data:

	Amounts per year (000s)
Revenue before rent revenue..	$1,200
Expenses before income tax...	920
Income before rent revenue and income tax	$ 280

Rent revenue:

For accounting purposes ($60 ÷ 3 years) = $20 ⎤
For income tax purposes (taxable all in 19X1) = $60 ⎦ → TEMPORARY DIFFERENCE, $40.

Note: Simplifying assumptions: *(a)* no changes in the temporary difference, *(b)* no carrybacks and carryforwards, *(c)* no changes in tax rates and *(d)* no constraint on recognizing a deferred tax asset. These topics are discussed later in the chapter.

Step 2—Reconciliation of accounting income and taxable income:

	19X1	19X2	19X3	19X4	19X5
Accounting income before rent and income tax....................	$280	$280	$280	$280	$280
Rent revenue for accounting purposes	20	20	20	–0–	–0–
Pretax Accounting Income (as defined in *FASB Standard 96*)	300	300	300	280	280
Temporary difference (rent revenue) (step 3).....................	40°	(20)r	(20)r	–0–	–0–
Taxable income ...	$340	$280	$280	$280	$280
Income tax rate ...	×30%	×30%	×30%	×30%	×30%
Income tax payable (shown on tax return).......................	$102	$ 84	$ 84	$ 84	$ 84

Step 3—Schedule of temporary differences between accounting and taxable income:

Temporary differences:

	19X1	19X2	19X3	19X4	19X5
Rent revenue (in statement of income)	$ (20)	$ (20)	$ (20)	$–0–	$–0–
Rent revenue (in tax return)	(60)	–0–	–0–	–0–	–0–
Temporary difference ...	$ 40	$ (20)	$ (20)	$–0–	$–0–

Step 4—Conversion of temporary differences to tax amounts and to compute the balance in the deferred tax asset account each period:

	19X1	19X2	19X3	19X4	19X5
Temporary difference (from step 3 × 30%, deferred tax asset)	$ 12°	$ (6)r	$ (6)r	$–0–	$–0–
Add beginning balance (debit)	0	12	6	–0–	–0–
Total, ending balance (debit)	$ 12	$ 6	$ 0	–0–	–0–

Step 5—Journal entry to record income taxes at end of year:

	19X1	19X2	19X3	19X4	19X5
Income tax expense (payable minus deferred)	90*	90	90	84	84
Deferred income tax asset (from step 4)†	12°				
Income tax payable (from step 2).............................		6r	6r		
	102	84	84	84	84

* Proof, $300 × 30% = $90; etc., from step 2.

† The credits to the deferred income tax asset account years 19X2 and 19X3 (the reversing periods) reduce the account balance to zero.

° = Originating difference.

r = Reversing difference.

tax asset (a debit balance) is reported on the statement of financial position as an asset (because there is a future taxable advantage to be realized).

Spreadsheet for a Deferred Income Tax Asset. Interperiod income tax allocation requires recognition in a company's accounts of a deferred tax amount when there are temporary differences that do not exactly offset. Temporary differences will result in recognition of either, or both: (1) a deferred tax liability (a credit balance) as illustrated in Exhibit 23–3, or (2) a deferred tax asset (a debit balance).

Exhibit 23–4 illustrates the computations and recording of a deferred tax asset. This exhibit continues the Simple Case, which is adapted by disregarding depreciation and using instead **rent revenue collected in advance.** Notice that the originating entry is a collection of revenue in advance which is reported on the tax return when collected before it is recognized in accounting; it reverses during the next two years. The collection in advance causes a deferred tax asset, which is a deductible amount because the income tax on the rent revenue is paid in advance. This illustration reflects the same characteristics shown in Exhibit 23–3, except for "asset" and "debit" instead of liability and credit.

A Limitation on Deferred Tax Assets

FASB Standard 96 specifies a limit on the amount that can be recorded as a deferred tax asset. No limit is specified for deferred tax liabilities. The reasons for this inconsistent rule are *(a)* such an asset lacks real value and *(b)* conservatism. *FASB Standard 96*, par. 17, states: "Deferred Tax Assets—Recognize a deferred tax asset for the tax benefit of net deductible amounts that could be realized by loss carryback from future years (1) to reduce a current deferred tax liability and (2) to reduce taxes paid in the current or a prior year. (No asset is recognized for any additional net deductible amounts in future years.)" When future deductible amounts (i.e., deferred income tax asset) exceed future taxable amounts (i.e., deferred income tax liability) a **net** deferred income tax asset could exist. This rule means that the deferred tax asset recognized cannot exceed the sum of *(a)* the current **deferred** tax liability plus *(b)* any carryback to the current and the prior two years' income tax payable amounts. To analyze the effect of this limitation refer to Simple Company, Exhibit 23–4, as follows:

	19X1	19X2	19X3
Current deferred tax liability	$–0–	$–0–	$–0–
Current income taxes paid or payable	102	84	84
Total limit on tax asset	102	84	84
Deferred tax asset	12°	6^{r}	6^{r} = zero
Total asset in excess of the limit	$–0–	$–0–	$–0–

Conclusion: Recognize the deferred tax asset amount of $12 because it is less than the current income taxes paid or payable (19X1 is year 1 for Simple Company). However, if the current income taxes paid or payable at the end of 19X1 was $10, only $10 of the $12 deferred tax amount could be recognized.

This simple example is not typical because it does not involve carryback and carryforward procedures for deductible amounts referred to in the above quotation from *FASB Standard 19*. Application of the deferred income tax limitation is discussed later, starting on page 1223 (ESY Corporation).

Application of the Enacted Tax Laws or Rates

FASB Standard 96, par. 17f, specifies that estimated net taxable amounts that are scheduled to occur in each future year be computed by applying **currently enacted tax rates and laws.** Estimates of future tax rates cannot be used. Application of the enacted tax rates in interperiod income tax allocation involves three different situations:

1. The enacted tax rate (specified by current tax law) is **constant** from year to year.

2. The enacted tax rates (specified by current tax law) are **different for some or all of the future years.**
3. The enacted tax rate or rates are **changed by a newly enacted tax law.** This situation requires a catch-up entry.

Situation 1—In this case the cumulative temporary difference for each year is multiplied by the enacted constant tax rate to compute the deferred tax liability or asset. For example, assume that XY Corporation had a $300,000 temporary tax difference for deferred gross margin on installment sales (a taxable amount) at the end of 1986. This temporary difference will reverse equally during 1987, 1988, and 1989. Assuming an enacted corporate income tax rate of 48%, the related deferred tax liability at the end of 1986 would be $144,000 (a credit). The annual change and cumulative balance in the deferred income tax liability account would be as follows:

	1986	1987	1988	1989
Tax return basis	$300,000	$ -0-	$ -0-	$ -0-
Accounting basis	-0-	100,000	100,000	100,000
Temporary difference (a taxable amount)	$300,000[o]	$100,000[r]	$100,000[r]	$100,000[r]
Tax rate (constant)	× 48% [a]	× 48%	× 48%	× 48%
Deferred tax liability	$144,000 cr.	$ 48,000 dr.	$ 48,000 dr.	$ 48,000 dr.
Cumulative balance in the deferred tax liability account[b]	$144,000 cr.	$ 96,000 cr.	$ 48,000 cr.	$ -0-

[o] = Originating difference; [r] = reversing difference.
[a] The rate used here must be consistent with the reversing tax rates otherwise it will not reverse to zero.
[b] 1987: ($300,000 − $100,000) × 48% = $96,000; 1988: ($300,000 − $100,000 − $100,000) × 48% = $48,000.

Situation 2—In this situation the currently enacted tax rates do not change during the reversing period, but these currently enacted tax the rates are not the same for all years. To illustrate, the data for XY Corporation are used, except that the currently enacted tax rates are: 1987, 46%; 1988, 40%; and 1989, 34%. The related deferred tax liability at the end of 1986 would be computed as follows: ($100,000 × 46% = $46,000) + ($100,000 × 40% = $40,000) + ($100,000 × 34% = $34,000) = $120,000. The annual change and cumulative balance in the deferred tax liability account would be computed as follows:

	1986	1987	1988	1989
Temporary difference (a taxable amount)	$300,000[o]	$100,000[r]	$100,000[r]	$100,000[r]
Tax rate (varies)	[a]	× 46%	× 40%	× 34%
Deferred tax liability	$120,000 cr.[b]	$ 46,000 dr.	$ 40,000 dr.	$ 34,000 dr.
Cumulative ending balance in the deferred tax liability account[c]	$120,000 cr.	$ 74,000 cr.	$ 34,000 cr.	$ -0-

[o] = Originating difference; [r] = reversing difference
[a] The rate used here must be consistent with the reversing tax rates otherwise it will not reverse to zero.
[b] $46,000 + $40,000 + $34,000 = $120,000.
[c] $120,000 − $46,000 = $74,000; $74,000 − $40,000 = $34,000; and $34,000 − $34,000 = $ -0-.

Situation 3—In this situation the enacted tax rate or rates are changed by a newly enacted tax law; that is, the rates already used are changed. In this situation *(a)* the newly enacted rate or rates must be used in the computations and *(b)* a **catch-up entry** must be made to adjust the cumulative deferred tax amount from the old tax basis to the new tax basis. To illustrate, assume that effective January 1, 1987, the president signed a new tax law that changed the corporate tax rate from 48% (i.e., Situation 1) to 34% (constant until another tax rate is enacted). When a newly enacted tax rate occurs, its effect on the deferred tax amount must be reflected in income tax expense (whether a debit or a credit) in the period in which the new rate is enacted. Refer to Situation 1 to ascertain that the deferred tax liability balance at the end of 1986 was $144,000. This amount must be recomputed based on the newly enacted tax rate as follows:

	1986	1987	1988	1989
Temporary difference (a taxable amount)	$300,000[o]	$100,000[r]	$100,000[r]	$100,000[r]
Tax rate (newly enacted)	× 34%*	× 34%	× 34%	× 34%
Deferred tax liability	$102,000 cr.	$ 34,000 dr.	$ 34,000 dr.	$ 34,000 dr.

* The rate used here must be consistent with the reversing tax rates.

Adjustment required in the deferred tax liability account:

Prior balance	$144,000 cr.
Required balance	102,000 cr.
Decrease	$ 42,000 dr.

January 1, 1987, catch-up entry:

Deferred tax liability	42,000	
Income tax expense		42,000

Notice that if this entry is not made the deferred tax account will not reverse to zero.

Adjustment required in the deferred tax liability account:

	1986	1987	1988	1989
Prior balance	$144,000	$102,000	$68,000	$34,000
Catch-up entry effect	−42,000	−34,000	−34,000	−34,000
Cumulative ending balance as adjusted	$102,000	$ 68,000	$34,000	$ -0-

A newly enacted tax increase would be treated in the same way as a tax decrease. Notice that the "catch-up" adjustment for the change in the income tax rate is included in income tax expense in the period of change.

Restatement for tax rates as illustrated above is **limited to tax rates already enacted into law.** Expected or estimated future tax rates cannot be used under any circumstances.

Initial Adoption of the Provisions of *FASB Standard 96*

For the year of first application of *FASB Standard 96,* the balance in the deferred income tax liability, or asset, account must be restated to the balance that would have existed, had the provisions of *FASB Standard 96* been used in the past. This means a change in accounting principle "catch-up" adjustment must be made in conformity with *APB Opinion 20* (discussed in Chapter 24). To illustrate, assume Baker Company adopted *FASB Standard 96* starting in 19X6, at which time the deferred tax account balance was $25,000 (a debit). Computations in conformity with *FASB Standard 96* determined that the account should reflect a $12,000 credit balance. The following "catch-up" entry must be made:

Adjustment due to change in accounting principle (adoption of *FASB Standard 96*)	37,000*	
Deferred income tax liability ($25,000 + $12,000)		37,000

* This amount is reported on the statement of income in a manner similar to an extraordinary item.

Additional Issues Related to Income Tax Allocation

The prior section of this chapter conclude the discussion of the objectives and principles of interperiod income tax allocation. Also, the Simple Company case was concluded with its four simplifying assumptions: (1) no changes in the temporary differences during the allocation periods, (2) no carrybacks or carryforwards, (3) no changes in the enacted income tax rate(s), and (4) no constraint on recognition of deferred tax assets (see Exhibit 23–4).

The remaining sections of this chapter will discuss these simplifying assumptions and other related topics as follows:

1. Net operating tax loss carrybacks and carryforwards (NOLs).
2. Application of carryback and carryforward procedures in interperiod income tax allocation.
3. Analysis of net operating loss carrybacks and carryforwards (NOLs) for income tax allocation.
4. Interperiod tax-planning strategies.
5. Intraperiod income tax allocation.
6. Income tax effects of prior period adjustments.
7. Financial statement presentation and disclosure of deferred income taxes.
8. Investment tax credit (ITC).

Net Operating Tax Loss Carrybacks and Carryforwards (NOLs)

The prior discussions in this chapter excluded carryback and carryforward procedures for instructional convenience. However, they are an important aspect of interperiod income tax allocation. Interperiod income tax allocation applies carryback/carryforward procedures in **two ways:** (1) for **income tax purposes**—called **net operating** loss carrybacks and carryforwards (NOLs), and (2) for **accounting purposes** in analyzing temporary differences. This section discusses only net operating loss carrybacks and carryforwards. An understanding of net operating loss carrybacks and carryforwards is needed *(a)* to apply NOLs for income tax allocation and *(b)* to use the procedures for carryback and carryforward accounting purposes for temporary differences.

Net operating tax carrybacks and carryforwards (often called **net operating losses**—NOLs) as provided by income tax laws and regulations allow corporations that sustain a net operating loss for the current year to **carryback and/or carryforward** such losses for income tax purposes. These corporations receive a cash refund of prior taxes paid or a tax reduction in subsequent years. These are called **operating carrybacks** and **carryforwards.** Under the current law, at the end of the year of loss, the company must make an irrevocable choice of either the:

a. **Carryback-carryforward option**—A carryback of three years (in order of year starting with the oldest year) of such losses is permitted in order to secure a refund of prior taxes on income of an equivalent amount. If the loss is so large that the carryback provision does not fully absorb it, the remaining loss may be used as a carryforward (in order of year) until it is fully absorbed, with a limit of 15 years forward. The carryforward will result in a reduction of tax payable for each year to which it extends.
b. **Carryforward-only option**—A carryforward only for 15 years (in order of year) is permitted in order to reduce future income tax payments.

Assuming year D is the year of loss, these tax provisions may be diagrammed as shown below:

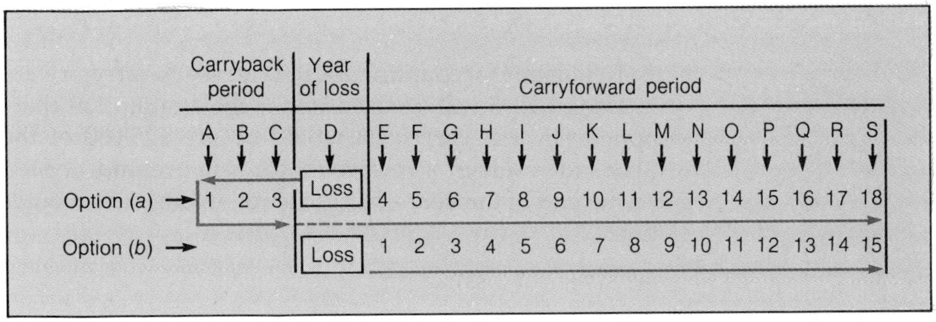

The accounting issue posed by income tax loss carrybacks and carryforwards is the extent to which in the year of loss any *(a)* carryback tax refunds and *(b)* potential carryforward tax benefits should be matched against the pretax loss of the period reported on the statement of income. To illustrate the accounting for tax loss carrybacks and carryforwards, the data for X Corporation shown in **Exhibit 23–5** is used. A carryforward period of seven years is used only for instructional convenience.

Based on the data given in Exhibit 23-5, should option *(a)* or option *(b)* be selected? The choice between the two options, which must be made at the end of year of loss, is critical because the two options have different cash flow effects. That is, the corporation must weigh the benefit of a certain cash refund (from the carryback) against the likelihood of increases in future tax rates. Such increases may make the carryforward-only option more attractive. The carryforward-only option should be selected only if the corporation expects to earn sufficient income in future years to absorb the loss and is able to do so quickly enough to offset the present value advantage of the carryback options. Therefore, a choice between the two options involves a projection of future tax rates and future income amounts.

Accounting for the Carryback-Carryforward Option. When an operating loss follows a three-year period of net income sufficient to offset that loss, the resultant loss carryback will produce a refund (or income tax payable offset) of at least some of the taxes paid during that three-year period. Because the carryback refund or offset is certain, the **tax effect** should be recorded in the accounts and reflected in the financial statements for the loss period.

Exhibit 23–5
Carryback and carryforward illustrative data—X Corporation.

	Actual (carryback)			Loss	Estimated (carryforward)						
Year	A	B	C	D	E	F	G	H	I	J	K
Income (loss) - in $000s	$5	$9	$11	$(30)	$5	$5	$50	$55	$60	$75	$100
Tax rate (%)	20	20	20		20	20	40	40	40	40	45
Tax paid - in $000s	$1	$1.8	$2.2		$1	$1	$20	$22	$24	$30	$45

To illustrate accounting for the carryback-carryforward option, the data given in Exhibit 23–5 will be used under the assumption that X Corporation selected option *(a)*. The carryback would absorb $25,000 of the loss (i.e., $5 + $9 + $11) and result in a receivable for a tax refund of $5,000 ($1 + $1.8 + $2.2). At the end of the year of loss, the following entry would be made by X Corporation:

19D (year of loss):

Receivable for income tax refund (loss carryback)	5,000	
Gain, income tax refund from loss carryback (closed to income summary; not extraordinary)		5,000

The effect of the above entry would cause X Corporation to *(a)* report a $5,000 receivable on its 19D statement of financial position and *(b)* reduce the reported loss from $30,000 to $25,000 for 19D. Because the carryback did not fully absorb the $30,000 loss, there is a potential carryforward tax benefit relating to the $5,000 unabsorbed loss (under option [*a*]). Although this **unabsorbed loss,** in the usual case, will be carried forward, it will not be recognized (i.e., not accrued) in the accounts in the year of loss because its realization as a future income tax deduction is uncertain.

In 19E, the effect of the tax reduction would be recorded as follows:*

Income tax payable ($5,000 × 20%)	1,000	
Gain, tax saving from loss carryforward		1,000

* Assuming the following entry was already made ($5,000 × 20%):

Income tax expense	1,000	
Income tax payable		1,000

Accounting for the Carryforward-Only Option. When a taxpayer sustains a tax loss and expects higher income in the future than in prior years, election of the carryforward-only option [*(b)* above] usually is elected. Because the realization of a future income tax deduction is typically uncertain, the effects of a loss carryforward are not recognized (i.e., not accrued) in the year of loss. The annual **tax benefit** of the loss is recognized as a **gain** in each future year as the benefits occur.

To illustrate using the data given in Exhibit 23–5, assume X Corporation selected the carryforward-only option. The actual pretax incomes and tax rates were (000s): 19E, $4, 20%; 19F, $6, 22%; and 19G, $60, 40% (relatively close to the estimates given in Exhibit 23–5). The related entries and computations would be as follows:

19D (year-end for year of loss):

No entry, that is, the income tax **carryforward** is not accrued because its realization is uncertain (i.e., it cannot be estimated beyond any reasonable doubt). However, if material in amount, it should be explained in a disclosure note.

Year-end (to record income tax each year):

	19E		19F		19G	
Income tax expense	800		1,320		24,000	
Gain (loss carryforward)*		800		1,320		8,000
Income tax payable						16,000

* Prior to *FASB 96* this would have been an extraordinary gain.

Computations:

Income tax expense: 19E, ($4,000 × 20%); 19F, ($6,000 × 22%); 19G, ($60,000 × 40%).

Gain (tax offset on $30,000 carryforward):

Year	Carryforward used	Tax rate	Gain
19E	$ 4,000	× 20% =	$ 800
19F	6,000	× 22% =	1,320
19G	20,000	× 40% =	8,000

Income tax payable (net of carryforward offset):

Year	Actual pretax income	Carryforward offset	Taxable income	Tax rate	Tax payable
19E	$ 4,000 −	$ 4,000	= $ -0-	× 20% =	$ -0-
19F	6,000 −	6,000	= -0-	× 22% =	-0-
19G	60,000 −	20,000	= 40,000	× 40% =	16,000

In the X Corporation case, option *(b)* appears preferable because the cash saved (income tax benefit of the loss) amounted to $10,120 compared to a maximum of $6,000 under option *(a)*. This difference resulted because the carryforward-only option took advantage of a 22% tax rate in 19F and a 40% tax rate in 19G (as opposed to 20% under the carryback-carryforward option). This conclusion must be tempered with the element of uncertainty implicit in option *(b)*. That is, the actual results may differ substantially from the estimates, even though in this illustration the actual results were relatively close to the estimates. Additionally, in assessing the comparative advantages of one option over the other (i.e., in the year of loss), the future projections should be discounted to present values because the cash flows under the two options occur at different times.

The Economic Recovery Tax Act of 1981 lengthened the carryforward period from 7 to 15 years. The Tax Reform Act of 1986 did not change the carryback and carryforward provisions discussed above. This concludes the discussion of net operating carrybacks and carryforwards (NOLs) in conformity with the current income tax laws. Next, the discussion returns to the primary topic—income tax allocation.

Application of Carryback and Carryforward Procedures in Interperiod Income Tax Allocation

In the prior discussions and illustrations (e.g., Exhibit 23–4) the carryback and carryforward provisions of *FASB Standard 96* were disregarded for instructional convenience. The most complex aspect of interperiod income tax allocation is the application of a carryback and carryforward procedure and the deferred tax asset limitation. The carryback/carryforward procedure is used in the **analysis** of temporary differences (i.e., taxable amounts and deductible amounts) for deferred tax **accounting** purposes. It is independent of the net operating loss carryback and carryforward (NOL) discussed in the prior section, but it uses that model or procedure and conforms to the tax requirement of a 3-year limit on carrybacks and a 15-year carryforward. Basically, *FASB Standard 96* uses the carryback/carryforward procedure essentially as follows:

1. Determine the taxable amounts for future years (i.e., deferred tax liabilities).
2. Determine the deductible amounts for future years (i.e., deferred tax assets).
3. Deferred tax **asset** amounts recognized (after carrybacks) are **limited** to the current income tax payable amount plus any tax refundable amounts for the two prior years as permitted under the three-year carryback rule.
4. In analyzing temporary differences the carryback/carryforward procedure is applied only to deductible amounts to offset taxable amounts and current income taxes payable. The carryback cannot exceed three consecutive years back and the carryforward cannot exceed the taxable amounts (and not more than 15 years forward).

In view of the complexities and some of the misconceptions of deferred tax liabilities and assets, the following direct quotations from *FASB Standard 96* are provided (emphasis supplied):[9]

Annual Computation of a Deferred Tax Liability or Asset
17. In concept, this Statement requires determination of the amount of taxes payable or refundable in each future year **as if a tax return were prepared** for the net amount of temporary differences that will result in taxable or deductible amounts in each of those years. That concept is illustrated by the following procedures.

a. Estimate the particular future years in which temporary differences will result in taxable or deductible amounts.
b. Determine the **net** taxable or deductible amount in each future year.
c. Deduct **operating loss carryforwards for tax purposes** (as permitted or required by tax law) from net taxable amounts that are scheduled to occur in the future years included in the loss carryforward period. (Authors' note—this relates primarily to NOLs.)

[9] *FASB Standard 96*, par. 17.

d. **Carryback or carryforward (as permitted or required by law) net deductible amounts occurring in particular years to offset net taxable amounts that are schedule to occur in prior or subsequent years.** (Authors' note—this relates primarily to temporary differences).

Deferred Tax Assets

e. Recognize a deferred tax asset for the tax benefit of **net deductible amounts** that could be realized by loss carryback from future years (1) to reduce a current deferred tax liability and (2) to reduce taxes paid in the current or a prior year.* (No asset is recognized for any additional net deductible amounts in future years.)

* Note—"prior year" refers to any taxes refundable for the two prior years permitted under the three-year carryback rule.

Deferred Tax Liabilities

f. Calculate the amount of tax for the remaining **net taxable amounts** that are scheduled to occur in each future year by applying presently enacted tax rates and laws for each of those years to the type and amount of net taxable amounts scheduled for those years.
g. Deduct **tax credit carryforwards for tax purposes** (as permitted or required by law) from the amount of tax (calculated above) for future years that are included in the carryforward periods. (No asset is recognized for any additional amount of tax credit carryforward).
h. **Recognize a deferred tax liability for the remaining amount of taxes payable for each future year.**

Determination of temporary differences taking into account carryback and carryforward procedures requires that the **income tax consequences be estimated for the future periods over the duration of the reversing periods of each pretax temporary difference already or currently originated.** The objective is to prepare the annual entry to record income tax expense, deferred income tax, and income tax payable. The complete process (an expansion of the five steps given on page 1207) involves seven steps as follows:

Step 1 *(FASB 96, par. 17)*	Collect accounting and income tax data for the current and future years. Focus on temporary differences; these will cause taxable and deductible amounts in future years.
Step 2 *(FASB 96, par. 17a)*	Estimate the particular future years in which temporary differences will result in taxable and/or deductible amounts.
Step 3 *(FASB 96, par. 17b)*	Determine the net taxable or net deductible amount in each future year. Prepare a reconciliation of pretax accounting income and taxable income. Also compute income taxes payable for the current year. Prepare a **schedule of temporary differences,** which is an analysis to determine the deferred tax liability and deferred tax asset. The schedule of temporary differences is set up with **columns** for the current and future reversing years. Primary side captions are set up for the following amounts: *(a)* pretax accounting income, *(b)* each temporary difference, *(c)* preliminary net taxable (deductible) amounts,

(*d*) net taxable (deductible amounts), (*e*) carrybacks and carryforwards, (*f*) NOLs, and (*g*) net taxable amount after carrybacks and carryforwards. Enter data for (*a*), (*b*), and (*c*).

Step 4 *(FASB 96, par. 17d)* Offset—Carryback or carryforward **net deductible** temporary-difference amounts occurring in particular future years to **offset** net taxable amounts. Compute the last line.

Step 5 *(FASB 96, par. 17c)* Deduct net operating loss carryforwards for income tax purposes (i.e., NOLs) to compute the net taxable (deductible) amount for each year—net taxable amount after carrybacks and carryforwards.

Step 6 *(FASB 96, par. 17e–h)* Compute the amount of any deferred tax asset to be recognized and the deferred tax liability to be recorded. The schedule of temporary differences provides the pretax differences which are multiplied by the current enacted income tax rates.

Step 7 Based on the results in step 6, prepare the current year-end journal entry to record income taxes:

a.	Income tax expense $(d + c - b)$	\$	
b.	Deferred tax asset	\$	
c.	Deferred tax liability		\$
d.	Income tax payable		\$

Carryback and carryforward procedures for temporary differences are not applied when:

a. There are no temporary differences for deductible items and no current income taxes payable or paid.

b. When there are temporary differences for deductible items (i.e., deferred tax assets) but they are already fully offset against taxable items (deferred tax liabilities).

The schedule of temporary differences (steps 3, 4, and 5) is the most critical and complex step because it must provide selected data that are multiplied by the enacted tax rates to develop the journal entry to record income taxes.

FAS Corporation—To illustrate the process outlined above for analyzing carrybacks and carryforwards the FAS Corporation case is used. The steps are separately identified in the discussions that follow.

Step 1—FAS Corporation case data: The first year of operations is year 1 and the reversing time span is through year 6. The enacted income tax rate is 40% for each year.[10] The temporary differences are (1) installment sales, \$1,500 and (2) estimated expenses, \$1,300. The details are as follows:

[10] This case was adapted from *FASB Standard 96*, par. 38, to illustrate "offsetting" by using carrybacks and carryforwards.

Step 2—Amount of temporary differences at the end of year 1:

Temporary differences:		
Taxable amount—gross margin on installment sales:		
Accounting basis (year 1)	$3,300	
Income tax basis (taxed as collected; year 1, $1,800)	1,800	
Temporary difference—will be taxable during years 2–6 at $300 per year		$1,500
Deductible amount—estimated expenses accrued:		
Accounting (recorded at end of year 1)	1,300	
Taxable (all on year 5 tax return)	-0-	1,300
Net temporary difference		$ 200
Taxable income (tax return, 19X1)		$ 900
Pretax accounting income		$1,100

Step 3—Reconciliation of pretax accounting income and taxable income at the end of year 1 and computation income tax payable (see page 1206)*:

Pretax accounting income	$1,100
Temporary differences at end of year 1:	
Gross margin on installment sales (taxable in years 2–6)	−1,500
Estimated expense accrued (taxable in year 5)	+1,300
Taxable income (in tax return, year 1)	$ 900
Income tax rate	× 40%
Income tax payable	$ 360

* Alternatively, this reconciliation can start with taxable income and end with pretax accounting income, in which case the signs reverse.

This reconciliation serves a useful purpose for step 3 because it summarizes the basic case data including the overall effect of each of the two temporary differences. Notice that this step involves only year 1 amounts. The two temporary differences start in year 1 but each one has a different reversing time period.

Before proceeding be sure that you understand the following: *(a)* the meaning of pretax accounting income and taxable income, *(b)* when each of the two temporary differences, $1,500 and $1,300, **originated,** and *(c)* that each of these two differences will **reverse** during the six-year time span.

Steps 4 and 5—Schedule of temporary differences: This schedule, shown below, is the "key" in the entire process because it shows the *(a)* timing of the originating and reversing amounts, *(b)* net taxable (deductible) amounts for each year, *(c)* carrybacks and carryforwards, and *(d)* deferred asset and liability differences needed to prepare the year-end entry to record current income taxes. Notice the columns for the current year and the future reversing years and the appropriate side captions for each line. The reconciliation data developed in step 3 was transferred to the schedule of temporary differences for analytical purposes. Also, notice that the line for step 5 provides for the deduction of NOLs when they exist.

Steps 4 and 5—Schedule of temporary differences and NOLs (FAS Corporation):

Items	Current year 1	Year 2	Year 3	Year 4	Year 5	Year 6
		Future years				
Pretax accounting income	$1,100					
Temporary differences:						
Taxable amount, gain on installment sales	(1,500)[o]	$300[r]	$300[r]	$300[r]	$ 300[r] ↑	$300[r]
Deductible amount, estimated expenses accrued	1,300[o]				(1,300)[r] ↓	
Taxable income (tax return)	$ 900[d]					
Net taxable (deductible) amount	$ 200	300	300	300	(1,000)	300
Net taxable (deductible) amount	$ 200	300	300	300	(1,000)	300
Step 4—Loss carryback (limit 3 years)	–0–[b]	(300) ←	(300) ←	(300) ←*	900	
Loss carryforward					100 **→	(100)
Step 5—Deduct net operating loss (NOLs)	–0–	–0–	–0–	–0–	–0–	–0–
Net taxable amount after carryback and carryforward	$ 200	–0–	–0–	–0–	–0–	$200[c]

o = Originating difference; r = reversing difference.
* Carryback available.
** Carryforward available.
b, c, d: See entry immediately below.

Steps 6 and 7—Computations (temporary differences × tax rate) and entry to record income taxes at the end of year 1:

a.	Income tax expense ($d + c - b$)	440*	
b.	Deferred tax asset (no carryback to current year)	–0–	
c.	Deferred tax liability ($200 × 40%)		80
d.	Income tax payable ($900 × 40%)		360

* Proof: Pretax income, $1,100 × 40% = $440.

For instructional purposes the lines in the above entry are lettered; these letters are shown in the schedule of temporary differences to indicate the sources of lines *b*, *c*, and *d* in the entry.

Analysis of carrybacks and carryforwards of deductile temporary differences. Completion of a schedule of temporary differences involves a careful analysis of the **reversals** of the future taxable (i.e., deferred tax liabilities) and future deductible amounts to apply the carryback and carryforward rules. Guidelines for this analysis are:

1. Carryback and carryforward procedures relate to the reversals of future taxable and deductible amounts.
2. Deductible amounts are subject to carryback and carryforward because they are offset against taxable amounts.
3. A deferred tax asset can be recognized only if, or the extent to which, it survives the carryback and carryforward rules (see page 1220).
4. The schedule of temporary differences must include a carryback and carry-

forward analysis if there are future deductible amounts. The schedule should be prepared to provide specific amounts for:

a. Taxable income (from the tax return).
b. Net temporary difference for the deferred tax liability.
c. Net temporary difference for the deferred tax asset.

To illustrate, the schedule of temporary differences for FAS Corporation identifies the originating and reversing amounts and applies the reversing characteristic of all temporary differences. The carryback and carryforward captions on the schedule are completed by focusing on the net **deductible** amount to determine the appropriate offsets against the periodic reversals of the taxable amounts.

The critical item on the above schedule is the $1,300 deductible amount estimated for year 5, which can be used for carryback and carryforward (called **offsetting**) against taxable amounts. The pointers in the schedule show that this $1,300 is used to offset $300 of taxable income for year 5 and $300 each year for three years back (years 2, 3, and 4). The remaining $100 can be used as a carryforward to year 6 because there is a $300 future taxable amount in existence. Notice that the $1,300 used for carryback and carryforward purposes in years 2 through 5 offset taxable amounts by the same amount. There was no carryback to year 1 (the fourth year back); therefore, no deferred tax asset can be recognized. However, there is a $100 carryforward to year 6 because there is a $300 taxable amount in existence. Finally, there is a $200 net taxable amount remaining in year 6 which must be reported in year 1 as a deferred tax liability.

The credit to **income tax payable** (or a debit in the case of a refund) is always the actual income tax currently payable because interperiod income tax allocation can never change income tax payable. Also, by definition in *FASB Standard 96,* income tax expense is computed as follows: income tax payable (from the tax return) plus any deferred tax liability minus any deferred tax asset. Therefore, the only determinations that must be made are for the deferred tax liability and deferred tax asset.

At the end of **each of the remaining years** the above process is repeated because *(a)* new temporary differences often arise, *(b)* the reversing time on current differences may be revised, *(c)* enacted rates may change, and *(d)* actual results for the remaining years often will be different from the original estimates. However, if none of these events occur, the year 1 schedules and computations can be easily updated for the remaining reversing years.

ESY Corporation—An additional spreadsheet illustration is presented in **Exhibit 23–6** because it includes some features of interperiod income tax not yet illustrated. These features are: *(a)* three temporary differences, *(b)* three different income tax rates, *(c)* two carrybacks and one carryforward, *(d)* an originating difference (depreciation) that is treated as a deductible amount, and *(e)* a deferred tax asset is recognized.[11]

The spreadsheet identifies each step in the process and shows all of the computations. Notice the flow of data from step 1 through step 7. For instructional purposes the spreadsheet identifies the originating and reversing entries to emphasize that all temporary differences reflect this characteristic. Also, pointers

[11] Adapted from *FASB Standard 96,* par. 42.

Exhibit 23–6
Analysis of temporary differences; carrybacks and carryforwards; ESY Corporation.

Step 1—Accounting and income tax data at end of year 1:
Pretax accounting income, $700; taxable income (tax return) $500.
Income tax rates: year 1, 40%; year 2, 35%, and years 3 through 7, 30%.
Temporary differences at end of year 1: Revenue on installment sales, $300; recognized for accounting at end of year; for income tax at end of year 2. Estimated litigation loss, $200; accrued (recorded) for accounting at end of year 1; for income tax at end of year 7 (when paid). There are no net operating losses (NOLs). Depreciation expense as follows:

	Year 1	Year 2	Year 3	Year 4	
Accounting depreciation (SL); 3-year life	$ 100*	$1,100	$1,100	$1,000* =	$3,300
Tax depreciation (accelerated)	(200)	(2,000)	(500)	(600) =	3,300
Temporary difference	$(100)[o]	$ (900)[o]	$ 600[r]	$ 400[r] =	-0-

o = Originating year; r = reversing year.
* Part of year, rounded.

Steps 2 and 3—Reconciliation of accounting income and taxable income:

			End of year 1
Pretax accounting income			$700
Taxable amounts:			
Revenue on installment sales recognized:			
Accounting basis (end of year 1)	$300		
Income tax basis (end of year 2)	-0-	−	300
Depreciation expense recognized:			
Accounting basis (end of year 1)	100		
Income tax basis (end of year 1)	200	−	100
Deductible amount:			
Litigation loss accrued, accounting basis (end of year 1)	200		
Litigation loss settled, income tax basis (end of year 7)	-0-	+	200
Taxable income (from tax return)			$500

Steps 4 and 5—Schedule of temporary differences:

	Year 1	Future: Year 2	Year 3	Year 4	Years 5–6	Year 7
Pretax accounting income (steps 2–3)	$700					
Temporary differences:						
Taxable amount, gain in installment sales	(300)[o]	300[r]				
Taxable amount, depreciation	(100)[o]	(900)[o]	$600[r]	$400[r]		
Deductible amount, estimated expenses	200[o]					$(200)[r]
Net temporary difference	(200)					
Taxable income (tax return)	$500[d]					
Preliminary net taxable (deductible) amount	$200	(600)	600	400		(200)
Net taxable (deductible) amount	$200	(600)	600	400		(200)
Loss carryback (limit 3 years)	500[*b] ←	500		(200) ←		200
Loss carryforward		100 →	(100)			
Net operating loss (NOLs)	-0-	-0-	-0-	-0-		-0-
Net taxable amount after carryback and carryforward	700	$-0-	$500[c]	$200[c]	$-0-	$ -0-

o = Originating difference; r = reversing difference.
b, c, d: See entry below.
* This carryback amount can never exceed taxable income shown above because of the limitation on the amount of deferred income tax asset that can be recognized. Also, this carryback amount algebraically must retain the same sign outside the matrix as inside.
Notice the horizontal and vertical consistency from the line "Net taxable (deductible) amount" to the bottom line "Net taxable amount after carryback and carryforward."

Exhibit 23–6
(concluded)

Steps 6 and 7—Journal entry to record income taxes at the end of year 1:

a.	Income tax expense (*d* + *c* − *b*)	210*		Net, $10 liability
b.	Deferred tax asset ($500 × 40%)	200**		
c.	Deferred tax liability ($500 × 30%) + ($200 × 30%)		210	
d.	Income tax payable ($500 × 40%)		200**	

* Proof: $700 × 30% = $210.
** These two amounts will be the same only when taxes payable and the carryback are the same.

are used to clarify the carrybacks and carryforwards. Each line in the journal entry (step 7) is keyed by letters to the exact source in the schedule of temporary differences.

The schedule of temporary differences is easy to develop except for the analysis of carrybacks and carryforwards. The carryback and carryforward lines on the schedule are developed by focusing on the net **deductible** amounts to determine offsets against the taxable amounts. Notice that the first deductible amount is at the end of year 2 (i.e., $600). This amount offsets the $500 taxable amount in year 1 and the remaining $100 is offset against the $600 taxable amount in year 3. Next, moving to the right, notice a $200 deductible amount in year 7. This amount is offset against the $400 taxable amount in year 4; it could not be used in years 5 and 6 because there were no taxable amounts (also, it cannot be carried back beyond year 4 because that is the third year back from year 7).

Notice that, after determining the carryback and carryforward effects, each column is summed to give the relevant pretax temporary differences needed to develop the journal entry for income taxes.

The authors designed the original self-contained spreadsheet shown in Exhibit 23–6 to encompass all aspects of interperiod income tax allocation in complex cases. This spreadsheet focuses on the analysis required and development of the end result—the **journal entry** at year-end to record income taxes. Also, the spreadsheet is very helpful because it contains four major internal checks of accuracy as follows:

a. **Steps 2 and 3**—reconciliation of taxable income, all temporary differences, and pretax accounting income.
b. **Steps 4 and 5**—each horizontal line is algebraically consistent.
c. **Steps 4 and 5**—the **total** line, "Net taxable (deductible) amount," is algebraically correct both vertically and horizontally. In particular, notice that the $200 amount on this line under year 1 vertically is the net temporary difference from above ($300 + $100 − $200) and horizontally ($600 + $400 − $600 − $200). This is a key check immediately prior to the carryback/carryforward analysis.
d. **Steps 4 and 5**—the final check in the schedule of temporary differences is on the carryback/carryforward analysis on the last line in this schedule. That is, the total of the column for year 1 ($700) should agree with horizontal sum ($500 + $200 = $700).

The spreadsheet merits careful study because it provides *(a)* an excellent overview of interperiod income tax allocation, and *(b)* an integrated and detailed analysis, consistent with the specifications of *FASB Standard 96*.

The credit to income taxes payable (or a debit in the case of a refund) is the annual taxes currently payable because the interperiod income tax allocation of temporary differences cannot change the tax return. Also, by definition in *FASB Standard 96*, income tax expense is computed as follows: income tax payable (from the tax return) plus any deferred tax liability minus any deferred tax asset. Therefore, the only determinations that must be made are for the deferred tax liability and deferred tax asset. Computations to compute the deferred tax asset and deferred tax liability are shown in the exhibit. The three different income tax rates complicate these computations. The computations are keyed to the schedule of temporary differences. Notice in step 7 of the exhibit that a proof of income tax expense is shown as pretax accounting income × 30%; the 40% rate was not used because for both years 1 and 2 the carrybacks and carryforwards eliminate taxable income for allocation purposes.

This case involved three different enacted tax rates—40%, 35%, and 30%. Notice that each period's tax rate is used in the computation of income tax payable and the deferred tax amounts. This means any tax rate change effect is included in income tax expense.

At the end of each of the remaining years the above process is repeated because *(a)* new temporary differences often arise, *(b)* the reversing time on current differences may be revised, *(c)* enacted tax rates may change, and *(d)* actual results for the remaining years will be different than the original estimates. However, if none of these events occurs, the year 1 schedules can be adapted for the remaining six years.

And finally, to summarize, the deferred asset limitation rule is applied as follows:

a. Disregard all carryforwards; the limitation rule applies only to carrybacks.

b. Recognize a deferred tax asset only when the deductible carryback amounts are in excess of the taxable amounts.

c. Measure the deferred tax asset as the excess in *(b)* that is a carryback to the current year. This carryback to the current year is limited to the amount of current taxes payable (and paid). Also, the carryback can extend to the two prior years (limited by the three-year rule) to any tax refundable amounts for those two years.

Analysis of Net Operating Loss Carrybacks and Carryforwards (NOLs) for Income Tax Allocation

A final spreadsheet and the related entries are presented to illustrate application of the NOLs (net operating losses) discussed on pages 1214–18. NOLs add considerable complexities such as income tax refunds and changes in future taxable amounts. A fundamental distinction is that **temporary differences do not change the total amount of income taxes otherwise payable** (see the prior FAS and ESY cases), **whereas NOLs do change total income taxes otherwise payable** (as in the NOL case below). However, the carryback (3 years) and carryforward (15 years) concept applies to both temporary differences and NOLs. This case for NOL Company is simplified by using only one temporary difference (depreciation) and one NOL (at the end of year 5).

Case Data (adapted from *FASB Standard 96,* par. 50)—NOL Company:

	Year 1	Years 2–4	Year 5	Year 6	Year 7
a. Pretax accounting income (NOL yr 5)	$2,000	$ 5,000	$(8,000)	$2,000	$7,000
b. Depreciation—accounting ($45,000 ÷ 15 years; originating)	3,000^{o}	9,000^{o}	3,000^{o}	3,000^{o}	3,000^{o}
—tax return (accelerated)	3,800	11,200	3,600	3,800	3,600
c. Taxable income (loss) (see Req. 1)	1,200	2,800	(2,800)	-0-	1,800

d. Other data: Tax rate, 40%; timing period, 15 years; no deductible amounts; pretax NOL of $8,000 shown on the year 5 tax return was: refundable carryback to years 2–4, $2,800; carryforwards to year 6, $600 and to year 7, $4,600.

e. Analysis of the temporary difference showed a $600 carryforward from year 5 to year 6 (explained later).

Required:

Prepare the income tax entry for each year. Support with (1) a reconciliation of pretax accounting income with taxable income and (2) a schedule of temporary differences (adapted to show each year for instructional purposes only).

Req. 1 Reconciliation of Pretax Accounting Income with Taxable Income—NOL Company

	Year 1	Years 2–4	Year 5	Year 6	Year 7	Years 8–15
Pretax accounting income (loss)	$2,000	$ 5,000	$(8,000)	$2,000	$7,000	$
Taxable amount (depreciation):						
Accounting basis	3,000	9,000	3,000	3,000	3,000	
Taxable basis	3,800	11,200	3,600	3,800	3,600	
Temporary difference	− 800°	−2,200^{o}	− 600°	− 800°	− 600°	+5,000^{r}
Total after temporary difference	1,200	2,800	(8,600)	1,200	6,400	
NOL (net operating loss):						
Carryback to years 2–4 ($2,800 refundable amount at end of year 5)						
Carryforward from year 5 to years 6 and 7			5,200* →	(600) →	(4,600)	
Temporary difference carryforward			600 →	(600)		
Taxable income (income tax return, and after NOL)	$1,200	$ 2,800**	$(2,800)	$ -0-	$1,800	

* $8,000 − $2,800 = $5,200.

** At the end of year 5 when the refundable amount of $2,800 is recognized this amount is, in effect, zero. However, the refundable amount does not change the tax returns for years 2–4.

Req. 2 Schedule of Temporary Differences and NOLs—NOL Company

	Year 1	Years 2–4	Year 5	Year 6	Year 7	Years 8–15
Pretax accounting income (loss)	$2,000	$ 5,000	$(8,000)	$2,000	$7,000	$(income)
Temporary differences:						
Taxable amount, depreciation[c]	(800)[o]	(2,200)[o]	(600)[o]	(800)[o]	(600)[o]	5,000[r]
Deductible amount	-0-	-0-	-0-	-0-	-0-	
Net taxable (deductible) amount for temporary differences	1,200	2,800	(8,600)	1,200	6,400	
Temporary differences:						
Carryback to years 2–4						
Carryforward to years 6 & 7[b]			600* →	(600)		
Net taxable (deductible) amount before NOL	1,200	2,800	(8,000)	600	6,400	
NOL (net operating loss, year 5):						
Carryback to years 2–4 ($2,800, step 1)						
Carryforward to years 6 & 7 ($8,000 − $2,800 refundable)			5,200* →	(600) →	(4,600)	
Taxable income (tax return)[d]	$1,200	$ 2,800	$(2,800)	-0-	$1,800	
d. Computation of income tax payable:						
Multiply by tax rate	× 40%	× 40%	× 40%	× 40%	× 40%	
Tax payable (receivable)	$ 480	$ 1,120	$(1,120)	-0-	$ 720	
c. Computation of deferred income tax liability (see analysis below):						
Net deferred difference (computed below)	$ (800)	$(2,200)	$ 3,000	$ -0-	$(5,000)	$5,000[r]
Multiply by tax rate	× 40%	× 40%	× 40%		× 40%	× 40%
Deferred tax liability	$ (320)	$ (880)	$(1,200)	$ -0-	$(2,000)	$2,000
Cumulative ending balance	$ (320)	$(1,200)	$ -0-	$ -0-	$(2,000)	$ -0-
Entries to record income taxes each year:						
a. Income tax expense (*d* + *c*)	800	2,000	2,320	-0-	2,720	
b. Deferred tax asset	-0-	-0-	-0-	-0-	-0-	
c. Deferred tax liability	320	880	1,200[c]	-0-	2,000	
d. Income tax payable	480	1,120	1,120[d]	-0-	720	

Year 5 has two entries to: *c*—eliminate the deferred tax and, *d*—record the refundable amount ($2,800 × 40% = $1,120). The exact formulation of these entries is given in the discussion which follows.

Analysis of temporary differences to compute deferred income tax (depreciation):

	Year 1	Years 2–4	Year 5	Year 6	Year 7	Years 8–15
Beginning cumulative balance	$ -0-	$ (800)	$(3,000)	$(3,600)	$(4,400)	$(5,000)
Ending cumulative balance	(800)	(3,000)	(3,600)	(4,400)	(5,000)	-0-
Current year change (as c above)	$ (800)[o]	(2,200)[o]	(600)[o]	(800)[o]	(600)[o]	5,000[r]
NOL carryforward to next year			$ 5,200	$ 4,600		
Net deferred difference (to c above)	$ (800)	$(2,200)	$ 3,000*	$ -0-**	$(5,000)†	$ 5,000[r]

* Year 5—Eliminate the beginning cumulative amount of $3,000 (i.e., $800 + $2,200) because the carryforward offset of $5,800 (i.e., $600 + $5,200) exceeds the ending cumulative temporary difference of $3,600 (i.e., $800 + $2,200 + $600). This means that the cumulative deferred tax amount (pretax) must be zero at the end of year 5. This is explained below.

** Year 6—There is no deferred amount this year because the total carryforward offset of $4,600 still exceeds the ending cumulative temporary difference of $4,400.

† Year 7—The cumulative temporary difference remaining for depreciation at the end of year 7 is $5,000 (the sum of the originating differences which have not been reversed) which will reverse in years 8–15. Therefore, the $5,000 difference must be recognized in year 7 because it is a taxable amount that will be offset in years 8–15.

Notice in the reconciliation (Req. 1) that the amounts each year-end for pretax accounting income and taxable income are the same as given in the case data (net of NOL effects). The schedule of temporary differences and NOLs (Req. 2) shows that the originating depreciation differences and the related entries for income taxes for years 1 through 4 are typical because they were not affected by the NOL at the end of year 5. The NOL at the end of year 5 had the following consequences:

Year 5—The NOL created an income tax refund of $1,120 (i.e., $2,800 taxable income of years 2–4 multiplied by the tax rate, 40%). This tax refund may be debited to cash, recorded as a receivable, or offset against income tax payable. NOL Company recorded this refundable amount as follows because a cash refund was not received:

Receivable for income tax refund (NOL)*	1,120	
Gain from income tax refund ($2,800 × 40%)		1,120

* There is no tax payable at the end of an NOL year.

Year 6—Carryforward from year 5 the remainder of the $8,000 net deductible amount; that is, $8,000 − $2,800 = $5,200 to year 6 as shown in the schedule of temporary differences.

Year 7—Carryforward from year 6 the remaining net deductible amount; that is, $5,200 − $600 = $4,600 to year 7 as shown in the schedule of temporary differences.

The net effects of these carryforwards are to reduce the net taxable amount for *(a)* year 6 to zero and *(b)* year 7 to $1,800.

The schedule of temporary differences and NOLs provides data to compute the deferred tax liability for each year. This **computation relates to temporary differences** (depreciation in this case). The depreciation originating differences (taxable amounts) cause deferred tax liabilities. There are no deferred tax assets because there are no carrybacks to year 1 and prior years. In years 1–4 taxable amounts for deferred tax liabilities are determined by the depreciation differences ($800 + $2,200 = $3,000 cumulative) because there are no offsets in those years. However, at the end of year 5 the $5,800 offset (i.e., $5,200, NOL + $600), temporary difference exceeds the $3,000 cumulative net deferred difference amount; therefore, there is no cumulative deferred taxable amount. This means that the deferred tax account balance must be reduced to zero at the end of year 5, which is based on the $3,000 net cumulative difference. The related entry at the end of year 5, standing alone, would be (see page 1228):

Deferred tax liability ($3,000 × 40%)	1,200	
Gain from reduction of deferred tax liability*		1,200

* Income tax expense in a NOL year usually reflects a zero balance.

For the same reason, at the end of year 6 ($4,600 compared with $4,400), no deferred tax liability can be recorded. However, a deferred tax liability must be recorded at the end of year 7 because the total cumulative depreciation difference (originating) of $5,000 remains as a taxable amount that will reverse during years 8–15. The entry at the end of year 7, standing alone, is as follows:

Income tax expense ($5,000 × 40%)	2,000	
Deferred tax liability		2,000

The above considerations and the related year-end entries to record income taxes are incorporated in Req. 2 shown above.[12]

Annual Analysis of Deferred Income Tax—The prior discussions in this chapter emphasized that the analysis and recording of deferred income taxes must be done at **each year-end** because each year stands alone. Pretax accounting income, taxable income, income taxes paid, and deferred income tax are known as of the end of the year immediately preceding the current year. In contrast, these amounts for the current and future years are unknown. Determination of the current year-end entry to record income taxes (including the effects of tax allocation) uses the prior data (for two years back), current data, and estimated future data. The estimated future data relates to temporary differences and NOL carryforwards. Income tax rates are not estimated because the currently enacted tax rates must be used for all future years until new actual rates are enacted. Also, pretax accounting income and taxable income are not estimated beyond the current year. In this regard, the NOL case above was unrealistic because the first line in the schedule of temporary differences showed pretax accounting income (as given) for each of the seven years; income tax payable by year also was given. In contrast, refer to Exhibit 23–6 (ESY Corporation) and FAS Corporation (p. 1220) for cases where the future pretax accounting income and taxable income amounts are not estimated. In those cases the schedule of temporary differences analyzed only the temporary differences.

To illustrate the analysis for a single year the NOL case above is used. The

[12] The schedule of temporary differences given above for NOL Company analyzed the carryforwards and carrybacks separately for temporary differences and NOLs for instructional purposes. However, these two different amounts may be combined with the same end results. For example, the combined basis for NOL Company would be as follows:

	Year 1	Years 2–4	Year 5	Year 6	Year 7	Years 8–15
Pretax accounting income (loss)	$2,000	$ 5,000	$(8,000)	$ 2,000	$ 7,000	$(income)
Temporary differences:						
Taxable amount, depreciation	(800)	(2,200)	(600)	(800)	(600)	5,000
Deductible amount	-0-	-0-	-0-	-0-	-0-	
Net taxable (deductible) amount	1,200	2,800	(8,600)	1,200	6,400	
Carryback to years 2–4						
Carryforward to years 6–7 . .			5,800* →	(1,200) →	(4,600)	
Taxable income (tax return) . . .	$1,200	$ 2,800	$(2,800)	-0-	$ 1,800	

* $8,600 − $2,800 = $5,800.

analysis in the schedule of temporary differences and NOLs and the resulting entry would be as shown below.

Schedule of Temporary Differences and NOLs, Year 5—NOL Company

	Cumulative	Year 5	Year 6	Year 7	Years 8–15
Pretax accounting income (loss)		$(8,000)	$	$	$
Temporary differences:					
Taxable amount, depreciation	(1–4) $(3,000)°	(600)°	(800)°	(600)°	5,000[r]
Deductible amount		–0–	–0–	–0–	
Net taxable (deductible) amount for temporary differences		(8,600)	(800)	(600)	
Temporary differences:					
Carryback					
Carryforward		600 →	800 →	600 →	(2,000)
Net taxable (deductible) amount before NOL		8,000	–0–	–0–	$ 3,000*
NOL (net operating loss):					
Carryback (years 2–4, refundable)	$ 2,800**				
Carryforward ($8,000 – $2,800)		5,200	–0–	–0–	$(5,200)*
Taxable income (tax return)	$ 2,800	$(2,800)	$ –0–	$ –0–	

Interpretation:
* No net cumulative deferred tax can be recognized at the end of year 5 because the carryforward needed ($5,200) exceeds the cumulative temporary difference (taxable amount) of $3,000. The deferred tax account must be reduced to zero.

Combined entry at end of year 5:

Income tax expense	–0–	
**Receivable for income tax refund (NOL) ($2,800 × 40%)	1,120	
Deferred tax asset	–0–	
Deferred tax liability ($3,000 × 40%; to reduce to zero)	1,200	
Gain from income tax refund (NOL)		1,120
Gain from reduction of deferred tax liability		1,200
Income tax payable		–0–

Cumulative balance in the deferred tax liability account: End of year 4, $3,000 and end of year 5, zero.

FASB Standard 96, par. 50, presents the NOL Company case and the related solution as quoted below for instructional purposes only:

The following example illustrates recognition of the tax benefit of an operating loss in the loss year and in subsequent carryforward years. The assumptions are as follows:

a. An operating loss occurs in year 5, and the enacted tax rate is 40 percent for all years.

b. The only difference between financial and taxable income results from use of accelerated depreciation for tax purposes. Differences that arise between the reported amount and the tax basis of depreciable assets in years 1–7 will result in taxable amounts before the end of the loss carryforward period from year 5.

c. Financial income, taxable income, and taxes currently payable or refundable are as follows:

	Year 1	Years 2–4	Year 5	Year 6	Year 7
Pretax financial income	$2,000	$ 5,000	$(8,000)	$ 2,000	$ 7,000
Depreciation differences	(800)	(2,200)	(600)	(800)	(600)
Loss carryback	—	—	2,800	—	—
Loss carryforward	—	—	—	(5,800)	(4,600)
Taxable income (loss)	$1,200	$ 2,800	$(5,800)	$(4,600)	$ 1,800
Taxes payable (refundable)	$ 480	$ 1,120	$(1,120)	$ —	$ 720

A liability for the deferred tax consequences that will result in taxable amounts in future years is calculated as follows:

	Year 1	Years 2–4	Year 5	Year 6	Year 7
Unreversed/differences:					
Beginning amount	$ —	$ 800	$ 3,000	$ 3,600	$4,400
Additional amount	800	2,200	600	800	600
Total	800	3,000	3,600	4,400	5,000
Tax loss carryforward	—	—	(5,800)	(4,600)	—
Net taxable amount	$800	$3,000	$ —	$ —	$5,000

	Year 1	Years 2–4	Year 5	Year 6	Year 7
Deferred tax liability (40 percent):					
At end of period	$320	$1,200	$ —	$ —	$2,000
At beginning of period	—	320	1,200	—	—
Deferred tax expense (benefit)	$320	$ 880	$(1,200)	$ —	$2,000

Total tax expense for each period is as follows:

	Year 1	Years 2–4	Year 5	Year 6	Year 7
Tax expense:					
Payable	$480	$1,120	$(1,120)	$ —	$ 720
Deferred	320	880	(1,200)	$ —	2,000
Total	$800	$2,000	$(2,320)	$ —	$2,720

In year 5, $2,800 of the loss is carried back to reduce taxable income in years 2–4, and $1,120 of taxes paid for those years is refunded. The $5,800 loss carryforward exceeds the $3,600 of temporary differences that will result in taxable amounts in future years. Therefore, the $1,200 deferred tax liability at the beginning of year 5 is eliminated.

In year 6, a portion of the loss carryforward is used to offset taxable income earned in year 6. The remaining $4,600 of loss carryforward at the end of year 6 exceeds the $4,400 of temporary differences, and there is no deferred tax liability.

In year 7, the loss carryforward is used up, and $720 of taxes are payable on net taxable income of $1,800. No loss carryforward offsets the $5,000 of temporary differences that will result in taxable amounts in future years, and a $2,000 deferred tax liability is recognized.

Changes in Estimates of Temporary Differences. Determination of originating temporary differences often involve estimates about the *(a)* timing of the reversing period and *(b)* amounts of the periodic reversal(s). If either of these estimates change during the timing period, the reversals must be changed. This means that a catch-up entry must be made to adjust the cumulative deferred tax amount from the old basis to the new basis (see page 1213, situation 3, for a similar procedure).

To illustrate, refer to the schedule of temporary differences for FAS Corporation (page 1222). Notice that a temporary difference of $1,300 for estimated expenses (a deductible amount) was originated in year 1 and reversed at the end of year 5. Now assume that at the beginning of year 3 the estimate was realistically changed to $1,400. The catchup entry would be as follows:

Deferred tax liability ($100 × 40%)*	40	
Income tax expense		40

* Debited because a higher deductible amount reduces the deferred taxable amount (a liability).

If this entry is not made, the deferred tax amount related to this item will not reverse to zero at the end of year 5.

Interperiod Tax-Planning Strategies

FASB Standard 96, par. 17, provides for the use of tax-planning strategies as follows (adapted):

> **Tax-planning strategies** that meet certain criteria (paragraph 19) are used for purposes of *estimating the years* in which temporary differences will result in taxable or deductible amounts. . . . By applying such a strategy:
>
> (1) Amounts may become deductible in a different year and thereby provide a tax benefit by offsetting . . . or by loss carryback.
>
> (2) Amounts may become taxable in a different year before a loss or tax credit carryforward expires . . . or in a particular year that maximizes the benefit of tax credits, for example, foreign tax credits.

Determining the reversing period(s) for some temporary differences often is difficult. The provision for the use of tax-planning strategies focuses on this problem. The objective of these strategies is to minimize the problem of individually scheduling the reversing periods for a number of temporary differences that have uncertain reversing periods. Strategies meeting the two criteria listed below can also be used to maximize the amount of deferred tax assets recognized or to minimize the amount of deferred tax liabilities recognized.

To illustrate a tax-planning strategy, assume that TS Corporation has a temporary difference related to installment sales (a deferred tax liability) as follows (in $000s):

Deferred gross margin on installment sales at the end of 19X1	$500
Reversal over the next five years; per year	$100

Tax-planning strategy—in 19X2, sell all of the related receivables at a discount. The sale of the receivables would mean that the $500 temporary difference would be reversed entirely in 19X2, which would result in the recognition of a deferred tax asset, or the reduction of a net deferred tax liability. To limit the use of tax-planning strategies for this latter purpose, the *Standard* provides strict guidelines for their use as follows:

> A tax-planning strategy (including elections for tax purposes that are required or permitted by the tax law) shall meet both of the following criteria:
> **a.** It must be a prudent and feasible strategy over which management has discretion and control. Management must have both the ability and the intent to implement the strategy, if necessary, to reduce taxes.
> **b.** It cannot involve significant cost to the enterprise, that is, significant expenses to implement the underlying transaction or significant losses as a result of changing the particular future years in which an asset is recovered or a liability is settled. The tax benefit derived from the strategy shall not be viewed as a reduction of the cost of the strategy for the purpose of determining whether that strategy gives rise to a significant cost.

Although the extent of use of tax-planning strategies will be significant, it is difficult to assess at this early date their full impacts on the recognition of deferred tax assets and liabilities.

Intraperiod Income Tax Allocation

Interperiod (i.e., among periods) income tax allocation is used to determine the total income tax amount for the accounting period. **Intraperiod** income tax allocation, as required by *APB Opinion 11,* involves deciding **how the total income tax amount, having already been determined, should be reported in the current financial statements.** This subject was reviewed in Chapter 3 (see Exhibit 3–8).

Intraperiod income tax allocation involves **reporting** rather than recording. It does not require additional journal entries. Also, it does not modify the entries previously illustrated for interperiod income tax allocation. Both types of income tax allocation must be applied. One is not an alternative to the other. However, interperiod allocation for the current period must precede intraperiod allocation because intraperiod tax allocation starts with total income tax expense for the period.

The basic concept underlying intraperiod income tax allocation is that the total income tax expense should be allocated to report a portion of the expense along with each of the major items on the financial statements that caused it (i.e., the tax effect follows the item that caused it). The primary financial statement items involved are: (1) income (loss) from continuing operations, (2) discontinued operations, (3) extraordinary items, (4) changes in accounting principle, and (5) prior period adjustments.

Two methods that are used to allocate the period's total income tax amount among the financial statements are the *(a)* average method and *(b)* specific method. The **average method** is simple because it applies the average tax rate to each pretax amount shown in the financial statements. To illustrate, Clay Corporation computed total income tax of $40,000 (based on interperiod tax allocation). The $40,000 is allocated under the average method as follows (in $000):

Taxable Items	Pretax amounts (given) ($000)	Income tax allocation using the average rate (40%)*	Net of tax
Statement of income:			
Income from continuing operations	$ 90.0	× 40% = $36.0	$54.0
Loss from discontinued operations	(6.0)	× 40% = (2.4)	(3.6)
Extraordinary gain	14.0	× 40% = 5.6	8.4
Change in accounting principle (debit)	(2.0)	× 40% = (.8)	(1.2)
Statement of retained earnings:			
Prior period adjustment, error correction (credit)	4.0	× 40% = 1.6	2.4
Total	$100.0	× 40% $40.0	$60.0

* Average tax rate: $40,000 ÷ $100,000 – 40%.

The **specific method** uses specific tax rates for the various taxable items, rather than a proportional allocation. Application of this method is simple when only one tax rate is assumed. In this case, which is not usual, each taxable item is multiplied by the single tax rate. However, when multiple tax rates exist, the assumption of order must be made so that the multiple tax rates are applied first to continuing operations, next to extraordinary items and finally to prior period adjustments. This ordering is complex when there are both taxable gains and losses. Exhibit 3–8 shows an application of the specific method (recommendation: restudy that exhibit).

The following data are used to compare the two methods: Pretax items: income before extraordinary items, $30,000; extraordinary loss, $10,000; and net pretax accounting income, $20,000. The corporate tax rates are: 20% on the first $25,000 of income, and 40% on income in excess of $25,000; total tax payable is $4,000. The intraperiod tax allocations, using each method, are as follows:

		Specific Method		Average Method*
Income before income tax and extraordinary items		$30,000		$30,000
Income tax allocated:	$25,000 × 20% = $5,000 5,000 × 40% = 2,000	(7,000)	$30,000 × 20%	(6,000)
Income before extraordinary items		23,000		(24,000)
Extraordinary loss		(10,000)		(10,000)
Income tax saving allocated: Take out in inverse order	$5,000 × 40% = $2,000 5,000 × 20% = 1,000	3,000	$10,000 × 20%	2,000
Net income		$16,000		$16,000

* Average tax rate: ($7,000 – $3,000) ÷ ($30,000 – $10,000) = 20%.

The specific method is viewed as preferable because it emphasizes continuing operations—income before extraordinary items—as the primary tax-incurring activity. In contrast, the average method gives all taxable components equal weight and is simple to apply. Companies typically use the average method for monthly and quarterly interim reports.

Income Tax Effects of Prior Period Adjustments

The correction of accounting errors of prior periods requires the recording of a prior period adjustment and sometimes income tax payable (or refundable). In such cases, the additional income tax paid (or refunded) is specified, which means that intraperiod allocation of such amounts is already known (also see Chapter 3, page 96).

FASB Standard 16, "Prior Period Adjustments," limits prior period adjustments to two items: *(a)* correction of an error in the financial statements of a prior period and *(b)* adjustments for income tax benefits related to preacquisition operating loss carryforwards of purchased subsidiaries.

If an error caused a misstatement of accounting income which was taxable in a prior period and if the misstated item had an income tax effect, a prior period adjustment would be needed to correct both the error and the income tax effect. In such a case, the company most likely would file an amended tax return to claim a refund or to pay additional taxes. To illustrate, INN Corporation understated depreciation expense on both the financial statements and the tax return in 19A by $10,000. At that time, the income tax rate was 40%. In 19C, the company discovered this error. At this time, the income tax rate was 45% (there was no error in 19B or 19C). Two entries (or a single combined entry) would correct the error in 19C:

Prior period adjustment (expense correction)	10,000	
Accumulated depreciation		10,000
Receivable for refund of 19A income tax ($10,000 × 40%)*	4,000	
Prior period adjustment (tax refund on expense correction)		4,000

* Depending on the circumstances this could be cash or income taxes payable.

The $6,000 debit balance in the Prior Period Adjustment account (i.e., $10,000 − $4,000) is closed to Retained Earnings and reported on the statement of retained earnings.

Notice that the tax rate in effect during the year when the error was made (i.e., 40%) was used, rather than the tax rate of the correction year (i.e., 45%). Any interest and/or penalties related to the extra income tax, and any interest related to any tax refunds, also would affect the net amount of the prior period adjustment.

Financial Statement Presentation and Disclosure of Deferred Income Taxes

Income tax expense is reported in the statement of income in conformity with intraperiod income tax guidelines. Income tax payable is reported on the statement of financial position as a current liability. **Deferred income tax** amounts are reported on the statement of financial position. *FASB Standard 96,* par. 24, specifies that the deferred income tax amount must be classified as follows:

1. Deferred income tax liability (a net credit balance):
   a. Current liability.
   b. Noncurrent liability.
2. Deferred income tax asset (a net debit balance):
   a. Current asset.
   b. Noncurrent asset.

Determining the Current and Noncurrent Components of Deferred Income Taxes

The basic rule for classifying a net deferred tax liability or a net deferred tax asset at the end of an accounting period is as follows:[13]

a. First compute the amount of the net deferred tax balance that is current. **This is the net taxable or deductible amount for the next year.**

b. The remaining balance is classified as noncurrent.

To illustrate, assume Stanford Company's records at the end of 1988 provided the following data:

	1988	1989	1990	1991	1992
Net taxable amount (net deferred liability)*	$400[o]	$100[r]	$100[r]	$100[r]	$100[r]
Multiply by tax rate	× 34%	× 34%	× 34%	× 34%	× 34%
Deferred tax amount	$136 cr	$ 34 dr	$ 34 dr	$ 34 dr	$ 34 dr
Cumulative balance in the net deferred tax liability account	$136	$102	$ 68	$ 34	$-0-

* This can be the "net" of all of the currently existing taxable and deductible amounts.
o = Originating difference; r = reversing difference.

The 1988 statement of financial position would report the $136 net deferred tax liability as follows:

Current liabilities:	
Deferred income tax liability (next year's amount)	$ 34
Long-term liabilities:	
Deferred income tax liability ($136 − $34)	102

Assuming no subsequent changes in the above data, the 1989 statement of financial position would report a net deferred tax liability of $102 as follows:

Current liabilities:	
Deferred income tax liability (next year's amount)	$ 34
Long-term liabilities:	
Deferred income tax liability ($102 − $34)	68

The disclosure notes to the financial statements should supplement the items reported in the financial statements (discussed above) with the following information:

---

[13] *FASB Standard 96*, par. 24, specification:
A deferred tax liability or asset shall be classified in two categories—the current amount and the noncurrent amount—in a classified statement of financial position. The current amount of a deferred tax liability or asset shall be the net deferred tax consequences of:

a. Temporary differences that will result in net taxable or deductible amounts during the next year.
b. Temporary differences related to an asset or liability that is classified for financial reporting as current because of an operating cycle that is longer than one year.
c. Temporary differences for which there is no related, identifiable asset or liability for financial reporting (paragraph 12) whenever *other* related assets and liabilities are classified as current because of an operating cycle that is longer than one year.

a. Current tax expense or benefit.
b. Deferred tax expense or benefit, exclusive of *(f)* below.
c. Investment tax credits.
d. Government grants (to the extent recognized as a reduction of income tax expense).
e. The benefits of net operating loss carryforwards (NOLs).
f. Adjustments of a deferred tax liability or asset for enacted changes in tax laws or rates or a change in the tax status of an enterprise.
g. Amounts and expiration dates of **operating** carrybacks and carryforwards.
h. Reconciliation of income tax expense attributible to continuing operations with pretax accounting income from continuing operations at current tax rates.

Investment Tax Credit (ITC)

The investment tax credit (ITC) is an income tax provision that encourages investments in new productive assets such as plant, machinery, and equipment. Prior to the Tax Reform Act of 1986, the law provided that taxpayers who acquired qualified assets could receive a 10% investment tax **credit** as a direct offset to income tax payable. This tax credit was important to investors because they could reduce their income tax payable for the year of purchase of a qualified asset by 10% of its full cost. The nature of a **tax credit,** as opposed to a **tax deduction,** is that a tax credit causes a direct dollar-for-dollar tax saving. A tax deduction decreases income tax only by the deduction amount multiplied by the income tax rate.

The first investment tax credit was provided by the Revenue Act of 1962. Its provisions were revised by the 1964 act, suspended in 1966, and restored in 1967. The Revenue Act of 1978 set the credit "permanently" at 10% of the cost of qualifying property. The Tax Reform Act of 1986 suspended the ITC.

At the time that the ITC was suspended, the two following alternative GAAP methods were acceptable under GAAP for recording and reporting the ITC:

a. **Flow-through (or current reduction) method**—Under this method, the full amount of the ITC is recorded and reported as a **direct reduction of income tax expense** of the period in which the related asset is acquired. Thus, the full amount of ITC "flows through" the **current** statement of income. As a result, it increases the reported income of the period of acquisition on a dollar-for-dollar basis. This method relates the ITC to the **purchase,** rather than the use, of the asset.
b. **Deferral (or allocated reduction) method**—Under this method, the total amount of the ITC is recorded as Deferred Investment Tax Credit (a contra account to the related asset account). It is then **allocated to each period over the life of the asset as a direct reduction of periodic income tax expense.** Thus, the ITC amount is allocated over the estimated useful life of the asset to which it relates. This method relates the ITC to **use** rather than to purchase of the asset.

This overview of the investment tax credit is given because many observers believe that the ITC will be restored in a few years.

Summary

This chapter discussed the two types of income tax allocation—interperiod (among accounting periods) and intraperiod (within the current period). The basic purpose of both types of allocation is to match income tax expense with the revenues, gains, expenses, and losses that caused the tax. To accomplish this purpose, interperiod income tax allocation is used to compute income tax expense for the current period; then intraperiod income tax allocates that amount to the major categories—income before extraordinary items, extraordinary items, discontinued operations, and prior period adjustments.

Interperiod tax allocation is much more complex than intraperiod tax allocation because *(a)* it must identify and measure temporary differences and *(b)* the allocation often involves long periods of time such as the life of a building.

Temporary differences are taxable items that are included in **both** the statement of income and the income tax return but in different years. This means that they will reverse or turn around in the future. *FASB Standard 96* defines income tax expense for an accounting period as income tax payable plus deferred income tax liability minus deferred income tax asset. Therefore, computation of the two latter amounts is the key problem in interperiod income tax allocation. The allocation is based on a schedule of temporary differences that involves carryback and carryforward procedures. The completed schedule of temporary differences provides specific amounts which are multiplied by the current enacted tax rates to prepare the **annual entry to record income taxes** as follows (assumed amounts):

Income tax expense	100,000	
Deferred tax asset	10,000	
Deferred tax liability		30,000
Income tax payable (from tax return)		80,000

The basic relationships involved in interperiod income tax allocation specified in *FASB 96* can be summarized as follows:

1. Taxable and deductible amounts (4 cases):

Item	Tax Return	Statement of Income	Explanation
Taxable Amounts—higher future tax; a liability:			
Case A—Revenues ⟶	after ⟶	before ⟶	Tax to be paid in the future; higher future tax.
Case B—Expenses ⟶	before ⟶	after ⟶	Expense is not tax deductible in future; higher future tax.
Deductible Amounts—lower future tax; an asset:			
Case C—Revenues ⟶	before ⟶	after ⟶	Tax is already paid; lower future tax.
Case D—Expenses ⟶	after ⟶	before ⟶	Expense is tax deductible in future; lower future tax.

2. Taxable income (tax return), Pretax Accounting Income (statement of income), and Temporary Differences:

		Temporary Differences				
Taxable income	+	Taxable amounts*	−	Deductible amounts**	=	Pretax accounting income
Example: $500	+	$400	−	$200	=	$700

or, inversely

Pretax accounting income	−	Taxable amounts	+	Deductible** amounts	=	Taxable income
Example: $700	−	$400	+	$200	=	$500

* Deferred tax liabilities
** Deferred tax assets

QUESTIONS

1. What are the two types of income tax allocation? Briefly distinguish between the two.
2. Relate the matching principle to interperiod income tax allocation.
3. Explain when deferred income tax can be either an asset or a liability.
4. Briefly define pretax accounting income and taxable income.
5. Define an income tax difference. Identify and briefly define the two types of differences.
6. XT Corporation *(a)* uses straight-line depreciation in its accounting and accelerated depreciation on its income tax return, and *(b)* holds a $50,000 investment in tax-free municipal bonds. What kind of tax difference is caused by each of these items? Explain.
7. Does the "deferred" caption in deferred income taxes mean that deferred income tax is always a long-term (noncurrent) item? Explain.
8. X Corporation has completed an analysis of its accounting income, taxable income, and the temporary differences. Taxable income is $100,000 and there are two temporary differences: *(a)* a deferred tax asset carryback to the current year of $15,000, and *(b)* a net deferred tax liability, after carrybacks and carryforwards of $20,000. The income tax rate is 32%. Give the entry to record income taxes and indicate how the amounts were determined.
9. On January 1, year 1, CD Corporation purchased an asset that cost $42,000, which has a seven-year life (no residual value). For accounting purposes it will be depreciated on the straight-line basis. For income tax purposes the machine will be depreciated over a three-year period. The income tax rate is 35%. Compute the following amounts: *(a)* depreciation each year for accounting purposes and tax purposes *(b)* temporary difference at the end of year 1, and *(c)* the related amount that would be reflected in the entry to record income taxes at the end of year 1.
10. Explain the difference between a deferred income tax liability and a deferred income tax asset.

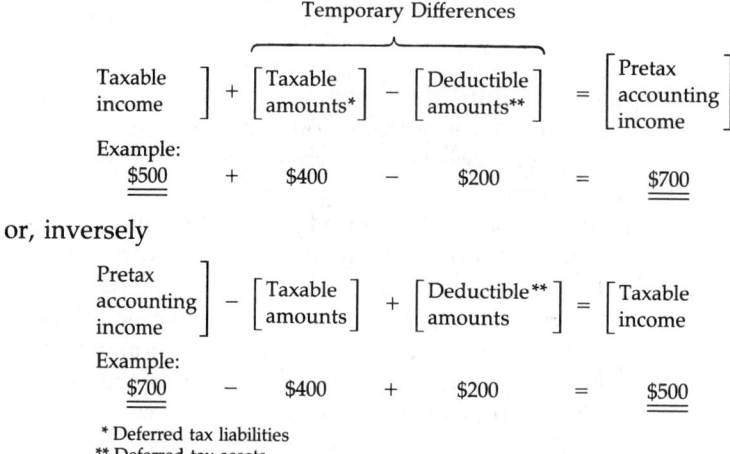

11. Explain the difference between a taxable amount and a tax deductible amount.
12. Define income tax net operating loss carrybacks and carryforwards (NOLs). Briefly explain the two options available to taxpayers.
13. In respect to net operating loss carrybacks and loss carryforwards (NOLs), which one involves greater certainty of realization of the benefit therefrom? How does this difference in certainty affect the accounting treatment for loss carrybacks and carryforwards?
14. Define an investment tax credit. How does it differ from a tax deduction?
15. Explain the limitation on recognizing a deferred income tax asset in interperiod income tax allocation.
16. RV Corporation's accounting and income tax records provided the following data at the end of 19A: Pretax accounting income, $60,000; deductible temporary differences, $14,000; taxable income, $51,000; and taxable temporary differences, $23,000. Prepare a reconciliation of pretax accounting income and taxable income.
17. Bye Corporation is preparing its 19X financial statements. Pretax amounts are: Income before extraordinary items, $300,000; extraordinary gain, $20,000; and prior period adjustment, $16,000 (a loss). Interperiod income tax computations showed income tax expense (including the prior period adjustment) of $104,880. How much income tax should be allocated to each of the three amounts assuming the average method of intraperiod income tax allocation is used?

EXERCISES

Exercises 23–1 to 23–12

E 23–1 **(Analysis of Interperiod Income Tax Deferrals)**

Listed below are six independent situations that require interperiod income tax allocation. For each item indicate with a check (√) whether the balance in the deferred income tax account would be a debit or a credit.

Item	The balance in the deferred income tax account would be a Debit	Credit
a. Construction contracts, percentage of completion for accounting and completed contract for income tax	______	______
b. Estimated warranty costs, accrual basis for accounting and future cash basis for income tax	______	______
c. Straight-line depreciation for accounting and accelerated depreciation for income tax	______	______
d. Unrealized gain (i.e., loss recovery), LCM recognized for accounting; and gain recognized only on later disposal of the asset for income tax	______	______
e. Rent revenue collected in advance, accrual basis for accounting, cash basis for income tax	______	______
f. Unrealized loss, LCM recognized for accounting and loss recognized only on later disposal of the asset for income tax	______	______

E 23–2 **(Terminology Overview)**

Listed below to the left are some terms frequently used in *FASB Standard 96.* Also, brief definitions are listed to the right. Match the definitions with the terms by entering the appropriate letters in the blanks.

Term		Brief definition
____	1. Deferred tax asset.	A. Income tax payable plus net deferred liability.
____	2. Taxable amount.	B. An amount used to compute income tax payable.
____	3. Permanent difference.	C. The difference between a deferred asset and a deferred liability when the latter is higher.
____	4. Schedule of temporary differences.	D. May result in a cash refund or a reduction of income tax payable.
____	5. Temporary difference.	E. An amount used to compute income tax expense.
____	6. Taxable income.	F. A deferred tax that has a net debit reported as an ________.
____	7. Net deferred liability.	G. A deferred tax amount that has a debit balance.
____	8. Income tax expense.	H. A tax difference that does not reverse or turn around.
____	9. Asset.	I. An allocation of tax among the components in the financial statement.
____	10. Net operating loss carryback (NOL).	J. A computation that is essential to compute the deferred tax amounts.
____	11. Intraperiod income tax allocation.	K. A pretax amount that represents a difference between financial accounting and tax return amounts that reverse or turn around.
____	12. Investment tax credit.	L. An income tax provision intended to encourage investments in new product-line assets.

E 23–3 (Reporting Deferred Income Tax on the Statement of Financial Position)

At the end of 19X5, Raleigh Corporation's deferred tax account had a $90,000 credit balance. The income tax rate was 30%. This credit balance was due only to the following pretax temporary differences:

a. Depreciation for accounting purposes, $200,000; for income tax purposes, $300,000. The related asset has a five-year remaining life.

b. Installment sale revenue; for accounting purposes, $600,000; for income tax purposes, $400,000. The collection period is the following four years with equal amounts each year.

Required:

Show how the deferred tax amount of $90,000 should be reported on the 19X5 statement of financial position. Show computations.

E 23–4 (Recording and Reporting Income Tax Consequences for a Two-Year Period; No Carrybacks or Carryforwards)

The records of Star Corporation provided the following data related to income tax allocation:

	19X1	19X2
Pretax accounting income	$200,000	$220,000
Taxable income (tax return)	220,000	200,000
Income tax rate	34%	34%

The deferred tax account showed a zero balance at the start of 19X1. There was only one temporary difference, a revenue, which was taxable in 19X1 but was recorded for accounting purposes in 19X2. There are no carrybacks nor carryforwards.

Required:

1. Give the journal entry to record the income tax consequences for each year.
2. Show how income tax expense, income tax payable, and deferred income tax should be reported on the financial statements each year.

E 23–5 (Interperiod Tax Allocation; a Revenue and an Expense; Carryback)
The records of TN Corporation, at the end of 19X1, provided the following data related to income taxes:

a. Gain on disposal of a special asset, $50,000; recorded for accounting purposes at the end of 19X1; reported for income tax purposes at the end of 19X3.
b. Estimated expense, $30,000, accrued for accounting purposes at the end of 19X1; reported for income tax purposes when paid at the end of 19X2.
c. Taxable income (from the tax return) at the end of 19X1, $100,000; the enacted income tax rate is 34%.

Required:
1. Did the gain and expense cause temporary differences? Explain why. Classify each item as deductible or taxable and explain why.
2. Prepare the following for 19X1: *(a)* reconciliation of taxable income with pretax accounting income and compute income taxes payable, *(b)* schedule of temporary differences (see Exhibit 23–4), and *(c)* entry to record income taxes at the end of the year at both gross and net.
3. Show the amounts that will be reported on the *(a)* statement of income and *(b)* statement of financial position for 19X1.

E 23–6 (Analyze a Tax Difference, Deferred Asset, Entries and Reporting)
Voss Corporation reported accounting income before taxes and rent revenue collected in advance of: 19A, $75,000, and 19B, $88,000. Taxable income for each year would have been the same as pretax accounting income except for the tax effects of $300 per month rent revenue collected in advance on October 1, 19A, for the six months ending March 31, 19B. Rent revenue is taxable in the year collected. The tax rate for 19A and 19B is 30%, and the year-end for both accounting and tax purposes is December 31. This is the only difference and it is not changed.

Required:
1. Is this a temporary difference? Why?
2. Using the steps shown in Exhibit 23–4, *(a)* reconcile accounting income with taxable income, *(b)* calculate income tax payable, *(c)* prepare a schedule of temporary differences, *(d)* compute the balance in the deferred tax asset account, and *(e)* prepare journal entries for each year-end
3. Prepare a partial statement of income for each year starting with pretax accounting income.
4. What amount of deferred income tax would be reported on the 19A and 19B statements of financial position?

E 23–7 (Analyze a Tax Liability; Entries and Reporting)
Stacy Corporation would have had identical income before taxes on both its income tax returns and statements of income for the years 19A through 19D except for an operational asset that cost $120,000 which was depreciated for income tax purposes using the following amounts: 19A, $48,000; 19B, $36,000; 19C, $24,000; and 19D, $12,000, whereas for accounting purposes, the straight-line method was used (i.e., $30,000 per year). Both the accounting and tax periods end December 31. The operational asset has a four-year estimated life and no residual value. Income before depreciation expense and income taxes for each of the four years were as follows (this is the only temporary difference and it is not changed):

	19A	19B	19C	19D
Accounting income before taxes and depreciation	$60,000	$80,000	$70,000	$70,000

Assume the average income tax rate for each year was 30%.

Required:

1. Is this a temporary difference? Explain why.
2. Using the steps shown in Exhibit 23–3, *(a)* reconcile accounting and taxable income, *(b)* calculate income tax payable, *(c)* compute the balance in the deferred tax liability account, and *(d)* prepare journal entries for each year-end.
3. For each year show the deferred income tax amount that should be reported on the statement of financial position.

E 23–8 (Operating Carryback-Carryforward (NOL) Options; Entries and Reporting; No Income Tax Allocation)

Tyson Corporation reported pretax income from operations in 19A of $80,000 (the first year of operations). In 19B, the corporation experienced a $40,000 pretax loss from operations (NOL). Assume an average income tax rate of 45%.

Required:

1. Assess Tyson's income tax situation for 19A and 19B separately. How should Tyson elect to handle the loss in 19B?
2. Based on your assessments in requirement (1), give the 19A and 19B income tax entries that Tyson should make. Disregard income tax allocations.
3. Show how all tax-related items would be reported on the 19A and 19B statement of income and statement of financial position.

E 23–9 (Operating Carryback-Carryforward (NOL) Options; Choice Required; Entries; No Income Tax Allocation)

Toner Corporation reported the following taxable income and loss: 19A, income, $10,000 (tax rate 20%), and 19B, $40,000 loss (tax rate 20%). At the end of 19B, Toner made the following estimates: 19C income, $4,000 (tax rate 20%); 19D income, $11,000 (tax rate 20%); and 19E income, $50,000 (tax rate 30%). On the basis of these estimates, which the company considered to be conservative, Toner elected the carryforward-only option. Disregard income tax allocations.

Required:

1. Give the income tax entry for 19A.
2. Give the income tax entry for 19B. Explain the basis for your response.
3. Give the income tax entry for 19C, assuming the actual income was $6,000 (tax rate, 20%).
4. Give the income tax entry for 19D, assuming the actual income was $13,000 (tax rate, 20%).
5. Give the entry for 19E, assuming the actual income was $45,000 (tax rate 35%).
6. Did Toner make a wise choice? Explain.

E 23–10 (Correction of Accounting Error Including Income Tax Consequences)

On January 1, 19X1, Cooper Corporation purchased a patent for $6,300. The patent had an estimated remaining economic life of seven years. During January 19X3, the newly employed accountant discovered that the full cost of the patent was debited to patent expense on the purchase date (for both accounting and income tax purposes). The income tax rate for 19X1 and 19X2 was 40%, and for 19X3, 34%. The annual accounting and tax periods end on December 31.

Required:

Give the entry(s) that should be made during January 19X3 to correct the error including the income tax consequences. Use an account titled Accumulated Amortization, Patent.

E 23–11 (Intraperiod Income Tax Allocation Methods)

Western Corporation's statement of income showed the following summarized pretax amounts:

Revenues	$300,000
Expenses	(220,000)
Income before extraordinary items	80,000
Extraordinary loss	(20,000)
Pretax income	$ 60,000

Income tax rates (for problem purposes only):
First $70,000 of taxable amount, 40%; remainder of taxable amount, 30%.

Required:

1. Complete the following comparative schedule:

	Specific method	Average method
Revenues Expenses Income before EO items Income tax allocated Extraordinary item Income tax allocated Net income (after tax)		

2. Was there a tax saving? How much?
3. Evaluate the two allocation methods.

E 23–12 (Intraperiod Tax Allocation Methods; with Prior Period Adjustment)

Boston Company's financial statements showed the following pretax amounts (summarized):

Pretax income before extraordinary items	$100,000
Extraordinary loss	20,000
Pretax income	80,000
Prior period adjustment (a credit)	5,000

The income tax rates were (assumed for illustrative purposes only): First $60,000, 40%, remaining income, 30%.

Required:

1. For comparative purposes, complete the following schedule:

	Specific method	Average method

Statement of income:
Income before EO items
  Income tax allocated
Extraordinary loss
  Income tax allocated
Net income (after tax)
Statement of retained earnings:
Prior period adjustment
  Income tax allocated
Net prior period adjustment		

2. Evaluate the two methods.

PROBLEMS

Problems 23–1 to 23–18

P 23–1 **(An Overview of Income Tax Allocation, Depreciation)**

The financial statements of Dakar Corporation for a four-year period reflected the following pretax amounts:

	19A	19B	19C	19D
Statement of income (summarized):				
Revenues	$110,000	$124,000	$144,000	$164,000
Expenses	(80,000)	(92,000)	(95,000)	(128,000)
Depreciation expense (straight-line)	(10,000)	(10,000)	(10,000)	(10,000)
Statement of financial position (partial):				
Machine (four-year life, no residual value), at cost	$ 40,000	$ 40,000	$ 40,000	$ 40,000

Dakar has an average tax rate of 40% each year and uses accelerated depreciation for income tax purposes as follows: 19A, $16,000; 19B, $12,000; 19C, $8,000; and 19D, $4,000.

Required:

1. Is this a temporary difference? Explain why.
2. Prepare the following for each year: *(a)* schedule to reconcile accounting and taxable incomes, *(b)* schedule to compute income tax payable, *(c)* schedule to compute deferred income tax, and *(d)* journal entry at each year-end to record income taxes.
3. For each year show the deferred income tax amount that should be reported on the statement of financial position.

P 23–2 **(Analyze Three Income Tax Items; Entries and Reporting)**

The statements of income for Victor Corporation for two years (summarized) were as follows:

	19A	19B
Revenues	$180,000	$200,000
Expenses	142,000	181,000
Accounting income before permanent and temporary differences	$ 38,000	$ 19,000
Taxable income (tax return)	$ 56,000	$ 11,000
Income tax rate, 40%.		

For tax purposes, the following income tax differences existed:

a. Expenses (given above) on the 19B statement of income include goodwill amortization of $10,000, which is not deductible for income tax purposes.
b. Revenues (given above) on the 19B statement of income include $10,000 rent revenue, which is taxable in 19A but was unearned at the end of 19A.
c. Expenses (given above) on the 19A statement of income include $8,000 of estimated warranty costs, which are not deductible for income tax purposes until 19B.

There were no other differences and these differences did not change.

Required:

1. Is each one of the three income tax consequences given above a temporary difference? Explain why.
2. Prepare the following for each year: *(a)* schedule to reconcile accounting and taxable

incomes, *(b)* schedule to compute income tax payable, *(c)* schedule to compute deferred income tax, and *(d)* journal entry at each year-end to record income taxes.

3. Show how the deferred income tax would be reported on the statements of income and financial position.

P 23–3 (Recording and Reporting the Income Tax Consequences of a Deferred Asset and a Deferred Liability)

The records of IW Corporation provided the following income-tax related information:

	19X1	19X2	19X3	19X4
Pretax accounting income	$90,000	92,000	95,000	98,000
Taxable income (tax return)	63,000	101,000	104,000	107,000
Income tax rate, 30%.				

The above amounts include only two temporary differences as follows (no other changes occurred):

a. Installment sales—for accounting purposes in 19X1, $30,000; included in the tax return, $10,000 each year, 19X2 through 19X4.
b. Cost of warranties—for accounting purposes, $4,000 in 19X1; deducted for income tax $1,000 each year, 19X1 through 19X4.

Required:

1. Prepare the following for each year: *(a)* schedule to reconcile accounting and taxable income and to compute income taxes payable, *(b)* schedule of temporary differences, *(c)* schedule to compute deferred income taxes, and *(d)* journal entry at the end of each year to record income taxes.
2. Show how income tax expense, deferred income tax, and income taxes payable should be reported on the financial statements for each year.

P 23–4 (Interperiod Tax Allocation; Depreciation and Goodwill Considered)

Fox Corporation purchased a machine on January 1, year 1, that cost $40,000. The machine had an estimated service life of five years and no residual value. Fox uses straight-line depreciation for accounting purposes and accelerated depreciation for the income tax return as follows: year 1, 30%, year 2, 25%, year 3, 20%, year 4, 15%, and year 5, 10%. Taxable income on the tax return for year 1 was $150,000. The year 1 statement of income showed a $15,000 deduction for amortization of goodwill; income tax regulations do not permit the amortization of goodwill for income tax purposes. There were no other factors to complicate the company's income tax computations during year 1. The income tax rate is 20% on the first $25,000 of taxable income and 40% on the excess.

Required:

1. Identify any temporary differences and explain the basis for your decisions. Also, identify any taxable amounts and deductible amounts and explain their effects on the analysis of the income tax differences.
2. Prepare the following at the end of year 1: *(a)* schedule to reconcile accounting income and taxable income and to compute income tax payable, *(b)* schedule of temporary differences, *(c)* schedule to compute deferred income taxes, and *(d)* journal entry to record income taxes at year-end.
3. Show the amounts for year 1 that should be reported on the statement of income and statement of financial position.

P 23–5 (Recording and Reporting Income Tax Consequences for Temporary Differences) The records of LA Corporation provided the following information: Taxable income based on tax return: 19X1, $47,600; income tax rate, 30%.
There were two temporary differences as follows:

a. December 1, 19X1, collected $2,400 rent in advance for 19X2. The $2,400 must be included on the 19X1 tax return.
b. On December 1, 19X1, the company recorded a $10,000 estimated expense that will be paid in 19X2 and included in the 19X2 income tax return.

Required:

1. Prepare a reconciliation of taxable income with pretax accounting income for 19X1.
2. Prepare a schedule of temporary differences for 19X1.
3. Give the entry to record income taxes at the end of 19X1. Show computations for each amount.
4. Show how the income tax consequences should be reported on the three required financial statements for 19X1 assuming 75% of the income tax payable was paid by the end of 19X1.

P 23–6 (Overview; Recording and Reporting a Deferred Tax Liability; Change in Tax Rate) The records of Ford Corporation provided the following data at the end of years 1 through 4 relating to income tax allocation:

	Year 1	Year 2	Year 3	Year 4
Pretax accounting income	$58,000	$70,000	$80,000	$88,000
Taxable income (tax return)	28,000	80,000	90,000	98,000

The above amounts include only one temporary difference; no other changes occurred. At the end of year 1 the company prepaid an expense of $30,000 which will be amortized for accounting purposes over the next three years (straight line). The full amount is included in year 1 for income tax purposes. At the end of year 1 the enacted tax rate was 35%. At the end of year 2 the enacted tax rate was changed to 30% to remain in effect through year 4.

Required:

1. Prepare a schedule of temporary differences at the end of year 1.
2. Give the entry to record income taxes at the end of year 1.
3. Give any entry that should be made in year 2 to reflect the change in the enacted income tax rate. If none is required, explain why.
4. Give the entry at the end of each year for years 2 through 4 assuming the new enacted tax rate is not changed.
5. Complete the following tabulation:

	Year 1	Year 2	Year 3	Year 4
Statement of income:				
Income tax expense				
Statement of financial position:				
Liabilities:				
Income tax payable				
Deferred income tax liability				

P 23–7 (Recording and Reporting Income Tax Consequences for a Four-Year Period) The records of Aris Corporation provided the following income tax allocation data:

	19X1	19X2	19X3	19X4
Taxable income (tax return)	$60,000	$80,000	$85,000	$ 75,000
Pretax accounting income	40,000	70,000	90,000	100,000
Income tax rate, 30%.				

The deferred tax account reflected a zero balance at the start of 19X1. There was only one temporary difference, an estimated expense, which was recorded (i.e., accrued) for accounting purposes in 19X1 and 19X2 but was deductible for tax purposes in 19X3 and 19X4.

Required:

1. Prepare a schedule to reconcile taxable and accounting income and to compute the temporary difference for each year.
2. Prepare a schedule of temporary differences at the end of 19X1.
3. Give the entry to record income taxes at the end of 19X1.
4. Give the entry at the end of each year for years 19X2 through 19X4, assuming the new enacted tax rate is not changed.
5. Complete the following tabulation:

	19X1	19X2	19X3	19X4
Statement of income:				
Statement of financial position:				

P 23–8 (Overview of the Concept of Interperiod Income Tax Allocation; Depreciation)
On January 1, 19X1, DEP Corporation purchased a special machine that cost $60,000. The machine has an estimated five-year life and no residual value. The company uses the straight-line method for accounting purposes and accelerated depreciation for tax purposes as follows: 19X1, $20,000; 19X2, $16,000; 19X3, $12,000; 19X4, $8,000; and 19X5, $4,000. The enacted income tax rates are 19X1 through 19X4, 30%; and 19X5, 35%. Taxable income (from the tax return): 19X1, $80,000; 19X2, $84,000; 19X3, $88,000; 19X4, $92,000; and 19X5, $96,000.
Depreciation on the special machine is the only timing difference.

Required:

1. Complete the following schedules:

	19X1	19X2	19X3	19X4	19X5
a. Temporary differences:					
Taxable income (tax return)					
Temporary differences:					
Depreciation, accounting					
Depreciation, income tax return					
Temporary difference					
b. Income tax payable					
c. Deferred income tax liability					

2. Use the following format to give the journal entry at each year-end for income taxes:

	Journal entry at year-end			Balance in the deferred tax account
	Taxes payable	Deferred tax	Tax expense	
Year	debit (credit)	debit (credit)	debit (credit)	debit (credit)
1				
2				
3				
4				
5				

P 23–9 (Reporting a Deferred Tax Asset)

Ajax Corporation began operations on January 1, 19X1. At the end of 19X1, the company had two temporary differences and the reversing period ends in 19X5. The two differences relate to (1) litigation loss and (2) depreciation. The company's records at the end of 19X1 showed pretax accounting income of $100 million, and the 19X1 income tax return shows taxable income of $95 million. An analysis of these two sources provided the following data about the two temporary differences at the end of 19X1 (in millions):

a. Depreciation of machinery acquired at start of 19X1 that cost $90. For accounting purposes, depreciate using the straight-line basis over years 19X1 through 19X5 ($18 per year).
   For income tax purposes the accelerated depreciation was as follows: 19X1, $30; 19X2, $24; 19X3, $18; 19X4, $12, and 19X5, $6 (total, $90).

b. Litigation loss accrual, recorded at the end of 19X1, $7. Accounting—the company was sued and an expected loss of $7 was recorded at the end of 19X1 and it is expected to be finally settled in 19X3 at which time it will be reported on the tax return; that is, the loss is deductible when the liability is paid.

At the end of 19X1 a reconciliation of pretax accounting income and taxable income (from the 19X1 tax return) was as follows:

	19X1 (pretax)
Taxable income (from the tax return)	$ 95
Temporary differences:	
a. Depreciation	12
b. Litigation loss	(7)
Pretax accounting income	$100
The tax rate is 30%.	

Required:

1. Prepare a schedule of temporary differences at the end of 19X1.
2. Give the 19X1 journal entry to record income taxes.
3. Show how the 19X1 tax related items should be reported in the financial statements.

P 23–10 (Analysis of Three Temporary Differences)

Triple Corporation started operations on January 1, 19A. At the end of 19A, the following income tax related data were available:

	19A	19B	19C
Taxable income (tax return)	$116,500	$	$
a. Gross margin on installment sales:			
Accounting	175,000		
Tax return	65,000	70,000	40,000
b. Rent revenue collected in advance:			
Accounting	6,000		
Tax return	4,000	2,000	
c. Estimated warranty expense:			
Accounting (accrued)	15,000	16,000	
Tax return	12,000	16,500	2,500
Income tax rate	30%	30%	30%

Required:

1. What kind of tax difference is represented by each one of the three income tax consequences given above? Explain. Also, identify the taxable and deductible amounts.
2. Prepare the following schedules related to income tax allocation for 19A:
   a. Schedule to reconcile taxable accounting income and taxable income.
   b. Schedule of temporary differences.

3. Give the entry at the end of 19A to record income taxes; show computations.
4. Show the items that should be reported on the 19A financial statements assuming 75% of taxes payable were paid.

P 23–11 (Analysis of Two Temporary Differences)

Cruse Corporation started operations on January 1, 19X1. At the end of 19X1 the data related to income taxes were as follows (in 000s):

Taxable income from the tax return	$2,850

Income tax consequences:

a. Gain on installment sale, $330—in 19X1 recognized for accounting purposes and will be included on tax return equally over 19X2, 19X3, and 19X4	(330)
b. Litigation loss, $270—in 19X1 accrued as expense for accounting purposes and will be included in the tax return in 19X4	270

Income tax rate, 30%.

Required:

1. Analyze each of the income tax consequences given above to determine whether each one is a temporary difference, a taxable or deductible amount, and a deferred tax liability or asset. Explain each determination.
2. Prepare the following schedules for 19X1: *(a)* reconciliation of taxable income and pretax accounting income, and *(b)* temporary differences.
3. Give the entry to record income taxes at the end of 19X1. Show computations.
4. Show the amounts that should be reported on the three required financial statements at the end of 19X1. Assume that 75% of the 19X1 income tax liability was paid before the end of 19X1.

P 23–12 (Comprehensive; Four Differences; Carryback and Carryforward)

Year 19X1 is the first year of operations for BG Corporation. The accounting and income tax periods end on December 31. The records of the company provided the following income tax-related data at the end of 19X1 (000s):

Taxable income (from the income tax return; tax rate, 30%), $330.

Temporary differences:

1. A $500 estimated litigation loss was accrued (i.e., recognized) at the end of 19X1 for accounting purposes; expected settlement date, end 19X4 for income tax purposes.
2. A $200 gain on a special installment sale, recognized for accounting purposes at the end of 19X1; included in income tax return as collected in equal amounts for 19X2 through 19X5.
3. A depreciable asset that cost $100 (estimated useful life five years and no residual value) is depreciated as follows:

	19X1	19X2	19X3	19X4	19X5
Accounting purposes	$ 20	$20	$20	$20	$20
Income tax purposes	(33)	(27)	(20)	(13)	(7)
Difference	$(13)	$ (7)	$ 0	$ 7	$13

4. Rent revenue collected in advance at the end of 19X1, $32; recognized for accounting purposes in 19X2 and 19X3. The full amount must be included in the 19X1 income tax return.

Required:

1. Analyze each of the four income tax consequences given above to determine whether each one is a temporary difference, a taxable or deductible amount, and a deferred asset or liability.

2. Prepare the following schedules for 19X1: *(a)* reconciliation of taxable income and pretax accounting income, and *(b)* temporary differences.
3. Give the entry to record income taxes at the end of 19X1. Show computations.
4. Show the amounts that should be reported on the three required financial statements at the end of 19X1. Assume that 75% of the 19X1 income tax liability was paid before the end of 19X1.

P 23–13 (Comprehensive; Four Differences; Carryback and Carryforward)

Year 19X1 is the first year of operations for OK Corporation. The accounting and income tax periods end on December 31. The records of the company provided the following income tax-related data at the end of 19X1 (000s):

Taxable income (from the income tax return; rate 40%), $150.
Temporary differences:

1. A $300 estimated expense was accrued (i.e., recognized) at the end of 19X1 for accounting purposes; expected settlement date, end 19X4 for income tax purposes.
2. A $200 gain on a special installment sale, recognized for accounting purposes at the end of 19X1; included in income tax return as collected in equal amounts for 19X2 through 19X5.
3. A depreciable asset that cost $200 (estimated useful life five years and no residual value) is depreciated as follows:

	19X1	19X2	19X3	19X4	19X5
Accounting purposes	$ 40	$ 40	$40	$40	$40
Income tax purposes	66	54	40	26	14
Difference	$(26)	$(14)	$ 0	$14	$26

4. Rent revenue collected in advance at the end of 19X1, $40; recognized for accounting purposes in 19X2 and 19X3. The full amount must be included in the 19X1 income tax return.

Required:

1. Analyze each of the four income tax consequences given above to determine whether each one is a temporary difference, a taxable or deductible amount, and a deferred asset or liability.
2. Prepare the following schedules for 19X1: *(a)* reconciliation of taxable income and pretax accounting income, and *(b)* temporary differences.
3. Give the entry to record income taxes at the end of 19X1. Show computations.
4. Show the amounts that should be reported on the three required financial statements at the end of 19X1. Assume that 75% of the 19X1 income tax liability was paid before the end of 19X1.

P 23–14 (Operating Carryback-Carryforward (NOL) Options; Entries)

The financial statements of Bayshore Corporation for the first four years of operations reflected the following pretax amounts:

	19A	19B	19C	19D
Statement of income (summarized):				
Revenue	$125,000	$155,000	$180,000	$230,000
Expenses	120,000	195,000	160,000	200,000
Pretax income (loss)	$ 5,000	$ (40,000)	$ 20,000	$ 30,000

Assume an average income tax rate of 30% during 19A and 19B and 40% in 19C and 19D, and that future incomes are uncertain at the end of each year. Management of Bayshore Corporation elects the carryback-carryforward option in order to "lock in" the immediate cash refund on the NOL carryback. Disregard income tax allocation.

Required:

1. Recast the above statements to incorporate the income tax effects. Show computations.
2. Give entries to record the NOL income tax effects for each year.
3. Explain the alternate option that Bayshore might have considered. What are the primary considerations that Bayshore should assess in making its choice?

P 23–15 (Operating Carryforward-Carryback (NOL) Options; Entries and Reporting)

The pretax financial statements of Gibson Corporation for the first two years of operation reflected the following amounts:

	19A	19B
Revenues	$295,000	$330,000
Expenses	320,000	315,000
Pretax income (loss)	$ (25,000)	$ 15,000

Assume an average tax rate of 20% for 19A and 19B.

Required:

Gibson will have to apply the NOL carryforward-only option because there are no piior earnings. Estimates of future earnings are uncertain.

a. Restate the above financial statements incorporating the income tax effects. Disregard income tax allocation.
b. Give entries to record the NOL income tax effects for 19A and 19B. Explain the basis for your entries.

P 23–16 (Operating Carryback-Carryforward (NOL) Options; Entries and Reporting)

Decker Corporation experienced a loss year in 19D. The company reported taxable income (loss) for 19A–19D and had average tax rates as follows:

	19A	19B	19C	19D
Taxable income (loss)	$8,000	$32,000	$15,000	$(65,000)
Income tax rate	30%	30%	35%	40%

There were no temporary differences in 19A–19D.

Required:

1. Record income taxes for 19D and 19E, assuming Decker elects the carryback-carryforward option. Also assume:
   a. For 19D, any receivable was collected early in 19E.
   b. For 19E, the company reported taxable income of $45,000 and pretax accounting income of $50,000 (a $5,000 credit timing difference). The income tax rate for 19E was 45%.
2. List the accounts and amounts that should be reported on the statements of income and financial position for each of the above requirements.

P 23–17 (Comprehensive; Taxable and Deductible Amounts with NOL Carryback and Carryforward)

Nary Company started operations on January 1, 19A. The accounting period ends on December 31. This problem encompasses a timing period of seven years of 19A through 19G. During this timing period the company had one taxable amount, two deductible amounts, and a net operating loss (NOL at the end of 19E). The enacted tax rate for each year is 40% and all dollar amounts are given in 000s.

Case Data	19A	19B-19D	19E	19F	19G
a. Pretax accounting income (loss)	$400	$500	$(700)	$70	$ 50
b. Taxable income (NOL)	300	545	(545)	30	(10)
c. Taxable amount—gross margin on an installment sale:					
Accounting basis (when sold)	200				
Income tax basis (as collected)		120	40	40	
d. Deductible amount—estimated expense accrued:					
Accounting basis	100			60	
Income tax basis		75	25		60

e. NOL (end of 19E), $700; refundable amount to 19B–19D from the end of 19E, $545.

Required:
Prepare the entry for income taxes for each year. Support the entries by preparing by year: (1) a reconciliation of pretax accounting and taxable income and (2) a schedule of temporary differences and NOL effects (adapted to show each year in order for instructional convenience).

P 23–18 (Taxable and Deductible Amounts, NOL; Annual Entry)
Refer to the data for Nary Company given in Problem 23–17. This problem uses those data without change. This problem focuses primarily on year 19E; therefore, disregard the future 19F and 19G amounts for pretax accounting income and any new temporary differences that start after 19E.

Required:
1. Prepare a schedule to reconcile pretax accounting income with taxable income for year-end 19E.
2. Prepare a schedule of temporary differences and NOLs for year-end 19E.
3. Give the combined entry at year-end 19E to record income taxes. Show the related computations.

24 ACCOUNTING CHANGES AND ERROR CORRECTIONS

OVERVIEW AND PURPOSE

An investor interested in buying or making a major investment in a company surely would want to examine the company's financial statements for several prior years. A reasonable expectation would be that those statements be accurate, comparable from year to year, and disclosure oriented so that no material items would escape the investor's scrutiny. A primary purpose of the examination of these statements would be to help assess the future cash flows of the company.

Accuracy, comparability, and full disclosure would be important because the summary of accounts and amounts shown in the financial statements can obscure major events. Companies, large and small, frequently change from one generally accepted accounting principle (GAAP) to another, such as changing the inventory method used from FIFO to LIFO. Also, accounting errors are sometimes made, discoverd later, and must be corrected. These changes and error corrections often are material in amount. If such changes and corrections are not uniformly recorded, reported, and disclosed, statement users may be misled. Historically, the accounting profession did not provide definitive guidelines for reporting GAAP changes and error corrections. As a consequence, a multitude of recording and reporting approaches was common, which tended to *(a)* minimize disclosure, *(b)* obscure their effects on the financial statements, and *(c)* avoid reductions in reported income by using direct changes to owners' equity. As a result, consistency and comparability often were sacrificed in the financial statements.

The purpose of this chapter is to discuss current GAAP requirements for recognizing and reporting accounting changes and error corrections. This chapter is organized as follows:

Part A: Accounting Changes

1. Classification of accounting changes and error corrections.
2. Change in accounting principle.
3. Change in accounting estimate.
4. Change in reporting entity.

Part B: Correction of Accounting Errors

1. Classification of accounting errors.
2. Fundamentals of error correction.
3. Correcting entries illustrated.

Supplement 24–A: Preparation of Financial Statements from Single-Entry and Other Incomplete Records

PART A: ACCOUNTING CHANGES

Accountants often encounter situations in which accounting changes must be made for substantive reasons. One main reason is that the *FASB Standards*, and to some extent, the SEC regulations, often mandate new or changed GAAP. A recent example is the new cash flow statement. Also, a company may decide to change from the completed contract method to the percentage-of-completion method of accounting for long-term construction contracts (Chapter 13). Perhaps the most common accounting change is a revised estimate of useful life and/or residual value of an operational asset. In addition, all companies discover prior accounting errors that must be corrected. Prior to GAAP guidelines for accounting changes, a common accounting practice was to report all change "credits" as gains on the statement of income and to report all change "debits" as corrections of the beginning balance of retained earnings. In this way the change "debits" were never reported on the statement of income. Another practice was called the **big bath** because the changes involving debits were deferred and later written off at one arbitrary date—usually when there was an eminent operating loss, which tended to obscure their impact. All of these practices were used to manipulate income. These practices posed recognition, reporting, and disclosure problems, which had to be resolved in ways which would enhance consistency, comparability, and full disclosure. The current GAAP guidelines for accounting changes and error corrections are specified in *APB Opinion 20*, "Accounting Changes," which was effective for fiscal years which began after July 31, 1971. This opinion has been supplemented by *FASB Standard 16*, "Prior Period Adjustments," June 1977 and later *Standards*. *APB Opinion 20* was issued to narrow the alternatives permitted by specifying the guidelines for recording, reporting, and disclosing the effects of accounting changes and error corrections.

Classification of Accounting Changes and Error Corrections

APB Opinion 20 defines three diverse types of accounting changes and one error correction. The *Opinion* specifies accounting guidelines for each type. The four types are:

A. **Accounting changes:**
   1. **Change in accounting principle**—This type of change occurs when a company changes from one generally accepted accounting principle to another generally accepted accounting principle (e.g., a change from straight-line depreciation to declining-balance depreciation).
   2. **Change in accounting estimate**—This type of change occurs when a company changes from one good faith estimate to another good faith estimate (e.g., a change in the estimated useful life, or estimated residual value, of a depreciable asset).
   3. **Change in reporting entity**—This type of change occurs when a company changes its composition from the prior period (e.g., the acquisition of a new subsidiary).

B. Correction of accounting errors—This case occurs in a reporting period when an accounting error is discovered that was made (and not corrected) in a prior reporting period. For example, in 19C the discovery that a depreciable asset purchased in 19A was incorrectly recorded at that time as an expense. Therefore, the asset was not recorded and no depreciation was subsequently recognized.

Recording and Reporting Accounting Changes

When an accounting change is made, there is a question about how the net dollar **effect of the change,** often called a **catch-up adjustment,** should be recorded in the accounts and reported in the financial statements. Another question is how the catch-up adjustment should be reported in the **comparative financial statements of the year of change.** These comparative financial statements will include the financial statements of *(a)* the year prior to the year of change and *(b)* the year of the change.[1] *APB Opinion 20* provides guidelines for measuring the amount of the catch-up adjustment. It sets forth three different **approaches** that should be used in accounting and reporting for the three types of accounting changes defined above. These approaches are as follows:

1. **Current approach**—This approach identifies the catch-up adjustment with the **current period;** that is, the period in which the accounting change is made. **The catch-up adjustment is reported as a separate item on the statement of income of the year of change.** it is reported between the captions "Income before extraordinary items" and "Net income." On the **comparative** financial statements of the year of change, the information reported for the prior year is repeated without change. For **comparability,** however, pro forma data must be reported (explained later).
2. **Prospective approach**—This approach **does not** compute or report a catch-up adjustment because it is not allocated to prior periods. Instead, the effects of the change are included in the **current and future reporting periods** (prospective means forward in time), by revising current and future allocations. On the **comparative** financial statements of the year of change, the prior year's reported information is repeated without change. Pro forma data are not reported under the prospective approach.
3. **Retroactive approach—This approach records and reports the catch-up adjustments and error correction as a correction of retained earnings.** The adjustment is called a **prior period adjustment** (*FASB Standard 16,* par. 11). That is, it carries the effect of the change back (i.e., retroactively) rather than to the current or future time period(s). On the **comparative** financial statements of the year of change, the information reported for the prior year must be **restated** to reflect the newly adopted principle.

The approach that is applied to each type of accounting change depends on the characteristics of that change. *APB Opinion 20* specifies when each of these approaches must be used as follows:

---

[1] Comparative financial statements usually present the financial statements of two consecutive years; however, the profession recommends three consecutive years. For practical reasons we illustrate a two-year time span.

Definitely know!!

Type	Approach required	Summary of the approach	
		Catch-up adjustment identified with	Comparative statements (results of prior year)
Accounting changes: 1. In accounting principles: *a.* Usual situations.	Current	Current statement of income (separate item).	Prior year's results carried forward (and pro forma).
b. Exceptions specified.	Retroactive	Retained earnings (adjustment of beginning balance; a prior period adjustment).	Prior year's results restated to new principle.
2. In accounting estimates.	Prospective	Catch-up adjustment not computed or reported.	Prior year's results carried forward.
3. In reporting entity.		Not discussed substantively in this text.	
Accounting errors: All kinds in prior periods	Retroactive	Retained earnings (adjustment of beginning balance; a prior period adjustment)	

With these fundamentals in mind, we proceed to a detailed discussion of changes in *(a)* accounting principle and *(b)* accounting estimate including application of the appropriate approach. These discussions focus on (1) **recording** in the accounts, (2) **reporting** on the financial statements, and (3) **disclosure.**

Change in Accounting Principle

A change in **accounting principle** occurs when a company changes from one generally accepted accounting principle to another generally accepted accounting principle. It involves a choice from among two or more generally accepted accounting principles. *APB Opinion 20* states that the term **accounting principle** includes "not only accounting principles and practices but also the methods of applying them." It **excludes** the adoption of a principle caused by events occurring for the first time or events that were previously immaterial in their effect. Examples of a change in accounting principle are:

1. A change from straight line to some other acceptable method of depreciation.
2. A change in inventory cost flow, such as from FIFO to average.
3. A change in accounting for long-term construction contracts from the completed contract method to percentage of completion.
4. A change from expensing certain costs to capitalizing those costs and depreciating them.
5. A change to or from the full costing method in the petroleum industry.
6. A change from the cost method to the equity method for long-term investments.

An underlying concept in accounting is that a generally accepted accounting principle once adopted should not be changed because consistency in application is desirable. Therefore, to make a change in principle the newly adopted principle must produce preferable financial statements that enhance their value to users. This usually means a better matching of expenses with revenues. When a change in accounting principle is made, the company must disclose the nature of the change and the justification for the change. Accounting for a change in accounting principle involves two different situations:

a. **Current approach for usual cases**—*APB Opinion 20* specifies that the **current approach** should be used for all changes in accounting principle other than a few specified exceptions.
b. **Specified exceptions**—*APB Opinion 20* specifies a few **exceptions** that must be accounted for using the **retroactive approach.**

Change in Accounting Principle—Current Approach (for usual cases)

APB Opinion 20 requires that **most** changes in accounting principle should be recognized by using the current approach. Under this approach, the cumulative effect of a change in accounting principle (i.e., the catch-up adjustment) is computed as the difference between application of each of the two principles for all periods affected by the change up to the **beginning of the period in which the change is made.** For example, if a company changed, at the start of the fourth year of the 10-year life of a machine, from straight-line to declining-balance depreciation, the cumulative effect of the change would be computed as the cumulative difference between the straight-line and declining-balance depreciation amounts on the machine for years 1–3.

The catch-up adjustment must be *(a)* **recorded** in the accounts as of the beginning of the year of change and *(b)* **reported** on the statement of income as a separate item **between** "Income before extraordinary items" and "Net income." The *Opinion* states that the adjustment is "not an extraordinary item but should be shown in a manner similar to an extraordinary item." Per share amounts must be shown for the cumulative adjustment reported.

Reporting on the **comparative** financial statements in the year of change must include: *(a)* the current year's statements based on the new principle, *(b)* the prior year's statements repeated without change, and *(c)* **pro forma** presentation based on the new principle. On this latter item, *APB Opinion 20* states that income before extraordinary items and net income also must be shown as supplementary information on a **pro forma basis** on the "face of the income statements for all periods presented as if the newly adopted accounting principle had been applied during all periods affected."[2] The purpose of this requirement is to enhance comparability and full disclosure by summarizing for statement users what the statement of income would have shown had the newly adopted principle been used during the prior periods reported on the comparative financial statements. The current approach is the only accounting change for which pro forma information is required by *APB Opinion 20.*

To illustrate the accounting and reporting **of the usual case of a change in**

---

[2] **Pro forma** is defined in *Webster's Ninth New Collegiate Dictionary* as "provided in advance to prescribe form." Pro forma statements are "as if" statements; the "as if" assumptions should be clearly stated.

Exhibit 24–1

Case to illustrate change in accounting principle: straight-line to declining-balance depreciation—current approach (usual cases).

Item	Reported in 19C*	19D trial balance prior to accounting change
Statement of financial position, December 31:		
Assets (not detailed)	$700,000	$823,400
Machinery (10-year life; no residual value)	200,000	200,000
Accumulated depreciation (straight line)	(60,000)	(60,000)†
Total	$840,000	$963,400
Liabilities	$340,000	$282,920
Contributed capital (100,000 shares)	300,000	300,000
Retained earnings	200,000	380,480
Total	$840,000	$963,400
Statement of income, year ended December 31:		
Revenues	$700,000	770,000
Expenses (includes 40% income tax)	(550,000)	(599,520)
Depreciation expense	(20,000)	
Income before extraordinary items	130,000	
Extraordinary gain (loss), net of tax	(6,000)	10,000
Net income	$124,000	
Earnings per share:		
Income before extraordinary items	$1.30	
Extraordinary gain (loss)	(.06)	
Net income	$1.24	

* The data are given in order of year to facilitate "tracing"; the actual statements always report the data in inverse order.

† The declining-balance method will be used for book and tax return purposes. The depreciation entry for 19D has not been recorded.

Exhibit 24–2

Change in accounting principle—current approach (usual cases).

Panel A—Computation of the Catch-Up Adjustment:

Analysis of the effect of the accounting change:

1. This is a change in **accounting principle** (not a specified exception); the **current approach** must be applied.
2. Computation of the catch-up adjustment:

From SL depreciation: Depreciation recorded to date years A, B, and C ($200,000 × 10% × 3 years)		$60,000
To DB depreciation: Depreciation that would have been recorded under DB:		
19A: $200,000 × 20%	$40,000	
19B: ($200,000 − $40,000) × 20%	32,000	
19C: ($200,000 − $40,000 − $32,000) × 20%	25,600	97,600
Catch-up adjustment—increase in accumulated depreciation to DB basis (pretax), (19A–19C)		$37,600
Catch-up adjustment, net of tax [$37,600 × (100% − 40%)]		$22,560

Panel B—Entries to Record the Change in Accounting Principle—Current Approach:

January 1, 19D—To record the catch-up adjustment—current approach:		
Adjustment due to change in accounting principle, depreciation (panel A)	22,560	
Income tax receivable ($37,600 × 40%)	15,040*	
Accumulated depreciation (panel A)		37,600
December 31, 19D—Adjusting entry to record DB depreciation (new basis):		
Depreciation expense [($200,000 − $97,600, Panel A) × 20%]	20,480	
Accumulated depreciation		20,480

* Assumes acceptable for tax purposes; if there had been no tax effects this line would be omitted.

Exhibit 24–2
(concluded)

Panel C—Comparative Financial Statements for 19D—Current Approach:

	19C—from prior year; no change	19D—based on new principle, DB
Statement of financial position:		
Assets (19D, $823,400 + $15,040)	$700,000	$838,440
Machinery (cost)	200,000	200,000
Accumulated depreciation (SL)	(60,000)	
DB: ($60,000 + $37,600 + $20,480)		(118,080)
Total	$840,000	$920,360
Liabilities	$340,000	$282,920
Contributed capital (100,000 shares)	300,000	300,000
Retained earnings	200,000	
19D: ($200,000 + income, $137,440)		337,440
Total	$840,000	$920,360
Statement of income:		
Revenues	$700,000	$770,000
Expenses (including 40% income tax)	(550,000)	(599,520)
Depreciation expense (panel B)	(SL) (20,000)	(DB) (20,480)
Income before extraordinary items and accounting change	130,000	150,000
Extraordinary gain (loss), net of tax	(6,000)	10,000
Adjustment due to accounting change (panel B)		(22,560)
Net income	$124,000	$137,440
Earnings per share (100,000 shares):		
Income before extraordinary items	$1.30	$1.50
Extraordinary items	(.06)	.10
Effect of accounting change		(.23)
Net income	$1.24	$1.37
Pro forma, DB amounts for comparability:		
Income before extraordinary items and accounting change:		
19C: $130,000 − [($25,600, DB − $20,000, SL) × 60%, net of tax = $3,360]	$126,640	
19D: No change; as above		$150,000
Earnings per share	$1.27	$1.50
Net income:		
19C: ($124,000 − $3,360, 19C above)	$120,640	
19D: ($137,440, net income above + $22,560, catch-up)		$160,000
Earnings per share	$1.21	$1.60

Note: At the beginning of 19D, the company changed from SL to DB depreciation. In the opinion of the management the new method better measures income. The aftertax effect of the change was to increase depreciation expense for 19D by $480 (i.e., $288 after tax) and decrease 19D income before extraordinary items by $22,848 (i.e., the adjustment amount $22,560 plus the current year depreciation difference $288) ($.23 per share) and 19C income by $3,360 ($.03 per share). The pro forma amounts have been restated to report income for 19C and 19D as though DB depreciation had been used in both years.

accounting principle (which always requires the current approach), a case is given in **Exhibit 24–1** that involves a change in the depreciation method from straight line to declining balance. **Exhibit 24–2** shows the accounting and reporting for this change in accounting principle.

On January 1, 19D, the company changed from straight-line (SL) to 200% declining-balance (DB) depreciation. Thus, the new depreciation rate is 20% (i.e., 10% × 200%) on the declining carrying value of the machinery.

Exhibit 24–2, panel A, computes the amount of the pretax catch-up adjustment of $37,600. This is the **cumulative difference,** up to the beginning of the current year, between the old and the new depreciation amounts. Panel B shows the *(a)* **catch-up entry** to record the change from straight-line to declining-balance (DB) depreciation and *(b)* the entry to record 19D **depreciation expense** of $20,480 (DB basis). In the catch-up entry, Accumulated Depreciation, Machinery is credited for the cumulative amount of $37,600 (i.e., $97,600 under DB − $60,000 under straight line) to adjust that amount to the new DB basis. Because the same depreciation method is used for both accounting and income tax purposes, Income Tax Receivable is debited for the income tax effect (i.e., $37,600 × 40% = $15,040). This amount would be claimed by the company as a refund on amended tax returns for the years 19A–19C. Adjustment Due to Change in Accounting Principle, Depreciation is debited for the aftertax amount of $22,560 (i.e., $37,600 − $15,040).

Because of the specific guidelines of *APB Opinion 20* regarding pro forma presentation, examine panel C carefully. Notice from the **comparative** financial statements that the 19C data are **unchanged** from the original 19C statements (i.e., they reflect the old SL basis), and the 19D data reflect the new DB basis. Because these two sets of data as reported on the 19D comparative statements are **not comparable,** the **pro forma** presentation is required. Notice that the pro forma presentation resolves this comparability problem by restating the 19C data to the new DB basis.

Also, notice that the catch-up adjustment is reported on the 19D statement of income immediately following the extraordinary item.

Change in Accounting Principle—Retroactive Approach (used for specified exceptions)

APB Opinion 20 (par. 27) states that **"certain changes in accounting principle are such that the advantage of retroactive treatment in prior year reports outweigh the disadvantages."** The main advantage of retroactive restatement is that it reports consistent financial statements and the statements are **comparable.** However, some accountants argue that the retroactive approach will undermine statement users' confidence in financial statements because the effects were in the previous financial statements which had not been "fairly presented."

The six exceptions to the current approach are:

1. A change from the LIFO inventory method to another inventory method—If inventory costs rise, the **catch-up adjustment** would require a **debit** to inventory and a **credit** to retained earnings.
2. A change in the method of accounting for long-term construction contracts (i.e., from percentage of completion to completed contract or vice versa).
3. A change to or from the "full cost" method in extractive industries.
4. A change in accounting principle related to a forthcoming issuance of capital stock by a closely held company.
5. A change from retirement/replacement accounting to depreciation accounting for railroad track structures *(FASB Standard 73).*
6. A change in accounting principle that is required by an APB or FASB

pronouncement (e.g., *FASB Standard 11,* "Accounting for Contingencies" and *FASB Standard 95,* "Statement of Cash Flows").

These exceptions, which relate to changes in accounting principle, often create catch-up amounts that are "credits." Credits increase reported income; therefore, some accounting changes were being made only to increase reported net income by using the current approach. The requirement to use the retroactive approach removed the opportunity to manipulate income with a large catch-up credit adjustment reported on the current statement of income.

These changes in accounting principle must be accounted for using the **retroactive approach** rather than the current approach. The retroactive approach requires two phases:

a. **Record** the catch-up adjustment as of the beginning of the year of change.
b. **Report** on a retroactive restated basis all of the financial statements included in the comparative statements issued for the year of change. Therefore, these statements will be **consistent and comparable** on the new basis. If the cumulative effect of the change (i.e., the catch-up adjustment) includes an amount that is attributable to years prior to those presented in the comparative statements, that part of the catch-up adjustment must be reported as an **adjustment of the beginning balance of retained earnings** for the first year presented.

Exhibit 24–3 shows a change in accounting principle—from inventory at LIFO to FIFO, which is one of the exceptions listed above. Panel A gives the case data. Panel B shows how the catch-up adjustment is computed, panel C gives the entry to record the catch-up adjustment, and panel D shows the comparative statements.

In panel A notice that the 19A ending inventory was: FIFO, $47,000, and LIFO, $45,000; therefore, there is a catch-up adjustment prior to the first year of the 19C comparative statements. Panel B shows an aftertax catch-up adjustment amount of $1,200 for **reporting** purposes and also an aftertax catch-up adjustment of $6,000 for 19C **recording** purposes. Following this computation, panel C gives the January 1, 19C (beginning of the year of change) **entry** to restate the accounts by recording the catch-up adjustment. Panel D shows all data reported in the 19C comparative statements (i.e., 19B and 19C) restated to the new FIFO basis. Notice the $1,200 catch-up adjustment reported in the 19C statement of retained earnings as an adjustment to the beginning balance. This adjustment relates to the 19A catch-up. Pro forma restatement is not needed. In the comparative statements, all amounts are comparable because they are now on the new FIFO basis. Notice that the 19B amounts reported are **different** from those originally reported (on the old LIFO basis).[3]

[3] In contrast, under the **current approach** shown in Exhibit 24–2, the catch-up adjustment (i.e., the cumulative effect of the accounting change) was recorded as a current-year adjustment and reported on the statement of income of the year of change. For this situation the pro forma statements were necessary to enhance comparability.

Exhibit 24–3
Change in accounting principle; LIFO to FIFO—retroactive approach (only for specified exceptions).

Panel A—Case Data (limited to only the data needed):

1. On January 1, 19C, X Company decided to change the inventory cost method from LIFO to FIFO for accounting and tax purposes. The reporting year ends on December 31, and the average income tax rate is 40%.
2. To provide data for the change, a computer run reflected the following selected data:

Item	19B FIFO	19B LIFO	19C—year of change FIFO	19C—year of change LIFO
a. Beginning inventory (from prior December 31)	$47,000	$ 45,000	$ 60,000	$50,000
b. Ending inventory	60,000	50,000	80,000	68,000
c. Income before extraordinary items (after tax)		160,000	176,000	
d. Retained earnings, beginning balance		86,000	169,000	
e. Extraordinary gains (losses), net of tax		3,000	(2,000)	
f. Dividends declared and paid		80,000	88,000	

Panel B—Computation of Catch-Up Adjustment:

	Pretax	Aftertax (60%)
At December 31, 19A: FIFO, $47,000 − LIFO, $45,000	$ 2,000	$1,200
At December 31, 19B: FIFO, $60,000 − LIFO, $50,000	10,000	6,000

Panel C—January 1, 19C, Entry to Correct the Beginning Inventory and to Record the Catch-Up Adjustment (retroactively):

Inventory (adjustment to FIFO; $60,000 − $50,000)	10,000	
Income tax payable (19A, $2,000 × 40%) + (19B, $8,000 × 40%)		4,000*
Retained earnings (adjustment for accounting change; $10,000 × 60%)		6,000

* If this change had no income tax effects this line would be omitted.

Panel D—Comparative Financial Statements (only those items affected by the change):

Items	19B FIFO basis	19C FIFO basis
Statement of financial position:		
Inventory (FIFO)	$ 60,000	$ 80,000
Statement of income:		
Income before extraordinary items	$164,800†	$176,000
Extraordinary item, net of tax	3,000	$ (2,000)
Net income	$167,800	$174,000
Earnings per share (100,000 shares):		
Income before extraordinary items	$1.65	$1.76
Extraordinary items	.03	(.02)
Net income	$1.68	$1.74
Statement of retained earnings:		
Beginning balance (19B, LIFO)	$ 86,000	
Add: Cumulative effect of accounting change (19A, $2,000 × 60%)	1,200	
Beginning balance (FIFO basis)	87,200	$175,000
Add: Net income (from above)	167,800	174,000
Deduct: Dividends declared and paid	(80,000)	(88,000)
Ending balance	$175,000	$261,000

† ($160,000 − 1,200 + $6,000) = $164,800.

Note: The 19C inventory valuation is at FIFO, LCM. At the beginning of 19C, the company changed from LIFO to FIFO inventory for accounting and tax purposes because FIFO more realistically measures net income. The aftertax effect of the change on 19C net income considering the effects on both the beginning and ending inventories, was an increase of $4,800 ($.048 per share). Retained earnings at January 1, 19C, was increased by $6,000. Pro forma amounts are not required by *APB Opinion 20* because the prior years' statements are restated to the new basis, which makes them comparable with the statements of the current year.

Change in Accounting Estimate

Accounting necessarily uses **estimates** because *(a)* certain essential facts are not known at the transaction date (e.g., which specific accounts receivable will be uncollectible), and *(b)* future developments and events cannot be known with certainty (e.g., warranty costs).

Estimates result from judgments that are based on specific assumptions and projections concerning future events. As the anticipated event draws nearer, it may be possible to **improve** on the prior estimates. Therefore, accountants often face the problem of what to do about improved estimates. *APB Opinion 20* specifies that new reliable estimates, if materially different from the prior estimate being used, should be adopted by revising the future amounts to be recorded and used in the financial statements. **Prior accounting results are not restated and pro forma disclosure is not used.** For example, during the first few years of a company's life, the estimated loss rate on uncollectible accounts may have a wide range of estimation error because of the lack of experience with collections. As time passes, the estimated rate often can be refined as additional information is developed.

The concept underlying a change in estimate is that changes in estimates are a inherent consequence of the necessity to make estimates when accrual basis accounting is used. When better estimates can be made, the new estimate must be used for the current and future periods because those are the periods explicit in the new estimates. It follows that the new estimates should not be used to change prior accounting based on prior estimates. Some accountants argue that comparability is adversely affected by using this approach, but most accountants disagree with this conclusion. Because of these characteristics, a change **from a prior good faith estimate to an improved estimate** is different from a change in accounting principle. Some examples of changes in accounting estimates are:

1. Change in the estimated residual value or useful life of an asset subject to depreciation, amortization, or depletion.
2. Change in the estimated loss rate on receivables.
3. Change in the estimated amortization period of a deferred charge.
4. Change in the estimated time over which revenue collected in advance will be earned.
5. Change in the expected warranty cost on goods sold under guarantee.

The definition of a change in estimate assumes that the original estimate and the new estimate both represent realistic and good faith determinations. These are based on the information available at the time the respective estimates are made. A change in estimate that does not meet these criteria must be classified as an "accounting error," defined and discussed in Part B of this chapter.

When a change in an estimate occurs, two problems arise. That is, how to *(a)* **record** the effect of the change of estimate in the accounts and *(b)* **report** the change on the comparative financial statements.

Because estimates are necessary in accounting and updated estimates occur frequently, it is reasonable to account for such changes **prospectively.** This approach means that the **new estimate** should be incorporated in revenue and expense determinations of the **current and future reporting periods** based on the existing balance in the related accounts when the new estimate is made. On this point *APB Opinion 20* states:

> The Board concludes that the effect of a change in accounting estimate should be accounted for in *(a)* the period of change if the change affects that period only, or *(b)* the period of change and future periods if the change affects both.

This means that a change in estimate does not involve a retroactive (or catch-up) adjustment. Therefore, **no entry is needed to record the change.** The only disclosure required by the *Opinion* is the effect of the change on income before extraordinary items, net income, and related per share amounts of the current period. This disclosure usually is made in a note to the financial statements.

In some situations, the same item may cause a concurrent change in accounting principle and change in estimate. When the effects of **each change can be clearly separated,** two changes should be recognized. However, when the two are indistinguishable, the one that clearly is dominant should be used; if neither is clearly dominant, a change in estimate should be assumed. For example, a major company changed its way of accounting for containers from recording them as inventory to recording (and depreciating) them as operational assets. This was a change in principle, however, it was properly classified as a change in estimate because the process of making the **new estimates,** and their future impact were clearly dominant in the change.[4]

To illustrate a typical **change in estimate,** assume a machine that cost $120,000 on January 1, 19A (no residual value) is being depreciated over a 10-year life. On the basis of new information available after 4 years' use, a 12-year life (instead of 10) appears more realistic. The change in the depreciation estimate, starting in 19E (fifth year), would be recognized as follows (assuming straight-line depreciation):

a. To compute annual depreciation for the current and subsequent years (no catch-up adjustment to be made):

Original cost of the asset	$120,000
Accumulated depreciation to date of change in estimate ($120,000 × 4/10)	48,000
Undepreciated balance at beginning of year of change in estimate	$ 72,000
Annual depreciation after change, $72,000 ÷ (12 − 4 = 8 years)	$ 9,000

b. Recording:

(1) January 1, 19E—No catch-up adjustment is computed or recorded.

(2) December 31—Adjusting entry for depreciation:

	19D		19E	
Depreciation expense	12,000		9,000	
Accumulated depreciation		12,000		9,000

[4] *APB Opinion No. 20,* par. 11, states that: "Distinguishing between a change in an accounting principle and a change in an accounting estimate is sometimes difficult. For example, a company may change from deferring and amortizing a cost to recording it as an expense when incurred because future benefits of the cost have become doubtful. The new accounting method is adopted, therefore, in partial or complete recognition of the change in estimated future benefits. The effect of the change in accounting principle is inseparable from the effect of the change in accounting estimate. Changes of this type are often related to the continuing process of obtaining additional information and revising estimates and are therefore considered as change in estimates for purposes of applying this *Opinion.*"

c. Reporting on **comparative** financial statements:

	19D	19E
Statement of income		
Depreciation expense	$ 12,000	$ 9,000
Statement of financial position		
Machine	$120,000	$120,000
Accumulated depreciation:		
19D: ($120,000 × 4/10 years)	(48,000)	
19E: ($48,000 + $9,000)		(57,000)
Carrying value	$ 72,000	$ 63,000

A disclosure note should be included in the financial statements. This note would explain the effect of the change in estimate on income and earnings per share if the amount of the change is material.

Change in Reporting Entity

Changes in reporting entity are recorded and reported using **retroactive restatement** as illustrated in Exhibit 24–3. That is, they "should be reported by restating the financial statements of all prior periods presented in order to show financial information for the new reporting entity for all periods." *APB Opinion 20*, paragraph 12, defines this type of accounting change as follows:

> One special type of accounting change in accounting principle results in financial statements which, in effect, are those of a different reporting entity. This type is limited mainly to *(a)* presenting consolidated or combined statements in place of statements of individual companies, *(b)* changing specific subsidiaries comprising the group of companies for which consolidated statements are presented, and *(c)* changing the companies included in combined financial statements. A different group of companies comprise the reporting entity after each change.

This type of change is discussed in detail in another textbook in this series.[5]

PART B: CORRECTION OF ACCOUNTING ERRORS

Classification of Accounting Errors

An accounting error is defined as the **incorrect recording and reporting of facts about the business that existed at the time an event or transaction was recorded.** *APB Opinion 20* states that, "Errors in financial statements result from mathematical mistakes, mistakes in application of accounting principles, or oversight or misuse of facts that existed at the time the financial statements were prepared." There are two types of accounting errors: (1) those that occur and are discovered in the **same** accounting period, and (2) those that occur in one accounting period and are discovered in a **later** accounting period. **When**

[5] C. H. Griffin, T. H. Williams, K. L. Larson, James R. Boatsman, and Timothy B. Bell, *Advanced Accounting*, 5th ed. (Homewood, Ill.: Richard D. Irwin, 1985).

an accounting error is discovered, it should be corrected as of the discovery date.

The type of error that occurs and is discovered in the same accounting period is not difficult to correct because the accounts have not been closed and the financial statements have not been issued. This type of error can be corrected either *(a)* by reversing the incorrect entry and then recording the correct entry or *(b)* by making a single correcting entry designed to correct the account balances.

In contrast, *APB Opinion 20* deals with errors that affect the financial statements of one period and are discovered in a later period. This type of error is more complex because one or more past periods are involved (and the past financial statements have been issued). The current period usually is involved, and often one or more future periods will be affected as well. Because of these complexities, and opportunities to manipulate accounting values by selective ways of correcting errors, the *Opinion* provides specific guidelines for correcting accounting errors (see pages 1257–58).

Examples of accounting errors, as distinguished from changes in accounting principles or changes in estimates, are:

a. Use of an inappropriate or unacceptable accounting principle. Thus, a change from an unacceptable accounting principle, or one incorrectly applied, to a generally accepted one would require the correction of an error (not a change in accounting principle).

b. Intentional use of an unrealistic accounting estimate. That is, the misapplication in the accounts and on the financial statements of known information at the date of the decision related to the estimate. Thus, the adoption of an unrealistic depreciation rate, when discovered later, requires the correction of an error (not a change in accounting estimate).

c. Misstatement of an accounting value, such as for inventory, operational assets, liabilities, or owners' equity.

d. Failure to recognize accruals and/or deferrals.

e. Incorrect classification of an expenditure as between expense and asset.

f. Incorrect or unrealistic allocations of accounting values, such as in the allocation of overhead costs during the construction of operational assets for self use.

g. Failure to record a completed transaction.

h. Mathematical errors involved in the accounting process.

i. Recording revenues before the earnings process is completed.

Fundamentals of Error Correction

APB Opinion 20 (pars. 36 and 37) and *FASB Standard 16*, "Prior Period Adjustments," provide guidelines for the correction of accounting errors on their **discovery date.** Fundamentally, correction of errors uses the **retroactive approach.** Thus, accounting errors included in the financial statements of a prior period and discovered in the current period require that all of the cumulative effects of the error be computed up to the beginning of the current period. **An entry then is made to correct the beginning balance of Retained Earnings and all other existing accounts affected by the error.** The cumulative effect of an error on the net income of prior periods should be **recorded** as of the discovery date in a separate account—Prior Period Adjustment—Correction of Accounting Error. This PPA account is closed directly to Retained Earnings and corrects the beginning balance of that account for the current period.

A prior period adjustment, in accordance with *FASB Standard 16,* is **reported** on the statement of retained earnings as a retroactive adjustment of the beginning balance. As to disclosure, *APB Opinion 20* states: "The nature of an error in previously issued financial statements and the effect of its correction on income before extraordinary items, net income, and the related per share amounts should be disclosed in the period in which the error was discovered and corrected." Financial statements of subsequent periods need not repeat the disclosures. In other words, in this last sentence the profession says, correct, report, disclose, then drop it! On comparative financial statements, all errors must be corrected for each year presented.

Correcting Accounting Errors Illustrated

Exhibit 24–4 illustrates the correction of errors that occurred in each of two prior years; these errors affected the statements of income and statements of retained earnings. Panel A presents the case data. Panel B gives the entry to correct the errors, on a **retroactive basis, as required for error corrections.** Panel C shows the reporting on the current year's comparative financial statements. The correcting entry in the year of discovery, 19F, as given in panel B, is recorded net of income tax because these two errors involved items that affected taxable income; therefore, Income Tax Receivable is debited. Accumulated depreciation is corrected, and a **prior period adjustment (i.e., retroactive basis) is recorded at the net of tax amount of $6,000.**

The comparative statements of income and statements of retained earnings for 19E and 19F, as shown in panel C, reflect the amounts that would have been reported had the errors in 19D and 19E not occurred (notice that 19F income was correct). **For comparative statement purposes, the 19E statement of income, and the 19E and 19F statements of retained earnings must be restated to reflect the amounts that would have been reported had the errors not occurred.** Therefore, 19E net income was restated from $45,000 to $42,000; that is, for the net-of-tax error due to understatement of depreciation expense for 19E only [i.e., $5,000 × (100% − 40%) = $3,000].

Both the 19E and 19F statements of retained earnings must be restated. The 19E statement must first reflect the cumulative amount of the error (as a PPA) as of the beginning of 19E. Thus, for this purpose the 19D error, net of tax, is reported as a PPA [i.e., $5,000 × (100% − 40%) = $3,000]. Note that this is **not** the amount of the PPA recorded in panel B (it is different by the amount of the 19E error, $3,000). The 19E corrected net income ($42,000) is then added to the corrected balance. The dividend is deducted to derive the corrected 19E ending balance of retained earnings. This balance is carried forward as the 19F beginning balance.

Exhibit 24–4 **does not show a pro forma presentation.** It is not needed for comparability purposes in view of the restatement of the prior year's statements. For this reason, *APB Opinion 20* does **not** require a pro forma presentation for error corrections. The only instance in which the pro forma results are presented is for a change in accounting principle accounted by using the current approach.

Exhibit 24–4
Correction of an accounting error (depreciation).

Panel A—Case Data:

1. The accounting records of Easie Company reflected the following data:

	19E	19F
Sales revenue	$450,000	$480,000
Cost of goods sold	(300,000)	(310,000)
Depreciation expense	(20,000)	(25,000)
Remaining expenses	(55,000)	(65,000)
Income tax (40% average rate)	(30,000)	(32,000)
Net income (for year ended December 31)	$ 45,000	$ 48,000
Balance in retained earnings, January 1	$135,000	$165,000
Dividends declared and paid	15,000	17,000

2. During June 19F, the company discovered that **depreciation expense** for 19D and 19E was understated each year by $5,000 for both accounting and income tax purposes; total pretax understatement, $10,000.

Panel B—Correcting Entry (retroactive approach—required for error corrections):
June 19F—To correct the accounts and record the cumulative effect of the error on discovery date:

Prior period adjustment, depreciation correction [($5,000 × 2 years) × (100% − 40%)]	6,000	
Income tax receivable (amended return) [($5,000 × 2 years) × 40%]	4,000*	
Accumulated depreciation ($5,000 × 2 years)		10,000

* If this error had no income tax implications, this line would drop out.

Panel C—Reporting on the 19F Statement of Income and Statement of Retained Earnings:

Step 1—Restate the 19E statement of income to incorporate the correction of that year's depreciation expense and income tax.

Step 2—Prepare the 19F statement of income. There were no errors in 19F; therefore, use the data given in Panel A.

Comparative statement of income—for the years ended December 31, 19E (restated), and 19F:

		19E restated (step 1)		19F (step 2)	
Sales revenue			$450,000		$480,000
Cost of goods sold		$300,000		$310,000	
Depreciation expense (see Note)	$20,000 + $5,000	25,000		25,000	
Remaining expenses		55,000		65,000	
Income tax expense (40% average rate)	$30,000 − ($5,000 × 40%)	28,000	408,000	32,000	432,000
Net income	$45,000 − ($5,000 × 60%)		$ 42,000		$ 48,000

Comparative statement of retained earnings—for the years ended December 31, 19E, and 19F (restated):

Step 3—Correct the 19E statement of retained earnings. Note that the PPA is for the 19D error because the 19E error was corrected in the 19E statement of income above. The statement of financial position will reflect the $10,000 increase in accumulated depreciation recorded in panel B above.

Step 4—Prepare the 19F statement by bringing forward the corrected beginning balance from 19E.

	19E (step 3)	19F (step 4)
Beginning balance (for 19E amount, see panel A)	$135,000	$159,000
Deduct: PPA, accounting error, 19D [$5,000 × (100% − 40%)]	(3,000)	
Beginning balance corrected	132,000	
Add: Net income (per corrected income statement immediately above)	42,000	48,000
Deduct: Dividends declared and paid (see panel A)	(15,000)	(17,000)
Ending balance	$159,000	$190,000

Note: Prior period adjustment—During 19F, an error was discovered in which depreciation expense of $5,000 (aftertax effect on net income, $3,000) was understated each year, 19D and 19E. Accordingly, for comparative statement purposes, the 19E statement of income was restated to reflect a $3,000 decrease in net income. Also, the 19E statement of retained earnings was restated by (1) a prior period adjustment for the 19D error, and (2) the restated 19E net income; the net effect was to reduce the 19F beginning balance of retained earnings by $6,000, from $165,000 to $159,000.

Analysis of Accounting Errors

Efficient analytical procedures should be used for correcting multiple accounting errors. Correcting entries must be determined and appropriate notes prepared to augment the statement disclosure. This section presents some analytical techniques that are useful for these purposes as well as for problem-solving purposes for students, professional examination candidates, and others.

It is helpful in the analysis of accounting errors that are **discovered in subsequent accounting periods** to classify them according to their effects on the periodic financial statements. There are three types of accounting errors:[6]

a. **Errors that affect only the statement of financial position (SFP)**—This type involves incorrect designation and classification of assets, liabilities, or stockholders' equity accounts when originally recorded. These include recording premium on capital stock issuances as a credit to retained earnings and classifying a short-term liability as a long-term liability. Correction of "SFP only" errors involves a transfer from one **permanent** account to another **permanent** account and no prior period adjustment is involved. In this case, statements of financial position for future periods usually would be in error until the respective account balances are corrected. Alternatively, if the error was made in **preparing** the SFP, rather than in the accounts, correction can be made by *(a)* reissuance of the SFP and *(b)* correct reporting of the reissued SFP on the next set of comparative financial statements.

b. **Errors that affect only the statement of income**—This type involves incorrect designation or classification of revenues, gains, expenses, and losses when initially **recorded.** These include a credit to a gain account that should have been credited to a revenue account, or the improper classification of a gain or loss as extraordinary. In this case, financial reports of future periods would be unaffected whether or not the error is corrected (because all temporary accounts are closed each period and retained earnings is unaffected by this error). Therefore, the correction can be made by *(a)* reissuance of the statement of income and *(b)* correct reporting of the reissued statement of income on the next set of **comparative** financial statements.

c. **Errors that affect both the statement of financial position and statement of income**—This type of error can be further classified on the basis of the effects on the **current and future financial statements** as follows:
   (1) **Counterbalancing errors**—This kind of error (also called a **self-correcting error**) will be automatically corrected or offset over a consecutive two-year period. The income of one reporting period will be overstated or understated, with the opposite effect occurring in the next

---

[6] There are some exceptions to the discussion of counterbalancing and noncounterbalancing errors as follows: *(a)* Practically all errors eventually are counterbalancing; for example an operational asset that has errors in depreciation will self-correct when the asset is sold or discarded. This is the reason we have assumed a two-year self-correction period. *(b)* The way that the amount is computed for the depreciation, depletion, or intangible amortization determines the self-correcting event. For example, if the periodic estimate of bad debts based on a percent of credit sales is incorrect, it would not self-correct the next year; however, if based on a percent of accounts receivable it would self-correct. Similarly, errors in depreciation expense would not self-correct if based on the usage for the current year; if based on the total amount needed in the accumulated depreciation account it would self-correct.

period. For example, the overstatement of 19A ending inventory **overstates** 19A income. Because of the consequent overstated 19B beginning inventory, 19B income is understated. Thus, the 19A error was self-corrected at the end of 19B—19B assets and retained earnings are correct.

Most errors that affect both the statement of income and SFP are self-correcting over a consecutive two-year period. Counterbalancing errors, as defined above, that are **discovered more than two years after the error was made** do not require a correcting entry. However, the two statements of income and financial position for the first reporting period that have already been issued would continue to be incorrect unless reissued. In contrast, if such errors are **discovered during the second year of the two-year cycle,** a correcting entry in the second year is required.

Two examples of counterbalancing errors and their effects are:

(a) Errors in adjusting entries for accruals and deferrals—Errors of this type include errors in adjusting for prepaid expenses, accrued expenses, revenues collected in advance, and revenues earned but not yet collected. Such errors cause the statement of income of the period in which the error was made to be incorrect. There is an equal misstatement in the opposite direction on the statement of income of the following period. To illustrate, assume the correct amount of accrued wages payable was understated at the end of 19A. Instead, Wage Expense was debited and Cash was credited when these wages were paid early in the next period. The effects of this error are:

19A	19B
19A statement of income: Wage expense understated Income overstated	19B statement of income: Wage expense overstated (because Wage expense was debited when the wages were paid) Income understated
19A statement of financial position: Current liabilities (wages payable) understated Retained earnings overstated	19B statement of financial position: No misstatements

(b) Errors in the merchandise inventory—Errors of this type are counterbalancing because the ending inventory of the current period is the beginning inventory of the following period. Likewise the beginning and ending inventories have opposite effects on income of the two periods. To illustrate, assume the ending inventory for 19A is understated. The effects of this error are:

19A	19B
19A statement of income: Ending inventory understated Cost of goods sold overstated Income understated	19B statement of income: Beginning inventory understated Cost of goods sold understated Income overstated
19A statement of financial position: Assets (inventory) understated Retained earnings understated	19B statement of financial position: No misstatements

(2) **Noncounterbalancing errors**—This kind of error, which is **not** self-correcting over a two-year cycle, continues to affect account balances for a long period of time if not corrected. Therefore, one or more statement of financial position accounts continue to be reported in error. Examples of noncounterbalancing errors are:

(a) Over- or understatement of depreciation expense; the accumulated depreciation and retained earnings balances are in error until corrected or until the asset is disposed of or fully depreciated. Also, the statements of income are in error for all of the reporting periods in which incorrect amounts of depreciation expense were recorded.

(b) Recognition of an expenditure (which should be debited to an asset account) as an expense, or vice versa, results in incorrect asset balances, expense amounts, and retained earnings until corrected or until the asset is disposed of or fully depreciated.

Correction of noncounterbalancing errors usually requires recognition of a **prior period adjustment** to correct for the **cumulative effect** of the errors in net income and in retained earnings.

Correcting Entries Illustrated

Correcting entries vary depending on the following:

a. Whether the error is counterbalancing or noncounterbalancing.
b. The period of time between the date the error was made and the date that the error was discovered.
c. Whether the temporary accounts have been adjusted and/or closed for the year that the error was discovered.

Six situations are given below that involve both counterbalancing and noncounterbalancing errors. For each situation, the correcting entry is given (assuming no income tax effects). As illustrated in Exhibit 24–4, when an error made in a prior period is corrected, the cumulative effect of the error is reported in the discovery (i.e., current) period as a **prior period adjustment.** Because prior period adjustments are closed to Retained Earnings, the prior period adjustment corrects the **beginning balance** of that account for the current year.

Situation 1: Error in merchandise inventory. The ending inventory for 19A was understated by $1,000.

Case A—The 19A error was found at the end of 19B (before books were adjusted and closed for 19B).

Analysis: Income for 19A was understated by $1,000; thus, retained earnings at the start of 19B is understated by this amount. Also, the **beginning** inventory for 19B is understated by $1,000.

Correcting entry during 19B to restate the 19B beginning inventory:

Inventory, beginning	1,000	
Prior period adjustment (retained earnings)		1,000

Case B—Assume that the 19A inventory error was found during 19C instead of 19B; the 19B books were closed.

Analysis: Counterbalanced at the end of 19B; income for 19A was understated by $1,000, and income for 19B was overstated by the same amount. Therefore, Retained Earnings and all other statement of financial position accounts are correct at the end of 19B. **No correcting entry is needed in 19C.** Restate 19A and 19B financial statements to a correct basis for all subsequent reporting purposes.

Situation 2: Error in both purchases and inventory. A $2,000 credit purchase in 19A was not recorded until 19B when payment was made; also the goods were **not** included in the 19A ending inventory.

Case A—The two 19A errors were discovered in 19B (before books were closed for 19B).

Analysis: In 19A, both purchases and ending inventory were understated by the same amount; therefore, because they have opposite effects on cost of goods sold and income, the income reported for 19A was correct. However, on the 19A year-end statement of financial position both inventory and payables were understated by $2,000. Also, in 19B, both inventory (beginning) and purchases are in error.

Correcting entry in 19B:

Inventory, beginning	2,000	
Purchases (periodic inventory system)		2,000

Case B—Assume that the two 19A errors were discovered in 19C instead of 19B; the 19B books were closed.

Analysis: Both errors **counterbalanced** in 19B; therefore, no correcting entry is needed in 19C. Restate 19A and 19B financial statements to a correct basis for all subsequent reporting purposes.

Situation 3: Error in prepaid expense. A five-year fire insurance policy was acquired on January 1, 19A. The five-year premium of $500 was paid and debited in full to insurance expense in 19A. No adjustment was made to recognize the asset at the end of 19A.

Case A—The error was discovered at the end of 19B (before books were closed for 19B).

Analysis: In 19A, insurance expense was overstated and income understated by $400. Also in 19A, both prepaid insurance and retained earnings were understated by $400. No insurance expense for 19B has been recorded because the full $500 was expensed in 19A.

Correcting entry at the end of 19B:

Prepaid insurance ($500 × ⅘)	400	
Prior period adjustment (retained earnings)		400

Adjusting entry for insurance expense:

Insurance expense ($500 ÷ 5 years)	100	
Prepaid insurance		100

Case B—Assume that the 19A error was discovered in 19C instead of 19B:

Correcting entry in 19C:

Prepaid insurance ($500 × 3/5)	300	
Prior period adjustment (retained earnings)		300

Adjusting entry for insurance at the end of 19C:

Insurance expense ($500 ÷ 5 years)	100	
Prepaid insurance		100

Situation 4: Error in accrued expense. Accrued property tax payable of $100 for 19A was not recorded. The tax was paid early in 19B and was recorded as expense when paid.

Case A—The 19A error was discovered at the end of 19B (before books were closed for 19B).

Analysis: In 19A, tax expense was understated and income overstated. Also, liabilities were understated and retained earnings overstated by $100. Tax expense for 19B is overstated by $100 because the expense was not recorded until payment was made in 19B.

Correcting entry at end of 19B:

Prior period adjustment (retained earnings)	100	
Tax expense		100

Case B—Assume that the 19A error was found during 19C instead of 19B; the 19C books are not closed.

Analysis: The error **counterbalanced** in 19B because 19A income was overstated. Also, 19B income was understated by the same amount. **No correcting entry is needed for 19C.** Restate 19A and 19B financial statements to a correct basis for all subsequent reporting purposes.

Situation 5: Error in revenue earned but not yet collected. Interest receivable of $75 earned by the end of 19A was not recorded. The interest was collected in 19B and recorded as revenue when collected.

Case A—The error was discovered at the end of 19B (before books were closed).

Analysis: In 19A, both interest revenue and net income were understated. On the statement of financial position, receivables and retained earnings were understated. In 19B, interest revenue is overstated because it was recorded when the collection was made in 19B.

Correcting entry at end of 19B:

Interest revenue	75	
Prior period adjustment (retained earnings)		75

Case B—Assume that the 19A error was discovered during 19C instead of 19B; the 19C books are not closed.

Analysis: The error **counterbalanced** in 19B because 19A income was understated and 19B income was overstated by the same amount. **No correcting entry is needed in 19C.** Restate 19A and 19B financial statements to a correct basis for all subsequent reporting purposes.

Situation 6: Expense capitalized as an asset when incurred. On January 1, 19A, $500 was expended for ordinary repairs; the $500 was debited to the Machinery account, which was being depreciated 10% per year.

Case A—The 19A error was discovered at the end of 19B (before books were adjusted for 19B).

Analysis: For 19A, repair expense was understated and depreciation expense overstated. Also, income was overstated by the difference. On the statement of financial position, assets were overstated and retained earnings overstated by $500 × 90% = $450.

Correcting entry at end of 19B:

Accumulated depreciation (for 19A; $500 × 10%)	50	
Prior period adjustment (retained earnings, $500 × 90%)	450	
Machinery		500

Case B—Assume that the 19A error was discovered during 19C instead of 19B (before the adjustment for depreciation expense was made for 19C).

Correcting entry during 19C:

Accumulated depreciation (for 19A and 19B; $500 × 10% × 2 years)	100	
Prior period adjustment (retained earnings; $500 × 80%)	400	
Machinery		500

These illustrations indicate the care that must be taken in analyzing and correcting errors. Fundamental to the analysis are the following:

1. A clear understanding of how the **incorrect entry** was made, or whether a needed entry was omitted.
2. A determination of what the **correct entry** should have been and when it should have been made.
3. Development of a **correcting entry** needed at the discovery date to bring all of the accounts affected by the error into agreement with their correct balances by taking into account all effects of the error between the date of the error and the discovery date.

Worksheet Techniques for Correcting Errors

Usually errors can be analyzed and appropriate accounting can be developed without a worksheet. However, when errors are numerous and complicated, a worksheet approach often is helpful. An efficient worksheet usually can be designed to meet the needs of the particular situation.[7] In the remainder of this section of the chapter two different worksheets that are often used will be presented.

Exhibit 24–5 shows a worksheet useful for *(a)* computing correct income for each of several periods and *(b)* providing data for the correcting entries in the year of correction. Panel A gives the case data. Panel B shows the worksheet, and panel C gives the combined correcting entry. A separate correcting entry could be made for each of the five errors with the same result.

Another group of problems commonly requires recasting of incorrect account balances to develop correct statements of income and financial position and statement of retained earnings. **Exhibit 24–6** shows a worksheet designed for this purpose. It concentrates on the statements of income and financial position, and the statement of retained earnings. A separate worksheet would have to be designed for the statement of cash flows (SCF) as shown in Chapter 19.

Supplement 24–A discusses the preparation of financial statements from incomplete records. The analyses and the worksheet presented are also adaptable to correcting errors.

Summary

This chapter discussed two topics—accounting changes and error correction. Accounting changes are classified as follows: *(a)* change in accounting principle, such as a change from straight-line to declining-balance depreciation, *(b)* change in estimate, such as a change in the estimated useful life of an operational asset from 20 years to 15 years, and *(c)* change in reporting entity, such as a change to preparing consolidated statements (not discussed in this book). An accounting change is recorded and reported using one of three approaches. The **current approach** recognizes the cumulative effect of the change (called the **catch-up** adjustment) as a separate item on the current statement of income between "income before extraordinary items" and "net income"; also, pro forma data must be reported. In the **prospective approach** the cumulative effect of the change is included only in the current and future reporting periods (no catch-up adjustment is recorded). When the **retroactive approach** is used, catch-up adjustment is recorded and reported as an adjustment of the beginning balance of retained earnings.

Accounting errors made in prior reporting periods must be corrected when discovered. The net effect of such an error is recorded and reported as a prior period adjustment (to the beginning balance of retained earnings). Accounting errors are classified as *(a)* counterbalancing, if they self-correct over two consecutive reporting periods, such as an error in the ending inventory, and *(b)* noncounterbalancing, if they do not self-correct in two reporting periods, such as depreciation.

Full disclosure of accounting changes and error correction is required. The emphasis in recording and reporting accounting changes and error correction is on comparability, consistency, full disclosure, and the matching principle.

---

[7] A reasonable skill in worksheet design often is quite helpful in tackling problems on examinations.

Exhibit 24–5
Worksheet to correct net income.

Panel A—Case Data:

1. The first audit of Company X, covering years 19A, 19B, and 19C, discovered the following errors (the books for 19C, but not 19D, have been closed):

Error	19A	19B	19C
a. Prepaid expense (i.e. asset) not recognized at each year-end (i.e., the amount was incorrectly expensed when the cash was paid one year earlier). Example: Prepaid interest expense	$100	$300	$400
b. Revenue collected in advance at year-end (i.e., the revenue was incorrectly recognized each year-end as earned when the cash was collected earlier). Example: Rent revenue collected one year in advance	300	500	100
c. Accrued expenses incurred but not recognized by each year-end (was not recognized until paid the next period). Example: Wages payable	600	800	500
d. Accrued revenue (earned but not collected) not recognized at each year-end (i.e., the revenue had been earned by year-end but was uncollected; the revenue was incorrectly recognized as earned in the next period when collected). Example: Rent revenue receivable	500	400	600
e. Depreciation expense understated. Example: Depreciation expense not recorded at each year-end	200	200	200

2. Reported pretax income, uncorrected for the above errors, was 19A, $5,000; 19B, $7,000; and $6,000. The accounting year ends December 31.

Panel B—Worksheet to Compute Correct Income at Each Year-End:

Item	Income		
	19A	19B	19C
Reported income (pretax)	$5,000	$7,000	$6,000
Corrections:			
a. Prepaid interest expense not recognized as asset:			
19A	+100	−100	
19B		+300	−300
19C			+400*
b. Rent revenue collected in advance not recognized as liability:			
19A	−300	+300	
19B		−500	+500
19C			−100*
c. Accrued wages not recognized in:			
19A	−600	+600	
19B		−800	+800
19C			−500*
d. Accrued rent revenue not recognized in:			
19A	+500	−500	
19B		+400	−400
19C			+600*
e. Depreciation understated:			
19A	−200		
19B		−200	
19C			−200*
Correct income (pretax)	$4,500	$6,500	$6,800

* Requires correcting entry, January 19D.

Exhibit 24–5
(concluded)

Panel C—Correcting Entry During January 19D, Year of Correction (books already closed for 19C):

a.	Prepaid interest expense	400	
d.	Rent receivable	600	
	Prior period adjustment (correction of errors)†	200	
b.	Rent revenue collected in advance		100
c.	Accrued wages payable		500
e.	Accumulated depreciation		600

† Because the books have been closed for 19C, the amount ($200) of this prior period adjustment to Retained Earnings is the cumulative effect of all errors through 19C, which did not self-correct. For items *a–d,* the 19A and 19B errors self-corrected in 19B and 19C. However, for item *e,* none of the amounts self-corrected. Therefore, the cumulative adjustment to the January 1, 19D, balance of Retained Earnings would be a debit of $200 [i.e., from Panel B, col. 19C, $400 − $100 −$500 + $600 − ($200 × 3)].

SUPPLEMENT 24–A: PREPARATION OF FINANCIAL STATEMENTS FROM SINGLE-ENTRY AND OTHER INCOMPLETE RECORDS

Most businesses maintain a record of all transactions based on the "double-entry" system. However, **many small businesses,** especially sole proprietorships, maintain only a single-entry system that records the "bare essentials." In some cases only records of cash, accounts receivable, accounts payable, and taxes paid may be maintained. Records of operational assets, inventories, expenses, revenues, and other elements usually considered essential in an accounting system may not be kept, except in memorandum form. However, such incomplete data, plus other information that often can be assembled, usually can be analyzed to provide a reasonably complete statement of income and financial position.

Preparation of Statement of Financial Position from Single-Entry Records

Single-entry records usually provide little information about assets (other than cash and accounts receivable). Therefore, preparation of the SFP in such situations involves identification and measurement of various assets and liabilities. The cost of the operational assets must be determined or estimated from available data. Canceled checks, receipts, bills of sale, papers transferring title to real estate, and other similar records provide the needed data. Once the cost of each operational asset is determined, depreciation can be computed. The amount of merchandise, supplies, and other inventories on hand may be obtained by actual count. If original cost cannot be determined, merchandise and supplies can be recorded at current replacement cost.

Similarly, notes payable and other liabilities (except accounts payable for which there is generally an invoice from the seller) must be obtained from memoranda, correspondence, and even by consultation with creditors.

Exhibit 24–7 shows the preparation of a SFP and computation of income or loss for the period in a simple situation. Panel A presents the case data. Panel B shows the SFP. Owner's equity is the difference between total assets and total liabilities. Panel C computes the net income or loss for the period. It is the difference between ending and beginning owner's equity adjusted for owner investments and withdrawals. The following schedule shows the procedure

Exhibit 24–6

Worksheet to correct statements of income, financial position and retained earnings.

Panel A—Case Data:

Uncorrected and unadjusted trial balance at December 31, 19B—as shown in first two columns of the worksheet.
Additional data: *(a)* Merchandise inventory, December 31, 19A, overstated, $4,000 (periodic inventory); *(b)* prepaid advertising of $2,000 at December 31, 19B, not recorded; *(c)* prepaid insurance of $2,000 at December 31, 19B, not recognized because the entire premium, paid on June 1, 19B, was debited to expense; *(d)* accrued sales salaries of $1,000 at December 31, 19A, not recorded; *(e)* accrued utilities expense of $1,000 at December 31, 19B, not recorded (classify as general expense); *(f)* no provision was made for doubtful accounts—the amounts should have been 19A, $1,000, and 19B, $3,000 (classify as general expense); *(g)* depreciation expense was not recorded prior to 19B, $15,000, 19B, $5,000 (classify as general expense); *(h)* cash shortage at end of 19B, $1,000 (classify as general expense); *(i)* premium on capital stock is included in the amount credited to the Capital Stock account; and *(j)* 19B ending inventory correctly determined, $32,000.

Panel B—Worksheet to Correct Statements of Income, Financial Position, and Retained Earnings

Account	Uncorrected trial balance		Correcting and adjusting entries		Statement of income		Statement of retained earnings		Statement of financial position	
	Debit	Credit	Debit	Credit	Debit	Credit	Debit	Credit	Debit	Credit
Cash	9,000			*(h)* 1,000					8,000	
Receivables	20,000								20,000	
Allowance for doubtful accounts				*(f)* 4,000						4,000
Inventory, beginning*	30,000			*(a)* 4,000	26,000					
Equipment	60,000								60,000	
Accumulated depreciation				*(g)* 20,000						20,000
Accounts payable		5,000								5,000
Capital stock, par $10, 7,500 shares outstanding		76,000	*(i)* 1,000							75,000
Retained earnings, beginning		25,000						25,000		
Prior period adjustments:										
Inventory (CGS) correction			*(a)* 4,000				4,000			
Salary expense correction (19A)			*(d)* 1,000				1,000			
Bad debt expense correction			*(f)* 1,000				1,000			
Depreciation expense correction			*(g)* 15,000				15,000			

Sales revenue		130,000				130,000				
Purchases	90,000				90,000					
Selling expenses	17,000			*(b)* 2,000	14,000					
				(d) 1,000						
General expenses	10,000		*(e)* 1,000	*(c)* 2,000	18,000					
			(f) 3,000							
			(g) 5,000							
			(h) 1,000							
	236,000	236,000								
Prepaid advertising			*(b)* 2,000						2,000	
Prepaid insurance			*(c)* 2,000						2,000	
Utilities payable				*(e)* 1,000						1,000
Inventory, ending*						32,000			32,000	
Contributed capital in excess of par				*(i)* 1,000						1,000
Net income					14,000			14,000		
Retained earnings balance							18,000			18,000
			36,000	36,000	162,000	162,000	39,000	39,000	124,000	124,000

*Alternative entries could be made for the beginning and ending inventories with the same results.

Exhibit 24–7

Incomplete records—preparation of the statement of financial position and computation of income (loss).

Panel A—Case Data:

1. Brown Company was organized by A. A. Brown on January 1, 19A; on this date the owner invested $4,500 cash in the business. During 19A, no formal records were kept.
2. Additional data for 19A:
   a. December 31, cash on hand and on deposit, $2,345—from count of cash and bank statement.
   b. December 31, merchandise inventory, $1,550—Count made by Brown, costed at current replacement cost because purchase invoices were not available.
   c. Office and store equipment acquired on January 1, 19A, $500—from invoice found in the files.
   d. Brown agreed that a depreciation rate of 5% per annum, with no material amount of residual value, was reasonable.
   e. Note receivable, dated December 31, 19A, $50—This note, signed by a customer for goods purchased, was in the files.
   f. December 31, accounts receivable, $90—Brown maintained a Charge Book that listed four customers as owing a total of $90; Brown was positive that the bills were outstanding. You called the customers for verification.
   g. December 31, accounts payable, $240—The "unpaid invoices" file contained two invoices that totaled to this amount; Brown assured you that they were the only unpaid invoices.

Panel B—Statement of Financial Position Prepared from Incomplete Data:

BROWN COMPANY
Statement of Financial Position
At December 31, 19A

Assets			**Liabilities**	
Current assets:			Current liabilities:	
Cash		$2,345	Accounts payable	$ 240
Accounts receivable		90	Long-term liabilities	None
Notes receivable, trade		50	Total liabilities	240
Merchandise inventory		1,550		
Total current assets		4,035	**Owner's Equity**	
Property and equipment:			A. A. Brown, proprietorship ($4,510 − $240)	4,270
Office and store equipment	$500			
Less: Accumulated depreciation	25	475	Total liabilities and owner's equity	$4,510
Total assets		$4,510		

Panel C—Income (Loss) Computed:

BROWN COMPANY
Computation of Net Loss
For the Year Ended December 31, 19A

Owner's equity, January 1, 19A	$4,500
Owner's equity, December 31, 19A	4,270
Net loss for period	$ 230

for determining income when investments or withdrawals have occurred during the period:

	Computation where there was	
	An income	A loss
Owner's equity, end of period	$8,000	$5,500
Owner's equity, beginning of period	7,100	6,300
Change increase (decrease)	900	(800)
Add: Withdrawals during period	1,200	1,000
	2,100	200
Deduct: Additional investments during period	500	300
Income for period	$1,600	
Loss for period		$ (100)

Preparation of the Statement of Income from Incomplete Data

Income or loss for the period can be computed as shown in the preceding section. However, knowing only the amount of income or loss does not identify the components of income needed by financial statement users. For example, banks and other credit grantors usually request a statement setting out the details of operations. The Internal Revenue Service requires a detailed statement of revenues and expenses for income tax purposes.

It is possible to prepare an itemized statement of income in the conventional form from single-entry records and supplemental data without converting the records to double-entry form. Much of the needed detail may be obtained through an analysis of the cash receipts and disbursement records. The preparation of a statement of income from single-entry data is illustrated in **Exhibit 24–8.** Panel A presents the case data. Panel B illustrates schedules used to compute sales revenue, purchases, depreciation, and other expenses, respectively. Panel C shows the related statement of income.

Worksheets for Problems from Single-Entry and Other Incomplete Records

The preceding example (Exhibit 24–8) suggests the need for a worksheet approach to reduce clerical work and minimize errors and omissions. A worksheet provides several internal checks on accuracy. Also, it recognizes each group of transactions in terms of their debit and credit effects. To provide a "track record," such worksheets should be accompanied by explanations and computations of the analyses involved.

Exhibit 24–9 shows a worksheet designed to develop statements of income and financial position based on incomplete records. Panel A presents the case data. Panel B illustrates the worksheet. The entries on the worksheet should be studied carefully. Each entry is explained in panel C of the exhibit.

Limitations of Single-Entry Record Keeping

Single-entry record keeping is used by many small businesses, by nonprofit organizations, by persons acting in a fiduciary capacity as administrators or executors of estates, and by many individuals for their personal affairs. Even some regular systems of record keeping recommended for retail outlets by

Exhibit 24–8
Preparation of statement of income from incomplete data.

Panel A—Case Data:

	19A Jan. 1	19A Dec. 31
Account balances:		
Accounts and trade notes receivable (no doubtful accounts)	$35,000	$48,000
Inventory (from physical count)	6,900	8,700
Building and equipment (appraised at estimated cost less depreciation)	17,000	17,400
Prepaid expenses (from memoranda)	100	110
Accounts payable (from files)	8,100	9,200
Notes payable (for equipment, from files)		500
Cash on hand (from cash register)	60	110
Liability for accrued expenses (from memoranda)	120	150
Salaries paid		7,000

	19A
Analysis of bank statements:	
Bank overdraft, 1/1/19A	$ 2,800
Deposits during year:	
Collections on account	42,000
Additional capital contributions by owner	10,000
Checks drawn during year for:	
Purchases (goods for resale)	26,000
Expenses	6,000
Salaries of employees	7,000
Withdrawals by owner	3,000
Purchase of equipment	340

Panel B—Computation of Statement of Income Items:

1. Sales revenue:		
Accounts and trade notes receivable, 12/31/19A		$ 48,000
Cash collected from customers and deposited		42,000
Increase of cash on hand ($110 − $60)		50
Less: Accounts and trade notes receivable, 1/1/19A		(35,000)
Sales revenue for the year, 19A		$ 55,050
2. Purchases:		
Accounts and trade notes payable, 12/31/19A		$ 9,200
Payments to creditors for purchases		26,000
Less: Accounts payable, 1/1/19A		(8,100)
Purchases for the year, 19A		$ 27,100
3. Depreciation expense:		
Net balance of buildings and equipment, 1/1/19A		$ 17,000
Purchases of equipment during 19A:		
By issue of note payable		500
By cash payment		340
Balance before depreciation		17,840
Less: Net balance on 12/31/19A (after 19A depreciation)		(17,400)
Depreciation expense for the year, 19A		$ 440
4. Remaining expenses:		
Expenses paid in cash during 19A		$ 6,000
Add: Expenses accrued on 12/31/19A		150
Prepaid expenses on 1/1/19A		100
Total		6,250
Deduct: Expenses accrued on 1/1/19A	$120	
Prepaid expenses on 12/31/19A	110	(230)
Other expenses for the year, 19A		$ 6,020

Exhibit 24–8
(concluded)

Panel C—Statement of Income for 19A:

Statement of Income
For Year Ended December 31, 19A

Sales revenue (panel B, item 1)		$55,050
Cost of goods sold:		
Inventory, 1/1/19A (given)	$ 6,900	
Purchases (panel B, item 2)	27,100	
Goods available for sale	34,000	
Less inventory, 12/31/19A (given)	8,700	
Cost of goods sold		25,300
Gross margin on sales		29,750
Less: Expenses:		
Depreciation (panel B, item 3)	440	
Other expenses (panel B, item 4)	6,020	
Salaries (given)	7,000	13,460
Net income		$16,290

trade associations and by manufacturers are maintained on a single-entry basis. One such system is used by a large number of small retail druggists. Single-entry records are used in the interest of simplicity. They are usually less expensive to maintain than double-entry systems because they do not require the services of a trained person. In fact, single-entry records are maintained by the proprietor or someone closely associated with the activities being recorded.

Single-entry record keeping usually is inadequate except where operations are especially simple and the volume of activity is small. Some of the more important disadvantages of single-entry systems are as follows:

1. Data may not be available to the management for effectively planning and controlling the business.
2. Lack of systematic and precise record keeping may lead to inefficient administration and reduced control over the affairs of the business.
3. Single-entry records do not provide a check against clerical errors, as does a double-entry system. This is one of the most serious defects of single-entry records.
4. Single-entry records seldom make provision for recording all transactions. Many internal transactions (i.e., those normally reflected through adjusting entries), in particular, often are not recorded.
5. Because no accounts are provided for many of the items appearing in both the statement of financial position and statement of income, omission of important data always is a possibility.
6. In the absence of detailed records of all assets, lax administration of those assets may occur.
7. Theft and other losses are less likely to be detected.

Exhibit 24–9
Worksheet to develop a detailed statement of income based on incomplete records.

Panel A—Case Data:

1. Main Company has been in business two years and has kept only incomplete records. An accountant prepared a statement of financial position at December 31, 19A, and a statement of financial position has been completed by "inventorying all assets and liabilities at December 31, 19B." These SFP accounts are entered on the worksheet as shown in panel B.
2. Additional data for 19B, developed in various ways as follows:
   a. Main kept no record of cash receipts and disbursements, but an analysis of canceled checks provided the following summary of payments: accounts payable, $71,000; expenses, $20,700; and purchase of equipment, $3,700. No checks appeared to be outstanding.
   b. Main stated that $100 cash was withdrawn regularly each week from the cash register for personal use. No record was made of these personal withdrawals.
   c. The $5,000 bank loan was for one year, the note was dated July 1, 19B, and 6% interest was deducted from the face amount (cash proceeds, $4,700).
   d. Main stated that equipment listed in the January 1 SFP at $900 was sold for $620 cash.
   e. The bank reported that it had credited Main with $4,000 during the year for customers' notes that Main left for collection.
   f. One $400 note on hand December 31, 19B, was past due and appeared worthless. Therefore, this note was not included in the $3,000 notes receivable listed in the December 31, 19B, SFP. Assume no allowance for doubtful accounts; bad debts are written off directly to expense because of immateriality.

Panel B—Worksheet to Develop Statement of Income (Main Company):

Account	Beginning balances 1/1/19B	Interim entries Debit	Interim entries Credit	Statement of income	Ending balances 12/31/19B
Debit accounts:					
Cash	10,000	(c) 4,700	(a) 95,400		22,000
		(d) 620	(b) 5,200		
		(e) 4,000			
		(h) 103,280			
Notes receivable	5,000	(g) 2,400	(e) 4,000		3,000
			(f) 400		
Accounts receivable	61,000	(i) 112,680	(g) 2,400		68,000
			(h) 103,280		
Inventories	25,000	(j) 27,000	(j) 25,000		27,000
Prepaid expenses	500	(c) 150	(k) 500		200
		(k) 50			
Furniture and equipment (net)	10,600	(a) 3,700	(d) 900		12,400
			(l) 1,000		
Expenses		(a) 20,700	(k) 50	21,000	
		(k) 500	(n) 800		
		(n) 650			
Interest expense		(c) 150		150	
Loss on sale of equipment		(d) 280		280	
Loss on worthless note		(f) 400		400	
Depreciation expense		(l) 1,000		1,000	
Purchases		(m) 77,000		77,000	
Net income		(o) 14,850		14,850	
	112,100			114,680	132,600
Credit accounts:					
Bank loan payable			(c) 5,000		5,000
Accounts payable	30,000	(a) 71,000	(m) 77,000		36,000
Accrued expenses payable	800	(n) 800	(n) 650		650
Main, owner's equity	81,300	(b) 5,200	(o) 14,850		90,950
Sales revenue			(i) 112,680	112,680	
Income summary (inventory change)		(j) 25,000	(j) 27,000	2,000	
	112,100	476,110	476,110	114,680	132,600

Exhibit 24–9
(concluded)

Panel C—Explanation of Entries on Worksheet (Main Company):

a. To record cash payments shown by analysis of canceled checks.

b. To record Main's cash withdrawals of $100 per week for 52 weeks.

c. To record bank loan of $5,000 less $300 interest of which $150 was prepaid as of December 31, 19B.

d. To record sale of equipment (cost less depreciation, $900) for $620 cash.

e. To record $4,000 notes receivable collected by bank.

f. To record write-off of bad note, $400.

g. To record notes from customers, computed as follows (data taken directly from worksheet).

Notes collected	$ 4,000
Note written off	400
Notes on hand, 12/31/19B	3,000
	7,400
Less: Notes on hand, 1/1/19B	5,000
Notes receivable (received on accounts)	$ 2,400

h. Cash collected from customers (notice that it does not matter whether the collection was at time of sale or on account) is computed as follows from data shown in the Cash account on the worksheet:

Cash paid out ($95,400 + $5,200)	$100,600
Cash balance, 12/31/19B	22,000
	122,600
Cash collected from all sources other than from customers: ($4,700 + $620 + $4,000)	9,320
	113,280
Less: Cash balance, 1/1/19B	10,000
Cash collected from customers	$103,280

i. Sales are computed by finding the only "missing entry" in **accounts receivable,** which entry is for sales on account. (Balance in notes receivable has already been reconciled on the worksheet.)

Note received on account (item *g*)	$ 2,400
Cash collected from customers (item *h*)	103,280
Ending balance of accounts receivable	68,000
Total credits and balance	173,680
Less: January 1 balance	61,000
Total debits for the year (sales revenue)	$112,680

j. To close the January 1 inventory and to record the December 31 inventory (to income summary).

k. To adjust the balance of prepaid expenses and to increase the prepaid expense balance as of December 31 to $200 as given.

l. To set up the depreciation expense for the period. All entries have been made in the Furniture and Equipment account on the worksheet except the 19B depreciation credit. Depreciation is computed as follows:

Furniture and equipment, 1/1/19B	$ 10,600
Equipment purchased	3,700
	14,300
Less: Equipment sold	900
	13,400
Less: Balance of furniture and equipment, 12/31/19B	12,400
Depreciation expense for the period	$ 1,000

m. Purchases are computed by finding the missing entry in accounts payable on the worksheet as follows:

Payments on accounts payable	$ 71,000
Balance of accounts payable, 12/31/19B	36,000
	107,000
Less: Accounts payable, 1/1/19B	30,000
Purchases for the period	$ 77,000

n. To transfer the beginning balance ($800) of accrued expenses payable to expense and to record accrued expenses payable as of December 31. Note that entry *a* on the worksheet transfers all of the expenses paid in cash during 19B to the Expense account. As a result, the beginning and ending balances of Accrued Expense Payable, respectively, are entered in the Expense account.

o. To close net income to owner's equity. The net income may be computed by analyzing the changes in capital from January 1 to December 31, 19B, as illustrated previously or by extending the balances in the temporary accounts to the Income Statement column and then computing the difference between the debits and credits. One computation serves as a check on the other.

QUESTIONS

Part A

1. Distinguish among the following: *(a)* change in principle, *(b)* change in estimate, *(c)* change in reporting entity, and *(d)* accounting error.
2. What are the three basic ways to account for the effects of accounting changes and error corrections?

3. Complete the following schedule:

	Method of reflecting the effect*		
	(1) ______	(2) ______	(3) ______
a. Change in estimate	______	______	______
b. Change in principle	______	______	______
c. Correction of error	______	______	______

* Identify these three captions; then enter appropriate check on each line.

4. What are pro forma statements? Why are they used in respect to some accounting changes?
5. Explain the basic difference between an accounting change and an error correction.
6. Why are the effects of changes from LIFO to other inventory flow methods required to be accounted for retroactively when changes to LIFO from another method are reflected as changes in the income of the year the change is made?
7. Other than changing from LIFO to another inventory flow method (which must be reflected retroactively), what other types of accounting changes must be accorded retroactive treatment rather than being accounted for using the current basis?
8. *APB Opinion 20* deals with three types of accounting changes in addition to error corrections. The three types of accounting changes involve *(a)* principles, *(b)* estimates, and *(c)* reporting entities. Using these letters and the letter *(d)* for error corrections, identify each of the following types of change:
   (1) A lessor discovers while a long-term capital lease term is in progress that an estimated material unguaranteed residual value of the leased property has probably become zero.
   (2) A corporation with foreign subsidiaries has used the cost method of accounting for its investments in the subsidiary companies since they were acquired because economic conditions in the countries in which the subsidiary companies operate have been unstable and exchange of foreign currency into dollars has been restricted. Under changed, improved conditions, it has become feasible for the controlling entity to prepare consolidated statements instead, thereby eliminating the foreign investment account from the statement of financial position of the corporation.
   (3) After 5 years of use, an asset originally estimated to have a 15-year life is now to be depreciated on the basis of a 20-year life.
   (4) Because of inability to estimate reliably, a contractor began business using the completed contract method. Now that reliable estimates can be made, the percentage-of-completion method is adopted.
   (5) Office equipment purchased last year is discovered to have been debited to Office Expense when acquired. Appropriate accounting is to be applied at the discovery date.
   (6) A company that has been using the FIFO inventory method now is changing to LIFO.
   (7) A company which used 1% of sales to estimate its bad debt expense discovers losses are running higher than expected and changes to 2½%.

Part B

9. What is the difference between a counterbalancing and a noncounterbalancing error? Basically, why is the distinction significant in the analysis of errors?
10. Complete the schedule below by entering a plus to indicate overstatement, a minus to indicate understatement, and a zero if no effect.

	Effect of error on			
	Net income	Assets	Liabilities	Owners' equity
a. Ending inventory for 19A understated:				
19A financial statements	______	______	______	______
19B financial statements	______	______	______	______
b. Ending inventory for 19B overstated:				
19B financial statements	______	______	______	______
19C financial statements	______	______	______	______
c. Failed to record depreciation in 19A:				
19A financial statements	______	______	______	______
19B financial statements	______	______	______	______
d. Failed to record a liability resulting from revenue collected in advance at end of 19A; instead, credited revenue in full erroneously:				
19A financial statements	______	______	______	______
19B financial statements	______	______	______	______

11. Give two examples of each of the following types of errors:
    a. Affects statement of income only.
    b. Affects statement of financial position only.
    c. Affects both statement of income and statement of financial position.

EXERCISES

Part A: Exercises 24–1 to 24–6

E 24–1 (Overview; Types of Accounting Changes and Errors)
Analyze each case and enter one letter code under each column (type and approach) to indicate the basic accounting for each case.

Case (event or transaction)	Type P = Principle E = Estimate R = Entity AE = Error	Approach C = Current R = Retroactive P = Prospective
1. Recorded expense, $870; should be $780	AE	R
2. Changed useful life of a machine	E	P
3. Changed from single company to consolidated financial statements	R	?
4. Changed from straight-line to accelerated depreciation	P	C
5. Change in residual value of an intangible operational asset	E	P
6. Changed from cash basis to accrual basis in accounting for bad debts	AE	R
7. Changed from percentage-completion to completed-contracts for long-term construction contracts	P	R
8. Changed from LIFO to FIFO for inventory	P	R
9. Changed both the useful life and method of depreciation (which predominates) for an operational asset	______	______
10. Changed to a new accounting principle required by the FASB	______	______

E 24–2 (Change in Estimated Useful Life; Entries; Reporting)
Stacy Corporation has been depreciating equipment over a 10-year life on a straight-line basis. The equipment, which cost $24,000, was purchased on January 1, 19A. It has an estimated residual value of $6,000. On the basis of experience since acquisition, the management has decided to depreciate it over a total life of 14 years instead of 10, with no change in the estimated residual value. The change is to be effective on January 1, 19E. The annual financial statements are prepared on a comparative basis (19D and 19E presented). 19D and 19E income before depreciation and any change effects for 19D and 19E were $49,800, and $52,800, respectively. Disregard income tax considerations.

Required:

1. Identify the type of accounting change involved and analyze the effects of the change. Which approach should be used—current, prospective, or retroactive? Explain.
2. Prepare the entry, or entries, to appropriately reflect the change in the accounts for 19E, the year of the change.
3. Illustrate how the change should be reported on the 19E financial statements, which include 19D results for comparative purposes (shares of common stock outstanding, 100,000).

E 24–3 (Change in Estimated Useful Life; Entries; Reporting)
On January 1, 19A, Mavis Company purchased a machine that cost $40,000. The estimated useful life was 12 years with an estimated residual value of $4,000. Starting on January 1, 19F, the company revised its estimates as follows: Total useful life, 18 years, and total residual value, $2,900. The company uses straight-line depreciation, and the reporting period ends December 31.

Required:

1. What kind of accounting change is this? How should it be accounted for—current, retroactive, or prospective? Explain.
2. Give all entries required in 19E and 19F related to this case. Disregard income tax considerations.
3. Show what related 19E and 19F amounts should be reported on the comparative 19F statement of income and statement of financial position.

E 24–4 (Change in Estimated Useful Life; Entries; Reporting)
Bite Corporation has been depreciating equipment over a 10-year life using the SYD method. The equipment was acquired January 1, 19A, and cost $68,000 (estimated residual value, $13,000). The company decided to change to straight-line depreciation, effective as of the beginning of 19E, with no change in the estimated useful life or the residual value. The annual accounting period ends December 31. The annual financial statements are prepared on a comparative basis (19D and 19E presented). Income before depreciation and prior to giving effect to this change was 19D, $55,000, and 19E, $57,500. Shares of stock outstanding were 100,000. Disregard income tax considerations.

Required:

1. Identify the type of accounting change involved and analyze the effects of the change. Which approach should be used—current, prospective or retroactive? Explain.
2. Prepare the entry, or entries, to appropriately reflect the change in the accounts in 19E, the year of the change, including the 19E adjusting entry.
3. Show how the change should be reported on the 19E financial statements which include 19D results for comparative purposes.

E 24–5 (Change SYD Depreciation to Straight-Line; Change Useful Life; Entries)
XY Sales Company has made several accounting changes to improve the matching of expenses with revenue. Assume it is the end of 19H, and that the accounting period

ends on December 31. The books have not been adjusted or closed at the end of 19H. Among the changes were the following:

a. Machinery that cost $25,000 (estimated useful life 10 years, residual value $3,000) has been depreciated using the SYD method. Early in the eighth year (19H), it was decided to change to straight-line depreciation (with no change in residual value or estimated life).

b. A patent that cost $8,500 is being amortized over its legal life of 17 years. Early in the 6th year (19H) since its acquisition, it was decided that the economic benefits would not last longer than 13 years from date of acquisition.

Required:

1. For each of the above situations, identify the type of accounting change that was involved, and briefly explain how it should be accounted for.
2. Give the appropriate entry to record the change and the 19H adjusting entry in each instance. Show computations and disregard income tax considerations. If no entry is required in a particular instance, explain why.

E 24–6 (Change from LIFO to FIFO; Entries; Reporting)

On January 1, 19D, Baker Company decided to change the inventory costing method used from LIFO to FIFO. The annual reporting period ends on December 31. The average income tax rate is 30%. The following related data were developed:

	LIFO basis	FIFO basis
Beginning inventory, 19C	$15,000	$15,000
Ending inventory:		
19C	20,000	35,000
19D		38,000
Net income:		
19C: LIFO basis	40,000	
19D: FIFO basis		45,000
Retained earnings:		
19C beginning balance	60,000	
Dividends declared and paid:		
19C	32,000	
19D		35,000
Common shares outstanding, 10,000.		

Required:

1. Identify the type of accounting change involved. Which approach should be used—current, prospective, or retroactive? Explain.
2. Give the entry(s) to record the effect of the change.
3. Complete the following schedule:

	FIFO basis	
	19C	19D
Comparative statement of financial position:		
Inventory	$	$
Retained earnings		
Comparative statement of income:		
Net income:		
19C		
19D		
Earnings per share		
Statement of retained earnings:		
Beginning balance		
Cumulative effect of accounting change		
Beginning balance restated		
Net income		
Dividends declared and paid		
Ending balance		

Part B: Exercises 24–7 to 24–15

E 24–7 (Errors, Analysis and Overview)
Indicate the effect of the errors and transactions listed below on income for 19A and 19B. Respond by placing one check mark for 19A and one for 19B under the appropriate heading. Each item is independent of the others.

Error	Income—19A			Income—19B		
	Over-stated	Under-stated	No effect	Over-stated	Under-stated	No effect
a. Ending inventory, 19A, overstated.	✓				✓	
b. Depreciation expense, 19B, understated.	✓				✓	
c. Did not recognize the inventory of office supplies at the end of 19A.			✓			✓
d. Did not amortize goodwill in 19A; amortization was recorded in 19B.	✓				✓	
e. Debited the cost of a depreciable asset to an operating expense account on January 1, 19A.		✓				
f. Merchandise purchased on credit in 19A was neither recorded nor included in the 19A inventory. Not sold in 19B.						
g. Did not include a large residual value on a depreciable asset, acquired in 19A (10-year life).		✓			✓	
h. Unpaid wages not accrued at the end of 19A.	✓				✓	
i. Did not record bad debt estimate in 19A.	✓					✓
j. Merchandise purchased on credit in 19A was not recorded, but was included in the 19A ending inventory.						
k. Wrote off a bad debt in 19A (not an error).						
l. Sold merchandise at a profit in 19A on credit; did not record it as sales revenue until 19B.						
m. Did not recognize interest payable in 19A.						
n. Did not amortize premium on bonds payable in 19A.						
o. Sold treasury stock at a gain (not an error).						

E 24–8 (Analysis of Eight Errors; Correcting Entries; Correct Pretax Income)
The 19E statement of income of Burke Corporation has just been tentatively completed. It reflects pretax income for 19E of $85,000. The accounts have not been closed for the year ended December 31, 19E. A review of the company's files and records revealed the following errors that have not been corrected:

a. Patent amortization of $3,000 per year was not recorded in 19D and 19E.
b. The 19C ending inventory was overstated by $4,000.
c. Machinery acquired on January 1, 19A (year 1), at a cost of $26,000, is being depreciated

on the straight-line basis over 10 years. The good faith estimate of its residual value of $6,000 has not been included in the computation of depreciation expense.

d. Accrued wages of $1,500 at December 31, 19D, were not recognized.

e. A $1,000 cash shortage during 19E was debited to Retained Earnings.

f. Ordinary repairs on the machinery in *(c)* above of $7,000, incurred during January 19E, were debited to the machinery account.

g. During 19E, treasury stock that cost $8,000 was sold for $11,000. The difference was credited to extraordinary gain. The company uses the cost method to account for treasury stock.

Required:

1. Give the correcting entry, if needed, for each of the above errors. Explain the basis and show computations for each item. Ignore income tax considerations.
2. Compute the correct pretax income amount for 19E. Set up an appropriate schedule that reflects each change and the "Correct 19E pretax income."

E 24–9 (Analysis of Four Errors; Correcting Entries; Correct Pretax Income)

Travis Corporation has just completed its financial statements for the reporting year ended December 31, 19X5. The pretax income amount is $160,000. The accounts have not been closed for December 31, 19X5. Further consideration and review of the records revealed the following items related to the 19X5 statements:

a. On January 1, 19X1, a machine was acquired that cost $10,000. The estimated useful life was 10 years, and the residual value was $2,000. At the time of acquisition, the full cost of the machine was incorrectly debited to the land account. Use straight-line depreciation.

b. On January 1, 19X3, a long-term investment of $18,000 was made by purchasing a $20,000, 8% bond of XT Corporation. The investment account was debited for $18,000. Each year, starting on December 31, 19X3, the company has recognized and reported investment revenue on these bonds of $1,600. The bonds mature in 10 years from date of purchase. Assume any amortization would be straight line and the net method is used to record the investment.

c. The 19X4 ending inventory was overstated by $7,000 (periodic inventory system).

d. A $11,000 credit purchase of merchandise occurred on December 18, 19X4. Because the merchandise was on hand on December 31, 19X4, it was included in the 19X4 ending inventory. The purchase was recorded on January 18, 19X5, when the invoice was paid.

Required:

1. Prepare any correcting and adjusting entries that should be made on December 31, 19X5, and reported on the 19X5 statement of income. Ignore income tax.
2. Compute the correct pretax income for 19X5. Set up an appropriate schedule that reflects each change and the "Correct pretax income, 19X5."

E 24–10 (Error; Comparative Statements; Correcting Entry; Reporting)

Bar Corporation had never been audited prior to December 31, 19D, the current year. Prior to the arrival of the auditor, the company accountant prepared comparative financial statements with 19C and 19D shown thereon. The accounts for 19D have not been closed. The auditors discovered that an invoice dated January 19A for $9,000 (paid in cash at that time) was debited to 19A operating expenses, although it was for the purchase of equipment. The equipment has an estimated useful life of 10 years and no estimated residual value.

Reported incomes reflected on the financial statements prepared by the company (prior to discovery of the error) were: 19A, $11,000; 19B, $22,000; 19C, $30,000; and 19D, $33,000. Shares of common stock outstanding, 100,000. Disregard income tax considerations.

Required:
1. Identify the type of change or correction involved and analyze the effects of the change or correction, as appropriate.
2. Give the entry, or entries, to appropriately record the change or correction in the accounts for 19D, the year of the change.
3. Show how the change or correction should be reported on the 19D comparative financial statements.

E 24–11 (Four Errors; Corrections Before and After Closing Compared; Entries)
Give the journal entries needed to correct the accounts, and the subsequent adjusting entry, for each of the errors described below assuming (1) the errors were discovered on December 31, 19B, before the books were adjusted or closed; and (2) the errors were discovered in January 19C (after the books for 19B were adjusted and closed). Assume each item is material. Disregard income tax considerations.

a. Merchandise that cost $6,000 was received on December 28, 19A, and was included in the ending inventory of 19A, but the credit purchase was not recorded in the purchases journal until January 13, 19B.
b. An entry was made on December 30, 19B, to write-off of organization expense as follows (assume only one year's amortization was justified for 19B; amortization per year, $1,000):

General expense	5,000	
Deferred organization expense		5,000

c. Discount of $3,300 on a long-term bond investment purchased on May 1, 19A, was written off directly and in full to Retained Earnings on that date. These bonds mature on July 1, 19J. Use straight-line amortization.
d. Machinery that cost $900 was purchased and debited in full to Repair Expense on June 30, 19A. The depreciation rate on machinery is 10% per year on cost (no residual value; depreciation is calculated on the number of months held).

E 24–12 (Errors; Prior Years Adjustments Not Recorded; Entries to Correct for Current Year)
You are auditing the accounts of Sun Merchandising Corporation for the year ended December 31, 19B. You discover that the adjustments made in the previous audit for the year 19A were not entered in the accounts by Sun's bookkeeper; therefore, the accounts are not in agreement with the audited amounts as of December 31, 19A. The following adjustments were included in the 19A audit report:

a. Invoices for merchandise purchased on credit in December 19A, not entered on the books until payment of $6,000 was made in January 19B; not included in the December 31, 19A, inventory. The company uses a periodic inventory system.
b. Invoices for merchandise received on credit in December 19A were not recorded in the accounts until payment was made in January 19B; the goods were included in the 19A ending inventory, $9,000.
c. Allowance for doubtful accounts for 19A was understated by $1,000 because bad debt expense in 19A was not recorded.
d. Selling expense for 19A was not recorded in the accounts until paid in January 19B, $2,500.
e. Accrued wages of $2,000 at December 31, 19A, were not recorded in the accounts until paid in January 19B.

f. Prepaid insurance at December 31, 19A, understated by $300 because this amount was included in 19A expense. The insurance policy expires on December 31, 19B.

g. Income tax expense for the last part of the year ended December 31, 19A, of $1,200 was not recorded until paid in January 19B.

h. Depreciation of $4,500 was not recorded for 19A.

Required:
You have the uncorrected and unadjusted trial balance dated December 31, 19B. Give the journal entry for each of the above items that should be made to the trial balance before using it for further 19B audit purposes. Disregard income tax implications.

E 24–13 **(Analysis of Four Accounts; Compute Correct Ending Balances)**
The accounts and financial statements of Slo Company have never been audited. A preliminary examination has shown numerous errors. Also, the files and supporting documentation are not available in some cases and unclear in others. As a consequence, you have been asked to compute the ending 19B balances of the four accounts identified below based on the data given. Each item is independent of the others. Show computations.

a. Wage expense, $__________.
Data: Amount paid during 19B, $15,000; accrued on December 31, 19A, $1,000; and accrued on December 31, 19B, $2,000.

b. Rent revenue, $__________.
Data: Amount collected during 19B, $8,000; unearned (collected in advance), $500 on December 31, 19A, and $300 on December 31, 19B; earned but not collected, $200 on December 31, 19A, and $600 on December 31, 19B.

c. Sales revenue, $__________.
Data: Cash account, balance, December 31, 19A, $26,000; balance, December 31, 19B, $33,000; and total disbursements for 19B, $39,000. All cash receipts were from customers. Accounts receivable: balance, December 31, 19A, $40,160; and balance, December 31, 19B, $59,000. Accounts written off during 19B as uncollectible, $960.

d. Purchases (net of cash discounts), $__________.
Data: Accounts payable balance on December 31, 19A, $28,320, and on December 31, 19B, $33,000; payments made on accounts during 19B, $46,000. Credit purchases are recorded net of cash discount whether taken or not.

E 24–14 **(Adjusting Entries Not Made for Three Years; Compute Pretax Incomes; Correcting and Adjusting Entries)**
Bowler Company has failed to recognize accruals and prepayments since organization three years previously. The pretax income, accruals, and prepayments at year-end are given below:

	Amounts incorrectly reported at year-end		
	19A	**19B**	**19C**
Reported pretax income (loss)	$14,000	$(7,000)	$15,000
Items not recognized at year-end (i.e., no adjusting entry was made for these items):			
a. Prepaid expense (insurance premium for the following year was debited in full to expense when paid)	200	280	109
b. Accrued expense (wages incurred but not yet paid)	250	225	247
c. Rent revenue collected in advance but not yet earned (revenue credited in full when rent was collected in advance)	325	360	293
d. Interest revenue earned but not yet collected	275	230	196

Required (disregard income tax considerations):

1. Compute the correct pretax income for each year. Set up an appropriate worksheet to reflect each change.
2. Give the entry to correct each item assuming the errors were discovered at year-end 19C (books were not closed for 19C).
3. Give the entry to correct each item assuming the errors were discovered early in 19D, after the 19C books were closed, but prior to any 19D entries related to these items.

E 24–15 (Based on Supplement 24–A; Incomplete Records; Worksheet to Develop Statement of Income and Statement of Financial Position)

On January 2, 19A, Star Retail Company was organized. During 19A, the company paid trade creditors $49,062 in cash and had an ending inventory per count (FIFO basis) of $9,563. Balances available on December 31, 19A, were the following: accounts payable, $16,125; expenses, $2,450 (no depreciation); M. Lane (sole proprietor), capital (representing beginning balance of cash on January 2, 19A), $45,000; accounts receivable, $13,188; and sales, $50,000. There were no withdrawals. All sales and purchases were on credit. The company is not subject to income tax.

Required:

1. Complete a worksheet to develop a correct statement of income and statement of financial position. Use a format similar to the following:

Accounts	Statement of financial position Jan. 2, 19A	Interim entries		Statement of income	Statement of financial position Dec. 31, 19A
		Debit	Credit		
Cash					
Accounts receivable					
Purchases					
Expenses					
Accounts payable					
M. Lane, capital					
Sales revenue					
Income summary					
Net gain (loss)					

2. Prepare a proof of the ending cash balance.

PROBLEMS

Part A: Problems 24–1 to 24–5

P 24–1 (Change from Declining Balance to Straight-Line Depreciation; Entries; Reporting)

On January 1, 19A, KLM Corporation purchased equipment that cost $23,000; the estimated useful life was 10 years with no estimated residual value. The company uses 200% declining-balance depreciation; however, at the start of 19F, the company decided to switch to straight-line depreciation (no change in useful life or residual value). At December 31, 19E, the annual financial statements reported the following correct amounts:

Depreciation expense (DB)	$ 1,884*
Accumulated depreciation (DB)	15,463
Shares of common stock outstanding, 10,000.	

* 19F, $1,507.

Net income before depreciation and before the effects of the accounting change was 19E, $40,000; and 19F, $47,000. Disregard income tax considerations.

Required:

1. What type of accounting change is this? What approach should be used—current, prospective, or retroactive? Explain.
2. Prepare the 19F (i.e., the year of change) entries to appropriately reflect the change; also prepare the 19F adjusting entry.
3. Show how the change and the amount of depreciation should be reported on the 19F comparative statement of income. Also, show how the asset should be reported on the 19F comparative statement of financial position including any required pro forma disclosure.

P 24–2 (Change from Straight Line to SYD; Income Tax; Entries; Reporting)

CRT Company purchased a machine on January 1, 19A, for $240,000. At the date of acquisition, the machine had an estimated useful life of 10 years with an estimated residual value of $20,000. The machine is being depreciated on a straight-line basis for financial reporting (i.e., accounting) purposes, but for income tax purposes, an accelerated method is used because of its cash flow advantage. On January 1, 19D, CRT changed, for financial reporting purposes, to an accelerated method of depreciation for this machine (with no change in estimated useful life or residual value). The accelerated depreciation amounts were: 19A, $40,000; 19B, $36,000; 19C, $32,000; and 19D, $28,000. The annual accounting period ends December 31. The annual financial statements are presented on a comparative basis (19C and 19D presented). CRT has an average income tax rate of 40% (for problem purposes only). Pretax income before depreciation and prior to giving effect to this change was 19C, $90,000; and 19D, $98,000. There are 10,000 shares of common stock outstanding.

Required:

1. Identify the type of accounting change involved. Which approach should be used—current, prospective, or retroactive? Explain.
2. Give the entry to appropriately reflect the accounting change in 19D, the year of change, including the 19D adjusting entry. Hint: Debit deferred income tax (to recognize income tax).
3. Show how the change should be reported on the 19D comparative statement of financial position (19C and 19D).
4. Prepare the comparative statement of income for 19D (19C and 19D), starting with pretax income before depreciation and prior to the effects of the change.

P 24–3 (Change from Completed Contract to Percentage of Completion; Entries; Reporting)

Modern Construction Company began operations on January 1, 19A. During 19A and 19B, the company used the completed contract (CC) basis to account for its long-term construction contracts.

At the start of 19C, the company changed to the percentage of completion (PC) basis.

The following data are available:

	19A		19B		19C	
Income (net of 30% income tax rate)	$70,000 (CC)		$120,000 (CC)		$185,000 (PC)	
Dividends	-0-		50,000		90,000	
Retained earnings (ending balance)	70,000 (CC)		140,000 (CC)			
Inventory of construction in process, net	CC	PC	CC	PC	CC	PC
of billings (ending balance)	$150,000	$165,000	$250,000	$350,000	$280,000	$360,000
Shares outstanding, 100,000.						

Required:

1. Identify the type of accounting change involved. How should it be accounted for—current, retroactive, prospective? Explain. Hint: The inventory of work in process must be adjusted.
2. Give the entry on January 1, 19C, to record this accounting change in 19C, the year of change (net of income tax).
3. Show how the following should be reported on the 19C comparative:
   a. Statement of financial position—inventory of construction in process and ending balance of retained earnings.
   b. Statement of income—starting with income before extraordinary items.
   c. Statement of retained earnings—starting with beginning balance (CC). The ending 19C balance of retained earnings is $305,000.

P 24–4 (Two Assets; Useful Life and Residual Value Changed; Entries; Reporting)

On January 1, 19A, TV Company purchased a machine that cost $78,000. The estimated useful life was 20 years with an estimated residual value of $8,000. Starting on January 1, 19H, the company revised its estimates to 16 years for total life and $9,000 for residual value.

The company also owns a patent that cost $34,000 when acquired on January 1, 19E. It is being amortized over its legal life of 17 years (no residual value). On January 1, 19H, the patent is estimated to have a total useful life of only 13 years (no residual value). The company uses the straight-line method for both of these assets. The annual reporting period ends December 31. Disregard income tax considerations.

Required:

1. What kinds of accounting changes are involved? How should each change be accounted for—current, retroactive, or prospective? Explain.
2. Give all entries required in 19G and 19H related to these changes.
3. Show what amounts related to these changes should be reported on the comparative 19H statement of income and statement of financial position.

P 24–5 (Analysis of Three Accounting Changes: Principle, Current; Retroactive; Estimate, Prospective)

During 19D, Sugarland Corporation completed an analysis of its operational assets with the purpose of updating its accounting procedures used to compute depreciation, inventory costing, and amortization each reporting period. The annual reporting period ends December 31. Decisions have been made concerning the three different assets listed below (designated Cases A, B, and C for convenience). The indicated accounting changes are to be implemented starting January 1, 19E, the fifth year of operations for this new company. Disregard income tax considerations.

Case A

Machine A, acquired on January 1, 19A, at a cost of $60,000, is being depreciated straight line over an estimated 10-year useful life; residual value is $5,000. On January 1, 19E, the company will start using SYD depreciation (with no other changes).

Required:

1. Identify the type of accounting change and the approach that should be used—current, retroactive, or prospective. Explain.
2. Give the following entries:
   a. Depreciation adjusting entry at the end of 19D.
   b. 19E entry to record the accounting change in 19E. Explain.
   c. Depreciation adjusting entry at the end of 19E.
3. Explain:
   a. How the catch-up adjustment (i.e., the change effect) recorded in Requirement 2 is reported on the 19E comparative financial statements.
   b. How the 19D financial statement amounts are reported in the 19E comparative statements.

Case B

On January 1, 19E, the company changed from LIFO to FIFO for inventory costing purposes. The ending inventory for 19D was: LIFO basis, $12,000, and FIFO basis, $17,000. Ending inventory for 19E, FIFO basis, was $19,000.

Required:

1. Identify the type of accounting change and the approach that should be used—current, retroactive, or prospective. Explain.
2. Give the entry to record the catch-up adjustment (i.e., the change effect) in the year of change.
3. Explain:
   a. How the catch-up adjustment (i.e., the change effect) recorded in Requirement 2 is reported in the 19E comparative financial statements.
   b. How the 19D statement of income amounts are reported on the 19E comparative statements.

Case C

A patent, purchased for $17,000 on January 1, 19A, is being amortized (straight line) over its legal life of 17 years; there is no residual value. On January 1, 19E, the company decided to change to a more realistic total useful life of 12 years.

Required:

1. Identify the type of accounting change and the approach that should be used—current, retroactive, or prospective. Explain.
2. *(a)* Compute any catch-up adjustment and give the entry (if any) to record this accounting change in 19E, the year of change. Explain. Give the adjusting entries to record patent amortization for *(b)* 19D, and *(c)* 19E.
3. Explain:
   a. How any catch-up adjustment should be reported in the 19E comparative financial statements.
   b. How the 19D financial statement amounts are reported in the 19E comparative statements.

Part B: Problems 24–6 to 24–13

P 24–6 **(Eight Errors; Analysis and Correction; Entries)**

General Sales Company recently was acquired by a new owner who has decided to "clean up" the prior accounting records during the current reporting period which ends December 31, 19X9. The accounts have been partially adjusted but not closed for 19X9. The following additional items have been discovered:

a. The merchandise inventory at December 31, 19X8, was overstated by $10,000 (periodic inventory system).

b. During January 19X7, extraordinary repair on machinery was debited to Repair Expense; the $15,000 should have been debited to Machinery, which is being depreciated 15% per year on cost (no residual value).

c. A patent that cost $9,350 has been amortized (straight line) for the past 7 years (excluding 19X9) over its legal life of 17 years. It is now clear that its economic life will not be more than 12 years from the initial acquisition date.

d. At the end of 19X8, sales revenue collected in advance of $3,000 was included in 19X8 sales revenue. It was earned in 19X9.

e. Paid $8,000 during January 19X7 for ordinary repairs on a machine that was acquired during January 19X7. The repairs were erroneously capitalized. The machine has an estimated life of five years and no residual value. Assume straight-line depreciation.

f. The rate used for bad debts has been ½% of credit sales, which has proven to be too low; therefore, for 19X9 and thereafter, the rate used will be 1% of credit sales. The amount of the expense recorded per year under the old rate was 19X7, $800; and 19X8, $1,000 (the amount for 19X9 has not been entered in the accounts because the adjusting entries have not been made). Credit sales for 19X9 exceeded 19X8 credit sales by 20%.

g. During January 19X7, a five-year insurance premium of $750 was paid, which was debited in full to Insurance Expense at that time.

h. At the end of 19X8, accrued wages payable of $1,800 were not recorded; they were first recorded when paid early in 19X9. Unpaid wages at the end of 19X9 were $2,100.

Required:

1. For each of the above additional items identify if it is an error correction or an accounting change, and briefly explain how each should be accounted for.
2. Give the appropriate pretax entry to record any change or correction, and give any adjusting entry needed in each instance at the end of 19X9. Show computations. If no entry is needed, explain why.

P 24–7 (Error; Depreciation, Income Tax; Correcting Entries)

On January 3, 19A, Young Sales Company purchased a machine that cost $15,000. Although the machine has an estimated useful life of 10 years and an estimated residual value of $3,000, it was debited to expense when acquired. It is now December 19D, and the error has been discovered. The average income tax rate is 30%, and straight-line depreciation is used.

Required:

1. Give the entry to correct the accounts at the end of 19D assuming the books have not yet been closed for 19D. Also give the adjusting entry for depreciation for 19D. The income tax return was correct and there was no deferred income tax related to this transaction.
2. Assume instead that the income tax return also was incorrect because of this error; therefore, additional income tax must be paid, including a 10% penalty for each year an amount of tax was underpaid, less 10% each year on any amount of tax that was overpaid. Give the entry to correct the accounts, including the income tax effects, at the end of 19D, and the adjusting entry for depreciation for 19D. Round amounts to the nearest dollar.

P 24–8 (Correction of Errors, Comprehensive; Entries; Compute Correct Net Income and Retained Earnings)

Victor Wholesale Company was organized as a partnership on January 1, 19A; its five years of existence has involved a steady growth in assets, revenue, and incomes. The reporting period ends December 31. The 19E accounts have been adjusted but are not yet closed. Since this is a partnership, it does not pay income tax. The net income for each of the five years was as follows (in thousands):

	19A	19B	19C	19D	19E
Income before extraordinary items	$12	$27	$47	$60	$83
Extraordinary item, gain (loss)	—	—	—	(10)	—
Net income	$12	$27	$47	$50	$83

Partners' withdrawals through 19D, $100.

The company's records and reports are maintained by the company's bookkeeper. Although a part-time person has assisted in this area for the past two years, numerous problems have arisen with respect to the financial reports prepared for the owners and the local bank. The bank has been the primary source of borrowed funds. The owners currently are making plans to *(a)* expand the business and *(b)* contract for the construction of a large building to replace the rented space now used. In view of the anticipated financing needs, the company has engaged an outside CPA to *(a)* update all of the prior financial statements and *(b)* advise on the installation of a computerized accounting system.

During the March 19F examination of the 19A through 19E financial records, the CPA discovered the following accounting and reporting errors:

a. A forklift vehicle (used for moving inventory inside the warehouse) that was purchased for $8,500 on January 1, 19C, was debited in full to expense. It has an estimated useful life of eight years and a $500 residual value. The company uses straight-line depreciation.

b. The ending inventory of goods in the warehouse was overstated $10,000 at the end of 19B due to an arithmetic error. Also, the 19D ending inventory was overstated by $2,000 for the same reason. The company uses a periodic inventory system and FIFO.

c. Extraordinary repairs of $6,000 were debited in full to repair expense late in December, 19C. The equipment repaired was being depreciated over a four-year remaining life, straight line.

d. Prepaid insurance not recognized at year-end was as follows: 19B, $100; 19C, $150; 19D, $160; 19E, $180.

e. Merchandise purchased on credit (ownership passed) in one year but not recorded as a purchase until payment was made in the following year, but these items were correctly included in the ending inventory (periodic inventory system) as follows: 19A, $700; 19B, $1,000; 19C, $1,200; 19D, $1,400 and 19E, $2,000. The accounts payable are not yet paid for 19E.

f. The company recognized revenue on credit sales only when the cash was collected. Sales revenues related to credit sales that were collected in a subsequent accounting period were as follows: 19A, $4,000; 19B, $7,000; 19C, $10,000; 19D, $14,000; and 19E, $18,000. The receivable is not yet collected for 19E.

g. During 19E, recorded an $800 cash shortage as a debit to retained earnings.

h. Accrued selling expenses were not recorded in the accounts until actually paid; such expenses were: 19A, $2,000; 19B, $2,700; 19C, $3,100; 19D, $4,000; and 19E, $4,400. The payable for 19E is not yet paid.

i. An allowance for doubtful accounts has never been established. The CPA made the following estimates of additions to the allowance account (net of write-offs): 19A, $1,600; 19B, $1,200; 19C, $1,200; 19D, $1,700; and 19E, $1,600.

Required (ignore income tax considerations):

1. Give all correcting and adjusting entries that should be made on March 31, 19F (date of discovery of errors and omissions). The 19E accounts have been adjusted (except when indicated otherwise) but have not yet been closed.
2. Compute net income for 19E. Set up an appropriate schedule that reflects each change.
3. Compute the ending 19E balance in total partners' capital. Set up a schedule that reflects each change.

P 24–9 (Errors; Set up Worksheet to Correct Income; Correcting Entries)

Jackson Company did not recognize all accruals and deferrals in the accounts for a three-year period. In addition, numerous other errors were made in computing pretax income. The income amounts for each of the past three years are given in the tabulation below along with a list of the items that were not properly recognized and reported. All of these errors were discovered in February 19D after the 19C adjusting and closing entries.

Items to be corrected	19A	19B	19C
a. Reported pretax income (loss)	$4,000	$(3,500)	$10,000
Items not recognized correctly at each year-end:			
b. Accrued wages, not recorded	400	250	300
c. Rent revenue collected in advance, not recorded	100		200
d. Prepaid insurance, not recognized (was debited to expense)	320	410	120
e. Interest revenue earned but not collected (recognized as revenue when the cash was received)	170	140	
f. Annual depreciation overstated (by year)		1,000	1,200
g. Estimated annual expense for doubtful accounts understated (by year)	170	200	190
h. Goods purchased on credit on Dec. 31, were included in ending inventory; but the purchase was not recorded until payment was made the following year, before discovery date (periodic inventory system)	460	210	150
i. Sales on credit on Dec. 31 not recorded until the following year when the cash was collected, before discovery date; the goods were not included in ending inventory	290	770	390
j. Ending inventory overstated each year	130	240	290
k. Checks written; not mailed on Dec. 31 as payment on accounts payable; not recorded until the next year	1,100	1,500	1,400*
l. Bad debts that should have been written off each year to allowance for doubtful accounts by year-end (have not been written off to date; not cumulative)	800	950	1,170

* Not yet mailed or recorded for 19C by discovery date; the checks were mailed after discovery date.

Required:

1. You are to set up a worksheet to correct income for each year. Set up column headings similar to those shown in the tabulation. Key and briefly identify the errors under the first column and enter amounts under the respective years as plus or minus so that the last line will report correct pretax income. All items are pretax and are material in amount. Disregard income tax effects.
2. Give the correcting entry (if any should be made) on date of discovery (i.e., February 19D). For each item, code the entries with the letters given in the above tabulation.

P 24–10 (Errors; Worksheet to Correct Pretax Income; Entries)

L. Long established a retail business in 19A. Early in 19D, Long entered into negotiations with S. Short with the intent to form a partnership. You have been asked by Long and Short to check Long's books for the past three years to help Short evaluate the earnings potential of the business.

The net incomes reported on statements submitted to you were as follows:

	Year ending 12/31		
	19A	**19B**	**19C**
Income, pretax	$9,000	$10,109	$8,840

During the examination of the accounts, you found the data given below:

	For year ended Dec. 31		
	19A	**19B**	**19C**
Omissions from the books:			
a. Accrued expenses at end of year	$2,160	$2,094	$4,624
b. Earned (uncollected) revenue at end of year	200	—	—
c. Prepaid expenses at end of year	902	1,210	1,406
d. Unearned revenue (collected in advance) at end of year	—	610	—
Goods in transit at end of year omitted from inventory:			
e. Purchase for which the entry had been made (ownership passed)	—	2,610	—
f. Purchase for which the entry had not been made (ownership not passed) . . .		—	1,710

Other points requiring consideration:

g. On January 1, 19C, sold operational equipment for $4,500 that originally cost $5,000 on January 1, 19A. Cash was debited for $4,500 and equipment was credited for $4,500. The asset sold was depreciated in 19A and 19B but not 19C on the basis of a 10-year life and no residual value.

h. No allowance for bad debts has been set up. An analysis of accounts receivable as of December 31, 19C, indicates that the allowance account should have a balance of $2,000, of which $500 relates to 19A, $700 to 19B, and $800 to 19C.

Required:

1. You have decided to set up a worksheet to correct net income for each of the three years. Use column headings similar to those in the above tabulation and analyze each item separately.
2. Give the correcting entry, if any, for each item that should be made on date of discovery (that is, early January 19D). For each item, code the entries with the letters given for each item in the above data.

(AICPA adapted)

P 24–11 (Errors; Worksheet to Develop Correct Statement of Income and Statement of Financial Position)

The records of Davis Corporation have never been audited. At the end of 19K, the company prepared the following financial statements (summarized):

Statement of income:	
Sales and service revenue	$600,000
Expenses:	
Cost of goods sold	(350,000)
Distribution expenses	(120,000)
Administrative expenses	(60,000)
Pretax income	70,000
Income taxes	(21,500)
Net income	$ 48,500
Statement of financial position:	
Assets:	
Cash	$ 23,000
Accounts receivable (net)	40,000
Inventory (periodic system)	110,000
Property, plant, and equipment (net)	160,000
Patent	8,000
Other assets	9,000
Total assets	$350,000
Liabilities:	
Accounts payable	$ 80,000
Income taxes payable	15,000
Notes payable, long term (8%)	40,000
Total liabilities	135,000
Stockholders' equity:	
Common stock, par $10	145,000
Retained earnings (including 19K net income)	80,000
Dividends declared and paid	(10,000)
Total stockholders' equity	215,000
Total liabilities and stockholders' equity	$350,000

The company is negotiating a large loan for expansion purposes. The bank has requested that an audit of the company be performed. During the course of the audit, the following facts were determined:

a. The inventory at December 31, 19J, was overstated by $10,000.

b. The inventory at December 31, 19K, was overstated by $20,000.

c. The property, plant, and equipment was underdepreciated in 19J by $9,000 and in 19K by $12,000 (report this depreciation as a separate expense).

d. A three-year insurance premium of $900 paid on January 1, 19J, was debited in full to Administrative Expense at that time.

e. Accrued wages (an element of Administrative Expense) were not recorded as follows: 19J, $800; and 19K, $1,000.

f. The patent, which originally cost $17,000, is being amortized to Administrative Expense over a 17-year life (including 19K). Evidence clearly indicates that its economic life will approximate 14 years from date of acquisition.

g. Service revenues earned but not yet collected were not recognized when earned, as follows: 19J, $5,000; and 19K, $7,500. Revenue is recognized when collection is made.

h. A delivery truck purchased in January 19K, at a cost of $13,000, was debited to Distribution Expense at that time. The truck has an estimated useful life of 10 years and an estimated residual value of $2,000. The company uses straight-line depreciation (report depreciation on this truck as a Distribution Expense). The balance in the Allowance for Doubtful Accounts is sufficient to cover this bad debt.

i. Uncollectible account receivable from a bankrupt customer should be, but has not been, written off, $8,500.

j. Common stock outstanding, 12,000 shares.

Required:
Set up a worksheet to develop corrected amounts for the 19K statements of income and financial position. Complete the worksheet and key your entries. Assume the income tax expense amount is correct despite the above items. *Suggestion:* Set up pairs of columns for Trial Balance, Entries, Statements of Income, Retained Earnings, and Financial Position. Also, you will need four lines for property, plant, and equipment; six for retained earnings; and three for administrative expense.

P 24–12 **(Based on Supplement 24–A; Incomplete Records; Worksheet to Develop Statement of Income and Statement of Financial Position)**
Stanley Company has maintained single-entry records. In applying for a much-needed loan, a set of financial statements was required. An analysis of the records for 19C provided the following data:

Cash receipts:	
Cash sales	$130,000
Collections on credit sales	43,000
Collections on trade notes	1,000
Purchase allowances	1,500
Miscellaneous revenue	250
Cash payments:	
Cash purchases	84,500
Payments to trade creditors	34,100
Payment on mortgage on 7/1/19C plus prepayment of one year's interest of $1,020 to 7/1/19D	4,020
Sales commissions	7,200
Rent expense	2,400
General expenses (including interest)	14,590
Other operating expenses	29,800
Sales returns ($3,000, including $1,000 cash)	1,000
Insurance (renewal 3-year premium, April 1)	468
Operational assets purchased	1,500

	Balances	
	1/1/19C	12/31/19C
Cash	$14,100	$10,172
Accounts receivable	13,000	18,000
Trade notes receivable	2,000	1,500
Inventory	10,000	18,400
Prepaid insurance	39	?
Prepaid interest expense	600	510
Trade accounts payable	26,500	23,800
Income taxes payable		1,984
Accrued operating expenses payable	600	400
Operational assets (net)	35,400	33,290
Other assets	11,861	11,861
Common stock	40,000	40,000
Mortgage payable (6%, dated 7/1/19A)	20,000	?

No operational assets were sold during the year.

Required:
Prepare a worksheet to provide data for a detailed statement of income for 19C and a statement of financial position at the end of 19C. Show how the amounts for the various entries were developed. *Suggestion:* Set up columns for Balances, January 1, 19C; Interim Entries—Debit and Credit; Statement of Income; and Statement of Financial Position, December 31, 19C (use a "debits-over-credits" format).

P 24–13 **(Based on Supplement 24–A; Incomplete Records; Analysis to Compute Income)**
The following data were taken from the records of Rooster's Sporting Goods Store:

	Balances	
	1/1/19A	12/31/19A
Accounts receivable	$ 2,300	$ 3,900
Notes receivable (trade)	1,500	2,000
Interest receivable	90	70
Prepaid interest on notes payable	75	60
Inventory	9,255	10,400
Prepaid expenses (operating)	100	130
Store equipment (net)	8,500	8,600
Other assets	—	500
Accounts payable	1,700	1,900
Notes payable (trade)	11,000	11,500
Notes payable (equipment)	—	500
Accrued interest payable	40	30
Accrued expenses (operating) payable	170	210
Interest revenue collected in advance	30	40

An analysis of the checkbook, canceled checks, deposit slips, and bank statements provided the following summary for the year:

Balance, 1/1/19A		$ 4,200
Cash receipts:		
Cash sales	$23,000	
On accounts receivable	7,600	
On notes receivable	1,000	
Interest revenue	160	31,760
Cash disbursements:		
Cash purchases	11,800	
On accounts payable	2,400	
On notes payable (trade)	500	
Interest expense	560	
Operating expenses	14,130	
Miscellaneous nonoperating expenses	970	
Other assets purchased	500	
Withdrawals by Rooster	2,400	(33,260)
Balance, 12/31/19A		$ 2,700

Required:

1. Compute income by analyzing the changes in the owner's equity account.
2. Prepare a detailed statement of income with supporting schedules; show computations.

CASE

C 24–1 **(Analysis of Three Accounting Changes)**

A business entity may change its method of accounting for certain items. The change may be classified as a change in accounting principle, accounting estimate, or reporting entity.

Listed below are three independent, unrelated situations relating to accounting changes.

Situation 1: Able Company determined that the depreciable lives currently used for its operational assets were too long to best match the cost of using the assets with the revenue produced. At the beginning of the current year, the company decided to reduce the depreciable lives of all of its existing operational assets by five years.

Situation 2: On December 31, 19G, Baker Company owned 51% of the voting stock of Allen Company, at which time Baker reported its investment using the cost method due to political uncertainties in the country in which Allen was located. On January 2, 19H, the management of Baker Company was satisfied that the political uncertainties had been resolved and the assets of the company were in no danger of nationalization. Accordingly, Baker will prepare consolidated financial statements for Baker and Allen for the year ended December 31, 19H.

Situation 3: Charlie Company decided in January 19H to adopt the straight-line method of depreciation for plant equipment. The straight-line method will be used for new acquisitions as well as for previously acquired plant equipment for which depreciation in the past has been provided on a declining balance basis (DB).

Required:

For each of the situations described above, provide the information indicated below.

a. Type of accounting change.
b. Manner of reporting the change under current GAAP including a discussion, for situations 1 and 3 only, of how amounts are computed.
c. Effect of the change on the statements of financial position and of income (situations 1 and 3 only).
d. Note disclosures which would be necessary.

(AICPA adapted)

25 FINANCIAL REPORTING AND CHANGING PRICES

OVERVIEW AND PURPOSE

This chapter discusses inflation—a subject that you already understand in some respects. For example, you know that as inflation increases it requires more dollars (or more units in any currency) to buy the same amount of goods and services as before. Simply, as inflation occurs the dollar becomes cheaper; that is, its purchasing power decreases. You also know that the aggregation of 1935 dollars (a period of deflation) to 1980 dollars (a period of high inflation) is like adding apples and bananas! Such aggregation also is like adding dollars to German marks and French francs because these units likewise are not equivalents. This lack of equivalence is prevalent in financial statements when dollars with different purchasing power units are aggregated—the higher the inflation (or deflation) the more pronounced the inequivalence.

You also understand the implications of significant inflation for investors, debtors, and creditors. For example, if you invest $10,000 cash in vacant land and five years later sell it for $18,000 cash, there is an $8,000 economic (real) gain only if *(a)* the opportunity to earn interest on your $10,000 investment is disregarded and *(b)* there was no inflation during the five-year period. In fact, if inflation doubled during the period, you would suffer a $2,000 loss in purchasing power (disregarding the lost interest). As another example, you know that with inflation debtors gain, and creditors lose purchasing power because debts are paid (and collected) with the same number, but cheaper, dollars.

Financial statements are burdened with all of these problems—lack of equivalence, asset (i.e., investment) valuation, and debtor-creditor inflation gains and losses. This chapter discusses some alternative approaches used to resolve these problems in accounting. We believe you will find them to be interesting and challenging. This chapter is organized as follows:

Part A: Basic Concepts and the Historical Cost/Constant Dollar (HC/CD) Reporting Model

1. Basic concepts—a continuing controversy.
2. Alternative models in financial statements.
3. Historical cost constant dollar (HC/CD) reporting.
4. An overview of HC/CD reporting.

Part B: The Current Cost/Constant Dollar (CC/CD) Model

1. Objectives of the CC/CD model.
2. Measuring the effects of current cost price changes.
3. Preparation of CC/CD financial statements, stated in end-of-period CDs.
4. Usefulness of CC/CD financial statements.
5. FASB suggested disclosure requirements for changing prices.

PART A: BASIC CONCEPTS AND THE HISTORICAL COST/CONSTANT DOLLAR (HC/CD) REPORTING MODEL

Basic Concepts—A Continuing Controversy

The accounting profession traditionally has accepted historical cost as the basis for financial statements. Under this model, historical costs (and revenues) usually are measured when there is a completed transaction. That is, the realization concept is dominant. This model produces reliable and relevant information for statement users when there is no (or insignificant) inflation.

The significant inflationary trend during the late 1970s and early 1980s caused many accountants and other interested observers to call for supplementary information about the impact of changing prices on financial statements, or a change in the fundamental basis of the accounting model from historical cost to current cost. They argued that the historical cost basis model ignores the economic facts of life. However, the accounting profession has tenaciously supported the historical cost basis for financial reporting primarily because of its objectivity and consistency and also for several practical reasons. Most accountants support the historical cost model and generally support the position that supplementary information should be provided about the effects of price changes on a business. However, this position leads to the next controversy; that is, what kind of supplementary information should be provided. For example, *FASB Standard 89*, par. 4 states in a dissent:

> that inflation causes historical cost financial statements to show illusory profits and mask erosion of capital—is virtually undisputed. Specific price changes are inextricably linked to general inflation, and the combination of general and specific price changes seriously reduces the relevance, the representational faithfulness, and the comparability of historical cost financial statements.

The scope and complexity of this controversy and the long-term concerns of accountants about it are indicated in the following chronology of selected milestones:

1918 Livingston Middleditch, Jr., "Should Accounts Reflect the Changing Value of the Dollar?" *Journal of Accountancy* 25 (February 1918), pp. 114–20. The controversy starts!

1936 Henry W. Sweeney, *Stabilized Accounting* (New York: Harper & Row, 1936). This was the first book on the subject; it explains "Constant Dollar Accounting."

1963 "Reporting the Financial Effects of Price-Level Changes," Accounting Research Study No. 6 (New York: AICPA, 1963). Recommended supplementary disclosure of the effects of price level changes.

1969 "Financial Statements Restated for General Price-Level Changes," *Accounting Principles Board Statement No. 3* (New York: AICPA, 1969). Recommended supplementary disclosure of financial statements for general price level changes.

1976 "Disclosures of Certain Replacement Cost Data," Accounting Series Release No. 190 (Washington, D.C.: Securities and Exchange Commission, 1976). Required supplementary general price level disclosures about inventories and operational assets for large "listed" companies.

1979 "Financial Reporting and Changing Prices," *Statement of Financial Accounting Standards No. 33* (Stamford, Conn.: FASB, 1979). Required large companies to disclose supplementary information about the effects of changing prices.

1986 "Financial Reporting and Changing Prices," *Statement of Financial Accounting Standards No. 89* (Stamford, Conn.: FASB, 1986). Supersedes the prior *FASB Standards* on this topic. Supplementary disclosure of price change effects is "recommended, but not required."

This continuing controversy is implied in *FASB Standard 89,* which explains that the statement was adopted by the affirmative vote of four members, with three dissenting votes. The remainder of this chapter discusses the two main approaches that have been proposed for supplementary disclosure: (1) historical cost/constant dollar (acronym, HC/CD), and (2) current cost/constant dollar (CC/CD).

Current Status of Supplementary Disclosure of the Effect of Price Changes on Financial Statements

FASB Standard 33 (issued September 1979) provided the guidelines for supplementary disclosure of current cost, constant dollar (CC/CD) information. These disclosures were **required** for publicly held companies that, at the beginning of the year, had either *(a)* inventories and tangible operational assets (e.g., property, plant, and equipment) of more than $125 million (before deducting accumulated depreciation), or *(b)* total assets of more than $1 billion (after deducting accumulated depreciation). *FASB Standard 33,* as it was promulgated, was experimental; its paragraph 14 stated the following:

> The measurement and use of information on changing prices will require a substantial learning process on the part of all concerned. The Board makes no pretense of having solved all of the implementation problems. Rather, it encourages experimentation within the guidelines of this Statement and the development of new techniques that fit the particular circumstances of the enterprise.

Six years later *FASB Standard 89* (issued December 31, 1986) superseded *Standard 33* (and the eight related statements), and changed "required" to "encouraged," as follows:

> In 1979, *FASB Standard No. 33, "Financial Reporting and Changing Prices,"* was issued as an experiment in requiring supplementary information on the effects of inflation and changes in specific prices. At that time the Board committed itself to review the results of the requirements within five years. The Board has completed that review and has concluded that further supplementary disclosures should be encouraged, but not required.
>
> A business enterprise that prepares its financial statements in U.S. dollars and in accordance with U.S. generally accepted accounting principles is encouraged, but not required, to disclose supplementary information on the effects of changing prices. Appendix A provides measurement and presentation guidelines for disclosure. Entities are not discouraged from experimenting with other forms of disclosure.

FASB Standard 89 has an extensive appendix that provides guidance if a company desires to continue reporting current cost/constant dollar (CC/CD) supplementary disclosures. Part B will discuss those disclosures.

Numerous reasons have been given to explain why the FASB changed its position from "required" to "encouraged." *FASB Standard 89* gives no reasons; however, the dissenting members imply some. The reasons usually cited focus on the following: *(a)* inflation is no longer a problem, *(b)* the required disclosures are not useful, or at least they fail the cost/benefit test, *(c)* strong pressure was exerted by both businesses and the accounting profession, and *(d)* the pronouncements are difficult to understand and apply with confidence. Consistent terminology has been a real problem. For example, even in *FASB Standard 89,* there is no specific definition of "current cost" or "functional currency," even though those terms are used frequently in the statement.

Since the Great Depression of the 1930s, the aggregate price of commodities and services in the United States has increased steadily. This means that the general purchasing power of the dollar has been decreasing.

A dollar will command a certain amount of **real** goods and services in the marketplace at a given time. As aggregate prices change, the value of a dollar changes; it will command a different quantity of real goods and services. **General purchasing power** is the capacity of the monetary unit to purchase some general collection of commodities and services (i.e., a typical "market basket"). When the general level of prices **increase** (i.e., the general purchasing power of the dollar **decreases**), it is called **inflation.** When the general level of prices **decreases** (i.e., when the general purchasing power of the dollar **increases**), it is called **deflation.**[1]

This part of the chapter discusses historical cost/constant dollar (HC/CD) reporting and provides background for the discussion in Part B of current cost/constant dollar (CC/CD) reporting. Before discussing these two models, we must consider two topics—general and specific price indexes and monetary and nonmonetary items.

General and Specific Price Indexes

The basic concept that supports the incorporation of inflation effects in financial statements is the conversion of historical cost (HC) dollars to constant dollars (CD) using a general price level index (GPL index). The conversion is done by multiplying a historical cost (HC) amount by a general price level (GPL) restatement ratio. The numerator of the restatement ratio is the GPL index number on the date of the financial statements and the denominator is the GPL index number that existed on the date of the transaction that caused the item to be recorded. For example in 19X1, equipment was purchased for $100,000 (HC) when the GPL index was 127. When the 19X2 statement of financial position was prepared the GPL index was 159. The conversion formula and its application is as follows:

$$\text{HC amount} \times \frac{\text{GPL index at end of current period}}{\text{GPL index on transaction date}} = \text{HC/CD amount}$$

Statement of financial position (HC)	Statement of financial position (HC/CD)	
Equipment, $100,000 ×	159/127*	= $125,200

* Conversion index: 159/127 = 1.252.

[1] Because inflation has been pervasive, our discussions, illustrations, and assignment material are primarily in the context of rising prices; however, the concepts discussed also apply to deflation.

A **price index** is a relative measure of the prices of a given commodity or group of goods and/or services at a specific date. As the prices of the goods and services components of the index change, the "value" of the index changes. The base date usually is assigned a percentage index value of 100, or, alternatively, is stated as a decimal, 1.00. There are two basic types of price indexes: (1) **general** price level (GPL) indexes and (2) **specific** price level indexes.

General Price Level Indexes. **A general price level** (GPL) index is computed as **the average of a broad category of goods and services** sometimes called the **market basket.** The most widely known general price level (GPL) indexes now available are the gross national product, implicit price deflator, consumer price index, and wholesale price index. For **CD financial reporting,** use of the consumer price index for all Urban Consumers (CPI-U) is recommended.[2] The CPI-U is published in *Monthly Labor Review* by the U.S. Department of Labor. Annual average indexes for the CPI-U are presented below (the base year is 1967 = 100).

Year	Annual average CPI-U index	Annual inflation rate	Year	Annual average CPI-U index	Annual inflation rate
1950	72.1		1978	195.3	7.6
1955	80.2	2.2%*	1979	217.7	11.5
1960	88.7	2.0*	1980	247.0	13.5
1965	94.5	1.3*	1981	272.3	10.2
1967	100.0	2.9*	1982	288.6	6.0
1970	116.3	5.2*	1983	297.4	3.0
1975	161.2	9.1	1984	311.1	4.6
1976	170.5	5.8	1985	322.2	3.5
1977	181.5	6.5	1986	335.0**	4.0

* Annual compound rate for the period specified.
** Tentative.

Specific Price Indexes. A specific price index is computed as an average of a single good or service (e.g., lumber) or a single group (e.g., food) from among the broad categories of goods and services available. The price of a single good or service is affected by both supply and demand and general inflation. The construction of a specific price index is shown below to enhance your understanding of index numbers:

Component	Component prices at— Jan. 1	Dec. 31	Relative change
Meat (per pound)	$3.00	$3.41	+13.7%
Potatoes (per pound)	.65	.63	− 3.1
Green vegetable (per pound)	.70	.77	+10.0
Beverage (per quart)	.80	.83	+ 3.8
Total	$5.15	$5.64	

Computation of indexes:
Price index for food:
January 1 (base date) 5.15/5.15 = 1.000
December 31 5.64/5.15 = 1.095

[2] The FASB required the use of the CPI-U in *FASB Standard 33* and recommended in *FASB Standard 89* that it be used in the future.

The food price index shown above is a **specific price index.** It encompasses a single group of goods (i.e., food) from among the broad categories of goods and services available. Also, it shows that the prices of the individual components of an index seldom, if ever, increase or decrease proportionately with each other. Therefore, an index for a **group** of components reflects the **average** price movement for that particular group. For example, the price of potatoes decreased while the prices of the other items increased. Overall, food prices, as reflected by this hypothetical index, increased by 9.5% during the year.

In the discussions which follow you will learn why only the GPL index is used with the HC/CD model and why both indexes are used with the CC/CD model.

Timing of Index Numbers

For accounting purposes either end-of-year index or average-year index units (i.e., dollars) may be used to restate the nonmonetary items on the statement of financial position. The above illustrations have used end-of-year index units. Many accountants, including these authors, prefer end-of-year index units because *(a)* the restated amounts are representative of the latest prices, and *(b)* the monetary assets and liabilities are already in year-end dollars without conversion. Advocates of using average-year index units to restate make the point that although the statement of income amounts are nonmonetary, many of them do not have to be restated at average-year for the units because they are incurred evenly through the year. However, this advantage is mitigated because the monetary items that are already in year-end units must be indexed back to midyear. Further, the average-year restatement of monetary items causes the HC and HC/CD amounts to be different. *FASB Standard 89,* par. 7, recommends use of either "average-for-the-year or end-of-year units of constant purchasing power."

Monetary and Nonmonetary Items

Another primary concept in the conversion of historical cost dollars (HC) to constant dollars, using the GPL index numbers, is the distinction between *(a)* monetary items, which by their characteristics, are always stated in current dollars, and *(b)* nonmonetary items, which by their characteristics, must be converted to current dollars.

Monetary items are assets and liabilities, such as cash, receivables and payables, that are stated in a **fixed number of dollars.** The fixed number of dollars does not change regardless of changes in prices. Examples of monetary items include cash, accounts receivable, notes receivable, and other receivables stated in a fixed number of dollars; and accounts payable, notes payable, bonds payable, and other payables stated in a fixed number of dollars. Neither inflation nor deflation affects the **number of dollars** to be received or paid for a monetary item, although the "value" of those dollars is changed (i.e., with inflation the dollars become cheaper). **Monetary items are reported only on the statement of financial position.**

Nonmonetary items are financial statement items that are stated in a number of dollars that is **not** fixed. All items that are not classified as monetary are classified as nonmonetary. **The number of dollars they command changes.** Examples of nonmonetary items include inventories, operational assets, investments in stock, and common stock outstanding. **Nonmonetary items are reported on the statement of financial position along with monetary items. All revenues,**

expenses, gains, and losses reported on the statement of income are nonmonetary items.

Exhibit 25–1 shows the list of items and their classifications as monetary or nonmonetary adapted from *FASB Standard 89.* This exhibit emphasizes that in some cases the distinction between monetary and nonmonetary items is not easy to make. **Notice that the monetary/nonmonetary distinction is not related in any way to whether the item is current or noncurrent.** For instructional convenience, we sometimes abbreviate monetary as "M" and nonmonetary as "NM."

An important distinction between monetary and nonmonetary items in HC/CD reporting is that **monetary items are not restated on the HC/CD** statement of financial position. This is because the number of dollars that monetary items command does not change when the GPL changes. In contrast, **nonmonetary items are restated on the HC/CD** statement of financial position. This is because the number of dollars reflected in the HC of nonmonetary items can change when the GPL changes. That is, their CD equivalent amounts may differ from their HC amounts.

Another important distinction is that **monetary items cause purchasing power gains and losses when the GPL changes.** Purchasing power gains and losses arise because monetary items are **fixed** in terms of the number of dollars they command. For example, if $10,000 is borrowed when the GPL index is 150 and is repaid when the GPL index is 165, the borrower experiences a purchasing power **gain** of $1,000 because the $10,000 repaid is in dollars of lower purchasing power (i.e., cheaper dollars). For the same reason, the lender experiences a purchasing power **loss** of $1,000. This economic effect can be diagrammed as follows:

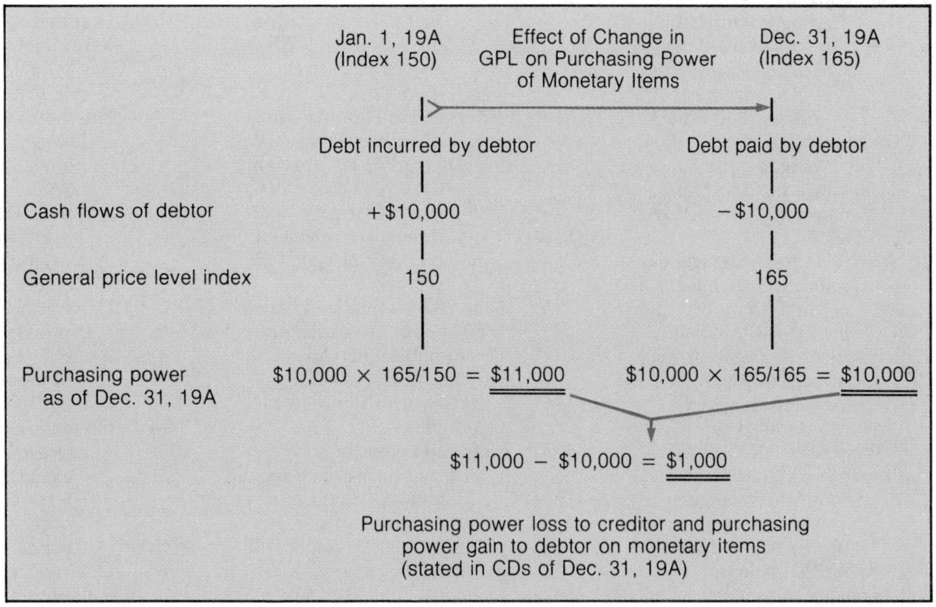

The overall economic effect of GPL changes on monetary items (i.e., purchasing power gains and losses) means that HC/CD reporting **must compute the net purchasing power gain or loss** each reporting period. This purchasing power

Exhibit 25–1

Monetary (M) and nonmonetary (NM) items.

Item	Classification
Assets:	
Cash on hand and demand bank deposits (dollars)	M
Time deposits (dollars)	M
Foreign currency on hand and claims to foreign currency	M
Securities:	
Common stocks (not accounted for on the equity method)	NM
Common stocks represent residual interests in the underlying net assets and earnings of the issuer.	
Preferred stock (convertible or participating)	(a)
Preferred stock (nonconvertible, nonparticipating)	M
Future cash receipts are likely to be substantially unaffected by changes in specific prices.	
Convertible bonds	(b)
Bonds (other than convertibles)	M
Trading account investments in fixed-income securities owned by banks, investment brokers, and others	M
Accounts and notes receivable	M
Allowance for doubtful accounts and notes receivable	M
Variable rate mortgage loans: The terms of such loans do not link them directly to the rate of inflation. Also, there are practical reasons for classifying all loans as monetary	M
Inventories used on contracts	(c)
Inventories (other than inventories used on contracts) and commodity inventories (other than those described below)	NM
Loans to employees	M
Prepaid insurance, advertising, rent, and other prepayments	(d)
Long-term receivables	M
Refundable deposits	M
Advances to unconsolidated subsidiaries	M
Equity investment in unconsolidated subsidiaries or other investees	NM
Pension, sinking, and other funds under an enterprise's control	(e)
Property, plant, and equipment	NM
Accumulated depreciation of property, plant, and equipment	NM
Portion of the carrying amount of lessors' assets leased under noncancelable operating leases that represent claims to fixed sums of money	NM
Cash surrender value of life insurance	M
Purchase commitments—portion paid on fixed-price contracts	NM
An advance on a fixed-price contract is the portion of the purchaser's claim to nonmonetary goods or services that is recognized in the accounts; it is not a right to receive money.	
Advances to supplier—not on a fixed-price contract	M
Such advances are rights to receive credit for a sum of money, not claims to a specified quantity of goods or services.	
Deferred income tax charges	M
Offsets to prospective monetary liabilities.	
Patents, trademarks, licenses, and formulas	NM
Goodwill	NM
Deferred property and casualty insurance policy acquisition costs related to unearned premiums	NM
Other intangible assets and deferred charges	NM
Liabilities:	
Accounts and notes payable	M
Accrued expenses payable (wages and so forth)	M
Accrued vacation pay	(f)
Cash dividends payable	M
Obligations payable in foreign currency	M
Sales commitments—portion collected on fixed-price contracts	NM
An advance received on a fixed-price contract is the portion of the seller's obligation to deliver goods or services that is recognized in the accounts; it is not an obligation to pay money.	
Advances from customers—not on a fixed-price contract	M
Such advances are equivalent to loans from customers and are not obligations to furnish specified quantities of goods or services.	
Accrued losses on firm purchase commitments	M
In essence, these are accounts payable.	
Deferred revenue	(g)
Refundable deposits	M
Bonds payable and other long-term debt	M
Unamortized premium or discount and prepaid interest on bonds or notes payable	M
Such items are inseparable from the debt to which they relate—a monetary item.	
Convertible bonds payable	M
Until converted, these are obligations to pay sums of money.	
Accrued pension obligations	(h)
Obligations under warranties	NM
These are nonmonetary because they oblige the enterprise to furnish goods or services or their future price.	
Deferred income tax credits	M
Cash requirements will not vary materially due to changes in specific prices.	

Exhibit 25–1
(concluded)

Item	Classification
Deferred investment tax credits	NM
These are not to be settled by payment of cash and are related to nonmonetary assets.	
Life insurance policy reserves	M
These represent portions of policies' face values that are now deemed liabilities.	
Property and casualty insurance loss reserves	M
Unearned property and casualty insurance premiums	NM
These are nonmonetary because they are principally obligations to furnish insurance coverage. The dollar amount of payments to be made under that coverage might vary materially due to changes in specific prices.	
Deposit liabilities of financial institutions	M
Minority interests in consolidated subsidiaries	NM
Equity:	
Capital stock of the enterprise or of its consolidated subsidiaries subject to mandatory redemption at fixed amounts	M

(a) Circumstances may indicate that such stock is either monetary or nonmonetary. Refer to convertible bonds.
(b) If the market values the security primarily as a bond, it is monetary; if it values the security primarily as stock, it is nonmonetary.
(c) They are, in substance, rights to receive sums of money if the future cash receipts on the contracts will not vary due to future changes in specific prices. Goods used on contracts to be priced at market upon delivery are nonmonetary.
(d) Claims to future services are nonmonetary. Prepayments that are deposits, advance payments, or receivables are monetary because the prepayment does not obtain a given quantity of future services, but rather is a fixed-money offset.
(e) The specific assets in the fund should be classified as monetary or nonmonetary. Refer to listings under securities above.
(f) If to be paid at the wage rates as of the vacation dates and if those rates may vary, accrued vacation pay is nonmonetary.
(g) If an obligation to furnish goods or services is involved, deferred revenue is nonmonetary. Certain "deferred income" items of savings and loan associations are monetary.
(h) Fixed amounts payable to a fund are monetary; all other amounts are nonmonetary.
Source: Adapted from *FASB Standard No. 89* (1986), par. 96.

gain or loss is not computed on nonmonetary items. We will discuss purchasing power gains and losses in more detail in the next section and in Part B.

Alternative Models in Financial Statements

The central problem of including price changes in financial statements is whether the historical cost model (HC) under GAAP or a current cost (CC) model should be used. A directly related question is what **measurement unit** (in dollars) should be used. Three alternative measurement units for accounting are: historical cost-basis dollars, general price level dollars, and specific price level dollars. These alternatives can be outlined as follows:

a. **Historical cost model (HC)**—the historical cost basis amounts recorded under GAAP:
   1. **Measurement in historical cost basis dollars** with no restatement for price level changes. This is the current GAAP model discussed in the prior chapters.
   2. **Measurement in constant dollars (CD).** This model uses and retains the historical costs, but restates those costs in common dollars by using **general price level (GPL) index** numbers. This model is identified herein as the HC/CD model.

b. **Current cost model (CC)**—current replacement costs at financial statement date (with specified constraints):
   1. **Measurement in specific price level dollars.**

2. **Measurement in constant dollars** (CD) by using general price level index numbers. This model is identified herein as the CC/CD model.

The historical cost basis (a1 above), as required by current GAAP, must be used in the primary financial statements. For supplemental disclosure, *FASB Standard 89* now encourages use of the current cost/constant dollar (CC/CD) model (b2 above).[3] The restatement, or conversion, of HC and CC to constant dollars involves detailed procedures. To help you understand the CC/CD model, discussed in Part B, we first discuss the HC/CD model in Part A (a2 above). This background discussion will facilitate your understanding of the steps used to implement the CC/CD model presented in Part B.

Historical Cost/Constant Dollar (HC/CD) Reporting Model

The objective of the HC/CD model is to report the HC financial statement elements in dollars of equivalent purchasing power (CDs). As a result, it makes all of the reported amounts comparable in terms of the measuring unit. The restatement of each HC amount to its HC/CD equivalent amount uses two GPL index values for each item restated—one is as of the transaction date when the item was first recorded and the other one is as of the date of the financial statement.

Historical cost (HC) financial statements aggregate historical dollar amounts representing assets, liabilities, owners' equity, revenues, expenses, gains, and losses, just as though each dollar had the same purchasing power. However, if prices were changing during the periods when those dollars were recorded, such dollars would have unequal purchasing power—that is, they would lack equivalence.

For example, a building was acquired at a cost of $400,000 in 1969 (say, when the general price level [GPL] index was 100). Another building was acquired at a cost of $900,000 in 1988 (the current year) when the general price index was 200.[4] The total balance in the Buildings account of $1,300,000 (HC dollars) in 1988 would include a mixture of dollars of different purchasing power, which is adding them as if they were equivalents. In contrast, a historical cost/constant dollar (HC/CD) reporting model converts these historical cost amounts to constant dollars (also called current dollars) as follows:

	HC restated in 1988 CD
1988 building (already in 1988 dollars)	$ 900,000
1969 building (restated to 1988 dollars, $400,000 × 200/100)	800,000
Total HC in 1988 CDs (equivalent dollars)	$1,700,000*

* This amount is reported on the supplemental HC/CD statement of financial position instead of the $1,300,000, which is reported on the traditional HC statement of financial position.

The change in prices also would affect the depreciation expense on the old building in a similar manner. For example, assume the annual HC depreciation on the 1969 building is $20,000. This amount would be restated to 1988 CDs

[3] For the first time the FASB, in *Standard 89*, pars. 11 and 30, calls constant dollars "Constant purchasing power units." Using this terminology we would abbreviate HC/CPP and CC/CPP. Throughout this chapter we will use the "CD" designation.

[4] General price level (GPL) index numbers were discussed on page 1313 under the caption, "General and Specific Price Indexes."

Exhibit 25–2
General price level (GPL) ratios for relevant dates; AB Company.

Date	GPL index	CD restatement ratio
1/1/19A	127	159/127
3/31/19B	138	159/138
12/31/19E	147	159/147
3/31/19F	149	159/149
6/30/19F	151	159/151
9/30/19F	154	159/154
12/31/19F	159	159/159
Period		
Average, 4th quarter 19E	146	159/146
Average, 4th quarter 19F	157	159/157
Average, full year 19F	152*	159/152

* (147 + 149 + 151 + 154 + 159) ÷ 5 = 152.

as: $20,000 × 200/100 = $40,000. This $20,000 difference in expense causes HC pretax income to be greater by $20,000 than the HC/CD restated amounts. This example shows that the relevance of many amounts on most HC financial statements may be reduced due to the effects of changing prices.

The "key" to CD restatement involves identification of *(a)* monetary and nonmonetary items, *(b)* the transaction date for each nonmonetary item, *(c)* the GPL index for each of these dates, and *(d)* the GPL index on the date of the financial statements.

The transaction date is the date when the item was originally recognized. Transaction dates relate to assets, liabilities, owners' equity, revenues, gains, expenses, losses, and any other transactions. Items that experience numerous transactions during the reporting period, such as sales revenue, often are assumed to occur evenly throughout the period. This assumption provides a practical basis for using an average GPL index value for the denominator in the restatement ratio.

The numerator of the restatement ratio is the GPL index on the current statement of financial position date and the denominator is the GPL index that existed on the transaction date. The relationship between these two indexes is called the **restatement** or **conversion ratio.** All nonmonetary items are restated, while nonmonetary items are not restated.

Comprehensive Illustration of the Preparation of HC/CD Financial Statements

Preparation of HC/CD statements involves the following five steps: (1) Collect the basic data—the HC financial statements and the relevant GPL index ratios. (2) Classify each item on the statement of financial position and statement of income as either monetary or nonmonetary. (3) Prepare the HC/CD statement of financial position. (4) Prepare the HC/CD statements of income and retained earnings. (5) Compute the purchasing power gain or loss on monetary items and complete the statement of income. Next, we will discuss and illustrate each step for AB company for the year ended December 31, 19F.

Step 1. Collect the basic data for AB Company.

The relevant index ratios are given in **Exhibit 25–2** and **Exhibit 25–3** gives the 19F HC financial statements for AB Company. **These statements are to be converted to the HC/CD basis.**

Exhibit 25–3

Summary of transactions and financial statements for 19F—AB Company.

Panel A—Summary of Transactions During 19F:

a. Sales of $144,000 were made evenly during the year (assume all on credit).
b. Purchases of $85,000 were made evenly during the year (assume all on credit).
c. The equipment is depreciated 4% per year with no residual value; the equipment was bought on January 1, 19A, when the GPL index was 127.
d. The long-term investment in common stock of Smith Company was acquired for $25,000 on March 31, 19B, when the GPL index was 138. On December 30, 19F, when the GPL index was 159, half of these shares (i.e., cost of $12,500) were sold for $15,000 cash.
e. General expenses (including interest) of $20,000 were accrued and paid evenly during the year.
f. Collections on accounts receivable, $135,000, were made evenly during the year.
g. Payments on accounts payable, $80,000, were made evenly during the year.
h. A $10,000 cash dividend was declared at midyear when the GPL index was 151. It was paid one month later.
i. Parking garage was acquired January 1, 19F, when the GPL index was 147; issued 12% note payable, $50,000; interest paid quarterly.
j. Parking garage is depreciated 4% per year with no residual value.
k. Issued common stock for cash on September 30, 19F, when the GPL index was 154; cash received, $60,000. The initial $100,000 of common stock was issued on January 1, 19A, when the GPL index was 127.
l. Income tax of $10,000 was accrued evenly during the year. For instructional convenience, assume that all of it will be paid in 19G.
m. The December 31, 19F, inventory was $25,000 (FIFO basis; LCM = cost).

Panel B—Financial Statements—AB Company:

Comparative Statement of Financial Position, HC, at December 31, 19F:

		12/31/19F HC (from books)	12/31/19E HC (from books)
	Assets		
M	Cash	$136,000	$ 36,000
M	Accounts receivable (net)	33,000	24,000
NM	Inventory (FIFO)	25,000	20,000
NM	Investment in common stock	12,500	25,000
NM	Equipment	100,000	100,000
NM	Accumulated depreciation, equipment	(24,000)	(20,000)
NM	Parking garage	50,000	—
NM	Accumulated depreciation, parking garage	(2,000)	—
	Total assets	$330,500	$185,000
	Liabilities		
M	Accounts payable	$ 45,000	$ 40,000
M	Income tax payable	10,000	—
M	Note payable, 12%	50,000	—
	Stockholders' Equity		
NM	Common stock, nopar	160,000	100,000
NM	Retained earnings	65,500	45,000
	Total liabilities and stockholders' equity	$330,500	$185,000

M = Monetary item.
NM = Nonmonetary item.

Exhibit 25–3
(concluded)

Statement of Income
HC, for the Year Ended December 31, 19F
(all items are NM)

	HC (from books)
Sales revenue	$144,000
Gain on sale of investment	2,500
Total revenues and gains	146,500
Cost of goods sold*	80,000
General expenses (including interest)	20,000
Depreciation expense, equipment	4,000
Depreciation expense, garage	2,000
Income tax expense	10,000
Total expenses	116,000
Net income	$ 30,500

* Cost of goods sold (FIFO):

Inventory, beginning (1/1/19F)	$ 20,000
Purchases (all on credit)	85,000
Goods available for sale	105,000
Inventory, ending (12/31/19F)	(25,000)
Cost of goods sold	$ 80,000

Statement of Retained Earnings
HC, for the Year Ended December 31, 19F
(all items are NM)

Beginning balance, January 1, 19F	$ 45,000
Add: Net income for 19F	30,500
Deduct: Dividends declared during 19F	(10,000)
Ending balance, December 31, 19F	$ 65,500

Step 2. Classify items on the financial statements as either monetary or nonmonetary (Exhibit 25–3).

The classifications M and NM are shown in Exhibit 25–3, panel B. Notice that both monetary and nonmonetary items appear on the statement of financial position, but all items on the statements of income and retained earnings are nonmonetary.

Step 3. Prepare the HC/CD statement of financial position (Exhibit 25–4).

The objective of CD restatement of **HC statement of financial position** is to report the HC of assets, liabilities, and owners' equity at their **current CD equivalents.** For AB Company, this is in December 31, 19F, dollars. Therefore, the numerator of all CD restatement ratios is the GPL index as of the statement of financial position date. The denominators vary, depending upon when the individual item was acquired (i.e., its **transaction date**). Thus, for AB Company all numerators are 159, and the denominators vary as discussed below.

a. **Monetary items**—Because monetary items have fixed amounts that are not affected by GPL changes, their HC and HC/CD amounts are the same. Therefore, **monetary items are not restated on the HC/CD statement of financial position.** Notice in Exhibit 25–4 that the HC of each monetary item is extended to the last column, HC/CD.

Exhibit 25–4
HC/CD restated statement of financial position—AB Company.

Panel A—Summary of Acquisition Dates and GPL Index Values for Nonmonetary Items:

a. Ending 19F inventory was acquired evenly throughout the fourth quarter; GPL index, 157.
b. Investment in common stock of Smith Company was acquired March 31, 19B; GPL index, 138.
c. Equipment was acquired on January 1, 19A; GPL index, 127.
d. Accumulated depreciation, equipment, restated on same basis as related asset account.
e. Parking garage was acquired on January 1, 19F; GPL index, 147.
f. Accumulated depreciation, parking garage, restated on same basis as related asset account.
g. Original issue of common stock, $100,000, on January 1, 19A; GPL index, 127. Subsequent issuance of common stock, $60,000, on September 30, 19F; GPL index, 154.

Panel B—Statement of Financial Position

AB COMPANY
HC/CD Statement of Financial Position
At December 31, 19F

	HC (from books)	CD restatement ratio[a]	HC/CD
Assets			
Cash	$136,000	Monetary	$136,000
Accounts receivable (net)	33,000	Monetary	33,000
Inventory	25,000	159/157	25,325
Investment in common stock	12,500	159/138	14,400
Equipment	100,000	159/127	125,200
Accumulated depreciation, equipment	(24,000)	159/127	(30,048)
Parking garage	50,000	159/147	54,100
Accumulated depreciation, parking garage	(2,000)	159/147	(2,164)
Total assets	$330,500		$355,813
Liabilities			
Accounts payable	$ 45,000	Monetary	$ 45,000
Income tax payable	10,000	Monetary	10,000
Note payable, 12%	50,000	Monetary	50,000
Stockholders' Equity			
Common stock, nopar	160,000	*b*	187,120
Retained earnings[c]	65,500	Bal. amt.	63,693
Total liabilities and stockholders' equity	$330,500		$355,813

a. The CD restatement ratios are rounded to three decimals.
b. Original common stock restatement (GPL index at issuance, 127):

$100,000 × (159/127)	$125,200
19F common stock issuance restatement (GPL index at issuance, 154):	
$60,000 × (159/154)	61,920
Common stock restated in CDs	$187,120

c. The 19F beginning HC/CD balance is $47,180.

b. **Nonmonetary items**—The **nonmonetary items are restated on the HC/CD statement of financial position** as shown in Exhibit 25–4 because their prices can change as the GPL changes. The restatement ratio for each nonmonetary item uses the GPL index as of the restatement date as the numerator and the GPL index at transaction date as the denominator. The **transaction** (i.e., acquisition) **dates** and related GPL index ratios are reported for convenience in Exhibit 25–4, panel A. Two nonmonetary items listed there warrant further explanations:

(1) **Common stock, nopar**—AB Company first issued common stock for cash on January 1, 19A, when the GPL index was 127. AB Company subsequently issued additional stock on September 30, 19F, when the GPL index was 154. Therefore, the two separate issuances must be restated as shown in note *(b)* of Exhibit 25–4.

(2) **Retained earnings**—HC/CD retained earnings can be computed as a **balancing amount,** as shown for AB Company in Exhibit 25–4. The amount, $63,693, is computed (and verified) in Exhibit 25–5.

These procedures complete the preparation of the HC/CD statement of financial position of AB Company. Notice the following: *(a)* total assets increased when HC amounts are restated to CDs, and *(b)* retained earnings decreased when restated to CDs.

Step 4. Prepare the HC/CD statements of income and retained earnings (Exhibit 25–5).

The objective of CD restatement of the **HC statement of income** is to report the HC revenues, expenses, gains and losses restated to **their CD equivalents** because **all items on the statement of income are nonmonetary.** For AB Company, restatement is to December 31, 19F, dollars. The numerator of all CD restatement ratios is the GPL index at year-end (i.e., 159). The denominators of the restatement ratios vary according to the **transaction date** (i.e., when the depreciable assets were acquired or when current expenses were incurred). Thus, for AB Company, all numerators are 159, and the denominators vary as discussed below (for basic data, see Exhibit 25–3, panel A).

a. **Sales revenue** increased net monetary assets (i.e., accounts receivable) **evenly** during 19F. Therefore, the denominator of the CD restatement ratio is the **average** GPL index value for the year. The numerator is the index at December 31, 19F. Thus, sales revenue is restated by the CD index ratio 159/152.

b. **Gain on sale of investment** [Exhibit 25–3, item *(d)*] requires CD restatement of the HC entry to record the sale on December 30, 19F, when the GPL index was 159, as shown in note *(a)* of Exhibit 25–5. Therefore, the cash received is restated by the CD ratio of 159/159. The HC amount of the investment is restated by the ratio of 159/138 because the GPL index at date of acquisition, March 31, 19B, was 138. The resulting HC/CD gain of $600 is a balancing amount. It represents a weighted average of the CD equivalents of the cash received and the cost of the investment sold.

c. **Cost of goods sold** requires multiple HC/CD restatements as shown in note *(b)* of Exhibit 25–5. Based on the FIFO assumption [Exhibit 25–3, panel A, item *(m)*], the beginning inventory was acquired during the fourth quarter of the preceding year when the **average** GPL index was 146 (Exhibit 25–2). Therefore, it is restated by the CD ratio, 159/146. Purchases decreased net monetary assets (i.e., increased accounts payable or decreased cash) **evenly** during 19F. Because the purchases were made evenly during 19F, the **average** GPL index of 152 is used. Therefore,

Exhibit 25–5
HC/CD restated statements of income and retained earnings—AB Company.

AB COMPANY
HC/CD Statement of Income
For Year Ended December 31, 19F

	HC (from books)	CD restatement ratio	HC/CD
Sales revenue	$144,000	159/152	$150,624
Gain on sale of investment	2,500	*(a)*	600
Total revenues and gains	146,500		151,224
Cost of goods sold	80,000	*(b)*	85,365
General expenses (including interest)	20,000	159/152	20,920
Depreciation expense, equipment	4,000	159/127	5,008
Depreciation expense, garage	2,000	159/147	2,164
Income tax expense	10,000	159/152	10,460
Total expenses	116,000		123,917
Net income	$ 30,500		
HC/CD income before purchasing power loss on net monetary items			27,307
Purchasing power loss on net monetary items (Exhibit 25–6)			(264)
HC/CD income			$ 27,043

[(a)] Entry to record sale of investment (12/30/19F):

	HC Dr.	HC Cr.	CD ratio	HC/CD Dr.	HC/CD Cr.
Cash	15,000		159/159	15,000	
Investment in common stock ($25,000 ÷ 2)		12,500	159/138		14,400
Gain on sale of investment		2,500	Bal. amt.		600

[(b)] Cost of goods sold:

	HC	CD ratio	HC/CD
Inventory, 1/1/19F	$ 20,000	159/146	$ 21,780
Purchases	85,000	159/152	88,910
Goods available for sale	105,000		110,690
Inventory, 12/31/19F (see Exhibit 25–4)	(25,000)	159/157	(25,325)
Cost of goods sold	$ 80,000		$ 85,365

HC/CD Statement of Retained Earnings for the Year Ended December 31, 19F.

	HC/CD
Beginning balance January 1, 19F, HC/CD balance from prior year, ($43,619* × 159/147)	$ 47,180
Add: Net income for 19F (above)	27,043
Deduct: Dividends, 19F ($10,000 × 159/151)	(10,530)
Ending balance, December 31, 19F*	$ 63,693

* See Exhibit 25–4.

purchases are restated by the CD ratio, 159/152. Based on the FIFO assumption, ending inventory was acquired evenly during the fourth quarter of 19F, when the average GPL index was 157. This amount is restated by the ratio, 159/157.

If AB Company had used LIFO, the denominators of the CD ratios applied to beginning and ending inventory would have been based upon the dates those costs were incurred. In some cases, those dates may have been in the distant past. If AB had used the average cost method for inventory, the denominators of the CD ratios for beginning and ending inventory would have been average GPL index values for 19E and 19F, respectively. For all three of the inventory cost flow methods, the CD restatement of purchases would be the same because the cost flow method does not affect the timing of purchases.

d. **General expenses** decreased net monetary assets (i.e., decreased cash or increased payables) evenly during 19F. Therefore, the HC amount is restated by the average CD ratio for the year, 159/152.
e. **Depreciation expense,** equipment, occurred evenly during 19F. However, the HC/CD amount of depreciation expense is based upon the HC/CD amount of the related asset. Therefore, depreciation expense on equipment is restated by the **same ratio applied to equipment,** 159/127, because the assets were acquired and decreased net monetary assets on January 1, 19A, when the GPL index was 127.
f. **Depreciation expense,** parking garage, is CD restated by the ratio, 159/147, because the garage was acquired on January 1, 19F, when the GPL index was 147.
g. **Income tax expense** decreased net monetary assets (i.e., increased income tax payable) evenly during 19F. Therefore, it is restated by using the average CD restatement ratio, 159/152.
h. **Purchasing power loss on net monetary items** of $264 is computed in Exhibit 25–6 and is discussed in step 5.

The statement of retained earnings is restated as follows:

a. The beginning balance is restated to express it in current dollars. The restatement ratio is computed by dividing the ending index for the current year (159) by the ending index for the prior year (147).
b. Net income is carried from the HC/CD statement of income.
c. The dividend restatement ratio is computed by dividing the ending index for the current year (159) by the index on the transaction date (midyear, 151).

Step 5. Compute the purchasing power gain (loss) on net monetary items for 19F (Exhibit 25–6).

The concept that underlies computation of the gain (loss) on net monetary items is that the company began 19F with a net monetary asset (or liability) amount and during the year completed transactions that increased or decreased its monetary assets and liabilities. The beginning net monetary asset amount (i.e., monetary assets minus monetary liabilities), plus the increases and minus the decreases of net monetary assets that occurred during the year, equals the ending **net** monetary asset (or **net** monetary liability) amount. When all of these amounts are restated (i.e., beginning balance, increases, decreases, and ending balance) into their CD equivalents at December 31, 19F, the difference between the total *(a)* HC and *(b)* HC/CD **ending** net monetary assets is an **economic** measure of the company's success (a gain) or lack of success (a loss) in using monetary items during the year. This difference between HC and HC/CD ending balances considers both the amounts and the timing of all net monetary effects on the entity during the period, relative to the changes in

Exhibit 25–6
Computation of purchasing power gains and losses on monetary items—AB Company.

AB COMPANY
Computation of Purchasing Power Gain (Loss) on Net Monetary Items
For Year Ended December 31, 19F

	HC	CD restatement ratio	HC/CD
Net monetary items—increases (decreases):			
1. Total beginning net monetary assets	$ 20,000*	159/147	$ 21,640
2. Increases in net monetary assets during 19F from:			
Sales revenue	144,000	159/152	150,624
Sale of investment	15,000	159/159	15,000
Sale and issuance of common stock	60,000	159/154	61,920
3. Decreases in net monetary assets during 19F from:			
Purchases	(85,000)	159/152	(88,910)
General expenses (including interest)	(20,000)	159/152	(20,920)
Income tax expense	(10,000)	159/152	(10,460)
Cash dividends declared†	(10,000)	159/151	(10,530)
Parking garage acquisition	(50,000)	159/147	(54,100)
4. Total ending net monetary assets:			
HC	$ 64,000‡		
HC/CD			$ 64,264
5. Purchasing power gain (loss) on net monetary items; to statement of income, HC, $64,000 − HC/CD, $64,264; a positive remainder is a gain and a negative remainder is a loss			$ (264)

* Computation from 19E statement of financial position (Exhibit 25–3): Cash, $36,000 + Accounts receivable, $24,000 − Accounts payable, $40,000 = $20,000 (may be positive or negative; positive in this case).

† Declaration date, not payment date is relevant to the CD restatement of cash and property dividends because on declaration date, the entity incurs a monetary liability and, hence, decreases net monetary assets. Subsequent payment has no effect on net monetary assets because payment involves monetary items only (i.e., Dr. Dividends Payable; Cr. Cash).

‡ Computation from 19F statement of financial position (Exhibit 25–3): Cash, $136,000 + Accounts receivable, $33,000 − Accounts payable, $45,000 − Income tax payable, $10,000 − Note payable, $50,000 = $64,000 (may be positive or negative; positive in this case). This exhibit demonstrates that usually it is not necessary to compute the purchasing power gain (loss) on each separate monetary item; rather, they can be combined as shown.

the GPL that occurred during that period. Therefore, it is viewed as a measure of the HC/CD **purchasing power gain (or loss) on net monetary items** during the period.

In Exhibit 25–6, AB Company began 19F with $20,000 of net monetary assets; on the beginning date, the GPL index was 147. Therefore, because the GPL index at December 31, 19F, was 159, the **total** beginning balance of $20,000 must be restated by using the CD restatement ratio, 159/147. The **increases and decreases** in all of the monetary items must be restated individually to CDs of December 31, 19F, by using the index at that date (i.e., 159) as the numerator. The denominator must be the index at the transaction date of each item. Sales of goods and services, operational assets, and common stock, whether for cash or on account, cause net monetary assets to increase. In contrast, purchases, expenses, declaration of dividends, and acquisitions of nonmonetary assets, whether for cash or on account, cause net monetary assets to decrease. Exhibit 25–6 shows the CD restatement of such items. Observe in Exhibit 25–6 that the **purchasing power gain (loss) is computed to be the remainder of the ending HC amount minus the ending HC/CD amount.** A positive remainder is a purchasing power gain, and a negative remainder is a purchasing power loss. The logic of this relationship can be explained using Exhibit 25–6. If AB Company had kept pace exactly with general inflation during 19F, the net monetary assets should have been $64,264 at the end of 19F. However, on December 31, 19F, AB Company actually had net monetary assets of only $64,000. The difference of $264 (i.e., HC, $64,000 minus HC/CD, $64,264) is a purchasing power **loss.** The purchasing power gain (loss) is reported on the HC/CD statement of income (Exhibit 25–5).

This completes the HC/CD conversion process. The company now has two sets of statements: one on the HC basis (which is used as the primary set of financial statements) and the other on the HC/CD basis (which can be presented as a supplemental disclosure).

An Overview of HC/CD Reporting

HC/CD reporting retains the traditional HC results but restates the measuring unit to current year CDs. Therefore, it enables users of financial statements to compare HC amounts in a common measuring unit. The HC/CD model also reports the purchasing power gain (or loss) on net monetary items. This is an economic gain (or loss) which is not reported when HC accounting only is used. The HC model does not measure the effects of holding monetary assets or liabilities during periods of general price changes.

HC/CD reporting does not report current values because the GPL indexes used for HC/CD restatements ignore the **specific price changes** of the individual assets of the entity. Only by coincidence would an HC/CD amount equal the market value (either current market value or current cost) of each individual asset of the entity.[5]

FASB Standard 89 does not "encourage" use of the HC/CD model. Rather, it encourages use of a current cost/constant purchasing power model. This model often is designated as a current cost/constant dollar (CC/CD) model. The discussion in this part of the chapter did not consider the CC/CD model because it combines two separate concepts—current cost and constant dollar. Part B discusses this integrated model.

PART B: THE CURRENT COST/CONSTANT DOLLAR (CC/CD) MODEL

FASB Standard 89 (issued December 1986), par. 11, states that:[6]

> In addition to the information required by paragraphs 7–10, an enterprise shall provide the information specified in paragraphs 12 and 13 if income from continuing operations on a **current cost/constant purchasing power** basis would differ significantly from income from continuing operations in the primary financial statements.

---

[5] This coincidence would likely occur only on an aggregate company basis and not on an account-by-account basis, and most likely for the type of entity that is so well diversified that changes in the aggregate of the specific price change effects of its individual assets and liabilities paralleled changes in the GPL index.

[6] Although "current cost/constant purchasing power" (CC/CPP) is appropriately descriptive, for consistency we will continue to use the acronym "CC/CD."

Part A emphasized that *(a)* the GAAP historical cost basis model (HC) does not report the effects of inflation (or deflation) nor current costs. Part A also emphasized that the historical cost-constant dollar (HC/CD) model retains HC, but changes the measuring unit from HC at transaction date (called **nominal dollars**) to constant current dollars based on the general price level (GPL) index at the end of the current year. **Significantly, the current cost/constant dollar model discussed in this part of the chapter has two special features—it replaces the historical cost basis (HC) with a current cost basis (CC) and also applies the constant dollar (CD) concept. These two concepts provide an integrated model, current cost/constant dollar (CC/CD).** This means that a CC/CD statement of financial position reports the current cost of each asset (instead of HC). The statement of income reports expenses at CC rather than HC. **Thus, CC accounting changes the attribute measured from historical cost to current cost.**[7]

Objectives of the CC/CD Model

The CC/CD model has two interrelated objectives; one relates to the statement of financial position and the other to the statement of income. On the statement of financial position, the objective of the CC/CD model is to report **the lower of *(a)* the current cost of replacing each asset (or asset group, or *(b)* the net recoverable amount of each asset or asset group.**[8]

Current Cost. *FASB Standard 89* does not give a specific definition of current cost. Instead, paragraphs 16–26 define current cost for each type of nonmonetary asset essentially as follows:

a. **Inventory**—current cost of purchasing or producing the inventory owned.
b. **Property, plant, and equipment**—current cost of acquiring the same service potential as embodied in the asset or group of assets owned.
c. **Specialized assets such as natural resources**—current market buying price or current cost of finding and developing.
d. **Remaining assets**—generally use historical cost, if not significant in amount, because the FASB model focuses on inventory and property, plant, and equipment. Some of these assets are already at current cost for all practical purposes.

Guidelines for Measuring Current Cost. The *FASB Standard 89* measurement guidelines can be summarized as follows:

1. Assets used (*FASB Standard 89*, par. 18):
   a. By measuring the current cost of a new asset that has the same service potential as the used asset had when it was new (the current cost of the asset as if it were new) and deducting an allowance for depreciation.

---

[7] Edgar O. Edwards and Philip W. Bell, *The Theory and Measurement of Business Income* (Berkeley: University of California Press, 1961).

[8] This constraint is ever-present in accounting. It applies to HC amounts in the traditional HC accounting framework, as well as to HC/CD, CC, and CC/CD amounts because under GAAP, assets generally should not be reported at amounts in excess of their net realizable value, and expenses are measured accordingly.

   b. By measuring the current cost of a used asset of the same age and in the same condition as the asset owned.
   c. By measuring the current cost of a new asset with a different service potential and adjusting that cost for the value of the difference in service potential due to differences in life, output capacity, nature of service, and operating costs.
2. Groups of directly related assets (par. 19)—current cost may be determined on the basis of single items or groups of related items as appropriate in the circumstances.
3. Some approaches that may be used to determine current cost (par. 19):
   a. Indexation
      (1) Externally generated price indexes for the class of goods or services being measured
      (2) Internally generated price indexes for the class of goods or services being measured
   b. Direct pricing
      (1) Current invoice prices
      (2) Vendors' price lists or other quotations or estimates
      (3) Standard manufacturing costs that reflect current costs

Net Recoverable Amount. Paragraphs 29 and 30 define net recoverable amount as the net amount of cash expected to be recoverable from the use or sale of each asset or group of assets. Recoverable amount may be **measured** as: *(a)* **use value** if the asset is not to be sold, or *(b)* **current market value** if the asset is about to be sold.

On the **statement of income,** the objective of the CC/CD model is to report **distributable income.** This is the amount the company can distribute in dividends without reducing the future operating capacity of the entity. This objective is accomplished by measuring expenses at the CC of the assets and services used in the revenue earnings process. Proponents of CC/CD reporting argue that the resultant income (i.e., revenues minus expenses measured at CC, all stated in CDs) measures the **distributable** income of the entity in constant dollars.

The importance of CC/CD income as a measure of distributable income can be seen by comparing it to HC income. During periods of rising prices, HC depreciation usually is less than CC depreciation because of the increase in the cost of operational assets. When the lower amount of HC depreciation is matched against revenue, HC income exceeds CC/CD income. A similar effect occurs when the costs of inventory and other nonmonetary assets are expensed. If a company were to distribute all of its HC income, part of the dividends would not be paid from income as intended but instead would erode the contributed capital of the entity. This erosion appears to be a significant problem. A relevant study indicated that many companies paid dividends in 1980 and 1981 in excess of CC/CD operating income (after tax) for those years.[9]

The CC/CD model uses both specific price indexes and a general price level index. A **specific price index** relates to a single good or service, or to a narrow

[9] R. Evans and R. Freeman, "*Statement 33* Disclosures Confirm Profit Illusion in Primary Statements," *FASB Viewpoints* (Stamford, Conn.: FASB, June 1983).

group of goods or services. In contrast, a GPL index relates to an average of all commonly used goods and services.

The CC/CD statement of income also reports two new values: *(a)* the purchasing power gain or loss (i.e., general price level changes) on net monetary items (as in HC/CD reporting), and *(b)* changes in the CC of the nonmonetary items, net of inflation (i.e., specific price level changes).

Measuring the Effects of Current Cost Price Changes

Under the CC/CD model, the following price change effects are measured and reported for the current period:

1. **On monetary (M) items**—Purchasing power gains (losses) on monetary items are measured by using the GPL index (as discussed in Part A).
2. **On nonmonetary (NM) items**—For each nonmonetary item, its total **change in current cost** (CC) during the period is the difference between its beginning CC and its ending CC.[10] This total change in CC is subdivided as follows:
   a. **Change in CC of nonmonetary (NM) items due to general inflation**—This is the **general** price level effect. It is the difference between beginning CC and that amount restated to CDs on the year-end date, by using the **GPL index.** The change in CC of NM items due to general inflation is positive in the case of inflation and negative in the case of deflation.
   b. **Change in CC of nonmonetary (NM) items, net of general inflation**—This is measured as the **total** change in current cost **minus** the change due to **general inflation.** The change in CC of NM items **net** of general inflation can be positive or negative depending on the relationship between the change in the CC of the particular NM item relative to the change in the CC of that item due to general inflation. The change in CC is sometimes called a holding gain or loss on NM items.

The effects of CC price changes can be shown by the following example. Assume that the current cost of land was $100,000 on January 1, 19A, when the GPL index was 150. On December 31, 19A, the current cost of the land is $112,000 and the GPL index is 165. The total increase in CC during 19A measured in nominal dollars (i.e., before adjusting for inflation) is $12,000 (i.e., $112,000 − $100,000). This change in CC is subdivided into two parts:

a. **Increase in CC due to inflation**—To compute this amount, the beginning CC must be restated in terms of common dollars. The 1/1/19A CC, restated to 12/31/19A dollars, is:

$$\$100{,}000 \times \frac{165}{150} = \$110{,}000$$

The increase in CC caused solely by a change in the general price level is $10,000 (i.e., $110,000 − $100,000).

---

[10] For assets acquired during the current period, **beginning** current cost is the CC at the transaction date, which is the same as the HC on that date. For assets sold or used during the period, ending current cost is current cost on the date the asset is sold or used.

b. **Increase in CC, net of general inflation**—This amount is determined by subtracting the beginning CC (in end-of-year dollars), $110,000, from the ending CC (in end-of-year dollars), $112,000, to compute the increase in CC, net of inflation, $2,000.

In this example, the specific price of land increased faster than the general rate of inflation, resulting in an increase in CC after removing the effects of an increasing GPL.

This example can be diagrammed as follows:

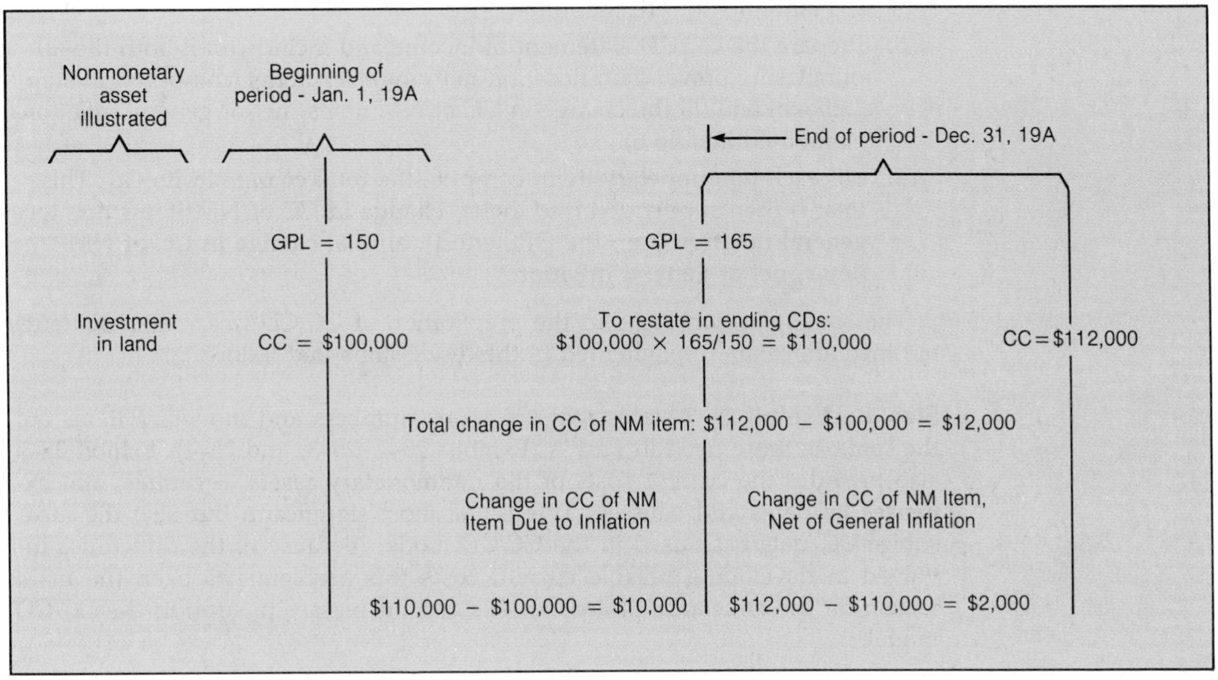

Preparation of CC/CD Financial Statements, Stated in End-of-Period CDs

FASB Standard 89, pars. 7–13, provides guidelines for presenting supplemental information on the effects of changing prices for those enterprises wishing to provide such information as supplements to their primary HC financial statements. This supplemental information would be in the form of *(a)* specified minimum CC information or *(b)* CC/CD financial statements. The discussion and illustrations in this section assume that **comprehensive** CC/CD financial statements are prepared as **supplements** to the HC statements. This approach establishes a foundation for you to learn the concepts and application procedures of the CC/CD model. Also, this approach provides the data needed for the specified minimum CC/CD reporting requirements of *FASB Standard 89* for enterprises willing to provide this information.

Preparation of CC/CD financial statements involves measurement of the CC of each financial statement item and restatement of all such CC amounts to end-of-period CDs.

To illustrate a comprehensive application of the CC/CD concepts, the situation used in Part A, for AB Company (Exhibit 25–3), is adapted. The six application steps to prepare CC/CD financial statements are:

1. Collect the basic data for the company.
2. Identify each financial statement item as either **monetary** or **nonmonetary** (as in Part A).
3. Compute the purchasing power gain (loss) on net monetary items (as in Part A).
4. Prepare the CC/CD statement of financial position by substituting CC/CD amounts for HC amounts.
5. Prepare the CC/CD statement of income and include on it both the *(a)* purchasing power gain (loss) on net **monetary** items (computed in step 2 above) and *(b)* the change in CC of NM items, net of general inflation (computed in step 6).
6. For each **nonmonetary** item, compute the **total change in its CC.** This total is then subdivided into the *(a)* **change in CC of NM items due to general inflation** (i.e., the GPL effect), and *(b)* **change in CC of NM items, net of general inflation.**

The six application steps in the preparation of CC/CD financial statements outlined above are implemented in the discussions that follow.

Step 1. Exhibit 25–7 states that the index numbers and monetary items are the same as those used in Part A (Exhibits 25–2, 25–3, and 25–4). Exhibit 25–7 also provides the current costs of the **nonmonetary assets, revenues, and expenses** by dates and sources. This is the most significant, but also the most subjective, data base used in the CC/CD model. Because of the difficulties involved in developing reliable current costs this problem has been the main reason for the reluctance of accountants and businesses to support the CC/CD model.

Steps 2 and 3. These steps require classification of each financial statement item as either monetary or nonmonetary and computation of the purchasing power gain (loss) on net **monetary items.** These steps were discussed for AB Company in Part A. For AB Company, the **purchasing power loss on net monetary items** during 19F was $264 (Exhibit 25–6) and was reported on the HC/CD statement of income (Exhibit 25–5). This purchasing power loss is reported on the CC/CD statement of income following CC/CD income from continuing operations (illustrated in Exhibit 25–9).

Step 4. Prepare the CC/CD statement of financial position. The CC/CD statement of financial position of AB Company at December 31, 19F, stated in CDs at that date for all items, is shown in **Exhibit 25–8.** The reported **monetary** amounts are the **same** at HC, HC/CD, and CC/CD, which is a typical situation. Therefore, these amounts were taken directly from Exhibit 25–3 or 25–4. The 19F ending CC/CD amounts for the **nonmonetary** assets (i.e., inventory, investment, and operational assets) are given in Exhibit 25–7. The CC/CD amount for contributed capital is the HC amount restated in end-of-period dollars (as

Exhibit 25–7
Selected current cost (CC) data—AB Company, 19F.

General Price Level (GPL) Index Numbers—given in Exhibit 24–2.

Monetary Items—given in Exhibit 25–3.

Nonmonetary Assets, Revenues, and Expenses by Dates:

Item	Source of CC data	Current cost
December 31, 19E:		Current cost (in CDs of 1/1/19F)
Assets (beginning balances):		
Inventory	From prior period, 19E	$ 20,500
Investment in common stock of Smith Company	From prior period, 19E	33,000
Equipment	From prior period, 19E	175,000
Accumulated depreciation (equipment)	From prior period, 19E	(35,000)
Retained earnings (credit)	From prior period, 19E	97,822
December 31, 19F:		Current cost (in CDs of 12/31/19F)
Assets (ending balances):		
Inventory	Suppliers' price lists	$ 26,000
Investment in common stock	Quoted market price	15,000
Equipment (acquired 1/1/19A)	Indexed, specific	196,000
Accumulated depreciation (equipment)	$196,000 × 24%[a]	(47,040)
Parking garage (acquired 1/1/19F)	Professional appraisal	56,000
Accumulated depreciation (PG)	$56,000 × 4%[b]	(2,240)
During 19F (revenues and expenses occurred evenly throughout the year):		Current cost (in average CDs of 19F)
Sales revenue	HC, Exhibit 24–3	$144,000
Cost of goods sold	Suppliers' price lists	86,000
Depreciation expense (equipment)	Computed[c]	7,420
Depreciation expense (PG)	Computed[d]	2,120
General expenses (including interest)	HC, Exhibit 24–3	20,000
Income tax expense	HC, Exhibit 24–3	10,000

Computations:
[a] $24,000 ÷ $100,000 (i.e., HC depreciation ÷ HC) = 24% depreciated to date; $196,000 × 24% = $47,040.
[b] $2,000 ÷ $50,000 (i.e., HC depreciation ÷ HC) = 4% depreciated to date; $56,000 × 4% = $2,240.
[c] Current cost depreciation expense for the year based on average current cost of equipment: ($175,000 + $196,000) ÷ 2 = $185,500; $185,500 × 4% (depreciation rate per year) = $7,420.
[d] Current cost depreciation expense for the year based on average current cost of parking garage: ($50,000 + $56,000) ÷ 2 = $53,000; $53,000 × 4% (depreciation rate per year) = $2,120.

in HC/CD reported in Exhibit 25–4). The amount of retained earnings is computed as a balancing amount.[11]

Step 5. Prepare the CC/CD statement of income and statement of retained earnings. The CC statement of income for AB Company for 19F, stated in CDs of December 31, 19F, is given in **Exhibit 25–9.** Sales revenue, general expenses, and income tax expense are as computed in Exhibit 25–5 because these amounts occurred evenly throughout 19F and did not involve **nonmonetary** assets. Notice the restatement of retained earnings in Exhibit 25–8; it also is a proof of the restated statement of financial position and statement of income.

[11] Alternatively, total stockholders' equity can be used as the balancing amount.

Exhibit 25–8
CC/CD Statements of financial position and retained earnings—AB Company.

AB COMPANY
CC/CD Statement of Financial Position
At December 31, 19F

		Source (exhibit)	CC/CD (in CDs of 12/31/19F)
	Assets		
M	Cash	25–3	$136,000
M	Accounts receivable (net)	25–3	33,000
NM	Inventory	25–7	26,000
NM	Investment in common stock of Smith Co.	25–7	15,000
NM	Equipment	25–7	196,000
NM	Accumulated depreciation, equipment	25–7	(47,040)
	Parking garage	25–7	56,000
NM	Accumulated depreciation, parking garage	25–7	(2,240)
	Total assets		$412,720
	Liabilities		
M	Accounts payable	25–3	$ 45,000
M	Income tax payable	25–3	10,000
M	Note payable, 12%	25–3	50,000
	Stockholders' Equity		
NM	Common stock, nopar	25–4	187,120
NM	Retained earnings	Bal. amt.*	120,600
	Total liabilities and stockholders' equity		$412,720

AB COMPANY
CC/CD Statement of Retained Earnings (also a Proof of Accuracy)
For Year Ended December 31, 19F
(Stated in CDs of December 31, 19F)

	CC/CD (in CDs of 12/31/19F)
Retained earnings, 1/1/19F (from prior year, Exhibit 25–7; $97,822 × 159/147)	$105,807
Add: CC/CD income (Exhibit 25–9)	25,323
Deduct: CC/CD dividends 19F ($10,000 × 159/151)	(10,530)
CC/CD retained earnings, 12/31/19, in CDs of same date	$120,600*

M = Monetary item; same as HC and HC/CD amount; NM = Nonmonetary item.
* Total assets ($412,720) minus sum of total liabilities and common stock ($45,000 + $10,000 + $50,000 ÷ $187,120) = $120,600.

Cost of goods sold and depreciation expense involve **nonmonetary** assets (inventory, equipment, and the parking garage). Their CC amounts are based on the **average CCs** of those assets during 19F, as shown in Exhibit 25–7. To illustrate, the average CC of **equipment** was $185,500 [i.e., ($175,000 + $196,000) ÷ 2; see Exhibit 25–7], and 4% of the asset was depreciated during 19F. Therefore, CC depreciation on the equipment of AB Company was $7,420 (i.e., $185,500 × 4%). CC depreciation on the parking garage is computed in a similar manner.

For **cost of goods sold,** the company could keep two sets of records, one at HC and the other at CC based on suppliers' price lists. For AB Company, it is assumed that the CC of goods sold, stated in average 19F dollars, was $86,000.

Exhibit 25–9
CC/CD statement of income—AB Company.

AB COMPANY
CC/CD statement of Income
For Year Ended December 31, 19F

	Source (exhibit)	CC nominal dollars	CD restatement ratio*	CC/CD (in CDs of 12/31/19F)
Revenues and gains:				
Sales revenue	25–5	$144,000	159/152	$150,624
Expenses and losses:				
Cost of goods sold	25–7	86,000	159/152	(89,956)
General expenses (including interest)	25–5	20,000	159/152	(20,920)
Depreciation expense, equipment	25–7	7,420	159/152	(7,761)
Depreciation expense, parking garage	25–7	2,120	159/152	(2,218)
Income tax expense	25–5	10,000	159/152	(10,460)
CC/CD income from continuing operations				19,309
Purchasing power gain (loss) on net **monetary** items	25–6			(264)
Total change in CC of **nonmonetary** items	25–10	Note A	$25,760	
Change in CC of NM items due to general inflation	25–10	Note A	19,482	
Change in CC of NM items, net of general inflation	25–10			6,278
CC/CD comprehensive income				$ 25,323

Note A: The price change effects of **nonmonetary** assets are as follows (computed in Exhibit 25–10):

Nonmonetary asset	Change in CC total	Change in CC due to general inflation	Change in CC net of general inflation
Inventory	$ 6,500	$ 1,635	$ 4,865
Investment in common stock of Smith Co.	(3,000)	2,706	(5,706)
Equipment	16,380	11,139	5,241
Parking garage	5,880	4,002	1,878
Total	$25,760	$19,482	$ 6,278

* All CD restatement ratios are rounded to three decimals.

All of the revenue and CC expense measures are multiplied by the **CD restatement ratio,** 159/152, to restate each item from average dollars of 19F (because they occurred evenly during 19F) to CDs of December 31, 19F. This attains comparability with all other amounts in the CC/CD 19F financial statements.

The CC/CD financial statements of AB Company report no **gain or loss on the sale of the investment in common stock** of Smith Company (see Exhibit 25–3). This is because the sale proceeds ($15,000 in this example) are the same as the CC of the investment sold at the date of sale. Exhibit 25–7 shows that the CC of the investment shares at December 31, 19F (or on any date) would be determined by the quoted market price of the shares. The quoted market price also would determine the sale proceeds. Therefore, at CC, no gain or loss would result from the sale.

Income from continuing operations for AB Company (i.e., $19,309) is computed as the difference between CC revenues and CC expenses. The last phase of the preparation of the CC/CD statement of income is to include *(a)* the purchasing power gain (loss) on net **monetary items and** *(b)* the two price change effects on **nonmonetary items**—change in CC of NM items due to general inflation and change in CC of NM items, net of general inflation. For AB Company (Exhibit 25–9), these three amounts are set in a box for emphasis. The fundamental nature of each amount may be summarized as follows:

1. Price change effect of **net monetary** items—The **purchasing power gain (loss) on net monetary items** occurs when monetary items are held during a period in which the GPL changes. When this situation occurs, the company experiences a purchasing power gain or loss because the number of dollars related to each monetary item is fixed during the period. However, the "value" of each of those dollars changes. This kind of gain or loss was discussed and illustrated in Part A. During 29F, AB Company experienced a purchasing power loss on net monetary items of $264, as computed in Exhibit 25–6.
2. Price change effects of **nonmonetary assets**—Price changes cause two different effects on nonmonetary assets. One is the effect of **general inflation** due to a change in the **GPL,** and the other is the effect of a **price change net of general inflation** related to each individual asset (see the diagram on page 1331). **Both** of these price change effects occur when the **specific** price of a nonmonetary asset changes more or less than the change in the **GPL** during the period. Step 6 explains the analysis of these price change effects.

Step 6. This step relates only to **nonmonetary assets.** It involves computation of the two price change effects related to nonmonetary assets. These two amounts are as follows:

a. Change in CC of NM items during the period due to **general inflation only.**
b. Change in CC of NM items during the period, net of general inflation. This effect occurs only when the **specific** price change of the item is more or less than the change in CC due to general inflation. This amount sometimes is called a "holding gain or loss on NM items," due to CC **price changes.**

Exhibit 25–10 shows how to compute these two price change effects.

The computational format shown in Exhibit 25–10 is the same for each nonmonetary asset. **The reasoning underlying the computations is similar to that applied to compute the purchasing power gain or loss on net monetary assets.** That is, the changes during the period in the CC amount of each nonmonetary asset are analyzed using the beginning balance and the additions and deductions during the period to derive the ending balance.

For **inventory,** the computed ending CC balance was $19,500 (Exhibit 25–10). This CC balance reflects CC amounts that occurred at different dates. Therefore, it reflects dollars that are not comparable. For example, the CC of beginning inventory (i.e., $20,500) was measured on the beginning date, and each dollar of this amount is **not** comparable with each dollar reflected in the CC amounts

Exhibit 25–10

Computation of price change effects of nonmonetary assets—AB Company, 19F.

Nonmonetary assets	Source	CC at transaction date	Restated to CDs	CC at 12/31/19F
Inventory:				
Beginning balance	25–7	$ 20,500	159/147 = $ 22,181	
Add—purchases during 19F	25–5	85,000	159/152 = 88,910	
Deduct—cost of goods sold for 19F	25–7	(86,000)	159/152 = (89,956)	
1. Ending inv. at CC at transaction dates.		$ 19,500		
2. Ending inv. at CC restated to CDs.			$ 21,135	
3. Ending inventory at year-end CC.	25–7			$ 26,000
Changes in CC during 19F:				
Total increase (decrease) in CC (3 – 1)				$26,000 – $19,500 = $6,500
Change in CC due to inflation (2 – 1)				$21,135 – $19,500 = $1,635
Change in CC, net of inflation (3 – 2)				$26,000 – $21,135 = $4,865
Investment in common stock of Smith Co.:				
Beginning balance	25–7	$ 33,000	159/147 = $ 35,706	
Add—acquisitions—none				
Deduct—sale on 12/30/19F, at CC when sold	25–3	(15,000)	159/159 = (15,000)	
1. Ending balance at CC at transaction dates.		$ 18,000		
2. Ending balance at CC restated to CDs.			$ 20,706	
3. Ending balance at year-end CC.	25–7			$ 15,000
Changes in CC during 19F:				
Total increase (decrease) in CC (3 – 1)				$15,000 – $18,000 = $(3,000)
Change in CC due to inflation (2 – 1)				$20,706 – $18,000 = $ 2,706
Change in CC, net of inflation (3 – 2)				$15,000 – $20,706 = $(5,706)
Equipment:				
Beginning balance (net of depreciation)	25–7	$140,000	159/147 = $151,480	
Add—acquisitions—none				
Deduct—depreciation during 19F	25–7	(7,420)	159/152 = (7,761)	
1. Ending balance at CC at transaction dates.		$132,580		
2. Ending balance at CC restated to CDs.			$143,719	
3. Ending balance at year-end CC.	25–7			$148,960
Changes in CC during 19F:				
Total increase (decrease) in CC (3 – 1)				$148,960 – $132,580 = $16,380
Change in CC due to inflation (2 – 1)				$143,719 – $132,580 = $11,139
Change in CC, net of inflation (3 – 2)				$148,960 – $143,719 = $ 5,241
Parking garage:				
Beginning balance (net of depreciation)	25–7	$ -0-	$ -0-	
Add—acquisition on 1/1/19F, CC at acquisition date	25–3	50,000	159/147 = 54,100	
Deduct—depreciation during 19F	25–7	(2,120)	159/152 = (2,218)	
1. Ending balance at CC at transaction dates.		$ 47,880		
2. Ending balance at CC restated to CDs.			$ 51,882	
3. Ending balance at year-end CC.	25–7			$ 53,760
Changes in CC during 19F:				
Total increase (decrease) in CC (3 – 1)				$53,760 – $47,880 = $5,880
Change in CC due to inflation (2 – 1)				$51,882 – $47,880 = $4,002
Change in CC, net of inflation (3 – 2)				$53,760 – $51,882 = $1,878

of purchases and cost of goods sold, which occurred evenly during the period. Because of this noncomparability, each of these three CC amounts must be restated to CDs. Exhibit 25–10 provides the restatement to CDs of the year-end date.[12]

To compute the three CC price change effects (i.e., total, general inflation, and net), a series of comparisons is made as shown in Exhibit 25–10. Computation of the price change effect for **each nonmonetary asset** is:

1. **Total change in CC of NM items**—The total change in CC of each nonmonetary asset is computed as the difference between:
   a. Its actual CC at the end of the period, which automatically is stated in end-of-period CDs (i.e., for inventory, $26,000), and
   b. Its ending balance at CC when the balance or transaction occurred (i.e., $19,500 for inventory).

   Thus, for inventory the total change in CC during 19F was $6,500 (i.e., $26,000 − $19,500). The general inflation and net of inflation price change effects, explained below, must sum algebraically to this total price change effect.
2. **Change in CC of NM items due to general inflation (GPL)**—The change in CC due to general inflation (of each nonmonetary asset) is computed as the difference between:
   a. Its ending balance at CC when the balance or transaction occurred (i.e., $19,500 for inventory), and
   b. Those amounts restated in end-of-period CDs (i.e., $21,135 for inventory).

   Thus, for **inventory** the change in CC due to general inflation during 19F was $1,635 (i.e., $21,135 − $19,500).
3. **Change in CC of NM items, net of general inflation**—The change in CC, net of general inflation, is computed for each nonmonetary asset as the difference between:
   a. Its actual CC at the end of the period (i.e., $26,000 for inventory), and
   b. The ending balance at CC when the balance or transaction occurred (i.e., beginning balance plus additions minus deductions during the period) restated to end-of-period CDs (i.e., $21,135 for inventory). Thus, for inventory the change in CC, net of general inflation, during 19F was $4,865 (i.e., $26,000 − $21,135).

Notice that each computation in Exhibit 25–10 follows the pattern described above for inventory.

During 19F, the current costs of the inventory, equipment, and parking garage of AB Company increased faster than did the GPL.[13] Their respective changes in CC, net of general inflation, were $4,865, $5,241, and $1,878, as shown in Note A of Exhibit 25–9. During 19F, the CC of the investment in common

[12] Use of annual average GPL index numbers also is acceptable for the numerator of the CD index ratios, in which case all items on the financial statements would be stated in annual average, rather than end-of-period, CDs.

[13] For example, reference to Exhibit 25–7 indicates that the CC of equipment (excluding depreciation) increased by 12% (i.e., from $175,000 to $196,000), while the GPL index increased by 8.2% (i.e., from 147 to 159) during 19F.

stock **decreased** from $33,000 to $30,000 (note that half of the investment shares were sold on December 30, 19F). Because the GPL **increased** during 19F, the change in CC, net of general inflation, on the investment was a **negative** (a loss) $5,706 (i.e., – $3,000 – $2,706). For AB Company during 19F, the total change in CC, net of general inflation, of all its nonmonetary assets was $6,278, as shown in Exhibit 25–9.

Usefulness of CC/CD Financial Statements

The potential usefulness of CC/CD data can be summarized as follows:

1. **CC/CD income from continuing operations** may be useful for assessing future net cash flows of an enterprise. The resulting **CC/CD income from continuing operations** may be a good predictor of future CC/CD income from continuing operations. CC/CD income provides more up-to-date information about the current costs of the company's assets used up in production than the corresponding HC or HC/CD amounts. Also, CC/CD income from continuing operations is an approximation of "distributable income." This amount is the maximum an enterprise can pay in dividends and maintain its physical operating capacity by retaining sufficient internally generated funds to replace worn-out assets.
2. The **increase or decrease in the CCs** of the **nonmonetary assets** held by the enterprise may be useful for assessing the future net cash flows of the enterprise because a change in the CCs of assets represents a change in the financial investment. Because an enterprise expects to earn a return on that investment, information on **changes in CCs** may represent a basis for assessing **changes in future cash flows.**[14]
3. The **separation of CC/CD comprehensive income into its operating** (i.e., income from continuing operations) **and holding** (i.e., increases or decreases in CCs of nonmonetary assets) **components** may be useful information for predicting the future net cash flows of the entity. The results of operating and holding activities may be affected by different economic forces. Also, these two measures may be used in different ways to predict future cash flows. It is easier to evaluate the prospective impacts of the various factors affecting operating income and CC changes if the two items are separated than if they are aggregated as in HC and HC/CD reporting.[15]
4. The CC/CD statement of financial position presents assets, liabilities, and stockholders' equity at current cost. This provides users with an estimate of the amount required currently to replace the entity's assets in their

---

[14] For a discussion of the contrary position that CC changes cannot be used to predict changes in future cash flows, see L. Revsine, *Replacement Cost Accounting* (Englewood Cliffs, N.J.: Prentice-Hall, 1973), pp. 142–64; and R. A. Samuelson, "Should Replacement Cost Changes Be Included in Income?" *The Accounting Review*, April 1980, pp. 254–68.

[15] A contrary position (i.e., that operating and holding activities are inseparable and, hence, cannot be evaluated separately) is presented by P. Prakash and S. Sunder, "The Case Against Separation of Current Operating Profit and Holding Gain," *The Accounting Review*, January 1979, pp. 1–22.

present condition. It also helps investors and others make better estimates of the value of a company.

5. Conceptually, the CC/CD model is far superior to the current GAAP, HC model except for one major problem; that is, the necessity to develop reliable current costs on a going-concern basis that satisfies the cost-benefit constraint. The impact these changes have on accounting income is well documented. A relevant study of companies disclosing constant dollar and current cost information found that for 1981 the average return on investment (i.e., operating income divided by net assets) on a historical cost (HC) basis was 14.3%. However, it was only 2.9% and 2.5% on the historical cost/constant dollar (HC/CD) and current cost/constant dollar (CC/CD) bases. Direct comparison of the steel and computer industries provides further evidence of the relevance of alternative accounting models. The steel industry showed an 11.7% return on investment (ROI) on a HC basis, while showing only a .6% and .1% ROI on the HC/CD and CC/CD bases, respectively. For the same three measures, the computer industry showed a 16.7% (HC), 6.7% (HC/CD), and 13.3% (CC/CD) ROI.[16] Alternative accounting models appear to be relevant in evaluating the profitability of a business. However, the controversy about their usefulness continues.[17]

FASB Suggested Disclosure Requirements for Changing Prices

FASB Standard 89, Appendix A, recommends the following disclosures of current cost/constant dollar (CC/CD) information:

1. Five-year comparison of 10 selected HC/CD items, in either average for the year or end-of-year units of constant purchasing power. The 10 selected items are illustrated in **Exhibit 25–11.**
2. Additional disclosures for the current year:
   a. Components of income from continuing operations for the current year on a current cost basis.
   b. Difference between the amounts in the primary statements on the current cost basis for cost of goods sold and depreciation, depletion, and amortization expense.
   c. Separate amounts for the current cost or lower recoverable amounts for inventory and property plant and equipment.
   d. Principal types of information used to compute the current cost of cost of goods sold; and depreciation, depletion, and amortization expense.
   e. Any differences between the primary statements and the HC/CD amounts for the depreciation methods, estimates of useful life, and

[16] K. Evans and R. Freeman, "*Statement 33* Disclosures Confirm Profit Illusion in Primary Statements," *FASB Viewpoints* (Stamford, Conn.: FASB, June 1983).

[17] W. Beaver and W. Landsman, "Incremental Information Content of *Statement 33* Disclosures," *FASB Research Report* (Stamford, Conn.: FASB, 1983), consider whether HC/CD or CC/CD disclosures influence security prices.

Exhibit 25–11
Five-year comparison of selected financial data (CC/CD).

Five-Year Comparison of Selected Financial Data
Adjusted for Effects of Changing Prices
In Thousands of Dollars,
Except for Per Share Amounts

	Year Ended December 31				
	19X6	19X5	19X4	19X3	19X2
1. Total revenue:					
As reported	$275,500	$239,800	$219,100	$194,800	$193,100
Adjusted for general inflation[a]	275,500	247,500	240,000	235,500	265,000
2. Income (loss) from operations:					
As reported	22,995	11,097	4,756	9,977	11,847
Adjusted for specific price changes[a]	4,839	1,660	(2,102)	(4,663)	1,261
3. Purchasing power gain from holding net monetary liabilities[a]	2,449	7,027	5,432	1,247	6,375
4. Excess of increase in specific prices of assets over increase in the general price level[a]	20,458	2,292	3,853	8,597	3,777
5. Foreign currency translation adjustment:					
As reported	(295)	(276)	(396)	(138)	76
Adjusted for specific price changes[a]	(624)	(386)	(454)	(293)	127
6. Net assets at year-end:					
As reported	47,700	28,000	20,179	18,819	11,980
Adjusted for specific price changes[b]	92,027	67,905	60,409	56,966	55,705
7. Per share information:					
Income (loss) from operations:					
As reported	$ 15.33	$ 7.40	$ 3.17	$ 6.65	$ 7.90
Adjusted for specific price changes[a]	3.23	1.11	(1.40)	(3.11)	.84
8. Cash dividends declared:					
As reported	2.00	2.00	2.00	2.00	2.00
Adjusted for general inflation[a]	2.00	2.06	2.19	2.42	2.75
9. Market price at year-end:					
As reported	36	38	41	23	25
Adjusted for general inflation[a]	35	39	43	27	32
10. Average consumer price index[c]	298.4	289.1	272.4	246.8	217.4

[a] In average 19X6 dollars.
[b] Net assets adjusted for specific price changes include inventory and property, plant, and equipment at current cost and all other items as they are reported in the primary financial statements. No adjustment has been made for the lower tax basis applicable to the current cost amounts included in net assets.
[c] For purposes of this illustration, although the years for which information has been provided are nonspecific, the actual 1979–83 average index numbers have been applied.
Source: *FASB Standard No. 89,* p. 30.

residual values. **Exhibit 25–12** shows an illustrative report from *FASB Standard 89* designed to satisfy these reporting needs.

Summary

This chapter discusses accounting for changing prices, conformity with the latest FASB pronouncement *(Standard 89)* with primary emphasis on *(a)* general price level effects related to the current GAAP historical cost basis accounting model and *(b)* the concept of a current cost basis with constant dollar measurement units as a replacement for historical costs.

Two kinds of price indexes were defined: *(a)* general price level (GPL) indexes,

Exhibit 25–12
Statement of income from continuing operations (CC/CD).

Statement of Income from Continuing Operations Adjusted for Changing Prices[a]
For the Year Ended December 31, 19X6
(in thousands)

	As reported in the primary statements	Adjusted for changes in specific prices (current cost)
Net sales and other operating revenues	$275,500	$275,500
Cost of goods sold	197,000	205,408
Depreciation expense	10,275	20,023
Other operating expenses	14,685	14,685
Interest expense	7,550	7,550
Income tax expense	22,995	22,995
	252,505	270,661
Income from continuing operations	$ 22,995	$ 4,839
Gain from decline in purchasing power of net amounts owed[b]		$ 2,449
Increase in specific prices (current cost) of inventory and property, plant, and equipment held during the year[c]		$ 25,846
Effect of increase in general price level		5,388
Excess of increase in specific prices over increase in the general price level		$ 20,458
Foreign currency translation adjustment[d]	$ (295)	$ (624)

[a] The condensed financial information in this schedule compares selected information from the primary financial statements with information that reflects effects of changes in the specific prices (current cost) of inventory and property, plant, and equipment expressed in units of constant purchasing power. The current cost amounts for inventory and cost of goods sold reflect actual manufacturing costs incurred in 19X6. The current cost amounts for major components of property, plant, and equipment were determined by applying specific price indexes to the applicable historical costs. For assets used in U.S. operations, producer price indexes and factory mutual building indexes were used; for assets used in foreign operations, appropriate indexes for each country were used. The current cost information is expressed in average 19X6 dollars as measured by the CPI-U.

[b] The purchasing power gain on net amounts owed is an economic benefit to the enterprise that results from being able to repay those amounts with cheaper dollars.

[c] During 19X6, the specific prices (current cost) of inventory increased by $9,108 and of property, plant, and equipment by $16,738. The total increase of $25,846 exceeded the increase necessary to keep pace with general inflation. At December 31, 19X6, the current cost of inventory was $65,700 and of property, plant, and equipment, net of accumulated depreciation, was $89,335 (both measured in December 31, 19X6 units of purchasing power). Those amounts are higher than the amounts in the primary statements of $63,000 for inventory and $45,750 for property, plant, and equipment, net of accumulated depreciation; therefore, it is reasonable to expect income from continuing operations on a current cost basis for 19X7 to remain significantly below that reported in the primary statements.

[d] Current cost amounts for foreign operations are measured in their functional currencies, translated into dollar equivalents using the average exchange rate for the year, and restated into constant units of purchasing power using the CPI-U. Essentially, the foreign currency translation adjustment is the effect of changes in exchange rates during the year on shareholders' equity. The negative translation adjustment indicates that, overall, the dollar has increased in value relative to the functional currencies used to measure the foreign operations of the enterprise.

Source: *FASB Standard No. 89,* p. 26.

which represent a broad "market basket" used to measure inflation and deflation, and *(b)* specific price indexes that relate to price changes of a single good or service (or to small groups). Monetary and nonmonetary items were carefully defined because in preparing inflation adjusted (GPL) financial statements **monetary** items are not restated, while **nonmonetary** items are restated. Monetary items are cash, cash instruments, receivables, and debts; they are not restated because they call for a specific number of dollars that does not change even though the general price level changes. In contrast, nonmonetary items such as operational assets are free to change in terms of the number of dollars that they will command; their prices tend to change as the GPL changes.

Part A discussed the historical cost, constant dollar (HC/CD) model. This model retains the historical cost attribute, but it changes the measurement unit from transaction cost (called **nominal cost**) to a constant and current (year-end) cost. In this way it attains equivalence in the measuring unit because all costs are measured in the same dollars the same across time.

Part B discusses current cost (CC) as a replacement for historical cost (HC). The model is called **current cost/constant dollar** (CC/CD). This model reports the statement of financial position and statement of income amounts at current cost measured in constant units—the ending or average price level for the current period. The primary CC/CD problem is measuring the current cost of each item which is a very complex and subjective process.

QUESTIONS

Part A

1. What is the price phenomenon known as inflation? What is the opposite phenomenon called? How would each affect you if you received an equal amount from an educational trust fund set up by your parents 20 years ago?
2. "When prices are going up, they all go up; when they drop, they all drop." Comment on this statement.
3. What indexes measure changes in the general purchasing power of the U.S. dollar? What index has been prescribed for preparation of CD financial statements?
4. Among sales, cost of goods sold, salaries, and depreciation expense, during a period of rapidly changing prices, which would most nearly be at the current price basis under the conventional historical cost (HC) model and which would not be on a current price basis? Give reasons for your response.
5. When prices are changing rapidly, why may financial statements prepared on the HC basis be deficient in some respects?
6. When general prices are rising and depreciation expense is computed on the conventional HC basis, what is likely to be true with respect to the availability of resources that would be required for replacement of the depreciable assets?
7. Under the CD restatement approach, financial statement items are classified as monetary or nonmonetary. Briefly, by which criterion can these two categories be distinguished?
8. Indicate, with explanations where necessary, whether the following items are monetary or nonmonetary: *(a)* stocks held as investments, *(b)* bonds held as investments, *(c)* deposits in domestic banks, *(d)* merchandise inventory, *(e)* accounts and notes receivable, *(f)* machinery and equipment, *(g)* accounts and notes payable, *(h)* preferred stock, *(i)* retained earnings, and *(j)* deferred credit related to income taxes.
9. During its most recent accounting period, XY Company had a larger balance of cash and receivables than monetary liabilities; general prices rose steadily. Would this condition cause a purchasing power gain or loss on net monetary items?
10. If prices rise steadily over an extended period of time, indicate whether the following items would cause a purchasing power gain, a purchasing power loss, or neither purchasing power gain nor loss on net monetary items:

a. Maintaining a balance in a checking account.
b. Owing bonds payable.
c. Owning land.
d. Amortizing goodwill.
e. Holding common treasury stock.

11. The valuation basis used in conventional HC financial statements is—
    a. Market value.
    b. Original cost.
    c. Replacement cost.
    d. A mixture of costs and values.
    e. None of the above.
12. A company begins the fiscal year with a $10,000 net monetary asset position, has an even outflow of monetary assets of $25,000 during the year, and ends the year with a net monetary liability position of $15,000. If the GPL index is 120 at the beginning of the year, 125 average for the year, and 132 at the end of the year, what is the purchasing power gain or loss during the year?

Part B

13. "The HC/CD accounting model changes the unit of measure but retains the attribute measured relative to the conventional accounting model, whereas CC/CD changes both the attribute measured and the unit of measurement." Evaluate this statement.
14. What are the advantages and disadvantages of CC/CD reporting in relation to HC/CD reporting?
15. Why are increases or decreases in the current costs of nonmonetary assets in CC reporting defined in relation to the GPL?
16. How does the recognition of increases or decreases in the CC of nonmonetary assets under the CC/CD model affect the ability of an entity to "manipulate its earnings" by selling selected assets that have increased or decreased in value?
17. Distinguish between the current cost and replacement cost of an asset.
18. How does the net realizable value, or recoverable amount, of an asset affect current cost accounting?
19. The current cost of land is $50,000 on January 1, 19A, and $55,000 on December 31, 19A. If the GPL index was 100 and 110 on January 1 and December 31, respectively, what was the increase in the current cost of land, net of inflation, during 19A (stated in dollars as of December 31, 19A)?
20. Assume that in question 19 the GPL index remained unchanged during 19A; it was 100 on January 1, 19A and December 31, 19A. What was the increase in the current cost of land, net of inflation, during 19A (stated in dollars as of December 31, 19A)?

EXERCISES

Part A: Exercises 25–1 to 25–10

E 25–1 (Overview Questions about HC/CD Disclosures)

Select the best answer in each of the following. Give the basis for your response:

1. In preparing HC/CD financial statements, monetary items consist of:
    a. Cash items plus all receivables with a fixed maturity date.

b. Cash, other assets expected to be converted into cash and current liabilities.
c. Assets and liabilities whose amounts are fixed by contract or otherwise in terms of dollars, regardless of price level changes.
d. Assets and liabilities classified as current on the balance sheet.
e. None of the above.

2. In preparing HC/CD financial statements, a nonmonetary item would include:
   a. Accounts payable in cash.
   b. Long-term bonds payable.
   c. Accounts receivable.
   d. Allowance for doubtful accounts.
   e. None of the above.
3. An accountant who recommends the restatement of financial statements for GPL changes should not support this recommendation by stating that:
   a. Purchasing power gains and losses should be recognized.
   b. Historical dollars are not comparable to present-day dollars.
   c. The conversion of asset costs to a constant dollar basis is a useful extension of the original cost basis of asset valuation.
   d. Assets should be valued at their replacement cost.
4. During a period of deflation, an entity usually would have the greatest gain in general purchasing power by holding:
   a. Cash.
   b. Plant and equipment.
   c. Accounts payable.
   d. Mortgages payable.
   e. None of the above.
5. CD restatement of HC financial statements to reflect GPL changes reports nonmonetary assets at:
   a. Lower of cost or market (LCM).
   b. Current appraisal values.
   c. Costs adjusted for purchasing power changes.
   d. Current replacement cost.
   e. None of the above.
6. An unacceptable practice for reporting HC/CD information is:
   a. The inclusion of general purchasing power gains and losses on monetary items in the price level statement of income.
   b. The inclusion of extraordinary gains and losses in the HC/CD statement of income.
   c. The use of charts, ratios, and narrative information.
   d. The use of specific price indexes to restate inventories, plant, and equipment.
   e. None of the above.

(AICPA adapted)

E 25–2 (Analysis of HC Statement Items, Comparability)

Some items on conventional historical cost basis financial statements are expressed in current period dollars (or nearly so), while other items are normally expressed in dollars of prior periods.

Required:

1. Name the principal statement of financial position items that likely would not be expressed in current period dollars. If any part of your answer depends on the accounting procedures employed, explain.
2. Name the principal items in the statement of income that likely would not be expressed in current period dollars (or nearly so). If any part of your answer depends on the accounting procedures used, explain.

3. Name the principal items in the statement of cash flows-indirect method that likely would not be expressed in current period dollars. If any part of your answer depends on the accounting procedures used, explain.

(AICPA adapted)

E 25–3 **(Prepare HC/CD Statement of Financial Position and Statement of Income)** Banner Corporation is completing its fifth year of operations (19E). Comparative statements of financial position (HC basis) at year-end 19D and 19E are as follows:

	December 31	
	19D	19E
Cash and receivables	$250,000	$325,000
Inventories	187,500	162,500
Future plant site	62,500	62,500
Fixtures	210,000	270,000
Accumulated depreciation	(50,000)	(74,000)
	$660,000	$746,000
Current liabilities	$ 75,000	$137,500
Long-term liabilities	150,000	125,000
Capital stock	400,000	400,000
Retained earnings	35,000	83,500
	$660,000	$746,000

The statement of income (HC basis) for the year ended December 31, 19E, follows:

Sales revenue		$1,000,000
Cost of goods sold:		
Beginning inventory	$187,500	
Purchases	625,000	
Goods available	812,500	
Ending inventory	162,500	
Cost of goods sold		650,000
Gross margin		350,000
Expenses:		
Operating expenses except depreciation	120,000	
Depreciation expense	24,000	144,000
Income before taxes		206,000
Income tax expense		87,500
Net income		$ 118,500

A dividend of $70,000 was declared at year-end. At midyear, additional fixtures costing $60,000 were purchased. The annual rate of depreciation on fixtures is 10% of cost. Inventories are on a FIFO basis. When the capital stock was issued at various times, the average GPL index was 130.312. The original fixtures of $150,000 and the future plant site were acquired during the first year of operations when the relevant GPL index was 120. Other GPL index data are as follows: 12/31/19E, 163.8; 12/31/19D, 150; Average for 19E, 157.5; Average for 19D, 146.25.

Assume the beginning inventory was acquired at average 19D prices. Purchases, sales, operating expense, and income taxes occurred or accrued evenly throughout the year.

Required (round all CD restatement ratios to three decimals):

1. Prepare an HC/CD statement of financial position as of December 31, 19E, and HC/CD statement of income for 19E. Determine the purchasing power gain or loss on net monetary items and present a separate schedule detailing its computation.
2. Give the gross and net carrying values of the fixtures and of the future plant site for the HC/CD statement of financial position as of December 31, 19D. Give the

19E, HC/CD statement of retained earnings as proof of the statement of financial position.

E 25–4 (Analysis of GPL Index Numbers; Investment)

Becker Corporation sold one third of its long-term investment in the common stock of another company (carried at cost) and made the entry shown in Column A below:

	Column A		Column B	
Cash	31,000		31,000	
Investment in stock		25,000		28,750
Gain on sale of investment		6,000		2,250

In preparing HC/CD statements, the transaction of column A was restated as shown in column B.

Required (round restatement ratios to five decimal places):

1. If the GPL index was 138 when the transaction recorded above occurred, at what level was it when the stock was acquired? Show computations.
2. Assume the remaining two thirds of the stock is sold later for $60,000 when the GPL index is 147. Give entries paralleling those above in columns A and B.
3. If the stock prices and GPL index values given were unchanged, what other factors, if any, would cause entries reflected in columns A and B to differ at the time of either the first or second sale?

E 25–5 (HC/CD of Individual Items on the Statement of Financial Position and Statement of Income)

Bertrand Company is preparing financial statements on the HC/CD basis. Selected data are as follows:

1. GPL index data: 1/1/19A, 115; 12/31/19A, 120; 6/30/19B, 126; 12/31/19D, 168; Average for 19E, 174; 12/31/19E, 180.
2. Property, plant and equipment acquisition and depreciation data.
   a. Land acquired January 1, 19A, at a cost of $90,000.
   b. Building acquired December 31, 19A, at a cost of $120,000; by year-end, 19D and 19E, respectively, accumulated depreciation on the building amounted to $44,000 and $48,000.
   c. Equipment costing $168,000 was acquired June 30, 19B; by December 31, 19D, accumulated depreciation amounted to $109,200; depreciation recorded for 19E was $8,400.
   d. New equipment, added during 19E at a time when the index was at an average value for the year, cost $58,000; depreciation recorded on this new equipment for 19E amounted to $4,350.
3. Monetary items: At the start of 19E, total monetary assets amounted to $120,000, while total monetary liabilities amounted to $180,000. At the end of 19E, total monetary assets amounted to $140,000, while total monetary liabilities were $190,000.

Required:

Use the numbers below for identification and compute the amounts for each numbered item. Round CD restatement ratios to five decimal places.

A. On the HC/CD statement of financial position as of December 31, 19E, carrying values for each would be—
   1. Land.
   2. Building (gross amount).
   3. Accumulated depreciation—building.
   4. Original equipment (gross amount).

5. New equipment (gross amount).
6. Accumulated depreciation on equipment (original).
7. Accumulated depreciation on equipment (new).
8. Total monetary assets.
9. Total monetary liabilities of income.

B. On the HC/CD statement of income for the year ended December 31, 19E, amounts reported would be—
   10. Depreciation expense (original equipment).
   11. Depreciation expense (new equipment).
   12. Depreciation expense (building).
   13. Sales revenue (if sales of $400,000 were made evenly throughout 19E).

E 25–6 (HC/CD Restatement; Seven Questions; an Overview)

Select the best answer in each of the following questions. Items are independent of one another except where indicated otherwise. Give the basis, including computations, for your choice.

The following information is applicable to items 1 through 3:

Equipment purchased for $120,000 on January 1, 19A, when the price index was 100, was sold on December 31, 19C, at a price of $85,000. The equipment originally was expected to last six years with no residual value and was depreciated on a straight-line basis. The GPL index at the end of 19A was 125; 19B, 150; and 19C, 175.

1. HC/CD (CDs as of December 31, 19A) financial statements prepared at the end of 19A would include:
   a. Equipment, $150,000; accumulated depreciation, $25,000; and no gain or loss.
   b. Equipment, $150,000; accumulated depreciation, $25,000; and a gain, $30,000.
   c. Equipment, $150,000; accumulated depreciation, $20,000; and a gain, $30,000.
   d. Equipment, $120,000; accumulated depreciation, $20,000; and a gain, $30,000.
   e. None of the above.
2. HC/CD (CDs as of December 31, 19B) financial statements prepared at the end of 19B should include depreciation expense of:
   a. $35,000.
   b. $30,000.
   c. $25,000.
   d. $20,000.
   e. None of the above.
3. The HC/CD (CDs as of December 31, 19C) statement of income prepared at the end of 19C should include:
   a. A gain of $35,000.
   b. A gain of $25,000.
   c. No gain or loss.
   d. A loss of $5,000.
   e. None of the above.
4. If land were purchased at a cost of $20,000 in January 19A when the GPL index was 120 and sold in December 19F when the GPL index was 150, the selling price that would result in no gain or loss on a HC/CD basis would be:
   a. $30,000.
   b. $24,000.
   c. $20,000.
   d. $16,000.
   e. None of the above.
5. If land were purchased in 19A for $100,000 when the GPL index was 100 and sold at the end of 19G for $160,000 when the GPL index was 170, the HC/CD (CDs as of the end of 19G) statement of income for 19G would show:
   a. A purchasing power gain of $70,000 and a loss on sale of land of $10,000.
   b. A gain on sale of land of $60,000.
   c. A purchasing power loss of $10,000.
   d. A loss on sale of land of $10,000.
   e. None of the above.

6. If the base year is 19A (when the GPL index = 100) and land is purchased for $50,000 in 19C when the GPL index is 108.5, the cost of the land restated to 19A general purchasing power (rounded to the nearest whole dollar) would be:
   a. $54,250.
   b. $50,000.
   c. $46,083.
   d. $45,750.
   e. None of the above.
7. Assume the same facts as in item 6. The cost of the land restated to December 31, 19G, general purchasing power when the GPL index was 119.2 (rounded to the nearest whole dollar) would be:
   a. $59,600.
   b. $54,931.
   c. $46,083.
   d. $45,512.
   e. None of the above.

(AICPA adapted)

E 25–7 (Effects of GPL Price Changes on an Investment)

An investor bought land for $90,000 in 19A when the index measuring general purchasing power of the dollar was 110. Assuming a gain on sale of the land is taxable at a capital gains rate of 25%, at what price would the land have to be sold on each of the following dates for the investor to maintain the equivalent purchasing power after taxes (round answer to the nearest dollar)? In each instance, the GPL index number on the date of sale was as follows: 10/1/19B, 120; 5/1/19C, 129; 7/1/19D, 140; 12/1/19E, 154.

E 25–8 (HC/CD; Nine Questions; an Overview)

Select the best answer in each of the following. Give the basis for your response.

1. The valuation basis used in HC financial statements is:
   a. Market value.
   b. Original cost.
   c. Replacement cost.
   d. A mixture of costs and values.
   e. None of the above.
2. When preparing HC/CD financial statements, it would not be appropriate to use:
   a. Cost or market, whichever is lower, in the valuation of inventories.
   b. Replacement cost in the valuation of plant assets.
   c. The HC basis in reporting income tax expense.
   d. The actual amounts payable in reporting liabilities on the statement of financial position.
   e. Any of the above.
3. Gains and losses on nonmonetary assets usually are reported in HC financial statements when the items are sold. Gains and losses on the sale of nonmonetary assets should be reported in HC/CD financial statements:
   a. In the same period, but the amount will probably differ.
   b. In the same period and the same amount.
   c. Over the life of the nonmonetary asset.
   d. Partly over the life of the nonmonetary asset and the remainder when the asset is sold.
   e. None of the above.
4. A practice for presenting HC/CD information that is not acceptable is the:
   a. Use of charts, ratios, and narrative information.
   b. Use of GPL indexes to restate inventories, plant, and equipment.
   c. Inclusion of purchasing power gains and losses on monetary items in the HC/CD statement of income.
   d. Inclusion of extraordinary gains and losses in the HC/CD statement of income.
   e. None of the above.

5. For purposes of restating financial statements for changes in the general level of prices, monetary items consist of:
   a. Assets and liabilities whose amounts are fixed by contract or otherwise in terms of dollars regardless of price level changes.
   b. Assets and liabilities that are classified as current on the statement of financial position.
   c. Cash items plus all receivables with a fixed maturity date.
   d. Cash, other assets expected to be converted into cash, and current liabilities.
6. Following are four observations regarding the amounts reported in HC/CD financial statements. Which observation is valid?
   a. The HC/CD amount reported for an asset usually approximates its current market value.
   b. The HC/CD amounts are not departures from historical cost.
   c. When inventory increases and prices are rising, last-in, first-out (LIFO) inventory accounting has the same effect on financial statements as HC/CD amounts.
   d. When inventory remains constant and prices are rising, LIFO inventory accounting has the same effect on financial statements as HC/CD amounts.

Items 7, 8, and 9 are based on the following information:

The general price level index at the end of each of the following years was: 19A, 100; 19B, 110; 19C, 115; 19D, 120; and 19E, 140.

7. In December 19D, Russel Corporation purchased land for $300,000. The land was held until December 19E, when it was sold for $400,000. The HC/CD (CDs as of December 31, 19E) statement of income for the year ended December 31, 19E, should include how much gain or loss on this sale?
   a. $20,000 loss.
   b. $20,000 purchasing power loss.
   c. $50,000 gain.
   d. $100,000 gain.
8. On January 1, 19B, the Silver Company purchased equipment for $300,000. The equipment was being depreciated over an estimated life of 10 years on the straight-line method, with no estimated residual value. On December 31, 19E, the equipment was sold for $200,000. The HC/CD (CDs as of December 31, 19E) statement of income for the year ended December 31, 19E, should include how much gain or loss from this sale?
   a. $10,600 loss.
   b. $16,000 gain.
   c. $20,000 gain.
   d. $52,000 loss.
9. An analysis of the Gallant Corporation's Machinery and Equipment account as of December 31, 19E, follows:

Machinery and equipment:	
Acquired in December 19B	$400,000
Acquired in December 19D	100,000
Balance	$500,000
Accumulated depreciation:	
On equipment acquired in December 19B	$160,000
On equipment acquired in December 19D	20,000
Balance	$180,000

An HC/CD (CDs as of December 31, 19E) statement of financial position prepared as of December 31, 19E, should include machinery and equipment net of accumulated depreciation of:
   a. $284,848.
   b. $360,000.
   c. $398,788.
   d. $448,000.

(AICPA adapted)

E 25–9 (HC/CD; First Period; Financial Statements)

When items in the following HC trial balance were acquired, the GPL index was 150.

Cash	$ 7,500	
Equipment	10,000	
Accumulated depreciation		$ 2,000
Liability		1,900
Capital stock		13,600
Retained earnings		-0-
Total	$17,500	$17,500

Transactions during the first half of the current accounting year follow GPL index values prevailing at the time are indicated parenthetically.

Jan.	10	A payment of $800 on the liability balance is made (160).
Feb.	15	Revenue for services is billed to customers, $2,500 (175).
Mar.	1	Four fifths of the revenue billed is collected (180).
Apr.	20	Land is purchased for $8,000 cash (190).
May	5	General expenses are paid, $500 (185).
June	30	Recorded six months' depreciation on the equipment that has a 10-year life and no residual value (200).

Required:

1. Enter the initial balances, then record the six months' transactions directly in ledger accounts; also enter the date and the GPL index number parenthetically.
2. At the close of the six-month period, prepare both HC and HC/CD (CDs as of June 30) statements of financial position and statements of income, using the CD restatement procedures as illustrated in the chapter. Calculate the purchasing power gain or loss on net monetary items. Since no average for the six-month period is given, it will be necessary to apply, to each transaction and balance, a specific CD restatement ratio. For example, if a $660 transaction occurred when the price index was 165, in June 30 terms (when the index was 200), the restatement would be calculated as $660 × 200/165 = $800. Round all calculations to nearest dollar. Prepare a proof of the HC/CD ending balance of retained earnings.

E 25–10 (Analytical; Purchasing Power Gain or Loss on Monetary Items)

An incomplete computation of purchasing power gain or loss on net monetary items is given below.

	HC	HC/CD
Total beginning excess of monetary assets over monetary liabilities	$121,000	$132,000
Increases during the year:		
Sales revenue	$287,500	$300,000
Sale of common stock	106,200	108,000
Total increases	$393,700	$408,000
Decreases during the year:		
Purchases	$197,800	$206,400
Expenses	33,120	34,560
Cash dividend declared	20,000	20,000
Total decreases	$250,920	$260,960

Additional data: Sales, purchases, and expenses occurred evenly throughout the year. The GPL index at year-end was 120.

Required (support each answer; show how it was derived):

1. What was the index value when the period began?
2. What was the average index value for the year?

3. What was the index value when the stock was sold?
4. Assuming prices rose steadily, when was the dividend declared?
5. What was the purchasing power gain or loss on net monetary items?

Part B: Exercises 25–11 to 25–17

E 25–11 **(CC/CD; Analysis of Inventory and Cost of Goods Sold)**
The following information is available regarding the inventory of Spruce Corporation:

	HC	CC (at transaction or balance date)
January 1, 19C, balance	$ 45,000	$ 50,000
Purchases during 19C	300,000	300,000
December 31, 19C, balance	82,000	95,000

Purchases were made evenly during 19C. Merchandise that sold evenly during 19C had an average current cost of $25 per unit (10,800 units sold). GPL index information during 19C was: January 1, 19C, 100; Average for 19C, 115; December 31, 19C, 132.

Required (round ratios to three decimal places).

1. Set up and complete a schedule of inventory changes in the current cost (CC) of inventory and compute *(a)* total increase in CC *(b)* increase in CC, due to general inflation, and *(c)* decrease in CC, net of general inflation. Suggestion: set up three column headings: CC at transaction or balance date; CC restatement ratio, and CC/CD (in CDs as of 12/31/19C). Also, indicate what items would be reported on the CC/CD financial statements.
2. Assume the CC/CD income from continuing operations is $40,000 and the purchasing power loss on net monetary items is $12,000. Complete the HC/CD statement of income for Spruce Corporation.

E 25–12 **(CC/CD; Nau Bought Inventory for $40 and Sold it for $68; What Was the Real Gain?)**
The controller of Nau Company is discussing a comment you made in the course of presenting your audit report.

> ". . . and frankly," Franklin continued, "I agree that we, too, are responsible for finding ways to produce more relevant financial statements that are as reliable as the ones we now produce.
>
> "For example, suppose the company acquired a finished item of inventory for $40 when the general price level index was 110. And, later, the item was sold for $68 when the general price level index was 121 and the current cost at the date of sale was $54. We could calculate a 'holding gain' (i.e., an increase in the current cost of the item)."

Required:

1. Explain to what extent and how current costs already are used within GAAP to value inventories (excluding CC/CD).
2. Calculate the amount of the "holding gain" (i.e., the increase in the CC of inventory, net of the effects of general inflation) in Franklin's example.
3. Why is the use of current cost for both inventories and cost of goods sold preferred by some accounting authorities to the use of FIFO or LIFO?

(AICPA adapted)

E 25–13 **(CC/CD; Analysis of Equipment)**
Wood Company acquired equipment on January 1, 19A, at a cost of $100,000. On December 31, 19C, the current cost of the equipment was $140,000, and on December 31, 19D, the current cost was $170,000. Both current cost amounts are estimated before

deducting associated accumulated depreciation. The equipment is being depreciated on a straight-line basis over a 10-year period with no residual value. GPL index data are as follows: January 1, 19A, 105; December 31, 19C, 120; December 31, 19D, 128; 19D average, 124.

Required (round all CD restatement ratios to three decimal places):

1. Compute the CC of the equipment, net of accumulated depreciation, on December 31, 19C, and December 31, 19D.
2. Compute CC depreciation expense for 19D.
3. Compute for equipment 19D: *(a)* the total change in CC, and *(b)* the change in CC due to general inflation at December 31, 19D. Set up captions for: CC at transaction or balance date, CD restatement ratio, and CC/CD.
4. Assume the CC/CD income from continuing operations is $95,000 and the purchasing power loss on net monetary items is $11,000. Complete the HC/CD statement of income for Wood Company.

E 25–14 (CC/CD; FIFO versus LIFO)

Signal Corporation purchased all of the shares of Flag Corporation (it will be a subsidiary) on January 1, 19D, at a cost of $150,000. Flag Corporation had cash and receivables of $10,000; finished goods inventory, $50,000; building, $125,000, with accumulated depreciation, $60,000; and land, $15,000; all amounts reflect the HC basis. Flag Corporation had no liabilities at the time of the acquisition, and the GPL index was 109.

It is now December 31, 19D, and the GPL index is 122. The December 31, 19D, statement of financial position data of the purchased company are as follows, with HC and CC/CD data in comparative form:

FLAG CORPORATION
Statement of Financial Position—HC and CC/CD
December 31, 19D

	HC	CC/CD
Cash and receivables	$ 15,000	$ 15,000
Finished goods inventory	65,000	75,000
Building	125,000	150,000
Accumulated depreciation, building	(65,000)	(78,000)
Land	10,000	30,000
Total assets	$150,000	$192,000
Liabilities	$ 25,000	$ 30,000
Owners' equity	125,000	162,000
Total equities	$150,000	$192,000

Required:

1. Which item on the CC/CD statement of financial position is reported incorrectly? Why?
2. Does the fact that CC data are presented for the building mean that the building could be sold on December 31, 19D, for $150,000? for $72,000? Explain.
3. Which inventory method (i.e., LIFO, FIFO, average, etc.) would yield an ending inventory cost closest to the CC/CD amount? Respond to the same question for cost of goods sold.

E 25–15 (CC/CD; Inventory and Cost of Goods Sold)

Action Hardware acquired its beginning inventory on January 1, 19A, for $56,000. Goods were sold evenly during 19A, and cost of goods sold on a current cost basis was $250,000. Inventory on December 31, 19A, was $45,000 on the HC basis and $59,000 on the CC basis. Purchases totaled $200,000 and were made evenly during 19A. The GPL index was 150 on January 1, 19A, 180 on December 31, 19A, and averaged 168 during 19A.

Required (round all CD restatement ratios to three decimal places):

1. Compute for inventory the 19A change in CC, *(a)* total, *(b)* due to CC general inflation, and *(c)* net of general inflation (in CDs of December 31, 19A). Set up column headings for: CC at transaction date or balance date, CD restatement ratio, and CC/CD.
2. Assume the CC/CD income from continuing operations is $180,000 and the purchasing power gain on net monetary items is $20,000. Complete the HC/DC statement of income for Action Hardware Corporation.

E 25–16 (CC/CD; Prepare Financial Statements)

Quality Transport Company transfers freight from its home office in Tuscon, Arizona, to cities throughout the United States. Thus, it is a service-oriented enterprise and has no merchandise inventory. On January 1, 19C, the HC statement of financial position of Quality Transport was as follows:

QUALITY TRANSPORT COMPANY
Statement of Financial Position
January 1, 19C

Assets	
Cash and receivables	$12,000
Trucks	80,000
Accumulated depreciation	(–0–)
	$92,000
Liabilities and Owners' Equity	
Current liabilities	$10,000
Long-term liabilities	30,000
Owners' equity	52,000
	$92,000

Assume for simplicity that all revenues and all expenses occur evenly during the year. The trucks are new on January 1, 19C, are expected to remain in service for five years, and will be depreciated on a straight-line basis with no estimated residual value. GPL indexes were 100 at January 1, 19C, 102 at February 15, 19C, 104 for average of 19C, and 108 at December 31, 19C. Current cost (CC) of the trucks at December 31, 19C, was $88,000 before deducting accumulated depreciation.

Historical cost (HC) transactions for 19C included the following:

1. Payment on February 15, 19C, of the $10,000 beginning balance of current liabilities.
2. Service revenue of $100,000, of which $70,000 is collected in cash.
3. Depreciation of $16,000.
4. Other expenses of $75,000, of which $35,000 is unpaid at December 31, 19C. The $35,000 of liabilities are "current."

Required (round all CD restatement ratios to three decimals):

1. Prepare the CC/CD (CDs as of December 31, 19C) statement of financial position of Quality Transport Company at December 31, 19C.
2. Prepare the CC/CD (CDs as of December 31, 19C) statement of income for Quality Transport Company for the year ended December 31, 19C.

E 25–17 **(CC/CD; Analysis of Changes in Land Costs)**
Waco Development Corporation acquired land on January 1, 19A, for $500,000. On June 30, 19E, half of the land was sold for $800,000. The following current cost data regarding the land are available:

	CC of land	GPL index
January 1, 19E	$1,400,000	150
June 30, 19E		162
19E—average		160
December 31, 19E	850,000*	171

* After sale of land.

Required (round all CD restatement ratios to three decimal places):

1. Compute for land the 19E change in CC, *(a)* total, *(b)* due to general inflation, and *(c)* net of general inflation (in average CDs of 19E). Set up column headings for: CC at transaction or balance date, CD restatement ratio, and CC/CD.
2. Assume the CC/CD income from continuing operations is $800,000 and that the purchasing power loss on net monetary items is $15,000. Complete the HC/CD statement of income for Waco Development Corporation.

PROBLEMS

Part A: Problems 25–1 to 25–8

P 25–1 **(Prepare HC/CD Statement of Financial Position, Statement of Income, and Statement of Retained Earnings)**
The items reflected in the September 30 trial balance given below were acquired when the relevant GPL index was 105.0 except for capital stock, which was 105.2377 (to avoid rounding error).

Cash	$ 27,235	
Land	79,085	
Accounts payable		$ 2,570
Capital stock		100,000
Retained earnings		3,750*
	$106,320	$106,320

* HC/CD on this date, $4,165.

The following transactions were computed during the first quarter of the current accounting year:

Date	GPL index	Data
Oct. 1	110	Purchased machinery costing $9,600 on account.
15	120	Paid for machinery purchased on October 1.
31	135	Billed customers for services rendered, $8,000.
Nov. 15	140	Paid $1,230 of the initial liability balance.
30	145	Collected half of the billed revenue.
Dec. 10	150	Paid general expense of $5,700.
31	160	Recorded three months' depreciation on machinery, which has a five-year life with no residual value.

Required:

1. Enter the initial balances, and then record the transactions for the first quarter directly into ledger accounts; also include, in parentheses, the GPL index number prevailing when each transaction occurred.
2. As of the close of the quarter, prepare the statements of financial position and income on the HC basis and the HC/CD (CDs as of December 31) basis using the GPL index number procedures illustrated in the chapter. Show calculation of the purchasing power gain or loss on net monetary items. Prepare a statement of retained earnings at HC and HC/CD (the HC/CD beginning balance is $6,058). No average index value for the period is given. Therefore, it will be necessary to apply to each transaction a specific CD restatement ratio. For example, if a $360 transaction occurred when the index was 120, in December 31 terms, this would convert to $360 × 160/120 = $480. Round all calculations to the nearest dollar.

P 25–2 **(HC/CD; Property, Plant, and Equipment on the Statement of Financial Position and Statement of Income)**

Chase Corporation is preparing financial statements for 19E on an HC/CD basis. Selected data are as follows:

1. GPL index numbers:
   1/1/19A, 92; 12/31/19A, 95; 6/30/19B, 100; 12/31/19B, 106; 12/31/19D, 145; Average for 19E, 150; 12/31/19E, 155.
2. Property, plant, and equipment acquisition and depreciation data:
   a. Land acquired January 1, 19A, at a cost of $68,000.
   b. Building acquired December 31, 19A, at a cost of $380,000; by year-end 19D and 19E, respectively, Accumulated Depreciation—Building account reflected balances of $22,800 and $30,400.
   c. Fixtures costing $77,000 were acquired June 30, 19B; on these, accumulated depreciation recorded by year-end 19D and 19E amounted to $19,250 and $26,950.
   d. Additional fixtures were purchased in midyear 19E for $30,000 when the index was 150; by year-end, depreciation recorded on the newest fixtures amounted to $2,250.
3. Monetary assets: At the start of 19E, total monetary assets were $87,000 and total monetary liabilities were $31,900. At the end of 19E, total monetary assets were $100,200 and total monetary liabilities were $46,000.

Required:

Use the numbers given below for identification and compute the amounts that would appear on HC/CD (CDs as of December 31, 19E) financial statements. Round CD restatement ratios to five decimal places.

A. On the HC/CD statement of financial position as of December 31, 19E, the carrying values would be:
   1. Land.
   2. Building (gross amount).
   3. Old fixtures (gross amount).
   4. New fixtures (gross amount).
   5. Accumulated depreciation—building.
   6. Accumulated depreciation—old fixtures.
   7. Accumulated depreciation—new fixtures.
   8. Total monetary assets.
   9. Total monetary liabilities.
B. On the HC/CD statement of income for the year ended December 31, 19E, amounts reported would be:

10. Depreciation expense (building).
11. Depreciation expense (new fixtures).
12. Depreciation expense (old fixtures).
13. Purchases (assume purchases of $302,000 were made evenly throughout 19E).

P 25–3 **(Overview of HC/CD; Six Analytical Questions)**

Select the best answer in each of the following. Justify your choices.

1. A company was formed on January 1, 19B. Selected balances from its HC statement of financial position at December 31, 19B, were as follows:

Accounts receivable	$ 70,000
Accounts payable	60,000
Long-term debt	110,000
Common stock	100,000

At what amounts should these selected accounts be shown in an HC/CD (CDs as of December 31, 19B) statement of financial position at December 31, 19B, if the general price level index was 100 at December 31, 19A, and 110 at December 31, 19B?

	Accounts receivable	Accounts payable	Long-term debt	Common stock
a.	$70,000	$60,000	$110,000	$100,000
b.	70,000	60,000	110,000	110,000
c.	70,000	60,000	121,000	110,000
d.	77,000	66,000	121,000	110,000

2. Baker Company reported sales of $2,000,000 in 19B and $3,000,000 in 19C made evenly throughout each year. The GPL index during 19A remained constant at 100, and at the end of 19B and 19C it was 102 and 104, respectively. What should Baker report as sales revenue for 19C, restated for CD (in CDs as of the end of 19C) changes?

a. $3,000,000.
b. $3,029,126.
c. $3,058,821.
d. $3,120,000.

3. On January 2, 19C, the Mannix Corporation mortgaged one of its properties as collateral for a $1,000,000, 12% five-year loan. The mortgage note payable was interest-bearing, and the interest rate was realistic. During 19C, the GPL increased evenly, resulting in a 5% rise for the year.

In preparing an HC/CD (CDs as of the end of 19C) statement of financial position at the end of 19C, at what amount should Mannix report the five-year mortgage note?

a. $950,000.
b. $1,000,000.
c. $1,025,000.
d. $1,050,000.

4. The HC statement of financial position of Post Company showed the original cost of depreciable assets as $5,000,000 at December 31, 19A, and $6,000,000 at December 31, 19B. These asset costs are being depreciated on a straight-line basis over a 10-year period with no residual value. Acquisitions of $1,000,000 were made on January 1, 19B. A full year's depreciation was taken in the year of acquisition.

Post presents HC/CD financial statements as supplemental information to its HC financial statements. The December 31, 19A, depreciable assets balance (before accumulated depreciation) restated to reflect December 31, 19B, purchasing power was $5,800,000. What amount of depreciation expense should be shown in the HC/CD (CDs as of December 31, 19B) statement of income for 19B if the GPL index was 100 at December 31, 19A, and 110 at December 31, 19B?

a. $600,000.
b. $660,000.
c. $670,000.
d. $690,000.

5. If a constant unit of measure during a period of inflation is used, the general purchasing power of the dollar in which some expenses are measured (for assets systematically allocated among several accounting periods) may differ significantly from the general purchasing power of the dollar in which revenue is measured. Which of the following accounting procedures minimizes this effect?
   a. Allowance method of accounting for bad debts.
   b. Income tax allocation.
   c. Accelerated depreciation.
   d. Valuing inventory at the LCM.

6. Land was purchased for $20,000 when the GPL index was 115. When the index was 138, the land was sold for $25,000. Ignoring taxes on the transaction, the landowner, for having bought and sold the land, is economically (i.e., in terms of purchasing power):
   a. Worse off.
   b. Better off.
   c. In the same position.

(AICPA adapted)

P 25–4 (HC/CD Overview; Six Analytical Questions)

Select the best answer in each of the following. Justify your choices. For questions 1–4 below, use the following GPL data (round CD restatement ratios to three decimals): 12/31/19A, 165; 3/31/19B, 171; 6/30/19B, 175; 9/30/19B, 180; 12/31/19B, 186; 3/31/19C, 190; 6/30/19C, 194; 9/30/19C, 198; 12/31/19C, 201.

1. On January 1, 19B, P Corporation had as its only asset $7,000 in cash (no liabilities). On March 31, 19B, P Corporation paid $5,000 for a machine that will have a 10-year life and no residual value. On September 30, 19B, P Corporation purchased merchandise inventory on account for $1,000. At an even rate during the three months ended December 31, 19B, P Corporation paid off the $1,000 on the inventory and sold half the inventory for $650 cash. If these are the only transactions P Corporation entered into during 19B, the company will report for 19B (in terms of CDs as of 12/31/19B) a purchasing power gain or loss on net monetary items of:
   a. Loss of $365.
   b. Loss of $426.
   c. Gain of $365.
   d. Gain of $426.

2. Assume that P Corporation's January 1, 19B, owners' equity consisted of capital stock of $7,000. On its HC/CD (CDs as of 12/31/19B) statement of income for the year ended December 31, 19B, P Corporation will report net income (loss)—ignoring the purchasing power gain or loss on net monetary items—of:
   a. $(276).
   b. $(264).
   c. $(255).
   d. $253.

3. On its December 31, 19B, HC/CD (CDs as of 12/31/19B) statement of financial position P Corporation will report cash of:
   a. $1,650.
   b. $2,080.
   c. $1,285.
   d. $2,904.

4. You are in the process of preparing the 19C, HC/CD financial statements (assume that you have been given the necessary transaction data involving revenues and expenses for 19C). In particular, you are now "rolling forward" the January 1, 19C, HC statement of financial position in order to obtain the January 1, 19C, HC/CD owners' equity balance stated in December 31, 19C, dollars—as a test of the accuracy of your other HC/CD restatements. Assuming that the beginning cash balance arose on the beginning date, the correct January 1, 19C, owners' equity stated in December 31, 19C, dollars would be:

a. $7,197.
b. $7,322.
c. $7,777.
d. $7,975.
e. None of the above.

5. Under HC/CD reporting, purchasing power gains are earned during inflation on:
   a. Net monetary assets.
   b. Net monetary liabilities.
   c. Nonmonetary assets.
   d. Nonmonetary liabilities.
6. Which of the following items is a nonmonetary item?
   a. Marketable securities—bonds to be held to maturity.
   b. Accounts receivable.
   c. Accounts payable.
   d. Preferred stock stated at liquidation value.
   e. Unearned revenue.

P 25–5 **(HC/CD Financial Statements)**

Falvey Corporation prepared the following comparative statements of financial position (HC basis) at the close of its fourth year of operations (19D):

	December 31	
	19C	19D
Cash	$ 30,000	$ 41,400
Receivables (net)	74,000	99,000
Inventory	25,000	39,000
Land	100,000	100,000
Building	320,000	320,000
Accumulated depreciation, building	(38,400)	(51,200)
Fixtures	90,000	120,000
Accumulated depreciation, fixtures	(40,500)	(58,500)
Total	$560,100	$609,700
Current liabilities	$ 55,000	$ 80,000
Bonds payable	45,000	45,000
Common stock	250,000	250,000
Retained earnings	210,100*	234,700
Total	$560,000	$609,700

* At HC/CD on this date, $230,722.

The statement of income (HC basis) for 19D was as follows:

Sales revenue		$950,000
Cost of goods sold:		
Beginning inventory	$ 25,000	
Purchases	584,000	
Goods available	609,000	
Ending inventory	39,000	
Cost of goods sold		570,000
Gross margin		380,000
Expenses:		
Administrative	125,000	
Depreciation, building	12,800	
Depreciation, fixtures	18,000	
Distribution	100,000	255,800
Income before taxes		124,200
Income tax expense		49,600
Net income		$ 74,600

A $50,000 dividend was declared at year-end. Fixtures costing $30,000 were purchased on January 2, 19D. Fixtures are depreciated 15% per year on cost. Inventories are on a FIFO basis; assume the ending inventory was acquired at the average GPL prevailing during 19D. When the common stock was issued and the land, buildings, and original fixtures were acquired, the GPL was 112.5. Other GPL index data are as follows: 12/31/19D, 135; 12/31/19C, 125; Average for 19D, 129.8.

The beginning inventory was acquired at 19C year-end prices. Purchases, sales, administrative expenses (which include interest), distribution, and income taxes accrued evenly throughout 19D. The building is depreciated over a 25-year life; no residual value, straight-line basis.

Required (round CD restatement ratios to three decimals):

1. Prepare an HC/CD statement of financial position as of December 31, 19D, and an HC/CD statement of income for 19D (CDs as of December 31, 19D). Show computation of the purchasing power gain or loss on net monetary items for the year. Prepare a proof of retained earnings.
2. Indicate the gross and net carrying values of land, fixtures, and building for the HC/CD (CDs as of December 31, 19C) statement of financial position as of December 31, 19C.

P 25–6 **(HC/CD Financial Statements)**

Wagner Company prepared the following comparative statement of financial position (HC basis) at the close of its 10th year of operations (19J):

	December 31	
	19I	**19J**
Cash	$ 75,000	$101,000
Receivables (net)	215,000	195,000
Inventory	135,000	127,000
Land	150,000	150,000
Building	240,000	240,000
Accumulated depreciation, building	(56,000)	(64,000)
Machinery	225,000	280,000
Accumulated depreciation, machinery	(115,000)	(137,500)
Total	$869,000	$891,500
Current liabilities	$124,000	$137,000
Long-term liabilities	75,000	81,000
Bonds payable	60,000	60,000
Common stock	350,000	350,000
Retained earnings	260,000*	263,500
Total	$869,000	$891,500

* At HC/CD on this date, $277,070.

The common stock was issued, and the land was bought in 19A, when the GPL index was 104. The building was acquired early in 19C when the GPL index was 107; it has an estimated 30-year life and no residual value and is depreciated on a straight-line basis. Machinery is depreciated 10% per year on cost with no residual value. The first machine was bought at a cost of $50,000 in 19B when the GPL index was 106; a second machine was acquired for $100,000 in 19D when the index was 108.5; a third machine was bought in 19H when the index was 117. A full year's depreciation is taken in the year of acquisition unless the purchase is at year-end. At year-end 19J, machinery costing $55,000 was acquired.

On January 2, 19J, an $85,000 dividend was declared and paid when the GPL index was 121. Assume the beginning inventory was acquired when the GPL index was 107; the ending inventory should be restated to CDs on the assumption the index was 125 when it was bought.

Sales, operating expenses, income taxes, and purchases occurred evenly during 19J. Relevant GPL index data (aside from that already given) are as follows: 12/31/19I, 121;

12/31/19J, 127; Average for 19J, 125. The statement of income (HC basis) for the year 19J was as follows:

Sales revenue		$1,275,000
Cost of goods sold:		
Inventory, January 1	$135,000	
Purchases	850,000	
Goods available	985,000	
Inventory, December 31	127,000	
Cost of goods sold		858,000
Gross margin		417,000
Expenses:		
Operating (excluding depreciation)	210,000	
Depreciation, building	8,000	
Depreciation, machinery	22,500	240,500
Income before taxes		176,500
Income tax expense		88,000
Net income		$ 88,500

Required (round all CD restatement ratios to three decimals):
Prepare a statement of income for 19J and a statement of financial position as of December 31, 19J, on an HC/CD (CDs as of December 31, 19J) basis. Show computations of the purchasing power gain or loss on net monetary items. Prepare a proof of retained earnings.

P 25–7 (HC/CD Financial Statements)
Cuisine Corporation's statements of financial position (HC basis) at December 31, 19B and 19C were as follows:

	December 31	
	19B	**19C**
Cash	$ 8,000	$ 7,600
Accounts receivable (net)	19,000	31,000
Inventory	20,000	18,000
Equipment	21,000	29,400
Accumulated depreciation	(11,000)	(17,400)
	$57,000	$68,600
Accounts payable	$24,000	$29,000
Common stock	25,000	30,000
Retained earnings	8,000*	9,600
	$57,000	$68,600

* HC/CD on this date, $9,359.

The statement of income (HC basis) for the year ended December 31, 19C, was as follows:

Sales revenue		$80,000
Beginning inventory	$20,000	
Purchases	42,000	
Goods available	62,000	
Ending inventory	18,000	
Cost of goods sold		44,000
Gross margin		36,000
Expenses:		
Salaries	15,000	
Other (icluding income tax)	9,000	
Depreciation	6,400	30,400
Net income		$ 5,600

Original equipment was acquired and original common stock was issued on January 1, 19A. New equipment was acquired on January 1, 19C. Equipment is being depreciated over a six-year life by the SYD method with an assumed zero residual value. When the first equipment was acquired and the original stock was issued, the GPL index was 94.

The company uses the LIFO inventory method; the beginning inventory for 19C is below the level at which the company began operations (January 1, 19A). Salaries and other expenses were incurred evenly over the year, and purchases and sales occurred evenly over the year. The additional common stock was sold on June 30, 19C. Dividends were declared and paid at midyear and year-end in equal amounts of $2,000 per payment. GPL price index data are as follows: 12/31/19B, 120; Midyear 19C and average, 126; 12/31/19C, 132.

Require (Round to the nearest $10):

1. Prepare the 19C statement of financial position to show HC and HC/CD.
2. Prepare the 19C statement of income to show HC and HC/CD. Give the schedule to compute the 19C purchasing power gain or loss on monetary items.
3. Give a proof of the 19C ending balance in retained earnings.

P 25–8 **(HC/CD; Analyze Equipment Accounts for Three Years; Compute Purchasing Power Gain or Loss on Monetary Items)**

Cutter Retail Corporation was organized during 19A. Cutter's management has decided to supplement its December 31, 19D, HC financial statements with HC/CD financial statements. The following trial balance (HC basis) and additional information have been furnished:

CUTTER RETAIL CORPORATION
Trial Balance
December 31, 19D

	Debit	Credit
Cash and receivables (net)	$ 540,000	
Short-term investments (common stock)	400,000	
Inventory	440,000	
Equipment	650,000	
Accumulated depreciation, equipment		$ 164,000
Accounts payable		300,000
6% first-mortgage bonds, due 19V		500,000
Common stock, $10 par		1,000,000
Retained earnings, 12/31/19C	46,000	
Sales revenue		1,900,000
Cost of goods sold	1,508,000	
Depreciation	65,000	
Other operating expenses including interest	215,000	
	$3,864,000	$3,864,000

a. Monetary assets (cash and receivables) exceeded monetary liabilities (accounts payable and bonds payable) by $445,000 at December 31, 19C.
b. Purchases ($1,840,000 in 19D) and sales are made evenly throughout the year.
c. Depreciation is computed on a straight-line basis, with a full year's depreciation being taken in the year of acquisition and none in the year of retirement. The depreciation rate is 10%, and no residual value is anticipated. Acquisitions and retirements have been made evenly over each year, and the retirements in 19D consisted of assets purchased during 19B that were scrapped. An analysis of the Equipment account reveals the following:

Year	Beginning balance	Additions	Retirements	Ending balance
19B	—	$550,000	—	$550,000
19C	$550,000	10,000	—	560,000
19D	560,000	150,000	$60,000	650,000

d. The bonds were issued in 19B, and the short-term investment in common stock was purchased evenly over 19D. Other operating expenses, including interest, are assumed to be incurred evenly throughout the year.

e. Assume the values of the GPL index were as follows:

Annual averages	GPL index	Quarterly averages	GPL index
19A	113.9	19C, 4th	123.5
19B	116.8	19D, 1st	124.9
19C	121.8	2d	126.1
19D	126.7	3d	127.3
		4th and year-end	128.5

Required (round CD statement ratios to three decimals):

1. Prepare a schedule to convert the Equipment account balance at December 31, 19D, from HC to HC/CD (CDs as of 12/31/19D) amounts.
2. Prepare a schedule to analyze, at HC, the Equipment—Accumulated Depreciation account for the year 19D.
3. Prepare a schedule to analyze, at HC/CD (CDs as of 12/31/19D), the Equipment—Accumulated Depreciation account for the year 19D.
4. Prepare a schedule to compute Cutter's purchasing power gain or loss on its net monetary items for 19D (ignore income tax implications).

(AICPA adapted)

Part B: Problems 25–9 to 25–13

P 25–9 **(CC/CD; Analyze Fleet of Trucks, Statement of Income)**

Brown Hauling Company maintains a fleet of trucks for use in its business. Information regarding the acquisition dates and cost of these trucks is provided below:

Total cost	Date acquired	GPL index
$80,000	January 1, 19A	100
60,000	January 1, 19B	115
50,000	June 30, 19C	125

Trucks are depreciated on a straight-line basis over a five-year life with residual value estimated to be zero. The acquisition on June 30, 19C, was depreciated for one-half year in 19C.

A schedule of the current cost of the trucks (before deducting accumulated depreciation) is given below as of January 1, 19D, and December 31, 19D:

Trucks acquired in:	CC on 1/1/19D	CC on 12/31/19D
19A	$100,000	$125,000
19B	80,000	90,000
19C	60,000	80,000

Additional GPL index data are as follows: January 1, 19D, 130; 19D—average, 135; December 31, 19D, 140.

Required (round all CD restatement ratios to three decimal places):

1. Compute the current cost of the trucks, net of accumulated depreciation, on January 1, 19D, and December 31, 19D.

2. Compute 19D depreciation expense for the trucks on a current cost basis.
3. Prepare a schedule that shows *(a)* the total 19D change in CC, *(b)* change in CC, due to general inflation, and *(c)* change in CC, net of general inflation (in CDs as of 12/31/19D). Set up column headings for CC at transaction or balance date, CD restatement ratio, and CC/CD.
4. Assume the CC/CD income from continuing operations is $150,000 and the purchasing power loss on net monetary items is $12,000. Complete the HC/CD statement of income for Brown Company.

P 25–10 **(CC/CD; Prepare Financial Statements; Comprehensive)**
Palmer Company prepared the following comparative statement of financial position (HC basis) at the close of its 10th year of operations (19J):

	December 31	
	19I	19J
Cash	$ 60,000	$101,000
Receivables (net)	175,000	195,000
Inventory	135,000	127,000
Land	150,000	150,000
Building	240,000	240,000
Accumulated depreciation, building	(48,000)	(56,000)
Machinery	280,000	280,000
Accumulated depreciation, machinery	(196,000)	(224,000)
Total	$796,000	$813,000
Current liabilities	$124,000	$137,000
Long-term liabilities	75,000	81,000
Bonds payable	60,000	60,000
Common stock	350,000	350,000
Retained earnings	187,000	185,000
Total	$796,000	$813,000

The common stock was issued, and the land was bought in 19A, when the GPL index was 104. The building was acquired late in 19C when the GPL index was 107; it has an estimated 30-year life and no residual value and is depreciated on a straight-line basis. Machinery is depreciated 10% per year on cost with no residual value. The machinery was bought late in 19B when the GPL index was 106.

On January 2, 19J, and $85,000 dividend was declared and paid. Sales, operating expenses, income taxes, and purchases occurred evenly during 19J. Relevant GPL index data (aside from that already given) are as follows: 12/31/19I, 121; 12/31/19J, 127; Average for 19J, 125.

The statement of income (HC basis) for the year 19J was as follows:

Sales revenue		$1,275,000
Cost of goods sold:		
Inventory, January 1	$135,000	
Purchases	850,000	
Goods available	985,000	
Inventory, December 31	127,000	
Cost of goods sold		858,000
Gross margin		417,000
Expenses:		
Operating, excluding depreciation	210,000	
Depreciation, building	8,000	
Depreciation, machinery	28,000	246,000
Income before taxes		171,000
Income tax expense		88,000
Net income		$ 83,000

Current cost data are as follows:

	December 31	
	19I	19J
Nonmonetary assets (in CDs of the balance date):		
Inventory	$160,000	$135,000
Land	185,000	200,000
Building	270,000	270,000
Accumulated depreciation, building	(54,000)	(63,000)
Machinery	300,000	330,000
Accumulated depreciation, machinery	(210,000)	(264,000)
Retained earnings (credit) from prior period	220,000	
Expenses (in average of CDs of 19J):		
Cost of goods sold		$897,000
Depreciation expense, building		9,000
Depreciation expense, machinery		31,500
Sales revenue and all other expenses		Same as HC

Required (round all CD restatements ratios to three decimals):

1. Prepare the CC/CD (CDs as of 12/31/19J) statement of financial position for the company at December 31, 19J.
2. Prepare the single-step CC/CD (CDs as of 12/31/19J) statement of income for the company for the year ended December 31, 19J, with all supporting computations.
3. Prove the accuracy of the CC/CD ending balance of retained earnings.

P 25–11 (CC/CD; Analysis of Inventory; Statement of Income)

The following information regarding the historical and current cost of Control Corporation's inventory is available:

	HC	CC*
January 1, 19A, inventory	$ 10,000	$ 10,000
19A purchases	100,000	100,000
19A cost of goods sold	80,000	90,000
December 31, 19A, inventory	30,000	50,000
19B purchases	120,000	120,000
19B cost of goods sold	95,000	115,000
December 31, 19B, inventory	55,000	75,000

* Current cost at transaction or balance date.

GPL index data are as follows: January 1, 19A, 110; 19A—average, 118; December 31, 19A, 125; 19B—average, 132; December 31, 19B, 140. Sales and purchases occurred evenly during 19A and 19B. Sales and purchases occurred evenly during 19A and 19B.

Required (round all CD restatement ratios to three decimal places):

1. Prepare a schedule of the total 19A change in CC, change in CC due to general inflation, and change in CC, net of general inflation (in average CDs of 19A) for inventory.†
2. Assume the CC/CD income from continuing operations is $80,000 and that the purchasing power loss on net monetary items is $10,000. Complete the CC/CD statement of income for 19A for Control Company.
3. Prepare a schedule of the total 19B change in CC, change in CC due to general inflation, and change in CC, net of general inflation (in average CDs of 19B) for inventory.†
4. Assume the CC/CD income from continuing operations is $90,000 and that the purchasing power gain on net monetary items is $7,000. Complete the CC/CD statement of income for 19B for Control Company.

† Set up three column headings, CC at transaction or balance date, CD restatement ratio, and CC/CD.

5. Does the cost flow assumption used for inventory (i.e., LIFO, FIFO) affect the computation of changes in current cost? Explain.

P 25–12 (CC/CD; Analysis of Land; Change in CC; Statement of Income)

Easley Development Corporation maintains records for its land acquisitions on both historical and current cost bases. The following schedule reflects land acquisitions and sales for the period 19B through 19D:

Date	HC of acquisition (sale)	Balance in account (at HC)	CC of acquisition (sale)	Balance in account (at CC)
1/1/19B	$50,000	$50,000	$50,000	$ 50,000
12/31/19B		50,000		75,000
1/1/19C	40,000	90,000	40,000	115,000
12/31/19C		90,000		130,000
1/1/19D	(50,000)	40,000	(85,000)	45,000
12/31/19D		40,000		65,000

The land sold on January 1, 19D, was acquired on January 1, 19B, and sold for $85,000. All current costs are given in CDs as of the balance or transaction date. Additional GPL index data are: 1/1/19B, 100; 12/31/19B–1/1/19C, 120; 12/31/19C–1/1/19D, 138; 12/31/19D, 150.

Required (round all CD restatement ratios to three decimal places):

1. Prepare a schedule of the total change in CC, change in CC due to general inflation, and change in CC, net of general inflation (in CDs as of 12/31/19D) for land in *(a)* 19A, *(b)* 19B, and *(c)* 19D; set up three column headings, CC at transaction or balance date, CD restatement ratio, and CC/CD.
2. Assume the 19D CC/CD income from continuing operations is $70,000 and that the purchasing power loss on net monetary items is $13,000. Complete the 19D HC/CD statement of income for Easley Corporation.

P 25–13 (CC/CD; Analysis of Equipment CC Changes; Statement of Income)

The following information regarding the historical and current cost of equipment for Weller Corporation is available:

Date of acquisition (retirement)	Original cost	CC on 12/31/19A	CC on 12/31/19B	CC on 12/31/19C
1/1/19A	$100,000	$140,000	$160,000	$110,000*
6/30/19A	80,000	120,000	145,000	170,000
1/1/19B	40,000		50,000	64,000
1/1/19C	50,000			55,000
12/31/19C	(60,000)			
Total	$210,000	$260,000	$355,000	$399,000

* After retirement on 12 /31/19C.

When equipment was sold on December 31, 19C, it had a CC (before deducting accumulated depreciation) of $70,000. Equipment is depreciated over a 10-year life, with an estimated residual value of zero. GPL index data are: January 1, 19A, 108; June 30, 19A, 112; December 31, 19A, 120; December 31, 19B, 135; 19B average, 128; December 31, 19C, 150; 19C average, 142.

Required (round all CD restatement ratios to three decimals):

1. Compute depreciation expense on a CC basis for 19B (in average CDs for 19B) and 19C (in average CDs for 19C).
2. Compute the CC of equipment, net of accumulated depreciation, on the following dates:

a. December 31, 19A (in CDs as of 12/31/19A).
b. December 31, 19B (in CDs as of 12/31/19B).
c. December 31, 19C (in CDs as of 12/31/19C).

3. Prepare a schedule for equipment of the total change in CC, change in CC due to general inflation, and change in CC, net of general inflation for:
   a. 19B (in CDs as of 12/31/19B).
   b. 19C (in CDs as of 12/31/19C).
4. Assume the 19C CC/CD income from continuing operations is $350,000 and that the purchasing power loss on net monetary items is $22,000. Complete the 19C CC/CD statement of income for Weller Corporation.

CASES

C 25–1 (HC versus HC/CD Financial Statements)

The primary financial statements of U.S. companies are currently prepared on a stable-dollar assumption (historical cost) even though the general purchasing power of the dollar has declined considerably because of inflation in recent years. To account for this changing value of the dollar, many accountants argue that financial statements should be restated for general price level changes. Three independent, unrelated statements regarding HC/CD financial statements follow. Each statement contains some fallacious reasoning.

Statement I: The accounting profession has not seriously considered HC/CD financial statements before because the rate of inflation usually has been so small from year to year that the restatements would have been immaterial in amount. HC/CD financial statements represent a departure from the historical cost basis of accounting. Financial statements should be prepared from facts, not estimates.

Statement II: If financial statements were restated for GPL changes, depreciation expense in the earnings statement would permit the recovery of dollars of current purchasing power and thereby equal the cost of new assets to replace the old ones. GPL restated (i.e., HC/CD) data would yield statements of financial position amounts closely approximating current values. Furthermore, management can make better decisions if HC/CD financial statements are published.

Statement III: When restating financial data for GPL changes, a distinction must be made between monetary and nonmonetary assets and liabilities, which, under the HC basis of accounting, have been identified as "current" and "noncurrent." When using the HC basis of accounting, no purchasing power gain or loss on net monetary assets is recognized in the accounting process, but when financial statements are restated for GPL changes, a purchasing power gain or loss will be recognized on monetary and nonmonetary items.

Required:

Evaluate each of the independent statements and identify the areas of fallacious reasoning in each. Explain why the reasoning is incorrect. Complete your discussion of each statement before proceeding to the next statement.

(AICPA adapted)

C 25–2 (HC versus HC/CD Financial Statements)

In this situation, HC/CD statements, as supplements to the conventional cost basis statements, are presented. Knowing that you have studied accounting, a friend, who owns common stock in several companies, drops their latest annual reports before you with a look that hovers between dismay and bewilderment.

Your friend begins "I used to think that I understood a little about these reports, but now that the companies have all gone to this price level accounting, the only things clear to me are the nice pictures of company employees and products!" Upon your inquiry, you find that the following points bother your friend:

a. Most of the companies reported higher net income on their HC statements than on their HC/CD statements, while at the same time the latter statements showed the assets to be larger in amount.
b. Some of the companies reported purchasing power gains on net monetary liabilities concurrent with operating gains; others reported general purchasing power losses on net monetary assets concurrent with operating gains; yet all of the companies were subject to the same degree of general inflation.
c. The statements, prepared on an HC/CD basis, showed that even the amount of cash reported for last year had changed. Your friend wonders whether the companies discovered overages or shortages of cash or are somehow "juggling the figures."
d. Your friend realizes that the prices of most things are rising and wonders whether the increased values of certain assets on the HC/CD statements represent what the items are worth. At the same time, your friend noticed that some assets are carried at identical amounts on both sets of statements (i.e., both HC and HC/CD statements).

Required:

1. Explain the specifics that are confusing your friend in such a way that a knowledgeable nonaccountant can understand them.
2. To cope with the effects of price changes, aside from HC/CD statements, what alternative accounting could be used? Describe them briefly and cite some of their pros and cons.
3. What is your assessment of the usefulness of HC/CD financial statements? Give reasons for your answer.

C 25–3 (CC/CD Comprehensive Income)

(Note: This case contains questions over theoretical material that is covered only indirectly in the chapter). In this chapter, changes in the current costs of nonmonetary assets are presented as elements of CC/CD comprehensive income (i.e., on the statement of income). Many accountants favor reporting these current cost changes as a direct element of owners' equity, thereby bypassing the statement of income. This issue has not been resolved.

Required:

List and discuss arguments for reporting the changes in the current costs of nonmonetary assets on the statement of income versus reporting them as separate elements of owners' equity on the statement of financial position. List and discuss arguments for reporting the current cost changes on nonmonetary assets as separate elements of owners' equity on the statement of financial position.

C 25–4 (HC/CD versus CC/CD)

Checker Corporation, a manufacturer with large investments in property, plant and equipment, began operations in 1940. The company's history has been one of expansion in sales, production, and physical facilities. Recently, some concern has been expressed that the HC financial statements do not provide sufficient information for decisions by investors. After consideration of proposals for various types of supplementary financial statements to be included in the 1988 annual report, management has decided to present an HC/CD statement of financial position as of December 31, 1988, and an HC/CD statement of income and retained earnings for 1988.

Required:

1. On what basis can it be contended that Checker's HC financial statements should be restated for changes in the general price level (GPL)?
2. Distinguish between HC/CD financial statements and CC/CD financial statements.
3. Distinguish between monetary and nonmonetary assets and liabilities as the terms are used in the HC/CD reporting model. Give examples of each.
4. Outline the procedures Checker should follow in preparing the proposed HC/CD statements.
5. Indicate the major similarities and differences between the proposed HC/CD statements and the corresponding HC statements.
6. Assuming that in the future Checker will want to present comparative HC/CD statements, can the 1988 HC/CD statements be presented in 1989 without adjustment? Explain.

(AICPA adapted)

APPENDIX: 1987 Financial Statements of The Kimberly-Clark Company as included in the annual report, fiscal year ended December 31, 1987

OVERVIEW AND PURPOSE

This Appendix is included for reference and study purposes throughout the 24 chapters.

This particular annual report was selected because (1) it is comprehensive, (2) it includes a broad array of transactions, notes, company programs, and display schedules, and (3) it is characterized by a comparatively high level of clarity and understandable disclosure notes.

ANNUAL REPORT

KIMBERLY-CLARK 1987

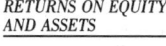

As 1987 began, we said we had a clear shot at achieving net income of $3.50 per share. Also, we expressed confidence that we would make substantial progress toward reaching our announced objective of a sustainable 18 percent return on average stockholders' equity by 1990.

On behalf of the employees of Kimberly-Clark and its affiliated companies, it is a privilege for me to report that our confidence was justified. Their stewardship of your capital produced record 1987 results — even better than forecasted — with earnings per share of $3.73 and return on average stockholders' equity of 18.6 percent.

ADJUSTED CAPITALIZATION AT YEAR-END
($ Millions)

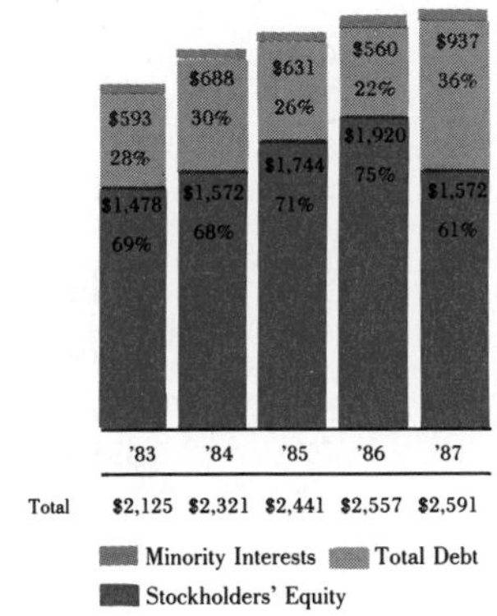

RETURNS ON EQUITY AND ASSETS

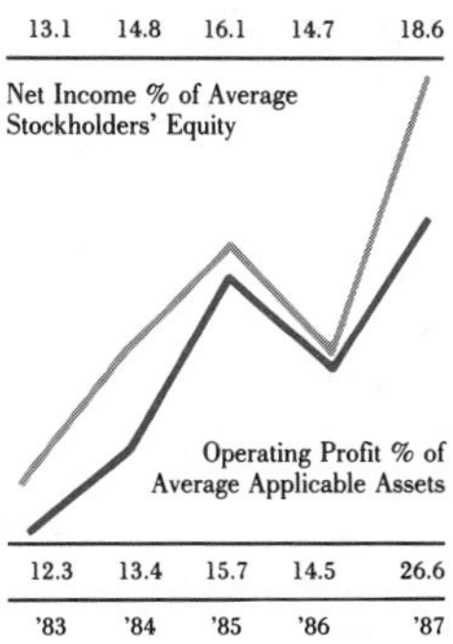

Sales, net income and net income per share increased over 1986 by 14 percent, 21 percent and 27 percent, respectively.

The early attainment of a return on average stockholders' equity exceeding 18 percent reflected not only the improvement in operating results and the plan announced at the beginning of the year to repurchase today's equivalent of six million shares of the company's common stock, but also an identical repurchase plan which was announced shortly after the October 19 stock market crash and completed in December. (Continued on page 2)

FINANCIAL HIGHLIGHTS

(Millions of dollars except per share amounts)	Year Ended December 31 1987	1986	1985	Change 1987 vs. 1986	Change 1986 vs. 1985
RETURN ON INVESTMENT					
Net Income Return on Average Stockholders' Equity	18.6%	14.7%	16.1%	+27%	− 9%
Operating Profit Return on Average Assets*	16.6%	14.5%	15.7%	+14%	− 8%
OPERATING RESULTS					
Net Sales	$4,884.7	$4,303.1	$4,072.9	+14%	+ 6%
Operating Profit	586.1	484.9	486.3	+21%	0%
Income Before Income Taxes	534.1	433.0	439.3	+23%	− 1%
NET INCOME	325.2	269.4	267.1	+21%	+ 1%
WORKING CAPITAL	138.9	228.1	163.6	−39%	+39%
CAPITALIZATION					
Stockholders' Equity	1,571.9	1,919.9	1,743.9	−18%	+10%
Total Assets	3,885.7	3,676.0	3,503.8	+ 6%	+ 5%
Long-Term Debt	686.9	426.3	509.2	+61%	−16%
CASH FLOW					
Capital Spending	247.3	282.4	425.8	−12%	−34%
Depreciation	186.0	169.3	140.3	+10%	+21%
Cash Provided by Operations	656.6	434.5	583.5	+51%	−26%
PER SHARE BASIS					
Net Income	3.73	2.93	2.92	+27%	0%
Dividends Declared	1.44	1.24	1.16	+16%	+ 7%
Book Value	19.60	20.89	19.04	− 6%	+10%
Market Value	50.00	40.00	33.50	+25%	+19%

Average assets excluding investments in equity companies.

Distribution of Revenue Received

(Millions of dollars)	1987		1986		1985		Change 1987 vs. 1986	Change 1986 vs. 1985
	Year Ended December 31							
Wages, Salaries and Benefits	$1,151	24%	$1,088	25%	$1,003	25%	+ 6%	+ 8%
Manufacturing Materials	1,416	29	1,285	30	1,107	27	+10	+16
Other Manufacturing Costs	746	15	536	12	581	14	+39	− 8
Other Business Costs	903	18	827	19	828	20	+ 9	−
Income, Payroll and Other Taxes	344	7	298	7	287	7	+15	+ 4
Dividends	125	3	114	3	106	3	+10	+ 7
Retained Earnings	200	4	155	4	161	4	+29	− 3
Net Sales	$4,885	100%	$4,303	100%	$4,073	100%	+14%	+ 6%

Summary of Selected Financial Data

(Millions of dollars except per share amounts)	1987	1986	1985	1984	1983
	Year Ended December 31				
Net Sales	$4,884.7	$4,303.1	$4,072.9	$3,616.2	$3,274.3
Operating Profit	586.1	484.9	486.3	374.9	315.4
Share of Net Income of Equity Companies	35.3	37.0	31.7	22.7	26.8
Earnings Before Extraordinary Item	325.2	269.4	267.1	217.5	188.8
Per Share	3.73	2.93	2.92	2.39	2.10
Net Income	325.2	269.4	267.1	225.0	188.8
Per Share	3.73	2.93	2.92	2.47	2.10
Cash Dividends Declared Per Share	1.44	1.24	1.16	1.10	1.05
Total Assets	3,885.7	3,676.0	3,503.8	3,172.6	2,903.9
Long-Term Debt	686.9	426.3	509.2	541.5	505.9
Stockholders' Equity	1,571.9	1,919.9	1,743.9	1,572.2	1,477.7

REVIEW OF LIQUIDITY AND CAPITAL RESOURCES

Cash provided by operations increased 51 percent in 1987. Major factors affecting the increase were:

- Record 1987 earnings,
- Lower operating working capital, and
- Timing of income tax payments.

During 1987, the company repurchased 13 percent of its common stock on the open market.

- 12 million shares were acquired at a total cost of $632 million, or an average cost of $52.63 per share.
- After completing the share repurchase programs, the company retired 14.5 million shares of common stock held in treasury.

In 1987, long-term debt increased $261 million or 61 percent. Noteworthy changes in long-term financings during the year were:

- $100 million of 9⅛ percent notes were issued in the U.S. public market in the second quarter.
- $200 million of commercial paper was classified as long-term debt at year-end because it was refinanced by issuance of long-term obligations in the first quarter of 1988.

The ratio of total debt to adjusted capital increased to 36 percent at the end of 1987, compared with 22 percent a year earlier. The ratio is expected to be close to the company's target range of 28 to 32 percent by the end of 1988. (Adjusted capital is the sum of total debt, minority owners' interests in subsidiaries and stockholders' equity.)

The company's long-term debt securities have a double-A rating, and its commercial paper is rated in the top category. Unused credit facilities, capacity to issue long-term debt and the ability of operations to generate cash are believed adequate to fund working capital, capital spending and other needs in the foreseeable future.

Dividends were increased for the 15th consecutive year. The quarterly rate was increased by 16 percent to 36 cents per share from 31 cents per share in 1986.

CONSOLIDATED STATEMENT OF INCOME

Kimberly-Clark Corporation and Subsidiaries

(Millions of dollars except per share amounts)	*Year Ended December 31* 1987	1986	1985
NET SALES	$4,884.7	$4,303.1	$4,072.9
Cost of products sold	3,065.9	2,712.2	2,511.5
Distribution expense	181.2	166.2	168.9
GROSS PROFIT	1,637.6	1,424.7	1,392.5
Advertising, promotion and selling expense	674.9	595.2	576.3
Research expense	110.5	111.0	109.4
General expense	266.1	233.6	220.5
OPERATING PROFIT	586.1	484.9	486.3
Interest income	7.2	5.6	6.0
Other income	26.2	22.8	20.5
Interest expense	(65.6)	(62.8)	(59.0)
Other expense	(19.8)	(17.5)	(14.5)
INCOME BEFORE INCOME TAXES	534.1	433.0	439.3
Provision for income taxes *(Note 2)*	230.5	186.5	189.4
INCOME BEFORE	303.6	246.5	249.9
Share of net income of equity companies *(Note 11)*	35.3	37.0	31.7
Minority owners' interests in subsidiaries' net income	(13.7)	(14.1)	(14.5)
NET INCOME	$ 325.2	$ 269.4	$ 267.1
NET INCOME PER SHARE	$ 3.73	$ 2.93	$ 2.92

See Notes to Financial Statements.

CONSOLIDATED STATEMENT OF CHANGES IN FINANCIAL POSITION

Kimberly-Clark Corporation and Subsidiaries

(Millions of dollars)	*Year Ended December 31* 1987	1986	1985
OPERATIONS			
Net income	$ 325.2	$ 269.4	$ 267.1
Noncash items included in income:			
Depreciation	186.0	169.3	140.3
Deferred income taxes	85.0	52.6	87.2
Unremitted net income of equity companies	(17.2)	(14.0)	(17.7)
Minority owners' interests in subsidiaries' net income	13.7	14.1	14.5
Other	18.6	3.0	6.6
Cash provided by income	611.3	494.4	498.0
Changes in operating working capital *(Note 9)*	45.3	(59.9)	85.5
Cash provided by operations	656.6	434.5	583.5
INVESTING			
Capital spending	(247.3)	(282.4)	(425.8)
Disposals of property	34.5	18.8	15.7
Other	(20.8)	20.6	(4.4)
Cash used for investing	(233.6)	(243.0)	(414.5)
CASH PROVIDED BEFORE FINANCING	$ 423.0	$ 191.5	$ 169.0
FINANCING SUMMARY			
Cash dividends paid	$(124.1)	$(112.0)	$(104.8)
Acquisitions of common stock for the treasury	(632.2)	(1.0)	(.7)
Changes in debt payable within one year	116.0	11.7	(24.3)
Increases in long-term debt	314.9	35.2	20.7
Decreases in long-term debt	(54.3)	(118.1)	(53.0)
Increase in cash and cash equivalents	(43.3)	(7.3)	(6.9)
NET DECREASE IN FINANCING	$(423.0)	$(191.5)	$(169.0)

See Notes to Financial Statements.

Authors' note: The Statement of Cash Flows prescribed by FASB 9 to replace this statement was effective for fiscal years ending after July 15, 1988.

CONSOLIDATED BALANCE SHEET

Kimberly-Clark Corporation and Subsidiaries

(Millions of dollars)	*December 31* 1987	1986
ASSETS		
CURRENT ASSETS		
Cash and cash equivalents	$ 89.7	$ 46.4
Accounts receivable *(Note 9)*	519.9	455.2
Inventories *(Note 9)*	525.4	531.3
Total current assets	1,135.0	1,032.9
PROPERTY		
Land	25.6	24.7
Timberlands	56.3	55.9
Buildings	621.7	591.3
Machinery and equipment	2,961.4	2,765.5
Construction in progress	103.0	66.8
	3,768.0	3,504.2
Less accumulated depreciation	1,431.2	1,241.2
Net property	2,336.8	2,263.0
INVESTMENTS IN EQUITY COMPANIES (Note 11)	264.8	243.8
DEFERRED CHARGES AND OTHER ASSETS	149.1	136.3
	$3,885.7	$3,676.0

See Notes to Financial Statements.

(Millions of dollars)	*December 31* 1987	1986
LIABILITIES AND STOCKHOLDERS' EQUITY		
CURRENT LIABILITIES		
Debt payable within one year *(Note 4)*	$ 250.0	$ 134.0
Accounts payable and accrued liabilities *(Note 9)*	619.9	577.6
Accrued income taxes	96.7	64.7
Dividends payable	29.5	28.5
Total current liabilities	996.1	804.8
LONG-TERM DEBT (Note 4)	686.9	426.3
DEFERRED INCOME TAXES	548.2	448.5
MINORITY OWNERS' INTERESTS IN SUBSIDIARIES	82.6	76.5
STOCKHOLDERS' EQUITY (Notes 5, 6, and 8)		
Common stock — $1.25 par value — authorized 300.0 million shares; issued 81.0 million shares at December 31, 1987 and 95.5 million shares at December 31, 1986	101.2	119.3
Additional paid-in capital	144.5	168.5
Cost of common stock in treasury	(39.3)	(61.8)
Unrealized currency translation adjustments	(85.9)	(163.8)
Retained earnings	1,451.4	1,857.7
Total stockholders' equity	1,571.9	1,919.9
	$3,885.7	$3,676.0

NOTES TO FINANCIAL STATEMENTS

NOTE 1. ACCOUNTING POLICIES

Kimberly-Clark Corporation's accounting policies conform to generally accepted accounting principles. Significant policies followed are described below.

Basis of Presentation

The consolidated financial statements include the accounts of Kimberly-Clark Corporation and all significant subsidiaries which are more than 50 percent owned and controlled. Investments in nonconsolidated companies which are at least 20 percent owned are stated at cost plus equity in undistributed net income. These companies are referred to as equity companies.

Investment Tax Credits

The Tax Reform Act of 1986 eliminated the U.S. investment tax credit retroactive to January 1, 1986. Certain assets, however, were entitled to the investment tax credit under the transition rules of the Act. Investment tax credits are treated as reductions of income tax expense in the year in which the credits arise.

Start-Up and Preoperating Expenses

Significant expenses incurred in bringing new or expanded facilities into operation are recorded as deferred charges and amortized to income over periods of not more than five years.

Advertising and Promotion Expenses

Advertising expenses are charged to income during the year in which they are incurred. Promotion expenses are charged to income over the period of the promotional campaign.

Net Income Per Share

Net income per share is based on the weighted average number of common shares outstanding, which were 87.2 million, 91.8 million and 91.5 million for the years ended December 31, 1987, 1986 and 1985, respectively.

Inventories

Most U.S. inventories which qualify to be valued at cost on the Last-In, First-Out (LIFO) method for U.S. income tax purposes are so valued for accounting purposes. The balance of the U.S. inventories and inventories of consolidated operations outside the U.S. are valued at the lower of cost on the First-In, First-Out (FIFO) method or market.

Property and Depreciation

Property, plant and equipment are stated at cost. Depreciable property is generally depreciated on a straight-line or unit-of-production method for accounting purposes and on an accelerated method for income tax purposes. The cost of property sold or retired is credited to the asset account, and the related depreciation is charged to the accumulated depreciation account. Profit or loss resulting from the sale or retirement is included in income.

NOTE 2. INCOME TAXES

Provisions for income taxes were as follows:

(Millions of dollars)	*Year Ended December 31* 1987	1986	1985
Current income taxes:			
United States	$ 67.0	$ 81.7	$ 74.1
State	14.6	12.7	15.6
Other countries	66.3	52.5	42.1
Investment tax credits	(2.4)	(13.0)	(29.6)
	145.5	133.9	102.2
Deferred income taxes due to:			
Depreciation			
United States	47.4	63.8	72.2
State	13.3	7.2	9.1
Other countries	19.2	1.7	(3.6)
Obsolescence allowance			
United States	(2.1)	(4.6)	(3.5)
State	(.7)	(.3)	(.5)
Other			
United States	4.3	(13.4)	9.8
Other	3.6	(1.8)	3.7
	85.0	52.6	87.2
Total	$230.5	$186.5	$189.4

Income before income taxes included $190.8 million in 1987, $105.3 million in 1986 and $80.0 million in 1985 representing income from subsidiaries outside the U.S.

An analysis of the Corporation's effective income tax rates follows:

	% of Income Before Taxes 1987	1986	1985
Federal statutory rates	40.0%	46.0%	46.0%
State income taxes, net of federal income tax benefit	2.7	2.6	3.1
Investment tax credits	–	(2.7)	(6.7)
Non-U.S. rates over (under) federal statutory rate	.4	(1.2)	(.5)
All other factors — net	.1	(1.6)	1.2
Effective income tax rates	43.2%	43.1%	43.1%

Income taxes have not been provided on $545.4 million of unremitted net income of operations outside the U.S. which had been permanently invested as of December 31, 1987.

NOTES TO FINANCIAL STATEMENTS

NOTE 3. RETIREMENT PLANS AND TRUSTS

The Corporation and most of its major subsidiaries have defined benefit retirement plans covering substantially all their salaried and hourly employees. All plans are noncontributory except for Kimberly-Clark Limited (United Kingdom). Retirement benefits are based on years of service and generally on the average compensation earned in the highest five of the last 15 years of service except for the United Kingdom plan which bases benefits on the highest year during the last five years. Benefits are paid from pension trusts and, in certain cases, are supplemented by direct payments by the Corporation. The funding practice is to contribute to trusts at least the minimum amount required by governmental agencies. Assets of the trusts are comprised principally of common stocks, high-grade corporate and government bonds, guaranteed income contracts and cash investments.

Statement of Financial Accounting Standards (SFAS) No. 87, Employers' Accounting for Pensions, was adopted for the principal North American plans effective January 1, 1986, and for the United Kingdom plan effective January 1, 1987. The effect of adopting SFAS No. 87 in North America was to reduce 1986 pension expense by $11.1 million and to increase net income and net income per share by $5.4 million and 6 cents, respectively. The effect of adopting SFAS No. 87 in the United Kingdom was to reduce 1987 pension expense by $4.1 million and to increase net income and net income per share by $2.7 million and 3 cents, respectively.

The components of pension expense were as follows:

	Year Ended December 31		
(Millions of dollars)	1987	1986	1985
Benefits earned	$30.9	$24.1	$ –
Interest on projected benefit obligation	73.1	61.9	–
Amortization of transition adjustment	(.9)	.2	–
Special early retirement benefits*	3.3	5.4	–
Pension expense determined under accounting pronouncements other than SFAS No. 87	1.4	3.2	29.1
	107.8	94.8	29.1
Less expected return on plan assets (Actual return on plan assets was $143.7 million in 1987 and $83.0 million in 1986.)	83.7	67.4	–
Pension expense	$24.1	$27.4	$29.1

**Special early retirement benefits were offered to eligible employees at Spruce Falls Power and Paper Company, Limited in 1987 and at Terrace Bay and Longlac, Ont., in 1986.*

The funded status of the principal plans follows:

(Millions of dollars)	December 31 1987	December 31 1986
Actuarial present value of plan benefits:		
Vested	$639.6	$606.7
Nonvested	18.6	20.7
Accumulated benefit obligation	$658.2	$627.4
Projected benefit obligation	$836.2	$796.6
Plan assets at fair value	936.1	769.7
Plan assets in excess of (less than) projected benefit obligation	$ 99.9	$ (26.9)
Consisting of:		
Favorable (unfavorable) actuarial experience not being amortized	$ 77.7	$ (31.6)
Unamortized transition adjustment	13.0	9.7
Net prepaid (accrued) pension expense	9.2	(5.0)
Total	$ 99.9	$ (26.9)

The projected benefit obligation was based on assumed discount rates of 10% to 10.5% in 1987 and 9% to 10% in 1986 and assumed long-term rates of compensation increases of 6% to 7.5% in 1987 and 5.25% to 7.5% in 1986.

The assumed average long-term rate of return on pension assets was 11% in 1987 and 1986. The transition adjustment is being amortized to pension expense on the straight-line method over 14 to 18 years.

NOTES TO FINANCIAL STATEMENTS

NOTE 4. DEBT

The major issues of long-term debt were:

(Millions of dollars)	December 31 1987	1986
Kimberly-Clark Corporation		
Commercial paper to be refinanced	$200.0	$ –
9⅛% Notes due 1997	100.0	–
12% Notes due 1994	100.0	100.0
11½% Sinking Fund Debentures due 2013	60.5	60.5
10.35% Notes due 1987	–	25.0
11⅛% Notes due 1990	99.8	99.8
6⅞% to 9.67% Pollution Control and Industrial Development Revenue Bonds maturing to 2005	33.8	33.8
Other	18.1	15.3
	612.2	334.4
Subsidiaries		
Bank loans in various currencies at variable rates (8% to 11% at December 31, 1987) maturing to 1993	54.3	92.1
Bank loans in various currencies at fixed rates (9% to 18% at December 31, 1987) maturing to 1996	12.0	13.9
Other	16.5	15.6
	695.0	456.0
Less current portion	8.1	29.7
Total	$686.9	$426.3

At December 31, 1987, $200 million of commercial paper was classified as long-term debt. In January 1988, the Corporation issued $100 million of First Series Medium-Term Notes due in four to six years, with interest rates from 8.35% to 8.75%. The proceeds from this financing were used to retire $100 million of commercial paper. Also, $100 million of commercial paper will be repaid with the proceeds from a January 1988 offering of $100 million principal amount of 9½% Sinking Fund Debentures due in 2018.

Maturities of long-term debt, including the medium-term notes described above, are $23.8 million in 1989, $121.7 million in 1990, $53.5 million in 1991 and $62.1 million in 1992.

At December 31, 1987, the Corporation had $475 million of revolving credit facilities with a group of U.S. banks. These facilities, which were unused at December 31, 1987, permit borrowing at competitive interest rates and are available for general corporate purposes, including backup for commercial paper borrowings. The Corporation pays commitment fees on the unused portion but may cancel the facilities without penalty at any time prior to their expiration on October 1, 1989.

Debt payable within one year:

(Millions of dollars)	December 31 1987	December 31 1986
Commercial paper	$212.9	$ 78.0
Current portion of long-term debt	8.1	29.7
Other short-term debt	29.0	26.3
Total	$250.0	$134.0

NOTE 5. FOREIGN CURRENCY TRANSLATION

Assets and liabilities of foreign operations are translated into U.S. dollars at period-end exchange rates except for operations in the highly inflationary economies of Mexico, Brazil and Colombia where the functional currency is the U.S. dollar. Gains or losses on such translations are reflected as unrealized currency translation adjustments in stockholders' equity. Income and expense accounts are translated into U.S. dollars at rates of exchange in effect each month.

Unrealized currency translation adjustments:

(Millions of dollars)	1987	1986
Balance, January 1	$(163.8)	$(179.2)
Adjustments for the year:		
Canadian Dollar	21.3	3.8
British Pound	30.6	2.4
French Franc	12.3	7.9
German Mark	5.5	5.8
Other	8.2	7.8
	77.9	27.7
Sale of Jujo Kimberly K.K. (Japan)	–	(12.3)
Balance, December 31	$ (85.9)	$(163.8)

The net loss reflected in the determination of net income pertaining to currency transactions and translation of balance sheets of operations in hyperinflationary economies was $13.4 million in 1987 and $3.5 million in 1985, compared to a gain of $.7 million in 1986.

NOTES TO FINANCIAL STATEMENTS

NOTE 6. EQUITY PARTICIPATION PLANS

The 1976 and 1986 Plans provide for awards of participation shares and stock options to key employees of the Corporation and its subsidiaries. The Plans are more fully described in the Corporation's proxy statement.

At maturity, participation shares result in cash payments determined by the increase in the book value of the Corporation's common stock. Participants are not entitled to dividends on the participation shares, but their accounts are credited with dividend shares which are payable in cash to the participant at the time the related participation shares become payable. Neither participation nor dividend shares are shares of common stock.

Data concerning participation shares and dividend shares follow:

Participation and Dividend Shares	1987	1986	1985
Outstanding — Beginning of year	2,037,492	1,873,674	1,651,250
Awarded	46,000	269,000	300,400
Dividend shares credited — net .	108,930	102,118	90,366
Matured or forfeited	(404,667)	(207,300)	(168,342)
Outstanding — End of year	1,787,755	2,037,492	1,873,674

Stock options are granted at not less than market value, become exercisable over a period of three years from date of grant and expire 10 years after the date of the grant. Stock appreciation rights (SARs) have been granted to certain participants which allow them, in lieu of option exercise, to receive cash equal to the difference between the option price and the market price of the Corporation's common stock at the date of conversion. As a condition of SAR conversion, a participant is required to exercise an equal number of option shares.

Data concerning stock options and SARs follow:

	1987 Price Range	*Number of Options* 1987	1986	1985
Outstanding — Beginning of year	$12.00-43.81	1,706,556	1,499,438	1,513,718
Granted	$56.44	12,000	538,000	300,400
Exercised*	$12.00-43.81	(277,440)	(313,542)	(232,534)
Cancelled or expired	$30.44-43.81	(18,300)	(17,340)	(82,146)
Outstanding — End of year*	$12.00-56.44	1,422,816	1,706,556	1,499,438
Exercisable	$12.00-43.81	930,556	939,876	1,083,798

**Options outstanding on December 31, 1987, 1986 and 1985 included 33,650 shares, 128,920 shares and 138,820 shares, respectively, with related stock appreciation rights. Price ranges for shares exercised in 1986 were $10.06 to $30.44 and in 1985 were $10.06 to $24.44.*

At December 31, 1987, the number of additional shares of common stock of the Corporation available for option and sale under the 1986 Plan was 2,461,600 shares; in the aggregate, the number of such shares available plus the number of participation shares which could be awarded at such date under the 1986 Plan was 3,161,800 shares. The 1976 Plan has expired and no additional grants will be made under that Plan. Amounts expensed under the Plans in 1987, 1986 and 1985 were $8.8 million, $5.4 million and $6.0 million, respectively.

NOTE 7. LEASES

Future minimum rental payments under operating leases as of December 31, 1987 were:

(Millions of dollars)	
Year Ending December 31:	
1988	$15.9
1989	10.0
1990	6.7
1991	3.9
1992	3.2
Thereafter	21.2
Total	$60.9

Consolidated rental expense under operating leases was $52.5 million in 1987, $48.0 million in 1986 and $44.5 million in 1985.

NOTES TO FINANCIAL STATEMENTS

NOTE 8. STOCKHOLDERS' EQUITY

Changes in common stock issued, treasury stock, additional paid-in capital and retained earnings are shown below:

	Common Stock Issued		*Treasury Stock*		*Additional Paid-In*	*Retained*
(Millions of dollars except share amounts)	*Shares*	*Amount*	*Shares*	*Amount*	*Capital*	*Earnings*
Balance at December 31, 1984	95,453,272	$119.3	4,038,770	$ (67.1)	$165.7	$1,541.3
Exercise of stock options	–	–	(232,534)	2.9	.8	–
Purchased for treasury	–	–	27,812	(.7)	–	–
Net income	–	–	–	–	–	267.1
Cash dividends declared	–	–	–	–	–	(106.2)
Balance at December 31, 1985	95,453,272	119.3	3,834,048	(64.9)	166.5	1,702.2
Exercise of stock options	–	–	(313,542)	4.1	2.0	–
Purchased for treasury	–	–	23,154	(1.0)	–	–
Net income	–	–	–	–	–	269.4
Cash dividends declared	–	–	–	–	–	(113.9)
Balance at December 31, 1986	95,453,272	119.3	3,543,660	(61.8)	168.5	1,857.7
Exercise of stock options	–	–	(277,440)	4.3	1.9	–
Purchased for treasury	–	–	12,012,790	(632.2)	–	–
Retirement of treasury shares	(14,500,000)	(18.1)	(14,500,000)	650.4	(25.9)	(606.4)
Net income	–	–	–	–	–	325.2
Cash dividends declared	–	–	–	–	–	(125.1)
Balance at December 31, 1987	80,953,272	$101.2	779,010	$ (39.3)	$144.5	$1,451.4

On April 16, 1987, the stockholders adopted an amendment to the Corporation's Restated Certificate of Incorporation: (a) increasing the authorized shares of common stock from 100 million shares to 300 million shares and the authorized shares of preferred stock from 10 million shares to 20 million shares; (b) reducing the par value of the common stock from $2.50 per share to $1.25 per share; and (c) splitting each issued share of common stock into two shares of common stock. Accordingly, all numbers of common shares and per share data for the current and prior periods presented in these financial statements have been restated to reflect the stock split.

During 1987, the Corporation completed the acquisition of 12 million shares of its common stock for $631.6 million under two separate six million share repurchase programs announced on January 27 and October 21, 1987.

On December 17, 1987, the board of directors authorized the retirement of 14.5 million shares of treasury stock which became authorized but unissued shares.

The Corporation has 20 million shares of authorized preferred stock with no par value, none of which has been issued.

At December 31, 1987, unremitted net income of equity companies included in consolidated retained earnings was $226.5 million.

NOTE 9. SUPPLEMENTARY DATA (Millions of dollars)

Summary of Cash Flow Effects of Changes in Operating Working Capital	*Year Ended December 31* 1987	1986	1985
Accounts receivable	$ (64.7)	$ (14.5)	$ (28.4)
Inventories	5.9	(54.3)	(3.0)
Accounts payable and accrued liabilities . .	42.3	13.0	82.6
Accrued income taxes	32.0	(15.0)	31.7
Currency rate changes	29.8	10.9	2.6
Changes in operating working capital	$ 45.3	$ (59.9)	$ 85.5

Summary of Accounts Receivable and Inventories	*December 31* 1987	1986
Accounts Receivable:		
From customers	$490.5	$440.3
Other	39.3	25.4
Less allowances for doubtful accounts and sales discounts	(9.9)	(10.5)
Total	$519.9	$455.2
Inventories By Major Class:		
At the lower of cost on the First-In, First-Out (FIFO) method or market:		
Raw materials	$173.3	$169.1
Work in process	122.6	116.6
Finished goods	241.7	262.7
Supplies and other	107.4	104.9
	645.0	653.3
Excess of FIFO cost over Last-In, First-Out (LIFO) cost	(119.6)	(122.0)
Total	$525.4	$531.3

Inventories which were valued on the LIFO method at December 31, 1987 and 1986, were $190.4 million and $229.8 million, respectively.

NOTES TO FINANCIAL STATEMENTS

NOTE 9. (Continued)

Summary of Accounts Payable and Accrued Liabilities	*December 31* 1987	1986
Accounts payable to suppliers	$191.2	$165.9
Other accounts payable	90.4	80.0
Total accounts payable	281.6	245.9
Accrued advertising and promotion expense	69.4	96.2
Accrued salaries and wages	85.7	87.1
Accrued pension expense	17.4	23.1
Other accrued liabilities	165.8	125.3
Total	$619.9	$577.6

Other	*Year Ended December 31* 1987	1986	1985
Maintenance and repairs expense	$247.4	$234.7	$211.2
Advertising expense	87.0	89.9	92.5
Interest capitalized	1.5	3.3	13.9

Please refer to the discussion of New Accounting Standards on page 17 of the Operating/Financial Review for information concerning the effects of recently issued accounting rules not yet adopted by the company.

NOTE 10. UNAUDITED QUARTERLY DATA

(Millions of dollars except per share amounts)	1987				1986			
	Fourth	*Third*	*Second*	*First*	*Fourth*	*Third*	*Second*	*First*
Net sales	$1,253.9	$1,223.2	$1,224.4	$1,183.2	$1,113.2	$1,065.0	$1,087.7	$1,037.2
Gross profit	414.1	410.5	404.2	408.8	337.5	348.4	373.0	365.8
Operating profit	157.8	146.5	139.6	142.2	117.3	112.9	122.9	131.8
Net income	82.2	84.1	83.8	75.1	64.3	63.0	68.8	73.3
Net income per share	$ .99	$ .98	$ .94	$ .82	$ .70	$ .68	$ .75	$ .80

NOTE 11. PRODUCT CLASS AND GEOGRAPHIC DATA

The business and products of the Corporation and its subsidiaries are described on the inside front cover of this report. For reporting purposes, products are assigned to three product classes. Class I principally includes household and institutional tissues; feminine, infant and incontinence care products; industrial and commercial wipers; hospital and home health care products; and related products and by-products. Class II principally contains premium business and correspondence papers, tobacco industry papers and products, newsprint and other printing papers, technical and specialty papers, and related products and by-products. Class III comprises aircraft services, air transportation, and other miscellaneous products and services.

Information about consolidated operations by product class and geographic area, as well as data for equity companies, is presented in the tables below and on the following pages:

Consolidated Operations by Product Class

(Millions of dollars)	*Sales* 1987	1986	1985	*Operating Profit* 1987	1986	1985
Class I	$3,808.7	$3,369.7	$3,171.8	$433.9	$362.6	$361.2
Class II	1,000.4	876.4	855.9	177.3	144.9	162.1
Class III	125.3	98.8	118.3	13.1	9.0	2.1
Combined	4,934.4	4,344.9	4,146.0	624.3	516.5	525.4
Interclass sales	(49.7)	(41.8)	(73.1)	–	–	–
Unallocated expenses	–	–	–	(38.2)	(31.6)	(39.1)
Consolidated	$4,884.7	$4,303.1	$4,072.9	$586.1	$484.9	$486.3

(Millions of dollars)	*Assets* 1987	1986	1985	*Depreciation* 1987	1986	1985	*Capital Spending* 1987	1986	1985
Class I	$2,765.0	$2,680.7	$2,489.9	$144.4	$134.5	$110.1	$180.8	$210.3	$364.1
Class II	709.3	652.6	616.2	30.5	27.6	23.6	43.0	64.4	35.6
Class III	84.9	69.0	77.3	2.9	2.3	1.8	9.1	6.6	9.6
Combined	3,559.2	3,402.3	3,183.4	177.8	164.4	135.5	232.9	281.3	409.3
Unallocated	363.7*	329.2*	393.5*	8.2	4.9	4.8	14.4	1.1	16.5
Interclass assets	(37.2)	(55.5)	(73.1)	–	–	–	–	–	–
Consolidated	$3,885.7	$3,676.0	$3,503.8	$186.0	$169.3	$140.3	$247.3	$282.4	$425.8

**Included investments in equity companies of $264.8 million, $243.8 million and $253.8 million in 1987, 1986 and 1985, respectively.*

NOTES TO FINANCIAL STATEMENTS

NOTE 11. (Continued)

Consolidated Operations by Geographic Area

	Sales			*Operating Profit*			*Assets*		
(Millions of dollars)	1987	1986	1985	1987	1986	1985	1987	1986	1985
United States	$3,475.8	$3,112.7	$3,042.2	$417.4	$393.7	$419.5	$2,252.5	$2,261.5	$2,098.1
Canada	646.3	560.8	543.8	88.7	39.4	36.6	622.3	572.1	568.0
Europe	673.9	561.8	436.6	77.1	55.9	40.8	496.2	379.0	349.3
Latin/South America	60.6	41.6	44.6	15.5	6.4	9.7	61.0	55.6	51.2
Far East	150.9	120.5	109.9	25.6	21.1	18.8	119.7	102.3	84.2
Combined	5,007.5	4,397.4	4,177.1	624.3	516.5	525.4	3,551.7	3,370.5	3,150.8
Intergeographic sales*	(122.8)	(94.3)	(104.2)	–	–	–	–	–	–
Unallocated expenses	–	–	–	(38.2)	(31.6)	(39.1)	–	–	–
Unallocated assets**	–	–	–	–	–	–	363.7	329.2	393.5
Intergeographic assets	–	–	–	–	–	–	(29.7)	(23.7)	(40.5)
Consolidated	$4,884.7	$4,303.1	$4,072.9	$586.1	$484.9	$486.3	$3,885.7	$3,676.0	$3,503.8

**Included sales of $99.0 million, $75.8 million and $85.9 million by operations in Canada to other geographic areas and all other intergeographic sales (primarily United States) of $23.8 million, $18.5 million and $18.3 million in 1987, 1986 and 1985, respectively.*
***Included investments in equity companies of $264.8 million, $243.8 million and $253.8 million in 1987, 1986 and 1985, respectively.*

	Net Income			*Kimberly-Clark's Share of Net Income*		
(Millions of dollars)	1987	1986	1985	1987	1986	1985
United States	$187.8	$176.2	$200.7	$187.8	$176.1	$200.5
Canada	45.0	18.4	17.4	38.4	10.9	8.2
Europe	45.9	36.3	17.5	44.3	34.6	16.4
Latin/South America	8.9	2.3	3.5	8.3	1.7	2.9
Far East	16.0	13.3	10.8	11.1	9.1	7.4
Consolidated	$303.6	$246.5	$249.9	$289.9	$232.4	$235.4

Sales of products between classes and geographic areas are made at market prices and are referred to as interclass sales and intergeographic sales.

Assets reported by product class and geographic area represent assets which are directly used and an allocated portion of jointly used assets. These assets include receivables from other product classes or geographic areas, and are referred to as interclass or intergeographic assets. Assets and expenses that cannot be associated with classes or geographic areas are referred to as unallocated assets or unallocated expenses.

With the exception of 1987, which benefited from increased pulp selling prices, the company's pulp manufacturing mill at Terrace Bay, Ont., has been unprofitable for the past nine years. The related woodlands operation at Longlac, Ont., has been unprofitable for all nine years.

In 1986, a survival plan was adopted. Two key features of the plan were to control manufacturing costs at the pulp mill and the woodlands operation and to resolve environmental issues. Since inception of the survival plan, total employment at the two operations has been reduced by more than 400 people. Other labor issues, however, remain a concern. Negotiations with the woodworkers union began early in the fourth quarter and a union contract with pulp mill employees expires on April 30, 1988. In 1987, the government of Ontario issued a new environmental control order which expires in October 1989.

Although mill operations have improved, the technological difficulties of complying with environmental regulations, including those contained in the control order, coupled with the excessive wood costs and the uncertain outcome of the labor negotiations, leave management of the Corporation unable to predict whether full recovery of the approximately $300 million net carrying amount of the facilities will occur.

Equity Companies' Data by Geographic Area

(Millions of dollars)	*Current Assets*	*Non-current Assets*	*Current Liabilities*	*Non-current Liabilities*	*Stock-holders' Equity*	*Net Sales*	*Gross Profit*	*Operating Profit*	*Net Income*	*Kimberly-Clark's Share of Net Income*
December 31, 1987										
Latin/South America	$273.8	$389.4	$104.2	$ 53.6	$505.4	$543.9	$189.7	$128.8	$60.1	$26.2
Far East and Australia	54.7	94.7	45.3	35.6	68.5	197.3	69.9	31.5	15.4	7.7
Africa	35.3	33.1	24.1	18.3	26.0	108.9	34.3	8.7	3.5	1.4
Total	$363.8	$517.2	$173.6	$107.5	$599.9	$850.1	$293.9	$169.0	$79.0	$35.3
December 31, 1986										
Latin/South America	$237.1	$374.3	$ 60.5	$ 74.4	$476.5	$431.6	$134.3	$ 85.8	$45.9	$20.1
Far East and Australia*	47.8	70.8	39.4	23.8	55.4	333.0	135.1	33.7	23.0	15.5
Africa	29.1	29.9	19.2	17.7	22.1	86.8	28.2	8.5	3.6	1.4
Total	$314.0	$475.0	$119.1	$115.9	$554.0	$851.4	$297.6	$128.0	$72.5	$37.0
December 31, 1985										
Latin/South America	$245.1	$383.8	$ 64.8	$ 93.1	$471.0	$446.2	$154.5	$101.3	$56.6	$24.6
Far East and Australia	86.3	121.8	97.4	24.5	86.2	289.5	109.5	26.2	11.3	5.6
Africa	20.5	24.3	14.5	13.3	17.0	81.5	27.2	8.6	3.8	1.5
Total	$351.9	$529.9	$176.7	$130.9	$574.2	$817.2	$291.2	$136.1	$71.7	$31.7

**In December 1986, the Corporation sold its interest in Jujo Kimberly K.K. (Japan).*

The name and the percent of common stock owned of each company are shown on page 38.

INDEPENDENT AUDITORS' OPINION/AUDIT COMMITTEE CHAIRMAN'S LETTER

INDEPENDENT AUDITORS' OPINION

Kimberly-Clark Corporation, Its Directors and Stockholders:

We have examined the consolidated balance sheets of Kimberly-Clark Corporation and Subsidiaries as of December 31, 1987 and 1986, and the related consolidated statements of income and changes in financial position for each of the three years in the period ended December 31, 1987. Our examinations were made in accordance with generally accepted auditing standards and, accordingly, included such tests of the accounting records and such other auditing procedures as we considered necessary in the circumstances.

In our opinion, such consolidated financial statements of Kimberly-Clark Corporation and Subsidiaries present fairly the financial position of the companies at December 31, 1987 and 1986, and the results of their operations and the changes in their financial position for each of the three years in the period ended December 31, 1987, in conformity with generally accepted accounting principles applied on a consistent basis.

Deloitte Haskins & Sells

Certified Public Accountants
Dallas, Texas

January 27, 1988

AUDIT COMMITTEE CHAIRMAN'S LETTER

The Audit Committee is selected by the board of directors and consists of five outside directors. The members of the Audit Committee are shown on page 39 of this annual report. The committee met three times during the year ended December 31, 1987.

The Audit Committee oversees the financial reporting process on behalf of the board of directors. As part of that responsibility, the committee recommended to the board of directors, subject to stockholder approval, the selection of the Corporation's independent public accountants. The Audit Committee discussed the overall scope and specific plans for audits with the internal auditor and Deloitte Haskins & Sells. The committee also discussed the Corporation's consolidated financial statements and the adequacy of its internal controls. The committee met regularly with the Corporation's internal auditor and Deloitte Haskins & Sells, without management present, to discuss the results of their examinations, their evaluations of the Corporation's internal controls, and the overall quality of the Corporation's financial reporting. The meetings also were designed to facilitate any private communication with the committee desired by the internal auditor or independent public accountants.

Rev. John P. Raynor, S.J.
Chairman, Audit Committee

January 27, 1988

MANAGEMENT'S RESPONSIBILITY FOR FINANCIAL REPORTING

Management of Kimberly-Clark is responsible for conducting all aspects of the business, including preparation of all information in this annual report and the audited financial statements. These financial statements have been prepared using generally accepted accounting principles considered appropriate in the circumstances to present fairly the Corporation's financial position, its results of operations and changes in financial position on a consistent basis.

As can be expected in a complex and dynamic business environment, some financial statement amounts are based on management's estimates and informed judgments. Even though estimates and judgments are used, readers of Kimberly-Clark's financial information should be aware of the measures that have been taken to ensure the integrity of this financial report. These measures include an effective control-oriented environment, in which the Internal Audit Department plays an important role, independent audits and an Audit Committee of the board of directors which oversees the quality of financial reporting.

One characteristic of a control-oriented environment is a system of internal controls which provides reasonable assurance that assets are safeguarded, transactions are appropriately authorized, recorded and reported, and that financial statements are reliable and fraudulent financial reporting is prevented or detected. This system is supported with written policies and procedures, and the Internal Audit Department monitors the system to help ensure that it is working effectively.

In addition, the Corporation has adopted policies with respect to conducting business affairs in a lawful and ethical manner in each country in which it does business, to potential conflicts of interest, and to confidentiality of information and business ideas. Internal controls have been developed and instituted to provide assurance that these policies are followed.

The financial statements have been audited by independent accountants, Deloitte Haskins & Sells, whose report appears on the facing page. Their examination included a review of the system of internal controls, tests of the accounting records and other auditing procedures which they considered necessary to form an opinion as to the fairness of the financial statements. In the course of their examination, the independent accountants were given unrestricted access to all financial records and related data, including minutes of all meetings of stockholders and the board of directors and all committees thereof. Furthermore, management believes that all representations made to the independent accountants during their audit were valid and appropriate.

Information about the Audit Committee is contained in the Audit Committee Chairman's letter shown on the facing page.

During the examinations conducted by both the independent accountants and the Internal Audit Department, management received recommendations to strengthen or modify internal controls as business develops and changes. Management has adopted or is in the process of adopting all such recommendations which are cost effective in the circumstances. Management believes that the Corporation's internal control system is adequate to accomplish the objectives for which it was designed.

Darwin E. Smith
Chairman of the Board and
Chief Executive Officer

Brendan M. O'Neill
Senior Vice President and
Chief Financial Officer

January 27, 1988

INDEX

n = footnote.

ARB No.	Date Issued	Title
29	Feb. 1979	Reporting Tax Benefits Realized on Disposition of Investments in Certain Subsidiaries and Other Investees
30	Sept. 1979	Accounting for Involuntary Conversions of Nonmonetary Assets to Monetary Assets
31	Feb. 1980	Treatment of Stock Compensation Plans in EPS Computations
32	Mar. 1980	Application of Percentage Limitations in Recognizing Investment Tax Credit
33	Aug. 1980	Applying *FASB Statement 34* to Oil and Gas Producing Operations Accounted for by the Full Cost Method
34	Mar. 1981	Disclosure of Indirect Guarantees of Indebtedness of Others
35	May 1981	Criteria for Applying the Equity Method of Accounting for Investments in Common Stock
36	Oct. 1981	Accounting for Exploration Wells in Progress at the End of a Period
37	July 1983	Accounting for Translation Adjustments upon Sale of Part of an Investment in a Foreign Entity
38	Aug. 1984	Determining the Measurement Date for Stock Options, Purchase, and Award Plans Involving Junior Stock

Financial Accounting Standards Board (FASB) *Technical Bulletins* (1979–87)

79–1	Dec. 1979	Purpose and Scope of FASB Technical Bulletins and Procedures for Issuance—To Provide Guidance Concerning the Application of Official Pronouncements of the FASB, APB, and ARBs
79–2	Dec. 1979	Computer Software Costs
79–3	Dec. 1979	Subjective Acceleration Clauses in Long-Term Debt Agreements
79–4	Dec. 1979	Segment Reporting of Puerto Rican Operations
79–5	Dec. 1979	Meaning of the Term "Customer" as It Applies to Facilities
79–6	Dec. 1979	Valuation Allowances Following Debt Restructure
79–7	Dec. 1979	Recoveries of a Previous Writedown under a Troubled Debt Restructuring Involving a Modification of Terms
79–8	Dec. 1979	Applicability of *FASB Statements 21* and *33* to Certain Brokers and Dealers in Securities
79–9	Dec. 1979	Accounting in Interim Periods for Changes in Income Tax Rates
79–10	Dec. 1979	Fiscal Funding Clauses in Lease Agreements
79–11	Dec. 1979	Effect of a Penalty on the Term of a Lease
79–12	Dec. 1979	Interest Rate Used in Calculating the Present Value of Minimum Lease Payments
79–13	Dec. 1979	Applicability of *FASB Statement 13* to Current Value Financial Statements
79–14	Dec. 1979	Upward Adjustment of Guaranteed Residual Values
79–15	Dec. 1979	Accounting for Loss on a Sublease Not Involving the Disposal of a Segment
79–16	Dec. 1979	Effect of a Change in Income Tax Rate on the Accounting for Leveraged Leases
79–17	Dec. 1979	Reporting Cumulative Effect Adjustment from Retroactive Application of *FASB Statement 13*
79–18	Dec. 1979	Transition Requirement of Certain FASB Amendments and Interpretations of *FASB Statement 13*
79–19	Dec. 1979	Investor's Accounting for Unrealized Losses on Marketable Securities Owned by an Equity Method Investee
80–1	Dec. 1980	Early Extinguishment of Debt through Exchange for Common or Preferred Stock
81–1	Feb. 1981	Disclosure of Interest Rate Futures Contracts and Forward and Standby Contracts
81–2	Feb. 1981	Accounting for Unused Investment Tax Credits Acquired in a Business Combination Accounted for by the Purchase Method
81–3	Feb. 1981	Multiemployer Pension Plan Amendments Act of 1980
84–4	Feb. 1981	Classification as Monetary or Nonmonetary Items
81–5	Feb. 1981	Offsetting Interest Cost to Be Capitalized with Interest Income
81–6	Nov. 1981	Applicability of *FASB Statement 15* to Debtors in Bankruptcy Situations
82–1	Jan. 1982	Disclosure of the Sale or Purchase of Tax Benefits through Tax Leases
82–2	Mar. 1982	Accounting for the Conversion of Stock Options into Stock Incentive Plans as a Result of the Economic Recovery Tax Act of 1981
83–1	July 1983	Accounting for the Reduction in the Tax Basis of an Asset Caused by the Investment Tax Credit
84–1	Mar. 1984	Accounting for Stock Issued to Acquire the Results of a Research and Development Arrangement
84–2	Sept. 1984	Accounting for the Effects of the Tax Reform Act of 1984 on Deferred Income Taxes Relating to Domestic International Sales Corporations
84–3	Sept. 1984	Accounting for the Effects of the Tax Reform Act of 1984 on Deferred Income Taxes for Life Insurance Enterprises
84–4	Oct. 1984	In-Substance Defeasance of Debt
85–1	Mar. 1985	Accounting for the Receipt of Federal Home Loan Mortgage Participating Preferred Stock
85–2	Mar. 1985	Accounting for Collateralized Mortgage Obligations (CMOs)
85–3	Nov. 1985	Accounting for Operating Leases with Scheduled Rent Increases
85–4	Nov. 1985	Accounting for Purchases of Life Insurance

ARB No.	Date Issued	Title
82	Nov. 1984	Financial Reporting and Changing Prices: Elimination of Certain Disclosures (an amendment of *FASB Statement 33*)
83	Mar. 1985	Designation of AICPA Guides and Statement of Position on Accounting by Brokers and Dealers in Securities, by Employee Benefit Plans, and by Banks as Preferable for Purposes of Applying *APB Opinion 20* (an amendment of *FASB Statement 32* and *APB Opinion 30*, and a recission of *FASB Interpretation 10*)
84	Mar. 1985	Induced Conversions of Convertible Debt (an amendment of *APB Opinion 26*)
85	Mar. 1985	Yield Test for Determining whether a Convertible Security Is a Common Stock Equivalent (an amendment of *APB Opinion 15*)
86	Aug. 1985	Accounting for the Costs of Computer Software to Be Sold, Leased, or Otherwise Marketed
87	Dec. 1985	Employers' Accounting for Pensions
88	Dec. 1985	Employers' Accounting for Settlements and Curtailments of Defined Benefit Pension Plans and for Termination of Benefits
89	Dec. 1986	Financial Reporting and Changing Prices
90	Dec. 1986	Regulated Enterprises: Accounting for Abandonments and Disallowances of Plant Costs (as amendment of *FASB Statement 71*)
91	Dec. 1986	Accounting for Nonrefundable Fees and Costs Associated with Originating or Acquiring Loans and Initial Direct Costs of Leases (an amendment of *FASB Statements 13, 60,* and *65*, and a recission of *FASB Statement 17*)
92	Aug. 1987	Regulated Enterprises—Accounting for Phase-In Plans (an amendment of *FASB Statement 71*)
93	Aug. 1987	Recognition of Depreciation by Not-for-Profit Organizations
94	Oct. 1987	Consolidation of All Majority-Owned Subsidiaries (an amendment of *ARB 51*, with related amendments of *APB Opinion 18* and *ARB 43*, Chapter 12)
95	Nov. 1987	Statement of Cash Flows
96	Dec. 1987	Accounting for Income Taxes
97	Dec. 1987	Accounting and Reporting by Insurance Enterprises for Certain Long-Duration Contracts and for Realized Gains and Losses from the Sale of Investments
98	May 1988	Accounting for Leases: Sale-Leaseback Transactions involving Real Estate; Definition of the Lease Term; Initial Direct Costs of Direct Financing Leases (an amendment of *FASB Statements 13, 66,* and *91*, and a recission of *FASB Statement 26* and *Technical Bulletin 79–11*)

Financial Accounting Standards Board (FASB) *Interpretations* (1974–85)

1	June 1974	Accounting Changes Related to the Cost of Inventory
2	June 1974	Imputing Interest on Debt Arrangements Made under the Federal Bankruptcy Act
3	Dec. 1974	Accounting for the Cost of Pension Plans Subject to the Employment Retirement Income Security Act of 1974
4	Feb. 1975	Applicability of *FASB Statement 2* to Business Combinations Accounted for by the Purchase Method
5	Feb. 1975	Applicability of *FASB Statement 2* to Development Stage Enterprises
6	Feb. 1975	Applicability of *FASB Statement 2* to Computer Software
7	Oct. 1975	Applying *FASB Statement 7* in Financial Statements of Established Operating Enterprises
8	Jan. 1976	Classification of a Short-Term Obligation Repaid Prior to Being Replaced by a Long-Term Security
9	Feb. 1976	Applying *APB Opinions 16* and *17* When a Savings and Loan Association or a Similar Institution Is Acquired in a Business Combination Accounted for by the Purchase Method
10	Sept. 1976	Application of *FASB Statement 12* to Personal Financial Statements
11	Sept. 1976	Changes in Market Value after the Balance Sheet Date
12	Sept. 1976	Accounting for Previously Established Allowance Accounts
13	Sept. 1976	Consolidation of a Parent and Its Subsidiaries Having Different Balance Sheet Dates
14	Sept. 1976	Reasonable Estimation of the Amount of a Loss
15	Sept. 1976	Translation of Unamortized Policy Acquisition Costs by a Stock Life Insurance Company
16	Feb. 1977	Clarification of Definitions and Accounting for Marketable Equity Securities That Become Nonmarketable
17	Feb. 1977	Applying the Lower of Cost or Market Rule in Translated Financial Statements
18	Mar. 1977	Accounting for Income Taxes in Interim Periods
19	Oct. 1977	Lessee Guarantee of the Residual Value of Leased Property
20	Nov. 1977	Reporting Accounting Changes under AICPA Statements of Position
21	Apr. 1978	Accounting for Leases in a Business Combination
22	Apr. 1978	Applicability of Indefinite Reversal Criteria to Timing Differences
23	Aug. 1978	Leases of Certain Property Owned by a Governmental Unit or Authority
24	Sept. 1978	Leases Involving Only Part of a Building
25	Sept. 1978	Accounting for an Unused Investment Tax Credit
26	Sept. 1978	Accounting for Purchase of a Leased Asset by the Lessee during the Term of the Lease
27	Nov. 1978	Accounting for Loss on a Sublease
28	Dec. 1978	Accounting for Stock Appreciation Rights and Other Variable Stock Option or Award Plans